Stephen David Ricks
3235 Withers Avenue
Lafayette, California 94549

A HISTORY OF GREECE

A

HISTORY OF GREECE

TO THE

DEATH OF ALEXANDER THE GREAT

BY

J. B. BURY, D.Litt., LL.D., F.B.A.

SOMETIME REGIUS PROFESSOR OF MODERN HISTORY, AND FELLOW OF
KING'S COLLEGE, IN THE UNIVERSITY OF CAMBRIDGE

THIRD EDITION

Revised by RUSSELL MEIGGS,
Fellow of Balliol College, Oxford

MACMILLAN
ST MARTIN'S PRESS

First Edition July 1900
Reprinted October 1900, 1902, 1904, 1906, 1908, 1909, 1911, 1912
Second Edition 1913.   *Reprinted* 1914, 1916, 1917, 1920, 1922
1924, 1927, 1929, 1931, 1938, 1941, 1945
Third Edition 1951.   *Reprinted* 1951, 1952, 1955, 1956, 1959
1963, 1966, 1967, 1970

Published by

MACMILLAN AND CO LTD
London and Basingstoke
Associated companies in New York Toronto
Dublin Melbourne Johannesburg and Madras

SBN   333   08484   5   (hard cover)

Printed in Great Britain by
R. & R. CLARK LTD
Edinburgh

PREFACE TO THIRD EDITION

THE first edition of this History of Greece was published in 1900, on the eve of Sir Arthur Evans' dramatic excavations at Cnossus in Crete. In the second edition, published in 1913, Bury re-wrote the first chapter in the light of the new evidence. Outside Chapter I a few minor changes only were made.

In the period since 1913 excavation and discussion have advanced considerably our understanding of mainland Greece before the coming of the Dorians. In the present edition, while the section on early Crete has been left substantially unchanged, the Greek sections of the first chapter have been again re-written, incorporating where possible Bury's material in a revised setting. The accumulation of new evidence over the past two generations and the further sifting of old evidence have also demanded widespread revision in the other chapters.

For technical reasons the plates of the book have been altered only where changes were necessary. This often imposed unwelcome restrictions on the reviser and may excuse some unevenness of style. Passages that have been re-written to introduce new material are enclosed in square brackets.

The notes have been largely recast. Those of the first edition reflected current controversies in British and foreign periodicals; many of Bury's views, then highly controversial, have now been generally accepted and need no defence. Modern writing on Greek history, in books and periodicals, has grown extensively, but to-day's reader is well provided with guides: the bibliographies in the Cambridge Ancient History, of which Bury was himself chief editor until his death, and in other works, justify economy in references to modern works. The emphasis in the new notes has therefore been concentrated on the ancient sources: in particular I have followed the principle established by Bury of illustrating the text, wherever possible, by surviving inscriptions. Several changes have also been made in the illustrations.

Throughout my revision I have tried to preserve the individual character of Bury's work and particularly to make no change in the scale or emphasis of his History.

I am grateful to Miss H. L. Lorimer and to Professor A. J. B. Wace, who allowed me to see proofs of their books before publication; to Mr. T. J. Dunbabin for much profitable discussion; and to Professor Sir J. D. Beazley and Mr. Bernard Ashmole for judicious help in the selection of new illustrations. I have also good cause to repeat Bury's warm tribute to the printers, Messrs. R. and R. Clark.

R. M.

PREFACE TO FIRST EDITION

In determining the form and character of this book, I have been prompted by two convictions. One is that while, in writing a history based on the original authorities and from one's own personal point of view, it is natural and certainly easier to allow it to range into several volumes, its compression into a single volume often produces a more useful book. In the case of a new history of Greece, it seemed worth while to undertake the more laborious task. The other opinion which I venture to hold is this. So far as history is concerned, those books which are capable of enlisting the interest of mature readers seem to me to be best also for informing younger students. Therefore, while my aim is to help education, this book has in view a wider circle than those merely who are going through a course of school or university discipline.

It was a necessary consequence of the limitations of space which I imposed upon myself, that literature and art, philosophy and religion, should be touched upon only when they directly illustrate, or come into some specially intimate connexion with, the political history. It will be found that I have sometimes interpreted this rule liberally ; but it is a rule which could be the more readily adopted as so many excellent works dealing with art, literature, and philosophy are now easily accessible. The interspersion, in a short political history, of a few unconnected chapters dealing, as they must deal, inadequately with art and literature seems useless and inartistic.

The existence of valuable handbooks, within the reach oi
all, on constitutional antiquities has enabled me, in tracing the
development of the Athenian state or touching on the institutions
of other cities, to omit minor details.   The reader must also seek
elsewhere for the sagas of Hellas, for a geographical description
of the country, for the topography of Athens.   On the topography of Athens, and on the geography of Greece, he will find
excellent works to his hand.

There are two cautions which I must convey to the reader,
and it will be most convenient to state them here.   The first
concerns the prehistoric age, which is the subject of the first
chapter of this work.   The evidence gathered by the researches
of archaeologists on the coasts and islands of the Aegean during
the last twenty years, as to the civilisation of prehistoric Greece,
brought historians face to face with a set of new problems, for
which no solutions that can be regarded as certain have yet been
discovered.   The ablest investigators differ widely in their views.
Fresh evidence may at any hour upset tentative conclusions and
force us to seek new interpretations of the data.   The excavations
which are now to be undertaken in Crete, at last restored to its
own Greek world, may lead to unexpected results that may
transform the whole question.   Thus prehistoric Greece cannot
be treated satisfactorily except by the method of discussion, and
in a work like this, since discussion lies outside its scope, a
writer can only describe the main features of the culture which
excavation has revealed, and state with implied reserve the chief
general conclusions, which he considers probable, as to the corre-
lation of the archaeological evidence with the literary traditions
of the Greeks.   He must leave much vague and indefinite.   The
difficulty of the problems is increased by the circumstance that
the literary evidence concerning the doings and goings of the
early Greek folks is largely embedded in myth and harder to
extract from its bed than buried walls or tombs from their
coverings of earth.   The importance of the pre-Greek inhabitants
of Greece, the mixed ethnical character of the historical Greeks,

the comparatively early date of the "Ionian" migration, the continuity of Aegean civilisation, the relation of the so-called "Mycenaean" culture to the culture described by Homer,— these are the main points which I have been content to emphasise.[1]

The second caution applies to all histories of Greece that have been written since the days of Ephorus. The early portion of Greek history, which corresponds to the seventh and sixth centuries B.C., is inevitably distorted and placed in a false perspective through the strange limitations of our knowledge. For at that time (as well as in the centuries immediately preceding, which are almost quite withdrawn from our vision) the cities of the western coast of Asia Minor formed the most important and enlightened part of the Hellenic world, and of those cities in the days of their greatness we have only some disconnected glimpses. Our knowledge of them hardly begins till Persia advances to the Aegean and they sink to a lower place in Greece. Thus the pages in which the Greeks of Asia should have the supreme place are monopolised by the development of elder Greece ; and the false impression is produced that the history of Hellas in the seventh and sixth centuries consisted merely or mainly of the histories of Sparta and Athens and their immediate neighbours. Darkness also envelops the growth of the young Greek communities of Italy and Sicily during the same period. The wrong, unfortunately, cannot be righted by a recognition of it. Athens and Sparta and their fellows abide in possession. *Les absents ont toujours tort.*

In the Notes and References at the end of the volume I have indicated obligations to modern research on special points. Here I must acknowledge my more general obligations to the histories of Grote, Freeman (*History of Sicily*), Busolt, Beloch, E. Meyer (*Geschichte des Altertums*), and Droysen. Though other histories of high reputation, both English and foreign, have

---

[1] It has been a disappointment to me that Professor Ridgeway's promised work on the "Mycenaean" age has not yet appeared.

been respectfully consulted, it is to those mentioned that I am chiefly indebted. But I owe perhaps a deeper debt to the writings of one who, though he has never written a formal history of Greece, has made countless invaluable contributions to its study—Professor U. von Wilamowitz-Möllendorff. With some of his conclusions I do not agree, but I would express here deep sympathy with his methods and admiration for the stimulating virtue of his writings.

Several friends have been good enough to help me. The book has had the advantage of the criticisms of a master of the subject, Mr. Mahaffy, who most kindly read through the proof-sheets. The first chapter is enriched by a small map of the " Mycenaean " sites of Crete, marked for me by Mr. J. L. Myres. Mr. Cecil Smith assisted me in the matter of illustrations taken from antiquities in the British Museum ; and Professor Percy Gardner superintended the preparation of some photographs from busts in the Oxford Galleries.

All the plans and many of the maps (including Bactria and North-Western India) were roughly sketched by myself and then properly drawn by the skilful chartographers Messrs. Walker and Boutall. In the case of a plan or map that is not current, I have stated in the List of Illustrations to what work I am in-debted. Nearly all the reproductions of coins are from coins in the British Museum.

My obligations to Messrs. R. and R. Clark will be understood by those who have had the good fortune to have had works printed at their press.

J. B. BURY.

CONTENTS

INTRODUCTORY

CHAPTER I

THE BEGINNINGS OF GREECE AND THE HEROIC AGE

CHAPTER II

THE EXPANSION OF GREECE

CHAPTER III

GROWTH OF SPARTA

CHAPTER IV

THE UNION OF ATTICA AND THE FOUNDATION OF
THE ATHENIAN DEMOCRACY

CHAPTER V

GROWTH OF ATHENS

CHAPTER VI

THE ADVANCE OF PERSIA TO THE AEGEAN

CHAPTER VII

THE PERILS OF GREECE.   THE PERSIAN AND PUNIC
INVASIONS

CHAPTER VIII

THE FOUNDATION OF THE ATHENIAN EMPIRE

CHAPTER IX

THE ATHENIAN EMPIRE UNDER THE GUIDANCE OF PERICLES

CHAPTER X

THE WAR OF ATHENS WITH THE PELOPONNESIANS

$(431$-421 B.C.$)$

CHAPTER XI

THE DECLINE AND DOWNFALL OF THE ATHENIAN EMPIRE

CHAPTER XII

THE SPARTAN SUPREMACY AND THE PERSIAN WAR

CHAPTER XIII

THE REVIVAL OF ATHENS AND HER SECOND LEAGUE

CHAPTER XIV

THE HEGEMONY OF THEBES

CHAPTER XV

THE SYRACUSAN EMPIRE AND THE STRUGGLE WITH CARTHAGE

CHAPTER XVI

RISE OF MACEDONIA

CHAPTER XVII

THE CONQUEST OF PERSIA

CHAPTER XVIII

THE CONQUEST OF THE FAR EAST

ILLUSTRATIONS

PRINTED IN THE TEXT

MAPS AND PLANS

INTRODUCTORY

GREECE AND THE AEGEAN

THE rivers and valleys, the mountains, bays, and islands of Greece
will become familiar, as our story unfolds itself, and we need not
enter here into any minute description. But it is useful at the very
outset to grasp some general features which went to make the history
of the Greeks what it was, and what otherwise it could not have
been. The character of their history is so intimately connected with
the character of their dwelling-places that we cannot conceive it
apart from their land and seas.

Of Spain, Italy, and Illyricum, the three massy promontories of *The*
which southern Europe consists, Illyricum in the east would have *Illyrian*
closely resembled Spain in the west, if it had stopped short at the *(or Balkan)*
north of Thessaly and if its offshoot Greece had been sunk beneath *peninsula.*
the waters. It would then have been no more than a huge block of
solid land, at one corner almost touching the shores of Asia, as
Spain almost touches the shores of Africa. But Greece, its southern
continuation, has totally different natural features, which distinguish
it alike from Spain the solid square and Italy the solid wedge, and make
the eastern basin of the Mediterranean strikingly unlike the western.
Greece gives the impression of a group of nesses and islands. Yet in *Character*
truth it might have been as solid and unbroken a block of continent, *of Greece :*
on its own smaller scale, as the massive promontory from which it
juts. Greece may be described as a mountainous headland broken
across the middle into two parts by a huge rift, and with its whole *the Gulf of*
eastern side split into fragments. We can trace the ribs of the frame- *Corinth ;*
work, which a convulsion of nature bent and shivered, for the service,
as it turned out, of the human race. The mountains which form *the moun-*
Thessaly's eastern barrier, Olympus, Ossa, and Pelion ; the mountains *tain ribs ;*
of the long island of Euboea ; and the string of islands which seem
to hang to Euboea as a sort of tail, should have formed a perpetual
mountainous chain—the rocky eastern coast of a solid promontory.

Æ

Again, the ridges of Pindus which divide Thessaly from Epirus find their prolongation in the heights of Tymphrestus and Corax, and then, in an oblique south-eastward line, deflected from its natural direction, the chain is continued in Parnassus, Helicon, and Cithaeron, in the hills of Attica, and in the islands which would be part of Attica, if Attica had not dipped beneath the waters. In the same way the mountains of the Peloponnesus are a continuation of the mountains of Epirus. Thus restoring the framework in our imagination and raising the dry-land from the sea, we reconstruct, as the Greece that might have been, a lozenge of land, ribbed with chains of hills stretching south-eastward far out into the Aegean. If nature had given the Greeks a land like this, their history would have been entirely changed ; and by imagining it we are helped to understand how much they owed to the accidents of nature. In a land of capes and deep bays and islands it was determined that waterways should be the ways of their expansion. They were driven as it were into the arms of the sea.

imaginary reconstruction.

The most striking feature of continental Greece is the deep gulf which has cleft it asunder into two parts. The southern half ought to have been an island—as its Greek name, "the island of Pelops," suggests—but it holds on to the continent by a narrow bridge of land at the eastern extremity of the great cleft. Now this physical feature had the utmost significance for the history of Greece ; and its significance may be viewed in three ways, if we consider the existence of the dividing gulf, the existence of the isthmus, and the fact that the isthmus was at the eastern and not at the western end. 1. The double effect of the gulf itself is clear at once. It let the sea in upon a number of folks who would otherwise have been inland mountaineers, and increased enormously the length of the seaboard of Greece. Further, the gulf constituted southern Greece a world by itself ; so that it could be regarded as a separate land from northern Greece—an island practically, with its own insular interests. 2. But if the island of Pelops had been in very truth an island, if there had been no isthmus, there would have been from the earliest ages direct and constant intercourse between the coasts which are washed by the Aegean and those which are washed by the Ionian Sea. The eastern and western lands of Greece would have been brought nearer to one another, when the ships of trader or warrior, instead of tediously circumnavigating the Peloponnesus, could sail from the eastern to the western sea through the middle of Greece. The disappearance of the isthmus would have revolutionised the roads of traffic and changed the centres of commerce ; and the wars of Grecian history would have been fought out on other lines. How important the isthmus was may perhaps be best illustrated by a

Im-PORTANT GEOGRAPH-ICAL FEATURES. 1. The Great Inlet (Gulf of Corinth).

modern instance on a far mightier scale. Remove the bridge which joins the southern to the northern continent of America, and contemplate the changes which ensue in the routes of trade and in the conditions of naval warfare in the great oceans of the globe. 3. Again, if the bridge which attached the Peloponnesus to the mainland had been at the western end of the gulf, the lands along either shore of the inlet would have been accessible easily, and sooner, to the commerce of the Aegean and the orient; the civilisation of north-western Greece might have been more rapid and intense; and the history of Boeotia and Attica, unhooked from the Peloponnesus, would have run a different course.

The character of the Aegean basin was another determining *II. The* condition of the history of the Greeks. Strewn with countless *Aegean.* islands it seems meant to promote the intercourse of folk with folk. The Cyclades, which, as we have seen, belong properly to the framework of the Greek continent, pass imperceptibly into the isles which the Asiatic coast throws out, and there is formed a sort of island bridge, inviting ships to pass from Greece to Asia. The western coast of Lesser Asia belongs, in truth, more naturally to Europe than to its own continent; it soon became part of the Greek world; and the Aegean might be considered then as the true centre of Greece.

The west side of Greece too was well furnished with good *The west.* harbours, and though not as rich in bays and islands as the east, was a favourable scene for the development of trade and civilisation. It was no long voyage from Corcyra to the heel of Italy, and the inhabitants of western Greece had a whole world open to their enterprise. But that world was barbarous in early times and had no civilising gifts to offer; whereas the peoples of the eastern seaboard looked towards Asia and were drawn into contact with the immemorial civilisations of the Orient. The backward condition of western as contrasted with eastern Greece in early ages did not depend on the conformation of the coast, but on the fact that it faced away from Asia; and in later days we find the Ionian Sea a busy scene of commerce and lined with prosperous communities which are fully abreast of Greek civilisation.

The northern coast of Africa, confronting and challenging the *III.* three peninsulas of the Mediterranean, has played a remarkable part *Position of* in the history of southern Europe. From the earliest times it has *Greece in* been historically associated with Europe, and the story of geology *regard to* illustrates the fitness of this connexion. Western Europe and *Africa.* northern Africa were once in days long past united together *Land-* by bridges of continuous land; and this ancient continent, which *bridges in* we might call Europo-Libya, was perhaps inhabited by peoples of a *the Medi-* *terranean* *in the*

pliocene homogeneous race, who were severed from one another when the
period: ocean was let in and the Mediterranean assumed its present shape.
(1) *at* Sicily, a remnant of the old land-bridge, has always been for Italy a
Gibraltar; step to, or a step from, Africa; while Spain needs no island to
(2) *Italy—* bridge her strait.
Sicily—
Tunis.   Greece is a land of mountains and small valleys; it has few
IV. Greece plains of even moderate size and no considerable rivers.   It is
suitable for therefore well adapted to be a country of separate communities, each
small protected against its neighbours by hilly barriers; and the history of
states. the Greeks, a story of small independent states, could not have been
wrought out in a land of dissimilar formation.   The political history
of all countries is in some measure under the influence of geography;
but in Greece geography made itself pre-eminently felt, and fought
along with other forces against the accomplishment of national unity.
The islands formed states by themselves, but, as seas, while like
mountains they sever, may also, unlike mountains, unite, it was less
difficult to form a sea than a land empire.   In the same way, the
hills prevented the development of a brisk land traffic, while, as we
have seen, the broken character of the coast and the multitude of
islands facilitated intercourse by water.

Climate   There is no barrier to break the winds which sweep over the
and pro- Euxine from the Asiatic continent towards the Greek shores and
ductiveness. render Thrace a chilly land.   Hence the Greek climate has a certain
severity and bracing quality, which promoted the vigour and energy
of the people.   Again, Greece is by no means a rich and fruitful
country.   It has few well-watered plains of large size; the cultivated
valleys do not yield the due crop to be expected from the area; the
soil is good for barley but not rich enough for wheat to grow freely.
Thus the tillers of the earth had hard work.   And the nature of
the land had consequences which tended to promote maritime enterprise.   On one hand, richer lands beyond the seas attracted the
adventurous, especially when the growth of the population began
to press on the means of support.   On the other hand, it ultimately
became necessary to supplement home-grown corn by wheat imported
from abroad.   But if Demeter denied her highest favours, the vine
and the olive grew abundantly in most parts of the country, and their
cultivation was one of the chief features of ancient Greece.

CHAPTER I

THE BEGINNINGS OF GREECE AND THE HEROIC AGE

SECT. I. THE ORIGIN OF THE GREEKS

[Less than a century ago Greek mythology, and in particular the great epics of Homer, were the only witnesses to the history of Greece before the coming of the Dorians. When Schliemann, inspired by Homer, set out to find the remains of Agamemnon's kingdom in Mycenae he opened a new epoch. But the dramatic discovery of the great wealth of the Mycenaean shaft graves, while throwing tantalising light on the Homeric poems, soon raised a series of problems which encouraged archaeologists to carry their work farther and farther afield. It was not long before the Homeric poems took a very secondary place in the study of the early history of Greece and the Aegean.

Since Schliemann's day a long series of excavations, increasingly scientific in spirit, has widened the horizon and extended our knowledge so that to-day a provisional historical account can be given. The limitations of archaeology should, however, be clearly recognised. Excavations can find evidence of destruction and changes in culture. The inference from this evidence is primarily the historian's problem, and we are still in a stage where most inferences can be only working hypotheses to be further tested as new evidence is offered. Any account of the second millennium B.C. written to-day must be substantially different from an account written even twenty years ago. There is little doubt that in a further twenty years the story will be further modified. Moreover even with the evidence available to-day a short account involves simplification, which necessarily involves some degree of distortion. In particular, changes are made to seem more abrupt than they are likely to have been, and dates which can at best be approximate carry a false air of precision.

In the Neolithic period Greece was settled with an agricultural population stretching from Thessaly to the south of the Peloponnese, *Early* knowing nothing of metals and their working. Early in the third *Helladic* millennium a new culture known as the early Helladic, the first phase of *culture.* the Bronze Age, enters Greece and it is almost certainly brought by a new population which is found also in the Aegean islands and in south-west Asia Minor. This people has left its clearest traces in non-Greek place-names that survived in historical Greece (the suffixes *nt* and *ss* being the clearest examples). These names are found in south and central Greece in such towns as Corinth, Tiryns and in the rivers Kephissus and Ilissus. They predominate in Crete and are common in the islands. In Asia Minor, where *nth* becomes *nd*, Halicarnassus and Alinda are but two of many examples. Traces of this language are also seen in certain names of plants and birds in later Greek, some of which have passed into our language, for example hyacinth and narcissus. This new people spread widely from the south into Greece but did not enter Thessaly where the neolithic civilisation continued. They introduced the use of copper, and small quantities of gold and silver have also been found, showing that they had connections abroad. Their pottery was of a high quality, with attractive linear designs in bright colours, but still hand-made.

The At some time near 2000 B.C. there are signs of a new people enter-*coming of* ing Greece. A new style of pottery, the Middle Helladic, is intro-*the Greeks.* duced, made on the wheel with different shapes and no affinities with Aegean culture. The surface is grey and polished, usually plain without designs : the pots seem to imitate and to derive from metal vases. In many of the earlier settlements the break in culture is marked by destruction. The typical house-room of the early Helladic culture had a rough apsidal end ; square shapes now come to predominate and the developed form of the primary dwelling is the megaron known to Homer, a large hall with its entrance in the main axis and a hearth standing free of the walls. The new influences, whatever their ultimate origin, come no longer from the Aegean and the east but from the north, and there is a fair measure of agreement that it was this invasion which brought the Greek language into Greece. For there is yet no evidence of any other large-scale movement into Greece before the Dorian invasion that followed the collapse of Mycenaean power ; and the dialect in historical times of Arcadia in the Peloponnese, which was not occupied by the Dorians, shows that the Greek language was established in Greece before the Dorians came.

The next archaeological period, known for convenience as the late

Helladic, begins about 1600 B.C. but marks a change in culture rather than of population. For some two hundred years Crete exercised a dominant influence on the culture of the Greeks, and to Crete we must first turn.]

SECT. 2. AEGEAN CIVILISATION. CRETE

About the Greeks in the early centuries of their settlement we know *Aegean* very little. We know much more of a great non-Greek island civilisa- *civilisa-* tion which, towards 1600 B.C., was to exercise a powerful influence *tion.* on the Greek mainland. It is only recently that we have become aware of this " Aegean " civilisation, as it is called, which had grown steadily in Crete and in Melos and other islands of the Aegean, from remote

FIG. 1.—Two sides of a white steatite Seal, with writing (Crete).

beginnings in the stone age, until towards the end of the third millennium Crete entered upon a period of power and brilliancy *Crete.* which rivals in interest the more famous civilisations of Egypt and Babylon. The monuments which reveal the great age of Crete have been dug out of the earth ; and although Greek tradition remembered that Crete was once a strong sea power, no one suspected that this island had been the home of a life and art highly developed and various, and the centre of a culture which spread far over the Mediterranean Sea.

In the course of the third millennium Crete had passed from the age of stone into the age of metal. The remains of a homogeneous culture have been found all over the island, but the leading settlements, the seats of the most powerful rulers, were Gnossus and Phaestus. Nearly at the middle of the north *Cnossus* coast, the hill of Cnossus is situated a few miles from the sea, *and* close to the banks of a stream (Cairatos). About 2000 B.C., a *Phaestus ;* great palace was erected on this hill ; and at Phaestus in the

FIG. 2A.—Store-jars in the Palace of Cnossus.

FIG. 2B.—Vase with octopuses, Cnossus.

south of the island, a palatial residence arose much about the *the first* same time. These palaces endured for several centuries; and in *palaces,* this period the development of Cretan art was marked by the *c. 2000 B.C.* perfection of polychrome (many-coloured) pottery. At first the surface of the vase was covered with a black glaze on which was painted a bold decorative pattern in white, red, and orange. Later a more pictorial style was introduced. The painter took his subjects from plant and marine life, and represented octopus, dolphin, papyrus, lily with fine effect. The decoration of pottery was strongly influenced in this later phase by the large-scale paintings in palaces and houses. We have some beautiful examples of what Cretan artists could do, such as a fresco picture of a monkey, who is painted in blue, picking white crocuses and placing them in a vase.

One of the most interesting facts about the civilisation of the *Systems of* Cretans is that they could write. We find first a method of picture *writing.* writing, in which each pictorial symbol, such as an ox head, or a *(1) Hiero-* gate, or an eye, represented a word; [1] but at a later period there was *glyphic* likewise used a system of " linear " signs, of which each probably *(before* stood for a syllable. A table of drink offerings, inscribed with *(2) Early* signs of this kind, was found in the cave of Mount Dicte, already *linear* a holy place and afterwards to be associated with the birth of *(before* Zeus.[2] *1600 B.C.).*

We have no clue to the language of these documents. It seems *Language.* unlikely that it was Indo-European; it seems most likely that it was cognate with the tongues of the Lycians and other ancient peoples of western Asia Minor. In eastern Crete a strange language was still spoken in late times when the rest of the island had become Greek; we have some slight records of it which can be read but cannot be interpreted; and it would be natural to suppose that this was the same language which prevailed in the pre-Hellenic period.

It was about 1700 B.C. that the end of this brilliant period of *End of* Cretan history was marked by the partial destruction of the palaces *first palace* of Cnossus and Phaestus. [It seems probable that this was the *of Cnossus,* consequence of a violent earthquake and not of invasion, for no traces *c. 1700 B.C.* of burning have been found, and the disaster was soon repaired. The palaces were rebuilt on a grander scale and Crete now entered on the most brilliant period of her history. Cretan prosperity is seen not only in the new magnificence of the palaces but in the evidence of increasing population throughout the island.]

---

[1] A most remarkable document of pictorial writing found in Crete is a small terra-cotta disc from Phaestus, entirely covered on both sides with picture-characters running in a continuous spiral line. It seems to have been intended for use as a die; and it has been conjectured that the text is a religious hymn. But there is reason for thinking that it is not of Cretan origin, but was imported, perhaps from Lycia.   [2] See below, p. 71.

"Cycladic" civilisation.

Melos.

Aegean civilisation attained its highest bloom in Crete, but it had developed independently in the islands of the Archipelago, especially in Melos, where its continuous growth can be traced in the important settlement of Phylakopi. Melos produces obsidian, which in the stone age and later was in great request for the manufacture of knives and spear-points, and her export of this product, which was taken for instance to Egypt, may explain her early prosperity. Remains have been found which show that the eastern coast of Greece was not unaffected by this insular civilisation.

Troy (the hill now called Hissarlik, "fortress").

The oldest city.

We have still to glance at a great stronghold which towards the end of the third millennium stood on the hill of Troy, commanding the entrance of the Hellespont. It was not the first city that had been reared on that illustrious hill, which rises to the height of about 160 feet, not far from the banks of the Scamander. The earliest settlement, fortified by a rude wall of unwrought stone, can still be traced; and some of its primitive earthware and stone implements have been found. An axe-head of white nephrite seems to show that in those remote days there was a line of traffic, however slow and uncertain, between the Mediterranean and the Far East; for this white jade must have come from Central Asia.

The SECOND CITY.

On the ruins of this primeval city arose a great fortress, girt with a wall of sun-baked brick, built on strong stone foundations. There were three gates, and the angles of the walls were protected by towers. The inhabitants of this city lived in the stone and copper age; bronze was still a rarity. Their pottery was chiefly hand-made. But a treasure of golden ornaments, wrought by skilful craftsmen, shows

FIG. 3.—Ivory figurine of a Boy God, S. Crete.

Fig. 4.—The Plain of Troy

that the place was wealthy. The most important feature to be noted is the outline of the palace in this ancient city. Here at the very outset of Aegean civilisation we find the general plan of the main part of the house very similar to that of the great palaces which were built at Mycenae and other Greek centres more than a thousand years later. From an outer gate we pass through a courtyard, in which an altar stood, into a square preliminary chamber ; and from it we enter the great hall, in the centre of which was the hearth.[1]

Destroyed,
c. 2300
B. C.
An enemy's hand destroyed the castle by fire, and no tradition of its existence has survived. When we come down seven or eight centuries, to the famous city of which it was the precursor, we shall learn the probable secret of the prosperity of its kings.

CHRONO-
LOGY:
Relative;
It may be asked how, without the guidance of literary records, we can fix the successive stages of Aegean civilisation in an ordered series and assign approximate dates to its periods. When we have started with the capital division of time between the age of stone and the age of bronze, the potter's art is the chief clue for establishing a relative chronology within each of those ages. The clay vessels, from the most simple and primitive moulded by hand to the most artistic and elaborate wrought by wheel, can be arranged in a definite series ; and thus the things which are found in the same stratum as a particular class of sherds can be assigned to a definite place in this succession. Such things, found in association with particular stages in the development of pottery, may then become themselves additional criteria for dating remains. The history of Cretan civilisation from the end of the stone age has by this means been arranged in three chief ages, called Early, Middle, and Late " Minoan," and each of these has been subdivided into three periods.[2]

Absolute.
It is to the intercourse of Crete with Egypt that we are indebted for the means of determining roughly the absolute dates of its history, or, in other words, of correlating its chronology with the general

---

[1] In an adjacent building we find not only the preliminary chamber ($\pi\rho\delta\delta\omega\mu\omega$s), but the vestibule outside it, as described by Homer.

[2] [The chronology of Minoan civilisation, with only minor modifications, is still based on the framework established by Sir Arthur Evans :

Early Minoan B.C. 2600-1800
Middle Minoan B.C. 1800-1600
Late Minoan B.C. 1600-1100

The dates are approximate only and the transitions are not abrupt. Periods also overlap, since the pace of development was slower in the more backward parts of the island. Within Late Minoan 1400 B.C., the date of the destruction of Cnossus, marks the beginning of a sharp decline.]

FIG. 5.—Lower Balustrade of Staircase, Palace of Cnossus

chronology of the world. Thus a polychrome Cretan vessel found in the tomb of King Senusert III. (Sesostris) at Egyptian Abydos enables us to conclude that the Second period of the Middle Minoan age was approaching its close about B.C. 1880. Again, the statuette of an Egyptian in diorite stone, inscribed with his name in Egyptian characters, was found in a court of the Cnossian palace, and its style makes it probable that it was wrought under the XIIth or XIIIth Dynasty, perhaps in the second half of the nineteenth century B.C.[1]

The later palace of Cnossus. In this last phase of Cretan greatness, from *c.* 1600-1400 B.C., Cnossus became the dominant power in the island. The palace had been rebuilt on a grander scale, and adapted to more sumptuous needs, though there was no change in the general architectural style ; and about 1500 B.C. it seems to have been extensively remodelled. It covered an area of about five acres. It was not fortified by an exterior wall ; its lords seem to have trusted to their ships for defence against foreign invaders. To the east and to the west of a great central court were extensive labyrinths of rooms and passages, and the remains of staircases show that in some parts the building rose to the height of three or four storeys. The principal halls were lit at one end by open shafts or "light-wells," walled in on three sides, and on the fourth open to the hall from which they were separated by two or three columns. There were bathrooms, and there was an excellent system of drainage by pipes, superior perhaps to any of the contrivances that have been since in use till quite recent times. If the palace had merely served as the habitation of the royal household it need not have been so large ; but it was much more. It was the seat of a government which controlled not merely the neighbouring regions or even the island, but a maritime empire. The administration of this empire was conducted on careful business lines as is shown by the financial documents found in the archives. We may fairly surmise that there existed a well-developed system of administrative machinery which needed considerable room for its offices. The rich tributes which the kings derived from their dependencies were stored in the palace, and various industries were carried on within its walls for the private needs of the monarch and also probably for purposes of commerce. The discovery of an olive press and great jars for oil-storage suggests that not only did the palace supply itself with the oil required for its cooking and its lamp-fuel, but that the king himself may have traded in oil, which seems at this time to

---

[1] The dates of the XIth, XIIth, and following dynasties have been much disputed, but the view has recently gained ground that the XIIth (to which "Sesostris" belongs) began about 2000 B.C., and the XIth may be placed about 2160-2000 B.C.

FIG. 6A.—Throne Hall, Royal Villa of Cnossus.

FIG. 6B.—Painted Jar with papyrus reliefs (Cnossus).

have been one of the principal Cretan exports. Then there was accommodation for the sculptors and painters who were employed in the royal service ; there is evidence that the paints were manufactured on the spot, and a sculptor's workshop has been discovered.

Throne Room. One of the most notable rooms in this spacious palace was the Chamber of the Throne, entered through an anteroom from the central court. The throne is a stone seat adorned with a painted design, and on either side are benches along the wall. Here the king may have sat in council with his ministers. Adjoining this apartment was a room open to the air, containing a tank, and its *Paintings.* walls showed a picture of Egyptian character, a landscape with river, sedge, and palms. Most of the principal chambers and corridors were decorated with fresco paintings, representing solemn processions, gay groups of men and women, scenes of town-life, less often *Fashions.* of war. The fashions of the time are vividly portrayed in a series of miniature frescoes, showing us women, idling in courts or on balconies, with their hair elaborately dressed, wearing costumes which look as if they had been modelled on quite modern fashions, puffed sleeves, flounced skirts, bodices tightly drawn in round the waist. One of the most striking pictures which have survived is that of a tall, handsome cupbearer, evidently belonging to the same race as the *(Thothmes* Cretans (Keftiu) who are represented in a painting of Egyptian Thebes *B.C. 1500-* as bringing offerings to King Thothmes III. in the fifteenth century. *1450.)* Near the northern entrance to their palace the later lords of Cnossus constructed a theatre, capable of holding about 400 *Theatres.* spectators. This was not a new thing ; a theatre of an earlier period has been discovered in the palace of Phaestus. The orchestral area in these early theatres was not circular as in those of later times, but rectangular ; and the performances were probably religious dances in honour of the great Cretan goddess, and perhaps boxing *Bull fights.* matches. The space was not large enough for bull fights, which seem to have been a favourite amusement of the Cretans if we may judge from scenes depicted on wall-paintings and gems, which present acrobats grappling with bulls. Women took part in this dangerous sport. In one painting we see a girl in the air caught on the horns of a bull. The kings had also quieter recreations. A magnificent inlaid gaming board of very beautiful design was found in the palace, made of pieces of ivory overlaid with gold foil, and crystals coloured alternately blue and white by means of bluepaste (*kyanos*) and silver foil on which they were set.[1]

[1] Another Aegean gaming table, made of ivory, was found at old Salamis (Enkomi) in Cyprus ; and some crystal plaques in one of the graves on the acropolis of Mycenae are surmised to be the remains of a similar board. What appear to be ivory pieces for playing the unknown game have also been found in the Cnossian palace.

Fig. 7.—A Gaming-Board, Palace of Cnossus.

The royal villa at Cnossus. Beneath the great palace, close to the river bank and about 130 yards east of the northern entrance gate, was a smaller building which, it has been conjectured, may have been used by the king as a summer retreat. On its smaller scale it seems to have been as sumptuous as the greater dwelling. Here was found, fallen from a room on an upper storey, a superb painted jar, showing the highest point to which the art of the Cnossian potters could attain in the sixteenth century. The decoration, displaying sprays of papyrus and rosettes, is effected by the combination of colour and relief. Here, too, there was a throne-room—a remarkable pillared hall, more than 12 yards long, resembling in its arrangement the Roman basilica or law-court.

The palace of Phaestus. The rebuilding of the palace of Phaestus fell perhaps in the sixteenth century. Like that of Cnossus it was unfortified, and it was built on a very similar plan, and in the same fashion of architecture. Here, too, there was a large court in the centre, surrounded by pillared reception halls and store-rooms, and a smaller court in the west of the building. The residence of Phaestus was distinguished by an imposing entrance, with a flight of twelve steps forty-five feet broad ; and though it was much smaller in extent than the rival palace of Cnossus, and its walls were not adorned with such rich and various paintings, its external appearance seems to have been more imposing, for it was built upon the top of a hill and dominated the wide valley of the Mesara. About two miles off, at a place now called Hagia Triada, a well-built house has been found which seems to have served as a pleasure-residence for the potentates of the neighbouring palace.[1]

Cretan towns. Not far from the palace of Cnossus there must have been a populous town. Whole Cretan towns have been excavated in eastern Crete, and much has been found to illustrate the town life of the common people and the artisans ; for instance, the house of a carpenter, with all his tools, his chisels, saws, awls, and nails.[2] But of the appearance of a flourishing town, such as Cnossus must have been, we can better gain an idea from the façades of private houses which are represented on mosaic plaques of porcelain discovered in the palace. The houses were of several storeys ; some had two doors, others one ; the windows above might have four or six panes ; and there seem to be unwindowed openings in the upper storeys,

---

[1] It is remarkable that while valuable art treasures of the sixteenth century have been found at Hagia Triada, few objects of interest have been unearthed at Phaestus itself.

[2] At Gournia (ancient name unknown), which seems to have been burned down about 1500 B.C. Palaikastro, where the plan of a town has also been laid bare, was the ancient Heleia.

which might serve the purposes of balconies. These Cretan houses show considerable likeness to contemporary houses in Egypt.

There seems to be no evidence that there were public temples in *Religion.* Crete at this period. [The sacred places were in caves and on the peaks of certain mountains. Here the people brought offerings and celebrated some form of public cult; but there were also domestic sanctuaries in palaces and private houses. Religion centred round the forces of nature and nature-daemons in the form of animals are often represented by the Cretan artist. The chief divinity seems to have been a nature-goddess, mistress of animals, who is sometimes repre- *Mother-* sented as guarded by lions, sometimes associated with doves, who *Goddess.* symbolised the descent of a deity; she was served by priestesses.] She was closely connected with a male divinity, whether her consort or her son, who seems to have been subordinate to her. In later times the Greeks conceived this god as Zeus, son of Rhea and nurtured in the Idaean cave. Both the goddess and the god were associated with the double-axe, a fetish in which the deity was supposed to dwell. We find the same worship of the double-axe in western Asia Minor among the Carians. This symbol was so frequently represented on the walls of the Cnossian palace that it might almost be called the palace of the *Labyrinth.* double-axe; and, as the Carian name for the double-axe was *labrys*, it has been suggested that the palace was known as the *labyrinthos*. This would explain the origin of the curious Greek legend that Minos, king of Cnossus, kept in a labyrinth the monstrous Minotaur who devoured the tribute of youths and virgins brought from overseas. The intricate plan of the palace might well suggest a maze.

We have seen that the art of writing was long familiar to the Cretans. *Later* In this later period a new and more advanced system of linear signs *linear* was in use. The kings kept accurate records and accounts. Hundreds *writing.* of written documents have been found in the Cnossian palace, consisting of small rectangular tablets of clay, which were preserved in wooden boxes secured by seals. As we have no clue to the language they cannot be read; but the numerical symbols can be identified. The arithmetical system was decimal, and there were signs for fractions. It has been inferred from the frequent occurrence of numerals, and from the insertion of figures representing objects, that many of the documents are accounts relating to the stores. The *Weights,* Cretans possessed a system of weights, and here they seem to have been indebted, through whatever intermediate channel, to the kingdom of Babylonia, for their standard was derived from what is known as the light Babylonian talent. And they had a metal currency. *Money.* Pieces of gold and silver, and bronze ingots have been found, which can only have been used for the purpose of exchange.

The power and splendour of the kings of Cnossus were at their

Extent of
Cretan
power and
influence.
height in the fifteenth century. These kings were undoubtedly the richest and most powerful in Crete, and it is not improbable that they now exercised overlordship over the rulers of Phaestus and over the other towns of the island, in many of which striking remains of Aegean civilisation have been unearthed. Their fleets controlled the Aegean sea ; they dominated the islands ; and their civilisation spread, as we shall see, to the mainland of Greece. But Cretan influence radiated to more distant shores, by trade and even by colonisation. The commercial intercourse with Egypt, which had existed from primitive times, became probably more regular and frequent ; oil and pottery were exported to the lands of the Nile ;

Keftiu,
Egyptian
name for
Cretans.
" the kings of the country of the Keftiu and the isles of the great sea " brought offerings to the great monarchs of the XVIIIth Dynasty. And the influence of Egypt can be traced in the Cretan culture of the time. The Philistines who settled in southern Palestine are now supposed to have been colonists from Crete ;[1] and remains found in Sicily and Spain testify that the island of Minos sent products and offshoots of its civilisation far to the west.

Minos.
The later Greeks associated the Cretan supremacy in the Aegean with the name of the great sea-lord Minos. There is, however, a difficulty about Minos. In Homer he appears as an Achaean ruler in Crete, two generations before the Trojan War (that is, in the thirteenth century). It was thought by some Greeks in later times that there were two kings of this name, of whom the earlier reigned towards the end of the fifteenth century. But there is no early evidence for the existence of the supposed Minos I.[2]

SECT. 3. MYCENAEAN CIVILISATION (1600-1100 B.C.)

The
records of
Mycenaean
civilisa-
tion.
[The highly developed civilisation of Crete began to exercise a dominant influence on the Greek mainland from about 1600 B.C., and the first clear evidence comes from the shaft graves of Mycenae. Mycenae was well placed to be a centre of power in an insecure age. Some twelve miles inland, at the north-east corner of the Argive plain, it had good corn land to support it, a strong defensive and strategic position, and a good water-supply. Built on a hill rising some 900 feet above sea-level, it overlooked the Argive plain and commanded

[1] Minoa was an ancient name of Gaza. The same name, in Amorgos, Siphnos, and Paros, is a record of Cretan rule over the Aegean islands.

[2] So far as the Catalogue in *Iliad* ii. may be regarded as preserving a record of the relative resources of the Greek states *c.* 1200 B.C., it does not suggest that Crete at this time had an exceptionally strong fleet. Crete sent 80 ships, less than Pylos which sent 90, not to speak of Argolis (180, besides 50 lent to the Arcadians) and Thessaly (220).

CRETE
(c. 2000 - 1000 B.C.)

Stadia
0   50   100   200   300

English Miles
0   5   10   20   30   40   50

Eleutherna

Axoso

Sybrita
Pantamodio
Shiviakin
Kamares
Kastamanitzao
Kastelo

Knossos
Kalokla
Tuleta
Kourtes
Legortino

Milato
Mallia
Ag. George
Kaprana Omales
Psychro Tsermiado
Papura
Godi
Fortezz
Gournia
Pachio
Katsoudi
Pseira
Prachsos
Petras
Siteia
Palaikastro
Zakro
Goudouras
Pyrgos
Erganos
Kastri
Sphachiandres

Christos Mallia
Kalamafke
Ketaton
K. Aivi

Arctinia
Stalkano

Ag. Onuphrios

Kourtes

Phaestos

Legortino

Longitude East 25° of Greenwich

Walker & Boutall sc.

FIG. 8.

Fig. 9A.—Gravestone with Chariot (Acropolis of Mycenae).

easy routes to the Isthmus. There are no traces of settlement on the site in Neolithic times, but it was occupied early in the Bronze Age and became a flourishing centre in the Middle Helladic period. On the hill-top was built the King's palace and a small area was probably surrounded by a strong wall. Outside the wall, on the lower slope of the hill, was a spreading cemetery, part of which was used as the burial ground of the royal dynasty. Shafts were *The shaft* sunk in the rock. The body, elabor- *graves of* ately dressed, was laid at the bottom *Mycenae* of the shaft and beside the body prized possessions to accompany the dead. The graves were covered with stone slabs and over them were set up tombstones with linear designs or figured scenes of war and the chase in low relief, the first monumental sculpture of the Greek mainland. The graves are six in number, contain the remains of nineteen persons, and cover a period of roughly one hundred years (*c.* 1600-1500). Their most astonishing feature is the great wealth and the wide contacts that they witness in vessels of gold and silver, golden jewelry, richly decorated daggers, amber and faience beads, fine pottery. The men's faces were covered with golden masks ; the children were wrapped in sheet gold. Who were these princes, and whence came their wealth ? The problem looms large, because we have no such series of graves elsewhere in Greece of the time. The later raising of the level at this point when the cemetery was no longer used for burial has guarded the graves from robbers, and the treasures therefore stand out in more splendid isolation.

FIG. 9B.—Inlaid Dagger-blade with Nilotic scene (Mycenae).

The finest gold and silver cups, the choicest pottery and seals are undoubtedly the product of Cretan craftsmen, and such Cretan influence can be seen spreading through Greece in the succeeding period. A Cretan control of the Greek mainland with Cretan over-lords in the most accessible fortresses provides an attractive solution and is still held by some. But the arguments against such a view seem decisive. The contents of the graves suggest a barbaric splendour very different from the Cretan way of life. The types represented in the death masks are, in some cases at least, almost certainly not Cretan. The gravestone reliefs have no parallel in Crete and the megaron of the contemporary Mycenaean palaces is not found in the Cretan palaces. Though the large body-shield, well known from Homer's description, is shared with Crete, the graves have preserved a helmet faced with slivers of boars' tusks, a type which is confined to the mainland. Amber which came from the head of the Adriatic is much prized in Mycenae at this time, but little is found in Crete. It is probable that Cretan craftsmen rather than Cretan princes came to Greece, perhaps following the earthquake at Cnossus. What seems a sudden access of wealth might be explained by a successful raid on Crete or the development of power and foreign contacts. The dynasty of the shaft graves may have been newcomers from the north, but there is no sign of a general invasion at this date and the question must be left open until more evidence accumulates.

One other significant development is found in this phase. When the shaft-grave cemetery was abandoned a new type of royal tomb was built of striking magnificence, the so-called tholos tomb, normally built into the side of a hill. A passage of approach, the *dromos*, leads through a portal into a round vaulted chamber. This chamber, of beehive shape, is formed by rings of well-joined stones, which grow narrower as they rise and are crowned by a roof-stone. The type, first developed perhaps at Mycenae, spreads through southern and central Greece and is reserved for princes : the great noble families meanwhile built more modest square chamber-tombs, based on the same ideas.

For some two hundred years Cretan influence on pottery and metal work predominated in Greece and traces of it have been found at most of the centres to which Homer attributes wealth and power, at Orcho-menus and Thebes in Boeotia, at Amyclae in Lacedaemon, and in the Pylian Kingdom of Nestor.

In pottery Cretan subjects and shapes are taken over by the main-land potter. At first the subjects, mainly drawn from plant and marine life, are treated naturalistically and a single theme covers the whole vessel. Later the design becomes more conventionalised and the area of the vase is divided into panels. Mainland vases of the period are found outside Greece and even reach as far as Egypt.

With the third and last archaeological period, the late Helladic, we *Collapse* come to rather firmer ground.   About 1400 B.C. there is evidence of *of Cretan* widespread destruction in Crete.   The royal palace of Cnossus was *power* laid in ruins and here and at other places fire accompanied the destruction.   The evidence of fire suggests a sack rather than an earthquake, and whereas Cnossus and Phaestus had earlier recovered from earthquake their power was now broken.   The invaders have left but scanty traces of their settlement on the island, and there is no sharp break in culture, but the steady deterioration in building and craftsmanship shows that the glory of Crete has departed.

That the invaders came from the mainland is probable but not certain.   What is certain is that with the fall of Cnossus and the *Growing* collapse of Crete, Mycenaean power and wealth develop rapidly both *power of* inside and outside Greece.   Nor was wealth confined to Mycenae. *Mycenae.* A common civilisation spreads through Greece and has left traces of its magnificence at widely scattered points.   From 1400-1200 Greece was wealthier and probably more united than it was to be again for more than 500 years.

In this phase of greatness Mycenae almost certainly played the dominant role.   The strength of her position has already been seen. The use she made of that position is best attested in the period after 1400 B.C.   It was during the fourteenth century (probably soon after 1350 B.C.) that the protected area of Mycenae's hill was enlarged. *New* The new walls, averaging some six metres in thickness, were, for most *fortifica-* of the circuit, constructed of huge irregular blocks of limestone, *tions at* packed with small stones and clay.   Where extra strength was required *Mycenae.* or appearance was particularly important, blocks of conglomerate were used, hammer-dressed and laid in regular courses.   The most striking feature of the new wall was the western gate, ensconced in a corner of the wall which at this point ran in south-eastward and then turned outward due west, thus enclosing and commanding the approach to the gate.   The lintel of the doorway is formed by a huge square block of stone, and the weight of the wall resting on it is lightened by the device of leaving a triangular space.   This opening is filled by a sculptured relief in hard limestone representing two lionesses standing opposite each other on either side of a pillar, on whose pedestal their forepaws rest.   They are, as it were, watchers who ward the castle, and from them the gate is known as the Lion Gate.   The composition admirably fits the space and, with strict economy, combines realism of treatment with a strong architectural sense.   The unknown artist, working with crude tools of bronze, has created a masterpiece.   To protect the gate a strong bastion was

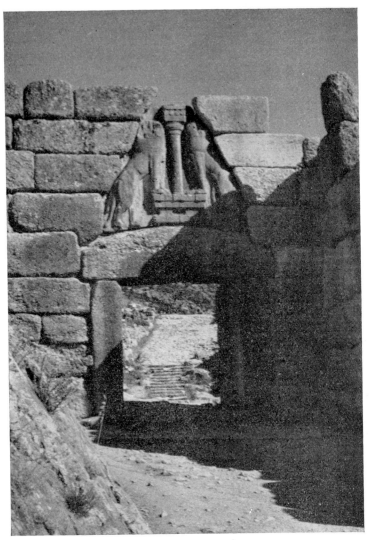

Fig. 10.—Lion Gate, Mycenae.

built on the west to threaten the shieldless side of an attacking enemy. The line of the new wall cut across the cemetery which had been outside the earlier settlement, but the shaft graves of the royal dynasty were enclosed within the circuit. At this point the ground level was raised, the gravestones carefully re-erected, and the area enclosed in a circle of upright stone slabs to mark its religious character. On the top of the citadel the King's palace was thoroughly reconstructed and enlarged and, by bold terracing and levelling, the architect adapted the difficult site to his ambitious plan, so that the most important apartments could be laid out in the most suitable and commanding positions. The detailed plan of the palace cannot be recovered but the main sequence of Throne Room, Great Court, and Megaron, preceded by columned porch and vestibule, can be traced. These public quarters were gaily decorated. Fragments of frescoes show women, elaborately dressed, in procession, others are decorated with spirals, lotus and rosettes. The floors of vestibule and megaron were covered with painted stucco with coloured linear designs, bordered with blocks of gypsum. To the north of the megaron were the domestic

quarters and evidence has been found of store-rooms and a shrine. The fortified area was reserved for the King's palace, the houses of his chief retainers, and humbler quarters for guards, craftsmen, and workers. The rest of the population lived in unwalled settlements on the neighbouring hills.

It is to roughly this time that *" Treasury* the greatest of the tholos tombs *of Atreus."* should be dated, the so-called Treasury of Atreus. What marks it out from its predecessors, apart from its great size, is the fine workmanship of its walling, the monumental character of the entrance, and the magnificent proportions and decoration of the chamber. The entrance passage or *dromos* which runs into the side

FIG. 11A.—Column from the portal of the " Treasury of Atreus " (Mycenae).

of the hill, floored with cement, is six metres wide and thirty-six metres long. The walls of the passage, over ten metres high at the inner end, are built of well-coursed blocks of conglomerate and, at the west end, are irregularly bonded with the face of the tomb. The doorway into the tholos is 5·4 m. high and 2·7 wide, narrowing at the top. It is framed by two tall engaged half-columns of green stone, carved in relief with a zigzag pattern of spirals, beading, and flutes crowned with capitals of a similar pattern. In a relieving triangle over the door, reminiscent of the Lion Gate, was set a large block of red stone chosen for its decorative effect and probably linked by a design which cannot be precisely recovered, with two smaller half-columns

FIG. 11B.—Restoration of the " Treasury of Atreus " (inside).

continuing the line of the lower pair that frame the door. The doorway is 5·4 m. deep and the inner lintel is formed by a massive block of conglomerate, calculated to weigh about a hundred tons. This huge block, brought into place no doubt by rollers along the hillside rather than raised from below, overlaps considerably the jambs on either side and is clearly intended to sustain at each end the downward lateral thrust of the upper vault, one sign among many of the considerable skill of the architect. The tholos, which is 14·5 m. across and 13·2 m. high, is built of large blocks of conglomerate hammerdressed and laid in regular courses, narrowing gradually to the summit

GULF OF CORINTH

Sicyon

CORINTH

New-Corinth

Korakou
CORINTH

Acrocorinth

Cenchreai

Phlius

(Neochóri)

Cleonai

Nemea

(Chiliomódi)

(H. Vasilios)

Tenea

Treton M.

(Cléniai)

(Stepháni)

(Hagi. eri)

Elias

MYCENAE

Cephalari

(Phichtia)

(Dervenaki)

Sziro

(Limnaes)

(Kutsopódi)

Inachus

Heraion

(Chéli)

(Chónika)

Midea

ARACHNAION

Larisa
ARGOS

TIRYNS

THE ARGIVE PLAIN

Stadia
0   50   100

Nauplia

(Pronia)

English Miles
0 1 2 3 4 5   10

Tolon

Asine

GULF OF ARGOS

FIG. 12A.

where the chamber is crowned with a large roof-stone. The stones
of the walls are roughly triangular in shape, with only the inner
surface prepared : in the heart of the wall the spaces are filled with
small stones and clay, and to make the structure water-tight the upper
part of the dome, which stood above the level of the hill, was covered
with clay. The walls of the vaulted chamber were decorated with a
pattern of bronze rosettes, and a door, similar to that of the main
portal, admits to a side-chamber hewn in the rock, its walls decorated
with sculptured alabaster plates.

*Mycenae
and the
Argive
plain.*
　　　The immediate sphere of Mycenae's influence can be clearly
traced. From the same period as the building of the new palace and
city wall date the remains of a network of prepared roads radiating

FIG. 12B.—Prehistoric Road (Argolis).

from Mycenae, marked by the bridges that carried them over streams
and culverts and by low embankments on hillsides. Northwards three
roads ran to the isthmus fortresses, the two western joining at Cleonae,
the eastern going by Tenea ; from the other side of the Corinthian
gulf roads ran to the fortresses of Boeotia. Southwards traces have
been found of a road going to the site of the later temple of Hera, and
the other settlements on the borders of the Argive plain were doubtless
linked up by similar roads. For Mycenae's special domain was the
Argive plain guarded at crucial points by fortresses under vassal
princes. The Larissa above Argos guarded the entry from the west,
Tiryns held guard over the open coast-line of the gulf. Nauplia, at
the south-west corner, was a useful port, and on the east side of the
plain there was a settlement at Prosymna, the site of the later Heraeum,
and princes ruled at Dendra-Midea which guarded the route to
another settlement at Asine. Reflections of Mycenae's wealth have
been found at all these sites and tholos tombs from Dendra-Midea

have recently yielded particularly rich treasures. But of them all Tiryns has the longest history and the most revealing monuments. *Tiryns.* Tiryns stands on a long low rock about a mile and a half from the sea and was probably occupied before Mycenae. The ruins of the great palace still enable us to trace the main ground plan in its final phases. The south and higher end of the hill was surrounded with a strong wall of fortification and within the walls was built the great palace. The main entrance, on the east side, was approached by a

Fig. 13.—Fortification Wall, Asine.

long passage between the inner wall of the fortress and the wall of the palace. A portico leads into a large courtyard from which an inner gate gives entrance to an inner courtyard with an altar. From this inner courtyard a vestibule and fore-hall lead into the main megaron with its central hearth, surrounded by four wooden pillars to support a flat roof. Beside the large megaron, and approached separately, with a separate courtyard, is a much smaller megaron. The view that this represents the women's megaron we may discard, for in Mycenaean art there is no evidence of the segregation of the sexes typical of classical Greece. We should think rather perhaps of the large megaron as the public reception room, and the smaller as the private quarters of the royal family. While the megaron is the central feature marking a sharp difference from the palaces of Crete, there

LOWER CITADEL

Entrance Passage

MIDDLE CITADEL

Main Gate

Back Entrance to Harem

Megaron

Megaron

Hearth

Preliminary Hall

Vestibule

Courtyard

Courtyard

Altar

Postern

Inner Gate

Outer Gate of the Palace

Large Courtyard

Gallery Store Houses

THE PALACE
or
UPPER CITADEL
of
TIRYNS

Scale of Yards
0 5 10   20   30

Fig. 14A.

FIG. 14B. —Frieze, alabaster and cyanus, of Palace of Tiryns.

are a number of rooms, including a bathroom, built beside the megaron more reminiscent of the arrangement of the palace of Cnossus and, as at Cnossus, there are traces of stairs showing that some parts of the palace had one or more upper storeys.   More reminiscent of Crete are the frescoes on the walls and the patterned decoration of the floors, inspired from Crete if not the work of Cretans.   The hill was monopolised by the palace, the people lived in the plain below.

Mycenaean culture in Greece.   While we can be reasonably certain that the princes of the Argolid owed allegiance to Mycenae, we can only conjecture how far afield in Greece this power reached and what form it took.   Homer pictures the Achaean princes as recognising the overlordship of Agamemnon of Mycenae, and, however loose the structure may have been, common enterprises under a single command are not unlikely.   Some such union, as we shall see, is suggested by foreign records.   Whatever the political relation between the princes of the various strongholds in Greece, it is clear that they enjoyed a common culture whose main centre of influence was Mycenae.   Striking remains of this period have been found widely spread throughout Greece.   At Athens there are remains of a palace and a fortress wall on the Acropolis, with a tholos tomb below, and other strongholds in Attica.   In Boeotia remains of a palace with some traces of wall-paintings have been found on the Cadmeia, the citadel of historical Thebes ; while at Orchomenos the " golden " the palace remains yielded wall-paintings comparable with those of Tiryns, representing sports of the bull-ring and other themes from the Cretan painters' repertoire.   Here too was a rich tholos tomb rivalling the most ambitious from Mycenae, which had a second chamber covered by a stone ceiling adorned with a curious design in low relief, an arrangement of meandering spirals and   fan - shaped leaves bordered by rosettes, producing the effect of a carpet.   Similar remains have been found in the territory of Corinth, in Messenia and in the western cities of Odysseus' Homeric realm. And now for the first time this advanced culture penetrates southern Thessaly and leaves its mark at Iolcos and other sites.

FIG. 15.—Gold Cup from Vapheio.

The pottery of this period (from 1400 B.C.) marks a break with the strong Cretan influence.   The naturalistic designs of plant and sea life are abandoned and the surface is divided into panels. Human figures appear, and simple linear designs become more common, recalling the period that preceded Minoan influence. Though a common style can be seen the manufacture of this pottery was distributed over several cities with local variations, most marked in character at Rhodes and Cyprus ; and it was carried far afield, outside as well as inside Greece. New types of armour also appear. The large figure - of - eight shield which covered the whole body, cumbersome and unwieldy, has passed out of date, to survive in religious dedications. At first it was succeeded by the tower shield, in appearance like the vertical section of a cylinder, with straight sides and rectangular base, curved at the top, to protect the face, guarding the sides but not coming below the knee. The tower shield in turn was soon succeeded by the smaller and more wieldy round shield, probably

FIG. 16A.—Thrusting Swords (L.), Cut-and-thrust Sword (R.), Mycenae.

FIG. 16B. — Gold Intaglio with combat of warriors, showing shape of shield.

introduced from the east. Swords too have changed. In the shaft graves they are mainly of Cretan type, designed for thrusting, but by the fourteenth century the more dangerous cut-and-thrust sword has been introduced, and to meet the new sword metal helmets gradually replace leather. But by the thirteenth century the sword is no longer the main weapon of attack. In Homer's epics and in classical times

FIG. 17A. — Warrior Vase (Mycenae).

the thrusting spear has taken its place. On a Mycenaean vase of the late thirteenth century we get a glimpse of the new equipment. A woman watches a file of soldiers proceeding to battle. They wear metal plumed helmets and carry in their right hands the long thrusting spear. The shield, round and small, but with a segment cut from the bottom, is carried on the left arm. The upper part of the body is protected by a leather corselet, and the legs are protected by leather leggings to be replaced in the later hoplite phalanx by metal greaves. Weapons were still made of bronze. Iron was a precious metal,

FIG. 17B.—Painted Gravestone with warriors (Mycenae, lower town).

reserved for rings and jewelry. The princes went forth to war in two-horsed war chariots which consisted of a board to stand on and breastwork of wicker.

It was an age of sharp contrasts. Dominating the community was the king's palace, magnificently furnished, the scene of lavish hospitality for his chief retainers and his guest friends from abroad, the scene of banqueting and minstrelsy. In this splendour the nobles shared with their women, for in Mycenaean living seclusion of the women of the house was unknown. The men wore long hair, tied or plaited. Razors have been found in the tombs, but in contrast with the Cretans who always shaved, they often let the beard grow. It is not certain that they even went naked with mere loin aprons, like Cretans; their normal dress was the close-fitting chiton and skirt. The women of the nobility wore tight-fitting jackets with open bosoms and wide gown skirts, flounced and pleated. They wore their hair high coiled in rings, letting the ends fall behind, with bands round the brow. They delighted in jewelry, especially of gold, necklaces, bracelets, and earrings. The men, to judge from the vivid scenes on seals, were great hunters and they delighted in chariot races and other contests. It was a gay society and there is little trace of morbid undercurrents in their religion or their burial customs.

Fig. 18.—Gem showing Female Dress.

Burial customs.

Though nearly all the tholos tombs have long since been plundered, the Mycenaean attitude to death can be inferred from many of the better-preserved chamber tombs. The body, fully dressed, was carried into the tomb on a wooden bier and left on the floor. By the side of the corpse were placed arms and other valued possessions and jars to contain wine, oil, and grain. The door of the tomb chamber was then sealed and the mourners held a commemorative feast outside, the ceremony apparently ending with a libation followed by the shattering of the cups on the door. The entrance passage was then filled with earth and a stone marker set up to identify the site. When the next member of the family died, the tomb was opened again and the new body laid to rest with the same accompaniments. Little respect was paid to the earlier burials and, as the chamber floor became filled, the bones were swept aside or thrown into the entrance passage: valuable objects from earlier burials were also apparently taken away without scruple. It seems that the spirit was considered to leave the body when the flesh had decomposed. Until then the dead must have his possessions and food for the long journey to the nether world, and the door must be sealed to prevent escape. But once the spirit had departed no sanction attached to the bones.

Religion.

Of Mycenaean religion we can say less. No temples have been found though palaces contained domestic shrines. From figured representations, however, the most important deity seems to have been a mother goddess, resembling in conception the great mother goddess of Anatolia and the Cretan goddess. Perhaps a cult already existed of the goddesses who were worshipped later at Eleusis, for an exquisite ivory from the palace shrine at Mycenae depicts two female figures and a boy, suggesting the triple cult at Eleusis of Demeter, Persephone, and Iakchos, personifying the beneficent powers of nature.

Mycenae was not self-sufficient.   She grew her own barley, olives, and vines and had ample supplies of good building stones and clay for pottery.   But the raw material for her weapons came from without, copper for bronze perhaps from Cyprus, for arrow-heads flint from Egypt, and obsidian from the island of Melos.   For the refinements of living she relied primarily on the east, whence came her gold and

FIG. 19.—Ivory group, Mycenae.   ? Demeter, Persephone, Iakchos.

silver and the ivory which the Mycenaean craftsman, taking his lessons from Syria and Phoenicia, used with such delicacy and skill.   Writing was used by the Mycenaeans, and fragments of Cretan linear script *Mycenaean* have survived on pottery and, more important, in a large find of clay *writing* tablets from the palace at Pylos.   Attempts to reconcile the pottery *and* scratchings with the Greek language have not been convincing and it *language.* appears that the language of the Pylos tablets is at least akin to the Cretan.   That the common language of the country was Greek is a

Aegean Civilisation,
in the second millennium B.C.

Stadia
0   500   1000

English Miles
0   50   100

FIG. 20.

Walker & Boutall sc.

reasonable inference from the surviving dialects of the lands not occupied by the later invaders from the north, but it is possible that the official language of court documents was taken over from Crete.

The rich life of the nobility, given to fighting and banqueting, was not shared by the common people. They lived in unprotected villages, worked the fields, laboured on the buildings, and waited on their masters. It was a far cry to the democratically shared wealth and splendour of Periclean Athens.

The distribution of Mycenaean pottery shows contacts with the *Mycenaean* west in Sicily and south Italy, but the main stream of Mycenaean *influence* penetration is towards the wealthier east. With the fall of Cnossus, *spreads abroad.*

FIG. 21.—Ivory Box from Encomi, Cyprus.

Greek goods penetrated the eastern Mediterranean in increasing volume. Mainland vases had already found their way to Egypt before 1400, but at Tel-el-Amarna in the second quarter of the fourteenth century the finds are so numerous as to suggest a settlement of Greeks, and similar evidence comes from Gurob. A more solid reflection of the eastward movement is the settlement of Rhodes and Cos from the mainland early in the fourteenth century, and the colonisation, or at least widespread settlement, in Cyprus, rich in copper. Greeks probably settled along the coast of Caria and Pamphylia, but the great Cilician plain, a more attractive area for settlement, was for long closed by the Hittite fortresses of Mersin at the western edge, and Tarsus in the centre. While Egypt with its wealth of gold from Nubia, its papyrus so useful in the making of sails and ropes, and its many luxuries was always a dazzling goal to the Greeks, the north Syrian coast was also a useful centre where goods could be exchanged. Here, at Ugarit (Ras-Shamra), the Greeks established themselves in a foreign quarter of the town and harbour. The settlement goes back to the fifteenth century and may have been established by Cretans or Greeks under strong Cretan influence; but from the fourteenth century mainland influence predominates and we may imagine Greeks exchanging there the products of the Aegean for the luxuries of the east such as gold, ivory, and textiles,

FIG. 22.—Siege-scene on a silver vessel; shield above in left corner (Mycenae).

and making for distribution in the Near East the bronze cut-and-thrust sword which the Mycenaeans had recently adopted. For Ugarit was a brisk trading centre resembling the sixth-century Tyre, vividly described by Ezekiel, trading with Egypt and the rich lands of Mesopotamia. From Ugarit and other Syrian ports Greek merchandise found its way to the hinterland of Syria and south to Palestine, where the finds of Mycenaean sherds are steadily increasing.

While the main thrust seems to have been into the eastern Mediterranean it is probable that the Greeks also turned their attention to the western coast of Asia Minor, but here archaeologists have had less opportunity and we must wait until the coastal sites can be systematically explored. At Miletus there was certainly a Greek settlement in this period, at Colophon probably, and possibly Phocaea ; Samos we should expect to be included in this sphere and there is reason to believe that it was. But for Chios we have no evidence, and though Lesbos has been more fully investigated and has yielded Mycenaean sherds there is no evidence for settlement. So far as our evidence goes at present it seems that the sphere in the north-west later occupied by the Aeolian migration was not settled by Greeks in this period.

This striking penetration of the east suggests enterprise and power *Achaeans* and there is some reason to believe that it was not the work of inde- *and* pendent adventurers. Such is the natural interpretation of a series of *Hittites.* important documents from the imperial archives of the Hittites. The Hittites had established themselves as the dominant people in Asia Minor about 2000 B.C. with their capital at Boghazkoi. At roughly the time of the fall of Cnossus they were reaching the height of their power and even penetrating southwards to compete with Egypt for the control of the rich lands of Syria. The struggle which ensued between the two powers weakened both, and the Hittite empire in Asia Minor collapsed about 1200 B.C. under an invasion from the north, or revolt from within. Their capital was looted and destroyed but a substantial part of the imperial archives inscribed on clay tablets has been preserved and deciphered.

These documents refer frequently to the King of Ahhiyava and his relations with the Hittite King. The contexts in which the King-dom of Ahhiyava appears make it clear that this Kingdom is on the coast or over the seas, and nearly all scholars are now agreed that we have here the first documentary evidence for the Achaeans, the name most commonly applied to the Greeks by Homer. One of the main problems raised by these documents is the identification of place-names. Very few can be securely identified and the location of incidents in which the Achaeans are involved should be postponed until further evidence makes the picture clearer. But though at the best we can make only attractive guesses about detailed incidents, the general style of the correspondence is important to the historian. The powerful King of the Hittites, a world power of the first rank, addresses the Achaean King as " brother " and with some respect. On one tablet the King of Ahhiyava was even recognised as a great King on a level with the Kings of Egypt, of Mitanni, and Assyria (though the entry for some reason was later erased). At some point on the periphery of the Hittite empire, probably in south-west Asia Minor, the brother of the King of Ahhiyava is in control, but he has to recognise his rule as a gift of the Hittite King. Negotiations are delicate, the Achaeans encroach upon the territory of the Lycians, the threat of counteraction follows. All is patched up again. We hear of enemies of the Hittite King banished to Ahhiyava, but also of protests against the reception of disloyal servants of the Hittite King. The presents of the King of Ahhiyava are welcome at the great king's court. The god of the King of Ahhiyava is summoned for help when the Hittite king is ill. Relations, to judge from the records, were first established in the fourteenth century and end late in the thirteenth. They are outwardly friendly but often strained. We feel that the Achaeans are making the most of their opportunities without risking an open breach. The last reference is a protest from the Hittite King against an Achaean raid on Cyprus towards the end of the thirteenth century.

These records, fragmentary and tantalising as they are, show clearly that the King of Ahhiyava wielded considerable power and could be held responsible for the actions of his vassals in the east, strengthening the impression that the ruler of Mycenae controlled, however loosely, a great part of the Greek world.

Unsettlement in the Near East.
Towards the end of the thirteenth century Egyptian records take up the story. Egypt, worn out by her long struggle with the Hittites, was temporarily exhausted, and appeared to be an easy prey. In 1221 King Merneptah had to face a league of invaders. The King of Libya seems to have led the invasion, but the bulk of the attackers came from the north. They include the Lukka, Achaïwasha, Shardana, Turseni, and Pulesati. The Achaïwasha are almost certainly Achaeans and with them were Lycians, and perhaps peoples later known as Etruscans, Sardinians, Sikels, and Philistines. The raiders were defeated and dispersed, but a generation later Rameses III. has to face a new invasion. The Achaeans are not among his enemies but the Danuna may be the Danaoi, a name sometimes used for the Greeks, whom tradition later connected with the Argolid and with Egypt.

The raiders had left a trail of destruction behind them as they pressed towards Egypt. Mersin and Tarsus, the Hittite fortresses guarding the plain of Cilicia, were destroyed; Ugarit and other cities along the Syrian and Phoenician seaboards met a similar fate. Many of the raiders, driven back from Egypt, found new homes in the lands they had ravaged. It was probably at this time that the Philistines occupied their coastal strip of Palestine; Greeks may have settled on the ruins of Mersin and Tarsus in Cilicia, and Danuna are later found at Kara Tepe, some hundred miles inland from Tarsus.

The collapse of the Hittite and Egyptian empires left a vacuum in the Near East. The raids on Egypt are symptoms which mark the breakdown of the balance of power and a period of growing anarchy and insecurity. Greek trade with the Near East has left few traces after the middle of the thirteenth century. The confusion of the raids severed the sea lanes. Many of the older Greek settlements were probably abandoned or engulfed. The Greek chapter at Ugarit closed with the sack of the city. At Miletus and Colophon there is a sub-

FIG. 23.—A Gallery in the palace, Tiryns

stantial gap between Mycenaean settlement and later colonisation. An even clearer break is seen at Rhodes where the Mycenaean settlers seem to have migrated *en masse*, perhaps to Cyprus. Cyprus, however, retained its Greek colour though for long it remained cut off from the Aegean world. Not until the eighth century were Greeks to sail freely again in the eastern Mediterranean.

Mycenae herself had already passed her prime; the end of the thirteenth and twelfth centuries are a period of decline. In the thirteenth century we find her strengthening her fortifications and enclosing under protection her water supply and perhaps building a large granary for reserves of grain. At Tiryns the lower slope of the hill is surrounded by a wall to serve as a fortified refuge in need for the people, and a strong bastion is built to strengthen the walls in the south; it includes store-chambers, useful in time of siege. Similar signs of preparation are seen at Athens in the strengthening of the Acropolis.

SECT. 4. THE TROJAN WAR

The Trojan War.

It is in this last phase of declining strength that the siege and sack of Troy, immortalised by the *Iliad*, can be placed. In the poetic tradition Agamemnon, lord of Mycenae, calls on the Achaean princes throughout Greece, who own allegiance to him, to avenge the rape of Helen stolen from his brother Menelaus by Trojan Paris. The combined fleet sails from Aulis on the Euboean strait and lands on the Asiatic shore. The Achaeans build a strong base camp on the Trojan plain, and for ten years with fluctuating fortunes, helped and hindered by gods and goddesses, they lay siege to Troy. Disaster threatens the Achaeans when Achilles quarrels with Agamemnon and leaves the fight; his return is decisive. The city is finally taken by a cunning ruse and sacked. Thucydides, reviewing the campaign as a historian who had also been a general, explains the length of the siege. " The invading army was limited by the difficulty of obtaining supplies to such a number as might be expected to live on the country in which they were to fight. After their arrival at Troy, when they had won a battle (as they clearly did, for otherwise they could not have fortified their camp), even then they appear not to have used the whole of their force, but to have been driven by want of provisions to the cultivation of the Chersonese and to pillage. And in consequence of this dispersion of their forces, the Trojans were enabled to hold out against them during the whole ten years, being always a match for those who remained on the spot. Whereas if the besieging army had brought abundant supplies, and, instead of betaking themselves to agriculture or pillage, had carried on the war persistently with all their forces, they would easily have been masters of the field and have taken the city; since, even divided as they were, and with only a part of their army available at any one time, they held their ground. Or, again, they might have regularly invested Troy, and the place would have been captured in less time and with less trouble." The tradition of the Trojan War cannot be proved by archaeology, but at least the evidence of archaeology is consistent with tradition. The latest excavations at Troy have somewhat modified earlier conclusions, it is true, but the crucial point is not affected. At roughly the time when Greeks were first penetrating Greece, Troy, with new settlers, revived its power and wealth. The new settlement, Troy VI, was in close touch with mainland Greece and shared its early pottery styles. In the period of Mycenaean power (from 1400) the import of Mycenaean ware was brisk. This city was destroyed by

FIG. 24A.—Troy, Sixth City (view from east tower). Prehistoric wall on the left (Roman foundations on right).

earthquake about 1300 B.C., but no change of culture occurred. The town was rebuilt from the fallen material and imports from the mainland, though reduced in scale, continued. This settlement (VIIa) was destroyed and fired after about 100 years. The next stage shows a new influence dominant in pottery, derived probably from the north. Greek tradition had no doubt of the historical truth of the war against Troy, and was fairly confident that it could be dated to the first quarter of the twelfth century. With this date the archaeological evidence conforms. The Greeks sacked and burnt Troy and, as the epic story tells us, departed without settlement. If we ask the reason for the expedition, we are left to guess. It is possible that, especially with the growing insecurity in the east, the Greeks turned of necessity to the north for the metals, and perhaps the food, that they needed. The legend of the Argonauts and the Golden Fleece of Colchis may reflect such voyages of severely practical exploration. Troy had owed its power and wealth to its strategic position. Before ships were strong and swift enough to master the dangerously fast current of the Hellespont, Troy commanded the land route from the north Aegean to the southern shores of the Bosphorus and Black Sea. When ships could make the voyage, a hostile Troy would have made the passage of the Hellespont permanently insecure. It is also possible that the Greeks wanted to plant settlements in northern Asia Minor and could not settle securely until Troy was broken.

Whatever the motive of the expedition the fruits were not gathered. There is no evidence of large-scale Greek penetration into the Hellespont and Euxine at this period, and no trace of settlement in northern Asia Minor before the Dorian invasion. The reason no doubt is that the Mycenaean Greeks had to face a growing insecurity on the mainland. Before the end of the twelfth century Mycenae, Pylos, and many other centres had been destroyed. At Mycenae clear traces of the disaster can be seen. The buildings were first plundered and then systematically fired, leaving a wilderness of charred ruins. For a long period the site was abandoned until in the ninth century traces are found of new occupation, with a small temple marking the site and preserving the orientation of the palace shrine. This iron-age settlement also had a melancholy end when the Argives, jealous of its independence, destroyed it towards the middle of the fifth century. Thucydides, writing a generation after this destruction, had no conception of the great days of Mycenae and would have marvelled more than did Schliemann at the great wealth of the princes of the Mycenaean Age.

The destruction of the Mycenaean centres in Greece marks the end of a century of dissolution. If we review the scene when the Hittites made peace with Egypt in the early thirteenth century, we see Egypt secure within her own borders and her political frontiers extended into Syria; the Hittites, ruling from Boghazkoi, dominant in Asia Minor; Troy commanding the Hellespont, with her power reaching along the western fringe of Asia Minor and the north coast of the Aegean; Greece a land of strong principalities recognising the primacy of Mycenae. In all these centres there was wealth and power: little more than a hundred years later they were all broken. Egypt, already weakened by her long struggle with the Hittites, had been further crippled by a series of land and sea raids from west and north, and for many centuries was to be a powerless spectator of events. Boghazkoi lay in ruins, and Asia Minor entered on a confused period of small-scale powers until the incoming Phrygians consolidated an empire in the north and centre, to be followed by the Lydians in the west. But, though the power of the Hittites was eclipsed in Asia Minor, the principalities that they had established in Syria in the days of their greatness carried on the Hittite traditions and provided one of the fertilising elements for Greek craftsmen when Greek traders once again sailed into the eastern Mediterranean. The breaking of the Hittite and Egyptian empires also gave opportunity to the Phoenician cities of the coast to play a greater part in Mediterranean seafaring. Troy never recovered its power : the settlements that followed on the Greek sack were poor and powerless. When the Aegean world settled down again the hill of Hissarlik was no longer a strategic site ; Sestos and Abydos on the two shores commanded the Hellespont. Greece entered on a dark age, but, when the new invaders had been assimilated, she was to enter a new spring on the way to a more glorious summer ; but the centres of power were to be transferred from Mycenae to Sparta and Athens.]

FIG. 24B.—Late Mycenaean Vase, from Encomi, Cyprus.

FIG. 25.—Inlaid Dagger-blade with lion-hunt (Mycenae).

SECT. 5. THE HOMERIC POEMS

[The material remains of the period that follows the destruction of the great Mycenaean centres bear eloquent witness to the completeness of the collapse. The architect no longer designs on a monumental scale, for there are no wealthy princes to command his services and the necessary labour ; there is little sign even of building in permanent materials. The craftsman, restricted to a narrower world, lacks the precious materials and the skilled refinement of his predecessors. The burials of the period are those of an impoverished society. But memories of Mycenaean greatness and the age of heroes were kept alive in song.

The deeds of Achaean princes were celebrated by minstrels in Mycenaean palaces and the stories were handed down and added to by nameless bards in the bleak period that followed, until the greatest of them all conceived an epic on a grand scale which eclipsed his predecessors. Homer, who sang of the Achaean war against Troy and the wrath of Achilles, lived long after the Trojan War : he himself tells us that he is composing in an age of lesser men. Herodotus thought that he lived in the ninth century, but the material background of the *Iliad* points more strongly to the eighth century. Homer, however, had a long tradition behind him ; the epic style and language had already been fashioned, the outlines of the story were fixed. Stock epithets, recurrent lines, whole passages he could take and adapt, while the artistic structure of the work could be wholly his own.

And so Homer gives us vivid reflections of a period as remote from his own day as the Elizabethans from ourselves. In the great catalogue of the Achaean forces in the second book he passes in review the main centres of Achaean power, many of which were deserted or mere villages in his own day. He describes a helmet which had gone out of fashion before Mycenae fell—" And Meriones gave Odysseus a bow and quiver, and a sword, and on his head set a helmet made of leather, and with many a thong was it stiffly

FIG. 26A.—Gold Cup with hawks (Mycenae).

wrought within, while without the white teeth of a boar of flashing tusks were arranged thick set on either side, well and cunningly, and in the midst was fixed a cap of felt " : just such a helmet was discovered in a tholos tomb at Dendra in the Argolid. A gold cup with hawks poised at the handles, buried in one of the shaft graves at Mycenae, has something in common with the famous cup of Nestor *Cup of* in the *Iliad*, " a rightly good cup, embossed with studs of gold, and *Nestor.* four handles there were to it, and round each two golden doves were feeding, and to the cup were two feet below." Though Homer lives in the iron age, the swords of his heroes are still of bronze, and, though chariots have passed out of date in fighting, they are retained as a traditional element in heroes' battles.

FIG. 26B.—Gold-leaf Image (Mycenae).

But there is much more of the Mycenaean world that has been forgotten. No mention is made in the *Iliad* of the great tholos tombs, the most striking achievement of the Mycenaean architect ; and the burial customs of the poem bear little resemblance to Mycenaean remains. In the Mycenaean period bodies were buried and not burnt ; in the *Iliad* cremation is implied throughout as the normal rule. It seems also that Homer regarded his Achaean heroes as illiterate. The only possible reference to writing in the *Iliad* is in the story of Bellerophon who carries from Argos to Lycia " deadly symbols in a folded tablet ", and the strangeness of the expression suggests something most unusual ; but the Mycenaean palace at Pylos has yielded a large collection of clay tablets and writing has been found on several Mycenaean vessels. Perhaps Homer was conscious that the Greeks had only lately borrowed their alphabet from the Phoenicians and did not realise that earlier Greeks had learnt to write from the Cretans. Though much of the Homeric geography is faithful to the Mycenaean period, there are passages that betray a much later age. When Hera is made to say " Of a surety three cities are there that be dearest far to me, Argos and Sparta and wide-wayed Mycenae," she implies a period after the Dorian invasion, for in the Mycenaean world Argos was of little account beside Mycenae, and Amyclae held the dominance in Laconia that only later passed to Sparta. The prominence of Phoenicians in the *Odyssey* also points to a date long after the Trojan War. Sidon and Tyre were then of little account : in the eighth century, possibly already in the ninth, they were playing an important part in Mediterranean trade.

Homer's material world.

But it is in the material objects mentioned in the poem that Homer most clearly betrays his own age. In Mycenaean days iron was still a precious metal, used primarily for jewelry ; in Homer it is common, and used even for axes, pruning hooks, and knives. The fighting tactics and weapons of the *Iliad* strain the patience of scholars, especially those who look for uniformity. There are traces of Bronze Age equipment and practice, but the main descriptions seem to mirror the practice of the ninth and eighth centuries, as illustrated in the geometric vases of the period : but to make confusion worse confounded there are also echoes of the later hoplite phalanx which may be later additions. It is difficult to reconcile the Homeric house with the palace remains of the Mycenaean world, and Homer never mentions wall paintings which are one of the most striking features of the palaces that we know. In Mycenaean times there is no evidence of temples and large cult statues : in the *Iliad* they are both implied. The dress fasteners of the Mycenaeans were plain and simple, not unlike our safety-pins : the intricate animal design of the brooch of Odysseus recalls the orientalising style of the eighth and seventh centuries.

Though reflections of the culture of Mycenae remain, the material world of Homer's *Iliad* is predominantly the world of the eighth century. He is not only a witness to the glories of the past : he reflects also the reawakening of the present. But before that reawakening could come, the Greek world was to know a long period of disturbance and poverty.]

Sect. 6. Political and Social Organisation of the Early Greeks

The Homeric poems give us our earliest glimpse of the working *Old Aryan* of those political institutions which were the common heritage of *institu-* most of the children, whether children by adoption or by birth, of the *tions.* Aryan stock,—of Greek, Roman, and German alike. They show us the King at the head. But he does not govern wholly of his own will ; he is guided by a Council of the chief men of the community whom he consults ; and the decisions of the Council and King deliberating together are brought before the Assembly of the whole people. Out of these three elements—King, Council, and Assembly—the constitutions of Europe have grown ; here are the germs of all the various forms of monarchy, aristocracy, and democracy.

But in the most ancient times this political organisation was weak *Family or-* and loose. The true power in primitive society was the family. When *ganisation.* we first meet the Greeks they live together in family communities. Their villages are habitations of a *genos*, that is, of a clan, or family *γένος,* in a wide sense ; all the members being descended from a common *gens.* ancestor and bound together by the tie of blood. Originally the chief of the family had the power of life and death over all who belonged to the family ; and it was only as the authority of the state grew and asserted itself against the comparative independence of the family, that this power gradually passed away. But the village communities are not, as they were in the Asian foreworld, isolated and independent; they are part of a larger community which is called the *phylē* or tribe. The tribe is the whole people of the kingdom, in the kingdom's simplest form; and the territory which the tribe inhabited was called its deme. When a king became powerful and won sway over the demes of neighbouring kings, a community consisting of more than one tribe would arise; and, while each tribe had to merge its separate political institutions in the common institutions of the whole state, it would retain its separate identity within the larger union.

It was usual for several families to group themselves together into a society called a *phratra* or brotherhood, which had certain common religious usages. The organisation of clan and tribe, with the intermediate unit of the phratry, was a framework derived from Aryan forefathers, shared at least by other Aryan races. For we find the same institutions among the Romans and among the Germans. The clan is the foundation of Roman society; the Julian *gens*, for instance, has exactly the same social significance as the *genos* of the Alcmaeonids of Attica. The *phylē* is the Roman tribe; and the phratry corresponds to the Roman *curia*, and to our own English *hundred*. The importance of the brotherhood is illustrated by Homer's description of an outcast, as one who has no "brothers" and no hearth.

The importance of the family is most vividly shown in the manner in which the Greeks possessed the lands which they conquered. The soil did not become the private property of individual freemen, nor yet the public property of the whole community. The king of the tribe or tribes marked out the whole territory into parcels, according to the number of families in the community; and the families cast lots for the estates. Each family then possessed its own estate; the head of the family administered it, but had no power of alienating it. The land belonged to the whole kin, but not to any particular member. The right of property in land seems to have been based, not on the right of conquest, but on a religious sentiment. Each family buried their dead within their own domain; and it was held that the dead possessed for ever and ever the soil where they lay, and that the land round about a sepulchre belonged rightfully to their living kinsfolk, one of whose highest duties was to protect and tend the tombs of their fathers.

The king was at once the chief priest, the chief judge, and the supreme war-lord of the tribe. He exercised a general control over religious ceremonies, except in cases where there were special priesthoods; he pronounced judgment and dealt out justice to those who came to his judgment-seat to have their wrongs righted, and he led

Marginal notes:

φυλή, tribus.

δῆμος.

See Orteg.
γ Gass.
Φράτρα.

Clan, phratry, and tribe were Aryan institutions.

Curia

Family property in land.

The Basileus or king.

forth the host to war. He belonged to a family which claimed
descent from the gods themselves. His relation to his people was
conceived as that of a protecting deity ; " he was revered as a god
in the deme." The kingship passed from sire to son, but it is probable that personal fitness was recognised as a condition of the kingly
office, and the people might refuse to accept a degenerate son who
was unequal to the tasks that his father had fulfilled. The sceptred *σκηπτ-*
king had various privileges—the seat of honour at feasts, a large and *οῦχος*
choice share of booty taken in war and of food offered at sacrifices. *βασιλεύς.*
A special close of land was marked out and set apart for him as a
royal domain, distinct from that which his family owned.

The royal functions were vague enough, and a king had no power *The bulê or*
to enforce his will if it did not meet the approval of the heads of the *council.*
people. He must always look for the consent and seek the opinion
of the deliberative Council of the Elders. Strictly, perhaps, the
members of the Council ought to have been the heads of all the
clans, and they would thus have represented the whole tribe, or all
the tribes if there were more than one. But we must take it for
granted, as an ultimate fact, which we have not the means of explaining, that certain families had come to hold a privileged position above
the others—had, in fact, been marked out as noble, and claimed *Class of*
descent from Zeus ; and the Council was composed of this nobility. *nobles.*
In the puissant authority of this Council of Elders lay the germ of
future aristocracy.

More important than either King or Council for the future growth *Agora, or*
of Greece was the Gathering of the people, out of which democracy *Gathering*
was to spring. All the freemen of the tribe—all the freemen of the *of the folk.*
nation, when more tribes had been united—met together, not at
stated times, but whenever the king summoned them, to hear and
acclaim what he and his councillors proposed. To hear and acclaim,
but not to debate or propose themselves. As yet the Gathering of *The army*
the folk for purposes of policy had not been differentiated from the *is the*
Gathering for the purpose of war. The host which the king led forth *assembly.*
against the foe was the same as the folk which assented, by silence or
applause, to the declarations of his will in the Agŏra. The Assembly
was not yet distinguished as an institution from the army ; and if
Agamemnon summons his host to declare his resolutions in the plain
of Troy, such a gathering is the Agora in no figurative sense, it is
no mere military assembly formed on the model of a political
assembly ; it is in the fullest sense the Assembly of the people—the
fellow institution of the Roman *comitia*, our own *gemot*, derived all
three from the same old Aryan gatherings.

The king's
The king was surrounded by a body of Companions, or retainers, *Com-*
who were attached to him by personal ties of service, and seem often *panions.*

to have abode in his palace. The Companions are the same institution as the thanes of our English kings. And if kingship had held its ground in Greece, the Companions might possibly, as in England, have developed into a new order of nobility, founded, not on birth, but on the king's own choice for his service.

Though the monarchy of this primitive form, as we find it reflected in the Homeric lays, generally passed away, it survived in a few outlying regions which lagged behind the rest of the Hellenic world in *Survival of* political development. Thus the Macedonian Greeks in the lower *old form of* valley of the Axius retained a constitution of the old Homeric type *monarchy in Mace-* till the latest times—the royal power continually growing. At the *donia.* close of the tale of Greek conquest and expansion, which began on the Cayster and ended on the Hyphasis, we shall come back by a strange revolution to the Homeric state. When all the divers forms of the rule of the few and the rule of the many, which grew out of the *Alexander* primitive monarchy, have had their day, we shall see the Macedonian *the Great.* warrior, who is to complete the work that was begun by the Achaean conquerors of Troy, attended by his Companions like Agamemnon or Achilles, and ruling his people like an Achaean king of men.

The constitutional fabric of the Greek states was thus simple and loose in the days of Homer. Perhaps few large communities had come into Greece, but larger communities were constantly formed in the course of the conquest. In the later part of the royal period a new movement is setting in which is to decide the future of Greek *Beginning* history. The city begins to emerge and take form and shape out of *of the CITY:* the loose aggregate of villages. The inhabitants of a plain or valley *10th to 9th* are induced to leave their scattered villages and make their dwellings *cent. B.C.* side by side in one place, which would generally be under the shadow of the king's fortress. At first the motive would be to gain the protection afforded by joint habitation in unsettled times ; just as we find in an earlier age villages grouped under the citadel of Mycenae. Sometimes the group of villages would be girt by a wall ; sometimes *Some* the protection of the castle above would be deemed enough. The *peoples* change from village to city life was general, but not universal ; many *(e.g. the* communities continued to live in villages, and did not form cities till *Eleans)* long afterwards. The movement was promoted by the kings ; and it *continue to* is probable that strong kings often brought it about by compulsion. *live in* But in promoting it they were unwittingly undermining the mon- *villages.* archical constitution, and paving the way for their own abolition. A city-state naturally tends to be a republic.

The state In the heroic age, then, the state had not fully emerged from the *not yet* society. No laws were enacted and maintained by the state. Those *differen-* ordinances and usages which guided the individual man in his conduct, *tiated.* *(θέμιστες.)* and which are necessary for the preservation of any society, were maintained by the sanction of religion.   There were certain crimes which the gods punished.   But it was for the family, not for the whole community, to deal with the shedder of blood.   The justice which the king administered was really arbitration.   A stranger had no right of protection, and might be slain in a foreign community, unless he was bound by the bond of guest friendship with a member of that community, and then he came under the protection of Zeus the Hospitable.   Wealth in these ages consisted of herds and flocks ; for, though the Greeks were tillers of the soil and had settled in a country which was already agricultural, the land was not rich enough to bestow wealth.   The value of a suit of armour, for instance, or a slave was expressed in oxen.   Piracy was a common trade, as was inevitable in a period when there was no organised maritime power strong enough to put it down.   So many practised this means of livelihood that it bore no reproach ; and when seamen landed on a strange strand, the natural question to ask them was : " Outlanders, whence come ye ? are ye robbers that rove the seas ? "

Man-slaughter avenged by kinsfolk.

Attitude to strangers.

(Zeus Xenios.)

Wealth.

Piracy.

SECT. 7. THE DORIAN CONQUEST

The heroic age of Greece may be said to have come to an end within two generations after the Trojan War.   A dark period of about two centuries followed, which were marked by the disappearance of the old civilisation, by the expansion of the Greek race over the Aegean, and by wide political changes in the mother country.   The transition to the new period corresponds to the transition from the bronze to the iron age.

Iron age.

[In the Mycenaean culture iron is still a rare article of luxury, used mainly for rings and jewelry.   In the transitional period that follows the collapse of Mycenae iron, probably introduced from the east, increasingly replaces bronze in weapons and tools.   Under the strain of insecurity cremation takes the place of burial and in the Homeric epics has obscured the earlier ritual.   The Mycenaean fashions in pottery gradually give way to a style dominated by geometric decoration, which crowds the surface of the vase.   But whereas a common style was spread through Greece in the days of Mycenae's greatness and in the Protogeometric period which follows, the styles of geometric pottery, after the transitional period, are strictly localised and differ appreciably in the main centres of production.   It was an age of restricted horizons.

Changes in culture.

Though a general decline in Mycenaean civilisation was setting in before Mycenae fell, the general cultural collapse was accentuated by invasion and the consequent upheaval of population that followed. Greek tradition kept alive the memory of the Dorian invasion, but

Tradition.

legend, invention, and propaganda distorted the details. Already by the fifth century the coming of the Dorians was being interpreted as a reinstatement of the Heraclids rather than an invasion of newcomers. Eurystheus, according to this version, exiled from Mycenae the sons of Heracles and their followers. After various wanderings they found refuge and help in Attica. With the Athenians they fought and defeated the followers of Eurystheus and killed the king. But Atreus, who succeeded to the kingship of Mycenae, led the forces of the Peloponnese to the Isthmus. Hyllus, son of Heracles, challenged the chosen of the enemy to single combat: if he won, the Heraclids should inherit the Kingdom of Mycenae; if he were defeated, they should not return to the Peloponnese for a hundred years. Hyllus was slain by Echemus, an Arcadian king; the Heraclids withdrew, but returned to their heritage after a hundred years had passed. They were led by three Heraclid brothers, Temenus, Aristodemus, and Cresphontes, who divided their conquests into the three kingdoms of Argos, Sparta, and Messenia. This concoction we may dismiss as patriotic fiction; but Herodotus, who reflects this tradition, gives also a version of the Dorian movement which may be closer to history. " In the time of King Deucalion the Dorians lived in Phthiotis; in the time of Dorus son of Hellen they occupied the land under Ossa and Olympus, which was called Histiaeotis. From Histiaeotis they were expelled by Cadmeians and dwelt in Pindus, being called Macedonians. Thence again they moved to Dryopis (historic Doris) and from Dryopis they came to the Peloponnese and were called Dorians." That Doris had been their temporary home was believed as early as the seventh century, for Tyrtaeus wrote of Sparta: " Zeus has granted this city to the Heraclids with whom, leaving wind-swept Erineus (in Doris), we came to the broad island of Pelops." But the movement was more widespread and less homogeneous than this tradition suggests. The invaders came from the north and north-west and formed part of a widespread movement that also took Illyrian peoples into Italy. The main stream of the invaders of Greece came through Epirus, but the precise details of their movements cannot yet be disentangled, and matter less than the final results on the map of Greece.

Distribution of Greek dialects. More reliable for the shape of the invasion than legends, which are often inconsistent, is the distribution of dialects which we know from later inscriptions. Two groups of dialects, closely related, the north-western and the Dorian, represent the invaders; the Arcadian, Aeolic, and Ionic dialects derive from the Greeks of the pre-Dorian period. The north-western dialect is spread along the northern shores of the Corinthian gulf through Locris, Doris, Phocis, Aetolia into Acarnania and the islands at the mouth of the gulf. Across the water it is the language of the narrow coastal strip of Achaea and of

Elis. These peoples played little part in the history of classical Greece. In Aetolia Homer spoke of " Pleuron by the sea and rocky *Aetolia.* Calydon," and the myth of Meleager and the hunting of the Calydonian boar became a part of the heritage of the national legend of Greece. But Mycenaean culture has left little mark on this land of hills and valleys. Aetolia kept pace with mainland Greece in the period of settlement following the invasions, but in the age of colonisation and rapid progress it fell behind. It remained a land of villages, dangerous to the invader, but without influence on the main current of events. Locris suffered eclipse and was split by the establishment of *Locris.* the Phocians, dividing the Locrians into three separate communities, the Ozolian Locrians on the Corinthian gulf, to the west of Phocis ; the other two divisions on the Euboean sea, to the north-east. Doris *Doris.* played a rather more important part in the development of Greece, for its territory lay near Delphi, the " rocky threshold of Apollo " which was to become the most important religious centre in the Greek world. Tradition said that this small territory was the last halting-place of the Dorians before they invaded the Peloponnese and it was recognised as the mother-country of Dorians everywhere. The tradition may be true, though classical Doris is not strictly Dorian in language, cult, or customs. It was at any rate convenient, for a claim to the championship of Delphic Apollo was not to be despised.

Of those who spoke the north-western dialect the richest prize fell to the invaders of Elis. They settled first in the Peneus Valley, *Elis.* " Hollow Elis," a land of rich pasture, famous for its horses and good arable. Later they extended their dominion south to the Alpheus Valley, penetrating the religious centre of Olympia which they transformed by the establishment of the great Olympic festival early in the eighth century. But the Eleans, though good fighters when it was necessary to defend themselves, had no far-reaching ambitions. In their fertile territory they remained primarily a conservative agricultural community independent of trade and colonisation. They did not feel the economic stresses that led to friction and progress elsewhere. The Dorians proper, whose distinguishing marks are the three Dorian tribes, Hylleis, Dymanes, Pamphyloi, and the cult of Apollo Pythaeus, occupied the main seats of power in the Peloponnese, in the Argolid, Laconia, Messenia, Corinth, and Megara. They also occupied the southern islands, Cythera, Melos, Thera, Crete and Rhodes, Cos, and the south-west corner of Asia Minor.

Though remnants of the early population could be identified later in scattered pockets, only one large area in the Peloponnese remained free from invasion. The peoples of mountainous Arcadia, the least *Arcadia.* inviting of lands to an invader, retained the pre-conquest speech and in historical times spoke the same language as the Greeks of Cyprus,

recalling a time when their language was spread throughout the
southern coastlands of the Peloponnese.

Attica and   North of the Peloponnese Attica and Euboea retained the Ionic
Euboea. dialect, confirming the Athenian tradition that their land though
attacked was not occupied, and became a refuge for dispersed peoples
and a pierhead for further emigration. Further north the mixed
Thessaly dialects of Thessaly and Boeotia confirm the tradition of two further
and invasions arising from the main disturbances. In both these countries
Boeotia. the mixed dialect shows that an Aeolic population was invaded by
peoples speaking a north-western dialect. In Boeotia the two races
seem to have amalgamated ; in Thessaly the conquered peoples were
reduced to serfdom and were known as the Labourers working for
overlords who ruled in the strong centres of Pharsalus, Pagasae,
Larissa, and Pherae.

The pressure of the great invasions had come from the north and
north-west. Arcadia was left as an island of independence. Elsewhere in the Peloponnese the invaders became the dominant force in
Argos. history. The first centre of Dorian power was in the Argolid, the
immediate sphere of Mycenae's rule, and from the Argolid Phlius on
the upper Asopus and Sicyon on the Corinthian gulf were occupied.
Argos replaced Mycenae as the centre of power. Temenos in tradition was the leader of these invaders and, recalling her priority in
conquest, Argos throughout her history aspired to the hegemony of
the Peloponnese. She had her days of greatness, but often she had
to struggle hard even for the control of her own plain. In the
Argolid the earlier population was submerged but not enslaved and
they probably provided the bulk of the agricultural labour, in time
intermarrying and even being admitted into the citizen body.

Laconia.   It was different in Laconia. Here invasion came later, but the
conquest was more rigorous. The native population was enslaved
and worked the land for their Dorian masters. Further west a thin
stream of Dorians may have penetrated Messenia, but their number
was too small to dominate the land and Messenia was later to be
conquered by the Dorians of Laconia.

The   Corinth and Sicyon were also occupied by the Dorians and, per-
Isthmian haps last of the mainland cities, Megara. From Corinth the Doric
states. dialect was later taken to Corcyra and her other colonies along the
north-western seaboard. In Sicyon, Corinth, and Megara, though the
Dorians predominated, the native population was not submerged and
when later tyrants arose they were to obtain strong support from the
pre-Dorians. The island of Aegina in the Saronic Gulf, which was
to play a leading role in Greek trade and for long challenge Athens,
also became a Dorian land. It was occupied from Epidaurus after the
mainland conquerors had settled down. When Pindar, speaking of

Aegina, says " the Dorian host of Hyllus and Aegimius came here and made our city," he is making full use of poetic license.

Such may have been the general pattern of the sweeping changes that transformed Greece. To attempt a chronological framework is more hazardous. Literary traditions varied substantially about the direction and composition of the invaders, but they felt far less doubt about their date. Even Thucydides, most critical of historians, could say without hesitation that the Boeotians came into their later home in the sixtieth year after the Trojan War, and that in the eightieth year the Dorians occupied the Peloponnese.

FIG. 27.—Attic Protogeometric Vase.

Archaeology is here an embarrassment, undermining faith but not yet confident enough to construct a historical record of events. We should expect to find evidence of destruction at the great Mycenaean settlements accompanied by a change in material products and in customs, marking the path of the invaders. And there was indeed a time when the introduction of the geometric style of pottery, of iron, and cremation were thought to be the archaeological clues. But the progress of excavation has shown that the problem is much more complex. A wave of destruction of the Mycenaean palaces at Mycenae, Pylos, and other centres has certainly left its traces, and can be dated, where we should expect it, in the twelfth century. But it is not accompanied by a change in culture. In pottery there is no sharp break between Mycenaean and geometric; the one decays and the other gradually evolves, through sub-Mycenaean and protogeometric; it develops in Greece and is not brought from without, for throughout this transitional phase the leading centre of production is Attica which always boasted of its continuity with the past. Similarly it is

Archaeological evidence.

in Attica that the first cremations on the mainland are found, and the practice seems to be introduced from the east, finding a receptive background in the insecurity that accompanied the collapse of Mycenae. Nor is iron introduced from the north: it too is first found in Attica, is probably of eastern origin, and only gradually comes into general use. It is likely enough that the invaders had not reached any high standard of material culture but took over and adapted what they found. They did, however, maintain contact

FIG. 28.—Oriental Gold Pendant, eighth century (found in Aegina).

with the areas from which they came, and northern influences can be seen in the bronzes found in Dorian lands as late as the eighth and seventh centuries.

For large-scale Dorian elements archaeology provides no evidence in the century following the destruction of the Mycenaean fortresses. In Sparta, where excavation should have yielded firm results, Dorian settlement seems to date only from the tenth century. No signs of Dorian occupation in Corinth have yet been found from the eleventh century. Argos still awaits systematic exploration.

The evidence of Homer. So much for archaeology. Of the literary sources Homer, who wrote before the systematisers had been busy, deserves special respect.

In Homer's world, as has often been pointed out, there is a gap north of Olympus. It may be here, as later tradition said, that the Dorians had established themselves before the Trojan war and before they moved into the Pindus mountains. To Homer they are, however, known already in Crete and Rhodes. It may well be that this was the first stage of the Dorian movement though the main Dorian occupation of Crete and Rhodes came later from the Peloponnese. The Dorian invasion proper came after the Trojan War and, for most of its early course, probably by land. But the central problem remains. How do we reconcile the main body of Greek literary tradition with the archaeological evidence of a long break between destruction and large-scale Dorian settlement ? It seems as if the first invaders moved on when their work of destruction was done, or were absorbed by the existing inhabitants. Steady infiltration from the north may have followed, but perhaps organised movements leading to the dominance of the invaders did not develop for over a hundred years. Any such hypothesis, however, can only be tentative. Not until the period has been systematically attacked by archaeologists looking in the right places, particularly in the Argolid, for the evidence that is needed can we hope to lighten substantially the dark ages of early Greece.

It is not until the eighth century that we begin to see clear signs of a renaissance. By then Greece has settled down, contact is once again being established with the east and with the west, and Dorian states are to play a leading part in shaping the progress of Greek civilisation.

Sect. 8. Expansion of the Greeks to the Eastern Aegean

[Greek tradition associated with the Dorian invasion a great emigration of the dispossessed across the Aegean, which planted the Greek language and Greek customs in Asia. But, like the Dorian invasion, this movement has been simplified and distorted and we cannot yet recover the pattern. Already in Herodotus' day the story of the foundation of the Ionian cities had been schematised. It was said that they derived from the twelve centres of historic Achaea, which stretched along the south shore of the Corinthian gulf. Dis-possessed by the invaders, they had fled to Attica and thence sailed east to establish their twelve cities on the western coast of Asia Minor. But Herodotus himself knew that the story was more complex than that. He knew that the settlers were not of common origin, that they included Abantes from Euboea, Minyans from Orchomenos, Dryopes, and many other stocks. And local traditions in these Ionian cities retained memories of their diverse origins : an early poet of Colophon, *Tradition of Ionian origins.*

Mimnermus, who lived at the end of the seventh century, reminded his fellow citizens : " when we left the city of Neleian Pylos and came in our ships to Asia of our longing and when in lovely Colophon with the might of arms we settled." Such traditions suggest an uncoordinated stream of refugees fleeing before invaders, and if we could fix the date of this emigration we might in turn illuminate the *Chrono-* Dorian invasion itself. But the vital centres in Asia Minor have been *logy.* only fitfully excavated, and not until their lower levels have been systematically explored can we hope to retrace the main outlines of the movement. But such evidence as we have from Asia Minor is consistent with the late date suggested for the Dorian invasion. Greek settlement in Samos seems to date from the tenth century.

Evidence It may even be that the occupation of the coastal lands was a *of* process spreading over some two centuries. For Thucydides seems *Thucy-* to imply a date in the eighth century for the Ionian colonisation from *dides.* Athens. " A considerable time elapsed before Hellas became finally settled ; after a while, however, she recovered tranquillity and began to send out colonies. The Athenians colonised Ionia and most of the islands ; the Peloponnesians the greater part of Italy and Sicily, and various places in Hellas." Perhaps a disordered emigration in the tenth and ninth centuries from scattered points was followed by a more ordered movement in the early eighth century from Athens. But, whenever it ended, the origin of the movement was immediately connected with the Dorian invasion. It succeeded because, after the breaking of the Hittite empire at the end of the thirteenth century, there was no longer any strong power to deny the Greeks a foothold.

Physical The western coast of Asia Minor was well suited to Greek settle- *character* ment and encouraged the individual development of separate city *of coast of* states, as did the mountain barriers of Greece that separate plain from *Asia* plain. A series of river valleys are divided by mountain chains which *Minor.* run out into promontories so as to form deep bays ; and the promontories are continued in islands. The valleys of the Hermus and the Caicus are bounded on the north by a chain of hills which run out into Lesbos ; the valley of the Hermus is parted from that of the Cayster by mountains which are prolonged in Chios ; and the valley of the Cayster is separated from the valley of the Maeander by a chain which terminates in Samos. South of the Maeander valley there are bays and islands, but the mountains of the mainland are broken by no rivers. The climate is temperate, the rainfall sufficient, and the river valleys provided natural routes into the interior which were to prove a powerful incentive to trade when secure conditions were established inland and wealthy and powerful kingdoms developed.

To the north settled the Aeolians. Tradition connected their settlement with Thessaly and Boeotia and their dialect confirms this origin. *The* They settled on the island of Lesbos and the opposite coastland of the *Aeolians.* Troad, which for much of its history remained in the Lesbian sphere. Further south they occupied strong places which they could defend— Pitane, Myrina, Cyme, Aegae, old Smyrna. They pressed up the rivers, and on the Hermus they founded Magnesia under Mount Sipylus. All this, needless to say, was not done at once. It must have been the work of many years, and of successive expeditions from the mother country.

The Aeolians were to play a less prominent part in history than the emigrants who occupied the coast to the south. These were the Ionians, many of whom could claim kinship with the people of Attica. *The* Simplified tradition, encouraged later by Athenian pretensions, re- *Ionians.* corded that the Ionian cities were established formally from Athens and took their fire from the Athenian hearth. It is indeed probable that the main body of settlers came through Attica when, before the Dorians, the Ionian-speaking peoples fled from the Peloponnese. But others doubtless sailed direct from the Peloponnese—from the Saronic Gulf, the Argolid, and other coastal districts into which the Dorians came. The two-pronged peninsula between the Hermus and Cayster rivers, with the off-lying isle of Chios, the valleys of the Cayster and Maeander with Samos and the peninsula south of Mount Latmos, were studded with communities which came to form a group distinct from the Aeolians to the north.]

But it would probably be a mistake to regard these two groups *Distinction* as well defined from the first. To begin with, it is possible that they *of the two* overlapped chronologically. The latest of the Aeolian settlements *groups and* may have been founded subsequently to the earliest of the Ionian. *their over-* In the second place, the original homes of the settlers overlapped. *lappings.* Though the Aeolian colonists mainly came from the lands north of Mount Oeta—apart from those who came from Aetolia—they included some settlers from the coasts of Boeotia and Euboea. Thus Cyme in Aeolis derived its name from Euboean Cyme. And, on the other hand, though the Ionian colonies were chiefly derived from the coasts of Attica and Argolis—apart from some contingents from Crete and other places in the south—there were also some settlers from the north. Thirdly, the two groups ran into each other geographically. Phocaea, for example, which is geographically in Aeolis, standing on the promontory north of the Hermus river, was included in Ionia. Its name shows that some of the men who colonised it were Phocians. And some of the places in north Ionia—Teos, for instance—had received Achaean settlements first, and were then re-settled by Ionians. In Chios, which was afterwards fully in Ionia, a language of Aeolic complexion was once spoken.

GREEK COLONIES
in the
EASTERN AEGEAN.

Stadia
0   100   200   300   400   500

English Miles
0   10   20   30   40   50

Troy, Ilium (Hissarlik)
R. Scamander
Mt. Ida
PHRYGIA

Methymna
Lesbos
Bresa
Mytilene

Pitane
R. Caïcus
MYSIA

Myrina
Aegae
Phocaea   Cyme
R. Hermus
Magnesia
Mt. Sipylus
Old Smyrna

Chios
Erythrae
Clazomenae
Teos
Lebedus
Colophon
R. Cayster
Mt. Tmolus
LYDIA

Ephesus
Magnesia
R. Maeander

Samos
Icaria
Mt. Mycale
TEMPLE OF THE
HELICONIAN POSEIDON
Priene
Myus
Miletus
Mt. Latmus
CARIA

Patmos
Leros
Halicarnassus
Termera
Cos
Cnidus
Astypalaea
Nisyros
Syme
Amorgos
Anaphe
Telos
Camirus
Chalce
Rhodes
Ialysos
Rhodes

Carpathus

Walker & Boutall sc.

FIG. 20.

Of the foundation of the famous colonies of Ionia, of the order in *Ionian* which they were founded, and of the relations of the settlers with *colonisa-* the Lydian natives, we know as little as of the settlements of the *tion.* Achaeans. Clazomenae and Teos arose on the north and south sides of the neck of the peninsula which runs out to meet Chios ; and Chios, on the east coast of her island, faces Erythrae on the mainland—Erythrae, " the crimson," so called from its purple fisheries, the resort of Tyrian traders. Lebedus and Colophon lie on the coast as it retires eastward from Teos to reach the mouth of the Cayster ; and there was founded Ephesus, the city of Artemis. By the streams of the Cayster was a plain called " the Asian meadow," which destiny in some odd way selected to bestow a name upon one of the continents of the earth. South of Ephesus and on the northern slope of Mount Mycale was the religious gathering-place of the Ionians, the temple of the Heliconian Poseidon, which, when once the Ionians became conscious of themselves as a sort of nation and learned to glory in their common name, served to foster a sense of unity among all their cities from Phocaea in the north to Miletus in the south. Samos faces Mount Mycale, and the worship of Hera, which was the religious feature of Samos, is thought to point to men of Argos as participators in its original foundation. South of Mycale the cities of Myus and Priene were planted on the Maeander. Then the coast retires to skirt Mount Latmos and breaks forward again to form the promontory, at the northern point of which was Miletus with its once splendid harbour. There was one great inland city, Magnesia on the Maeander, which must not be confused with the inland Aeolian city, Magnesia on the Hermus. Though counted to Ionia, it was not of Ionian origin, for it was founded by the Magnētes of Thessaly. And settlers from Euboea and Boeotia took part in the colonisation of Ionia, as well as the Ionians of Argolis and

---

[1] The following list will illustrate the Ionian colonisation. Phocaea—Phocians ; Clazomenae—Cleonae and Phlius ; Samos—Argolis ; Chios—Euboea ; Erythrae —Boeotia and Euboea ; Teos (first, Achaeans from Thessaly)—Attica and Boeotia ; Lebedos—Boeotia ; Colophon—Pylus (in Messenia) ; Ephesus—Argolis, and various ; Priene—Cadmeans and Arcadians ; Myus—Attica ; Miletus— Attica. These twelve cities were called the Ionian dodecapolis. The best test of Ionian race was the celebration of the feast of *Apaturia* ; and the fact that this feast was not held at Ephesus and Colophon shows that the Ionian element in these cities was very small. The Ionian dialect embraces the idioms which were spoken in Euboea, the Cyclad islands, and the Ionian colonies. Euboean speech was much influenced by neighbouring dialects (especially the Boeotian) ; but the language of the Cyclades is close enough to that of Ionia, one of the chief differences being that Ionia lost the *spiritus asper*. Herodotus says that there were four distinct sub-dialects in Ionia itself. He probably refers to the speech of the common people. So far as the evidence of inscriptions goes, the local differences in the written language were insignificant.

Attica.[1] The old inhabitants—Leleges, Maeonians, Carians—probably offered no prolonged resistance to the invaders, and in some places, as the Carians for example at Miletus, they mixed with the Greek strangers.

The colonists carried with them into the new Greece beyond the seas traditions of the old civilisation which in the mother country was being overwhelmed by the Dorian invaders ; and those traditions helped to produce the luxurious Ionian civilisation which meets us some centuries later when we come into the clearer light of recorded history. And they carried with them their minstrelsy, their lays of Troy, celebrating the deeds of Achilles and Agamemnon and Odysseus. The heroic lays of Greece entered upon a new period in *Homer* Ionia, where a poet of supreme genius arose, and the first and *(c.*850 *B. C.).* greatest epic poem of the world was created. [Homer's date was disputed in antiquity and has been disputed ever since, but there is a growing consensus of opinion in favour of the eighth century, for reasons that we have already seen.[1] He probably lived in Chios, for such was the tradition as early as the sixth century and the Homeridae of Chios derived their origin from him and may at first have been his direct descendants. He seems to have visited the scene of the fighting he describes with a keen eye for significant detail and he was personally familiar with the geography of the north Aegean. He gives us a local touch when he describes the sun as rising over the sea. The historical importance of Homer is his witness to the early flowering of Ionia after the great emigration. The conscious art of his epic, his keen imagination, and his sense of form show a striking maturity which could not be paralleled on the mainland in his day. In the *Iliad* he took as his main argument the wrath of Achilles leading up to the death of Hector, and wrought into his epic many other episodes derived from the old lays on the theme of Troy. Tradition made Homer the author of both the great epics, the *Odyssey* as well as the *Iliad.* Whether this is so or not, no great length of time need separate the composition of the two poems.

The material background of the *Iliad* shows a broadening horizon, when contact was again being established with the eastern Mediterranean, and the effect of such contact on Homer's imagination is well illustrated by his description of the shield of Achilles. The shield, wrought in bronze, tin, silver, and gold, is round and has a ringed space in the centre, encompassed by three concentric girdles. In the middle is the earth, the sea, and the heaven, with " the unwearied sun and the moon at her full, and all the stars wherewith heaven is crowned." The subject of the first circle is Peace and War. Here are

[1] See pp. 50-53.

scenes in a city at peace—banquets, brides borne through the streets
by torchlight to their new homes, the elders dealing out justice;
there is another city besieged, and scenes of battle. The second circle
shows scenes from country life at various seasons of the year : plough-
ing in spring, the ploughman drinking a draught of wine as he reaches
the end of the black furrow ; a king watching reapers reaping in his
meadows, and the preparations for a harvest festival ; a bright vintage
scene, " young men and maids bearing the sweet fruit in wicker
baskets," and dancing, while a boy plays a lyre and sings the song of
Linus ; herdsmen with their dogs pursuing two lions which had carried
off an ox from the banks of a sounding river ; a pasture and shepherds'
huts in a mountain glen. The whole was girdled by the third, outmost
circle, through which " the great might of the river Oceanus " flowed—
rounding off, as it were, the life of mortals by its girdling stream.
Individual scenes from this shield can be paralleled from the work of
Cretan and Mycenaean craftsmen, but neither in Crete nor on the
Greek mainland have such decorated shields nor such elaborate
compositions been found from the Mycenaean period. It seems that
Homer was inspired by the orientalising bronze shields of his own day
such as have been found in Crete, but he has gone far beyond his
models and infused the composition with a sense of balance and form
which is essentially Greek.]

Homer preserved the memory of the Trojan War as a great *The* Iliad
national enterprise. The *Iliad* was regarded as something of far *a national*
greater significance than an Ionian poem ; it was accepted as a *epic.*
national epic, and was, from the first, a powerful influence in promoting among the Greeks community of feeling and tendencies
towards national unity.

[It was followed, perhaps at no long interval, by the *Odyssey*, *The Epic*
which tells of the wanderings of Odysseus after the fall of Troy, and *Cycle, c.*
which tradition also attributed to Homer. The *Odyssey* reflects the *750-600*
age of bold sea journeys which prepared the way for colonisation and *B.C.*
is a fitting complement to the story of battling armies. The pre-
eminence of Homer led to the dominance of the Trojan story in epic
tradition, and he was followed by a long line of lesser poets who dealt
with events that preceded or followed those described in the *Iliad*.
Along with the *Iliad* and *Odyssey* they formed a chronological series
which came to be known as the Epic Cycle.]

The Ionic settlements did not complete the Greek colonisation *New Doris*
of Asia Minor. The Dorian conquest of the eastern Peloponnesus *in Asia*
was followed by a Dorian expansion beyond the seas and a colonisa- *Minor.*
tion of the Asiatic coast, to the south of Ionia. The Carians had
spread over this region down to the border of Lycia and had pressed
the older inhabitants into the promontory which faces the island

The Leleges of Calymna. Here the Leleges participated in the latest stages of
confined the Aegean civilisation, as we know by the pottery and other things
to the which have been discovered at Termera in chamber-tombs. These
Myndian round tombs, not hewn out of the earth, like the vaulted sepul-
promon- chres of Mycenae, but built above ground, are found in many parts
tory. of the peninsula and remain as the most striking memorial of the
Chamber- Leleges.
tombs at
Termera
(Assarlik);   The bold promontories below Miletus, the islands of Cos and
"late My- Rhodes, were occupied by colonists from Argolis, Laconia, Corinth,
cenaean." and Crete. [Cnidus was the most important settlement, making with
Cos and the three cities of Rhodes (Lindus, Ialysus, Camirus) a Dorian
pentapolis. These settlements were independent, but they kept alive
their communion of interest and sentiment by the common worship
of the Triopian Apollo. Thesis was no small part of the Dorian
achievement. Rhodes was to be a pioneer in the reopening of the
sea-ways to east and west, planting settlements as far afield as in
France and Spain ; Cnidus could boast a wealthy treasury at Delphi
and an important part in the opening up of the Adriatic ; Cos was to
be famous for her school of medicine. Inland was settled Dorian
Halicarnassus, but she early lost her place in the common Dorian
festival ; for, as the names of her citizens show, the population had
a strong Carian admixture and the language of her documents is
Ionian ; but Halicarnassus could claim Herodotus among her citizens,
and many colourful characters before and after him.]

Caria.   The Carians were a vigorous people. They impressed themselves
upon their land, and soon men began to forget that it had not been
always Caria. They took to the sea and formed a maritime power
of some strength, so that in later ages a tradition was abroad that
there was once upon a time a Carian sea-supremacy, though no one
could mention anything that it had achieved. The Carians also
claimed to have made contributions to the art of war by introducing
shield-handles, and the crested helmet, and the emblazoning of
shields—claims which we cannot test.

The Greek fringe of western Asia Minor was complete. It was
impossible for Doris to creep round the corner and join hands with
Lycia. Pamphylia ; for the Lycians presented an insuperable barrier. The
Lycians were not a folk of Aryan speech, as a widely-spread error
supposed them to have been ; their language is related to the Carian.
Their proper name was Trm̃mili ; but the name Lycian seems to
have been given them by others as well as by the Greeks, who
recognised in the chief Tremilian deity their own Apollo Lykios.[1]

---

[1] This fact need not exclude the view (now generally accepted) that the **Luku**,
who appear as invaders of Egypt in the reigns of Ramses II. and **Mernptah**,
were Lycians.

Fig. 30A.—Table of Offerings, with inscription, found in the Dictaean Cave (Crete).

But, though Lycia was not colonised, the Aegean was now entirely
within the Greek sphere, excepting only its northern margin, where
Greek enterprise in the future was to find a difficult field. It is important to observe that the process by which Asiatic Greece was
created differs in character from the Dorian invasion of the Peloponnesus. The settlements of Ionia and Doris are examples of
colonisation. Bands of settlers went forth from their homes to find
new habitations for themselves, but they left a home-country behind

FIG. 30B.

them. The Dorian movements, on the other hand, partake of the
character of a folk-wandering. The essential fact is that a whole
people dispersed to seek new fields and pastures. For the paltry
remnant which remained in the sequestered nook beyond Parnassus
could not be called the parent people except by courtesy ; the people,
as a whole, had gone elsewhere.

[In this period of the breakdown of a civilisation and violent dis-
location of peoples some of the refugees from the Greek mainland
may have penetrated as far as the island of Cyprus and reinforced the
Greek settlements of the Mycenaean Age. But in the slow years of
settlement and recovery this distant island was cut off from the Greek
world, and carried on Mycenaean traditions in her pottery and material
culture. She retained too the language her settlers had brought from

Greece and her antique syllabary even when the rest of the Greek world adopted the Phoenician alphabet. Typical of her conservatism was the long survival into the fifth century and beyond of a kingship tracing direct descent from Mycenaean days. But cut off from the Greek world the Greeks of Cyprus could not maintain their dominance in the island. By the ninth century the Phoenicians had planted settlements. The culture of Cyprus reflects the mixture of races, but the Greeks kept their national consciousness and were proud to renew their associations with the Aegean world when Greek traders in the eighth century again began to sail regularly into the eastern Mediterranean. Cyprus was to become for a long period a battle-ground between Greek and Semite. Salamis became the champion of Hellenism ; Citium and Amathus were the chief centres of Phoenician influence. It was Amathus later that led the opposition to the Greek revolt from Persia in the island ; it was at the siege of Citium that the Athenian Cimon died. There are few more striking demonstrations in Greek history than the attempt in the early fourth century of Evagoras of Salamis, with the limited resources of a small island, to challenge the great Persian empire and to make Cyprus more Greek than Greece.]

If we look back now upon the early history of the Greeks, we see that though we can establish a probable chronology, there is only a single date which can lay claim to precision, and this concerns an event of minor importance—an Achaean raid on Egypt. For all the leading changes and movements we must be content with approximate limits :— *Chronology.*

[Greek-speaking peoples occupy Greece   .   .   *c.* 2000 B.C.
Crete leading power in Aegean .   .   .   *c.* 2200-1400 B.C.
Cretan influence dominant in Greeks .   .   *c.* 1600-1400 B.C.
Fall of Cnossus   .   .   .   .   .   *c.* 1400 B.C.
The Great Age of Mycenae   .   .   .   *c.* 1400-1200 B.C.
Achaean raids and settlements in Eastern
     Mediterranean .   .   .   .   .   *c.* 1350-1200 B.C.
Achaeans join in raid on Egypt   .   .   .   1223 B.C.
Trojan War   .   .   .   .   .   Early 12th century B.C.
Destruction of Mycenae, Pylos, etc. .   Middle 12th century B.C.
Large-scale Dorian settlement in Pelo-
     ponnese .   .   .   .   .   .   from *c.* 1000 B.C.
Colonisation of west coast of Asia Minor .   after *c.* 1000 B.C.]

Sect. 9. Fall of Greek Monarchies and Rise of the Republics

What the kings did for Greece. Under their kings the Greeks had conquered the coasts and islands of the Aegean, and had created the city-state. These were the two great contributions of monarchy to Grecian history. In forwarding the change from rural life in scattered thorps to life in cities, the kings were doubtless considering themselves as well as *Effects of city-life.* their people. They thought that the change would consolidate their own power by bringing the whole folk directly under their own eyes. But it also brought the king more directly under the eye of his folk. The frailties, incapacities, and misconduct of a weak lord were more noticed in the small compass of a city ; he was more generally criticised and judged. City-life too was less appropriate to the patriarchal character of the Homeric " shepherd of the people." Moreover, in a city those who were ill-pleased with the king's rule were more tempted to murmur together, and able more easily to conspire. Considerations *Decline of* like these may help us to imagine how it came about that throughout *monarchy :* the greater part of Greece in the eighth century the monarchies were *causes.* declining and disappearing, and republics were taking their place. It is a transformation of which the actual process is hidden from us, and we can only guess at probable causes ; but we may be sure that the deepest cause of all was the change to city-life. The revolution was general ; the infection caught and spread ; but the change in different states must have had different occasions, just as it took different shapes. In some cases gross misrule may have led to the violent deposition of a king ; in other cases, if the succession to the sceptre devolved upon an infant or a paltry man, the nobles may have taken it upon themselves to abolish the monarchy. In many places perhaps the change was slower. The kings who had already sought to strengthen their authority by the foundation of cities must have sought also to increase or define those vague powers which belonged to an Aryan ruler—sought, perhaps, to act of their own freewill without due regard to the Council's advice. When such attempts at magnifying the royal power went too far, the elders of the Council might rise and gainsay the king, and force him to enter into a contract with his people that he would govern constitutionally. Of the existence of such contracts we have evidence. The old monarchy lasted into late times in remote Molossia, and there the king was obliged to take a solemn oath to rule his people according to law. In other cases the rights of the king might be strictly limited, in consequence of his seeking to usurp undue authority ; and the imposition of limitations might go on until the office of king, although maintained in name, became in fact a mere magistracy in a state wherein the real power had passed elsewhere. Of the survival of monarchy in a limited form we have an example at Sparta ; of its survival as a mere magistracy we have an example at Athens. And it should be observed that the functions of the monarch were already restricted by limits which could easily be contracted further. Though he was the supreme giver of dooms, there might be other heads of clans or tribes in the state who could give dooms and judgment as well as he. Though he was the chief priest, there were other families than his to which certain priesthoods were confined. He was therefore not the sole fountain of justice or religion.

There is a vivid scene in Homer which seems to have been painted *Episode of* when kings were seeking to draw tighter the reins of the royal power. *Thersites* The poet, who is in sympathy with the kings, draws a comic and *(in* Iliad odious caricature of the " bold " carle with the gift of fluent speech, ii.). who criticises the conduct and policy of the kings. Such an episode could hardly have suggested itself in the old days before city-life had begun ; Thersites is assuredly a product of the town. Odysseus, who rates and beats him, announces, in another part of the same scene, a maxim which has become as famous as Thersites himself : " The sovereignty of many is not good ; let there be one sovereign, one king." That is a maxim which would win applause for the minstrel in the banquet-halls of monarchs who were trying to carry through a policy of centralisation at the expense of the chiefs of the tribes.

Where the monarchy was abolished, the government passed into *Rise of the* the hands of those who had done away with it, the noble families of *republics.* the state. The distinction of the nobles from the rest of the people is, as we have seen, an ultimate fact with which we have to start. When the nobles assume the government and become the rulers, an *Rule of the* aristocratic republic arises. Sometimes the power is won, not by *nobles.* the whole body of the noble clans, but by the clan to which the king belonged. This was the case at Corinth, where the royal family of the Bacchiads became the rulers. In most cases the aristocracy and the whole nobility coincided ; but in others, as at Corinth, the aristocracy was only a part of the nobility, and the constitution was an oligarchy of the narrowest form.

At this stage of society the men of the noble class were the nerve and sinew of the state. Birth was then the best general test of excellence that could be found, and the rule of the nobles was a true aristocracy, the government of the most excellent. They practised the craft of ruling ; they were trained in it, they handed it down from father to son ; and though no great men arose—great men are dangerous in an aristocracy—the government was conducted with knowledge and skill. Close aristocracies, like the Corinthian, were apt to become oppressive ; and, when the day approached for aristocracies in their turn to give way to new constitutions, there were signs of grievous degeneration. But on the whole the Greek republics flourished in the aristocratic stage, and were guided with eminent ability.

The rise of the republics is about to take us into a new epoch of history ; but it is important to note the continuity of the work which was to be done by the aristocracies with that which was accomplished by the kings. The two great achievements of the aristocratic age are the planting of Greek cities in lands far beyond the limits of the Aegean sea, and the elaboration of political machinery. The first of these is simply the continuation of the expansion of the Greeks around the Aegean itself. But the new movement of expansion is distinguished, as we shall see, by certain peculiarities in its outward forms,—features which were chiefly due to the fact that city-life had been introduced before the colonisation began. The beginning of colonisation belonged to the age of transition from monarchy to republic ; it was systematically promoted by the aristocracies, and it took a systematic shape. The creation of political machinery carried on the work of consolidation which the kings had begun when they gathered together into cities the loose elements of their states. When royalty was abolished or put, as we say, " into commission," the ruling families of the republic had to substitute magistracies tenable for limited periods, and had to determine how the magistrates were to be appointed, how their functions were to be circumscribed, how the provinces of authority were to be assigned. New machinery had to be created to replace that one of the three parts of the constitution which had disappeared. It may be added that under the aristocracies the idea of law began to take a clearer shape in men's minds, and the traditions which guided usage began to assume the form of laws. In the lays of Homer we hear only of the single dooms given by the kings or judges in particular cases. At the close of the aristocratic period comes the age of the lawgivers, and the aristocracies had prepared the material which the lawgivers improved, qualified, and embodied in codes

Two achievements of aristocracies :
1. Coloni-sation (see below, Chap. II. sects. 1-3).

2. Political organisation.

Growth of law.

SECT. 10. PHOENICIAN INTERCOURSE WITH GREECE

[During the Mycenaean Age the Greeks had been a great seafaring people. They had traded and settled in the eastern Mediterranean and had brought back the luxuries of Syria and Egypt to the palaces of their kings and nobles. The great sea-raids, combined with the weakening of Mycenaean power, had severed these sea lanes, and it was not for some four centuries that they were once again opened up by the Greeks. It was the Phoenicians who first, perhaps in the ninth

Period of Phoenician trade with Greece.

century, re-established contact between the eastern Mediterranean and the Aegean world.] They were the traders of the city-states of Sidon and Tyre on the Syrian coast, men of that Semitic stock to which Jew, Arab, and Assyrian alike belonged. These coast-landers, born merchants like the Jews, seem to have migrated to the shores of the Mediterranean from an older home on the shores of the Red Sea. The Greeks knew these bronzed Semitic traders by the same name, Phoenikes or " red men," which they had before applied to the Cretans. This led to some confusion in their traditions. We have seen how the Cretan Cadmus and Europa were transferred to Phoenicia in the legend.

We have no warrant for speaking of a Phoenician sea-lordship in the Aegean. We shall see in the next chapter how the men of Tyre *No* and Sidon made a new Phoenicia in the western Mediterranean; *Phoenician* but on the shores of the Aegean they seem to have made no serious *settlements* attempts, or at least to have succeeded in no attempts, to plant per- *only some* manent settlements, except at Camirus in Rhodes, and possibly in *trading* the island of Cythera. It may be that they had stations at the purple *stations.* fisheries of Cos and Nisyros and Erythrae and elsewhere; it has been supposed that they were the first to tap the gold-mines of Siphnos and Thasos and even the silver-mines of Attica. It has been held that there were Phoenician settlements on the Isthmus of Corinth, under the Acropolis of Athens, and even at inland Thebes. There is no assurance or probability that such settlements were ever made. The Phoenicians, doubtless, had marts here and there on coast or island; but there is no reason to think that Canaanites ever made homes for themselves on Greek soil or introduced Semitic blood into the population of Greece. It was not here that the struggle was to be fought out between Baal and Zeus. Their ships were ever winding in and out of the Aegean isles from south to north, bearing fair naperies from Syria, fine-wrought bowls and cups from the work-shops of Sidonian and Cypriot silversmiths, and all manner of luxuries and ornaments; and this constant commercial intercourse lasting for two centuries is amply sufficient to account for all the influence that Phoenicia exerted upon Greece. In the worship of Aphrodite and other Greek goddesses we see the influence of the cult of Syrian Astarte. It is a mistake to suppose that the Phoenician god Melkart was taken into Greek mythology as Melicertes, but he was identified *Iavan* (= in many places with the Greek god Heracles. The briskest trade was *Iāvones),* perhaps driven with the thriving cities of Ionia, and the Phoenicians *oriental* adopted the Ionian name, and diffused it in Syria, as the general *name for* designation of all the Greeks. [But before the end of the eighth *Greeks.* century the Greeks themselves were taking part in this trade. As their Mycenaean predecessors had established themselves at Ras

Shamra on the north Syrian coast, so they now set up a small trading post at Al Mina at the mouth of the Orontes through which they traded Greek pottery and other wares for the tapestries, ivory, precious metals, and other luxury goods that came to the Syrian coast.]

The Greek These things were of slight concern compared with one inestim-
alphabet able service which the Phoenicians rendered to Hellas and thereby to
(derived Europe. They gave the Greeks the most useful instrument of civilisa-
from the tion, alphabetic writing. It was perhaps at the beginning of the ninth
Phoeni- century, hardly later, that the Phoenician alphabet was moulded to
cian) in- the needs of the Greek language. In this adaptation the Greeks
vented 10th showed their genius. The alphabet of the Phoenicians and their
to 9th cent. Semitic brethren is an alphabet of consonants ; the Greeks added
the vowels. They took some of the consonantal symbols for which
their own language had no corresponding sounds, and used these
superfluous signs to represent the vowels. Several alphabets, differ-
ing in certain details, were diffused in various parts of the Hellenic
world, but they all agree in the main points, and we may suppose
that the original idea was worked out in Ionia. In Ionia, at all
events, writing was introduced at an early period, and was perhaps
used by poets of the ninth century. Perhaps the earliest example
of a Greek writing that we possess is on an Attic jar of the seventh
century ; it says the jar shall be the prize of the dancer who dances
more gaily than all others.[1] But the lack of early inscriptions is
what we should expect. The new art was used for ordinary and
literary purposes long before it was employed for official records.
It was the great gift which the Semites gave to Europe. [And the gift
is reflected in our word " bible," which, through the Greek $\beta \upsilon \beta \lambda \acute{\iota} o \nu$
(book) and $\beta \acute{\upsilon} \beta \lambda o s$ (papyrus), is derived from the Phoenician town of
Byblos where Egyptian papyrus was first perhaps obtained by the
Greeks.]

SECT. 11. GREEK RECONSTRUCTION OF EARLY GREEK HISTORY

We must now see what the Greeks thought of their own early
history. Their construction of it, though founded on legendary
tradition and framed without much historical sense, has considerable
importance, since their ideas about the past affected their views of
the present. Their belief in their legendary past was thoroughly
practical ; mythic events were often the basis of diplomatic transactions ; claims to territory might be founded on the supposed conquests
or dominions of ancient heroes of divine birth.[2]

[1] $\grave{o}s$ $\nu \hat{\upsilon} \nu$ $\grave{o} \rho \chi \eta \sigma \tau \hat{\omega} \nu$ $\pi \acute{a} \nu \tau \omega \nu$ $\grave{a} \tau a \lambda \acute{\omega} \tau a \tau a$ $\pi a \acute{\iota} \zeta \epsilon \iota$
$\tau o[\hat{\upsilon}] \tau o$ $\delta \epsilon \kappa \hat{a}[\nu]$ $\mu \iota \nu$ (?)
[2] Grote has illustrated this from our own history. The belief in the descent

At first, before the growth of historical curiosity, the chief motive *Gene-* for investigating the past was the desire of noble families to derive *alogies.* their origin from a god.   For this purpose they sought to connect their pedigrees with heroic ancestors, especially with Heracles or with the warriors who had fought at Troy.   The Trojan war was, with some reason, regarded as a national enterprise ; and Heracles— who seems originally to have been specially associated with Argolis —was looked on as a national hero.   The consequence was that the Greeks framed their history on genealogies and determined their chronology by generations, reckoning three generations to a hundred years.   The later Homeric poets must have contributed a great deal *Poets of the* to the fixing of the mutual relations of legendary events ; but it was *Epic Cycle.* the poets of the school of Hesiod in the eighth century who did *Hesiodic* most to reduce to a historical system the legends of the heroic age. *school.* Their poems are lost, but they were worked up into still more complete and elaborate schemes by the prose logographers or "story- *The logo-* writers" of the sixth and fifth centuries, of whom perhaps the most *graphers.* influential were Hecataeus of Miletus and Acusilaus of Argos.   The original works of the logographers have also perished, but their teaching has come down to us fully enough in the works of later compilers and commentators.

In the first place, it had to be determined how the various *Classifica-* branches of the Greek race were related.   As soon as the Greeks *tion of the* came to be called by the common name of Hellenes,[1] they derived *Greek race.* their whole stock from an eponymous ancestor, Hellēn, who lived in Thessaly.[2]   They had then to account for its distribution into a number of different branches.   In Greece proper they might have searched long, among the various folks speaking various idioms, for some principle of classification which should determine the nearer and further degrees of kinship between the divisions of the race, and establish two or three original branches to which every community could trace itself back.   But when they looked over to the eastern Greece on the farther side of the Aegean, they saw, as it were, a reflection of themselves, their own children divided into three homogeneous groups—Aeolians, Ionians, and Dorians.   This gave a simple classification ; three families sprung from Aeolus, Ion, and Dorus, who must evidently have been the sons of Hellen.   But there was one difficulty.   Homer's Achaeans had still to be accounted for ;

of the kings of England from Brute the Trojan was still robust in the seventeenth century.   It figured in a state document drawn up in A.D. 1301 to uphold the rights of the English crown in the dispute with Scotland.

[1] See below, p. 106.

[2] Hellen and his sons were placed in Thessaly because the Hellenes of Homer lived in Thessalian regions.   Hellen was variously represented as the son of Zeus and the son of Deucalion (who was the son of Prometheus and Pandora).

they could not be affiliated to Aeolians, or Ionians, or Dorians, none of whom play a part in the *Iliad.* Accordingly it was arranged that Hellen had three sons, Aeolus, Dorus, and Xuthus ; and Ion and Achaeus were the sons of Xuthus.[1] It was easy enough then, by the help of tradition and language, to fit the ethnography of Greece under these labels ; and the manifold dialects were forced under three [2] artificial divisions.

The Dorian conquest conceived as the Return of the Hera-clidae.

The two great events on which everything turned and to which all other events were related were the Trojan war and the Dorian conquest of the Peloponnesus. A most curious version of the Dorian conquest was invented in Argos and won its way into general belief ; it is a striking illustration of the motives and methods of the Greeks in reconstructing their past. The Temenids, the royal family of Argos, derived themselves from Aegimius, to whom the foundation of the Dorian institutions was ascribed. But as the fame and glory of Heracles waxed great, the Temenids desired to connect themselves with him. The problem was solved with wonderful skill. The eponymous ancestors of the three Dorian tribes, Hyllus, Pamphylus, and Dyman, were naturally regarded as the sons of Aegimius. According to the new story Hyllus was really the son of Heracles. It was said that Heracles fought against the Lapiths for Aegimius who was Dorian king in Thessaly, and that he received a third of the kingdom as a reward for his valiant service. On his death his children were protected by Aegimius, who adopted Hyllus, and confirmed him in the possession of his father's third. The sons of Hyllus failed in their attempts to recover the possessions of Heracles in the Peloponnesus ; the achievement was reserved for his great-grandchildren, Temenus, Cresphontes, and Aristodemus. With a Dorian host they crossed from Naupactus, under the guidance of a one-eyed Aetolian man named Oxylus, and conquered all the Peloponnesus except Arcadia. They gave Elis to Oxylus for his pains. Those of the Achaean inhabitants of the peninsula, who did not migrate beyond the sea, retreated to the northern coast-land— the historical Achaea. The other three parts of the Peloponnesus fell by lot to the three brothers, Messenia to Cresphontes, Laconia to Aristodemus, and Argos to Temenus. An explanation was added how there were two royal houses at Sparta. Aristodemus died prematurely, and Laconia was divided between his twin sons Eurysthenes and Procles.[3]

[1] The motive for making Ion and Achaeus brothers may have been the belief that in consequence of the Dorian invasion Achaeans and Ionians had together left the Peloponnesus and colonised Asia Minor.

[2] Not four, for the Achaeans had been partly dorized and partly ionized.

[3] See below, p. 121. Agis and Eurypon, the ancestors of the royal families, the Agids and Eurypontids, were made sons of Eurysthenes and Procles.

Thus the Dorian invasion was justified as a recovery of usurped rights ; and the royal houses of Argos and Sparta renounced their Dorian origin and connected themselves by blood with Heracles, who was associated with the pre-Dorian lords of Argolis.

Every place in Greece had its own local legends, which grew up quite independently. Sometimes they were adapted and modified to suit the legendary scheme of the poets and "story-writers" ; but often they lived on, unscrupulously accepted notwithstanding all incompatibilities. In several cases we find in the poems of Homer and Hesiod legends which are inconsistent with those which became currently accepted. Thus Cadmus was the founder of Thebes according to the current legend ; but in the *Odyssey*, Thebes is built by Amphion and Zethus. The origin of Corinth was traced on one hand to Ephyre, daughter of Ocean ; on the other to Sisyphus, the son of Aeolus. The received genealogy of pre-Dorian Argos had no connexion with Hellen and his sons. Argos derived its origin from Inachus—a personification of the stream of Inachus which flows by the town—who, like most rivers, was regarded as a son of Ocean ; Argos was his great-grandson ; Io, from whom the Danaoi were descended, was his daughter. Thus it emerges that the pre-Dorian Argives were not Hellenes, for they were not derived from Hellen. If the legend had been true to history they should have been traced from Ion, as there was probably a large Ionian element in Argolis.

But for most of the Greeks connexions with Hellen and his sons *The* were manufactured. It was to Aeolus that most descents were *Aeolids:* traced. He had seven sons and five daughters, and it was not difficult to work out more or less plausible connexions. Aetolian legends fastened themselves on to his daughter Calyce. His son Sisyphus founded Corinth. The Thessalian heroes, Admetus and Jason, were derived from another son, Cretheus. Perhaps the most *The* interesting instance is the genealogy which was established for the *Neleids.* Codrid families of Miletus and other cities of Ionia. They traced up their lineage to Poseidon and at the same time derived themselves from Hellen. The story was that Salmoneus, son of Aeolus, had a daughter who bore to Poseidon twin sons, Pelias and Neleus. As Pelias won the Thessalian kingdom of Iolcus, Neleus went forth from the land and founded a kingdom for himself at Pylus in the south-west of the Peloponnesus. He was succeeded by Nestor, who in his old age bore a part in the Trojan war. Nestor's fourth successor Melanthus was ruler of Pylus when the Dorians came down into the Peloponnesus, and he retreated before their attack to Athens, where Νειλεύς he became king and was the father of Codrus. Then Neleus, a son (*Ionic*), Νηλεύς of Codrus, led the Ionian migration to Asia Minor. Thus a number (*Aeolic*).

of different traditions were wrought into a narrative, which, originating in Ionia, was accepted in Attica and influenced the ideas of the Athenians about a part of their own early history.

The Greeks were not content that their legends should be confined to the range of their own country and their own race ; and, in curious contrast with that exclusive pride which drew a hard and fast line between Greek and barbarian, they brought their ancestors and their myths into connexion with foreign lands. Thus the myth *Egypt.* of Io made the Danaoi of Argos cousins of the Egyptians. By her amour with Zeus, Io became the grandmother of Danaus and Aegyptus, the eponymous ancestors of the two peoples. Cadmus, the *Phoenicia.* name-sire of the Cadmeians of Thebes, was represented as a Phoenician, who went forth from his own land in quest of his sister *Phrygia.* Europa and settled in Boeotia. The tale which gained widest belief made Pelops son of the Phrygian Tantalus, king of Sipylus, whence he migrated to the Peloponnesus and founded the royal line of Argos, *Colchis.* from which Agamemnon was sprung. A Corinthian legend brought the early history of Corinth into connexion with Colchis, representing Aeetes, offspring of the Sun, as the first Corinthian king, and his daughter Medea as heiress to the land. The true home of the Greeks before they won dominion in Greece had passed clean out of their remembrance, and they looked to the east, not to the north, as the quarter from which some of their ancestors had migrated.

Legend of the Amazons Of the legends which won sincere credence among the Greeks, and assumed as we may say a national significance, none is more curious or more obscure in its origin than than of the Amazons. A folk of warrior women, strong and brave, living apart from men, were conceived to have dwelt in Asia in the heroic age, and proved themselves worthy foes of the Greek heroes. An obvious etymology of their name, " breastless," suggested the belief that they used to burn off the right breast that they might the better draw the bow. *In the* Iliad In the *Iliad* Priam tells how he fought against their army in Phrygia ; *(iii.186 and* and one of the perilous tasks which are set to Bellerophon is to *vi. 152).* march against the Amazons. In a later Homeric poem, the Amazon *In the* Penthesilea appears as a dreaded adversary of the Greeks at Troy. *Aethiopis.* To win the girdle of the Amazon queen was one of the labours of Heracles. All these adventures happened in Asia Minor ; and, though this female folk was located in various places, its original and proper home was ultimately placed on the river Thermodon near the *Amazon* Greek colony of Amisus. But the Amazons attacked Greece itself. *invasion of* It was told that Theseus carried off their queen Antiope, and so they *Attica.* came and invaded Attica. There was a terrible battle in the town of Athens, and the invaders were defeated after a long struggle. At the feast of Theseus the Athenians used to sacrifice to the Amazons ;

there was a building called the Amazoneion in the western quarter of the city; and the episode was believed by such men as Isocrates and Plato to be as truly an historical fact as the Trojan war itself. The battles of Greeks with Amazons were a favourite subject of Grecian sculptors; and, like the Trojan war and the adventure of the golden fleece, the Amazon story fitted into the conception of an ancient and long strife between Greece and Asia.

The details of the famous legends—the labours of Heracles, the Trojan war, the voyage of the Argonauts, the tale of Cadmus, the life of Oedipus, the two sieges of Thebes by the Argive Adrastus, and all the other familiar stories—belong to mythology and lie beyond our present scope. But we have to realise that the later Greeks believed them and discussed them as sober history, and that many of them had a genuine historical basis, however slender. The story of the Trojan war has more historical matter in it than any other; but we have seen that the Argonautic legend and the tale of Cadmus contain dim memories of actual events. It is quite probable that the heroic age witnessed rivalry and war between Thebes and Argos.

Two powerful generating forces of these historic myths had been the custom of families and cities to trace their origin to a god, and the instinct of the Greeks to personify places, especially towns, rivers, and springs. Then, when men began both to become keenly conscious of a community of race and language, and to speculate upon the past, attempts were naturally made to bring the various myths of Greece into harmony; since they were true, they must be reconciled. Ultimately they were reduced into chronological systems, which were based upon genealogical reckonings by generations. Hecataeus of Miletus counted a generation as forty years; but it was more usual to reckon three generations to a hundred years. According to the scheme which finally won the widest acceptance, Troy was taken in 1184 B.C., and the Dorians invaded the Peloponnesus under the leadership of the Heraclids in 1104 B.C., and both these dates accord more closely than one might expect, considering the method by which they were obtained, with the general probabilities of the case.

LEADING DATES ACCORDING TO THE SYSTEM OF ERATOSTHENES
(*c.* 220 B.C.)

Cadmus	.	.	.	B.C.	1313
Pelops	.	.	.	,,	1283
Heracles	.	.	.	,,	1261-1209
Argonauts	.	.	.	,,	1225
Seven against Thebes			.	,,	1213
Fall of Troy	.	.	.	,,	1184

LEADING DATES ACCORDING TO THE SYSTEM OF ERATOSTHENES
(*c*. 220 B.C.)—*continued*

Thessalian conquest ⎱
Boeotian   ,,   ⎰   .   .   B.C. 1124
Aeolic migration ⎰
Return of Heraclidae   .   .   ,, 1104
Death of Codrus   .   .   .   ,, 1044
Ionic migration   .   .   .   ,, 1044
Lycurgus at Sparta.   .   .   ,,   885

NORTHERN
GREECE.

Stadia
0   100 200 300 400 500 600

English Miles
0   10   20   30   40   50   60

FIG. 21.

Walker & Boutall sc.

CHAPTER II

THE EXPANSION OF GREECE

SECT. 1. CAUSES AND CHARACTER OF GREEK COLONISATION

THE expansion of the Greeks beyond Greece proper and the coasts of the Aegean, the plantation of Greek colonies on the shores of Thrace and the Black Sea, in Italy and Sicily, even in Spain and Gaul, began it is uncertain when, and was completed in the sixth century. But it must not be regarded as a single or isolated phenomenon. It was the continuation of the earlier expansion over the Aegean islands and the coast of Asia Minor, the details of which were forgotten by the Greeks themselves, and are consequently unknown to us.

Difference of Greek and Phoenician colonisation. The cause of Greek colonisation is not to be found in mere trade interests. These indeed were in most cases a motive, and in some of the settlements on the Black Sea they were perhaps a leading motive. But the great difference between Greek and Phoenician colonisation is that, while the Phoenicians aimed solely at promoting their commerce, and only a few of their settlements, notably Carthage, became more than mere trading-stations or factories, Greek colonisation satisfied other needs than desire of commercial profit. It was the expression of the adventurous spirit which has been poetically reflected in the legends of the "Sailing of the Argo" and the "Home-coming of Odysseus" — the same spirit, not to be expressed in any commercial formula, which prompted English colonisation.

Causes of Greek colonisation: (1) trade; (2) the land-system; Trade, of course, sometimes paved the way. [Greek pottery, made before the age of colonisation, has been found widely distributed in Italy and Sicily and, in many cases, at or near the sites where the Greeks later established colonies.] Colonists followed in the paths of trade. The adventurous, the discontented, and the needy were always to be found. But in the case of the early colonies at least, it was not over-population of the land, so much as the nature of the land-system, that drove men to emigrate. In various ways, under the family system, which was ill suited to independent and adventurous spirits, it would come about that individual members were excluded from a share in the common estate, and separated from their kin. Such lacklands were ripe for colonial enterprise. Again, the political circumstances of most Greek states in the eighth and seventh centuries favoured emigration. We have seen that at this time the aristocratic form of government generally pre- *(3) political conditions* vailed. Sometimes a king was formally at the head, but he was really no more than the first of peers ; a body of nobles were the true masters. Sometimes there was an aristocracy within an aristocracy ; or a large clan, like the Bacchiads at Corinth, held the power. In all cases the distinction between the members of the ruling class and the mass of free citizens was widened and deepened. It was the tendency of the rulers to govern in their own interest and oppress the multitude, and they cared little to disguise their contempt for the mass of the people. At Mytilene things went so far that the Penthilids, who had secured the chief power, went about in the streets, armed with clubs, and knocked down citizens whom they disliked. Under these conditions there were strong inducements for men to leave their native city where they were of little account and had to endure the slights, if nothing worse, of their rulers, and to join in the foundation of a new *polis* where they might themselves rule. The same inducement drew nobles who did not belong to the inner oligarchical circle. In fact, political discontent was an immediate *Colonisa-* cause of Greek colonisation ; and conversely it may be said that *tion a* colonisation was a palladium of aristocracy. If this outlet had not *security to* existed, or if it had not suited the Hellenic temper, the aristocracies *aristocratic* might not have lasted so long, and they wisely discerned that it was *states.* their own interest to encourage colonisation.

But while we recognise the operation of general causes we must *Special* not ignore special causes. We must, for instance, take into account *causes.* the fact that Miletus and the south Ionian cities were unable to expand in Caria, as the north Ionian cities expanded in Lydia, because the Carians were too strong for them ; and Lycia presented the same kind of barrier to Rhodes. Otherwise, perhaps neither Rhodes nor Miletus would have sent settlers to distant lands.

Wherever the Greek went, he retained his customs and language, and made a Greek " polis." It was as if a bit of Greece were set down on the remote shores of the Euxine or in the far west on the wild coasts of Gaul or Iberia. The colony was a private enterprise, *Relation of* but the bond of kinship with the " mother-city " was carefully fostered, *the colony* and though political discontent might have been the cause which *to the* drove the founders forth, yet that solemn departure for a distant land, *mother-city.*

where a new city-state, protected by the same gods, was to spring up, always sealed a reconciliation. The emigrants took fire from the public hearth of their city to light the fire on that of their new home. Intercourse between colonies and the mother-country was specially kept up at the great religious festivals of the year, and various marks of filial respect were shown by the daughter to the mother. When, as frequently befell, the colony determined herself in turn to throw off a new shoot, it was the recognised custom that she should seek the *oecist* or leader of the colonists from the mother-city. Thus the Megarian colony, Byzantium, when it founded its own colony, Mesembria, must have sought an oecist from Megara. The political importance of colonisation was sanctified by religion, and it was a necessary formality, whenever a settlement was to be made, to ask the approbation of the Delphic god. The most ancient oracular god of Greece was Zeus of Dodona. The Selli, his priests and "interpreters," are

Oracles.   mentioned in the *Iliad;* and in the *Odyssey* Dodona appears as a place to which a king of the west might go to ask the will of Zeus "from the lofty oak," wherein the god was conceived to dwell. But the oak-shrine in the highlands of Epirus was too remote to become the chief oracle of Greece, and the central position of Delphi enabled the astute priests of the Pythian Apollo [1] to exalt the authority of their god as a true prophet to the supreme place in the Greek world. There were other oracular deities who foretold the future ; there was, not far off, Trophonius at Boeotian Lebadea ; there was Amphiaraus in the land of the Graii, not yet Boeotian. But none of these ever became even a rival of the Delphian Apollo, who by the seventh century at least had won the position of adviser to Greece.[2]

Conscious-ness of Greek unity promoted by colonisa-tion,   It is worthy of notice that colonisation tended to promote a feeling of unity among the Greek peoples, and it did so in two ways. By the wide diffusion of their race on the fringe of barbarous lands, it brought home to them more fully the contrast between Greek and barbarian, and, by consequence, the community of the Greeks. The
through (1) *intercourse with non-Greeks ;*   Greek dwellers in Asia Minor, neighbours of not-Greek peoples, were naturally impressed with their own unity in a way which was strange to dwellers in Boeotia or Attica, who were surrounded on all sides by Greeks and were therefore alive chiefly to local differences. With the diffusion of their sons over various parts of the world, the
(2) *joint enterprises.*   European Greeks acquired a stronger sense of unity. In the second place, colonisation led to the association of Greeks of different cities. An oecist who decided to organise a party of colonists could not always find in his own city a sufficient number of men willing to take

---

[1] The Delphic oracle is also mentioned in the *Odyssey*, for instance in viii. 80.

[2] The influence of the oracle is another question. See below, p. 161.

part in the enterprise. He therefore enlisted comrades from other cities; and thus many colonies were joint undertakings and contained a mixture of citizens of various nationality. This feature was not indeed confined to the later epoch of colonisation; it is one of the few facts about the earlier settlements on the Asiatic coast of which we can be certain.

Sect. 2. Colonies on the Coasts of the Euxine, Propontis, and North Aegean

The voyage of the Argonauts in quest of the golden fleece com- *Legend of* memorates in a delightful legend the memorable day on which Greek *the Argo.* sailors for the first time burst into the waters of the Euxine Sea. Accustomed to the island straits and short distances of the Aegean, they fancied that when they had passed the Bosphorus they were embarking on a boundless ocean, and they called it the " Main," *Pontos.* Even when they had circumnavigated its shores it might *The Pontos* still seem boundless, for they knew not where the great rivers, the *(Black* Ister, the Tanais, the Danapris, might lead. The little preliminary *Sea).* sea into which the Hellespont widens, to contract again into the narrow passage of the Bosphorus, was appropriately named the " vestibule of the Pontus "—*Propontis.* Full of creeks and recesses, *Propontis.* it is happily described by Euripides as the " bayed water-key of the boundless Sea." The Pontus was a treacherous field for the barques of even experienced mariners, and it was supposed to have received for this reason its name " Euxine," or Hospitable, in accordance with a habit of the Greeks to seek to propitiate adverse powers by pleasant names.[1] It was when the compass of the Euxine was still unknown, and men were beginning shyly to explore its coasts, that the tale of *Signifi-* the wanderings of Odysseus took form. He was imagined to have *cance of the* sailed from Troy into the Pontus, and, after having been driven about Odyssey. in its waters, to have at last reached Ithaca by an overland journey through Thrace and Epirus. In the *Odyssey,* as we have it now, compounded of many different legends and poems, this is disguised; the island of Circe has been removed to the far west, and the scene of the Descent to the Underworld translated to the Atlantic Ocean. But Circe, the daughter of the Sun, and sister of King Aeetes who possessed the golden fleece, belongs to the seas of Colchis; and the world of shades beyond the Cimmerians is to be sought near the Cimmerian Bosphorus. The mention of Sicily in *(Straits of* some of the later parts of the poem, and the part played by Ithaca, *Azov).* which, with the other islands of the Ionian Sea, lay on the road to the western Mediterranean, reflect the beginning of the expansion of

[1] But this explanation is by no means certain.

Greece in that direction. But the original wanderings of Odysseus were connected, not with the west, but with the exploration of the Euxine.

A mist of obscurity hangs about the beginnings of the first Greek cities which arose on the Pontic shores. Here Miletus was the pioneer. Merchants carrying the stuffs which were manufactured from the wool of Milesian sheep may have established trading-stations along the southern coast. Flax from Colchis, steel and silver, slaves were among the chief products which their wool bought. But the *Megarian colonies:* work of colonisation beyond the gate of the Bosphorus can hardly have fully begun until the gate itself was secured by the enterprise of Megara, which sent out men, in the first part of the seventh century, *Byzan-tium;* to found the towns of Chalcedon and Byzantium. Byzantium could command the trade of the Black Sea, but the great commercial and *[660 B.C.]* political importance of her situation was not fully appreciated until a thousand years had passed, when she became the rival and successor of Rome and took, in honour of her second founder, the name Constantinople. This is the first appearance of the little state of Megara in Greek history; and none of her contemporaries took a step that was destined to lead to greater things than the settlement on the Chalcedon; Bosphorus. The story was that Chalcedon was founded first, before the Megarians perceived the striking advantages of the opposite shore, and the Delphic oracle, which they consulted as a matter of course, chid them as "blind men." Westward from Byzantium Selymbria; they also founded Selymbria, on the north coast of the Propontis; Heraclea. eastward they established "Heraclea in Pontus," on the coast of Bithynia.

Milesian colonies: The enterprise of the Megarians stimulated Miletus, and she determined to anticipate others in seizing the best sites on the Pontic shore. At the most northerly point of the southern coast a strait-necked cape forms two natural harbours, an attractive site for Sinope; settlers, and here the Milesians planted the city Sinope.[1] Farther east, half-way to that extreme eastern point of the sea where the Phasis flows out at the foot of Mount Caucasus, arose another Mile-Trebizond; sian colony, Trapezus. At the Bosphorus the Milesians had been anticipated by Megara, but they partly made up for this by planting Abydos; Abydos on the Hellespont opposite Sestos, and they also seized a jutting promontory on the south coast of the Propontis, where a narrow neck, as at Sinope, forms two harbours. The town was Cyzicus. named Cyzicus, and the peninsula was afterwards transformed into

---

[1] This city claimed to date from the eighth century, to have been swept away in the invasion of the Cimmerians, and to have risen again in the seventh; but it is highly improbable that any of the Pontic cities were older than the towns of the Bosphorus and Propontis.

FIG. 32.

Expansion of Greece in the
PROPONTIS AND PONTUS

Stadia
0   500   1000   1500

English Miles
0   50   100   150   200

Walker & Boutall sc.

Phocaean colony: Lampsacus.

an island ; the tunny-fish on the coins of the city shows what was one of the chief articles of her trade. Lampsacus, at the northern end of the Hellespont, once a Phoenician factory, was colonised by another Ionian city, Phocaea, about the same time, and the winged sea-horse on Lampsacene coins speaks of naval enterprise which led afterwards to wealth and prosperity. The foundation of Parion was due to a joint undertaking of Miletus and Erythrae ; and Clazomenae joined Miletus in planting Cardia at the neck of the Thracian Chersonese, in the important position of an advance fort against Thrace. On the southern side of the Hellespont the lands of the Scamander invited the Greeks of Lesbos, and a number of small Aeolian settlements arose.

Milesian and Erythraean colony: Parion. Cardia.

Other settlements on the Pontus: Dioscurias, Phasis, Panticapaeum, Tanais, Heraclea, Olbia, Odessus, Mesembria.

Greek settlements also sprang up in the more remote parts of the Euxine. Dioscurias and Phasis were founded in the far east, in the fabled land of Colchis. On the Tauric Chersonesus or " peninsula " (now the Crimea), Panticapaeum was founded over against Phanagoria at the entrance to the Maeotic lake, and Tanais at the mouth of the like-named river. Heraclea, or Chersonesus, on the western side of the peninsula, was destined to preserve the municipal forms of an old Greek city for more than a thousand years. Olbia at the mouth of the Dnieper, Odessus, Istrus, Mesembria were only some of the Greek settlements which complete the circuit of the Black Sea.

Worship of Achilles in the Pontus.

This sea and the Propontis were the special domain of the sea-god Achilles, whose fame grew greater by his association as a hero with the legend of Troy. He was worshipped along the coasts as " lord of the Pontus " ; and in Leuce, the " shining island " near the Danube's mouth, the lonely island where no man dwelled, he had

Ποντ-άρχης. *Temple at Leuce.*

a temple, and the birds of the sea were said to be its warders.

Chalcidian colonisation.

FIG. 33.—Early coin of Potidaea (obverse). Poseidon riding ; star [legend : Π].

If Miletus and Megara took the most prominent part in extending the borders of the Greek world eastward of the Hellespont, the north-western corner of the Aegean was the special domain of Euboea. The barren islands of Sciathus and Peparethus were the bridge from Euboea to the coast of Macedonia, which, runs out into a huge three-pronged promontory. Here Chalcis planted so many towns that the whole promontory was named Chalcidice. Some of

Chalcidice.

Corinthian colony: Potidaea.

the chief cities, however, were founded by other states, notably Corinthian Potidaea on the most westerly of the three prongs, which was called Pallene. Sithonia was the central prong, and Acte, ending in Mount Athos, the eastern. Some of the colonies on

Pallene were founded by Eretria, and those north of Acte by Andros, which was dependent on Eretria. Hence we may regard this group of cities as Euboean, though we cannot regard it as Chalcidian. On the west side of the Thermaic Bay, two Euboean colonies were planted, Pydna and Methone, on Macedonian soil.   *Pydna and Methone.*

Sect. 3. Colonies in the Western Mediterranean

The earliest mention of Sicilian and Italian regions in literature is to be found in some later passages of the *Odyssey*, which should perhaps be referred to the eighth century. There we meet with the Sicels, and with the island of Sicania ; while Temesa, where Greek traders could buy Tuscan copper, has the distinction of being the first Italian place mentioned by name in a literary record. By the end of the seventh century Greek states stood thick on the east coast of Sicily and round the sweep of the Tarentine Gulf. These colonies naturally fall into three groups :

(1) The Euboean, which were both in Sicily and in Italy.
(2) The Achaean, which were altogether on Italian soil.
(3) The Dorian, which were, with few exceptions, in Sicily.

The oldest stories of the adventures of Odysseus were laid, as we have seen, in the half-explored regions of the Black Sea. Nothing shows more impressively the life of this poetry, and the power it had won over the hearts of the Greek folks, than the fact that when the navigation of the Italian and Sicilian seas began, these adventures were transferred from the east to the west ; and in the further growth of this cycle of poems a new mythical geography was adopted. At a time when the Greeks knew so little of Italy that the southern promontories could be designated as "sacred islands,"[1] the straits of Messana were identified with Scylla and Charybdis, Lipara became the island of Aeolus, the home of the Cyclopes was found in the fiery mount of Aetna. Then Scheria, the isle of the Phaeacians, was fancied to be Corcyra ; an entrance to the under-world was placed at Cumae ; and the rocks of the Sirens were sought near Sorrento. And not only did the first glimpses of western geography affect the transmutation of the *Odyssey* into its final shape, but the *Odyssey* reacted on the geography of the west. That the promontory of Circei in Latin territory bears the name of the sorceress of Colchis, is an evidence of the spell of Homeric song. Odysseus was not the only hero who was borne westward with Greek ships in the eighth century. Cretan Minos and Daedalus, for example, had links with Sicily. Above all, the earliest navigation of the western seas was ascribed to Heracles, who reached the limits of the land of the setting sun,   *Odysseus in the west.*

[1] The expression is preserved in the Catalogue of the Hesiodic Theogony.

and stood on the ledge of the world looking out upon the stream of Oceanus. From him the opposite cliffs which form the gate of the Mediterranean were called the Pillars of Heracles.

EUBOEAN COLONIES : The earliest colony founded by Greek sailors in the western seas was said to have been Cyme on the coast of Campania. Tradition
Cyme. assigned to it an origin before 1000 B.C., a date which modern
Its date. criticism has called in question. [But the tradition that it was the first Greek colony may still be true, for the pottery in the earliest graves of the colonists is earlier than that from Syracuse and suggests a foundation date before the middle of the eighth century. It had an
Founders. unique position.] Chalcis, Eretria, and Cyme a town on the eastern coast of Euboea, which at that time had some eminence but afterwards sank into the obscurity of a village, joined together, and enlisted for their expedition some Graeans who dwelled on the opposite mainland in the neighbourhood of Tanagra. The colonisers settled first on the island of Pithecusae, and soon succeeded in establishing themselves on a rocky height which rises above the sea just where the Italian coast is about to turn sharply eastward to encircle the bay
Site. of Naples. The site was happily chosen. It was a strong post, and though there was no harbour, the strangers could haul up their ships on a stretch of sand below. But when trade developed and larger merchantmen were built an open strand was no longer adequate. The Cumaeans then occupied the harbour which was just inside the
Dicae- promontory, and established there the town of Dicaearchia, which
archia. afterwards became Puteoli; farther east they founded Naples, " the
Neapolis. new city."

The people in whose midst this outpost of Greek civilisation was planted were the Opicans, one of the chief branches of the Italic
Importance race. The colonists were eminently successful in their intercourse
of Cyme in with the natives; and the solitary position of Cyme in these regions
European —for no Greek settlement could be made northward on account of
history. the great Etruscan power, and there was no rival southward until the later plantation of Posidonia—made her influence both wide and noiseless. Her external history is uneventful; there are no striking wars or struggles to record; but the work she did holds an important and definite place in the history of European civilisation. To the
Italian Euboeans of Cyme we may say that we owe the alphabet which we
alphabet. use to-day, for it was from them that the Latins learned to write. The Etruscans also got their alphabet independently from the same masters, and, having modified it in certain ways to suit themselves,
Intro- passed it on to the Oscans and Umbrians. Again, the Cymaeans
duction of introduced the neighbouring Italian peoples to a knowledge of the
Greek gods. Greek gods and Greek religion. Heracles, Apollo, Castor, and Polydeuces became such familiar names in Italy that they came to

be regarded as original Italian deities. The oracles of the Cymaean Sibyl, prophetess of Apollo, were believed to contain the destinies of Rome.

To Cyme, too, western Europe probably owes the name by which *Origin of* she calls Hellas and the Hellenes. The Greeks, when they first *the name* came into contact with Latins, had no common name ; Hellenes, the *Greece—* name which afterwards united them, was as yet merely associated with a particular tribe. It was only natural that strangers should extend the name of the first Greeks with whom they came in contact to others whom they fell in with later, and so to all Greeks whatsoever. But the curious circumstance is that the settlers of Cyme were *from the* known, not by the name of Chalcis or Eretria or Cyme itself, but by *Boeotian* that of Graia. *Graii* was the term which the Latins and their *Graeans.* fellows applied to the colonists, and the name *Graeci* is a derivative of a usual type from Graii. It was doubtless some trivial accident which ruled that we to-day call Hellas " Greece," instead of knowing it by some name derived from Cyme, Eretria, or Chalcis. The west has got its " Greece " from an obscure district in Boeotia ; Greece itself got its " Hellas " from a small territory in Thessaly. This was accidental. But it was no accident that western Europe calls Greece by a name connected with that city in which Greeks first came into touch with the people who were destined to civilise western Europe and rule it for centuries.

The next settlement of the Euboean Greeks was on Sicilian, not *Sicily ; its* Italian, ground. The island of Sicily is geographically a continuation *position in* of Italy—just as the Peloponnesus is a continuation of the great *history.* eastern peninsula ; but its historical importance depends much more on another geographical fact. It is the centre of the Mediterranean ; it parts the eastern from the western waters. It has been thus marked out by nature as a meeting-place of nations ; and the struggle between European and Asiatic peoples, which has been called the " Eternal Question," has been partly fought out on Sicilian soil. There has been in historical times no native Sicilian power. The greatness of the island was due to colonisation—not migration— from other lands. Lying as a connecting link between Europe and Africa, it attracted settlers from both sides ; while its close proximity to Italy always rendered it an object of acquisition to those who successively ruled in that peninsula.

The earliest inhabitants of the island were the Sicans. They *SICANS.* believed themselves to be autochthonous, and we have no record at what time they entered the island or whence they came or to what race they belonged. The nature of things makes it probable that they entered from Italy. From them the island was called Sicania. The next comers were the Sicels, of whom we can speak *SICELS.*

with more certainty. As we find Sicels in the toe of Italy, we know that tradition correctly described them as settlers from the Italian peninsula, and there is some slight evidence to show that they spoke the same language as that group of Italic peoples, to which the Latins belonged. The likeness of the names Sicel and Sican has *Were* naturally led to the view that these two folks were akin in race and *Sicans and* language. But likeness of names is deceptive ; and it is a remarkable *Sicels* fact that the Greeks, who were only too prone to build up theories *kinsfolk ?* on resemblances of words, always carefully distinguished the Sican *Answer* from the Sicel as ethnically different. Still a connexion is possible, *uncertain.* if we suppose that the Sicels were Sicans who remaining behind in Italy had in the course of centuries become Italicised by intercourse with the Latin and kindred peoples, and then, emigrating in their turn to the island, met without recognition the brethren from whom they had parted in the remote past. But all this is uncertain. The Sicels, however, wrested from the Sicans the eastern half of the island, which was thus cut up into two countries, Sicania in the west, Sicelia in the east. In the *Odyssey* we read of Sicania ; perhaps the Greeks of Cyme knew it by this name. At a very early time Sicania was invaded by a mysterious people named *ELY-* Elymians, variously said to have come from Italy and from the *MIANS.* north of Asia Minor. The probability is that they were of Iberian race. They occupied a small territory in the north-west of the island.

These were the three peoples who inhabited this miniature continent, soon about to become the battlefield of Greek and Phoenician. The Sicels were the most numerous and most import- *Sican* ant. The only Sican town of any significance in historical times *places.* was *Hykkara* on the north-west promontory. *Minôa*, originally Sican on the south coast, became Greek. *Camicus*, at some dis- tance inland in the same region, was in early days an important *Elymian* stronghold. The Elymian settlements at *Segesta* and *Eryx* became *towns.* of far greater importance than the Sican. The eastern half of the *Sicel towns.* isle, the original Sicelia, was thickly set with Sicel fortresses from *Cephaloedium* (the modern Cefalù), at the centre of the northern coast, to *Motyca*, an inland town in the south-eastern corner. Among the most famous were *Agyrium*, *Centuripa*, *Morgantina*, and above all *Henna*.

PHOE- At an early age merchants from Phoenicia planted factories on *NICIANS :* the coasts of the island. At first they did not make any settlements of a permanent kind,—any that could be called cities. For Sicily *Colonies in* was to them only a house to call at, lying directly on their way to *Spain* the land of the farthest west, when they went forth to win the golden *(Gades).* treasures of Tarshish and planted their earliest colony, Gades, outside *Africa.*

FIG. 34.

SICILY
and
MAGNA GRAECIA.

Stadia
0 100 200 300 400 500   1000

English Miles
0   50   100

Walker & Boutall sc.

Sican Settlements......Μυκκαρα
Sicel   „   ......Henna
Elymian   „   ......SEGESTA
Phoenician „   ......MOTYA
Greek {Euboean (Ionian)....Cyme
       Dorian.................SYRACUSE
       Achaean & mixed......Sybaris

the straits which divide Europe from Africa.   Their next colonies were
on the coast of Africa over against Sicily, and this settlement had a
decisive influence on the destinies of the island.   The Phoenician
trading-stations on the east coast of Sicily were probably outposts
of old Phoenicia, but some at least of those in the west seem to
(Hippo,   have come from the new and nearer Phoenicia.   The settlements
Utica.)   of Hippo and Utica, older than Carthage, were probably the parents
Stations in of the more abiding Phoenician settlements in Sicily.[1]   In the east
Sicily.   of the island the Phoenicians had no secure foothold.   They were
not able to dispossess the Sicel natives, or to make a home among
them ; they appeared purely in the guise of traders.   Hence when
the Greeks came and seriously set to work to plant true cities, the
Phoenicians disappeared and left no traces to show that they had ever
been there.

GREEKS.   Sicilian, like Italian history, really opens with the coming of the
Greeks.   They came under the guidance of Chalcis and the auspices of
Apollo.   It was naturally on the east coast which faces Greece that
the first Greek settlement was made, and it is to be noticed that of
the coasts of Sicily the east is that which most resembles in character
the coast-line of Greece.   The site which was chosen by the Chalcidians,
Naxos   and the Ionians of Naxos who accompanied them, was not a striking
[*tradi-*   one.   A little tongue of land, north of Mount Aetna, very different
tional date, from the height of Cyme, was selected for the foundation of Naxos.
735 *B.C.*].   Here, as in the case of Cyme, the Chalcidians who led the enterprise
surrendered the honour of naming the new city to their less prominent
fellow-founders.   The first of all the Greek towns of Sicily, Naxos was
Its destruc- not destined to live for much more than three hundred years.   It was
tion.   to be destroyed not by the fire of the dangerous mountain which dominated it, but by a human foe. A sort of consecration was always attached
to Naxos as the first homestead of the Hellenes in the island which
The altar   was to become a brilliant part of Hellas.   To Apollo Archēgĕtes an
of Apollo   altar was erected on the spot where the Greeks first landed,—driven,
Archegetes. as the legend told, by contrary winds, through Apollo's dispensation,
to the Sicilian shores.   It was the habit of ambassadors from old
Greece as soon as they arrived in Sicily to offer sacrifice on this

---

[1] See below, p. 102.   There is no clear evidence for the date of the Phoenician
colonies in western Sicily.   It might be argued that they were later than the Greek
colonies, on the ground that the Phoenicians, if their colonisation had begun
earlier than Greek colonisation, would have occupied the excellent sites which the
Greeks seized.   But this argument is not conclusive.   For one thing, the Sicels
had to be reckoned with.   It was probably an easier task to gain a footing on
Sican soil ; and the Phoenicians may have tried and failed on Sicel soil where the
Greeks succeeded.   Or again, if Phoenician city-settlements grew out of mere
factories. the Greeks may have abolished such factories, which might, if they had
been left to themselves, have grown into cities.

altar. In the fertile plain south of Aetna the Chalcidians soon after- Catane
wards founded Catane, close to the sea and protected by a low range [728 *B.C.*].
of hills behind, but under the power of Aetna which was to unmake
the place again and again ; and inland Leontini at the south end of Leontini
her plain between two hills, with an eastern and a western acropolis. [728 *B.C.*].
These sites, Leontini certainly if not Catane, were wrested from the
Sicels. The Chalcidians also won possession of the north-east
corner, and thus obtained command of the straits
between the island and the mainland. Here
Cymaeans and Chalcidians planted Zancle on a low
rim of land, which resembles a reaping-hook and
gave the place its name. The haven is formed by
the curving blade ; and when Zancle came in after-
days to mint money she engraved on her coins a
sickle representing her harbour and a dolphin
floating within it. Some 200 years later, under the
influence of Anaxilas of Rhegium, new immigrants
were brought in including Messenians, and ultimately the old local name was ousted in favour of
Messana. From Zancle the Euboeans established

Zancle [*c.*
715 *B.C.* ?]
(ζάγκλον,
δάγκλον)

FIG. 35.—Coin of
Zancle, early (ob-
verse). Harbour
of Zancle, with a
dolphin [legend :
ΔANK(λαίων)].   = *Messêné*

the fortress of Mylae on the other side of the north-eastern promontory ; Mylae.
and in the middle of the seventh century they founded Himera, the Himera
only Greek city on the northern coast, destined to [648 *B.C.*].
live for scarce two centuries and a half, and then
to be swept away by the Phoenician. It was
important for Zancle that the land over against
her, the extreme point of the Italian peninsula,
should be in friendly hands, and therefore the men
of Zancle incited their mother-city to found
Rhegion ; and in this foundation Messenians took Rhegion.
part.

FIG. 36.—Coin of
Himera,   early
(obverse). Cock.

    While this group of Chalcidian colonies was *DORIAN*
being formed in north-eastern Sicily, Dorian Greeks *COLONIES :*
began to obtain a footing in south-eastern Sicily, which history
decided should become the Dorian quarter. The earliest of the
Dorian cities was also the greatest. Syracuse, destined to be the Syracuse
head of Greek Sicily, was founded by Corinthian emigrants under [*trad. date,*
the leadership of Archias before the end of the eighth century. Some- 734 *B.C.*].
where about the same time Corinth also colonised Corcyra ; the Corcyra
Ionian islands were half-way stations to the west. Which colony was [*trad. date,*
the elder, we know not ; tradition did not attempt to decide, for it 734 *B.C.*].
placed both in the same year. Force was needed for both enterprises.
Eretrians had to be driven from Corcyra, Sicels from Syracuse.

    The great Haven of Syracuse, with its island and its hill, formed the most striking site on the east coast, and could not fail to invite the

The Island, Ortygia. earliest colonists. [The island of Ortygia, already well known to Greek traders, was first occupied and the colony was soon to spread extensively on the mainland opposite. There is an alternative

tradition in Ephorus that Syracuse was not founded until a generation later than Naxos, but the earlier date has the earlier and more reliable testimony of Thucydides. By holding Syracuse Corinth effectually prevented any Chalcidian expansion south of Leontini.]

Fig. 37.—Coin of Syracuse, early (obverse). Head of Arethusa ; dolphins [legend : ΣΥΡΑϙΟ-ΣΙΟΝ].

At an early date Megarians also sailed into the west to find a new home. After various unsuccessful attempts to establish themselves, they finally built their city on the coast north of Syracuse, beside the hills of Hybla, and perhaps Sicel natives joined in founding the western *Megara*. It was

Megara *(Hyblaean)* [*trad. date,* 728 *B.C.*]. the most northerly Dorian town on the east coast. But, like her mother, the Hyblaean Megara was destined to found a colony more famous than herself. In the middle of the seventh century the Megarians sent to their metropolis to invite co-operation in planting

Selinus [628 *B.C.*]. a settlement in the south-western part of the island. This settlement, which was to be the farthest outpost of Greek Sicily, was Selinus, the town named of wild celery as its own coins boasted, situated on a low hill on the coast. Megara had been occupied with the good-will of the Sicel ; Selinus was probably held at the expense of the Sican. In the meantime the south-eastern corner was being studded with Dorian cities, though they did not rise by any means so rapidly as the Chalcidian in the north. The Sicels seem to have offered a

Rhodian Gela [*trad. date,* 688 *B.C.*]. stouter resistance here. At the beginning of the seventh century, Gela—the name is Sicel—was planted by Rhodian colonists with Cretans in their train. This city was set on a long narrow hill which stretched between the sea and an inland plain. At a later time

Syracusan Acrae *and* Casmenae *and* Camarina [595 *B.C.*]. Acrae and Casmenae were founded by Syracuse. They were over-shadowed by the greatness of the mother-city, and never attained as much independence as more distant Camarina which was planted from the same metropolis about half a century later.

Geloan Acragas (*Roman Agrigentum*) [580 *B.C.*]. The latest Dorian colony of Sicily was only less conspicuous than the first. The Geloans sought an oecist from their Rhodian metropolis and founded, half-way between their own city and Selinus, the lofty town of Acragas, which soon took the second place in Greek Sicily and became the rival of Syracuse. [The acropolis, standing back from the coast, covered an area which to-day satisfies a town of

25,000, but occupation soon extended down the hill. The walls enclose an area of 900 acres and they date from within a generation of the foundation. The small harbour was some distance from the

Fig. 38.—Temple of Apollo, Segesta.

town: " flock-feeding Acragas " never became a maritime power. But the surrounding country of hill and valley was well suited to olive, vine and grazing and an easy track led to the rich corn land of the interior.]

In planting their colonies and founding their domination in

E

The Sicans. Sicily, the Greeks had mainly to reckon with the Sicels. In their few foundations in the farther west they had to deal with the Sicans. These older inhabitants were forced to retire from the coasts, but they lived on in their fortresses on the inland hills. The island was too large and its character too continental to invite the newcomers to attempt to conquer the whole of it. With the Phoenicians the Greeks had no trouble. Their factories and temples had not taken root in the soil, and on the landing of a stranger who was resolved to take root they vanished. But they did not abandon the western corner of the island, where the Greeks did not attempt to settle.

Three Phoenician cities: Panormus, Solus, Motya. There they maintained three places which now assumed the character of cities. These were Panormus, Solus, and Motya—the Haven, the Rock, and the Island. Panormus or " All-haven " in a fertile plain is protected on the north by Mount Hercte, now the Pilgrim Mount, and on the east by Solus. Motya is on an island in a small bay on the west coast.

The Elymians and their towns. The Elymian country lay between Motya and Panormus. The chief town of the Elymians, Segesta (which in Greek mouths became Egesta), was essentially a city, while Eryx farther west, high above the sea but not actually on it, was their outpost of defence. On Eryx they worshipped some goddess of nature, soon to be identified with the Greek Aphrodite. The Elymians were on good terms with the Phoenicians, and western Sicily became a Phoenician corner. While the inland country was left to Sicel and Sican, the coasts were to be the scene of struggles between Phoenician and Greek. In the seventh century this struggle was still a long way off, Sicily was still large enough to hold both the Greek and the Canaanite in peace. The first great trial of strength was to coincide with the Persian invasion of Greece.

ACHAEAN COLONIES. Original meaning of the name Italy. The name by which we know the central of the three great peninsulas of the Mediterranean did not extend as far north as the Po in the time of Julius Caesar, and originally it covered a very small area indeed. In the fifth century Thucydides applies the name Italy to the modern Calabria—the western of the two extremities into which the peninsula divides. This extremity was inhabited, when the Greeks first visited it, by Sicels and Oenotrians. But the heel was occupied by peoples of that Illyrian race which had played, as we dimly see, a decisive part in the earliest history of the Greeks. The Illyrian was now astride of the Adriatic ; he had reached Italy before the Greek. The Calabrians, who gave their name to the heel, were of Illyrian stock ; and along with these were the

Messapioi or Metapioi. Messapians, some of whose brethren on the other side of the water seem to have thrown in their fortunes with the Greeks and penetrated into Locris and Boeotia and perhaps into the Peloponnesus. It was on the seaboard of the Sicels and Oenotrians that the Achaeans of the Peloponnesus, probably towards the close of the eighth century, found a field for colonisation. It has been already remarked that the Ionian islands are a sort of stepping-stone to the west, and just as we find Corinthians settling in Corcyra, so we find Achaeans settling in Zacynthus. The first colonies which they planted in Italy were perhaps Sybaris and Croton, famous for their wealth and their rivalry. Sybaris on the river Crathis, in an unhealthy but most fruitful plain, soon extended her dominion across the narrow peninsula and, founding the settlements of Laos and Scidros on the western coast, commanded two seas. Thus having in her hands an overland route to the western Mediterranean, she could forward to her ports on the Tyrrhenian sea the valuable merchandise of the Milesians, whom Chalcidian jealousy excluded from the straits between Italy and Sicily. Thus both agriculture and traffic formed the basis of the remarkable wealth of Sybaris, and the result was an elaboration of luxury which caused the Sybarite name to pass into a proverb. Posidonia, famous for its temples and its roses, was another colony on the western sea, founded from Sybaris. It is said to have been formed by Troezenians who were driven out from that city by the Achaeans.

Sybaris [trad. date, 721 B.C.].

Posidonia.

Fig. 39. — Early coin of Poseidonia (obverse). Poseidon with trident.

A good way to the south of Sybaris you come to Croton, before the coast, in its southern rend, has yet reached the Lacinian promontory, on which a stately temple of Hera formed a central place of worship for the Greek settlers in Italy. Unlike the other Achaean colonies, Croton had a good harbour, the only good harbour on the west side of the gulf, but her prosperity, like that of her fellows, rested not on maritime traffic but on the cultivation of land and the rearing of cattle. The Delphic god seems to have taken a more than wonted interest in the foundation of this city, if we may judge from the Delphic tripod which appears on its earliest coins. Like Sybaris, Croton widened its territory and planted colonies of its own. On the Tyrrhenian sea, Terina and Temesa were to Croton what Laos and Scidros were to Sybaris.[1]

Croton [trad. date, 703 B.C.].

Caulonia, perhaps also a Crotoniate settlement, was the most southerly Achaean colony and was the neighbour of the western Locri. This town was founded in the territory of the Sicels, it is not certain by which of the three Locrian states ; perhaps it was a

Caulonia.
Locrian colonies.
Epizephyrian Locri.

---

[1] Another colony of Croton was Pandosia, and it conquered the Ionian town of Scylletion (Scylacium).

joint enterprise of all three. It was agricultural, like its Achaean neighbours, and like them it pushed over to the western sea and

Medma.
Hip-
ponion.

founded Medma and Hipponion on the other coast.

The Achaeans and Locrians might quarrel among themselves, but they had more in common with each other than either had with the Dorians, and we may conveniently include Locri in the Achaean

FIG. 40.—Early coin of Caulonia. Obverse: Apollo with bough, small figure on his arm; stag [legend: ΚΑΤΛΟ]. Reverse: incuse, back of these figures.

group. Thus the southern coast of Italy would have been almost a *Dorian* homogeneous circle if a Dorian colony had not been established in a *colonies.* small sheltered bay at the extreme north point of the gulf to which it *Taras* gave the name it still bears, Taras or Tarentum. Taras was remark-*[trad. date,* able as the only foreign settlement ever made by the greatest of all *707 B.C.].* the Dorian peoples. [The site had long been in contact with the Greek world. There are traces of settlement from the Aegean in the Mycenaean period and contact was maintained after the Dorian invasion. But the Spartan colony was founded at the end of the First Messenian War. The story runs that in the war with the Messenians, when the Spartans were for many years absent from home, the women bore sons to Helots, and that this progeny, called Partheniae or "Maidens' Children," conspired against the state, and being driven out of the country were directed by the oracle to settle at Taras. But even if there was some non-Dorian blood in the colonists, the official Spartan origin of the colony was not questioned in antiquity, and archaeological evidence shows that the relations between Sparta and Taras were close. Laconian geometric pottery has been found on the site and imports continued in the sixth century. The cults of the colony are almost exclusively Spartan, and the dialect is predominantly Dorian.

FIG. 41.—Coin of Taras, fifth century (reverse). Taras on a dolphin; shell [legend: ΤΑΡΑΣ].

Phalan- Phalanthus, who was reported to be the leader of the colonists, and *thus—* who appears on the coinage riding a dolphin, has by some been *Poseidon.* regarded as a local sea-god but he may well be a historical figure.]

The prosperity of the Tarentines depended partly on the cultivation of a fruitful territory, but mainly on their manufacturing industry.

Their fabrics and dyed wools became renowned, and their pottery
was widely diffused.   Taras in fact must be regarded as an industrial
rather than as an agricultural state.   Her position brought her into
contact with inhabitants of the Calabrian peninsula, and she had a
foe in the Messapian town of Brentesion.   She founded the colonies *Brun-*
of Callipolis and Hydrus on the eastern coast where she had no *dusium.*
Greek rivals.   But on the other side, her possible advance was foreseen and hindered by the prudence of the Sybarites.   They feared
lest the Dorian city might creep round the coast and occupy the
fertile lands which are watered by the Bradanus and the Siris.   So *Achaean*
they induced the Achaeans of old Greece to found a colony at Meta- Metapontion on the Bradanus, a place which had derived its name from $_{Meta-}^{pontion,}$
Messapian settlers ; and this the most northerly of the Achaean *pontum*
cities flourished as an agricultural community and cut off the west- *(= "place*
ward expansion of Taras.   But in the meantime another rival seized *of the*
the very place from which the Achaeans had desired to exclude the $_{pians,"\;or}^{Meta-}$
Dorians.   [In the middle of the seventh century Colophonians, fleeing *Messa-*
before Lydian pressure, planted a colony at Siris, and this Ionian *pians*).
state threatened to interrupt the Achaean line of cities and cut off Siris.
Metapontion from her sisters.   " No land so fair as the land by the
waters of Siris " wrote Archilochus, but the colony was short-lived.
There are reasons for thinking, though the evidence is not clear, that
a hundred years later the place was destroyed by its Achaean neighbours and became an Achaean town.]   Siris, like Sybaris, Croton,
and Locri, had her helpmate, though not a daughter, on the Tyrrhenian sea.   By the persuasion of common interest she formed a close *Pyxus*
connexion with Pyxus ; the two cities issued common coins ; and *(Poli-*
perhaps organised a rival overland route.   *castro*).

Thus the western coast of the Tarentine gulf was beset with a
line of Achaean cities, flanked at one extremity by Western Locri, on
the other by Dorian Taras.   The common feature, which distinguished
them from the cities settled by the men of Chalcis and Corinth, was
that their wealth depended on the mainland, not on the sea.   Their
rich men were landowners, not merchants ; it was not traffic but
rich soil that had originally lured them to the far west.   The un-
warlike Sicels and Oenotrians seem to have laid no obstacles in the
way of their settlements and to have submitted to their rule.   The
Iapygians and Messapians of Calabria were of different temper, and
it is significant that it was men from warlike Sparta who succeeded
in establishing Taras.   But there were destined to be bitter and costly
struggles with the natives.

These cities, with their dependencies beyond the hills, on the ἡ μεγάλη
shores of the Tyrrhenian sea, came to be regarded as a group, and Ἑλλάς
the country came to be called Great Hellas.   We might rather have $_{Graecia}^{(Magna}$).

looked to find it called Great Achaia, by contrast to the old Achaean lands in Greece ; but here, as in other cases, it is the name of a lesser folk which prevails. If the Hellenes, the old Greek inhabitants of the plain of the Spercheus, had been conquered by the Achaeans, the conquest was forgotten, and the two peoples had gone forth together to found new cities in the west ; and here the Hellenic name rose to celebrity and honour. It was no small thing in itself that the belt of Greek settlements on the Tarentine gulf should come to be called

Great Hellas. But it was a small thing compared with the extension of the name Hellenes to designate all peoples of Greek race. There was nothing to lead the Greeks of their own accord to fix on Hellenes as a common name ; if they had sought such a name deliberately, their natural choice would have been Achaeans, which Homer had already used in a wide sense. The name must have been given to them from without. Just as the barbarian peoples in central Italy had taken hold of the name of the Graii, so the barbarians in the southern peninsulas took hold of the name of the Hellenes, and used it to denote all settlers and strangers of the same race. Such a common name, applied by barbarian lips to them all alike, brought home to Greek traders the significance of their common race ; and they adopted the name themselves as the conjugate of *barbarians.* So the name Hellenes, obscure when it had gone forth to the west, travelled back to the east in a new sense, and won its way into universal use. The fictitious ancestor Hellên became the forefather of the whole Greek race ; and the fictitious ancestors of the Dorians, Ionians, and Aeolians were all derived from him. The original Hellenes lost their separate identity as completely as the original Aeolians and Ionians had lost theirs ; but their name was destined to live for ever in the speech of men, while those of their greater fellows had passed into a memory.

SECT. 4. GROWTH OF TRADE AND MARITIME ENTERPRISE

The age of the aristocratic republics saw the face of the Greek world completely transformed. The colonial expansion of Greece eastward and westward was itself part of this transformation, but it also helped signally to bring about other changes. For, while the colonies were politically independent of their mother-states, they re-acted in many ways on the mother-country.

We have seen how the system of family property was favourable to colonial enterprise. But the colonists, who had suffered under that system, were not likely to introduce it in their new settlements, and thus the institution of personal landownership was probably first established and regulated in the colonies. Their example reacted

on the mother-country, where other natural causes were also gradually undermining the family system.   In the first place, as the power
of the state grew greater the power of the family grew less ; and
when the head of the state, whether king or republican government,
was felt as a formidable authority, the prestige of the head of the
family, overshadowed by the power of the state, became insensibly
weaker.   In the second place, it was common to assign a portion of
an estate to one member of the family, to manage and enjoy the undivided use of it ; and although it did not become his and he had no
power of disposing of it, yet the natural tendency would have been to
allow it on his death to pass to his son on the same conditions.   It
is clear that such a practice tended to the ultimate establishment of
personal proprietorship of the soil.   Again, side by side with the undivided family estate, personal properties were actually acquired.   At
this period there was much wild unallotted land, " which wild beasts
haunt," especially on the hill-slopes, and when a man of energy reclaimed a portion of this land for tillage, the new fields became his
own, for they had belonged to no man.   We can thus see generally
how inevitable it was that the old system should disappear and the
large family estates break up into private domains ; but the change
was not accomplished by legislation, and the gradual process by which
it was brought about is withdrawn from our eyes.   It was only when
private landownership had become an established fact, that the law
came in and recognised it by regulating sales of land and allowing
men to bequeath it freely.

The Boeotian poet Hesiod has given us a picture of rural life in *The life of*
Greece at this period.   He was a husbandman himself near Ascra, *farmers in*
where his father, who had come as a stranger from Cyme in Aeolis, *Boeotia,*
had put under cultivation a strip of waste land on the slopes of *8th century,*
Helicon.   The farm was divided between his two sons, Perses and *in Hesiod's*
Hesiod, but in unequal shares ; and Hesiod accuses Perses of win- *Works and*
ning the larger moiety by bribing the lords of the district.   But *Days.*
Perses managed his farm badly and it did not prosper.   Hesiod
wrote his poem the *Works* to teach such unthrifty farmers as his
brother true principles of agriculture and economy.   His view of life
is profoundly gloomy, and suggests a condition of grave social distress
in Boeotia.   This must have been mainly due to the oppression of
the nobles, " gift-devouring " princes as he calls them.   The poet
looks back to the past with regret.   The golden age, the silver, and
the bronze, have all gone by, and the age of the heroes who fought
at Troy ; and mankind is now in the iron age, and " will never cease
by day or night from weariness and woe."   " Would that I did not
live in this generation, would that I had died before, or were born
hereafter ! "   The poem gives minute directions for the routine of the

husbandman's work, the times and tides of sowing and reaping, and the other labours of the field, the fashion of the implements of tillage ; and all this is accompanied by maxims of proverbial wisdom.

Historical significance of Hesiod's poem.   Apart from the value of his poem as a social picture, Hesiod has a great significance as the first spokesman of the common folk. In the history of Europe, his is the first voice raised from among the toiling classes and claiming the interest of mankind in their lot.   It is a voice indeed of acquiescence, counselling fellow-toilers to make the best of an evil case ; the stage of revolt has not yet been reached. But the grievances are aired, and the lords who wield the power are exhorted to deal just judgments, that the land may prosper.   The new poet is, in form and style, under the influence of the Homeric poems, but he is acutely conscious that he is striking new notes and has new messages for men.   He comes forward, unlike Homer, in his own person ; he contrasts himself with Homer when he claims that the Muses can teach truth as well as beautiful fiction.   In

The Theogony   another poem, the *Theogony*, we are told that the daughters of Zeus taught Hesiod as he fed sheep on the hill-sides of Helicon ; they gave him for staff a branch of bay.   The staff was now the minstrel's emblem ; for the epic poems were no longer sung to the lyre, but were recited by the " rhapsode " standing with a staff in his hand.   Then the Muses breathed into the shepherd of Ascra the wizard power of declaring the future and the past, and set him the task of singing the race of the blessed gods.   In the *Theogony* he performs this task. He sings how the world was made, the gods and the earth, the rivers and the ocean, the stars and the heaven ; how in infinite space which

Hesiod's cosmic system.   was at the beginning there arose Earth and Tartarus and Love the cosmic principle ; and it is notable how he introduces amongst the eldest-born powers of the world such abstractions as love itself, memory, sleep.   These speculations on the origin of the universe, and the attempt to work up the popular myths into a system, mark a new stage in the intellectual development of Greece.   There were

Hesiodic school.   other works composed by various bards who merged their identities under Hesiod's name ; and, as we have seen,[1] these Hesiodic poems had a decisive influence in moulding the ideas of the Greeks as to the early history of their race.

Boeotia was always an unenterprising country of husbandmen, and Hesiod had no sympathy with trade or foreign venture, though his father had come from Aeolis.   But the growth of trade was the most important fact of the time, and here too the colonies reacted on the mother-country.   By enlarging the borders of the Greek world they invited and facilitated the extension of Greek trade and promoted the

[1] Above, p. 79.

growth of industries.   Hitherto the Greeks had been mainly an agricultural and pastoral people ; many of them were now becoming industrial.   They had to supply their western colonies with oil and wool,
with metal and pottery, and they began to enter into serious competition
with the Phoenician trader and to drive eastern goods from the market.

Greek trade moved chiefly along water-ways, and this is illus- *Roads in*
trated by the neglect of road-making in Greece.   There were no *Greece.*
paved roads, even in later times, except the Sacred Ways to fre-
quented sanctuaries like that from Athens to Eleusis and Delphi, or
that from the sea-coast to Olympia.   Yet the Greeks were still
timorous navigators, and it was deemed hazardous to sail even in the
most familiar waters, except in the late summer.   Hesiod expresses *Danger of*
in vivid verses the general fear of the sea : " For fifty days after the *navigation.*
solstice, till the end of the harvest, is the tide for sailing ; then you
will not wreck your ship, nor will the sea wash down your crew,
unless Poseidon or Zeus wills their destruction.   In that season
winds are steady and Ocean kind ; with mind at rest, launch your
ship and stow your freight ; but make all speed to return home, and
await not the new wine and the rain of the vintage-tide, when the
winter approaches, and the terrible South-wind stirs the waves, in
fellowship with the heavy autumnal rain of Zeus, and makes the sea
cruel."   About this time, however, an important advance was made
in seacraft by the discovery of the anchor.

Seafaring states found it needful to build warships for protection *Develop-*
against pirates.   The usual type of the early Greek warship was the *ment of*
penteconter or "fifty-oar," a long, narrow galley with twenty-five *ship-*
benches, on each of which two oarsmen sat.   The penteconter hardly *building.*
came into use in Greece before the eighth century.   The Homeric
Greeks had only smaller vessels of twenty oars, but we can see in *The pente-*
the Homeric poems the penteconter coming within their ken as *conter.*
a strange and wonderful thing.   The ocean deity, Briareos, called
by the name of the Aegean, appears in the *Iliad;* and he is *Aegaeeus.*
probably no other than the new racer of the seas, sped by a hundred
hands.   In the *Odyssey* the Phaeacians, who are the kings of seacraft, have ships of fifty oars.   But before the end of the eighth
century a new idea revolutionised shipbuilding in Phoenicia.   Vessels
were built with two rows of benches, one above the other, so that *The*
the number of oarsmen and the speed were increased without adding *bireme.*
to the length of the ship.   The " bireme," however, never became
common in Greece, for the Phoenicians had soon improved it into the
" trireme," by the superposition of another bank of oars.[1]   The

[1] The secret of building this kind of galley has been lost.   Modern shipwrights cannot reproduce a trireme.   In later times the Greeks built ships of
many banks—five, ten, even forty.

The trireme comes into more general use in Greece not long before 500 B.C. The beak (embolos).

trireme, propelled by 170 rowers, was ultimately to come into universal use as the regular Greek warship, though for a long time after its first introduction, probably in the sixth century, the old penteconters were still generally used ; but the unknown shipwright who invented the bireme deserves the credit of the new idea. Whatever naval battles were fought in the seventh century were fought mainly, we may be sure, with penteconters. But penteconters and triremes alike were affected by the new invention of the bronze ram on the prow, a weapon of attack which determined the future character of Greek naval warfare.

Tradition of an ancient naval battle between Corinth and Corcyra (664 B.C.).

The Greeks believed that the first regular sea-fight between two Greek powers was fought before the middle of the seventh century between Corinth and her daughter city Corcyra. If the tradition is true, we may be sure that the event was an incident in a struggle for the trade with Italy and Sicily and along the Adriatic coasts. The chief competitors, however, with Corinth in the west were the Euboean cities, Chalcis and Eretria. In the traffic in eastern seas the island city of Aegina, though she had no colonies of her own, took an active part, and became one of the richest mercantile states of Greece. Athens too had ships, but her industries were still on a comparatively small scale, and it was not till a much later period that her trade was sufficient to involve her in serious rivalry with her neighbours. But the most active of all in industry and commerce were the Greeks of Ionia.

SECT. 5. INFLUENCE OF LYDIA ON GREECE

The Greeks of the Asiatic coast were largely dependent, for good or evil, on the adjacent inland countries. The inland trade added to their prosperity, but at any moment if a strong barbarian power arose their independence might be gravely menaced. At the beginning of the seventh century active intercourse was maintained between the Greeks and the kingdoms of Phrygia and Maeonia.

Dedication of Midas (c. 700 ?).

The Phrygian king Midas dedicated a throne to the god of Delphi ; both the Phrygians and the Lydians adopted the Greek alphabet, while the Greeks adopted their modes of music and admitted Phrygian legends into Greek mythology.

The Maeonian dynasty (so-called Heraclidae) of Lydia.

A considerable Phrygian element had won its way into Lydia, and had gained the upper hand. In the Homeric poems we nowhere read of Lydians but only of *Maeonians*, and there can be no doubt that this name represents the Phrygian settlers or conquerors. A Maeonian dynasty ruled in Lydia at the beginning of the seventh century, and the king bears a Maeonian name, Candaules, "hound-choker." The Aryan conquerors—conquerors, that is, who spoke an

Aryan tongue—had occupied the throne for centuries; and Greek tradition afterwards derived the origin of the family of Candaules from Heracles himself. But they had become degenerate, and Gyges, *Usurpation* a native Lydian, of the clan of the Mermnadae, succeeded in slaying *of Gyges* Candaules and seizing the crown. This revolution ushered in a new *687-652* period for the Lydian, as it was now called, no longer Maeonian, *B.C.* kingdom. The dominion of the Maeonian sovereign had probably extended southward to the valley of the Maeander. Gyges extended *His* his power northward to the shores of the Propontis, where he founded *conquests.* Dascylion, and conquered the Troad. But he also designed to make the Aegean his western boundary and bring the Greek cities under his lordship. He pressed down the valley of the Hermus against Smyrna; down the valley of the Cayster against Colophon; down the valley of the Maeander against Miletus and Magnesia. Of these enterprises only the faintest hints have come down to us. It may be that Colophon was actually captured, and perhaps Magnesia; but the other cities beat back the enemy. The poet Mimnermus sings how a warrior, perhaps his own grandfather, wrought havoc in the ranks of the Lydian horsemen in the plain of the Hermus.

But the plans of Gyges against his Greek neighbours were suddenly interrupted by a blow, which descended, as it were from the other side of the world, upon Greeks and Lydians alike. The regions round about Lake Maeotis, on the northern coast of the *Cimmerian* Black Sea, were inhabited by the Cimmerians, who appear in the *invasions.* marvellous wanderings of Odysseus. They were now driven forth from their abodes, to which, however, their name clung and still *(Crimea.)* clings, by a Scythian folk, the Scolotae, who came from the east. Homeless, the Cimmerians wandered to the opposite side of the Euxine; but whether they travelled by the eastern or the western route, by the Caucasus or by the Danube, is not known for certain. On one hand, they seem to have appeared first in eastern Asia Minor; on the other, they seem to have associated with themselves some Thracian peoples—the Trerians, Edonians, and Thynians. The truth may be that they came round by the eastern coast; and that afterwards, when they made their incursions into western Asia Minor, they invited allies from Thrace to help them. Having defeated the Milesians of Sinope, they chose this place to be their chief settlement. They ventured to attack the great Assyrian empire, and *Cim-* King Assarhaddon himself tells how " I smote the Cimmerian Teuspa *merians* with all his army." But they overthrew the realm of Phrygia under *defeated by* its last king Midas, and towards the middle of the seventh century *Assyrians,* they attacked Lydia. To meet this danger, Gyges sought help from *679 B.C.* Assyria. The warlike Assarhaddon had been succeeded at Nineveh by Assurbanipal, a peaceful and literary prince, whose refined luxury is caricatured in the Greek conception of Sardanapalus. The lord of Lydia acknowledged the overlordship of the lord of Assyria. He gained a victory over the Cimmerians, and sent their chiefs in chains to Nineveh. But he did not long brook to be the vassal of another sovereign. He threw off his allegiance to Assyria, and sent Ionian and Carian mercenary soldiers to Egypt, to help that country also to free itself from Assyrian dominion. At this moment, perhaps, Gyges was at the height of his power. His wealth was famous, and he too, like Phrygian Midas, sent gifts—among them, six golden mixing-bowls—to the Delphian god. The poet Archilochus, who witnessed his career, makes one of his characters declare that he "cares not for the wealth of golden Gyges."

Power and wealth of Gyges.

FIG. 42.—East Greek Vase. *c.* 600 B.C.

But the Cimmerians presently renewed their attack, and fortune changed. Gyges was slain in battle; his capital Sardis was taken, except the citadel; and it was some satisfaction

Death of Gyges.

to Assurbanipal to record that Lydia was in the hands of the Cimmerians. It was not long before they swooped down upon the Greek cities. Callinus, a poet of Ephesus, heard the trample of their horses and roused his fellow-citizens to battle; Ephesus defied their attack, but the temple of Artemis outside the walls was burned down. They and their allies from Thrace destroyed Magnesia on the Maeander. The barbarians made a deep impression. But the danger passed away. Ardys succeeded Gyges on the Lydian throne, and he finally not only drove out the Cimmerians from the land, but perhaps succeeded in extending his power into Cappadocia, as far as the Halys. [The expulsion of the Cimmerians was of profound importance to the Greeks no less than to the Lydians. For the

Cimmerian attack on Ionia.

Ardys, king of Lydia.

Greek cities depended largely on the Lydian kingdom for their prosperity. Sardis provided a market and an incentive for Greek craftsmanship and the Lydian kings protected and encouraged the trade that came along the great caravan routes across Asia Minor. Had the Cimmerians established themselves permanently, western Asia Minor would have relapsed into a new dark age. Happily the invasion was a passing whirlwind only, doing much temporary damage, but little permanent harm. Herodotus, comparing it with the later subjection by Croesus, could describe it as a plundering raid.]

In the meantime Lydia had made an invention which revolution- *Lydian* ised commerce. It is to Lydia that Europe owes the invention of *coinage.* coinage. The Babylonians, Phoenicians, and Egyptians made use of weighed gold and silver as a medium of exchange, a certain ratio being fixed between the two metals. A piece of weighed metal becomes a coin when it is stamped by the State and is thereby warranted to have its professed weight and purity. This step was first taken in Lydia, where the earliest money was coined somewhere about the beginning of the seventh century, probably by Gyges. These Lydian coins were *Electron* made of the native white gold, or *electron*—a mixture of gold and *staters.* silver in which the proportion of gold was greater. A bar of the white gold of Sardis was regarded as ten times the value of a silver bar, and three-fourths of the value of a gold bar, of

the same weight.[1] Miteus and Samos soon adopted the new invention, which then spread

Fig. 43.—Coin of Halicarnassus, sixth century. Obverse: stag [legend: ΦΑΝΟΣ ΕΜΙ ΣΕΜΑ]. Reverse: incuse.

to other Asiatic towns. Then Aegina and the two great cities of Euboea instituted monetary systems, and by degrees all the states of Greece gave up the primitive custom of estimating value in heads of cattle, and most of them had their own mints. As gold was very rare in Greece, not being found except in the islands of Siphnos and Thasos, the Greeks coined in silver. This invention, coming at the very moment when the Greeks were entering upon a period of great commercial activity, was of immense importance, not only in facilitating trade, but in rendering possible the accumulation of capital. Yet it took many generations to supersede completely the old methods of economy by the new system.

The Greeks had derived their systems of weight from Babylonia *The* and Phoenicia. But, when Aegina and the Euboean cities fixed the *Aeginetan* standard of their silver coinage, they did not adopt the silver standard *and Euboic silver standards.*

---

[1] The Lydians had two scales: one for domestic intercourse, based on a standard which they derived from Babylonia, and one for foreign commerce, based on a standard derived from Phoenicia through the Greeks.

of either of those countries. The heavier statêr (as the standard silver coin was named) of Aegina weighed 194 grains, and this system was adopted throughout the Peloponnese and in northern Greece. The lighter statêr of Euboea weighed 130 grains, which was the Babylonian standard of gold. This system, at first confined to Euboea, Samos, and a few other places, was adopted in the seventh century by Corinth in a modified form, and afterwards by Athens.[1] [From Corinth it spread to Corcyra and her other colonies in the north-west, and, in a modified form, to the cities of south Italy. These

Religious character of Greek coinage.

FIG. 44.—Coin of Cyzicus, fifth century (obverse). Kneeling Heracles with bow and club ; tunny-fish.

cities, having no easy access to supplies of silver, often melted down Corinthian coins for reminting, and in some surviving specimens traces of the Corinthian Pegasus can still be seen.

It was highly characteristic of the Greeks that their coinage was from the first secular in character ; it was the work of merchants and magistrates, not of priests. And so the types of Greek coins are rarely religious. Some states chose their civic badge such as the bee of Ephesus, the lion's scalp of Samos ; others made good propaganda by illustrating their exports—the tunny fish of Cyzicus, the silphium of Cyrene, the grapes of Maronea; others recalled local legends, the Pegasus of Corinth, the labyrinth of Cretan Cnossus. In sixth-century Athens, when aristocrats were struggling for power the coin types often represent the heraldic devices of the competing families of nobles. Coin types offered an attractive field for the artist and nowhere was the opportunity more richly exploited than in the western colonies.]

SECT. 6. THE OPENING OF EGYPT

Thus the merchants of Miletus and her fellows grew rich. They were the intermediaries between Lydia and the Mediterranean ; while the Lydians carried *their* wares to the interior parts of Asia Minor and the far east. Their argosies sailed to the far west, as well as to the coasts of the Euxine. But a new field for winning wealth was opened to them, much about the same time as the invention of coinage revealed a new prospect to the world of commerce. The jealously guarded gates of Egypt were unbarred to Greek trade.

Assyrian conquest of Egypt, c. 672. Egypt recovers independence, c. 655.

The greatest exploit of the Assyrian monarch Assarhaddon was the conquest of Egypt. The land had been split up into an endless number of small kingdoms, and the kings continued to govern as vassals of Assyria. But the foreign domination did not last for much more than a quarter of a century. One of the kings, Psammetichus of Sais, in Lower Egypt, probably of Libyan stock, revolted against

[1] See below, p. 183.

Assurbanipal, who, in the last year of his reign, was occupied in subduing an insurrection of the Elamites of Susiana.   We have seen how mail-clad soldiers of Ionia and Caria were sent by the lord of Lydia to assist Psammetichus.   With the help of these "bronze *Psam-* men who came up from the sea," he reduced the other kings and *metich I.* brought the whole of Egypt under his sway.   This Libyan dynasty kept Sais as their capital, and their power was supported by foreign mercenaries, Greeks and Carians, Syrians and Phoenicians.   A *Fort of* fortress was built at Daphnae—for so Greek speech graciously altered *Defenneh,* into Greek shape the Egyptian name Defenneh—and entrusted to *c. 570 B.C.* Greek mercenaries.   Relics of this foreign garrison have been dug up among the ruins of Daphnae.   Psammetichus and his successors completely departed from the narrow Egyptian policy of the Pharaohs, and were the forerunners in some respects of the Greek dynasty of the Ptolemies, who three centuries hence were to rule the land.   They opened Egypt to the trade of the world and allowed Greeks to settle permanently in the country.   Necho, the son of Psammetichus, connected the Red Sea with the Nile by a canal, and began a work, which it was reserved for our own time to achieve, the cutting of a channel through the isthmus which parts the Red Sea from the Mediterranean.   His war-fleets sailed both in the Cypriot and in the Arabian seas ; and a party of Phoenician explorers sent out by him accomplished the circumnavigation of Africa —a feat which two thousand years later was regarded as a wild dream.

The Milesians founded a factory on the western or Canobic *Founda-* channel of the Nile, not very far from Sais ; and around it a Greek *tion of* city grew up, which received the name of Naucratis, " sea-queen." *Naucratis.* This colony became the haven of all Greek traders ; for though at first they seem to have moved freely, restrictions were afterwards placed upon them and they were not permitted to enter Egypt except by the Canobic mouth.   At Naucratis, the Milesians, the Samians, and the Aeginetans had each their own separate quarter and their own sanctuaries ; all the other Greek settlers had one common enclosure called the Hellenion, girt by a thick brick wall and *c. 620 B.C.* capable of holding 50,000 men.   Here were their market-place and their temples.   All the colonists of Naucratis were Greeks of the Asiatic coast, whether Ionians, Dorians, or Aeolians, excepting alone the Aeginetans.

Egypt, as we see, offered a field not only for traders but for *Greek* adventurous soldiers, and thus helped to relieve the pressure of over- *soldiers at* population in Ionia.   At Abusimbel in Upper Egypt we have a relic *Abusimbel* of the Greek mercenaries, who accompanied King Psammetichus *[Psam-* II., Necho's successor, in an expedition against Ethiopia.   Some of *metich II., 594-89 B.C.].*

They write
their
names.

them scratched their names on the colossal statues of the temple; and the very triviality of this relic, at such a distance of time, perhaps makes it the more interesting.

SECT. 7. CYRENE

Founda-
tion of
Cyrene,
c. 630 *B.C.*

Not long after Egypt was thrown open to Greek trade, there arose to the west of Egypt a new Greek city. Civil dissension in the island of Thera between the older population, who called themselves by the obscure name of Minyae, and the later Dorian settlers led to an emigration of the Minyae—some Dorians among them; and the exiles, having increased their band by Cretan adventurers, sailed for the shores of Barca. They made their first settlement on the little island of Platea off the coast; their second on the opposite coast of the mainland; and when this too proved a failure, they founded their abiding settlement about eight miles from the sea near an abundant spring of water, on two white hills, which commanded the encompassing plain. The city was named Cyrene, and it was the only Greek colony on the coast of Africa which attained to eminence and wealth. The man who led the island folk to their new home became their king; his name seems to have been

Arcesilaus.

FIG. 45.—Coin of
Cyrene, early (ob-
verse). Silphion;
silphion seed;
lion's head.

Aristoteles, but he took the strange name of Battus, which is said to mean "king" in the Libyan language, while its resemblance to the Greek word for "stammer" gave rise to the legend that Battus I. stammered in his speech. His son was Arcesilas; and in the line of the Cyrenaean kings Battus and Arcesilas succeeded each other in alternation. Under Battus II. the new city was reinforced by a large incoming of new settlers whom he invited, chiefly from the Peloponnese and Crete; and this influx changed the character of the place, since the original "Minyan" element was outnumbered. The lands which the Greeks

took from the Libyan inhabitants were made fruitful by the winter rains; Pindar describes them as plains over which dark clouds hover. [The chief source of the wealth of the Cyrenaean kings was the royal monopoly in the export of silphium, a plant which acquired a high repute for medicinal virtues and was richly prized throughout the Greek world. In the early days of the Greek colony it grew luxuriantly in the district; but it was already dying out in the Roman period and is now extinct. There was also excellent pasturage, and the men of Cyrene became famous for rearing horses and for skill as riders and charioteers. Cyrene's sheep too were famous.

On a fine Laconian cup we can see Arcesilas II. himself watching the *The* wool being weighed and packed. It was in the reign of this king *Arcesilas* that Barca was founded, farther west. He quarrelled with his *vase.* brothers, and they left Cyrene and founded a town for themselves.]

Cyrene held her head high in the Greek world though she was somewhat apart from it. A Cyrenaean poet arose, and continued the

FIG. 46.—The Arcesilas Vase.

Odyssey and described the last adventures of Odysseus. His poem *The* was accepted by Greece as winding up the Epic Cycle which was Telegony associated with the name of Homer. His work was distinguished *of Eu-* by local pride and local colouring. He gave Odysseus a son *gammon,* Arcesilaus, and connected the royal line of Cyrene with the great *c. 600 B.C.* wanderer. And he introduced a flavour of those Libyan influences which modified Cyrenaean civilisation, just as the remote cities of the Euxine received influences from Scythia.

Sect. 8. Popular Discontent in Greece

Increase of trade and industry.

Slavery.

The advance of the Greeks in trade and industry produced many consequences of moment for their political and social development. The manufactures required labour, and a sufficient number of free labourers was not to be had. Slaves were therefore indispensable, and they were imported in large numbers from Asia Minor and Thrace and the coasts of the Euxine. The slave-trade became a profitable enterprise, and the men of Chios made it their chief pursuit. The existence of household slaves, generally war-captives, such as we meet in Homer, was an innocent institution which would never have had serious results ; but the new organised slave-system which began in the seventh century was destined to prove one of the most fatal causes of disease and decay to the states of Greece.

Decrease of importance of agriculture.

Wealth becomes a power in politics.

At first the privileged classes of the aristocratic republics benefited by the increase of commerce ; for the nobles were themselves the chief speculators. But the wealth which they acquired by trade undermined their political position. For, in the first place, their influence depended largely on their domains of land ; and when industries arose to compete with agriculture, the importance of land necessarily declined. In the second place, wealth introduced a new political standard ; and aristocracies resting on birth tended to transform themselves into aristocracies resting on wealth. The proverb "money makes the man" now came into vogue. As nobility by birth cannot be acquired, whereas wealth can, such a change is always a step in the direction of democracy.

The voice of the people begins to be heard.

On the other hand, the poorer freemen at first suffered. How heavily the transition from the old systems of exchange to the use of money bore upon them, we shall find illustrated when we come to the special history of Athens. But their distress and discontent drove them into striving for full political equality, and in many cases they strove with success. The second half of the seventh century is marked in many parts of Greece by struggles between the classes ; and the wiser and better of the nobles began themselves to see the necessity of extending political privileges to their fellow-citizens. The centralisation in towns, owing to the growth of industries and the declining importance of agriculture, created a new town population and doubtless helped on the democratic movement.

Archilochus.

In this agitated period lived a poet of great genius, Archilochus of Paros. It has been truly said that Archilochus is the first Greek "of flesh and blood" whom we can grasp through the mists of antiquity. Son of a noble by a slave mother he left Paros to seek a better livelihood in its recently established colony of Thasos. But he had no love of the sea and sang of the " bitter gifts of Poseidon " and the mariner's prayers for " sweet home." In Thasos he was involved in party struggles which rent the island. It has been thought that he witnessed at Thasos an eclipse of the sun at noontide which he describes, the eclipse of the 6th of April 648 B.C., but it is very doubtful whether he is really referring to this eclipse. All the evils of all Hellas are here, he exclaims ; and " Thasos is not a fair place nor a desirable, like the land round the stream of Siris." He announces that he is " the servant of the lord of battle and skilled in the delicious gift of the Muses." But when he fought in a war which the Thasians waged with the Thracians of the opposite coast, he ran for his life and dropped his shield ; "never mind, he said, I will get me another as good." Poor, with a stain on his birth, tossed about the world, soured by adversity, Archilochus in his poetry gave full expression to his feelings, and used it to utter his passionate hatred against his enemies, such as the Parian Lycambes, for instance, who refused him his daughter Neobule. Had fortune favoured him, he would have been a noble of the nobles ; ill-luck drove him to join the movement against aristocracy. His poems present a complete contrast to the epic style and even to Hesiod. He addressed himself to the people ; used colloquial language ; and perfected iambic and trochaic measures for literary purposes. His influence may be judged from the fact that his poems were recited by the rhapsodes along with Homer and Hesiod.

The ills of Greece, which were reflected in the poems of Archilochus, were to lead to the development of equality and freedom. But success in the struggle would in most cases depend on military efficiency ; and a revolution in the art of warfare, which was brought about at the same period, was therefore of immense importance. This takes us to the history of Sparta.

FIG. 47.—Electron coin of Lydia (beginning of seventh century). Obverse : striated surface. Reverse : oblong and two square sinkings.

FIG. 48.—Greek Hoplite.

CHAPTER III

GROWTH OF SPARTA. FALL OF THE ARISTOCRACIES

SECT. I. SPARTA AND HER CONSTITUTION

Origin of the Spartan state.

THE Dorian settlers from the north, who took possession of the valley of the Eurotas, established themselves in a number of village communities throughout the land, and bore the name of Lacedaemonians. In the course of time, a city-state grew up in their midst and won dominion over the rest. The town was formed by the union of five villages[1] which, after their union, still continued to preserve their identity, as separate units within the larger unity. The city was called Sparta, and took the dominant place in Laconia which had been formerly held by Amyclae.

Subject communities; perioikoi.

The other Lacedaemonian communities were called the *perioeci*, or " dwellers round about " the ruling city, and, though they were free and managed their local affairs, they had no political rights in the Spartan state. The chief burdens which fell on them were military service and the farming of the royal domains.

Conservative spirit of Sparta.

The Spartans were always noted for their conservative spirit. Hence we find in their constitution, which was remarkable in many ways, survivals of an old order of things which existed in the days of Homeric poetry, but has passed away in most places when trustworthy history begins. The most striking of these survivals was royalty; Sparta was nominally ruled by kings.

[1] Pitane, Messoa, Limnae, Konoûra, and Dyme.

This conservative spirit of the Spartans rendered them anxious to *Spartan* believe, and others willing to accept the view, that their constitution *belief in the* had existed from very ancient times in just the same shape and *antiquity* feature which it displayed in the days of recorded history. We are, *of the con-stitution.* however, forced to suspect that this was not the case. There can be little doubt that the Spartan state developed up to the end of the seventh century on the same general lines as other Greek states, though with some remarkable peculiarities. There can be little doubt that, like most other states, it passed through the stages of royalty and aristocracy ; and that the final form of the constitution was the result of a struggle between the nobles and the people. The remarkable thing was that throughout these changes hereditary kingship survived.

The machine of the Spartan constitution, as we know it when it was fully developed, had four parts : the Kings, the Council, the Assembly, and the Ephors. The first three are the original institutions, which were common, as we saw, to the whole Greek race ; the Ephors were peculiar to Sparta and states derived from Sparta.

We saw that towards the end of the Homeric period the powers *I. The* of the king were limited, and that this limited monarchy then died *kings.* out, sometimes leaving a trace behind it, perhaps in the name of a magistracy—like the king-archon at Athens. In a few places it survived, and Sparta was one of them. But, if it survived here, its powers were limited in a twofold way. It was limited not only by the other institutions of the state, but by its own dual character. For there *Origin of* were two kings at Sparta, and had been since the memory of *the dual* men. It seems possible that the origin of this double kingship lay *kingship.* in the coalition of two distinct communities, each of which had its own king. One tribe dwelt about Sparta, and its kings belonged to the clan of the Agidae. The other tribe, we may guess, was settled somewhere in southern Laconia, and its royal clan was that of the *(At* Eurypontidae. These two tribes must have united to form a large *Amyclae ?)* city-state at Sparta ; and the terms of the union may have been that neither tribe should give up its king, but two kings, with coequal authority, should rule over the joint community. The kingship passed from father to son in the two royal houses of the Agids and Eurypontids ; and if the Agid kings possessed a slight superiority in public estimation over their colleagues, this may have been due to the fact that the Eurypontids were the strangers who migrated to Sparta.[1] According to a pedigree which was made out for them in later days, when the myth of the Return of the Heraclidae had become current, both dynasties traced themselves back to Heracles.

It seems probable that it was partly because there were two kings,

[1] The relation of the five villages to these two communities must remain obscure ; and also the question of the coalition of yet another tribe or clan, (?) the Aegidae, who, however, did not retain their own king.

Limitation of the royal powers. the one a check upon the other, that kingship was not abolished in Sparta, or reduced to a mere magistracy. But the powers of the kings were largely curtailed; and we may suppose that the limitations were introduced by degrees during that epoch in which throughout Greece generally, monarchies were giving way to aristocratic republics. Of the religious, military, and judicial functions, which belonged to them and to all other Greek kings, they lost some and retained others.

Religious functions.   They were privileged to hold certain priesthoods;[1] they offered solemn sacrifices for the city every month to Apollo; they prepared the necessary sacrifices before warlike expeditions and battles; they were priests, though not the sole priests, of the community.

Military functions.   They were the supreme commanders of the army. They had the right of making war upon whatever country they chose, and penalties were laid on any Spartan who presumed to hinder them. In the field they had unlimited right of life and death; and they had a bodyguard of a hundred men. It is clear that these large powers

c. 500 B.C. were always limited by the double nature of the kingship. But at a later period it was defined by law that only one of the kings, to be chosen on each occasion by the people, should lead the army in time of war, and moreover they were made responsible to the community for their conduct in their campaigns.

Judicial functions.   But while they enjoyed this supreme position as high-priests and leaders of the host, they could hardly be considered judges any longer. The right of dealing out dooms like the Homeric Agamemnon had passed away from them; only in three special cases had they still judicial or legal powers. They presided at the adoption of children; they decided who was to marry an heiress whose father had died without betrothing her; and they judged in all matters concerning public roads.

      There were royal domains in the territory of the *perioeci* from which the kings derived their revenue. But they also had perquisites at public sacrifices; on such occasions they were (like Homeric kings) given the first seat at the banquet, were served first, and received a double portion of everything, and the hides of the

Funeral honours. slaughtered beasts. The pious sentiment with which royalty, as a hallowed institution, was regarded, is illustrated by the honours which were paid to the kings when they died. "Horsemen," says Herodotus, "carry round the tidings of the event through all Laconia, and in the city women go about beating a cauldron. And at this sign, two free persons of each house, a man and a woman, must put on mourning garb, and if any fail to do this great pains are imposed." The funeral was attended by a fixed number of the perioeci, and it was part of the stated ceremony that the dead king

---

[1] Of Zeus Lacedaemon and Zeus Uranios.

should be praised by the mourners as better than all who had gone before him. Public business was not resumed for ten days after the burial. The king was succeeded by his eldest son, but a son born before his father's accession to the kingship had to give way to the eldest of those who were born after the accession. If there were no children, the succession fell to the nearest male kinsman, who was likewise the regent in the case of a minority.

The *gerontes* or elders whom we find in Homer advising the king and also acting as judges have developed at Sparta into a body of fixed number, forming a definite part of the constitution, called the *gerusia*. This Council consisted of thirty members, including the two kings, who belonged to it by virtue of their kingship. The other twenty-eight must be over sixty years of age, so that the council was a body of elders in the strict sense of the word. They held their office for life and were chosen by acclamation in the general assembly of citizens, whose choice was supposed to fall on him whose moral merits were greatest ; membership of the Council was described as a " prize for virtue." The Council prepared matters which were to come before the Assembly ; it exercised, as an advising body, a great influence on political affairs ; and it formed a court of justice for criminal cases. *II.* Gerusia, *or Council of Elders (or Gerontia).*

But though the Councillors were elected by the people, they were not elected from the people. Nobility of birth retained at Sparta its political significance ; and only men of the noble families could be chosen members of the Council. And thus the Council formed an oligarchical element in the Lacedaemonian constitution.

Every Spartan who had passed his thirtieth year was a member of the *Apella*, or Assembly of Citizens, which met every month between the bridge of Babyka and the stream of Knakion. In old days, no doubt, it was summoned by the kings, but in historical times we find that this right has passed to the ephors. The assembly did not debate, but having heard the proposals of kings or ephors, signified its will by acclamation. If it seemed doubtful to which opinion the majority of the voices inclined, recourse was had to a division. The people elected the members of the Gerusia, the ephors and other magistrates ; determined questions of war and peace and foreign politics ; and decided disputed successions to the kingly office. Thus, theoretically, the Spartan constitution was a democracy. No Spartan was excluded from the apella of the people ; and the will of the people expressed at their apella was supreme. " To the people," runs an old statute, " shall belong the decision and the power." But the same statute granted to the executive authorities— " the elders and leaders "—a power which restricted this apparent supremacy of the people. It allowed them " to be dissenters, if the people make a crooked decree." It seems that the will of the people, declared by their acclamations, did not receive the force of *III.* Apella, *or Assembly of the People.*

law, unless it were then formally proclaimed before the assembly was formally dissolved. If the elders and magistrates did not approve of the decision of the majority of the assembly, they could annul the proceedings by refusing to proclaim it—" seceding " and dissolving the meeting, without waiting for the regular dissolution by king or ephor.

Ephorate.   The five ephors were the most characteristic part of the political constitution of Sparta. The origin of the office is veiled in obscurity ; it was supposed to have been instituted in the first half of the eighth century.[1] But we must distinguish between the first institution of the office and the beginning of its political importance. It is probable that, in the course of the eighth century, the kings finding it impossible to attend to all their duties were constrained to give up the civil jurisdiction, and that the ephors or "overseers" were appointed for this purpose.[2] The number of the ephors would seem to be connected with the number of the five demes or villages whose union formed the city ; and perhaps each one of the ephors was assigned originally to one of the villages. But it cannot have been till the seventh century that the ephors won their great political power. They must have won that power in a conflict between the nobility who governed in conjunction with the kings, and the people who had no share in the government. In that struggle the kings represented the cause of the nobility, while the ephors were the representatives of the people.[3] A compromise, as the result of such a conflict, is implied in the oaths which were every month exchanged between the kings and the ephors. The king swore that he would observe the laws of the state in discharging his royal functions ; the ephor that he would maintain the royal power undiminished, so long as the king was true to his oath. In this ceremony we have the record of an acute conflict between the government and people. The democratic character of the ephorate appears from the fact that any Spartan might be elected. The mode of election, which is described by Aristotle as " very childish," was practically equivalent to an election by lot. When the five ephors did not agree among themselves, the minority gave way.

[1] The Alexandrines seem to have had an ephor-list reaching as far back as 757 B.C. ; but we cannot build much on this. It is perhaps of more importance that the ephorate existed in the Laconian colony at Thera ; but what most of all proves its antiquity is its close inter-connexion with the whole framework of the Spartan constitution.

[2] We have no knowledge of the local institutions in the towns of the *perioeci*, which would probably throw some light on details of the Spartan constitution. Polemon's work, *On the Cities in Lacedaemon*, has unfortunately not survived.

[3] The Eurypontid kings probably smoothed the way for the compromise. It has been suggested that such names as Archi*damos*, which occur among the Eurypontids but not among the Agids, allude to their popular attitude.

The ephors entered upon their office at the beginning of the Laconian year, which fell on the first new moon after the autumnal equinox. As chosen guardians of the rights of the people, they were called upon to watch jealously the conduct of the kings. With this object two ephors always accompanied the king on warlike expeditions. They had the power of indicting the king and summoning him to appear before them. The judicial functions which the kings lost passed partly to the ephors, partly to the Council. The ephors were the supreme civil court; the Council, as we have seen, formed the supreme criminal court. But in the case of the Perioeci the ephors were criminal judges also. They were moreover responsible for the strict maintenance of the order and discipline of the Spartan state, and, when they entered upon office, they issued a proclamation to the citizens to "shave their upper lips and obey the laws."

This unique constitution cannot be placed under any general head, cannot be called kingdom, oligarchy, or democracy, without misleading. None of these names is applicable to it, but it participated in all three. *Character of Spartan constitution.* A stranger who saw the kings going forth with power at the head of the host, or honoured above all at the public feasts in the city, would have described Sparta as a kingdom. If one of the kings themselves had been asked to define the constitution, it is probable that he would have regretfully called it a democracy. Yet the close Council, taken from a privileged class, exercising an important influence on public affairs, and deferring to an Assembly which could not debate, might be alleged to prove that Sparta was an oligarchy. The secret of this complex character of the Spartan constitution lies in the fact that, while Sparta developed on the same general path as other states and had to face the same political crises, she overcame each crisis with less violence and showed a more conservative spirit. When she ought to have passed from royalty to aristocracy, she diminished the power of the kings, but she preserved hereditary kingship as a part of the aristocratic government. When she ought to have advanced to democracy, she gave indeed enormous power to the representatives of the people, but she still preserved both her hereditary kings and the Council of her nobles.

Sect. 2. Spartan Conquest of Messenia

In the growth of Sparta the first and most decisive step was the conquest of Messenia. The southern portion of the Peloponnesus is divided into two parts by Mount Taygetus. Of these, the eastern part is again severed by Mount Parnon into two regions: the vale of the river Eurotas, and the rugged strip of coast between Parnon and the sea. The western country is less mountainous, more fruitful, and *Messenia.*

THE
PELOPONNESUS.

Stadia
0 50 100   200   300   400   500

English Miles
0   5 10   20   30   40   50

Longitude East 22° of Greenwich

Walker & Boutall sc.

Fig. 49.

blessed by a milder climate, nor is it divided in the same way by a mountain chain; the hills rise irregularly, and the river Pamisus waters the central plain of Stenyclarus where the Greek invaders are said to have fixed their abode. The natural fortress of the country was the lofty rock of Ithome which rises to the west of the river. It is probable that under its protection a town grew up at an early period, whose name Messene was afterwards transferred to the whole country.

The fruitful soil of Messenia, " good to plant and good to plough," *Early con-* as a Spartan poet sang, could not but excite the covetousness of her *quest of* martial neighbours. The First Messenian War may be dated to the *Messenia.* last quarter of the eighth century. Legends grew up freely as to its causes and its course. All that we know with certainty is that the Spartan king, under whose auspices it was waged, was named Theopompus; that it was decided by the capture of the great fortress of Ithome; and that the eastern part of the land became Laconian. A poet writing at the beginning of the seventh century would have naturally spoken of Messene or Pherae as being " in Lacedaemon." When the Second War broke out towards the end of the seventh century, it was either history or legend that the previous war had lasted twenty years. Legends grew up around it in which the chief *Legend of* figure was a Messenian hero named Aristodemus. The tale was *Aristo-* that he offered his daughter as a sacrifice to save his country, in *demus.* obedience to the demand of an oracle. Her lover made a despairing effort to save her life by spreading a report that the maiden was about to become a mother, and the calumny so incensed Aristodemus that he slew her with his own hand. Afterwards, terrified by evil dreams and portents, and persuaded that his country was doomed, he killed himself upon his daughter's tomb. All this is later romance; but the conquest of Messenia is historical and of fundamental importance in Sparta's development.

As the object of the Spartans was to increase the number of the *Condition* lots of land for their citizens, many of the conquered Messenians *of the Mes* were reduced to the condition of Helots, and servitude was hard *senians.* though their plight might have been harder, for they paid to their lords only one-half of the produce of the lands which they tilled. The Spartan poet Tyrtaeus describes how the Messenians endured the insolence of their masters :—

> As asses worn by loads intolerable,
> So them did stress of cruel force compel,
> Of all the fruits the well-tilled land affords,
> The moiety to bear to their proud lords.

For some generations they submitted patiently, but at length, when

Their rebellion: "Second War" (c. end of 7th cent.).

victorious Sparta felt secure, a rebellion was organised in the northern district of Andania. The rebels were supported by their neighbours in Arcadia and Pisatis, and they are said to have found an able and ardent leader in Aristomenes, sprung from an old Messenian family. The revolt was at first successful. The Spartans fared ill, and their young men experienced the disgrace of defeat. The hopes of the serfs rose, and Sparta despaired of recovering the land.

Tyrtaeus.

But a leader and a poet arose amongst them. The lame Tyrtaeus is recorded to have inspired his countrymen with such martial vigour that the tide of fortune turned, and Sparta began to retrieve her losses and recover her reputation. Some scraps of the poems of Tyrtaeus have been preserved, and they supply the only trustworthy material we have for the history of the Messenian wars ; and he won such fame by the practical successes of his art that at a later time the Athenians sought to claim him as one of their sons and gave out that Sparta, by the counsel of an oracle, had sent for him. The warriors advanced to battle singing his " marches " to the sound of flutes, while his elegies, composed in the conventional epic dialect, are said to have been recited in the tents after the evening meal. But we learn from himself that his strategy was as effective as his poetry, and the Messenians were presently defeated in the Battle of the Great Foss. They then retired to the northern stronghold of Eira on the river Nedon, which plays the same part in the second war that Ithome played in the first, while Aristomenes takes the place of Aristodemus. As to Eira, indeed, we possess no record on the contemporary authority of Tyrtaeus, whose extant fragments notice none of the adventures, nor even the name, of the hero Aristomenes. Yet Eira may well have been the place where the last stand was made ; for the Spartans had rased the fortifications of Ithome, which is not mentioned in connexion with the second war.

Capture of Eira.

At Eira the defenders were near their Arcadian supporters and within reach of Pylos which seems not to have been yet Lacedaemonian. But Eira fell ; legend says that it was beleaguered for eleven years. Aristomenes was the soul of the defence, and his wonderful escapes

Tales of Aristo-menes.

became the argument of a stirring tale. On one occasion he was thrown, with fifty fellow-countrymen, captured by the Spartans, into a deep pit. His comrades perished, and Aristomenes awaited certain death. But by following the track of a fox he found a passage in the rocky wall of his prison and appeared on the following day at Eira. When the Spartans surprised that fortress, he made his escape wounded to Arcadia. He died in Rhodes, but two hundred and fifty years later, on the field of Leuctra, he reappeared against the Spartans to avenge his defeat.

Those Messenians who were left in the land were mostly reduced again to the condition of Helots, but the maritime communities and even a few in the interior remained free, as perioeci, in the possession of their estates. Many escaped to Arcadia, while some of the inhabitants of the coast-towns may have taken ship and sailed to other places.

At this time Sparta, like most other Greek states, suffered from domestic discontent. There was a pressing land question, with which Tyrtaeus dealt in a poem named *Eunomia*, or *Law and Order*. This question was partly solved by the conquest of the whole land of Messenia, which may have given opportunity for a new distribution of land and perhaps the incorporation of new citizens who had helped in the war but were not of pure Spartan descent, and so did not enjoy full privileges. *Pressure of population on the land.*

The Messenian war, as recorded by Tyrtaeus, shows us that the power of the privileged classes had already been undermined by a great change in the method of warfare. The fighting is done, and the victory won, by regiments of mailed foot-lancers, who march and fight together in close ranks. [The secret had been discovered that the well-drilled phalanx of hoplites, as they were called, was superior to the aristocratic method of fighting on horse, or the hurling of spears at long range, such as is seen on geometric vases of the ninth and eighth centuries. The change in tactics was bound up with a change in armour. The two throwing spears were replaced by a single thrusting spear, metal corselet and metal greaves were added, and the shield was no longer strapped to the body but held securely on the left arm, valuable in the clash of the two battle lines, useless in retreat.] The progress of metal-smiths in their trade, which accompanied the general industrial advance of Greece, rendered possible this transformation in the art of war. Every well-to-do citizen could now provide himself with an outfit of armour and go forth to battle in panoply. The transformation was distinctly levelling and democratic; for it placed the noble and the ordinary citizen on an equality in the field. We shall not be wrong in connecting this military development with those aspirations of the people for a popular constitution, which resulted in the investment of the ephorate with its great political powers. *Revolution in warfare: the hoplites.* *Political significance of this change.*

[The new tactics were probably borrowed from the Carians and are seen first on Corinthian and Attic vases of the early seventh century. It was probably with them that Pheidon revived the power of Argos.] They spread rapidly through Greece and their natural tendency everywhere was to promote the progress to democracy. It is significant that in Thessaly, where the system of hoplites was not introduced and cavalry was always the kernel of the army, democratic ideas never made way, and the peasants remained a depressed class.

SECT. 3. INTERNAL DEVELOPMENT OF SPARTA AND HER INSTITUTIONS

Character
of Sparta
in early
times.

In the seventh century one could not have foretold what Sparta was destined to be. Her nobles lived luxuriously, like the nobles of other lands ; the individual was free, as in other cities, to order his life as he willed. She showed some promise of other than military interests. Lyric poetry was transported from its home in Lesbos to find for a while a second home on the banks of the Eurotas. Songs to be sung at banquets, at weddings, at harvest feasts, and at festivals of the gods, by single singers or choirs of men or maidens, were older than memory could reach ; but with the development of music and the improvement of musical instruments the composition of these songs became an art, and lyric poetry was created. The lyre of seven strings was an ancient invention, but it was attributed to

Terpander
(c. 700
B.C.).
[Feast of
Carnean
Apollo.)

Terpander of Lesbos, who was at all events an historical person, and both a poet and a musician. He visited Sparta, and is said to have instituted the musical contest at the Carnea, the great festival of Lacedaemon. His music was certainly welcomed there, and Sparta soon had a poet, who, though not her own, was at least her adopted, son. Alcman from Lydian Sardis made Sparta his home, and we have some fragments of songs which he composed for choirs of Laconian maidens. Sparta had her epic poet too in Cinaethon. But this promise of a school of music and poetry was not to be fulfilled.

Material
culture.

[Excavation has added colour and detail to the pictures of early Sparta drawn from literary sources. Imports of ivory, often carved, amber, scarabs, gold and silver jewelry show that Sparta had wide contacts in the seventh century ; and Laconian craftsmen in ivory, bone, and pottery could compare with the best in Greece. In the sixth century the stream of imports gradually dries up, but Laconian pottery, which is found as far afield as Sardis and Etruria, reaches its peak in the second quarter of the sixth century and rapid deterioration only sets in after *c.* 550. While other states developed industrial and artistic production Sparta gradually lost the material refinements of living. But though there is no sudden break in the development to suggest that the decline in culture was the result of formal enactment, the ultimate cause was the retention by Sparta of an obsolete currency of iron bars. The new silver coinage spread rapidly through mainland Greece at the end of the seventh century. The conservatism of Sparta was deliberate choice.

Army
reform.

That Sparta was taking careful stock of her position after the crushing of the Messenian revolt is suggested by the reorganisation in her army. In the fighting against the Messenians, as a papyrus fragment of Tyrtaeus shows, the Spartan army is still brigaded in three Dorian tribal contingents. At the battle of Plataea in the Persian war there were five divisions based on the five *Obai* or villages; and there are already signs of the new order in the early sixth century. The long-drawn-out struggle with the Messenians had exposed military weakness: the army was reorganised and dangerous social innovations were avoided.]

When Sparta emerges into the full light of history we find her *Trans-* under an iron discipline, which invades every part of a man's life *formation* and controls all his actions from his cradle to his death-bed. Every- *of Sparta* thing is subordinated to the art of war, and the sole aim of the state *(7th-6th* is to create invincible warriors. The martial element was doubtless, *cent.).* from the very beginning, stronger in Sparta than in other states; and as a city ruling over a large discontented population of subjects and serfs, she must always be prepared to fight; but we shall probably never know how, and under what influences, the singular Spartan discipline which we have now to examine was introduced. Nor can we, in describing the Spartan society, distinguish always between older and later institutions.

The whole Spartan people formed a military caste; the life of a Spartan citizen was devoted to the service of the state. In order to carry out this ideal it was necessary that every citizen should be freed from the care of providing for himself and his family. *Land:* The nobles owned family domains of their own; but the Spartan *private* community also came into possession of common land, which was *and public.* divided into a number of lots. Each Spartan obtained a lot, which *Lots.* passed from father to son, but could not be either sold or divided; thus a citizen could never be reduced to poverty.[1] The original *The* inhabitants, whom the Lacedaemonians dispossessed and reduced to *Helots.* the state of serfs, cultivated the land for their lords. Every year the owner of a lot was entitled to receive seventy medimni of corn for (105 himself, twelve for his wife, and a stated portion of wine and fruit. *bushels?*. All that the land produced beyond this, the Helot was allowed to retain for his own use. Thus the Spartan need take no thought for his support; he could give all his time to the affairs of public life. Though the Helots were not driven by taskmasters, and had the right of acquiring private property, their condition seems to have been hard; at all events, they were always bitterly dissatisfied and ready to rebel, whenever an occasion presented itself. The system of Helotry was a source of danger from the earliest times, but especially after the conquest of Messenia; and the state of constant

[1] In the fourth century, however, some Spartans had been impoverished, from what cause is unknown.

Krypteia.

military preparation in which the Spartans lived may have been partly due to the consciousness of this peril perpetually at their doors. The *Krypteia* or secret police was instituted—it is uncertain at what date—to deal with this danger. Young Spartans were sent into the country and empowered to kill every Helot whom they had reason to regard with suspicion. Closely connected with this system was the remarkable custom that the ephors, in whose hands lay the general control over the Helots, should every year on entering office proclaim war against them. By this device, the youths could slay dangerous Helots without any scruple or fear of the guilt of manslaughter. But notwithstanding these precautions serious revolts broke out again and again. A Spartan had no power to grant freedom to the Helot who worked on his lot, nor yet to sell him to another. Only the state could emancipate. As the Helots were called upon to serve as lightarmed troops in time of war, they had then an opportunity of exhibiting bravery and loyalty in the service of the city, and those who conspicuously distinguished themselves might be rewarded by the city with the meed of freedom. Thus arose a class of freedmen called *neodamōdes*, or new demesmen. There was also another class of persons, neither serfs nor citizens, called *mothōnes*, who probably sprang from illegitimate unions of citizens with Helot women.

Neodamōdes and Mothōnes (or Mothakes).

Education (ἀγωγή).

Thus relieved from the necessity of gaining a livelihood, the Spartans devoted themselves to the good of the state, and the aim of the state was the cultivation of the art of war. Sparta was a large military school. Education, marriage, the details of daily life were all strictly regulated with a view to the maintenance of a perfectly efficient army. When a child was born it was submitted to the inspection of the heads of the tribe, and if they judged it to be unhealthy or weak, it was exposed to die on the wild slopes of Mount Taygetos. At the age of seven years, the boy was consigned to the care of a state-officer, and the course of his education was entirely determined by the purpose of inuring him to bear hardships, training him to endure an exacting discipline, and instilling into his heart a sentiment of devotion to the state. The boys, up to the age of twenty, were marshalled in a huge school formed on the model of an army. The captains and prefects who instructed and controlled them were young men who had passed their twentieth year, but had not yet reached the thirtieth, which admitted them to the rights of citizenship. Warm friendships often sprang up between the young men and the boys whom they were training.

(Paidonómos.)

Iranes.

At the age of twenty the Spartan entered upon military service and was permitted to marry. But he could not yet enjoy home-life; he had to live in " barracks " with his companions, and could only pay stolen and fugitive visits to his wife. In his thirtieth year, having completed his training, he became a " man," and obtained the full rights of citizenship. The *Homoioi* or peers, as the Spartan citizens were called, dined together in tents in the Hyacinthian Street. These public messes were in old days called *andreia*, or " men's meals," and in later times *phiditia*. Each member of a com- Phiditia mon tent made a fixed monthly contribution, derived from the pro- duce of his lot, consisting of barley, cheese, wine, and figs, and the members of the same mess-tent shared the same tent in the field in time of war. These public messes are a survival, adapted to military purposes, of the old custom of public banquets, at which all the burghers gathered together at a table spread for the gods of the city. Of the organisation of the Spartan hoplites in early times we have *Army.* no definite knowledge. Three hundred " horsemen," chosen from the Spartan youths, formed the king's bodyguard ; but though, as their name shows, they were originally mounted, in later times they fought on foot. The light infantry was supplied by the Perioeci and Helots.

Spartan discipline extended itself to the women too, with the pur- *Spartan* pose of producing mothers who should be both physically strong and *women.* saturated with the Spartan spirit. The girls, in common with the boys, went through a gymnastic training ; and it was not considered immodest for them to practise their exercises almost nude. They enjoyed a freedom which was in marked contrast with the seclusion of women in other Greek states. They had a high repute for chastity ; but if the government directed them to breed children for the state, they had no scruples in obeying the command, though it should involve a violation of the sanctity of the marriage-tie. They were, proverbially, ready to sacrifice their maternal instincts to the welfare of their country. Such was the spirit of the place.

Thus Sparta was a camp in which the highest object of every man's life was to be ready at any moment to fight with the utmost efficiency for his city. The aim of every law, the end of the whole social order was to fashion good soldiers. Private luxury was strictly forbidden ; Spartan simplicity became proverbial. The individual man, entirely lost in the state, had no life of his own ; he had no problems of human existence to solve for himself. Sparta was not a place for thinkers or theorists ; the whole duty of man and the highest ideal of life were contained in the laws of his city. Warfare being the object of all the Spartan laws and insti- *Motive of* tutions, one might expect to find the city in a perpetual state of war. *Spartan* One might look to see her sons always ready to strive with their *discipline.* neighbours without any ulterior object, war being for them an end in itself. But it was not so ; they did not wage war more lightly than other men ; we cannot rank them with barbarians who care

F

only for fighting and hunting. We may attribute the original motive of their institutions, in some measure at least, to the situation of a small dominant class in the midst of ill-contented subjects and hostile serfs. They must always be prepared to meet a rebellion of Perioeci or a revolt of Helots, and a surprise would have been fatal. Forming a permanent camp in a country which was far from friendly, they were compelled to be always on their guard. But there was something more in the vitality and conservation of the Spartan constitution than precaution against the danger of a possible insurrection. It appealed to the Greek sense of beauty. There was a certain completeness and simplicity about the constitution itself, a completeness and simplicity about the manner of life enforced by the laws, a completeness and simplicity too about the type of character developed by them, which Greeks of other cities never failed to contemplate with genuine, if distant, admiration. Shut away in "hollow many-clefted Lacedaemon," out of the world and not sharing in the progress of other Greek cities, Sparta seemed to remain at a standst'1; and a stranger from Athens or Miletus in the fifth century visiting the straggling villages which formed her unwalled unpretentious city must have had a feeling of being trans ported into an age long past, when men were braver, better, and simpler, unspoiled by wealth, undisturbed by ideas. To a philosopher, *Greek ad-* like Plato, speculating in political science, the Spartan state seemed *miration of* the nearest approach to the ideal. The ordinary Greek looked upon *Sparta.* it as a structure of severe and simple beauty, a Dorian city stately as a Dorian temple, far nobler than his own abode but not so comfortable to dwell in. If this was the effect produced upon strangers, we can imagine what a perpetual joy to a Spartan peer was the contemplation of the Spartan constitution; how he felt a sense of superiority in being a citizen of that city, and a pride in living up to its ideal and fulfilling the obligations of his nobility. In his mouth "not beautiful" meant "contrary to the Spartan laws," which were believed to have been inspired by Apollo. This deep admiration for their constitution as an ideally beautiful creation, the conviction that it was incapable of improvement—being, in truth, wonderfully effective in realising its aims—is bound up with the conservative spirit of the Spartans, shown so conspicuously in their use of their old iron coins [1] down to the time of Alexander the Great.

It was inevitable that, as time went on, there should be many fallings away, and that some of the harder laws should, by tacit agreement, be ignored. The other Greeks were always happy to point to the weak spots in the Spartan armour. From an early period it seems to have been a permitted thing for a citizen to acquire land in

[1] The *obel* and the *pelanor*.

addition to his original lot. As such lands were not, like the original lot, inalienable, but could be sold or divided, inequalities in wealth necessarily arose, and the " communism " which we observed in the life of the citizens was only superficial. But it was specially provided by law that no Spartan should possess wealth in the form of gold or silver. This law was at first eluded by the device of depositing money in foreign temples, and it ultimately became a dead letter; Spartans even gained throughout Greece an evil reputation for avarice. By the fourth century they had greatly degenerated, and those who wrote studies of the Lacedaemonian constitution contrasted Sparta as it should be and used to be with Sparta as it was. *Degeneration of Sparta.*

There is no doubt that the Spartan system of discipline grew up by degrees; yet the argument from design might be plausibly used to prove that it was the original creation of a single lawgiver. We may observe how well articulated and how closely interdependent were its various parts. The whole discipline of the society necessitated the existence of Helots; and on the other hand the existence of Helots necessitated such a discipline. The ephorate was the keystone of the structure; and in the dual kingship one might see a cunning intention to secure the powers of the ephors by perpetual jealousy between the kings. In the whole fabric one might trace an artistic unity which might be thought to argue the work of a single mind. And until lately this was generally believed to be the case; many still maintain the belief. A certain Lycurgus was said to have framed the Spartan institutions and enacted the Spartan laws about the beginning of the ninth century. *Unity of the constitution.* *Vulgar date of Lycurgus 885 B.C.*

But the grounds for believing that a Spartan lawgiver named Lycurgus ever existed have been questioned. The earliest statements as to the origin of the constitution date from the fifth century, and their discrepancy shows that they were mere guesses, and that the true origins were buried completely in the obscurity of the past. Pindar attributed the Lacedaemonian institutions to Aegimius, the mythical ancestor of the Dorian tribes; the historian Hellanicus regarded them as the creation of the two first kings of Sparta, Procles and Eurysthenes. The more critical Thucydides, less ready to record conjectures, contents himself with saying that the Lacedaemonian constitution had existed for rather more than 400 years at the end of the Peloponnesian war. Herodotus states that the Spartans declared Lycurgus to have been the guardian of one of their early kings, and to have introduced from Crete their laws and institutions. But the divergent accounts of this historian's contemporaries, who ignore Lycurgus altogether, suggest that it was only one of many guesses and not a generally accepted tradition. It may be added that if the old Spartan poet Tyrtaeus had mentioned Lycurgus as a lawgiver, *Statements of Pindar, Hellanicus, Thucydides [c. 804], and Herodotus.* *Silence of Tyrtaeus.*

his words would certainly have been quoted by later writers ; and therefore it is argued that he knew nothing of such a tradition.

Lycurgus deified.　Hence the theory has arisen that Lycurgus (*Lyco-vorgos*) was not a man ; he was only a god. He was an Arcadian deity or " hero,"—perhaps some form of the Arcadian Zeus Lycaeus, god of the wolf-mountain ; and his name meant " wolf-repeller." He was worshipped at Lacedaemon where he had a shrine, and it is conjectured that his cult was adopted by the Spartans from the older inhabitants whom they displaced. He may have also been connected with Olympia, for his name was inscribed on a very ancient *Quoit of Iphitus.*　quoit—the so-called quoit of Iphitus—which was preserved there, and perhaps dated from the seventh century. The belief that this deity was a Spartan lawgiver, promoted by the Delphic oracle, gradually gained ground and in the fourth century generally prevailed. Aristotle believed it, and made use of the old quoit to fix the date of the Lycurgean legislation to the first half of the eighth century. But while everybody regarded Lycurgus as unquestionably an historical personage, candid investigation confessed that nothing certain was known concerning him, and the views about his chronology were many and various.

SECT. 4. THE CRETAN CONSTITUTIONS

Ancient Greek students of constitutional history were struck by some obvious and remarkable resemblances between the Spartan and the Cretan states, and it was believed by many that the Spartan constitution was derived from Crete, though there are notable differences

as well as notable likenesses. It will be convenient to glance here at the political condition of this island, to which we shall seldom have to recur, since, owing to its geographical situation and the lack of political union, it was isolated and withdrawn from the main course of Greek history.

FIG. 50.—Early coin of Gortyna (obverse). Europa on bull.

Genuine Cretans.　In a passage in the *Odyssey* the inhabitants of Crete are divided into five classes : Achaeans, Eteo-Cretans, Cydonians, Dorians, and Pelasgians. Of these the Eteo-Cretans may represent the original people who dwelled in the island before the Greeks came, like the Eteo-Carpathians of Carpathus. They survived chiefly in the eastern part of the island, and they continued to speak their own tongue in historical times, writing it, however, not in their ancient linear script but in Greek characters. A specimen of it—but we have no key to the meaning—has been preserved in some inscriptions found at Praesus, their most important city. The people of Cydonia were perhaps also a remnant of the old population. The Achaeans and Pelasgians point to Thessaly, and there are some links which seem to connect Cretan towns with Perrhaebia. We may consider it probable that early settlers from Thessaly found their way to Crete.

But the most important settlers belonged to the Dorian branch of the Greek race, easily recognised by the three tribes, Hylleis, Pamphyli, and Dymanes, which always accompanied its migrations. These three tribes can be traced in many Cretan cities, and we saw that this island was one of the first places to receive the Dorian wanderers. But at a later time there seems to have been a further infusion of the "Dorian" element. New settlers came from Argolis and Laconia and mingled with the older inhabitants, refounding many cities. Thus Gortyn in the south of the island, in the valley of the river Lethaeus, was re-settled; and her neighbour Phaestos, dis- (Od. iii. tinguished by a mention in Homer, was invaded 293.) by newcomers from Argolis. "Well-built Lyttus," in its central site, also of Homeric fame, and Polyrrhenion, "rich in sheep," in the north-western corner, a haunt of the divine huntress Dictynna, were both colonised from Laconia. Cnossus "the great city" of Minos, Cnossus "the broad," was repeopled by Dorians, and though it never attained to its former (Od. xix. splendour, it remained the leading city in Crete. 178; Il.

Fig. 51.—Coin of xviii. 590.) Cnossus, early (obverse). Minotaur [legend: KNOΣ].

The island then, colonised first by a folk closely akin to those who conquered Lacedaemon and Argos, colonised again by those very conquerors, may be said to be doubly "Dorian"; and there is thus a double reason for resemblances between Laconian and Cretan institutions. In the Cretan cities themselves there were of course many local divergences, but the general resemblances are so close, wherever we can trace the facts, that for our purpose we may safely follow the example of the ancients in assuming a general type of Cretan polity.

The population of a Cretan state consisted of two classes, warriors and serfs. In a few cases where one city had subjugated another, the people of the subject city held somewhat the same position as the Laconian Perioeci and formed a third class, but these cases were exceptional. In general, one of the main differences between a *The serfs.* Cretan state and Sparta was that the Cretan state had no perioeci. There were two kinds of serfs, *mnoitai* and *aphamiotai*. The *mnoites* belonged to the state, while the *aphamiotes*, also called *clarotes* or "lot-men," were attached to the lots of the citizens, and belonged to the owners of the lots. These bondsmen cultivated the land themselves and could possess private property, like the Spartan Helots, but though we do not know exactly what their obligations were, they seem to have been in some ways in a better condition than the bondsmen of Laconia. If the *pastas* or lord of a Cretan serf died childless, the serf had an interest in his property. He could contract a legal marriage, and his family was recognised by law. The two privileges from which he was always jealously excluded were the carrying of arms and the practice of athletic exercises in the gymnasia. Unlike the Helots, the Cretan serfs found their condition tolerable, and we never hear that they revolted. The geographical conditions of the Cretans enabled them to excuse their slaves from military service.

Of the monarchical period in Crete we know nothing. In the sixth century we find that monarchy has been abolished by the aristocracies, and that the executive governments are in the hands of boards of ten annual magistrates, entitled *kosmoi*. The *kosmoi* were chosen from certain important clans (*startoi*), and the military as well as the other functions of the king had passed into their hands.

(Gerusia.) They were assisted by the advice of the Council of elders which was elected from those who had filled the office of *kosmos*. The resolves of the *kosmoi* and Council were laid before the *agorai* or general assemblies of citizens, who merely voted and had no right to propose or discuss.

Comparison of Crete and Sparta.

There is a superficial resemblance between this constitution, which prevailed in most Cretan cities, and that of Sparta. The Cretan *agora* answers to the Spartan *apella*, the Cretan to the Spartan *gerusia*, and the *kosmoi* to the ephors. The most obvious difference is that in Crete there was no royalty. But there is another important difference. The democratic feature of the Spartan constitution is absent in Crete. While the ephors were chosen from all the citizens, in a Cretan state only certain noble families were eligible to the office of *kosmos;* and, as the *gerusia* was chosen from the *kosmoi*, it is clear that the whole power of the state resided in a privileged class consisting of those families or clans. Thus the Cretan state was a close aristocracy.

Cretan education.

The true likeness between Sparta and Crete lies in the circumstance that the laws and institutions of both countries aimed at creating a class of warriors. Boys were taught to read and write, and to recite certain songs ordained by law ; but the chief part of their training was bodily, with a view to making them good soldiers. At the age of seventeen they were admitted into "herds," *agelai*, answering to the Spartan *buai*, which were organised by sons of noble houses and supported at the expense of the state. The members of these associations went through a training in the public gymnasia or *dromoi*, and hence were called *dromeis*. Great days were held, on which sham fights took place between these "herds" to the sound of lyres and flutes. The *dromeus* was of age in the eyes of the law, and he was bound to marry, but his wife continued to live in the house of her father or kinsmen, until he passed out of the state of a *dromeus* and became a "man." The men dined at public messes called *andreia*, corresponding to the Spartan *phiditia*, but the boys were also permitted to join them.[1] These meals were not defrayed altogether, as at Sparta, by the contributions of the members, but were partly at least paid for by the state ; and the state also made provision for the sustenance of the women. The public income, which defrayed these and other such burdens and maintained the worship of the gods, must have been derived from public land cultivated by the mnoites, and distinct from the land which was apportioned in lots among the citizens.

We see then that in the discipline and education of the citizens, in the common meals of the men, in general political objects, there is a close and significant likeness between Sparta and Crete. But otherwise there are great differences. (1) In Crete there were, as a rule, no Perioeci ; (2) the Cretan serfs lived under more favourable conditions than the Helots, and were not a constant source of danger; (3) kingship did not survive in Crete, and consequently (4) the functions which in Sparta were divided between kings and ephors were in Crete united in the hands of the *kosmoi ;* (5) the Cretan state was an aristocracy, while Sparta, so far as the city itself was concerned, was a limited democracy ; a difference which clearly reveals itself in (6) the modes of electing *kosmoi* and ephors ; (7) there is a more advanced form of communism in Crete, in so far as state stores contribute largely to the maintenance of the citizens. If one city had become dominant in Crete and reduced the others to subjection, the resemblance between Laconia and Crete would have been much greater. A class of Cretan perioeci would have forthwith been formed.

SECT. 5. THE SUPREMACY AND DECLINE OF ARGOS. THE OLYMPIAN GAMES

The rebellion of Messenia had been especially formidable to Sparta, because the rebels had been supported by two foreign powers, Arcadia and Pisa. Part of Arcadia seems to have been united at this time under the lordship of the king of the Arcadian Orchomenus.

---

[1] The citizens were divided into *hetairiai*, and each *hetairia* had its own *andreion*.

The king of Pisa on the Alpheus had recently risen to new power and honour with the help of Argos ; and Argos itself had been playing a prominent part in the peninsula under the leadership of *Pheidon of Argos (middle of 7th century).* her king Pheidon. The reign of this king was the last epoch of Argos as an active power of the first rank. We know little about him, but his name became so famous that in later times the royal house of distant Macedonia, when it reached the height of its success in Alexander the Great, was anxious to connect its line of descent with Pheidon.[1] Under his auspices a system of measures *Phei-donian measures.* was introduced into Argos and the Peloponnesus. These measures were called after his name *Pheidonian*, and were likewise adopted at Athens ; they seem to have been closely connected with the Aeginetan system of weights. But the only clear action of Pheidon is his expedition to the west. He led an Argive army across Arcadia to the *Pheidon at Olympia.* banks of the Alpheus, and presided there over the celebration of the Olympian festival, which is now for the first time heard of in the history of Greece.

The Altis at Olympia The *altis* or sacred grove of Olympia lay, under the wooded mount of Cronus, where the river Cladeus flows into the Alpheus, in the angle between the two streams. It was dedicated to the worship of Zeus ; but the spot was probably sacred to Pelops, before Zeus claimed it for himself, and Pelops, degraded to the rank of a hero, kept his own sacred precinct within the larger enclosure. The sanctuary was in *belongs to the Pisans.* the territory of Pisa, and it is possible that the care of the worship and the conduct of the festivals belonged originally to the Pisan community. But the men of Elis, the northern neighbours of Pisa, set their hearts on having the control of the Olympian

FIG. 52.—Coin of Elis, early (reverse). Victory with wreath [legend : FΑ(λείων).

sanctuary, which, though it is not once mentioned, as Delphi and Dodona are mentioned, in the poems of Homer, must by the seventh century have won a high prestige in the Peloponnesus and drawn many visitors. As Elis was stronger *Usurped by Eleans, 572 B.C.* than Pisa, the Eleans finally succeeded in usurping the conduct of the festival. Games were the chief feature of the festival, which was held every fourth year, at the time of the second full moon after midsummer's day. The games at first included foot-races, boxing, and wrestling ; chariot-races and horse-races were added later. Such contests were an ancient institution in Greece. We know not how far back they go, or in what circumstances they were first introduced, but the funeral games of Patroclus, described in the

[1] In the interest of genealogy, he was placed more than a century before the time in which he really reigned.

OLYMPIA.

Scale of Yards

0   50   100   200

a.a. Treasure-Houses
1. *Sicyon (5th. Cent.)*
4. *Syracuse (end of 6th. Cent.)*
5. *Epidamnos*
6. *Byzantium*
7. *Sybaris (6th. Cent.)*
8. *Cyrene (early 6th. Cent.)*
9. *Selinus (late 6th. Cent.)*
10. *Metapontion*
11. *Megara (late 6th. Cent.)*
12. *Gela (6th. Cent.)*

Walker & Boutall sc.

Fig. 53.

Iliad, permit us to infer that they were a feature of Ionian life in the ninth century. We can see but dimly into the political relations of Pheidon's age; but we can discern at least that Sparta lent her countenance to Elis in this usurpation, and that Argos, jealous of the growing power of Sparta, espoused the cause of Pisa. This *Pheidon* was the purpose of king Pheidon's expedition to Olympia. He *restores* took the management of the games out of the hands of Elis and *Olympia to* restored it to Pisa. And for many years Pisa maintained her rights. *Pisa.* She maintained them so long as Sparta, absorbed in the Messenian strife, had no help to spare for Elis; and during that time she did what she could to help the foes of Sparta. But when the revolt was suppressed, it was inevitable that Elis should again, with Spartan help, win the control of the games, for Argos, declining under the successors of Pheidon, could give no aid to Pisa.

The temple When king Pheidon held his state at Olympia, the most *of Hera* impressive shrine in the altis was the temple of Hera and Zeus; and *and Zeus* this is the most ancient temple of which the foundations are still *(Heraeum).* preserved on the soil of Hellas. It was built of sun-baked bricks, upon lower courses of stone, and the Doric columns were of wood. The days of stone temples were at hand; but it was not till two centuries later that the elder shrine was overshadowed by the great stone temple of Zeus. The temple of Hera is supposed by some to have been founded in the eleventh or tenth century; it is hardly likely to be so old; but it was certainly very old, like the games of the place. The mythical institution of the games was ascribed to Pelops or to Heracles; and, when the Eleans usurped the presi- *The tradi-* dency, the story gradually took shape that the celebration had been *tional first* revived by the Spartan Lycurgus and the Elean Iphitus in the year *Olympiad,* 776 B.C., and this year was reckoned as the first Olympiad. From *776 B.C.* that year until the visit of Pheidon, the Eleans professed to have presided over the feast; and their account of the matter won its way into general belief.

The games It is possible that king Pheidon reorganised the games and *become* inaugurated a new stage in the history of the festival. At all events, *Pan-* by the beginning of the sixth century the festival was no longer an *hellenic.* event of merely Peloponnesian interest. It had become famous wherever the Greek tongue was spoken, and, when the feast-tide came round in each cycle of four years, there thronged to the banks of the Alpheus, from all quarters of the Greek world, athletes and horses to compete in the contests and spectators to behold them. During the celebration of the festival a sacred truce was observed, and the men of Elis claimed that in those days their territory was inviolable. The prize for victory in the games was a wreath of wild olive; but rich rewards always awaited the victor when he returned

Fig. 54.—Temple of Hera, Olympia.

home in triumph and laid the Olympian crown in the chief temple of his city.

Geographi-cal position of Olympia, facing westward.
It may seem strange that the greatest and most glorious of all Panhellenic festivals should have been celebrated near the western shores of the Peloponnesus. One might have looked to find it nearer the Aegean. But situated where it was, the scene of the great games was all the nearer to the Greeks beyond the western sea ; and none of the peoples of the mother-country vied more eagerly or more often in the contests of Olympia than the children who had found new homes far away on Sicilian and Italian soil. This nearness of Olympia to the western colonies comes into one's thoughts, when standing in the sacred altis one beholds the terrace on the northern side of the precinct, and the scanty remains of the row of twelve treasure-houses which once stood there. For of those twelve treasuries five at least were dedicated by Sicilian and Italian cities. Thus the Olympian festival helped the colonies of the west to keep in touch with the mother-country ; it furnished a centre where Greeks of all parts met and exchanged their ideas and experiences ; it was one of the institutions which expressed and quickened the consciousness of fellowship among the scattered folks of the Greek race ; and it became a model, as we shall see, for other festivals of the same kind, which concurred in promoting a feeling of national unity.

The treasuries.

Festival promotes national feeling in Greece.

[The final success of Sparta in the long struggle with Messenia laid the foundation of Spartan supremacy. Corinth had been rich and powerful in the eighth century under the Bacchiads, and her power, after temporary eclipse, was to reach new heights under the Cypselid tyranny, but the end of the tyranny marked the end of Corinth's greatness. In the early seventh century Pheidon reassembled the lot of Temenos and made Argos for a generation the dominant power. But less than a hundred years after the subjugation of Messenia, the Spartans become the strongest state in the Peloponnesus, and the Argives sink into the position of a second-rate power—always able to maintain their independence, always a thorn in the side of Sparta, always to be reckoned with as a foe and welcomed as a friend, but never leading, dominant, or originative. Sparta owed her greatness to the hardness of her soldier citizens and the stability of her institutions. But the conservatism which maintained her power for more than three centuries led finally to her eclipse.]

Decline of Argos and rise of Sparta.

SECT. 6. DEMOCRATIC MOVEMENTS. LAWGIVERS AND TYRANTS

It is clear that there is no security that equal justice will be meted out to all, so long as the laws by which the judge is supposed

to act are not accessible to all.   A written code of laws is a condition *Demand*
of just judgment, however just the laws themselves may be.   It *for written*
was therefore natural that one of the first demands the people in *laws.*
Greek cities pressed upon their aristocratic governments, and one of
the first concessions those governments were forced to make, was
a written law.   It must be borne in mind that in old days deeds
which injured only the individual and did not touch the gods or the
state, were left to the injured person to deal with as he chose or
could.   The state did not interfere.   Even in the case of blood-
shedding, it devolved upon the kinsfolk of the slain man to wreak
punishment upon the slayer.   Then, as social order developed along
with centralisation, the state took justice partly into its own hands ;
and the injured man, before he could punish the wrong-doer, was
obliged to charge him before a judge, who decided the punishment.
But it must be noted that no crime could come before a judge, unless
the injured person came forward as accuser.   The case of blood-
shedding was exceptional, owing to the religious ideas connected
with it.   It was felt that the shedder of blood was not only impure
himself, but had also defiled the gods of the community ; so that, as
a consequence of this theory, manslaughter of every form came under
the class of crimes against the religion of the state.

The work of writing down the laws, and fixing customs in legal *Early law-*
shape, was probably in most cases combined with the work of re- *givers (7th*
forming ; and thus the great codifiers of the seventh century were *century).*
also lawgivers.   Among them the most famous were the misty
figures of Zaleucus who made laws for the western Locrians, and
Charondas the legislator of Catane ; the clearer figure of the
Athenian Dracon, of whom more will be said hereafter, and, most
famous of all, Solon the Wise.   But other cities in the elder Greece
had their lawgivers too, men of knowledge and experience ; the
names of some are preserved but they are mere names.   It is
probable that the laws of Sparta herself, which she afterwards
attributed to a god, were first shaped and written down at this
period.   The cities of Crete too were affected by the prevalent
spirit of law-shaping, and some fragments are preserved of the early
laws of Gortyn, which were the beginning of an epoch of legislative
activity culminating in the Gortynian Code which has come down to
us on tablets of stone.

In many cases the legislation was accompanied by political *Political*
concessions to the people, and it was part of the lawgiver's task to *struggles :*
modify the constitution.   But for the most part this was only the *democratic*
beginning of a long political conflict ; the people striving for freedom *movements.*
and equality, the privileged classes struggling to retain their
exclusive rights.   The social distress, touched on in a previous

chapter, was the sharp spur which drove the people on in this effort towards popular government. The struggle was in some cases to end in the establishment of a democracy; in many cases, the oligarchy succeeded in maintaining itself and keeping the people down; in most cases, perhaps, the result was a perpetual oscillation between oligarchy and democracy—an endless series of revolutions, too often sullied by violence. But though democracy was not everywhere victorious—though even the states in which it was most firmly established were exposed to the danger of oligarchical conspiracies—yet everywhere the people aspired to it; and we may say that the chief feature of the domestic history of most Greek cities, from the end of the seventh century forward, is an endeavour, here successful, yonder frustrated, to establish or maintain popular government. In this sense then we have now reached a period in which the Greek world is striving and tending to pass from the aristocratic to the democratic commonwealth. The movement passed by some states, like Thessaly,—just as there had been some exceptions, like Argos, to the general fall of the monarchies; while remote kingdoms like Macedonia and Molossia were not affected.

Rise of new unconstitutional monarchies in some states. As usually, or at least frequently, happens in such circumstances, the popular movement received help from within the camp of the adversary. It was help indeed for which there was no reason to be grateful to those who gave it; for it was not given for love of the people. In many cities feuds existed between some of the power-holding families; and, when one family was in the ascendant, its rivals were tempted to make use of the popular discontent in order to subvert it. Thus discontented nobles came forward to be the leaders of the discontented masses. But when the government was overthrown, the revolution generally resulted in a temporary return to monarchy. The noble leader seized the supreme power and maintained it by armed might. The mass of the people were not yet ripe for taking the power into their own hands; and they were generally glad to entrust it to the man who had helped them to overthrow the hated government of the nobles. This new kind of monarchy was very different from the old; for the position of the monarch did not rest on hereditary right but on physical force.

The tyrannis. Such illegitimate monarchs were called tyrants, to distinguish them from the hereditary kings, and this form of monarchy was called a tyrannis. The name "tyrant" was perhaps derived from Lydia, and first used by Greeks in designating the Lydian monarchs; Archilochus, in whose fragments we first meet "tyrannis," applied it to the sovereignty of Gyges. The word was in itself morally neutral and did not imply that the monarch was bad or cruel; there was nothing self-contradictory in a good tyrant, and many tyrants were beneficent. But the isolation of these rulers, who, being without the support of legitimacy, depended on armed force, so often urged them to be suspicious and cruel, that the tyrannis came into bad odour ; arbitrary acts of oppression were associated with the name ; and " tyrant " inclined to the evil sense in which modern languages have adopted it. For the Greek dislike of the tyrannis there was however a deeper cause than the fact that many tyrants were oppressors. It placed in the hands of an unconstitutional ruler arbitrary control, whether he exercised it or not, over the lives and fortunes of the citizens. It was thus repugnant to the Greek love of freedom, and it seemed to arrest their constitutional growth. As a matter of fact, this temporary arrest during the period when the first tyrannies prevailed may have been useful ; for the tyrannis, though its direct political effect was retarding, forwarded the progress of the people in other directions. And even from a constitutional point of view it may have had its uses at this period. In some cases, it secured an interval of repose and growth, during which the people won experience and knowledge to fit them for self-government.

The period which saw the fall of the aristocracies is often called *No such* the age of the tyrants. The expression is unhappy, because it might *thing in* easily mislead. The tyrannis first came into existence at this period ; *Greek his-* there was a large crop of tyrants much about the same time in *tory as an* different parts of Greece ; they all performed the same function of *age of* overthrowing aristocracies, and in many cases they paved the way *tyrannies.* for democracies. But on the other hand, the tyrannis was not a form of government which appeared only at this transitional crisis, and then passed away. There is no age in the subsequent history of Greece which might not see, and did not actually see, the rise of tyrants here and there. Tyranny was always with the Greeks. It, as well as oligarchy, was a danger by which their democracies were threatened at all periods.

Ionia seems to have been the original home of the tyrannis, and *Tyrants in* this may have been partly due to the seductive example of the rich *Asiatic* court of the Lydian " tyrants " at Sardis. But of the Ionian tyrannies *Greece.* we know little. We hear of factions and feuds in the cities, of aristocratic houses overthrown and despotisms established in various states. A tyrant of Ephesus marries the daughter of the Lydian monarch Alyattes. The most famous of these tyrants was Thrasy- *Thrasy-* bulus of Miletus, under whose rule that city held a more brilliant *bulus, c.* position than ever. Abroad, he took part in planting some of the *610 B.C.* colonies on the Black Sea, and successfully resisted the menaces of Lydia. At home, he developed the craft of tyranny to a fine art.

In Lesbian Mytilene we see the tyrannis and also a method by *Mytilene* which it might be avoided. Mytilene had won great commercial prosperity ; its ruling nobles, the Penthilids, were wealthy and luxurious and oppressed the people. Tyrants rose and fell in rapid

Myrsilus, tyrant.

Alcaeus (c. 600-570 B.C.).

Pittacus

holds office of aesymnetes [first years of 6th cent. ?].

FIG. 55.—Early coin of Methymna in Lesbos (reverse). Head of Pallas [legend: ΜΑΘΥΜ- ΝΑΙΟΣ].

succession ; the echoes of hatred and jubilation still ring to us from relics of the lyric poems of Alcaeus. "Let us drink and reel, for Myrsilus is dead." The poet was a noble and a fighter ; but in a war with the Athenians on the coast of the Hellespont he threw away his shield, like Archilochus, and it hung as a trophy at Sigeum. He plotted with Pittacus against the tyrant, but Pittacus was not a noble and his friendship with Alcaeus was not enduring. Pittacus however, who distinguished himself for bravery in the same war with Athens, was to be the saviour of the state. He gained the trust of the people and was elected ruler for a period of ten years in order to heal the sores of the city. Such a governor, possessing supreme power but for a limited time, was called an aesymnētes. Pittacus gained the reputation of a wise lawgiver and a firm, moderate ruler. He banished the nobles who opposed him, among others the two most famous of all Lesbians, the poets Alcaeus and Sappho. At the end of ten years he laid down his office, to be enrolled after his death in the number of the Seven Wise Men. The ship of state had reached the haven, to apply a metaphor of Alcaeus, and the exiles could safely be allowed to return.

This was the brilliant period of the history of Lesbos, and a few surviving fragments of its two great poets, who struck new notes and devised new cadences of lyric song, give a glimpse of the free and luxurious life of the Aeolian island. The radiant genius of Sappho was inspired by her passionate attachments to young Lesbian maidens ; the songs of Alcaeus, mirroring the commotions of party warfare, rang with the clatter of arms and the clinking of drinking-cups.

SECT. 7. THE TYRANNIES OF CENTRAL GREECE

The three Isthmian tyrannies.

About the middle of the seventh century, three tyrannies arose in central Greece in the neighbourhood of the Isthmus : at Corinth, at Sicyon, and at Megara. In each case the development was different, and is in each case instructive. In Sicyon the tyranny is brilliant and beneficent, in Corinth brilliant and oppressive, in Megara short-lived and followed by long intestine struggles.

I. CORINTH.

[In the eighth and early seventh centuries Corinth had been the wealthiest city on the Greek mainland. Her situation commanding the land route north and south and the narrow stretch of isthmus, which linked the Aegean with the Corinthian Gulf and offered the safest route to the west, encouraged the development of trade. Already by the middle of the eighth century Corinthian pottery, Corinthian perfumes, and other products were being widely distributed in Italy and Sicily. Corinth's potters were the first mainlanders to exploit the opportunities offered by renewed contact with the east and to enrich their repertoire with a wide range of oriental motifs. Her early power is witnessed by the foundation of Corcyra and Syracuse and even more by the change in the nature of imports to the west which follows the first wave of colonisation. In the early stages of this trade pottery from many widely scattered production centres in the Aegean and on the mainland was being carried to the west. By the beginning of the seventh century Corinth seems to have won a virtual monopoly which lasted until the rise of Athenian export towards the middle of the sixth century. But the rise of Argos under Pheidon overshadowed Corinth and towards the

Fig. 56.—Corinthian Vase, with hoplites, from Etruria. *c.* 650 B.C.

middle of the seventh century she was only able to hold her own in a sea battle with her colony Corcyra. The weakening in the leadership of Corinth invited challenge from within.]

The ruling clan of the Bacchiads was overthrown by Cypselus, who had put himself at the head of the people. A characteristic legend was formed at an early time about the birth of Cypselus, suggested by the connexion of his name with κυψέλη, a jar. His mother was a Bacchiad lady named Labda, who, being lame and consequently compelled to wed out of her own class, married a certain Eetion, a man of the people. Having no children and consulting the Delphic oracle on the matter, Eetion received this reply :—

Cypselus: legend of his birth and name.

> High honour is thy due, Eetion,
>   Yet no man doth thee honour, as were right.
> Labda thy wife will bear a huge millstone,
> Destined to fall on them who rule alone,
>   And free thy Corinth from their rightless might.

The prophecy came to the ears of the Bacchiads and was confirmed to them by another oracle. So, as soon as Labda's child was born, they sent ten men to slay it. When the men came to the court of Eetion's dwelling they found that he was not at home, and they asked Labda for the infant. Suspecting nothing, she gave it to one of them to take in his arms, but, as he was about to dash it to the ground, the child smiled at him and he had not the heart to slay it. He passed it on to the second, but he too was moved with pity; and so it was passed round from hand to hand, and none of the ten could find it in his heart to destroy it. Then giving the infant back to the mother, and going out into the courtyard, they reviled each other for their weakness, and resolved to go in again and do the deed together. But Labda listening at the door overheard what they said, and hid the child in a jar, where none of them thought of looking.[1] Thus the boy was saved, but the men falsely reported to the Bacchiads that they had performed their errand.

The Bacchiads were banished and their property confiscated; dangerous persons were executed, and Cypselus took the reins of government into his own hands. Of the rule of Cypselus himself we know little; he is variously represented as harsh and mild. His son Periander succeeded, and of him more is recorded. The general features of the Cypselid tyrannis were a vigorous colonial and commercial policy, and the encouragement of art.

Colonial policy of the Cypselids.

One of the earliest triumphs of Cypselus was probably the reduction of Corcyra, which had formed a fleet of its own and had grown to be a rival of its mother in the Ionian seas. It has already been mentioned that the earliest battle of ships between two Greek states was supposed to have been fought between Corinth and Corcyra. The attempt of Corinth to form a colonial empire was an interesting experiment. The idea of Cypselus corresponded to our modern colonial system, in which the colonies are in a relation of dependence to the mother-country, and not to that of the Greeks, in which the colony was an independent sovereign state. Geographical conditions alone rendered it out of the question to apply the new principle to Syracuse, but the success at Corcyra was followed up by a development of Corinthian influence in the north-west of Greece. The Acarnanian peninsula of Leucas was occupied and made into an island by piercing a channel through the narrow isthmus. Anactorion was founded on the south side of the Ambracian gulf, and inland, on the north side, Ambracia. Apollonia was planted on the coast of Epirus; and farther north Corcyra, under the auspices of her mother-city, colonised Epidamnus. At a later period, and in another

Corinth makes Corcyra subject.

Leucas. Anactorion. Ambracia. Apollonia. Epidamnus.

[1] The hiding in the jar is illustrated by Euphronius' picture of Eurystheus hiding from Heracles in a jar.

quarter of the Greek world, a son of Periander founded Potidaea in the Chalcidic peninsula.

Cypselus and Periander did their utmost to promote the com- *Trade.* mercial activity of their city. In the middle of the eighth century the rival Euboean cities, Chalcis and Eretria, were important merchant states. But fifty years later they had somewhat declined, *Decline of* to the profit of Corinth and Aegina. Their decline was brought *Eretria* about by their rivalry, which led to an exhausting war for the Lelan- *and* tine plain. [This war was singled out by Thucydides in his summary *Chalcis.* account of early Greek history for its large scale and widespread *War of the* alliances. We hear that Miletus supported Eretria, while Samos *Lelantine* and Thessaly were allied to Chalcis; Thucydides implies that other *Plain (end* states also were involved. The decision was reached on land in *of 8th* Euboea but the struggle seems to have assumed the wider aspect of *cent.).* a trade war with repercussions in the east and west. The expulsion of Megarian colonists from Sicilian Megara may have been one incident, a Samian raid on Aegina another. Eretria suffered most. She lost her share of the Lelantine plain; her control over the islands of Andros, Tenos, and Ceos was undermined; her continental territory, the plain of Oropus, passed in the sixth century at the latest under the power of Thebes. Corinth perhaps enjoyed the most solid fruits of victory. For though the date of the war is highly controversial, the end of the eighth century seems to provide the most probable setting, and it is about this time, as has been seen, that Corinth won a virtual monopoly of western trade.]

The decline of Chalcis was followed by a radical change in the foreign policy of Corinth. This city had formerly cultivated the alliance of Samos. She now deserted this alliance and formed a friendship with her old foe Miletus. The cause of this change was, at least in great measure, the natural sympathy of tyrannies. Thrasy-bulus the powerful tyrant of Miletus sympathised with Periander the powerful tyrant of Corinth. [This change in policy is reflected in changes in the currents of trade. Corinthian wares are more widely distributed in the east. Miletus enters the western market, formerly a Corinthian preserve, through Sybaris.]

The foreign relations of Periander extended to Egypt, and there are two indications of his inter-course with the Egyptian monarchs Necho and Psammetichus II. His nephew and successor was called after the last-named king. Moreover we may guess that the canal works of Necho suggested to Periander under-takings of the same kind—the small canal which he actually cut at

Fig. 57.—Coin of Corinth, 6th-5th cent. (obverse). Helmeted head of Goddess.

Egyptian name of Peri-ander's nephew.

Peri-ander's canals.

Leucas, and the great canal which he designed to cut through the isthmus of Corinth itself. But a Greek tyrant had not at his command the slave-labour of which an Egyptian king disposed, and the design fell through—an enterprise more than once attempted since, but not accomplished till our own day. Had Periander had the resources to carry out his idea, the subsequent history of Greek military and naval operations would have been largely changed.

(Tyrants patrons of art and literature.) Dithyramb.
While the most successful of the tyrants, like Periander, furthered material civilisation, they often manifested an interest in intellectual pursuits, and did something for the promotion of art. A new form of poetry called the *dithyramb* was developed at Corinth during this period, the rude strains which were sung at vintage-feasts in honour of Dionysus being moulded into an artistic shape. The discovery was attributed to Arion, a mythical minstrel, who was said to have leaped into the sea under the compulsion of mariners who robbed him, and to have been carried to Corinth on the back of a dolphin, the fish of Dionysus.

Invention of roof-tiles.
In architecture, Corinthian skill had made an important contribution to the development of the temple. In the course of the seventh century men began to translate into stone the old shrine of brick and wood ; and stone temples arose in all parts of the Greek world—the lighter " Ionic " form in Ionia, the heavier " Doric " in the elder Greece. By the invention of roof-tiles, Corinthian workmen rendered it practicable to give a considerable inclination to the roof ; and thus in each gable of the temple a large triangular space was left, inviting the sculptor to fill it with a story in marble. The pediment, as we name it, was called by the
ἀετός. Pottery.
Greeks the " eagle " ; and thus it was said that Corinth had discovered the eagle. [Corinthian pottery, which had developed remarkably under the Bacchiads, won even wider markets under the tyrants ; but quantity seems to have undermined quality. The controlled vigour and imagination of the Proto-Corinthian and early Corinthian styles is gradually replaced by fluent mediocrity ; and not long after the fall of the tyranny the finer quality of Attic black-figure vases was beginning to eclipse the Corinthian potter. By the end of the sixth century Attic pots had virtually conquered the western market, once almost a Corinthian preserve ; though the continued friendship of Corinth with Athens suggests that the Athenians may have used Corinthian ships to carry their goods to the west until the fifth century.

Corinthian thêsauros at Delphi.
The dedicatory offerings of the Cypselids at Delphi and Olympia were rich and remarkable. The treasure-house of the Corinthians at Delphi was ascribed to Cypselus. More famous, on account of the legend which was in later times attached to it, was a large chest of cedar-wood, which was dedicated, probably by Periander, in the

shrine of Hera at Olympia. It was called the chest of Cypselus, and *So-called* was said to have been the place in which Labda hid her child. This *"Chest of* story overlooked the fact that a chest was an obvious place to search *Cypselus"* in, and fabricated the theory that the Corinthians called a chest a *(c. 600* "jar." Three sides of the chest were ornamented with mythological *B.C.).* scenes which ran round in five bands. It was still in existence eight *Seen and* centuries later, and a traveller who saw it then has left a minute *described* description, which enables us to form a notion how Greek art in the *by* days of Periander attempted the treatment of legend. [The seven *Pausanias* great columns of limestone which for long were almost the only sign *(2nd cent.* *A.D.).*

FIG. 58.—Pillars of Temple of Apollo at Corinth, *c.* 550 B.C.

to mark the site of ancient Corinth, were until recently thought to be a relic of Periander's rule. But systematic exploration of the foundations has shown that this Temple of Apollo dates from a generation *Temple of* after the fall of the tyranny.] *Apollo.*

Judged by a modern standard, the government of Periander was *Periander* strict, though in accordance with the practice in other cities and with the Greek views of the time. There were laws forbidding men to *Laws* acquire large numbers of slaves or to live beyond their income ; sup- *restricting* pressing excessive luxury and idleness ; hindering country people *individual* from fixing their abode in the city. *liberty.*

In his home-life Periander was unlucky. He married Melissa,
Tyranny at the daughter of Procles, who had made himself tyrant of Epi-
Epidaurus. daurus. It was believed that he put her to death, and this led to
Tale of an irreconcilable quarrel with his son Lycophron. The story is that
Lycophron, Procles invited his two grandchildren, Lycophron and an elder
son of brother, to his court. When they were departing he said to them,
Periander. " Do ye know, boys, who killed your mother ? " The elder was
dull and did not understand ; but the words sank into the heart
of Lycophron, and henceforward he showed dislike and suspicion
Periander towards his father. Periander, pressing him, discovered what
reduces Procles had said ; and the affair ended, for the time, in a war with
Epidaurus. Epidaurus in which Procles was captured, and the banishment of
Lycophron Lycophron to Corcyra. As years went on and Periander was
at Corcyra. growing old, seeing that his elder son was dull of wit, he desired
to hand over the government to Lycophron. But the son was im-
placable, and did not deign even to answer his father's messenger.
Then Periander sent his daughter to intercede, but Lycophron replied that he would never come to Corinth while his father was
there. Periander then decided to go himself to Corcyra and leave
Corinth to his son, but the Corcyraeans were so terrified at the
idea of having the tyrant among them that they slew Lycophron
in order to foil the plan. For this act Periander chastised them
heavily.

c. 586 *B.C.* The great tyrant died and was succeeded by his nephew Psammetichus, who having ruled for a few years was slain. With him the
End of the tyranny of the Cypselids came to an end, and an aristocracy of
tyranny. merchants was firmly established. At the same time the Cypselid
colonial system partly broke down, for Corcyra became independent
and hostile, while the Ambraciots set up a democracy. But over
her other colonies Corinth retained her influence, and was on
friendly terms with all of them.

II. The natural sympathy of tyrannies affected the relations of
MEGARA. Corinth and Megara. Some time after the inauguration of the
Cypselid tyranny, a similar constitutional change occurred at Megara,
and a friendship sprang up between the two cities. The mercantile
development of Megara, famous for her weavers, had enriched the
nobles, who held the political power and oppressed the peasants with
Theagenes, a grinding despotism. Then Theagenes arose as a deliverer and
c. 640 *B.C.* made himself tyrant. The example of Cypselus, and probably his
direct influence and help, had something to do with the enterprise
of Theagenes. Having obtained a bodyguard, Theagenes surprised
and massacred the aristocrats. His term of tyranny was marked by
one solid work, the construction of an aqueduct. He was overthrown
and did not, like Cypselus, transmit his power to his descendants.

Then followed a political struggle between the aristocracy, which
had regained its power, and the people. But the time for an un-
mitigated aristocracy had gone by; the dêmos could not be ignored
or brushed aside. Concessions were wrung from the government.
The economical condition of the peasants was relieved by a measure
which forced the capitalists to pay back the interest which they had
extorted, while the political disabilities were relieved by extending
citizenship to the country population and admitting the tillers of the
soil to the Assembly. These conflicts and social changes are reflected
in the poems of Theognis, who meditated and lamented them. He *Theognis.*
sang in the early part of the sixth century, pouring out his heart to
Cyrnus, a young noble of the Polypaid family.[1] He had made an
unsuccessful voyage, lost his land and fortune, and consequently his
influence. He judges severely the short-sighted, greedy policy of
his own caste, and sees that it is likely to lead to another tyranny.
On the other hand, his sympathies are with an aristocratic form of
government, and he discerns with dismay the growth of democratic
tendencies, and the changed condition of the country folk, whom he
regarded with true aristocratic contempt. The exclusiveness of the
nobility was breaking down in the new circumstances, and mixed
marriages were coming in. He cries :

> Unchanged the walls, but, ah, how changed the folk !
> The base, who knew erstwhile nor law nor right,
> But dwelled like deer, with goatskin for a cloak,
> Are now ennobled ; and, O sorry plight !
> The nobles are made base in all men's sight.

It was not long before the importance of Megara as a power in *Megara*
Greece dwindled. The war with Athens which resulted in the loss *loses*
of the island of Salamis was decisive for her own decline and for the *Salamis.*
rise of her rival.[2]

The rise of a tyranny in agricultural Sicyon seems to have occurred *III.*
much about the same time as at mercantile Corinth. We know *Sicyon.*
nothing of the circumstances. The name of the first founder, who *Ortha-*
was of low birth, is said to have been Orthagoras.[3] The first of the *goras* (?).
house of whom we have any historical record is Cleisthenes, who *Cleisthenes*
ruled in the first quarter of the sixth century. His hostility to Argos, *c. 590.*
which claimed lordship over Sicyon, the part he took in the Sacred
War of Delphi, and the splendour of his court are the chief facts of

---

[1] The Theognidea are a collection of poems of various ages—drinking songs,
moral and political apophthegms. Those addressed to Cyrnus are from the
genuine Theognis.

[2] See below, p. 190.

[3] Cleisthenes was the son of Aristonymus, the son of Myron, the son of
Andreas, according to Herodotus, who does not mention Orthagoras.

which we know. He was engaged in an Argive war. He would not permit rhapsodists to recite the Homeric poems at Sicyon, because there was so much in them about Argos and Argives; and he did away with the worship of the Argive hero Adrastus, whose cult in Sicyon had been conspicuous. It is also stated that not wishing that the tribes of Sicyon and Argos should have the same

Story of the
new
phylae :
Hyatai,
Oneatai,
Choireatai,
and
Archelaoi.
names, he substituted for the Dorian tribes—Hylleis, Pamphyli, Dymanes—the insulting names Swine-ites, Assites, and Pigites, and called his own tribe Archelaoi, "Rulers"; and that this nomenclature endured for sixty years after his death, when the old Dorian names were restored and Archelaoi changed to Aigialeis. In this form the story seems highly unlikely, for such a change would have been a greater slight to the mass of the Sicyonians than to the Argives. But it is quite possible that the tyrant changed the name of his own tribe Aigialeis to Archelaoi, and we can understand how the story might have arisen out of a word spoken in jest: "I have changed my Goats ($A\mathit{i}\gamma\iota$-$\alpha\lambda\epsilon\hat{\iota}s$) into Rulers of the folk; I have a mind to change those Argive *Hy*-lleis and the rest of them into Swine and Asses."

Cleisthenes married his daughter Agarista to an Athenian noble, Megacles, of the famous family of the Alcmaeonids. A legend is told of the wooing of Agarista which illustrates the tyrant's wealth and hospitality and the social ideas of the age. On the occasion of an Olympian festival at which he had himself won in the chariot-race, Cleisthenes made proclamation to the Greeks that all who aspired to the hand of his daughter should assemble at Sicyon, sixty days hence, and be entertained at his court for a year. At the end of the year he would decide who was most worthy of his daughter. Then there came to Sicyon all the Greeks who had a high opinion of themselves or of their families. From Sybaris and Siris in the far west, from Epidamnus and Aetolia, Arcadia and Elis, Argos and Athens, Euboea and Thessaly, the suitors for the hand of Agarista came. Cleisthenes tested their accomplishments for a year. He tried them in gymnastic exercises, but laid most stress on their social qualities. The two Athenians, Hippocleides and Megacles, pleased him best, but to Hippocleides of these two he most inclined. The day appointed for the choice of the husband came, and Cleisthenes sacrificed a hundred oxen and feasted all the suitors and all the folk of Sicyon. After the dinner, the wooers competed in music and general conversation. Hippocleides was the most brilliant, and, as his success seemed assured, he bade the flute-player strike up and began to dance. Cleisthenes was surprised and disconcerted at this behaviour, and his surprise became disgust when Hippocleides, who thought he was making a decisive impression, called for a table and

danced Spartan and Athenian figures on it. The host controlled his
feelings, but, when Hippocleides proceeded to dance on his head, he
could no longer resist, and called out, " O son of Tisander, you have
danced away ·our bride." But the Athenian only replied, " Hippocleides careth not," and danced on. Megacles was chosen for
Agarista and rich presents were given to the disappointed suitors.

SECT. 8. THE SACRED WAR. THE PANHELLENIC GAMES

The most important achievement of Cleisthenes, and that which
won him most fame in the Greek world, was his championship of
the Delphic oracle.

The temple of Delphi, or Pytho, lay in the territory of the
Phocian town of Crisa.[1] A Delphic Hymn tells how Apollo came
" to Crisa, a hill facing to westward, under snowy Parnassus ;
a beetling cliff overhangs it, beneath is a hollow, rugged glen. *Site of*
Here," he said, " I will make me a fair temple, to be an oracle for *Delphi*
men." The poet's picture is perfect. The sanctuary of " rocky
Pytho " was terraced on a steep slope, hard under the bare sheer cliffs
of Parnassus, looking down upon the deep glen of the Pleistus ; an
austere and majestic scene, supremely fitted for the utterance of the
oracles of God. The city of Crisa lay on a vine-tressed hill to the *Site of*
west of the temple, and commanded its own plain which stretched *Crisa.*
southward to the sea. The men of Crisa claimed control over the
Delphians and the oracle, and levied dues on the visitors who came
to consult the deity. The Delphians desired to free themselves from
the control of the Crisaeans, and they naturally looked for help to
the great league of the north, in which the Thessalians, the ancient
foes of the Phocians, were now the dominant member. The folks *The*
who belonged to this religious union were the " dwellers around " the *Amphi-*
shrine of Demeter at Anthela, close to the pass of Thermopylae ; *ctionic*
and hence they were called the *Amphictiones* of Anthela or Pylae. *league.*
The league was probably old ; it was formed, at all events, before the
Thessalians had incorporated Achaean Phthiotis in Thessaly ; for the
people of Phthiotis were an independent member of the league, which
included the Locrians, Phocians, Boeotians, and Athenians, as well
as the Dorians, Malians, Dolopians, Enianes, Thessalians, Perrhae-
bians, and Magnetes. The members of the league were bound not to
destroy, or cut off running water from, any city which belonged to it.

The Amphictions espoused warmly the cause of Apollo and his

---

[1] Crisa and Cirrha are different forms of the same name, and mean the same
town. After the destruction of Crisa the name was applied to the port where the
pilgrims used to land—mentioned simply as λιμήν in the Hymn to the Pythian
Apollo, a work of the seventh century.

FIG. 59.—Site of Delphi.

Delphian servants, and declared a holy war against the men of Crisa *The Sacred* who had violated the sacred territory.[1] And Delphi found a champion *War.* in the south as well as in the north. The tyrant of Sicyon across *c. 590 B.C.* the gulf went forth against the impious city. It was not enough to conquer Crisa and force her to make terms or promises. As she was situated in such a strong position, commanding the road from the sea to the sanctuary, it was plain that the utter destruction of the city was the only conclusion of the war which could lead to the assured independence of the oracle. The Amphictions and Sicyonians took the city after a sore struggle, rased it to the ground, and slew the indwellers. The Crisaean plain was dedicated to the god ; solemn and heavy curses were pronounced against whosoever should till it. The great gulf which sunders northern Greece from the Peloponnesus, and whose old name " Crisaean " testified to the greatness of the Phocian city, received, after this, its familiar name " Corinthian " from the city of the Isthmus.

One of the consequences of this war was the establishment of a *Conse-* close connexion between Delphi and the Amphictiony of Anthela. *quences* The Delphic shrine became a second place of meeting, and the league *for the* was often called the Delphic Amphictiony. The temple was taken *ctiony.* under the protection of the league ; the administration of the property of the god was placed in the hands of the Hieromnemones or sacred councillors, who met twice a year in spring and autumn, both at Anthela and at Delphi. Two Hieromnemones were sent as its representatives by each member of the league. The oracle and the priestly nobles of Delphi thus won a position of independence ; their great career of prosperity and power began. The Pythian games *Pythian* were now reorganised on a more splendid scale, and the ordering of *games* them was one of the duties of the Amphictions. The festival became, *[first* like the Olympian, a four-yearly celebration, being held in the middle *Pythiad,* of each Olympiad ; gymnastic contests were introduced, whereas *582 B.C.]* before there had been only a musical competition ; and money-prizes were abolished for a wreath of bay. Cleisthenes won the laurel in the first chariot-race in the new hippodrome which was built in the plain below the ruins of Crisa. Hard by was the stadion or racecourse in which the athletes ran and wrestled ; and it was not till after many years had passed that the new stadion was built high up above Delphi itself, close under the cliffs. Cleisthenes was remembered as having taken a prominent part both in the Sacred War and in the institution of the games ; and he commemorated the occasion of his victory by founding Pythian games at Sicyon, which afterwards, by a stroke of the irony of history, became associated with the hated hero Adrastus. [The Sicyonian treasury whose foundations can be seen at Delphi

[1] It is said that Solon the Athenian took an active part in urging on the war.

was built at the end of the sixth century, but it replaced an earlier building which was probably the gift of Cleisthenes. Fragments of the metopes of this earlier building have been recovered, showing that in the days of her great tyrant Sicyon's craftsmen were among the best of the day, with a rhythmic style which distinguished them from other mainland schools.]

Isthmian games (586 or 582).

Nemean games (? 576).

Much about the same time two other Panhellenic festivals were instituted at Isthmus and at Nemea. It is uncertain whether the Isthmian games in honour of Poseidon were founded by Periander, or in commemoration of the abolition of tyranny at Corinth after the death of Psammetichus. The games in honour of Nemean Zeus were administered by the little town of Cleonae, and seem to have been established by the influence of Argos. Both the Isthmian and the Nemean festivals were two-yearly. Thus from the beginning of the sixth century four Panhellenic festivals are celebrated, two in the Peloponnesus, one on the isthmus, one in the north ; and throughout the course of Grecian history the prestige of these gatherings never wanes.

Growth of Hellenic unity: displayed by

These four Panhellenic festivals helped to maintain a feeling of fellowship among all the Greeks ; and we may suspect that the promotion of this feeling was the deliberate policy of the rulers who raised these games to Panhellenic dignity. But it must not be overlooked that the festivals were themselves only a manifestation of a tendency towards unity, which had begun in the eighth century. We have already seen how this tendency was promoted by colonisation, and confirmed by the introduction of a common name for the Greek race. About the middle of the seventh century, we meet the name " Panhellenes " in a poem of Archilochus, and the phrase " Panhellenes and Achaeans " occurs in a passage, which may be still earlier, in the Homeric Catalogue of the Ships. The Panhellenic idea, the conception of a common Hellenic race with common interests, was encouraged by the poetical records of the heroic age. The Trojan war was remembered as a common enterprise, in which northern and southern Greece had joined ; and the ancient poets had called the whole host " Achaeans " or " Argives " indifferently. The Homeric poems were a bond among all men of Greek speech, and the memory of Troy was an ingredient in a sentiment which, though we cannot call it national, was distinctly a sentiment of community. The feeling of community was also displayed in the recognition of the Pythian Apollo as the chief and supreme oracle of Greece. The growth of the prestige of the Delphic god might almost have been used as a touchstone for measuring the growth of the feeling of community. As a meeting-place for pilgrims and envoys from all quarters of the Greek world, Delphi served to keep

(1) a common name ;

(2) the conception of the Trojan war as Panhellenic ;

(3) the Panhellenic position of Delphi (the " common hearth " of Greece) ;

distant cities in touch with one another, and to spread news; purposes which were effected in a less degree by the Panhellenic festivals. The tendencies to unity were also shown by the leagues, chiefly of a religious kind, which were formed among neighbouring states. The maritime league of Calauria is an instance; [1] the northern Amphictiony of Anthela is another; and we shall presently have a glimpse of the Ionic federation of Delos. In the second half of the sixth century we find the cities of south Italy bound together in some form of loose confederacy, which was indicated in the character of their coinage. We shall soon see Sparta uniting a large part of the Peloponnesus in a confederacy under her presidency.

(4) the Panhellenic games; (5) partial minor religious leagues.

These tendencies to unity never resulted in a political union of all Hellas. The Greek race never became a Greek nation; for the Panhellenic idea was weaker than the love of local independence. But an ideal unity was realised; it was realised in those beliefs and institutions which we have just been considering. They fostered in the hearts of the Greeks a lively feeling of fellowship and a deep pride in Hellas; though there was no political tie. And it is to be noted that the Delphic oracle made no efforts to promote political unity, though unintentionally it promoted unity of another kind. If it had made any such efforts, they would certainly have failed; for the oracle had little influence in initiation. Greek states did not ask Apollo to originate or direct their policy; they only sought his authority for what they had already determined.

Nature of Delphic influence.

We saw that the Boeotians were a member of the northern Amphictiony. The unity of Boeotia itself had taken the form of a federation, in which Thebes was the dominant power, being not only the federal capital, but—at all events in later times—being represented by two members on the board of Boeotarchs, as the federal magistrates were called, whereas each of the other districts returned only one Boeotarch. Its religious centre—for like all old Greek federations it was religious before it became political—was the sanctuary of Poseidon at Onchestus. In the seventh century it did not yet include all Boeotia; Orchomenus still resisted. But at length Thebes forced Orchomenus to join, and in the course of the sixth century the Graian land of Oropus was annexed. The unity of Boeotia, thus completed, had its weak points; its maintenance depended upon the power of Thebes; some of the cities were reluctant members. Above all, Plataea chafed: she had kept herself pure from mixture with the Boeotian settlers, and her whole history—of which some remarkable episodes will pass before us—may be regarded as an isolated continuation of the ancient struggle between the elder Greek inhabitants of the land and the Boeotian conquerors.

The Boeotian confederacy.

Orchomenus joins Boeotian league (? c. 600 B.C.), [see below, p. 218]. Position of Plataea.

[1] See below, p. 177. For the Ionic league of Delos, see p. 198.

BOEOTIA.

Stadia
0 10 20 40 60 80 100

English Miles
0   2   4   6   8   10

EUBOEA

Euboean Sea

Euripus

Chalcis

Euripus

Aulis

Anthedon

Larymna

Upper Larymna

Harma

Mycalessus

Acraephnium

L. Hylica

Hyettus

Copae

Copaic Lake

Onchestus

THEBES

Tanagra

Delium

Mount Parnes

Asopus R.

R. Ismenus

Erythrae

Hysiae

Eleutherae

ATTICA

LOCRIS

Opus

Orchomenus

Abae

Cephisus

Chaeronea

Lebadea

Coronea

Haliartus

Ascra

Thespiae

Leuctra

Plataea

Mount Cithaeron

Creusis

Corinthian Gulf

Mount Helicon

Thisbe

Corsiae

Bulis

PHOCIS

Longitude East 23° of Greenwich

23°

38° 30′

38° 30′

Walker & Boutall sc.

FIG. 60.

CHAPTER IV

THE UNION OF ATTICA AND THE FOUNDATION OF THE ATHENIAN DEMOCRACY

SECT. I. THE UNION OF ATTICA

WHEN recorded history begins, the story of Athens is the story of Attica, the inhabitants of Attica are Athenians. But Attica, like its neighbour Boeotia and other countries of Greece, was once occupied by a number of independent states. Some of these little kingdoms are vaguely remembered in legends which tell of the giant Pallas who ruled at Pallene under the ...orth-eastern slopes of Hymettus, of the dreaded Cephalus lord of the southern region of Thoricus, or of Porphyrion of mighty stature whose domain was at Athmonon unde Mount Pentelicus. The hill of Munychia was, in the distant past, an island, and was crowned by a stronghold ; the name *Piraeus* has been supposed to preserve the memory of days when the lords of Munychia looked across to the mainland and spoke of the "opposite shore." At a later stage we find neighbouring villages uniting themselves together by political or religious bonds. Thus in the north, beyond Pentelicus, Marathon and Oenoe and two other towns formed a *tetrapolis*. Again Piraeus, adjacent Phaleron, and two other places joined in the common worship of the god Heracles, and were called the Four-Villages. Of all the lordships between Mount Cithaeron and Cape Sunium the two most important were those of Eleusis and Athens, severed from one another by the hill-chain of Aegaleos.

Tetra-kômoi

It was upon Athens, the stronghold in the midst of the Cephisian plain, five miles from the sea, that destiny devolved the task of working out the unity of Attica. This Cephisian plain, on the south side open to the Saronic gulf, is enclosed by hills, on the west by Aegaleos, on the north-west by Parnes, on the east by Hymettus, while the gap in the north-east, between Parnes and Hymettus, is filled by the gable-shaped mass of Pentelicus. The river Cephisus flows not far from

*The
Acropolis.*

Athens to westward, but the Acropolis was girt by two smaller streams, the Ilīsus and the Eridănus.[1] We have seen that it had been occupied as an abode of men in the third millennium, and that in the bronze age it was one of the strong places of Greece. There still remain pieces of the wall of grey-blue limestone with which the Pelasgian lords of the castle secured the edge of their precipitous hill.[2] The old wall was called the Pelargikon, but in later times this name was specially applied to the ground on the north-western slope. The Acropolis is joined to the Areopagus by a high saddle, which forms its natural approach, and on this side walls were so constructed that the main western entrance to the citadel lay through nine successive gates. At the north-western corner a covered staircase led down to the well of Clepsydra, which supplied the fortress with water ; and on the north side there were two narrow " postern " descents into the plain, much steeper than that at Tiryns. We may take it that all these constructions were the work of the Pelasgians and were inherited by their Greek successors.

*Remains of
Pelasgic
wall on
S. W. and
S. E. of
Acropolis.*

*Ennea-
tylon.*

*The
Cecròpes.*

*(Tradi-
tional date
of Cecrops,
1581 B.C.)*

The first Greeks who won the Pelasgic acropolis were probably the Cecropes, and, though their name was forgotten as the name of an independent people, it survived in another form. For the later Athenians were always ready to describe themselves as the sons of Cecrops. This Cecrops was numbered among the imaginary prehistoric kings of Athens ; he was nothing more than the fabulous ancestor of the Cecropes. But the time came when other Greek dwellers in Attica won the upper hand over the Cecropes, and brought with them the worship of Athena. It was a momentous day in the history of the land when the goddess, whose cult was already established in many other Attic places, took possession of the hill which was to be pre-eminently, and for all time, associated with her name. The Acropolis became Athēnai ; the folks—whether Cecropes or Pelasgians—who dwelled in the villages around it, on the banks of the Ilīsus and Eridănus, became Athenians. The god whom the Cecropes worshipped on the hill, Poseidon Erechtheus, was forced to give way to the goddess. Legend told that Athena and Poseidon had disputed the possession of the Acropolis, and that each had set a token there, the goddess her sacred olive-tree, the god a salt-spring. The dethroned deity was not banished ; there was a conciliation, characteristic of the Greek temper, between the old and the new. Erechtheus in the shape of a snake is permitted still to live on the hill of Athena, and the oldest temple that was built for the goddess, harboured also the god. In later times Athenian

*Athens
derives its
name from
Athena.*

*Legendary
contest of
Poseidon
and
Athena.*

[1] This stream no longer exists, but its bed has been traced.

[2] Remains of prehistoric houses, and perhaps of the royal palace (see above, p. 25), have also been found on the north side of the Acropolis.

"history" transformed Erechtheus into a hero, and regarded him, *Athenians*
like Cecrops, as one of the early kings.   *called*

There was another god who was closely associated in Attic legend *Erech-*
with Athena, and Athens was distinguished by the high honour   *theidae.*
in which she held him.   This was Hephaestus, the divine smith,   *Athenian*
the master and helper of handicraftsmen, the cunning giver of   *worship of*
wealth.   But we cannot say how far back his worship in Attica   *Hephae-*
goes, or when his special feasts were instituted.   It is probable that *stus.*
                                                                  Feasts :
                                                                  Hephaestia
                                                                  and
                                                                  Chalkeia.

FIG. 61.—Athena and Poseidon on a vase painted by Amasis.

his honour grew along with the prosperity of the craftsmen.   An
Athenian poet calls his countrymen "sons of Hephaestus," and,
according to one myth, it was from his seed that all the earth-born
inhabitants of Attica were sprung.   At the feast of Apaturia, in
the last days of autumn, when children were admitted into the
Phratries by a solemn ceremony, the fathers used to light torches at
the hearth and sing a hymn to the lord of fire.

The next great step in Attic history was the union of the land. *The*
We cannot be certain at what time this union took place ; it recedes *Athenian*
beyond the beginnings of recorded history ; and we can only dimly *conquest of*
                                                                 Attica.

G

discern how it was brought about. When the lords of the Acropolis had subdued their own Cephisian plain, from Mount Parnes to the hill of Munychia, from the slopes of Hymettus to Aegaleos, they were tempted to extend their power eastward into the " Midlands " beyond Mount Hymettus, and subdue the southern " acté," or wedge of land which ends in the lofty cape of Sunium. The completion of this conquest was possibly the first great achievement of Athens, and the second was probably the subjugation of the north-eastern plain of Marathon and the " tetrapolis." Thus the first stage in the union of Attica is the reduction of the small independent sovereignties throughout all the land, except the Eleusinian plain in the west, under the loose overlordship of Athens.

The Synoecism of Attica.

(Feast of Synoikia.)

In the course of time the feeling of unity in Attica became so strong that all the smaller lordships, which formed parts of the large state, but still retained their separate political organisations, could be induced to surrender their home governments and merge themselves in a single community with a government centralised in the city of the Cephisian plain. The man of Thoricus or Aphidnae or Icaria now became a citizen of Athens and his political rights must be exercised there. The memory of this *synoecism* was preserved in historical times by an annual feast, and it was fitting that it should be so remembered, for it determined the whole history of Athens.

Historical importance of this constitutional change.

From this time forward she is no longer merely the supreme city of Attica. She is neither the head of a league of partly independent states, nor yet a despotic mistress of subject-communities. She is not what Thebes is to become in Boeotia, or what Sparta is in Laconia. If she had been, and she might well have been, either of these things, her history would have been gravely altered. She is the central city of an united state ; and to the people of every village in Attica belong the same political rights as to the people of Athens herself. The man of Marathon or the man of Thoricus is no longer an Attic, he is an Athenian. It is generally supposed that the synoecism was the work of one of the kings. It was undoubtedly the work of one man ; but it is possible that it belongs to the period immediately succeeding the abolition of the royal power.

Theseus.

In after-times the Athenians thought that the hero Theseus, whom they had enrolled in the list of their early kings,[1] was the author of the union of their country. But at the period when that union was brought about Theseus was not a national hero. He was a local god, worshipped in the Marathonian district and in the east

[1] Old Attic tradition (preserved by Herodotus) counted only four kings before Theseus, viz. Cecrops, Erechtheus, Pandion, and Aegeus. The four Cleisthenic tribes (see next chapter) which were named after Attic kings were named after these four. The augmentation of the list was due to Hellanicus.

ATTICA.

Stadia
0   20   40   60   80
English Miles   5   10

FIG. 62.

coastlands of Attica ; he had not yet won the importance which he was to possess hereafter in Athenian myth and history.

SECT. 2. FOUNDATION OF THE ATHENIAN COMMONWEALTH

The early history of the Athenian constitution resembles that of most other Greek states, in the general fact that a royalty, subjected

FIG. 63.—Codrus, going forth to his last battle, bids a friend farewell (Bologna cylix).

to various restrictions, passes into an aristocracy.   But the details of the transition are peculiar, and the beginning of the republic seems to have been exceptionally early.   The traditional names of the Attic kings who came after the hero Theseus are certainly in some cases, and, it may be, in most cases, fictitious, the most famous of them being the Neleid Codrus,[1] who was said to have sacrificed

---

[1] Codrus was regarded by the Ionian cities as the leader of the Ionian colonisation ; and therefore, as Athens claimed to be the mother city of the Ionian colonies, Codrus must needs be connected with Attica and made into an Athenian king.   He was made the son of Melanthus, the eponymous hero of Melaenae. Now many Ionian families connected their origin with Messenia and the Neleids

himself to save his country on the occasion of an attack of invaders
from the Peloponnesus. The Athenians said that they had abolished
royalty, on the death of Codrus, because he was too good to have a
successor—a curious reversal of the usual causes of such a revolution.
But this story is a late invention.[1]   The first limitation of the royal
power effected by the aristocracy was the institution of a *polemarch*
or military commander. The supreme command of the army, which
had belonged to the king, was transferred to him and he was elected
from and by the nobles. The next step seems to have been the *Fall of the*
overthrow of the royal house by the powerful family of the Medontids. *kings.*
The Medontids did not themselves assume the royal title, nor did
they abolish it. They instituted the office of *archon* or regent, and *Rule of the*
this office usurped the most important functions of the king. *regents for*
Acastus, the Medontid, was the first regent. We know that he was *life.*
an historical person ; the archons of later days always swore that *(Tradi-*
tional date
they would be true to their oath even as Acastus. He held the post *of Medon,*
for life, and his successors after him ; and thus the Medontids 1088 *B.C.*)
resembled kings, though they did not bear the kingly name. But
they fell short of royalty in another way too ; for each regent was
elected by the community ; the community was only bound to elect
a member of the Medontid family. The next step in weakening the *Ten-yearly*
power of this kingly magistrate was the change of the regency from *regents*
a life office to an office of ten years. This reform is said to have *(tradi-*
tional date
been effected about the middle of the eighth century. It is uncertain 753-2
at what time the Medontids were deprived of their prerogative and *B.C.*).
the regency was thrown open to all the nobles. With the next step
we reach firmer ground. The regency became a yearly office, and *Annual*
from this time onward an official list of the archons seems to have *regents,*
been preserved. 683-2 *B.C.*

But meanwhile there were still kings at Athens. The Medontids *Mainte-*
had robbed the kings of their royal power, but they had not done *nance of*
away with the kings ; there was to be a king at Athens till the latest *the title*
Basileus
days of the Athenian democracy. It seems probable that, as some
historical analogies might suggest, the Medontids allowed the shadow

---

of Pylos ; and it therefore became necessary to Athens, for the full establishment
of her maternal relation to Ionia, to bring Neleids from Pylos to Attica.
Consequently the hero Melanthus was explained to be a Neleid prince, a
descendant of Nestor (see above, pp. 82-3). It was said that the Athenian king
Thymoetes — the eponymous ancestor of the clan of the Thymoetadae — was
compelled on account of his cowardice to resign the royal power to the brave
stranger Melanthus.

[1] The popular story of Codrus visiting the camp of the Peloponnesians in
peasant's dress, and seeking a quarrel in order that the enemy might slay him—
an oracle having predicted that they would take Athens if they did not slay king
Codrus—is also late. According to the older tradition Codrus fell in battle.

of royalty to remain in the possession of the old royal house, so that for some time there would have been life-kings existing by the side of the life-regents ; it is not likely that from the very first the kingship was degraded to be a yearly office, filled by election. This, however, was what it ultimately became. The title remained when the power had long since vanished.

The whole course of the constitutional development is uncertain ; for it rests upon traditions, of which it is extremely hard to judge the value. But, whatever the details of the growth may have been, two important facts are to be grasped One is that the fall of royalty, which does not imply the abolition of the royal name, happened in Athens at an earlier period than in Greece generally. The other is that the Medontids were not kings, but archons—the chiefs of an aristocracy. The great work of the Medontids was the foundation of the Athenian commonwealth ; and perhaps one of their house is to be remembered for another achievement, not less great, which has been already described, the union of Attica.

Origin of the four Ionian tribes.

That union need not be older than the ninth century, and it is possible that the same republican movement which led to the downfall of the old royal house of the Acropolis, led to the synoecism of Attica, the concentration in Athens of political control and government. The organisation of the Athenian state was based on the four Ionian tribes, which are found also in east Greek states of Ionian origin, and go back far beyond the Dorian invasion. The curious names of these tribes—Geleontes, Argadeis, Aigicoreis, and Hoplētes—seem to have been derived from the worship of special deities ; for instance, Geleontes from Zeus Geleon. But the original meanings of the names had entirely passed away, and the tribes were affiliated to Apollo Patrōos, the paternal Apollo, from whom all Athenians claimed descent. The Brotherhoods seem to have been reorganised and arranged under the tribes—three to each tribe ; so that there were twelve brotherhoods in the Attic state. At the head of each tribe was a " tribe-king."

Twelve phratries. Phylo-basileus.

The γένη.

We can see the clan organisation at Athens better than elsewhere. The families of each clan derived themselves from a common ancestor,[1] and most of the clan names are patronymics. The worship of this ancestor was the chief end of the society. All the clans alike worshipped Zeus Herkeios and Apollo Patrōos ; many of them had a special connexion with other public cults. Each had a regular administration and officers, at the head of whom was an " archon." To these clans only members of the noble families belonged ; but the other classes, the peasants and the craftsmen,

[1] And were therefore called *Homogalaktes*, " milk-fellows," descended from common *mothers*.

formed similar organisations founded on the worship not of a common *The*
ancestor, for they could point to none, but some deity whom they *orgeōnes*
chose.   The members of these were called *orgeōnes*.   This innova- *or*
tion heralds the advance of the lower classes to political importance. *thiasōtai.*

The brotherhoods, composed of families whose lands adjoined, *Phratriae.*
united their members in the cult of Zeus Phratrios and Athena Phratria.
In early times only clansmen belonged to the brotherhoods, but
here again a change takes place in the seventh century, and orgeones
are admitted.   The organisation was then used for the purposes of
census.   Every child whose parents were citizens must be admitted
into a brotherhood ; and, if this rite is neglected, he is regarded
as illegitimate.   It should be observed that illegitimacy at Athens
did not deprive a man of political rights, but he could not lay claim
by right of birth to his father's inheritance.

At a much late. time the constitutional historians of Athens *Later mis-*
made out that the clans were artificial subdivisions of the brother- *apprehen-*
noods.   They said that each tribe was divided into three brother- *sion.*
hoods, each brotherhood into thirty clans, and it was even added that
each clan comprised thirty men.   This artificial scheme is true, so
far as the relation of the tribe to the brotherhood is concerned ; but
it is not true in regard to the clan, and is refuted by the circumstance
that the tribes consisted of others than clansmen.

Sect. 3. The Aristocracy in the Seventh Century

Early in the seventh century, then, the Athenian republic was an *The aris-*
aristocracy, and the executive was in the hands of three annually elected *tocracy.*
officers, the archon, the king, and the polemarch.   The archon was *The magis-*
the supreme judge in all civil suits.   When he entered on office, he *trates :*
published a declaration that he would, throughout the term of his *Archon ;*
archonship, preserve the property of every citizen intact.   At a later
time this sphere of judicial power was limited and he judged mainly
cases in which injured parents, orphans, heiresses were involved.
He held the chief place among the magistrates, having his official
residence in the Prytaneum where was the public hearth, and his
name appeared at the head of official lists, whence he was called
epōnymus ; though the archonship was a later institution than
that of polemarch, as is shown by the fact that no old religious
ceremonies were performed by the archon, such as devolved upon
the polemarch as well as upon the king.   But the conduct of
festivals instituted at later times was entrusted to him.   Such
was the Thargelia, the late-May feast of the first-fruits, the chief
Athenian feast of Apollo, introduced from Delos probably in the
seventh century ; such was the great Dionysia, which, as we shall

Polemarch; see, were founded in the sixth.   The polemarch had judicial duties, besides being commander-in-chief of the army.   He held a court in the Epilykeion on the banks of the Ilisus, and judged there all cases in which non-citizens were involved.   Thus what the archon was for citizens, the polemarch was for the class of foreign settlers who *Basileus.* were called "metics."   The king had his residence in the royal Stoa in the Agora.   His functions were confined to the management of the state-religion, and the conduct of certain judicial cases connected with religion.   He was president of the Council, and thus had considerable power and responsibility in the conduct of the judicial functions of that body.

The Council, called of the Areopagus.   The Bulê or Council was the political organisation through which the nobles carried out, at Athens as elsewhere, the gradual abolition of monarchy.   This Council of Elders — a part as we saw of the Aryan inheritance of the Greeks—came afterwards to be called at Athens the Council of the Areopagus, to distinguish it from other councils of later growth.   This name was derived from one of the Council's most important functions.   According to early custom, which we find reflected in Homer, murder and manslaughter were not regarded as crimes against the state, but concerned exclusively the family of the slain man, which might either slay the slayer or accept a compensation.   But gradually, as the worship of the souls of the dead and the deities of the underworld developed, the belief gained ground that he who shed blood was impure and needed cleansing. Accordingly when a murderer satisfied the kinsfolk of the murdered by paying a fine, he had also to submit to a process of purification, and satisfy the Chthonian gods and the Erinyes or Furies, who were, in the original conception, the souls of the dead clamouring for vengeance.   This notion of manslaughter as a religious offence necessarily led to the interference of the state.   For when the member of a community was impure, the stain drew down the anger of the gods upon the whole community, if the unclean were not driven out.   Hence it came about that the state undertook the conduct of criminal justice.   The Council itself formed the court, and the proceedings were closely associated with the worship of the *Semnai.* These Chthonian goddesses had a sanctuary, which served as a refuge for him whose hand was stained with bloodshed, on the northeast side of the Areopagus, outside the city wall.   It is possible that the association of this hill with the god Ares is merely due to a popular etymology, for he had no shrine here ; but the correct explanation of the name *Areiospagos* is not known.[1]   On this

[1] One suggestion is that the name is derived from Athena Areia, who had an altar on the hill, another that it means the hill of the *Arai,* "curses," a name of the Semnai in Aeschylus.

rugged spot, apart from but within sight of the dwellings of men, the Council held its sittings for cases of murder, violence with murderous intent, poisoning, and incendiarism. The accuser stood on the stone of Insolence, the accused on the stone of Reckless- *(ὕβρις.)* ness, each a huge unhewn block. This function of the Council, *(ἀναίδεια.)* which continued to belong to it after it had lost its other powers, procured it the name of the Areopagus.

During the period of the aristocracy, the Council was the governing body of Athens. We may be certain that the magistrates were always members ; but otherwise we do not know how it was composed, and therefore can form no clear idea how the constitution worked. The Council doubtless exercised direct control over the election of the chief magistrates ; but we need have small doubt that the king, the archon, and the polemarch were either elected by the Ecclesia consisting of the whole body of citizens entitled to vote, or at all events were chosen by the Council out of a limited number nominated by the Assembly.

As an achievement of the aristocracy we may regard the annexa- *Conquest of* tion of Eleusis. The Eleusinian kingdom bound in by Athens *Eleusis.* on one side and Megara on the other—its little bay locked by Megarian Salamis—did not play any part in any portion of Greek history of which we have the faintest record. But of its independent existence we have a clear echo in a hymn which tells the Eleusinian story of Demeter. That goddess, wandering in quest of her lost *The* daughter Persephone, came to Eleusis, where she was hospitably *coming of* entertained by the king, and would have made his infant son *Demeter.* immortal but for the queen's want of faith. This poem is thought to have been composed in the seventh century, and, if so, the days when Eleusis was independent had not yet passed out of men's memories then.

The middle of the seventh century is marked by a further constitutional change, which is the result of various social changes. The aristocracy of birth is forced to widen into an aristocracy of wealth. The general causes of this change are to be found in the new economical conditions which have been already pointed out as affecting the whole Greek world in the seventh century. But to understand their operation and political consequences at Athens, we must look more closely into the classes of the Attic population and the social structure.

Under the rule of the kings and the aristocracies, the free *Three* population fell into three classes : the *Eupatridae* or nobles ; [1] the *classes :* *Georgi* or peasants who cultivated their own farms ; and the *1. Eupa-* *tridai,*

[1] The generic name must be distinguished from the particular family of the *2. Georgoi,* Eupatridae.

3. Demi-urgoi.

Demiurgi (public workers), those who lived by trade or commerce. The Eupatrids originally lived in the country, and many Attic places were called from their families, such as Paeonidae or Butadae. After the synoecism, many of them came to live in the city. The Demiurgi had their settlements in the neighbourhood of the city—for example,

Kerameis.

there was the quarter of the "potters" north of the Areopagus—and also villages in the country, such as *Pelekes* or *Daedalidae*. But

Freemen without civic rights.

besides these classes of citizens, who had the right of attending the Assembly, there was a mass of freemen who were not citizens. Among these we can distinguish the agricultural labourers, who, having no land of their own, cultivated the estates of the nobles. In return for their labour they retained one-sixth of the produce

Hekte-moroi *or* Pelatai.

and were hence called "Sixth-parters" (Hektemoroi). [1] There were also the craftsmen who were employed and paid by the Demiurgi, and doubtless small retail dealers and others.

Although Attica seems to have taken no part in the colonising movements of the eighth and seventh centuries, the Athenians shared in the trading activities of the period and were profoundly affected by the economical revolution in the Greek world. The cultivation of the olive was becoming a feature of Attica, and its oil

Pottery.

a profitable article of exportation. At the same time Attic potters were actively developing their industry on lines of their own, and Attic pottery was in the course of another century to become disseminated throughout the Mediterranean countries from Tuscany to

The Dipylon vases (9th and 8th centuries).

Cyprus. Jars of this age have been found in tombs near the Dipylon gate on the north-west side of Athens, and these Dipylon vases, as they are called, give us a glimpse of the Attic civilisation of the period. We not only see a new style of vase-painting, with geometrical ornament and a symmetrical arrangement of the space at the painter's disposal; but in the pictures of funeral processions we can observe with what pomp and cost the Attic nobles buried their dead. In the graves where these vases were found, offerings were laid beside the dead, pottery and sometimes gold ornaments; and the sepulchral pit was surmounted not by a mound but by a tall clay jar with an opening below through which drink offerings could be

c. 650 *B.C.* (?).

poured. Though eastern influences had already introduced the custom of burning the dead, burial was continued. Ionia also influenced Athenian dress. The woollen peplos fastened with a pin was given up and the Ionian sleeved tunic or chiton, of linen, took its place.

It would be interesting if we might see in the rude representations of ships on some of the Dipylon vases an illustration of the beginnings of Attic seamanship. The sea traffic of Athens must

[1 For a different explanation of Hektemoroi, see notes.]

have been rapidly growing in the first half of the seventh century. It is easy to see how the active participation of Athens in trade began to undermine the foundations of the aristocracy of birth, by introducing a new standard of social distinction. The nobles engaged in mercantile ventures with various success, some becoming richer, and others poorer; and the industrial folk increased in wealth and importance. The result would ultimately be that wealth would assert itself as well as birth, both socially and politically; and in the second half of the seventh century we find that, though the aristocracy has not been fully replaced by a *timocracy*, or constitution, in which political rights depend entirely on wealth, all

FIG. 64.—Dipylon Vase, with ship (British Museum).

the conditions are present for such a transformation. For we find the people divided into three classes according to their wealth. The principle of division was the annual yield of landed property, in corn, oil, or wine. The highest class was the *Pentacosiomedimni*. Before this name had any official meaning it was perhaps in popular use to designate those large proprietors whose income reached five hundred medimni of corn, at a time when oil and wine had not been much cultivated. When it acquired an official sense, it was defined to include those whose land produced at least so many measures (medimni) of corn and so many measures (metrētae) of oil or wine as *together* amounted to five hundred measures. The second class included those whose property produced more than three hundred but less than five hundred such measures. These were called

Three classes:

1. Pentacosiomedimni.

2. Hippês.

Knights, and so represented roughly those who could maintain a horse and take their part in war as mounted soldiers. The minimum income of the third class was two hundred measures, and their name, *Teamsters*, shows that they were well-to-do peasants who could till their land with a pair of oxen. The chief magistracies of archon, king, and polemarch were confined to the first class, but the principle was admitted that a successful man, although not a Eupatrid, was eligible for the highest offices if his income amounted to 500 medimni. It was natural that the rating should be expressed in terms of wealth derived from land ; but it is not a necessary inference that the handi-craftsmen were entirely excluded, or that in order to win political rights they were forced to purchase estates.

3. Zeu-gitae.

At first this concession of the Eupatrids to their fellow-citizens did not practically amount to much. Most of the richest men in the state still belonged to the old clans ; but the recognition of wealth as a political test could not fail to undermine ultimately the privileges of birth. The organisation of the lower classes into bodies resembling the Clans of the nobles, and their admission into the Brotherhoods, have been mentioned. It is probable that the institution of the *Thesmothetae* also marks a step in the self-assertion of these classes. The Thesmothetae were a college of six judges, who managed the whole judicial system of Athens. It was their duty to examine, and call attention to defects in, the laws, and to keep a record of judicial decisions ; and they seem to have taken cognisance of all cases which belonged to the scope of the Council of Areopagus, except trials for murder. In fact, it looks as if they were practically a committee of that Council. They were elected annually, and it has been plausibly supposed that the number of six was determined by the fact that they originated in a compromise between the orders, three being Eupatrids, two Georgi, and one a Demiurgos. They were soon associated with the three chief magistrates, the archon, basileus, and polemarch ; and the nine came to form a sort of college and were called the Nine Archons. Each of the Nine when he entered on his office took an oath that he would act in accordance with the laws, and vowed that if he committed any injustice he would dedicate in gold a man's statue of life-size. It was a penalty which no archon could have discharged.

Six Thes-mothetae (? 650-630 B.C.).

" Nine archons."

Outside these classes were the smaller peasants who had land of their own, of which, however, the produce did not amount to two hundred measures of corn or oil, and the humbler handicraftsmen. These were called *Thêtes*, the name being perverted from its proper meaning of "labourers." The Thêtes were citizens, but had no political rights. Yet they were beginning to win a certain public importance. The conditions of a growing maritime trade led to

Thêtes.

the development of a navy.　As the sea power grew, a new organisation was found necessary, and there can be little doubt that the duty of serving as marines in the penteconters mainly devolved upon the Thêtes.　This gave them a new significance in the state, a significance which would strengthen their claim to political rights when the time for pressing that claim should come.　We shall see hereafter how closely connected was the democracy of Athens with her sea power ; and we can hardly be wrong in surmising the faint foreshadowings of that connexion at the very beginning of her naval history.　Each of the four tribes was divided, for this purpose, *Nau-* into twelve districts called *Naucrariae ;* each naucraria was probably *crariae.* bound to supply a ship.　Thus the fleet consisted of forty-eight ships. *Council of* The administration was directed by a body of naucrari, at the head *naucrari :* of which were presidents; and the organisation might be found con- *prytanies.* venient for other than naval purposes.　Thus the naucrari formed *(4 ?)* an important administrative council.

We see then that, in the middle of the seventh century, society *Recapitu-* in Attica is undergoing the change which is transforming the face of *lation.* all the progressive parts of Hellas ; wealth is competing with descent as a political test ; and the aristocracy of birth seems to be passing into a timocracy.　The power is in the hands of the three chief archons, who always belong to the class of wealthy nobles, and the Council of Areopagus, which is certainly composed of Eupatridae. But the classes outside the noble Clans, the smaller proprietors and the merchants, are beginning to assert themselves and make their weight felt ; possibly the institution of the thesmothetae is due to their pressure.　They also obtain admission into the Brotherhoods, which had been hitherto exclusive.　Attic trade is rapidly growing. The commercial development promotes these democratic tendencies, and has also led to the creation of a fleet, which, since the poorest class of citizens are required to man it, renders that class important and prepares the way for its political recognition.

As yet, however, the naval establishment of Athens was but *The* small compared with her neighbours Chalcis and Corinth, or her *worship of* daughter cities of Ionia.　And Aegina, which had come for a while *Poseidon at* under the influence of Argos, outstripped her.　It is interesting to *Calauria.* find these two cities, Athens and Aegina, which were in later times to be bitter rivals for the supremacy in their gulf, in the seventh century taking part in an association for maintaining the worship of Poseidon in the little island of Calauria, over against Troezen. Other coast towns of the Saronic and Argolic bays—Epidaurus, Troezen, Hermione, Nauplia, Prasiae—belonged to this sacred union ; and the Boeotian Orchomenus, by virtue of the authority which she still possessed over the sailors of Anthedon, was also a member.

There was no political significance in the joint Calaurian worship of

Temple at Calauria (? end of 7th cent.). these maritime towns ; their seamen propitiated Poseidon at Calauria, just as they sacrificed to Panhellenic Zeus on the far-seen Mountain of Aegina. And they were not grudging votaries. They built a house for the sea-god in his island ; its foundations have been recently uncovered, and it is one of the earliest stone temples whose ruins have been found in Greece.

Money. Attica, like the rest of the Greek world, was disturbed in her economic development by the invention of money. She had naturally been brought into close commercial relations with her neighbour Aegina, which at this time began to take a leading part in maritime enterprise. Accordingly we find Athens adopting the Aeginetan coinage, and using a system of weights and measures which was almost, if not quite, identical with the Aeginetan. The introduction of money, which was at first very scarce, and led to the accumulation of capital in the chests of successful speculators, was followed by a period of transition between the old system of the direct exchange of commodities and the new system of a metallic medium ; and this transitional period was trying to all men of small means. But the inevitable economic crisis did not come at once, though all conditions of social distress were present, and a conflict between the rich and

Conspiracy of Cylon. c. 632 B.C. the poor was drawing steadily near. An event happened about thirty years before the end of the century which shows that the peasants were still loyal to the existing constitution.

The example of tyranny was infectious, and, as it flourished at the very door of Athens—in Megara and Corinth,—it was unlikely that some attempt should not be made at Athens too. A certain Cylon, of noble family, married the daughter of Theagenes, tyrant of Megara ; and, under Megarian influence and with Megarian help, he tried to make himself master of the city. Consulting the Delphic oracle, he was advised to seize the Acropolis on the greatest festival of Zeus. Cylon, an Olympic victor himself, had no doubt that the feast of Olympia was meant ; but when his plot failed, it was explained that the oracle referred to the Athenian feast of the Diasia in March, which was celebrated outside the city. Cylon enlisted in his enterprise a number of noble youths, and a band of Megarian soldiers were sent by Theagenes ; he had no support among the people. He succeeded in seizing the Acropolis, but the sight of foreign soldiers effectually quenched any lurking sympathy that any of the Athenians might have felt for an effort to overthrow the government. The Council of the naucraries summoned the husbandmen from the country, and the summons was readily obeyed. Cylon was blockaded in the citadel, and, after a long siege, when food and water began to fail, he escaped with his brother from the fortress. The rest were soon constrained to capitulate. They sought refuge in the temple of Athena Polias, and left it when the archons promised to spare their lives. But Megacles, of the Alcmaeonid family, was archon this year; and at his instigation the pledge was disregarded, and the conspirators were put to death. Some feud among the clans may have been at work here. The city was saved from a tyrant, but it had incurred a grave pollution. Such a violation of a solemn pledge to the suppliants who had trusted in the protection of the gods was an insult to the gods themselves; and the city was under a curse till the pollution should be removed. This view was urged by the secret friends of Cylon and those who hated the Alcmaeonids. And so it came to pass that while Cylon, his brother, and their descendants were condemned to disfranchisement and perpetual banishment, the Alcmaeonids and those who had acted with them were also tried on *Banish-* the charge of sacrilege and condemned to a perpetual exile, with con- *ment of the* fiscation of their property. And the bodies of those of the clan *Alcmae-* who had died between the deed of sacrilege and the passing of this *onids.* sentence were exhumed and cast beyond the boundary of Attica. The banishment of the Alcmaeonids had consequences in the distant future, and we shall see how it comes into the practical politics of Athens two hundred years later. The tale is also told that the city required a further purification, and that a priest named Epimenides *Epi-* came from Crete and cleansed it. But it has been thought doubtful *menides.* whether Epimenides is more than a mythical name like Orpheus, since another story brings him to Athens again, for similar purposes of atonement, more than a century afterwards; and then both tales are conciliated by ascribing to the seer a miraculous sleep of a hundred years.

In the course of the next ten years, the state of the peasants seems to have changed considerably for the worse. The outbreak of a war with Megara, in consequence of the plot of Cylon, aggravated the distress of the rural population; for the Attic coasts suffered from the depredations of the enemy, and the Megarian market was closed to the oil-trade. Whether the peasants, who groaned under the existing system, found leaders and extorted concessions from the government, or whether the ruling classes themselves saw the danger, and tried to prevent it by a timely concession, it was at all events decided that a code of law should be drawn up *Dracon's* and written down. Probably men had been clamouring long to *Code,* obtain this security for life and property; and what the thesmothetae *621 B.C.* may have already done by recording judicial decisions in writing was not enough. Dracon was appointed an extraordinary legislator (Thesmothetes), and empowered to codify and rectify the existing law. We know only the provisions of that part of his criminal law which dealt with the shedding of blood ; for these provisions were not altered by subsequent legislation. In later times it was thought that Dracon revealed to the Athenians how harsh their laws were, and his name became proverbial for a severe lawgiver. An Athenian *(Demādes.)* orator won credit for his epigram that Dracon's laws were written not in ink but in blood. This idea arose from the fact that certain small offences, such as stealing cabbage, were punished by death. A broader view, however, of Dracon's code will modify this view. He drew careful distinctions between murder and various kinds of accidental or justifiable manslaughter. In Dracon's laws we *The* meet a body of fifty-one judges, called the *Ephetae.* They were *Ephetae.* chosen from the Eupatrids, but it is not clear whether they formed a part of the Council of the Areopagus or were a wholly distinct body. Those cases of bloodshed which did not come before the court of the Areopagus were tried by the Ephetae, in case the shedder of blood was known. According to the nature of the deed the Ephetae held their court in different places : in the temple of the Delphinian Apollo, in the Palladion at Phaleron, or at Phreatto, a tongue of land on the Munychian peninsula. This last court was used in the case of those who were tried for manslaughter committed abroad, and as they might not set foot on the soil of their country, they had to answer the charge standing in a boat drawn up near the shore. When the shedder of blood was not known, the case came before the King in the Prytaneum.

It is unfortunate that we are not informed of Dracon's other legislation. We know that the laws relating to debtors were stringent ; the creditor could claim the person of the insolvent debtor. In general, he was bound to provide for the interests of the rich power-holding class ; but it was at all events an enormous gain for the poor that those interests should be defined in writing.

SECT. 4. THE LEGISLATION OF SOLON AND THE FOUNDATION OF DEMOCRACY

Dracon's code was something, but it did not touch the root of the evil. Every year the oppressiveness of the rich few and the impoverishment of the small farmer were increasing. Without capital, and obliged to borrow money, the small proprietors mortgaged their lands, which fell into the hands of capitalists, who lent money at ruinous interest. It must be remembered that money was still very scarce,[1] and that the peasants had now to purchase all their needs

[1] The value of silver at this time may be judged from the fact that a sheep cost a drachma, a bushel of barley a drachma, an ox five drachmae.

in coin. Even in Attica the small peasant could not cope with the larger proprietor. Thus the little farms of Attica were covered with stones, on which the mortgage bonds were written ; the large estates grew apace ; the black earth, as Solon said, was enslaved.

The condition of the free labourers was even more deplorable. *The Hek-*
The sixth part of the produce, which was their wage, no longer *temoroi,*
sufficed, under the new economical conditions, to support life, and they were forced into borrowing from their masters. The interest was high, the laws of debt were ruthless, and the person of the borrower was the pledge of repayment and forfeited to the lender in *reduced to* case of inability to pay. The result was that the class of free *slavery.* labourers was being gradually transformed into a class of slaves, whom their lords could sell when they chose.

Thus while the wealthy few were becoming wealthier and greedier, the small proprietors were becoming landless, and the landless freemen were becoming slaves. And the evil was aggravated by unjust judgments, and the perversion of law in favour of the rich and powerful. The social disease seemed likely to culminate in a political revolution. The people were bitter against their remorseless oppressors, and only wanted a leader to rebel. To any student of contemporary politics, observing the development in other states, a tyranny would have seemed the most probable solution. A tyranny had already, once at least, and probably more than once, been averted ; and now, as it happened, the masses obtained a mediator, not a demagogue, a reform, not a revolution. The tyranny, though it was ultimately to come, was postponed for more than thirty years. The mediator in the civil strife was Solon, the son of Execestides, a *Solon.* noble connected with the house of the Medontids. He was a merchant, and belonged to the wealthiest class in the state. But he was very different from the Attic Eupatrids, rustic squires, of old fashions and narrow vision. We may guess that he had not been a home-keeping youth, but had visited the eastern coasts of the Aegean, whither mercantile concerns might have taken him. At all events, he had learned much from progressive Ionia. He had imbued *His Ionic* himself with Ionic literature, and had mastered the art of writing *culture.* verse in the Ionic idiom ; so that he could himself take part in the intellectual movement of the day and become one of the sages of Greece. He was a poet, not because he was poetically inspired, like the Parian Archilochus of an earlier, or the Lesbian Sappho of his own, generation ; but because at that time every man of letters was a poet ; there was no prose literature. A hundred years later Solon would have used prose as the vehicle of his thoughts. His mode-rate temper made him generally popular ; his knowledge gave him authority ; and his countrymen called upon him, at last, to set their house in order. We are fortunate enough to possess portions of poems—political pamphlets—which he published for the purpose of guiding public opinion ; and thus we have his view of the situation in his own words. He did not scruple to speak plainly. The social abuses and the sad state of the masses were clear to everybody, but Solon saw another side of the question ; and he had no sympathy with the extreme revolutionary agitators who demanded a redistribution of lands. The more moderate of the nobles seem to have seen the danger and the urgent need of a new order of things ; and thus *Solon's archonship,* it came to pass that Solon was solicited to undertake the work of reform. He definitely undertook the task and was elected archon,[1] *594-3 or 592-1 B.C.* with extraordinary legislative powers, for the purpose of healing the evils of the state, and conciliating the classes.

Solon's inaugura- tory act: the Sei- sachtheia. Instead of making the usual declaration of the chief magistrate, that he would protect the property of all men undiminished, he made proclamation that all mortgages and debts by which the debtor's person was pledged were annulled, and that all those who had become slaves for debt were free. By this proclamation in that summer, memorable for the rescue of hundreds of poor wretches into liberty and hope, the Athenians "shook off their burdens," and this first act of Solon's social reform was called the *Seïsachtheia.* The great deliverance was celebrated by a public feast.

The character of the remedial measures of Solon is imperfectly known. After the cancelling of old debts he passed a law which forbade debtors to be enslaved. He fixed a limit for the measure of land which could be owned by a single person, so as to prevent the growth of dangerously large estates. And he forbade the exportation of Attic products of the earth, except oil. For it had been found that so much corn was carried to foreign markets, where the prices were higher, that an insufficient supply remained for the population of Attica. It is to be observed that at this time the Athenians had not yet begun to import Pontic corn.

All these measures hit the rich hard, and created discontent with the reformer ; while, on the other hand, he was far from satisfying the desires and hopes of the masses. He would not confiscate and redistribute the estates of the wealthy, as many wished. And, *The Hektemors.* though he rescued the free labourer from bondage, he made no change in the Sixth-part system, so that the condition of these landless freemen was improved only in so far as they could not be enslaved,

---

[1] The year of Solon's archonship is either 594-3 or 592-1 B.C. : there is evidence for both, perhaps the earlier is the more probable. In any case it seems certain that Solon's legislative activity extended over more than a single year, and likely that he was commissioned as an extraordinary lawgiver (nomo- thetês) to revise the constitution.

and in so far as the law limiting exportation affected prices. And Solon was too discreet to attempt to interfere seriously with the conditions of the money market by artificial restrictions. He fixed no maximum rate of interest, and his monetary reforms must be kept strictly apart from his social reforms. Hitherto the Athenians did not coin money of their own. They used the Aeginetan currency. Solon inaugurated a native coinage, but he adopted the Euboic, not the Aeginetan, standard. Thus 100 of the new Attic drachmae were equivalent in value to about 70 Aeginetan drachmae. The Attic coinage introduced by Solon is to be brought into connexion, not with the domestic reform, but with the foreign policy of Athens, to which new prospects were opening. The old coinage attached her to Aegina, with which her relations were strained, and to her foe Megara ; the new system seemed to invite her into the distant fields beyond the sea, where Chalcis and Corinth had led the way in opening up a new world. A generation later, a new monetary reform introduced a distinct Attic standard, slightly higher than the Euboic. [Other measures also show that Solon, himself a merchant, looked to the development of trade to improve the general economy of Athens. Citizenship was granted to foreign craftsmen who settled with their families in Attica, and fathers had to teach their sons a trade if they were to demand support in their old age.] *Attic coinage begins; Euboic standard.*

Attic standard introduced by Pisistratus.

What Solon did to heal the social sores of his country entitled him to the most fervent gratitude, but it was no more than might have been done by any able and honest statesman who possessed men's confidence. His title to fame as one of the great statesmen of Europe rests upon his reform of the constitution. He discovered a secret of democracy, and he used his discovery to build up the constitution on democratic foundations. The Athenian commonwealth did not actually become a democracy till many years later ; but Solon not only laid the foundations, he shaped the framework. At first sight, indeed, the state as he reformed it might seem little more than an aristocracy of wealth—a timocracy—with certain democratic tendencies. He retained the old graduation of the people in classes according to property. But he added the Thêtes as a fourth class, and gave it certain political rights. On the three higher classes devolved the public burdens, and they served as cavalry or as hoplites. The Thetes were employed as light-armed troops or as marines. It is probable that Solon made little or no change in regard to the offices which were open to each class. Pentacosiomedimni were alone eligible to the archonship, and for them alone was reserved the financial office of Treasurer of Athena. Other offices [1] were open to the Hippês and the Zeugitae, but the distinction *Solon's reform of the Constitution.*

The four classes.

[1] The offices of the Pôlêtai (who farmed out public contracts, *e.g.* mines), the Eleven (heads of the executive of justice), the Kôlakretai (financial officers).

Ecclesia opened to the Thetes.

in privilege between them is unknown. The Thetes were not eligible to any of the offices of state, but they were admitted to take part in the meetings of the Ecclesia, and this gave them a voice in the election of the magistrates.

The popular courts.

The opening of the Assembly to the lowest class was indeed an important step in the democratic direction ; but it may have been only the end of a gradual process of widening, which had been going on under the aristocracy. The radical measure of Solon, which was the very corner-stone of the Athenian democracy, was his constitution of the courts of justice. He constituted a court out of all the citizens, including the Thetes ; and as the panels of judges were enrolled by lot, the poorest burgher might have his turn. Any magistrate on laying down his office could be accused before the people in these courts ; and thus the institution of popular courts invested the people with a supreme control over the administration. The people, sitting in sections as sworn judges, were called the *Heliaea*,—as distinguished from the Ecclesia, in which they gathered to pass laws or choose magistrates, but were required to take no oath. Having in its hands both the appointment of the magistrates and the control of their conduct, the people possessed theoretically the sovereignty of the state ; and the meting out of more privileges to the less wealthy classes could be merely a matter of time. At first the archons were not deprived of their judicial powers, and the heliaea acted as a court of appeal ; but by degrees the competence of the archons was reduced to the conduct of the proceedings preliminary to a trial, and the heliaea became both the first and the final court.

The constitution of the judicial courts out of the whole people was the secret of democracy which Solon discovered. It is his title to fame in the history of the growth of popular government in Europe. Without ignoring the tendencies to a democratic development which existed before him, and without, on the other hand, disguising the privileges which he reserved to the upper classes, we can hardly hesitate to regard Solon as the founder of the Athenian democracy. It must indeed be confessed that there is much in the scope and intention of his constitution which is difficult to appreciate, because we know so little of the older constitution which he reformed. Thus we have no definite record touching the composition of the Council of the Areopagus, touching its functions as a deliberative body and its relations to the Assembly, or touching the composition of the Assembly itself. We can, however, have little doubt that under the older commonwealth the Council of Elders exerted a preponderant influence over the Assembly, and that the business submitted to the Assembly, whether by the magistrates or in whatever way introduced, was previously discussed and settled by the *Solon's* Council. The founder of popular government could not leave this *treatment* hinge of the aristocratic republic as it was. He must either totally *of the* change the character of the Council and transform it into a popular *Areopagus.* body, or he must deprive it of its deliberative functions in regard to the Assembly. Solon deprived the Council of Elders of these deliberative functions, so that it could no longer take any direct part in administration and legislation. But on the other hand he assigned to it a new and lofty rôle. He constituted it the protector of the constitution, and the guardian of the laws, giving it wide and undefined powers of control over the magistrates, and a censorial authority over the citizens. Its judicial and religious functions it retained. In order to bring it into harmony with the rest of his constitution, Solon seems to have altered the composition of the Council. Henceforward, at least, the nine archons at the end of their year of office became life-members of the Council of the Areopagus ; and this was the manner in which the Council was recruited. Thus the Areopagites were virtually appointed by the people in the Assembly.

Having removed the Council of the Areopagus to this place of *The new* dignity, above and almost outside the constitution, Solon was obliged *Council of* to create a new body to prepare the business for the Assembly. *Four* Such a body was indispensable, as the Greeks always recognised ; and *Hundred.* it is clear that in its absence enormous powers would have been placed in the hands of the magistrates, on whom the manipulation of the Assembly would have entirely devolved. The "probuleutic" Council which Solon instituted consisted of four hundred members ; a hundred being taken from each of the four tribes, either chosen by the tribe itself or, more probably, picked by lot. All citizens of the three higher classes were eligible ; the Thetes alone were excluded. In later days this Council—or rather a new Council which took its place—gained a large number of important powers, which made it to all intents an independent body in the state, but at first its functions seem to have been purely "probuleutic," and it has therefore rather the aspect of being merely a part of the organisation of the Assembly. It must always be remembered that it does not represent the Council of Elders of the Aryan foreworld ; it does not correspond to the Gerusia of Sparta or the Senate of Rome. But it takes over certain functions which had before formed part of the duty of the Council of elders ; it discusses beforehand the public matters which are to be submitted to the Assembly.

The use of lot for the purpose of appointing public officers was a *Lot.* feature of Solon's reforms. According to men's ideas in those days, lot committed the decision to the gods, and was thus a serious method of procedure—not a sign of political levity, as we should regard it now. But a device which superstition suggested was approved by the reflexions of philosophical statesmen ; and lot was recognised as a valuable political engine for security against undue influence and for the protection of minorities. It was doubtless as a security against the undue influence of clans and parties that Solon *Mixed* used it. He applied it to the appointment of the chief magistrates *method of* themselves. But, religious though he was, he could not be blind to *election* the danger of taking no human precautions against the falling of the *and lot.* lot upon an incompetent candidate. He therefore mixed the two devices of lot and election. Forty candidates were elected, ten from each tribe, by the voice of their tribesmen ; and out of these the nine archons were picked by lot. It is probable that a similar mixed method was employed in the choice of the Four Hundred Councillors.

Danger in Solon sought to keep the political balance steady by securing that *the tribes* each of the four tribes should have an equal share in the government. *and clans* He could hardly have done otherwise, and yet here we touch on the weak point in the fabric of his constitution. The gravest danger ahead was in truth not the strife of poor and rich, of noble lord and man of the people, but the deep-rooted and bitter jealousies which existed between many of the clans. While the clan had the tribe behind it and the tribe possessed political weight, such feuds might at any moment cause a civil war or a revolution. But it was reserved for a future lawgiver to grapple with this problem. Solon assuredly saw it, but he had no solution ready to hand ; and the evil was closely connected with another evil, the local parties which divided Attica. For these dangers Solon offered no remedy, and therefore his work, though abiding in the highest sense, did not supply a final or even a brief pacification of the warring elements in the state. He is said to have passed a law—so clumsy, so difficult to render effective, that it is hard to believe that such an enactment was ever made—that in the case of a party struggle every burgher must take a side under pain of losing his civic rights. Solon, if he was indeed the author of such a measure, sought to avert the possible issues of political strife by forcing the best citizens to intervene ; it was a safeguard, a clumsy safeguard, against the danger of a tyranny.

It is interesting to observe that in some directions Solon extended and in others restricted the freedom of the individual. He restricted it by sumptuary laws and severe penalties for idleness ; he extended it by an enactment allowing a man who had no heirs of his body to will his property as he liked, instead of its going to the next of kin.[1]

---

[1] This measure, we may probably assume, simply legalised an usage which had been introduced in practice long before.

One of Solon's first acts was to repeal all the legislation of Dracon, except the laws relating to manslaughter.   His own laws were inscribed on wooden tables set in revolving frames called *axŏnes*, *Preserva-* which were numbered, and the laws were quoted by the number of *tion of* the axon.   These tablets were kept in the Public hall.   But copies *Solonian* were made on stone pillars, called in the old Attic tongue *kyrbeis*, *laws.* and kept in the Portico of the King.   Every citizen was required to take an oath that he would obey these laws ; and it was ordered that the laws were to remain in force for a hundred years.

Solon had done his work boldly, but he had done it constitu- *Solon's* tionally.   He had not made himself a tyrant, as he might easily *modera-* have done, and as many expected him to do.   On the contrary, one *tion.* purpose of his reform was to forestall the necessity, and prevent the possibility, of a tyranny.   He had not even become an aesymnetes— a legislator (like Pittacus) who for a number of years supersedes the constitution in order to reform it, and rules for that time with the absolute power of a tyrant.   He had simply held the office of archon, invested, indeed, with extraordinary powers.   To a super- ficial observer caution seemed the note of his reforms, and men were surprised, and many disgusted, by his cautiousness.   His caution *His* consisted in reserving the highest offices for men of property, and *caution.* the truth probably is that in his time no others would have been fitted to perform the duties.   But Solon has stated his own principle that the privileges of each class should be proportional to the public burdens which it can bear.   This was the conservative feature of his legislation ; and, seizing on it, democrats could make out a plausible case for regarding his constitution as simply a timocracy.   When he laid down his office he was assailed by complaints, and he wrote elegies in which he explains his middle course and professes that he performed the things which he undertook without favour or fear. " I threw my stout shield," he says, " over both parties."   He re- fused to entertain the idea of any modifications in his measures, and thinking that the reforms would work better in the absence of the reformer, he left Athens soon after his archonship and travelled for ten years, partly for mercantile ends, but perhaps chiefly from curiosity, to see strange places and strange men.

Though the remnants of his poems are fragmentary, though the *Character* recorded events of his life are meagre, and though the details of his *of Solon.* legislation are dimly known and variously interpreted, the personality of Solon leaves a distinct impression on our minds.   We know enough to see in him an embodiment of the ideal of intellectual and moral excellence of the early Greeks, and the greatest of their wise men.   For him the first of the virtues was moderation, and his motto was " Avoid excess."   He was in no vulgar sense a man of the world, for he was many-sided—poet and legislator, traveller and trader, noble and friend of the people. He had the insight to discern some of the yet undeveloped tendencies of the age, and could sympathise with other than the power-holding classes. He had meditated too deeply on the circumstances of humanity to find power a temptation ; he never forgot that he was a traveller between life and death. It was a promising and characteristic act for a Greek state to commit the task of its reformation to such a man, and empower him to translate into definite legislative measures the views which he expressed in his poems.

The sequel.   Solon's social reforms inaugurated a permanent improvement. But his political measures, which he intended as a compromise, displeased many. Party strife broke out again bitterly soon after his archonship, and only to end, after thirty years, in the tyranny which it had been his dearest object to prevent. Of this strife we know little. It took the form of a struggle for the archonship, and two years are noted in which, in consequence of this struggle, no *Years of* archons were elected, hence called years of *anarchy*. Then a certain *anarchia,* archon, Damasias, attempted to convert his office into a permanent *589-8 (?)* tyranny and actually held it for over two years. This attempt *and 584-3* *(?) B.C.* frightened the political parties into making a compromise of some *Damasias,* sort. It was agreed [1] that ten archons should be chosen, five *583-581* Eupatrids, three Georgi, and two Demiurgi, all of course possessing *B.C.* the requisite minimum of wealth. It is unknown whether this *581-580* arrangement was repeated after the year of its first trial, but it *B.C.* certainly did not lead to a permanent reconciliation.

Two   The two great parties were those who were in the main satisfied *ţarties :* with the new constitution of Solon, and those who disliked its democratic side and desired to return to the aristocratic government which he had subverted. The latter consisted chiefly of Eupa- *the Plain* trids and were known as the men of the Plain. They were led by *(πεδιακοί);* Lycurgus, and numbered among them the clan of the Philaidae— distinguished as the clan of Hippoclides, the wooer of Agarista, and destined to become more distinguished still as that of more than *the Coast* one Cimon and Miltiades. The opposite party of the Coast included *(πάραλοι).* not only the population of the coast, but the bulk of the middle classes, the peasants as well as the Demiurgi, who were bettered by the changes of Solon. They were led by Megacles, son of Alcmaeon, the same Megacles who married Agarista. For one of Solon's

[1] We learn this from Aristotle's 'Αθηναίων Πολιτεία, and there is no longer any doubt about the reading. This unique arrangement superseded the Solonian constitution.

measures was an act of amnesty which was couched in such terms that, while it did not benefit the descendants of Cylon, it permitted the return of the Alcmaeonidae. Their position severed them from the rest of the Eupatrids and associated them with the party which represented Solon's views.

FIG. 65.—Attic Kouros, *c.* 600 B.C.

CHAPTER V

SECT. 1. THE CONQUEST OF SALAMIS AND NISAEA

IN the midst of these domestic troubles and party struggles, there were a few statesmen who found time to attend to foreign affairs, and saw that the time had come for Athens to take a new step in her political career. Under her aristocracy, Athens had enjoyed a long period of development which may be called peaceful, if we compare the growth of some other states; and this prepared her to take her place in the general scene of Greek history. Though Attica was a poor country, scantily watered and with light soil, her prosperity in the oil trade might encourage her to look forward to becoming rich. But, if she was ever to become a political power, there was one thing to be achieved at all hazards. Every Athenian who stood on his strong hill and looked south-westward could see what this was. He *Salamis.* descried, lying close to his own shore, an island which was not his own. And, if he walked across Mount Aegaleos, he saw how this foreign island blocked up the bay of what was now his own Eleusis. Almost equally distant from Athens and Megara, parted by a narrow water from both, Salamis in the hands of either must be a constant *Rivalry of* menace to the other. The possession of Salamis must decide the *Megara.* future history of both Megara and Athens. At this period Megara with her growing colonial connexions was a strong state and a formidable neighbour; and her expanding trade must have been *Megarian* viewed with alarm and jealousy by Athenian statesmen. A struggle *war (c. 629* with Megara, sooner or later, was inevitable, and the Cylonian con- *B.C.).* spiracy, as we saw, furnished an occasion of war. Theagenes could not easily brook the slaughter of his men in violation of the promise which had been given to them, and he sent his ships to harry the Attic coasts. The Athenians sought to occupy Salamis, but all their efforts to gain a permanent footing failed, and they abandoned the attempt in despair. Years passed away. At length Solon saw that the favourable hour had come. It was, perhaps, a quarter of a century after the year of his lawgiving ; he had returned from his travels and was living at Athens, one of the Council of the Areopagus. Megara was now weaker than in the days of Theagenes, and, whether she had given any new cause of offence to Athens or not, Solon and his friends decided that it was time to strike. The great legislator came forward now, not as before to assuage strife but to stir up to conquest. He composed a stirring poem which *Solon's* began : " I came myself as a herald from lovely Salamis, but with *poem on* song on my lips instead of common speech." He blamed the peace *Salamis.* policy of the "men who let slip Salamis," as dishonourable ; and cried, "Arise and come to Salamis, to win that fair island and undo our shame." The poem of Solon was intended to have the effect which in later times, when "common speech" had been perfected to a fine art, would have been wrought by the eloquence of an orator in the Assembly. His appeal moved the hearts of his countrymen to a national effort, and an Athenian army went forth to lay the first stone of their country's greatness.

An intimate friend of Solon took part in the enterprise,—Pisis- *Pisistratus* tratus, son of Hippocrates, whose home and estates were near *(pole-* Brauron. It has been thought that Pisistratus was the polemarch of *march),* the year, but it is more probable that he was only a general sub- *c. 570-65* ordinate to the polemarch. He helped the expedition to a successful *B.C.* issue. Not only was the disputed island wrested from Megara, but *Conquers* he captured the port of Nisaea over against the island. We may *Salamis* conjecture that Nisaea was surprised first, and that its capture *and* *Nisaea.* enabled the Athenians to occupy Salamis. Thus, though Pisistratus was associated with the conquest of Nisaea, not with the conquest of Salamis, it was to him, along with his friend Solon who inspired the enterprise, that the great achievement was really due. The seizure of her port was a great shock to the trade of Megara. It was indeed afterwards restored, when peace was made through the mediation of Sparta ; but the hopes of Athenian policy, which its possession aroused, are reflected in the legend, created at this time, that Nisus the Megarian hero was a son of Pandion an early Athenian king. The two states agreed to submit their disputes to the arbitration of Sparta, and the award of the Spartans gave the island to Athens. In setting forth her case, Athens based her claims on a verse in Homer which she interpreted as proving that Salamis had formerly belonged to her (*Iliad* ii. 558). There is no reason to suppose that there was any truth in this prehistoric claim. But the fact of the appeal to Homer is interesting as showing the weight carried by Homer's authority. But Salamis now became permanently annexed to Attica. The island was afterwards divided in lots among

Cleruchs in Athenian citizens, who were called *cleruchs* or "lot-holders." Salamis,
Salamis. unlike Eleusis, was not incorporated in Attica, though it was nearer
Athens. There have been found fragments of a document inscribed
on a stone-pillar, perhaps (but it is difficult to judge the dates of
early Attic writings) eighty years or so later than the conquest,—a
decree of the people which concerns the settlement of Salamis; one
Athenian of the earliest scriptured stones of Athenian history, and the earliest
decree. example we possess of a decree of the Athenian people. [The new
settlers on the island were to pay the same taxes as the "Athenians"
and to serve in the army, but they were to dwell on their farms in
the island, and were not to let their lots to others under pain of a
fine.]

The conquest of Salamis was a decisive event for Athens. Her
territory was now rounded off; she had complete command of the
landlocked Eleusinian bay; it was she who now threatened Megara.

SECT. 2. ATHENS UNDER PISISTRATUS

The conqueror of Nisaea was the hero of the day. By professing
democratic doctrines and practising popular arts, he ingratiated himself with those extreme democrats who, being bitterly opposed to the
nobles and not satisfied by the Solonian compromise, were outside
both the Plain and the Coast. Pisistratus thus organised a new
party which was called the Hill, as it largely consisted of the poor
The hillsmen of the highlands of Attica; but it also included the hektemors,
Hillsmen for whom Solon had done little, and many discontented men, who
(Diakrioi). preferred radical measures to the barrenness of oligarchic faction.
Pisistratus With this party at his back, Pisistratus aimed at no less a thing than
seizes the grasping the supreme power for himself. One day he appeared
tyranny, in the agora, wounded, he said, by a foul attack of his political foes—
561-0 B.C. his foes because he was a friend of the people; and he showed wounds
Archonship
of Comeas. which he bore. In the Assembly, packed by the Hillsmen, a body-
(κορυνη- guard of fifty clubsmen was voted to him on the proposal of Aristion.
φόροι.) We have a monument, which we may associate with the author of this
memorable act, in a sepulchral slab discovered near Brauron, on
The stele of which is finely wrought in very low relief the portrait of "Aristion"
Aristion. standing armed by his tombstone; and it is hardly too bold to recognise in this contemporary sculpture the friend of Pisistratus, when
we remember that the home of the Pisistratid family was at Brauron.
Having secured his bodyguard—the first step in the tyrant's progress
—Pisistratus seized the acropolis, and made himself master of the
state.

It was the fate of Solon to live long enough to see the establishment of the tyranny which he dreaded. We know not what part he

had taken in the troubled world of politics since his return to Athens. The story was invented that he called upon the citizens to arm themselves against the tyrant, but called in vain ; and that then, laying his arms outside the threshold of his house, he cried, " I have aided, so far as I could, my country and the constitution, and I appeal to others to do likewise." Nor has the story that he refused to live under a tyranny and sought refuge with his Cyprian friend the king of Soli, any good foundation. We know only that in his later years he enjoyed the pleasures of wine and love, and that he survived but a short time the seizure of the tyranny by Pisistratus.

Death of Solon (c. 560-59 B.C.).

The discord of parties had smoothed the way for the schemes of Pisistratus ; but his success led in turn to the union of the two other parties, the Plain and the Coast, against him, and at the end of about five years they succeeded in driving him out. But new disunion followed, and Megacles the leader of the Coast seems to have quarrelled not only with the Plain but with his own party. At all events, he sought a reconciliation with Pisistratus and undertook to help him back to the tyranny on condition that the tyrant wedded his daughter. The legend is that the partisans of Pisistratus found in Paeania, an Attic village, a woman of loftier than common stature, whom they arrayed in the guise of the goddess Athena. Her name was Phye. Then heralds, on a certain day, entered Athens, crying that Pallas herself was leading back Pisistratus. Presently a car arrived bearing the tyrant and Phye ; and the trick deceived all the common folk.

First exile of Pisistratus (556-5 B.C.).

Legend of Phye.

First restoration and second tyranny (550-49 B.C.?).

But the coalition of Pisistratus with Megacles was not more abiding than that of Megacles with Lycurgus. By a former wife [1] Pisistratus had two sons—Hippias

FIG. 66.—Stele of Aristion.

[1] Her name is unknown. Pisistratus had also married Timonassa, an Argive woman, whom, being a foreigner, Attic law did not recognise as a legal wife. The sons of Timonassa, Iophon and Hegesistratus, were therefore technically

and Hipparchus; and as he desired to create a dynasty, he feared that, if he had offspring by a second wife, the interests of his older sons might be injured and family dissensions ensue. So, though he went through the form of marriage with the daughter of Megacles, as he had promised, he did not treat her as his wife. Megacles was enraged when the tyrant's neglect reached his ears; he made common cause with the enemies of Pisistratus and succeeded in driving him out for the second time, perhaps in the same year in which he had been restored.

Second exile (550-49 B.C. ?). The second exile lasted for about ten years, and Pisistratus spent it in forming new connexions in Macedonia. On the Thermaic gulf he organised the inhabitants of the neighbourhood of Rhaecelus into some sort of a city-state. He exploited the gold mines of Mount Pangaeus near the Strymon, and formed a force of mercenary soldiers, thus providing himself with money and men to recover his position at Athens. He was supported by Lygdamis, the tyrant of Naxos, and by the friendship of other Greek states, such as Thessaly, which he had cultivated in the days of his power. The aristocracy of Eretrian horsemen were well-disposed to him, and their city was an admirable *Second restoration and third tyranny (540-39-528-7 B.C.)* basis for an attack upon Athens. When he landed at Marathon, his adherents flocked to his standard. The citizens who were loyal to the constitutional government marched forth, and were defeated in battle at Pallene. Resistance was at an end, and once more Pisistratus had the power in his hands. This time he kept it.

The rule of Pisistratus may be described as a constitutional tyranny. He did not stop the wheels of the democracy, but he guided the machine entirely at his own will. The constitution of Solon seems to have been preserved in its essential features, though in some details the lapse of time may have brought modifications. Thus it is possible that even before the first success of Pisistratus the assessment according to measures of corn and oil had been converted into an assessment in money. And as money became more plentiful the earlier standards for the division of classes ceased to have the old significance. A man who at the beginning of the sixth century just reached the standard of the first class was passing rich; fifty years later he would be comparatively poor. But it was not to the interest of the tyrant to raise the census for political office. Various measures of policy were adopted by him to protect his position, while he preserved *(1) Influence on the magistracies.* the old forms of government. He managed to influence the appointment of the archons, so as to secure personal adherents, and one of his own family generally held some office. The tyrant kept up a

illegitimate, but socially, doubtless, no stain was attached to them. Hegesistratus seems to have been afterwards legitimised and made a citizen; perhaps it was on this occasion that he received his other name Thessalus.

standing force of paid soldiers—among them, perhaps, Scythian *(2) Mer-* archers, whom we see portrayed on Attic vases of the time. And *cenaries.* he kept in his power, as hostages, the children of some noble families *(3) Host-* which he suspected. Most indeed of his more prominent opponents, *ages.* including the Alcmaeonids, had left Attica, and the large estates which they abandoned were at his disposal.

These estates gave him the means of solving a problem which Solon had left unsolved, and of satisfying the expectations of a large number

FIG. 67.—Olive-harvest. Whipping the trees.

of his supporters. He divided the vacant lands into lots and gave *Land dis-* them to those who had most need. They became peasant proprietors, *tribution.* and they had to pay only the land-tax, amounting to one-tenth of *The* the produce. Land was also given to many needy people who idled *land-tax.* in the city, and loans of money to start them. The tax of a tenth, imposed on all estates, formed an important source of the tyrant's revenue, and it is generally supposed that he introduced it. But this is not probable. We may take it that this land-tax was an older institution which continued under Pisistratus, until either he or his sons were able, through an increase of revenue from other sources, to reduce it to onetwentieth. It has been plausibly suggested that this increase of revenue came from the silver mines of Laurion, which now perhaps began to be more effectively worked. His possessions on the Strymon were another mainstay of the finance of Pisistratus. He exerted himself to improve agriculture, and under his influence the olive, which had long ago found a home in Attica, was planted more widely.

Under Pisistratus Athens rested from the distractions of party strife, and the old parties gradually disappeared. The development of industry and trade and the tyrant's land policy gave the people a tranquil period of economical and political development. And as the free forms of the constitution were preserved, the masses, in the Assembly and in the Law-courts, received a training in the routine at least of public affairs, which rendered them fit for the democracy which was to ensue when the tyranny was overthrown.

Foreign policy.

Abroad it was the consistent policy of Pisistratus to preserve peaceful relations with other states. Aegina indeed was openly the rival of Athens, and humbled Megara could hardly be aught save sullen. But Athens was on friendly terms with both the rival powers of the Peloponnesus, Sparta and Argos ; and Thebes, and Thessaly, and the Eretrian knights had helped the tyrant in the days of his adversity. His influence extended to the banks of the Strymon and the coast of Macedonia, as we have already seen ; and he had a sub-servient friend in Lygdamis of Naxos, whom he had installed as tyrant over the Naxian people. Corinth, later to be Athens' most bitter enemy, was still friendly.

Athens on the Propontis : the war for Sigeum.

It was doubtless with the object of injuring the Megarian trade in Pontic corn, and gaining some counterpoise to Megarian power in the region of the Propontis, that Athens made her first venture in distant seas. It was about forty years before Pisistratus became tyrant that Athens seized the Lesbian fortress of Sigeum on the shore of the Troad at the entrance to the Hellespont. The friend-ship of Miletus, mother of many Pontic colonies, favoured this enter-prise, which however involved Athens in a conflict with Mytilene whose power and settlements extended along the shores of the straits. Mytilene, failing to recover the fortress, built another, the Achilleon, close by, which cut off the Athenians from the sea. It has been already told how the statesman Pittacus was engaged in this war and slew an Athenian commander in single combat, and how the poet Alcaeus threw away his shield. It would seem that while Athens was absorbed in her party conflicts at home, Sigeum slipped from her hands, and that the recapture of it was one of the achievements of Pisistratus. The tyrant showed the importance he attached to it

535-27 B.C.) by installing one of his sons as governor. The statesmen who first sent Athenian soldiers to the shores of the Hellespont had in truth opened up a new path for Athenian policy, and Pisistratus pursued

Acquisi-tion of the Thracian Chersonese (559-6 ?). Miltiades.

that path. It was not long before a much greater acquisition than Sigeum was made in the same region ; but this acquisition, though made with the good-will, and even under the auspices, of Pisistratus, was made by one who was his political rival and opponent. Miltiades, son of Cypselus, belonged to the noble family of the Philaids, and

was one of the leaders of the Plain.   It was after the usurpation of
Pisistratus, that as he sat one day in the porch of his country-house
at Laciadae on the road from Athens to Eleusis, he saw a company
of men in Thracian dress, and armed with spears, passing along the
road.   He called out to them, invited them into his house, and proffered them hospitality.   They were Dolonci, natives of the Thracian
Chersonese, and they had come to Greece in search of a helper, who
should have the strength and skill to defend them against their
northern neighbours, who were pressing them hard in war.   They
had gone to Delphi, and the oracle had bidden them invite the man
who first offered them entertainment after they left the shrine.   Miltiades, thus designated by the god, obeyed the call of the Thracians,
not reluctant to leave his country fallen under a tyrant's rule.

The circumstances of the foundation of Athenian power in the
Chersonese were thus wrought by the story-shaping instinct of the
Greeks into a picturesque tale.   The simple fact seems to have been
that the Dolonci applied directly to Athens, inviting the settlement
of an Athenian colony in their midst.   Pisistratus was well pleased
to promote Athenian influence on the Hellespontine shores ; and the
selection of Miltiades was not unwelcome to him, since it removed
a dangerous subject.   We may feel no doubt that it was as a representative of the Athenian state that Miltiades went forth, blessed by
the Delphic oracle, to the land of his Thracian guests.   But the oecist
who went forth, as it was said, to escape tyranny, became absolute
ruler in his new country.   He ruled as a Thracian prince over the
Dolonci ; he ruled as a tyrant over his Athenian fellow-settlers.   He
protected the peninsula against invasions from the north by a wall
which he built across the neck from Cardia to Pactye.   We hear of
his war with Lampsacus and his friendship with the king of Lydia.

It is not too much to say that Pisistratus took the first steps on
the path which led Athens to empire.   That path had indeed been
pointed out to him by nameless predecessors ; but his sword conquered Salamis ; under his auspices Athens won a footing on both
shores of the Hellespont.   We cannot estimate too highly the states- *Importance*
manship which sought a field for Athenian enterprise in the regions *of the*
of the Propontis.   The Ionian cities had forestalled Athens in venturing *settlements on the*
into the vast spaces of the eastern sea and winning the products of *Hellespont.*
its shores.   But though she entered into the contest late, she was
destined to outstrip both her friend Miletus, and Megara her foe.
Many years indeed were still to run before her ships dominated the
Euxine ; but it was much that she now set her posts as a watcher on
either side of the narrow gate

Where the sea-ridge of Helle hangs heavier, and east upon west waters
break.

Pisistratus strongly asserted the claim of Athens to be the mother and leader of the Ionian branch of the Greek race. The temple of Apollo in Delos, the island of his mythical birth, had been long a religious centre of the Ionians on both sides of the Aegean. There, as an ancient hymn sang, "the long-robed Ionians gather with their children and their wives," to honour Apollo with dance and song and games : "a stranger who came upon the Ionians in their throng, seeing the men and the fair-girdled women and the swift ships and all their wealth, would say that they were beings free for ever from death and eld." Pisistratus "purified" the sacred spot by digging up all the tombs that were within sight of the sanctuary and removing the bones of the dead to another part of the island.

Thus Athens took the famous Ionian festival under her special care. It was said, and has been believed by many both in ancient and in modern times, that Pisistratus or his enlightened son Hipparchus did a yet more important thing for the great Ionic epics, the *Iliad* and the *Odyssey*. The story is that a commission of literary men was appointed to collect and write down and revise the two poems of Homer, and it has thus been supposed that it was due to the initiative of the tyrants and the labours of the learned men whom they employed that the poems were for the first time written down. If this were so, it would be difficult to explain how the Athenians a generation before, in their dispute with Lesbos over the possession of Sigeum, could appeal to Homer as to the part they had played in the Trojan War, in the absence of a generally recognised text of the *Iliad*. As to the special verse in the Catalogue which they quoted to establish their claim to Salamis (see above, page 191) against Megara, it was alleged by Megarians in later times that it was spurious, having been fabricated and inserted by the Pisistratean commission in the interests of Athens. This accusa- tion had a certain plausibility, because Onomacritus, who was the most prominent member of the commission, was not above suspicion in the matter of forgery. He was a teacher of the Orphic religion, and assisted Hippias, the tyrant's eldest son, in editing a collection of the oracles of soothsayers. But he was detected in introducing into the collection an oracle which he had invented, and was banished from Athens. The whole story, however, of the Homeric com- mission of Pisistratus, implying that our texts of the two poems only go as far back as the sixth century, is without good foundations and is highly improbable.

Pisistratus was indeed interested in Homer in another way. He made Homeric recitations a feature of the great Panathenaic festival, and he made a rule that the rhapsodes who competed should follow strictly the order of the poems in choosing the pieces they recited.   The Panathenaic feast had been remodelled, if not *The Pan-* founded, shortly before he seized the tyranny, and, on the pattern of *athenaic* the national gatherings at Olympia and Delphi, was held every fourth *feast.* year.   It was celebrated with athletic and musical contests, but the *Temples of Athena* (1) centre and motive of the feast was the great procession which went *on the site* up to the house of Athena on her hill, to offer her a robe woven by *of the later* the hands of Athenian maidens.   The "rich fane" of Athena, *Erech-* wherein she accorded Erechtheus a place, had the distinction of *theum = house of* passing into the Homeric poems.   [It was situated on the Acropolis, *Athena* north of the later Parthenon and close to the site of the old royal *and* palace.   Of the original temple but few blocks remain, for early in *Erech-* the tyranny of Pisistratus, or shortly before, it was rebuilt and *theus,* surrounded by a Doric colonnade.   Many of the lowest stones of the *(2) temple of Athena* walls, still lying in their places, show us the site and shape of this *Polias.* temple ; and some of its sculptures have survived.]   The triangular *Peristasis and* gables displayed what Attic sculptors of the day could achieve. *pediments* Hitherto the favourite material of these sculptors had been the soft *added* marly limestone of the Piraeus, and by a curious stroke of luck some *probably* striking specimens of such work—Zeus encountering the three-headed *in Pisis-* Typhon, Heracles destroying the Hydra—have been partly preserved, *tratean age. Pedi-* the early efforts of an art which a hundred and fifty years would *mental* bring to perfection.   But now—in the second half of the sixth *sculptures* century—Greek sculptors have begun to work in a nobler and harder *(? c. 600* material ; and on one of the pediments of the renovated temple of *B. C.).* Athena Polias the battle of the Gods and Giants was wrought in *Use of* Parian marble.   Athena herself in the centre of the composition, *marble in* slaying Enceladus with her spear, may still be seen and admired. *sculpture.* *Gigan-*

But the tyrant planned a greater work than the new sanctuary on *tomachy in* the hill.   Down below, south-eastward from the citadel, on the banks *the Pisis-* of the Ilisus, he began the building of a great Doric temple for the *tratean* Olympian Zeus.   He began but never finished it, nor his sons after *pediment.* him.   So immense was the scale of his plan that Athens, even when she reached the height of her dominion and fulfilled many of the aspirations of Pisistratus, never ventured to undertake the burden of completing it.   A full completion was indeed to come, though in a *Completed* shape far different from the old Athenian's plan ; but not until *by the* Athens and Greece had been gathered under the wings of a power *Emperor* which had all Europe at its feet.   The richly ornamented capitals of *Hadrian.* the few lofty pillars which still stand belong to the work of the Roman emperor, but we must remember that the generations of Athenians, with whom this history has to do, saw only plain Doric columns there, the monument of the wealth and ambition of the tyrant who had done more for their city, with his wide-ranging plans, than they cared to think.

Pisistratus was indeed scrupulous and zealous in all matters concerned with religion, and his sons more than himself. But no act of his was more fruitful in results than what he did for the worship of Dionysus. In the marshes on the south side of the Areopagus the bacchic god had an ancient sanctuary, of which the foundations have

The Lenaeum; the temple of Dionysus in Limnae.

FIG. 68.—Athena slaying a Giant (from a pediment of the old temple of Athena on the Athenian acropolis).

been recently uncovered; but Pisistratus built him a new house at the foot of the Acropolis, and its ruins have not yet wholly disappeared. In connexion with this temple Pisistratus instituted a new festival, called the Great Dionysia of the City, and it completely overshadowed the older feast of the Winepress (Lenaea), which still continued to be held in the first days of spring at the temple of the Marshes. The chief feature of the Dionysiac feasts was the choir of satyrs, the god's attendants, who danced around the altar clothed in goat-skins, and sang their "goat song." But it became usual for the leader of the dancers, who was also the composer of the song, to separate himself from his fellows and hold speech with them, assuming the character of some person connected with the events which the song celebrated, and wearing an appropriate dress. Such performances, which at the rural feasts had been arranged by private enterprise, were made an official part of the Great Dionysia, and thus taken under state protection, in the form of a "tragic" contest, two or more choruses competing for a prize. It was the work of a generation to develop these simple representations into a true drama, by differentiating the satyric element. Legends not connected with *Differen-* Dionysus were chosen for representation, and the dancers appeared, *tiation of* not in the bacchic goat-dress, but in the costume suitable for their *tragedy* part in the story. This performance was divided into three acts; *from* the dancers changed their costumes for each act; and only at the end *drama.* did they come forward in their true goat-guise and perform a piece *(Trilogy.)* which preserved the original satyric character of "tragedy." Then *(Satyric* their preponderant importance was by degrees diminished, and a *drama.)* second actor was introduced; and by a development of this kind, hidden from us in its details, the goat song of the days of Pisistratus grew into the tragedy of Aeschylus.

The popularity of the worship of Dionysus at Athens in the *Dionysiac* days of Pisistratus might be observed in the workshops of the *subjects on* potters. No subject was more favoured than Dionysiac scenes by *vases.* the artists—Exekias and his fellows—who painted the black-figured jars of this period. There is another thing which the student of *Heracles on* history may learn among the graceful vessels of the potters of *black-* Athens. On the jars of the Pisistratean age the deeds of Heracles *figured* are a favourite theme, while Theseus is little regarded. But before the *amphorae,* golden age of vase-painting sets in, about the time of the fall of *etc. (c. 570-* the Pisistratids, Theseus has begun to seize the popular imagination *510 B.C.).* as the great Attic hero, and this is reflected in paintings on the cups *Theseus on* of Euphronius and the other brilliant masters of the red-figured *red-figured* style. If we remember that Theseus was specially associated with *cylixes,* the hill country of north Attica, which was the stronghold of the *etc. (c. 510-* Pisistratean party, we may be tempted to infer that the glorification *470 B.C.).* of Theseus was partly due to the policy of Pisistratus.

But besides caring for the due honours of the gods, the tyrant busied himself with such humbler matters as the improvement of the water-supply of Athens. West and south-west of the Acropolis, in the rocky valley between the Areopagus and the Pnyx, his water- *Aqueaucts.* works have recently come to light. A cistern there received the waters which an aqueduct conveyed from the upper stream of the Ilisus. It is indeed on this side of Athens, south and west of the oldest Athens of all, that the chief stone memorials of the age of Pisistratus stood, apart from what he may have built on the Acropolis itself.

SECT. 3. GROWTH OF SPARTA, AND THE PELOPONNESIAN LEAGUE

While a tyrant was moulding the destinies of Athens, the growth of the Spartan power had changed the political aspect of the Peloponnesus. About the middle of the sixth century Sparta won successes against her northern neighbours Tegea and Argos ; and in consequence of these successes she became the predominant power in the peninsula.

Tegeate war, c. 560-50 (?).

Legend of the conquest of Tegea and the bones of Orestes.

Eastern Arcadia is marked by a large plain, high above the sea-level ; the villages in the north of this plain had coalesced into the town of Mantinea, those in the south had been united in Tegea. Sparta had gradually pressed up to the borders of the Tegean territory, and a long war was the result. This war is associated with an interesting legend based on the tradition that the Laconian hero Orestes was buried in Tegea. When the Spartans asked the Delphic oracle whether they might hope to achieve the conquest of Arcadia, they received a promise that the god would give them Tegea. Then, on account of this answer, they went forth against Tegea with fetters, but were defeated ; and bound in the fetters which they had brought to bind the Tegeates were compelled to till the Tegean plain. Herodotus professed that in his day the very fetters hung in the temple of Athena Alea, the protectress of Tegea. War went on, and the Spartans, invariably defeated, at last consulted the oracle again. The god bade them bring back the bones of Orestes, but they could find no trace of the hero's burying-place, and they asked the god once more. This time they received an oracle couched in obscure enigmatic words :

> Among Arcadian hills a level space
>   Holds Tegea, where blow two blasts perforce
> And woe is laid on woe and face to face
>   Striker and counter-striker ; there the corse
> Thou seekest lies, even Agamemnon's son ;
> Convey him home and victory is won.

This did not help them much. But it befell that, during a truce with the Tegeates, a certain Lichas, a Spartan man, was in Tegea and entering a smith's shop saw the process of beating out iron. The smith in conversation told him that wishing to dig a well in his courtyard he had found a coffin seven cubits long and within it a corpse of the same length, which he replaced. Lichas guessed at once that he had won the solution of the oracular enigma, and returning to Sparta communicated his discovery. The courtyard was hired from the reluctant smith, the coffin was found, and the bones brought home to Laconia. Then Tegea was conquered, and here we return from fable to fact. The territory of the Arcadian city was not treated like Messenia; it was not incorporated in the territory of Lacedaemon. It became a dependent state, contributing a military contingent to the army of its conqueror; and it bound itself to harbour no Messenians within its borders. [The recovery of the bones of Orestes is to be interpreted as Spartan propaganda. The tyrants of Corinth and Sicyon had pursued a strong anti-Dorian policy. Sparta, in extending her influence through the Peloponnese, did not wish to raise issues of race. Later the Spartan King Cleomenes could say at Athens: " I am no Dorian, but Achaean."]

At this period the counsels of Sparta seem to have been guided by Chilon, whose name became proverbial for wisdom. It was much about the same time, perhaps shortly after the victory over Tegea, *Sparta* that Sparta at length succeeded in rounding off the frontier of Laconia *conquers* on the north-eastern side by wresting the disputed territory of *Thyreatis,* Thyreatis from Argos. The armies of the two states met in the *c. 550 B.C.* marchland, but the Spartan kings and the Argive chiefs agreed to decide the dispute by a combat between three hundred chosen champions on either side. The story is that all the six hundred were slain except three, one Spartan and two Argives; and that while the Argives hurried home to announce their victory, the Spartan— Othryades was his name—remained on the field and erected a trophy. In any case, the trial was futile, for both parties claimed the victory and a battle was fought in which the Argives were utterly defeated. Thyreatis was the last territorial acquisition of Sparta. She changed her policy, and instead of aiming at gaining new territory, she endeavoured to make the whole Peloponnesus a sphere of Lacedaemonian influence. This change of policy was exhibited in her dealing with Tegea.

The defeat of Argos placed Sparta at the head of the peninsula. *The Pelo-* All the Peloponnesian states, except Argos and Achaea, were enrolled *ponnesian* in a loose confederacy, engaging themselves to supply military con- *confederacy* tingents in the common interest, Lacedaemon being the leader. The *and* meetings of the confederacy were held at Sparta, and each mem- *Sparta's* ber sent representatives. Corinth readily joined; for Corinth was *supremacy.* naturally ranged against Argos, while her commercial rival, the island state of Aegina, was a friend of Argos. Periander had already inflicted a blow upon the Argives by seizing Epidaurus and thus cutting off their nearest communications with Aegina. The other Isthmian state, Megara, in which the rule of the nobles had been restored, was also enrolled. Everywhere Sparta exerted her influence to maintain oligarchy, everywhere she discountenanced democracy; so that her supremacy had important consquences for the constitutional development of the Peloponnesian states.

In northern Greece the power of the Thessalians was declining; and thus Sparta became the strongest state in Greece in the second half of the sixth century. She was on the most friendly terms with Athens throughout the reign of Pisistratus; but the tyrant was careful to maintain good relations with Argos also. With Argos herself indeed Athens had no cause for collision; but the rivalry which existed between Athens and Aegina naturally ranged Athens and *Athenian* Argos in opposite camps. [Earlier, probably near the middle of the *attack on* seventh century, Athens had landed forces in Aegina and had been *Aegina* heavily defeated with Argive help. The policy of Pisistratus avoided a *(first half* conflict with his island neighbour and courted the friendship of Argos.] *of 7th cent. ?).*

Sect. 4. Fall of the Pisistratids and Intervention of Sparta

Death of When Pisistratus died, his eldest son Hippias took his place. *Pisistratus* Hipparchus helped him in the government, while Thessalus took *(528-7* little or no share in politics. [The new rule opened with a gesture of *B.C.).* political reconciliation, for a fragment of an Athenian archon list *His sons* shows that the Alcmaeonid Cleisthenes, whose family went into exile *and their* after the battle of Pallene, was archon in 525, and was followed in office *court.* by the Philaid Miltiades, whose family had also been hostile to the tyranny. The reconciliation, however, did not last long. Cleisthenes was soon in exile again, and Miltiades in the Chersonese.] The general policy of Pisistratus, both in home and foreign affairs, was continued. But the court of Athens seems to have acquired a more distinctive literary flavour. Hippias, who was a learned student of oracles, and Hipparchus were abreast of the most modern culture. The eminent poets of the day came to their court. Simonides of Ceos, famous for his choral odes; Anacreon of Teos, boon companion, singer of wine and love; Lasus of Hermione, who made his *ὕμνος* mark by novelties in the treatment of the dithyramb, and amused his *ἀσιγμος.* leisure hours by composing " hissless hymns," in which the sound *s* did not occur—all these were invited or welcomed by Hipparchus. One of the most prominent figures in this society was Onomacritus, a religious teacher,[1] already mentioned in connexion with the alleged edition of Homer.

[1] See below, p. 317.

The first serious blow aimed at the power of the tyrants was due *Conspiracy* to a personal grudge, not to any widespread dissatisfaction; but *of Har-* nevertheless it produced a series of effects which resulted in the *modius and* fall of the tyranny. It would seem—but conflicting accounts of *Aristo-* the affair were in circulation—that Hipparchus[1] gave offence to *giton.* a comely young man named Harmodius and his lover Aristogiton. It is said that Hipparchus was in love with Harmodius, and, when his wooing was rejected, avenged himself by putting a slight on the youth's sister, refusing to allow her to "bear a basket" in the Panathenaic procession. Harmodius and Aristogiton then formed (514 *B.C.*) the plan of slaying the tyrants, and chose the day of that procession, because they could then, without raising suspicion, appear publicly with arms. Very few were initiated in the plot, as it was expected that when the first blow was struck, the citizens would declare themselves for freedom. But, as the hour approached, it was observed that one of the conspirators was engaged in speech with Hippias in the outer Ceramicus. His fellows leapt hastily to the conclusion that their plot was betrayed, and, giving up the idea of attacking Hippias, rushed to the market-place and slew Hipparchus near the *Murder of* Leokorion. Harmodius was cut down and Aristogiton was afterwards *Hippar-* captured, tortured, and put to death. *chus.*

At the time no sympathy was manifested, little perhaps felt, for *Harsh rule* the conspirators. But their act led to a complete change in the *of Hippias.* government of Hippias. Not knowing what ramifications the plot might have, or what dangers might still lurk about his feet, he became a hard and suspicious despot. He fortified Munychia, to have a post on the shore, from which he might at any hour flee overseas, and he began to turn his eyes towards Persia, where a new power had begun to cast its shadow over the Hellenic world. Then many Athenians came to hate him, and longed to shake off the reins of tyranny; and they began to cherish the memory of Harmodius and Aristogiton as tyrant-slayers.

The overthrow of the tyranny was chiefly brought about by the *Temple of* Alcmaeonids, who desired to return to Athens, and could not win *Delphi* their desire so long as the Pisistratids were in power. They had *built by* taken care to cultivate an intimacy with the priesthood of Delphi, *Alcmaeon-* which they now turned to account. The old sanctuary of Apollo *ids.* had been burned down by a mischance, and it was resolved to build a new temple at the enormous cost of 300 talents. A Panhellenic 548-7 *B.C.* subscription was organised, and by this means about a quarter of the needed money was raised; the rest was defrayed from the resources of Delphi. The Alcmaeonids undertook the contract for the work, and the story went that a frontage of Parian marble was added at their own

---

[1] According to another story, Thessalus.

expense, poros-stone having been specified in the agreement. The temple was not unworthy of the greatest shrine of Hellas. An Athenian poet has sung of the "glancing light of the two fair faces" of the pillared house of Loxias, and has vividly described sculptured metopes with heroes destroying monsters, and a pediment with the gods quelling the giants.[1] It must have been about the time when the new temple was approaching its completion, or soon after, that to the holy buildings of Delphi was added one *Siphnian* of the richest of all. The islanders of Siphnos spent some of the *Treasury.* wealth which they dug out of their gold and silver mines, in making themselves a treasury at the mid-centre of the earth, and its remains show us the richness of its decoration. Perhaps this building marks the height of Siphnian prosperity. Before a hundred years had passed, their supply of precious metal was withdrawn ; their miners had got below the sea-level, and the water filtering in cut them off from the sources of their wealth.

Large sums of money passed through the hands of the Alcmaeonids during the building of the temple, and their enemies said that this enabled them to hire mercenaries for their design on Attica. Their first attempt was a failure. They and other exiles seized Leipsydrion, a strong position on a spur of Mount Parnes looking down on Paeanidae and Acharnae ; but they were too few to take the field by themselves, and the people had no desire to drive out the tyrant for the sake of setting up an oligarchy of nobles. They were soon forced to abandon their fortress and leave Attica. Convinced that they could only accomplish their schemes by foreign help, they used their influence with the Delphic oracle to put pressure on Sparta. Accordingly, whenever the Spartans sent to consult the god, the response always was : "First free Athens."

It has already been said that the Pisistratids cultivated the friendship of Sparta, and after his brother's murder Hippias was more anxious than ever not to break with her. But the diplomacy of the Alcmaeonids, of whose clan Cleisthenes, son of Megacles, was at this time head, supported as it was by the influence of Delphi, finally prevailed, and the Spartans consented to force freedom upon Athens. Perhaps they thought the dealings of Hippias with Persia suspicious ; he had married his daughter Archedice to a son of the tyrant of Lampsacus, who was known to have influence at the Persian court.

The A first expedition of the Spartans under Anchimolius was utterly *Spartans* routed with the help of a body of Thessalian cavalry ; but a second *invade* *Attica.* led by king Cleomenes defeated the Thessalians, and Hippias was

---

[1] Euripides, in the *Ion*, 185 *sqq.*

Fig. 69.—Frieze from the Siphnian treasury at Delphi.

Fall of the Pisistratids, 510 B.C. (archonship of Harpactides). blockaded in the Acropolis. When his children, whom he was sending secretly into safety abroad, fell into the hands of his enemies, he capitulated, and, on condition that they were given back, undertook to leave Attica within five days. He and all his house departed to Sigeum; and a pillar was set up on the Acropolis, recording the sentence which condemned the Pisistratids to perpetual disfranchisement (*atimia*).

Thus the tyrants had fallen, and with the aid of Sparta Athens was free. It was not surprising that when she came to value her liberty she loved to turn away from the circumstances in which it was actually won and linger over the romantic attempt of Harmodius and Aristogiton, which might be considered at least the prelude to the fall of Hippias. A drinking-song, breathing the spirit of liberty, celebrated the two friends who slew the tyrant; Harmodius and Aristogiton became household words. A skilful sculptor Antenor wrought a commemorative group of the two tyrant-slayers, and it was set up, not very many years later, above the market-place.

Athens in the Peloponnesian league. The Athenian republic had to pay, indeed, something for its deliverance. It was obliged to enter into the Peloponnesian league, of which Sparta was the head; and thus Sparta acquired a certain right of interference in the affairs of Athens. This new obligation was destined to lead soon to another struggle.

SECT. 5. KING CLEOMENES AND THE SECOND SPARTAN INTERVENTION

The birth of Cleomenes, and how he became king. It is necessary here to digress for a moment to tell of the strange manner of the birth of king Cleomenes, who liberated Athens. His father king Anaxandridas was wedded to his niece, but she had no children. The Ephors, heedful that the royal family of the Agids should not die out, urged him to put her away, and when he gainsaid, they insisted that he should take a second wife into his house. This he did, and Cleomenes was born. But soon afterwards his first wife, hitherto childless, bore a son, who was named Dorieus. When the old king died, it was ruled that Cleomenes as the eldest should *Dorieus.* succeed, and Dorieus, who had looked forward to the kingship, was forced to leave Sparta. He went forth to seek his fortune in lands beyond the sea; having attempted to plant a settlement in Libya, he led an expedition of adventure to the west; he took part in a war of Croton with Sybaris, and then fared to Sicily, with *(c. 510 B.C.)* the design of founding a new city in the south-west country, yet he did not bring his purpose to pass, for he fell in a battle against the Carthaginians and their Elymian allies. It must also be told that after the birth of Dorieus his mother brought Anaxandridas two

FIG. 70.—Harmodius and Aristogiton (copy of group by Critias and Nesiotes).

other sons, Leonidas and Cleombrotus, both of whom we shall meet hereafter.

Situation at Athens, 510-8 B.C.

After the expulsion of the tyrant, the Athenians had to deal with the political problems, whose solution, fifty years before, had been postponed by the tyranny. The main problem was to modify the constitution of Solon in such a way as to render it practicable. The old evils which had hindered the realisation of Solon's democracy reared their heads again as soon as Hippias had been driven out and the Spartans had departed. The strife of factions, led by noble and influential families, broke out ; and the Coast and Plain seem to have risen again in the parties of the Alcmaeonid Cleisthenes [1] and

Isagoras archon, 508-7 B.C.

his rival Isagoras. As Cleisthenes had been the most active promoter of the revolution, Isagoras was naturally supported by the secret adherents of the tyrant's house. The struggle at first turned in favour of Isagoras, who was elected to the chief magistracy ; but it was only for a moment. Cleisthenes won the upper hand by enlisting on his side superior numbers. He rallied to his cause a host of poor men who were outside the pale of citizenship, by promising to make them citizens. Thus the victory of Cleisthenes—and the victory of Cleisthenes was the victory of reform—was won by the threat of physical force ; and in the year of his rival's archonship he introduced new democratic measures of law. Isagoras was so far outnumbered that he had no recourse but appeal to Sparta. At his instance the Lacedaemonians, who looked with disfavour on democracy, demanded that the Alcmaeonids, as a clan under a curse,[2] should be expelled from Attica ; and Cleisthenes, without attempting resistance, left the country. But this was not enough. King Cleo-

---

[1] Tree showing the relationships of eminent Alcmaeonids in the sixth and fifth centuries :

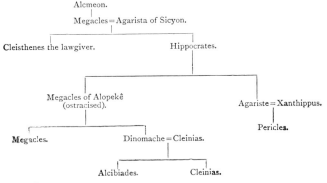

```
                        Alcmeon.
                           |
                Megacles = Agarista of Sicyon.
                           |
      ┌────────────────────┴───────────────┐
Cleisthenes the lawgiver.            Hippocrates.
                                          |
         ┌────────────────────────────────┴──────────┐
   Megacles of Alopekê                          Agariste = Xanthippus.
      (ostracised).                                        |
         |                                             Pericles.
   ┌─────┴──────────────────┐
Megacles.            Dinomache = Cleinias.
                              |
                    ┌─────────┴──────────┐
               Alcibiades.           Cleinias.
```

[2] See above, p. 179.

menes entered Attica for the second time ; he expelled 700 families
pointed out by Isagoras, and attempted to dissolve the new constitution and to set up an oligarchy.   But the whole people rose in *Spartans*
arms ; Cleomenes, who had only a small band of soldiers with him, *besieged*
was blockaded with Isagoras in the Acropolis, and was forced to *in the*
capitulate on the third day "in spite of his Spartan spirit."[1]   Clei- *Acropolis.*
sthenes could now return with all the other exiles and complete
his work.   The event was a check for Lacedaemon.   It was the
first, but it was not the last, time that Athenian oligarchs sought
Spartan intervention and Spartan men-at-arms held the hill of Athena.

Sect. 6. Reform of Cleisthenes

Solon created the institutions, and constructed the machinery, of
the Athenian democracy.   We have seen why this machinery would
not work.   The fatal obstacle to its success was the political strength
of the clans ; and Solon, by retaining the old Ionic tribes, had therewith retained the clan organisation as a base of his constitution.   In
order therefore to make democracy a reality, it was indispensable *Need of a*
to deprive the clans of political significance and substitute a new *new or-*
organisation.   Another grave evil during the past century had been *ganisation*
the growth of local parties ; Attica had been split up into political
sections.   The memorable achievement of Cleisthenes was the
invention of a totally new organisation, a truly brilliant and, as the
event proved, practical scheme, which did away with the Ionic
tribes, abolished the political influence of the phratries and clans, and *Abolition*
superseded the system of the Naucraries ; thus removing the danger *of old*
of the undue preponderance of social influence or local parties, and *tribes.*
securing to the whole body of citizens a decisive and permanent
part in the conduct of public affairs.

Taking the map of Attica as he found it, consisting of between
one and two hundred demes or small districts, Cleisthenes distinguished three regions : the region of the city, the region of the *Three*
coast, and the inland.   In each of these regions he divided the *regions.*
demes into ten groups called *trittyes*, so that there were thirty such *Thirty*
trittyes in all, and each trittys was named after the chief deme *trittyes.*
which was included in it.   Out of the thirty trittyes he then formed
ten groups of three, in such a way that no group contained two *Ten tribes.*
trittyes from the same region.   Each of these groups constituted
a tribe, and the citizens of all the demes contained in its three
trittyes were fellow-tribesmen.   Thus Kydathenaion, a trittys of the *Distribu-*
city region, was combined with Paeania, a trittys of the inland, and *tion of*
Myrrhinus, a trittys of the coast, to form the tribe of Pandionis. *demes*
                                                                      among the
[1] ὅμως Λακωνικὸν πνέων, Aristoph. *Lys.* 276.   *tribes.*

The ten new tribes thus obtained were called after eponymous heroes chosen by the Delphic priestess.[1] The heroes had their priests and sanctuaries, and their statues stood in front of the senate-house in the Agora.

Both the tribes and the demes were corporations with officers, *Demarchs.* assemblies, and corporate property. The demarch or president of (λῃξιαρ- the deme kept the burgess list of the place, in which was solemnly χικὸν entered the name of each citizen when he reached the age of seven- γραμμα- teen. The organisation of the army depended on the tribes, each τεῖον.) of which contributed a regiment of hoplites and a squadron of horse. The trittys had no independent constitution of this kind, no corporate existence, and consequently it appears little in official *Importance* documents. But it was the scarce visible pivot on which the Clei- *of the* sthenic system revolved, the link between the demes and the tribes. *trittys* By its means a number of groups of people in various parts of Attica, without community of local interest, were brought together at Athens, *Effect of the* and had to act in common. The old parties of Plain, Hill, and Coast *new system;* were thus done away with; there was no longer a means of local *contrast* political action. Thus an organisation created for a purely political *with the* purpose was substituted for an organisation which was originally *old.* social and had been adapted to political needs. The ten new tribes, based on artificial geography, took the place of the four old tribes, based on birth. The incorporate trittys, which had no independent existence, but merely represented the relation between the tribe and the deme, took the place of the independent and active phratry. And the deme, a local unit, replaced the social unit of the clan. This scheme of Cleisthenes, with the artificial trittys and the artificially formed tribe, might seem almost too artificial to last. The secret of its permanence lay in the fact that the demes, the units on which it was built up, were natural divisions, which he did not attempt to reduce to a round number.

It must have taken some time to bring this reform into full working order. The first list of demesmen on the new system decided the deme of all their descendants. A man might change his home and reside in another deme, but he still remained a member of the deme to which he originally belonged. Henceforward in official documents men were distinguished by their demes instead of, as heretofore, by their fathers' names.[2] All Attica was included in this system except Eleutherae and Oropus on the frontier, which were treated as subject districts and belonged to no tribe.

---

[1] Names of the ten tribes: Erechtheis, Aegeis, Pandionis, Leontis, Acamantis, Oeneis, Cecropis, Hippothontis, Aeantis, Antiochis.

[2] At a later period it became customary to give the father's name as well as the deme.

The political purpose and significance of this reorganisation, which entitles its author to be called the second founder of the democracy, lay in its connexion with a reformed Council. As the existing Council of Four Hundred had been based on the four Ionic tribes, Cleisthenes devised a Council of Five Hundred based on his ten new tribes. Each tribe contributed fifty members, of which each deme returned a fixed number, according to its size. They were probably appointed annually by lot from a number of candidates chosen by each deme; but the preliminary election was afterwards abolished, and forty years later they were appointed entirely by lot. All those on whom the lot fell were proved, as to the integrity of their private and public life, by the outgoing Council, which had the right of rejecting the unfit. They took an oath when they entered upon office that they would "advise what is best for the city"; and they were responsible for their acts, when they laid it down.

Close connexion of this organisation with the Council. New council of Five Hundred and One (460 B.C.).

This Council, in which every part of Attica was represented, was the supreme administrative authority in the state. "In conjunction with the various magistrates it managed most of the public affairs." An effective control was exerted on the archons and other magistrates, who were obliged to present reports to the Council and receive the Council's orders. All the finances of the state were practically in its hands, and ten new finance officers called *apodektai* (one from each tribe) acted under its direction. It seems, moreover, from the very first to have been invested with judicial powers in matters concerning the public finance, and with the right of fining officials. Further, the Council acted as a ministry of public works, and even as a ministry of war. It may also be regarded as the ministry of foreign affairs, for it conducted negotiations with foreign states, and received their envoys. It had no powers of declaring war or concluding a treaty; these powers resided solely in the sovereign Assembly. But the Council was not only an administrative body, it was a deliberative assembly, and had the initiative in all lawmaking. No proposal could come before the Ecclesia unless it had already been proposed and considered in the Council. Every law passed in the Ecclesia was first sent down from the Council in the form of a *probuleuma*, and, on receiving a majority of votes in the Ecclesia, became a *psephisma*. Again, the Council had some general as well as some special judicial functions. It formed a court before which impeachments could be brought, as well as before the Assembly, and in these cases it could either pass sentence itself or hand them over to another court.

(1) Administrative functions.

(2) Deliberative functions.

(3) Judicial functions. (εἰσαγγελίαι.)

It is obvious that the administrative duties could not conveniently be conducted by a body of five hundred constantly sitting. Accordingly the year of 360 days was divided into ten parts, and

The Prytaneis and the civil year. the councillors of each tribe took it in turn to act as a committee for carrying on public business during a tenth of the year.[1] In this capacity, as members of the acting committee of fifty, the councillors were called *Prytaneis* or presidents, the tribe to which they belonged was said to be the *presiding*, and the divisions of this artificial year were called *prytanies*. It was incumbent on the *Epistates.* chairman, along with one trittys, of the committee, to live permanently during his prytany in the Tholos, a round building, where the presidents met and dined at the public expense. The Tholos or Skias was on the south side of the Agora, close to the Council-hall. The old prytaneion still remained in use as the office of the archon and the hearth of the city.

The Cleisthenic cycle, and the adjustment of the official and the civil years. Cleisthenes invented an ingenious arrangement for bringing his official year into general harmony with the civil year, so that the beginning of the one should not diverge too far from the beginning of the other. The civil year was supposed to begin as nearly as possible to the first new moon after the summer solstice ; and the difference between the lunar twelvemonth and the solar revolution was provided for by a cycle of eight years, in the first, third, and sixth of which additional months were intercalated. The ordinary year consisted of 354, the intercalated of 384 days. Cleisthenes, taking 360 as the number of days in his official year, was also obliged to intercalate, but not so often. He adopted a cycle of five years, and once in each cycle an intercalary month of 30 days was introduced. But this month was not always inserted in the same year of the cycle. It was here that Cleisthenes brought his quinquennial into line with the octennial system. The extraordinary official month was intercalated in the first year of the official cycle that coincided with an intercalary year of the civil cycle. The new institution of Cleisthenes began to work in 503-2 B.C.—the first year of an octennial cycle. The first Cleisthenic year began on the 1st of Hecatombaeon, the first month of the civil calendar ; it would not begin on that day again till forty years hence.[2]

In opening the citizenship to a large number of people who had hitherto been excluded, Cleisthenes was only progressing along the path of Solon. He seems to have retained the Solonian restrictions on eligibility for the higher offices of state. It is just possible that he may have set the knights, in this respect, on a level with the

---

[1] At the same time some changes must have been made in the organisation of the Ecclesia, but we do not know what they were. As we find it working in later times, the Assembly met four times regularly in each prytany, and, when necessary, extraordinary meetings were held.

[2] It is convenient to observe that the first year of a Cleisthenic quinquennium begins always in a year B.C. ending in 3 or 8 (503, 498, 493 B.C., etc.).

Pentacosiomedimni ; but the two lower classes were still excluded
from the archonship ; the third class remained ineligible for another *[Till* **458-7**
half-century. But this conservatism of Cleisthenes might be easily *B.C.]*
misjudged. We must remember that since the days of Solon time
itself had been doing the work of a democratic reformer. The
money value of five hundred medimni was a much lower rating at
the end than it had been at the beginning of the sixth century.
Trade had increased and people had grown richer.

     The new tribes of Cleisthenes led to a change in the military *Military*
organisation. Each of the ten tribes was required to supply a *reforms.*
regiment of hoplites and a squadron of horsemen ; and the hoplites
were commanded by ten generals [1] whom the people elected from *Ten*
each tribe. The office of general was destined hereafter to become *generals.*
the most important in the state ; but at first he was merely the commander of the tribal regiment.

     The Athenian Council instituted by Cleisthenes shows that *The*
Greek statesmen understood the principle of representative govern- *Council a*
ment. That Council is an excellent example of representation with *popular*
a careful distribution of seats according to the size of the electorates ; *representa-*
and it was practically the governing body of the state. But though *tive body.*
Greek statesmen understood the principle, they always hesitated to
entrust to a representative assembly sovereign powers of legislation.
The reason mainly lay in the fact that, owing to the small size of the
city-state, an Assembly which every citizen who chose could attend
was a practicable institution ; and the fundamental principle, that
supreme legislative power is exercised by the people itself, could be
literally applied. But while we remember that the Council could not
legislate, although its co-operation was indispensable to the making
of laws, we may say that its function will be misunderstood if it be
either conceived as a sort of Second Chamber or compared to a body
like the Roman Senate. It was a popular representative assembly,
and from it were taken (though on a totally different principle) committees which performed in part the administrative functions of our
" Government." It had a decisive influence on legislation ; and here
the influence of the Council on the Ecclesia must be rather compared
to the influence of the Government on our House of Commons. But
the ratification given by the Assembly to the proposals sent down by
the Council was often as purely formal as the ratification by the
Crown of bills passed in Parliament. [The Areopagus still retained
important powers but, as most of its members had been the nominees
of the tyrants, its prestige was temporarily weakened.]

---

   [1] The office of stratêgos, as commander of a τάξις, was much older; but the
institution of the ten stratêgoi (501 B.C.) was a consequence of the reforms of
Cleisthenes.

Sect. 7. First Victories of the Democracy

The Athenian republic had now become a democracy in a fuller sense, and the new government was hardly established before it was called upon to prove its capacity. King Cleomenes, who was the greatest man in Greece at the time, could not rest without attempting to avenge the humiliation which he had recently endured at the hands of the Athenian people. The man who had pulled down one tyrant now proposed to set up another. Isagoras, who had hitherto aimed at establishing an oligarchy, now, it would seem, came forward as an aspirant to the tyrannis. Cleomenes arranged with the Boeotians and the Chalcidians a joint attack upon Attica. While the Lacedaemonians and their allies invaded from the south, the Boeotians were to come down from Mount Cithaeron, and the men of Chalcis were to cross the Euripus ; the land was to be assailed on three sides at the same moment.

506 B.C. : the Pelo- ponnesians invade Attica,
The Peloponnesian host under the two kings, Cleomenes and Demaratus, passed the isthmus and occupied Eleusis ; and the Athenians marched to the Eleusinian plain. But the peril on this side passed away without a blow. The Corinthians, on second thoughts, disapproved of the expedition, as unjust, and returned to Corinth. At this time Aegina was the most formidable commercial rival of Corinth, and it therefore suited Corinthian interests to encourage the rising power of Aegina's enemy. This action of the Corinthians disconcerted the whole army, and the situation was aggravated by the discord between the Spartan leaders, Cleomenes

and retire.
and Demaratus. In the end the army broke up, and there was nothing left for Cleomenes but to return home. His attempt to thrust a tyranny had been as unsuccessful as his previous attempt to thrust an oligarchy upon Athens. For the second time the Athenian democracy had been saved from Spartan coercion. A hundred years hence, indeed, that coercion was to befall her ;

(404 B.C.)
Cleomenes is the forerunner of Lysander, who will amply avenge him.

Plataea supported by Athens against Thebes.
The Theban leaders of Boeotia had readily concurred in the Spartan plan, for they had a recent cause of offence against Athens. The town of Plataea, on the Boeotian slope of Mount Cithaeron, was determined to retain her independence and hold aloof from the Boeotian league, which was under the supremacy of Thebes. The Plataeans applied in the first instance to Sparta ; but as Sparta was

510-9 B.C.
unwilling to interfere, they sought and obtained the help of Athens. This was the beginning of a long friendship between Athens and Plataea, based on mutual interest. Plataea depended on the support

of Athens to maintain her independence in Boeotia ; while it suited Athens to have a small friendly power on the other side of Cithaeron—a sort of watch-tower against Thebes. The Athenians went to the protection of Plataea, but the threatened conflict was averted by the intervention of Corinth. The Corinthian arbitration *Hysiae* ruled that Boeotian cities which did not wish to join the league *becomes* must not be coerced. But, as they were departing, the Athenians *Athenian.* were treacherously attacked by the Thebans, and, winning a victory, they fixed the river Asopus as the southern boundary of the territory of Thebes. The Athenians acquired, by this expedition, a post in Boeotia itself—the town of Hysiae, on the northern slope of Cithaeron.

On the approach of the Peloponnesian army, the Boeotians had *Athenians* seized Hysiae, and crossing the pass of Cithaeron above it had taken *defeat the* Oenoe on the upper Attic slopes. When Cleomenes and the Pelopon- *Boeotians* nesians retreated, the Athenian army marched northward to check *(506 B.C.),* the knights of Chalcis who were ravaging the northern demes of Attica. The Boeotian forces then withdrew into their own land and moved northwards too, in order to join the Chalcidians. But the Athenians, who must have been generalled by an able polemarch, succeeded in encountering their two foes singly. They intercepted the Boeotians near the straits and won a complete victory. Then they crossed the straits, for the Chalcidians had retired to their island, and fought another battle, no less decisive, with the horse-men of Chalcis. The defeat of the Chalcidians was so crushing that *and the* they were forced to cede to Athens a large part of that rich Lelantine *Chal-* plain whose possession in old days they had disputed so hotly with *cidians.* Eretria. But this was not all. A multitude of Chalcidians and Boeotians had been made prisoners ; they were kept fettered in bitter bondage until their countrymen ransomed them at two minas a man. We cannot withhold our sympathy from the Athenian people if they dealt out hard measure to those whom the Spartan king had so unjustly stirred up against them. The "gloomy iron chains" in which "they quenched the insolence" of their foes were proudly preserved on the Acropolis, and with a tithe of the ransom they dedicated to Athena a bronze chariot.

A portico commemorative of this victory was set up within the *Stoa at* sanctuary of Delphi. "The Athenians dedicated the portico, with *Delphi.* the arms and figureheads which they took from their foes"—so runs the dedicatory inscription found in recent years on a step of the ruined building. It would appear from this that the Athenians cap-tured and destroyed the ships of Chalcis. If the victory had been some twenty years later, Athens would have added them to her own fleet ; but she had not yet come to discern that her true element was the sea.

*Cleruchies
of Chalcis.*
The democracy had not only brilliantly defended itself, but had won a new territory. The richest part of the Chalcidian plain was divided into lots among two thousand Athenian citizens, who transported their homes to the fertile region beyond the straits—probably under the same conditions as the cleruchs of Salamis.

These outsettlers retained all their rights as citizens; they remained members of their demes and tribes. The Salaminians were so near Athens that it was easier for them than for most of the inhabitants of Attica to attend a meeting of the Ecclesia; and the plain of Chalcis was not farther than Sunium from Athens.

*Acquisi-
tion of
Oropus
(which
remains
under
Athens till
412 B.C.).
The land
of the Graes
(see above,
p. 161):
under
Eretria till
some date
subsequent
to Lelan-
tine war,
then
annexed to
Boeotia.*
And not only beyond the sea was new territory acquired, but on the borders of Attica itself. This at least is the only occasion to which we can well assign the annexation of the march district of Oropus, the land of the people who gave to the Hellenic race its European name. It had come under the sway of Eretria, had adopted the Eretrian dialect which it was to retain throughout all future vicissitudes, and was the last part of Boeotia to be annexed by the Boeotian power of Thebes. This fertile little plain was destined to be a constant subject of discord between Boeotia and Athens, as it had before been a source of strife between Eretria and Boeotia; but it was now to remain subject to Athens for nearly a hundred years. Subject to Athens, not Athenian; the men of Oropus, like the men of Eleutherae, never became Athenian citizens.

CHAPTER VI

THE ADVANCE OF PERSIA TO THE AEGEAN

SECT. I. THE RISE OF PERSIA AND THE FALL OF THE LYDIAN KINGDOM

WHILE the Greeks were sailing their own seas, and working out in their city-states the institutions of law and freedom, untroubled by any catastrophe beyond the shores of the Mediterranean, great despotic kingdoms were waxing and waning in the east. In the seventh century, the mighty empire of Assyria was verging to its end ; the power destined to overthrow it had arisen. But the story of Assyria lies outside the story of Greece, since the Greeks, except in one outlying corner, came into no immediate contact with the lords of Nineveh. The Greek, as well as the Phoenician, communities of Cyprus were involved in the fortunes of the Syrian coastland. When in the last quarter of the eighth century *Sargon,* Sargon, under whose sceptre Assyria reached the summit of her *king of* power, had conquered the lands of the sea-coast—the Phoenicians *Assyria,* and the Philistines—seven kings who lived "at a distance of seven 722-705 days in the middle of the western sea" trembled before him and *B.C.* offered their submission. They were the kings of Yatnan, as the Assyrians called Cyprus, and their act of fealty is recorded for us by *The stele of* Sargon himself on a pillar which he set up "in a valley of the land *Sargon (set* of Yatnan." Among the monarchs who submitted there were doubt- *up at* less Greeks as well as Phoenicians, and a generation later we have *Cition),* the names of ten Cypriote kings who were subject to Assarhaddon *709 B.C.* and to Assurbanipal—Assarhaddon the great conqueror who volun- *Cypriote* tarily abdicated his throne, and Assurbanipal the peaceful sovereign, *vassals of* whom the Greeks remembered as Sardanapalus. Among the names *Assar-* of the vassals whom inscriptions of these two kings enumerate are *haddon* those of Eteandros of Paphos and Pylagoras of Cition.[1] But if the *(681-668 B.C.) and Assur- bānipal (c. 668-626 B.C.).*

[1] The other eight are the kings of Idalion, Salamis, Soli, Curion, Tamassus, a Cypriote Carthage (Kartihadaasti), Ledron (near Leucosia), and Nurii (?).

The Medes.

FIG. 72.—Stele of king Sargon at Cition
(Berlin Museum).

story of Assyria touches only a remote fringe of the Hellenic world, it is otherwise with the story of those who destroyed the Assyrian empire. The Medes and Persians, folks of Aryan speech like the Greeks, were marked out by destiny to be the adversaries of the Greeks throughout the two chief centuries of Grecian history.

The land of Media lies east of Assyria. Its ancient history is shrouded in mist; but there are some reasons for guessing that in the second millennium it was part of a great Aryan kingdom which stretched far north-eastwards over the plains of Bactria, peopled by the Iranian branch, as it is called, of the Aryan stock. The Iranians worshipped the same gods of heaven and light as the other folks of their kindred; but their sun-worship developed into a very different shape from the religion of Zeus. They regarded the element of fire with deeper reverence than other sun-worshippers; they dreaded to pollute it by the touch of a dead body or the overflow of boiling water; their land was full of temples with altars of perpetual fire. But the religion of the fire-worshippers had been moulded into an almost philosophical form by their prophet Zoroaster, who, though his name is encompassed with legend and it is uncertain when he lived, was assuredly a real man and not a creation of myth. He diffused among the Iranians the doctrine that the world is the perpetual scene of a deadly strife between the powers of light and darkness, between Ormuzd, the Great Lord, and Ahriman, the principle of evil.

It was towards the .end of the eighth century that the Medes *Deioces* rebelled against the yoke of Assyria. They were led by Deioces, *(Da-* and after a struggle Media gained her independence, and the deliverer *yaukku)* was elected king by the free vote of his people. He had not only *founds* freed but had united his countrymen, and he set the seal on the *kingdom of* union of Media by building the great city of Ecbatana. His treasury *Media, c.* and palace were in the centre of a fortress girdled by seven walls; *700 B.C.* and he is said to have lived in this stronghold, withdrawn from the sight of his people, who could approach him only by written petitions.

The first successors of Deioces had enough to do in resisting the *Phraortes* efforts of Assyria to recover her power over Media. But presently *(c. 650-25* a king arose who was strong enough to extend his sway beyond the *B.C.) con-* borders of his own land. Phraortes conquered the hilly land of *quers* Persia in the south; and thus a large Aryan realm was formed *Persia.* stretching from the Caspian to the Persian Gulf, east of Assyria and Babylonia. The next step was to conquer Assyria itself; and Cyaxares, the successor of Phraortes, prepared for the enterprise by a new organisation of the Median army. It was no hopeless task, for the Assyrian empire had been breaking up. Egypt had thrown *New* off the yoke of the kings of Nineveh; and Nabopolassar had just *kingdom of* arisen to do for Babylonia what Deioces had done for Media. Nabo- *Babylonia.* polassar and Cyaxares joined hands; and the united forces of Media *Nabo-* and Babylonia defeated the Assyrian army. The conquerors divided *polassar,* the empire. The south-western portion up to the borders of Egypt went *625-605.* to Babylonia; Assyria itself and the lands stretching westward into *Fall of* Asia Minor were annexed to Media. *Nineveh,* *612 B.C.*

The restored kingdom of Babylonia, under Nebucadnezar, the *Babylonia* successor of its founder, rose into wonderful fame and brilliance. *under* He drove the Egyptians out of Syria, smiting them in the great *Nebucad-* battle of Carchemish; he stormed Jerusalem and carried the Jews *nezar, 604-* into captivity; he made Tyre on its rock tremble though he failed *562 B.C.* to take it; he invaded and overran Egypt. But more famous than his conquests abroad were his mighty works in his own land. He made Babylon the greatest city in the world; and the stray Greeks who visited it came back with amazing stories of the palaces and temples, and the "hanging gardens," a terraced park which was constructed by Nebucadnezar, though report ascribed it to the mythical queen Semiramis. But the gigantic walls which girt the city were the mightiest monument of Nebucadnezar; Greek travellers said that the circuit was more than fifty miles. It seems certain that few men have done more than this lord of Babylon to increase the sum of human misery, if we imagine the lives of countless thralls forced under the pitiless lash to spend their flesh and blood in unceasing and unsparing labour. Nebucadnezar went down to his grave, full of honours, after a long reign. He knew well on what side danger was to be feared for his kingdom. One of his works of fortification was a wall from the Tigris to the Euphrates, north of Babylon, to defend Babylonia against Media, her northern neighbour.

The exploits of the great Babylonian king affected Greece little.[1] The Greeks of Cyprus must have caught the echoes of the clash of arms at Carchemish; they must have been stirred by the tidings of the storming of Jerusalem and excited by the siege of Tyre. But the changes which had befallen the east were brought nearer to the ken of Greece by the advance of Media. Cyaxares drew under his power the eastern parts of Asia Minor as far as the banks of the Halys, and this river became the boundary between Media and Lydia. The conquest of Lydia was the next aim in the expansion of the Median *War of* power, and a pretext was found for declaring war. In the sixth *Lydia and* year of the war a battle was fought, but in the midst of the *Media:* combat the day was turned suddenly to night; and the darkening of *battle:* the sun made such a deep impression on the minds of the combatants *eclipse* that they laid down their arms and a peace was concluded. But the *of sun,* solar obscuration of this May day has another association which has *May 28,* a deeper interest for Europe than the warfare of Lydian and Mede. *585 B.C.,* It was the first eclipse of which European science foretold when it *predicted* should betide. Thales of Miletus, the father of Greek, and thereby *by Thales.* of European, philosophy and science, had studied astronomy in Egypt; and he was able to warn the Ionians that before such a year had passed—his lore could not tell the day or the hour—the sun *Beginnings* would be darkened. Thales was not only the first man of science; *of Greek* he was also the first philosopher: science and philosophy were not *science and* yet separated. If he looks over the ages to Copernicus, Newton, *philosophy.* and Laplace, he looks likewise to Descartes, Berkeley, and Kant. He sought for a common substance, a single principle which should explain the variety of nature and reduce the world to unity and system; it is a small matter that he found this principle in water;[2] it is his eternal merit to have sought it.

[1] Greek mercenaries, indeed, took service under him, including the brother of the poet Alcaeus.

[2] Yet not so small. It was much to have fixed on fluid substance, and rejected the vulgar fallacy of ascribing to hardness a greater reality.

The Lydian king Alyattes wedded his daughter to Astyages, who succeeded to the throne of Media, and the kingdom of Lydia was saved for a generation, to enjoy the most brilliant period of its history.   When Lydia recovered from the Cimmerian invasion, king *Reign of* Ardys renewed the efforts of Gyges to reduce the Greek cities of the *Ardys in* coast.   His chief success seems to have been the capture of Priene. *Lydia;* His successors, Sadyattes and Alyattes, carried on a weary war against Miletus.   They harried the Milesian territory every year, destroying the corn crops, and defeated the Milesians in two battles ; but the strong walls of the coast-city defied them, as they had no fleet.   At length Alyattes made peace with Miletus ; possibly it was *of Alyattes.* the outbreak of the war with Media that forced him to this step.   At all events, he seems to have behaved liberally to his foes.   He built two temples to Athena in the place of one which had been burned down when he was devastating the Milesian land.   This act of reparation was quite in accordance with the reverence for the gods of Greece which the Lydian monarchs invariably displayed.   The story is that, when Alyattes fell ill and consulted Apollo at Delphi, the oracle enjoined upon him to restore the temple.   Ionian Miletus was saved, but the famous Achaean city of Smyrna was not only captured but destroyed, and in this volume its name will occur no more. Alyattes also conquered Bithynia, and drove the remnant of the Cimmerians out of Asia.   He might think that Lydia would now take rank with one of the great monarchies of the south or the east, and he built himself an enormous sepulchre, an earth-mound on stone foundations, which in size at least might match the monuments of Egyptian or Babylonian kings.

It was reserved for Croesus, the son of Alyattes, to carry out *Reign of* fully the design of subjugating the cities of Eastern Greece.   He *Croesus,* attacked and subdued the cities, Ionian and Aeolian, one after *560-546* another, all except Miletus, whose treaty with his father he respected, *B.C.* while Miletus on her part saved her freedom by withholding all help from her sister cities.   The Dorian states of Caria were also forced to submit, and the empire of Croesus extended from the Halys to the Aegean.   We saw before that Lydia exercised a distinct influence on the Greeks of Asia, but perhaps their influence upon her was even greater.   The Greek language spread in Lydia, and we may suspect that it was heard in Sardis as much as the native idiom ; the Greek gods were revered ; the Greek oracles were appealed to.   The kings were benefactors of Hellenic sanctuaries.   In the new temple of Artemis, which arose at Ephesus during his reign, Croesus was the donor of the sculptured reliefs which encircled the Ionic pillars, and fragments of the three words, which recorded the gift "Dedicated by King Croesus," can still be read on the bases of the columns.   Hence the

FIG. 73.—Ivory Priest and Priestess, from the Temple of Artemis
at Ephesus, *c.* 600 B.C.

Greeks never regarded the Lydians as utter barbarians; and they always cherished a curious indulgence and sympathy for Croesus, though he had enslaved and ruled as despot the cities of Asiatic Hellas.   The court of Sardis was in truth more oriental than Hellenic, not only in wealth and luxury, but also in its customs, for instance, polygamy and the infliction of cruel punishments. Croesus carded alive a man who had opposed his succession to the throne.   The Ionians had marvelled at the treasures of golden Gyges, but the untold wealth of Croesus became proverbial.   It was furnished largely by the tributes of the Greek cities, as well as by the white gold of the Pactolus and the products of the mines of Pergamon.   Croesus was the first to introduce, instead of the white gold money, a coinage of two metals, pure gold and silver, bearing to each other the fixed proportion of 3 to 40.

There is no more striking proof of the political importance of *Croesus* the oracle of Delphi at this period than the golden offerings dedicated *and* by Croesus, offerings richer than even the priestly avarice of the *Delphi.* Delphians could have dared to hope for.   Wealthy though the lord of Lydia was, genuine as was his faith in the inspiration of the oracle, he might hardly have sent such gifts if he had not wished to secure the political support of Apollo and believed that Apollo's support was worth securing.   His object was to naturalise himself as a member of the Greek world; to appear, not as an outsider, but as an adopted son of Hellas, ruling over the Greeks whom he had subdued and those whom he still hoped to subdue.   Nothing would be more helpful than the good word of the Delphic oracle to compass such a reputation.   Moreover, if one of the Asiatic cities contemplated rebellion, a discouraging reply from the oracle, which would assuredly be consulted, might stand the despot in good stead.

Having extended his sway to the coast, Croesus conceived the idea of making Lydia a sea-power and conquering the islands.   It was a perfectly feasible plan; and it was not till unforeseen events had frustrated it that the islanders could have found much comfort in the epigram that a Lydian king sailing against them with a fleet would be like themselves advancing against Lydia with a host of cavalry.   The tale afterwards shaped itself that one of the wise men of Greece—it mattered little whether he was alive at the time or not —used this witticism to dissuade Croesus from the enterprise.   But Croesus was diverted from his western designs by something graver than an epigram.   Events of great moment were happening in the *Fall* east.   His brother-in-law Astyages was hurled from the throne of *of Median* Media by a hero, who was to become one of the world's mightiest *Dynasty.* conquerors.   The usurper was Cyrus the Great, of the Persian family *Cyrus.* of the Achaemenids.   The revolution signified indeed little more

[margin note:] See Dio- Sio. IX. 25 Herodotus I. 27

than a change of dynasty ; the Persians and Medes were peoples of the same race and the same faith ; the realm remained Iranian as before. But the Persians seem to have been the noblest part of the Iranian race ; their bravery, temperance, and love of truth extorted the admiration of the Greeks.

The fall of Astyages was an opportunity for the ambitious Lydian to turn his arms to the east. The restoration of his brother-in-law was indeed a sufficient plea ; and he might have good cause to fear that if he were not the first to strike, the Persian usurper would soon advance to the conquest of Lesser Asia. But Croesus certainly cherished hopes of extending the Lydian power into the interior parts of Asia, if not of succeeding himself to the Median throne. In undertaking such an enterprise he had to fear his Greek subjects, who might take advantage of his absence to throw off his yoke, and might even intrigue with the Persian. That the Greeks of Ionia had been long accustomed to regard Media as a resort against Lydia and to intrigue with the Median kings is shown by the word *medism*. For if such intriguing had first come into fashion after the rise of Persia and the fall of Lydia, the name chosen to designate it would naturally have been *persism*. Desirous of probing the hidden event of the future, Croesus consulted some of the oracles of Greece. There can be no question that the Delphic god gave him an answer which was meant to encourage him in his enterprise. It is said that the answer was that if he crossed the Halys he would destroy a mighty empire—an answer which need not have been that which was actually given, but may have been circulated afterwards to justify the oracle when the expedition failed. But it is the policy of the oracle, not its methods of evasion, which has historical significance. The spirit of Delphi was favourable to Hellenic freedom, and it saw in the proposed expedition the probability of a long war with Persia and a chance for the eastern Greeks of retaining their independence. It did not foresee the complete conquest of Lydia and the subjection of the Greeks to a power which was utterly barbarian. The oracle took the occasion, however, to bring about a union between Croesus and the Lacedaemonians, by bidding him seek the aid of the most powerful state of Greece. An alliance was concluded, but led to nothing, and Lacedaemon sent no help. [Egypt and Babylon, who could not afford to see the balance of power destroyed, joined the alliance but events moved too swiftly for them.]

Croesus, at the head of an army which included a force of Ionian Greeks, crossed the fateful Halys and invaded Cappadocia. He took the ancient city of Pteria, and in its neighbourhood fought an indecisive battle with the host of Medes and Persians which Cyrus had led against him. But the host of Cyrus seems to have been far

Policy of Delphi.

Diod. Sic. ix. 31

For another version see Diod. Sic. ix. 32

superior in numbers, and Croesus retired before him into Lydia. Under the walls of the capital the invader won a decisive victory, *Capture of* and after a short siege Sardis was stormed and plundered.   The life *Sardis,* of Croesus was spared.   Cyrus had given strict injunctions that he 546 *B.C.* was on no account to be slain in the struggle of the capture ; and the story went that a soldier, not recognising him, was about to cut him down, when the king's son, who had been dumb from birth, suddenly burst out into speech : " O man, slay not Croesus."

This was not the only tale which adorned the fall of the Lydian king.   The capture of Sardis was an eventuality of which no one had seriously thought.   So great had been the wealth and might of Croesus, so dizzy the height of his power, that none deemed his overthrow possible ; and the sheer and sudden fall into nothingness made perhaps a deeper and more abiding impression on the imagination of Hellas than any other historical event.   It was the most illustrious example that the Greeks had ever witnessed of their favourite doctrine that the gods visit with jealousy men who enjoy too great prosperity.   And the personality of Croesus himself crept into their sympathies—the admirer of Hellenic art and wisdom, the adorer of Hellenic gods, the generous giver out of his abundant wealth.   Never more than for the memory of Croesus did Greece put forth the power of that genius, which she possessed in such full measure, of weaving round an event of history tales which have a deep and touching import as lessons for the life of men.

Cyrus built a great pyre—so the story is told by Herodotus—and *Story of* placed thereon Croesus bound in chains, with fourteen Lydian boys. *Croesus* And as Croesus was standing on the pile, in this extreme pass, there *and Solon* came into his mind a word which Solon had said to him, that no *Diod. J.* man could be called happy so long as he was alive.   For the Athenian *IX. 2, 27* statesman had visited the court of Sardis in his travels—the art of the tale-weaver had no precise regard for the facts of time—and when he had seen the royal treasures and the greatness of the kingdom Croesus asked him whom he deemed the happiest of men.   Solon named some obscure Greeks who were dead ; and when the king, unable to hide his wonder and vexation, exclaimed, " Is our royal fortune so poor, O Athenian stranger, that you set private men before me ? " the wise Greek had discoursed on the uncertainty of life and the jealousy of the gods.   Then Croesus, remembering this, groaned aloud and called thrice on the name of Solon.   But Cyrus heard him call, and bade the interpreters ask him on whom he was calling.   For a while Croesus would not speak, then he said : " One whom I would that all tyrants might meet and converse with."   Pressed further he named Solon the Athenian, and repeated the wise man's words.   The pyre was already alight, but when Cyrus heard the answer of his prisoner he reflected that he too was a man, and he commanded that the fire should be quenched and the victims set free. The flames were already blazing so strong and high that the men could not quench them. Then Croesus cried to Apollo for help, and the god sent

Fig. 74.—Croesus on the pyre (Attic vase).

clouds into the clear sky, and a tempestuous shower of rain extinguished the fire.

Such is the tale as we read it in the history of Herodotus, who may have heard it at Athens. But we can almost see the story in the making. For, before the episode of Solon was woven in, the fate of Croesus had been wrought into a legend; this legend is related in a poem of Bacchylides. When the day of doom surprised the king, "he would not abide to endure the bitterness of bondage,

The story of the fate of Croesus, as told by Bacchylides.

but he raised a pyre before the palace court, and gat him up thereon with his wife and his weeping daughters. He bade the slippered thrall kindle the timber building ; the maidens screamed, and stretched their arms to their mother. But as the might of the fire was springing through the wood, Zeus set a sable cloud above it and quenched the yellow flame. Then Apollo bore the old man with his daughters to the land of the Hyperboreans, to be his abiding place, for his piety's sake, because his gifts to Pytho were greater than all men's gifts." The moral of the tale clearly was, Bring gifts to Delphi ; and we can hardly doubt that it originated under Delphic influence. But in the city of Solon it was transformed by a touch of genius into one of the great stories of the world.

As for Croesus it is probable that his life was spared, and it is possible that he spent his remaining days in Media, unconscious that a mythical association with the famous Athenian lawgiver would be his best assured claim on the memory of future ages. *Fate of Croesus.*

SECT. 2. THE PERSIAN CONQUEST OF ASIATIC GREECE

The kingdom of Lydia had performed a certain function in the development of Greece. Besides the invention of coinage, which was its one great contribution to the civilisation of mankind ; besides the influence which its luxury and "tyranny" exercised on Ionia ; the mere existence of the Lydian realm, in its intermediate position between Greece and the east, was of considerable importance as a bulwark against the great oriental empires. It kept Greece from coming into direct contact with the empire of Assyria ; it kept Greece for sixty years from coming into direct contact with the empire of Media. When the barrier is swept away, a new period is opened in Grecian history. The Greeks now stand face to face with the power of a monarch whose dominion stretches far away beyond the Euphrates, beyond the Tigris, into lands which are totally unknown to them. The Asiatic Greeks are now to exchange subjection to a lord of Sardis for subjection to a potentate who holds his court in a city so distant that the length of the journey is told by months. This distance of the centre from the extremities of the empire was of the utmost significance. The king was obliged to leave his conquests in Asia Minor to the government of his satraps ; and the Greeks were unable to exercise any influence upon him, as they might have done if he had ruled from Sardis or some nearer capital. This was all the more unfortunate, on account of another difference which distinguished the Persian from the Lydian kingdom. While the Lydians were outside the Aryan family, the Persians and Medes spoke a language of the same stock as that of the Greeks. It may be

I

thought that if the Persians had come under Greek influence, Iranian history would have taken a different course. For the Persians were a people marked out to fall under the influence of others and not to hew an independent path for themselves. In their own highlands, like the Spartans in the Laconian vale, they might live unspotted from the world, a valiant, simple, and truthful race; but when they once went forth to conquer and to rule, it was their inevitable doom to be led captive by their captives and to adopt the manners and ideals of more intellectual and original peoples. If Cyrus had transported the centre of his empire to the west, the Greeks might have been the teachers of their Persian speech-fellows; but such an idea would have occurred to no Mede or Persian. Consequently the new Iranian kingdom fell under the relaxing influences of the corrupt Semitic civilisations of Babylonia and Assyria; and it had soon become a despotism so typically oriental that it is hard to remember that the ruling peoples spoke a tongue akin to the Greek. Hence the struggle of two hundred years, upon which we are now entering, between Greece and Persia, though strictly and literally it was a struggle between Aryan peoples,—peoples, that is, of Aryan speech,—assumes the larger character of strife between Europe and Asia, between east and west, between Aryan and non-Aryan; and takes its place as the first encounter in that still unclosed debate which has arrayed Europe successively against Babylonian, Phoenician, Saracen, and Turk.

Disunion of Ionia. At the beginning of the campaign against Lydia, Cyrus had invited the Ionians who were in the army of Croesus to change sides. They had refused to " medize," not perhaps from loyalty to the rule of the Lydian, under which they chafed, but because they did not anticipate his utter overthrow and therefore feared his vengeance. This refusal annoyed Cyrus; and when, after the fall of Sardis, the Greek cities made overtures to the conqueror, he declined to make any conditions. Only with Miletus, which had not been subject to Lydia and had stood aloof from the contest, did he conclude a sort of treaty like that in which Croesus had recognised her independence. The others prepared to defend themselves. Cyrus himself had greater projects which recalled him to the far east; and he committed the lesser task of reducing the Asiatic Greeks to the lieutenants whom he left in Lydia. The want of unity among the Ionians was disastrous. They might meet in their Panionic assembly, but they seem to have been without the ability or the organisation to carry out any plan of common action. The most powerful of all the states, Miletus had gone her own path and stood quite apart. One of her citizens, Thales, the astronomer and philosopher, whom we have met before, is said to have ventured himself into the speculations of political, as well as of celestial, science.   He saw the weakness of Ionia in its disunion, and the futility of the loose league of the Panionion ; and he made the remarkable proposal that Ionia should form itself into an united nation, with one Hall of Council as well as one place of Assembly, each city surrendering her sovereignty and becoming merely a town or deme of the state ; and he suggested Teos as the fitting place for the capital.   The idea, whether it was put forward by Thales or not, was assuredly suggested by the political development of Attica, the mother country of the Ionians.   It was an idea which the proposer can hardly have hoped to persuade the Ionians to adopt, but it had its value as a comment on the disunion of the Greeks in the one part of Greece where, above all others, there was needed a closer unity and a solid serried front, to resist the aggression of the great barbarian powers.   Another proposal, which was made in one of the ineffectual meetings of the Panionion, receives the approval of the historian Herodotus.   Bias, a statesman of Priene, advised all the Ionians to sail forth together to the west, to the great island of Sardinia, and there found an Ionian city-state, and live happy and free.   This proposal illustrates the terror and despair of Ionia at the prospect of Persian rule.

Disunited, the Asiatic Greeks were an easy prey.   Harpagus, the *Persian* general of Cyrus, reduced them one after another ; tribute was im- *conquest of* posed upon them and the burden of serving in the Persian armies, *Greeks of* when such service was required ; but no restrictions were placed *Asia.* upon the freedom of their commerce.   To the inhabitants of two cities, exile seemed more endurable than this new slavery and they acted in the spirit of Bias.   The people of Phocaea, or the more part of them, embarked in their penteconters and sailed to the island of Corsica, where their own settlement of Alalia received them.   The Teians did likewise, but found a nearer home on the coast of Thrace, where they founded Abdera.

One common effort indeed the Aeolians and Ionians made for *Asiatic* their defence.   They made a common appeal to the most powerful *Greeks* state in the mother country.   They sent an embassy to Lacedaemon, *appeal to* but the Spartans, whose horizon was bounded by the Peloponnesus, *Sparta.* did as little for them as they had done for Croesus.   Sparta had the curiosity, however, to send a ship to Ionia, to spy out the condition of the country and the power of Cyrus.   The story is that one of her reconnoitrers went up to Sardis and standing before the Persian king forbade him to work harm to any Greek community, "since the Lacedaemonians will not permit it."   The anecdote was doubtless invented by those who liked a jest at the expense of Sparta ; but, if Cyrus might well ask "who are the Lacedaemonians?" his successors learned the answer to their cost.

Fall of Babylon, 538.

The conqueror of Lydia returned to the east to subdue the mightier power of Babylon. The conquest occupied some years; then the greatest city on earth was taken; and Cyrus took to himself the title of "king of Babel, Sumer, and Accad, and of the four quarters of the world," thus formally entering into the Babylonian inheritance. The dominion of Cyrus the Great extended in the east over Armenia and Hyrcania, Parthia and Bactria, and into the midst of Afghanistan; from the coasts of the Aegean to the banks of the Jaxartes. But his conquests lie outside our history. His last enterprise was the subjugation of the Massagetae, a Scythian folk near the

Death of Cyrus.

Aral lake, and one story says that he was slain in battle against them, and that the savage queen placed his head in a basin of blood. All we know with certainty is that his body was buried in Persia, and two hundred years hence we shall visit his tomb at Pasargadae, in the company of a conqueror who was mightier even than he.

SECT. 3. PERSIAN CONQUEST OF EGYPT. POLYCRATES OF SAMOS

The subjugation of Lydia and the Greek sea-board carried the borders of the Iranian empire, under its new dynasty, farther westward than the Assyrian conquest had ever reached. Two lords of Sardis had indeed acknowledged the overlordship of the kings of Nineveh; but that relation had been of brief duration and slight significance, and Lydia can hardly be said to have ever formed a part of the Assyrian dominion. In subduing the Greeks of the coast, at all events, Cyrus broke entirely new ground; they had never paid submission in any shape to Assyria. But while he far outpassed the utmost limits of Assyria in some directions, he left unconquered the great kingdom of the south, which had once been part of the

Persian conquest of Egypt by Cambyses.

Assyrian empire. But his son Cambyses repaired the omission; it was inevitable that the new lords of Syria should seek to bring Egypt under their subjection. We saw how Egypt, like Media itself and Babylonia, threw off the Assyrian yoke and entered upon a new

Amasis (Aahmes), 569 B.C.;

period of national prosperity under enlightened rulers. King Amasis who climbed the throne by a revolution maintained his power by a bodyguard of Ionian and Carian mercenaries, like a Greek tyrant. An Egyptian writing tells us how he loved the strong "wine of Kelebi of Egypt." He built great temples to the Egyptian gods like

a phil-Hellene.

the Pharaohs of old; but in his patronage of Greece he may be compared to Croesus. He sent gifts to the Greek sanctuaries; he subscribed generously to the rebuilding of the temple at Delphi; he married a Greek princess of Cyrene; under him Naucratis rose to

Naucratis.

the rank of a city, though the only city where Greeks were allowed to trade. He had extended his sway over the island of Cyprus when the power of Babylonia was declining; but the Cypriots threw off his yoke when Cyrus entered into the Babylonian heritage, and made their submission to the Persian. Amasis trembled at the *Death of* rise of the new power in the east, and he lived to witness with dis- *Amasis,* may the preparations of Cambyses; but he died a few months before *525 B.C.* the invasion, and the blow fell upon his son, Psammetichus. A *(Psam-* fierce battle near Pelusium delivered Egypt into the hands of the *metichus* Persians. The conqueror led his army up the Nile, and perhaps he *III.)* extended the southern frontier of the Egyptian kingdom on the side *Battle of* of Nubia. The Egyptians said that he planned the conquest of all *525 B.C.* Ethiopia and was compelled to return through want of provisions, so *Ethiopian* that his enterprise came to nothing. But the Egyptians hated Cam- *expedi-* byses, who openly scoffed at their religion; and it is possible that *tion of* they may have represented as an inglorious failure what was really a *Cambyses.* successful effort to secure the southern frontier. The conquest of *Voluntary* Egypt, which became a Persian satrapy, led to the submission of *submission* Greek Cyrene, even as the conquest of Lydia had led to the sub- *of Cyrene.* jection of the Greeks of the neighbouring coasts.

Amasis and his son might have hoped, when the Persian danger *Polycrates* threatened, that they could depend on the support of a powerful *tyrant of* Greek friend, the lord of Samos. In that island, *Samos.* not long after the Persian conquest of Ionia, a certain Polycrates and his two brothers had estab- lished a joint tyranny over the state, with the help of Lygdamis of Naxos. But Polycrates removed his brothers by death and banishment and became sole tyrant. He organised a fleet of a hundred pente- conters and made Samos a strong power; as the FIG. 75.—Early Ionian mainland had fallen under Persian dominion, Coin of Samos he had perhaps the strongest Greek sea-power in the (obverse). Part Aegean and with it controlled the important religious of a bull. centre of Delos. His luxurious court was brightened by the presence of the Bacchic poet Anacreon. He completed the building of the great temple of Hera, but the most famous of his works was the aqueduct which supplied the city with water from a spring beyond a hill. The engineering skill of the Megarian architect Eupalinus —who perhaps also constructed the waterworks of Pisistratus at Athens—carried the duct through the hill by a tunnel. In all that he put his hand to, Polycrates prospered; he defied the power of Persia; he extended his influence over some of the Ionian cities under Persian sway. It was natural that he and Amasis of Egypt should form a close alliance, based on the common interest of antagonism to Persia. But when the hour of peril came, when Cambyses moved upon Egypt, the Samian tyrant altered his policy. He felt that his *526 B.C.*

navy was unequal to coping with the joint armaments of Phoenicia and Cyprus, and, instead of coming to the aid of his old friend's son, he sent forty ships to increase the fleet of the invader. These ships, however, never reached Egypt. The tyrant had manned them with those Samians whom he most suspected of hating himself and his tyranny; but his trick recoiled. At the island of Carpathus the crew took the resolve of sailing back to Samos and overthrowing the despot. Defeated in a battle they sought the aid of Sparta, and their appeal was strongly backed by the Corinthians, whose trade *Spartan* probably suffered from the pirate ships of Polycrates. The Lace-*attack on* daemonians sent an armament to besiege Samos; it was their first *Samos.* expedition to the east, and it was a failure. Despairing of taking the city, and repulsed in a conflict, they returned home.

We cannot charge Polycrates with perfidy in espousing the cause of Persia against Egypt, since we are ignorant of his relations, not only with Psammetichus, but with Amasis in the last years of *Story of* that monarch's reign. We might indeed gather from the story of *the ring of* the ring of Polycrates, that the alliance had ceased to exist, and that *Polycrates.* it was Amasis who had broken it off. Amasis hearing of his friend's marvellous prosperity, never varied by a reverse, wrote him a letter, expressing misgivings at a good fortune so great and enduring that it could not fail to draw down the envy of heaven, and counselling Polycrates to cast away whatever possession it would give him the most pain to lose: "Cast it away utterly, out of the world." Poly-crates, taking the words to heart, manned a penteconter, and having rowed out to sea, cast into the waves the most precious thing he had, an emerald ring engraved by the gem-cutter Theodorus. A few days later a fisherman came to his house and presented him with a huge fish; the ring was found inside it. Polycrates wrote to Amasis an account of what had happened, and Amasis, when he read the letter, discerned that it was impossible for any man to deliver another from that which was destined to befall him. Convinced therefore that Polycrates would come to no good end, and not wishing to have to grieve for a friend's misfortune, Amasis broke off the tie of guest-friendship which bound them. The forecast of the Egyptian was *Death of* fulfilled. Soon after his repulse of the Lacedaemonian attack, *Polycrates,* Polycrates fell into a trap laid for him by the Persian satrap of *c. 523 B.C.* Sardis, and was seized and crucified.

SECT. 4. IONIA UNDER DARIUS

Death of King Cambyses was recalled from Egypt by a rebellion. He *Cambyses,* had put to death, on suspicions of disloyalty, his brother Smerdis, to *522 B.C.* whom he had entrusted the regency of some of the eastern provinces;

and a usurper had arisen, pretending to be the dead Smerdis, to whom he bore a remarkable likeness. Cambyses went in haste to crush the false Smerdis. But, as he passed through Syria, he "found death by his own hand," as is related in a great writing on the rock of Behistun. The next heir to the Persian throne was a *Accession* certain Hystaspes, who was satrap of Parthia and had a son named *of Darius* Darius. But Hystaspes made no attempt to secure his right, and *(Dârajava* the false Smerdis established himself so firmly that, as Darius wrote *huš), 521* afterwards in that famous inscription of the rock, "No Persian nor *B.C.* Mede dared to oppose him."   But Darius had different thoughts from his father ; and conspiring with six nobles he killed the usurper and became king himself. In the first years of his reign his force and ability were proved in the task of quelling rebellions which broke out in almost all parts of the wide realm which Cyrus had put together. Elam, Babylonia, Media, Armenia revolted ; a new false *(Babylon* Smerdis arose ; Babylon had to be twice besieged. Having *taken,* established his power firmly and crushed all resistance, Darius *(1) Feb.* recorded for future ages the hardly won successes of his first years, *520 B.C.,* in an inscription on the lofty rock of Behistun on the upper course of *(2) 519* the river Choaspes. The writing is in the Persian, the Susic, and *Inscription* the Babylonian languages. *of Bagistan.*

By wedding Atossa, the daughter of Cyrus and widow of her *Atossa.* brother Cambyses, Darius linked himself closely to the family of his predecessors. He proceeded to reorganise the administration of his dominion. He extended the system of satrapies or governments, and the whole realm was divided into twenty such satrapies. West *Western* of the Halys, the old kingdom of Lydia consisted of three provinces, *satrapies :* but subject to two satraps : the Ionian and the Lydian under one *1. (a)* governor who resided at Sardis ; the Phrygian which included the *Ionian,* Greek cities of the Propontis under a governor whose seat was at *(b) Lydian,* Dascylion. These satraps did not interfere in the local affairs of *2. Phry-* the Greek cities, which were ruled by despots ; and the despots might *gian.* do much as they pleased, so long as they paid tribute duly and *Tyrants* furnished military contingents when required. The despots liked the *under* Persian rule which secured their power, and this explains the note- *Persian* worthy fact that the Greeks of Asia Minor made no attempt to shake *rule.* off the Persian yoke during the troubles which ushered in the reign of Darius. It is possible too that their condition under the rule of Cambyses was better than under Darius ; for Darius is said to have instituted a fixed yearly tribute instead of irregular contributions. Commerce, however, was furthered by this king's monetary reforms, and by his improvement of the road-system in Persia. He adopted the bimetallic coinage which Croesus had introduced in Lydia ; the chief piece of Persian gold money was always known in Greece by

The Royal
Road. the name *daric.* The Royal Road, by which the messengers between Susa and Sardis came and went, was divided into stages marked off by regular stations. Its length was over 1500 miles, and the way was counted a three months' journey for a man on foot. A Greek who had to visit Susa would land at Ephesus, and in three days reach Sardis. The road ran through the heart of Phrygia, by the tomb of Midas the golden king, past Pessinus and Ancyra and across the Halys to Pteria the ancient Cappadocian city which Croesus took, then across the Halys again, southward to Mazaka and Comana, to cross the Taurus and reach the Euphrates at Samosata. Beyond the Euphrates, it skirted the mountains which bound Mesopotamia on the north, passing Nisibis and reaching the Tigris at Nineveh, the ruined capital of Assyria. Beyond Arbela, it went south-eastward to the river Choaspes and Susa. A good and safe road, carefully maintained, brought central Asia nearer to the Aegean, and helped to open the east to western curiosity. The construction of the Royal Road must have had an incalculable effect in widening Greek ideas of geography. Its influence is shown by the importance which it assumed on the first Greek maps. Conceived as a straight line

Early
maps.
running east and west, it plays on one of the maps which were used by Herodotus practically the same part which is played in the modern Atlas by the Equator. The longitudes were determined by the conception that the Nile and the Danube, the two greatest rivers known within the range of the Greek world, were in the same meridian—the Danube being supposed to flow from north to south. This meridian line passed through Sinope. It was a principle of the early Greek geographers who arose about the end of the sixth century in Ionia that the features of the earth were symmetrically arranged. The attempt to apply mathematical principles to a small portion of the earth, very imperfectly observed, necessarily produced maps which to our fuller knowledge appear grotesque. But it would be hard to overestimate the intellectual activity of the Ionian investigators who made the new departure, Anaximander and

Anaxi-
mander.
Hecataeus, both citizens of Miletus. Anaximander constructed the first map, and Hecataeus wrote a Geography which served as a "text to Anaximander's map." Hecataeus was himself a traveller—he composed the earliest guide-book to the wonders of Egypt; and he could supplement his own observations by second-hand material gathered, in the great centre of trade where his home was, from travellers and strangers. This development of geography in Ionia was certainly forwarded by the Royal Road, and so far the Persian conquest of eastern Greece was an advantage to European civilisation.

Europe owes so much to the Ionian intellects which at this period were breaking new paths of progress that we may linger a moment

longer over the movement of intellectual discovery before resuming the march of events. It was a movement of the most interesting kind, in which the instinct for speculation and the thirst for positive knowledge were closely united. For Anaximander, the first charto-grapher, map-making is only part of his wider work as a physical philosopher. Dissatisfied with the theory of Thales who found the first principle of the universe in water, he sought it in a more general conception which he designated, negatively, as the "Unlimited" —unlimited, that is, by qualities, and so capable of differentiation into all the kinds of definite matter which our senses perceive. Hecataeus is the founder of Greek history. He partly breaks with *Hecataeus* the old traditions, and criticises the Hesiodic school of theology. *the logo-* The heroes who appeared in legend as sons of the gods he regards *grapher.* as the bastard sons of women who, to shield their shame, ascribed the fatherhood to Zeus or Apollo. "The stories of the Greeks," he says, "are, in my opinion, manifold and absurd." Thus reason was asserting itself against authority in the religious sphere ; and Hecataeus was one of the pioneers. But more effective than he in *Xeno-* pressing the claims of reason was another Ionian, his contemporary, *phanes (see* Xenophanes of Colophon ; and we shall have to consider the *below,* importance of his work in another connexion.   *Chap. VII.*
sect. 14).

The remoteness of Susa from the Greek seas, and the home-sickness of Greeks whom any chance transported to the far east, find an illustration in the curious story of the physician Democedes of *The story* Croton. This man's skill had earned high salaries, as public physician *of Demo-* at Aegina and Athens, and higher still in the service of Polycrates *cedes.* of Samos. He was carried off as a prisoner to Susa, in consequence of a series of troubles which followed the death of that tyrant ; and he was taken from his dungeon to try his craft for Darius, who had sprained a foot in the chase. His success gained him the king's favour, and there was nothing which he might not ask except the one thing which he desired, permission to return to Greece. One day he was summoned by Queen Atossa who was suffering from a tumour on the breast, and he made her swear that if he cured her she would do what he asked. Acting by his directions, she stirred up the king to cherish the project of conquering the Greeks, and suggested that he should send spies under the conduct of Democedes to travel through Greece and bring back a report. These counsels of the daughter of Cyrus carried weight with Darius, according to the story ; and the plan of Democedes succeeded. He promised to return to Susa, and Darius gave him rich presents for his kinsfolk ; the Persians who accompanied him were privately charged to see that he did not escape. When they came to Taras,—for the story assumes that Italiot Greece was included in the programme of the journey,—the lord of that city arrested the Persians as spies, and kept them in prison until Democedes had time to escape to his native town. When the Persians were released they followed him to Croton, but the Crotoniats refused to give him up ; a Persian invasion of Italy was a contingency which they might reasonably risk. Such is the strange story, blended of fact and fiction, which men told of the first Greek physician who practised at the court of Susa. He was not the last ; *(Ctesias.)* we shall meet hereafter a more famous leech, who did not yearn back to Greece and wrote the history of his adopted country.

SECT. 5. THE EUROPEAN EXPEDITION OF DARIUS : CONQUEST OF THRACE

Diod. Sic.
X. 19. 5

Cyrus had conquered the eastern coasts of the Mediterranean ; Cambyses had completed and secured that conquest on the south side by the subjection of Egypt ; it remained for Darius to complete and secure his empire on the north side by the reduction of Thrace. The possession of the adjacent part of the European continent was of like importance to the lord of Asia Minor, as the possession of the adjacent part of the African continent to the lord of Syria. Having spent eight years in setting his house in order, Darius prepared for his European expedition. It seems probable that his original design was first to subdue the Thracian peoples as far as the Danube, so as to make that river the northern boundary of his empire, and secondly to extend his power westward over Macedonia. The Thracian race was warlike and the country is mountainous, so that the Persian enterprise was serious and demanded large forces and careful pre- c. 512 B.C. cautions. The skill of a Samian architect named Mandrocles was employed to throw a bridge of boats across the Bosphorus, north of Byzantium ; and, when the Persian host had passed over, Darius ordered two pillars to be set up on the European side, inscribed with the names of the various peoples composing his army, in Greek and cuneiform characters. These pillars were seen by the historian Herodotus. And in the temple of Hera at Samos there was to be seen another monument of the crossing into Europe. Mandrocles spent a part of the reward which Darius gave him in setting up there a painting in which the bridge and the crossing over, with Darius seated in a prominent place, were portrayed. He inscribed on it four verses to this effect : " Having bridged the fishy Bosphorus, Mandrocles dedicated to Hera a memorial of his raft-bridge. A crown he set upon his own head, and glory upon the men of Samos ; for the work he wrought pleased king Darius." A large fleet was also furnished by the Greek subjects of Persia, to sail along the Thracian coast of the Black Sea as far as the mouths of the Danube.

and to support and co-operate with the army. The contingents of the various Greek cities were commanded by their despots, prominent among whom were Histiaeus of Miletus, Hippoclus of Lampsacus, and Miltiades of the Thracian Chersonesus.

No details of the warfare in Thrace are preserved. We are told that many tribes submitted, and the Getae signalised their love of freedom by refusing to surrender it without a struggle. It seems probable, however, that the Thracians made some preparations to meet the invader. North of the Danube, in the lands which are now called Walachia and Moldavia (between the Danube, the Carpathians, and the Pruth), lived tribes which were allied in many respects to the tribes south of the river. The Greeks included these tribes under the general name of Scythian, which they applied to the whole series of peoples who dwelled between the Carpathians and the Caucasus. While the most easterly of that series approximated in language to the Persian, the most westerly approximated to the Thracian. Nothing was more natural than that the people south of the Danube, threatened by an Asiatic invasion, should have taken steps to gain help from their neighbours on the north, to oppose the Persian advance. Such help would have been readily given, and Darius doubtless became aware before he reached the Danube that the hostility of the Scythian beyond the Danube—whose frozen waters invited them to cross in winter—might be a frequent trouble to Persian rule in Thrace. The Greek fleet sailed up the mouth of the river and a bridge of boats was thrown across. Darius and his army marched over into Scythia. But both the king's purpose and *Why* what he did, in this remote corner of the world, are hidden in a cloud *Darius* of legend. That he may have wished to make a hostile demonstra- *crossed the* tion and strike terror into the restless neighbours of Thrace is *Danube.* probable ; but it is not the whole explanation. We may rather suppose that the chief object of the diversion beyond the Danube was to lay hands upon the gold mines of Dacia, which was then the land of the Agathyrsi, and to secure a route of communication between that land and the mouth of the Danube. For three facts seem to emerge from the mist. The first is that the Agathyrsi were active in opposing the march of the Persians ; the second, that he erected forts on a river named the Oaros,—a name otherwise unknown, but evidently a tributary of the Danube ; the third, that his communications with the fleet which awaited his return were for some time cut off, and the Greek commanders were tempted to sail away and leave him in the lurch. He afterwards showed his gratitude to them for the loyalty with which they supported him in this expedition. The fact is that it would have been entirely contrary to their own interests to inflict a blow on the power which maintained despotism in the Greek cities of Asia Minor.   But their loyalty at this juncture was all the more precious to the Persian king when he found on returning through Thrace that Byzantium, Perinthus, and Chalcedon had revolted. These revolts forced him to avoid the Bosphorus.   He marched to the Thracian Chersonese and crossed the Hellespont, but left behind him an army under Megabazus, which was ultimately to complete the conquest of Thrace, and immediately to reduce the Greek cities *Persian* along the northern coast of the Propontis and the Aegean.   Mega-*sway in* bazus established Persian dominion actually as far as the Strymon, *Europe.* and nominally even farther west ; for the Paeonians, between the Strymon and the Axius, were conquered, and Macedonia acknow-ledged allegiance to the Great King.

The Persian dominion over the eastern part of the Balkan peninsula lasted for about fifteen years, and it was increased by the acquisition of the islands of Lemnos and Imbros.   The excursion of Darius beyond the Danube, so far as it was intended to make an impression on the Scythians, seems to have been ineffective.   Shortly *c. 496 B.C.* afterwards we find the Scythians raiding Thrace and driving Miltiades from the Chersonese.

Legend of The European expedition of Darius had thus been a distinct *Scythian* success, which might fearlessly be set beside the Egyptian expedi-*xpedition.* tion of Cambyses.   But it has come down to us in a very different and totally fabulous shape.   It is represented as not primarily an expedition against Thrace, but as an attempt to execute the mad project of incorporating the Scythians of the steppes of southern Russia in the Persian empire.   In this story, which is told with all the art of Herodotus, Thrace appears merely as the way to Scythia ; and the actual conquest of Thrace sinks into insignificance beside the ignominious failure of the Persian army to achieve the ultimate end of their wild enterprise, the conquest of Scythia.   Darius, whose purpose is said to have been to take vengeance on the Scythians for their invasion of Media a hundred years before, dispatches the Greek fleet to the Ister simply for the purpose of throwing a bridge of boats across the river.   His first idea was to break down the bridge when he had passed over and send the ships home ; but by the advice of a prudent Greek he changed his plan.   He took a cord, in which he tied sixty knots, and said to the Greek captains : " Untie one of these knots every day, and remain here and guard the bridge till they are all untied.   If I have not returned at the end of that time, sail home."   The Greek historian Herodotus then con-ducts Darius with his vast host through the steppes of Scythia "as it were through fairyland," without any regard to the rivers which had to be crossed, the leagues which had to be traversed, the want of supplies.   He carries him to regions beyond the Don, and transports

the river Oaros, on which Darius built his forts, from the neighbourhood of the Danube to the neighbourhood of the Maeotic sea ;
placing this imaginary march of the Persians in the midst of a
poetical picture of the Scythian folks and the Scythian land.
In returning to the Danube the Persians found themselves in sore
straits, chased and harassed by the barbarians, and meanwhile the
sixty days had passed.   The Ionians waited at the river beyond the
ordained time, and presently a band of Scythians arrived urging them
to destroy the bridge, so that they might ensure the destruction of
Darius and gain their own freedom.   Miltiades the tyrant of the
Chersonese strongly advocated the proposal of the Scythians, but the
counter-arguments of Histiaeus of Miletus prevailed, for he pointed
out that the power of the despots in the cities depended on the
Persian domination.   They pretended however to fall in with the
Scythian proposal, and destroyed a part of the bridge on the
northern side, so that the Scythians went their ways, satisfied that
the retreat of Darius would be cut off.   A little later, Darius
arrived in the dark hours of the night, and was filled with terror
when he could discover no bridge.   An Egyptian with a loud voice
shouted the name " Histiaeus ! " across the water, and Histiaeus,
who was himself keeping guard, heard the cry, brought up his
boats, and renewed the missing portion of the bridge.   Thus
Darius, after an ignominious retreat, was saved by the good offices
of Histiaeus ; whereas, if the advice of Miltiades had been adopted,
the subsequent Persian invasion of Greece might never have taken
place.

Thus Greek imagination, inspired by Greek prejudice, has
changed a reasonable and successful enterprise into an insane and
disastrous expedition ; and the transmutation was so skilfully wrought
that the fiction was taken for history until the other day.

SECT. 6. THE IONIC REVOLT AGAINST PERSIA

The Persian conquest of Thrace and Macedonia was a step,
though there is no reason for supposing it an intentional step, towards
a Persian attempt to conquer Greece.   The attempt on Greece was
not made till more than twenty years later ; and for the first twelve
years after the return of Darius from Thrace, nothing occurred
which seemed likely to bring on a great struggle between Asiatic
autocracy and European freedom.   Hippias, the banished tyrant of
Athens, repaired to Sardis and tried to induce the satrap Artaphernes
to aid him in recovering his power.   Artaphernes went so far as to
threaten the Athenians; envoys from Sardis said at Athens : " Take

back Hippias, if you look for safety." But he did nothing to enforce his menace.

It was in consequence of events in which Hippias had no part that the expedition of the Persians against Athens was at last undertaken. The condition of politics in the island of Naxos led indirectly to an insurrection of the subject Greeks against the Persian power ; and the part which Athens and other Greek cities played in connexion with this revolt was the proximate cause of the Persian expeditions against Greece.

Histiaeus,   In return for services rendered during the Thracian expedition Histiaeus of Miletus was rewarded by Darius with a boon of his own *512 B.C.;* requesting. He asked for Myrcinus, a town with fertile land on the lower Strymon—near the place where the famous Amphipolis was to be built at a later date—where he desired to found a colony. He seems to have accompanied Megabazus in his western march, and he set to work to fortify the place at once. Myrcinus was in the neighbourhood of silver-mines, and there was abundance of wood suitable for shipbuilding. The Persian general thought it would be impolitic to allow a Greek colony to be planted in such a position, and communicated his views to the king who was still at Sardis ; *at Susa,* and Darius sending for Histiaeus, on the plea that he was a friend *511 B.C.* whose company was indispensable, carried him off to Susa, with the full purpose of never allowing him to return to the Aegean. Thus the schemes of Histiaeus were cut short, and he spent twelve years in regrets at the court of Susa before he had an opportunity of resuming his connexion with the politics of the Aegean.

Arista-   Miletus was governed by his son-in-law Aristagoras, a man whose *goras of* ability fell short of his ambition, but famous in history as the *Miletus ;* originator of the revolt of the Ionian Greeks. To this man came a number of Naxian oligarchs, who had been expelled from their city by a democratic rising, begging for help to put down the people and *his Naxian* gain possession of the populous and wealthy island. Aristagoras *enterprise ;* discerned in the request a means for his own aggrandisement ; but without Persian assistance the enterprise did not seem feasible. He therefore went up to Sardis, and unfolded to Artaphernes a project of reducing all the Cyclades and then perhaps Euboea itself, a project of which the occupation of Naxos was to be the first step. Artaphernes readily entered into the plan, the consent of Darius was obtained, and 200 ships under the command of Megabates were placed at the *its failure.* disposal of the Milesian. There is little doubt that the enterprise would have been entirely successful but for a quarrel between Aristagoras and Megabates. The Persian admiral spitefully warned the Naxians of the approaching danger ; the islanders made such effectual preparations that they stood a siege of four months, and, as there was then no likelihood of reducing the city, the fleet returned to Ionia. This failure was fatal to the prospects of Aristagoras. He resolved to retrieve his fortunes by inciting a revolt of the Asiatic 499 *B.C.* Greeks against the Persian power.

The story was that his father-in-law Histiaeus, weary of his long *Was* exile beyond the Tigris, instigated Aristagoras to this step, by a secret *Histiaeus* message branded on the head of a faithful slave. This message is *concerned* said to have reached Aristagoras just at the moment when he was *in the Ionic* meditating a rebellion and to have decided him. The motive of *revolt?* Histiaeus in desiring the revolt is supposed to have been the conviction that Darius would send him down to Ionia to restore order. But the story sounds improbable. Histiaeus, detained at Susa because he was already deemed dangerous to Persian interests in the Aegean, would rather have had reason to fear that a revolt promoted by his son-in-law would prove fatal to his credit with Darius. It was a surprising thing that Darius was afterwards induced to send down such a near relative of Aristagoras, and we may suspect that the story that Histiaeus instigated the rebellion was suggested by his subsequent conduct—possibly even invented by himself.

There were the seeds of revolt in Ionia and it would be superficial to suppose that the rebellion was due to the ambition of Greek despots. Its indispensable condition was the widespread hatred of a despotic constitution, which smouldered in the cities; and the despotic constitutions were part of the Persian system. An ambitious despot was indeed the means of calling this feeling into action; but in order to do so he had first to cease to be a despot. [The issue by the rebel cities of a confederate coinage shows a wide measure of unity and determination in the revolt.]

The initial step in promoting the rebellion was to set up democracies in the Greek States and drive out the tyrants. Aristagoras himself resigned his position in Miletus, and in most cases the change seems to have been accomplished without the shedding of blood. Mytilene was an exception; there the tyrant had earned such deep hatred that he was stoned to death.

The next step was to obtain help from free Greece against the *Arista-* Persian power. Aristagoras undertook the mission. He went first *goras at* to Sparta, but the Spartans refused to send help to free Ionia from *Sparta;* Persian oppression, even as they had before refused to aid her against Persian invasion. In later days a delightful story was told of his visit. He went to king Cleomenes and showed him a map of the earth, graven on bronze, displaying the countries of the known world, the seas, and the rivers. Cleomenes had never seen a map before, and the plausible Ionian tried to convince him that Sparta ought to aspire to the conquest of the Persian empire. Cleomenes was impressed, but deferred his reply till the third day, and then asked Aristagoras the distance from Ionia to Susa. "Three months," said Aristagoras off his guard, and he would have described the road, but the king cut him short with the command, "Begone from Sparta, Milesian stranger, before the sun sets." Aristagoras made yet another attempt. Entering the house of Cleomenes as a suppliant, he sought to bribe him. Beginning with ten talents, he gradually raised his offers till he reached fifty. Then Gorgo, the king's daughter, a child of eight or nine years, cried out, "Father, the stranger will corrupt you"; and moved by her words Cleomenes left the room.

at Athens and Eretria. 498 B.C. The Milesian stranger fared better at Athens and Eretria. Both these cities sent succour; Athens twenty ships—ships, says Herodotus, with the solemnity due to the historical significance of the moment, "which were the beginning of ills between Greeks and barbarians."

Advice of Hecataeus. The prospects of success seemed unfavourable to those who were acquainted with the vast resources of the Persian empire. When Aristagoras consulted with the men of leading at Miletus, the geographer Hecataeus had tried to dissuade him. Seeing that Aristagoras and the others had made up their minds and disparaged his arguments, Hecataeus gave a second-best counsel: "If you do revolt, seize the treasure of the temple of Apollo at Didyma, and become masters of the sea; for if you do not, the enemy will." But the advice was not taken.

The Greeks at Sardis. With his Athenian and Eretrian allies, Aristagoras marched up to Sardis and occupied the city, but they did not take the citadel. While they were there, a fire broke out and the town was burned to the ground. The Greeks left the smoking ruins and marched back to the coast; but near Ephesus they were met by a Persian force and defeated. The Athenians straightway returned home; and with this battle the part played by Athens in the Ionic revolt comes to an end. [The election of Hipparchus, a Pisistratid, to the archonship in 496 suggests a strong reaction against the anti-Persian policy.] But the brief episode was to bring serious consequences upon Athens in the future. The burning of Sardis was important, not so much for the course of the revolt itself as for what the revolt was to lead to. It irrevocably compromised two states of European Greece in the eyes of Persia. The story is that Darius, being told that Athenians had helped to burn Sardis, asked, "The Athenians—who are they?" He then called for a bow and shooting an arrow into the air, invoked heaven that it might be given to him to punish the Athenians. Moreover he bade one of his slaves to say to him three times at dinner, "Sire, remember the Athenians." The story has no historical value, but it has artistic significance in the narrative of Herodotus.

Part played by Athenians in the revolt.

Anecdote of Darius and the Athenians.

The revolt extended southwards to Caria and to Cyprus, north- *The revolt* wards to the Propontis. In Cyprus all the cities except Amathus *in the* threw off the Persian yoke. The Greek fleet sailed east and controlled *south.* the seas, but the Cyprians were defeated on land and the island came again under Persian control. The Hellespontine towns were also subdued. In Caria the insurgents, after suffering two serious defeats, succeeded in destroying a Persian army.

But Aristagoras was a man of slight spirit. Seeing that Persia *Flight of* prospered in dealing with the rebellion, he despaired of his cause and *Arista-* fled to Myrcinus in Thrace. It is said that he called a meeting of his *goras.* adherents, to decide what they should do and whither they should flee. In that assembly it was proposed to sail to the distant shores of Sardinia ; and here again Hecataeus is related to have offered advice, which Aristagoras and his friends rejected—the establishment of a fortress in the neighbouring island of Leros, from which, if fortune favoured, they might easily return to Miletus. Aristagoras soon met his fate at the siege of a Thracian town. His death did not affect the course of the rebellion, in which he had played a sorry part. He has hardly left the stage when his father-in-law appears ; *Reappear-* but the rôle of Histiaeus is even less important than that of *ance of* Aristagoras. This adventurer persuaded, or professed that he had *Histiaeus ;* persuaded, Darius to send him down to the coast, by promising to suppress the insurrection before he changed his tunic, and to annex Sardinia to the dominion of the Great King. This promise of Histiaeus, though it may not be true to fact, is thoroughly character-istic of the Greek adventurers of that time, deceiving themselves and others with speculations on the re-mote island of Sardinia. When he came down to Sardis, Histiaeus found that he was deeply suspected by the satrap Artaphernes, and feeling himself unsafe he fled to Chios. There he embraced the cause of the rebels, asserting that *he* had instigated FIG. 76. — Early the revolt, and perhaps spreading the famous story coin of Chios (ob- of the message written on the slave's head. Having verse). Sphinx ; obtained some ships from Lesbos he adopted the jar.

congenial business of piracy, occupying Byzantium and seizing the ships that attempted to pass the straits, as long as the revolt lasted. *his fate,* In the end he was taken prisoner and crucified by Artaphernes.   *493 B.C.*

The main and decisive event of the war was the siege of Miletus on which the Persians at length concentrated all their efforts. *494 B.C.* The town was blockaded by the Persian fleet, said to number 600 *Battle of* ships, which had just reduced Cyprus. The Greek fleet was stationed *Lade and* off the island of Lade. It is said to have numbered 353 ships, but *capture of* they were ill disciplined, and the contingents were not united under a *Miletus.*

single command, nor animated by a common spirit. In the battle which ensued, the Lesbians and Samians deserted; the men of Chios fought splendidly but they were too few. Miletus was then taken by storm; the men were slain and the women and children sent up to Susa. The temple of Apollo at Didyma, one of the chief oracular sanctuaries of the Greek world, was surrendered by the Branchidae, its hereditary priests, and was burnt down.

Temple of the Branchidae.

We may suspect that the burning of Apollo's shrine was not approved of by Darius himself. The respect which the king of kings felt for the oracular god is attested in a letter of admonition which he addressed to a satrap of Phrygia. The text of a Greek version of this letter is partly preserved on a stone, and records the remarkable testimony of the king that Apollo always " told the truth to the Persians."

Letter of Darius to Gadates.

The capture of Miletus was followed by the reduction of Caria, where the rebels had for a time prospered, and by the conquest of the islands. Presently the Phoenician navy appeared in the waters of the Hellespont; and the attempt of eastern Greece to regain her independence was completely crushed.

End of revolt.

[For over a hundred years the eastern Greeks had been under increasing pressure, first from Lydia and then from Persia. But from the suffering of Ionia the rest of the Greek world profited. Faced by growing insecurity in the east, individuals and groups left their homes for more congenial surroundings. Already under the Lydian dominance Colophonians had founded Siris in south Italy: we have seen how, when Persia attacked, Phocaeans and Teans sailed to make new homes in Corsica and in Thrace. A stream of emigration followed through discontent with Persian rule or local tyranny, and in the crisis of the collapse of the great revolt, Samians, Milesians, Phocaeans and no doubt others sailed to the west. Among the emigrants of this long period were craftsmen and philosophers. Pythagoras abandoned Polycrates' tyranny in Samos and settled in Croton to spread his teaching in the south Italian cities and influence their politics. Xenophanes of Colophon came to Elea, to be the founder of a famous line of philosophers. The influence of east Greek craftsmen is no less marked. It is seen clearly at Acragas in Sicily from the late sixth century and was responsible for the brilliant coinage of Gelo at Leontini and Syracuse. Another Pythagoras came also from Samos to Rhegium to become one of the most famous sculptors of the age.]

Influence of east Greeks.

The crushing of the Ionian revolt had a profound effect in Athens. Though the Athenians had withdrawn from the movement in Ionia at an early stage, the tidings of the fall of Miletus produced at Athens a deep feeling of disappointment and sympathy, which found expression some time afterwards in the punishment of Phrynichus,

Capture of Miletus, Phryni- chus fined.

a tragic poet, who made the catastrophe of Miletus the theme of a drama. The Athenians fined him for having recalled to their minds *their own* misfortunes. But in the meantime there had been won for them, from the Persian, what was destined to become afterwards

FIG. 77.—Rider in oriental costume, with Μιλτιαδες καλος.
Attic bowl, *c.* 510 B.C.

a lasting possession. Miltiades, the tyrant of the Chersonese, *Miltiades.* sympathised with the rebels and during the revolt seized for Athens *Lemnos* the isles of Lemnos and Imbros. *and Imbros become Athenian.*

Sect. 7. Second and Third European Expeditions of Darius. Battle of Marathon

Having suppressed the rebellion, Persia had three things to do. Greek Asia was to be reorganised; Persian Europe was to be re-conquered; and those free Greek states which had made war on Persia and occupied Sardis were to be punished.

Reorgan-
isation of
Ionia.

Artaphernes caused the territories of the Ionian cities to be measured and surveyed, and regulated the tributes accordingly. It was also ordained that the cities should no longer have the right of making war upon one another. But there was more to be done. The revolt had taught Persia that the system of tyrannies did not answer; and it was now resolved to make an experiment of the opposite policy. The despots were abolished and democratic governments were set up. The world may well have been surprised to see the great despotism of all favouring the institution of democracy; it was a concession to the spirit of the Greeks, which reflects credit on the wisdom of Darius.

Thrace and
Macedonia
conquered
by Mar-
donius,
492 B.C.

The king's son-in-law, Mardonius, was sent to reassert Persian supremacy in Thrace and Macedonia; and through Macedonia he proposed to advance into Greece in order to punish the two cities which had helped the Ionian rebels. A fleet sailed along the coast and subdued the island of Thasos on its way. Thrace was reduced, and Macedonia, then under king Alexander, submitted—a submission which was to be avenged in distant days to come by a descendant and a namesake. But the Greek expedition could not be carried out, since a disaster had befallen the fleet which was partly wrecked in a storm off the perilous promontory of Athos. Mardonius returned; he had lost many ships, but he had fulfilled the more important parts of his task.

Darius
prepares an
expedition
against
European
Greece.

But Darius was sternly resolved that Athens and Eretria should not escape without chastisement. Their connexion with the burning of Sardis had deeply incensed him; it seemed an insult which the Great King's pride could not let pass unnoticed. Moreover Hippias, the banished tyrant, was at the court of Susa, urging an expedition against the city which had cast him out. It was decided that the new expedition should not be sent by way of Thrace and Macedonia, but should move straight across the Aegean sea. The cities of the Persian seaboard were commanded to equip warships and transports for cavalry, and heralds were sent to the chief cities of free Greece that were not at war with Persia, requiring the tokens of submission, earth and water. In most cases the tokens were given; and among others by Aegina, the enemy of Athens. The command of the army was entrusted to Datis and Artaphernes, a nephew of Darius; and they were accompanied by the aged tyrant Hippias, who hoped to rule once more over his native country. The armament—600 galleys strong, according to Herodotus—setting sail from Samos, made first for Naxos, the island where Aristagoras had failed. The inhabitants abandoned the city and fled up into the hills; and the Persians burned the town. The sacred island of Delos was scrupulously spared; but soon after the Persians had departed, it was shaken by an earthquake, and the unwonted event was noted as a

sign of coming troubles.   Having sailed from isle to isle, subduing *Persians*
the Cyclades, the fleet went up the channel between Euboea and *subdue*
Attica, and, reducing Carystus by the way, reached the territory of $\frac{Cyclades}{and}$
Eretria.   It is strange to find that Athens and Eretria had made no *Carystus,*
common preparations to meet a common danger.   Eretria was
severed from Attica only by a narrow water, and yet there was no
joint action.   Athens indeed directed the colonists whom she had
settled in the territory of her dependency Chalcis to assist their
Eretrian neighbours, but she sent no other help.   We hear of sharp
engagements outside the walls of the Euboean city, but within seven
days it was delivered over to the invaders by the treachery of some *burn*
leading burghers.   The flames which consumed the temples of *Eretria.*
Eretria were a small set off against the flames of Sardis.   The
inhabitants were enslaved.   Of all the Greek towns which were
involved in the strife between Europe and Asia, none was more ill-
fated than Eretria.

The Persian generals had accomplished the lesser half of their
task ; it now remained to deal with the other city which had defied
their king.   Crossing over the strait they landed their army in the *land in*
bay of Marathon.   For the second time an exiled tyrant of Athens *Attica.*
came down from Eretria to recover his power.   The father had
come, fifty years before, with but a few mercenaries ; the son came
now with the forces of Asia.   Yet so far as winning support at
Athens was concerned, the foreign host was the weakest argument of
Hippias.   The house of the Pisistratids had many bitter enemies,
but none was more bitter than one who had also known what it was
to rule as a tyrant, Miltiades, son of Cimon.   We have seen how he *Miltiades.*
returned from the Chersonese after the Ionic revolt.   His enemies
accused him of the crime of oppressive rule in the Chersonese, but
he was acquitted by his fellow-citizens, to whom he had brought
the gift of Lemnos and Imbros.   His hatred of the Pisistratids
was natural ; they had put to death his father Cimon, celebrated as
a victor in the Olympian chariot-race.   It is not surprising that
Miltiades, who was active as a party man, who was known to be a
hot foe of the tyrants, who had probably more first-hand knowledge
of the Persians than any other man at Athens, was chosen as the
strategos of his tribe.   He was the soul of the resistance which his
country now offered to the invader.

Athens had changed much since Hippias had been cast out, *Energy of*
though a generation had not passed.   Athenian character had been *free*
developed under free democratical institutions.   It has been said *Athens.*
that if the Athenians had not been radically different from their
former selves Hippias would easily have recovered Athens.   In other
words, if the Persian invasion had happened twenty years sooner,

the same stand would not have been made against it as Athens now made ; the liberty of Greece would have succumbed. But it was no mere accident that the blow had not been aimed twenty years sooner. The Persian invasion was brought about by the same political causes which enabled Athens to withstand it. The Ionian Greeks would not have risen in revolt but for the growth of a strong sentiment against tyrannies,—the same cause which overthrew the Pisistratids and created Marathonian Athens. On the other hand, if the Ionic revolt had broken out before the expulsion of Hippias, Athens would have taken no part in it, and the Persian invasion of Greece might not have followed.

Philippides sent to Sparta. As the story is told by our historian, one would almost think that the enemy had already landed on Attic soil before the Athenians bethought themselves how they were to defend their city and their land. A fast runner was dispatched in hot haste to Lacedaemon to bear the news of the fall of Eretria and the jeopardy of Athens. The Lacedaemonians said that they would help Athens but religious scruples forbade them to come at once ; they must wait till the full moon had passed. But when the full moon had passed, it was too late. The Plataeans alone, faithful to their new alliance, sent help and fought with the Athenians.

Calli-machus. The whole army of the Athenians may have numbered about 9000. The commander-in-chief was Callimachus, the polemarch of the year ; and the grave duty of organising the defence rested upon him and the ten generals of the tribal regiments, who formed a Council of War. Fortunately for Athens, Callimachus seems to have been willing to hearken to the counsels of Miltiades ; and the joint authority of the polemarch and the most influential general outweighed the scruples of their less adventurous colleagues. The enemy had landed near Marathon and clearly intended to advance

Decision to march to Marathon. on unwalled Athens by land and sea. The question was whether the Athenian army should await their approach and give them battle within sight and reach of the Acropolis, or should more boldly go forth to find them. This was a question which it devolved upon the Athenian people itself to decide. The hour when the Assembly met to deliberate on this question was the most fateful moment in the whole episode. Miltiades proposed that the army should march to Marathon and meet the Persians there. To have proposed and carried this decree is probably the greatest title of Miltiades to his immortal fame.

Field of Marathon. The plain of Marathon, stretching along a sickle-shaped line of coast, is girt on all other sides by the hills which drop down from Pentelicus and Parnes. In the northern part, and on the extreme south, the soil is marshy, and the plain is cleft into two halves by the path of a torrent coming down from the hills through the northern valley, in which the village of Marathon is situated.   Two roads lead from Athens to Marathon.   The main road, turning eastward, passes between the mountains of Hymettus and Pentelicus ; and, traversing the deme of Pallene, skirting Mount Pentelicus, and then turning due north when it reaches the coast, it enters the plain of Marathon from the south.   The other road, which is somewhat shorter but more difficult, continues northward, past the deme of Cephisia, and, running into the hills north of Pentelicus, finds two issues in the Marathonian

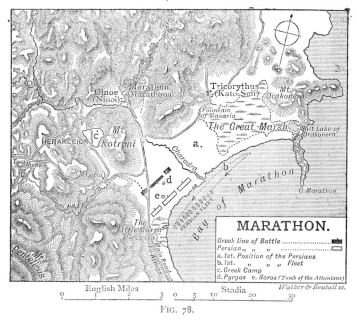

FIG. 78.

plain.   It divides into two paths which encircle the hill of Kotroni: the northern path goes on to Marathon and descends into the plain from the north along the banks of the torrent ; the other, passing by a sanctuary of Heracles, and descending the valley of Avlona, issues in the plain at its south-western corner, close to the village which is now called Vraná.

Callimachus took the northern road by Cephisia, and encamped *Athenian* in the valley of Avlona, not far from the shrine of Heracles.   The *position.* choice of this admirable position was more than half the victory. The Athenians were themselves unassailable, in the lower valley,

Persian position.

except at a great disadvantage; and they commanded not only the mountain road by which they had come, but also the main road and the southern gate of the plain; for the Persians in attempting to reach that gate would be exposed to their flank attack. At this period Athens had accomplished strategists, and the brilliant campaign against Boeotia and Chalcis, sixteen years before, has prepared us for the ability which her commanders now displayed in the presence of a graver peril. The Persians had encamped on the north side of the torrent-bed, and their ships were riding at anchor beside them. It was to their interest to bring on a pitched battle in the plain as soon as possible. On the other hand, the Athenians had everything to gain by waiting in their impregnable position; if they waited long enough they might hope for help from Sparta. Help from another quarter had already come. When they reached the sanctuary of Heracles they were joined by a band of 1000 Plataeans, who, in gratitude for the protection of Athens against the Theban yoke, now came to help her in the hour of jeopardy.

Persians prepare to move.

Some days passed, and then, as the Greeks remained immovable, the Persians would wait no longer. Having embarked a part of the army, including the whole body of their cavalry, they made ready to move upon Athens by land and sea. The land force must follow the main road by Pallene, and was therefore prepared for battle, in case the Greeks should attack them before they defiled from the plain. Another critical moment had come for the Athenians, but the polemarch and the generals had probably decided already what should be done when this contingency arose. That Miltiades, as before in the Assembly so now in the camp, urged the boldest course, we may well believe; but the supreme direction belonged to the polemarch, and he decided to attack the enemy as they marched southward.

Tactics of the Athenians.

Callimachus, whether he acted of his own wit or by the counsel of others, showed now a skill in tactics as consummate as the skill in strategy which we have already witnessed. Outnumbered by the foe, if the Athenian line had formed itself in equal depth throughout, it would have swept the Persian centre into the sea, but then it would have been caught in a trap, between the sea and ships on one side and the Persian wings, which would have closed in, on the other. Accordingly Callimachus made his own centre long and shallow, so that it would cover the whole Persian centre, while his wings of the normal depth would be opposed to the wings of the enemy.

Battle of Marathon (Sept.).

The long Persian line crossed the bed of the torrent and advanced along the shore. A large portion was detached to mask the Greek position—a precaution which was dictated by elementary principles of strategy, in order either to prevent or to repel a flank attack. With these troops to cover them, the rest of the host might march securely past. The Greek army had perhaps already appeared in the recess of the hills at the mouth of the valley of Avlona. Callimachus himself led the right wing; the Plataean allies were posted on the extreme left. Among those who fought for their country on this day we must notice one who, though he held no post of command, was destined to hold a greater place in Athenian history than any of his fellow-warriors, Themistocles, the son of Neocles, who fought in the regiment of the Leontid tribe. Another of world-wide fame, Aeschylus the tragic poet, also bore shield and spear, and charged the Medes, on this memorable day. When the Greeks drew near to the line of the enemy, they were met by volleys of arrows from the eastern archers, and to escape this danger they advanced at a run into close quarters. The hoplites did not fail the generals; their valour secured the victory which masterly strategy and tactics had prepared. All fell out as had been foreseen. The Athenian centre was driven back towards the hills by the enemy's centre, where the best troops, including the Persians themselves, were stationed; but the Athenian wings completely routed the wings of their foe. Then, closing in—and leaving the vanquished to reach their ships if they could—they turned upon the victorious Persians, who were following the retreating Greek centre. Here again they were utterly victorious, breaking up the array of the enemy and pursuing them in confusion to the shore, where all who escaped the sword were picked up by the ships. Only a portion of the Persian army had been engaged; the main body doubtless embarked as soon as they saw the first signs of the disruption of the force on which they had relied to cover them from the enemy.

It was not a long battle. The Athenian loss was small, 192 slain; and the Persian loss was reckoned at about 6400, a number whose very moderation stamps it as probably near the truth. Datis and Artaphernes had still an immense host, which might retrieve the fortune of the campaign; Athens was not yet out of danger. The Persian squadron sailed down the straits and rounded Cape Sunium, while the victorious army, leaving one regiment on the field of their triumph to guard the slain and the spoils, marched back to defend Athens. They halted outside the city near the shrine of Heracles in Cynosarges, on the banks of the Ilisus, and they beheld the fleet *Persians* of the enemy riding off Phaleron. But it did not put into shore, and *near* presently the whole squadron began to draw out to sea. Datis had *Phaleron:* abandoned his enterprise. Perhaps he had sailed within sight of *return to* Athens only on the chance of finding it undefended; and, when he *Asia.* saw that the army was there, shrank from another conflict with the

Arrival of the Spartans.

hoplites. But a Spartan army, 2000 strong, cannot have been far from Athens now ; it had set out on the day after the full moon, and it reached Athens soon after the battle. We may guess that tidings of the approach of the Spartans, if not their actual presence, had something to do with the sudden departure of the invaders, who, though they had received an unlooked-for check, had not endured an overwhelming defeat.

The Spartans arrived too late for the battle. They visited the field desiring to gaze upon the Persian corpses, and departed home praising the exploit of the Athenians. The scene of the battle is still marked by the mound which the Athenians raised over their own dead ; Callimachus was buried there, and Cynegirus (a brother of the poet Aeschylus), who was said to have seized a Persian galley and held it until his arm was severed by an axe. Legend grew up quickly round the battle, and there was no historian to record at the time what had actually happened ; so that, when a generation had passed, the facts were partly forgotten, and partly transfigured. Three motives were at work in this transfiguration : the love of the marvellous, the vanity of the Athenians, and the desire of his family to exalt the services of Miltiades. Gods and heroes fought for Athens, ghostly warriors moved among the ranks. The panic terror of the Persians at the Greek charge was ascribed to Pan, and the worship of this god was revived in a cave consecrated to him under the north-west slope of the Acropolis. Out of this grew a story which added a charming incident to the chain of Marathonian memories. The fast runner Philippides, speeding through Arcadia on his way to seek Spartan help, had been accosted by Pan himself, who had asked why the Athenians neglected his worship, and promised them favours in the future. But the supernatural can be easily allowed for. It was more serious that the extraordinarily brilliant strategy and tactics, to which the success was chiefly due, should have faded out of the story, and that Marathon should have been regarded as entirely a soldiers' battle. It was soberly asserted and believed that those wonderful warriors had taken their enemy aback by advancing against them for a whole mile at a run. Miltiades, who was doubtless the heart and soul of the campaign, was raised by the Marathonian myth to be the commander-in-chief on the day of battle ; and it was explained that the chief command each day devolved upon the generals in rotation. This was an arrangement which came into force a few years later, when the polemarch lost his importance ; but it supplied the legend with a ready means of setting aside Callimachus in favour of Miltiades. We need not follow the myth further. The battle of Marathon was caught up into a cloud of glory, which obscured the truth of the events ; and historical criti-

The mound of Marathon.

The Marathonian myth.

Worship of Pan.

cism has been able to rescue only the barest outline. Callimachus in particular received less than his due, overshadowed by the fame of Miltiades ; [but chance has preserved the name of Callimachus on a base which once carried an Ionic column mounted by a figure of Victory. Perhaps it was vowed by the polemarch before battle, and set up after his death by his son.]

One mysterious incident connected with the battle must be numbered among those historical puzzles which have never been cleared up. " When the Persians were already in their ships," a shield was flashed, as a signal to them, on the summit of Pentelicus. Who held up the shield, and what did the signal mean ? The popular explanation, in later days, was that it invited the Persians to sail straight for Athens, and the enemies of the Alcmaeonids said that they were the treacherous authors of the signal. Herodotus doubted the explanation, but he was convinced that the flashing of the shield was a well-attested fact. *The flashing of the shield.*

[Due thanksgiving was made for the victory at the great religious centre of Delphi. On the expulsion of the tyrants the Athenians, mindful of Apollo's help, had built a little Doric treasury of Pentelic marble. It seems to have been a gem of architecture, worthy of the severe grace of the sculptured reliefs which ran round the inside of the building and have been safely preserved under its ruins. The sculptures represent the deeds of Theseus and of Heracles, and the battle of the gods and giants. After Marathon a long base was built in front of the treasury to carry trophies of the battle. *The Athenian treasury of Delphi.*

The victory was also commemorated at Athens. Two large fragments of a marble base have been discovered, with two epigrams commemorating Marathon, of which the lower was not part of the original design and was inscribed later. An attractive hypothesis has been built round this strange procedure. In the life of Aeschylus we are told that in a public competition for an elegy on the Marathon dead Simonides was the victor ; Aeschylus, soured by defeat, went to Sicily. It has been suggested that Simonides' epigram was first inscribed on the monument and that it was later decided to add his rival's. On this interpretation the base will have carried a stele recording the names of the dead. The mood of thanksgiving was also expressed on the Acropolis. Under the Periclean temple of Athena, the so-called Parthenon, have been found remains of an earlier temple which was never completed. Some of the drums from its columns can still be seen built into the north wall of the Acropolis ; and its ground-plan has been recovered from surviving blocks. Excavation has shown, from pottery fragments at the level of the foundations, that this temple was begun in the eighties, but it was fired by the Persians, during Xerxes' invasion ten years after Marathon, when they sacked the city. *Memorial at Athens.* *The Acropolis.*

No attempt was made to renew the work until peace had been made with Persia in the middle of the century; and the new architect abandoned the old design. To the same period also probably belongs a monumental entrance to the Acropolis, the old Propylon, which was to be superseded by the magnificent Propylaea designed by Mnesicles during the ascendancy of Pericles. The victory was also *Coinage.* commemorated on the Athenian coinage by the placing of an olive crown on Athena's head, and by the addition of a waning moon to the reverse to indicate the time of the battle.]

Picture of the battle in the Poikilē Stoa. The descendants of the Marathonian warriors derived perhaps their most vivid idea of the combat from a picture of it which was painted about a quarter of a century later—one of the famous battle-pictures in the Portico of Frescoes in the market-place. In one scene the Athenians and Plataeans advanced against the trowsered barbarians; in a second the Persians in their flight pushed each other into the marsh; and in the last, the Phoenician ships were portrayed and the Greeks slaying the foemen who were striving to reach the ships. Callimachus, Miltiades, Datis and Artaphernes, Cynegirus seizing the prow of a ship, could all be recognised; and Theseus, who was believed to have given phantom aid to the warriors, seemed to rise out of the earth. High above the raging strife, the artist—Micon was his name—showed the gods and goddesses as they surveyed, from the tranquillity of Olympus, the prowess of their Greeks smiting the profane destroyers of the holy places of Eretria.

What the victory of Marathon meant. The significance of the victory of Marathon, as a triumph for Athens, for Greece, for Europe, cannot be gainsaid; but we must take care not to misapprehend its meaning for Greece and for Athens herself. That significance is unmistakable even if we minimise the immediate peril which was averted. The Asiatic invader had perhaps not yet come to annex; he had come only to chastise; it was enough for him if the rest of the Greeks looked on with respectful awe, while he meted out their doom to the two offending cities. His work in Euboea had been purely a work of demolition; he had not sought to annex territory or add a satrapy to the Persian dominion. The Cyclad islands and Carystus had indeed been compelled to submit to the formal authority of the Great King; but it is not proved that Darius thought of reducing the western coasts of the Aegean to the subject condition of Ionia. Thus the danger which menaced Athens may not have been subjection to an Asiatic despot. Nor was she threatened by the doom of destruction and slavery which befell Eretria. The Persian army had come to restore Hippias; and assuredly Darius did not purpose to restore his friend to a city of smouldering temples. The Athenians would be condemned to bow beneath the yoke of their own tyrant; they would not become, like their Eretrian fellows, the bondmen of a barbarian master. To be delivered over to an aged despot, thirsting for power and vengeance, embittered by twenty years of weary exile,—this was the punishment of the Athenians, and this was the fate which they escaped by their valour on the field of Marathon. If they had lost that battle and the rule of the Pisistratids had been restored, the work of twenty years ago would have had to be done again ; but that it would have been done again there can be hardly a doubt. The defeat of the Athenians would have arrested, it would not have closed, their development. It might even be argued that it would have saved Greece the terrible trial of the later Persian invasion ; if that invasion was undertaken solely to wipe out the ignominy of the repulse at Marathon. Probably, if Datis had been victorious, the subsequent attempt of Persia to conquer Greece would have assumed a different shape. But the attempt would assuredly have been made. The history of the world does not depend on proximate causes. The clash of Greece and Persia, the effort of Persia to expand at the cost of Greece, were inevitable. From the higher point of view it was not a question of vengeance ; where Darius stopped, the successors of Darius would undoubtedly go on. The success of Marathon inspirited Greece to withstand the later and greater invasion ; but the chief consequence was the effect which it wrought upon the spirit of Athens herself. The enormous prestige which she won by the single-handed victory over the host of the Great King gave her new self-confidence and ambition ; history seemed to have set a splendid seal on her democracy ; she felt that she could trust her constitution and that she might lift her head as high as any state in Hellas. The Athenians always looked back to Marathon as marking an epoch. It was as if on that day the gods had said to them, Go on and prosper.

The great battle immortalised Miltiades ; but his latter end was not good. His services at Marathon could not fail to gain for him increased influence and respect at Athens. His fellow-citizens granted *Expedition* him, on his own proposal, a commission to attack the island of Paros. *to Paros.* For the Parians had furnished a trireme to the armament of Datis, and had thereby made war upon Athens. Miltiades besieged the city of Paros for twenty-six days but without success, and then returned home wounded. The failure was imputed to criminal *Condemna-* conduct of the general ; his enemies, jealous of his exploits in the *tion of* Marathonian campaign, accused him of deceiving the people ; and he *Miltiades.* was fined fifty talents, a heavy fine. It is not known what his alleged wrongdoing was ; but afterwards, when the legend of Miltiades grew and the part which he played in the campaign of Marathon was unduly magnified, it was foolishly said that he persuaded the

Athenians to entrust the fleet to him, promising to take them to a
land of gold, and that he deceived them by assailing Paros to gratify
a private revenge.   At Paros itself, in the temple of Demeter, the
tale was told that, when the siege seemed hopeless, he corrupted a
priestess of the goddess, named Timo, and that, coming to meet her
in a sanctuary to which only women were admitted, he was seized
with panic and in his flight, leaping the fence of the precinct, hurt
his leg.   Certain it is that he returned wounded to Athens, however

His death.   he came by the chance ; appeared on a couch at his trial ; and died
soon after his condemnation.

Sect. 8. Struggle of Athens and Aegina

Hostility of   At this time Aegina was the strongest naval power in the Aegean.
Aegina   Hostile feeling had long been the rule between her and Athens, and
and
Athens,   soon after the fall of the Pisistratids the island had been involved
506 *B.C.*   in the quarrel between Athens and Thebes.   Legend said that the

(πόλεμος
ἀκήρυκτος),
498 *B.C.*

nymphs Aegina and Theba were sisters ; but it
was more than sisterly sympathy which drove
Aegina to declare a state of standing war—a war
without herald, as the Greeks called it—against
her continental neighbour.   Her ships ravaged
Phaleron and the Attic coast.   It was to be expected that Aegina would side with the Persian
when he sailed against her foe, and would cordially

Fig. 79.—Coin of
Aegina,   early
(obverse).   Sea-
turtle.

desire the humiliation of Athens.   The Athenians
had some reason to fear that she would give the
invader not only her goodwill but her active help.

Appeal of   Accordingly, the Athenians sought the intervention
Athens to   of Sparta, complaining that Aegina was medizing and betraying
Sparta ;   Greece out of enmity to Athens.   The complaint was listened to
coercion of   at Sparta, and king Cleomenes, proceeding to Aegina, seized ten
Aegina   hostages and deposited them with the Athenians.   By this means
(before
491 *B.C.*).   the hands of Aegina were tied ; she was hindered from lending
help to the Persians or hampering the men of Athens in their
preparations to meet the invaders.

This appeal of Athens to Sparta to interfere and exercise coercion
in the common interests of Hellas, and the implied recognition of
Sparta as the leading power, has been supposed to mark a climax
in that feeling of deference towards her which had been growing
up both within and without Greece.   The episode has been described
as "the first direct and positive historical manifestation of Hellas as
an aggregate body with Sparta as its chief."   This description is an
exaggeration ; for we must not lose sight of the fact—which is too

often forgotten, and which Athens took pains to forget—that Athens was, like Aegina, a member of the Peloponnesian league, and the appeal to the head of the league was therefore a matter of course.

The prestige of Sparta had indeed been confirmed and increased *Defeat of* by a decisive victory which she had won a few years before over her *Argos.* old rival Argos. The battle was fought at Sêpeia, near the hill of 494 B.C. Tiryns. According to the story, the Argive generals acted with extraordinary folly and were easily overreached by Cleomenes. They listened for the commands which the herald proclaimed to the army of their enemies, and then issued those same commands to their own men. Learning this, Cleomenes gave secret orders that, when the herald gave the word for dinner, the soldiers should pay no heed but stand prepared for battle. The Argives dined in accordance with the command of the Spartan herald, and were immediately fallen upon and destroyed by their enemies. The disaster lamed the power of Argos for more than twenty years.

The episode of the hostages of Aegina brought to a final issue the *Feud of the* great scandal of Sparta, the bitter feud of her two kings, Cleomenes *Spartan* and Demaratus. King Demaratus entered into a private compact *kings.* with the Aeginetans to thwart the intervention of king Cleomenes. Accordingly Cleomenes incited Leotychidas, the next heir of the Eurypontid line to which Demaratus belonged, to challenge the legitimacy of his rival's birth. A trial was held ; a curious story touching the birth of Demaratus was manufactured and attested ; and an oracle came from Delphi, declaring that Demaratus was not the son of his reputed father. Leotychidas consequently became king ; Demaratus fled to the court of Darius—refuge of fallen potentates—where as the friend of medizing Aegina he found a good *mit Land-* reception. Then Cleomenes and his new colleague went to Aegina *dasitz aus-* and seized the hostages. *gestattet*

But the means which Cleomenes used to ruin Demaratus recoiled *Fate of* upon himself. It was discovered that he had tampered with the *Cleomenes.* Pythian priestess at Delphi to bring about the dethronement of his enemy, and fearing the public indignation at this disclosure he fled first to Thessaly and then returned as far as Arcadia, where he conspired against his country. The Spartan government deemed it politic to invite him to return, and he accepted their offer of pardon. But his adventures had unhinged his mind ; he became a violent madman, striking with his stick every one who approached, and his kinsfolk placed him in chains under the guard of a Helot. One day, having forced his keeper by means of threats to give him [? c. 489 a sword, he wounded himself horribly and died. B.C.]

Such was the curiously inglorious end of king Cleomenes, who, if he had not been a Spartan, might have been one of the greater figures in Grecian history. But his ambition was cabined and his abilities hampered by the Spartan system; whenever, if left to himself he might have pursued an effective policy, he was checked by the other king or the Ephorate. On important occasions during his life, Sparta was called upon to take action in foreign affairs; and on each occasion we find that the policy of Cleomenes falls short of the mark owing to the opposition of his royal colleague. Even as it is, he dominates in Spartan history for more than twenty years.

War of Athens and Aegina. After his death, the Aeginetans sent envoys to Sparta, demanding the restoration of the hostages whom he and the other king Leotychidas had delivered over to Athens. Leotychidas had been the accomplice of Cleomenes in deposing Demaratus, and was consequently at this time under the shadow of public displeasure. The Spartans were ready, it is said, to hand him over to the Aeginetans as a prisoner, but the envoys preferred to ask that he should go with them to Athens and compass the restoration of the hostages. The Athenians flatly refused the demand. Aegina resorted to reprisals, and a war broke out. It began with the conspiracy of an Aeginetan citizen, named Nicodromus, who undertook with the help of Athens to overthrow the oligarchical government of his city. His plan failed because the Athenians came a day too late. The delay was due to the necessity of increasing their squadron of fifty ships by a loan of twenty more from Corinth. These ships gained a victory and landed troops on the island to besiege the town. But the Aeginetans on their side obtained some troops from Argos, and overcame the Athenians. This defeat caused disorder in the fleet, which was then attacked and routed by the islanders. But the double repulse was not decisive, and warfare was protracted between the two cities by desultory plundering raids on their respective coasts. The necessity of protecting Attica from Aeginetan depredations, the ambition perhaps of ultimately reducing Aegina to subjection or insignificance, sensibly accelerated the conversion of Athens into a naval power.

487 B.C.

SECT. 9. GROWTH OF THE ATHENIAN DEMOCRACY

The Athenian constitution underwent several important modifications in the course of the twenty years which followed its reform by Cleisthenes; and there is reason for thinking that some of the changes which tradition ascribed to Cleisthenes were really not introduced by him. Under his scheme, the power of the archons remained very great; they were usually men deliberately elected for their ability; and if the Council of Cleisthenes was a check upon them, they also were a check upon it. The natural development of

Change in method of appointing archons.

things was to strengthen the Council and weaken the magistrates. And at length, some years after Marathon, this step was taken by means of a change in the mode of appointment. Henceforward they were appointed by lot. Five hundred men were elected by the demes—in the same way in which the Council itself was elected— and out of this body of five hundred the nine archons were taken by lot. The result of any system of lot in the appointment to offices is to secure average honesty and exclude more than average ability. Henceforward the chances against any prominent statesmen holding the office of chief archon are very small. It is obvious that the political importance of the chief magistracy now disappears. It is also obvious that a polemarch appointed by lot could no longer hold the post of commander-in-chief. That post must pass to those who were deliberately picked out as competent to hold it. The powers of the polemarch were therefore vested, not in a new officer, but in the body of the ten strategi who were hitherto elected each by his own tribe. Either now or not many years later a reform was introduced by which the whole people elected the Generals, one from each tribe. [Later still, probably when Pericles dominated the political scene, and his continuous re-election seemed likely to deprive all other men of ability in his tribe of hope of the Generalship, it was made possible for one of the tribes to have two representatives on the Board of Ten.] There is no reason, however, to suppose that it ever became the practice at the election of the Generals to assign to one of the ten a position of supreme authority over all his colleagues during their whole term of office. That would have been a reinstitution of the polemarch in another form. The danger of a divided command was avoided by a simpler expedient. Whenever the people voted a military or naval expedition, they decreed which of the Generals should conduct it, and assigned a position of leadership or presidency to one of those whom they chose. But this superior command was limited to the conduct of the particular expedition ; and the General to whom it was assigned exercised it only over those of his colleagues who were specially associated with him. Special powers of a wider kind were only voted in an extreme emergency, as for Pericles when the Peloponnesians invaded Attica in 431 or for Alcibiades in the crisis of the Ionian war.

487-6 B.C.

Polemarch superseded by the Ten Generals.

We have no record touching the attitude of Cleisthenes to the venerable council of the Areopagus, nor do we hear anything about that body for a generation after the fall of the Pisistratids. But a new institution was originated during this period which weakened the position of the Areopagus by depriving it of its most important political function—that of guarding the constitution and protecting the state against the danger of a tyranny. The institution of

Ostracism. Diod. Sic. XI. 55

ostracism is traditionally ascribed to Cleisthenes, but it was not made use of till two years after the battle of Marathon. The ordinance of the *Ostrakismos* was that in the sixth prytany of each civil year the question should be laid before the Assembly of the people whether they willed that an ostracism should be held or not. If they voted in the affirmative, then an extraordinary Assembly was summoned in the market-place in the eighth prytany. The citizens were grouped in tribes, and each citizen placed in an urn a piece of potsherd (*ostrakon*) inscribed with the name of the person whom he desired to be "ostracized." The voting was not valid unless 6000 votes at least were given, and whoever had most ostraka against him was condemned to leave Attica within ten days and not set foot in it again for ten years. He was allowed however to retain his property, and remained an Athenian citizen.

By this institution the duty of guarding against the dangerous ambitions of influential citizens was transferred from the paternal council of the Areopagus to the sovereign people itself.[1] If this clumsy and, it must be owned, oppressive institution was established by Cleisthenes, it would follow that for about fifteen years the Assembly declined every year to make use of it, though it is stated that the chief object of Cleisthenes was to banish a relation of the Pisistratids, Hipparchus the son of Charmus. And in fact this Hipparchus was ultimately banished, by the first ostracism that was ever practised; and in the following year Megacles, who though an Alcmaeonid had espoused the cause of the Pisistratid faction, suffered the same fate. In these acts, as well as in the constitutional reform affecting the archonship, we must see the work of the progressive democratic statesmen, of whom the three most prominent were Xanthippus, Aristides, and Themistocles. These leaders, however, had separate policies and separate parties, and the people were persuaded to ostracise Xanthippus, and, two years later, Aristides. It is clear that in these cases there was no fear or danger of a tyranny, but that ostracism was used as a convenient engine for removing the opposition of a statesman who hampered the adoption of a popular measure. We cannot guess on what question Xanthippus stood in the way of Aristides or Themistocles, but it is possible that the ostracism of Aristides was connected with the bold naval policy which it was the great merit of Themistocles to have originated and carried through. An excellent anecdote is told of the ostracism of Aristides " the Just,"

Ostracism of Hipparchus, 487 B.C.; of Megacles, 486 B.C.;

of Xanthippus, 484 B.C.; of Aristides, 482 B.C.

[1] It is important to note that the law of ostracism did not leave it to the discretion of the Council of Five Hundred whether the question should be proposed to the Assembly or not, but ordained that it should be proposed as a matter of course at a fixed time every year. This was an additional safeguard to the people.

as he was called.   On the day of the voting an illiterate citizen
chanced to be close to Aristides who was unknown to him by sight,
and requested him to write down the name " Aristides " on the
ostrakon.   " Why," said Aristides, doing as he was asked, " do you
wish to ostracise him ? "   " Because," said the fellow, " I am tired
of hearing him called ' the Just.' "

Sect. 10. Athens to be a Sea-power

But the greatest statesman of this critical period in the history of *The work*
Athens, greater than either of his two rivals, Xanthippus and Aris- *of Themis-*
tides, greater than the hero of Marathon himself, was Themistocles, *tocles.*
the son of Neocles.   It may be said that he contributed more than
any other single man to the making of Athens into a great state.
The pre-eminent importance of his statesmanship was due in the
first place to his insight in discerning the potentialities of his city
and in grasping her situation before any one else had grasped it ; and
then to his energy in initiating, and his adroitness and perseverance in
following, a policy which raised his city, and could alone have raised
her, to the position which she attained before his death.   In the
sixth century the Athenians were a considerable naval power, as Greek
naval powers then went ; but the fleet was regarded as subsidiary to
the army.   The idea of Themistocles was to sacrifice the army to the
navy and make Athens a sea-state—the strongest sea-state in Greece.
The carrying out of this policy in the face of scepticism and opposition was the great achievement of Themistocles.   He began the
work when he was archon and thus already a man of some promi- *493-2 B.C.*
nence, two or three years before the battle of Marathon, by carrying
a measure through the Assembly for the fortification of the peninsula
of Piraeus.   Hitherto the wide exposed strand of Phaleron was the
harbour where the Athenians kept their triremes, hauled up on the
beach, unprotected against the surprise of an enemy, but within
sight of the Acropolis.   At that time, after the quelling of the Ionic
revolt, Persian warships were cruising about the Aegean, and the
possibility of an attack on Phaleron seems to have opened the eyes
of the Athenians to the need of reforming their naval establishment.
The hostility of Aegina was a nearer and more pressing motive.
The Athenians had not to seek far for a suitable port.   It seems *Harbours*
strange that they had not before made use of "the Piraeus," the *of Piraeus.*
large harbour on the west side of the peninsula of Munychia, which
could be supplemented by the two smaller harbours on the east
side, Munychia and Zea.   But the Piraeus was somewhat farther
from the city, and was not within sight of the Acropolis like Phaleron.

So long, therefore, as there was no fortified harbour, Phaleron was safer. The plan of Themistocles was to fortify the whole circuit of the peninsula by a wall, and prepare docks in the three harbours for the reception of the warships. The work was begun, but it was interrupted by the Persian invasion, and by the party struggles after Marathon. Then the war with Aegina broke out, and this, combined with the fear of another Persian invasion, helped Themistocles *Increase* to carry to completion another part of his great scheme—the increase *of fleet.* of the fleet. A rich bed of silver had been recently discovered at *(Cama-* Maronea, in the old mining district of Laurion, and had suddenly *reza.)* brought into the public treasury a large sum, perhaps a hundred 483-2 B.C. talents. It was proposed to distribute this among the citizens, but 482 B.C. Themistocles persuaded the Assembly to apply it to the purpose of building new ships. Special contributions for the same object must have been made soon afterwards ; more ships were built ; and two years later we find Athens with nearly 200 triremes at her command—a navy which could be compared with those of Syracuse and Corcyra. The completion of the Piraeus wall was not attempted at this period, but was accomplished, as we shall see, after the final repulse of the Persians from the shores of Greece.

FIG. 80.—Greek Trireme.

CHAPTER VII

THE PERILS OF GREECE.   THE PERSIAN AND PUNIC INVASIONS

THE SECOND PERSIAN WAR.

WE have now reached the threshold of the second and the greater Persian invasion—the second and the greater triumph of Hellas. The significance of this passage in their history was not lost upon the Greeks.   Their defence of Europe against the barbarians of Asia, the discomfiture of a mighty oriental despot by a league of their free states, the defeat of a vast army and a large fleet by their far smaller forces,—these surprises made an enduring impression upon the Greek mind, and were shaped by Greek imagination into a wonderful dramatic story at a time when the critical instinct had not yet developed.   No tale is more delightful than this tale as Herodotus tells it, when we take it simply as a tale ; and none illustrates better the story-shaping genius of the Greeks.   The historical criticism of it is another matter : we have to seek to extract what actually happened out of the bewildering succession of daring exaggerations, naïve anecdotes, fictitious motives, oracles, not to speak of miracles ; in most of which the reflected light of later events is visibly altering the truth, while much is coloured by the prejudices and leanings of the Athenians, from whom Herodotus seems to have derived a great part of his record.

SECT. I. THE PREPARATIONS AND MARCH OF XERXES

The chief event in Persia during the ten years which elapsed between the first and second invasions of Greece was the death of king Darius.   After the unexpected repulse of his forces at Marathon, he had determined to repeat the experiment and begun to make some preparations.   Four years passed and then a revolt broke out in the province of Egypt which demanded immediate attention.   But its suppression was delayed in consequence of the king's death, and was only accomplished under Xerxes, son of Atossa, who succeeded to the throne.   The question then arose whether the design of an

(490-80 B.C.)

Revolt— (486-5 B.C.) Egypt Death of H. vii.1 Darius, 485 B.C.

Xerxes accession N throne H. vii.3

*Subjuga-
tion of
Egypt,
484-3 B.C.*

expedition against Greece, to avenge those who fell at Marathon and redeem the fame of Persian arms, should be carried out. It is related that Xerxes was himself undecided, but was over-persuaded by the impetuous counsels of his cousin Mardonius. On the other hand, his uncle Artabanus appears in the pages of Herodotus as the prudent and experienced adviser who weighs all the obstacles and foresees failure. Xerxes, swayed hither and thither between these opposing counsels, is finally determined to yield to the wishes of Mardonius by the peremptory command of a dream, which overcomes even the scruples of Artabanus. In this manner does Herodotus pretend to take us behind the curtain of the council chamber at Susa, representing—in the light of later events—the advice of Mardonius as youthful and foolish, although that advice merely amounted to the execution of the design which, according to Herodotus himself, the old and experienced Darius had initiated and prepared. Nevertheless the contrast of Mardonius and Artabanus, and the dreams divinely sent with evil purpose, are, though not historical, a most effective dramatic introduction to the episode of the invasion. Further pressure was brought to bear on the king by Greeks who visited his court—envoys from the Aleuad princes of Thessaly and members of the Pisistratid family who brought with them the seer Onomacritus to impress Xerxes by favourable oracles.

*Canal of
Athos,
483 B.C.*

It was clear that the expedition must consist of a joint attack by sea and land. Preparations were begun by the difficult enterprise of digging a canal (about a mile and a half long) across the isthmus of Mount Athos. On the occasion of the expedition of Mardonius to Thrace and Macedonia, it will be remembered that a large part of the fleet had been wrecked in rounding that dangerous headland. But was it necessary for the fleet to venture on this occasion within the proximity of Cape Athos? Might it not sail straight across the Aegean to Greece? On these grounds Herodotus suggested that the cutting of Athos was undertaken for display rather than from necessity. This is an unsound criticism. It was a fundamental principle of Persian strategy in these expeditions that the army and navy should co-operate and never lose touch. The Thracian expedition of Darius, the Macedonian expedition of Mardonius, the Greek expedition of Xerxes illustrate this principle. The canal of Athos was intended to ensure that the ships should safely accompany the land forces along the coasts of Thrace.[1] It seems to be established that the work was completed and used, although later writers threw doubts on the "velification" of Athos. When it was finished, the

[1] Once through Athos the fleet was sheltered from the dangerous north-east winds, and it was not necessary to cut through the flat-shored promontories of Sithonia and Pallene.

workmen proceeded to lay a bridge over the Strymon for the passage of the army, and preparations were made all along the line of route for the feeding of a vast host.

Xerxes came down from Susa to Sardis in the autumn. He met the oriental contingents of his army at Critalla in Cappadocia. At Celaenae it is recorded that Pythius, the richest man in the empire, entertained at his own cost the king and the whole army. His wealth amounted to four million gold darics, all but seven thousand, and Xerxes bestowed upon him seven thousand to make up the full sum. Xerxes spent the winter at Sardis. Pythius was so pleased with the king's graciousness that when the army was about to start for the Hellespont in the following spring he ventured to prefer the request that the eldest of his five sons who were serving in the army might be permitted to remain behind. Great was the king's wrath at what he regarded as the insolent demand of a "slave." The body of the eldest son was cut in two; one half placed at each side of the gate of Sardis, through which the army was about to march forth. The anecdote illustrates the severity with which personal military service was enforced. *481 B.C. Story of Pythius.*

It is impossible to suppose that the whole army wintered in Sardis with the king; it is probable that the place of mustering was at the Hellespont across which two bridges had been constructed, in the neighbourhood of Sestos and Abydos, by Phoenician and Egyptian engineers. But the strength of these bridges was not sufficient, and a tempest destroyed them. The wrath of Xerxes at this catastrophe was violent. He not only beheaded the engineers, but commanded that 300 lashes should be inflicted on the waters of the Hellespont. Those who carried out this strange order addressed the sea as they scourged it in these words: "O bitter water, our lord lays this punishment upon thee, for having done him wrong, who never did wrong to thee. King Xerxes will cross thee, whether thou wilt or not. Just is it that no man sacrifices to thee, for thou art a treacherous and briny river." These words are blamed by Herodotus as "un-Greek and impious." The reconstruction of the bridges was entrusted to new engineers. Two lines of ships were moored across the strait by anchors at prow and stern. The line nearer to the Propontis consisted of 360, the other of 314, triremes and pente-conters mixed. Over each of these lines of ships six huge cables—two of flax, four of papyrus—were stretched; and in three places gaps were left between the ships and under the cables for small trading craft to pass between the Euxine and the Aegean. Planks were laid across the cables and kept in their places by a second layer of cables above. On this foundation a road was made with wood and earth, and at each side palisades were set, high enough to *Crossing of the Hellespont, April, 480 B.C. Herodotus VII. 35* prevent the animals which passed over from seeing the water. On a marble throne erected on the shore Xerxes is said to have witnessed the passage of his army, which began at the first moment of sunrise. The troops crossed under the lash, and the crossing was accomplished in two days. But when the size of the Persian host was magnified, in later years, to the impossible figure of five millions, the story was that the crossing of the Hellespont required seven days and seven nights—the favourite number of fiction—without a moment's pause.

Description of Persian forces. The army was joined by the fleet at Doriscus in Thrace. Fleet and army were henceforward to act together. In the plain of Doriscus Xerxes reviewed and numbered his forces. "What nation of Asia," asks Herodotus, "did not Xerxes lead against Hellas?" He enumerates forty-six peoples, with a picturesque description of their array. The Persians themselves, who were under the command of Otanes, wore coats of mail and trowsers; they had wicker shields, large bows, and short spears. The Medes, Cissians, and Hyrcanians were attired in the same way. Then there were Assyrians with brazen helmets, linen cuirasses, clubs, lances, and short swords; Bactrians with cane bows; trowsered Sacae with pointed hats, and carrying axes; Indians clad in cotton, Caspians in goatskin; Sarangians wearing dyed garments and high boots; Ethiopians clad in lion skins or leopard skins and armed with arrows whose stone points transport us to a primitive age; Sagartians with dagger and lasso; Thracians with foxskin caps; Colchians with cowskin shields. The fleet was furnished by the Phoenicians, Egyptians, Cypriotes, Cilicians, Pamphylians, Lycians, Carians, and subject Greeks. It is said to have consisted of 1207 warships, with 3000 smaller vessels. A curious story was told of the numbering of the army. Ten thousand men were packed together in a close space; a line was drawn round them, and a wall built. All the infantry passed successively into this enclosure. It was filled 170 times, so that the whole number of fighting men was 1,700,000. The number of the cavalry was 80,000, and there were some additional troops not included. Adding to these the crews of the ships—counting 200 to each larger and 80 to each smaller vessel—the total was obtained of 2,317,000 men. This enormous number was further increased by fresh contingents which joined during the march through Thrace and Macedonia. Besides the fighting men were a vast number of servants, sutlers, camp-followers, whom Herodotus considered to be quite as numerous as the soldiers. The whole host would consequently have reached to upwards of 5,000,000, not including eunuchs and concubines.

Fabulous numbers. It is needless to say that these numbers are wholly fabulous. The facts which Herodotus states as to the number of the fighting men are false, and the principle of his conjecture that the total number of the host was double that of the fighting men is also fallacious. The picked body of 10,000 troops, called the Immortals, had the privilege of travelling comfortably with their wives and baggage ; but this was an exceptional privilege, and it cannot be supposed that the mass of the troops were accompanied by servants. There is reason for supposing that the land forces may have amounted to perhaps 180,000. A larger force than that would have been un-manageable in a small mountainous country, and the difficulties of provisioning even this were formidable. The number of the fleet must also be considerably reduced—perhaps to 800 triremes.

From Doriscus, Xerxes proceeded to Therma with his fabulous host, in three divisions, drinking rivers dry in their march. At the crossing of the Strymon, near the place called the Nine Roads, he sacrificed nine native youths and virgins. At Therma he was *August,* rejoined by his fleet.   480 B.C.

Most of the incidents which Herodotus recounts concerning this *Tendencies* march of Xerxes are pleasing stories, designed to illustrate the his- *of the* torian's general view as to the great stuggle of Greek and barbarian. *Greek story.* The cruelty of Xerxes to Pythius, his barbarity and impiety in scourging the Hellespont, serve to characterise the barbarian and the despot. The enormity of the host which rolled over the straits to deluge Europe enhances the danger and the glory of Hellas. And to signify by a solemn portent the destined discomfiture of the Persian host, it is stated that as Xerxes was setting forth from Sardis the sun was darkened. No eclipse was visible at Sardis in the spring of 480. In 481, however, a total eclipse was visible at Sparta. The tradition which Herodotus follows has moved it forward to heighten the dramatic effect.

SECT. 2. PREPARATIONS OF GREECE

In the meantime Greece was aware of the preparations of the Great King for her enslavement, and was making her counter-preparations. The digging at Athos had warned her betimes, and the coming down of the king to Sardis showed that the danger was imminent. Xerxes is said to have dispatched from Sardis heralds to all the Greek states, except Athens and Sparta, to demand earth and water. These two cities now joined hands to resist the invasion. They were naturally marked out as the leaders of Greece in Greece's greatest crisis ; Sparta by virtue of that generally acknowledged headship which we have already seen, Athens by the prestige which she had won in resisting the Mede at Marathon. They jointly *Autumn* convened an Hellenic congress at the Isthmus to consult on the *481 B.C.*

measures to be taken for common resistance to the threatened invasion. We have already observed certain indications of the growth of a Panhellenic feeling ; but this is the first instance of anything that can be called a deliberate Panhellenic policy. It is an "attempt to combine all the scattered cities of the Greek world to withstand the power of Persia. It is a new fact in Grecian history, opening scenes and ideas unlike to anything which has gone before—enlarging prodigiously the functions and duties connected with that headship of Greece which had hitherto been in the hands of Sparta, but which

The congress at Isthmus. is about to become too comprehensive for her to manage." [1] A large number of cities sent delegates to the congress, which was called the *Synedrion of Probuloi* or Congress of Representatives. It met at the Isthmus—a meeting-place marked out by its central position—under the presidency of Sparta. There the states which were represented, thirty-one in number, bound themselves together in a formal confederation by taking a solemn oath that they would

Diod. Sic. XI. 3 "tithe those who uncompelled submitted" to the barbarian, for the benefit of the Delphic god. This was a way of vowing that they would utterly destroy such traitors. A great many states, the

Policy of the northern states. Thessalians, most of the Boeotian cities, besides the smaller peoples of northern Greece—Locrians, Malians, Achaeans, Dolopians, and others—took no part in this congress. Their inaction by no means

Comment on their action by Diod. Sic. XI. 3 meant that they had made up their minds to "medize." They were only waiting to see how things would turn out, and, considering their geographical position, their policy might be justified by the natural instinct of self-preservation. These northern states would be first invaded by the Persian, and it was hopeless for them to think of withstanding him alone. Unless they could absolutely rely on Sparta and her confederates to support them in defending the northern frontier of Thessaly, nothing would be left for them but to submit. And with this prospect, it would have been imprudent for them to compromise themselves by openly joining the confederacy. Events proved that if they had seriously relied on that confederacy throwing all its strength into the defence of northern Greece, they would have been cruelly deceived. And, as we shall see, they were ready to resist so long as there were hopes of support from the stronger states. In some cases there were parties or classes who were favourable to the Persian cause, for example, the oligarchs of Thebes and the Aleuadae of Thessaly.

One of the great hindrances to joint action was the existence of domestic disputes. There were feuds of old standing between Thessaly and Phocis, Argos and Lacedaemon, Athens and Aegina.

[1] Grote.

The Congress attempted to reconcile such feuds, and Athens and
Aegina laid aside their enmity to fight together for Grecian freedom.
Another important question concerned the command of the confederate forces.   The claim of Sparta to the leadership of the army *Question of*
was at once admitted.   The question as to the fleet was not so clear. *leadership.*
Sparta was not a naval power, and Athens, which would furnish more
ships than any other state, had a fair claim.   But the other cities
were jealous of Athens ; they declared that they would submit only
to a Spartan leader.   The Athenian representatives, when they saw
the feeling of the allies, at once yielded the point.

The Congress made some other provisions.   While spies were
sent to observe the preparations of Xerxes in Asia Minor, envoys
went forth to various Greek states to enlist new confederates—to
win over Argos, which had sent no delegates to the Isthmus ; and to
obtain promises of assistance from Crete, Corcyra, and Syracuse. *Appeal to*
None of these embassies led to anything.   Gelon, the great tyrant of *Syracuse.*
Syracuse, was himself absorbed by the prospect of an attack of the
Carthaginians, and, even if he had wished, could have sent no aid to
the mother-country.

When the military preparations for the defence of Greece were
made, and the generals appointed, the Congress of Representatives
probably met again in spring, and then consigned the conduct of (480 *B.C.*).
affairs to the military congresses of the commanders who used to
meet together and decide on each movement under the presidency of
the Spartan leaders.   King Leonidas was leader of the confederate
army, and Eurybiadas, a Spartan who did not belong to either of the
royal families, was commander of the confederate fleet.

The Greeks had abundance of time for their preparations—for
strengthening their defences and building new ships.   Athens
probably threw herself with more energy into the work than any
other city.   One wise measure shows that she had risen to a full *Athens re-*
apprehension of the truth that a solemn hour in her history had *calls*
arrived.   She recalled those distinguished citizens whom the vote *ostracized*
of ostracism had driven into banishment during the last ten *statesmen,*
years.   Aristides and Xanthippus returned home ; their feuds with *spring,*
Themistocles were buried in the presence of the great danger ; and *480 B.C.*
the city seems to have soon shown its confidence in their patriotism
by choosing them as Generals.   These leaders will each play his
part in the coming struggle. D. Sic. XI. 5-11

SECT. 3. BATTLES OF THERMOPYLAE AND ARTEMISIUM

About the time when Xerxes reached the Hellespont, the
Thessalians sent a message to the confederacy, suggesting that the

Northern passes left open. pass of Tempe should be defended against the invading army. Accordingly 10,000 hoplites were sent. But when they arrived at the spot they found that there were other passes from Macedonia into Thessaly, by which the Persians would be more likely to come. There were the passes of Volustana and Petra which descended into the valley of the river Titaresius, and it was by one of these that Xerxes actually marched. Ten thousand hoplites were not enough to defend the three passes and certain strong elements in Thessaly had no intention of opposing the Persians. It seemed useless and dangerous to occupy this advanced post. Hence the defence of Tempe was abandoned, and the troops left Thessaly. This desertion necessarily drove all the northern Greeks—between Tempe and Thermopylae—to submit to Xerxes.

Thermo-pylae, natural features. The next feasible point of defence was Thermopylae, a narrow pass between the sea and mountain, separating Trachis from Locris. It was the gate to all eastern Greece south of Mount Oeta. At the eastern and at the western end the pass, in those days, was extremely narrow, and in the centre the Phocians had constructed a wall as a barrier against Thessalian incursions. Near the western end was Anthela, the meeting-place of the amphictionic council, while on the Locrian side one emerged from the defile near the village of Alpenoi. The retreat of the sea, and consequent enlargement of the Malian plain, have so altered the appearance of this memorable pass that it is hard to recognise its ancient description; the hot sulphur springs from which it derived its name and the sheer mountain are the two permanent features. It was possible for an active band of men, if they were debarred from proceeding by Thermopylae, to take a rough and steep way over the mountains and so reach the Locrian road at a point east of Alpenoi. It was therefore needful for a general who undertook the defence of Thermopylae to secure this path, lest a detachment should be sent round to surprise him in the rear.

Greek troops at Thermo-pylae. The Greeks determined to defend Thermopylae, and Leonidas marched thither at the head of his army. He had about 7000 men, including 4000 from Peloponnesus, 1000 Phocians, 400 Thebans, 700 Thespians, and the Locrians in full force. It is possible that there may have been some other Boeotians who are not mentioned. Of the Peloponnesians more than half were Arcadians. Mycenae, free at this moment from Argive control, sent 80 men. There were Corinthians and Phliasians; 1000 Laconians, and 300 Spartans. So far as the Peloponnesians were concerned, this was only a small portion of their forces, and we may suspect that but for Athens they would have abandoned northern Greece entirely and concentrated themselves at once on the defence of the

Isthmus. But they were dependent on Athens because her fleet was so strong, and they were therefore obliged to consider her interests. To surrender Thermopylae and retire to the Isthmus meant the surrender of Attica. But the hearts of the Spartans were really set on the ultimate defence of the Isthmus, and not on the protection of the northern states ; their policy was narrow and Peloponnesian. They attempted to cover this selfish and short-sighted policy by the plea that they were hindered from marching forth in full force by the celebration of the Carnean festival, and that the Peloponnesians were delayed by the Olympic games ; they alleged that the soldiers of Leonidas were only an advance guard, the rest would soon follow. Yet the feasts did not interfere with the movement of the confederate fleet.

Policy of Sparta.

Not so Diod. Sic. XI. 5. Only a many were taken that the whole army — l dstryd.

As the land arm and the sea arm of the Persian force always operated together, it was necessary that while the Greek hoplites held the pass under Mount Oeta, the Greek triremes should oppose the Persian fleet in the straits between Euboea and the mainland. The Persians would naturally attempt to sail between Euboea and Magnesia into the Malian gulf, and thence, accompanying the advance of the army, along the western shore of the long island, to the Euripus. The object of the Greeks was to prevent this, and support the garrison of Thermopylae by controlling the Malian gulf.

Position of Greek fleet. D. Sic. XI. 12–13

The Greek fleet, which numbered 324 triremes and 9 pente-conters—the Athenians contributing 200—chose its station near Artemisium on the north coast of Euboea. Three ships were sent forward to reconnoitre in the Thermaic gulf, and two of them were destroyed by the Persians. This was the first collision in the war. The incident is said to have so depressed the Greeks that the whole squadron sailed back to the Euripus ; but this is highly unlikely, for it was bound to remain at the mouth of the Malian gulf, so long as Leonidas held Thermopylae. It was however necessary that the Euripus should be guarded. For there was the possibility that the Persians might send round a detachment by the south of Euboea and so cut off their retreat. As fifty-three Athenian ships were absent during the first conflicts at Artemisium, it may be supposed that they were deputed to the service of keeping watch at the Euripus.

in D. S. XII. 280 ships. 140 Ath.

In the month of July the Persian army arrived at Ther-mopylae, and the Persian navy at the Magnesian coast between Casthanaea and Cape Sepias. Their ships were so many that they could not all be moored at the shore, and had to range themselves in eight lines parallel to the coast. While they were in this unsafe position a great storm rose and destroyed a considerable number of their ships. Thus the gods intervened, to lessen the inequality between the Persian and the Greek forces. Encouraged by this disaster, the Greek fleet returned to its station at Artemisium. In this account of Herodotus, the main fact is that the Persians suffered serious loss by a storm off the Magnesian coast. But the loss is exaggerated in proportion to the exaggeration of the original size of the fleet, and the movements of the Greeks are probably misrepresented. The story goes on that cowed by the numerical superiority of the Persians, even after their losses, the Greek commanders wished to retreat again and were restrained from doing so by Themistocles. The Euboeans were naturally anxious that the fleet should remain where it was, as a protec-

FIG. 81.

tion to themselves, and to secure this they gave Themistocles thirty talents. Of this sum Themistocles distributed eight in bribes to his colleagues and kept the rest. The facts of the case throw doubt on this story, which was perhaps suggested by what happened some weeks later at Salamis. For Eurybiadas and the Peloponnesians were bound to stay at Artemisium so long as the land army was at Thermopylae.

After the storm the Persians took up their station at Aphetae. They determined to cut off the Greek retreat, and secretly sent a squadron of 200 vessels to sail round Euboea. The news of this movement was brought to the Greek camp by Scyllias of Scione, the most remarkable diver of his time, who plunged into the sea at

Aphetae and did not emerge above water till he reached Artemisium
at a distance of ten miles.   Herodotus, indeed, hesitates to accept this
tale, and records his private belief that Scyllias arrived at Artemisium
in a boat.   The Greeks decided that when midnight had passed they
would sail to meet the ships which were sailing to the Euripus, but
in the afternoon they attacked the enemy, just to see how they
fought, and they succeeded in capturing thirty Persian ships.   The *Persian*
night was very stormy ; the gods had again intervened to aid Greece. *losses.*
The 200 ships, having rounded the southern cape of Euboea,
were wrecked off the dangerous coast known as the Hollows.
Immediately afterwards the fifty-three Attic ships which had not
yet appeared at Artemisium arrived there, and at the same time
came the news of the disaster.   The Greeks consequently gave up
the intention of retreating.   There was some further fighting, with loss
on both sides ; with no decisive advantage, according to the Greek
account, but we may suspect that the Persians had the best of it.

Meanwhile Leonidas had taken up his post at Thermopylae, *Battle of*
and the Phocians, who knew the ground, had undertaken the *Thermo-*
defence of the bye-road over the mountains.   The old Phocian wall *pylae.*
in the centre of the pass was repaired.   It was a serious matter for
even such a large army as that which was now encamped in the
Malian plain to carry the narrow way of Thermopylae against
6000 determined men.   For four days Xerxes waited, expecting
that they would retreat, awed by the vision of his mighty host.
On the fifth he attacked ; and in the engagements which took place
at the west end of the pass the Hellenic spearmen affirmed their
distinct superiority to the Asiatic archers.   On the following day the
result was the same ; the Immortals themselves made no impression
on the defenders.   Herodotus says that Xerxes "sprang thrice
from his throne in agony for his army."   It was then decided to
send round the Immortals — hardly the whole 10,000 — under
their commander Hydarnes, by the mountain road to take the
Greeks in the rear.   A Malian Greek named Epialtes guided the
band and so won the name of having betrayed Greece.   At dawn
they reached the highest point of the path, where the Phocians
were posted.   The Phocians fled to the heights, and the Persians
went on paying no attention to them.   Meanwhile deserters
informed Leonidas of the Persian stratagem.   He hastily called a
council of war.   The exact plan of action which was decided on is
unknown.   We only know that the Spartans, Thebans, and
Thespians remained in the pass, while the rest of the Greeks retired
southward.   It was afterwards represented that they had deserted
the defence of the position and returned home.   But in that case,
it was foolish, if splendid, of Leonidas to hold the pass between foes

on both sides. The rational courses were either for the whole garrison to abandon the pass, or else, just as the Persians aimed at enclosing the Greeks, so to enclose the band of Hydarnes. We may suspect that this second plan was actually adopted. While part of the force, including Leonidas and the Spartans, remained in the pass, the rest (we may suppose) placed themselves at some distance east of the point where the mountain path descended to the road, so as to take Hydarnes in the rear. Of the 1400 who stood in the pass, some had to guard the eastern entrance against Hydarnes, others the western against the main army. Leonidas and his 300 undertook the western side. But they were no longer content with merely repelling assaults ; they now rushed out upon the enemy. Their charge was effective, but Leonidas himself was slain, and a Homeric battle raged over his body. Two brothers of Xerxes fell. Many Persians were driven into the sea. But at length the defenders were forced back behind the wall. They drew together on a hillock where they made a last stand, to be surrounded and slain by overwhelming numbers. For the Immortals, having in the meantime routed the Greeks in their rear, had now forced their way into the pass. It was said that 4000 Greeks fell.

For another version might look to seed Diod. Siculus XI.10 [marginal note]

The valiant defence of Thermopylae made a deep impression upon Greece, and increased the fame of the Spartans for bravery. It was represented as a forlorn defence—Leonidas and his band devoting themselves to certain death, and clinging to their posts from that sense of military duty which was inculcated by the Spartan system from early youth. The brave Thespians would not desert the Spartans ; while the Thebans are represented as detained by Leonidas against their will, because they were suspected of secret medism. The malicious tale adds that, having taken only a perfunctory part in the defence, the Thebans advanced to the enemy and asked for quarter, declaring that they were friends of the Great King and had come to Thermopylae against their will. Their lives were spared, but all, including the commander, were forced to suffer the shame of being branded as bad slaves. It is certain that this contrast between the Thespians and Thebans was invented in the light of the subsequent medism of Thebes. Nor is it clear that the defence of Thermopylae, although eminently heroic, was, until the very end, desperate. If, as we suspected, an effort was made to meet the Immortals, then, if that effort had been more effectual, it might have been possible to hold the pass ; and in that case a naval battle must have decided whether the Persians or the Greeks would be forced to retreat.

Behaviour of Thebans. [margin]

A column was afterwards erected at Sparta with the names of Leonidas and his 300. Among them was to be read the name

Econium Sprites &c. XI.11 D. Sic. [marginal note]

of Diēnekes, reputed as the author of a famous *mot*, which displayed the lightheartedness of a Spartan soldier in the hour of peril. When it was observed to him that the Persian host was so enormous that their arrows hid the sun, he replied, "So much the better, we shall fight in the shade."

The news of Thermopylae speedily reached the fleet at Artemisium. *Retreat of* The Greeks forthwith weighed anchor and sailed through the Euripus *Greek fleet.* to the shores of Attica.

SECT. 4. BATTLE OF SALAMIS *Diod . Siculus XI. 14-8*

Having thus succeeded in breaking through the inner gate of 480 *B.C* Hellas, and slain the king of the leading state, Xerxes continued his *(August)*. way and passed from Locris into Phocis and thence into Boeotia, *Sic. XI. 14* meeting with no resistance. The Thebans and most of the other Boeotians now, unable to do otherwise, submitted to the Persians. The loss of Thermopylae forced them to this course, as the abandonment of Tempe had forced the Thessalians.

In later days a story was told at Delphi that a Persian band *Delphic* detached itself from the main host in Phocis, in order to proceed *legend.* to Pytho and plunder the shrine of the god. "I think," says *D.Sic. XI. 14* Herodotus, "that Xerxes knew its treasures better than his own." The Delphians fled up into the heights of Parnassus, leaving only sixty men and the prophet Acĕrătus in the temple. They did not remove the treasures, for the god said that he would protect his own. As soon as the barbarians approached, marvels began to happen. The prophet saw the sacred arms, which no man might touch, lying in front of the temple, carried out by some mysterious means. And when the Persians came to the shrine of Athena Pronaea, which stood not far from the Castalian fountain, lightning flashed; two crags rent from Parnassus fell with a loud crash, crushing many of them; and a war-whoop was heard from Athena's temple. The barbarians fled in terror, and told how two hoplites of superhuman size pursued them. These were Phylacus and Autonous, the native heroes of Delphi. Such was the legend told at Delphi of the Persian invasion.

When the Athenians returned from Artemisium they found that *The* the main body of the Peloponnesian army was gathered at the *Athenians* Isthmus and engaged in building a wall from sea to sea, instead of *leave* advancing to the defence of Boeotia as had been previously arranged. *Attica.* Thus Boeotia and Attica were unprotected. Themistocles and his *D.Sic XI. 15* Athenian colleagues decided to evacuate Athens. They made a proclamation that all the citizens should embark in the triremes, and that all who could should convey their families and belongings to places of safety. This was done. The women and children were transported to Troezen, Aegina, and Salamis. The council of Areopagus helped at this crisis by distributing from the treasury of Athena eight drachmae to each citizen who embarked. At the same time the great natural strength of the Acropolis, though its walls had been demolished after the expulsion of the tyrants, encouraged the hope that it might be held against the Persians, and a small garrison was left to defend it. This bold and wise policy of embarkation was dictated by the circumstances, but it was supposed to have been based on an oracle, which foretold the utter destruction of Attica with the sole exception of a " wooden wall." The wooden wall was interpreted to mean the ships. And to suit this view it was represented that the garrison left on the Acropolis was merely a handful of poor citizens who remained behind and barricaded themselves there, because they adopted the more literal interpretation of a wooden barricade. This explanation of the oracle was perhaps suggested by subsequent events.

While the Athenians were thus showing that they were not bound to their soil, the allied fleet had stationed itself in the bay of Salamis, and it was reinforced by new contingents, so that it reached the total strength of 378 triremes and seven penteconters. The army at the Isthmus was now placed under the command of Cleombrotus, brother of Leonidas and guardian of his son Pleistarchus, who was still a child.

c. Sept. 17.   Xerxes arrived at Athens about the same time that his fleet sailed into the roadstead of Phaleron. He found the town empty, but for the small band which had entrenched itself on the Acropolis. *Persians* Persian troops occupied the lower height of the Areopagus, which is *capture the* severed from the Acropolis by a broad saddle, and succeeded in *Acropolis.* setting the wooden barricade on fire by means of burning arrows. The garrison rolled stones down on them, and such is the natural strength of the Acropolis that the siege lasted two weeks. Then the Persians managed to ascend on the precipitous north side by the secret path which emerged close to the shrine of Aglaurus. The Greeks were slain, the temples plundered and burnt.

Will the After the fall of the Acropolis the Greek generals held a council *Greek fleet* of war, and it was carried by the votes of the majority that they *fight at* should retreat to the Isthmus and await there the attack of the *Salamis* Persian fleet. The advantage of this seemed to be that they would *or the* there be in close touch with the land forces and have the Peloponnesus *Isthmus?* as a retreat in case of defeat ; whereas at Salamis they would be entirely cut off. This decision meant the abandonment of Aegina, Salamis, and Megara ; and it was strenuously opposed by the Aeginetans, Athenians, and Megarians. Themistocles determined to

thwart it.   He went privately to Eurybiadas and convinced him
that it would be much more advantageous to fight in the narrow
waters of the Salaminian channel than in the open bay of the Isthmus,
where the superior speed and number of the hostile ships would tell.
A new council was summoned at which, it is said, hot words passed
between the Athenian and the Corinthian general.   When Themistocles opened the debate without waiting for the formal introduction
of Eurybiadas, the Corinthian Adeimantus said, " O Themistocles,
those who stand up too soon in the games are whipped."   "Yes,"
was the reply, " but those who start late are not crowned."   It
is recorded that Themistocles, in order to carry his point, had to
threaten that the Athenians, who were half the fleet, would cease to
co-operate with their allies and seek new homes in some western
land, if the retreat to the Isthmus were decided.   Themistocles won
his way ; and when it was resolved to fight in Salaminian waters, the
heroes of the island, Ajax and Telamon, were invoked, and a ship
was sent to Aegina to fetch the other Aeacid heroes.

Of all the tales of signs and marvels which befell in these *What*
memorable days none perhaps was more attractive to the Athenians *Demaratus*
than the experience of two Greek exiles as they walked in the *and*
Thriasian plain.   One was an Athenian named Dicaeus, and his com- *Dicaeus*
panion was none other than Demaratus, the Spartan king, who had *saw in the*
sought refuge at the Persian court.   As they went, they saw a great *Thriasian*
dust afar off near Eleusis, such a dust as they thought might be *plain.*
raised by a host of thirty thousand men ; and then they heard a voice
suddenly from the midst of the dust, and it sounded like the cry
of the mystic Iacchus which is cried at the Eleusinian festival.
Demaratus asked his companion what it might be.   " It is a token,"
said Dicaeus, " of some great disaster to the King's host.   For since
the plain is desolate of men, it is clear that the thing which uttereth
the cry is divine,—and it is a thing coming from Eleusis to help the
Athenians.   If it turn to the Peloponnese, the peril menaces the
army of the land, but if it wend toward the ships, then are the
King's ships endangered."   " Peace," said Demaratus, " for if these
words of thine come to the King's ears, thou shalt lose thy head."
Then the dust, wherein the voice was, turned to a cloud, and rising
aloft moved towards the Greek fleet at Salamis ; and so they knew
that the fleet of Xerxes was doomed.

Meanwhile the Persians too had deliberated and determined to
fight.   According to a Halicarnassian story told by Herodotus, the
Carian queen Artemisia alone gave sound advice—not to risk a sea
fight but either to wait for the Greek fleet to disperse from want of
provisions, or to advance by land into the Peloponnesus.

The southern entrance to the narrow sound between Salamis and

Attica is blocked by the islet of Psyttalea and the long promontory which runs out from Salamis towards the mainland. The Greek fleet was anchored close to the town of Salamis, north of this promontory. It would be best for the Greeks if they could lure the Persian fleet to enter the Salaminian bay so that its flank would be exposed as it sailed through the narrow waters. It would be best for the Persians if they could force the Greeks out into the open sea. Xerxes foresaw the possibility that his enemies might attempt to escape at night, and to prevent this he moved his armament so as to enclose the ingresses of the two straits on either side of Psyttalea,

FIG. 82.

and landed troops on that island, to rescue Persians and kill Greeks who should happen to swim to its shores in the expected battle. These movements, carried out in the afternoon, alarmed the Greeks; the Peloponnesian commanders brought pressure to bear on Eurybiadas; another council was called, and Themistocles saw that the *Artifice of* hard-won result of his previous exertions would now be overthrown. *Themis-* He therefore determined on a bold stroke. Leaving the council, he *tocles* dispatched a slave named Sicinnus to the Persian camp bearing a *to bring on* message from himself, as a well-wisher to Xerxes, that the Greeks *a battle.* purposed to sail away in the night. If they were prevented from doing so, a Persian victory was certain, owing to the disunion which existed in the Hellenic camp. If the Persians attacked the Greeks where they were, the Athenians would turn against their allies.   This message was believed, and Xerxes took his measures at nightfall to hinder the Greek fleet from escaping by the western straits between Salamis and the Megarid.   He sent his 200 Egyptian ships to round the southern promontory of Salamis and place themselves so that they could bar the straits.   And he decided to attack in the morning—a fatal decision, which only the prospect of the treachery of some of his foes could have induced him to take.

The Greek generals meanwhile were engaged in hot discussion. Suddenly Themistocles was called out from the council.   It was his rival Aristides who had sailed across from Aegina and brought the news that the fleet was surrounded by the enemy.   Themistocles made Aristides inform the generals of what had happened, and the tidings was presently confirmed by a Tenian ship which deserted from the Persians.   There is no reason to question the sensational incident that Aristides brought the news ; but we need not suppose that this was his first return from ostracism.   It seems probable that he had been sent with the ship which fetched the Aeacids from Aegina and that he was one of the ten strategoi.

Themistocles had managed that a naval battle should be fought *Position of* at Salamis, and under the conditions most favourable to the Greeks. *fleets on* The position and tactics of the two armaments have been the *day before* subject of much debate.   According to the poet Aeschylus, who *battle.* was an eyewitness of the battle, the Persian ships were drawn up in three lines outside the entrance into the sound.   The extreme left wing was composed of the Ionian Greeks, while the right, towards the Piraeus, was the Phoenician squadron on which Xerxes chiefly relied.   The Greek fleet was drawn up behind the promontory of Cynosura and facing northward ; the Athenians on the left, near the town of Salamis ; the Aeginetans probably near them ; and the Lacedaemonians on the right.   On the opposite mainland shore, under Mount Aegaleos, a high throne was erected, from which Xerxes could survey the battle and watch the conduct of his men.

At break of day the Persians began to advance into the straits. *The battle,* The three lines converted their formation into three columns, and *c. Sept. 20.* the Phoenicians led the way through the opening between Psyttalea and the mainland.   The Ionians on the left would naturally move through the smaller channel between Psyttalea and Salamis.   When the Phoenicians came into view, the Athenian squadron immediately advanced, assailed them in the flank, and cut them off from the rest of the fleet, driving them towards the Attic shore.   The other Persian divisions crowded through the straits, and a furious mellay ensued, which lasted till nightfall.   There was no room for the exercise of tactical skill in the crowded, narrow waters, where the fairway (between Cynosura and Attica) is little more than a mile in breadth. The valour of the Aeginetans was conspicuous. They seem to have completed the discomfiture of the Phoenicians, and to have dispersed the Ionians.

Causes of Persian defeat.   The Persians, under the eyes of their king, fought with great bravery, but they were badly generalled and the place of the combat was unfavourable to them. By sunset the great armament of Xerxes was partly destroyed, partly put out of action. Aristides, who with a force of Athenian hoplites was watching events on the shore of Salamis, crossed over to Psyttalea and killed the barbarians who had been posted there by Xerxes.

Anecdote of Artemisia.   Among the anecdotes told about this battle the most famous is that which was current at Halicarnassus, of the signal bravery and no less signal good fortune of the Carian queen Artemisia. She saved herself by the stratagem of attacking and sinking another Carian vessel. Those who stood round Xerxes observed the incident, but supposed the destroyed trireme to be Greek. "Sire," they said, "seest thou how Artemisia has sunk an enemy's ship." And Xerxes exclaimed, "My men have become women, my women men."

SECT. 5. CONSEQUENCES OF SALAMIS

Movements of the Persians after the defeat,   The Greek victory of Salamis was a heavy, perhaps a decisive, blow to the naval arm of the Persian power. The wrath of Xerxes against the Phoenicians was boundless. On them he had relied, and to their infidelity he ascribed the loss of the battle; his threats so frightened the remnant of the Phoenician contingent that they deserted. But the prospects of the ultimate success of the invasion were still favourable. The land army had met with no reverse, and was overwhelmingly superior in numbers. The only difficulty was to keep it supplied with provisions, and in this respect the loss of the command of the sea was a serious misfortune. The Greeks represented Xerxes as smitten with wild terror, fleeing back overland to the Hellespont and hardly drawing breath till he reached Susa. This dramatic glorification of the victory misrepresents the situation.

and the cause thereof.   Xerxes personally was in no jeopardy. The real danger lay not in Attica but in Ionia. The Persians had good reason to fear the effect which the news of the crushing defeat of their navy might have upon the Greeks of Asia, and if Xerxes dreaded anything, he dreaded the revolt which actually came to pass in the following year. It was all-important for him to secure his line of retreat, while he had no intention of relinquishing his enterprise of conquering Greece. These considerations explain what happened. The Persian fleet was immediately dispatched to the Hellespont to guard the bridge and the line of retreat. The land forces were placed under the command of Mardonius, who, as the season was now advanced, determined to postpone further operations till the spring and to winter in Thessaly. A force of 60,000 men was detached to accompany Xerxes to the Hellespont.

When he arrived the bridge was no longer there. Either it had been destroyed by storm or perhaps its ships had been used as transports. The fleet took him across to Abydos, and he proceeded to Sardis which he made his headquarters. The convoy of 60,000 soldiers returned to the main army in Thessaly, and on their way they laid siege to two towns, which afterwards became famous, on the Pallene isthmus, Olynthus and Potidaea. Olynthus, then a *Olynthus* Bottiaean town, was taken and handed over to the Chalcidians who *becomes* had remained faithful to Persia. Potidaea successfully withstood a *a Greek* siege of three months. *town :* *480 B.C.*

Meanwhile the Greeks had failed to follow up their victory. Cleombrotus was about to advance from the Isthmus with the purpose of aiming a blow at the retreating columns of the Persian forces before they reached Boeotia. But as he was sacrificing, before setting out, *Eclipse of* two hours after noon on the second of October, the sun was totally *the sun,* eclipsed, and this ill-omen made him desist from his plan and march *Oct. 2,* back to the Peloponnesus. Themistocles tried to induce the naval *480 B.C.,* commanders to follow up their advantage by sailing after the Persian *2 P.M.* fleet to the Hellespont, that they might deal it another blow and break down the bridge. It might be expected that, if this were done, the Greeks of Ionia would revolt. But the Peloponnesians would not consent to sail to a distant part of the world, while the Isthmus was still threatened by the presence of the Persian army. The story goes that, having failed to get his advice adopted, Themistocles, with that characteristic adroitness which won the admiration of his contemporaries, determined to utilise his failure. The faithful Sicinnus was sent to Xerxes to assure the monarch of the goodwill of Themistocles, who had dissuaded the Greeks from pursuing the Persian fleet. Themistocles might expect that Xerxes, having been deceived before, would now disbelieve his announcement and therefore hasten back with all speed to reach the Hellespont, if possible, before the Greeks. But on a later day of his life, when he was an exile, he claimed Persian gratitude for this service. It was even represented that, with extraordinary longsightedness or treachery, he had in his view the contingency of being driven to seek Persian help or protection against his countrymen. But the tale need not be seriously criticised ; it has all the appearance of an invention suggested by subsequent adventures of the subtle Athenian.

The island of Andros and the Euboean city Carystus had furnished

Andros and Carystus. contingents to the Persian fleet. Just as the Athenians, after the battle of Marathon, had sailed against Paros and demanded a war contribution, so now the Greeks acted against Andros and Carystus. They failed at Andros, just as Miltiades had failed at Paros; they devastated the territory of Carystus.

Prizes of bravery to the warriors of Salamis. Great was the rejoicing in Greece over the brilliant victory which was so little hoped for. The generals met at Isthmus to distribute the booty, and adjudge rewards. The Aeginetans received the choice lot of the spoil on account of their pre-eminent bravery, and dedicated in the temple of Delphi, on Apollo's express demand, three golden stars set on a mast of bronze. For bravery the Athenians were adjudged the second place. Prizes were also proposed for individuals who had distinguished themselves for valour, or for wisdom. In adjudging the prizes for wisdom, each captain wrote down two names in order of merit and placed his tablet on the altar of Poseidon at Isthmus. The story is that each wrote his own name first and that of Themistocles second, and that consequently there was no prize, for a second could not be given, unless a first were also awarded. This ingenious anecdote reflects the reputation for cleverness which had been won by Themistocles.

The epitaphs. The Corinthians who fell in the battle were buried in Salamis, and their sepulchral stélé was inscribed with a simple distich telling the stranger that "Salamis the isle of Ajax holds us now, who once dwelled in the city of Corinth between her waters." The stone has been recently found. This is only one of many epitaphs composed by nameless authors in those days of joy and sorrow in various parts of Greece, all marked by the simplicity of a great age, whose reserve, as has been said truly, is the pride of strong men under the semblance of modesty. In later days, insensible to such reserve, it became the fashion to improve these epitaphs by the addition of boastful verses, which have imposed, till recently, upon posterity; and the epitaphs thus disfigured were all said to be the workmanship of the poet Simonides. The exposure of these two deceptions increases our admiration for Hellas at the time of the invasion. There were men everywhere capable of writing a simple appropriate inscription for a grave, and the tombstones of the fallen were not used for superfluous boasts.

But the triumph of Hellas had nobler memorials than the unassuming verses of the tombs. The barbarian invasion affected art and literature, and inspired the creation of some of the great works of the world. Men seemed to rise at once to the sense of the high historical importance of their experience. The great poets of the day wrought it into their song; the great plastic artists alluded to it in their sculptures. Phrynichus had now a theme which he could

treat without any dread of another fine.   Aeschylus, who had himself *The*
fought against the Mede, made the tragedy of Xerxes the argument *Phoenissae*
of a drama, which still abides the one great historical play, dealing *of Phryni-*
with a contemporary event, that exists in literature.   But the Persian *chus.*
war produced, though not so soon, another and a greater work than *The*
the *Persians ;* it inspired the "father of history" with the theme of *Persians of*
his book—the contest of Europe with Asia.   The idea was afloat in *Aeschylus,*
the air that the Trojan war was an earlier act in the same drama,— *acted*
that the warriors of Salamis and Plataea were fighting in the same *472 B.C.*
cause as the heroes who had striven with Hector on the plain of *Herodotus.*
Troy.   Men might see, if they cared, this suggestion in the
scenes from the two Trojan wars, which were wrought by the *Sculptures*
master sculptors of Aegina to deck the pediments of the temple of *in the*
Athena, whose Doric columns still stand to remind us that Aegina *Aeginetan*
once upon a time was one of the great states of Greece.   And in *temple of*
other temples, friezes and pediments spoke in the conventional *Aphaea.*
language of sculptured legend—by the symbols of Lapiths and
Centaurs, Gods and Titans—of the struggle of Greek and barbarian.

Sect. 6. Preparations for another Campaign

The words of the poet Aeschylus, that the defeat of the Persian *Prospects of*
sea-host was the defeat of the land-host too, were perfectly true for *Greece.*
the hour.   But only for the hour.   The army, compelled after
Salamis to retreat to the north, spent the winter in the plains of
Thessaly, and was ready for action, though unsupported by a fleet,
in the following spring.   The liberty of Greece was in greater
jeopardy than ever, and the chances were that the success of Salamis
would be utterly undone.   For in the first place the Greeks,
especially the Lacedaemonians and Athenians, found it hard to act
together.   This had been shown clearly the year before, eminently
on the eve of the Salaminian battle.   The Peloponnesian interests of
the Lacedaemonians rendered them unwilling to meet the enemy in
northern Greece ; while the northern Greeks, unless they were
supported from the Peloponnesus, could not attempt a serious
resistance, and were therefore driven to come to terms with the
barbarians.   And, in the second place, if these difficulties were
overcome and a Panhellenic force were opposed to the Persians,
the chances were adverse to the Greeks ; not from the disparity of
numbers, but from the deficiency of the Greeks in cavalry.

In spring Mardonius was joined by Artabazus and the troops who *479 B.C.*
had conducted Xerxes to the Hellespont.   The total number of the
forces now at the disposal of Mardonius is unknown ; it may perhaps
have been 120,000.   Meanwhile the Persian fleet, weakened by the

absence of the Phoenician ships, was collected at Samos, with the purpose of guarding Ionia; and a Greek squadron of 110 ships gathered at Aegina under the command of the Spartan king *Inactivity* Leotychidas, for the purpose of defending the coasts of Greece, but *of Greek* not intending to assume the offensive. With great difficulty some *fleet.* envoys from Chios induced Leotychidas to advance as far as Delos, but he could not be moved to sail farther east with a view to the liberation of Ionia, for " Samos seemed as far away as the Pillars of Heracles," and he dreaded the Persian waters teeming with unknown dangers. It seems probable that Athenian policy was working upon the Spartan admiral's inexperience in military affairs. The object of the Athenians was to secure their own land against a second Persian occupation. They therefore desired the protection of the fleet for their coasts; but there was a more important consideration still. If the fleet took the offensive and gained another naval victory, the Peloponnesus would be practically secured against a Persian attack, defended at once by a victorious navy and the fortifications of the Isthmus. The result would be that the Peloponnesians would refuse to take any further part in the defence of northern Greece and would leave Athens a prey to the army of Mardonius. It was therefore the policy of the Athenians to keep the fleet inactive until the war should have been decided by a battle on land; and for this reason they equipped only a few of their ships.

Mardonius Mardonius, well aware of this fatal division of interests between *tempts* the Athenians and Peloponnesians, made a politic attempt to with-*Athens.* draw Athens from the Greek league. He sent an honourable Diod. ambassador, King Alexander of Macedon himself, with the most Siov.28 generous offers. He undertook to repair all the injuries suffered by Athens from the Persian occupation, to help her to gain new territory, and asked only for her alliance as an equal and independent power. In a desolated land, amid the ruins of their city and its temples, knowing well that their allies, indifferent to the fate of Attica, were busy in completing the walls of Isthmus, the Athenians might be sorely tempted to lend an ear to these seductive overtures. Had they done so, the fate of Peloponnesus would have been sealed, —as the Lacedaemonians knew. Accordingly envoys were sent from Sparta to counteract the negotiations of Alexander, and to offer Athens material help in the privations which she was suffering. Tempting as the proposals of Mardonius sounded, and good reason as they had to depend little on the co-operation of their allies, the Athenians were constrained by that instinct of freedom which made them a great *The* people, to decline the Persian offer. " Tell Mardonius," they said to *answer* Alexander, " that the Athenians say : so long as the sun moves in his *of Athens.* present course, we will never come to terms with Xerxes." This

See also
Diod-Sic. XI. 28

answer utters the spirit of Europe in the "eternal question" between the East and West—the spirit of the Senate when Hannibal was at the gates of Rome, the spirit of Roman and Goth when they met the riders of Attila on the Catalaunian Plain.

Thus the embassy of Alexander ought to have strengthened *Difficulty* rather than weakened the Greek league. It ought to have made *of moving* the Lacedaemonians more actively conscious of the importance of *Sparta to action.* Athenian co-operation, and consequently readier to co-operate with Athens. It enabled Athens to exert stronger pressure on the Peloponnesians, with a view to the defence of northern Greece ; and the Spartan envoys promised that an army should march into Boeotia. But still stronger pressure was needed to overcome the selfish policy of the Peloponnesians. Soon after the embassy of Alexander they had completed the walling of the Isthmus, and, feeling secure, they took no thought of fulfilling their promise. The Spartans alleged in excuse the festival of the Hyacinthia, just as the year before they had pleaded the Carnea. And in the meantime Mardonius had set his army in motion and advanced into Boeotia, with the purpose of reoccupying Attica. Once more the Athenians had been cruelly deceived by their allies ; once more they had to leave their land and remove their families and property to the refuge of Salamis. Mardonius reached Athens without burning or harrying ; he still hoped to detach the Athenians from the Greek cause ; herein lay his best chance of success. If they would now accept his former offers he would retreat from their land, leaving it unravaged. But even at this extremity, under the bitter disappointment of the ill-faith of their allies, the Athenians rejected the insidious propositions which were laid by an envoy before the Council of the Five Hundred at Salamis. Immediately the three northern states which had not yielded to the Mede, Athens, Megara, and Plataea, sent ambassadors to Sparta, to insist upon an army marching at once to oppose Mardonius in Attica—a tardy redemption of their promises—with the threat that otherwise there would be nothing for it but to come to terms with the foe. Even now the narrow Peloponnesian policy of the Ephors almost betrayed Greece. For ten days, it is said, they postponed answering the ambassadors, and would have ultimately refused to do anything, but for the intervention of a man of Tegea, named Chileos, who impressively pointed out that the alliance of the Athenian naval power with the Persians would render the Isthmian fortifications on which the Ephors relied absolutely useless. One would have fancied that this was obvious even to an Ephor, without a prophet from Tegea to teach him. However it happened, the Lacedaemonian government suddenly changed its policy and dis- *Sparta* patched a force of 5000 Spartans, each attended by some Helots, to *acts.*

northern Greece.   Never since, never perhaps before, did so large a body of Spartan citizens take the field at once.   They were followed by 5000 perioeci, each attended by one Helot.   It was clear that Sparta had risen at last to an adequate sense of the jeopardy of the Peloponnesus.   The command was entrusted to Pausanias, who was acting as regent for his child-cousin Pleistarchus, son of the hero of Thermopylae.   At the Isthmus, the Lacedaemonian army was joined by the troops of the Peloponnesian allies, and by contingents from Euboea, Aegina, and western Greece ;[1] in the Megarid they were reinforced by the Megarians, and at Eleusis by Aristides in command of 8000 Athenians and 600 Plataeans.   It was entirely an army of foot soldiers, and the total number, including light armed troops, may have approached **100,000.**   The task of leading this host devolved upon Pausanias.

Movements of Mardonius.   The strong fortress of Thebes, which he had abundantly supplied with provisions, was the base of Mardonius; and once the Greek army was in the field, he could not run the risk of having his communications with his base broken off and finding himself shut up in Attica, a land exhausted by the devastation of the preceding autumn.   Accordingly he withdrew into Boeotia, having completed the ruin of Athens, and having sent a detachment to make a demonstration in the Megarid.   He did not take the direct route to Thebes, but marching northward to Decelea and by the north side of Mount Parnes he reached Tanagra and the plain of the Asopus.   Marching up this stream, westward, he came to the spot where it is crossed by the road from Athens to Thebes, at the point where that road descends from the heights of Cithaeron.   The river Asopus was the boundary between the Theban and Plataean territories, and the destruction of Plataea was probably an object of the Persians.   But the main purpose of Mardonius in posting himself on the Asopus was that he might fight with Thebes behind him.   The Persians had every cause to be sanguine.   Not only had they superior, though not overwhelmingly superior, forces, but they had a general who was far abler than any commander on the side of the Greeks.   Mardonius was not anxious to bring on a battle.   He fully realised that his true strategy was to do as little as possible ; he knew that the longer the army of the Greeks remained in the field, the more would its cohesion be relaxed through the jealousies and dissensions of the various contingents.   We need not take too seriously the story which the Greeks were afterwards fain to believe, that at this moment there was a

Diod. Sic. VI. 28-29

[1] (a) Peloponnesian : from Tegea, Orchomenus, Corinth, Sicyon, Phlius, Epidaurus, Troezen, Hermione, Lepreon, Mycenae, and Tiryns. (b) Euboean : from Chalcis, Eretria, and Styra. (c) West Greek : from Ambracia, Leucas, Anactorion, Paleis in Cephallenia.

certain dispiritedness and foreboding of disaster in the Persian camp. An anecdote told by one of the guests at a Theban banquet was thought to illustrate this gloomy mood. Attaginus, a Theban general, made a feast in honour of Mardonius. A hundred guests were present, arranged on double couches, a Persian and a Boeotian on each. Thersander of Orchomenus was among the guests, and in after-days he told the historian Herodotus that his Persian couch-fellow spoke these words to him : " Since we have now shared the same table and wine, I wish to leave thee a memorial of my opinion ; that being forewarned thou mayest look to thine own welfare. Seest thou these Persians feasting,—and the host which we left encamped by the river ? In a little while thou shalt see few of all these remaining." The Persian shed tears as he spoke, and Thersander rejoined : " It behoves thee to tell this to Mardonius " ; but the Persian said : " Stranger, man cannot avert what God hath ordained. No one would believe me. Many of us Persians know it and follow the army under constraint. No human affliction is worse than this : to know and to be helpless."

Mardonius had taken up his position and constructed a fortifica- *Strategic* tion on the north bank of the river Asopus, before the Greek army *policy of* had crossed Cithaeron. His plan was to act on the defensive. He *Mardonius.* would wait for the Greeks to attack him, so that the issue might be *XI. 30* tried in a plain when he would be able to reap the full advantage of his superiority in cavalry. It would, on the contrary, be to the interest of the Greeks, when they descended from Cithaeron, if they could by any means entice the enemy to give battle on the rough and high ground south of the river where cavalry would be of little use. *Diod. Sic.*

SECT. 7. BATTLE OF PLATAEA   Diod. Sic. XI.3

The field on which the fate of Greece was decided is bounded on *August,* the north by the river Asopus, on the south by Mount Cithaeron. 479 *B.C* The town of Plataea stood in the south-west of this space, on the most westerly of six ridges which connect the lower heights of the moun- tain with the plain. Three roads descended here into Boeotia : on the *The roads* extreme east the road from Athens to Thebes ; in the centre, that *of Cithae-* from Athens to Plataea ; on the west, that from Megara to Plataea. *ron.* The Greek army took the most easterly way, which after a gradual ascent on the Attic side reaches the fortress of Eleutherae and the pass of the Oak's Heads, and then descends steeply into the Boeotian land. They found when they reached the other side that the road passed through the Persian camp, and they were forced to take up *First* a position at the foot of the pass. Their right wing, consisting of the *position of* Spartans and Tegeates, rested on the high bastion of the mountain *the Greeks.*

which rises above the town of Erythrae; their centre on lower
ground close to the town; and the left wing, where the Athenians
and Megarians were posted, was advanced right down to the foot of
the descent. Thus the position of the Greeks was astride the road
to Thebes. The only assailable point was the left wing, and against
it Mardonius sent cavalry under the command of Masistius. Sore
bestead by the darts and arrows of the enemy, and with no cavalry to
aid them, the Megarians required succour. Three hundred Athenians
(for the Athenians were also on the left wing) went down to the
scene of battle, and the fortune of the day was at last changed
when the general Masistius, a conspicuous figure in the fight, fell
from his wounded charger. He was slain with difficulty by a spear
which pierced his eye, for his armour was impenetrable; and the
Persian horsemen, after a furious and fruitless charge to recover the
body of their leader, abandoned the attack. The camp of the
Persians was filled with loud wailing and lamentation—echoing, says
Herodotus, all over Boeotia—for the death of Masistius.

But this success was far from dealing any solid advantage to
the Greeks or serious injury to their foes. The Persians were well
content to remain where they were; their great host still lay north
of the Asopus. The Greeks, in order to obtain a better water
supply, and knowing that there was no chance that the Persians
would attack them in their present position, decided to occupy lower
ground in the territory of Plataea. In order to do this they moved
north-westward along the spurs of Cithaeron, past the towns
of Erythrae and Hysiae. To understand the operations which
ensued, it is to be observed that the region between Cithaeron and
the Asopus falls into two parts separated by a depression in the
ground. The southern part is marked by the six ridges already
mentioned and the streams which divide them; while the northern
tract is also hilly, being marked by three ridges between which
rivulets flow into the Asopus. Westward the depression opens out
into flat land, the only flat land here, which stretches northward from
Plataea to the river and is traversed by the road to Thebes.

Second
position of
the Greeks.
The Greek army ultimately arranged itself in order of battle
between the Theban road and the Moloeis, a tributary stream of the
Asopus. Their position was marked by the spring of Gargaphia,
which afforded an abundant supply of fresh water, and the temple of
the hero Androcrates. We are told that a dispute arose between
the Tegeates and the Athenians for the occupation of the west wing,
and that the Lacedaemonians decided in favour of the Athenians,
who (as we have seen) were under the command of Aristides. The
Tegeates were stationed next the Lacedaemonians on the right.
Pausanias had now lost control of the eastern passes across Mount

Cithaeron.   The Persian general, as soon as the Greeks had left
their first position, promptly occupied the roads, and cut off a provision
train which was on its way to supply the Greek army.   The Greek
general hoped every day that the enemy would attack ; but Mardonius,

FIG. 83.

apart from cavalry skirmishing, remained persistently on the defensive.
   It would seem that the Greeks remained about two days inactive
in this weak position, harassed by the Persian cavalry, which crossed
the river, hovered on the ridges, discharged darts into the camp, and
finally succeeded in choking up the waters of the Gargaphia spring.

The only course open to the Greeks was to fall back upon the mountain, and either take up a position on the ridges between Hysiae and

The Greeks Plataea, or seek to regain their former position at the foot of the
fall back. main pass.   For they could not venture to cross the Asopus and
brave the Persian cavalry.   Pausanias held a council of war, and
it was determined that the army should fall back to a position
between Hysiae and Plataea, and that one division should move up
the mountain slope to recover command of the pass from Plataea to
Athens.   The whole movement was to be carried out at night.
Perhaps Pausanias had received information that the Persian commander was growing impatient and was contemplating an attack.
In any case his plan of retreat proved fortunate, and though it was
not executed with precision, the Persians, even as at Salamis, were
induced to give battle in conditions chosen by their enemy and
unfavourable to themselves.   We might understand why Mardonius
decided to abandon the defensive strategy to which hitherto he had
adhered, if we knew something of the intrigues and divisions in the
Persian camp.   There seems to have been disastrous rivalry between
himself and his second in command, Artabazus, who in the ensuing
battle did simply nothing, and probably desired that Mardonius
should not win the glory of victory.

The   A little to the south-east of Plataea, a spur of Cithaeron was
Island. inclosed by the two branches of a stream which met again at the
(The foot of the ridge, and went by the name of the Island.   It was
stream of arranged that the Athenians should now occupy the centre next the
Oeroe.) Lacedaemonians, and they were instructed to retreat to this ridge.
The scheme was carried out, as it was planned, by the left wing,
who took up their post in front of the temple of Hera, which was
just outside the walls of Plataea.   But the Athenians, for some
unexplained reason, failed to obey orders, and remained where
they were in a dangerous and isolated position.   The Lacedaemonians too seem to have wasted the precious hours of the
short night.   Their delay is ascribed to the obstinacy of the
commander of one of the Spartan divisions, who had not been
present at the council of war, and refused to obey the order to
retreat.   His name was Amompharĕtus ; he was a man of blame-
less valour, and Pausanias could not persuade himself to leave
him behind.   But the morning was approaching, and at length
Pausanias began his march, convinced that his stubborn captain
would follow when he found himself deserted.   And so it fell out.

(A little When they had moved about ten stades, the Spartans saw that
more than Amompharetus was coming, and waited for him.   But the day had
a mile.) dawned ; the Persians had perceived that the Greek position
was deserted, and Mardonius decided that now was the moment

to attack when the forces of the enemy were divided. His cavalry came up and prevented the Lacedaemonians from proceeding. It *The battle.* was on the slopes under Hysiae, near the modern village of Krie-kouki, that Pausanias was compelled to turn and withstand the Persian horsemen, who were speedily supported by the main body advancing under Mardonius himself. The Persians threw up a light barricade of their wicker shields, from behind which they discharged innumerable arrows. Under this fire the Greeks hesitated; for the victims were unfavourable. At length Pausanias, looking towards the temple of Hera, invoked the goddess; and after his prayer the prophets obtained good omens from the sacrifices. The Lacedae-monians no longer held back. Along with the Tegeates who were with them they carried the barricade and pressed the Persians back-ward towards the temple of Demeter which stood on a high acclivity above them. In this direction the battle raged hotly; but the discipline of the best spearmen of Greece approved itself brilliantly; and, when Mardonius fell, the battle was decided.

The Lacedaemonians and Tegeates had borne the brunt of the day. At the first attack, Pausanias had dispatched a hasty messenger to the Athenians. As they marched to the scene they were attacked by the Greeks of the left wing of the enemy's army, who effectually hindered them from marching farther. Meanwhile the tidings had reached the rest of the Greek army at Plataea, that a battle was being fought and that Pausanias was winning it. They hastened to the scene, but the action was practically decided before their arrival; some of them were cut off, on the way, by Theban cavalry. The defeated host fled back across the Asopus to their fortified camp; the Greeks pursued, and stormed it. The tent of Mardonius was plundered by the men of Tegea, who dedicated in *Spoils.* the temple of Athena Alea in their city the brass manger of his horses; while his throne with silver feet and his scimitar were kept by the Athenians on the Acropolis, along with the breastplate of Masistius, as memorials of the fateful day. The body of Mardonius was respected by Pausanias, but it was mysteriously stolen, and none ever knew the hand that buried it. The slain Greek warriors, among whom was the brave Amompharetus, were buried before the gates of Plataea, and the honour of celebrating their memory by annual sacrifice was assigned to the Plataeans, who also agreed to commemorate the day of the deliverance of Hellas by a " Feast of Free- *Festival of* dom " every four years. Pausanias called the host together, and in *Eleutheria.* the name of the Spartans and all the confederacy guaranteed to Plataea political independence and the inviolability of her town and territory. The hour of triumph for Plataea was an hour of humilia-tion for Thebes. Ten days after the battle the army advanced

Fest: Plut. Arist. 19ᴬ 21ᴵ⁻² Diod. Jio. Munro, Cambridge Ancient Hist. 4 XI. 28 p.339 ff.

Action 89. Th. H. IX. 86-8; Diod. Sic. XI. 33³

HISTORY OF GREECE   CHAP.

against the chief Boeotian city and demanded the surrender of the leaders of the medizing party.   On a refusal, Pausanias laid siege to the place, but presently the leaders were given up, by their own wish, for they calculated on escaping punishment by the influence of bribery.   But Pausanias caused them to be executed, without trial, at Corinth.   A Theban poet who sympathised with the national effort of Hellas might well feel "distressed in soul."

(Pindar.)

The battle had been won simply and solely by the discipline and prowess of the Spartan hoplites.   The plans of the exceptionally able commander, who was matched indeed with a commander abler than himself, were frustrated once and again through the want of unity and cohesion in his army, through the want apparently of tactical skill—most of all perhaps through the half-heartedness of the Athenians.   Never do the Athenians appear in such an ill light, as in the campaign of Cithaeron ; and in no case have they exhibited so strikingly their faculty of refashioning history, in no case so successfully imposed their misrepresentations on the faith of posterity. They had no share in the victory ; but they told the whole story afterwards so as to exalt themselves and to disparage the Spartans. They represented the night movements planned by Pausanias as a retreat before an expected attack of the enemy, and they invented an elaborate tale to explain how the attack came to be expected. Mardonius, they said, growing impatient of the delay, called a council of war, and it was decided to abandon defensive tactics and provoke a battle.   Then Alexander of Macedon showed at this critical moment that his real sympathies were with Hellas and not with his barbarian allies.   He rode down to the outposts of the Athenians, and, shouting, we must suppose, across the river, revealed the decision of the Persian council of war.   Thus made aware of the Persian resolve to risk a battle, the Spartans proposed to the Athenians to change wings, in order that the victors of Marathon might fight with the Persians, whose ways of warfare they had already experienced, while the Spartans themselves could deal better with the Boeotians and other Greeks, with whose methods of fighting they were familiar.   The proposal was agreed to, and as day dawned the change was being effected.   But the enemy perceived it, and immediately began to make a corresponding change in their own array.   Seeing their plan frustrated, the Greeks desisted from completing it ; and both the adversaries resumed their original positions. Mardonius then sent a message to the Lacedaemonians, complaining that he had been deeply disappointed in them, for though they had the repute of never fleeing or deserting their post, they had now attempted to place the Athenians in the place of danger.   He challenged them to stand forth as champions for the whole Greek

The legend of the battle; Athenian misrepresentations.

host and fight against an equal number of Persians. To this pro-posal the Spartans made no reply. Then Mardonius began his cavalry operations which led to the retreat of the Greeks from their second position. The three striking incidents of this malicious tale, the night-visit of Alexander, the fruitless attempt of the Spartans to shirk the responsibility of their post on the right wing, the challenge of Mardonius, are all improbable in themselves ; but nevertheless this story was circulated and believed, and has received a sort of consecration in the pages of Herodotus.

SECT. 8. BATTLE OF MYCALE AND CAPTURE OF SESTOS

The battle of Cithaeron shares with Salamis the dignity of being *Signifi-* decisive battles in the world's history. Pindar links them together *cance of* as the great triumphs of Sparta and Athens respectively, battles *battle of* "wherein the Medes of the bent bows were sore afflicted." Not-*Plataea* withstanding the immense disadvantage of want of cavalry, the Lacedaemonians had turned at Plataea a retreat into a victory. The remarkable feature of the battle was that it was decided by a small part of either army. Sparta and Tegea were the actual victors ; and on the Persian side, Artabazus, at the head of 40,000 men, had not entered into the action at all. On the death of Mardonius, that general immediately faced about and began without delay the long march back to the Hellespont. Never again was Persia to make a serious attempt against the liberty of European Greece ; "a god," said a poet of the day—and the poet was a Theban—"turned away the stone of Tantalus imminent above our heads." For the following century and a half, the dealings between Greece and Persia will only affect the western fringe of Asia, and then the balance of power will have so completely shifted that Persia will succumb to a Greek conqueror, and Alexander of Macedon will achieve against the Asiatic monarchy what Xerxes failed to achieve against the free states of Europe.

One memorial of this victory of Europe over Asia has survived *its memo-* till to-day. The votive offering which the Greeks sent to Delphi *rial.* was a tripod of gold set upon a pillar of three brazen serpents, *The tripod* with the names of the Greek peoples who offered it inscribed upon *at Delphi.* the base. The pillar still stands in Byzantium, whither it was transferred by the emperor Constantine when he refounded the city as Constantinople, his new eastern capital. The immense booty which was found in the Persian camp was divided, when portions had been set apart for the gods and for the general who had led the Greeks.

The achievement of the Hellenic army under Mount Cithaeron, which rescued Greek Europe from the invader, was followed in a

Main memorials of Plataea H. 8. 82¹ 9. 81¹ Thuc. 1. 132²⁻³
Pausanias 5. 23¹ X. 139 ; Nepos, Paus 1³⁷¹ Aristod. 4¹, 9,
Demosthenes Ix '97-8 ; Diod. XI. 33²

Battle of Mycale (middle of August, 479 B.C.).

Diod. Sic. XI.34–37

few days by an achievement of the Hellenic fleet which delivered the Asiatic Greeks from their master. The Greek fleet was still at Delos. We saw that it was the policy of the Athenians to remain inactive at sea until a battle had been fought on land. For a naval victory would probably have meant the retreat of the Spartans from northern Greece, on the calculation that the enemy would not attack Peloponnesus without the co-operation of the fleet. But the armament at Delos was drawn into action by a message from the Samians, seeking to join the Greek league, and begging help against the Persian. For the Persian fleet was at Samos, and hard by at Cape Mycale a large Persian army, including many Ionian troops, was encamped. The Samian request was granted; Leotychidas sailed to the island, and on his approach the Persian ships withdrew to the shelter of Cape Mycale and their army. The Greeks landed; attacked, carried, and burned the enemy's camp. Their victory was decided by the desertion of the Ionians, who won their freedom on this memorable day. Mycale followed so hard upon Plataea, that the belief easily arose that the two victories were won on the same afternoon. There is more to be said for the tradition that as the Athenians and their comrades assailed the entrenchments on the shore of Mycale the tidings of Plataea reached them and heartened them in their work.

Return of Sp.
H. IX.114
Th. I.89²
Diod. XI.37

The Athenians and Ionians, led by the admiral Xanthippus, followed up the great victory by vigorous action in the Hellespont, while the Peloponnesians with Leotychidas, content with what they had achieved, returned home. The difference between the Athenian and the Spartan character, between the cautious policy of Sparta and the imperial instinct of Athens, is here distinctly and, it is not too much to say, momentously expressed. The Lacedaemonians were unwilling to concern themselves further with the Greeks of the eastern and north-eastern Aegean; the Athenians were both capable of taking a Panhellenic point of view, and moved by the impulse to extend their own influence. The strong fortress of Sestos, which stands by the straits of Helle, was beleaguered and taken; and with this event Herodotus closes his history of the Persian wars. The independence of the Hellespontine regions was a natural consequence of the victory of Mycale, but its historical significance lies in the fact that it was accomplished under the auspices of Athens. The fall of Sestos is the beginning of that Athenian empire, to which Pisistratus and the elder Miltiades had pointed the way.

Capture of Sestos. 478 B.C.

At. I. βασιοφ Sestos: H. IX.114²–121, Thucid. I.8.9², Diod. XI.37⁴–⁵, Aristot. 4'

Sect. 9. Gelon Tyrant of Syracuse

While the eastern Greeks were securing their future development against the Persian foe, and were affirming their possession of the

Aegean waters, the western Greeks had been called upon to defend themselves against that Asiatic power which had established itself in the western Mediterranean and was a constant threat to their existence. The Greeks had indeed, on their side, proved a formidable check *Struggle of* and hindrance to the expansion of the dominion and trade of Carthage. *Greek and* The endeavours of this vigorous Phoenician state to secure the queen- *Phoenician in western* ship of the western seas, from Africa to Gaul, from the coast of Spain *Mediter-* to the shores of Italy, depended largely for their success on her close *ranean in* connexion and identity of interests with her sister-towns in Sicily ; *sixth cen-* and secondly, on her alliance with the strong pirate power of Etruria. *tury.* The friendly Phoenician ports of western Sicily—Motya, Panormus, and Solus—were an indispensable aid for the African city, both for the maintenance of her communications with Tuscany and for the prosecution of designs upon Sardinia and Corsica. In Corsican waters as well as in Sicily, the Phoenician clashed with the Greek. It was in the first quarter of the sixth century that Dorian adventurers *The enter-* from Cnidus and Rhodes sought to gain a foothold in the barbarian *prise of* corner of Sicily, at the very gates of the Phoenicians. The name of *Pentathlus,* their leader was Pentathlus. He attempted to plant a settlement on *c. 580 B.C.* Cape Lilybaeum, hard by Motya,—a direct menace to the communications between Motya and Carthage. The Phoenicians gathered in arms, and they were supported by their Elymian neighbours ; the Greeks were defeated and Pentathlus was slain. It was not the destiny of Lilybaeum to be the place of a Hellenic city ; but long afterwards it was to become illustrious as the site of a Punic stronghold which would take the place of Motya, when Motya herself had been destroyed by a Greek avenger of Pentathlus. After their defeat *Foundation* the men of Pentathlus, casting about for another dwelling-place, *of Lipara.* betook themselves to the volcanic archipelago off the north coast of Sicily, and founded Lipara in the largest of the islands. This little state was organised on communistic principles. The soil was public *Collectiv-* property : a certain number of the citizens were set apart to till it for *ism.* the common use ; the rest were employed in keeping watch and ward on the coasts of their little home against the descents of Tuscan rovers. This system was indeed subsequently modified : the land was portioned out in lots, but was redistributed every twenty years.

The attempt of Pentathlus, the occupation of the Liparaean group, *Cartha-* the recent settlement of Acragas, pressed upon Carthage the need of *ginian* stemming the Greek advance. Accordingly we find her sending an *expedition* army to Sicily. The commander of this expedition, precursor of *to Sicily* *under* many a greater, was Malchus ; and it is possible that he was opposed *Malchus,* by Phalaris, who established a tyranny at Acragas. There was a long *c. 560-50* war, of which we know nothing except that the invader was successful *B.C.* and Greek territory was lost to the Phoenician. [Soon afterwards

Abt. Phalaris D Jio. IX. 18 ; Lucian Phalaris 1.4 ; Pindar Pythian Odes 1.95

Carthaginian armies were closing Sardinia, rich in metals and corn, to the Greeks and establishing themselves securely in the island.] In the northern seas Carthage was also confronted by the Greeks. The Phocaeans of Massalia planted colonies and won influence on the coast of Spain. Moreover the new Phocaean settlement at Alalia in Corsica was a challenge to Carthage in what she regarded as her own domain. But Greek Alalia was short-lived. Carthage and her powerful Etruscan allies nearly annihilated the Phocaean fleet; and the crews which escaped were only able to rescue their families and goods. Alalia was deserted; Corsica fell under the power of the Etruscans, and the coasts of Sardinia were gradually appropriated by Carthage. Thus the chance of establishing a chain of Greek settlements between Massalia and Sicily was frustrated.

The Phocaeans: of Massalia; of Alalia.

Battle of Alalia, c. 535 B.C.

It now remained for Carthage to establish and extend Phoenician power in Sicily. We have seen how Dorieus, son of a Spartan king, made an attempt to do somewhat the same thing which the Cnidian adventurer had essayed—to gain a footing in Sicily within the Phoenician circle. He too failed; but such incidents brought home to Carthage the need of dealing another and a mightier blow at the rival power in Sicily. She was occupied with the conquest of Sardinia and with a Libyan war, and the struggle was postponed; but the hour came at last, and the Carthaginians put forth all their power to annihilate colonial Greece at the very time when the Great King had poured forth the resources of Asia against the mother-country. It was, in the first instance, an accident that the two struggles happened at the same moment. The causes which led to the one were independent of the causes which led to the other. But the exact moment chosen by Carthage for her attack upon Sicily was probably determined by the attack of Xerxes upon Greece; and although the two struggles ran each its independent course, there is no reason to question the statement that the courts of Susa and Carthage exchanged messages, through the mediation of the Phoenicians, and were conscious of acting in concert against the same enemy.

(See above, p. 208.)

Sicily menaced by Carthage.

In the second decade of the fifth century Greek Sicily was dominated by four tyrants. Anaxilas of Rhegium had made himself master of Zancle, which from this time forward is known as Messana, and he thus controlled both sides of the straits, which he secured against the passage of Etruscan pirates. Terillus, his father-in-law, was tyrant of Himera. Over against this family group in the north stood another family group in the south: Gelon of Syracuse and his father-in-law Theron of Acragas.

Tyrants in Sicily.

Gelon had been the general of Hippocrates, a tyrant of Gela, who had extended his sway, whether as lord or over-lord, over Naxos,

Zancle, and other Greek cities, and had aimed at winning Syracuse. *Hippo-* Hippocrates had defeated the Syracusans on the banks of the *crates,* Helorus, and would have seized their city, if it *tyrant of* had not been for the intervention of Corinth *Gela.* and Corcyra. But Syracuse was forced to *[Battle* cede her dependency, Camarina, to the victor. *of the* Hippocrates died in besieging Hybla ; and the *Helorus,* men of Gela had no mind to allow his sons *492 B.C.]* to continue their father's tyranny. But Gelon, son of Deinomenes, a general who had often *Gelon,* led the cavalry of Gela to victory, espoused *tyrant of* the cause of his master's heirs, and as soon *Gela,* as he had gained possession of the city brushed *491 B.C. ;* them aside and took the tyranny for himself. The new lord of Gela achieved what his pre-decessors had vainly striven to accomplish.

FIG. 84.—Coin of Gela, early (obverse). Bull with human head, forepart[legend: ΓΕΛΑΣ.]

The *Gamori* or nobles of Syracuse had been driven out by the commons, and they appealed to Gelon to restore them. The *wins Syra-* Syracusan people, unable to resist the forces which Gelon brought *cuse :* against them, made terms with him, and he established his power in Syracuse over oligarchs and democrats alike. It seems probable that Gelon was either at once or at a later stage of his rule appointed formally " General with full powers "; we find his brother Hieron, *his position* who succeeded to his position, addressed by the poet Bacchylides *there.* as " General " of the Syracusan horsemen.

The tyrant of Gela now abandoned his own city and took up his abode in Syracuse, making it the centre of a dominion which embraced the eastern part of the island. Gela had for a short space enjoyed the rank of the first of Sicilian cities ; she now surrendered it to Syracuse, which was marked out by its natural site for strength and domination. Gelon may be called the second founder of Syra- *He enlarges* cuse. Soon after the occupation of Ortygia settlement had extended *Syracuse;* to the mainland where there was ample room for expansion between *his walls* the coast and the heights of Epipolae. This district, Achradina, had *and docks;* been linked in the sixth century with the island by a mole. Gelon compassed the mainland settlement, much enlarged, with a wall. Ortygia remained the " acropolis." The chief gate of Syracuse was now in the new wall of Gelon, close to the Harbour ; and near it a new agora was laid out, for the old agora in the Island no longer sufficed. Hard by docks were built, for Syracuse was to become a naval power. Until now, in spite of the natural advantages of her position, she had been less wealthy and powerful than Acragas and Gela ; her supremacy had been local only. Henceforward she was to become and remain by far the greatest Greek city in the west.

his court and class-prejudice;   Gelon, belonging to a proud and noble family, sympathised and most willingly consorted with men of his own class, and looked with little favour on the people, whom he described in a famous phrase as "a thankless neighbour." He held court at Syracuse like a king, surrounded by men of noble birth. He tolerated the Syracusan commons; he was not unpopular with them; but he showed elsewhere what his genuine feelings were. One of his first needs was to find inhabitants to fill the spaces of his enlarged town. For this

his treatment of other cities;   purpose he transplanted men on a large scale from other places of his dominions. His own town Gela was sacrificed to the new capital; the half of its citizens were removed to Syracuse. Harder was the fate of luckless Camarina, which was now for the second time blotted out from the number of Greek cities. Two generations had hardly passed since she had been swept away by the Syracusan republic; and now the Syracusan tyrant carried off all the inhabitants and made them burgesses of the ruling state. Megara, the next-door neighbour of Syracuse on the north, and Euboea higher up the coast, also contributed to swell the population of Gelon's capital. Megara became an outpost of Syracuse, while Euboea was so entirely blotted out that its very site is uncertain. But in both these cases the policy of Gelon strikingly displayed the prejudice of his class. He admitted the nobles of Megara and Euboea to Syracusan citizenship; he sold the mass of the commons in the slave market. In abolishing cities and transplanting populations Gelon set an example which we shall see followed by later tyrants. He also invited new settlers from elder Greece, and he gave the citizenship to 10,000 mercenary soldiers.

his family.   Gelon was supported in his princely power by his three brothers, Hieron, Polyzālus, and Thrasybulus. He entered into close friendship with Theron, his fellow-tyrant, who made Acragas in wealth a power second only to Syracuse itself. Theron, like Gelon, was a noble, belonging to the family of the Emmenids, and his rule was said to have been mild and just. Gelon married Damareta, the daughter of Theron; and Theron married a daughter of Polyzalus. The brilliant lords of Syracuse and Acragas, thus joined by close bonds, were presently associated in the glorious work of delivering Greek Sicily from the terrible danger which was about to come against her from over-seas.

Diod. Sic. XI. SECT. 10. THE CARTHAGINIAN INVASION OF SICILY,
AND THE BATTLE OF HIMERA

    A quarrel between Theron of Acragas and Terillus tyrant of Himera led up to the catastrophe which might easily have proved

Battle ✓ same day as Thermop. : Diod. Sic. XI. 24. 1
"   "   "   ✓   " Sal.   : Herod. 7. 166

fatal to the freedom of all the Sicilian Greeks. The ruler of Acragas *Terillus* crossed the island and drove Terillus out of Himera. The exiled *invites in-* tyrant had a friend in Anaxilas of Rhegium; *tervention* but Rhegium was no match for the combined *of Car-* power of Acragas and Syracuse, and so Terillus *thage.* sought the help of Carthage, the common enemy of all.

Carthage was only waiting for the opportunity. She had been making preparations for a descent on Sicily, and the appeal of Terillus merely determined the moment and the point of her attack. Terillus urging the Phoenician against Himera plays the same part as Hippias urging the Persian against Athens, but in neither case is a tyrant's fall the cause of the invasion. The motive of the Carthaginian expedition against Sicily at this particular epoch is to be found in a

FIG. 85.—Coin of Rhegion, fifth century (reverse). The Rhegine People seated [legend: ΡΕΓΙΝΟΣ].

far higher range of politics than the local affairs of Himera or the interests of a petty despot. There can hardly be a doubt that *Carthage* the Great King and the Carthaginian republic were acting in concert, *and Persia.* and that it was deliberately planned to attack, independently but at Diod. Sic. the same moment, eastern and western Greece. While the galleys XI. 1. 20 of the elder Phoenicia, under their Persian master, sailed to crush

the elder Hellas, the galleys of the younger Phoenician city would cross over on her own account against the younger Hellas. In the Phoenicians of Tyre and Sidon, Xerxes had willing intermediaries to arrange with Carthage the plan of enslaving or annihilating Hellas. The western island mattered little to Xerxes; but it mattered greatly to him that the lord of Syracuse should be hindered

FIG. 86.—Coin of Himera, from sending a powerful succour in men and fifth century (obverse). ships to the mother-country. We have already Himera, the nymph, seen how the mother-country sought the help sacrificing at altar; satyr of Gelon, and how the danger of Sicily forced bathing himself at a hot him to refuse. spring.

When the preparations were complete, *The Punic* Hamilcar, the shophet of Carthage, sailed with a large armament *armament.* and landed at Panormus; for the call of Terillus determined that the recovery of Himera should be the first object. It is said that the army consisted of ~~300,000 men, conveyed by more than 200~~ So Diod. ~~galleys and 3000 transports;~~ but we can lay no stress on these figures. Sic. XI. 20.2 From Panormus this great host moved along the coast to Himera, accompanied by the warships, and proceeded to besiege the city, which Theron was himself guarding with a large force. Hamilcar made two camps in front of the town. The sea camp lay on the low ground between the hill of Himera and the beach; the land

FIG. 87.

camp stretched along the low hills on the western side of the town. A sally of the besieged resulted in loss, and Theron sent a message to Syracuse to hasten the coming of his son-in-law. With 50,000 foot-soldiers and 5000 horsemen Gelon marched to the rescue without delay. He approached the town on the east side and formed a strong camp on the right bank of the river.

The decisive battle was brought about in a strange way, if we *Battle of* can trust the story. Hamilcar determined to enlist the gods of his *Himera,* foes on his own side. He appointed a day for a great sacrifice to 480 B.C. Poseidon near the shore of the sea. For this purpose it was needful *So in Diod.* to have Greeks present who understood how the sacrifice should be per- *Sic. XI. 21·2* formed. Accordingly Hamilcar wrote to Selinus, which had become a dependency of Carthage, bidding that city send horsemen to the Punic camp by a fixed day. The letter fell into the hands of Gelon, and he conceived a daring stratagem. On the morning of the appointed day a band of Syracusan horsemen stood at the gate of the sea camp, professing to be the expected contingent from Selinus. The Carthaginians could not distinguish strangers of Syracuse from strangers of Selinus, and they were admitted without suspicion. They cut down Hamilcar by the altar of Poseidon, and they set fire to the ships. All this was visible from the high parts of the town above them, and men posted there signalled to Gelon the success of the plan. The Greek commander

Fig. 88.—Coin of Selinus, fifth century (obverse). River Selinus sacrificing at altar; cock, bull, leaf of selinon [legend: ΣΕΛΙΝΟΣ].

immediately led his troops round the south side of the city against the land camp of the enemy. There the battle was fought, a long and desperate struggle, in which the scale was finally turned in favour of the Greeks by a body of men which Theron sent round to take the barbarians in the rear. The victory was complete; the great expedition was utterly destroyed; the chief himself was slain.

But of the death of that chieftain the Carthaginians had another *Legend of* and a far grander tale to tell. This tale does not explain how the *Hamilcar's* battle was brought about. It simply gives us a splendid picture. *death.* The battle rages "from the morning till the late evening," and *Her. 7. 179* during that long day Hamilcar stands at the altar of Baal, in his camp by the sea. A great fire devours the burnt-offerings to the god; victim after victim, whole bodies of beasts and perhaps of men, are flung into the flames, and the omens are favourable to Carthage. But as he is pouring out a drink-offering, he looks forth, and behold his army is put to flight. The moment for a supreme sacrifice has come; he leaps into the fire and the flames consume him. The offering of his life did not retrieve the day; but hereafter Himera was destined to pay a heavy penalty for the death of Hamilcar.

The common significance of the battles of Salamis and Himera, *On Sig.* or the repulse of Asia from Europe, was appreciated at the time and *See Hdt.* naïvely expressed in the fanciful tradition that the two battles were *Sic. 23* fought on the same day. But Himera, unlike Salamis, was immedi-ately followed by a treaty of peace. Carthage paid the lord of Syracuse 2000 talents as a war indemnity, but this was a small treasury

FIG. 89.—Syracusan Decadrachm (Demaretean). Reverse: Chariot crowned by Victory; below, the lion of Carthage in flight.

The Damaretean decadrachms.

compared with the booty taken in the camp. Out of a portion of that spoil a beautiful issue of large silver coins was minted and called " Damaretean," after Gelon's wife ; and some pieces of this memorial of the great deliverance of Sicily are preserved.

SECT. 11. SYRACUSE AND ACRAGAS UNDER HIERON AND THERON

The enlargement of Acragas, 479-2 B.C.

Theron and Acragas had played an honourable part in the deliverance of Sicily, though it was a part which was second to that of Gelon and Syracuse. Theron survived the victory by eight years, and during that time he was engaged in doing for Acragas what had been already done for Syracuse by his fellow-tyrant. [The area enclosed by the early walls of Acragas needed no enlargement. Theron's task lay in rebuilding the city and particularly its temples on a more magnificent scale. He laid the foundations of the greatness of Acragas in the fifth century but it was not till long after his death that the temples he planned were completed.] In all this work, and in the watercourses which he also constructed, Theron had slave-labour in abundance—the barbarians who had been captured after the battle of Himera. Theron placed rescued Himera under the government of his son Thrasydaeus, who however, unlike Theron himself, proved an oppressor and was hated by the citizens.

Meanwhile Gelon died, and left the fruits of his enterprise and *Death of*
statesmanship to be enjoyed by his brother Hieron. While Hieron *Gelon and*
was to have the sovereign power, Gelon desired that Polyzalus, whom *succession*
he ordered to marry his widow Damareta, should have the supreme *of Hieron,*
command of the Syracusan army. The idea of this dual system was *478 B.C.*
unwise; and it necessarily led to fraternal discord. Polyzalus was *Diodorus*
popular at Syracuse, and his double connexion with Theron secured *Siculus XI.*
him the support of that tyrant. To Hieron he seemed a dangerous *38*
rival, and in the end he was compelled to seek refuge at Acragas.
This led to an open breach between Hieron and Theron, but it did
not come to actual war, and it is said that the lyric poet Simonides,
who was a favourite at both courts, acted as peacemaker.

Hieron may be said to have completed the work of Himera by *Hieron*
the defeat which he inflicted upon the Etruscans at Cyme. The *defeats the*
Etruscans were the other rival power which, besides the Cartha- *Etruscans.*
ginians, threatened the " Greater Greece " of the west. [The posses- *Diod.*
sion of Cyme was an important Etruscan objective for it threatened *Sic.*
the communications of Etruria with her growing dominion in Cam- *XI. 51*
pania. Soon after the naval victory at Alalia the Etruscans made a
formidable land attack on Cyme, but Aristodemus, who had emerged
from faction as a tyrant, saved the city. This check was followed by
the driving of the Etruscan kings from Rome and the eclipse of
Etruscan power in Latium, confirmed by the victory of the Latin
allies, strongly supported by Cyme, over the Etruscans at Aricia.
The cutting of the land route emphasised the need for securing the
sea passage along the Italian coast, and some years later an Etruscan
fleet sailed against Cyme. Hieron, realising the issues at stake, *Battle of*
brought up a Syracusan fleet. The Etruscans were decisively defeated *Cyme,*
and no longer menaced the development of western Greece.] From *474 B.C.*
the booty Hieron sent a bronze helmet to Olympia; and this precious
memorial of one of the glorious exploits of Greece is now in the great
London collection of antiquities. More precious still is the song in *Pindar's*
which Pindar of Thebes immortalised the victory. *First*

It is perhaps from the hymns of Pindar that we win the most *Pythian.*
lively impression of the wealth and culture of the courts of Sicily in *Att. to Simon-*
the fifth century. Pindar, like other illustrious poets of the day, *ides (frag. 106*
Simonides and Bacchylides, and Aeschylus, visited Sicily, to bask *Edmonds*
in the smiles, and receive the gifts, of the tyrant. The lord of *Victories of*
Syracuse—or king, as he aspired to be styled—sent his race-horses *Sicilian*
and chariots to contend in the great games at Olympia and Delphi, *tyrants*
and he employed the most gifted lyric poets to celebrate these *in Pan-*
victories in lordly odes. Pindar and Bacchylides were sometimes *hellenic*
set to celebrate the same victory in rival strains. These poets *games.*
give us an impression of the luxury and magnificence of the royal

courts and the generosity of the royal victors. Syracuse, on whose adornment her tyrants could spend the Punic spoils, and Acragas, "fairest of the cities of men," seemed wonderful to the visitors from elder Greece. Yet amid all their own magnificence and amid their absorbing political activity, the princes of this younger western world coveted above all things that their names should be glorious in the mother country. They still looked to the holy place of Delphi as the central sanctuary of the world, and they enriched it with costly dedications. The golden tripods, which Gelon and his brothers dedicated from Punic treasure, became, like the other golden things of

Fig. 90.—Helmet dedicated by Hiero (in British Museum). [Inscription: Ἱάρων ὁ Δεινομένεος καὶ τοὶ Συρακόσιοι τῷ Δὶ Τυρ(ρ)άν' ἀπὸ Κύμας]

Delphi, the loot of robbers; but we are reminded of that fraternal union by a precious bronze charioteer, which was dug up recently in the ruins of the Delphic sanctuary. It was dedicated by Polyzalus, perhaps in honour of a Pythian victory.

Ideals of Pindar. It were easy to be blinded by the outward show of these princely tyrants, which the genius of Pindar has invested with a certain dignity. But Pindar, himself born of a noble family, cherished the ideas and prejudices of a bygone generation. He belonged to a class, he wrote chiefly for a class, whose day was past: nobles whose sole aim in life was to win victories at the public games. These men were out of sympathy with the new ideas and the political tendencies of their own age ; they were belated survivals of an earlier society. Pindar sympathised with them. He liked aristocracies best ; he accepted monarchy even in the form of tyranny ; but democracy he regarded as the rule of a mob's passions. The despots of Sicily and Cyrene supported the national games of Greece, and that was in truth their great merit in the eyes of the poet. The chariot-race, the athletic contests, seen in the midst of a gay crowd, then the choral dance and song in honour of the victory, and the carouse,

FIG. 91.—Bronze Charioteer, Delphi.

FIG. 92.—Coin of Cyrene, fifth century (obverse). Head of Zeus Ammon [legend: ΚΥΡΑ].

in the hall perhaps of some noble Aeginetan burgher, these were "the delightful things in Hellas" which to Pindar were the breath of life. He was religious to the heart's core ; and all these things were invested with the atmosphere of religion. But allowing for this, we feel that he takes the games too seriously, and that when Aeschylus was wrestling with the deep problems of life and death, the day was past for regarding an Olympian victory as the grandest thing in the world. We must not be beguiled by Pindar's majestic art into ascribing to the tyrants any high moral purpose. It was enough that they should aspire to an Olympian crown, and incur the necessary outlay, and seek immortality from the poet's craft; the poet could hardly dare to demand a higher purpose.

Diod. Sic.
XI. 49

Fair as the outside of a Syracusan state might seem to a favoured visitor who was entertained in the tyrant's palace, underneath there was no lack of oppression and suspicion. The system of spies which Hieron organised to watch the lives of private citizens, tells its own tale. One of his most despotic acts was his dealing with the city of

*Founda
tion of
Aetna.*

Catane. He deported all the inhabitants to Leontini, peopled the place with new citizens, and gave it the name of Aetna. His motive was partly vanity, partly selfish prudence. He aspired to be remembered and worshipped as the founder of a city; and he also intended Aetna to be a stronghold of refuge to himself or his dynasty, in case a day of jeopardy should come. His son Deinomenes was installed as "King of Aetna." But the Dorian city of Aetna, so cruelly founded, though it was celebrated in lofty phrases by Pindar and had the still higher honour of supplying the motive of a play of Aeschylus, had but a short duration; it was soon to become Catane again.

Diod. Sic.
XI. 53

At Acragas, the mild rule of Theron seems to have secured the love and trust of his fellow-citizens; but at Himera he showed what a tyrant might do, by slaughtering without any mercy those who had showed their discontent at the rule of his son. Neither the Syra-

*Death of
Theron,
472-1 B.C.
Thrasy-
daeus: his
war with
Hieron,
and
his fate.
471-0 B.C.
Death of
Hiero,
467 B.C.*

cusan nor the Acragantine dynasty endured long. After Theron's death, Thrasydaeus misruled Acragas, as he had already misruled Himera. But for some unknown reason he had the folly to go to war with Hieron, who discomfited him in a hard-fought battle. This defeat led to his fall. Himera became independent, and Acragas adopted a free constitution. The deliverance of Syracuse came about five years later. When Hieron died, his brother Thrasybulus took the reins of government, and, being a less able and dexterous ruler than Hieron, he soon excited a revolution by his executions and confiscations. The citizens rose in a mass, and obtaining help from other Sicilian cities besieged the tyrant and his mercenaries in Syracuse. He was ultimately forced to surrender and retired into private life in a foreign land. Thus the tyranny at Syracuse came to an end, and the feast of *Eleutheria* was founded to preserve the memory of the dawn of freedom.

*Republics
in Sicily.*

The rule of the despots seems to have wiped out the old feud between the nobles and the commons. But a new strife arose instead. The old citizens, nobles and commons alike, distrusted the new citizens, whom Gelon had gathered together from all quarters. A civil war broke out; for some time, the old citizens were excluded from both the Island and Achradina; but in the end all the strangers

were driven out, and the democracy of Syracuse was securely established.   One good thing the tyrants had done.   They had obliterated
the class distinctions which had existed before them ; and thus the
cities could now start afresh on the basis of political equality for all.
The next half-century was a period of weal and prosperity for the
republics of Sicily, especially for the greatest among them, Syracuse
and Acragas, and for Selinus, freed from the Phoenician yoke.   At
Acragas the free people carried to completion the works which
their beneficent tyrant had begun.   The stately row of temples
along the southern wall belongs to this period.   " It was a grand
conception to line the southern wall, the wall most open to the
attacks of mortal enemies, with this wonderful series of holy places
of the divine protectors of the city.   It was a conception due, we
may believe, in the first instance, to Theron, but which the democracy fully entered into and carried out." [1]   But her sacred buildings
brought less glory to Acragas than the name of the most illustrious
of her sons.   The poet and philosopher Empedocles was reared in *Em-*
what he describes as the "great town above the yellow river of *pedocles.*
Acragas."   He was not only a profound philosopher, an inspired
poet, a skilful physician, but he had lent his hand to the reform of
the constitution of his city.   Unhappily his personality is lost in the
dense covert of legends which quickly grew up around him.   The
true Empedocles who, banished from his home, died quietly in the
Peloponnesus, becomes the seer and magician who hurled himself
into the bowl of Aetna that he might become a god.   A god indeed
he proclaims himself to be, going about from city to city, crowned
with Delphic wreaths, and worshipped by men and women.

    For a time indeed the Siceliots were threatened with a remark- *Ducetius*
able danger, the revival of the native power of the Sicels.   This *and the*
revival was entirely due to the genius of one man, and the danger *Sicels,*
disappeared on his death.   Ducetius organised a federation of the *460-440*
                                                                     B.C.
Sicel towns, and aspired to bring the Greek cities under Sicel rule. *His cities :*
He displayed his talent in the foundation of new cities, which survived (1)
the failure of his schemes.   His first settlement was on the hill-top *Menaenum*
of Menaenum, overlooking the sacred lake and temple of the Palici. *(Mineo),*
                                                                     (2) Palica,
As his power and ambitions grew, he descended from the hill and (3) *Kalê*
founded Palica close to the national sanctuary, to be the political *Aktê.*
capital of the nation.   He captured Aetna, gained a victory over
the Acragantines and Syracusans, but was subsequently defeated by *His*
Syracuse, and on this defeat his followers deserted him, and the *failure,*
fabric which he had reared collapsed.   He boldly took refuge *450 B.C.*
himself at the altar in the Syracusan market-place ; his case was
debated in the Assembly ; and by an act of clemency, which we

<hr>

[1] Freeman.

FIG. 93.—? Return of Persephone. ? From Locri.

might hardly expect, he was spared and sent to Corinth. Five years later we find him again in Sicily, engaged in the congenial work of founding a third city, Kalê Aktê or Fairshore, on the northern coast, with the approbation of Syracuse. It is uncertain whether he dreamed of repeating his attempt at a national revival or had become convinced that the fortune of the Sicel lay in Helleni-zation. His foundations were more abiding than those of Hieron ; one of them, Mineo, survives to-day. The career of Ducetius exhibited the decision of destiny that the Greek was to predominate in the island of the Sicels.

SECT. 12. RELIGIOUS MOVEMENTS IN THE SIXTH CENTURY

In the latter part of the sixth century, the expansion of the Persian power had suspended a stone of Tantalus over Hellas, and it seemed likely that Greek civilisation might be submerged in an oriental monarchy. We have seen how Greek generals, Greek spearmen, and Greek seamen averted this calamity. We have now to see how another danger was averted, a danger which, though it is not like the Persian invasion written large on the face of history, threatened Greece with a no less terrible disaster. This danger lay in the dissemination of a new religion, which, if it had gained the upper hand, as at one time it seemed likely to do, would have pressed with as dead and stifling a weight upon Greece as any oriental superstition. Spiritually the Greeks might have been annexed to the peoples of the orient.

The age of Solon witnessed not only a social and political move-*Beginning* ment among the masses in various parts of Greece, but also an intel-*of rational-* lectual and spiritual stirring. There was an intellectual dissatisfac-*ism.* tion with the theogony of Hesiod as an explanation of the origin of the world ; and the natural philosophy of Thales and his successors came into being in Ionia. But there was also a moral dissatisfaction with the tales of religious mythology, as they were handed down by the epic bards ; and this feeling took the form of interpreting and modifying them, so as to make them conform to ethical ideals. The poet Stesichorus was a pioneer in this direction, and it was he who first imported into the legend of the house of Atreus—the murder of Agamemnon by his wife, and the murder of Clytaemnestra by her son—the terrible moral significance which Aeschylus and the Attic tragedians afterwards made so familiar. Further than this, men began to feel a craving for an existence after death, and intense *Religious* curiosity about the world of shades, and a desire for personal contact *movement.* with the supernatural. Both the scientific and the religious move-ments have the same object—to solve the mystery of existence ; but the religious craving demanded a short road and immediate satisfaction. The craving led to the propagation of a new religion, which began to spread about the middle of the sixth century. We know not where it originally took shape, but Attica became its most active centre, and it was propagated to western Hellas beyond the sea.

Elements in the Orphic religion. Based partly on the wild Thracian worship of Dionysus, this religion was called Orphic from Orpheus, poet and priest, who was supposed to have been born in Thrace and founded the bacchic rites ; and it exercised a deep influence over not only the people at large, but even the thinkers of Greece. The Orphic teachers elaborated a theology of their own ; a special doctrine of the future world ; peculiar rites and peculiar rules of conduct. But they took up into their system, so far as possible, the old popular beliefs. The Orphic religion might almost be described as based on three institutions : the worship of Dionysus, the mysteries connected with the gods of the underworld, and the itinerant prophets ; but Dionysus, the underworld, and the art of the seer and purifier, all acquired new significance in the light of the Orphic theology.

Dionysiac worship. It was perhaps as early as the eighth century that the worship of Dionysus was introduced into northern Greece, and various legends record the opposition which was at first offered to the reception of the stranger. His orgies spread, especially in Boeotia and Attica. The worshippers gathered at night on the mountains, by torchlight, with deer-skins on their shoulders and long ivy-wreathed wands in their hands, and danced wildly to the noise of cymbals and flutes. Men and women tore and devoured the limbs of the sacred victims. They desired to fall, and they often fell, especially the women, into a sort of frenzied ecstasy, in which their souls were thought to be in mystic communion with Dionysus. It was probably the influence of the Dionysiac worship that induced the Delphic god [1] to give his oracles through the mouth of a woman cast into a state of divine frenzy.

Itinerant seers. Men could also deal with the supernatural world through the mediation of seers. Wise men and women, called *bakids* and *sibyls*, attached to no temple or sanctuary, travelled about and made their livelihood by prophesying, purifying, and healing. They practised these three arts through their intimacy with the invisible world of spirits ; to which the causes of disease and uncleanness were ascribed. Epimenides was one of the most famous and powerful of these wizards ; we saw how he was called upon to purify Athens.

Mysteries. Mysteries, connected with the cult of the deities of the under-

---

[1] Dionysus was worshipped from of old at Delphi, and was identified with Apollo. This identity comes out strikingly in the hymn to Dionysus Paean by a Locrian poet (338 B.C.), recently discovered at Delphi.

world, supplied another means of approaching the supernatural. The Homeric bards of Ionia may have lived in a society where life yielded so many pleasures that men could look forward with equanimity and resignation to that colourless existence in the grey kingdom of Persephone, which is described in the epics. But the conditions of life were very different in the mother-country in the eighth century. The strife for existence was hard, and the Boeotian poet must have echoed the groans of many a wretched wight when he cried

> The earth is full of ills, of ills the sea.

It was a time when men were ready to entertain new views of a future world, suggesting hopes that a tolerable existence, unattainable here, might await them there. These new hopes which begin to take shape in the course of the seventh century were naturally connected with the religion of the deities of the underworld. In Homer we find Persephone as queen in the realm of the ghosts, but we meet there no hint of a connexion between her worship and that of Demeter, the goddess of the fruits of the earth. But as the earth which yields the sustenance of men's life also receives men into her bosom when they die, Demeter and Persephone came to be associated in many local cults throughout Greece, and there grew up the legend of the rape of Persephone, which was specially developed at Eleusis and was the subject of the Eleusinian Hymn to Demeter, composed in the seventh century. At Eleusis this *chthonian* cult acquired a peculiar character by the introduction of a new doctrine touching the state of souls in the life beyond the grave.

In the days of Eleusinian independence, the kings themselves *The Eleusinian religion.* were the priests of the two goddesses. When Eleusis became part of the Athenian state, the Eleusinian worship was made part of the Athenian state-religion ; a temple of the two goddesses was built under the Acropolis and called the Eleusinion ; and the Eleusinian Mysteries became one of the chief festivals of the Attic year, conducted by the king. The Mysteries, which were probably of a very simple nature in the seventh century, were subsequently transformed under Athenian influence. Two points in this transformation are especially to be noted. The old Eleusinian king Triptolemus is made more pro- (1) *Triptolemus.* minent, and is revered as the founder of agriculture, sent abroad by Demeter herself to sow seed and instruct folk in the art. But far more important is the association of the cult of Iacchus with the (2) *Iacchus.* Eleusinian worship. Iacchus was a god of the underworld, who had a shrine in Athens. In the Mysteries he was borne to Eleusis and solemnly received there every year. He was originally distinct from the mystic Dionysus, with whom he was afterwards identified.

FIG. 94. —Relief, with Demeter, Triptolemus, and Persephone
(Eleusis : fifth century).

The Mysteries seem to have consisted of a representation in *The rites* dumb show of the story of Persephone and Demeter.   Mystic spells *at Eleusis.* were uttered at certain moments in the spectacle, and certain sacred gear was exhibited.   There was no explanation of any system of doctrine ; the initiated were seers not hearers.   When the scheme of the Mysteries was fully developed the order of the festival, which took place in September, was on this wise.[1]   On the first day, the cry was heard in the streets of Athens—

> Seaward, O mystae, mystae, to the sea !

And the initiated went down to the shore and cleansed themselves in the sea water.   Hence the day was called ἅλαδε μύσται.   The next two days were occupied with offerings and ceremonies at Athens, and on the fourth, the image of Iacchus was taken forth from his shrine and carried in solemn procession along the Sacred Way, over *(By the pass* Mount Aegaleos to Eleusis.   The Mystae, as they went, sang the *of Daphne.)* song of Iacchus, and reached the temple of the goddesses, under the Eleusinian acropolis, late at night, by the light of torches.   The great day was when they assembled in the Hall of Initiation, and *(Tele-* sat around on the tiers of stone-seats.   The Hierophant, who always *sterion.)* belonged to the Eleusinian royal family of the Eumolpids, displayed the secret things of the worship.   Beside him the Torch-holder, the Herald, and the Priest of the Altar, conducted the mystic ceremonies. The Mysteries are mysterious still, so far as most of the details are concerned.   Yet we may perhaps say that no definite dogma was taught, no systematic interpretation was laid on the legends ; but the " acts " were calculated to arouse men's hopes, mysterious enough to *(τὰ* impress their imaginations, and vague enough to suggest to different *δρώμενα.)* minds different significances.   The rites gave to many an assurance of future weal and even to harder reasoners a certain sense of possibilities in the unknown.   And it was believed that the Mystae had an advantage over the uninitiated not only here but hereafter,—an interest as it were with the powers of the other world.   So it is said in the old Eleusinian Hymn :

> Bliss hath he won whoso these things hath seen,
>   Among all men upon the earth that go ;
> But they to whom those sights have never been
>   Unveiled have other dole of weal and woe,
> Even dead, shut fast within the mouldy gloom below.

The Eleusinian Mysteries became Panhellenic.   All Greeks, not impure through any pollution, were welcome to the rites of initiation,

---

[1] The feast of the greater Mysteries is referred to.   The lesser Mysteries were celebrated early in the year at Agrae, a suburb of Athens.

women were not excluded by their sex, nor slaves by their condition. It is probable that the development of the Mysteries owed a good deal to the Pisistratids ; and the ground plan of the Hall of Ceremonies, which was erected in their time, can be traced at Eleusis.

SECT. 13. SPREAD OF THE ORPHIC RELIGION

Orphic cosmogony. The Orphic teachers promulgated a new theory of the creation of the world—a theory which may have derived some suggestions from Babylonia. They taught that Time was the original principle ; that then Ether and Chaos came into being ; that out of these two elements Time formed a silver egg, from which sprang the first-born of the gods, Phanes god of light ; the development of the world is the self-revelation of Phanes. It was necessary to bring this cosmogony into connexion with Greek theology. Accordingly, Zeus swallows Phanes and thereby becomes the original force from which the world has to be developed anew. The Thracian god, Dionysus *Myth of Dionysus Zagreus.* Zagreus, is the son of Zeus and Persephone—and thus closely connected with the underworld. Zeus gives him the kingdom of the universe, while he is still a boy ; but he is pursued by the Titans, and when, after many escapes, he takes the shape of a bull, he is rent in pieces by them, but Athena saves his heart. Zeus swallows *Origin of the human race.* it, and afterwards brings forth the new Dionysus. The Titans, still wet with the blood of their victim, he strikes with lightning, and the race of men springs from their ashes. So that the nature of men is compact of Titanic and Dionysiac elements, good and bad. The motive of the myth was to awaken in the human soul a consciousness of its divine origin, and help it on its way back to the divine state. To escape from the prison or tomb of the body, to become free from the Titanic elements, penalties and purifications are necessary, and the soul has to pass through a cycle of incarnations. In the intervals between these incarnations which recur at fixed times the soul exists in the kingdom of Hades. To attain a final deliverance, a man must live ascetically according to rules which the Orphics prescribed, and be initiated in the orgies of Dionysus. Thus they prescribed abstinence from animal food, and imposed necessary ceremonies of purification. They taught the doctrine of judgment after death, and rewards and punishments in Hades, according to men's deeds in the body.

Thus the Orphics reintroduced, as it were, into Greece the Thracian Dionysus, who seemed almost another god when brought face to face with the Dionysus who had been hellenized and sobered since his admission into the society of the Greek gods of Olympus. They adopted and developed the ideas of the Eleusinian Mysteries ; and in a poem on the Descent of Orpheus into Hades they described the geography of the underworld. They also aspired to take the place of the old prophets and purifiers ; and they sought out and collected the oracles which those prophets had disseminated. Their doctrines were published in poems which were intended to supersede the Theogony of Hesiod ; and the surviving fragments of these works show more poetical power than the compositions of the later successors of Homer.

The Orphics in Attica. Onomacritus. The Orphic religion found a welcome at Athens, and was encouraged by Pisistratus and his sons. Onomacritus, one of the most eminent Orphic teachers, reputed the author of a poem on the " Rites of Initiation," won great credit and influence at the court of the tyrants. We saw how he was supposed to have taken part in preparing an edition of Homer, in which it was suspected that he and his collaborators made interpolations ; and how another interpolation led to his banishment, when he was detected in making an addition of his own to a collection of ancient oracles, which were ascribed to the mythical poet Musaeus.

Pythagoras : goes to Croton, c. 530 B.C.; his scientific work ; Diod. Sic. X. 5— The Orphic doctrines were taken up by a man of genius, Pythagoras of Samos, who went to Italy and settled at Croton, where he was well received. His philosophy had two sides, the philosophic and the religious. He made important discoveries in mathematics and the theory of music ; he recognised the spherical form of the earth, and his astronomical researches led to a considerable step, taken by his followers, in the direction of the Copernican system— the distinction of real and apparent motions. The Pythagoreans knew that the motion of the sun round the earth was only apparent, but they did not discover the revolution of the earth on its axis. They conceived a fire in the centre of the universe, round which the earth turns in twenty-four hours ; the five known planets also revolving round it ; and the moon and the sun, in a month and a year respectively. We never see the fire, because we live on the side of the earth which is always turned away from it. The whole world is warmed and lit from that fire—the " hearth of the universe." Pythagoras sought to explain the world, spiritual and material, by numbers ; and, though he could plausibly defend the idea in general, its absurdity was evident when carried out in detail. His great achievement was the creation of mathematical science.

he founds a brotherhood ; its Orphic character ; At Croton he founded a religious sect or brotherhood, organised according to strict rules. The most important doctrine was the transmigration of souls, and the ascetic mode of life corresponded to that of the Orphic sects. In fact, the Pythagoreans were practically an Orphic community. Their brotherhood, which did not exclude women, obtained adherents not only in Croton but in the neighbouring cities, and won a decisive political influence in Italiot Greece.

its political influence. But this influence was exerted solely in the interests of oligarchy; it would seem indeed that the nobles became members of the religious organisation, in order to use it as an instrument of political power. It was during the ascendency of the Pythagoreans that a war broke out between Croton and its neighbour Sybaris, which was then subject to a tyranny. The men of Croton harboured the exiles whom Telys, the despot of Sybaris, drove out, and refused his demand for their surrender. Telys led forth a large host; a battle was fought; and the Sybarites were routed. Then the victors captured Sybaris and utterly blotted it out. New cities were to arise near the place; one was for a few months to resume its name; but the old Sybaris, which had become proverbial throughout Greece for its wealth and luxury, disappeared so completely that its exact site is unknown. The destruction of the rival city was the chief exploit of the Pythagorean oligarchy of Croton; but a strong opposition arose in Croton against the government and against the Pythagorean order. Pythagoras himself found it prudent to escape from the struggle by leaving Croton, and he ended his life at Metapontion. The democratic party was led by Cylon, but the Cylonians did not get the upper hand till more than half a century had passed; and the Pythagorean order flourished in Croton and the neighbouring cities. At length a sudden blow dissolved their power. One day forty brethren were assembled at Croton in the house of Milon. Their opponents set the building on fire, and only two escaped. It was a signal for a general persecution throughout Italy; everywhere the members of the society were put to death or banished.

War of Sybaris and Croton.

FIG. 95.—Coin of Sybaris, before 510 B.C. (obverse). Bull [legend : ΣΥ].

Destruction of Sybaris, 511-10.

Pythagoras leaves Croton, c. 510-9 (?).

Suppression of the Pythagoreans, c. 450.

At the time of the fall of the Pythagoreans, the Orphic religion was no longer a danger to Greece. It was otherwise in the lifetime of Pythagoras himself. Then it seemed as if the Orphic doctrines had been revealed as the salvation which men's minds craved; and, if those doctrines had taken firm hold of Greece, all the priesthoods of the national temples would have admitted the new religion, become its ministers, and thereby exercised an enormous sacerdotal power. Nor would the Orphic teachers have failed, if there had not been a powerful antidote to counteract their mysticism. Even as it was, they exercised a permanent influence, stimulating the imaginations of poets, like Aeschylus and Pindar, and diffusing a vivid picture of the world of Hades, which has affected all subsequent literature.

SECT. 14. IONIAN REASON

The antidote to the Orphic religion was the philosophy of Ionia. In Asiatic Greece, that religion never took root ; and most fortunately the philosophical movement—the separation of science from theology, of "cosmogony" from "theogony"—had begun before the Orphic movement was disseminated. Europe is deeply indebted to Ionia for having founded philosophy ; but that debt is enhanced by the fact that she thereby rescued Greece from the tyranny of a religion interpreted by priests. We have met Thales and Anaximander already. Pythagoras, although he and his followers made important advances in science, threw his weight into the scale of mysticism ; affected by both the religious and the philosophical movements, he sought to combine them ; and in such unions the mystic element always wins the preponderance. But there were others who pursued, undistracted, the paths of reason, and among these the most eminent and influential were Xenophanes and Heraclitus.

No man was more active in the cause of reason than Xenophanes of Colophon, who, after the Persian subjugation of Ionia, migrated to Elea, where he died in extreme old age. But he spent his long life in wandering about the world, and none saw and heard more of many lands and many men than he. The feeble resistance of Ionia to the invader had disgusted him with the Greeks, and produced a reaction in his mind against their religion and their ideals. His experience of many lands helped him to cast away national prejudices, and he spent his strength in warring against received opinions. In the first place he attacked the orthodox religion and showed up the irrational side of gods made in the image of men. If oxen or horses or lions, he said, had hands to make images of their gods, they would fashion them in the shape of oxen, horses, and lions. In the next place, he protested against the accepted teachers of the Greeks, the poets Homer and Hesiod, whom Greece regarded as inspired. All they have taught men, he said, is theft, adultery, and mutual deceit. Again, he ridiculed the conventional ideals of Greek life, the ideal, for instance, of the athlete. He deprecated the folly which showed great honours to a victor in a race or a contest. "Our wisdom is better than the strength of human animals and horses." He carried about and spread his revolutionary ideas from city to city in the guise of a musician, attended by a slave with a cithern. But he was not merely destructive ; he had something to put in the place of the beliefs which he overthrew. He constructed a philosophy of which the first principle was god—not like mortals in either form or mind—which he identified with the whole cosmos.

*Xeno-
phanes
(after
545 B.C.).*

and which was thus material, existing in space, and not excluding the existence of particular subordinate gods animating nature. He was also distinguished as a geologist; he drew conclusions from fossils as to the past history of the earth. As a fearless thinker, seeking to break through national prejudices, he is one of the most attractive of the pioneers of Greek thought.

But what especially concerns us here is that Xenophanes rejected Orpheus as utterly as he rejected Hesiod. He would have nothing to do with mysticism and divine revelation; he regarded the Orphic priests as impostors, and he inveighed strongly against Pythagoras. We can hardly over-value his services in thus actively fighting the battle of reason, and diffusing ideas which counteracted not only the comparatively harmless superstitions of the vulgar but also the more serious and subtle danger of the Orphic religion. Long before he died, Greek philosophy had become a living power which no religion would stifle, a waxing force which would hinder sacerdotalism from ever turning back the stream of progress.

Heraclitus. The rationalism of Xenophanes affected Heraclitus of Ephesus, a man of very different temper. Heraclitus heartily despised the vulgar—he was an aristocrat in politics—and he wrote in a hard style, for the few. In old age he retreated to the woods to end his life, having deposited the book of his philosophy in the temple of Artemis. A man of greater genius than any of the Ionian philosophers who preceded him, he thought out the "doctrine of the flux," which exercised an immense influence on his successors. This principle was the constant change in all things; existence is change; "we are and we are not." But the process of change observes a certain law; nature has her measures; and thus, while he had developed the doctrine of relativity—"good and bad," he said, "are the same"—he had a basis for ethics. His influence was both subversive and conservative, according as one took hold of the doctrine of the flux or the fixed law of the world.

Par-menides. The pantheistic principle of Xenophanes was taken up at Elea by Parmenides, who gave it a new metaphysical meaning. He assumed an eternal unchanging Being, and treated it with the scientific method which he learned from the Pythagoreans. One of the most important services of Parmenides and his followers was their argument that sense is deceptive and leads us into self-contradiction. Here, they said, was the capital error of Heraclitus, who founded his system on the senses.

The religious danger averted. With Parmenides and Heraclitus, philosophy in the strict sense, metaphysics as we call it, was fully founded. We have not to pursue the development here; but we have to realise that the establishment of the study of philosophy was one of the most momentous facts in the history of the Greeks. It meant the triumph of reason over mystery; it led to the discrediting of the Orphic movement; it ensured the free political and social progress of Hellas. A danger averted without noise or bloodshed, not at a single crisis but in the course of many years, is a danger which soon ceases to be realised; and it is perhaps hard to imagine that in the days of Pisistratus the religion which was then moving Greece, and especially Attica, bid fair to gain a dominant influence and secure a fatal power for the priests. The Delphic priesthood had, doubtless, an instinct that the propagation of the Orphic doctrines might ultimately redound to its own advantage. Although the new religion had arisen when the aristocracies were passing away and had addressed itself to the masses, it is certain that, if it had gained the upper hand, it would have lent itself to the support of aristocracy and tyranny. The tyrants of Athens might have made an Orphic priesthood an useful instrument of terror; and the brotherhood of Pythagoras was an unmistakable lesson to Greece what the predominance of a religious order was likely to mean.

We may say, with propriety, that a great peril was averted from Greece by the healthful influence of the immortal thinkers of Ionia. But this, after all, is only a superficial way of putting the fact. If we look deeper, we see that the victory of philosophy over the doctrines of priests was simply the expression of the Greek spirit, which inevitably sought its highest satisfaction in the full expansion of its own powers in the free light of reason.

The sixth century, the most critical period in the mental development of the Greeks, came to be known afterwards as the age of the Seven Sages.[1] The national instinct for shaping legends chose out a number of men who had made some impression by their justice and prudence, and, regardless of dates, invented an ideal community among them, as if they had formed a sort of college; and brought them into connexion with great people, like Lydian kings. Periander, the tyrant of Corinth, was curiously added to the list, which included Solon and Thales. To them were attributed wise maxims like "Know thyself," "Avoid excess," "It is hard to be virtuous." The spirit, which the legend ascribes to these sages and which the lives of Solon and Pittacus displayed, reflects the wisdom, which sought to solve, or rather to evade, the everlasting problem of the discrepancy between man's ideal of justice and the actual ordering of the world, by enjoining a life of moderation. But it is not without significance that, when the Orphic agitation had abated, Greece should have enshrined the worldly wisdom of men who stood wholly aloof from mystic excitements and sought for no revelation, in the fiction of the Seven Sages.

Legend of the Seven Sages.

See Diod. Sic. IX. 1—

[1] Solon, Periander, Chilon of Sparta, Pittacus, Bias, Thales, Cleobulus of Lindus.

D. Sic. IX. 5.—16   D. Sic. IX II.—12

[handwritten] Myson the Malian sometimes in place of Periander, who I rejected because o turned s, harsh tyrant D. S. IX. 7

FIG. 96.—Themistocles.

CHAPTER VIII

THE FOUNDATION OF THE ATHENIAN EMPIRE

SECT. I. THE POSITION OF SPARTA AND CAREER OF PAUSANIAS

THE Persian war, in its effects on Greece, illustrates the operation of a general law which governs human societies. Pressure from without, whether on a nation or a race, tends to promote unity and cohesion within. In the case of a nation the danger of foreign attack increases the sense of unity among individual citizens and strengthens the central power. In the case of a race, it tends to weld the individual communities into a nation or a federation. In the latter case, the chance of realising a complete or permanent unity depends partly on the strength and the duration of the external pressure, partly upon the degree of strength in the instinct for independence which has hitherto hindered the political atoms from cohesion. The Persian danger produced a marked tendency towards unity, but the pressure was acute only for a few years, and lasted in any form only for a few decades. On the coast of Asia, where the danger was permanent, a union was made.

Now on these principles a philosopher might have predicted that an Hellenic union, whether whole or partial, whether of short or of long duration, would follow the repulse of the Persians; he might have predicted that such a great joint effort would react upon the domestic development of the victorious peoples. But no one could have foreseen what shape the union would take or how the reaction would be directed. The course of Grecian affairs entered upon a new and unexpected way. For the last forty years, Sparta had been *The position of Sparta;* the predominant power in continental Greece. She had become the head of a Peloponnesian League, and had intervened with effect in Greek affairs beyond the limits of the Peloponnesus. Her headship in the common resistance to Persia was recognised without murmur or dispute by the allies of northern Greece ; in fact, her peninsular league may be said to have widened into the Panhellenic confederacy of the Isthmus.   Her admirals had been commanders-in-chief at Salamis and at Mycale ; and, if it were said that those naval victories could not be ascribed to Lacedaemonian skill or enterprise, Sparta could point to Thermopylae where her king had been gloriously defeated, to Cithaeron where her general and her spearsmen had won what was after all the decisive contest of the war.   A political prophet would therefore have been tempted to predict that Sparta, universally acknowledged before the war to be the leading state of Greece, would after the war be able to convert leadership into dominion.   A great national enterprise, conducted under her auspices to a splendid conclusion, must immensely increase the moral strength of her position, and might justly stimulate her ambition ; moral power, by dexterous management, can soon be converted into material strength ; in short, after the battle of Plataea, the Greek world seemed to lie at Sparta's feet.   If such calculations were made, they were doomed to disappointment.   Lacedaemon had not the means, and the Lacedaemonian government had not the brains or the spirit to create the means, of carrying out an effective imperial policy.

For a state which aspired to a truly imperial position in Greece *not a sea-* must inevitably be a sea-power.   This was determined by the *power ;* geographical and commercial conditions of the Greek world.   So long as the Asiatic Greeks belonged to the Persian dominion, so long as the eastern waters of the Aegean were regarded as a Persian sea, Sparta might indeed hold a dominant position in a Hellas thus restricted. But when the world of free Hellenic states once more extended over the Aegean to the skirts of Asia and to Thrace, Sparta unless she became a sea-power could not extend her influence over this larger sea-bound Greece.   She might retain her continental position, but her prestige must ultimately be eclipsed and her power menaced by any city which won imperial authority over the islands and coasts of the Aegean.   This was what happened.

The Spartans were a people unable to adapt themselves to new *her limita-* conditions.   Their city, their constitution, their spirit were survivals *tions.* from mediaeval Greece.   The government was conservative by tradition ; reforms were unwelcome ; a man of exceptional ability was regarded with suspicion.   They continued to drill their hoplites in the fifth century as they had done in the sixth ; the formation of a navy would have seemed to them as unpractical an idea as an expedition against the capital of Persia.   And if we follow their conduct of the recent war, we see that their policy was petty and provincial.   They had generally acted at the last moment ; they had never shown the power of initiation ; their view was so limited by the smaller interests of the Peloponnesus that again and again they almost betrayed the national cause. Failing to share in the progress of Greece, utterly wanting in the imperial instinct and the quality of imagination which accompanies it, the city of Lacedaemon was not marked out to achieve a political union of the Hellenic states. She was, however, able to prevent a rival from achieving it ; but not before that rival had completely thrown her into the shade.

History of these critical years ill-known. Unfortunately the events of the years succeeding the battle of Plataea are but very slightly known. Herodotus, who, about half a century later, completed the story, compact of fiction and history, of the Persian war, ends his work at the capture of Sestos. In the meantime the events of that full and momentous half-century had not been recorded, except by bits and scraps ; the dates became confused, the details were forgotten ; and, when Thucydides, some years after Herodotus, came to investigate the history of this period, the result of his research was a meagre narrative, in a very uncertain chronological setting. The growth of the Athenian empire is the central fact of the period ; but before tracing it, we must pause—it will not be for long—over the misfortunes of Sparta.

Career of Pausanias. Pausanias, the son of Cleombrotus, had shown, it must be allowed, remarkable military ability in conducting the campaign of Plataea. But his talents as a politician were not equal to his talents as a general. Leaping into fame by his victory, he was led into attempting to play a part for which he was too slight a man. Sparta sent him out, in command of a squadron of ships supplied by her allies, to continue the work of emancipating the eastern Greeks. He sailed first to Cyprus and was successful in delivering the greater part of the island from Persian rule. He then proceeded to Byzantium and expelled the Persian garrison. But here his conduct became ambiguous ; he began to play a game of his own. He connived at the escape of some kinsmen of Xerxes who were in the city ; and he committed various acts of insolence and oppression to the Greeks. He behaved more as a tyrant than as a general ; and he completely ruined all chances that his country had of remaining at the head of the confederacy which the Persian invasion had called into being. The eastern Greeks placed themselves under the protection and headship of Athens. This step was inevitable ; the maritime power of Athens marked her out to be leader in the prosecution of the war beyond the sea. But the conduct of Pausanias at Byzantium may well have been the occasion of the formal transference of the leadership of the confederacy from Sparta to Athens. At Sparta itself the reports of the doings of the general aroused alarm and anxiety. He

Th. I 131, Plut. Cim. 6b; Diod. xi. 60²;
Justin ix. 13

Them.'s
dealings in
the Aegean
325

VIII   THE FOUNDATION OF THE ATHENIAN EMPIRE

was recalled to answer the charges.   It was said that he wore Persian *His*
dress, and was attended by an Asiatic bodyguard in his journey *medism;*
through Thrace.   For he had indeed been intriguing with the Persian *Plut. Them.*
court.   The victor of Plataea offered to enslave his own city and the *21³⁻⁴*
rest of Hellas to Xerxes, and to seal the compact by marrying his
daughter.   His overtures were welcomed by the Great King ; and
Pausanias, being a small man and elated by vanity, was unable to
refrain from betraying, in little things, his treacherous designs.   The *recalled*
Persian intrigue, however, could not at this time be proved against *and*
him ; he was punished only for some acts of injury which he had *acquitted.*
done to particular persons.   He was not sent out again ; but he sub- *Proceeds to*
sequently hired a trireme for himself and returned to the scene of his *Byzantium*
former intrigues.   He resumed possession of Byzantium and thus *on his own*
controlled the inner gate of the Euxine ; and he succeeded almost *account,*
immediately in capturing Sestos, which gave him control of the outer *477 B.C.*
gate also.   This was too much for the Athenians who were extending *Takes*
their political and commercial interests in those regions, and they *Sestos ;*
sent out a squadron under Cimon, the son of Miltiades, who *driven out*
recovered Sestos and drove Pausanias out of Byzantium.   The *by Cimon,*
Spartan government, hearing that he was intriguing in the Troad, sent *476 B.C.*
a herald commanding him to return home.   He obeyed the summons, *Recalled to*
believing that he could compass an acquittal by bribes ; but it seems *Sparta.*
that he was already devising a daring and dangerous plan against *T I 95⁵,*
the constitution of his own city.   The Ephors threw him into prison ; *128³.*
but it was difficult to procure evidence of his guilt.   He was released
and challenged inquiry.   Everybody knew that he had not only *Nep. Paus.*
negotiated with Persia but that he had prepared the way for a revolt *2⁶⁻³¹*
of the Helots by promising them emancipation.   He dreamed of *Aristod.*
converting the Spartan state into a true monarchy.   But there were *6²⁻³*
not clear enough proofs to act upon, until a confidential servant turned
informer.   Pausanias had entrusted him with a letter to Artabazus,
but the man, who had noticed that none of the messengers who
had been previously dispatched on the same errand, ever returned,
broke the seal and read in the letter the order for his death.   He
showed the letter to the Ephors, and they, wishing to have proof
against Pausanias from his own mouth, contrived a stratagem.   A
hut with a partition was erected at the sanctuary of Taenarus.   They
concealed themselves in one room and the man remained in the
other as a suppliant.   Pausanias came to discover why he was there ;
the man told him of the letter and reproached him.   In the conversation, Pausanias admitted the whole truth.[1]   But he received

---

[1] This anecdote has its improbabilities.   The device would have been difficult
of execution owing to the long distance of Taenarus from Sparta.   Nor is it easy
to see why the Ephors should hesitate to act on the letter.

M

Detection and Death: T. i. 132-4; Diod. XI. 45; Nepos Paus. iii. 5? 79-10; Diod. XI. 45 Nep. Paus. 4-5 Plut. Them 23+; Cim. 6?, Aristo? ch.; Justin ii. 15 11-16 Pausanias iii. 17 7-

a hint of his danger and fled to the temple of Athena of the Brazen House. He took refuge in a small covered building adjoining the shrine. The Ephors had the doors built up and starved him to

The curse of Athena of the Brazen House. (c. 471 B.C. ?).

death. As he was dying they brought him out, and by the command of the Delphic god he was buried at the entrance to the sacred enclosure. But the starvation within the precincts was an offence against the goddess and brought a curse upon the Spartans. To expiate this they dedicated two brazen statues to Athena of the Brazen House.

Judgement of Pausanias, XI. 46?

Debate on the loss of hegemony Diod. XI. 50 Sending of Dorcis.

Though the adventures of Pausanias are of no great consequence, his career is typical of the Spartan abroad; and it throws some light on years of which we know very little. The Spartan government had sent out another general to replace Pausanias in the Hellespont, but the allies would have no more dealings with Spartan generals; and Sparta made no further attempt to win back the allegiance which

Thuc. i. 95 Plut. Aris. 23? Xen. Hell. VI 534

FIG. 97.—Coin of Pharsalus, fifth century (obverse). Head of Pallas.

the Aegean and Asiatic Greeks had transferred to Athens. On the other hand, she made some attempts at extending her power on the mainland and forming a continental federation. She cast her eyes upon Thessaly, and perhaps hoped that if she brought the far north under her sway, she could extend her influence southward to the Crisaean gulf and form a Lacedaemonian empire on the basis of the Amphictionic league of northern Greece. She sent forth an army under king Leotychidas, who landed in the Pagasaean bay, and showed that he could have

Lacedaemonian expedition against Thessaly: 476 B.C.

Leotychidas' exile Her. VI. 72 Paus. iii. 5⁶ 79-10

easily subjugated the Thessalian states. But like many a Spartan general, he could not resist silver and gold; and the Aleuad princes saved their power by bribing the invader. His guilt was evident, and when he returned home he was condemned to death. He saved himself by fleeing to Tegea, where Athena's sanctuary was ever the refuge of a Spartan king in the day of danger. It is possible that Sparta gained some influence in Thessaly by this enterprise, in which she employed the Peloponnesian fleet; but she made no conquest. Nor did her attempt to reorganise the Amphictionic federation prosper better. She proposed to expel from this league all those states which had joined the Mede—this was aimed at Thebes and Thessaly; and even the states which had not joined the federation against the Mede—this was aimed at Argos. But through the influence of Themistocles, who represented Athens, the proposal was thrown out. The activity of Themistocles in defeating the designs of Sparta at this period is reflected in the story that he tried to induce the Athenians to set fire to the Peloponnesian fleet in Thessalian waters.

Lacedaemonian attempt to annex the Amphictionic league (476 B.C. ?); thwarted by Themistocles.

Plut. Themistocles 203-4; Her. VII. 213²

Sparta was unable to prosecute any further plans of empire beyond her own peninsula; she was soon compelled to fight for her position within the Peloponnesus itself. Argos had now recovered somewhat from the annihilating blow which had been dealt her by king Cleomenes, and was entering upon a new constitutional development which was ultimately to shape itself into a democracy. Most of the small towns, which had taken advantage of the prostration of their mistress to throw off her yoke, such as Hysiae and Orneae, were brought back to their allegiance. It might have been harder *Argos* to cast out the slave lords of Tiryns from their Cyclopean fortress; *recovers* but a prophet from Phigalia came and stirred them *Tiryns* up against Argos; they took the offensive, endured *(468-7* a defeat, and Tiryns was recovered. Thus re-arising, *B.C. ?).* Argos was able to support the Arcadian cities in a combination against the power of Sparta. She entered into alliance with Tegea, but outside the walls of that *Battle of* city the joint forces of the two allies were smitten by *Tegea,* the hoplites of Lacedaemon. Yet the city was not taken, and the epitaph of the fallen warriors told how "their bravery hindered the smoke of blazing Tegea from mounting to the sky." Soon after this we find all the Arcadian cities leagued against Sparta,—all except the Mantineans who were never ready to join hands with their Tegeate neighbours. This time Argos sent no help. The Arcadian league sustained a crushing defeat at Dipaea, and Tegea was forced to submit. Thus, through the energy of the young king Archidamus, Sparta maintained her position, but there were grave causes of anxiety for the future. She had to behold the synoecism of the villages of Elis into a city with a democratic constitution; that was a danger in the west. Regenerate Argos was a danger in the east. And even in Arcadia, Sparta was constrained reluctantly to recognise the new synoecism of the Mantinean villages, as a mark of gratitude to the community for holding aloof from the Arcadian league.

FIG. 98.—Coin of Arcadia, fifth century (reverse). Head of Despoena [legend: AP-ΚΑΔΙΚΟΝ].

FIG. 99.—Coin of Elis, fifth century (obverse). Flying eagle [legend: FΑΛΕΙΟ].

Thus it was not given to Sparta to strike out a new path; the Persian war left her much where she was before. She had, if anything, diminished rather than increased her prestige, and she had shown the world that she was destined to remain in the old Peloponnesian groove. In the meantime another city had been advancing with rapid strides along a new path, compassing large enterprises, and establishing a large empire.

Handwritten top margin:

formation of Delian League: Thuc. 1.95², 6 96. Her. VIII. 3².
Diod. XI. 46⁹-47; Aris. ΑΘΠ. 23²⁻⁵; Plut Arist 23-5¹, Cim 6²⁻³
Nepos, Arist. ⸱⸱⸱ Isocrates VII. 17, VIII 76 XII 52, Dem.
III. 34

SECT. 2. THE CONFEDERACY OF DELOS

The lukewarmness of Sparta, exhibited in her failure to follow up the battle of Mycale, had induced the Ionian and other Asiatic Greeks to place themselves under the leadership of Athens. <u>Thus was formed the voluntary confederacy on which an Athenian empire was to rise.</u> The object was not only to protect the rescued cities from reconquest by the barbarian, but also to devastate the country of the Great King, in order to obtain by rapine a set-off against the expenses and losses of the war. The treasury of the league was established in the sacred island of Delos, the ancient centre of Ionian worship, and it was hence called the Confederacy of Delos. The recapture of Sestos was its first achievement.

<u>The league included the Ionian and Aeolian cities of Asia</u>; the islands adjacent to the coast from Lesbos to Rhodes; a large number of towns on the Propontis, and some in Thrace; most of the Cyclades; and Euboea except its southern city Carystus. It was a league of sea-states, and <u>therefore the basis of the contract was that each state should furnish ships to the common fleet.</u> But most of the members were small and poor; many could not equip more than one or two ships; many could do no more than contribute a part of the expense to the furnishing of a single galley. To gather together a number of small and scattered contingents at a fixed time and place was always a matter of difficulty; nor was such a miscellaneous armament easily managed. It was therefore arranged that the smaller states, instead of furnishing ships, should pay a yearly sum of money to a common treasury. It is uncertain how the amount of these payments was fixed. It seems probable that a calculation was made that all the states, which undertook to pay in money, ought to have been able to contribute between them 100 ships; and that the annual sum of 460 talents was taken as the equivalent of this contribution. Then a careful estimate was made of the resources and capacities of each city; and that sum was proportionally distributed among them. The valuation of the wealth of the confederate cities and the determination of the "contribution" of each was a work of great difficulty; and it was devolved upon Aristides, whose discretion, and the respect in which he was held, fitted him eminently for the task. His valuation remained substantially in force for more than fifty years. Thus from the very beginning the Confederacy consisted of two kinds of members, those who furnished ships and those who paid an equivalent in money— a *phoros*, as it was called; and the second class was for the larger. For besides those who could only furnish a ship or two, or even part

*Left margin printed notes:*

Confederacy of Delos; its purpose (winter 478-7 B.C.) (above, p. 325).

Original Extension of League

(φóρος.) *The Phoros fixed and assigned by Aristides.*

Left margin handwritten notes:

Thuc. i
iii. 10³
vi. 76
Th. V I 96²

Oath of All
ΑΘ.Π 235
Plut

Tribute
560.D. 5. XI 47
Th. 96.
460: Plut. 24.3

T. i. 96, V. 18.5 ΑΘ Π 23⁵

Bottom handwritten notes:

Diod. XI. 47¹⁻², Plut. Aris. 24, 26³; Nepos, Aristides 3¹
Diod. XI. 47¹⁻², Demos. XXIII. 209, Aeschines iii. 258, Ando K II
Paus. viii 52², Aelian VH XI. 9

of a ship, many of the larger cities preferred the system of money payments, which did not oblige their burghers to leave home. The tribute was received by ten Athenian officers, who bore the title of *Hellenotamiae,* "treasurers of the Greeks." The Council of the Confederates met at Delos, where the treasury was, and each member had an equal voice. The large number of votes enabled Athens easily to control the proceedings of the Council; she could influence the smaller states, and the number of these votes overcame the weight of any opposition which the larger states could offer. As leader of the Confederacy, Athens had the executive entirely in her hands, and it was of the highest significance that the treasurers were not selected from the whole body of Confederates but were Athenian citizens. Thus from the first Athens held in her hands the means of gradually, and without any violent revolution, transforming the naval union into a naval empire.

The Council.

*Thuc. i.
96[2] 97[1]
cf. Diod.
xi. 70[1]*

While the name of Aristides is connected most closely with the foundation of the Confederacy, there is no doubt that it was due to his rival Themistocles that Athens took the tide of fortune at the flood. Themistocles had made his city a sea-power; and this feat approved him the greatest of all her statesmen. He was a man of genius. The most reserved of all historians, Thucydides, turns aside to praise his unusual natural gifts: his power of divining what was likely to happen, and his capacity for dealing with difficult situations.

*Desc. v Then
Dial. S.c.
vi. 58·59
Them.
i. 138[3]*

We should have expected that the guidance of the policy of Athens, the organisation of the new Confederacy, would have been entirely entrusted to Themistocles. Half a century later, when the democratic development of Athens had advanced farther, this would probably have been the case. But at this time a man without powerful connexions could not long maintain his influence over the people. Themistocles had no party behind him, and the exceptional ability of the man is shown by nothing so much as by the fact that in spite of this disadvantage he played such a great part. His rivals, Aristides and Xanthippus, inherited prestige and position; and Xanthippus had married into the Alcmaeonids, the family of Megacles and Cleisthenes. They are the leaders at Plataea and Mycale; the name of Themistocles does not appear in the second year of the Persian war. The circumstance that Themistocles was not a party leader, that there was no protracted period during which Athens submitted to his influence, might easily lead us to underrate his importance. Though he was not formally or officially the founder of the Confederacy, yet, when Athens undertook the leadership and entered upon the new paths which then opened out before her, she was under the spell of a spirit of which he had been the clearest and earliest interpreter. But his influence had not yet passed away; and, while

*Position of
Themis-
tocles; he
has no
party to
support
him.*

the fleet was building an empire in the east, there was work for him to do amid the ruins of Athens.

SECT. 3. THE FORTIFICATION OF ATHENS AND THE PIRAEUS

The Acropolis too far from the coast. Themistocles, as we saw, made Athens a sea-power. Under his guidance she threw her chief energy into the development of a navy; but, if she had followed that guidance more fully, she would have now cut herself more boldly adrift from the ties which attached her to the continent. It often occurred to the Athenians to regret that Athens was not an island; "if we were islanders," they thought, "we could defy the world." There would always be the Boeotian and the Megarian frontiers. But, if a series of strong fortresses had been regularly maintained on these frontiers, and if Athenian politicians had resolutely eschewed a continental policy, it might have been possible to spend practically all their strength on their ships. In any case, when Athens decided to enter upon a new career, her true policy would have been to come down to the Piraeus. She should have left her old city round the Acropolis and migrated to the shore of the sea which was henceforward to shape her history. The position of the Acropolis was a fatality for Athens; it was too far from the sea and at the same time too near. If it had been as far from the coast as Acharnae, the citizens would almost certainly at this period have transferred their hearths and temples to the hill of Munychia and the shores of the Piraeus. But it was near enough to admit of tolerably quick communication with the harbour; and this geographical circumstance at once saved the old town and weakened the new city. Expediency will induce a monarch, but nothing except necessity will persuade a free people, to take the momentous resolution of leaving the spot where the homes and temples of the community have stood for centuries—the place associated with their dearest memories, their hopes and their fears.

Themis. / walls : Thuc. i 90. Pir. T. i 93. Diod. XI. 4 Plut. Them. 19 Nep. Them. 6 Gorgias 455 d-e. Had Themistocles been a tyrant, we may venture to suppose that he would have left Athens unfortified, built his palace on Munychia, and made Piraeus the centre of government—the city; so that in a few years the old town would have sunk into decay. But since Athens was to remain as before, notwithstanding the new development, and since this new development made the Piraeus of greater strategic importance, it became necessary to fortify and defend two towns within five miles' distance of each other.

The walls of Athens. After Plataea, the Athenians brought back their families and goods to their desolate habitation. Little of the old town wall was still standing, and they proceeded to build a new wall. The work

Rebuilding √ city walls : Thuc. 90-32 ; Diod. XI. 39-40 ; Aris. Ath. 23 ; Plut. Them. 19 ; Nepos, Themistocles 6 was done in haste ; the material of older buildings and even grave-stones were used.   The traces of haste can be detected in some of the remains of this wall of Themistocles, near the Dipylon Gate in the north-west of the city.   For it was by the advice and under the inspiration of Themistocles that the work was wrought.   It embraced a larger circuit than the old enclosure which Pisistratus had destroyed ; on the south side it followed the heights of the Pnyx group of hills, and approached the Ilisus.   The Peloponnesians looked with jealousy at the rise of the Athenian walls.   The activity of Athens in the Persian war and her strong navy made them suspect her ambitions. But they could not prevent her from strengthening her town.   The Lacedaemonians sent an embassy, to deprecate fortifications, and to invite the Athenians instead of fortifying their own town to join Sparta in demolishing all fortifications in Greece.   But they were not in a position to do more than remonstrate.   As the name of Themistocles was associated with the wall, it was inevitable that an anecdote should be circulated, to illustrate the resources and wiles of the Attic Odysseus.   At his suggestion, the Spartan envoys were sent back *The trick* with the answer that the Athenians would send an embassy.   When *of Themis-* they were gone, he started himself, as one of the ambassadors, but *tocles.* his colleagues were to remain behind till the wall had reached the *Diod XI.* lowest defensible height.   In the meantime, the whole population, *89⁵–90⁴* men, women, and children, were to press on the work.   Having arrived at Sparta, he delayed presenting himself before the assembly, and when he was asked why, he said that his colleagues had been detained and that he expected them every day.   Meanwhile persons arriving from Athens assured the Spartans that the wall was being built.   Themistocles asked them not to be deceived by such rumours, but to send men of their own to discover whether it was true.   At the same time he sent a message to Athens, with instructions that the envoys from Sparta should be detained till he and his colleagues had returned.   The wall had now reached a sufficient height ; and, the other ambassadors having arrived, Themistocles appeared before the assembly, and declared that Athens had walls and could defend her people.   In future, he said, if the Lacedaemonians or their allies have any communication to make, they must deal with us as with men who are capable of deciding their own and Greece's interests. The Lacedaemonians had to put as good a face on the matter as they could.   The story has significance in representing Athens as now formally declaring herself the peer of Sparta.

The fortification of Piraeus was likewise taken in hand.   A thick wall was built all round the Munychian peninsula, keeping close to the sea, and was continued along the north side of the harbour of Cantharus,—or the Harbour, as it was simply called,—

and out to the promontory of Eetionea. The entrances to this chief Harbour and to the two small havens of Munychia and Zea on the east side of the peninsula were fortified by moles.

In the course of the next twenty years the Athenians came to see the disadvantage of the two towns, which ought to have been one. It was borne in upon their statesmen that in the case of an enemy invading Attica with a powerful army, the communications between Athens and the Piraeus might be completely severed, and the folk of the city be cut off from their ships. In order to meet this danger— which would have been most simply met by deserting Athens—a new device was imagined. It was resolved to transform the two towns into a double town, girt by a continuous line of fortification. Two diverging walls were built, to connect Athens with the sea. The northern joined the Piraeus wall, near the Harbour, the southern ran down to the roadstead of Phaleron. By these Long Walls, costly to build and costly to defend, Athens sought to rectify a mistake and adapt her topography to her rôle of mistress of the sea.

The Long Walls, 458 B.C.

But though this device of Athens to conciliate her past history with her future seems clumsy enough, it answered its purpose fairly well. Her naval power was based upon the only sure foundation, a growing naval commerce. This, in its turn, depended upon the increase of Attic industries, which may be estimated by the enormous number of resident aliens or metics, who settled in Athens or Piraeus for the purpose of manufacture and trade. These metics, who seem to have ultimately approached the number of 10,000, were liable to the same ordinary burdens as the citizens, and, when a property-tax was imposed in time of war, they were taxed at a higher rate. We may well believe that Themistocles was concerned to encourage the growth of a class of inhabitants who were directly or indirectly so profitable to the community. But in our scanty and vague records of this momentous period, it is impossible to define the activity of Themistocles.

The μέτοικοι.

He may have wished to introduce a system by which a certain number of triremes should be added to the fleet every year; but this idea was not adopted; new ships were built from time to time according as they were needed. But a new system of furnishing them was introduced. The state supplied only the hull and some of the rigging; the duty and expense of fitting the galley, launching it complete, and training the oarsmen, were laid upon the most wealthy burghers, each in his turn. This public burden was called the trierarchy, and the trierarch, who sailed with his ship, was responsible for the good repair of the trireme at the end of the period of his office. One hundred and seventy oarsmen composed of hired foreigners and slaves, and partly of the poorest class of the citizens, propelled each galley; there was a crew of twenty men, to manage

Introduction of the trierarchy.

Crew: 170 oarsmen, twenty hypêretai,

Increase in Democracy after Salamis Aris. Pol. 1274ᵃ ₵ 1304ᵃ 22 the vessel, including the *keleustes* who set the time to the oarsmen ; *ten* and there were, besides, ten soldiers. *epibatai.*

As their navy was from henceforth to be the chief arm of their military power, the Athenians were obliged to make a necessary *Change* change in the constitution of their highest military command. Two *in the* courses were open to them. They might leave the board of generals *stratêgia.* as it was, each general being the captain of the hoplites of his own tribe, and institute a new board of admirals. If this arrangement had been made, it would have been necessary to assign to the admirals a higher authority, for the purpose of conducting joint operations by land and sea, so that the position of generals would have been reduced to that of subordinate officers. The other course was to make the generals supreme commanders by land and sea alike— and such had been their virtual position during the Persian invasion. This second plan was adopted, and as a logical consequence the *(See above,* generals were no longer elected by each tribe, but by the whole *p. 261.)* people, though normally each tribe was represented on the Board of Ten. The old duties of the generals as commanders of the tribal regiments were undertaken for the infantry by new officers called taxiarchs and for the cavalry by the phylarchs.

[The fortification of the city and her harbour was the chief, but it was not the only, work that the masons of Athens were set to do. When Mardonius withdrew from Athens before the battle of Plataea he had completed the destruction begun when the city was first captured by the Persians in the previous year. The Athenians returned to find most of their public and private buildings levelled to the ground. After the fortifications had been made secure the most pressing problem was to build living quarters for the citizens *Rebuilding* and to restore such buildings as were essential to the carrying on of *of the* public business. It was on the buildings round *city.* the Agora and in the rest of the city below the Acropolis that rebuilding was first concentrated. The temples of the Acropolis had also been *Temples* destroyed, but the main debt to the gods was to be repaid by a later generation. The old temple of Athena Polias, which housed the sacred image of the goddess, was probably brought back into immediate use by temporary improvisation, but no attempt was made to restore the building in its previous form nor to replace the sculptures which had been shattered in the collapse of the temple. Together with fragments of dedica-

Fig. 100.—Coin of Athens, fifth century (reverse). Owl and spray of olive [legend : AΘE].

tions, sculptures from other buildings, and miscellaneous material from the ruins, they were cleared from the site and used as filling to raise the level of the Acropolis, and to preserve thereby for posterity a vivid picture of one of the finest phases of Athenian art. The great new temple of Athena, which had been begun after Marathon, and had been destroyed before it was completed, was not continued. Not until peace had been made with Persia did Athena receive her new home, when the Parthenon arose on the foundations which were intended for a building of wholly different proportions.]

SECT. 4. OSTRACISM AND DEATH OF THEMISTOCLES

For some years Themistocles divided the guidance of public affairs with Aristides and Xanthippus. He superintended the building of the walls, and we have already seen how he effectually opposed the designs of Sparta. But the man of genius had his weaknesses. Like most Greek statesmen, he was accessible to bribes, and perhaps he would hardly have cared to tell how he had become a rich man. It was more serious that his vanity betrayed him into committing public indiscretions. He built near his own house a shrine to *(Artemis* " Artemis wisest in Council," on the ground that the counsels which *Aristo-* he had offered his country had been wiser than all others. In them-*bule.)* selves such things were of little importance ; but they conduced to unpopularity and gave opponents a handle for attack. The time and the immediate causes of the banishment of Themistocles are uncertain. Perhaps he tried to carry through measures which were too revolutionary for Aristides, though Aristides was a decided democrat. [More probably his continuous opposition to Sparta was *Ostracism* attacked by the philo-Laconian Cimon whose victories gave him *of Themis-* great influence in the Assembly. Appeal was made to ostracism *tocles.* and the verdict went against Themistocles. Many sherds bearing *c. 472 B.C.* his name have been found and one deposit found in a well filling is of particular interest. It contains 190 sherds with Themistocles' name, written by a few hands only. These were perhaps sherds prepared by his enemies for distribution, and it is interesting to note that they were all from vases of good quality. The deposit probably dates from an ostracism before 480, but his enemies are not likely to have been more scrupulous now.] The exiled statesman took up his abode in Argos and carried his anti-Spartan propaganda through the Peloponnese. The presence there of such a crafty and active enemy was not agreeable to Sparta, and he was not left long in peace. When the Persian intrigues of Pausanias were disclosed, the Lacedaemonians discovered that Themistocles was implicated in the scandal. But though Themistocles held communications with Pausanias, communications of a compromising kind, it is not in the least likely that he was really guilty of any design to betray

Greece to Persia; it is rather to be presumed that those communications were concerned with the schemes of Pausanias against the Spartan constitution. He was accused of high treason against his country; men were sent to arrest him and bring him to trial; and he fled to Corcyra. The Corcyraeans refused to keep him and he crossed over to Epirus, pursued by Lacedaemonian and Athenian officers. He was forced to stop at the house of Admetus king of the Molossians, though his previous relations with this king had not been friendly. In these western lands, we seem to be translated into a far older time and to visit the homestead of a Homeric king. Admetus was not at home, but Themistocles supplicated the queen and she directed him to take her child and seat himself by the hearth. When the king returned, Themistocles implored his protection; and Admetus hospitably refused to give him up to the pursuers. The Athenians, disappointed of their prey, condemned him as a traitor to outlawry, confiscating his property and dooming his descendants to loss of citizenship. Admetus sent the fugitive overland to Pydna in Macedonia. A vessel carried him to the shores of Ionia. For some years he lay hidden in towns on the Asiatic coast, but when Xerxes died and Artaxerxes came to the throne, he went up to Susa and intrigued at the Persian court. Thus circumstances drove him to follow the example of Pausanias; and, by a curious irony, the two men who might be regarded as the saviours of Greece, the hero of Salamis and the hero of Plataea, were perverted into framing plans for undoing their own work and enslaving the country which they had delivered. It may well have been, however, that Themistocles, who was an able and far-sighted man, merely intended to compass his own advantage at the expense of the Great King, and had no serious thought of carrying out any designs against Greece. He was, as we might expect, more successful than the Spartan schemer. He won high honour in Persia and was given the government of the district of Magnesia, where Magnesia itself furnished his table with bread, Lampsacus with wine, and Myus with meat.

Themistocles died in Magnesia, and the Magnesians gave him outside their walls the resting-place which was denied to him in his own country.[1] Nor were they content with this; they sought to associate his fame more intimately with their own city. They paid him the honour of a hero, and erected in their market-place a statue of the saviour of Greece, standing naked in the act of pouring a libation over an altar, below which lay a slain bull. It was not long before this scene was wilfully or ignorantly misunderstood and gave

Flight of Themistocles, to 471-0 B.C. Corcyra / Persia Thuc. i. 136-8; Diod. XI. 56; Plut. Them. 24-27; Nepos. Themis. 8-10; Arist. 10; Cic. Brut. 10.42; *Accession of Artaxerxes.* 464 B.C.

Death of Themistocles. *His statue.* Th. i. 138; Plut. 32.1,6; *Nepos, Th.* 10;

[1] It is said that relatives took his bones to Attica and buried them secretly; and it is supposed that his Attic sepulchre can be identified on the shore of the Munychian promontory.

Thuc. i. 138; Plut. Them. 32.4-6; Nepos Them. 10; Paus. i. 1.2; 10.8

Thuc. i. 138; Diod. XI. 58 1-3; Plut. Them. 31 4-7; Nepos Th. 10; Cic. Brutus 10-11. 42-43 De Amic. 12.42

Rumoured rise to a false story. Half a century after the death of Themistocles
suicide. it was popularly supposed that he had poisoned himself with bull's
blood ; and the absurd motive of despair at his inability to fulfil his
promises to the Persian king was assigned for his self-slaughter.
There can be little doubt that this tale, first circulated perhaps by
malicious tongues at Athens, was suggested by the bull and the
libation-dish in the monument of the Magnesian market-place.

Not so. Diod.
Sic. XI.58

SECT. 5. THE CONFEDERACY OF DELOS BECOMES AN ATHENIAN EMPIRE

Cimon
general of
confederate
fleet.
Capture of
Eion,
476-5 B.C.

The conduct of the war which the Confederacy of Delos was
waging against Persia had been entrusted to Cimon, the son of
Miltiades. We have seen already how he drove Pausanias out of
Sestos and Byzantium. His next exploit was to capture Eion, a town
near the mouth of the Strymon, and the most important stronghold
of the Persians west of the Hellespont. The place was defended to
the uttermost by Boges, its gallant commander, who refused all
overtures ; and when the food ran out he lit a great funeral pyre.
He slew his wife and his children, his concubines and his slaves, and
hurled them into the fire. He took all his gold and silver to the top
of the wall and flung it into the waters of the Strymon. Then he
leaped himself into the flames. Thus the Athenians captured a
strong coast-fortress, and they were tempted by the rich cornfields
and the forests of timber in the neighbourhood to make a permanent
settlement at Eion ; but the colonists whom they sent forth were
destroyed by the Thracian natives. The day for the establishment
of the Athenian power on the lower Strymon had not yet come.

Doriscus which commanded the mouth of the Hebrus was still in
Persian hands, the attempts of the Athenian fleet to take it were
successfully resisted, and we know not what befell it in the end.

Conquest of
Scyrus,
474-3 B.C.

Perhaps it fell into the hands of the Thracians. The next enterprise of Cimon was the reduction of the rocky island of Scyrus,
a stronghold of Dolopian pirates. While Athens was winning
posts on the fringe of the Aegean, it was no less necessary for her
to secure intermediate stations ; and the importance of Scyrus was
its position on the sea-road from Athens to western Thrace. The
rude inhabitants were enslaved, and their place was taken by Attic
settlers ; the island was in fact annexed to Attica. But Cimon won

Bones of
Theseus.

less glory by the conquest than by the discovery of the bones of
Theseus. There was a Delphic oracle which bade the Athenians take
up the bones of Theseus and keep them in an honourable resting-
place, and perhaps there was a legend that the hero was buried in
Scyrus. In any case, whether by chance or after a search, there was

found in the island a grave containing a warrior's corpse of heroic size. It was the corpse of Theseus; Cimon brought it back to Athens; and perhaps none of his exploits earned him greater popularity.

A few years later Cimon achieved what was the most brilliant success of his life. Hitherto he had been busy in the northern waters of the Aegean; it was high time that the fleet should sail southward and strike a blow against the Persian power in the seas of Rhodes and Cyprus. It was not only high time, it was imperative; for Xerxes had equipped a great armament—his last resistance to the triumph of Greek arms. Cimon delivered both the Greek and the native coast towns of Caria from Persian rule, and constrained the Lycian communities to enrol themselves in the Confederacy of Delos. Then at the river Eurymedon in Pamphylia he found the Persian army and the Persian fleet, overcame them in a double battle by land and sea, destroying 200 Phoenician ships, and then eliminated a reinforcing squadron sailing from Cyprus. This victory sealed the acquisition of southern Asia Minor, from Caria to Pamphylia, for the Athenian federation. *Carian and Lycian expedition of Cimon, ? 468 B.C.* *Diod. XI. ~~60~~, 4 Pl. Cim. 12 Battle of the Eurymedon. Thuc. i. 100 Diod. XI. 60³-62 Plut. 12-13 Nepos, Cim. 2²⁻³, Aristod. 11² Just. ii. 15²⁰*

The booty which was won in this battle was put to the use of fortifying the Athenian citadel which the Persians had dismantled. Themistocles, who laid his hopes on the Piraeus, would have been content that the Acropolis should have remained unwalled; but the conservative policy of Cimon decided otherwise. The south wall was now built out of the spoils of the Eurymedon.

It could not be said that the Confederacy of Delos had failed to do its work. The victory on the Pamphylian river freed Greece from all danger on the side of the Persian empire; and Cimon soon followed up his success by reducing some places on the Thracian Chersonese which were still held by the barbarians. But in the interval between the conquest of Scyrus and the battle of the Eurymedon, the confederate fleet had been set to do other work. It had been set to make war upon Greek states, which were unwilling to belong to the league. The first case was one of pure and simple coercion of a foreign city. Carystus, unlike the other cities of her island, had held aloof from the Confederacy; and this anomaly seemed intolerable to Athens, especially as the place was so near the shores of Attica. Carystus was subjugated, and made, in spite of herself, a member of the league. The second case was that of a confederate state which wished to be confederate no longer. Naxos seceded from the league, and the fleet of the allies reduced her by blockade. In the case of Carystus, the Confederacy could defend its act only by the plea of political necessity; in the case of Naxos, it could reasonably maintain its right of forcing the individual members to fulfil their obligations until the association should be dissolved by the *Cimon captures places on the Hellespont, B.C. (late summer). Reduction of Carystus, 472-1 B.C. Th. i. 98³ Hdt. ix. 105 Revolt and reduction of Naxos, 469 B.C. ? Th. i. 98⁴ 137²*

Plut. Themistocles 25²; Nep. Them 8ᵇ Aristod. 10³

common consent of all. But both acts alike seemed to be acts of tyrannical outrage on the independence of free states, and were an offence to public opinion in Greece. The oppression was all the worse, inasmuch as both Naxos and Carystus were deprived of their autonomy. They became in fact subjects of Athens. They are typical examples of the fashion in which the Athenian empire was built up. Athens was already forging the fetters with which she would bind her allies.

Revolt of Thasos, 465 B.C.

Thuc. i. 100
Diod. xi. 70
Plut. Cim.
14, Them.
25, Nepos Cim.

The victory of the Eurymedon left Athens free to pursue this inevitable policy of transforming the Confederacy into an empire. The most powerful confederate state on the Thracian coast was the island city of Thasos. Possessing a considerable fleet, it was doubtless one of those cities which contributed ships. Athens was making new endeavours to plant a settlement on the Strymon and to lay hands on the traffic in those regions. Her interests collided with those of the Thasians, whose prosperity largely depended upon their trade in Thrace. A dispute arose about a gold mine and the islanders revolted. They hoped for support both from Macedonia and from Thrace, since both those countries were interested in excluding Athens from the coast trade of the northern sea-board. They hoped too for help from Sparta ; but the Lacedaemonians were hindered from sending succour by a revolt of the Helots. The fleet of the Thasians was defeated by Cimon, and after a long blockade they capitulated. Their walls were pulled down, their ships were handed over to Athens, they gave up all claim to the mine and the mainland, and agreed to pay whatever tribute was demanded. [Meanwhile, however, Athenian and allied settlers had occupied the strategic point of Ennea Hodoi on the Strymon, but while penetrating up country to consolidate their position they were surrounded and annihilated by the native Thracians at Drabescus.]

FIG. 101.—Coin of Thasos, fifth century (obverse). Satyr and nymph [legend : (Θ)Α].

Surrender, 463 B.C.

i. 100, iv. 102
Diod. xi. 70
xii. 68
Her. ix. 75
Isoc. viii.
86
Pausanias i. 29

Three classes of confederates.

The typical instances of these three island cities, Carystus, Naxos, and Thasos, exhibit the methods which Athenian policy followed in numerous cases which are not recorded. There were now three classes of members in the Confederacy of Delos ; there were (1) the non-tributary allies which contributed ships ; (2) the tributary allies which were independent ; and (3) the tributary allies which were subject. As the Asiatic cities were declining in vigour, and disliked military service and absence from home, they mostly preferred to discharge their obligations by paying tribute. It was obviously for the interest of Athens that as many members as possible should contribute money, and as few as possible contribute ships. For the ships which the tribute money furnished out were simply an addition to her own fleet, because they were under her direct control. She consequently aimed at diminishing the members of the first class; and soon it consisted of only the three large and wealthy islands, Lesbos, Chios, and Samos. Again, it was to the interest of Athens to transfer the members of the second class into the third, and win control over the internal affairs of the cities. New members which were coerced to join were never allowed to preserve absolute autonomy; and all revolting cities were reduced to the condition of subjection. But the degrees of subjection were not the same. The position of each city was determined by a special agreement with Athens, and the terms of these treaties varied. As a rule, Athens prescribed to her subjects the general form of their constitutions, and it need hardly be said that these constitutions were always democratic. [The regulations imposed on Erythrae near the middle of the century have been *Erythrae,* partially preserved in a French traveller's copy of a stone now lost. *? 453-2 B.C.* Emphasis is laid on the appointment, with the aid of Athenian officers, of the Boule, the nerve centre of democratic government; precautions are taken against Medism; an Athenian garrison is to remain; Erythrae is to bring offerings to the Athenian festival of the Great Panathenaea.] But there was no general hard and fast system. Each city had its own individual arrangements, its own measure of restricted autonomy. The closer dependence of these tributary states on Athens was in many cases marked by the presence of an Athenian garrison and Athenian civil officers. But there was one burden which was common to all, the obligation of furnishing soldiers to the league in time of war. It was a duty which could be demanded only under certain defined conditions, but it was an innovation which altered the original character of the league as a merely maritime confederacy. It seems probable that Athens tried to extend the duty of military service to her autonomous allies, and that this policy caused revolts; a result which was not unwelcome to Athens, as it gave her opportunities to deprive them of autonomy. Ultimately, all the allies seem to have been liable to military service except the three states which furnished ships, Chios, Lesbos, and Samos.

As the process of turning the Alliance into an Empire advanced, Athens found herself able to discontinue the meetings of the Confederate assembly in the island of Delos. She could now act entirely as she deemed good without going through the form of consulting a body whose decisions must necessarily be hers, as the great majority of the members were her own subjects. [A further advance *Treasury* in imperialism was made when the treasury was moved from Delos *transferred* to Athens. The real as well as the declared reason may have been *to Athens,* *454 B.C.*

D i o d. XII 58, 40, 54³; 13. 213; Plut. Pericles 12¹

One-sixtieth as first-fruits to Athena.

the danger to the Aegean following the Athenian disaster in Egypt. But, however honest the motive, the transfer was to make more easy the use of league funds by Athens for her own purposes. The tribute money thus passed from the protection of the Ionian Apollo to the custody of the goddess of the Acropolis; and, in return for her safe keeping, one mina for every talent of the yearly tribute was paid into her own treasury.

The tribute.

(Quota lists.)

The Athenian empire in the middle of the century included most of the islands of the Aegean, with the important exceptions of Crete, Melos, and Thera, and most of the cities on and near the coast from Chalcidice in the north-west to Phaselis in the south-east. A careful record was made each year of the *aparche* paid to Athena, the account was audited by the Logistae for the Hellenotamiae, and the annual lists were inscribed on a large stone pillar prominently displayed on the Acropolis. Sufficient fragments of the first two pillars have been found for them to be reconstructed, so that, though gaps remain, we can tell with some accuracy how many states brought tribute each year and in many cases how much they paid. From 443-2 B.C. we find the cities arranged in five geographical districts, Thracian, Hellespontine, Ionian, Carian, Islands, but the Carian was soon merged in the Ionian.

Xen. Αθ.Π.3 [At the end of every fourth year, in the years of the Great Panathenaea, ~~the~~ assessment was revised by the Athenians, but the allies had an opportunity to plead in the Athenian courts for a lower assessment. No drastic change was made in the general level until the emergence of the great Peloponnesian war; and, at the assessment of 446, possibly as a measure of conciliation in a dangerous period, a large number of cities had their assessment lowered. In years when Athens was strong some 170 states brought tribute, but some of the lists before 446 are considerably shorter and a number of cities in Caria which were paying in the late fifties are not found again. There is therefore often a considerable gap between the amount of tribute actually received and the total assessment.]

Jurisdiction of Athens.

Calling of cases to Athens

Xen. Αθπ. ιι~18

Thuc. 1.7?

One of the most important restrictions on the independence of the cities was the jurisdiction which the Athenians asserted in criminal cases. It was natural that all disputes between Athens and any of her subjects should be decided at Athens; and it was not unreasonable that if the burgher of any allied community committed an act of treason against the empire he should be tried in the imperial city. But, with the growth of imperialism, Athens claimed further rights of jurisdiction. In her settlement with Chalcis after the revolt of 446, she enacted that all cases in which the penalty was death, banishment, or the loss of civic rights should be sent for judgment to Athens. In this as in other matters, there were various arrangements with the various cities; and some doubtless had more freedom than others, but from the middle of the century there was a general tendency towards closer control. Lawsuits arising out of breach of contract between citizens of Athens and citizens of the allied states normally were regulated by separate international agreements, and decided in the law-courts of the defendant's city. In this matter, and it was important, Athens could take the credit of not using her power for the furtherance of her own interests; and it may sometimes have happened that an Athenian was treated with somewhat less than fairness, when a subject folk had the chance of indulging their bitterness against one of their masters. [But this generosity was forgotten in the resentment caused by the use of Athenian courts for political cases. This proved an effective instrument of democratic control but it sharpened the opposition of allied oligarchs, who were the main sufferers. The democrats had less to fear and throughout the period of Athenian rule they remained strikingly loyal to Athens.]

The Athenian Empire was dissolved half a century after the translation of the treasury from Delos to Athens. The first principles *Athenian* of the political thought and political life of Greece were opposed to *empire* such an union. The sovereign city-state was the basis of the civilised *opposed to* · Hellenic world, and no city-state was ready, if it could help it, to *Greek* surrender any part of its sovereignty. In the face of a common danger, *political* cities might be ready to combine together in a league, each parting *sentiment.* with some of her sovereign powers to a common federal council but preserving the right of secession; and this was the idea of the Confederacy of Delos in its initial form. But even such a voluntary and partial surrender of sovereignty was regarded as a misfortune, so that when the motives which induced a city to join a federation became less strong and pressing, every member was anxious to gain its complete independence and resume the sovereign rights which it had laid down. Such being the free tendencies which swayed the peoples of Greece, it required a mighty arm and constant vigilance in a ruling state to keep her federation or empire together. An empire, however disguised, was always considered an injustice—a defiance to the political morality of Hellas. A Greek felt it a degradation of his dignity, or an infraction of his freedom, not to be the citizen of a free and sovereign city. And he felt this at many points if he belonged to one of the subject allies of Athens; since their self-government was limited in regard to domestic, as well as foreign, affairs. However liberal the general supervision of the mistress might be, the alliance with that mistress was a loss of the best of all good things, liberty, which means the right of governing one's self. If Athens had adopted the policy which was so successfully adopted by Rome, the policy of enlarging herself by admitting the citizens of smaller states to her own citizenship, she might have built up a more enduring fabric of empire. But such a plan was incompatible with the political notions of the Greeks.

SECT. 6. POLICY AND OSTRACISM OF CIMON

Antagonism of Dorian and Ionian. As the Persian War had brought out more vividly the contrast between Greek and barbarian and impressed the Greeks with the ideal unity of their race, so the Confederacy of Delos emphasised a division existing within the Greek race itself, the contrast of Dorian and Ionian. That division was largely artificial. It was the result of mistaken notions about the early history of Greece, and only within very restricted limits did it represent any natural line of cleavage in the Hellenic race. But it had come to be accepted as an axiom and was an important element in the situation. We must probably seek for the origin of the opposition between Dorian and Ionian, as a political doctrine, in the unity of the Peloponnesus. The actual geographical unity produced a political unity, when in the sixth century the Spartan power became dominant ; and this was reinforced by the conception of its ethnical unity, as mainly a Dorian country. The identity and exclusiveness of Peloponnesian interests had been apparent at the time of the Persian invasion ; and the Peloponnesus not only stood aloof from, but had the air of protesting against, the growth of the Athenian Confederacy. And this confederacy had taken upon itself from the very first an Ionian colour. Athens, believing that she was an Ionian city and the mother of the Ionians of Asia, was gathering her children about her. The shrine of the Delian Apollo, the great centre of Ionian worship, was chosen as the centre of the new Ionian union. The treasures of the league were in the Ionian Apollo's keeping ; and in his island the allies met to take counsel together. Thus the Dorian federation of the Peloponnesus under the headship of Sparta stood over against the Ionian federation of the Aegean under the headship of Athens.

FIG. 102. —Ostrakon cast against Cimon, son of Miltiades.

For some years the antagonism lay dormant. Sparta was still an ally of Athens against the Mede, and the danger from Persia had not passed away. But the preservation of peace was also due, in some measure, to the policy of the men who guided the fortunes of Athens, Aristides and Cimon.   The son of Miltiades had been at first regarded as a youth of little promise.   His grandfather was nicknamed " Simpleton "; and he was supposed to have inherited a wit poorer than that of the ordinary Athenian.   Fond of the wine-cup and leading a disorderly life, he was not a man of liberal educa-tion ; and a writer of memoirs, who knew him, described him as Peloponnesian rather than Athenian—uncultivated but honest and downright.   He lived with his step-sister Elpinice, and they both affected Lacedaemonian manners.   Aristides seems to have discerned his military ability and to have introduced him to public life.   His simplicity, geniality, and lavish hospitality rendered him popular ; his military successes confirmed his influence.   The two guiding principles of Cimon's policy were the prosecution of the war against Persia, and the maintenance of good relations with the Lacedac-monians.   He upheld the doctrine of dual leadership : Athens should be mistress of the seas, but she should recognise Sparta as the mistress on the continent.   Cimon's sympathy with Sparta and his connexions there became an important political fact, and undoubtedly helped to postpone a rupture between Sparta and Athens.

In this policy Aristides, the leader of the democracy, and Cimon, who was by no means in sympathy with the development of the democratic constitution, had pulled together.   After the ostracism of Themistocles they had the whole power in their hands, Cimon being continually re-elected as Strategos, and Aristides having the moral control of the sovereign Assembly.   On the death of Aristides, Cimon remained the most powerful statesman in Athens, but his want of sympathy with democracy rendered it impossible that he should retain this power in a state which was advancing on the lines along which Athens was moving now.   Younger statesmen arose and formed a party of opposition against Cimon and the oligarchs who rallied around him.   The two chief politicians of this democratic party were Ephialtes, a man of unquestioned probity, whom the oligarchs disliked and feared, and Pericles, the son of Xanthippus, who now began to play a prominent part in the Assembly.   After the conquest of Thasos, they charged Cimon with having received bribes from Alexander, the king of Macedon, who was supporting the Thasians, and with having failed to act against Macedonia as it was his duty to act.   The accusation appears not to have been pressed hard, and Cimon was acquitted.   But it was the first movement of an opposition which was speedily to bring about his fall.

Meanwhile Sparta herself had dealt a blow to his policy.   When the victory of the Eurymedon dispelled the fears of Persia which had hovered over Greece till then, Sparta felt herself free to unseal her dormant jealousy of Athens at the first suitable opportunity, and she saw her opportunity in the war with Thasos. But unforeseen events at home hindered her, as we saw, from actual intervention against Athens. The Spartan citizens lived over a perpetual volcano—the servitude of their Perioeci and Helots. The fire which Pausanias thought of kindling burst forth eight years after his death. An *Earth-* earthquake had laid in ruins the villages which composed the town *quake* of Sparta, and a large number of the inhabitants were buried in the *at Sparta,* convulsion. The moment was chosen by the Messenian serfs to *464 B.C.* shake off the yoke of their detested masters. They annihilated in *Revolt of* battle a company of 300 Spartans, but then they were smitten at *the Helots.* Isthmus, an unknown place in Messenia, and sought refuge in the stronghold of Ithome. On that steep hill, full of the memories of earlier struggles, they held out for a few years. The Spartans were driven to ask the aid of allies; Plataea, Aegina, and Mantinea sent troops to besiege Ithome. They even asked Athens herself to succour them in their distress.

Diod. Sic.
XI. 63

The democratic politicians lifted up their voices against the sending of any aid; and the event proved them to be perfectly right. *Expedition* But the Athenian folk listened to the counsels of Cimon, who drove *of Cimon to* home his doctrine of the dual leadership by two persuasive meta- *Messenia,* phors: "We must not leave Hellas lame; we must not allow *462 B.C.* Athens to lose her yoke-fellow." Cimon took 4000 hoplites to Messenia, but though the Athenians had a reputation for skill in besieging fortresses their endeavours to take Ithome failed. Then Sparta rounded and smote Athens in the face. She told the Athenians, alone of all the allies who were encamped around the hill, that she required their help no more. We are told that the Lacedaemonians were afraid "of the adventurous and revolutionary spirit" of the Athenians. But it is strange indeed that they should have dealt thus with a force which was both procured and com- manded by a friend so staunch as Cimon.

Athenians invited
Ithome.
1. 102; Plut.
Cim. 16-10
Diod. 64
Paus. 1. 29
iv. 246
Justin iii. 6

This incident exploded the Laconian policy of Cimon; it exposed the futility of making sacrifices to court Sparta's friendship, and it revealed the depth of Spartan jealousy. The opposition of Ephialtes and his party to the Messenian expedition received its justification. And meanwhile Ephialtes and Pericles had taken advantage of the absence of the conservative statesman to effect a number of radical reforms which were necessary to complete the democratic constitution. These reforms were extremely popular, and immensely increased the influence of the statesmen who carried them. When then Cimon returned with his policy discredited, they denounced him as a "Philo-Laconian," and felt that they could safely attempt to ostracize

Athen. dismissed
Ithome:
Thuc. 1. 102
Plut. Cim. 17
Diod. XI. 64
Paus. 1. 29
iv. 246-7

Athenian off alliance Sparta: Thuc. 1. 102; cf. Diod. Sic. XI. 64

him.   An ostracism was held, and Cimon was banished.   Soon *Ostracism* afterwards a mysterious crime was committed.   Cimon's chief *of Cimon,* antagonist Ephialtes was murdered, and no one ever ascertained *461 B.C.* with surety who the murderers were.   He had many bitter foes *Murder of* among the Areopagites whom he had attacked singly and collectively; *Ephialtes.* and there were perhaps some among them who would not have *Diod. XI. 77^b* hesitated to wreak such vengeance on their assailant. *Plut. Pericles 10⁷⁻⁸*

The Athenians had presently an opportunity of retaliating on *Capture of* Sparta for her contumely.   The blockade of Ithome was continued *Ithome,* and the rebels at last capitulated.   They were allowed to leave the *459 B.C.* Peloponnesus unharmed, on the condition that they should never return.   The Athenians who had helped to besiege them now found them a shelter.   They settled the Messenians in a new home at *Messenian* Naupactus, on the Corinthian Gulf, a place where they had recently *settled at* established a naval station.   In the Altis of Olympia we may still *Nau-* see a memorial of this "Third Messenian War"—the round base of *pactus.* a statue of Zeus which the Lacedaemonians dedicated as a thank- *Thuc. i. 103³.* offering for their victory; and we may read the inscribed verses in *Diod. XI. 84 ? Paus. iv. 24 ?* which they besought the lord Zeus of Olympus to accept the fair image graciously.

While the Lacedaemonians were wholly intent upon the long *Argos* siege of the Messenian fort, the Argives, free from the fear of attack *reduces and* on that side, had seized the occasion to lay siege to Mycenae.   In *destroys* the days of Argive greatness this stronghold can hardly have been *Mycenae* other than an Argive fortress, and it was probably after the great *(c. 462-0* victory of Cleomenes that with Spartan help the Mycenaeans won for *B.C.).* a brief space their ancient independence.   During that brief space *Diod. XI. 65* they had the glory of bearing a hand in the deliverance of Greece. *Paus. v. 23³* On the summit of their primeval citadel, they built a temple where *VII. 25⁵⁻⁶ ?* the old palace had stood; and they girdled the city below with a *VIII. 27¹ ?* wall.   They now defended the fortress for some time, but their *Strabo VIII. 6¹⁰* supplies were cut off and they were forced to submit.   The Argives *6¹⁹* let them depart whither they would and some found a refuge in Macedonia; but the old town was destroyed, all except the walls which were stronger than the forces of destruction.   Argos was once more mistress of her plain.

CHAPTER IX

THE ATHENIAN EMPIRE UNDER THE GUIDANCE OF PERICLES

SECT. I. THE COMPLETION OF THE ATHENIAN DEMOCRACY

General estimate of character. Thuc. ii. 65. Plutarch Pericles To the Greeks of Cimon's day it might have seemed that the Athenian constitution as it had been fixed by Cleisthenes and further reformed after the battle of Marathon was as democratic as it well could be. But the supreme people was to become in still fuller measure lord in its own house, under the guidance of Ephialtes, whose career was suddenly cut short, and of Pericles, son of Xanthippus, who was to be the most prominent figure in Greece for thirty years. The mother of Pericles belonged to the family, and bore the name, of the daughter of the Sicyonian tyrant, the Agarista whose wooing had been so famous. She was the niece of Cleisthenes the lawgiver, and sister of Megacles who had been ostracized as a friend of the Pisistratids. The young statesman had a military training, but he came under the influence of two distinguished teachers, to whom he owed much. One was a countryman of his own, Damon of Oa, one of the most intellectual Athenians of his day, and renowned as a master of the theory of music. The other was an outlander and a philosopher, Anaxagoras of Clazomenae, whose mechanical theory of the material universe, once for all set in motion by an act of unchangeable mind, freed Pericles from the superstitions of the multitude whom it was his task to guide. To these masters the statesman partly owed his intellectual aloofness ; but he did not owe them either his political ideas or the gift of lucid and persuasive speech which was essential to his success. He was indeed a striking contrast to Cimon, the loose and genial boon companion. He seldom walked abroad ; he was strict in the economy of his household ; he avoided convivial parties ; and jealously maintained the dignity of his reserve. His portrait was chiselled by Cresilas. It is something to have the round pedestal on which the original image was set, but we also possess a copy of the portrait. It shows us,

Pericles

See above, p. 210.

His teachers

His reserve.

Portrait.

᷄t the lofty " Olympian " statesman, but the passionless contempla-᷄ve face of the friend of Anaxagoras.

The most conservative institution in Athens was the Council of Areopagus, for it was filled up from the archons who were taken from the two richest classes in the state. This institution was incompatible with the development of democracy, and it was inevitable that it should be ended or mended. Ephialtes had prepared the way for an attack by accusing individual Areopagites of corruption and fraudulent practices ; and then, taking advantage of Cimon's absence in Messenia, he introduced a series of laws which deprived the ancient council of all its powers that had any political significance. Its right to punish the public ministers and officers if they violated the laws, its duties of supervising the administration and seeing that the laws were obeyed, were taken away and transferred to the people. The censorial powers

FIG. 103.—Pericles, copy of the portrait by Cresilas

which enabled it to inquire into the lives of private citizens were abolished. Nothing was left to the venerable body but its jurisdiction in homicidal cases, the care of the sacred olive-trees of Athena, and a voice in the supervision of the property of the Eleusinian deities. The functions which it lost passed to the Council of Five Hundred.

The Areo-pagus loses political power.

Arist. Pol.
1274ª 7
Aθ. π 25, 27'
35ª
Plvt. 812d
Cim. 108, 15²ᵈ
Per. 7ª '9ᵍ³⁵
Diod. xi 77ᵇ

Transference
v Cases /
Popular Law-
Courts : Arⁱˢᵗ·
Aθ. 25² Plvt.
Cim. 13²⁻ª Per.
9ᵍ

Cases ret. :
Dem. 23.22
₆₆
Lys. vii . 22
(Sacred olive-

the Assembly, and the popular law-courts. All impeachments for crimes which threatened the public weal were henceforward brought before the Council or the Assembly; and henceforward the people tried in their own courts officials who had failed to give a satisfactory account of their administration. [It was typical also of the new democracy that the expenditure on public works should now be publicly recorded for all to see.]

The Eumenides of Aeschylus, 458 B.C.

We have a notable monument of the excitement which this radical change caused at Athens, in a drama of Aeschylus which was performed a few years later. The *Eumenides* describes the trial of

FIG. 104.—The Athenian Acropolis.

Orestes on the hill of Ares for the murder of his mother, and the institution of the court of the Areopagus. The significance of the drama has been often misunderstood. It is no protest after the event; it is no cry to undo what had been done. On the contrary, Aeschylus, so far as his poetical motive permits him to suggest a criticism of recent events, approves of the reform. The Areopagus, he suggests, was instituted as a court, not as a council; its true purpose is to pass a judgment on homicides, like Orestes. The *Eumenides* was calculated to tranquillise those who, awed by the dark and solemn associations which hovered over the hill of Ares, regarded the attack upon it as an impiety.

The dismantling of the Areopagus was an indirect blow to the dignity of the archons, who, by virtue of their office, became Areopagites. About the same time another step was taken on the path of democracy by making the archonship a paid office. Once this was done, there was no longer any reason for confining the post to the two richer classes. The third class, the Zeugitae, were presently made eligible; perhaps in recognition of the part played by the hoplites in the stubborn battle of Tanagra which had confirmed the confidence of the new democracy.

Archonship becomes a paid office. Admission of Zeugitae to archonship, ΑΘΠ. 26³
458-7 *B.C.*

The two engines of the democratic development were lot and pay. Lot had been long ago introduced; but it had not been introduced in its purest form. The archons and other lesser officers, and the members of the council, were taken by lot from a select number of candidates; but these candidates were chosen by deliberate election. This mixed system was now abolished; the preliminary election was done away with; and the Council of Five Hundred, as well as the archons, were appointed by lot from all the eligible citizens. By this means every citizen had an equal chance of holding political office, and taking a part in the conduct of public affairs.

Lot.
Policy of State
Pay. Arist.
ΑΘΠ. 24 ₁₋₃
Plut. Per. 9

It is clear that this system could not work unless the offices were paid; for the poor citizens would have been unable to give up their time to the service of the state. Accordingly pay was introduced not only for the archonship, but for the members of the Council. The payment of state offices was the leading feature of the democratic reforms of Pericles.

Payment of offices. √ Council
Thuc. viii. 69⁴
Aris. ΑΘΠ. 29ᵈ

It was a feature which naturally won him popularity with the masses, especially when it was adopted in the case of the popular courts of justice. At the time of the attack on the Areopagus, Pericles carried a measure that the judges should receive a remuneration of an obol a day.[1] Though the measure had the immediate political object of gaining popular support for the attack on the Areopagus, it was a measure which was ultimately inevitable. The amount of judicial business was growing so enormously that it would have been impossible to find a sufficient number of judges ready to attend day after day in the courts without any compensation. But the easily earned pay attracted the poor and idle, who found it pleasant to sit in court listening to curious cases, their sense of self-importance tickled by the flattering respect of the pleaders. Every citizen who wished could place his name on a list from which the list of judges was selected by lot, so many from each tribe; and the courts were empanelled from this list.

Pay of the judges, c. 462-1 *B.C.*
Arist. Pol.
i 274ᵃ⁸
ΑΘΠ. 24³
27 3 5

It was now to the interest of every Athenian that there should be as few citizens as possible to participate in the new privileges and profits of citizenship. Accordingly, about ten years later the rolls of

Law of Limiting citizenship √
451-0 *B.C.*
Arist ΑΘΠ. 26¹

[1] There is some uncertainty whether the amount was one obol or two obols; perhaps the more probable view is that it was one.

Plut. Perikles
373

the burghers were stringently revised ; and a law was passed that the name of no child should be admitted whose father and mother were not Athenian citizens legitimately wedded.   It was a law which would have excluded Themistocles and Cleisthenes the lawgiver, whose mothers were foreigners.

The working of the law-courts.   It was a matter of course that in cases of a political character the judges of the heliaea should be swayed by their own political opinions and by the eloquence of the pleaders working upon their emotions. It was inevitable that the legal aspect of such cases should be often lost to sight, and the facts often misjudged.   It was an essential part of the democratic intention that the sovereign people should make its anger felt ; and if its anger were sometimes, like a king's anger, unfair, that could not be helped.   But it was far more serious that in private cases the ends of justice were liable to be defeated, not through intention but through ignorance.   We can have no better evidence as to the working of the popular courts than the speeches by which the pleaders hoped to influence the decisions of the judges.   Litigants at Athens had to plead their own cases ; there was no such institution as court-advocates.   But a man might learn off a speech which had been composed for him by another, and recite it in court.   Hence there arose a class of professional speech-writers, and many of their speeches have been preserved.   From these models of judicial eloquence we learn how pleaders expected to gain sentences in their favour.   They make a large use of arguments which are perfectly irrelevant to the case ; a plaintiff, for example, will try to demonstrate at great length that he has rendered services to the state and that his opponent has performed none.   There was thus no question of simply administering the law.   The judges heard each party interpreting the law in its own sense ; but they had themselves no knowledge of the law, and therefore, however impartial they sought to be, their decision was unduly influenced by the dexterity of an eloquent pleader, and affected by considerations which had nothing to do with the matter at issue.   And there was no appeal from their judgment.

Liturgies, or public burdens.   A feature of the Athenian democracy, not to be lost sight of, is that public burdens were laid upon the rich burghers, which did not fall upon the poor.   These were no regular taxes on income or capital, but burdens which were highly characteristic of ancient society, and which might fall to a man's lot only once or twice in his *The trierarchy.* life.   We have already seen how trierarchs were taken from the richer classes to equip and man triremes, in which they were themselves obliged to sail, and for which they were entirely responsible.   It was a duty which entailed not only an outlay of money, *The archi-theoria.* but a considerable sacrifice of time and trouble.   There were other burdens also.   For example, when the city sent solemn deputations on some religious errand, whether to the yearly feast of Apollo at Delos, or to one of the great Panhellenic festivals, or to the oracle of

FIG. 105.—Monument of Lysicrates, Athens.

Delphi, a wealthy citizen was chosen to eke out at his cost the money supplied for the purpose by the public treasury, and to conduct the deputation and equip it with magnificence worthy of the occasion. But none of the liturgies, as these public burdens were called, was more important or more characteristic of Athenian life than that of *The* providing the choruses for the festivals of Dionysus. Every year each *chorêgia.* tribe named one of its wealthy tribesmen to be a *chorêgos*, and his duties were to furnish and array a chorus and provide a skilled trainer to teach it the dances and songs of the drama which it was to perform. Rivalry spurred the *chorêgoi* to ungrudging outlay. He whose chorus was victorious in the tragic or the comic competition was crowned and received a bronze tripod, which he used to set up, inscribed with his own name and that of his tribe, upon a pillar, or sometimes upon a miniature round temple. On the east side of the Acropolis, leading to the theatre, a long street of these choregic monuments recorded the public spirit of the citizens, and this Street of Tripods showed, perhaps more impressively than any other evidence, how much significance the state attached to the theatre and the worship of Dionysus. Never was piety more fully approved as wisdom. The state's endowment of religion turned out to be an endowment of brilliant genius ; and the rich men who were called upon to spend their time and money in furnishing the dancers did service to the great masters of tragedy and comedy, and thereby served the whole world.

SECT. 2. WAR OF ATHENS WITH THE PELOPONNESIANS

Alliance of The banishment of Cimon was the signal for a complete change *Athens and* in the foreign policy of Athens. She abandoned the alliance with *Argos.* the Lacedaemonians and formed a new alliance with their enemies, Thuc. i. 102 4 Argos and Thessaly. The new friendship of the Athenian and Paus. i. 29 9 Argive peoples is reflected in the trilogy which Aeschylus composed iv. 34 7 about this time on the murder of Agamemnon and the vengeance (458 B.C.) of Orestes. The dramatist plays pointedly upon the alliance, and perhaps it is a not undesigned compliment to the new ally that he makes Agamemnon lord of Argos and not of newly-destroyed Mycenae. So far, indeed, as the main interests of Athens were concerned, she was not brought into direct collision with Sparta. But these interests forced her into deadly rivalry with two of Sparta's allies. The naval empire of Athens and the growth of her sea-power were rapidly extending her trade and opening new visions of commercial ambition in all quarters of the Greek world. She was competing with, and it seemed likely that she would outstrip, the two great cities of traffic, Corinth and Aegina. With Aegina there had already been a struggle, and now that Athens had grown in power and wealth another struggle was inevitable. The competition of

Athenian merchants with Corinth in the west was active, and it was about this time that an Athenian general took Naupactus from the Ozolian Locrians, and secured a naval station which gave Athens a considerable control over the mouth of the Corinthian Gulf. This was a blow which struck home ; Athens had now the means of intercepting and harassing the Corinthian argosies which sailed forth with merchandise for the far west. War was a question of months, and the occasion soon came.

Capture of Nau- pactus.

The Megarians, on account of a frontier dispute with Corinth, deserted the Peloponnesian league and placed themselves under Athenian protection. Nothing could be more welcome to Athens than the adhesion of Megara. Holding Megara, she had a strong frontier against the Peloponnesus, commanding the isthmus from Pagae on the Corinthian, to Nisaea on the Saronic, bay. Without any delays she set about the building of a double line of wall from the hill of Megara down to the haven of Nisaea, which faces Salamis, and she garrisoned these " Long Walls " with her own troops. Thus the eastern coast-road was under her control, and Attica had a strong bulwark against invasion by land.

Athens Thuc. i. 105²·
wins 106
Megara, Diod. xi.
459 B.C. 79⁻¹

Long Walls of Megara.

The occupation of Megara was a new offence to Corinth ; and it was an offence to the mistress of the Peloponnesian league. War soon broke out, but at first Sparta took no active part. On the events of the war we are ill-instructed. We find an Athenian squadron making a descent on Halieis, and receiving a setback from some Corinthian and Epidaurian troops. Then the little island of Cecryphalea, which lies between Aegina and the Argive shore, becomes the scene of a naval combat with a Peloponnesian fleet, and the Athenians prevail. At this point the Aeginetans enter the struggle. They saw that if Corinth sustained a severe defeat, their own fate was sealed ; Athens would become absolute mistress in the Saronic sea. A great naval battle was fought near Aegina ; the allies of both Aegina and Athens were engaged ; and the Athenians, having taken seventy ships, landed on the island and blockaded the town. Thereupon the Peloponnesians sent a force of hoplites to help the Aeginetans ; while the Corinthians, advancing over the heights of Geranea, descended into the Megarid, expecting that the Athenians would find it impossible to protect Megara and blockade Aegina at the same time. But they reckoned without a true knowledge of the Athenian spirit. The citizens who were below and above the regular military age were formed into an extraordinary army and marched to the Megarid under the strategos Myronides. A battle was fought ; both sides claimed the victory ; but, when the Corinthians withdrew, the Athenians raised a trophy. Urged by the taunts of their fellow-citizens, the Corinthian soldiers returned in twelve days and began

Battle of Th. i. 105ˢᵗ
Halieis, Diod xi.7
459-8 B.C. 656

Battle of Th. i. 105'
Cecry- Diod. xi. 78²
phalea. Justin iii. 6ᵗʰ

Battle of Thuc. i. 10
Aegina Diod. xi. 70
458 B.C. Justin
iii. 6 6-7

Battle in the Megarid, 458 B.C.

to set up a counter-trophy, but as they were at work the Athenians rushed forth from Megara and inflicted a severe defeat.

This warfare, round the shores and in the waters of the Saronic bay, is the prelude to more warfare in other parts of Greece ; but it is a prelude which has a unity of its own. Athens is opposed indeed to the Peloponnesian alliance ; but the war is, so far, mainly conducted by a concert of three states, whose interests lie in the neighbourhood of the Saronic Bay—Corinth, Epidaurus, and Aegina. These states have indeed the Peloponnesian league behind them, and are helped by "Peloponnesian ships" and "Peloponnesian hoplites" ; but at the same time, the war has not yet assumed a fully Peloponnesian character.

The year of these successes was a year of intense excitement and strain for Athens ; it might fairly be described as an *annus mirabilis* in her history. The victories of Cecryphalea and Aegina were won with only a portion of her fleet. For, in the very hour when she was about to be brought face to face with the armed opposition of rival Greek powers against the growth of her empire and the expansion of her trade, she had embarked in an enterprise beyond the limits of the Greek world. It was an expedition to Egypt, one of the most daring ventures she ever undertook.

Egyptian expedition. A fleet of 200 Athenian and Confederate galleys was operating against Persia in Cyprian seas, when it was invited to cross over to Egypt. The call came from Inaros, a Libyan potentate, who had stirred up the lands of the lower Nile to revolt against their Persian masters. The murder of Xerxes had been followed by troubles at the Persian court, and it was some time before Artaxerxes was safely seated on his throne ; the rebellion of Egypt was one of the consequences of this situation. The invitation of Inaros was most alluring. It meant that, if Athens delivered Egypt from Persian rule, she would secure the chief control of the foreign trade with the Nile valley and be able to establish a naval station on the coast ; by one stroke she would far outstrip all the rival merchant cities of Hellas. The nameless generals of the Aegean fleet accepted the call of the Libyan prince. As in the days of remote antiquity, the "peoples of the north" were now to help the Libyans in an attempt to overthrow the lords of Egypt. Of those remote episodes the Greeks knew nothing, but they might remember how Carian and Ionian adventurers had once placed an Egyptian king upon the throne. In another way, an attack on Egypt was a step in a new path. Hitherto the Confederate ships had sailed in waters which were wholly or partly Greek, and had confined their purpose to the deliverance of Greek cities or cities which, like the Carian and Lycian, were in close touch with Greek civilisation. The shores of Cyprus, where Greek and Phoenician were side by side, invited above other shores a squadron of Greek deliverers. But when the squadron crossed over to Egypt, it entered a new sphere and undertook a new kind of work. The Egyptian expedition was an attempt to carry the struggle with Persia into another stage—a stage in which Greece is the aggressor and the invader. This attempt was not destined to prosper; more than a century was still to elapse before the invasion of Xerxes would be avenged. But it is well to remember that the Athenians, in moving on Egypt, anticipated Alexander the Great, and that success was not impossible if Cimon had been their general.

The Athenians sailed up the Nile to find Inaros triumphant, *Capture of* having gained a great victory in the Delta over a Persian army *Memphis,* which had been sent to quell him. Sailing up they won possession 459 *B.C.* of the city of Memphis, except the citadel, the "White Castle," in *(autumn).* which the Persian garrison held out. After this achievement, we lose sight of the war in Egypt for more than two years, and beyond the protracted blockade of the White Castle we have no record how the Athenian forces were employed. But it was a fatal coincidence that the power of Athens should have been divided at this moment. With her full forces she might have inflicted a crushing blow on the Peloponnesians; with her full forces she might have prospered in Egypt. It was a triumph for the political party which had driven Cimon into banishment that, when half the Athenian fleet was on the banks of the Nile, the hostilities of Corinth and Aegina and their friends should have been so bravely repelled. Nothing impresses *Erechtheid* one more with the energy of Athens at this crisis than the stone *inscription,* which records the names of the citizens belonging to one of the 459-8 *B.C.* tribes, who fell in this memorable year :

> Of the Erechtheid tribe,
> These are they who died in the war, in Cyprus, in Egypt, in
> Phoenice, at Halieis, in Aegina, at Megara, in the same year ;

and the names follow.

The siege of Aegina was continued, and, within two years after *Fall of* the battle, the Aeginetans capitulated, and agreed to surrender their *Aegina,* fleet and pay tribute to Athens. Few successes can have been more 457-6 *B.C.* welcome or profitable to the Athenians than this. The island which *Enrolled in the Con-* offended their eyes and attracted their desires when they looked forth *federacy of* from their hill across the waters of their bay was at length powerless *Delos.* in their hands. They had lamed one of their most formidable commercial rivals ; they had overthrown one of the most influential cities of Dorian Greece. In the Confederacy, Aegina took her rank with Thasos as the richest of the subject states. For these two island cities the burden of yearly tribute was thirty talents, the largest sum paid at that time by any of the cities whose tribute we know, though much higher tributes were to be imposed later.

Lacedae-monian expedition to northern Greece,

457 B.C.

In the meantime events in another part of Greece had led the Lacedaemonians themselves to take part in the war, and had transported the main interest of the struggle from the Saronic Gulf to Boeotia. The errand of the Lacedaemonians was an errand of piety, to succour their mother people, the Dorians of the north, one of whose three little towns had been taken by the Phocians. To force the aggressors to restore the place was an easy task for a force which consisted of 1500 Lacedaemonian hoplites and 10,000 troops of the allies. The real work of the expedition lay in Boeotia. It was clearly the policy of Sparta to raise up here a powerful state to hold Athens in check; and this could only be effected by strengthening Thebes and making her mistress of the Boeotian federation. Accordingly Sparta now set up the power of Thebes again, revising the league, and forcing the Boeotian cities to join it. When the army had done its work in Boeotia, its return to the Peloponnesus was beset by difficulties. To march through the Megarid was dangerous, for the Athenians held the passes, and had redoubled their precautions. And it was not safe to cross the Corinthian Gulf— the way by which they probably had come—for Athenian vessels were now on the watch to intercept them. In this embarrassment they seem to have resolved to march straight upon Athens, where the people were now engaged on the building of Long Walls from the city to the harbour. This course was probably suggested by an Athenian party of oligarchs, who were always abiding an opportunity to overthrow the democracy.

Restoration of the hegemony of Thebes in Boeotia.

FIG. 106.—Coin of Thebes, fifth century (reverse). Heracles strangling snakes [legend : ΘΕ-ΒΑΙ(ΟΣ)].

Battle of Tanagra, 457 B.C. (summer).

The Peloponnesian army advanced to Tanagra, near the Attic frontier; but before they crossed the borders the Athenians went forth to meet them, 14,000 strong, including 1000 Argives, Thessalian cavalry and troops from the cities of the league. The story was later told that the banished statesman, Cimon, now came to the Athenian camp, pitched on Boeotian soil, and sought leave to fight for his country—against Sparta. The request was hastily referred to the Council of Five Hundred at Athens; it was not granted; and all that Cimon could do was to exhort his partisans to fight valiantly. This act of Cimon prepared the way for his recall; in the battle which followed, his friends fought so stubbornly that none of them survived. The story is doubtless fiction but its main point rings true. Cimon and his followers were first and foremost patriots; they were not the extremists who were prepared to betray the city to the Spartans in order to overthrow the new democracy and restore their own political position.   There was great slaughter on both sides; but the Thessalian horsemen deserted during the combat, and the Lacedaemonians gained the victory.   But the battle saved Athens, and the victory only enabled the victors to return by the Isthmus and cut down the fruit trees of the Megarid.   If Cimon's large following among the hoplites had been lukewarm at Tanagra the issue would have been very different.

The Lacedaemonians celebrated their victory by a golden shield which they set above the gable of the new temple of Zeus in the altis of Olympia, as a gift from the spoils of Tanagra.   But the victory did not even secure Boeotia.   Two months after the battle, the Athenians made an expedition into Boeotia under the command of Myronides. A decisive battle was fought at Oenophyta, and the Athenians became masters of the whole land except Thebes.   The Boeotian cities were not enrolled in the maritime Confederacy of Delos, but their dependence on Athens was expressed in the obligation of furnishing contingents to her armies.   At the same time the Phocians entered into the alliance of Athens, and the Opuntian Locrians were constrained to acknowledge her supremacy.   Such were the consequences of Oenophyta and Tanagra.   Athens could now quietly complete the building of her Long Walls.

These brilliant successes were crowned, as we have seen, by the capture of Aegina; and probably about the same time the acquisition of Troezen gave the Athenians an important post on the Argolic shore.   But in the far south their arms were not so prosperous. Since the capture of Memphis, no success seems to have been gained, and the White Castle still held out.   After an ineffectual attempt to induce Sparta to cause a diversion by invading Attica, king Artaxerxes sent a large army to Egypt under Megabyzus, who was supported by a Phoenician fleet.   Having won a battle, he drove the Greeks out of Memphis and shut them up in Prosopitis, an island formed by a canal which intersected the Canopic and Sebennytic channels of the Nile.   Here he blockaded them for eighteen months. At last he drained the canal and turned aside the water, so that the Greek ships were left high and dry, and almost the whole island was reconnected with the banks.   Thus the Persians were able to march across to the island.   The Greeks having burned their ships retreated to Byblos, where they capitulated to Megabyzus and were allowed to depart.   A tedious march brought them to friendly Cyrene, where they found means of returning to their homes.   Inaros who kindled the revolt was crucified, though his life had been spared by the terms of the capitulation.   Soon afterwards a relief squadron of fifty triremes

Conquest of Boeotia.

Battle of Oenophyta;
457 *B.C.*
(autumn).

Failure of the Egyptian expedition
456 *B.C.*

454 *B.C.*

arrived from Athens. It was attacked by the powerful Phoenician fleet in the Mendesian mouth of the Nile, and only a few ships escaped. The Persian authority was restored throughout the land; the day for Greek control of Egypt had not yet come.

But though the Athenians lost ships and treasure in this daring, ill-fated enterprise, their empire was now at the height of its power. They were even able to make the disaster in Egypt a pretext for converting the Delian confederacy into an undisguised Athenian empire. The triumphant Persian fleet might sail into the Aegean sea; Delos was not a safe treasury; the funds of the league must be removed to the Athenian Acropolis.

Extent of Athenian empire, 456-449 B.C.
The empire of Athens now included a continental as well as a maritime dominion. The two countries which marched on her frontiers, Boeotia and Megara, had become her subjects. Beyond Boeotia, her dominion extended over Phocis and Locris to the pass of Thermopylae. In Argos her influence was predominant, Aegina had been added to her Aegean empire, the ships of Aegina to her navy. Through the subjection of Megara, the conquest of Aegina, and the capture of Troezen, the Saronic bay had almost been converted into an Attic lake.

Expeditions to the Corinthian Gulf, 455 and 453 B.C.
The great commercial city of the isthmus was the chief and most dangerous enemy of Athens, and the next object of the policy of Pericles was to convert the Corinthian Gulf into an Attic lake also, and so hem in Corinth on both her seas. The possession of the Megarid and Boeotia, and especially the station at Naupactus, gave Athens control of the northern shores of the gulf, from within the gate up to the isthmus. But the southern seaboard was still entirely Peloponnesian; and outside the gate, on the Acarnanian coast, there were posts which ought to be secured. The general Tolmides made a beginning by capturing the Corinthian colony Chalcis, opposite Patrae. Then Pericles himself conducted an expedition to continue the work of Tolmides. Having failed to reduce Sicyon he laid siege to Oeniadae, an important and strong-walled mart on the Acarnanian coast, but was unable to take it. Though no military success was gained, the expedition created a sensation, and it seems to have led to the adhesion of the Achaean cities to the Athenian alliance. It is *Acquisition of Achaea between 453 and 446.* certain at least that shortly afterwards Achaea was an Athenian dependency; and for a few years Athenian vessels could sail with a sense of dominion in the Corinthian as well as in the Saronic bay.

SECT. 3. CONCLUSION OF PEACE WITH PERSIA

The warfare of recent years had been an enormous strain on the resources of Athens, but the Egyptian disaster indirectly enabled her

to secure more direct control of the tribute of the allies. She wanted
a relief from the strain, but after the expedition of Pericles three or
four years elapsed before peace was concluded. During that interval
there seems to have been a cessation from military operations. Then
Cimon, who may have been specially recalled to Athens, negotiated a
truce, which was fixed for five years, between the Athenians and
Peloponnesians. At roughly the same time Lacedaemon and Argos
concluded a treaty of peace for thirty years.

As soon as the peace was arranged, Athens and her allies were
able to resume their warfare against Persia, and to no man could
that warfare be more safely or fitly entrusted than to the hero of the
Eurymedon river. Pericles may have been well pleased to use
Cimon's military experience ; and an amicable arrangement seems to
have been made, Cimon undertaking not to interfere with the policy
of Pericles. Gossip said that Cimon's sister had much to do with
bringing to pass the reconciliation. " The charms as well as the
intrigues of Elpinice appear to have figured conspicuously in the
memoirs of Athenian biographers : they were employed by one party
as a means of calumniating Cimon, by the other for discrediting
Pericles." [1] But we need not heed the gossip. Women played no
part in the history of Athena's city.

The Phoenician fleet, which had put down the Egyptian rebellion,
was afterwards sent to re-establish the authority of Artaxerxes in the
island of Cyprus ; and accordingly Cimon
sailed thither with a squadron of 200 vessels.
He detached sixty to help a princelet who
had succeeded in defying the Persians in the
fens of the Delta of the Nile ; for the
Athenians, even after their calamity, had not
entirely abandoned the thought of Egyptian
conquest. Then he laid siege to Cition. It
was the last enterprise of the man who had
conducted the war against Persia ever since
the battle of Mycale. He died during the
blockade ; and his death marks the beginning
of a new period in which hostilities between
Greek and Persian slumber. But one final success was gained.
Raising the siege of Cition, because there was no food, the fleet
arrived off Salamis, and the Greeks gained a double victory by
sea and land over the Phoenician and Cilician ships.

But this victory did not encourage the Athenians to continue the
war. We have no glimpse of the counsels of their statesmen at this

FIG. 107.—Coin of Cition,
   fifth century (reverse).
   Seated lion ; ram's head
   [Phoenician   legend :
   l baal melek].

Margin notes:
Thuc. i.112
Diod. XI. 86
Pl. Cim. 18
Per. 10
Five Years' Truce.
Thirty Years' Peace of Argos and Sparta,
452-1 B.C.
Thuc. 5.19
28
Pericles and Cimon.
Campaign in Cyprus, and help sent to Egypt.
Thuc. i.112
Diod. XII. 3
46. Plut. Cim. 18-19 Per. 10
Them. 31
Nepos, Cimon. 3
Death of Cimon, 450-49 B.C.
Necessity of peace.

[1] Grote.

moment; but the facts of the situation enable us to understand their resolution to make peace with the Great King. The events of recent years had proved to them that it was beyond the strength of Athens to carry on war at the same time, in any effectual way, with the common enemy of all the Greeks and with her rivals among the Greeks themselves. It was therefore necessary to choose between peace with Persia and peace in Greece. But an enduring peace in Greece could only be purchased by the surrender of those successes which Athens had lately gained. Corinth would never acquiesce, until she had won back her old predominant position in her western gulf; so long as she was hemmed in, as Athens had hemmed her in, she would inevitably seize any favourable hour to strike for her release. Some Athenian politicians would have been ready to retreat from the positions which had been recently seized and of which the occupation was most galling to Corinth. But Pericles, who had won those positions, was a strong imperialist. The aim of his statesmanship was to increase the Athenian empire and to spread the political influence of Athens within the borders of Greece. He was unwilling to let any part of her empire go, for the sake of earning new successes against the barbarian. The death of Cimon, who had been the soul of the Persian war, may have helped Pericles to carry through his determination to bring that war to an end. And the Great King on his side was disposed to negotiate; for the Greek victory of Cyprian Salamis had been followed by a revolt of Megabyzus, the general who had quelled the insurrection of Egypt.

Policy of Pericles.

Peace with Persia negotiated, c. 448 B.C.

Accordingly peace was made with Persia. There is a dark mist about the negotiations, so dark that it has been questioned whether a formal treaty was ever concluded. But there can be no reasonable doubt that Athens came to an understanding with Artaxerxes, and that peace ensued; and it is equally certain that there was a definite contract, by which Persia undertook not to send ships of war into the Aegean, and Athens gave a similar pledge securing the coasts of the Persian empire against attack. An embassy from Athens and her allies must have waited on the Great King at Susa; and the terms of the arrangement must have been put in writing. But, whatever were the diplomatic forms of the agreement, both parties meant peace, and peace was maintained. It has been called the Peace of Callias; and we have a record which makes it probable that the chief ambassador was Callias, the richest man at Athens, and the husband of Cimon's sister.

Diod. XII. 2
4 + 6, 26
Plut. Cim. 13
Its authenticity
Plutarch Cimon

Kallias' embassy

Struggle of Greek and Phoenician in Cyprus.

The first act in the strife of Greece and Persia thus closes. All the cities of Hellas which had come under barbarian sway had been reunited to the world of free Hellenic states; except in one outlying corner. The island of Cyprus had been one of the prizes for which

Instances when treaty seems to have been disregarded:
Thuc. i. 115⁴ – 116³, iii. 31¹ 34² iv. 75¹ v. 1, Plut. Per. 20³
25²⁴, 26¹ could also b used r show b⟨⟩ treaty never existed

the Athenians had fought Persia. The victory of the Eurymedon had laid the foundation for a vigorous offensive in the east, and for more than ten years the winning of Cyprus had been one of the main objectives of Athenian policy. By the terms of the Peace Athens resigned her claims. The Greek cities of Cyprus were left to struggle with the Phoenicians as best they might; and the Phoenicians soon *Prevalence* got the upper hand and held it for many years. They tried to ex- *of Phoeni-* tirpate Greek civilisation from the island; but Greek civilisation was a *cians after* hardy growth, and we shall hereafter see Greek dynasties again in *the Peace.* power.

SECT. 4. ATHENIAN REVERSES. THE THIRTY YEARS' PEACE

The peace with Persia, however, was not followed by further *Athens* Athenian expansion within the defined limits; on the contrary, some *loses* of the most recent acquisitions of the Athenian empire began *Boeotia.* to fall away. Orchomenus and Chaeronea and some other towns ~~Thuc. i.113~~ in western Boeotia were seized by exiled oligarchs; and it was ~~iii.625 673~~ necessary for Athens to intervene promptly. The general Tolmides ~~iv.926 Diod~~ went forth with a wholly inadequate number of troops. He took ~~xi.6 7~~ and garrisoned Chaeronea, but did not attempt Orchomenus. On ~~Plut. Per.~~ his way home he was set upon by the exiles from Orchomenus and ~~18²⁻³~~ some others, in the neighbourhood of Coronea, and defeated. He *Coronea,* was himself slain; many of the hoplites were taken prisoners; ~~447 B.C.~~ and the Athenians in order to obtain their release resigned Boeotia. ~~Ale. I~~ Thus the battle of Coronea undid the work of Oenophyta. ~~Paus. i.27⁵~~

Athens had little reason to regret this loss; for dominion in ~~29¹⁴~~ Boeotia was not really conducive to the consolidation of her empire. To maintain control over the numerous city-states of the Boeotian country would have been a constant strain on her military re- sources, which would hardly have been remunerative. The loss of Boeotia was followed by the loss of Phocis and Locris. It was strange enough that Phocis should fall away. A few years before the Phocians had taken possession of Delphi. The Spartans had sent *Sacred* an army to rescue the shrine from their hands, and give it back to *War,* the Delphians; but as soon as the Spartans had gone, an Athenian ~~448 B.C.~~ army came, led by Pericles, and restored the sanctuary to the ~~Thuc. i.112⁵~~ Phocians. It was a Sacred War, but so conducted that it did not ~~Plut. Per.~~ make a breach of the Five Years' Truce. Yet, although their ~~21²³~~ position at Delphi seemed to depend on the support of Athens, the Phocians now deserted her alliance. The change was due to an oligarchical reaction in the Phocian cities, consequent on the oligarchical rising in Boeotia.

Revolt of
Euboia
Th. 114'
Diod. XII. 7
Plut. Per. 23
The defeat of Coronea dimmed the prestige of Athenian arms; and still more serious results ensued. <u>Euboea and Megara revolted at the same moment;</u> here too oligarchical parties were at work. Pericles, who was a General, immediately went to Euboea with the regiments of seven of the tribes, while those of the remaining three marched into the Megarid. But he had no sooner reached the island than he was overtaken by the news that the garrison in the

Loss of
Megara.
Thuc. i. 114¹⁻²
Diad. XII. 5
Plut. Per. 22
city of Megara had been massacred and that a Peloponnesian army was threatening Attica. He promptly returned, and his first object was to unite his forces with the troops in the Megarid, which were under the command of Andocides. But king Pleistoanax and the Lacedaemonians were, between them, commanding the east coast-road. Andocides was compelled to return to Attica by

March of
Andocides.
creeping round the corner of the Corinthian Gulf at Aegosthena and passing through Boeotia. The troops were guided by a man of Megara named Pythion, and the gratitude of the three tribes "whom he saved by leading them from Pagae, through Boeotia, to Athens" was recorded on his funeral monument. The stone has survived, and the verses written upon it are a touching reminiscence of a moment of great peril. But when the whole army united in Attica, the peril was passed. The return of Pericles had disconcerted king Pleistoanax, who commanded the Lacedaemonians, and having advanced only as far as the Thriasian plain he withdrew,

Reduction
of Euboea.
Thuc. i. 114³
Diod. XII. 6
Plut. Per. 23
deeming it useless to strike at Athens. Pericles was thus set free to carry out the reduction of Euboea. Histiaea, the city in the north of the island, was most hardly dealt with, probably because her resistance was most obstinate; the people were driven out, their territory annexed to Athens; and the new settlement of Oreos took the place of Histiaea. In other cases the position of each state was settled by an agreement; and the arrangements which were made with Chalcis are still preserved on stone. The alarm of the Athenians is reflected in reductions of tribute which they allowed to their subject states; they feared that the example of Euboea might spread.

Diod.
XII. 7 22²
Plut. Per. 23
The truce of five years was now approaching its end, and peace was felt to be so indispensable that they resigned themselves to purchasing a more durable treaty by considerable concessions. They had lost Megara, but they still held the two ports, Nisaea and Pagae.

The Thirty
Years'
Peace,
446-5 B.C.
Th. i. 87⁶
115¹, i. 2
iv. 21³
These, as well as Achaea and Troezen, they agreed to surrender, and on this basis a peace was concluded for thirty years between the Athenians and the Peloponnesians. All the allies of both sides were enumerated in the treaty, and it was stipulated that neither Athens nor Lacedaemon was to admit into her alliance an ally of the other, while neutral states might join whichever alliance they chose. Aegina was to remain tributary to Athens but her autonomy was guaranteed.

Diod. XII. 7, 26³, 28⁴, Plutarch Per. 24¹, Justin iii. 7¹

It was a humiliating peace for Athens, and perhaps would not have been concluded but for the alarm which had been caused by the inroad of the Peloponnesians into Attic territory. While the loss of Boeotia was probably a gain, and the evacuation of Achaea might be lightly endured, the loss of the Megarid was a serious blow. For, while Athens held the long walls and the passes of Geranea, she had complete immunity from Peloponnesian invasions of her soil. Henceforth Attica was always exposed to such aggressions. The attempt which she had made to win a land-empire had succeeded only for a brief space; the lesson was that she must devote her whole energy to maintaining her maritime dominion. It was a gloomy moment for the Athenians; and it must have required all the tact and eloquence of Pericles to restore the shaken confidence and revive the drooping spirits. Euboea at all events was safe, and men might look back over sixty years to that victory which had been won by *c. 507 B.C.?* their ancestors, in a critical hour, over a joint attack of the Boeotians and Chalcidians. On that occasion a bronze chariot had been dedicated to Athena from the tithe of the prisoners' ransom. Pericles now restored the monument. The parallel was close; for the rebellion of Euboea had been mainly instigated by the Boeotian oligarchs who freed their own land from Athenian control. The marble base on which the chariot stood, on the Acropolis, has been found, and a few letters of the inscribed verses, which Herodotus read and copied, can be made out. The recollection that the sons of the Athenians " quenched the insolence " of the Boeotians, as those verses have it, was indeed the only consolation that could be offered for the defeat of Coronea. While he made the most of the reduction of Euboea, Pericles may have also dwelt on the prospects of the Attic sea-empire. He may have elated them by words such as he is reported to have used at a later moment of despondency. " Of the two divisions of the world accessible to man, the land and the sea, there is one of which you are absolute masters, and have, or may have, the dominion to any extent you please. Neither the Great King nor any nation on earth can hinder a navy like yours from penetrating whithersoever you choose to sail." [1]

Sect. 5. The Imperialism of Pericles, and the Opposition to his Policy

The cities of the Athenian alliance might have claimed, when the Persian war was ended, that the " Confederacy " should be broken up and that they should resume their original and rightful freedom.

---

[1] Thucydides, ii. 62 (transl. Jowett).

Proposed Pan-hellenic Congress, ? 449 B.C.

[It was indeed a critical moment for Athens and it is probably at this time that, on the motion of Pericles, Athens addressed to the Greek world invitations to a Panhellenic Congress. She invited the Greek states to send representatives to Athens for the purpose of discussing certain matters of common interest: the restoration of the temples which had been burnt by the Persians, the payment of the votive offerings which were due to the gods for the great deliverance, and the taking of common measures for clearing the seas of piracy;—this was the programme which Athens proposed to the consideration of Greece. The invitation did not go to the west, for the Italiots and Siceliots were not directly concerned in the Persian war, but it went to all the cities of old Greece, and to the cities and islands which belonged to the Athenian empire. If the congress had been successful it would have inaugurated an amphictiony of all Hellas under Athenian leadership. But this type of panhellenism was not to the taste of Sparta and it is doubtful whether such a realist as Pericles can have been surprised when it miscarried. The Athenian envoys were rebuffed in the Peloponnese, the conference did not meet.

Pericles, however, now had a new sanction to maintain the empire. The Greek world had been invited to discuss other means of maintaining peace in the Aegean and had not responded. Athens would retain her empire resources to maintain her fleet. Her temples had to be rebuilt. They had been burnt in the common cause; they would be rebuilt from the common funds, the accumulated reserve of the League treasury.

Opposition to Pericles. This policy met with fierce opposition both inside and outside Athens. Inside Athens the opposition had found a new leader. Cimon had been primarily a general, with little flair for the subtleties of politics. His kinsman, Thucydides, son of Melesias, who now rallied the opponents of Pericles, was first and foremost a politician. He was the first to concentrate his supporters in assembly meetings and to organise a continuous and concerted opposition. Most of the party attacked the imperialist policy of Pericles because they realised that it was the foundation of extreme democracy, but there were among them some genuine panhellenists who had real sympathy with the allies and who distrusted any step that was likely to keep Athens and Sparta apart. The party had a strong case. They maintained that the tribute should be reserved for the purpose for which it had been levied, and that Athens had no right to use it for her own ends. " Greece is surely suffering sore insult and manifest tyranny, when she sees that with the monies contributed perforce for the war we are gilding and adorning our city like a wanton woman, decking her with costly statues and offerings and thousand-talent temples." But Pericles could claim that while Athens afforded protection to the allies she had the right to use their money ; and the ambitious building programme, with its promise of splendour for the city and profitable employment for the workers, was too popular with the masses to be defeated on a vote.

In the empire opposition was no less serious. The tribute quota *Discon-* lists show that even before the uprisings of 446 Athens had to weather *tent in the* a severe crisis. For the year 449-8 no list of quotas was inscribed on *empire.* the great pillar and the natural inference has been drawn that for this year, perhaps pending the outcome of the Congress, tribute was suspended. But whatever the explanation of the missing list, the normal system was resumed for the year 448-7. The list of this year gives clear evidence of widespread discontent. A considerable number of cities brought no tribute, others paid only part of what was due ; others paid late. The Athenian reaction, however, was vigorous. A decree was passed providing for the tightening up of collection : recognised seals were to be used by the allies to secure the money and a separate statement sent so that no plea could be made of loss in transit. The effect of the increased pressure can be seen in the list of the next year which includes not only a normal number of contributions, but also back payments by the defaulters of the previous year.

It is in this general context that two further acts of advanced imperialism should probably be placed.]

Among the measures which Pericles initiated to strengthen the *THE OUT-* empire of his city, none was more important in its results than the *SETTLE-* system of settling Athenian citizens abroad. Like measures of many *MENTS.* great statesmen, this policy effected the solution of two diverse problems. The colonies which were thus sent to different parts of the empire, served as garrisons in the lands of subject allies, and they also helped to provide for part of the superfluous population of Athens. The first of these Periclean *cleruchies* was established in the Thracian *Colonisa-* Chersonese, under the personal supervision of Pericles himself. Lands *tion of the* were bought from the allied cities of the peninsula, and a thousand *Cherso-* Athenian citizens, chiefly of the poor and unemployed, were allotted *nesus,* farms and assigned to the several cities. The payment for the land *447 B.C.* was made in the shape of a reduction of the tribute. At the same time Pericles restored the wall which Miltiades had built across the isthmus, to protect the country against the Thracians.

The out-settlements in the Chersonese—which were probably followed by out-settlements in Lemnos and Imbros, the island warders of the gate of the Propontis—were the most important of all. The same *Cleruchies* policy was at the same time adopted in Euboea and some of the *in Euboea,* islands of the Aegean, and in a mysterious place, the Thracian Brea, *Naxos,* which probably lay west of the Strymon. The original act of the *Andros,* *447 B.C. ;*

Brea (446 *B.C.?*). colonisation of Brea has been preserved, and the provision that all the settlers shall belong to the two poorest classes of the people, on the Solonian classification, illustrates the character of the Periclean cleruchies. The policy was naturally popular at Athens, since it provided for thousands of unemployed who cumbered the streets; and perhaps it may be regarded as one of the happiest strokes devised by Pericles for increasing his ascendency and confounding his opponents. But it was a policy which was highly unpopular among the allies, in whose territories the settlements were made; and it gave perhaps more dissatisfaction than any other feature of Athenian rule.

Enforcement of Athenian coinage [No less significant of Athens' imperial mood at this time is a decree enforcing the use of Athenian coins, weights, and measures throughout the greater part of the empire (the autonomous islands Samos, Chios, Lesbos, and Cyzicus with its currency of electron staters, useful for trade in the Euxine, were excluded). There had been an increasing tendency since the establishment of the Delian Confederacy for the smaller cities to adopt Athenian coinage with its wide commercial reputation, but many states still preferred to retain a coinage with their own state symbol. They were now forced to conform. Non-Attic coins were to be called in and brought to Athens to be reminted: henceforth Athenian coinage only must be used. This sweeping act may have facilitated the development of trade in the Aegean, but it increased still further the economic dominance of the Piraeus. Silver for coinage could be secured at several points: Athenian coinage had mainly to be bought with goods at Athens.]

Most Athenian citizens were naturally allured by a policy of expansion which made their city great and powerful without exacting heavy sacrifices from themselves. The day had not yet come when they were unwilling to undertake military service, and they were content as long as the cost of maintaining the empire did not tax their purses. The empire furthered the extension of their trade, and increased their prosperity. The average Athenian burgher was not hindered by his own full measure of freedom from being willing to press, with as little scruple as any tyrant, the yoke of his city upon the necks of other communities. So long as the profits of empire were many and its burdens light, the Athenian democracy would feel few searchings of heart in adopting the imperialism of Pericles.

Policy of Pericles. That imperialism was indeed of a lofty kind. The aim of the statesman who guided the destinies of Athens in these days of her greatness was to make her the queen of Hellas; to spread her sway on the mainland as well as beyond the seas; and to make her political influence felt in those states which it would have been unwise and perhaps impossible to draw within the borders of her empire. The full achievement of this ideal would have meant the union of all the Greeks, an union held together by the power of Athens, but having a natural support in a common religion, common traditions, common customs, and a common language.

[The firmness of Athens to the allies in the years immediately following peace with Persia helped her to survive the crisis of 446 without the disintegration of the empire, and the formal recognition of that empire in the peace by Sparta may well have discouraged the internal opposition to Pericles. In 443 their leader Thucydides was ostracised and a new phase of Athenian politics developed.]

SECT. 6. THE RESTORATION OF THE TEMPLES

With the collapse of the Panhellenic Congress it remained for Athens to carry out that part of the programme which concerned herself, and restore in greater splendour the temples of her city and her land. We shall miss the meaning of the architectural monuments which now began to rise under the direction and influence of Pericles, if we do not clearly grasp their historical motive, and recognise their immediate connexion with the Persian war. It devolved upon the city, as a religious duty, to make good the injuries which the barbarian had inflicted upon the habitations of her gods, and fully to pay her debt of gratitude to heaven for the defeat of the Mede. And seeing that Athens had won her great empire through that defeat, the gods might well expect that she would perform this duty on no small scale and in no niggardly spirit. In this, above all, was the greatness of Pericles displayed, that he discerned the importance of performing it on a grand scale. He recognised that the city by ennobling the houses of her gods would ennoble herself; and that she could express her own might and her ideals in no worthier way than by the erection of beautiful temples. His architectural plans went farther than this, and we can see that he was influenced by the example of the Pisistratids; but the chief buildings of the Periclean age, it should always be remembered, were, like the Athenian empire itself, the direct consequence of the Persian invasion.

One of the finest memorials of the Persian war had probably been completed before peace was made with Persia. This was the gigantic statue of Athena Promachos, wrought in bronze by Phidias. The goddess stood near the west brow of her own hill, looking southwestward, and her helmet and the tip of her lance flashing in the sun could be seen far off at sea. But the great transformation of the Acropolis began only after the peace. Nothing was so pressing as to carry to completion the new house of the goddess, which had been

The motive of the buildings at Athens under Pericles.

Use of tribute for buildings: Plut. Per. 12¹⁻³

Opposition to building: Plut. Per. 12¹⁻², 14

Perikl. buildings Plu. Per. 8³, 12-14

450-30 B.C

"Athena Promachos," before 450

THE ATHENIAN ACROPOLIS.

Scale of Yards

0   50   100

Walker & Boutall sc.

FIG. 108.

begun after Marathon but was destroyed by the Persians while
building was in process. The work was now resumed on the same
site and the same foundations; but it was resumed on an entirely
different plan, which was drawn up by the gifted architect Ictinus.
The new temple was slightly broader but considerably shorter
than it would have been if the old design had been carried out, and
instead of foreign Parian marble, native Attic from the quarries of
Pentelicus was employed. Callicrates, another expert architect,
superintended the execution of the plan which Ictinus had conceived.
It is not within our province to enter here into the architectural beauties
of this perfect Dorian temple, which came afterwards to be generally
known as the Parthenon. The building contained two rooms, between
which there was no communication. The eastern room into which
one entered from the pronaos was the temple proper, and contained
the statue of the goddess. It was about a hundred feet long, and
was hence officially called the *Hecatompedos*. The door of the
small western room was on the west side of the temple. This
chamber was perhaps designed for the habitation of invisible maidens
who attend the maiden goddess; it is at least certain that it was
called the *Parthenôn*. It is easy to imagine how a word which
designated as the room of the Maidens part of the house of the
Maiden, could soon come to be associated popularly with the whole
building, and the name Parthenon came to mean for the ordinary
ear, in defiance of official usage, the temple of Athena Parthenos, and
not the chamber of her virgins.

The goddess stood in her dwelling, majestic and smiling, her
colossal figure arrayed in a golden robe, a helmet on her head,
her right hand holding a golden Victory, and her left resting on her
shield, while the snake Erichthonius was coiled at her feet. It was
a wooden statue covered with ivory and gold—ivory for the exposed
flesh, gold for the raiment—and hence called *chryselephantine*. It
was wrought by the Athenian sculptor of genius who has given his
name to the plastic art of the Periclean age, Phidias, the son of
Charmides. He had already made his fame by the Athena Promachos
and another beautiful statue of the goddess of the city, which the outsettlers who went forth to colonise Lemnos dedicated on the Acropolis.
The Lemnian Athena was wrought in bronze and it revealed Athena
to her people in the guise of their friend, while the image of the
Parthenon showed her rather as their queen.

To Phidias too was entrusted the task of designing and carrying
out those plastic decorations which were necessary to the completion
of a great temple. With the metopes of the lofty entablature, from
which Centaurs and Giants stood out in high relief, the great master
had probably little to do. But in the two pediments and on the

Temple of Athena Polias (the "Parthenon"), 447-32 B.C.
Plut. Per. 13. 12
Strabo ix. 1
Paus. viii. 41

The statue of Athena by Phidias
Plut. Per. 24. 31
Strabo ix. 1. 16
Thuc. ii. 13
Diod. xii. 39, 40[3]

frieze which ran round the wall of the temple, within the colonnade, he left monuments of his genius and his skill, for mankind to adore. The triangle above the eastern portal was adorned with the scene of the birth of Athena, who has sprung from the head of Zeus, at the rising of the sun and the setting of the moon ; and Iris the heavenly messenger was shown, going forth to carry the good news to the ends of the world. The pediment of the western end was occupied with the passage in the life of the goddess, but specially appertained

FIG. 109.—Athena and Hephaestus, on the frieze of the Parthenon

to Attica—her triumph on the Acropolis in her contest with her rival Poseidon, for the lordship of the land. The olive which came forth from the earth by her enchantment was probably shown ; and we should like to believe that at the northern and southern ends reclined the two river gods, Eridanus and Ilisus, each at the side which was *The frieze* nearest his own waters. The subject of the wonderful frieze which *of cella.* encircled the temple from end to end was the most solemn of all the ceremonies which the Athenians performed in honour of their queen. At the great Panathenaic festival, every fourth year, they went up in

long procession to her temple to present her with a new robe.   The *The Pan-*
advance of this procession, starting from the western side, and *athenaic*
moving simultaneously along the northern and southern sides, to *procession.*
meet at the eastern entrance, was vividly shown on the frieze of the
Parthenon.   Walking along the peristyle and looking upwards,
the spectator saw the Athenian knights—beautiful young men—on
horseback, charioteers, citizens on foot, musicians, kine and sheep
led for sacrifice, stately maidens with sacred vessels, the nine
archons of the city, all advancing to the house of Athena where she
entertains the celestials on her feast-day.   The high gods are seated
on thrones, Zeus on one side of Athena, Hephaestus on the other ;
and near the goddess is a peplos—perhaps the old peplos—in the
hands of a priest.   The western side of the frieze is still in its place,
but the rest has been removed—the greater part to our own island.

Athena Polias had now two houses side by side on her hill.   For *The old*
the old restored temple was not destroyed, nor was her old image *temple.*
removed from it.   But in her character of Victory, yet another small
habitation, by the architect Callicrates, was decreed for her about the
same time, on the bastion which the hill throws out on its south- *Temple of*
western side.   It was an appropriate spot for the house of Victory. *Athena*
The Athenian standing on that platform saw Salamis and Aegina *Nike.*
near him ; his eye ranged along the Argolic coast, to the distant
citadel of Corinth and the mountains of the Megarid ; under the
shadow of Victory he could lose himself in reveries of memory and
dreams of hope.   The motive of the temple, as a memorial of the
Persian war, was written clear in the frieze.   Whereas the sculptures
of other temples of this period only alluded indirectly to that great
struggle, by the representation of mythical wars—such as the war of
Greek and Amazons, or of Lapiths and Centaurs, or of gods and
giants ; on the frieze of Athena Nike a battle between the Greeks
and Persians is portrayed.   It is the battle of Plataea ; for Greeks
are shown fighting in the Persian host.   The decree for the temple
was carried soon after the Peace of Callias, but the actual building
was delayed for some twenty years.

But there were other shrines of other gods in Athens and Attica, *The*
which had been wrecked by the Persians, and which were now to be *temple of*
restored.   From the west side of the Acropolis, as one looks down *Hephaestus*
on the western quarter of the city, no building is so prominent, or *(popularly*
can ever have been so prominent, as the Dorian temple of Pentelic *called the*
marble which crowns the hill of Colonus, and replaced an older *Theseum).*
temple of the limestone of Piraeus.   It is the temple which " the
sons of Hephaestus " built for their sire, the god of handicraftsmen,
who was always worshipped with special devotion at Athens—it is
significant that on the frieze of the Parthenon he sits next the lady

Fig. 110.—Temple of Athena Nike.

of the land.   This house of Hephaestus is the only Greek temple that is not a ruin.   About the same time, a marble temple of Poseidon *The temple* rose on the extreme point of southern Attica, the promontory of *of Sunium.* Sunium.   The Persian invasion had probably been fatal to the old temple of poros-stone.   Here the sea-god, "to whom men pray at (Σουνι- Sunium," seems to have had his own house, looking down upon his *άρατος.*) own domain.

At the other extremity of the Attic land, the shrine of the *The* goddesses of Eleusis had likewise been destroyed by the barbarians. *Eleusinian* The rebuilding had been soon begun, but, like the new temple *telesterion.* of Athena on the Acropolis, the work had been discontinued owing Plut. Per to the claims of war on the revenue of the state.   Under Pericles 137 it was taken up again and completed; Ictinus made the design Strabo and Coroebus carried it out.   The new Hall of Mysteries was built IX. 1 12 of the dark stone of Eleusis; one side of it was formed by the rock of the hill under which it was built; and the stone steps around the walls would have seated about 3000.   As the place was close to the Megarian frontier, a strong wall with towers was erected round the precincts of the shrine; so that the place had the aspect of a fortress.

[These splendid buildings required a large outlay of money, which was drawn mainly from the tribute reserve.   The opposition, as has

FIG. 111.—Coin of Erythrae, sixth century (obverse). Horseman with horse.

FIG. 112.—Coin of Cos, fifth century (obverse). Youth about to hurl quoit; tripod.

been seen, challenged this use of the allies' money for Athenian temples, but was overridden.   Expenditure, however, was not limited to temples and statues for the gods.   A programme of social building was also developed.   In the days of Cimon's ascendency the people still looked naturally to the aristocratic houses for patronage and Cimon in particular had a reputation for liberality: in the fully developed democracy the state provided for all its citizens the essential amenities of a citizen's life such as gymnasia and baths.   This side of the building programme has been overshadowed by the great works on the Acropolis, but it represents an important aspect of Periclean social policy. The extravagance of the social building programme was, we may think, a natural target for the opposition and one of the main issues which led to the ostracism of Thucydides. The most spectacular of the buildings, which were not primarily of a religious character, dates certainly from this time. A great Hall of Music or *Odeon*, intended for the musical contests which had recently been added to the Panathenaic celebrations, was erected on the east side of the Theatre of Dionysus. Its roof, made of the masts and yard-arms of captured Persian ships, was pointed like a tent, and *Cratinus* wits compared it to the helmet of Pericles the strategos. " The trial *on Pericles* by sherd is over," says some one in a play which the comic poet *(in the* Cratinus put on the stage at this time; " so here comes Pericles, *Thrattai).* our peak-headed Zeus, with the Odeon set on his crown."]

The new Though Cimon, when he constructed the southern wall of the *Propylaea.* Acropolis, also built a new entrance-gate facing south-westward, it was too small and unimposing to relieve the frowning aspect of the walled hill. A more worthy approach, worthy of the Parthenon, was devised by the architect Mnesicles and met the approbation of Pericles. The buildings designed by Mnesicles occupied the whole west side of the hill. In the centre, on the brow of the height and facing westward, was to be the entrance with five gates, and on either side of this two vast columned halls—reaching to the north and south brinks of the hill—in which the Athenians could walk sheltered from sun and rain. Thrown out on the projecting cliffs in front of these halls were to be two spacious wings, flanking the ascent to the central gate. But the plan of Mnesicles took no account of the sanctuaries on the south-western part of the Acropolis, on which his new buildings would encroach. The southern colonnade would have cut short the precinct of Artemis Brauronia and the adjacent southern wing would have infringed on the enclosure of Athena Nike. On the north side there were no such impediments. The priests of these goddesses raised objections to the execution of the architect's plan at the expense of their sacred precincts, and in consequence the grand idea of Mnesicles was only partly carried out. But even after the building had been begun, Pericles and his architect never abandoned the hope that the scruples of the priests might ultimately be overcome; and, while they omitted altogether the southern colonnade and reduced the proportions of the southern wing, they built in such a way that at some future time the structure might be easily enlarged to the measures of the original design. On the northern side, too, the idea of Mnesicles was not completed, but for a different reason. The covered colonnade was never built; it was left to the last, and, when the time came, Athens was threatened by a great war, and deemed it unwise to undertake any further outlay on building. But the north-western wing was built and was adorned *Pinaco-* with paintings. The greatest paintings that Athens possessed were *theca.* however not on the hill but in buildings below; and they belonged to a somewhat earlier age. It was Cimon who brought Polygnotus *Polygnotus* of Thasos to Athens, and it was when Cimon was in power that he, *at Athens,* in collaboration with Micon, another eminent painter, decorated with *c. 470-465.* life-size frescoes the new Theseum and the Anaceum, on the north *Poecile* side of the Acropolis, and the walls of the Painted Portico in the *Stoa.* market-place. We have already cast a glance at the picture of the Battle of Marathon. The most famous of the pictures of the Thasian master was executed, after he had left Athens, for the speech-hall of the Cnidians at Delphi. Its subject was the underworld visited by Odysseus.

If it was vain for Athens to hope that Greece would yield her any formal acknowledgment of headship, she might at all events have the triumph of exerting intellectual influence even in the lands which were least ready to admit her claims. And in the field of art she partly fulfilled the ambition of Pericles, who, when he could not make her the queen, desired that she should be the instructress, of Hellas. When Phidias had completed the great *Phidias* statue of Athena in gold and ivory, and had *goes to* seen it set up in the new temple, he went forth, *Olympia,* invited by the men of Elis, to make the image *c. 438 B.C.* for the temple of Zeus at Olympia. For five years in his workshop in the Altis the Athenian sculptor wrought at the "great chryselephantine god," and the colossal image which came from his hands was probably the highest creation ever achieved by the plastic art of Greece. The Pan-hellenic god, seated on a lofty throne, and clad in a golden robe, held a Victory in his right hand, a sceptre in his left. He was bearded, and his hair was wreathed with a branch of olive.

FIG. 113.—Coin of Elis, fifth century (obverse). Seated Zeus with eagle.

Many have borne witness to the impression which the serene aspect of this manifest divinity always produced upon the heart of the beholder. "Let a man sick and weary in his soul, who has passed through many distresses and sorrows, whose pillow is un-visited by kindly sleep, stand in front of this image; he will, I deem, forget all the terrors and troubles of human life." An Athenian had wrought, for one of the two great centres of Hellenic religion, the most sublime expression of the Greek ideal of godhead. Nor was *(E.g. temple* Phidias the only Athenian artist who worked abroad; we also find the *of Apollo at* architect Ictinus engaged in designing temples in the Peloponnesus. *Phigalia.)*

ATHENS and the PIRAEUS.

Stadia

0   5   10   15

English Miles

0   1   2

800 Yards

0   400

1. Acropolis
2. Areopagus
3. Agora
4. Temple of Hephaestus
5. Pnyx
6. Theatre of Dionysus
7. Temple of Olympian Zeus
8. Waterworks of Pisistratus
9. Theatre

Walker & Boutall sc.

ATHENS

CERAMICUS

To Eleusis

SACRED WAY

Barathrum

PIRAEIC GATE

MELITA

MELITE

Museum

DIPYLON GATE

ACHARNIAN GATE

DEMIAN GATE

SALE Velletta

PANATHENAIC GATE

DIOCHARIS GATE

Mt. Lycabettus

ITONIAN GATE

CYDATHENAEUM

NORTH WALL

MIDDLE WALL

PHALERIC WALL

R. Cephisus

Phalerum

Bay of Phalerum

THE PIRAEUS

The Harbour

ACTE

Munychia

Harbour of Munychia

Saronic Gulf

SECT. 7. THE PIRAEUS. GROWTH OF ATHENIAN TRADE

The Piraeus had grown enormously since it had been fortified by *The Piraeus.* Themistocles ; it was now one of the great ports and cheaping-towns "in the midst of Hellas," and Pericles took in hand to make it a greater and fairer place. There was one weak point in the common defences of Piraeus and Athens. Between Munychia and the extreme end of the southern wall which ran down to the strand of Phaleron, there was an unfortified piece of marshy shore, where an enemy might land at night. This defect might have been remedied by building a cross-wall, but a wholly different plan was adopted. A new long wall was built, running parallel and close to the *The middle* northern wall, and, like it, joining the fortification of Piraeus with the *Long* "upper city," as Athens was locally called. The southern or *Wall.* Phaleron wall consequently ceased to be part of the system of defence and was allowed to fall into disrepair. Round the three harbours shipsteads were constructed, in which the vessels could lie high and dry ; and on the wharfs and quays new storehouses and buildings of sundry kinds arose for the convenience of shipping and trade. On the east side of the great Harbour the chief traffic was carried on in the Place of Commerce. This mart was marked off by *Emporion.* boundary stones, some of which are still preserved, and was subject to the control of a special board of officers. The most famous of the buildings in the Place of Commerce was the colonnade known as the Deigma or Show-place, where merchants showed their wares. But Pericles was not content with the erection of new buildings ; the whole town, which crept up the slopes of Munychia from the quays of the great Harbour, was laid out on a completely new system, which created considerable interest in Greece. It was the rectangular system, on which the main streets run parallel and are cut by cross streets at right angles. The Piraeus was the first town in Europe where this plan was adopted, which we now see carried out on a large scale in many modern cities. The idea was due to Hippodamus, an architect of Miletus, a man of a speculative as well as practical turn, who tried with less success to apply his principles of symmetry to politics, and sketched the scheme of a model state whose institutions were as precisely correlated as the streets of his model town.

The increase of Athenian trade was largely due to the decline of the merchant cities of Ionia, as well as to the blow which was struck to Phoenician commerce by the victory of Greece over Persia. The decay of Ionian commerce is strikingly reflected in the tribute-records of the Athenian Confederacy, where the small sums paid by the

Ionians are contrasted with the larger tributes of the cities on the shores of the Propontis. Lampsacus contributes twice as much as Ephesus. Both trade and industry migrated from the eastern to the western and northern shores of the Aegean ; and as this change coincided with the rise of her empire, it was Athens that it chiefly profited. The population of Athens and her harbour multiplied ; and about this time the whole number of the inhabitants of Attica seems to have been about 315,000—perhaps more than twice as large as the population of the Corinthian state. But nearly half of these inhabitants were slaves ; for one consequence of the growth of manufactures was the inflowing of slave "hands" into the manufacturing towns. In towns where the people subsisted on the fruits of agriculture the demand for slaves remained small. It should be observed that, although Greece, and especially Athens, consumed large quantities of corn brought from beyond the seas, this did not ruin the agriculture of Greece ; the costs of transport were so great that home-grown corn could still be profitable.

Money plentiful.

Except in remote or unusually conservative regions, money had now entirely displaced more primitive standards of exchange and valuation. Most Greek states of any size issued their own coins, and their money at this time was in almost all cases silver. Silver had become plentiful, and prices had necessarily gone up. Thus the price of barley and wheat had become two or three times dearer than a hundred years before. Far more remarkable was the increase in the price of stock. In the days of Solon a sheep could be bought for a drachma ; in the days of Pericles, its cost might approach fifty drachmae. As money was cheap, interest should have been low ; but mercantile enterprise was so active, the demand for capital so great, and security so inadequate, that the usual price of a loan was twelve per cent.

Rise of prices.

Rate of interest.

(Tribute of Lampsacus, 12 tals.; of Ephesus, 6.)

SECT. 8. ATHENIAN ENTERPRISE IN ITALY

Athenian trade in the west.

In the far west Athens was spreading her influence and pushing her trade. She supplied Etruria with her black red-figured pottery, and there was a market for these products of her industry even in the remote valley of the Po. Her ships brought back metal-works from Tuscany, carpets and cushions from Carthage, corn, cheese and pork from Sicily. The Greek cities of Sicily had gradually adopted the Attic standard for their currency ; and in the little Italian republic on the Tiber, which was afterwards destined to make laws for the whole world, the fame of the legislation of Solon was so high that envoys were sent to Athens to obtain a copy of the code. Thus Athens had stepped into the place of Chalcis ; she was now the chief

Ionian trader with Italian and Sicilian lands.   Her rival in this western commerce was Corinth, but she was beginning to out-distance the great Dorian merchant-city.   In this competition Athens had one advantage.   By the possession of Naupactus she could control the entrance to the Corinthian gulf—a perpetual menace to Corinth; while the hatred which existed between Corinth and her colony Corcyra prevented this island from being as useful as it should have been to the Corinthian traffic with the west.   On the other hand, Corinth had the advantage of having important colonies in the west, with which she maintained intimate relations, especially Syracuse; and these maritime cities were centres of her trade and influence.   Next to Athens herself, Syracuse was probably the largest and most populous city in the Greek world.   Athens had no colonies and no such centres.   The disadvantage seems to have been felt by Themistocles, for there are several indications that he was interested in the west.   He named two of his daughters Sybaris and Italia and, before the battle of Salamis, threatened that the Athenians would emigrate to Siris, which had been destroyed by neighbours, if the Peloponnesians abandoned the narrow waters.   Corcyra also, on the western route, was under obligation to him.   But after the Persian invasion other men and other policies held the stage.   At length the opportunity came, when Pericles was at the head of affairs; here, as in other cases, it fell upon him to execute ideas of Themistocles.

The chance preservation of the fragment of a decree tells us that while Athens was reaching the height of her power in the First Pelo- *Alliance with Segesta,* ponnesian War she made alliance with Segesta in the west of Sicily. *458-7 B.C.* It is a reflection of her influence in the west and the foundation of her ultimate disaster in Sicily, but no military commitments were yet undertaken.   Some time after the peace with Persia we find Athens making alliances with Leontini in Sicily and Rhegium on the straits *Leontini* of Messena, but again the influence of Athenian prestige against any *and* growing threat from Syracuse rather than military help was secured *Rhegium.* by the alliance.   At roughly the same time an even better oppor-tunity offered.   The men of old Sybaris, who since the destruction of *Resettle-* their own city by Croton had dwelt in neighbouring cities, thought *ment of* that they might at length return to build a new Sybaris on the old *Sybaris.* site; but within five years their old foes, the men of Croton, drove them out.   They then invited Athens and Sparta to join them in *Founda-* founding a new city.   For Sparta the offer had no attraction; but *tion of* Athens seized her chance and a small band of Athenians and allies *New* was sent out. *Sybaris.*

But the men of old Sybaris were not content to stand on an equal footing with the colonists who had come to help them from the mother-country.   They thought that their old connexion with the place entitled them to a privileged position; they claimed an exclusive right to the most important offices in the state. Such claims could not be tolerated; a battle was fought; and the Sybarites were driven out. But, when the city was thus deplenished, there was a pressing need for men; and for the second time an appeal was made to Athens, but this time from her own children.

To the second appeal Athens, under the guidance of Pericles, responded by an enterprise on a still greater scale. All Greece was now invited to take part in founding a Panhellenic colony. In carrying out this project the right-hand man of Pericles was the Seer and Interpreter (*Exegete*) Lampon, who was closely connected with the Eleusinian worship, and was the highest authority in Athens on all matters pertaining to religion. He obtained from the Delphic god an oracle touching the new colony; it was to be planted where men could drink water by measure and eat bread without measure. At Athens the enemies of Pericles opposed the project, and especially the Panhellenic character which he sought to impress upon it.

Drapetides of Cratinus. Cratinus brought out a play deriding Lampon, and asking whether Pericles was a second Theseus who wanted to synoecize the whole of Greece. But Greece responded to the Athenian proposal, and the colony went forth under the guidance of Lampon. Not far from the *Colony of Thurii, 443 B.C.* site of Sybaris they found a stream gushing from a bronze pipe, which was locally known as the Bushel. Here clearly was the measured water to which the oracle pointed; while the land was so fruitful that it might well be said to furnish bread without measure. The place was named Thurii, and the new city was designed by Hippodamus, the architect who had laid out the Piraeus in rectangular streets. The constitution of Thurii was naturally a democracy; but though the influence of the Athenian model might be recognised, the colony adopted not the laws of Solon, but those of Zaleucus, the lawgiver of Locri. Some years after the foundation, the question was asked, Who was the founder? and the Delphic god himself claimed the honour. The coins of Thurii were stamped with Athena's head and an olive branch; and the place became, as it was intended, a centre of Athenian influence in Italy, although the Attic element in the population failed to maintain its predominance.

SECT. 9. ATHENIAN POLICY IN THRACE AND THE EUXINE

But Athens had greater and more immediate interests in the eastern sea where she succeeded Miletus than in the western where she challenged Corinth. The importance of the imports from the Pontus, especially corn, fish, and wood, was more vital than that of the wares which came to her from the west; and hence there was nothing of higher consequence in the eyes of a clear-sighted statesman than the assurance of the line of communication between Athens and the Euxine sea, and the occupation of strong and favourable points on the coasts of the Euxine itself.   The outer gate of the Euxine was secured by the possession of the Chersonese which Pericles strengthened, and the inner gate by the control of Byzantium and Chalcedon, members of the Athenian Confederacy.   In the Euxine, Athens relied on the Greek towns which, fringing the shores at distant intervals, looked to her for support against the neighbouring barbarians.   The corn-market in the Athenian agora was sensitive to every political movement in Thrace and Scythia ; and it was necessary to be ever ready to support the ships of trade by the presence of ships of war.   The growth of a large Thracian kingdom under Teres and his son Sitalces

FIG. 115.—Coin of Chalcedon, fifth century (o b v e r s e). Head of Ares. *Rise of Thracian kingdom, c. 450 B.C. Thuc. ii. 29 96-7*

demanded the attention of Athenian statesmen to these regions more pressingly than ever.   The power of Teres reached to the Danube, and his influence to the Dnieper ; for he married his daughter to the king of the neighbouring Scythians.

It was in order to impress the barbarians of the Euxine regions with a just sense of the greatness of the Athenian sea-power that Pericles sailed himself to the Pontus, in command of an imposing squadron.   Of that voyage we know little.   It is ascertained that he visited Sinope, and that in consequence of his visit the Athenians gained a permanent footing at that important point.   It is probable that he also sailed to the Cimmerian Bosphorus and visited the Archaeanactid lords of Panticapaeum, who were distinguished for many a long year by their abiding friendship to Athens in her good and evil days alike.   As Panticapaeum was the centre of the Euxine corn trade, this intimacy was of the highest importance.

Pericles visits the Euxine, c. 436 B.C. Plut. Per. 20 1-2

The union of the Thracian tribes under a powerful king constrained Athens also to keep a watchful eye upon the north coast of the Aegean and the eastern frontier of Macedonia.   The most important point on that coast both from a commercial and a strategic point of view was the mouth of the Strymon, where the Athenians possessed the fortress of Eion.   Not far from the mouth was the bridge over which all the trade between Thrace and Macedonia passed to and fro ; and up the Strymon valley ran the chief roads into the " Hinterland."   The mountains of the neighbourhood were famous for the veins of gold and silver stored in their recesses ; the Macedonian king Alexander had tapped a mine near Lake Prasias which yielded daily a silver talent.   In the days of Cimon, Athens had attempted to strengthen Eion by establishing a colony at the

Attempt to colonise the Nine Ways, 465 *B.C. Foundation of Amphipolis,* 437-6 *B.C.* Nine Ways, by the Strymon bridge. We saw how that attempt roused the opposition of Thasos, whose interests it menaced ; and, though Thasos was subdued, the colony of the Nine Ways was destroyed by the neighbouring barbarians. Thirty years later, Pericles resumed the project with greater success. Hagnon, son of Nicias, led forth a colony, of Athenians and allies, and founded a new city, surrounded on three sides by the Strymon-stream, and called its name Amphipolis. It flourished and became, as was inevitable, the most important place in the district. But a considerable proportion of the population was drawn from Greek cities of the neighbourhood, a local feeling grew up unfavourable to the mother-country, and the city was lost to Athens within fifteen years of its foundation.

SECT. 10. THE REVOLT OF SAMOS

Political position of Pericles. After the ostracism of Thucydides, Pericles reigned, the undisputed leader of Athenian policy, for nearly fifteen years. He ruled as absolutely as a tyrant, and folk might have said that his rule was a continuation of the tyranny of the Pisistratids. But his position was entirely constitutional, and it had the stablest foundation, his moral influence over the sovereign people. He had the power of persuading them to do whatever he thought good, and every year for fifteen years after his rival's banishment he was elected one of the generals. Although all the ten generals nominally possessed equal powers, yet the man who possessed the supreme political influence and enjoyed the confidence of the people was practically chief of the ten and had the conduct of foreign affairs in his hands. Pericles was not irresponsible ; for at the end of any official year the people could decline to re-elect him and could call him to account for his acts. When he had once gained the undisputed mastery, the only forces which he used to maintain it were wisdom and eloquence. Whatever devices he may have employed in his earlier career for party purposes, he rejected now all vulgar means of courting popularity or catching votes. He believed in himself ; and he sought to raise the people to his own wisdom, he would not stoop to their folly. The desire of autocratic authority was doubtless part of his nature ; but his spirit was fine enough to feel that it was a greater thing to be leader of freemen whom he must convince by speech than despot of subjects who must obey his nod. Yet this leader of democracy was disdainful of the vulgar herd ; and perhaps no one knew more exactly than he the weak points in a democratic constitution. There is no better equipment for the highest statesmanship than the temper which holds aloof from the public and shows a front of good-natured indifference towards unfriendly criticism ; and we may be sure that this quality in the temperament of Pericles helped to establish his success and maintain his supremacy.

Pericles was a man of finer fibre than Themistocles, but he was not like Themistocles a statesman of originative genius. He originated little ; he elaborated the ideas of others. He brought to perfection the sovereignty of the people which had been fully established in principle long ago ; he raised to its height the empire which had been already founded. As an orator he may have had true genius ; of that we cannot judge. It was his privilege to guide the policy of his country at a time when she had poets and artists who stand alone and eminent not only in her own annals and those of Greece, but in the history of mankind. The Periclean age, the age of Sophocles and Euripides, Ictinus and Phidias, was not made by Pericles. But Pericles, though not creative, was one of its most interesting figures. Perhaps his best service to Greece was one which is often overlooked : the preservation of peace for twelve years between Athens and her jealous continental neighbours—an achievement which demanded statesmanship of no ordinary tact.

In his military operations he seems to have been competent, though we have not material to criticise them minutely ; he was at least generally successful. Five years after the Thirty Years' *Revolt of* Peace, he was called upon to display his generalship. Athens was *Samos,* involved in a war with one of the strongest members of her Con- 440 *B.C.* federacy, the island of Samos. The occasion of this war was a Th̄uc. i.115- dispute which Samos had with another member, Miletus, about the 117 viii.76 possession of Priene. It appears that Athens, some years before, D̄iod xii 27 had settled the constitution of Miletus and placed a garrison in Plut. Per. the city ; and yet we now find Miletus engaged in a struggle with a 24 1-2 25-8 non-tributary ally, and, when she is worsted, appealing to Athens. The case shows how little we know of the various orderings of the relations between Athens and her allies and subjects. One would have thought the decision of such a case would have rested with Athens from the first. On the appeal, she decided in favour of Miletus, and Pericles sailed with forty-four triremes to Samos where he overthrew the aristocracy, carried away a number of hostages, and established a democratic constitution, leaving a garrison to protect it. The nobles who fled to the mainland returned one night, captured the garrison and handed them over to the Persian satrap of Sardis, with whom they were intriguing. They also recovered the hostages who had been lodged in the island of Lemnos. Athens *Revolt of* received another blow at the same time by the revolt of Byzantium. *Byzan-*

Pericles sailed speedily back to Samos and invested it with a *tium.* large fleet. Hearing that a Phoenician squadron was coming to assist the Samians, he raised the siege and with a part of his armament went to meet it. During his absence the Samians gained some successes against the Athenian ships which were anchored close to the harbour. At the end of two weeks Pericles returned ; either the Phoenicians had not appeared after all, or they had been induced *Siege and* to sail home. Well-nigh 200 warships now blockaded Samos, *reduction* and at the end of nine months the city surrendered. The Samians *of Samos,* undertook to pull down their walls, to surrender their ships, and pay *439 B.C.* a war indemnity which amounted to 1500 talents or thereabouts. They became subject to Athens and were obliged to furnish soldiers to her armies, but they were not made tributary.

The Athenian citizens who fell in the war received a public burial at Athens. Pericles pronounced the funeral oration, and it may have been on this occasion that he used a famous phrase of the young men who had fallen. The spring, he said, was taken out of the year.

Byzantium also came back to the confederacy. It had been a trying moment for Athens ; for she had some reason to fear Pelo-

FIG. 116. — Coin of Corinth, sixth century (obverse). Pegasus [legend: $Ϙ(ορινθίων)$].

ponnesian intervention. Sparta and her allies had met to consider the situation ; and the Corinthians afterwards claimed, whether truly or not, that they deprecated any interference, on the general principle that every state should be left to deal with her own rebellious allies. However the Corinthians may have acted on this occasion, it was chiefly the commercial jealousy existing between Athens and Corinth that brought on the ultimate outbreak of hostilities between the Athenians and Peloponnesians, which led to the destruction of the Athenian empire.

Temporary It seems that during the excitement of the *restrictions* Samian war, Pericles deemed it expedient to place some restraints *on Comedy.* upon the licence of the comic drama. What he feared was the effect which the free criticisms of the comic poets on his policy might have, not upon the Athenians themselves, but upon the strangers who were present in the theatre, and especially upon citizens of the subject states. The precaution shows that the situation was critical ; though the restraints were withdrawn soon afterwards, for they were contrary to the spirit of the time. Henceforward the only check on the comic poet was that he *might* be prosecuted before the Council of Five Hundred for "doing wrong to the people," if his jests against the officers of the people went too far.

Comedy had grown up in Athens out of the mummeries of masked revellers who kept the feasts of Dionysus by singing phallic songs and flinging coarse jests at the folk. It was not till *472-1 B.C.* after the Persian war that the state recognised it. Then a place was given at the great festival of Dionysus to comic competitions. To the three days which were devoted to the competitions of tragedies a fourth was added for the new contest.   The comic drama then assumed form and shape.   Magnes and Chionides were its first masters ; but they were eclipsed by Cratinus, the most brilliant comic poet of the age of Pericles.

There is no more significant symptom of the political and social health of the Athenian state in the period of its empire, than the perfect freedom which was accorded to the comic stage, to laugh at everything in earth and heaven, and splash with ridicule every institution of the city and every movement of the day, to libel the statesmen and even jest at the gods.   Such license is never permitted in an age of decadence even under the shelter of religious usage.   It can only prevail in a free country where men's belief in their own strength and virtue, in the excellence of their institutions and their ideals, is still true, deep, and fervent ; then they can afford to laugh at themselves. The Old Comedy is a most telling witness to the greatness of Athens.

Sect. 11. Higher Education.   The Sophists

Since the days of Nestor and Odysseus, the art of persuasive speech was held in honour by the Greeks.   With the rise of the democratic commonwealths it became more important, and the greater attention which was paid to the cultivation of oratory may perhaps be reflected in the introduction of a new class of proper names, which *New class* refer to excellence in addressing public assemblies.   The institutions *of names* of a Greek democratic city presupposed in the average citizen the *(e.g. Pyth-* faculty of speaking in public, and for any one who was ambitious for *agoras,* *Anax-* a political career it was indispensable.   If a man was hauled into a *agoras).* law-court by his enemies, and knew not how to speak, he was like an unarmed civilian attacked by soldiers in panoply.   The power of clearly expressing ideas in such a way as to persuade an audience, was an art to be learned and taught.   But it was not enough to gain command of a vocabulary ; it was necessary to learn how to argue, and to exercise one's self in the discussion of political and ethical questions.   There was a demand for higher education.

This tendency of democracy corresponded to the growth of that spirit of inquiry which had first revealed itself in Ionia in the field of natural philosophy.   The study of nature had passed into a *Science.* higher stage in the hands of two men of genius, whose speculations have had an abiding effect on science.   Empedocles distinguished the " four elements," and explained the development of the universe by the forces of attraction and repulsion which have held their place till to-day in scientific theory.   He also foreshadowed the doctrine of the survival of the fittest.   Democritus, of Abdera, a man of vast learning, originated the atomic theory, which was in later days popularised by Epicurus, and in still later by the Roman Lucretius. The scientific imagination of Democritus generated the world from atoms, like in quality but different in size and weight, existing in void space. Such advances in the explanation of nature implied and promoted a new conception of what may be called " methodized " knowledge, and this conception was applied to every subject. The second half of the fifth century was an age of technical treatises ; oratory and cookery were alike reduced to systems ; political institutions and received morality became the subject of scientific inquiry. Desire of knowledge had led the Greeks to seek more information about foreign lands and peoples ; they had begun both to know more of the world and to regard it with a more critical mind ; enlightenment was spreading, prejudices were being dispelled. Herodotus, who was far from being a sceptic, fully appreciates the instructiveness of the story which he tells, how Darius asked some Greeks for what price they would be willing to eat the dead bodies of their fathers. When they cry that nothing would induce them to do so, the king calls a tribe of Indians who eat their parents, and asks them what price *they* would accept to burn the bodies of their fathers. The Indians exclaim against the bare thought of such a horror. Custom, Pindar had said and Herodotus echoes, is king of the world ; and men began to distinguish between custom and nature. They felt that their own conventions and institutions required justification ; the authority of usage and antiquity was not enough ; and they compared human society with nature. The appeal to nature led indeed to very opposite theories. In the sight of nature, it was said, all are equal ; birth and wealth are indifferent ; therefore the state should be built on the basis of perfect equality. On the other hand, it was argued that in the state of nature the strong man subdues the weaker and rules over them ; therefore monarchy is the natural constitution. But it matters little what particular inferences were drawn ; for no attempt was made to put them into practice. The main point is that the questioning spirit was active ; there were clever men everywhere, who refused to take anything on authority ; who always asked, how do you know ? and claimed to discuss all things in heaven and earth.

It was in this atmosphere of critical inquiry and scepticism that Greece had to provide for the higher education of her youth, which the practical conditions of the democracy demanded. The demand was met by teachers who travelled about and gave general instruction in the art of speaking and in the art of reasoning, and, out of their encyclopaedic knowledge, lectured on all possible subjects. They received fees for their courses, and were called Sophists, of which name perhaps our best equivalent is "professors." Properly a sophist meant

The sophists.

one who was eminently proficient in some particular art—in poetry, for instance, or cookery. As applied to the teachers who educated the youths who were able to pay, the name acquired a slightly unfavourable colour—partly owing to the distrust felt by the masses towards men who know too much, partly to the prejudice which in Greece always existed more or less against those who gave their services for pay, partly too to the jealousy of those who were too poor to pay the fees and were consequently at a great disadvantage in public life compared with men whom a sophist had trained. But this haze of contempt which hung about the sophistic profession did not imply the idea that the professors were impostors, who deliberately sought to hoodwink the public by arguments in which they did not believe themselves. That suggestion—which has determined the modern meaning of "sophist" and "sophistry"—was first made by the philosopher Plato, and it is entirely unhistorical.

The sophists did not confine themselves to teaching. They wrote *Their* much; they discussed occasional topics, criticised political affairs, *writings.* diffused ideas; and it has been said that this part of their activity supplied in some measure the place of modern journalism. But the greatest of the professors were much more than either teachers or journalists. They not only diffused but set afloat ideas; they enriched the world with contributions to knowledge. They were all alike rationalists, spreaders of enlightenment; but they were very various in their views and doctrines. Gorgias of Leontini, Protagoras of Abdera, Prodicus of Ceos, Hippias of Elis, Socrates of Athens, each had his own strongly marked individuality. To Socrates, who has a place apart from the others, we shall revert in a later chapter. Prodicus of Ceos was a pessimist; and it was doubtless he whom the poet Euripides meant by the man who considered the ills of men to be more in number than their good things. It was Prodicus who invented the famous fable of Heracles at the cross-way choosing between virtue and pleasure. Of all the sophists Protagoras was perhaps the greatest. He first distinguished the parts of speech and founded the science of grammar for Europe. His activity as a teacher was chiefly at Athens, where

Prodicus.

Supplices 196.

FIG. 117.—Coin of Abdera, fifth century (reverse). *Prot-* Dionysus with *agoras.* wine-cup [legend: ΑΝΑΞΙΠΟΛΙΣ].

he seems to have been intimate with Pericles. The story that Pericles and Protagoras spent a whole day arguing on the theory of punishment—a question which is still unsettled—illustrates the services which the sophists rendered to speculation. The retributive theory of justice, which logically enough led to the trial and punishment of animals and inanimate things, was called in question; and a counter theory started that the object of punishment was to deter. Protagoras was a victim of the religious prejudices of the Athenians. He wrote a theological book, which he published by reading it aloud before a chosen audience in the house of his friend Euripides. The thesis of the work is probably contained in the first sentence : " In regard to the gods I cannot know that they exist, nor yet that they do not exist ; for many things hinder such knowledge,—the obscurity of the matter, and the shortness of human life." Protagoras may have himself *believed* in the gods ; what he asserted was that their existence could not be a matter of *knowledge*. Unluckily the book itself has perished. For a certain Pythodorus came forward as the standard-bearer of the state religion, and accused Protagoras of

His flight from Athens. (415 *B.C.*)

impiety. The philosopher deemed it wise to flee from Athens ; he sailed for Sicily and was lost at sea. When Euripides makes the choir of Thracian women in his play of *Palamedes* cry bitterly, " Ye have slain, O Greeks, ye have slain the nightingale of the Muses, the wizard bird that did no wrong," the poet was thinking of the dead friend who had come from the Thracian city. The sale of the book of Protagoras was forbidden in Athens, and all copies that could be found were publicly burned.

The case of Protagoras was not the only case of the kind. Years before, the philosopher Anaxagoras had been condemned for impiety ; years after, Socrates would be condemned. These cases show that the Athenians were not more enlightened than other peoples, or less prejudiced. The attitude of Protagoras to theology was perfectly compatible with a fervent devotion to the religion of the state ; but an Athenian jury was not sufficiently well-educated to discern this. When we admire the spread of knowledge and reasoning in the fifth century, we must remember that the mass of citizens was not reached by the new light ; they were still sunk in ignorance, suspicious and jealous of the training which could be got only by sons of the comparatively well-to-do, or those who were exceptionally intellectual.

Gorgias of Leontini.

Gorgias was a philosophical thinker and a politician, but he won his renown as an orator and a stylist. He taught Greece how to write a new kind of prose—not the cold style which appeals only to the understanding, but a brilliant style, rhythmic, flowery in diction, full of figures, speaking to the sense and imagination. In the inscription of a statue which his grand-nephew erected to him at Olympia, it is said : " No mortal ever invented a fairer art, to temper the soul for manlihood and virtue." Wherever he went he was received with enthusiasm ; we shall presently meet him as an ambassador at Athens.

Euripides.

The sophists were the chief, the professional expounders of the intellectual movement. But the exaltation of reason had a no less

powerful supporter in the poet Euripides.   He used the tragic stage *His*
to disseminate rationalism ; he undermined the popular religion from *critical*
the very steps of the altar.   By the necessity of the case he accom- *spirit.*
plished his work indirectly, but with consummate dexterity.   Aeschylus
and Sophocles had reverently modified religious legend, adapting it
to their own ideals, interpreting it so as to satisfy their own moral
standard.   Euripides takes the myths just as he finds them, and con-
trives his dramas so as to bring the absurdities into relief.   He does
not acquiesce, like the older tragic poets, in the ways of the gods with
men ; he is not content to be a resigned pessimist.   He will receive
nothing on authority ; he declines to bow to the orthodox opinions of
his respectable fellow-countrymen, on such matters as the institution of
slavery, or the position of women in society.   He refuses to endorse
the inveterate prejudice which prevailed even at Athens in favour of
noble birth.   But perhaps nothing is so significant as his attitude to
the contempt which the Greeks universally felt for other races than
their own.   Nowhere is Euripides more sarcastic than when, in his
Medea, he makes Jason pose as a benefactor of the woman whom
he has basely betrayed, on the ground that he has brought her out of
an obscure barbarian home, and enabled her to enjoy the privilege of
—living in Greece.

Yet we need not go to the most daring thinkers, to Euripides and
the sophists, to discern the spirit of criticism at work.   The Periclean
age has left us few more significant, and certainly no more beautiful,
monuments than a tragic drama which won the first prize at the great *The*
Dionysia a few years after the Thirty Years' Peace.   The soul of *Antigone,*
Sophocles was in untroubled harmony with the received religion ; *442 or*
but, living in an atmosphere of criticism and speculation, even he could *441 B.C.,*
not keep his mind aloof from the questions which were debated by the *March-*
thoughtful men of his time.   He took as the motive of his *Antigone* *April.*
a deep and difficult question of political and of ethical science—the
relation of the individual citizen to the state.   What shall a man do
if his duty of obedience to the government of his country conflicts with
other duties ?   Are there any obligations higher than that of loyalty
to the laws of his city ?   The poet answers that there are such,—for
instance, certain obligations of religion.   He justifies Antigone in her
disobedience to the king's decree.   The motive lends itself to dramatic
treatment, and never has it been handled with such consummate art
as by him who first saw its possibilities.   But it is worth observing
that the *Antigone*, besides its importance in the history of dramatic
poetry, has a high significance in the development of European
thought, as the first presentation of a problem which both touches
the very roots of ethical theory and is, in daily practice, constantly
clamouring for solution.

CHAPTER XI[1]

THE WAR OF ATHENS WITH THE PELOPONNESIANS
(431-421 B.C.)

THE empire and commercial supremacy of Athens had, as we have seen, swiftly drawn a war upon herself and Greece. That war had been indecisive; it had taught her some lessons, but it had not cooled her ambition or crippled her trade; and it was therefore inevitable that she should have to fight again. We have now to follow the second phase of the struggle, up to the culmination of that antagonism between Dorian and Ionian, of which the Greeks of this period never lost sight.

SECT. 1. THE PRELUDE OF THE WAR

The incidents which led up to the "Peloponnesian War" are connected with two Corinthian colonies, Corcyra and Potidaea: Corcyra which had always been an unfilial daughter; Potidaea which, though maintaining friendly relations with Corinth, had become a member of the Athenian Confederacy.

FIG. 118.—Coin of Corcyra, fifth century (obverse). Head of Hera [legend: KOP].

Incident of Epidamnus, 435 B.C., leads to war between Corcyra and Corinth.

(1) One of those party struggles in an insignificant city, which in Greece were often the occasion of wars between great states, had taken place in Epidamnus, a colony of Corcyra. The people, harassed by the banished nobles and their barbarian allies, asked help from their mother-city. Corcyra refused, and Epidamnus turned to Corinth. The Corinthians sent troops and a number of new colonists. The Corcyraeans, highly resenting this interference, demanded their dismissal, and when the demand was refused, blockaded the isthmus of Epidamnus. Corinth then made prepara-

---

[1] The citations from Thucydides in this chapter are taken from Jowett's translation.

Th. 1: 24

tions for an expedition against Corcyra ; and Corcyra in alarm sent envoys to Corinth, proposing to refer the matter for arbitration to such Peloponnesian states as both should agree upon. But the Corinthians refused the arbitration, and sent a squadron of seventy-five ships with 2000 hoplites against the Corcyraeans. The powerful *Corcyraean* navy of Corcyra consisted of 120 ships, of which forty were besieging *naval* Epidamnus. With the remaining eighty they won a complete victory *victory* over the Corinthians outside the Ambracian gulf ; and on the same *(435 B.C.,* day Epidamnus surrendered. During the rest of the year Corcyra *Surrender* had command of the Ionian sea and her triremes sailed about *of Epi-* damaging the allies of Corinth. *damnus.*

But Corinth began to prepare for a greater effort against her powerful and detested colony. The work of preparation went on for two years. The report of the ships she was building and the navies *434-3 B.C.* she was hiring frightened Corcyra. For, while Corinth had the Peloponnesian league at her back, Corcyra had no allies, and belonged neither to the Athenian nor to the Spartan league. It was her obvious policy to seek a connexion with Athens, and she determined to do so. The Corinthians hearing of this intention, tried to thwart *Corcyraean* it ; for they had good reason to fear a combination of the Athenian *and* with the Corcyraean navy. And so it came to pass that the envoys *Corinthian* of Corcyra and Corinth appeared together before the Assembly of *embassies* Athens. The arguments which Thucydides has put into their *at Athens.* mouths express clearly the bearings of the situation and the importance of the decision for Athens. The main argument for accepting the proffered alliance of Corcyra depends on the assumption that war is imminent. " The Lacedaemonians, fearing the growth of your empire, are eager to take up arms, and the Corinthians, who are your enemies, are all powerful with them. They begin with us, but they will go on to you, that we may not stand united against them in the bond of a common enmity. And it is our business to strike first, and to forestall their designs instead of waiting to counteract them." On this assumption, the alliance of Corcyra offers great advantages. It lies conveniently on the route to Sicily, and it possesses one of the only three considerable navies in Greece. " If the Corinthians get hold of our fleet, and you allow the two to become one, you will have to fight against the united navies of Corcyra and the Peloponnesus. But if you make us your allies, you will have our navy in addition to your own ranged at your side in the impending conflict." The reply of the Corinthian ambassadors was weak. Their appeal to certain past services that Corinth had rendered to Athens could hardly have much effect ; for there was nothing but jealousy between the two cities. They might deprecate, but they could not disprove, the notion that Athens

would soon have a war with the Peloponnesus on her hands. And
as for justice, Corcyra could make as plausible a case as Corinth.
The most cogent argument for Corinth was that if Athens allied
herself with Corcyra she would take a step which if not in itself
violating the Thirty Years' Peace would necessarily involve a
violation of it.

Defensive
alliance of
Athens
with
Corcyra.

After two debates the Assembly agreed to an alliance with
Corcyra, but of a defensive kind. Athens was only to give armed
help, in case Corcyra itself were threatened. By this decision she
avoided a direct violation of the treaty. Ten ships were sent to
Corcyra with orders not to fight unless Corcyra or some of the
places belonging to it were attacked. A great and tumultuous naval
engagement ensued near the islet of Sybota, between Leucimme, the
south-eastern promontory of Corcyra, and the Thesprotian mainland.
A Corcyraean fleet of 110 ships was ranged against a Corinthian of
150—the outcome of two years of preparation. The right wing of
the Corcyraeans was worsted, and the ten Athenian ships, which had
held aloof at first, interfered to prevent its total discomfiture. In
the evening the sudden sight of twenty new Athenian ships on the
horizon caused the Corinthians to retreat, and the next day they
declined battle. This seemed an admission of defeat, and justified
the Corcyraeans in raising a trophy; but the Corinthians also raised
a trophy, for they had come off best in the battle. They returned
home then, and on their way captured Anactorion, which Corcyra
and Corinth held in common. Corinth treated the Corcyraeans
who had been taken captive in the battle with great consideration.
Most of them were men of importance and it was hoped that through
them Corcyra might ultimately be won over to friendship with
Corinth. It will be seen afterwards that the hope was not ill-
founded.[1]

Battle of
Sybota,
433 B.C.
(autumn).

Revolt of
Potidaea
from
Athens.

(2) The breach with Corinth forced Athens to look to the
security of her interests in the Chalcidic peninsula, where Corinth
had a great deal of influence. The city of Potidaea, which occupies
and guards the isthmus of Pallene, was a tributary ally of Athens,
but received its annual magistrates from its mother-city, Corinth.
Immediately after the battle of Sybota, Athens required the
Potidaeans to raze the city-walls on the south side where they were
not needed for protection against Macedonia, and to abandon the
system of Corinthian magistrates. The Potidaeans refused; they
were supported by the promise of Sparta to invade Attica, in case
Potidaea were attacked by Athens. But the situation was compli-

Thuc. i. 56.
68, 71, 132.
(433 B.C.)
i. 56.
ii. 2¹
Diod. XII.
34·–7
37, 432 B.C.
Plut. Per. 29

---

[1] A report of the expenses of Athens on this Corcyraean expedition has been
partially preserved on a stone. The ships that sailed first and those that followed
are distinguished.

Perdiccas' Alliance w/ Athens : Thuc. 1.57²

cated by the policy of the Macedonian king, Perdiccas, who had been formerly the friend of Athens but was now her adversary, because she had befriended his brothers who were leagued against

Quarrel w/ Athens : Thuc. i. 57, 59² 61², 62². Diod. xii. 34²

him. He conceived and organised a general revolt of Chalcidice against Athens; and even persuaded the Chalcidians to pull down their cities on the coast and concentrate themselves in the strong inland town of Olynthus. The Bottiaeans also, centred on Spartolus, joined the rebels. Thus the revolt of Potidaea, while it has its special causes in connexion with the enmity of Athens and Corinth, under another aspect forms part of a general movement in that quarter against the Athenian dominion.

The Athenians began operations in Macedonia, but soon advanced against Potidaea and gained an advantage over the Corinthian general, Aristeus, who had arrived with some Peloponnesian forces. This battle has a particular interest; for a graven stone still speaks to us of the sorrow of Athens for the men who fell fighting foremost before Potidaea's walls and " giving their lives in barter for glory ennobled their country." The Athenians then invested the city. So far the Corinthians had acted alone. Now, seeing the danger of Potidaea, they took active steps to incite the Lacedaemonians to declare war against Athens.

Battle of Potidaea, c. Sept. 432 B.C. Thuc. i. ~~55-66~~ 62-3 Diod. xii. 34⁴ 37¹

FIG. 119.—Epitaph on Athenians who fell at Potidaea (British Museum).

Megarian Decree, 432 B.C., autumn.

Thuc. i. 67.

140 3 -4, 144

Diod. XII. 35.

Pericles knew that war was coming, and he promptly struck — not with sword or spear, but with a more cruel and deadly weapon. Megara had assisted Corinth at the battle of Sybota; the Athenians passed a measure excluding the Megarians from the markets and ports of their empire. The decree spelt economical ruin to Megara, and Megara was an important member of the Peloponnesian league; the Athenian statesman knew how to strike. The comic poet sang how

> The Olympian Pericles in wrath
> Fulmined o'er Greece and set her in a broil
> With statutes worded like a drinking catch :
>   No Megarian on land
>   Nor in market shall stand
> Nor sail on the sea nor set foot on the strand.[1]

First Assembly at Sparta.

The allies appeared at Sparta and brought formal charges against Athens of having broken the Thirty Years' Peace and committed various acts of injustice. Some Athenian envoys who were at Sparta—ostensibly for other business—were given an opportunity of replying. But arguments and recriminations were superfluous; it did not matter in the least whether Athens could defend this transaction or Corinth could make good that charge. For in the case of an inevitable war the causes openly alleged seldom correspond with the motives which really govern. It was not the Corcyraean incidents, or the siege of Potidaea, or the Megarian decree that caused the Peloponnesian War, though jointly they hastened its outbreak; it was the fear and jealousy of the Athenian power. The only question was whether it was the right hour to engage in that unavoidable struggle. The Spartan king, Archidamus, advised delay. " Do not take up arms yet. War is not an affair of arms, but of money which gives to arms their use, and which is needed above all things when a continental is fighting against a maritime power. Let us find money first, and then we may safely allow our minds to be excited by the speeches of our allies." But the ephors were in favour of war. Sthenelaidas, in a short and pointed speech, put the question, not, Shall we declare war? but Has the treaty been broken and are the Athenians in the wrong? It was decided that the Athenians were in the wrong, and this decision necessarily led to a declaration of war. But before that declaration was made, the approval of the Delphic oracle was gained, and a general assembly of the allies gathered at Sparta and agreed to the war.

Second Assembly.

Thucydides chose the setting well for his brilliant contrast between the characters and spirits and aims of the two great

[1] From Aristoph. *Acharnians*, transl. Tyrrell.

protagonists who now prepare to stand face to face on the stage of *The contrast, drawn by Thucy-dides,* Hellenic history. He makes the Corinthian envoys, at the first assembly in Sparta, the spokesmen of his comparison. " You have never considered, O Lacedaemonians, what manner of men are these Athenians with whom you will have to fight, and how utterly unlike *between the Athenians and Lacedae-monians.* yourselves. They are revolutionary, equally quick in the conception and in the execution of every new plan ; while you are conservative —careful only to keep what you have, originating nothing, and not acting even when action is most necessary. They are bold beyond their strength ; they run risks which prudence would condemn ; and in the midst of misfortune they are full of hope. Whereas it is your nature, though strong to act feebly ; when your plans are most prudent, to distrust them ; and when calamities come upon you, to think that you will never be delivered from them. They are im-petuous and you are dilatory ; they are always abroad, and you are always at home. For they hope to gain something by leaving their homes ; but you are afraid that any new enterprise may imperil what you have already. When conquerors, they pursue their victory to the utmost ; when defeated, they fall back the least. Their bodies they devote to the country, as though they belonged to other men ; their true self is their mind, which is most truly their own when employed in her service. When they do not carry out an intention which they have formed, they seem to have sustained a personal bereavement ; when an enterprise succeeds they have gained a mere instalment of what is to come ; but if they fail, they at once conceive new hopes and so fill up the void. With them alone to hope is to have, for they lose not a moment in the execution of an idea. This is the lifelong task, full of danger and toil, which they are always imposing upon themselves. None enjoy their good things less, because they are always seeking for more. To do their duty is their only holiday, and they deem the quiet of inaction to be as disagreeable as the most tiresome business. If a man should say of them, in a word, that they were born neither to have peace themselves nor to allow peace to other men, he would simply speak the truth."

On the present occasion, however, the Athenians did not give *Diplomatic futilities.* an example of that promptness in action which is contrasted in this passage with the dilatory habits of the Spartans ; we shall presently see why. It was the object of Sparta to gain time ; accordingly she sent embassies to Athens with trivial demands. She required the Athenians to drive out the " curse of the goddess," which rested on the family of the Alcmaeonidae. This was a raking up of history, two centuries old—the episode of Cylon's conspiracy ; the point of it lay in the fact that Pericles, on his mother's side, belonged to the accursed family. Athens replied by equally trivial demands

(*Above,
p. 326.*)

—the purification of the curse of Athena of the Brazen House, and of the curse of Taenarus, where some Helots had been murdered in the temple of Poseidon. These amenities, which served the purpose of Sparta by gaining time, were followed by an ultimatum, in the sense that Athens might still have peace if she restored the independence of the Hellenes. There was a peace party at Athens, but Pericles carried the day. "Let us send the ambassadors away"— he said—" giving them this answer : That we will not exclude the Megarians from our markets and harbours, if the Lacedaemonians will not exclude foreigners, whether ourselves or our allies, from Sparta ; for the treaty no more forbids the one than the other. That we will concede independence to the cities, if they were independent when we made the treaty, and as soon as the Lacedaemonians allow their subject states to be governed as they choose, not for the interest of Lacedaemon but for their own. Also that we are willing to offer arbitration according to the treaty. And that we do not want to begin the war, but intend to defend ourselves if attacked. This answer will be just and befits the dignity of the city. We must be aware, however, that the war will come ; and the more willing we are to accept the situation, the less ready will our enemies be to lay hands upon us." Pericles was in no haste to draw the sword ; he had delivered a blow already by the Megarian decree.

Athenian allies — 431 Thuc. ii. Diod. xii.

The peoples of Greece were parted as follows on the sides of the two chief antagonists. *Sparta* commanded the whole Peloponnesus, except her old enemy Argos, and Achaea ;[1] she commanded the Isthmus, for she had both Corinth and Megara ; in northern Greece she had Boeotia, Phocis, and Locris ; in western Greece, Ambracia, Anactorion, and the island of Leucas. In western Greece, *Athens* commanded the Acarnanians, Corcyra, and Zacynthus, as well as the Messenians of Naupactus ; in northern Greece she had Plataea ; and these were her only allies beyond her confederacy.

Resources of Athens and the Peloponnesians.

[Athens' strength lay in her fleet, large and well trained. In addition to the ships of Lesbos and Chios and the possible help from Corcyra she had 300 triremes of her own. Her fleet had a long tradition of active fighting and had maintained annual patrols in the Aegean even in peace. The nucleus of her crews was Athenian but the numbers needed were too large to be supplied from the citizen body alone, and a considerable proportion of her rowers were recruited in the islands, where men who had few chances to earn a livelihood at home were glad to earn good pay in a service with great traditions. On the Peloponnesian side the Corinthians alone were a naval power and their failure at Sybota had emphasised their weak-

[1] Pellene alone was on the Peloponnesian side.

ness. They had had little experience of fighting and their ships and crews were outclassed. On land, however, the Peloponnesians had an immense advantage. With their Boeotian allies they could put into the field at least 30,000 men without using reserves, and the Lacedaemonians were still the best hoplites in Greece. Against them the Athenians had a field force of 13,000 hoplites with 1200 cavalry, including mounted archers, and a reserve force, including metics, of 16,000.

Scarcely less important to Athens than her armed forces were her financial reserves. More than 1200 talents had been spent on crushing the revolt of Samos, and it was clear that war with the Peloponnesians would involve heavier and more expensive commitments. Pericles well knew that the efficiency of a navy depended in large part on regular and high pay and that war could not be financed on emergency measures; he had therefore deliberately aimed at maintaining a reserve for the inevitable clash. As war drew near special measures were taken to restrict expenditure. The building programme on the Acropolis was halted; further expenditure beyond a low annual limit from the reserve was made subject to a special vote of sanction in the Assembly. The treasures in money and kind of the other gods in the city below the Acropolis and throughout Attica were concentrated on the Acropolis, where they would be safe from invading Peloponnesians and readily available if the state needed to use them. After the Peace of Callias the principle had been established that the tribute could be used for Athenian purposes, and it was the accumulation of tribute that formed the bulk of the reserve. It had been given to the safe keeping of Athena and is described in documents as " the sacred moneys of Athena." Spending from this reserve for war purposes involved loans from the goddess; a strict record had to be kept and the interest on the debts was carefully calculated. In this reserve when war broke out there were some 6000 talents, and Athens could expect an annual income from home sources and the empire of some 1000 talents. From the experience of the Samian revolt Athens in 431 seemed likely to be able to finance war without resorting to extreme measures.

The Peloponnesians were in a much weaker position. They had no financial reserves and no common war chest. Their organisation was well adapted to land operations but they lacked the essential financial basis for naval warfare. The Corinthians could talk lightly of attracting the allies from the Athenian crews by higher pay, but in their hearts they knew that these were empty words. Not until Persian subsidies were secured could the Peloponnesians keep large fleets for long periods at sea.]

SECT. 2. GENERAL VIEW OF THE WAR.
THUCYDIDES

Perspective of the war of Athens with the Peloponnesians.   The war on which we are now entering is a resumption, on a somewhat greater scale, of the war which was concluded by the Thirty Years' Peace. Here too the Corinthians are the most active

FIG. 119A.—Promontory of Sunium.

instigators of the opposition to Athens. The Spartans are but half-hearted leaders, and have to be spurred by their allies. The war lasts ten years, and is concluded by the Peace of Nicias. But hostilities begin again, and pass for a time to a new scene of warfare, the island of Sicily. This war ends with the battle of Aegospotami, which decided the fate of the Athenian empire. Thus during fifty-five years Athens was contending for her empire with the Peloponnesians, and this conflict falls into three distinct wars : the first ending with the Thirty Years' Peace, the second with the Peace of Nicias, the third with the battle of Aegospotami. But while there is a break of thirteen years between the first war and the second, there is hardly any break between the second war and the third. Hence the second and the third, which have been united in the History of Thucydides, are generally grouped closely together and called by the common name of the "Peloponnesian War." This name is never used by Thucydides ; but it shows how Athenian the sympathies of historians have always been. From the Peloponnesian point of view the conflict would be called the "Attic War."

Three periods: (1) 460-445 B.C., (2) 431-421 ; (3) 420-404.

It will not be amiss to repeat here what the true cause of the struggle was. Athens was resolved to maintain, in spite of Greece, her naval empire ; and thus far she was responsible. But there is no reason to suppose that she had any design of seriously increasing her empire ; and the idea of some modern historians that Pericles undertook the war in the hope of winning supremacy over all Hellas is contrary to the plain facts of the case.

This war has attained a celebrity in the world's history which, considering its scale and its consequences, may seem unmerited. A domestic war between small Greek states may be thought a slight matter indeed, compared with the struggle in which Greece was arrayed against the might of Persia. But the Peloponnesian war has had an advantage which has been granted to no other episode in the history of Hellas. It has been recorded by the first and the greatest of Greek critical historians. To read the book which Thucydides, the son of Olorus, has bequeathed to posterity is in itself a liberal education ; a lesson in politics and history which is, as he aimed to make it, "a possession for ever." Only a few years can have separated the day on which Herodotus completed his work and the day on which Thucydides began his. But from the one to the other there is a sheer leap. When political events have passed through the brain of Herodotus, they come out as delightful stories. With the insatiable curiosity of an inquirer, he has little political insight ; he has the instinct of a literary artist, his historical methods are rudimentary. The splendid work of Herodotus has more in common with the epic poets who went before him than with the historians who came after

The History of Thucydides.

Contrast of Thucydides with Herodotus.

him. When he began to collect material for his history, the events of the Persian invasion were already encircled with a halo of legend, so that he had a subject thoroughly to his taste. It is a strange

FIG. 120.—Portrait head of Thucydides.

sensation to turn from the naïve, uncritical, entrancing story-teller of Halicarnassus to the grave historian of Athens. The first History, in the true sense of the word, sprang full-grown into life, like Athena from the brain of Zeus; and it is still without a rival,

Severe in its reserves, written from a purely intellectual point of view, unencumbered with platitudes and moral judgments, cold and critical, but exhibiting the rarest powers of dramatic and narrative art, the work of Thucydides is at every point a contrast to the work of Herodotus. Mankind might well despair if the science of criticism had not advanced further since the days of Thucydides; and we are not surprised to find that when he deals, on the threshold of his work, with the earlier history of Greece, he fails to carry his sceptical treatment far enough and accepts some traditions which on his own principles he should have questioned. But the interval which divides Thucydides from his elder contemporary Herodotus is a whole heaven; the interval which divides Thucydides from a critic of our own day is small indeed. Reserved as he is, Thucydides cannot disguise that he was a democrat of the Periclean school; he makes no secret of his admiration for the political wisdom of Pericles.

It must be granted that the incidents of the war would lose something of their interest, that the whole episode would be shorn of much of its dignity and eminence, if Thucydides had not deigned to be its historian. But it was not a slight or unworthy theme. It is the story of the decline and fall of the Athenian empire, and at this period Athens is the centre of ecumenical history. The importance of the war is not impaired by the smallness of the states, which were involved in it. For in these small states lived those political ideas and institutions which concerned the future development of mankind far more than any movements in barbarous kingdoms, however great their territory.

The war of ten years, which now began, may seem at first sight to have consisted of a number of disconnected and haphazard incidents. But both the Athenians and the Peloponnesians had definite objects in view. Their plans were determined by the nature of their own resources, and by the geography of the enemy's territories.

The key to the war is the fundamental fact that it was waged *Key to the* between a power which was mainly continental and a power which was *operations* mainly maritime. From the nature of the case, the land-power is *of the war.* obliged to direct its attacks chiefly on the continental possessions of the sea-power, while the sea-power has to confine itself to attacking the maritime possessions of the land-power. It follows that the small land army of the sea-power, and the small fleet of the land-power, are each mainly occupied with the work of defence, and are seldom free to act on the offensive. Hence the maritime possessions of the maritime power and the inland possessions of the continental power are not generally the scene of warfare. These considerations simplify the war. The points at which the Peloponnesians can attack Athens with their land forces are Attica itself and Thrace.

Accordingly Attica is invaded almost every year, and there is constant warfare in Thrace ; but the war is hardly ever carried into the Aegean or to the Asiatic coast, except in consequence of some special circumstance, such as the revolt of an Athenian ally.   On the other hand the offensive operations of Athens are mainly in the west of Greece, about the islands of the Ionian sea and near the mouth of the Corinthian gulf.   That was the region where they had the best prospect, by their naval superiority, of detaching members from the Peloponnesian alliance.   Thrace, Attica, and the seas of western Greece are therefore the chief and constant scenes of the war.   There are episodes elsewhere, but they are to some extent accidental.

Pericles had completely abandoned the policy of continental enterprise which had led up to the Thirty Years' Peace.   That enterprise had been a departure from the policy, initiated by Themistocles, of concentrating all the energy of Athens on the development of her naval power.   Pericles returned to this policy without reserve, and he appears, at the outbreak of the war, under the inspiration of the Salaminian spirit.   Athens is now to show the same extreme independence of her land, the same utter confidence in her ships, which she had shown when the Mede approached her borders.   " Let us give up lands and houses," said Pericles, " but keep a watch over the city and the sea.   We should not under any irritation at the loss of our property give battle to the Peloponnesians, who far outnumber us. Mourn not for houses or lands, but for men ; men may give these, but these will not give men.   If I thought that you would listen to me, I would say to you : Go yourselves and destroy them, and thereby prove to the Peloponnesians that none of these things will move you."   For " such is the power which the empire of the sea gives." [1]   This was the spirit in which Pericles undertook the war.

The policy of sacrificing Attica was no rash or perverse audacity ; it was only part of a well-considered system of strategy, for which Pericles has been severely blamed.   His object was to wear out the enemy, not to attempt to subjugate or decisively defeat.   He was determined not to court a great battle, for which the land forces of Athens were manifestly insufficient : on land Boeotia alone was a match for her.   He adopted the strategy of " exhaustion," as it has been called,—the strategy which consists largely in manœuvring, and considers the economy of one's own forces as solicitously as the damaging of the foe ; which will accept battle only under certain conditions ; which is always on the watch for favourable opportunities, but avoids great risks.   The more we reflect on the conditions of the struggle and the nature of the Athenian resources, the more fully will

[1] Jowett's translation.

the plan of Pericles approve itself as the strategy uniquely suitable to the circumstances.   Nor will the criticism that he neglected the land defences of Attica, and the suggestion that he should have fortified the frontier against invasions, bear close examination.   The whole Athenian land army would have been required to garrison both the Megarian and Boeotian frontiers, and there would have been no troops left for operations elsewhere.   Nor would it have been easy for a citizen army to abide on duty, as would in this case have been necessary, for a large part of the year.   It was quite in accord with the spirit of the patient strategy of Pericles that he refrained from the temptation of striking a blow at the enemy, when they had resolved on war but were not yet prepared.   One effective blow he had indeed struck, the decree against Megara ; to damage the foe commercially was an essential part of his method.   Within a few years this method would doubtless have been crowned with success and brought about a peace favourable to Athens, but for untoward events which he could not foresee.

Sect. 3.   The Theban Attack on Plataea

The declaration of war between the two great states of Greece was a signal to smaller states to profit by the situation for the gratification of their private enmities.   On a dark moonless night, in the early spring, a band of 300 Thebans entered Plataea, invited and admitted by a small party in the city.   Instead of at once attacking the chiefs of the party which supported the Athenian alliance, they took up their post in the agora and made a proclamation, calling upon the Plataeans to join the Boeotian league.   The Plataeans, as a people, with the exception of a few malcontents, were cordially attached to Athens ; but they were surprised, and in the darkness of the night exaggerated the numbers of the Thebans. They acceded to the Theban demand, but in the course of the negotiation discovered how few the enemies were.   Breaking down the party-walls between their houses, so as not to attract notice by moving in the streets, they concerted a plan of action.   When all was arranged, they barricaded the streets leading to the agora with waggons, and then attacked the enemy before dawn.   The Thebans were soon dispersed.   They lost their way in the strange town and wandered about, pelted by women from the house-tops, through narrow streets deep in mud, for heavy rain had fallen during the night.   A few clambered up the city wall and cast themselves down on the other side.   But the greater number rushed through the door of a large building, mistaking it for one of the town-gates, and were thus captured alive by the Plataeans.   A few escaped who reached an

Theban night attack on Plataea (March 431 B.C.).

unguarded gate, and cut the wooden bolt with an axe which a woman gave them.

The 300 were only the vanguard of a large Theban force which was advancing slowly in the rain along the eight miles of road which lay between Thebes and Plataea. They were delayed by the crossing of the swollen Asopus river, and they arrived too late. The Plataeans sent out a herald to them requiring them to do no injury to Plataean property outside the walls, if they valued the lives of the Theban prisoners. According to the Theban account, the Plataeans definitely promised to restore the prisoners, when the troops evacuated their territory. But the Plataeans afterwards denied this, and said that they merely promised (without the sanction of an oath) to restore the prisoners in case they came to an agreement after *Theban* negotiation. It matters little. The Plataeans as soon as they had *prisoners* conveyed all their property into the city, put their prisoners to death, *executed.* 180 in number. Even on their own showing they were clearly guilty of an act of ill faith, which is explained by the deep hatred existing *Athens* between the two states. A message had been immediately sent to *supports* Athens. The Athenians seized all the Boeotians in Attica, and sent *Plataea.* a herald to Plataea bidding them not to injure their prisoners ; but the herald found the Thebans dead. The Athenians immediately set Plataea ready for a siege. They provisioned it with corn ; removed the women, children, and old men ; and sent a garrison of eighty Athenians.

The Theban attack on Plataea was a glaring violation of the Thirty Years' Peace, and it hastened the outbreak of the war. Greece was now in a state of intense excitement at the approaching struggle of the two leading cities ; oracles flew about ; and a recent earthquake in Delos was supposed to be significant. Public opinion was generally favourable to the Lacedaemonians, who seemed to be the champions of liberty against a tyrannical city.

Both sides meditated enlisting the aid of Persia. The Lacedaemonians negotiated with the states of Italy and Sicily, for the purpose of obtaining a large navy to crush the Athenians. But this scheme also fell through ; the cities of the west were too busy with their own political interests to send ships and money to old Greece. Athens indeed had also cast her eyes westward ; and when she embraced the alliance of Corcyra, she seems to have been forming *Treaties of* connexions with Sicily. At all events, in the same year ambassadors *Athens* of Rhegium and Leontini appeared together at Athens ; and at the *with* same meeting of the Assembly alliances were renewed with both *Leontini* cities on the proposal of Callias. The object of Chalcidian Leontini *and with* was doubtless to gain support against Corinthian Syracuse ; while *Rhegium,* the motive of Rhegium may have been connected with the affairs of *433 B.C.*

Thuc. iii. 86?

Thurii, the rebellious daughter of Athens herself.   But these alliances led to no action of Athens in the west for six years to come.

SECT. 4. THE PLAGUE

When the corn was ripe, in the last days of May, king Archidamus *First in-* with two-thirds of the Peloponnesian army invaded Attica.   From the *vasion of* isthmus he had sent on Melesippus to Athens, if even at the last *Attica,* hour the Athenians might yield.   But Pericles had persuaded them $431\ B.C.$ to receive no embassies, once the enemy were in the field ; the envoy had to leave the borders of Attica before the sun set.   And Thucydides, after the manner of Herodotus, marks the formal commencement of the war by repeating the impressive words which Melesippus uttered as he stood on the frontier : " This day will be the beginning of many woes to the Greeks."   Archidamus then laid siege to Oenoe, a fortress on Mount Cithaeron, but failed to take it, and his delay gave the Athenians time to complete their preparations.   They brought into the city their family and their goods, while their flocks and herds were removed to the island of Euboea.   The influx of the population into the city caused terrible crowding.   A few had the homes of their friends, but the majority pitched their tents in the vacant spaces, and housed themselves, as the peace-party bitterly said, in barrels and vultures' nests.   They seized temples and shrines, and even the ancient enclosure of the Pelargicon on the north-west of the Acropolis was occupied, though its occupation was deprecated by a dark oracle.   Subsequently the crowding was relieved when the Piraeus and the space between the Long Walls were utilised.

Archidamus first ravaged the plain of Eleusis and Thria.   He then crossed into the Cephisian plain by the pass between Mounts Aegaleos and Parnes, and halted under Parnes in the deme of Acharnae, whence he could see, in the distance, the Acropolis of Athens.   The proximity of the invaders caused great excitement in Athens, and roused furious opposition to Pericles who would not allow the troops to go forth against them—except a few flying columns of horse in the immediate neighbourhood of the city.   Pericles had been afraid that Archidamus, who was his personal friend, might spare his property, either from friendship or policy ; so he took the precaution of declaring to his fellow-citizens that he would give his lands to the people, if they were left unravaged.   The invader presently advanced northward, between Parnes and Pentelicus, to Decelea, and proceeded through the territory of Oropus to Boeotia.

The Athenians meanwhile had been operating by sea.   They had sent 100 ships round the Peloponnesus.   An attack on Methone, on the Messenian coast, failed ; the place was saved by a daring

Athens wins Cephallenia and Sollion. Locrian expedition. Spartan officer, Brasidas, who by this exploit began a distinguished career. But the fleet was more successful further north. The important island of Cephallenia was won over, and some towns on the Acarnanian coast were taken. Measures were also adopted for the protection of Euboea against the Locrians of the opposite mainland. The Epicnemidian town of Thronion was captured, and the desert island of Atalanta, over against Opus, was made a guard

End of the Aeginetans. Aegina becomes part of Attica. station. More important was the drastic measure which Athens adopted against her subjects and former rivals, the Dorians of Aegina. She felt that they were not to be trusted, and the security of her positions in the Saronic gulf was of the first importance. So she drove out the Aeginetans and settled the island with a cleruchy of her own citizens. Aegina thus became, like Salamis, annexed to Attica. Just as the Messenian exiles had been befriended by Athens and given a new home, so the Aeginetan exiles were now befriended by Sparta and were settled in the region of Thyreatis, in the north of Laconia. Thyreatis was the Lacedaemonian answer to Naupactus.

When Archidamus left Attica, Pericles consulted for emergencies of the future by setting aside a reserve fund of money, and a reserve

£2,619,000 armament of ships. There had been as much as 9700 talents in the treasury, but the expenses of the buildings on the Acropolis and of

£1,620,000 the war at Potidaea had reduced this to 6000. It was now decreed that 1000 talents of this amount should be reserved, not to be touched unless the enemy were to attack Athens by sea, and that every year 100 triremes should be set apart, with the same object.

Funeral of those slain in the war. In winter the Athenians, following an old custom, celebrated the public burial of those who had fallen in the war. The bones were laid in ten cedar boxes, and were buried outside the walls in the Ceramicus. An empty bed, covered with a pall, was carried, for those whose bodies were missing. Pericles pronounced the funeral Panegyric. It has not been preserved; but the spirit and general argument of it have been reproduced in the oration which Thucydides, who must have been one of the audience, has put in his mouth.[1] It is a rare good fortune to possess a picture, drawn by a Pericles and a Thucydides, of the ideal Athens, which Pericles dreamed of creating.

The ideal Athens adumbrated by Pericles. "There is no exclusiveness," he said, "in our public life, and in our private intercourse. We are not suspicious of one another, nor angry with our neighbour if he does what he likes; we do not put on sour looks at him which, though harmless, are not pleasant. And we have not forgotten to provide for our weary spirits many relaxations from toil; we have regular games and sacrifices throughout

---

[1] We may fancy we can detect some phrases which fell from the lips of Pericles himself: such as '' The whole earth is the sepulchre of famous men," or '' Athens is the school of Hellas."

the year; at home the style of our life is refined; and the delight
which we daily feel in all these things helps to banish melancholy.
Because of the greatness of our city the fruits of the whole earth
flow in upon us; so that we enjoy the goods of other countries as
freely as of our own.

"Then again our military training is in many respects superior
to that of our adversaries. Our city is thrown open to the world,
and we never expel a foreigner or prevent him from seeing or learning
anything, of which the secret if revealed to an enemy might profit
him. We rely not upon management or trickery, but upon our own
hearts and hands. And in the matter of education whereas they
from early youth are always undergoing laborious exercises which
are to make them brave, we live at ease, and yet are equally ready
to face the perils which they face.

"If we prefer to meet danger with a light heart but without
laborious training, and with a courage which is gained by habit and
not enforced by law, are we not greatly the gainers? Since we do
not anticipate the pain, although, when the hour comes, we can be
as brave as those who never allow themselves to rest; and thus too
our city is equally admirable in peace and in war. For we are lovers
of the beautiful, yet simple in our tastes, and we cultivate the mind
without loss of manliness. Wealth we employ, not for talk and
ostentation, but when there is a real use for it. To avow poverty
with us is no disgrace; the true disgrace is in doing nothing to avoid
it. An Athenian citizen does not neglect the state because he takes
care of his own household; and even those of us who are engaged
in business have a very fair idea of politics. We alone regard a man
who takes no interest in public affairs, not as a harmless, but as a
useless character; and if few of us are originators, we are all sound
judges of a policy. The great impediment to action is, in our opinion,
not discussion, but the want of that knowledge which is gained by
discussion preparatory to action. For we have a peculiar power of
thinking before we act and of acting too, whereas other men are
courageous from ignorance but hesitate upon reflection."

Then the speaker goes on to describe Athens as the centre of
Hellenic culture and to claim that "the individual Athenian in his
own person seems to have the power of adapting himself to the most
varied forms of action with the utmost versatility and grace." And,
he continues, "we shall assuredly not be without witnesses; there
are mighty monuments of our power which will make us the wonder
of this and of succeeding ages; we shall not need the praises of
Homer or any other panegyrist whose poetry may please for the
moment, although his representation of the facts will not bear the
light of day. For we have compelled every land and every sea to

open a path for our valour, and have everywhere planted eternal memorials of our friendship and of our enmity. Such is the city for whose sake these men nobly fought and died; they could not bear the thought that she might be taken from them; and every one of us who survive should gladly toil on her behalf. I would have you day by day fix your eyes upon the greatness of Athens, until you become filled with the love of her; and when you are impressed by the spectacle of her glory, reflect that this empire has been acquired by men who knew their duty and had the courage to do it, who in the hour of conflict had the fear of dishonour always present to them, and who, if ever they failed in an enterprise, would not allow their virtues to be lost to their country, but freely gave their lives to her as the fairest offering which they could present at her feast. The sacrifice which they collectively made was individually repaid to them; for they received again and again each one for himself a praise which grows not old and the

FIG. 121.—Athena contemplating a stele (Acropolis Museum, Athens). *c.* 450 B.C.

noblest of all sepulchres—I speak not of that in which their remains are laid, but of that in which their glory survives and is proclaimed always and on every fitting occasion both in word and deed. For the whole earth is the sepulchre of famous men; not only are they commemorated by columns and inscriptions in their own country, but in foreign lands there dwells also an unwritten memorial of them, graven not on stone but in the hearts of men.   Make them your examples." [1]

The "Mourn-ing Athena." We are reminded of an earlier monument from the middle of the century.   A beautiful relief, found on the Acropolis, shows the helmeted lady of the land, leaning on her spear, with downcast head, and gazing gravely at a slab of stone.   It is an attractive interpretation that she is sadly engaged in reading the names of citizens who had recently fallen in defence of her city, perhaps in the First Peloponnesian War.

430 B.C., Invasion of Attica. Next year the Peloponnesians again invaded Attica, and extended their devastations to the south of the peninsula as far as Laurion. But the Athenians concerned themselves less with this invasion; they had to contend with a more awful enemy within the walls of their *The Great Plague.* city.   The Plague had broken out.   Thucydides, who was stricken down himself, gives a terrible account of its ravages and the demoralisation which it produced in Athens.   The art of medicine was in its first infancy, and the inexperienced physicians were unable to treat the unknown virulent disease, which defied every remedy and was aggravated by the over-crowding, in the heat of summer.   The dead lay unburied, the temples were full of corpses ; and the funeral customs were forgotten or violated.   Dying wretches were gathered about every fountain, seeking to relieve their unquenchable thirst. *Oracle : λοιμός or λιμός ?* Men remembered an old oracle which said that "a Dorian war will come and a plague therewith."   But the Greek for plague (*loimós*) was hardly distinguishable from the Greek for famine (*limós*)—at the present day they are identical in sound ; and people were not quite sure which was the true word.   Naturally the verse was now quoted with *loimos ;* but, says Thucydides, in case there comes another Dorian war and it is accompanied by a famine, the oracle will be quoted with *limos.*

Origin of the plague. The same historian—who has given of this pestilence a vivid description, unequalled by later narrators of similar scourges, Procopius, Boccaccio, Defoe—declares that the plague originated in Ethiopia, spread through Egypt over the Persian empire, and then reached the Aegean.   But it is remarkable that a plague raged at the same time in the still obscure city of central Italy which was afterwards to become the mistress of Greece.   It has been guessed with some plausibility that the infection which reached both Athens and Rome had travelled along the trade-routes from Carthage.   The Peloponnesus almost entirely escaped.   In Athens the havoc of *Effect of the plague on the Athenian population.* the pestilence permanently reduced the population.   The total number of Athenian burghers (of both sexes and all ages) was about

---

[1] Jowett's translation.

140,000 in the first quarter of the fifth century. Prosperity had raised it to 172,000 by the beginning of the war; but the plague brought it down below the old level which it never reached again.

Sea operations of Athenians. As in the year before, an Athenian fleet attacked the Peloponnesus, but this time it was the coasts of Argolis,—Epidaurus, Troezen, Hermione, Halieis. The armament was large, 4000 spearmen and 300 horse; it was under the command of Pericles; and it aimed at the capture of Epidaurus, while the Epidaurian troops were absent with their allies in Attica. The attempt miscarried, we know not why; and it is hard to forgive our historian for omitting all the details of this ambitious enterprise, which would have been, if it had succeeded, one of the most important exploits of the war.

[For Epidaurus occupied an invaluable strategic position. It would have been a useful base for raiding the territory of Corinth and Megara; it would have threatened Peloponnesian armies advancing into Attica; and it might have served as a tempting bait to Argos. For Epidaurus was part of the heritage of Temenos, and its independence was an index of Argive weakness. Should neutral Argos rejoin her old ally the balance of power would be decisively shifted in Athens' favour.

At the end of the summer hostilities broke out in the west of Greece. Before the war the inhabitants of Amphilochian Argos, driven out by the Ambraciots, had, with their allies the Acarnanians, appealed for help to Athens. Athens had sent Phormio with thirty ships to restore the position. The Ambraciots were sold into slavery and the city restored to Amphilochians and Acarnanians who became grateful allies. Now, taking advantage of the general unsettlement, the Ambraciots tried to recover the lost ground, but though they overran the countryside they could not take the city. A show of force by Athens was needed and Phormio was sent with twenty ships to hold guard at Naupactus. From this station he could watch the north-west and guard the entrance to the Crisaean Gulf.]

Surrender of Potidaea. In Thrace meanwhile the siege of Potidaea had been prosecuted throughout the year. The inhabitants had been reduced to such straits that they even tasted human flesh, and in the winter they capitulated. The terms were that the Potidaeans and the foreign soldiers were to leave the city, the men with one garment, the women with two, and a sum of money was to be allowed them. Athens soon afterwards colonised the place. The siege had cost 2000 talents.

Pericles deposed from office of general; Meanwhile the Athenians had been cast into such despair by the plague that they made overtures for peace to Sparta. Their overtures were rejected, and they turned the fury of their disappointment upon Pericles, who had returned unsuccessful from

Epidaurus.   He was suspended from the post of strategos to *tried and* which he had been elected in the spring; his accounts were called *fined* for and examined by the Council; and an exceptionally large court *(c. July,* of 1501 judges was impanelled to try him for the misappropriation *430 B.C.).* of public money.   He was found guilty of " theft " to the trifling amount of five talents; the verdict was a virtual acquittal, though he had to pay a fine of ten times the amount; and he was presently re-elected to the post from which he had been suspended.   He was in truth indispensable.   All the courage, all the patience, all the eloquence of the great statesman were demanded at this crisis.   He had to convince Athens that the privileges of her imperial position involved hardships and toils, and that it was dangerous for her to draw back.   The position of the Imperialist is always vulnerable to assaults on grounds of morality, and the peace party at Athens could make a plausible case against the policy of Pericles.   But the imperial instinct of the people responded, in spite of tem- porary reactions, to his call.   Athens was not destined to be guided *Death of* by him much longer.   He had lost his two legitimate sons in the *Pericles* plague, and he died about a year later.   In his last years he had been *(autumn* afflicted by the indirect attacks of his enemies.   Phidias was accused *429 B.C.).* of embezzling part of the public money devoted to the works on the *upon him.* Acropolis, in which he was engaged, and it was implied that Pericles *(1) Trial* was cognisant of the dishonesty.   Phidias was condemned.   Then *of Phidias.* the philosopher Anaxagoras was publicly prosecuted for holding and *(2) Trial of* propagating impious doctrines.   Pericles defended his friend, but *Anax-* Anaxagoras was sentenced to pay a fine of five talents, and retired to *(3) Trial of* continue his philosophical studies at Lampsacus.   The next attack *Aspasia,* was upon his mistress Aspasia, who was charged with impiety.   The *the mistress* pleading of Pericles procured her acquittal, and in the last year of his *of Pericles.* life the People passed a decree to legitimise her son.   The latest words *younger* of Pericles express what to the student of the history of civilisation is an *Pericles* important feature of his character—his humanity.   " No Athenian *legiti-* ever put on black for an act of mine."   Phidias: Plut. Per. 31²⁻⁵ *mised.* 326

Diod. xii.39ᴿ ; Diog. Laert. ii.5.19

SECT. 5.   THE SIEGE AND CAPTURE OF PLATÆA   Diod. xii.39²   *Third year*

In the next summer Archidamus was induced by the Thebans, *of the war,* instead of invading Attica, to march across Cithaeron and lay siege *429 B.C.* to Plataea.   Like Elis itself, the Plataean land was sacred,—in memory of the great deliverance of Hellas which had been wrought there; and the Spartan king, when he set foot upon it, called the gods to witness that the Plataeans had first done wrong.   He proposed to the Plataeans that they should evacuate their territory, until the end of the war; they might count their trees and their

Aspasia : Plut. Per. 32¹·⁵

possessions, and all should then be restored to them intact.   Having consulted Athens, which promised to protect them, the Plataeans refused, and Archidamus began the siege.   The Athenians, however, were true to the policy of avoiding continental warfare, and notwithstanding their promises sent no help.   Plataea was a very important position for the Peloponnesians to secure.   It commanded the road from Megara to Thebes, by which communications between the Peloponnesus and Boeotia could be maintained most easily without entering Attica.

Site of Plataea.

The visitor to Plataea must not suppose that the city which Archidamus besieged extended over the entire ground plan which now meets his eye.   For he sees the circuit of the city as it existed a century later, occupying the whole surface of the low triangular plateau on which the town stood.   The Plataea of Archidamus corresponds probably to the southern and higher part of the space occupied by the later town.   The wall of the older Plataea cannot have been much more than a mile long ; for the small garrison— 400 Plataeans and eighty Athenians—could never have maintained a longer line of defence in a place where nature had done almost nothing to assist them.

The mound.

Having surrounded the city with a palisade to prevent any one from getting out, Archidamus employed his army in building a mound against the southern wall.   They worked for seventy days and seventy nights.   The Plataeans endeavoured to counteract this by raising the height of their own wall, opposite the mound, by a structure of bricks set in a wooden frame.   They protected the workmen by screens of hide against burning arrows.   But as the mound rose higher and higher, a new device was tried.   They made a hole in the wall underneath and drew out the earth from the mound.   The Peloponnesians met this device by putting into the gap clay packed in baskets of reed ; this could not be drawn away quickly like the loose earth.   Another plan was then devised by the besieged.   They dug a subterranean mine under the wall to some distance beneath the mound, and drew the earth away as they had done before.   This effectually retarded the progress of the mound, for, though the besiegers were numerous, they had to carry the earth from a considerable distance.   The Plataeans resorted to yet another device.   From the two extremities of that portion of the wall which they had raised in height, they built an inner wall, in crescent shape, projecting inwards ; so that if the outer wall were taken, the Peloponnesians would have all their labour over again.   They also showed ingenuity in frustrating the battering-rams which the besiegers brought against the walls.   They placed two poles on the top of the wall, projecting over it ; to the ends of these poles they

Stratagems of the besieged. (1) Raising of the wall. (2) Removing the earth through wall ; (3) by a mine.

(4) The inner wall.

The battering-rams.

attached a huge beam by means of iron chains.   When the engine
approached, they let go the beam, which snapped off the head of the
battering-ram.   The besiegers then made an attempt to set the town   *The fire.*
on fire.   They heaped up faggots along the wall close to the mound,
and kindled them with brimstone and pitch.   If the prevalent south
wind had been blowing down the slopes of the mountain, nothing
would have saved the Plataeans from the tremendous conflagration
which ensued and rendered the wall unapproachable by the
besiegers.

When this device failed the Peloponnesians saw they would have   *Blockade,*
to blockade Plataea.   They built a wall of circumvallation, about   *autumn*
100 yards from the city, and dug two fosses one inside and one   *429 to*
outside this wall.   Then Archidamus left part of his army to maintain   *summer*
the blockade during the winter.   The blockaders, of whom about   *427.*
half were Boeotians, established a communication by means of fire
signals with Thebes.   At the end of another year, the Plataeans
saw that they had no longer any hope of help from Athens, and their
food was running short.   They determined to make an attempt to
escape.

The wall of the Peloponnesians looked like a single wall of   *Plan of*
immense thickness, but it actually consisted of two walls, 16 feet   *escape.*
apart.   The middle space, which served as quarters for the garrison,   *Winter*
was roofed over, and guard was kept on the roof.   Along the top   *(? Dec.)*
there were battlements on each side, and at every tenth battlement   *428 B.C.*
there was a tower which covered the whole width from wall to wall.
There were passages through the middle of the towers but not at the
sides.   On wet and stormy nights the guard used to leave the
battlements and retire under the shelter of the towers.   The escape
was attended with much risk and less than half the garrison
attempted it.   The plan was carefully calculated.   They determined
the height of the wall by counting and recounting the number of
layers of bricks in a spot which had not been plastered ; and then
constructed ladders of exactly the right length.   On a dark night,
amid rain and storm, they stole out, crossed the inner ditch, and
reached the wall unnoticed.   They were lightly equipped, and while
their right feet were bare the left were shod, to prevent slipping in
the mud.   Twelve men, led by Ammeas, ascended first, near two
adjacent towers.   They killed the guard in each tower, and secured
the passages, which they held until all their companions had mounted
and descended on the other side.   One of the Plataeans, in climbing
up on the roof, knocked a brick from one of the battlements ; its fall
was heard, and the alarm was given.   All the besiegers came out on
the wall, but in the blackness they could not discover what it was,
and no one dared to move from his own place.   Moreover the

Plataeans in the city distracted their attention, by sallying out on the side opposite to that on which their friends were escaping. The Peloponnesians lit their danger signals to Thebes, but this had also been foreseen by the Plataeans, who by lighting other beacons on their own wall confused the signals of their enemies. But what the Plataeans had most to fear was an attack from a band of 300 men, whose duty it was to patrol outside the wall. While the last of the Plataeans were descending, they arrived with lights. They were thus illuminated themselves and a good mark for the arrows and darts of the Plataeans who were standing along the edge of the outer ditch. This ditch was crossed with difficulty; it was swollen with rain and had a coat of ice too thin to bear. But all got over safely except one archer who was captured on the brink.

The escape was perhaps effected on the north side of the city. The fugitives at first took the road to Thebes, to put their pursuers off the scent, but when they had left Plataea about a mile behind them, they struck to the right and reached the road from Thebes to Athens near Erythrae. Two hundred and twelve men reached Athens; a few more had started but had turned back before they crossed the wall. This episode is an eminently interesting example of the survival of the fittest; for a melancholy fate awaited those *Surrender* who had not the courage to take their lives in their hands. In the *of Plataea,* following summer want of food forced them to capitulate at discretion *427 B.C.* to the Lacedaemonians. Five men were sent from Sparta to decide their fate. But their fate had been already decided through the influence of Thebes. Each prisoner was merely asked, " Have you in the present war done any service to the Lacedaemonians or their allies ? " The form of the question implied the sentence, and it was in vain that the Plataeans appealed to the loyalty of their ancestors to the cause of Hellas in the Persian war, or implored the Lacedaemonians to look upon the sepulchres of their own fathers buried in Plataean land and honoured every year by Plataea with the customary offerings. They were put to death, 200 in number, and twenty-five Athenians ; and the city was rased to the ground. The Peloponnesians now commanded the road from Megara to Thebes.

It is hard to avoid reproaching the Athenians for impolicy in not coming to the relief of their old and faithful ally, and maintaining a position so important for the communication between the Peloponnese and Boeotia. Their failure to bring succour at the beginning of the siege may be explained by their sufferings from the plague which still prevailed. And in the following year a more pressing danger diverted their attention, the revolt of a member of their maritime confederacy.

Sect. 6. Revolt of Mytilene

Archidamus had invaded Attica for the third time, and had just *Fourth* quitted it, when the news arrived that Mytilene and the rest of *year of the* Lesbos, with the exception of Methymna, had revolted. This was a *war,* great and, as it might seem to Athens, an unprovoked blow. It was *428 b.c.* not due to any special grievance. The oligarchical government of Mytilene confessed that the city was always well-treated and honoured by Athens. The revolt is all the more interesting and significant on this account. It was a protest of the Hellenic instinct for absolute autonomy against an empire such as the Athenian. The sovereignty of the Lesbian cities was limited in regard to foreign affairs ; their relations with other members of the confederacy were subject to control on the part of Athens ; and their ships were required for Athenian purposes. Such restraints were irksome, and as they had seen the free allies of Athens, most recently Samos, gradually transformed into subjects, they might fear that this would presently be their own case too. The revolt had been meditated for some years ; it was hastened in the end, before all the preparations were made— such as the closing of the harbour of Mytilene by a mole and chain —because the design had been betrayed to Athens by enemies in Methymna and Tenedos. The Athenians, on the first news, sent ships under Cleïppides to surprise Mytilene at a festival of Apollo, which all the inhabitants used to celebrate outside the walls ; but the Mytilenaeans received secret intelligence and postponed the feast. The Lesbians had a large fleet ; and the Athenians were feeling so severely the effects of the plague and of the war that the rebellion had a good prospect of success if it had been energetically supported by the Peloponnesians. Envoys who were sent to gain their help, *Lesbian* pleaded the cause of Lesbos at the Olympian games which were *envoys at* celebrated this year. At the most august of the Panhellenic festivals, *Olympia.* by the banks of the Alpheus, it was a fitting occasion to come forward among the assembled Greeks as champions of the principle of self-government which it is the glory of Greece to have taught mankind. And as Mytilene had no grievance beyond the general injustice of Athens in imposing external limitations on the autonomy of others, her assertion of that principle carried the greater weight. Lesbos was admitted into the Peloponnesian league, but no assistance was sent.

The revolt from Athens was accompanied by a constitutional change within the borders of Lesbos itself. Except Methymna in *Synoe-* the north, the other cities in the island—Antissa, Eresus, and *cism of* Pyrrha on her land-locked bay—agreed to merge their own political *Mytilene.*

individualities in the city of Mytilene.　By the constitutional process, known as synoecism, Mytilene was now to be to Lesbos what Athens was to Attica.　The citizens of Pyrrha, Eresos, and Antissa would henceforward be citizens of Mytilene.　Lesbos, with Methymna independent and hostile, would now be what Attica was before the annexation of Eleusis.

Autumn,
428 B.C.

Meanwhile the Athenians had blockaded the two harbours of Mytilene, and Paches soon arrived with 1000 hoplites, to complete the investment.　He built a wall on the land side of the city.　At this time the Athenians were in sore want of money, for their funds had been seriously strained, especially by the expenses of the siege of Potidaea.　As a measure of economy the hoplites sent from Athens to reinforce the besiegers were required to take the oars themselves. A small squadron was sent at the same time to the Carian district to levy tribute from states which had defaulted, a dangerous mission which met with no success.　The tribute of the empire was increased by a new, extraordinary, assessment and at home they resorted to the expedient of raising money by a property tax.

The
Eisphora
(property
tax),
428 B.C.

This tax, now introduced for the first time, differed both in object and in nature from the property tax of the sixth century. In the first place, it was not imposed permanently but only to meet a temporary crisis ; secondly, it was to be used for purely military purposes ; thirdly, it was imposed on all property and not merely on land.　Economical conditions had changed since the days of Pisistratus, and landed proprietors no longer formed the bulk of the

Probably a
tax on
capital.

richest men.　[The tax yielded, in the first year, 200 talents and was frequently reimposed.　The urgent need justified it, but it increased the bitterness of the oligarchs and helped to strain the allegiance of the moderates.　It was probably first introduced by Cleon, who was this year a member of the Council ; it became associated with the policy of the demagogues.]

427 B.C.,
first
months.

May.

Towards the end of the winter, the Spartans sent a man, his name was Salaethus, to assure the people of Mytilene that an armament would be dispatched to their relief.　He managed to elude the Athenians and get into the city.　The spirits of the besieged rose, and when summer came forty-two ships were sent under the command of Alcidas, and at the same time the Peloponnesians invaded Attica for the fourth time, hoping to distract the attention of the Athenians from Mytilene.　The besieged waited and waited, but the ships never came, and the food ran short.　Salaethus, in despair, determined to make a sally, and for this purpose armed the mass of the people with shields and spears.　But the people, when they got the arms, refused to obey and demanded that the oligarchs should bring forth the corn and that all should share it fairly; otherwise, they would surrender the city. This drove the *Surrender* government to anticipate the chance of a separate negotiation on the *of* part of the people; and they capitulated at discretion. Their fate *Mytilene.* was to be decided at Athens, and meanwhile Paches was to put no man to death.

The fleet of Alcidas had wasted time about the Peloponnesus, and *The* on reaching the island of Myconus received the news that Mytilene *expedition* was taken. He sailed to Erythrae and there it was proposed to *of Alcidas.* Alcidas that he should attack Mytilene, on the principle that men who have just gained possession of a city are usually off their guard. Another suggestion was that a town on the Asiatic coast should be seized and a revolt excited against Athens in the Ionian district. But these plans were far too good and daring for a Lacedaemonian admiral to adopt. He sailed southward, was pursued by Paches as far as Patmos, and retired into the Peloponnesian waters where he was more at home.

The ringleaders of the revolt of Mytilene were sent to Athens, and along with them the Spartan Salaethus, who was immediately put to death. The Assembly met to determine the fate of the *People of* prisoners, and decided to put to death not only the most guilty who *Mytilene* had been sent to Athens, but the whole adult male population, and *sentenced to* to enslave the women and children. A trireme was immediately *death.* dispatched to Paches with this terrible command.

The fact that the Athenian Assembly was persuaded to press the cruel rights of war so far as to decree the extinction of a whole population shows how deep was the feeling of wrath that prevailed against Mytilene. Many things contributed to render that feeling particularly bitter. The revolt had come at a moment when Athens was sore bestead, between the plague and the war. Every Athenian had a grudge against Mytilene; for his own pocket had suffered, through the tax which it had been necessary to impose. And the Imperial pride of the people had been wounded by the unheard-of event of a Peloponnesian fleet sailing in the eastern waters, of which Athens regarded herself as the sole mistress. But above all it was the revolt not of a subject, but of a free ally. Athens could more easily forgive the rebellion of a subject state which tried to throw off her yoke, than repudiation of her leadership by a nominally independent confederate. For the action of Mytilene was in truth an indictment of the whole fabric of the Athenian empire as unjust and undesirable. And the Athenians felt its significance. The mere unreasoning instinct of self-preservation suggested the policy of making a terrible example. It was another question whether this policy was wise.

The calm sense of Pericles was no longer there to guide and enlighten *New* the Assembly. We now find democratic statesmen of a completely *class of* *statesmen.*

different stamp coming forward to take his place. The Assembly is swayed by men of the people—tradesmen, like Cleon, the leather-merchant; Eucrates, the rope-seller; Hyperbolus, the lamp-maker. These men had not, like Aristides, Cimon, and Pericles, family connexions to start and support them; they had no aristocratic traditions as the background of their democratic policy. They were self-made; they won their influence in the state by the sheer force of cleverness, eloquence, industry, and audacity. A man like Cleon, the son of Cleaenetus, whom we now meet holding the unofficial position of leader of the Assembly, must, to attain that eminence, have regularly attended week after week in the Pnyx; he must have mastered the details of political affairs; he must have had the courage to confront the Olympian authority of Pericles, and the dexterity to make some palpable hits; he must have studied the art of speaking and been able to hold his audience. Cleon and the other statesmen of this new type are especially interesting as *the politicians whom the advanced democracy produced and educated.* It would be a grievous error and injustice to suppose that their policy was determined by mere selfish ambition or party malice. Nearly all we know of them is derived from the writings of men who not only condemned their policy but personally disliked them as low-born upstarts. Yet though they may have been vulgar and offensive in their manners, there is abundant evidence that they were able, and there is no proof that they were not generally honest, politicians. To those who regretted the dignity of Pericles, the speech of Cleon or Hyperbolus may have seemed violent and coarse; but Cleon himself could hardly have outdone the coarseness and the violence of the personalities which Demosthenes heaped on Aeschines in a subsequent generation.

These new politicians were for the most part strong imperialists, and Cleon seems to have taken fully to heart the maxim of Pericles, to keep the subject allies " well in hand." It was under his influence that the Assembly vented its indignation against Mytilene by dooming the whole people to slaughter. But when the meeting had dispersed, a partial reaction set in. Men began, in a cooler moment, to realise the inhumanity of their action and to question its policy.

Second meeting of the Assembly. The envoys of Mytilene, who had been permitted to come to Athens to plead her cause, seeing this change of feeling, induced the authorities to summon an extraordinary meeting of the Assembly for the following morning, to reconsider the decree. Cleon again came forward *Arguments* to support it on the grounds of both legal justice and good policy. *of Cleon.* Thucydides represents him as openly asserting the principle that a tyrannical city must use tyrannical methods, and rule by fear, chastising her allies without mercy. The chief speaker on the other side *Speech of* was a certain Diodotus, whose name has won immortality by his *Diodotus.*

action at this famous crisis.   Diodotus handled the question entirely as a matter of policy.   Cleon had deprecated any appeal to the irrelevant considerations of humanity or pity ; Diodotus, carefully avoiding such an appeal, deprecates on his own side with great force Cleon's appeal to considerations of justice.   The Mytilenaeans have deserved the sentence of death : certainly ; but the argument is entirely irrelevant.   The question for Athens to consider is not what Mytilene deserves, but what it is expedient for Athens to inflict. "We are not at law with the Mytilenaeans and do not want to be told what is just ; we are considering a matter of policy, and desire to know how we can turn them to account."   He then goes on to argue that as a matter of fact the penalty of death is not a deterrent, and that the result of such a severe punishment will be injurious to Athens.   A city which has revolted, knowing that whether she comes to terms soon or late the penalty will be the same, will never surrender ; money will be wasted in a long blockade ; and "when the place is taken, it will be a mere wreck."   Moreover, if the people of Mytilene, who were compelled to join with their oligarchical government in rebelling, are destroyed, the popular party will everywhere be alienated from Athens.

The reasoning of Diodotus, which was based on sound views of policy, must have confirmed many of the audience who had already been influenced by the emotion of pity.   But even still the Assembly was nearly equally divided, and the supporters of Diodotus won their motion by a very small majority.   The ship which bore the sentence of doom had a start of about a day and a night ; could it be overtaken by the trireme which was now dispatched with the reprieve ? The Mytilenaean envoys supplied the crew with wine and barley, and offered large rewards if they were in time.   The oarsmen continued rowing while they ate the barley, kneaded with wine and oil, and slept and rowed by turns.   The first trireme, bound on an unpleasant errand, had sailed slowly.   It arrived a little before the other. Paches had the decree in his hand and was about to execute it, when the second ship sailed into the harbour, and the city was saved.

The wrath of Athens against her rebellious ally was sufficiently gratified by the trial and execution of those Mytilenaeans who had been sent to Athens as especially guilty.

Having taken away the Lesbian fleet and rased the walls of Mytilene, the Athenians divided the island, excluding Methymna, into 3000 lots of which 300 were consecrated to the gods.   The rest they let to Athenian citizens as cleruchs, and the land was cultivated by the Lesbians, who paid an annual rent.

Sentence revoked.

Execution of Mytilenaean ring-leaders.

Cleruchy at Mytilene.

SECT. 7. WARFARE IN WESTERN GREECE. TRAGIC EVENTS IN CORCYRA

Course of events in western Greece. 429 B.C.

Thuc. ii. 6B

While the attention of Greece was directed upon the fortunes of Plataea and Mytilene, warfare had been carried on in the regions of the west, and the reputation of the Athenian navy had risen higher. The Ambraciots had persuaded Sparta to send an expedition against Acarnania; if the Peloponnesians firmly established themselves there, they might win the whole Athenian alliance in the west. Cnemus was sent with 1000 hoplites in advance; he made an attempt on the important town of Stratus but was forced to retreat. Meanwhile a Peloponnesian fleet was to sail from Corinth to support him. It consisted of forty-seven ships, and had to pass Phormio, who was guarding the entrance of the Corinthian gulf with only twenty. Phormio let them sail into the open sea, preferring to

First naval victory of Phormio.

attack them there. By skilful manœuvres he crowded the enemy's ships into a narrow space; a morning breeze helped him by knocking the ships against one another; and when they were in confusion the Athenians dashed in and gained a complete victory. The government at Sparta could not understand how skill could gain such an advantage over far superior numbers; they sent commissioners to make an inquiry; and Cnemus was told that he must try again and be

Second naval victory of Phormio.

successful. A reorganised Peloponnesian fleet took up a position at Panormus in Achaea, and Phormio was stationed at Rhion on the opposite coast. The object of Cnemus was to lure or drive the enemy into the gulf where their skill in handling their ships would be less decisive than in the open sea. With this purpose he sailed towards Naupactus, and Phormio in alarm sailed along the coast to

A defeat

protect the place. As the Athenian ships moved near the land in single file, the enemy suddenly swung round and rowed down upon them at their utmost speed. The eleven ships which were nearest Naupactus had time to run round the right Peloponnesian wing and escape; the rest were driven aground. Twenty Peloponnesian vessels on the right were in the meantime pursuing the eleven Athenian, which were making for Naupactus. A Leucadian ship was far in advance of the others, closely pursuing an Athenian which was lagging behind. Near Naupactus a merchant vessel lay in their way, anchored in the

turned into a victory at Naupactus.

deep water. The Athenian trireme rowed round it, struck her pursuer amidships, and sank her. This brilliant exploit startled the Peloponnesians who were coming up singing a paean of victory; the front ships dropped oars and waited for the rest. The Athenians, who had already reached Naupactus, saw the situation, and immediately bore down and gained another complete victory.

If this able admiral, Phormio, had lived, he might have extended Athenian influence considerably in western Greece. But, after a winter expedition which he made in Acarnania, he silently drops out of history, and, as we find his son Asopius sent out in the following *Asopius in* summer at the request of the Acarnanians, we must conclude that his *the west,* career had been cut short by death. Asopius made an unsuccessful *428 B.C.* attempt on Oeniadae, and was slain in a descent on Leucas. The peninsula of Leucas, and the Acarnanian Oeniadae, girt by morasses at the mouth of the river Achelous, were two main objects of Athenian enterprise in the west. Leucas was never won, but four *Oeniadae,* years later Oeniadae was forced to join the Athenian alliance. *424 B.C.*

Corcyra herself was to be the next scene of the war in the Ionian *Affairs at* Sea. The prisoners whom Corinth had taken in the Epidamnian *Corcyra,* war had been released on the understanding that they were to win *427 B.C.* over Corcyra from the Athenian alliance, and their intrigues were effectual in dividing the state and producing a sanguinary revolution. The question between the Peloponnesian and the Athenian alliance was closely bound up with the cleavage between the oligarchical and the democratic party. The intriguers in the Corinthian interest and their faction formed a conspiracy to overthrow the democratic constitution. Their first step was to prosecute Peithias, the leader of the people, on the charge of scheming to make Corcyra a subject of Athens. He was acquitted, and retorted by summoning their five richest men to take their trial for cutting vine-poles in the sanctuaries of Zeus and Alcinous. They were fined a stater for each pole : such a heavy fine that the culprits sat as suppliants in the sanctuary, imploring that they might pay by instalments. The prayer was *Murder of* refused, and in desperation they rushed into the senate-house and *the popular* slew Peithias and sixty others who were with him. *govern-*

The oligarchy now had the upper hand, and they attacked the *ment,* people, who fled to the acropolis and the Hyllaic harbour. The *427 B.C.* other harbour, which looks towards the mainland, along with the *Civil war* agora and the lower parts of the city were held by the oligarchs. *in Corcyra.* Next day reinforcements came to both sides : to the people, from other parts of the island ; and to the oligarchs, from the mainland. Fighting was soon resumed and the people had the advantage. In order to bar their way to the arsenal, the oligarchs set fire to the houses and buildings in the neighbourhood of the agora.

Next day twelve Athenian ships under Nicostratus arrived from *Arrival* Naupactus. He induced the two parties to come to an agreement, *of the* but the democrats persuaded him to leave five Athenian ships to *Athenians.* ensure the preservation of order, for they did not trust their opponents. Nicostratus was to take five Corcyraean ships instead, and the crews of them were chosen from the oligarchs ; they were in fact to be hostages for the behaviour of their fellows. But they feared they might be sent to Athens, and fled to the refuge of a temple. Nicostratus could not induce them to stir. The people regarded this distrust as a proof of criminal designs, and armed anew. The rest of the oligarchs then fled to the temple of Hera, but the democrats induced them to cross over to an islet off the coast.

Four or five days later a Peloponnesian fleet of fifty-three ships arrived under Alcidas, who had just returned from his expedition to Ionia. In a naval engagement outside the harbour the Corcyraeans fought badly, and the Athenians were forced to retreat; but the Peloponnesians did not follow up their success, and soon afterwards, hearing that an Athenian armament of sixty ships was on its way, returned home.

Cruel massacres by the democrats.

The democratic party was now in a position to wreak vengeance on its foes, who had gratuitously disturbed the peace of the city and sought to submit it to the yoke of its ancient enemy. The most vindictive and inhuman passions had been roused in the people by the attempt of the oligarchs on their liberty, and they now gave vent to these passions without regard to honour or policy The 400 suppliants had returned from the island, and were again under the protection of Hera. Fifty of them were persuaded to come forth to take their trial, and were executed. The rest, seeing their fate, aided each other in committing suicide; some hung themselves on the trees in the sacred enclosure. Eurymedon arrived with the Athenian fleet and remained seven days. During this time, the Corcyraeans slew all whom they suspected of being opposed to the democracy, and many victims were sacrificed to private enmity. "Every form of death was to be seen, and everything, and more than everything that commonly happens in revolutions, happened then. The father slew the son, and the suppliants were torn from the temples and slain near them; some of them were even walled up in the temple of Dionysus and there perished. To such extremes of cruelty did revolution go; and this seemed to be the worst of revolutions because it was the first." Eurymedon looked on and did not intervene.

While the democracy cannot be excused for these horrible excesses, the fact remains that the guilt of causing the revolution rests entirely with the oligarchs. The chief victims of the democratic fury deserve small compassion; they had set the example of violence. The occurrences at Corcyra made a profound impression in Greece, reflected in the pages of Thucydides. That historian has used the episode as the text for deep comments on the revolutionary spirit which soon began to disturb the states of the Greek

The revolutionary spirit.

world.   Party divisions were encouraged and aggravated by the
hope or fear of foreign intervention, the oligarchs looking to the
Lacedaemonians, and the democrats to the Athenians.   In time of
peace these party struggles would have been far less bitter.   This
acute observation is illustrated by a famous modern instance, the
French Revolution, where the worst outrages of the revolutionists
were provoked by foreign intervention.   In that great Revolution
too [1] we can verify the Greek historian's analysis of the effect of the
revolutionary spirit, when it runs wild, on the moral nature of men.
The revolutionists "determined to outdo the report of all who had
preceded them by the ingenuity of their enterprises and the activity
of their revenges.   The meaning of words had no longer the same
relation to things, but was changed by them as they thought proper.
Reckless daring was held to be loyal courage ; prudent delay was
the excuse of a coward ; moderation was the disguise of unmanly
weakness; to know everything was to do nothing.   Frantic energy was
the true quality of a man.   The lover of violence was always trusted
and his opponent suspected."   It was dangerous to be quiet and
neutral.   "The citizens who were of neither party fell a prey to
both ; either they were disliked because they held aloof, or men
were jealous of their surviving."   The laws of heaven as well as of
civilised societies were set aside without scruple amid the impatience
of party spirit, the zeal of contention, the eagerness of ambition, and
the cravings of revenge.   These are some of the features in the
delineation which Thucydides has drawn of the diseased condition
of political life in the city-states of Greece.

But the sequel of the Corcyraean revolution has still to be *Corcyraean*
recorded.   About 600 of the oligarchs who escaped the venge- *oligarchs*
ance of their opponents established themselves on Mount Istone *on Istone.*
in the north - east of the island, and easily becoming masters
of the open country they harassed the inhabitants of the city for two *427-5 B.C.*
years.   Then an Athenian fleet, of which the ultimate destination *Fall of*
was Sicily, under the command of Eurymedon and Sophocles, arrived *Istone,*
at Corcyra ; and the Athenians helped the democrats to storm the *425 B.C.*
fort on Mount Istone.   The oligarchs capitulated on condition that
the Athenian people should determine how they were to be dealt
with.   The generals placed them in the island of Ptychia, on the
understanding that, if any of their number attempted to escape, all
should be deprived of the benefit of the previous agreement.   But
the democrats apprehended that the prisoners would not be put to
death at Athens, and they were determined that their enemies should
die.   A foul trick was planned and carried out.   Friends of the

---

[1] Grote observed this.

prisoners were sent over to the island, who said that the generals had resolved to leave them to the mercy of the democrats, and advised them to escape, offering to provide a ship. A few of the captives fell into the trap and were caught starting. All the prisoners were immediately handed over to the Corcyraeans, who shut them *Massacre* up in a large building. They were taken out in batches of twenty, *of the* and made to march, tied together, down an avenue of hoplites, who *oligarchs.* smote and wounded any whom they recognised as a personal enemy. Three batches had thus marched to execution, when their comrades in the building, who thought they were merely being removed to another prison, discovered the truth. They called on the Athenians, but they called in vain. Then they refused to stir out of the building or let any one enter. The Corcyraeans did not attempt to force their way in. They tore off the roof, and hurled bricks and shot arrows from above. The captives, absolutely helpless, began to anticipate the purpose of their tormentors by taking their own lives, piercing their throats with the arrows which were shot down, or strangling themselves with the ropes of some beds which were in the place or with strips of their own dress. The work of destruction went on during the greater part of the night; all was over when the day dawned; and the corpses were carried outside the city. Thus ended the Corcyraean revolution, and the last scene was more ghastly even than the first. Eurymedon had less excuse, on this occasion, for refusing to intervene than he had two years before; since the prisoners had surrendered to the Athenians. It was said that he and Sophocles were ready to take advantage of the base trick of the democrats, because, unable to take the captives to Athens themselves, being bound for Sicily, they could not bear that the credit should fall to another. The oligarchical faction at Corcyra was now utterly annihilated, and the democrats lived in peace.

SECT. 8. CAMPAIGNS OF DEMOSTHENES IN THE WEST

Aetolian During the Corcyraean troubles, the war had not rested in *expedition,* western Greece. An Athenian fleet under the general Demo- *426 B.C.* sthenes had sailed round the Peloponnesus and attacked the "island" of Leucas. Demosthenes was an enterprising commander, distinguished from most of his fellows by a certain originality of conception. On this occasion, the idea of making a great stroke induced him to abandon the operations at Leucas,—though the Acarnanians thought he might have taken the town by blockade,— and engage in a new enterprise on the north of the Corinthian gulf. Most of the lands between Boeotia and the western sea—Phocis, Locris, Acarnania—were friendly to Athens. But the hostility of the uncivilised Aetolians rendered land operations in those regions dangerous. Demosthenes conceived the plan of reducing the Aetolians, so that he could then operate from the west on Doris and Boeotia, without the danger of his communications being threatened in the rear. His idea, in fact, was to bring the Corinthian gulf into touch with the Euboean sea. The Spartans, it is to be observed, were at this very time concerning themselves with the regions of Mount Oeta. The appeals of Doris on the south, and Trachis on *Colony of* the north, of the Oetaean range, for protection against the hostilities *Heraclea.* of the mountain tribes, induced the Lacedaemonians to send out a colony, which was established in Trachis not very far from the Pass of Thermopylae, under the name of Heraclea. A colony was an unusual enterprise for Sparta ; but Heraclea had a more important significance and intention than the mere defence of members of the amphictiony. It was a place from which Euboea could be attacked ; and it might prove of the greatest service, as an intermediate station, for carrying on operations in the Chalcidic peninsula. The fears which the foundation of Heraclea excited at Athens were indeed disappointed ; Heraclea never flourished ; it was incessantly assailed by the powerful hostility of the Thessalians, and its ruin was completed by the flagrantly unjust administration of the Lacedaemonian governors. But its first foundation was a serious event ; and it seems highly probable that Demosthenes, when he formed his plan, had before his mind the idea of threatening Heraclea from the south by the occupation of Doris. But his plan, attractive as it might sound, was eminently impracticable. The preliminary condition was the subjugation of a mountainous country, involving a warfare in which Demosthenes was inexperienced and hoplites were at a great disadvantage. The Messenians of Naupactus represented to him that Aetolia, a land of unwalled villages, could easily be reduced. But the Messenians had their own game to play. They suffered from the hostilities of their Aetolian neighbours and wanted to use the ambition of the Athenian general for their own purpose.

The Acarnanians, who were deeply interested in the defeat of Leucas, were indignant with Demosthenes for not prosecuting the blockade and refused to join him against Aetolia. Starting from Oeneon in Locris, the Athenians and some allies—not a large force—advanced into the country, hoping to reduce several tribes before they had time to combine. But the Aetolians had already learned his plans, and were already collecting a great force. The main chance of Demosthenes lay in the co-operation of the Ozolian Locrians, who knew the Aetolian country and mode of warfare and were armed in the Aetolian fashion. Demosthenes committed the error of not waiting for them. He was consequently unable to deal with the Aetolian javelin-men. At Aegition, rushing down from the hills they wrought havoc among the invaders who had captured the town. A hundred and twenty Athenian hoplites fell—"the very finest men whom the city of Athens lost during the war." Demosthenes did not dare to return to Athens. He remained at Naupactus, and soon had an opportunity of retrieving his fame.

The Lacedaemonians answered this invasion of Aetolia by sending 3000 hoplites under Eurylochus against Naupactus. Five

FIG. 122.—Silver Coin of Ambracia. Obverse—Flying Pegasus. Reverse—Head of Pallas (Corinthian helmet), and girl with a kottabos staff [legend (AM)ΠPAKIΩTAN].

hundred of these troops came from Heraclea, the newly-founded colony. Naupactus, ill-defended, was barely saved by the energy of Demosthenes, who persuaded the Acarnanians to send reinforcements. Eurylochus abandoned the siege, and withdrew to the neighbourhood of Calydon and Pleuron in southern Aetolia, for the purpose of joining the

Ambraciots in an attack upon Argos. Winter had begun when the Ambraciots descended from the north into the Argive territory and seized the fort of Olpae, which stands, a little north of Argos, on a hill by the sea, and was once used as a hall of justice by the Acarnanian league. Demosthenes was asked by the Acarnanians to be their leader in resisting this attack, and a message for help was sent to twenty Athenian vessels which were coasting off the Peloponnesus. The troops of Eurylochus marched from the south across Acarnania and joined their allies at Olpae. The Athenian ships arrived in the Ambracian gulf, and, with the reinforcements which they brought, Demosthenes gave battle to the enemy between Olpae and Argos, and by a skilfully contrived ambuscade annulled the advantage which they had in superior numbers. Eurylochus was slain, and the Peloponnesians delivered themselves from their perilous position—between Argos and the Athenian ships—by making a secret treaty with Demosthenes, in which the Ambraciots were not included. It was arranged that they should retreat stealthily without explaining their intention to the Ambraciots. It was good policy on the part of Demosthenes; for by this treacherous act the Lacedaemonians would lose their character in that part of Greece. The Peloponnesians crept out of Olpae one by one, pretending to gather herbs and sticks. As they got farther away, they stepped out more quickly, and then the Ambraciots saw what was happening and ran out to overtake them. The Acarnanians slew about 200

Ambraciots, and the Peloponnesians escaped into the land of Agraea. But a heavier blow was in store for Ambracia. Reinforcements of that city, ignorant of the battle, were coming to Olpae. Demosthenes sent forward some of his troops to lie in ambush on their line of march. At Idomene, some miles north of Olpae, there are two peaks of unequal height. The higher was seized in advance by the men of Demosthenes ; the Ambraciots when they arrived encamped on the lower. Demosthenes then advanced with the rest of his troops and attacked the enemy at dawn, when they were still half asleep. Most were slain, and those who escaped at first found the mountain paths occupied. Thucydides says that during the first ten years of the war "no such calamity happened within so few days to any Hellenic state," and he does not give the numbers of those who perished, because they would appear incredible in proportion to the size of the state. Demosthenes might have captured the city if he had pushed on, but the Acarnanians did not desire a permanent Athenian occupation at their doors ; they were content that their neighbour was rendered harmless. A treaty of alliance for 100 years was concluded between the Acarnanians, with the Amphilochians of Argos, and the Ambraciots. Neither side was to be required by the other to join against its own allies in the great war, but they were to help each other to defend their territories. Some time afterwards Anactorion, and then Oeniadae, were won *Anac-* over to the Athenian alliance.

torion,
425 B.C.
Oeniadae,
424 B.C.

SECT. 9. NICIAS AND CLEON. POLITICS AT ATHENS

The success against Ambracia compensated for the failure in Aetolia, and Demosthenes could now return to Athens. His dashing style of warfare and his bold plans must have caused grave mistrust among the older, more experienced, and more commonplace commanders. Nicias, the son of Niceratus, who seems to have already *Nicias.* won, without deserving, the chief place as a military authority at Athens, must have shaken his head over the doings of Demosthenes in the west. Nicias, a wealthy conservative slave-owner, who speculated in the silver-mines of Laurion, was one of the mainstays of that party which was out of sympathy with the intellectual and political progress of Athens, and bitterly opposed to the new politicians like Cleon who wielded the chief influence in the Assembly.

The ability of Nicias was irretrievably mediocre ; he would have been an excellent subordinate officer, but he had not the qualities of a leader or a statesman. Yet he possessed a solid and abiding influence at Athens, through his impregnable respectability, his superiority to bribes, and his scrupulous superstition, as well as his acquaintance with the details of military affairs. This homage paid to mediocre respectability throws light on the character of the Athenian democracy, and the strength of the conservative party. Nicias belonged to the advocates of peace and was well-disposed to Sparta, so that for several reasons he might be regarded as a successor to Cimon. But his political opponents, though they constantly defeated him on particular measures, never permanently undermined his influence. He understood the political value of gratifying in small ways those prejudices of his fellow-citizens which he shared himself; and he spared no expense in the religious service of the state. As Thucydides says, he thought too much of divination and omens. He had an opportunity of displaying his religious devotion and his liberality on the occasion of the purification of Delos, which was probably undertaken to induce Apollo to avert a recurrence of the plague. The dead were removed from all the tombs, and it was ordained that henceforth no one should die or give birth to a child on the sacred island. Those who were near to either should cross over to Rheneia. The Athenians revived in a new form the old festival, celebrated in the Homeric hymn to Apollo, the festival to which "the long-robed Ionians gathered, and made thee glad, O Phoebus, with boxing, dancing, and song." The games were restored, and horse-races introduced for the first time. Four years later the purification was perfected by the removal of all the inhabitants, and the Persians accorded them a refuge at Adramyttion.

Purification of Delos, 426 B.C.

Quadriennial festival established at Delos.

Conducting such ceremonies, Nicias was in his right place. Unfortunately such excellence had an undue weight; and it should be noted that this is one of the drawbacks of a city-state. In a large modern state, the private life and personal opinions of a statesman have small importance and are not weighed by his fellow-countrymen in the scale against his political ability, save in rare exceptional cases. But in a small city the statesman's private life is always before men's eyes, and his political position is distinctly affected, according as he shocks or gratifies their prejudices and predilections. A mediocre man is able, by judicious conforming, to attain an authority to which his brains give him no claim. Pericles was indeed so strong that his influence could survive attacks on his morality and his orthodoxy. Nicias maintained his position because he never shocked the public sense of decorum and religion by associating with an Aspasia or an Anaxagoras. The Athenian people combined in a remarkable degree the capacity of appreciating both respectability and intellectual power; their progressive instinct was often defeated by conservative prejudices.

Though Nicias was one of those Athenians who were not in full sympathy with the policy of Pericles and approved still less of the policy of his successors, he was thoroughly loyal to the democracy. But an oligarchical party still existed, secretly active, *The* and always hoping for an opportunity to upset the democratic *oligarchi-* constitution. This party, or a section of it, seems to have been *cal party.* known at this time as the "Young Party." It included, among οἱ νεώτεροι. others who will appear on the stage of history some years later, the orator Antiphon, who was now coming into public notice in *Antiphon.* connexion with some sensational lawsuits. Against the dark designs of this party, as well as against the misconduct of generals, Cleon was constantly on the watch; he could describe himself in the Assembly as the "people's watch-dog." But at present these oligarchs were harmless; so long as no disaster from without befell Athens, they had no chance; all they could do was to make common cause with the other enemies of Cleon, and air their discontent in anonymous political pamphlets. Chance has preserved us a work of *The pseudo-* this kind, written in one of these years by an Athenian of oligarchical *Xeno-* views. Its subject is the Athenian democracy, and the writer *phontic* *Ἀθηναίων* professes to answer on behalf of the Athenians the criticisms which *πολιτεία,* the rest of the Greeks pass on Athenian institutions. "I do not *c. 424 B.C.* like democracy myself," he says; "but I will show that from their point of view the Athenians manage their state wisely and in the manner most conducive to the interests of democracy." The defence is for the most part a veiled indictment; it displays remarkable acuteness, with occasional triviality. The writer has grasped and taken to heart one deep truth, the close connexion of the sea-power of Athens with its advanced democracy. It is just, he remarks, that the poor and the common folk should have more influence than the noble and rich; for it is the common folk that row the ships and make the city powerful, not the hoplites and the well-born and the worthy. Highly interesting is his observation that slaves and metics enjoyed what he considered unreasonable freedom and immunity at Athens: "Why, you may not strike one of them, nor will a slave make way for you in the street." And his malicious explanation is interesting too; the common folk dress so badly that you might easily mistake one of them for a slave or a metic, and then there would be a to-do if you struck a citizen. There is perhaps a touch of malice, too, in the statement that the commercial empire of Athens, which brought to her wharves the delicacies of the world, was affecting her language, as well as her habits of life, and filling it with foreign words.

An important feature in the political history of Athens in these years was the divorce of the military command from the leadership

Cleon's position. in the Assembly, and the want of harmony between the chief Strategoi and the Leaders of the People. The tradesmen who swayed the Assembly had no military training or capacity, and they were always at a disadvantage when opposed by men who spoke with the authority of a strategos on questions of military policy. Until recent years the post of General had been practically confined to men of property and good family. But a change ensued, perhaps soon after the death of Pericles, and men of the people were *Eupolis on the new generals.* elected. The comic poet Eupolis, in a play called the *Demes*—in which the great leaders, Miltiades and Themistocles, Aristides and Pericles, are summoned back to life that they may see and deplore degenerate Athens—meditates thus on the contrast between latter-day generals and their predecessors :

> Men of lineage fair
> And of wealthy estate
> Once our generals were,
> The noble and great,
> Whom as gods we adored, and as gods they guided and guarded the state.

> Things are not as then.
> Ah, how different far
> A manner of men
> Our new generals are,
> The rascals and refuse our city now chooses to lead us to war !

Cleon was a man of brains and resolution. Hitherto his main activity had been in the law-courts, where he called officers to account and maintained the safeguards of popular government. If he was to be more than an opposition leader, he must be ready to undertake the post of strategos ; and, supported by the experience of an able colleague, he need not disgrace himself. An understanding, therefore, between Cleon and the enterprising Demosthenes was one which seemed to offer advantages to both ; acting together they might damage both the political and the military position of Nicias.

Borrowing from the temple treasures. But before we pass to a famous enterprise, which was probably the result of such an understanding, we must note the great cost which the continuation of the war entailed. [More than 4000 talents had already been borrowed from the temple treasures and, though steps had been taken to increase revenue when Lesbos revolted, the drain was continuing and the end was not in sight. Cleon seems to have been particularly concerned with the financing of the war and it was no doubt under his influence that it was decided to strengthen *Increase of tribute.* the position at the expense of the allies. The decree providing for the new assessment was passed in the Assembly after the dramatic *Assessment of 425 B.C.* success at Sphacteria, but the main lines had probably been worked out by Cleon earlier. We possess numerous fragments of the stone recording the decree and, below it, the list of cities with their new assessment. The main character is clear: " Since the tribute has become too small, they (the jurors) shall join with the Council in making the current assessments. . . . They shall not assess a lower tribute on any city than it was paying before, unless because of impoverishment of the country there is a manifest inability to pay more." These instructions were faithfully followed. Many cities had their tribute doubled or trebled, few escaped increase. Cities that had long discontinued payment were included and more than 100 names were added of cities which are not known to have paid before, including a large group of cities in the Euxine and the stubborn island of Melos. The total of the assessment by these drastic measures was increased to nearly 1500 talents. But this total is in part illusory, for many of the cities waited on events and in the following years Athens was not able to display the necessary force overseas. Borrowings, though on a reduced scale, had to continue. A sharp increase in tribute was necessary to maintain the offensive, but it was an act of ruthless imperialism. It increased discontent among the allies who found sympathy from some of Cleon's opponents in Athens.]

While the allies were to be more heavily burdened Cleon raised *Cleon* the jurors' fee from two to three obols. It would be a mistake to *introduces* consider this measure a mere bid for popularity. We shall hardly *the "trio-* be wrong in regarding it as an attempt to relieve the distress which *bolon "—* the yearly invasions of Attica and losses of the harvests inflicted upon *fee of the* the poorer citizens. *dicasts* *(probably* *425-4 B.C.).*

Sect. 10. The Athenian Capture of Pylos

It was probably through the influence of Cleon that Demosthenes, *425 B.C.* though he received no official command, was sent to accompany the fleet of forty ships which was now ready to start for the west, under Eurymedon and Sophocles. We have already seen this fleet at Corcyra assisting the People against the oligarchical exiles who had established themselves on Mount Istone. Demosthenes accompanied the expedition without any official command. He had a plan in his head for establishing a military post in the western Peloponnesus ; and he was allowed to take advantage of the sailing of the fleet and use it according to his discretion. Arriving off the coast of Messenia, Demosthenes asked the commanders to put in at Pylos, but they had heard that the Peloponnesian fleet had already reached Corcyra, and demurred to any delay. But chance favoured the design of Demosthenes. Stress of weather drove them into the harbour of Pylos, and then Demosthenes pressed them to fortify the place. The task was easy ; for the place was naturally strong and there was an abundance of material, stone and timber, at hand.   The commanders ridiculed the idea.   " There are many other desert promontories in the Peloponnesus," they said, " if you want to waste the money of the city."   But the stormy weather detained the ships ; the soldiers were idle ; and at length, for the sake of something to do, they adopted the project of Demosthenes and fell to the work of fortifying Pylos.

Topo-graphy of Pylos and Sphacteria.   The features of the scene, which was now to become illustrious by a striking military episode, must be clearly grasped.   The high promontory of Pylos or Coryphasion was on three sides encompassed by water.   Once it had been an island, but at this time it was connected with the mainland on the north side by a low sand-bar.   If we go further back into prehistoric days, Pylos had been part of a continuous line of coast-cliff.   In this line three rents were made, which admitted the sea behind the cliff and isolated the islands of Pylos and Sphacteria.   Accumulation of sand gradually covered the most northern breach and reunited Pylos with the mainland, but the other openings were never filled up and Sphacteria still remains an island.   Originally Pylos and Sphacteria, when they had been severed, formed the sea-wall of one great land-locked bay ; but a curving sand-bar has gradually been formed, which now joins the mainland with the southern extremity of Pylos, and secludes a small lagoon of which Pylos forms the western side.   It is impossible to say whether the formation of this sand-bar had perceptibly begun in the time of Demosthenes ; but in any case it seems probable that it had not advanced so far as to hinder the waters behind Pylos from appearing to be part of a continuous bay. This north corner of the bay—now a marshy lagoon—was sheltered and afforded harbourage for ships ; the rest of the bay—the modern bay of Navarino—had no good anchorage ; but the whole sheet of water, by virtue of the northern corner, was called a harbour.   It follows from what has been said that there were two entrances into the bay : the narrow water which divides Pylos from Sphacteria, and the wide passage which severs the southern point of Sphacteria from the opposite mainland.   We must distinguish yet another smaller bay on the north side of the Pylos hill.   The sand-bar which there connects Pylos with the mainland is of lunar shape and forms the little circular basin of Buphras, dominated by the height of Pylos on the south and a far lower, nameless hill on the north.

Athenian fortifica-tions of Pylos.   The length of Pylos is less than a mile.   On the sea-side it was hard to land, and the harbour side was strongly protected by steep cliffs.   Only in three places was it found necessary to build walls :

(1) at the south-east corner, where the cliffs slope down to the channel for about 100 yards; (2) along the shore on the south-west side close to the entrance to the bay, for four or five hundred yards;

The Sieges of
PYLOS & SPHACTERIA

Stadia

1 Mile

a. *Prehistoric Wall round the top of Mt. Elias*
b. *The hollow*
c. *Point at which the Messenians landed to climb into the hollow*
d. *Probable landing place of the Athenians*

Walker & Boutall sc.

FIG. 123.

(3) the northern defence of the position consisted of a line of land cliffs, which required no artificial fortification except at the western extremity, where they decline before they reach the sea;

here another wall was built.   One of the soldiers present vividly
described to Thucydides the manner in which the fortifications were
wrought.   Being unprovided with iron tools they brought stones
which they picked out, and put them together as they happened to
fit ; if they required to use mortar, having no hods, they carried it on
their backs, which they bent so as to form a resting-place for it,
clasping their hands behind them that it might not fall off.[1]   In six
days the work was finished, and the fleet went on its way, leaving
Demosthenes with five ships to hold Pylos.

Arrival of   The Lacedaemonian army under Agis had invaded Attica earlier
Lacedae-   than usual, before the corn was ripe.   Want of food, wet weather,
monians by   and then perhaps the news from Pylos, decided them to return to
land and   Sparta after a sojourn of only two weeks within the Attic borders.
sea.   They did not proceed immediately to Pylos, but another body of
Spartans was sent on ; requisitions for help were dispatched to the
Peloponnesian allies ; and the sixty ships at Corcyra were hastily
summoned.   These ships succeeded in eluding the notice of the
Athenian fleet which had now reached Zacynthus.   In the meantime Demosthenes, beset by the Spartan troops, sent two of his
ships to overtake the fleet and beg Eurymedon to return to succour
him.

Siege of   The object of the Lacedaemonians was to blockade the hill of
Pylos.   Pylos by land and sea, and to prevent Athenian succours from
landing.   They probably established their camp on the north side of
Pylos, so that no ships entering the bay of Buphras could bring help
to the fort.   They were moreover afraid that the Athenians might
use the island of Sphacteria as a basis for military operations, and
accordingly Epitadas occupied Sphacteria with 420 Spartans and
their attendant Helots.   It would have been easy to block the
narrow entrance to the bay between Pylos and the island ; but there
was little use in doing so, as the Athenian ships would be able
to enter by the ingress at the south of the island, a passage about
three-quarters of a mile wide—far too wide to block with so small
a fleet.

Attack on   The Lacedaemonians then prepared to attack the place, before
Pylos   help could come to the Athenians.   Demosthenes posted the greater
part of his force to guard the northern line of defence and the south-
eastern corner ; while he himself with sixty hoplites and some
archers took his stand on the edge of the south-western shore, which
though rocky and perilous was the spot where the enemy had the
best prospect of effecting a landing.   Thrasymelidas was the name
of the Spartan admiral.   He had forty-three ships, which he brought

---

[1] Jowett's translation.

up in relays, the crews fighting and resting by turns. The great danger was that of running the vessels on reefs. Brasidas who commanded one of the ships was the leading spirit. " Be not sparing of timber," he cried to those who seemed to draw back from the rocks ; "the enemy has built a fortress in your country. Perish the ships, and force a landing." But in trying to disembark he was wounded and lost his shield. It was washed ashore and set up in the trophy which the Athenians afterwards erected. The Spartan attack which was renewed on two subsequent days was repelled.   *It repelled.* was a singular turn of fortune, says Thucydides,[1] which drove the Athenians to repel the Lacedaemonians, who were attacking them by sea from the Lacedaemonian coast, and the Lacedaemonians to fight for a landing on their own soil, now hostile to them, in the face of the Athenians. For in those days it was the great glory of the Lacedaemonians to be an inland people distinguished for their military prowess, and of the Athenians to be a nation of sailors and the first naval power in Hellas.

The fleet from Zacynthus, now augmented to fifty ships by some *Arrival of* reinforcements, at length arrived. But finding the shores of the bay *Athenian* of Buphras and the island of Sphacteria occupied, they withdrew for *fleet.* the night to the isle of Prote which was some miles distant. The next morning they returned, determined to sail into the harbour, if the enemy did not come out to meet them. The Lacedaemonians were preparing their ships for action, evidently intending to fight in the bay. The Athenians therefore rowed in by both entrances ; some of *Battle* the enemy's vessels which were able to come out to meet them were *in the* captured ; and a tremendous struggle ensued close to the shore. *harbour.* The Athenians were tying the empty beached ships to their own and endeavouring to drag them away, the Lacedaemonians dashed into the sea and were pulling them back. The Lacedaemonians knew that, if they lost their ships, the party on the island of Sphacteria would be cut off. Most of the empty ships were saved ; but the fleet was so far damaged and outnumbered that the Athenians were able to blockade Sphacteria.

The interest of the story now passes from Pylos to Sphacteria. *Second* The blockade of Demosthenes and his Athenians in Pylos by the *stage of the* Spartans has changed into a blockade of Epitadas and his Spartans *episode :* in Sphacteria by the Athenians. The tidings of this change in the *blockade of* situation caused grave alarm at Sparta and some of the ephors came *Sphac-* themselves to see what measures could be taken. They decided *teria.* that nothing could be done for the relief of the island, and obtained from the Athenian generals a truce for the purpose of sending

---

[1] Jowett's translation.

Truce. ambassadors to Athens to ask for peace. The terms of this truce were as follows : [1]—

The Lacedaemonians shall deliver into the hands of the Athenians at Pylos the ships in which they fought, and shall also bring thither and deliver over any other ships of war which are in Laconia ; and they shall make no assault upon the fort either by sea or land. The Athenians shall permit the Lacedaemonians on the mainland to send to those on the island a fixed quantity of kneaded flour, viz. two Attic quarts of barleymeal for each man, and a pint of wine, and also a piece of meat ; for an attendant half these quantities ; they shall send them into the island under the inspection of the Athenians, and no vessel shall sail in by stealth. The Athenians shall guard the island as before, but not land, and shall not attack the Peloponnesian forces by land or sea. If either party violate this agreement in any particular, however slight, the truce is to be at an end. The agreement is to last until the Lacedaemonian ambassadors return from Athens, and the Athenians are to convey them thither and bring them back in a trireme. When they return, the truce is to be at an end, and the Athenians are to restore the ships in the same condition in which they received them.

Athens rejects Spartan proposals of peace. In accordance with these terms, sixty ships were handed over and the ambassadors went to Athens. They professed the readiness of Sparta to make peace and pleaded for generous treatment on the part of Athens. At heart most of the Athenians were probably desirous of peace. But the Assembly was under the influence of Cleon, and he, as the opponent of Nicias and the peace-party, urged the Athenians to propose terms which could hardly be accepted. It might seem indeed an exceptionally favourable moment to attempt to undo the humiliation of the Thirty Years' Peace, and win back some of the possessions which had been lost twenty years ago. Not only Nisaea and Pagae, the harbours of the Megarid, but Achaea and Troezen, were demanded as the purchase of the lives of the Spartans in Sphacteria. The embassy returned to Pylos disappointed, and the truce came to an end. But the Athenians refused to give back the sixty ships, on the pretext of some slight infraction of the truce on the part of the Lacedaemonians.

Protracted blockade. The blockade proved a larger and more difficult matter than the Athenians had hoped. Reinforced by twenty more triremes from Athens, they lay round the island, both in the bay, and, except when the wind was too high, on the seaside ; and two ships kept continually cruising round in opposite directions. But their vigilance was eluded, and Sphacteria was secretly supplied with provisions.

---

[1] Jowett's translation of Thucydides.

Large sums were offered to any who succeeded in conveying meal, wine, or cheese to the island ; and Helots, who did such service, were rewarded with freedom. When a strong wind from the west or north drove the Athenian ships into the bay, the daring crews of provision-boats beat recklessly into the difficult landing-places on the seaside. Moreover some skilful divers managed to reach the shores of the island,—drawing skins with poppy-seed mixed with honey, and pounded linseed. But this device was soon discovered and prevented.

And besides the difficulty of rendering the blockade complete in a high wind, the maintenance of it was extremely unpleasant. As there was no proper anchorage, the crews were obliged to take their meals on land by turns,—generally in the south part of Sphacteria, which was not occupied by the Spartans. And they depended for their supply of water on one well, which was in the fort of Pylos. The supply of food was deficient,—for it had to be conveyed round the Peloponnesus. At home the Athenians were disappointed at the protraction of the siege, and grew impatient. They were sorry that *Impatience at Athens.* they had declined the overtures of the Lacedaemonians, and there was a reaction of feeling against Cleon. That statesman took the bold course of denying the reports from Pylos, and said—with a pointed allusion to the strategos Nicias—that if the Generals were men they would sail to the island and capture the garrison. "If I were commander," he added, "I would do it myself." The scene which follows is described in one of the rare passages where the most reserved of all historians condescends to display a little political animosity. Seeing that the people were murmuring at Cleon, Nicias stood up and offered, on the part of his colleagues, to give Cleon any force he asked for and let him try. Cleon—says Thucydides [1]—at first imagined that the offer of Nicias was only a pretence and was willing to go ; but finding that he was in earnest, he tried to back out and said that not he but Nicias was general. He was now alarmed, for he never imagined that Nicias would go so far as to give up his place to him. Again Nicias bade him take the command of the expedition against Pylos, which he formally gave up to him in the presence of the Assembly. And the more Cleon *Cleon sent* declined the proffered command and tried to retract what he had *as com-* said, so much the more the multitude, as their manner is, urged *mander to* Nicias to resign and shouted to Cleon that he should sail. At *Pylos.* length, not knowing how to escape from his own words, he undertook the expedition and, coming forward, said that he was not afraid of the Lacedaemonians and that he would sail without withdrawing

---

[1] Jowett's translation, to the end of the paragraph.

a single man from the city, if he were allowed to have the Lemnian and Imbrian forces now at Athens, the auxiliaries from Aenus who were targeteers, and four hundred archers from other places. With these and with the troops already at Pylos he gave his word that he would either bring the Lacedaemonians alive or kill them on the spot. His vain words moved the Athenians to laughter; nevertheless the wiser sort of men were pleased when they reflected that of two good things they could not fail to obtain one—either there would be an end of Cleon, which they would have greatly preferred, or, if they were disappointed, he would put the Lacedaemonians into their hands.

The story is almost too good to be true. But whether Cleon desired the command or had it thrust upon him against his will, his words which moved the Athenians to laughter were fully approved by the event. He chose Demosthenes as his colleague; and, invested with the command by a formal vote of the Assembly, he immediately set sail with special light-armed troops.

Nature of Sphacteria. In the meantime Demosthenes, wishing like Cleon to bring matters to an issue, was meditating an attack upon Sphacteria. This desert island is about two miles and three-quarters long. At the northern extremity rises a height, higher than the acropolis of Pylos over against it, and on the east side descending, a sheer cliff, into the water of the bay. Some of the Spartans had naturally occupied the summit, but the chief encampment of their small force was in the centre of the island, close to the only well; and an outpost was set on a hill farther to the south. An assault was difficult not only because the landing-places on both sides were bad, but because the island was covered with close bush, which gave the Spartans who knew the ground a great advantage. Demosthenes had experienced in Aetolia the difficulties of fighting in a wood. But one day, when some Athenians were taking their noonday meal *Burning of the wood.* on the south shore of the island, the wood was accidentally kindled, and, a wind arising, the greater part of the bush was burnt. It was then possible to see more clearly the position and the numbers of the Lacedaemonians, and, when Cleon arrived, the plan of attack *Athenian forces land on Sphacteria.* was matured. Embarking at night all their hoplites in a few ships, Cleon and Demosthenes landed before dawn on the south of the island, partly on the seaside and partly on the harbour side, near the spot where the Lacedaemonians had their outpost. The whole number of troops that landed must have been nearly 14,000, against which the Spartans had only 420 hoplites and perhaps as many Helots. And yet a high military authority described the Athenian enterprise as mad. The truth seems to be that it could hardly have succeeded if the Spartan commander had disposed his forces to the best advantage, posting watches at all possible landing-places and organising a proper system of signals.

The outpost was at once overpowered, and light-armed troops *The attack.* advanced towards the main Spartan encampment, along a high ridge on the harbour side of the island. Others moved along the low shore on the seaside; so that when the main body of the Spartans saw their outpost cut to pieces and began to move southward against the Athenian hoplites, they were harassed on either side by the archers and targeteers, whom, encumbered by their arms and in difficult ground, they were unable to pursue. And the attacks of these light-armed troops, as they grew more fully conscious of their own superiority in numbers and saw that their enemy was growing weary, became more formidable. Clouds of dust arose from the *Distress* newly burnt wood—so Thucydides reports the scene from the vivid *of the* description of an eye-witness—and there was no possibility of a *Spartans.* man's seeing what was before him, owing to the showers of arrows and stones hurled by their assailants which were flying amid the dust. And now the Lacedaemonians began to be sorely distressed, for their felt cuirasses did not protect them against the arrows, and the points of the javelins broke off where they struck them. They were at their wits' end, not being able to see out of their eyes or to hear the word of command, which was drowned by the cries of the enemy. Destruction was staring them in the face, and they had no means or hope of deliverance.[1]

At length it was determined that the only chance lay in retreating *Spartan* to the high hill at the north of the island. About a mile had to be *retreat to* traversed to the foot of the hill; but the ground was very difficult. *the hill* The endurance and discipline of the Spartan soldiers was con- *(now* spicuously displayed in this slow retreat which was accomplished, *Mt. Elias).* with but a small loss, under a burning sun, by men who were suffering from thirst and weary with the distress of an unequal battle. When they had reached and climbed the hill the battle assumed another aspect. On the high ground, no longer exposed on their flanks, and finding a defence in an old Cyclopean wall, which can still be traced round the summit, the Lacedaemonians were able to repel their assailants; and they were determined not to surrender. At length a Messenian captain came to the Athenian generals and *The* said that he knew a path by which he thought he could take some *Messenian* light-armed troops round to the rear of the Spartans. The hill on *plan.* its eastern side falls precipitously into the bay; but the fall is not direct. The summit slopes down into a hollow, about fifty yards wide, and then the hill rises again into the cliff which falls sheer into

[1] Jowett's translation.

the water.   But at the south end of the cliff there is a narrow gorge
by which it is possible to climb up into the hollow.   Embarking in a
boat on the eastern side of the island, the Messenians reached the
foot of the gorge and climbed up with difficulty, unseen by the
Spartans, who neglected what seemed an impracticable part of the
hill, and then ascending the summit suddenly appeared above the
Lacedaemonians, who were ranged in a semicircle below on the
western and northern slopes.   The Athenians now invited the defenders to capitulate, and with the consent of their friends on the
mainland they laid down their arms.   Two hundred and ninety-
two, of the four hundred and twenty, survived, and were brought to
Athens.   The high opinion which the Greek world held of the
Spartan spirit was expressed in the universal amazement which was
caused by this surrender.   Men had thought that nothing could induce the Lacedaemonians to give up their arms.

   Cleon had performed his promise ; he brought back the captives
within twenty days.   The success was of political rather than
military importance.   The Athenians could indeed ravage Lacedaemonian territory from Pylos, but it was a greater thing that they had
in the prisoners a security against future invasions of Attica and
a means of making an advantageous peace when they chose.   It
was the most important success gained in the war, and it was a
brilliant example of the valuable successes that can be gained, as it
were accidentally, in following that system of strategy which Pericles
had laid down at the beginning of the war.   This stroke of luck
increased the influence of Cleon.   It was necessary for Nicias to
do something to maintain his reputation.   Shortly afterwards he led
an army into the Corinthian territory, gained a partial victory at
Solygea, and then went on to the peninsula of Methone, between
Troezen and Epidaurus.   He built a wall across the isthmus and
left a garrison in Methone.   In the following year, he made the
more important acquisition of the island of Cythera, from which he
was able to make descents upon Laconia.   The loss of Cythera was
in itself more serious for Sparta than the loss of Pylos ; but owing
to the attendant circumstances the earlier event made far greater
stir.   The Athenians had now three bases of operation in the Peloponnesus—Pylos, Cythera, and Methone.

425 B.C.
Activity of Nicias.

424 B.C.
Capture of Cythera.

Victory *of Paeonius.*

   To none was the discomfit of the Spartans in Messenia sweeter
than to the Messenian exiles who had borne their part in the work
of that memorable day.   At Olympia there is a figure of Victory,
hovering aloft in the air, amid wind-blown drapery, while an eagle
flies below her.   It is the work of the sculptor Paeonius, and it was
dedicated by the Messenians in the Altis of Zeus, with part of the
spoil they stripped from the hated usurpers of their land.

FIG. 124.—The Nike of Paeonius (Olympia).

Sect 11. Athenian Capture of Nisaea

In each of the first seven years of the war, Attica was invaded, except twice ; on one occasion, the attack on Plataea had taken the place of the incursion into Attica, and, on another, the Peloponnesian army was hindered by earthquakes from advancing beyond the isthmus. Every year by way of reply the Athenians invaded the Megarid twice, in spring and in autumn. The capture of Pylos affected both these annual events. The invasion of Attica was discontinued, because Athens held the Spartan hostages ; and the elation of the Athenians at their success induced them to undertake a bolder enterprise against Megara.

Minoa, now a hill on the mainland but then an island, lay at the entrance to the harbour of Nisaea. It was separated from Nisaea by a narrow channel, protected by two projecting towers. Nicias had destroyed these towers, three years before, and had fortified Minoa, so as to blockade completely the port of Nisaea. The Megarians then depended entirely on the port of Pagae and their communications with the Crisaean Gulf. They were hard pressed ; their distress was vividly pourtrayed in the comedy of the *Acharnians* which was put on the stage two years later. The situation became
almost intolerable when a domestic sedition led to the expulsion of a small party who seized Pagae and cut off Megara from importing food on that side too. It became a question between allowing the exiles to return or submitting to Athens. Those who knew that the return of their rivals from Pagae would mean their own doom opened secret negotiations with Athens, and offered to betray Megara and Nisaea. The Long Walls and Nisaea were held by a Peloponnesian garrison. The generals Hippocrates and Demosthenes organised the enterprise. While a force of 4000 hoplites and 600 horse marched overland by Eleusis, the generals sailed to Minoa. When night fell, they crossed to the mainland. There was a gate in the eastern wall close to the spot where it joined the fortification of Nisaea, and near the gate there was a hollow out of which earth to make bricks had been dug. Here Hippocrates and 600 hoplites concealed themselves, while Demosthenes, with some light-armed Plataeans and a band of the youthful Peripoloi or Patrollers of Attica, took up a position still nearer the gate, in a sacred enclosure of the war-god, Enyalios. The conspirators had long matured their plan for admitting the Athenians. As no boat could openly leave the harbour, owing to the occupation of Minoa, they had easily obtained permission of the commander of the Peloponnesian garrison to carry out through this gate a small boat on a cart at night, for the alleged purpose of

privateering. They used to convey the boat to the sea along the ditch which surrounded Nisaea, and, after a midnight row, return before dawn, and re-enter the Long Walls by the same gate. This became a regular practice, so that they carried out the boat without exciting any suspicion, on the night fixed for executing the conspiracy. When the boat returned, the gate was opened, and Demosthenes, who had been watching for the moment, leapt forward and forced his way in, assisted by the Megarians. They kept the gate open till Hippocrates arrived with his hoplites, and, when these were inside, the Long Walls were easily secured, the garrison retreating into Nisaea. In the morning the main body of the Athenians arrived. A scheme for the betrayal of Megara had been concerted. The conspirators urged their fellow-citizens to sally forth and do battle with the Athenians ; they had secretly arranged that the Athenians should rush in, and had anointed themselves with oil, as a mark by which they should be known and spared in the assault. But their political opponents, informed of the scheme, immediately rushed to the gates and declared decisively that they should not be opened ; the battle would have to be first fought inside. The delay apprised the Athenians that their friends had been baffled, and they set about blockading Nisaea. Their energy was such that in two days the circumvallation was practically completed, and the garrison, in want of food (for their supplies were derived from Megara), capitulated. Thus the Long Walls, which they had built themselves, and the port of Nisaea had passed again into the hands of the Athenians. They were not, however, destined to take the city on the hill. The Spartan general Brasidas, who was recruiting in the north-east regions of the Peloponnesus for an expedition to Thrace, hastened to the relief of Megara and was joined by forces from Corinth and Boeotia, to whom the defence of Megara was vital. An indecisive skirmish took place ; the Athenians did not care to risk a battle and they resolved to be content with the acquisition of Nisaea. Soon afterwards there was a revolution in Megara. The exiles from Pagae were received back ; they soon got the power into their hands and murdered their enemies. A narrow oligarchical constitution was established. The new order of things, says Thucydides, lasted a very long time, considering the small number of its authors.

SECT. 12. ATHENS FAILS IN BOEOTIA

The recovery of Nisaea which had been lost by the Thirty Years' Peace was a solid success, and it seemed to the ambitious hopes of the two generals who had achieved it the first step in the recovery of all the former conquests of their city. Hippocrates and Demosthenes induced Athens to strive to win back what she had lost at Coronea. But Boeotia was not like Megara ; and an attempt on Boeotia was an unwise reversion to the early continental policy of Pericles, which Pericles had himself definitely abandoned. The dream of a second Oenophyta was far less likely to come true than the threat of a second Coronea. And the enterprise was a departure from the Periclean strategy, of which Nicias was the chief exponent, and it is significant that Nicias took no part in it. Moreover at this moment Athens, as we shall see, ought to have concentrated her forces on the defence of her Thracian possessions which were in grave jeopardy. The Boeotian, like the Megarian, plan was formed in concert with native malcontents who wished to overthrow the oligarchies in the cities, to establish democratical governments, and probably dissolve the Boeotian Confederacy. At this time the Confederacy was governed by eleven Boeotarchs, four of whom were chosen by Thebes, and a federal council representing the various districts of Boeotia and divided into four panels.

Plan for invading Boeotia.

The new Boeotian plan, in which Demosthenes was now concerned, did not involve such extensive operations and combinations as that which he had conceived when he invaded Aetolia. But the two plans resembled each other in so far as each involved operations from the Crisaean Gulf. Demosthenes, having sailed to Naupactus and gathered a force of Acarnanians, was to go on to secure Siphae, the port of Thespiae, on the shore of a promontory beneath Mount Helicon. On the same day, the Athenian army under Hippocrates was to enter Boeotia on the north-east and seize the temple of Apollo at Delium, which stood on the sea-coast over against the Lelantine plain in Euboea. At the same time Chaeronea, the extreme west town of the land, was to be seized by domestic conspirators. Thus on three sides the Boeotian government was to be threatened ; and the same day was fixed for the three attacks. But the scheme was betrayed by a Phocian, and frustrated by the Boeotarchs, who occupied Siphae and Chaeronea with strong forces, and made a general levy of the Boeotians to oppose the army of Hippocrates. It mattered little that Demosthenes made a mistake about the day fixed for the attack ; he found himself opposed by a Boeotian force and could only retire. None of the internal movements in the Boeotian cities, on which the Athenians had counted, took place.

Battle of Delium, 424 B.C.

Hippocrates, however, had time to reach and fortify Delium. He had a force of 7000 hoplites and over 20,000 light-armed troops. A trench, with a strong rampart and palisade, was drawn round the temple ; and at noon on the fifth day from their departure from Athens the work was completed. The army then left Delium,

to return home.   When they crossed the frontier and entered
the Athenian territory of Oropus, at about a mile from Delium,
the hoplites halted, to wait for Hippocrates, who had remained
behind to give final directions to the garrison of the temple ;
the light-armed troops proceeded on their way to Athens.   The
hoplites were interrupted in their rest by a message from Hippocrates,
ordering them to form instantly in array of battle, as the enemy
were upon them.   The Boeotian forces had been concentrated at
Tanagra, about five miles from Delium ; and they had been persuaded by Pagondas, one of the Theban Boeotarchs, to follow and
attack the Athenians in their retreat although they had left Boeotia.
After a rapid march, Pagondas halted where a hill concealed him
from the view of the Athenians and drew up his army.   It consisted
of 7000 hoplites—the same number as that of the enemy—1000
cavalry, and over 10,000 light-armed men.   The Thebans occupied the
right wing, in the unique formation of a mass twenty-five shields deep ;
the other contingents varied in depth.   The Athenian line was
formed with the uniform and regular depth of eight shields.
Hippocrates had arrived and was moving along the lines encouraging
his men, when the enemy, who had for some time been visible on the
crest of the hill, raised the Paean and charged down.   The extreme
parts of the wings never met, for watercourses lay between them.
But the rest pushed shield against shield and fought fiercely.   On
the right the Athenians were victorious, but on the left they could
not sustain the enormous pressure of the massed Theban force,
especially as the Thebans were probably man for man stronger than
the Athenians through a laborious athletic training.   But even the
victory on the right was made of none effect through the sudden
appearance of a squadron of cavalry, which Pagondas, seeing the
situation, had sent unobserved round the hill.   The Athenians
thought it was the vanguard of another army and fled.   Hippocrates
was slain and the army completely dispersed.

The battle of Delium confirmed the verdict of Coronea.

The Boeotians were left masters of the field, but Delium itself *Subsequent*
was still held by the invader.   This led to a curious negotiation. *negotia-*
The Athenians demanded their dead, and the Boeotians refused *tions.*
permission to take them unless they evacuated the temple of Apollo.
Now if there was an international custom which was universally
recognised among the Greeks, even among the barbarous Aetolians,
it was the obligation of the victor to allow his defeated opponents to
remove and bury their dead, unconditionally.   This custom had the
sanction of religious feeling and was seldom violated.   But in this
case the Boeotians had a pretext for departing from the usual
practice.   They alleged that the Athenians had on their side

violated the laws of Hellenic warfare by seizing and fortifying the sanctuary of Delium and living in it, as if it were unconsecrated,— using even the sacred water. There seems little doubt that the conduct of the Boeotians was a greater departure from recognised custom than the conduct of the Athenians. The herald of the Athenians made what seems a foolish reply, to the effect that Delium having been occupied by the Athenians was now part of Attic soil, and that they showed the customary respect for the temple, so far as was possible in the circumstances. " You cannot tell us to quit Boeotia," he said, " for the garrison of Delium is not in Boeotia." The Boeotians made an appropriate answer to the quibble : " If you are in Boeotia, take what is yours ; if you are in your own land, do as you like." The dead were not surrendered, and the Boeotians *Capture of* betook themselves to the blockade of Delium. They took the place *Delium,* by a curious device. They sawed in two and hollowed out a great *17 days* beam, which they joined together again very exactly, like a flute, *after the* *battle.* and suspended a vessel by chains at the end of the beam ; the iron mouth of a bellows directed downwards into the vessel was attached to the beam, of which a great part was itself overlaid with iron. This machine they brought up from a distance on carts to various points of the rampart where vine stems and wood had been most extensively used, and when it was quite near the wall they applied a large bellows to their own end of the beam and blew through it. The blast, prevented from escaping, passed into the vessel, which contained burning coals and sulphur and pitch ; these made a huge flame and set fire to the rampart, so that no one could remain upon it. The garrison took flight and the fort was taken.[1] The Boeotians no longer refused to surrender the dead, who included rather less than 1000 hoplites.

SECT. 13. THE WAR IN THRACE. ATHENS LOSES AMPHIPOLIS

The defeat of Delium eclipsed the prestige of Athens, but did not seriously impair her strength. Yet it was a fatal year ; and a much greater blow, entailing a permanent loss, was dealt her in her Thracian dominion.

The war in Thrace was always complicated by the neighbourhood of the kingdoms of Thrace and Macedonia. Before the fall of Potidaea the Athenians had formed an alliance with Sitalces, king of *The* Thrace, and made his son Sadocus an Athenian citizen. The realm *Thracian* of Sitalces extended from the Strymon to the Euxine, its coast-line *kingdom.*

[1] The description of the engine is a literal version of that of Thucydides. Jowett's translation.

began at Abdera and ended at the mouth of the Ister.   His revenue
of tribute both from Greek towns and barbarians amounted, in the
reign of his successor, to more than 400 talents—counting only what *£108,000.*
was paid in the shape of coin.   The alliance with Athens seems to
have lasted till the king's death.   An Athenian ambassador from
Thrace, in the *Acharnians* of Aristophanes, reports to the Assembly : *425 B.C.*

> We passed our time
> In drinking with Sitalces.   He's your friend,
> Your friend and lover, if ever there was one,
> And writes the name of Athens on his walls.[1]

Perdiccas, the shifty king of Macedonia, played a double game *Double*
between Athens and Sparta.   At one time he helped the Chalcidians *dealings of*
against Athens, at another he sided with Athens against her revolted *Mace-*
allies.   [In 429 combined operations had been planned between *donia.*
Athens and Sitalces.   Sitalces was to lead the Thracian tribesmen
against Perdiccas and to help in the reduction of the Chalcidic rebels.
A huge Thracian army was mustered and invaded Macedonia.   The
territory was laid waste, but for some reason which Thucydides does
not adequately explain the Athenian force did not arrive, and the
Thracians withdrew.]   Throughout all changes of fortune, the city of
Methone, situated to the south of the mouth of the Haliacmon, held
to Athens with unshaken fidelity, though the varying relations between
Athens and Perdiccas must have seriously affected the welfare of the
Methonaeans.   Some decrees relating to Methone have been pre- *Methone.*
served on a marble, adorned with a relief of the Athenian Demos
seated, stretching out his hand to the Demos of Methone, who stands
accompanied by a dog.

Perdiccas and the Chalcidians (of Olynthus) feared that the *Chal-*
success of Pylos might be followed by increased activity of the *cidians and*
Athenians in Thrace, and they sent an embassy to Sparta, request- *Macedonia*
ing help, and expressing a wish that Brasidas might be the com- *appeal to*
mander of whatever auxiliary force should be sent.   It was wise *Sparta.*
policy for Sparta to threaten her rival in Thrace at this juncture,
though the prospect of any abiding success was faint.   No Spartans
went, but 700 Helots were armed as hoplites ; the government was
glad to take the opportunity of removing another portion of this
dangerous element in the population.   Having obtained some
Peloponnesian recruits and having incidentally, as we have already
seen, saved Megara, Brasidas marched northward to the new colony
of Heraclea.

Brasidas was a Spartan by mistake.   He had nothing in common

---

[1] Frere.

Character of Brasidas. with his fellows, except personal bravery, which was the least of his virtues. He had a restless energy and spirit of enterprise, which received small encouragement from the slow and hesitating authorities of his country. He had an oratorical ability which distinguished him above the Lacedaemonians, who were notoriously unready of speech. He was free from political prejudices, and always showed himself tolerant, just, and moderate in dealing with political questions. Besides this, he was simple and straightforward ; men knew that they could trust his word implicitly. But the quality which most effectually contributed to his brilliant career and perhaps most strikingly belied his Spartan origin was his power of winning popularity abroad and making himself personally liked by strangers. In Greece, the Spartan abroad was a proverb for insolence and misbehaviour. Brasidas shone out, on a dark background, by his frank and winning manners.

Brasidas at Acanthus. His own tact and rapid movements, as well as the influence of Perdiccas, enabled Brasidas to march through Thessaly, which was by no means well disposed to the Lacedaemonians. When he reached Macedonia, Perdiccas required his assistance against Arrhabaeus, the king of the Lyncestians, in Upper Macedonia. Brasidas was impatient to reach Chalcidice, and he contrived to make a separate arrangement with Arrhabaeus and abstained from invading Lyncestis, to the disappointment of Perdiccas. He then marched against Acanthus, situated on the base of the peninsula of Acte. The mass of the Acanthians were perfectly content with the position of their city as a member of the Athenian Confederacy ; they had no grievance against Athens ; and they were unwilling to receive the overtures of Brasidas. They were, however, induced by a small party to admit Brasidas alone into the city, and give him a hearing in the Assembly. From his lips the Acanthians learned the Lacedaemonian programme, and Thucydides has given the substance of what he said. " We declared at the beginning of the war that we were taking up arms to protect the liberties of Hellas against Athens ; and for this purpose we are here now. You have a high repute for power and wisdom, and therefore a refusal from you will retard the good cause. Every city which joins me will retain her autonomy ; the Lacedaemonians have pledged themselves to me on this point by solemn oaths. And I have not come to be the tool of a faction, or to enslave the many to the few ; in that case we should be committing an act worse than the oppression of the Athenians. If you refuse and say that I have no right to thrust an alliance on a people against its will, I will ravage your land and force you to consent. And for two reasons I am justified in doing so. The tribute you pay to Athens is a direct and material injury to Sparta, for it contributes to strengthen her foe; and secondly, your example may prevent others from embracing freedom." When Brasidas retired, there was a long debate; much was said on both sides. The manner of Brasidas had produced a favourable impression; and the fear of losing the vintage was a powerful motive with many for acceding to his demand. The vote was taken secretly and the majority determined to detach themselves from Athens, though they had no practical grievance and were not enthusiastic for the change. Sparta's natural friends here as in other cities were the oligarchs.

Acanthus was an Andrian colony, and its action led to the adhesion of two other Andrian colonies, Stagira and Argilus; and the relations which Brasidas established with Argilus led to the capture of the most important of all Athenian posts in Thrace, and among the most important in the whole Athenian empire, the city of Amphipolis. This place, of which the foundation has been already recorded, had diminished the importance of Argilus and roused the jealousy of the Argilians; although some of the colonists were of Argilian origin. The coming of Brasidas offered Argilus an opportunity, for which she had been waiting, against the Athenians of Amphipolis. After a cold wintry night march, Brasidas found the Bridge of the Strymon defended only by a small guard, which he *(See above,* easily overpowered. Amphipolis was completely unprepared, but *p. 381.)* Brasidas did not venture to attack the city at once; he expected the gates to be opened by conspirators within, and meanwhile he made himself master of the territory.

That a place of such first-rate importance as Amphipolis should *Revolt of* be found unprepared at a time when an energetic enemy like Brasidas *Amphi-* was actively engaged against other Athenian cities in the neighbour- *polis* hood seemed a criminal negligence on the part of the two Strategoi to *(424 B.C.).* whom defence of the Thracian interests of Athens was entrusted. These were Thucydides, the son of Olorus, and Eucles. It was *Negligence* inexcusable in Eucles, who was in Amphipolis, to leave the Bridge *of Thucy-* without an adequate garrison; and it was considered culpable of *dides the* Thucydides, who had mining interests in the district, not to have *historian.* moved up the Athenian squadron from the island of Thasos. A message was sent at once to Thucydides; that officer hastened back with seven triremes and reached the mouth of the Strymon in the evening of the same day. But in the meantime Brasidas had offered the inhabitants of Amphipolis such easy terms that they were accepted. He promised every citizen who chose to remain equal political rights, without any loss of property; while all who preferred to go were allowed five days to remove their possessions. Had the Amphipolitans known how near Thucydides was, they would probably have declined to surrender. Thucydides arrived just too late. But he preserved Eion, at the mouth of the river, and repelled an attack of Brasidas.

The true blame for the loss of Amphipolis probably rests not on the General, who was in a very difficult position, but on the Athenians, who, instead of making adequate provision for the defence of Thrace, were misled by the new strategy of Demosthenes into the unsuccessful expedition to Boeotia. It must be remembered that Thucydides was responsible for the safety of the whole coast of Chalcidice and Thrace ; that at any moment he might be summoned to defend any part of it from Potidaea to the Chersonese ; that therefore either Eion or Thasos was a suitable centre for his headquarters ; and that Eion had the disadvantage of having no harbour.

his banish-ment.

It may be that we are indebted to the fall of Amphipolis for the great history of the war. The Athenians accused the neglect of their generals, as having cost them one of their most valuable possessions. Thucydides was sentenced to banishment, and it is probable that Cleon, to whom he bore no good-will, was instrumental in drawing down upon him a punishment which possibly was not deserved. But in his exile the discredited general became the greatest of Greek historians. If he had remained at Athens and continued his official career he might not have concentrated his whole mind on his history. By travelling in foreign lands, among the enemies of Athens and in neutral states, Thucydides gained a large knowledge of the Hellenic world and wrote from a wider point of view than he could have done if he had only had an Athenian experience. "Associating," he says himself, "with both sides, with the Peloponnesians quite as much as with the Athenians, because of my exile, I was thus enabled to watch quietly the course of events." Judged in this way, the fall of Amphipolis, a great loss to Athens, may have been a great gain to the world.

Reduction of Acte.

Having secured the Strymon, Brasidas retraced his steps and subdued the small towns on the high eastern tongue of Chalcidice. The Andrian Sane and another place held out, and their obscurity saved them. Brasidas hastened on to gain possession of Torone, the strongest city of Sithonia. A small party of the citizens invited and expected him ; but the rest of the inhabitants and the Athenian garrison knew nothing of his coming until the place was in his hands. Torone was a hill city by the sea. Besides its walls, it had the protection of a fort on a height which rose out of the water and was connected with the city by a narrow neck of land. This fortress, known as Lecythus, was occupied by an Athenian garrison. Brasidas halted within about half a mile from the city before daybreak. Seven bold soldiers, light-armed and carrying daggers, were secretly introduced by the conspirators. They killed the sentinels on the top

Capture of Torone, 424-3 B.C.

of the hill, and then broke down a postern gate, and undid the bars of the great gate near the market-place, in order that the men without might rush in from two sides. A hundred targeteers who had drawn near to the walls dashed in first, and when a signal was given Brasidas followed with the rest. The surprise was complete. Fifty Athenian hoplites were sleeping in the agora; a few were cut down; most escaped to the fort of Lecythus, which was held for some days and then captured.

Brasidas called an assembly of the Toronaeans, and spoke to them in words which sounded strange indeed falling from the mouth of an Hellenic victor. He told them that he had not come to injure the city or the citizens; that those who had not aided in the conspiracy to admit him would be treated on a perfect equality with the others; that the Lacedaemonians had never suffered any wrong from Torone; and that he did not think the worse of those who opposed him.

Sect. 14. Negotiations for Peace

In the meantime the Athenians had taken no measures to check *Athenian* the victorious winter-campaign of Brasidas. Their inactivity was *inactivity.* due to two causes. The disaster of Delium had disheartened them, and rendered the citizens unwilling to undertake fresh toil in Thrace. In Grecian history we must steadfastly keep in view that we are reading about citizen soldiers, not about professional soldiers; and that the temper of the time, whether of confidence or dismay, modifies all the calculations of military and political prudence. Secondly, the peace party, especially represented by the generals Nicias and Laches, took advantage of this depression to work in the direction of peace. The possession of the Spartan captives gave the means of coming to terms with Sparta at any moment, but it was clear that they could not now conclude a peace on such favourable terms as would have been possible a year before. If an able statesman, like Pericles, had at this time possessed the confidence and guided the counsels of the Athenians, he would have persuaded them to postpone all thoughts of peace until the success of Brasidas had been decisively checked and the prestige of Athens in some degree retrieved. This was obviously the true policy, which would have enabled Athens to win the full advantage of the captives of Sphacteria. It was a policy which Cleon, a far abler politician than any of his opponents, must have preached loudly in the Assembly. But the Athenians were not in a mood to weigh considerations of policy; they were swayed by the feelings of the hour, which were flattered by the arguments of the military experts; and they decisively inclined to peace.

Sparta desires peace.

The Lacedaemonians were more deliberately set on peace than the Athenians. Their anxiety to recover the Sphacterian captives increased, and on the other hand they desired to set a term to the career of Brasidas in Chalcidice. They wished to take advantage of the considerable successes he had already won, to extort favourable conditions from Athens before any defeat should undo or reverse his triumphs. Nor was the news of his exploits received at Sparta with unmixed feelings of pleasure. They were rather regarded with jealousy and distrust. The victories had not been won by an army of Spartan citizens, but by the brilliant un-Spartan qualities of Brasidas and a force of which the effectiveness entirely depended on its leader. Brasidas had broken through the fetters of Lacedaemonian method, and his fellow-citizens felt that he was a man of different fibre from themselves, and suspected and disliked him accordingly. Moreover the personal influence of king Pleistoanax was thrown weightily into the scale of peace. This king had been banished just before the Thirty Years' Peace, on the ground that he had taken bribes to spare Attica when he invaded it after the deliverance of Megara. He had lived for nearly twenty years in western Arcadia on the mountain of Lycaeon, beside the dread sanctuary of Zeus, of which it was told that whosoever entered it lost his shadow and died before the year was out. Even here Pleistoanax was afraid for his life. His house was half within the precincts, so that in case of danger he could retire into the sacred place without passing his door. But he had influence at Delphi, and whenever the Spartans consulted that oracle they were always bidden to take back into their own land the seed of the demi-god, the son of Zeus, or else they would have to plough with a silver share. The Lacedaemonians at length recalled him, and re-enthroned him as king with ancient and most solemn ceremonies. But his enemies now vexed him with the charge of having bribed the Pythian priestess to procure his recall. Pleistoanax conceived that such charges would fall to the ground if he satisfied the people by negotiating a permanent peace and restoring as speedily as possible the prisoners from their captivity in Athens to their impatient friends at home. And as a matter of fact, Sparta had everything to gain from making peace at once, unless she was prepared to adopt the Imperial policy of Athens, against which it had been hitherto her rôle to protest. Such a policy might for a time have met with some success if she had put her whole confidence in Brasidas, but must soon have been checked by the naval superiority of her rival.

One year's truce (March 423).

Pleistoanax and Nicias understood each other; and Nicias, a man of commonplace ability and possessed by one idea, played into the hands of Sparta. It was not, however, an easy matter to arrange the exact terms of a durable pacification, while it was important for Athens that the negotiation should be made before she experienced any further losses in Thrace. Accordingly the two states agreed on a truce for a year, which would give them time to arrange quietly and at leisure the conditions of a permanent peace. The truce and some of its conditions were suggested by Athens; the terms were drawn up at Sparta and accepted by the Spartan Assembly; and were then conveyed to Athens, where they were proposed for the acceptance of the Athenian Assembly by Laches. The clauses were the following: (1) Free access to the Delphic oracle was ensured to all. For Athens had been debarred from consulting it during the war. (2) Both parties guaranteed the protection of the treasures of Delphi. (3) During the truce both parties should keep what they had; the Athenians retaining Pylos, Cythera, Argolic Methone, Nisaea, and Minoa. (4) The Lacedaemonians were not to sail, even along their own coasts, in warships or in merchant vessels exceeding a certain size (twelve tons). (5) The free passage of envoys, for the purpose of arranging a peace, was provided for. (6) Neither party was to receive deserters; and (7) disputes, in case they arose, were to be decided by arbitration.

The truce was sworn to. But in the meantime an event hap-*Revolt of* pened in Chalcidice which was to disappoint the pacific calculations *Scione.* of the statesmen at Athens and Sparta. The city of Scione on the western prong of the Chalcidian fork revolted from Athens and invited Brasidas, much to that general's surprise. For it was far more hazardous for the towns on the peninsula of Pallene to defy the authority of Athens than for any others; since by the strong city of Potidaea, which stretched entirely across the narrow isthmus, they were isolated and as much exposed to the full force of Athenian power as if they had been islanders. The arrival of Brasidas and the words he spoke to them wound up the men of Scione to the highest pitch of enthusiasm; they set a golden crown on his head, as the liberator of Hellas, and their admiration for him personally was shown by casting garlands on him, as if he were a victorious athlete,—so great was his popularity.

At this point an Athenian and a Lacedaemonian commissioner arrived to announce the truce, which had in fact been concluded two days before Scione revolted. The Athenians refused to admit Scione to the benefit of the armistice until the authorities at home had been consulted. There was deep indignation at Athens when the news of the defection of Scione arrived; it was practically the rebellion of "islanders" relying on the land-power of Sparta. Cleon was able to take advantage of this exasperation and carry a decree that Scione should be destroyed and all the male inhabitants slain. This incident brings out in an interesting way the geographical difference between the three sea-girt promontories of Chalcidice as to their degrees of participation in the insular character. Acte, with its steep inhospitable shores, is far more continental than insular; Sithonia partakes of both natures more equally, is more strictly a half-island; Pallene is more an island than part of the mainland. And we see the political importance of such geographical differences. The loss of Scione produces an irritation at Athens which the loss of Torone could not inspire.

The revolt of Mende. The revolt of Scione was followed by that of the neighbouring town of Mende, and although this happened distinctly after the truce had been made, Brasidas did not hesitate to accept the alliance of Mende, his plea being that in certain points the Athenians themselves had broken the truce. The case of Mende differed from that of Scione; for the revolt was the doing not of the people but of an oligarchical faction. Brasidas was then obliged to join Perdiccas in another expedition against Arrhabaeus, king of the Lyncestians. The fact that the Macedonian monarch was contributing to the pay of the Peloponnesian army rendered it necessary for Brasidas to co-operate in an enterprise which was of no interest to the Greeks. Arrhabaeus was defeated in a battle, but a reinforcement of Illyrians came to his help, and the warlike reputation of Illyria was so great that their approach produced a panic among the Macedonians and *Perdiccas breaks with Brasidas.* the whole army of Perdiccas fled, leaving the small force of Brasidas to retreat as best it could. He was in great jeopardy, but effected his retreat successfully. The incident led to a breach between Brasidas and the Macedonians; Perdiccas changed sides once more, and proved his new friendship to Athens by preventing Lacedaemonian troops, which had been sent to join Brasidas, from crossing Thessaly.

The truce observed except in Thrace. Brasidas returned to Torone and found that an Athenian armament of fifty ships, under Nicias and Niceratus, had recovered Mende, and was besieging Scione. Everywhere else the truce was observed, and by tacit consent the hostilities in Thrace were not allowed to affect the rest of Greece. But it was inevitable that they should frustrate the purpose for which the truce had been concluded. It was impossible that negotiations with a view to the definitive peace should proceed in exactly the same way as had been originally contemplated; by the end of the year there was a marked change in public feeling at Athens and the influence of Cleon was again in the ascendant. If Nicias had played into the hands of Sparta, Brasidas had played into the hands of Cleon and effectually embarrassed the home government. His conduct first in regard to Scione and then in regard to Mende was indefensible and entirely

governed by personal considerations.   The gold crown of Scione
seems to have acted like a potent spell in arousing his ambition, and
he began to play a war-game of his own.   His policy was the more
unhappy, as he was perfectly aware that it was impossible to protect
the cities of Pallene against the fleets of their indignant mistress.
He effectually hindered the conclusion of peace, which his city
sincerely desired.   Brasidas and Cleon, Thucydides says, were the
chief opponents of the peace ; but while the motives of Brasidas
were purely personal, the policy of Cleon, whatever his motives may
have been, was statesmanlike.   He adopted the principle of Pericles
that Athens must maintain her empire unimpaired, and he saw that
this could not be done without energetic opposition to the progress
of Brasidas in Thrace.   The charge of Thucydides that Cleon desired
war because he could not so easily conceal his own dishonesty in
peace, does not carry the least conviction.   When the truce expired, *Summer*
Cleon was able to carry a resolution that an expedition should be *422 B.C.*
made to reconquer Amphipolis.   It does not appear whether he was
himself anxious for the command, in consequence of his previous
success at Pylos, or whether the opposition and lukewarmness of the
strategoi practically forced him into it.   But it is certain that all
possible difficulties were thrown in his way by Nicias and the peace
party, who in their hearts doubtless hoped for the complete failure of
his enterprise.

SECT. 15.   BATTLE OF AMPHIPOLIS AND PEACE OF NICIAS

Cleon set sail with thirty ships, bearing 1200 Athenian hoplites,
300 Athenian cavalry, as well as allies.   Taking some troops from
the force which was still blockading Scione, he gained a considerable
success at the outset by taking Torone and capturing the Lacedaemonian governor ; Brasidas arrived too late to relieve it.   Cleon
went on to the mouth of the Strymon and made Eion his headquarters,
intending to wait there until he had augmented his army by reinforcements from Thrace and Macedonia.

Not far from its mouth the stream of the Strymon expands into *Site of*
the lake Kerkinitis ; on narrowing again into its proper channel *Amphi-*
it is forced to bend to the westward in order to skirt a hill, and forms *polis.*
a great loop, before it disgorges its waters into the sea close to the
walls of Eion.   In this loop the high city of Amphipolis stood, water-
girt as its name implies,—the river serving as its natural defence, so
that it required artificial bulwarks only on the eastern side.   On the
right bank of the river, to the west of the town, rose the hill of
Cerdylion ; on the east were the heights of Pangaeus.   A ridge
joined Pangaeus with the hill of Amphipolis, and the wall of the

city crossed the ridge. The Strymon Bridge was outside the south-western extremity of the wall; but, since the place had passed into the hands of Brasidas, a palisade had been built connecting the wall with the bridge. Brasidas with some of his forces took up a commanding position on the hill of Cerdylion, from which he had a wide view of the surrounding country; while other troops remained in Amphipolis under the command of Clearidas, whom he had appointed governor. Their hoplites numbered about 2000.

The discontent and murmurs of his troops forced Cleon to move prematurely. The soldiers had grumbled at leaving Athens under an utterly inexperienced commander to face a general like Brasidas, and they were now displeased at his inaction. In order to do something, Cleon led his army to the top of the ridge, near the city wall, where he could obtain a view of the country beyond, and, as he saw Brasidas on Cerdylion, he had no fear of being attacked. But Brasidas was resolved to attack, before reinforcements should arrive; and, seeing the Athenians move, he descended from Cerdylion and entered Amphipolis. The Athenians, who had reached the ridge, could observe the whole army gathered within the city, and Brasidas himself offering sacrifice at the temple of Athena; and Cleon was presently informed that the feet of men and horses, ready to sally forth, could be seen under one of the gates. Having verified this fact for himself, Cleon gave the signal to wheel to the left and retreat to Eion; it was the only possible line of retreat, and necessarily exposed the unshielded side to an enemy issuing from the city. But he made the fatal mistake of not preparing his men for action, in case they should be forced to fight; he rashly calculated *Battle.* that he would have time to get away. Hence when Brasidas, with 150 hoplites, came forth from one of the gates, ran up the road, and charged the Athenian centre, the left wing, which was in advance, was struck with terror and took to flight. At the same time the rest of the garrison of Amphipolis, led by Clearidas, had issued from a more northerly gate and attacked the Athenian right. Here a stand was made, though Cleon, unused to the dangers of warfare, proved himself no better than many of his hoplites, who were said *Death of* to be the flower of the army. He fled, and was shot down by a *Cleon.* targeteer. But the bravery of Brasidas was doomed as well as the cowardice of Cleon by the equal decree of Death. As he was turning to assist Clearidas, he received a mortal wound and was *Death of* carried into the city. He lived long enough to be assured of the *Brasidas.* utter rout of the foe; but his death had practically converted the victory into a defeat. The people of Amphipolis gave him the honours of a hero; they made him their founder, and removed all the memorials of the true founder of their colony, the Athenian

Hagnon. Sacrifices were offered to Brasidas, and yearly games celebrated in his honour.

The death of Brasidas removed the chief obstacle to peace ; for no *Result of* man was competent or disposed to resume his large designs in Thrace. *the battle—* The defeat and death of Cleon gave a free hand to Nicias and the *peace.* peace party. The peace party were in truth far more responsible for the disaster than Cleon, whom they had placed in a false position. Thus the battle of Amphipolis led immediately to the conclusion of peace ; and the comic poet could rejoice in the destruction of the *(Aristo-* pestle and mortar—Cleon and Brasidas—with which the spirits of *phanes.)* War and Tumult had pounded the cities of Greece. But the desire of peace seems to have been even stronger at Sparta than at Athens, where there was a certain feeling, in spite of the longing for a rest from warfare, that the lustre of the city was tarnished and something strenuous should be done. Menaces of invading Attica were required to apply the necessary pressure ; though they could hardly have been seriously contemplated, as long as the captives were in an Athenian prison. Negotiations were protracted during autumn and winter, *422-1 B.C.* and the peace was definitely concluded about the end of March.

The Peace, of which Nicias and Pleistoanax were the chief *Peace of* authors, was fixed for a term of fifty years. Athens undertook to *Nicias,* restore all the posts which she had occupied during the war against *421 B.C.* the Peloponnesians : Pylos, Cythera, Methone, Atalanta, and *(March).* Pteleon in Thessaly. But she insisted upon retaining Sollion and Anactorion, and the port of Nisaea. The Lacedaemonians engaged to restore Amphipolis, and to relinquish Argilus, Stagira, Acanthus, Scolus, Olynthus, Spartolus, which cities, remaining independent, were to pay a tribute to Athens according to the assessment of Aristides. Moreover, the fortress of Panacton, in Mount Cithaeron, which the Boeotians had recently occupied, was to be restored to Athens. Certain towns in the possession of Athens, such as Torone, were to be dealt with at the discretion of Athens. All captives on both sides were to be liberated.[1]

[1] The details of this Treaty and of the Truce of 423 B.C. have been given fully by Thucydides, and are of great importance for the study of the diplomatic methods of the Greek states. Other clauses of the Peace of Nicias are as follows : The common temples of Greece are to be free to all. The autonomy of the Delphians and their temple is ensured. Controversies between the contracting parties are to be settled by legal means. The inhabitants of any city handed over to the Athenians are allowed to leave it and take their property with them. Argilus, Olynthus, etc., may become allies of Athens, if they voluntarily consent ; and Mecyberna, Sane, and Singe are to be independent. If any matter is forgotten in this contract, the Athenians and Lacedaemonians may make alterations by mutual agreement. The oaths to the Peace are to be renewed every year, and the terms are to be inscribed on pillars at Olympia, Delphi, Isthmus, and on the Acropolis of Athens, and in the Temple of Apollo at Amyclae.

Corinth,
Megara,
Boeotia
refuse to
accept the
Peace.

It appeared immediately that the situation was not favourable to a durable peace ; for, when the terms were considered at Sparta by a meeting of deputies of the Peloponnesian allies, they were emphatically denounced as unjust by three important states, Corinth, Boeotia, and Megara.   Corinth was indignant at the surrender of Sollion and Anactorion ; Megara was furious that Nisaea should be abandoned to the enemy ; and Boeotia was unwilling to hand over Panacton.   Yet Athens could hardly have demanded less.   The consequence was that the Peace was only partial ; those allies which were politically of most consequence refused to accept it, and they were joined by Elis ; the diplomacy of Nicias was a complete failure, so far as it aimed at compassing an abiding peace.   But since the deepest cause of the war lay in the commercial competition between Athens and Corinth, and since the interests of Sparta were not at stake, the treaty might seem at least to have the merit of simplifying the situation.

Cleon's
policy
justified,
if the
Periclean
imperial-
ism was
justified.

But, if we admit the justification of the imperial policy of Pericles, then the policy of vigorous action advocated by Cleon was abundantly justified.   It may safely be said that if the conduct of the state had rested entirely with Cleon, and if the military talents of the city had been loyally placed at his disposal, the interests of Athens (as Pericles understood them) would have been far better served than if Nicias and his party had been allowed to manage all things as they willed without the restraint of Cleon's opposition.   Few statesmen of the merit of Cleon have come before posterity for judgment at such a great disadvantage, condemned by Thucydides, held up to eternal ridicule by Aristophanes.   If we allow for the personal prejudice of Thucydides, these testimonies only show that Cleon was a coarse, noisy, ill-bred, audacious man, offensive to noblemen and formidable to officials—the watchful dog of the people.   Nothing is proved against his political insight or his political honesty.   The portrait of Aristophanes in the *Knights* carries no more historical value than nowadays a caricature in a comic paper.   He too had suffered from the assaults of Cleon, who

> had dragged him to the Senate House,
> And trodden him down and bellowed over him,
> And mauled him till he scarce escaped alive.[1]

The Peace,
421 *B.C.*

The Peace of Nicias was celebrated by a play of Aristophanes, which admirably expresses the exuberant joy then felt at Athens, but carefully avoids the suggestion of any noble sentiment that may have quickened the poet's delight in the accomplishment of the policy he

---

[1]. Frere.

had advocated.   So Cleon's friends might have said ; but we judge
Aristophanes unfairly, if we misapprehend the comic poet's function.
Comedy did not guide public opinion, but rather echoed it ; comedy
set up no exalted ideal or high standard of action.   The best hits
were those which tickled the man in the market-place and more or
less responded to his thoughts.   Aristophanes had his own political
prejudices and predilections ; but as a son of Athens he was assuredly
proud of the great place which her democracy had won for her
in the world.   It was the nature and the business of his muse to
distort in the mirror of comedy the form and feature of the age ; but
the poet who was inspired to write the verse

O rich and renowned, and with violets crowned, O Athens, the envied of
    nations !

cannot have been altogether out of sympathy with those who strove
to maintain the imperial position of his country.

FIG. 125.—Coin of Segesta, after 431 B.C. (reverse). River god with hunting-spears; two dogs; term [legend (invisible in reproduction): (ΕΓΕΣ)ΤΑΙΩΝ].

FIG. 126.—Coin of Catane, between 431 and 404 B.C. (obverse). Bay-wreathed Apollo; bell; crayfish [legend: ΚΑΤΑΝΑΙΩΝ].

CHAPTER XI

THE DECLINE AND DOWNFALL OF THE ATHENIAN EMPIRE

SECT. I. NEW POLITICAL COMBINATIONS WITH ARGOS

Sparta and Athens form a defensive alliance. SPARTA had good reasons for desiring peace; the prospect in the Peloponnesus gave her no little concern. Mantinea had been gradually enlarging her boundaries southwards; and that could not be permitted. Elis was sulky and hostile, because, in a quarrel with Lepreon, Sparta had supported her rival. Far more serious than these minor vexations was the circumstance that the treaty of peace with Argos was about to expire. It had been a consideration of supreme importance for Sparta, when she entered upon the war with Athens, that for the next ten years she was secure on the side of her old Peloponnesian rival. But there was now the chance that Athens and Argos might combine, and, as Argos had not agreed to renew the treaty, there was urgent need to come to terms with Athens. These reasons which recommended the peace to Sparta ought to have prevented Athens from consenting to it. The settlement was a complete failure. Not only did the Corinthians and the other chief allies refuse to accede to it, but the signatories found themselves unable to carry out the terms they had agreed upon. The Chalcidians refused to surrender Amphipolis, and the Spartans could not compel them. Athens therefore justly declined to carry out her part of the bargain. As a way out of this deadlock, the Spartans, impatient at all costs to recover the Sphacterian prisoners, conceived the device of entering into a defensive alliance with their old enemy This proposal, warmly supported by Nicias, was accepted, and the captives were at length restored,—Athens still retaining Pylos and Cythera.

This approximation between Sparta and Athens led directly

to the dissolution of the Peloponnesian league. Corinth, Mantinea, and *Disruption* Elis, considering themselves deserted by their leader, broke with her, *of Pelo-* and formed an alliance with Argos, who now enters upon the scene. *ponnesian* The Chalcidians of Thrace joined.   There was, however, little reason *league.* to fear or hope that the intimacy between Sparta and Athens could be long or strong, seeing that Athens insisted on keeping Cythera and Pylos until Amphipolis should be restored to her and the other states should accede to the Peace.   In the following year these un- 420 *B.C.* stable political combinations were upset by a change in the balance of parties at Athens, and by the triumph of the anti-Athenian war-party at Sparta.   The opposition to Nicias was led by Hyperbolus, *Hyper-* a man of the same class and same kind of ability as Cleon ; a comic *bolus.* poet—and no statesman was such a favourite butt of comedy as Hyper-bolus—described him as a Cleon in hyperbole.   But the party was now strengthened by the accession of a young man of high birth, brilliant intellect, and no morality, Alcibiades, son of Cleinias.   Educated by *Alcibiades.* his kinsman Pericles in democratic traditions, he was endowed by nature with extraordinary beauty and talents, by fortune with the inheritance of wealth which enabled him to indulge an inordinate taste for ostentation.   He had shocked his kinsfolk and outraged the city, not by his dissoluteness, but by the incredible insolence which accompanied it.   The numerous anecdotes of his petulance, which no one dared to punish, need not all be true ; but they illustrate the fact that undue respect for persons of birth and wealth had not dis-appeared in the Athenian democracy.   Alcibiades was feared and courted, and pursued by lovers of both sexes.   He fought with bravery at Delium, where his life was saved by his friend Socrates the philosopher.   It was a celebrated friendship.   Intellectual power and physical courage were the only points of likeness between them ; socially and morally, as well as in favour and fortune, they were as contrasted as two men well could be.   Though Socrates took no interest in politics, he was an unequalled dialectician, and an aspiring statesman found his society a good training for the business of political debate.   Alcibiades indeed had not in him the stuff of which true statesmen are made ; he had not the purpose, the perseverance, or the self-control.   An extremely able and dexterous politician he certainly was ; but he wanted that balance which a politician, whether scrupulous or unscrupulous, must have in order to be a great statesman.   Nor had Alcibiades any sincere belief in the democratic institutions of his country, still less any genuine sympathy with the advanced democratic party whose cause he espoused. When he said—as Thucydides makes him say—at Sparta, at a later stage of his career, that democracy is " acknowledged folly," he assuredly expressed what he felt in his heart.   Yet at this time his ultimate aim may have been to win such a place as that which Pericles had held, and rule his country without being formally her ruler. At all events he saw his way to power through war and conquest.

Alcibiades chosen strategos, 420 B.C. Alliance with Argos. Epidaurian War, 419 B.C.   The accession of Alcibiades was particularly welcome to the radical party, not so much on account of his family connexions, his diplomatic and rhetorical talents, but because he had a military training and could perform the functions of strategos. Unfitness for the post of strategos was, as we have seen, the weak point in the position of men like Hyperbolus and Cleon. When Alcibiades was elected a strategos and Nicias was not re-elected, the prospects of the radical party looked brighter. The change was immediately felt. Athens entered into an alliance with Argos, and her allies Elis and Mantinea, for a hundred years ;[1] and the treaty was sealed by a joint expedition against Epidaurus. Sparta assisted Epidaurus, and then the Athenians declared that the Lacedaemonians had broken the Peace.

418 B.C.   The new policy of Athens received a check by the return of Nicias to power and the refusal of the people to re-elect the adventurous Alcibiades ; but the alliance with Argos was not broken off. Sparta, alarmed by the activity of Argos against Epidaurus, resolved to *Spartan invasion of Argolis.* strike a blow, and sent forth in summer an army under king Agis to invade the Argive land. The allies gathered at Phlius, and Corinth, which had no longer any reason to hold aloof, sent a contingent. The Argive troops under Thrasyllus, with their Mantinean and Elean allies, were in every way inferior to the enemy ; yet concentrating close to Nemea, they could easily defend the chief pass from the north into the plain of Argos. But Agis outmanœuvred them. Sending the Boeotians along the main road by Nemea, he led his own troops by a difficult mountain path, from the west, and descended into the plain by the valley of the Inachus ; the Corinthians and Phliasians he sent over by another pass. Thus the Argives were hemmed in between two armies and cut off from their city. They left their position near Nemea and came down into the plain ; the Boeotians appear not to have followed. The soldiers of both Thrasyllus and Agis were confident of victory, but the generals were of another mind. Agis, as well as his antagonist, considered his position precarious, and consequently they came to terms, concluding a truce for four months. On both sides there was a loud outcry against the generals, and Thrasyllus was nearly stoned to death by his disappointed soldiers.

Athenian forces now arrived at Argos, 1000 hoplites and 300 cavalry, under Laches and Nicostratus, accompanied by Alcibiades as an ambassador. Alcibiades induced the allies to disregard the

---

[1] A fragment of the stone on which this treaty (given in full by Thucydides) was written was found near the Dionysiac Theatre.

Plain of
MANTINEA and TEGEA.

Scale.

Orchomenus

Mt Maenalus

R. Ophis

Mantinea

To Argos

To Argos

Mytika

(Tripolitza)

Hysiae

(Steno)

Tegea

Pallantium

To the Argive territory

Asea

R. Alpheus

To Sparta

To Sparta

Walker & Boutall sc.

To face page 461.

truce, on the technical ground that, not having been accepted by the Athenians, it was not valid. The allied troops accordingly crossed the mountains into Arcadia and won Orchomenus. The men of Elis then proposed to move against their own particular foes, the people of Lepreon ; and being out-voted they deserted their allies and marched home. The army, thus weakened by the loss of 3000 hoplites, was obliged to hasten southward to protect Mantinea, against which the Lacedaemonians under Agis, along with the men of Tegea, had meanwhile come forth.

And now, at length, a great battle was fought. The exact num- *Battle of* bers are not known, but must have approached 10,000 on each side. *Mantinea,* Coming round the hill of Scope, the spur of Mount Maenalus, which 418 *B.C.* projects into the plain between Tegea and Mantinea, at the point *(Scope =* where the territories of the two cities met, the Lacedaemonians found *hill of* *Mytika.)* the enemy drawn up for fight and proved their excellent discipline by a rapid formation in the face of the hostile line. They won the battle ; but their success was endangered, and its completeness diminished, by a hitch which occurred at the outset. There was a tendency in all Greek armies, when engaging, to push towards the right, each man fearing for his own exposed right side and trying to edge under the screen of his neighbour's shield. Consequently, an army was always inclined to outflank the left wing of the enemy by its own right. On this occasion, Agis observed that the Mantineans, who were on the right wing of the foe, stretched far beyond his own left wing, and fearing it would be disastrously outflanked and surrounded, gave a signal to the troops of his extreme left to make a lateral movement further towards the left ; and at the same time he commanded two captains on his right to move their divisions round to fill up the gap thus created. The first order was executed, but the two captains refused to move. The result was that the extreme left was isolated, and utterly routed, while a band of 1000 chosen Argives dashed through the gap. On the right, however, the Lacedaemonians were completely victorious over the Athenians and other allies. The Athenians would have been surrounded and utterly at the mercy of their foes, if Agis had not recalled his troops to assist his discomfited left wing. Both Laches and Nicostratus fell.

The Lacedaemonians returned home and celebrated the feast of *Results of* the Carnean Apollo in joy. The victory did much to restore the *the battle.* prestige of Sparta, which had dwindled since the disaster of Sphacteria. The public opinion of Greece had pronounced Sparta to be stupid and inert ; it now began to reconsider its judgment. But the victory had direct political results ; it transformed the situation in the Peloponnesus. One of those double changes which usually went together, a change in the constitution and a change in

Argos joins Sparta. foreign policy, was brought about at Argos. The democracy was replaced by an oligarchy, and the alliance with Athens was abandoned for an alliance with Sparta. Mantinea, Elis, and the Achaean towns also went over to the victor. Athens was again isolated.

Ostracism of Hyper- bolus, 418-7 B.C. It was probably at this juncture that the advanced democrats in Athens made an attempt to remove from their way the influential man who was their chief opponent, Nicias. It had been due to his counsels that Argos had not been more effectively supported ; there was probably a good deal of dissatisfaction at Athens ; and, when Hyperbolus proposed that a vote of ostracism should be held, he had good grounds to hope that there would be a decision against Nicias, and no apparent reason to fear for himself. He might calculate that most of the supporters of Nicias would vote against the more danger- ous Alcibiades. The calculation was so well grounded that it missed its mark ; for Alcibiades, seeing the risk which threatened him, deserted Hyperbolus and the democratic party, and allied himself with Nicias. So it came about that Hyperbolus was ruined by his own machination ; all the followers of Nicias and Alcibiades wrote *his* name on their sherds, and he was banished for ten years. His political career had ended. This was the last case of ostracism at Athens ; the institution was not abolished, but it became a dead letter.

The new alliance of the pious and punctilious Nicias, champion of peace, with the profane and unstable Alcibiades, bent on enterprises of war, was more unnatural than that between the high-born noble and the lamp-maker. But Nicias seems to have been to some small extent *417 B.C.* aroused from his policy of inactivity. We find him undertaking an expedition against Chalcidice, where nothing had been done since the *421 B.C.* Peace, except the capture of Scione and the execution of all the male inhabitants.

Conquest of Melos, 416 B.C. Nicias failed in an attempt on Amphipolis ; but in the following year an enterprise in the southern Aegean was attended with success. [The island of Melos had resolutely stood outside the Athenian empire, unlike her neighbour Thera who was compelled to pay tribute when war broke out. Athens probably demanded tribute from Melos at the same time ; but, far from complying, she actually contributed money to the Spartan fleet which sailed to the relief of Lesbos. In 426 Nicias took a small force to the island but, failing to secure a quick success, he withdrew. In 425 we find Melos listed in the Island panel with the high assessment of 15 talents, but still she stood firm. Now, under the influence of Alcibiades, the Athenians resolved to end the matter.] The town of Melos was invested in the summer by land and sea, and surrendered at discretion in the following winter. All the *Athenian cleruchs.* men of military age were put to death, the other inhabitants were enslaved, and the island was colonised by Athenians.

The conquest of Melos is remarkable, not for the rigorous treatment of the Melians, which is merely another example of the inhumanity which we have already met in the cases of Plataea,
Mytilene, Scione, but for the unprovoked aggressions of Athens, without any tolerable pretext.   By the curious device of constructing a *Emphasis*
colloquy between Athenian envoys and the Melian government, *laid by*
Thucydides has brought the episode into dramatic relief.   In this *Thucy-*
scene the Athenians assert in frank and shameless words the "law of *on the*
nature" that the stronger should rule over the weaker.   This was a *conquest*
doctrine which it was Hellenic to follow, but unusual to enunciate *of Melos.*
in all its nakedness ; and in the negotiations which preceded the
blockade no Athenian spokesmen would have uttered the undiplo-
matic audacities which Thucydides ascribes to them.   The historian
has artfully used the dialogue to indicate the overbearing spirit
of the Athenians, flown with insolence, on the eve of an enterprise
which was destined to bring signal retribution and humble their
city in the dust.   Different as Thucydides and Herodotus were in
their minds and methods, they had both the same, characteristically
Hellenic, feeling for a situation like this.   The check of Athens
rounded the theme of the younger, as the check of Persia had rounded
the theme of the elder, historian ; and, although Nemesis, who moves
openly in the pages of Herodotus, is not acknowledged by Thucydides, she seems to have cast a shadow here.

During the years immediately succeeding the Peace there are some
signs that the Athenians turned their attention to matters of religion,
which had perhaps been too much neglected during the war.   It may
have been in these years that they set about the building of a new *Temple of*
temple for Athena and Erechtheus, concerning which we shall hear *Athena*
again at a later stage.   It may have been at this time that Asclepius, *Polias*
the god of healing, came over with his snake from Epidaurus, and *(see below,*
established himself in a sanctuary under the south slope of the *The As-*
Acropolis.   And it was probably soon after the Peace that a resolu- *clepieum.*
tion was carried imposing a new tax upon the fruits of the earth for *The*
the maintenance of the worship of Eleusis.   The farmers of Attica *decree*
were required to pay $\frac{1}{600}$th of every medimnus of barley and $\frac{1}{1200}$th of *(medimnus*
every medimnus of wheat.   The same burden was imposed upon the *= 1½*
allies ; and the Council was directed to invite "all Hellenic cities whom *bushels),*
it seemed possible to approach on the matter " to send first-fruits *418 B.C.*
likewise.

SECT. 2. THE WESTERN POLICY OF ATHENS

During the fifth century the eyes of Athenian statesmen often
wandered to western Greece beyond the seas.   We can surprise some
oblique glances, as early as the days of Themistocles ; and we have

seen how under Pericles a western policy definitely began in alliances with Segesta, Leontini and Rhegium. One general object of Athens was to support the Ionian cities against the Dorian, which were predominant in number and power, and especially against Syracuse, the daughter and friend of Corinth. The same purpose of counteracting the Dorian predominance may be detected in the foundation of Thurii. But Thurii did not effect this purpose. The colonists were a mixed body; other than Athenian elements gained the upper hand; and, in the end, Thurii became rather a Dorian centre and was no support to Athens. It is to be observed that at the time of the foundation of Thurii, and for nigh thirty years more, Athens is seeking merely influence in the west, she has no thought of dominion. The growth of her connexion with Italian and Sicilian affairs was forced upon her by the conditions of commerce and the rivalry of Corinth.

Condition of Sicily, 427 B.C. The treaties with Leontini and Rhegium had led to no immediate interference in Sicily on the part of the Athenians. The first action came six years later, on an appeal for help from both cities. Leon-

FIG. 127.—Coin of Naxos, fifth century (reverse). Seated satyr with wine-cup [legend : NAΞION].

tini was struggling to preserve her independence against Syracuse, her southern neighbour. All the Dorian cities, with the exception of Acragas and Camarina, were on the side of Syracuse, while Leontini had the support of Rhegium, Catane, Naxos, and Camarina. The continued independence of the Ionian element in western Greece might seem to be seriously at stake. The embassy of the Leontines was accompanied by the greatest of their citizens, Gorgias, the professor of eloquence, whose fame and influence were Panhellenic. We may well believe that when the embassy arrived the Athenians were far more interested in the great man than in his mission; that they thronged in excitement to the Assembly, caring little what he said, but much how he said it. His eloquence indeed was hardly needed to win a favourable answer. Athens was convinced of the expediency of bringing Sicily within the range of her politics. It was important to hinder corn and other help being conveyed from thence to her Peloponnesian enemies; it was important to prevent Syracuse, the friend of Corinth, from raising her head too high; and already adventurous imaginations may have pressed beyond the thought of Athenian influence, and dreamed of Athenian dominion, in the west. Hyperbolus seems to have especially interested himself in the development of a policy in the western Mediterranean. Aristophanes ridicules him for contemplating an enterprise against Carthage herself.

A force of 20 ships was sent out, under the command of Laches. *Sicilian* It achieved little, but, if it had been followed up, might have led to *expedition* much.   Messana was induced to join Athens, who thus obtained free *under Laches,* navigation of the Straits.   The old alliance *427 B.C.* with Segesta was renewed, but a severe check was experienced in an attempt to take Inessa. The poor success of this expedition must partly at least be set down to the dishonesty of the general Laches and his treasurer.   Cleon seems to have called Laches to account for his defalcations, on his return ; and a comic poet jested how Laches ate up the Sicilian cheese —Sicily was famous for her cheeses—with the help of his treasurer, the cheese-grater.

FIG.   128. — Coin of Messana, fifth century (obverse).   Hare ; head of Pan ; syrinx [legend : MEΣΣANION].

The episode of Pylos and the operations *Expedition* at Corcyra may be regarded as causes which *of Eury-* ruined Athenian prospects in Sicily.   For *medon and* these affairs detained the fleet of 40 ships which was bound for the west *Sophocles,* under the command of Eurymedon and Sophocles, and the delay led *425 B.C.* to the loss of the one thing which the expedition of Laches had gained, the adhesion of Messana.   This city, cleft by adverse political parties, revolted ; and the fleet, when at last it came, accomplished nothing worthy of record.   Its coming seems rather to have been the occasion for the definite shaping of a movement among almost all the Sicilian states towards peace,—a movement unfavourable to the Athenian designs.   When the Athenian generals invited the cities to join in the war against Syracuse, they were answered by the gathering of a congress at Gela, where delegates *Congress* from all the Siceliot cities met to discuss the situation and consider *of Gela,* the possibility of peace.   The man who took the most prominent *424 B.C.* part at this remarkable congress was Hermocrates of Syracuse. He developed what has been justly described as a Siceliot policy. Sicily is a world by itself, with its own interests and politics, and the Greeks outside Sicily should be considered as strangers and not permitted to make or meddle in the affairs of the island.   Let the Sicilian cities settle their own differences among themselves, but combine to withstand intervention from Athens or any other external power.   Thus the policy of Hermocrates was neither local nor Panhellenic, but Siceliot.   It has been compared to the " Monroe doctrine" of the United States.   The policy, indeed, was never realised, and we shall see that Hermocrates himself was driven by circumstances to become eminently untrue to the doctrine which he preached.   But the Congress of Gela was not a failure ; [the Athenians had to accept the position and returned to Athens, where the assembly, flushed with the triumph of Sphacteria, fined Eurymedon and banished his two colleagues. Soon afterwards trouble arose in Leontini. The oligarchs, threatened by radical measures, called in Syracuse, drove out the democrats and then themselves transferred to Syracuse. Athens saw an opportunity to intervene and sent Phaeax, a prominent orator, with two colleagues, to build up a general alliance against Syracuse. The envoys, after a promising beginning, failed at Gela, and Athens, now moving to a peace mood, did no more until the year of the conquest of Melos.]

SECT. 3. THE SAILING OF THE SICILIAN EXPEDITION. FIRST OPERATIONS IN SICILY

Embassy of Segesta, 416 B.C In that year there arrived at Athens an appeal for help from Segesta, who was at war with her stronger southern neighbour, Selinus. The appeal was supported by the Leontine democrats, who had no longer a city of their own. Athens sent envoys to Sicily, for the purpose of reporting on the situation and spying out the resources of Segesta, which had undertaken, if the Athenians

FIG. 129.—Coin of Selinus, fifth century (obverse). River Hypsas sacrificing at altar; snake round the altar; lake-bird; leaf of selinon [legend : ΗΥΨΑΣ].

would send an armament, to provide the expenses of the war. The ambassadors returned with sixty talents of uncoined silver and glowing stories of the untold wealth of the people of Segesta. They described the sacred vessels of gold and the rich plate of the private citizens. Alcibiades and all the younger generation were in favour of responding to the appeal ; of vigorously espousing the causes of Segesta against Selinus, of the Leontines against Syracuse. Nicias wisely opposed the notion, and set forth the enormous cost of an expedition which should be really effective. The people, however, elated by their recent triumph over Melos, were fascinated by the idea of making new conquests in a distant, unfamiliar world ; the ordinary Athenian had very vague ideas of what Sicily meant ; and carried away by dreams of a western empire, he paid no more attention to the discreet counsels of Nicias than to vote a hundred triremes instead of the sixty which were originally asked for.

Athenians vote expedition to Sicily. But having committed the imprudence of not listening to Nicias when his caution was, from the highest point of view, wisdom, the people went on to commit the graver blunder of electing him as a commander of the expedition which he disapproved. He was

appointed as General along with Alcibiades and Lamachus.   This
shows how great was the consideration of his military capacity, and he
was doubtless regarded as a safe makeweight against the adventurous
spirit of his colleagues.   But though Nicias had shown himself
capable of carrying out that Periclean strategy which Athens had *(See above,*
hitherto adopted, his ability and temperament were wholly unsuited *p.* 400.)
for the conduct of an enterprise of conquest demanding bolder and
greater operations.

   When the expedition was ready to sail in the early summer, a *The*
mysterious event delayed it.   One morning in May it was found *mutilation*
that the square stone figures which stood at the entrance of *of the*
Hermae,
temples and private houses in Athens, and were known as Hermae, 415 *B.C.*
had been mutilated.   The pious Athenians were painfully excited.
Such an unheard-of sacrilege seemed an evil omen for the Sicilian
enterprise, and it was illogically argued that the act betokened
a conspiracy against the state.   The enemies of Alcibiades seized
the occasion and tried to implicate him in the outrage.   It was
said that a profane mockery of the Eleusinian Mysteries had
been enacted in his house,—a charge which may well have been
true ; and it was argued that he was the author of the present
sacrilege and prime mover in a conspiracy against the democracy.
It did not appear why a conspirator should thus advertise his plot.
But though the theory hardly hung together, it might be good
enough for an excited populace.   Alcibiades demanded the right
of clearing himself from the charge, before the fleet started.   In this
case, his acquittal was certain, as he was deemed necessary to the
enterprise ; and his enemies, aware of this, procured the postpone-
ment of his trial till his return.   The fleet then set sail, and in the *Sailing of*
excitement of its starting, the sacrilege was almost forgotten. *the fleet.*
Thucydides says that no armament so magnificent had ever before been
sent out by a single Greek state.   There were 134 triremes, and an
immense number of smaller attendant vessels ; there were 5100
hoplites ; and the total number of combatants was well over 30,000.
For cavalry they relied on their Sicilian allies ; only thirty horse
went with the fleet.

   A halt was made at Rhegium, where disappointments awaited
them.   Rhegium adopted a reserved attitude which the Athenians
did not expect.   The government said that their conduct must be
regulated by that of the other Italiot states.   This looks as if the
Italiots were aiming at a policy of joint interests, such as that which
the Siceliots had discussed at the Congress of Gela.   In the next
place, the Athenians had relied on the wealth of Segesta for supporting their expedition, and they now learned that their spies had been
deceived by simple tricks.   Gilt vessels of silver had been displayed

to them as solid gold; and the Segestaeans, collecting all the plate they could get from their own and other cities, had passed the same service from house to house and led the envoys to believe that each of the hosts who sumptuously entertained them possessed a magnificent service of his own.

This discovery came as an unwelcome surprise to soldiers and commanders alike. It was a serious blow to the enterprise, but no one, not even Nicias, seems to have thought of giving the enterprise up. What then was to be done? A council of war was held at Rhegium. Nicias advocated a course which involved risking and doing as little as possible,—to sail about, make some demonstrations, secure anything that could be secured without trouble, give any help to the Leontines that could be given without danger. Alcibiades proposed that active attempts should be made to win over the Sicilian cities by diplomacy, and that then, having so strengthened their position, they should take steps to force Selinus and Syracuse to do right by Segesta and Leontini. Both Nicias and Alcibiades kept in the forefront the ostensible object of the expedition, to right the wrongs of Leontini and Segesta. But Lamachus, who was no statesman or diplomatist but a plain soldier, regarded the situation from a soldier's point of view. Grasping the fact that Syracuse was the real enemy, the ultimate mark at which the whole enterprise was aimed, he advised that Syracuse should be attacked at once, while her citizens were still unprepared. Fortunately for Syracuse, the bold strategy of Lamachus did not prevail; he had no influence or authority except on the field; and, failing to convince his colleagues, who perhaps contemned him as a mere soldier, he gave his vote to the plan of Alcibiades.

The council of war at Rhegium.

Naxos and Catane were won over; the Athenian fleet made a demonstration in the Great Harbour of Syracuse and captured a ship. But nothing more had been done, when a mandate arrived from Athens recalling Alcibiades, to stand his trial for impiety. The people of Athens had reverted to their state of religious agony over the mutilation of the Hermae, and the mystery which encompassed it increased their terrors. A commission of inquiry was appointed; false informations were lodged; numbers of arrests were made. Andocides, a young man of good family, was one of the prisoners, and he at length resolved to confess the crime and give the names of his accomplices. His information was readily believed; the public agitation was tranquillised; and all the prisoners whom he accused were tried and put to death. He was himself pardoned, and soon afterwards left Athens. But it is not certain, after all, whether the information of Andocides was true; Thucydides declares that the truth of the mystery was never explained.

Recall of Alcibiades.

It was, indeed, never known for certain who the actual perpetrators *Meaning of* were ; so far the affair remained a mystery.   But the purpose of the *the Hermae* deed and the source of its inspiration can hardly be doubtful.   It *mystery.* was wrought on the eve of the Sicilian expedition, and can have had no other intention than to hinder the expedition from sailing, by working on the superstitions of the people.   If we ask then, who above all others were vitally concerned in preventing the sailing of the fleet, the answer is obvious, Corinth and Syracuse.   We are justified in inferring that the authors of the outrage—to us their names would be of only subordinate interest—were men suborned by Corinth, in receipt of Corinthian silver.   In the main point, the mutilation of the Hermae is assuredly no mystery.

The investigations in connexion with the Hermae led to the exposure of other profanations, especially of travesties of the Eleusinian mysteries, in which Alcibiades was involved.   His enemies of both parties deemed that it was the time to strike.   Thessalus, the son of Cimon, preferred the impeachment, which began thus : " Thessalus, son of Cimon, of the deme Laciadae, impeached Alcibiades, son of Cleinias, of the deme Scambonidae, of wrong-doing in respect to the two goddesses, Demeter and Core, by mimicking the mysteries and displaying them to his comrades in his own house, wearing a dress like that which a hierophant with the mysteries wears, and calling himself hierophant."   The trireme " Salaminia " was sent to summon Alcibiades to return, but with instructions to use no violence.   Alcibiades might have refused, but he did not do so.   He went with the Salaminia as far as Thurii, where he made his escape and went into voluntary exile.   The Athenians condemned him to death, along with some of his kinsfolk, and confiscated his property.

In Sicily, when Alcibiades had gone, the rest of the year was frittered away in a number of small enterprises, which led to nothing. At length, when winter came, Nicias aroused himself to a far more serious undertaking.   By a cunning stratagem he lured the Syracusan army to Catane for the purpose of making an attack on the Athenian camp, which they were led to believe they would take unawares, while in the meantime the Athenian host had gone on board the fleet and sailed off to the Great Harbour of Syracuse.   Nicias landed and fortified his camp on the south-west side of the harbour, near the point of Dascon, just south of the temple of the Olympian Zeus, which he was scrupulous to treat with profound respect.   When the Syracusans returned, a battle was fought, the first battle of the war. The Athenians had the disadvantage of having no cavalry whatever ; but the woeful want of discipline which prevailed in the ranks of the enemy outbalanced the advantage they had from 1200 horse.   A *Athenian* storm of rain and lightning aided the Athenians to discomfit their *victory.*

untrained antagonists; but the cavalry stood the Syracusans in good stead by protecting their retreat.

A success had now been gained, but the temper of Nicias forbade it to be improved. On the day ensuing, he ordered the whole army to embark and sail back to Catane. He had numbers of excellent reasons, —the winter season, the want of cavalry, of money, of allies; and in the meantime Syracuse was left to make her preparations. "The Athenian fleet and army was to go on falling away from its freshness and vigour. All Sicily was to get more and more accustomed to the sight of the great armada sailing to and fro, its energies frittered away on small and mostly unsuccessful enterprises, and, when it did strike something like a vigorous blow, not daring to follow it up." [1]

The winter was employed by both parties in seeking allies. The Sicels of the island for the most part joined Athens. Camarina, wooed by both Athens and Syracuse, remained neutral. It is in the Assembly of Camarina that Thucydides makes Hermocrates reassert the doctrine of a purely Siceliot policy, which he had formulated ten years before at Gela, while an Athenian envoy develops in its most naked form the theory of pure self-interest, reminding us of the tone which the Thucydidean Athenians adopted in the Melian dialogue. A train had been laid for the capture of Messana before Alcibiades had been recalled, but when the time came for making the attempt, it failed. Alcibiades began the terrible vengeance which he proposed to wreak upon his country by informing the Syracusan party in Messana of the plot.

It seemed, indeed, as if a fatality dogged Athens in her conduct of the expedition which she had so lightly undertaken. If she had committed the command to Alcibiades and Lamachus, without Nicias, it would probably have been a success, resulting in the capture of Syracuse. But, not content with the unhappy appointment of Nicias, she must go on to pluck the whole soul out of the enterprise by depriving it of Alcibiades. That active diplomatist now threw as much energy into the work of ruining the expedition as he had given *Alcibiades* to the work of organising it. He went to Sparta, and was present *at Sparta;* at the Assembly which received a Syracusan embassy, begging for *his speech.* Spartan help. He made a vigorous and effective speech. He exposed the boundless plans of Athenian ambition, aiming at conquests in the west (including Carthage), which should enable them to return and conquer the Peloponnesus. These had perhaps been the dreams of Alcibiades himself; but they had certainly never taken a definite shape in the mind of any sober Athenian statesman. Alcibiades urged the Spartans especially to take two measures: to send

[1] Freeman.

at once a Spartan general to Sicily to organise the defence,—a general was far more important than an army; and to fortify Decelea in Attica, a calamity which the Athenians were always dreading. "I know," said the renegade, "the secrets of the Athenians." Thucydides shows what defence Alcibiades might have made for his own vindictive—it can hardly be called treacherous—conduct. The description of the Athenian democracy as "acknowledged folly" may well have been a phrase actually used by Alcibiades. Intense hostility animated the exile, but, one asks, Did he act merely to gratify this feeling, or had he not further projects for his own career? If we might trust the speech which Thucydides ascribes to him, his ultimate aim was to win back his country. With Spartan help, presumably, he was to rise on the calamity of Athens, and, we may read between the lines, the "acknowledged folly' was to be abolished. One can hardly see a place for Alcibiades except as a second Pisistratus.

The speech of this powerful advocate turned the balance at a most critical point in the history of Hellas. The Lacedaemonians, who were wavering between the policies of neutrality and intervention, were decided by his advice, and appointed an officer named Gylippus to take command of the Syracusan forces. Corinth too sent ships to the aid of her daughter city.

Since the sailing of the expedition, Athens was in a mood of adventurous speculation and sanguine expectancy, dreaming of some great and wonderful change for the better in her fortunes. Aristophanes made this mood of his countrymen the motive of a fanciful comedy, entitled the *Birds*, which he brought out at the Great Dionysia. Some have sought to detect definite political allusions in the story of the foundation of Cloudcuckootown by the birds of the air, under the direction of two Athenian adventurers, Persuasive and his follower Hopeful; but this is to misapprehend the intention of the drama and to do wrong to the poet's art. The significance of the *Birds* for the historian is that it exhibits with good-humoured banter the temporary mood of the Athenian folk.

The Birds *of Aristophanes, 414 B.C., March to April.*

Sect. 4. Siege of Syracuse, 414 B.C.

The Island of Syracuse, the original settlement of Archias, always remained the heart and centre of the city. However the city might extend on the mainland opposite, the island was always what the Acropolis was to Athens, what Larisa was to Argos; it was even called the acropolis, a name which was never given to the hill. [The island had been connected in the sixth century by a mole with the mainland, and the city had gradually extended round the shore of the Little

414 B.C.

Harbour and up the slope towards the cliffs of Epipolae, forming the two districts of Achradina and Tyche which were enclosed by a circuit of walls. But the great plateau of Epipolae above the city, forming a large triangle with the high point of Euryalus as its vertex remained unoccupied. Earlier maps assign the district of Achradina to the east end of this plateau and assume that, when Dionysius later built his wall round Epipolae, the whole area had been occupied. But a thorough re-examination of the site and the literary sources has shown that what was thought to be the wall enclosing Achradina is in fact an old quarry, and that no evidence of occupation exists. Its dominating position made Epipolae a key point in the strategy of the siege.]

The Syracusans did something, though not perhaps as much as they might, to prepare for a siege. They reformed their system of military command and elected Hermocrates a general. They fortified the precinct of Apollo Temenites, which was just outside the wall of Achradina, and also strengthened Polichna, the fort south of the hill, near the shrine of Olympian Zeus.

The first brief operation of the Athenians against Syracuse had been made on the table-land west of the Great Harbour. With the second act, which began in the ensuing spring, the scene changes to the north, and the hostilities are enacted on the heights of Epipolae. Hermocrates had realised the necessity of guarding these heights. It was accordingly fixed that a great review should be held of all the fighting population, and a force of 600 was to be chosen for the guard of Epipolae. But the hour had almost passed. At the very moment when the muster was being held below in the meadows on the banks of the Anapus, the Athenians were close at hand. The fleet had left Catane the night before, steered for the bay on the north side of the Epipolae, and set down the army at a landing-place within less than a mile from the height of Euryalus.
The Athenians seize Epipolae. The soldiers hastened up the ascent, and were masters of Epipolae before the Syracusan host knew what was happening. The six hundred made an attempt to dislodge them, and were repulsed with great loss. The Athenians then fortified a place called Labdalon, near the north cliffs ; they have been criticised for not rather fortifying Euryalus.

The Athenian wall. The plan of the siege was to run a wall right across the hill, from the cliffs on the north to the harbour on the south. This would cut off communications by land, while the fleet which was stationed at Thapsus, ready to enter the Great Harbour, would cut off communications by sea. For this purpose, a point was chosen in the centre of the intended line of wall, and a round fort, "the Circle" (*kyklos*), was built there, from which the wall was to be constructed northward and southward. The Syracusans having made

The Athenian Siege of
SYRACUSE

Scale of Miles

0   1   2   3   4

1, 2 and 3, *Syracusan Cross Walls*
4, *Athenian Wall, based on circular fort*

Emery Walker Ltd., sc.

FIG. 130.

First Syracusan counter wall. a vain attempt to stop the building of the wall, set themselves to build a counter-wall, beginning at the Temenites and running west-ward, with a view to intercept the southern wall of the Athenians and prevent its reaching the harbour. The Athenians did not try to hinder them, and devoted themselves entirely to the building of their own wall north of the Round Fort; this seemed at first of greater consequence than the southern section, since they had to consider the maintenance of communications with their fleet at Thapsus. But though they were apparently not concerning them-selves with the Syracusan builders, they were really watching for a good opportunity. The carelessness of the Syracusans soon gave the looked-for chance. An attack was made on the counter-wall and it was utterly destroyed. The generals then began to look to the southern section of their own wall, and, without waiting to build it on the side of the Round Fort, they began to fortify the southern cliff, near the temple of Heracles, above the marshy ground on the north-west side of the great harbour.

The Syracusans then began a second counter-work, not on the hill, but over this low swampy ground, to hinder the Athenians from bringing their wall down from the cliff to the harbour. This work was not a wall, which would not have been suited to the swampy ground, but a trench with a palisade. At the break of day, the Athenians led by Lamachus descended into the swamp and destroyed the Syracusan works. But what was gained was more than undone by what followed. Troops sallied out of Syracuse; a battle was fought; and Lamachus—the hero Lamachus, as comic poets called him in derision while he lived, in admiration when he died—exposed *Death of Lamachus.* himself rashly and was slain. This was the third great blow to the prospect of Athenian success. Nicias had been appointed; Alcibiades had been recalled; now Lamachus was gone. To make things worse, Nicias himself was ill.

The southern Athenian wall advanced southward in a double line, and the fleet had now taken up its station in the Great Harbour. The Syracusans, not realising how much they had gained in the death of Lamachus, were prematurely in despair; they changed their generals, and were prepared to make terms. Nicias, strangely swerving from his wonted sobriety, was prematurely elated; he thought that Syracuse was in his hands, and made the fatal mistake of neglecting the completion of the wall on the north side. His neglect was the more culpable as he had received information of the help that was coming for Syracuse from the mother-country. But alike in his normal mood of caution and in his abnormal moment of confidence, Nicias was doomed to do the wrong thing.

All thought of capitulation was abandoned when a Corinthian

captain named Gongylus reached Syracuse with the news that
Corinthian ships and a Spartan general were on their way.   That
general had indeed given up the hope of being able to relieve
Syracuse, which, from the reports of Athenian success that had
reached him, was thought to be past helping ; but he had sailed on
to the coast of Italy with the aim of saving the Italiot cities.   At
Locri, Gylippus learned that Syracuse might still be saved, since the
northern wall was not yet completed.   He immediately sailed to
Himera and collected a land force, supplied by Gela, Selinus, and
Himera itself, and marched overland to Syracuse.   He ascended *Arrival of*
the hill of Epipolae by the same path on the north side which had *Gylippus.*
been climbed by the Athenian army when they seized the heights ;
and without meeting any opposition advanced along the north bend
of the hill to Tycha and entered the city.   Such was the result of
the gross neglect of Nicias.   If the wall had been finished, the
attempt of Gylippus would never have been made ; if Euryalus had
been fortified, the attempt would probably have failed.

Gylippus immediately undertook the command of the Syracusan
army, and inspired the inhabitants with new confidence.   He was as
unlike the typical Spartan as Nicias was unlike the typical Athenian.
He had all the energy and resourcefulness of Brasidas, without that
unique soldier's attractive personality.   He set himself instantly to
the work of the defence, and his first exploit was the capture of the
fort Labdalon.   But the great object was to prevent the Athenians
from hemming in the city by completing the northern section of
their wall, and this could be done only by building a new counter- *Third*
wall.   The Athenians themselves began to build vigorously, and *Syracusan*
there was a race in wall-building between the two armies.   As the *counter-*
work went on, attacks were made on both sides with varying success. *wall.*
In the end, the Syracusan builders prevailed ; the Athenian wall
was turned, and never reached the northern coast.   This was not
enough for Gylippus.   His wall was continued to reach Euryalus,
and four forts were erected on the western part of the hill, so that
Syracuse could now hinder help from reaching the Athenians by the
path by which Gylippus had himself ascended.   In the meantime
Nicias had occupied Plemmyrion, the headland which, facing the
Island, forms the lower lip of the mouth of the Great Harbour.   Here
he built three forts and established a station for his ships ; some of
which were now dispatched to lie in wait for the expected fleet from
Corinth.   The Syracusans made a sort of answer to the occupation
of Plemmyrion by sending a force of cavalry to the fort of Polichna
to guard the southern coast of the Harbour.   But, though the
Athenians commanded the south part of Epipolae and the entrance
to the Harbour, the Syracusan wall from Tycha to Euryalus had

completely changed the aspect of the situation for Syracuse from despair to reasonable hope.

The winter had now come and was occupied with embassies and preparations. Gylippus spent it in raising fresh forces in Sicily. Camarina, so long neutral, at length joined Syracuse, who had in fact all Greek Sicily on her side, except her rival Acragas, who persistently held aloof, and the towns of Naxos and Catane. Appeals of help were again sent to the Peloponnesus. Corinth was still unremitting in her zeal ; and Sparta had sent a force of 600 hoplites—Neodamodes and Helots. Thebes and Thespiae also sent contingents.

We must go back for a moment to Old Greece. The general war is being rekindled there, and the war in Sicily begins to lose the character of a collateral episode and becomes merged in the larger conflict, in which greater interests than those of Syracuse and Sicily are at stake. The Spartans had come to the conclusion that they had been themselves the wrong-doers in the earlier war, and the Athenian successes, especially the capture of Pylos, had been a retribution which they deserved. But now the Athenians had clearly committed a wrong in their aggression on Sicily, and Sparta might

413 B.C.
Occupation of Decelea by the Spartans.

with a good conscience go to war against her. The advice of Alcibiades to fortify Decelea was adopted : a fort was built and provided with a garrison under the command of king Agis. From Mt. Lycabettus at Athens one can see the height of Decelea through the gap between Pentelicus on the right and Parnes, of which Decelea is an outlying hill, on the left. It was a good position for reaching all parts of Attica, which could no longer be cultivated, and at the same time maintaining easy communications with Boeotia.

Appeal of Nicias for help.

But while the Peloponnesians were carrying the war once more to the very gates of Athens, that city was called upon to send forth a new expedition to the west on a scale similar to the first. Nicias wrote home a plain and unvarnished account of the situation. We are expressly told that he adopted the unusual method of sending a *written* despatch instead of a verbal message ; it was all-important that the Athenian Assembly should learn the exact state of the case. He explained that, since the coming of Gylippus and the increase of the numbers of the garrison, and the building of the counter-wall, the besiegers had become themselves besieged. They even feared an attack on their own element the sea, and their ships had become leaky and the crews fallen out of practice. Further successes of the enemy might cut off their supplies, now derived from the cities of Italy. One of two things must be done : the enterprise must be abandoned or a new armament, as strong as the first, must be sent out at once. Nicias also begged for his own recall, on the ground of the disease from which he suffered. The Athenian people repeated its previous recklessness by voting a second expedition, and by refusing to supersede Nicias, in whom they had a blind and touching trust. They appointed Eurymedon and Demosthenes as commanders of the new armament.

SECT. 5. THE SECOND EXPEDITION

" The original interference of Athens in the local affairs of Sicily, 413 *B.C.* her appearance to defend Segesta against Selinus and the Leontines against Syracuse, has grown into a gigantic struggle in which the greater part of the Hellenic nation is engaged. The elder stage of the Peloponnesian War has begun again with the addition of a Sicilian war on such a scale as had never been seen before. In that elder stage Sicilian warfare had been a mere appendage to warfare in Old Greece. Now Sicily has become the centre of the struggle, the headquarters of both sides." [1]

For Sicily itself, the struggle was now becoming a question of life and death, such as the Persian invasion had been for Greece. Syracuse, under the guidance of Hermocrates and Gylippus, put forth all her energy in the organisation of a fleet, and in the spring she had a navy numbering eighty triremes. The crews were inexperienced, but they could remember that it was under the pressure of the Persian danger that Athens herself had learned her sea skill. Gylippus determined to attack the Athenian station at *Sea battle.* Plemmyrion by land and sea. By sea the Syracusans were defeated, but while the naval battle was being fought in the harbour, a land force under Gylippus had marched round to Plemmyrion and captured the forts on the headland. The Athenian ships were thus forced back to their station close to their double wall on the north of the Harbour, of which the entrance was now commanded by the Syracusans. The Athenians were thus besieged both by land and sea, and could not venture to send ships out of the Harbour except in a number sufficient to resist an attack. Presently the new Syracusan sea-power achieved the important success of capturing off the Italian coast a treasure-fleet which was on its way from Athens.

At length the news came that the great fleet under Eurymedon and Demosthenes was on its way. It consisted of seventy-three triremes ; there were 5000 hoplites and immense numbers of light-armed troops. The chance of Syracuse lay in attacking the dispirited forces of Nicias before the help arrived, and it was obviously the policy of Nicias—a congenial policy—to remain in-

[1] Freeman.

active. The Syracusans made a simultaneous assault on the walls by land and on the naval station below the walls by sea. The land attack was beaten off, but two days' fighting by sea resulted in a *Syracusan* distinct victory for Syracuse. The Great Harbour was too small for *sea-victory.* the Athenians to win the advantage of their superiority in seaman-ship, and their ships were not adapted for the kind of sea-warfare which was possible in a narrow space. The effective use of the long light beaks depended on the possibility of manœuvring. The Syracusans had shaped the beaks of their vessels with a view to the narrow space, by making them short and heavy. On the day after the victory, the fleet of Eurymedon and Demosthenes sailed into the Great Harbour.

Fruitless Demosthenes saw at once that all was over, unless the Syra-*attacks* cusan cross-wall were captured. An attempt to carry it from the *on the* south was defeated, and the only alternative was to march round *Syracusan* *cross-wa.l.* the west end of the hill and ascend by the old path near Euryalus. It was a difficult enterprise, guarded as the west part of Epipolae was by the forts, as well as the wall, and by a picked body of 600 *(August.)* men who were constantly keeping watch. A moonlight night was chosen for the attempt. The Athenians were at first successful. One fort was taken and the six hundred under Hermocrates himself were repelled. But when one part of their force received a decisive check from the Thespians, the disorder spread to the rest, and they fell back everywhere, driven down the hill on the top of their comrades who had not yet reached the summit. Some, throwing away their shields, leapt from the cliffs. About 2000 were slain.

These failures damped the spirits of the army, and Demosthenes saw that no profit could be won by remaining any longer where they were. The only wise course was to leave the unhealthy marsh, while they had still command of the sea, and before the winter came. At Syracuse they were merely wasting strength and money. But though Demosthenes had the sense of the army and the sense of the other commanders with him, he could not persuade Nicias to adopt this course. The same quality of nature which had made Nicias oppose the counsel of Lamachus to attack Syracuse now made him oppose the counsel of Demosthenes to leave Syracuse. Fear of responsibility was the dominant note in the character of Nicias. He was afraid of " Pulydamas and the Trojan women," he was afraid of the censure, perhaps the condemnation, of the Athenian Assembly. Nor would he even accept the compromise of retiring to Catane and carrying on the war on a new plan. Demosthenes and Eurymedon being two to one, should have insisted on instant departure, but they foolishly yielded to the obstinacy of their senior colleague. In a few days, however, events overbore the resolution of Nicias himself. Gylippus

arrived at Syracuse with new contingents he had collected in the
islands ; and Peloponnesian and Boeotian succours, after a long roundabout journey by way of Cyrene, at length reached the Great
Harbour.   Nicias gave way and everything was ready for departure.
But on the night on which they were to start, the enemy suspecting *Eclipse of*
nothing, the full moon suffered an eclipse.   The superstitious army *the moon,*
regarded the phenomenon as a heavenly warning, and cried out for *Aug. 27.*
delay.   Nicias was not less superstitious than the sailors.   Unluckily
his best prophet, Stilbides, was dead, and the other diviners ruled
that he must wait either three days or for the next full moon.   There
was perhaps a difference of opinion among the seers, and Nicias *Departure*
decided to be on the safe side by waiting the longer period.   Never *postponed.*
was a celestial phenomenon more truly disastrous than that lunar
eclipse.   With the aid of Nicias, it sealed the doom of the Athenian
army.

Religious rites occupied the next few days.   But meanwhile the *Sea-fight*
Syracusans had learned of the Athenian intention to abandon the *in the*
siege ; their confidence was raised by the implied confession of *Harbour,*
defeat ; and they resolved not to be content with having saved their *Sept. 3.*
city, but to destroy the host of the enemy before it could escape.
So they drew up their fleet, seventy-six ships, in the Great Harbour
for battle ; and eighty-six Athenian ships moved out to meet them.
The Athenians were at a disadvantage as before, having no room for
manœuvring ; and, centre, right, and left, they were defeated.   The
general Eurymedon was slain.   The left wing was driven back on
the marshy north-west shore of the harbour, between their own wall
and Dascon.   A force under Gylippus endeavoured to advance along
the swamp of Lysimelea and prevent the crews of their ships from
landing, but he was driven off by the Etruscan allies of Athens who
had been sent to guard the shore here.   Then there was a battle for
the ships, and the Syracusans succeeded in dragging away eighteen.

The defeat completed the dejection of the Athenian army ;
the victory crowned the confidence of their enemies.   The one *Blocking*
thought of the Athenians was to escape,—the eclipse was totally *of the*
forgotten ; but Syracuse was determined that escape should be made *Harbour,*
impossible.   The mouth of the Great Harbour was barricaded by *Sept. 6-8*
a line of ships and boats of all kinds and sizes bound together by
chains and connected by bridges.   The fate of the Athenians
depended on their success in breaking through that barrier.   They
abandoned their posts on the hill and went on board their ships.
At this critical moment Nicias revealed the best side of his character. *Last battle*
He left nothing undone that could hearten his troops.   We are told *in*
that, after the usual speech, still thinking, " as men do in the hour of *Harbour,*
great struggles, that he had not done, that he had not said half *Sept. 9.*

enough," [1] he went round the fleet in a boat, making a personal appeal to the trierarch of each ship. " He spoke to them, as men will at such times, of their wives and children and the gods of their country; for men do not care whether their word sound commonplace, but only think that they may have some effect in the terrible moment." [2] The paean sounded, and the Athenian lines sailed forth together across the bay to attack the barrier. When they reached it, Syracusan vessels came out against them on all sides. The Athenians were driven back into the middle of the harbour, and the battle resolved itself into an endless number of separate conflicts. The battle was long and wavered. The walls of the Island, the slopes of Achradina above, were crowded with women and old men, the shores below with warriors, watching the course of the struggle. Thucydides gives a famous description of the scene; one would think that he had been an eye-witness. " The fortune of the battle varied, and it was not possible that the spectators on the shore should all receive the same impression of it. Being quite close and having different points of view, they would some of them see their own ships victorious; their courage would then revive, and they would earnestly call upon the gods not to take from them their hope of deliverance. But others, who saw their ships worsted, cried and shrieked aloud, and were by the sight alone more utterly unnerved than the defeated combatants themselves. Others again who had fixed their gaze on some part of the struggle which was undecided were in a state of excitement still more terrible; they kept swaying their bodies to and fro in an agony of hope and fear, as the stubborn conflict went on and on; for at every instant they were all but saved or all but lost. And while the strife hung in the balance, you might hear in the Athenian army at once lamentation, shouting, cries of victory or defeat, and all the various sounds which are wrung from a great host in extremity of danger." [3] Those motions of human passion, suspense, agony, triumph, despair, which swayed to and fro, in the breasts of thousands, round and over the waters of the Great Harbour on that September day, have been lifted out of the tide of time and preserved for ever by the genius of Thucydides.

In the end the Athenians gave way. They were driven back to the shelter of their own wall, chased by the foe. The crews of the remnant of the navy—which amounted to sixty ships—rushed on shore as best they could. The land forces were in a panic; no such panic had ever been experienced in an Athenian army. Thucydides compares the situation to that of the Spartans at Sphacteria. The generals did not even think of asking for the customary truce to bury

[1] Thucydides. [2] *Ibid.*

[3] Jowett's translation.

the corpses which were strewn over the waters of the bay.   Demosthenes proposed that they should make another attempt to pass the barrier at daybreak ; their ships were even now rather more numerous than those of the enemy ; but the men positively refused to embark. Nothing remained but to escape by land.   If they had started at once, they would probably have succeeded in reaching shelter at Catane or inland among the friendly Sicels.   But Hermocrates contrived a stratagem to delay their departure, so as to give him time to block the roads.   Taking advantage of the known fact that there were persons in Syracuse who intrigued with the besiegers, he sent some horsemen who rode up within earshot of the Athenian camp, and feigning to be friends stated that the roads were guarded and that it would be well to wait and set out better prepared.   The message was believed.   The Athenians remained the next day, and the Syracusans blocked the roads.

In his picture of the sad start of the Athenians on their forlorn retreat, Thucydides outdoes his wonderful powers of description. They had to tear themselves away from the prayers of their sick and wounded comrades, who were left to the mercy of the enemy.   They could hardly make up their minds to go.   The bit of hostile soil under the shelter of their walls had come to seem to them like their home.   Nicias, notwithstanding his illness, rose to this supreme occasion as he had never risen to another.   He tried to cheer and animate the miserable host—whose wretched plight was indeed of his own making—by words of hope.   They set forth, Nicias leading the van, Demosthenes the rear, along the western road which crosses the Anapus and passes the modern village of Floridia.   The aim was to reach Sicel territory first, and then get to Catane as they could ; for it would have been madness to attempt the straight road to Catane round the west of Epipolae under the Syracusan forts. The chief difficulty in their way was a high point called the Acraean cliff, approached by a rugged pass, which begins near Floridia. It was not till the fourth day that, having toiled along the pass under constant annoyance from darters and horsemen, they came in sight of the cliff, and found that the way was barred by a wall, with a garrison of Syracusan hoplites behind it.   To attempt to pass was impossible ; they retreated on Floridia in a heavy thunderstorm. They now moved southwards, and abandoning the idea of reaching the Sicel hill-land from this point, marched to the Helorine road, which would take them in the direction of Gela.   During the sixth day's march a sort of panic seems to have fallen on the rear of the army under Demosthenes ; the men lagged far behind and the army was parted in two.   Nicias advanced with his division as speedily as he could.   There were several streams to cross, and it was all-

Retreat of Athenians, Sept. 11.

Sept. 16.

R

important to press on before the Syracusans had time to block the passages by walls and palisades. The Helorine road approaches the

(R. Cassibile.)

shore near the point where the river Kakyparis flows into the sea. When they reached the ford, the Athenians found a Syracusan band on the other side raising a fortification. They drove the enemy

(R. Elanici, or Caval-lata ?)

away without much difficulty and marched as far as the river Erineos, where they encamped for the night. On the next morning a Syracusan herald drew near. He had news to tell. The rear of the army had been surrounded the day before, in the olive garden of Polyzalus, through which the Helorine road passed, and had been forced to surrender. The lives of the 6000 men were to be spared. Demosthenes did not condescend to make terms for himself, and when the capitulation had been arranged he sought death by his own hand, but the enemy, who desired to secure a captive general, intercepted the stroke. Having sent a messenger, under a truce, to assure himself of the truth of the tale, Nicias offered terms to the Syracusans—that the rest of the army should be allowed to go free on condition that Athens should repay the costs of the war, the security being a hostage for every talent. The terms were at once rejected. The Syracusans were bent on achieving the glory of lead-

Sept. 17.

ing the whole army captive. For that day the miserable army

Sept. 18.

remained where it was, worn out with want of food. Next morning they resumed the march and, harassed by the darts of the enemy,

(R. Fal-conara).

made their way to the stream of the Assinaros. Here they found a hostile force on the opposite steep bank. But they cared little for the foe, for they were consumed with intolerable thirst. They rushed down into the bed of the river, struggling with one another to reach the water. The Syracusans who were pursuing came down the banks and slaughtered them unresisting as they drank. The water was soon foul, but muddy and dyed with blood as it was, they drank notwithstanding and fought for it.

Athenians surrender.

At last Nicias surrendered. He surrendered to Gylippus, for he had more trust in him than in the Syracusans. The slaughter, which was as great as any that had been wrought in the war, was then stayed and the survivors were made prisoners. It seems that a great many of the captives were appropriated for their own use by the individual victors ; and their lot may have been comparatively light. But the

Treatment of the prisoners.

fate of the state-prisoners was cruel. Seven thousand were thrown into the stone-quarries of Achradina—deep, unroofed dungeons, open to the chills of night and the burning heat of the day—on a miserable allowance of food and water. The allies of the Athenians were kept in this misery for seventy days ; the Athenians themselves were doomed to endure the torture for six months longer, throughout the whole winter. Such was the vengeance which Syracuse wreaked

upon her invaders.   The prisoners who survived the ordeal were put
to work in the public prison or sold.   Some were rescued by young
men who were attracted by their manners.   Others owed mitigation
of their lot, even freedom, to the power which an Athenian poet
exercised over the hearts of men, in Sicily as well as in his own city.
Slaves who knew speeches and choruses of the plays of Euripides by
heart, and could recite them well, found favour in the sight of their
masters ; and we hear of those who, after many days, returned to
their Athenian homes and thanked the poet for their deliverance.

Some mystery has hung round the fate of the two generals, Demo- *Fate of*
sthenes and Nicias, but there is no doubt that they were put to death *Nicias and*
without mercy, and some reason to suppose that they were not *Demo-*
spared the pain of torture.   Hermocrates and Gylippus would have *sthenes.*
wished to save them, but were powerless in face of the intense feeling
of fury against Athens which animated Syracuse in the hour of
her triumph.   If a man's punishment should be proportionate not to
his intentions but to the positive sum of mischief which his conduct has
caused, no measure of punishment would have been too great for the
deserts of Nicias.   His incompetence, his incredible bungling, ruined
the expedition and led to the downfall of Athens.   But the blunders
of Nicias were merely the revelation of his own nature, and for his own
nature he could hardly be held accountable.   The whole blame rests
with the Athenian people, who insisted on his playing a part for which
he was utterly unsuited.   It has already been observed that one
dominant note of the character of Nicias was fear of responsibility.
Throughout the whole war there was no post which so absolutely
demanded the power of undertaking full responsibility as that of chief
commander in this great and distant expedition.   And yet Nicias
was chosen.   The selection shows that he was popular as well as
respected.   He was popular with his army, and he seems to have been
hardly a sufficiently strict disciplinarian.   It has been well said that
in the camp he never forgot that the soldiers whom he commanded
had votes in the Ecclesia which they might use against himself
when they returned to Athens.   Timid as a general, timid as a
statesman, hampered by superstition, the decorous Nicias was a
brave soldier and an amiable man, whose honourable qualities were
the means of leading him into a false position.   If he had been less
scrupulous and devout, and had been endowed with better brains,
he would not have ruined his country.   " Given the men a people
chooses," it has been said, " the people itself, in its exact worth and
worthlessness, is given."   In estimating the character of the Athenian
people, we must not forget their choice of this hero of conscientious
indecision.

So deep is the pity which the tragic fate of the Athenians excites in us that we almost forget to sympathise with the sons of Syracuse in the joy of their deliverance. Yet they deserve our sympathy; they had passed through a sore trial, and they had destroyed the powerful invader who had come to rob them of their freedom. To

Institution of the Assinarian games.

celebrate the anniversaries of their terrible victory they instituted games which they called Assinarian, after the river which had witnessed the last scene. In connexion with these games, some beautiful coins were struck. Perhaps there is nothing which enlists

The coin-engravers of Syracuse.

our affections for Syracuse so much as her coins. And it was at this very period that she brought the art of engraving coin-dies to perfection. Never in any country, in any age of the world, was the art of engraving on metal practised with such high inspiration and such consummate skill as in Sicily. No holy place in Hellas possessed diviner faces in bronze or marble than the faces which the Sicilian cities circulated on their silver money. The greatest of the Sicilian artists were Syracusan, and among the greatest of the Syracusan were Evaenetus and Cimon. The die-engraver's achievements may seem small, compared with the life-size or colossal works of a sculptor, yet, as creators of the beautiful, Evaenetus and his fellows may claim to stand in the same rank as Phidias. Their heads of Persephone and of the water-nymph Arethusa encircled by dolphins, their wonderful four-horsed chariots, seem to invest Syracuse with a glory

New issues of "Da-maratea," 412-406 B.C.

to which she hardly attained. In the years after the defeat of Athens there were several issues of large ten-drachm medallions, modelled on those "Damaratean" coins which had commemorated Gelon's victory at Himera.[1] The engraving of these was committed to Cimon and Evaenetus and a nameless artist—perhaps a greater than either—of whom a single medallion, an exquisite Persephone crowned with barley, has been found on the slopes of Aetna.

SECT. 6. CONSEQUENCES OF THE SICILIAN CATASTROPHE

Was the Sicilian expedition a foolish undertaking?

The Sicilian expedition was part of the general aggressive policy of Athens which made her unpopular in Greece. Unjust that policy was ; but this enterprise was not more flagrantly unrighteous than some of her other undertakings, and it had the plausible enough pretext of protecting the weaker cities in the west against the stronger. More fruitful is the question whether the expedition was expedient from a purely political point of view. It is often said that it was a wild venture, an instance of a whole people going mad, like the English people in the matter of the Crimean War. It is hard to see how this view can be maintained. If there were ever an enterprise of

[1] See above, p. 304.

which the wisdom cannot be judged by the result, it is the enterprise against Syracuse. All the chances were in its favour. If the advice of Lamachus had been taken and Syracuse attacked at once, there cannot be much doubt that Syracuse would have fallen at the outset. If Nicias had not let precious time pass and delayed the completion of the wall to the northern cliff of Epipolae, the doom of the city was sealed, Gylippus could never have entered. The failure was due to nothing in the character of the enterprise itself, but entirely to the initial mistake in the appointment of the general. And it was quite in the nature of things that the Athenian sea-power, predominant in the east, should seek further expansion in the west. An energetic establishment of Athenian influence in that region was recommended by the political situation. It must be remembered that the most serious and abiding hostility with which Athens had to reckon was the commercial rivalry of Corinth ; and the close alliance of Corinth with her Dorian daughters and friends in the west was a strong and adequate motive for Athenian intervention. The necessity of a counterweight to Corinthian influence in Sicily and Italy had long ago been recognised ; some attempts had been made to meet it ; and when peace with Sparta set Athenian forces free for service outside Greece and the Aegean, it was natural that the opportunity should be taken to act effectively in the west.

The infatuation of the Athenian people was shown not in willing *Cause of* the expedition, but in committing it to Nicias—instead of Demo- *the failure.* sthenes, who was clearly marked out for the task—and then in re- calling Alcibiades. These blunders seemed to point to something wrong in the constitution or its working. They did in fact show that an expedition of that kind was liable to be mismanaged when any of the arrangements connected with its execution depended on a popular assembly, or might be interfered with for party purposes. To Thucydides it was clear that the primary mistakes were political, not military.

And after the disaster of the Assinaros there was a feeling that some change must be made in the administration. Athens was hard pressed by the Lacedaemonian post at Decelea, which stopped cultiva- *Closing* tion and became a refuge for deserting slaves. Of these slaves, who *of the* numbered about 20,000, we can hardly doubt that many belonged to *mines of* the gangs which worked in the mines of Laurion. In any case, one *Laurion,* most disastrous effect of the seizure of Decelea was the closing of the *413 B.C.* mines ; since even southern Attica was at the mercy of the Lace- *Gold* daemonians. Thus one of the chief sources of Athenian revenue *coinage at* was cut off ; she was robbed of her supply of " Laureot owls " ; and *Athens* in a few years we find her melting gold dedicatory offerings to make *(407) ;* gold coins, and even coining in copper, thinly plated with silver. *copper* *coinage* *(406).*

Thus the treasury was at a low ebb, and there were no men to replace those who were lost in Sicily. It was felt that the committees of the Council of Five Hundred were hardly competent to conduct the city through such a crisis ; a smaller and more permanent body was required ; and the chief direction of affairs was entrusted to a board of Ten, named *Probuli*, which practically superseded the Council for the time being.

[Shortly before this a change had been made in the system of tribute payment. The fixed assessment was replaced by a tax of 5 per cent on all imports and exports carried by sea to or from the harbours of the empire. It was thought that this duty would produce a larger income than the tribute and it might seem a more equitable principle for payment, for it would be paid by those who had profited most from the growth of Aegean trade under the Athenian thalassocracy. Its effectiveness, however, depended on the requisite display of strength by Athens. No doubt there was considerable scope for disputing the amount due ; at all events the old system of tribute was restored as soon as the first substantial Athenian victory gave grounds again for confidence.]

The financial pressure was shown by the dismissal of a body of Thracian mercenaries who had arrived too late to sail to Sicily. They returned home under the conduct of Diitrephes, who was instructed to employ them, on the road, in any way he could against the enemy. Sailing northward between Euboea and the mainland, they disembarked on the coast of Boeotia, and reaching the small town of Mycalessus at daybreak, captured it. "Nothing was ever so unexpected and terrible." The Thracians showed their barbarity in massacring all the inhabitants,—nay, every living thing they saw. They broke into a boys' school and killed all the children.

Reforms did not avert the dangers which threatened Athens. The tidings of the great calamity which had befallen the flower of her youth in Sicily moved Hellas from end to end. The one thought of enemies, neutrals and subjects alike, was to seize the opportunity of shattering the power of Athens irretrievably. Messages came from some of the chief allies, from Euboea, from Lesbos, from Chios, to Agis at Decelea, to the ephors at Sparta, declaring that they were ready to revolt, if a Peloponnesian fleet appeared off their coasts. A fleet was clearly necessary to do the work that was to be done ; a naval policy was forced upon Sparta by the case. It was decided that a hundred ships should be equipped, of which half, in equal shares, were to be supplied by Sparta and Boeotia. Athens also spent the winter in building triremes, and fortified Cape Sunium to protect the arrival of her corn-ships.

King Agis while he was at Decelea possessed the right of sending troops wherever he chose. He received the overtures from Euboea and Lesbos and promised assistance. But Spartan interference in these islands was deferred owing to the more pressing demands of Chios, which were addressed directly to Sparta and were backed by the support of a great power, whose voice for many years had not been heard in the sphere of the politics of Hellas. Persia now *Persia* enters once more upon the stage of Greek history, aiming at the *comes on* recovery of the coast cities of Asia Minor, and for this purpose *the stage* playing off one Greek power against another. The Sicilian disaster *again.* suggested to Tissaphernes, the satrap of Sardis, and to Pharnabazus, the satrap of Hellespontine Phrygia, that it was the moment to wrest from Athens her Asiatic dominions. This must be done by stirring up revolt and by a close alliance with Sparta. Each satrap was anxious to secure for himself the credit of having brought about such a profitable alliance, and each independently sent envoys to Lacedaemon, Pharnabazus urging action in the Hellespont, Tissaphernes supporting the appeal of Chios. The Chian demand, which had the powerful advocacy of Alcibiades, carried the day.

In the following summer the rebellion against Athens actively *412 B.C.* began. The appearance of a few Spartan ships was the signal for the formal revolt of Chios, and then in conjunction with the Chian fleet *Revolt of* they excited Miletus, Teos, Lebedus to follow in the same path. *Athenian* Methymna and Mytilene lost little time in joining the movement and *allies.* were followed by Cyme and Phocaea. The Athenian historian has words of commendation for the city which played the chief part in this rebellion. " No people," says Thucydides, "as far as I know, except the Chians and Lacedaemonians (but the Chians not equally with the Lacedaemonians), have preserved moderation in prosperity, and in proportion as their city has gained in power have gained also in the stability of their government. In this revolt they may seem to have shown a want of prudence, yet they did not venture upon it until many brave allies were ready to share the peril with them, and until the Athenians themselves seemed to confess that after their calamity in Sicily the state of their affairs was hopelessly bad. And, if they were deceived through the uncertainty of human things, the error of judgment was common to many who, like them, believed that the Athenian power would speedily be overthrown." [1]

This successful beginning led to the Treaty of Miletus between *Treaty of* Sparta and Persia. In the hope of humbling to the dust her detested *Miletus.* rival, the city of Leonidas now sold to the barbarian the freedom of her fellow-Greeks of Asia. The Persian claim was that Athens had usurped the rights of the Great King for well-nigh seventy years over

---

[1] Jowett.

the Asiatic cities, and that arrears of tribute were owing to him for all that time. Sparta recognised the right of the Great King to all the dominion which belonged to him and his forefathers, and he undertook to supply the pay for the seamen of the Peloponnesian fleet operating on the Asiatic coast, while the war with Athens lasted. It may be said for Sparta that she merely wanted to get the money at the time, and had no intention of honourably carrying out her dishonourable undertaking, but hoped to rescue the Greek cities in the end. But the treaty of Miletus opened up a new path in Greek politics, which was to lead the Persian king to the position of arbiter of Hellas.

Warfare in 412-11 B.C.

Meanwhile Athens had not been idle. Straitened by want of money, she had been forced to pass a measure to touch the reserve fund of 1000 talents. She blockaded a Corinthian fleet, destined for Chios, on the Argolic coast ; she laid Chios itself waste, and blockaded the town ; she won back Lesbos, and gained some successes at Miletus. But Cnidus rebelled ; the Peloponnesians gained an advantage in a naval engagement at the small island of Syme, and this was followed by the revolt of Rhodes. This island was still divided between the territories of the three cities of Lindus, Ialysus, and Camirus, but a few years after the revolt the foundation of the island's future power

Battle of Syme (Jan.? 411).

was laid by the synoecism of the three communities in the common city of Rhodes. By the spring of 411 the situation was that Athens had her northern and Hellespontine confederacy intact, but that on the western coast of Asia little of importance remained to her but Lesbos, Samos, Cos, and Halicarnassus. She was confronted by a formidable Peloponnesian fleet, supported by Persia and by a considerable reinforcement from Sicily—twenty-two vessels under Hermocrates, the return of Syracuse for her deliverance.

FIG. 131.—Coin of Ialysus (Rhodes), fifth century (obverse). Part of winged boar ; helmet [legend : ΙΑΛΥΣΙΟΝ].

It could not be said indeed that all things had gone smoothly between Persia and Lacedaemon. Differences had arisen as to the amount of the subsidies, and a new treaty was concluded in which the rights of the king were less distinctly formulated. In the meantime

Alcibiades leaves Sparta, 412 B.C. (autumn).

Alcibiades had been cultivating the friendship of Tissaphernes at Miletus, and had on that account become an object of suspicion at Sparta. He had a bitter enemy in king Agis, whose wife he had seduced. Seeing that his life was in danger, he had left Miletus and gone to the court of the satrap, where he began a new series of machinations with a view to his own return to Athens. Indeed his work at Sparta had now been done, and political changes which were in the air at Athens invited the formation of new schemes. The man who had done much to bring about the alliance of Tissaphernes with Sparta now set himself to dissolve that union and bring about an understanding between the satrap and Athens.

Fig. 132.—Coin of Rhodes (obverse). Head of Helios.

Sect. 7. The Oligarchic Revolution

At Athens in these months there was distress, fear, and discontent. How deeply the people felt the pressure of the long war is uttered in the comedy of *Lysistrate* or "Dame Disbander" which the poet Aristophanes brought out at this crisis. The heroine unites all the women of the belligerent cities of Greece into a league to force the men to make peace. Under the ribald humour there pierces here and there a note of pathos not to be found in the poet's earlier peace plays, the *Acharnians* and the *Peace*. War is not a time for marrying and giving in marriage. "Never mind us married women," says Lysistrate; "it is the thought of the maidens growing old at home that goes to my heart." "Do not men grow old too?" asks a Probulos who argues with her. "Ah, but it is not the same thing. A man, though his hair be gray, can soon pick up a young girl; but a woman's season is short, and, if she miss her chance then, no one will marry her." The Lysistrate of Aristophanes, Jan.-Feb. 411 B.C.,

But the fear of Persia was the shadow which brooded darkest over Athens at this time, and there was also a lurking suspicion of treachery, a dread that the oligarchical party were planning a revolution or even intriguing with the enemy at Decelea. Two months after the *Lysistrate*, at the great feast of Dionysus, Aristophanes brought out a play whose plot had nothing to do with politics—the "Celebrants of the Thesmophoria." But the fears that were in the hearts of many were echoed by the poet, when his chorus called upon Athena, "the sole keeper of our city," to come as *the hater of tyrants*. Thesmophoriazusae (March to April, 411 B.C.).

Lovers of the democracy might well pray to the guardian lady of the city. The opportunity for which the oligarchs had waited so long had come at last. For outside their own ranks there was a large section of influential men who were dissatisfied with the existing forms of government and, though opposed to oligarchy, desired a modification of the constitution. There was a fair show of reason for arguing that the foreign policy had been mismanaged by the democracy, and that men of education and knowledge had not a The moderate revolutionists.

sufficient influence on the conduct of affairs. The chief of those who desired to see the establishment of a moderate polity—neither an extreme democracy nor an oligarchy, but partaking of both—was

*Thera-
menes.
ἡ πάτριος
πολιτεία
(Dracon's
constitu-
tion).*

Theramenes, whose father Hagnon was one of the Probuli. The watchword of Theramenes and his party was "the old constitution of our fathers." By this they meant not the constitution of Solon, but the constitution before Solon. They interpreted the whole history of Athens in accordance with their political views. They condemned Solon as the author of democracy, the first of a long line of mischievous demagogues; they made out that the Areopagus, and not Themistocles, was the hero of Salamis; they branded Aristides, founder of the Delian confederacy, for organising a system which fed 20,000 idlers on the allied cities; they represented Pericles as a man of no ideas of his own, but depending upon others to prompt him. After two centuries of evil government, the Athenians must go back to the times before Solon and revive in some new form the constitution of Dracon. This "constitution of Dracon," of which the chief feature was a Council of Four Hundred, had never existed; it was fathered upon Dracon by Theramenes and his friends.

The extreme oligarchs, though the ideal of Theramenes was not theirs, were ready in the first instance to act in concert with the moderate party for the purpose of upsetting the democracy. The

Antiphon.

soul of the plot was Antiphon of Rhamnus, an eloquent orator and advocate, who had made his mark in the days of Cleon. He was unpopular, on account of his undisguised oligarchical views; the historian Thucydides describes him as "a man who in virtue fell short of none of his contemporaries"; and by *virtue* is meant disinterested and able devotion to his party. Other active conspirators were Pisander, who had been in old days a partisan of Cleon, and Phrynichus, who was one of the commanders of the fleet stationed at Samos. The prospects of the movement were good; it was favoured by the Probuli and by most of the officers of the fleet. Moreover, the Athenians — as they had shown already by the appointment of the Probuli—were in a temper, with the fear of Persia before their eyes, to sacrifice their constitution if such a sacrifice would save the city. Alcibiades had entered into negotiations with the officers at Samos, promising to secure an alliance with Tissaphernes, but representing the abolition of democracy as a necessary condition. Most of the oligarchical conspirators were pleased with the scheme, and even the army was seduced by the idea of receiving pay from the Great King. Some indeed of the more sagacious thought they saw through the designs of Alcibiades; and Phrynichus, who aspired himself to be the leader of the revolution, detected a rival and tried by various intrigues to thwart him.

Alcibiades was certainly no friend of oligarchy; but it was his policy in any case to upset the existing democracy, which would never recall him.   If an oligarchy were established, he might intervene to restore the democracy, and in return for such a service all would be forgiven.   But he would have to be guided by events.

Pisander was sent to Athens to prepare the way for the return *Pisandros* of Alcibiades and a modification of the democracy.   The people *at Athens.* were at first indignant at the proposals to change the constitution and recall the renegade; the Eumolpidae denounced the notion of having any dealings with the profaner of the Mysteries.   But the cogent argument that the safety of Athens depended on separating Persia from the Peloponnesians, and that this could be managed only by Alcibiades, and that the Great King would not trust Athens so long as she was governed by a popular constitution, had its effect; and there was moreover powerful but secret influence at work through the Hetaeriae or political clubs.   It was voted that Pisander and other envoys should be sent to negotiate a treaty *(? Feb.)* with Tissaphernes and arrange matters with Alcibiades.

It appeared at once that Alcibiades had promised more than he *Sparta and* could perform.   There had indeed been a serious rupture between *Tissapher-* Tissaphernes and Sparta.   Lichas, a Spartan commissioner who *nes.* conferred with the satrap, denounced the terms of the treaties.   He pointed out the monstrous consequences of the clause which assigned to the king power over all the countries which his ancestors had held; for this would involve Persian dominion over Thessaly and other lands of northern Greece.   On such terms, he said, we will not have our fleet paid, and he asked for a new treaty.   Tissaphernes departed in anger.   But when it came to a question of union with Athens, Tissaphernes showed that he did not wish to break with the Peloponnesians.   He proposed impossible conditions to the Athenian envoys, and then made a new treaty with the Spartans, modifying the clause to which Lichas objected.   The territory which the Spartans recognised as Persian was now expressly confined to Asia.

But though the reasons for a revolution, so far as they concerned *The re-* Tissaphernes and Alcibiades, seemed thus to be removed, the pre- *volution at* parations had advanced so far that the result of the mission of *Athens.* Pisander produced no effect on the course of events.   The conspirators did not scruple to use menaces and even violence; Androcles, a strong democrat, who had been prominent in procuring the condemnation of Alcibiades, was murdered.   Some others of less note were made away with in like manner; and there was a general feeling of fear and mistrust in the city.   But there was a widespread conviction that the existence of Athens was at stake and that some change in the constitution was inevitable.   The news that Abydus

(End of April.)

(April to May, 411 B.C.)

and Lampsacus had revolted may have hastened the final act. The revolution was peaceably effected through the co-operation of the Ten Probuli. A decree was passed that the Probuli and twenty others chosen by the people should form a commission of thirty who should jointly devise proposals for the safety of the state and lay them before the Assembly on a fixed day. When the day came, the Assembly met at the temple of Poseidon at Colonus, about a mile from the town. After preliminary measures to secure impunity for a proposal involving a subversion of existing laws, a radical change was brought forward and carried. The sovereign Assembly was to consist in future not of the whole people, but of a body of about Five Thousand, those who were strongest physically and financially. A hundred men were to be chosen, ten by each tribe, for the purpose of electing and enrolling the Five Thousand. Pay for almost all public offices was to be abolished. To these revolutionary measures a saving clause was attached ; they were to remain in force "as long as the war lasts " ; and thus the people was more easily induced to pass them.

(May.)

Scheme of a polity.

But this was only preliminary ; a constitution had still to be framed. When the Five Thousand were elected, they chose a commission of one hundred men to draw up a constitution. The scheme which they framed is highly remarkable as a criticism on certain defects in the constitution which was now to be overthrown. The body of Five Thousand were not to act as an Assembly ; there was in fact to be no Assembly. The Five Thousand were to be divided into four parts, and each part was to act as Council for a year in turn. The Council would elect the higher magistrates from its own number. Thus the difficulties of administration which arose in the double system, where the Council's action was hampered by the Assembly, would be done away with ; and the inclusion of the generals and magistrates in the Council was a necessary consequence. Under the democracy, the holders of office could influence the Assembly against the Council ; under the new scheme there would be no room for such collisions.

Council of Four Hundred.

One fatal defect in this scheme was the size of the administrative body, and if it had been tried we may be sure that it would not have worked. But it was never tried. It passed the Assembly as a scheme to come into force in the future ; but in the meantime a further proposal of the Hundred commissioners enacted that the state should be administered by a Council of Four Hundred, in which each of the ten tribes was to be represented by forty members. It would seem, but it is not quite certain, that the election of the Council was managed in the following way. The Assembly which created it

5 proedroi. chose five men under the title of *presidents*, who were empowered to nominate one hundred councillors, and each of these councillors co-opted three others ; but both the presidents in their nomination and the one hundred councillors in their co-option were limited to a number of candidates who were previously chosen by the tribes.   The Four Hundred were instituted as merely a provisional government, but the entire administration was placed in their hands, the management of the finances, and the appointment of the magistrates.   The Five Thousand were to meet only when summoned by the Four Hundred, so that the Assembly ceased to have any significance, and the provisional constitution was an unadulterated oligarchy.   The Council of Four Hundred was proclaimed to be a revival of the imaginary constitution of Dracon, under which Athens flourished before demagogues led her into evil paths ; but the whole fabric of Cleisthenes, the ten tribes and the demes, was retained.   The existing Council of Five Hundred went *Council of* out of office before the end of the civil year, and seven days later the *Five* administration of the Four Hundred began.   Throughout these trans- *Hundred goes out* actions intimidation was freely used by the conspirators, and we are *of office,* 14 told that they went with hidden daggers into the council-chamber *Thargelion* and forced the Five Hundred to retire.   Thucydides admires the *(end of* ability of the men who carried out this revolution.   " An easy thing it *May);* certainly was not, one hundred years after the fall of the tyrants, to *Four* destroy the liberties of the Athenian people, who were not only a *Hundred enter on* free, but during more than one-half of this time had been an imperial, *office,* 22 people." [1] *Thargelion,* 411

It may be asked why a provisional government was introduced, *B.C.* instead of proceeding at once to the establishment of the permanent constitution which the Hundred commissioners had framed.   Here we touch upon the inwardness of the political situation : the two constitutions betray the double influence at work in the revolution.   The establishment of the Four Hundred was a concession made to Antiphon and the oligarchs by Theramenes and the moderates, who regarded it as only preliminary ; while the oligarchs hoped to render it permanent.

SECT. 8. FALL OF THE FOUR HUNDRED.   THE POLITY. THE DEMOCRACY RESTORED

For more than three months the Four Hundred governed the *Rule of the* city with a high hand, and then they were overthrown.   Their success *Four* had been largely due to the absence of so many of the most demo- *Hundred,* cratic citizens in the fleet at Samos ; and it was through the attitude *June-Sept.* of the fleet that their fall was brought about.   The sailors rose

[1] Jowett.

against the oligarchic officers and the oligarchs of Samos, who were conspiring against the popular party and had murdered the exile Hyperbolus. The chief leaders of this reaction were Thrasybulus and Thrasyllus, who persuaded the soldiers and sailors to proclaim formally their adhesion to the democracy and their hostility to the Four Hundred. The Assembly, which had been abolished at Athens, was called into being at Samos, and the army, representing the Athenian people, deposed the Generals and elected others. The Athenians at Samos felt that they were in as good a position as the Athenians at Athens, and they hoped still to obtain the alliance of Persia, through the good offices of Alcibiades, whose recall and pardon were formally voted. Thrasybulus fetched Alcibiades to Samos, and he was elected a General. The hoped-for alliance with Persia was not effected, but it was at least something that Tissaphernes did not use the large Phoenician fleet which he had at Aspendus against the Athenians, and that his relations with the Peloponnesians were becoming daily worse. He went to Aspendus, but he never brought the ships, and it was a matter of speculation what the object of his journey was. Thucydides records his own belief that Tissaphernes "wanted to wear out and to neutralise the Hellenic forces; his object was to damage them both, while he was losing time in going to Aspendus, and to paralyse their action and not strengthen either of them by his alliance. For if he had chosen to finish the war, finished it might have been once for all, as any one may see." [1] The Athenians at Samos now proposed to sail straight to Athens and destroy the Four Hundred. The proposal shows how much the fleet despised the Peloponnesian navy, which, under its incompetent admiral Astyochus, had been spending the summer in doing nothing. But to leave Samos would have been madness, and Alcibiades saved them from the blunder of sacrificing Ionia and the Hellespont. Negotiations were begun with the oligarchs at Athens, and Alcibiades expressed himself satisfied with the Assembly of Five Thousand, but insisted that the Four Hundred should be abolished.

As a matter of fact the overtures from Samos were welcome to the majority of the Four Hundred, who were dissatisfied with their colleagues and their own position. The nature of an oligarchy which supplants a democracy was beginning to show itself. "The instant an oligarchy is established," says Thucydides, "the promoters of it disdain mere equality, and everybody thinks that he ought to be far above everybody else. Whereas in a democracy, when an election is made, a man is less disappointed at a failure because he has not been competing with his equals." [1] Moreover, the

[1] Jowett.

Four Hundred were at first professedly established as merely a temporary government, preliminary to the establishment of a polity which would be less an oligarchy than a qualified democracy.   Such a polity was the ideal of Theramenes, and he was impatient to constitute it. Thus there was a cleavage in the Four Hundred, the extreme oligarchs on one side, led by Antiphon and Phrynichus, the moderate reformers on the other, led by Theramenes.   While the moderates had the support of the army at Samos behind them, the extreme party looked to the enemy for support and sent envoys to Sparta for the purpose of concluding a peace.   In the meantime they fortified Eetionea, the mole which formed the northern side of the entrance to the Great Harbour of Piraeus.   The object was to command the entrance so as to be able either to admit the Lacedaemonians or to exclude the fleet of Samos.

When the envoys returned from Sparta without having made *Movement* terms, and when a Peloponnesian squadron was seen in the Saronic *against the* gulf, the movement against the oligarchs took shape.   Phrynichus was *Four* slain by foreign assassins in the market-place.   The soldiers who were *Hundred.* employed in building the fort at Eetionea were instigated by Theramenes to declare against the oligarchy, and, after a great tumult at the Piraeus, the walls of the fort were pulled down, to the cry of " Whoever wishes the Five Thousand, and not the Four Hundred, to rule, let him come and help."   Nobody in the crowd really knew whether the Five Thousand existed as an actually constituted body or not.   When the fort was demolished, an Assembly was held in the theatre on the slope of Munychia ; the agitation subsided, and peaceable negotiations with the Four Hundred ensued.   A day was fixed for an Assembly in the theatre of Dionysus, to discuss a settlement on the basis of the constitution of the Five Thousand.   But on the very day, just as the Assembly was about to meet, the appearance of a Lacedaemonian squadron, which had been hovering about, off the coast of Salamis, produced a temporary panic and a general rush to the Piraeus.   It was only a fright, so far as the Piraeus was concerned, but there were other serious dangers ahead, as every one saw.   The safety of Euboea was threatened, and the Athenians depended entirely on Euboea, now that they had lost Attica.   The Lacedaemonian fleet —forty-two ships under Agesandridas—doubled Sunium and sailed to Oropus.   The Athenians sent thirty-six ships under Thymochares to Eretria, where they were forced to fight at once and were utterly defeated.   All Euboea then revolted, except Oreus in the north, *Revolt of* which was a settlement of Athenian cleruchs.   *Euboea*

At no moment perhaps—since the Persian War—was the situation *(early in* at Athens so alarming.   She had no reserve of ships, the army at *Septem-* Samos was hostile, Euboea, from which she derived her supplies, was *ber).*

lost, and there was feud and sedition in the city. It was a moment
which might have inspired the Lacedaemonians to operate with a little
vigour both by land and sea. Athens could not have resisted a combined attack of Agis from Decelea and Agesandridas at the Piraeus.
But the Lacedaemonians were, as Thucydides observes, very convenient enemies, and they let the opportunity slip. The battle of
Eretria struck, however, the hour of doom for the oligarchs. An

(Sept.)
" Polity"
or moderate
democracy
established
at Athens.
Assembly in the Pnyx deposed the Four Hundred, and voted that
the government should be placed in the hands of a body consisting
of all those who could furnish themselves with arms, which body
should be called the Five Thousand. Legislators (*nomothetae*) were
appointed to draw up the details of the constitution, and all pay for
offices was abolished. Most of the oligarchs escaped to Decelea,
and one of them betrayed the fort of Oenoe on the frontier of Boeotia
to the enemy. Two—Antiphon and Archeptolemus—were executed.

The chief promoter of the new constitution was Theramenes. It
was a constitution such as he had conceived from the beginning,
though apparently not actually the same as that which had been
proposed by the Hundred commissioners. Thucydides praises it as
a constitution in which the rule of the many and the rule of the few
were fairly tempered. It was the realisation of the ultimate intentions
of most of those who had promoted the original resolution. It is certain that Theramenes, from the very beginning, desired to organise a
polity, with democracy and oligarchy duly mixed ; his acquiescence in
a temporary oligarchy was a mere matter of necessity ; and the nickname of *Cothurnus*—the loose buskin that fits either foot—given to
him by the oligarchs was not deserved.

In the meantime the supine Spartan admiral Astyochus had been
superseded by Mindarus, and the Peloponnesian fleet, invited by
Battle of
Cynossema,
411 B.C.
Pharnabazus, sailed for the Hellespont. The Athenian fleet under
Thrasybulus and Thrasyllus followed, and forced them to fight in the
straits. The Athenians, with seventy-six ships, were extended along
the shore of the Chersonese, and the object of the Peloponnesians,
who had ten more ships, was to outflank and so prevent the enemy
from sailing out of the straits, and at the same time to press their
centre in upon the land. The Athenians, to thwart this intention,
extended their own right wing, and in doing so weakened the whole
line. The Peloponnesians were victorious on the centre, but
Thrasybulus, who was on the right wing, took advantage of their disorder in the moment of victory and threw them into panic. The
engagement on the Athenian left was round the Cape of
Cynossema, out of sight of the rest of the battle, and resulted after
hard fighting in the repulse of the Peloponnesians. This victory
heartened the Athenians ; it was followed immediately by the

recovery of Cyzicus, which had revolted. Mindarus had to send for the squadron which lay in the waters of Euboea; but only a remnant reached him: the rest of the ships were lost in a storm off Mt. Athos. Another Athenian success at Abydus closed the military operations of the year but, owing to lack of funds, the fleet had to disperse for the winter. Tissaphernes was ill satisfied with the success of Athens, and when Alcibiades paid him a visit at Sardis during the winter, he arrested him. But Alcibiades made his escape.

The Peloponnesians were now vigorously supported by Pharnabazus, who was a far more valuable and trustworthy ally than Tissaphernes. In the spring Mindarus laid siege to Cyzicus, and *Battle of* the satrap supported him with an army. The Athenian fleet of *Cyzicus,* eighty-six ships succeeded in passing the Hellespont unseen, and in *410 B.C.* three divisions, under Alcibiades, Theramenes, and Thrasybulus, took Mindarus by surprise. After a hard-fought battle both by land and sea, the Athenians were entirely victorious, Mindarus was slain, and about sixty triremes were taken or sunk. This annihilated the Peloponnesian navy. A laconic despatch, announcing the defeat to the Spartan ephors, was intercepted by the Athenians: "Our success is over; Mindarus is slain; the men are starving; we know not what to do." Sparta immediately made proposals of peace to Athens on the basis of the *status quo*. It would have been wise of Athens to accept the offer, and obtain relief from the pressure of the garrison at Decelea. But there is no doubt that the feeling in the navy was entirely against a peace which did not include the restoration of the power of Athens in the Aegean and Asia Minor; and the victory of Cyzicus seemed to assure the promise of its speedy recovery, notwithstanding the purse of Pharnabazus. The Spartan overtures were rejected.

The victory of Cyzicus led to a restoration of the unity of the *Restora-* Athenian state, which for a year had been divided into two parts, *tion of* centred in Athens and Samos. The democratic party at Athens, *Athenian* encouraged by the success of the thoroughly democratic navy, were *democracy.* able to upset the polity of Theramenes and restore the democracy with the unlimited franchise and the Cleisthenic Council of Five Hundred. The most prominent of the leaders of this movement was Cleophon the lyremaker, a man of the same class as Hyperbolus and Cleon, and endowed with the same order of talent. Like Cleon he was a strong imperialist, and he was now the mouthpiece of the prevailing sentiment for war. His financial ability seems to have been no less remarkable than that of Cleon. The remuneration of offices, which was an essential part of the Athenian democracy, was revived as a matter of course; but Cleophon instituted a new payment, for which his name was best remembered by posterity. *Diobelia.*

This was the "Two-obol payment." Though we know that it was introduced by Cleophon, it is not recorded for what purpose it was paid or who received it. Some have supposed that it was simply the wage of the judges,—that the old fee of three obols was revived in the reduced form of two obols. But this can hardly be the case. The two-obol payment is mentioned in a manner which implies that it was something completely novel. The probability is that it was a disbursement intended to relieve the terrible pressure of the protracted war upon the poor citizens whose means of livelihood was reduced or cut off by the presence of the enemy in Attica ; and we may guess that the pension of two obols a day was paid to all who were not in the receipt of other public money for their services in the field, on shipboard, or in the law courts. To give employment to the indigent by public works was another part of the policy of Cleophon, who herein followed the example of Pericles. In the first

The new temple of Athena Polias (so-called Erech-theum). years of this statesman's influence the building of a new temple of Athena on the Acropolis, [probably begun after the Peace of Nicias, but abandoned during the Sicilian expedition, was continued. It was close to the north cliff, on the site of the royal palace of Mycenaean days, and seems to have been designed to replace the oldest temple of Athena which held the ancient wooden statue of the goddess. This new temple Athena shared with Erechtheus and, though less magnificent than the Parthenon, it was the true centre of the city's worship of her patron goddess. Detailed accounts of the money paid to the craftsmen and labourers, citizens, metics, and slaves, who worked on the building and its sculptures, have survived and it is interesting to find that the sculptors of the panels of the frieze were paid at standard piece rates. That this graceful Ionic temple with the Porch of the Maidens should be completed in years of sore need is a striking tribute to Athenian resilience. And in this new confidence the old system of tribute was restored.]

FIG. 133.—Coin of Colophon, fifth century (o b v e r s e). A p o l l o wreathed with bay.

Recovery of Thasos ; occupation of Chryso-polis, 410 B.C. ; recovery of Colophon by Thrasyllus, 409 B.C. ; Athenians lose Pylus and Nisaea, 409 B.C. ; The years following the rejection of the Spartan overtures were marked by operations in the Propontis and its neighbourhood. The Athenians, under the able and strenuous leadership of Alcibiades, slowly gained ground. Thasos and Selymbria were won back. At Chrysopolis a toll station was established at which ships coming from the Euxine had to pay one-tenth of the value of their freight. Then Chalcedon was besieged and made tributary ; and finally Byzantium was starved into capitulation, so that Athens once more completely commanded the Bosphorus. Meanwhile Pharnabazus had made an arrangement to conduct Athenian envoys to Susa for the purpose of coming to terms with the Great King. Nearer home, Athens lost Nisaea to the Megarians ; *capture of* and Pylus was at length recovered by Sparta. *Chalcedon*

As the distinctive feature of the last eight years of the Pelo- *and Byzan-* ponnesian War was the combination between Persia and Sparta, we *tium,* 408. may divide this period into three parts, according to the nature of *Three* the Persian co-operation. During the first two years it is the satrap *periods of* Tissaphernes who supports the Peloponnesian operations, and Athens *union* loses nearly all Ionia. Then the satrap Pharnabazus takes the place *between* of Tissaphernes as the active ally of the Peloponnesians ; the military *Persia and* operations are chiefly in the Hellespont ; and Athens gradually *ponnesians:* recovers many of her losses. But the affairs of the west had begun (1) 412-11, to engage the attention of the Great King, Darius, who, aware that (2) 410-7, (3) 407-5.

the jealousy of the two satraps hinders an effective policy, sends down his younger son Cyrus to take the place of Tissaphernes at Sardis, with jurisdiction over Cappadocia, Phrygia, and Lydia. The government of Tissaphernes is confined to Caria. The arrival of Cyrus on the scene marks a new turning-point in the progress of the war.

It was a strange sight to see the common enemy of Hellas ranged along with the victors of Plataea against the victors of Salamis. It was a shock to men of Panhellenic feeling,

FIG. 134.—Coin of Elis (obverse). Head of Olympian Zeus laureate [legend : ΓΑΛΕΙΩΝ]. *Gorgias at Olympia, 408 B.C. (July to August).*

and it was fitting that at the great Panhellenic gathering at Olympia a voice of protest should be raised. Men of western Hellas beyond the sea could look with a calmer view on the politics of the east, and it was a man of western Hellas, the Leontine Gorgias himself, who lifted up an eloquent voice against the wooing of Persian favour by Greek states. " Rather," he said, " go to war against Persia."

SECT. 9. DOWNFALL OF THE ATHENIAN EMPIRE

Prince Cyrus was zealous ; but his zeal to intervene actively *Lysander.* and furnish pay to the Peloponnesian seamen might have been of little use, were it not for the simultaneous appointment of a new Spartan admiral, who possessed distinguished ability and inordinate ambition. This was Lysander, who was destined to bring the long war to its close. He gained the confidence of his seamen by his care for their interests, and he won much influence over Cyrus by being absolutely proof against the temptation of bribes,—a quality at which an oriental greatly marvelled. In prosecuting the aims of his ambition Lysander was perfectly unscrupulous, and he was a skilful diplomatist as well as an able general.

Alcibiades at Athens, summer, 407 B.C. While Cyrus and Lysander were negotiating, Alcibiades, after an exile of eight years, had returned to his native city. He had been elected strategos, and had received an enthusiastic welcome. Time had, in some measure, dulled the sense of the terrible injuries which he had inflicted on his country, and his share in the recent recovery of the Hellespontine cities had partly at least atoned. But it was rather hope for future benefits than forgiveness for past wrongs that moved the Athenians to let bygones be bygones. They trusted in his capacity as a general, and they thought that by his diplomatic skill they might still be able to come to terms with Persia. So a decree was passed, giving him full powers for the conduct of the war, and he was solemnly freed from the curse which rested upon him as profaner of the Eleusinian rites. He had an opportunity of making his peace with the divinities of Eleusis. Ever since the occupation of Decelea, which he had done so much to bring about, the annual procession from Athens along the Sacred Way to the Eleusinian shrine had been suspended, and the mystic Iacchus had been conveyed by sea.

(September.) Under the auspices of Alcibiades, who protected the procession by an escort of troops, the solemnity was once more celebrated in the usual way. It is possible that, if he had been bold enough to seize the opportunity of this tide of popularity, he might have established a tyranny at Athens; but he probably thought that such a venture would hardly be safe until he achieved further military or diplomatic successes. The opportunity was lost and did not recur. A slight incident completely changed the current of feeling in Athens.

Battle of Notion, spring, 406 B.C. An Athenian fleet was at Notion, keeping guard on Ephesus, and Lysander succeeded in defeating it and capturing fifteen ships. Though Alcibiades was not present at the battle, he was responsible, and lost his prestige at Athens, where the tidings of a decisive victory was confidently expected. New generals were appointed immediately, and Alcibiades withdrew to a castle on the Hellespont which he had provided for himself as a refuge in case of need. Conon succeeded him in the chief command of the navy.

The Peloponnesians during the following winter organised a fleet of greater strength than they had had for many years—140 ships; but Lysander had to make place for a new admiral, Callicratidas. The Peloponnesians at first carried all before them. The fort of Delphinion in Chios, and the town of Methymna in Lesbos were taken; Conon, who had only seventy ships, was forced into a battle outside Mytilene and lost thirty triremes in the action. The remainder were blockaded in the harbour of Mytilene. The situation was critical, and Athens did not underrate the danger. The gold and silver dedications in the temples of the Acropolis were melted to defray the costs of a new armament; freedom was promised to slaves, citizenship to resident aliens, for their services in the emergency; and at the end of a month Athens and her allies sent a fleet of 150 triremes to relieve Mytilene. Callicratidas, who had now 170 ships, left 50 to maintain the blockade and sailed with the rest to meet the foe. A great battle was fought near the islets *Battle of* of the Arginusae, south of Lesbos, and the Athenians were victorious. *Arginusae,* Seventy Spartan ships were sunk or taken, and Callicratidas was 406 *B.C.* slain. An untimely north wind hindered the victors from rescuing the crews of their wrecked ships, as well as from sailing to Mytilene to destroy the rest of the hostile fleet.

The success had not been won without a certain sacrifice; twenty- *Trial of* five ships had been lost with their crews. It was believed that many *the* of the men, floating about on the wreckage, might have been saved *generals.* if the officers had taken proper measures. The commanders were blamed; the matter was taken up by politicians at Athens; the generals were suspended from their office and summoned to render an account of their conduct. They shifted the blame on the trierarchs; and the trierarchs, one of whom was Theramenes, in order to shield themselves, accused the generals of not having issued the orders for rescue until the high wind made the execution impossible. We are not in a position to judge the question; for the decision must entirely depend on the details of the situation, and as to the details we have no certainty. It is not clear, for instance, whether the storm was sufficiently violent to prevent any attempt at a rescue. The presumption is, however, that the Athenian people were right in the conviction that there had been criminal negligence somewhere, and the natural emotion of indignation which they felt betrayed them into committing a crime themselves. The question was judged by the Assembly, and not by the ordinary courts. Two sittings were held, and the eight generals who had been present at Arginusae were condemned to death and confiscation of property. Six, including Thrasyllus and Pericles, son of the great statesman, were executed; the other two had prudently kept out of the way. Whatever were the rights of the case, the penalty was unduly severe; but the worst feature of the proceedings was that the Assembly violated a recognised usage [1] of the city by pronouncing sentence on all the accused together, instead of judging the case of each separately. Formally illegal indeed it was not; for the supporters of the generals had not the courage to apply the *Graphe Paranomon.* Protests had no effect on the excited multitude, thirsty for vengeance. It was an interesting incident that the philosopher Socrates, who happened on the fatal day to be one of the prytaneis,

[1] The principle was formulated in the Psephism of Cannōnus.

objected to putting the motion. All constitutions, democracy like oligarchy and monarchy, have their own dangers and injustices ; this episode illustrates the gravest kind of injustice which a primary Assembly, swayed by a sudden current of violent feeling and unchecked by any responsibility, sometimes commits,—and repents.

The victory of Arginusae restored to the Athenians the command of the eastern Aegean, and induced the Lacedaemonians to repeat the same propositions of peace which they had made four years ago after the battle of Cyzicus : namely, that Decelea should be evacuated and that otherwise each party should remain just as it was. Through the influence of the demagogue Cleophon, who is said to have come into the Assembly drunk, the offer was rejected. Nothing was left *Conspiracy* for the Spartans but to reorganise their fleet. Eteonicus had gathered *of the* together the remnants of the ships and gone to Chios, but he was *straw-* unable to pay the seamen, who were forced to work as labourers on *bearers at* *Chios.* the fields of Chian farmers. In the winter this means of support failed, and threatened by starvation, they formed a conspiracy to pillage the town of Chios. [The conspirators agreed to carry a reed-stick in order to recognise one another. Eteonicus discovered the plot, but there were so many reed-bearers that he shrank from an open conflict, and devised a stratagem. Walking through the streets of Chios, attended by fifteen armed men, he met a man who suffered from ophthalmia, coming out of a surgeon's house, and seeing that he had a reed-stick, ordered him to be put to death. A crowd gathered and demanded why the man was put to death ; the reply was, " Because he had a reed-stick." When the news spread, every reed-bearer was so frightened that he threw his reed away.] The Chians then consented to supply a month's pay for the men, who were immediately embarked.

This incident shows that money had ceased to flow in from *Lysander* Persia. It was generally felt that if further Persian co-operation was *in* to be secured and the Peloponnesian cause to be restored, the com-*command* mand of the fleet must again be entrusted to Lysander. But there *again,* *405 B.C.* was a law at Sparta that no man could be navarch a second time. On this occasion the law was evaded by sending Lysander out as secretary, but on the understanding that the actual command lay *His* with him and not with the nominal admiral. Lysander visited Cyrus *influence* at Sardis, asserted his old influence over him, and obtained the money *with Cyrus.* he required. With the help of organised parties in the various cities, he soon fitted out a fleet. An unlooked-for event gave him still greater power and prestige. King Darius was very ill, his death was expected, and Cyrus was called to his bedside. During his absence, Cyrus entrusted to his friend Lysander the administration of his satrapy, and the tribute. He knew that money was no temptation to this exceptional Spartan, and he feared to trust such power to a Persian noble.

With these resources behind him, Lysander speedily proved his ability.   Attacked at Ephesus by the Athenian fleet under Conon, he declined battle ; then, when the enemy had dispersed, he sailed forth, first to Rhodes, and then across the Aegean to the coast of Attica, where he had a consultation with Agis.   Recrossing the Aegean, he made for the Hellespont and laid siege to Lampsacus. The Athenian fleet of 180 ships reunited and followed him thither. Lampsacus had been taken before they reached Sestos, but they determined now to force him to accept the battle which he had refused at Ephesus, and with this view proceeded along the coast till they reached Aegospotami, " Goat's rivers," an open beach *Victory of* without harbourage, over against Lampsacus.   It was a bad position, *Lysander* as all the provisions had to be fetched from Sestos at a distance of *at Aegos-* *potami* about two miles, while the Peloponnesian fleet was in an excellent *(end of* harbour with a well-supplied town behind.   Sailing across the *summer,* strait, the Athenians found the enemy drawn up for battle but 405 *B.C.*). under orders not to move until they were attacked, and in such a strong position that an attack would have been unwise.   They were obliged to return to Aegospotami.   For four days the same thing befell.   Each day the Athenian fleet sailed across the strait and endeavoured to lure Lysander into an engagement ; each day its efforts were fruitless.   From his castle in the neighbourhood Alcibiades descried the dangerous position of the Athenians, and riding over to Aegospotami earnestly counselled the generals to move to Sestos.   His sound advice was received with coldness, perhaps with insult.   When the fleet returned from its daily cruise to Lampsacus, the seamen used to disembark and scatter on the shore.   On the fifth day Lysander sent scout ships which, as soon as the Athenian crews had gone ashore for their meal, were to flash a bright shield as a signal.   When the signal was given, the whole Peloponnesian squadron, consisting of about 200 galleys, rowed rapidly across the strait and found the Athenian fleet defenceless. There was no battle, no resistance.   Twenty ships, which were in a condition to fight, escaped ; the remaining 160 were captured at once.   It was generally believed that there was treachery among the generals, and it is possible that Adeimantus, who was taken prisoner and spared, had been bribed by Lysander.   All the Athenians who were taken, to the number of three or four thousand, were put to death.   The chief commander Conon, who was not among the unready, succeeded in getting away.   Greek ships usually unshipped their sails when they prepared for a naval battle, and the sails of the Peloponnesian triremes had been deposited at Cape

Abarnis, near Lampsacus. Informed of this, Conon boldly shot across to Abarnis, seized the sails, and so deprived Lysander of the power of an effective pursuit. It would have been madness for the responsible commander to return to Athens with the tidings of such a terrible disaster ; and Conon, sending home twelve of the twenty triremes which had escaped, sailed himself with the rest to the protection of Evagoras, the king of Salamis in Cyprus. Never was a decisive victory gained with such small sacrifice as that which Lysander gained at Aegospotami.

Situation at Athens. The tidings of ruin reached the Piraeus at night, and "on that night not a man slept." The city remembered the cruel measure which it had once and again meted out to others, as to Melos and Scione, and shuddered at the thought that even such measure might now be meted out to itself. It was hard for the Athenians to realise that at one blow their sea-power was annihilated, and they had now to make preparations for sustaining a siege. But the blockade was deferred by the policy of Lysander. He did not intend to attack Athens but to starve it into surrender, and with this view he drove all the Athenian cleruchs whom he found in the islands to Athens, in order to swell the starving population. Having completed the subjugation of the Athenian empire in the Hellespont and Thrace, and ordered affairs in those regions, Lysander sailed at length into the Saronic gulf with 150 ships, occupied Aegina, and blockaded the Piraeus. At the same time the Spartan king Pausanias entered Attica, and, joining forces with Agis, encamped in the Academe, west of the city. But the walls were too strong to attack, and at the beginning of winter the army withdrew, while the fleet remained near the Piraeus. As provisions began to fail, the Athenians made a proposal of peace, offering to resign their empire and become allies of Lacedaemon. The envoys were turned back at Sellasia ; they would not be received by the ephors unless they brought more acceptable terms ; and it was intimated that the demolition of the Long Walls for a length of ten stades was an indispensable condition of peace. It was folly to resist, yet the Athenians resisted. The demagogue Cleophon, who had twice hindered the conclusion of peace when it might have been made with honour, first after Cyzicus, then after Arginusae, now hindered it again when it could be made only with humiliation. An absurd decree was passed that no one should ever propose to accept such terms. But the danger was that such obstinacy would drive the enemy into insisting on an unconditional surrender ; for the situation was hopeless. Theramenes undertook to visit Lysander and endeavour to obtain more favourable conditions, or at all events to discover how matters lay. His real object was to gain time and let the people come to their senses.   He remained three months with Lysander, and when *Athens* he returned to Athens, he found the citizens prepared to submit on *submits.* any terms whatever.   People were dying of famine, and the reaction of feeling had been marked by the execution of Cleophon, who was condemned on the charge of evading military service.   Theramenes was sent to Sparta with full powers.   It is interesting to find that during these anxious months a decree was passed recalling to Athens an illustrious citizen, who had been found wanting as a general, but whose genius was to make immortal the war now drawing to its close—the historian Thucydides.

An assembly of the Peloponnesian allies was called together at Sparta to determine how they should deal with the fallen foe.   The general sentiment was that no mercy should be shown ; that Athens should be utterly destroyed and the whole people sold into slavery. But Sparta never felt the same bitterness towards Athens as that which animated Corinth and Thebes ; she was neither a neighbour nor a commercial rival.   The destruction of Athens might have been politically profitable, but Sparta, with all her faults, could on occasion rise to nobler views.   She resolutely rejected the barbarous proposal of the Confederacy ; she would not blot out a Greek city which had done such noble services to Greece against the Persian invader. That was more than two generations ago, but it was not to be forgotten ; Athens was saved by her past.   The terms of the Peace *Conditions* were : the Long Walls and fortifications of the Piraeus were to be *of Peace* destroyed ; the Athenians lost all their foreign possessions, but *imposed on* remained independent, confined to Attica and Salamis ; their whole *Athens.* fleet, with the exception of twelve triremes, was forfeited ; all exiles were allowed to return ; Athens became the ally of Sparta, pledged to follow her leadership.   When the terms were ratified, Lysander sailed into the Piraeus.   The demolition of the Long Walls immediately 404 *B.C.* began.   The Athenians and their conquerors together pulled them *April.* down to the music of flute-players ; and the jubilant allies thought that freedom had at length dawned for the Greeks.   Lysander permitted Athens to retain twelve triremes, and, having inaugurated the destruction of the fortifications, sailed off to reduce Samos.

It is not to be supposed that all Athenians were dejected and wretched at the terrible humiliation which had befallen their native city.   There were numerous exiles who owed their return to her calamity ; and the extreme oligarchic party rejoiced in the foreign occupation, regarding it as an opportunity for the subversion of the democracy and the re-establishment of a constitution like that which had been tried after the Sicilian expedition.   Theramenes looked forward to making a new attempt to introduce his favourite polity.   Of the exiles, the most prominent and determined was

Critias, son of Callaeschrus, and a member of the same family as the lawgiver Solon. He was a man of many parts, a pupil of Gorgias and a companion of Socrates, an orator, a poet, and a philosopher. A combination was formed between the exiles and the home oligarchs ; a common plan of action was organised ; and the chief *Institution* democratic leaders were presently seized and imprisoned. The inter-*of the* vention of Lysander was then invoked for the establishing of a new *Thirty* constitution, and awed by his presence, the Assembly passed *by the* *psephism of* a measure proposed by Dracontides, that a body of Thirty *Dracon-* should be nominated, for the purpose of drawing up laws and *tides* managing public affairs until the code should be completed. The *(summer,* oligarchs did not take the trouble to repeal the law which would 404). expose the proposer of the measure to prosecution by the Graphe Paranomon ; they felt sure of their power. Critias, Theramenes, and Dracontides were among the Thirty who were appointed.

Suspected The ruin of the power of Athens had fallen out to the advantage *oligarch-* of the oligarchical party, and it has even been suspected that the *ical* oligarchs had for many years past deliberately planned to place the *intrigues.* city at the mercy of the enemy, for the ulterior purpose of destroying the democracy. The part played by Theramenes in the condemnation of the generals who had the indiscretion to win Arginusae, the parts he subsequently played in negotiating the Peace and in establishing the oligarchy, the serious suspicions of treachery in connexion with the disaster of Aegospotami, have especially suggested this conjecture. The attempt of the Four Hundred on a previous occasion to come to terms with Sparta may be taken into account, and the comparatively lenient terms imposed on Athens might seem to point in the same direction. One thing seems certain. The oligarchic party had been distinctly aiming at peace, and the repeated opposition of Cleophon (impolitic, as we have seen) indicates that he suspected oligarchical designs. It must also be admitted that the conduct of the Athenians in fixing their station at Aegospotami, and delivering themselves to the foe like sheep led to the altar, argues a measure of folly which seems almost incredible, if there were not treachery behind ; and the suspicion is confirmed by the clemency shown to Adeimantus. It must, however, be acknowledged that it is hard to understand how the treason could have been effectually carried out without the connivance of Conon, the commander-in-chief ; yet no suspicion seems to have been attached to him. The whole problem of the oligarchic intrigues of the last eight years of the war remains wrapped in far greater mystery than the mutilation of the Hermae.

Sect. 10. Rule of the Thirty and Restoration of the Democracy

The purpose for which the Thirty had been appointed was to frame a new constitution; their powers, as a governing body, were only to last until they had completed their legislative work. The more part of them, however, with Critias, who was the master spirit, had no serious thoughts of constructing a constitution; they regarded this as merely a pretext for getting into power; and their only object was to retain the power in their own hands, establishing a simple oligarchy. In this, however, they were not absolutely unanimous. One of them at least, Theramenes, had no taste for pure oligarchy, but was still genuinely intent on framing a polity, tempered of both oligarchic and democratic elements. This dissension in the views of the two ablest men, Critias and Theramenes, soon led to fatal disunion.

Rule of the Thirty, c. Sept. 404 to May 403.

The first measures of the Thirty were, however, carried out with cordial unanimity. A Council of Five Hundred, consisting of strong supporters of oligarchy, was appointed, and invested with the judicial functions which had before belonged to the people. A body of Eleven, under the command of Satyrus, a violent, unscrupulous man, was appointed for police duties; and the guard of the Piraeus was committed to a body of Ten. The chief democrats, who on the fall of Athens had opposed the establishment of an oligarchy, were then seized, tried by the Council, and condemned to death for conspiracy. So far there was unanimity; but at this point Theramenes would have stopped. At such times, moderate counsels have small chance of winning, ranged beside the extreme policies of resolute men like Critias, who had come back in a bitter and revengeful spirit against democracy, relentlessly resolved to exercise an absolute despotism and expunge all elements of popular opposition. A polity on the broad basis which Theramenes desired was as obnoxious to Critias as the old democracy; into which, he was convinced, it would soon deviate. He and his colleagues were therefore afraid of all prominent citizens of moderate views, whether democratic or oligarchic, who were awaiting with impatience the constitution which the Thirty had been appointed to prepare,—the men on whom the polity of Theramenes, if it came into existence, would mainly rest.

First measures.

Disunion.

The Thirty had announced as part of their programme that they would purge the city of wrong-doers. They put to death a number of men of bad character, including some notorious informers; but they presently proceeded to execute, with or without trial, not only prominent democrats, but also men of oligarchical views who, though unfriendly to democracy, were also unfriendly to injustice and illegality. Among the latter victims was Niceratus, the son of Nicias.

Tyranny. To the motives of fear and revenge was soon added the appetite for plunder ; and some men were executed because they were rich, while many fled, happy to escape with their lives. Even metics, who had little to do with politics, were despoiled ; thus the speech-writer Lysias and his brother Polemarchus, who kept a lucrative manufactory of shields, were arrested, and while Lysias succeeded in making his escape, Polemarchus was put to death. And while many Athenians were removed by hemlock or driven into banishment, others were required to assist in the revolting service of arresting fellow-citizens, in order that they might thereby become accomplices in the guilt of the government. Thus the philosopher Socrates and four others were commanded with severe threats to arrest an honest citizen, Leon of Salamis. Socrates refused without hesitation to do the bidding of the tyrants ; the others were not so brave. Yet Socrates was not punished for his defiance ; and this immunity was perhaps due to some feeling of piety in the heart of Critias, who had been one of his pupil-companions ; a feeling which might be safely indulged, as the philosopher was neither wealthy nor popular.

Attitude of Thera-menes. To these judicial murders and this organised system of plundering, Theramenes was unreservedly opposed. The majority of the Council shared his disapprobation ; and he would have been able to establish a moderate constitution, but for the ability and strength of Critias. His representations, indeed, induced the Thirty to broaden the basis on which their power rested by creating a body of 3000 citizens, who had the privilege of bearing arms and the right of being tried by the Council. All outside that body were liable to be condemned to death by sentence of the Thirty, without a trial. The body of 3000 had practically no political rights, and were chosen so far as possible from known partisans of the government, the staunchest of whom were the thousand knights. This measure naturally did not satisfy Theramenes ; his suggestions had, in fact, been used with a purpose very different from his,—to secure, not to alter, the government.

The exiles. In the meantime the exiles whom the oligarchy had driven from Athens were not idle. They had found refuge in those neighbouring states—Corinth, Megara, and Thebes—which had been bitter foes of Athens, but were now undergoing a considerable change of feeling. Dissatisfaction with the high-handed proceedings of Sparta, who would not give them a share in the spoils of the war, had disposed them to look with more favour on their fallen enemy, and to feel disgust at the proceedings of the Thirty, who were under the aegis of Lysander. They were therefore not only ready to grant hospitality to Athenian exiles, but to lend some help towards delivering their city from the oppression of the tyrants.   The first step was made from Thebes.   Thrasybulus and Anytus, with a band of seventy *Thrasy-* exiles, seized the Attic fortress of Phyle, in the Parnes range, close *bulus seizes* to the Boeotian frontier, and put into a state of defence the strong *Phyle,* stone walls, whose ruins are still there.   The Thirty led out their *c. Dec. 404.* forces—their faithful knights and Three Thousand hoplites—and *First* sat down to blockade the stronghold.   But a timely snowstorm *expedition* broke up the blockade ; the army retired to Athens ; and for the next *of the* three months or more nothing further was done against Thrasy- *Thirty* bulus and the men of Phyle. *against*

Thrasy-

The oligarchs were now in a dangerous position, menaced with- *bulus,*

Dec. 404 or
Jan. 403.

FIG. 135.—View of Phyle.

out by an enemy against whom their attack had failed, menaced within by a strong opposition.   They saw that the influence of Theramenes, who was thoroughly dissatisfied with their policy, would be thrown into the scale against them, and they resolved to get rid of him.   Having posted a number of devoted creatures, *Death of* armed with hidden daggers, near the railing of the council-house, *Thera-* Critias arose in the assembled Council and denounced Theramenes *menes,* as a traitor and conspirator against the state,—a man who could not *c. Jan. 403.* be trusted an inch, in view of those repeated tergiversations which had won him the nickname of the " Buskin."   The reply of Theramenes, denouncing the impolicy of Critias and his colleagues, is said to have been received with applause by most of the Council, who really sympathised with him.   Critias, seeing that he would be acquitted by

the Council, resorted to an extreme measure. He struck the name of
Theramenes out of the list of the Three Thousand;[1] and then along
with his colleagues condemned him to death, since those who were
not included in the list could not claim the right of trial. Theramenes leapt on the sacred Hearth and appealed for protection to the
Council ; but the Council was stupefied with terror, and at the
command of Critias the Eleven entered and dragged the suppliant
from the altar. He was borne away to prison ; the hemlock was
immediately administered ; and when he had drunk, he tossed out a
drop that remained at the bottom of the cup, as banqueters used to
do in the game of kottabos, exclaiming, " This drop for the gentle
Critias ! " There had perhaps been a dose of truth in the reproaches
which the gentle Critias had hurled at him across the floor of the
council - chamber. Theramenes may have been shifty and unscrupulous where means and methods were concerned. But in his
main object he was perfectly sincere. He was sincere in desiring
to establish a moderate polity which should unite the merits of
both oligarchy and democracy, and avoid their defects. There can
be no question that he was honestly interested in trying this political
experiment. And the very nature of this policy involved an appearance of insincerity and gave rise to suspicion. It led him to oscillate
between the democratic and oligarchical parties, seeking to gain
influence and support in both, with a view to the ultimate realisation of his middle plan. And thus the democrats suspected him
as an oligarch, the oligarchs distrusted him as a democrat. In
judging Theramenes, it seems fair to remember that a politician
who in unsettled times desires to direct the state into a middle course
between two opposite extremes can hardly avoid oscillation more or
less, can rarely escape the imputation of the Buskin.

After the death of Theramenes, the Thirty succeeded in dis-
arming, by means of a stratagem, all the citizens who were not
enrolled in the list of the Three Thousand, and expelled them from
Spartan the city. But with a foe on Attic ground, growing in numbers every
garrison day, Critias and his fellows felt themselves so insecure, that they
occupies the took the step of sending an embassy to Sparta, to ask for a Lacedae-
Acropolis. monian garrison. The request was granted, and 700 men, under
Callibius, were introduced into the acropolis. The Thirty would
never have resorted to this measure except under the dire pressure
of necessity ; for not only was it unpopular, but they had to pay the
strangers out of their own chest.

[1] An appearance of legality seems to have been given to this act. A law was
passed — presumably on the spot — that persons who had opposed the Four
Hundred in 411 B.C., or taken part in destroying the fort at Eetionea, should be
excluded from the constitution.

It was perhaps in the first days of the month of May that it was *Second* resolved to make a second attempt to dislodge the democrats from *expedition* Phyle. A band of the knights and the Spartan garrison sallied *against Phyle,* forth ; but near Acharnae they were surprised at night and routed *beginning* with great loss by Thrasybulus. This incident produced considerable *of May,* alarm at Athens, and the Thirty had reason to fear that many of *403 B.C.* their partisans were wavering. Deciding to secure an eventual place of refuge in case Athens should become un- tenable, they seized Eleusis and put about 300 Eleusinians to death. This measure had hardly been carried out when Thrasybulus descended from Phyle and seized the Piraeus. He had now about 1000 men, but the Piraeus, without fortifications, was not an easy place to defend. He drew up his forces on the hill of Munychia, occupying the temples of *Artemis and the Thracian goddess Bendis, which* stood at the summit of a steep street ; highest of all stood the darters and slingers, ready to shoot over the heads of the hoplites. Thus posted, with his prophet by his side, Thrasybulus awaited the attack of the Thirty, who had led down all

Fig. 136.—Coin of Eleusis (reverse). Pig on torch; pig's head and ivy leaf below [legend : ΕΛ-ΕΥΣΙ].

their forces to the Piraeus. A shower of darts descended on their *Battle of* heads as they mounted the hill, and, while they wavered for a *Munychia* moment under the missiles, the hoplites rushed down on them, led by the prophet, who had foretold his own death in the battle and was the first to perish. Seventy of the enemy were slain ; among *Death of* them Critias himself. During the truce which was then granted for *Critias.* taking up the dead, the citizens on either side held some converse with one another, and Cleocritus, the herald of the Eleusinian Mystae, impressive both by his loud voice and by his sacred calling, addressed the adherents of the Thirty : " Fellow-citizens, why seek ye to slay us ? why do ye force us into exile ? us who never did you wrong. We have shared in the same religious rites and festivals ; we have been your schoolfellows and choir-fellows ; we have fought with you by land and sea for freedom. We adjure you, by our common gods, abandon the cause of the Thirty, monsters of impiety, who for their own gains have slain in eight months more Athenians than the Peloponnesians slew in a war of ten years. Believe that we have shed as many tears as you for those who have now fallen." This general appeal, and individual appeals in the same tone, at such an affecting moment, must have produced an effect upon the half- hearted soldiers of the Thirty, who had now lost their able and violent leader. There was dissension and discord not only among the Three Thousand and the Council, but among the Thirty themselves. It was felt that the government of the Thirty could no longer be maintained, and that if the oligarchy was to be rescued a new government must be installed. A general meeting of the

The first board of Ten.

Three Thousand deposed the Thirty and instituted in their stead a body of Ten, one from each tribe. One member of the Thirty was re-elected as a member of the new government, but the rest withdrew to the refuge which they had provided for themselves at Eleusis. The new body of Ten represented the views of those who were genuinely devoted to oligarchy, but disapproved of the extreme policy of Critias and his fellows. They failed to come to terms with Thrasybulus, who was every day receiving reinforcements both in men and arms ; the civil war continued ; and it soon appeared that it would be impossible for Athens to hold out against the democrats in the Piraeus without foreign aid.

Oligarchs appeal to Sparta (late spring, 403).
Sparta intervenes.

An embassy was accordingly dispatched by the Ten to Sparta; and about the same time the remnant of the Thirty at Eleusis sent a message on their own account for the same purpose. Both embassies represented the democrats at Piraeus as rebels against the power of Sparta. The Lacedaemonian government, through the influence of Lysander, was induced to intervene in support of the Ten. Lysander assembled an army at Eleusis, and forty ships were sent under Libys to cut off the supplies which the democrats received by sea. The outlook was now gloomy for Thrasybulus and his company ; but they were rescued by a disunion within the Lacedaemonian state. The influence of Lysander, which had been for the last years supreme, was perceptibly declining ; the king Pausanias was his declared opponent ; and many others of the governing class were jealous of his power, vexed at his arrogance, perhaps suspicious of his designs. The oligarchies which he had created at Athens and in the other cities of the Athenian empire had disgraced themselves by misgovernment and bloodshed ; and the disgrace was reflected upon the fame of their

Pausanias in command.

creator. Lysander had hardly begun his work when Pausanias persuaded the ephors to entrust to himself the commission of restoring tranquillity at Athens ; and Lysander had the humiliation of handing over to his rival the army which he had mustered. A defeat convinced Thrasybulus that it would be wise to negotiate ; and on the

Second board of Ten.

other hand Pausanias deposed the irreconcilable Ten, and caused it to be replaced by another Ten of more moderate views. Both parties then, the city and the Piraeus alike, submitted themselves to Spartan intervention, and Sparta, under the auspices of king Pausanias,

End of the civil war in Attica.

acquitted herself uncommonly well. A commission of fifteen was sent from Lacedaemon to assist the king, and a reconciliation was brought about. The terms were a general and mutual pardon for all past acts ; from which were excepted only the Thirty, the Ten who

had held the Piraeus under the Thirty, the Eleven who had carried out
the judicial murders perpetrated by the Thirty, and the Ten who had
succeeded the Thirty.   All these excepted persons were required
to give an account of their acts if they wished to remain at Athens.
Eleusis was to form an independent state, and any Athenian who
chose might migrate to Eleusis within a specified time.

The evil dream of Athens was at last over : a year and half of *September,*
oligarchical tyranny, and foreign soldiery on the Acropolis.   She owed *B. C.* 403.
her deliverance to the energy of Thrasybulus and the discretion of
Pausanias.   Pausanias displayed his discretion further by not
meddling with the reconciled parties in their settlement of the
constitution.   It was decreed, on the motion of Tisamenus, that *Nomothetes*
"lawgivers" should be appointed to revise the constitution, and that *appointed.*
in the meantime the state should be administered according to "the *Provisional*
laws of Solon and the institutions of Dracon."   The union of the two *arrange-*
names is significant of the conciliation.   Provisionally, then, the *ment.*
franchise was limited to those who belonged to the first three Solonian
classes—those who could at least serve as hoplites.   It is noteworthy
that there was an idea afloat of making the possession of landed
property a qualification for political rights.   But it was a totally
unpractical idea.   Such a test would have excluded rich men ; it
would have included many of the fourth class.   In the end, no new
experiment was tried.   The lawgivers restored the old democracy
with its unlimited franchise, and Athens entered upon a new stage of
her career.   The amnesty was faithfully kept ; the democrats did not *(See below,*
revenge themselves on the supporters of the oligarchical tyranny. *p.* 588.)
But it was easier to forgive than forget ; and for many years after the
reconciliation a distinction was drawn, though not officially, yet in the
ordinary intercourse of life, between the "men of the city" and the
"men of the Piraeus"—the men who had fought for freedom and
those who had fought against it.   That was almost inevitable ; and so
long as the oligarchs held Eleusis, there might even be some ground
for suspecting the loyalty of their old supporters.   After about two
years of independent existence, Eleusis was attacked by Athens ; the
Eleusinian generals were captured and put to death, and the town
resumed its old place as part of Attica.   Henceforward, for well-nigh
three generations, the Athenian democracy was perfectly secure from
the danger or fear of an oligarchical revolution.   That hideous night-
mare of the Thirty had established it on a firmer base than ever.

CHAPTER XII

THE SPARTAN SUPREMACY AND THE PERSIAN WAR

SECT I. THE SPARTAN SUPREMACY

Sparta drawn into founding an empire. SPARTA had achieved the task which she had been pressed to undertake, and had undertaken somewhat reluctantly, the destruction of the Athenian empire. It was a task which, though not imposed by the unanimous voice of Greece, appealed to a most deeply-seated sentiment of the Greeks, their love of political independence. The Athenian empire had been an outrage on that sentiment, and, apart from all calculations of particular interest, the humiliation of the great offender must have been regarded, even by those who were not her enemies, with an involuntary satisfaction. The avowed aim of Sparta throughout had been to restore their liberty to those states which had been " enslaved " by Athens, and protect the liberty of those whom her ambition threatened. Now that this object was accomplished as fully as could be desired, it would have been correct for Sparta to retire into her old position, leaving the cities which had belonged to the Athenian empire to arrange their own affairs,—if her deeds were to be in accordance with her professions. The alternative course for a state in the position of Sparta was to enter frankly upon the Athenian inheritance, and pursue the aims and policy of Athens as an imperial power. Other states might have adopted this course with advantage both to themselves and Greece ; for Sparta it was impossible. And so when Sparta, unable from the nature of her institutions and the character of her genius to tread in the footsteps of her fallen rival, nevertheless resolved to take under her own dominion the cities which she had gone forth to deliver from all dominion, she not only cynically set aside her high moral professions, but entered on a path of ambition which led to calamity for herself and distress for Greece. The main feature of Greek history for the thirty years after Aegospotami is Sparta's pursuit of a policy of aggrandisement beyond the Peloponnesus ; the opposition which this policy calls forth leads both to the revival of Athens as a great power and to the rise of Thebes. In the end Sparta is forced to retire into the purely Peloponnesian position for which her institutions fitted her. In the making of those institutions an activity beyond the Peloponnesus had not been contemplated; and they were too rigid to be adapted to the enlarged sphere of an Aegean dominion. Nothing short of a complete revolution in the Spartan state could have rendered her essay in empire a success; but the narrow Spartan system was too firmly based in the narrow Spartan character to suffer such a revolution.

We may wonder how far the general who had placed his country *Unfitness* in the position of arbitress of Greece appreciated the difficulty of *of Sparta* reconciling the political character of Lacedaemon with the rôle of an *for empire.* imperial city. Un-Spartan as he was in many respects, Lysander had possibly more enlightened views as to the administration of an empire than his countrymen. A story is told that when Callibius, the Spartan harmost of Athens, was knocked down by a young athlete whom he had insulted, and appealed to Lysander, he was told that he did not know how to govern freemen. To deal with freemen abroad was what the average Spartan could not do; and it was such men as Callibius that Lysander had to use for the establishment of the empire which he had resolved to found. In each of the cities which had passed from Athenian into Spartan control, a government of ten *De-* members was set up, and its authority was maintained by a Lacedae- *carchies.* monian *harmost* with a Lacedaemonian garrison. The cities were *Harmosts* thus given over to a twofold oppression. The foreign governors were (= "*regu-* rapacious and were practically free from home control; the native *lators*"). oligarchies were generally tyrannical, and got rid of their political opponents by judicial murders; and both decarchs and harmost played into each other's hands. Lysander exercised with a high hand and without farsightedness the dictatorship which was his for the time and might at any hour be taken from him. He was solely concerned to impose a firm military despotism on the states which had been rescued from the Athenian Confederacy.

It is obvious that the Athenian and Spartan empires had little in *Contrast* common. They were, first of all, sharply contrasted through the *between* fact that the Spartan policy was justified by no public object like *Athenian* that to which the Confederacy owed its origin. And this contrast *and* *Spartan* was all the more flagrant, considering that after the battle of Aegos- *empires.* potami there was the same demand for a Panhellenic confederacy, with the object of protecting the Asiatic Greeks from Persia, as there had been after the battle of Mycale. But so far from connecting her supremacy with such an object, Sparta had abandoned the Asiatic Greeks to the Great King as the price of Persian help. Athens had won her power as the champion of the eastern Greeks; Sparta had secured her supremacy by betraying them. In the second place, the methods of the two states in exercising their power were totally different. The grievances against Athens, though real, were mainly of a sentimental nature. Athens had deprived the Confederate cities of autonomy: there were few complaints of rapine or oppression. But under the Lacedaemonian supremacy men suffered from positive acts of injustice and violence, and might seek in vain at Sparta for redress. The spirit of the system which Lysander instituted may be judged from the statement that the will of any Spartan citizen was regarded as law in the subject states. The statement comes from a friend of Lacedaemon.

Lysander's recall.

The position of power which Lysander had attained in the eyes of the world, and enjoyed without moderation, could not fail to excite jealousy and apprehension at Sparta itself. He held a sort of royal court at Samos, and the Samians accorded him divine honours by calling after his name a feast which had hitherto been a feast of Hera. He was recalled to Sparta, and he obeyed the summons, bearing a letter from the satrap Pharnabazus to justify him. But when it was opened, instead of being an encomium, it was found to be a deed of accusation; and Lysander was covered with ridicule as the victim of a

403 B.C.

Persian trick. He was permitted to escape from the situation on the plea of visiting the temple of Zeus Ammon in the Libyan oasis, in accordance with a vow. But his work remained. Lacedaemon upheld her uncongenial military despotism, modifying Lysander's system only so far as not to insist on the maintenance of the decarchies, but to permit the cities to substitute other forms of government, under the aegis of the harmost. Diodorus, probably exaggerating considerably, tells us that more than 1000 talents were levied each year from the empire in tribute. The receipt of such an income was a political innovation, and its administration involved money transactions of a nature and on a scale which would have been severely condemned by "Lycurgus." The admission into the treasury of a large sum of gold and silver which had been brought to Sparta by Lysander was a distinct breach of the Lycurgean discipline. Thus, inflexible as the Spartan system was, the necessities of empire compelled it to yield at one point, and a point where attack is wont to be especially insidious.

404-371 B.C.

The supremacy of Sparta lasted for a generation, though with intervals in which it was not effective; and its history for more than half of the period is mainly determined by her relations with Persia. As it had been through Persia that she won her supremacy, so it

394 B.C.
387-6 B.C.

was through Persia that she lost it, and through Persia that she once more regained it.

Sect. 2. The Rebellion of Cyrus and the March of the Ten Thousand

We now come to an episode which takes us into the domestic *Cyrus and* history of Persia, out of the limits of Greek geography into the heart *Tissa-* of the Persian empire.   On the death of Darius, his eldest son *phernes.* Artaxerxes had succeeded to the throne, notwithstanding the plots of his mother Parysatis, who attempted to secure it for her younger and favourite son Cyrus.   In these transactions Tissaphernes had supported Artaxerxes, and when Cyrus returned to his satrapy in Asia Minor, Tissaphernes was set to watch him.   False suspicions and calumnies frequently lead to the actual perpetration of the crimes which they attribute ; and perhaps if he had not been suspected, Cyrus would not have formed the plan of subverting his brother and seizing the king-ship.   But it is far more likely that from the first Cyrus had hoped and resolved to succeed to his father's throne.   For his success he relied largely on an army of Greek mercenaries which he began to enlist. The revolutions which had passed over Greek cities in recent years, both in Asia and Europe, threw into the military market large numbers of strong men eager for employment and pay.   They were recruited for the prince's service by Clearchus, a Spartan, who had held the post of harmost, but had been repudiated and expelled by the ephors when he attempted to make himself tyrant of Byzantium, like a new Pausanias.   Moreover, the Lacedaemonian government, which owed much to Cyrus, was induced to support him secretly, and sent him—avowedly for another purpose—seven hundred hoplites. The army which Cyrus mustered when he set forth on his march to *Cyrus* Susa comprised a large body of oriental troops, and about 13,000 *takes the* Greeks, of which 10,600 were hoplites. *field,*

The purpose of the march was at first carefully concealed from *spring,* 401 *B.C.* the troops, nor was the secret communicated to any of the officers except Clearchus.   The hill tribes of Pisidia were often troublesome to Persian satraps, and their reduction furnished a convenient pretext. Among those who were induced, by the prospect of high pay under the generous Persian prince, to join this Pisidian campaign was Xenophon, an Athenian knight, who was one of the pupils and *Xenophon.* companions of the philosopher Socrates.   His famous history of the *Anabasis* or Up-going of the Greeks with Cyrus, and their sub-sequent retreat, has rendered the expedition a household word.   The charm of the *Anabasis* depends on the simple directness and fulness with which the story is told, and the great interest of the story con-sists in its breaking new ground.   For the first time we are privileged to follow step by step a journey through the inner parts of Asia Minor, into the heart of the Persian empire beyond the Euphrates and the Tigris. There is a charm of actuality in the early chapters, with their recurring phrases, like brief entries in a diary,—the days' marches from one city to another, the number of parasangs, and the lengths of the halts, all duly set out. " Hence Cyrus marches two stages, ten parasangs, to Peltae, an inhabited city ; and here he remained three days."

March through Asia Minor.

Setting forth from Sardis, Cyrus took the south-easterly road, which led across the upper Maeander to the Phrygian Colossae, where he was joined by the troops of one of his Greek captains, the Thessalian Menon ; and thence onward to Celaenae, where he awaited the arrival of Clearchus. So far, the march had been straight to the ostensible destination, the country of Pisidia ; but now Cyrus turned in the opposite direction, and, descending the Maeander, marched northward to Peltae and Ceramon Agora or Potters' Mart. Then eastward, to the city called Cayster-Plain, close to the fort of Ipsus. Here the Greeks demanded their arrears of pay, and Cyrus had no money to satisfy them. But he was relieved from the difficulty, which might well have proved fatal to his enterprise, by the Cilician queen Epyaxa, wife of Syennesis IV., who arrived well laden with money. Her coming must have been connected with private negotiations between Cyrus and the Cilician governor. As the route of Cyrus lay through Cilicia, a country barred on all sides by difficult passes, it was of the greatest moment for Cyrus to come to an understanding with the ruler ; and on the other hand it was the policy of Syennesis so to order his ways that whether Cyrus succeeded or failed he might in either event be safe. As the plan of Cyrus was still a secret, it was a prudent policy to entrust the delicate negotiations to no one less safe than the queen. Having pacified the demands of his Greek mercenaries, Cyrus proceeded (by Thymbrion and Tyriaeon) to Iconium ; and thence by the road, which describes a great southern curve through Lycaonia, to Tyana. The Greeks were allowed to plunder Lycaonia, a rough country with rough people, as they passed through it. The arrangement with Syennesis seems to have been that he should make a display of resisting Cyrus, and Cyrus make a display of circumventing him. To carry out this arrangement, Menon's division, accompanied by the queen Epyaxa, diverged from the route followed by the rest of the army, and crossed the Taurus into Cilicia by a shorter route. Perhaps they struck off at Barata and passed by Laranda, on a road that led to Soli. Thus Syennesis, who, as a loyal servant of the Great King, hastened to occupy the Cilician gates, the pass for which the main army of Cyrus was making, found himself taken in the rear by Menon. It was therefore useless to remain in the pass, and he retreated to a mountain strong-

Ceramon Agora (now Iskam Keui).

The march of the
TEN THOUSAND.

Route of the Ten Thousand..........

Longitude East 36° of Greenwich

Stadia
0   500   1000   1500

English Miles
0   100   200   300

Parasangs
0 10 20 30 40 50

Walker & Boutall sc.
To face page 518.

hold : what more could a loyal servant of the Great King be expected to do ? The army of Cyrus then coming up from Tyana, by Podandus, found the impregnable pass open, and descended safely to Tarsus, where it met Menon.   The city and palace of the prince of Cilicia were pillaged ; this perhaps was part of the pretence.   It was at all events safe now for Syennesis to enter into a contract with Cyrus (a compulsory contract, the Great King would understand) to supply some money and men.

It must have been dawning on the Greek troops for some time past, and at Tarsus they no longer felt any doubt, that they had been deceived as to their ultimate destination.   They had long ago passed Pisidia, the ostensible object of their march, and the true object was now clear to them.   They flatly refused to advance further.   It was a small thing to be asked to take the field against the forces of the Great King ; but it was no such light matter to be asked to undertake a march of three months into the centre of Asia.   To be at a distance of three months from the sea-coast was a terrible idea for a Greek. Clearchus, a strict disciplinarian—a man of grim feature and harsh voice, unpopular with his men—thought to repress the mutiny by severity ; but the mutiny was too general to be quelled by coercion. Then he resorted to a stratagem, which he carried out with admirable adroitness.   Calling his soldiers together, he stood for some time weeping before he spoke.   He then set forth the cruel dilemma in which their conduct had placed him : he must either break his plighted faith with Cyrus or desert them ; but he did not hesitate to choose ; whatever happened, he would stand by them, who were "his country, his friends, and his allies."   This speech created a favourable impression, which was confirmed when Cyrus sent to demand an interview with Clearchus and Clearchus publicly refused to go. But the delight of the troops was changed into perplexity when Clearchus asked them what they proposed to do : they were no longer the soldiers of Cyrus, and could not look to him for pay, provisions, or help.   He (Clearchus) would stand by them, but declined to command them or advise them.   The soldiers—some of them in the secret confidence of their captain—discussed the difficulty, and it was decided to send a deputation to Cyrus, to ask him to declare definitely his real

F IG. 137. — Daric (fourth century).   Obverse—Kneeling king with bow and spear.   Reverse—Incuse.

intentions.   Cyrus told the deputation that his purpose was to march against his enemy Abrocomas—Persian general in Syria— who was now on the Euphrates, and offered higher pay to the

Greeks, a daric and a half instead of a daric a month. The soldiers, finding themselves in an awkward pass, agreed to continue the march,—reluctant, but hardly seeing any other way out of the difficulty; though many of them must have shrewdly suspected that they would deal with Abrocomas on the Euphrates even as they had dealt with the hillmen of Pisidia.

Issus: new reinforcements. The march was now eastward by Adana and Mopsuestia, across the rivers Sarus and Pyramus, and then along the coast to Issus, where Cyrus found his fleet. It brought him 700 hoplites sent by the Lacedaemonians. Here too he was reinforced by 400 Greek mercenaries who had deserted from the service of the Persian general Abrocomas, the enemy of Cyrus, who had fled to the Euphrates, instead of holding the difficult and fortified passes from Cilicia into Syria, as a loyal general of the Great King should have done. So Cyrus now, with his Greek troops increased to the total number of 14,000, passed with as much ease through the Syrian gates, owing to the cowardly flight of Abrocomas, as he had before passed through the Cilician gates, owing to the prudent collusion of Syennesis. The Syrian gates are a narrow pass between the end of Mount Amanus and the sea, part of the coast road from Issus to Myriandrus. At Myriandrus the Greeks bade good-bye to the sea, little knowing how many days would pass, how many terrible things befall them, before they hailed it again. They crossed Mount Amanus by the pass of Beilan, which Abrocomas ought to have guarded, and in a twelve days' march, passing by the park and palace of Belesys, satrap of Syria, they reached Thapsacus and beheld the famous Euphrates.

Arrival at Thapsacus. Here a new explanation was necessary as to the object of the march, and Cyrus had at last to own that Babylon was the goal,—that the foe against whom he led the army was the Great King himself. The Greek troops murmured loudly and refused to cross the river; but their murmurings here were not like their murmurs at Tarsus, for they had guessed the truth long since; and their complaints were only designed to extort promises from Cyrus. The prince agreed to give each man a present of five minae at the end of the expedition— more than a year's pay at the high rate of a daric and a half. But while the rest of the Greeks were making their bargain, Menon stole

About August 1. a march on them, inducing his own troops to cross the river first— a good example, for which Cyrus would owe him and his troops particular thanks. Abrocomas had burned the ships, but the Euphrates was—a very unusual circumstance at that season—shallow enough to be forded; a fact of which Abrocomas was conceivably aware. The army accordingly crossed on foot and continued the march along the left bank; an agreeable march until they reached the river Chaboras, beyond which the desert of "Arabia" began:

a plain, Xenophon describes it, smooth as a sea, treeless ; only worm-
wood and scented shrubs for vegetation, but alive with all kinds of
beasts strange to Greek eyes, wild asses and ostriches, antelopes and
bustards.   The tramp through the desert lasted thirteen days, and
then they reached Pylae, at the edge of the land of Babylonia, fertile
then with its artificial irrigation, now mostly a barren wilderness.
Soon after they passed Pylae, they became aware that a large host
had been moving in front, ravaging the country before them.

Artaxerxes on his part had made somewhat tardy preparations to *Prepara-*
receive the invaders.   It seems indeed to have been hardly conceived *tions of*
at the Persian court that the army of Cyrus would ever succeed in *Arta-*
reaching Babylonia.   The city of Babylon was protected by a double *xerxes.*
defence against an enemy approaching from the north,—by a line
of wall and a line of water, both connecting the Euphrates with the
Tigris.   The enemy would first have to pass the Wall of Media,
100 feet high and 20 feet broad, built of bricks with bitumen cement;
and they would then have to cross the Royal Canal, before they could
reach the gates of Babylon.   To these two lines of defence a third
was now added, in the form of a trench about forty miles long, joining
at one end the Wall of Media and at the other the Euphrates, where
a space of not more than seven yards was left between the trench and
the river.   To defend a country so abundantly guarded by artificial
fortifications, the king was able to muster immediately an army of
about 40,000 ; but this did not seem enough when the danger became
imminent, and orders were sent to Media that the troops of that
province should come to the aid of Babylonia.   There was some
delay in the arrival of these forces, and Artaxerxes probably did not
wish to risk an action until their arrival had made his immense
superiority in numbers overwhelming.   This may explain the extraordinary circumstance that when the army of Cyrus came to the
foss which had been dug expressly to keep them out, they found it
undefended, and walked at their ease over the narrow passage between
the trench and the river.

But now it was hardly possible for Artaxerxes to let his foes *Battle of*
advance further, though there was still no sign of the troops from the *Cunaxa*
east.   Two days after passing the trench, the army of Cyrus reached *(summer,*
the village of Cunaxa, and suddenly learned that the king's host was *401).*
approaching.   The oriental troops under Ariaeus formed the left
wing of Cyrus, who himself occupied the centre with a squadron of
cavalry ; the Greeks were on the right, resting on the river Euphrates.
The Persian left wing, commanded by Tissaphernes, consisted of
cavalry, bowmen, and Egyptian footmen, with a row of scythe-armed
chariots in front.   The king was in the centre with a strong bodyguard of horse.   Cyrus knew the oriental character, and he knew

that if the king fell or fled, the battle would be decided and his own cause won. He accordingly formed a plan of battle which would almost certainly have been successful, if it had been adopted. He proposed that the Greeks should shift their position further to the left,—to a considerable distance from the river,—so that they might immediately attack the enemy's centre where the king was stationed. But Clearchus, to whom Cyrus signified his wishes, made decided objections to this bold and wise plan. Unable to rise, like Cyrus, to the full bearings of the situation, he ruined the cause of his master by pedantically or timorously adhering to the precepts of Greek drill-sergeants, that it is fatal for the right wing to allow itself to be outflanked. And besides the consideration which Cyrus had in view, the advantage of bringing about with all speed the flight of Artaxerxes, there was another consideration which would not have occurred to Cyrus, but which ought to have occurred to Clearchus. The safety of Cyrus himself was a matter of the first importance to the *Greeks* Greeks,—how important we shall see in the sequel. It was useless *victorious;* for the Greeks to cut down every single man in the Persian left, if while they were sweeping all before them the prince for whom they fought were slain. Cyrus did not press the matter, and left it to Clearchus to make his own dispositions. The onset of the Greeks struck their enemies with panic before a blow was struck. On the other side, the Persian right, which far outflanked the left wing of Cyrus, was wheeled round, so as to take the troops of Ariaeus in the rear. Then Cyrus, who was already receiving congratulations as if he were king on account of the success of the Greeks, dashed forward with his 600 horse against the 6000 who surrounded Artaxerxes. The impetuous charge broke up the guard, and, if the prince had kept command over his passions, he would have been the Great King within an hour. But unluckily he caught sight of his brother, whom he hated with his whole soul, amid the flying bodyguard. The bitter passion of hatred overmastered him, and he galloped forward, with a *Cyrus* few followers, to slay Artaxerxes with his own hand. He had the *slain.* satisfaction of wounding him slightly with a javelin ; but, in the mellay which ensued, he was himself wounded in the eye by a Carian soldier, and falling from his horse, was presently slain. The news of his death was the signal for the flight of his Asiatic troops.

The vivid narrative of Xenophon, who took part in the battle, preserves the memory of these remarkable events. At the time he saw little of the battle, and he could have known little of the arrange-*The work* ments and movements of the Persians. But before he wrote his own *of Ctesias.* book, he had the advantage of reading a book written by another Greek, who had also witnessed those remarkable events, but from the other side. This was Ctesias, the court physician, who was present

at the battle and cured Artaxerxes of the breast-wound which Cyrus
had dealt him.   The book of Ctesias is lost, but some bits of his
story have drifted down to us in the works of later writers who had
read it, and afford us a glimpse or two into the Great King's camp and
court about this eventful time.

For the Greek band, which now found itself in the heart of *Ability of*
Persia, girt about by enemies on every side, the death of Cyrus was *Cyrus ;*
an immediate and crushing calamity.   But for Greece it was probably *possible con-*
a stroke of good fortune,—though Sparta herself had blessed the *sequences of his success.*
enterprise.   Cyrus was a prince whose ability was well-nigh equal to
his ambition.   He had proved his capacity by his early successes as
satrap ; by the organisation of his expedition, which demanded an
exceptional union of policy and vigour, in meeting difficulties and surmounting dangers ; by his recognition of the value of the Greek soldier.
Under such a sovereign, the Persian realm would have thriven and
waxed great, and become once more a menace to the freedom of
the European Greeks.   Who can tell what dreams that ambitious
brain might have cherished, dreams of universal conquest to be
achieved at the head of an invincible army of Grecian foot-lancers ?
And in days when mercenary service was coming into fashion, the
service of Cyrus would have been popular.   Whatever oriental craft
and cruelty lurked beneath, he had not only a frank and attractive
manner, but a generous nature, which completely won such an
honest Greek as Xenophon, the soldier and historian.   He knew
how to appreciate the Greeks, as none of his country ever knew
before ; he recognised their superiority to the Asiatics in the military
qualities of steadfastness and discipline ; and this undisguised appreciation was a flattery which they were unable to resist.   If Cyrus had
come to the throne, his energy and policy would certainly have been
felt in the Aegean world ; the Greeks would not have been left for the
next two generations to shape their own destinies, as they did, little
affected by the languid interventions of Artaxerxes.   Perhaps the
stubborn stupidity of Clearchus on the field of Cunaxa, with his hard-
and-fast precepts of Greek drill-sergeants, saved Hellas from becoming a Persian satrapy.

But such speculations would have brought little comfort, could *Greeks*
they have occurred, to the 10,000 Greeks who, flushed with *refuse to*
the excitement of pursuit, returned to hear that the rest of their army *surrender.*
had been defeated, to find their camp pillaged, and then to learn on
the following morning that Cyrus was dead.   The habit of self-
imposed discipline which Cyrus knew so well how to value stood the
Greeks in good stead at this grave crisis ; and their easy victory had
given them confidence.   They refused to surrender, at the summons
of Artaxerxes.   For him their presence was extremely awkward,

like a hostile city in the midst of his land ; and his first object was at all hazards to get them out of Babylonia. He therefore parleyed with them, and supplied them with provisions. The only desire of the Greeks was to make all the haste they could homeward. By the road they had come it was nearly 1500 miles to Sardis ; but that road was impracticable ; for they could not traverse the desert again unprovisioned. Without guides, without any geographical know-ledge—not knowing so much as the course of the Tigris—they had no alternative but to embrace the proposal of Tissaphernes, who under-took to guide them home by another road, on which they would be able to obtain provisions. Following him—but well in the rear of his troops—the Greeks passed the Wall of Media, and crossed two navigable canals, before they reached the Tigris, which they passed by its only bridge, close to Sittace. Their course then lay north-ward, up the left bank of the Tigris. They passed from Babylonia into Media, and, crossing the lesser Zab, reached the banks of the greater Zab without any incident of consequence. But here the dis-trust and suspicion which smouldered between the Greek and the Persian camps almost broke into a flame of hostility, and Clearchus was driven into seeking an explanation with Tissaphernes. The frankness of the satrap disarmed the suspicions of Clearchus ; Tissa-phernes admitted that some persons had attempted to poison his mind against the Greeks, but promised to reveal the names of the calumni-ators, if the Greek generals and captains came to his tent the next day. Clearchus readily consented, and induced his four fellow-generals— Agias, Menon, Proxenus, and Socrates—to go to Tissaphernes, though such blind confidence was ill justified by the character of the crafty satrap. It was a fatal blunder—the second great blunder Clearchus had made—to place all the Greek commanders helplessly in the power *Treacherous* of the Persian. Clearchus had been throughout an enemy of the *seizure of* Thessalian Menon ; and it may be that he suspected Menon of *Clearchus and the* treason, and that his desire to convict his rival in the tent of Tissa-*generals.* phernes blinded his better judgment. The five generals went, with twenty captains and some soldiers ; the captains and soldiers were cut down, and the generals were fettered and sent to the Persian court, where they were all put to death.

Tissaphernes had no intention of attacking the Greek army. He had led them to a place from which it would be extremely difficult, if not impossible, to return to Greece, and he imagined that when they found themselves without any responsible commanders they would immediately surrender. But if in the first moments of dismay the prospect seemed hopeless, the Greeks speedily rallied their courage, chose new generals, and resumed their northward march. It was the Athenian Xenophon, a man of ready speech and great presence of mind, who did most to infuse new spirit into the army and guide it amidst the perils and difficulties which now beset it. Though he had no rank, being merely a volunteer, he was elected a general, and his power of persuasion, united with practical sense, won for him a remarkable ascendency over the men. He tells us how, on the first dreary night after the betrayal of the generals, he dreamed that he saw a thunderbolt striking his father's house and flames wrapping the walls about. This dream gave him his inspiration. He interpreted it of the plight in which he and his fellows were ; the house was in extreme danger, but the light was a sign of hope. And then the thought was borne in on him that it was foolish to wait for others to take the lead, that it would be well to make a start himself.

It was bold indeed to undertake a march of uncertain length— terribly long—without guides and with inexperienced officers, over unknown rivers and uncouth mountains, through the lands of barbarous folks. The alternative would have been to found a Greek city in the centre of Media ; but this had no attraction : the hearts of all were set upon returning to the Greek world. It would be long to tell the full diary of the adventures of their retreat ; it is a chronicle of courage, discipline, and reasonableness in the face of perils which nothing but the exercise of those qualities in an unusual measure would have been able to surmount. Their march to the Carduchian mountains, which form the northern boundary of Media, was harassed by the army of Tissaphernes, who however never ventured on a pitched battle. When they entered Carduchia, the *Kurdistan.* Greeks passed out of the Persian empire ; for the men of these mountains were independent, wedged in between the satrapies of Media and Armenia. The passage through this wild country was the most dangerous and destructive part of the whole retreat. The savage hillsmen were implacably hostile, and it was easy for them to defend the narrow precipitous passes against an army laden with baggage, and fearing, at every turn of the winding roads, to be crushed by rocky masses which the enemy rolled down from the heights above. After much suffering and loss of life, they reached the stream of the *Buhtan-* Centrites, a tributary of the Tigris, which divides Carduchia from *Tchai.* Armenia. The news of their coming had gone before ; and they found the opposite bank lined with the forces of Tiribazus, the Armenian satrap. The Carduchian hillsmen were hanging on their rear, and it needed a clever stratagem to cross the river safely. It was now the month of December, and the march lay through the snows of wintry Armenia. They had sore struggles with cold and hunger ; but they went unmolested, for they had made a compact with Tiribazus, undertaking to abstain from pillage. The direction of the march lay north-westward ; they crossed the two branches of the

They cross the Kara Su and Murad Su. Euphrates, and their route perhaps partly corresponded to that which a traveller follows at the present day from Tavriz to Erzerum. When they had made their way through the territories of the martial Chalybes and other hostile peoples, they reached a city—a sign that at last they were once more on the fringe of civilisation. It was the *Gumish.* city of Gymnias, a thriving place which perhaps owed its existence to neighbouring silver mines. Here they had a friendly welcome, and learned with delight that they were not many days' journey south of Trapezus. A guide undertook that they should have sight of the sea after a five days' march. "And on the fifth day they came to Mount Theches, and when the van reached the summit a great cry arose. *Reach the Euxine Sea.* When Xenophon and the rear heard it, they thought that an enemy was attacking in front; but when the cry increased as fresh men continually came up to the summit, Xenophon thought it must be something more serious, and galloped forward to the front with his cavalry. When he drew near, he heard what the cry was—*The Sea, the Sea!*" The sight of the sea, to which they had said farewell at Myriandrus, and which they had so often despaired of ever again beholding, was an assurance of safety at last attained. The night watches in the plains of Babylonia or by the rivers of Media, the wild faces in the Carduchian mountains, the bleak highlands of Armenia, might now fade into the semblances of an evil dream.

At Trapezus (first months of 400 B.C.). A few more days brought the army to Trapezus—to Greek soil and to the very shore of the sea. Here they rested for a month, supporting themselves by plundering the Colchian natives, who

dwelled in the hills round about, while the Greeks of Trapezus supplied a market. Here they celebrated games and offered their sacrifices of thanksgiving to Zeus Soter,—in fulfilment of a vow they had made on that terrible night on the Zab after the loss of their generals.

Ten thousand Greek soldiers dropt down from the mountains, like a sudden thunderbolt from heaven, were a surprise which must have caused strange perplexity to the Greeks of the coast,—

FIG. 138.—Coin of Trapezus (obverse). Male head.

to Trapezus and her sister Cerasus, and to their common mother Sinope. It was a somewhat alarming problem: more than a myriad soldiers, mostly hoplites, steeled by an ordeal of experience such as few men had ever passed, but not quite certain as to what their next step should be, suddenly knocking at one's gates. And they were not an ordinary army, but rather a democracy of ten thousand citizens equipped as soldiers, serving no king, responsible to no state, a law unto themselves, electing their officers and deciding all matters of importance in a sovereign popular assembly,—as it were, a great moving city, moving along the shores of the Euxine ; what might it, what might it not, do ?   For one thing, it might easily plant itself on some likely site within the range of Sinope's influence, and conceivably out-top Sinope herself.

The Ten Thousand themselves thought only of home—the Aegean and the Greek world.   Could they have procured ships at once, they would not have tarried to perplex Sinope and her daughter cities. To Xenophon, who foresaw more or less dimly the difficulties which *Xenophon* would beset the army on its return to Greece, the idea of seizing *thinks of* some native town like Phasis and founding a colony, in which he *founding a* might amass riches and enjoy power, was not unwelcome ; but when *new city.* it was known that he contemplated such a plan, though he never proposed it, he well-nigh forfeited his influence with the army.   In truth, a colony at Phasis, in the land of the Golden Fleece, founded by the practical Xenophon, might have been the best solution of the fate of the Ten Thousand.   The difficulties which they had now to face were of a different kind from those which they had so success-fully surmounted, demanding not so much endurance and bravery as tact and discretion.   Now that they were no longer in daily danger *Cohesion of* of sheer destruction, the motive for cohesion had lost much of its *the army.* strength.   If we remember that the army was composed of men of different Greek nationalities, brought together by chance, and that it was now united by no bond of common allegiance but was purely a voluntary association, the wonder is that it was not completely dis-organised and scattered long before it reached Byzantium.   It is true that the discipline sensibly and inevitably declined ; and it is true that the host dissolved itself at Heraclea into three separate bands, though only to be presently reunited.   But it is a remarkable spectacle, this large society of soldiers managing their own affairs, deciding what they would do, determining where they would go, seldom failing to listen to the voice of reason in their Assemblies, whether it was the voice of Xenophon or of another.

The last stages of the retreat, from Trapezus to Chalcedon, were accomplished partly by sea, partly by land, and were marked by delays, disappointments, and disorders.   It might be expected that *It reaches* on reaching Chalcedon the army would have dispersed, each man *Chalcedon.* hastening to return to his own city.   But they were satisfied to be well within the Greek world once more, and they wanted to replenish their empty purses before they went home.   So they still held together, ready to place their arms at the disposal of any power who would pay them.   To Pharnabazus, the satrap of the Helles-pontine province of Persia, the arrival of men who had defied the power of the Great King was a source of alarm.   He bribed the Lacedaemonian admiral Anaxibius, who was stationed at the Bosphorus, to induce the Ten Thousand to cross over into Europe.

At By-zantium. Anaxibius compassed this by promises of high pay ; but the troops, who were admitted into Byzantium, would have pillaged the city when they discovered that they had been deluded, if Xenophon's presence of mind and persuasive speech had not once more saved them from their first impulse. After this they took service under a Thracian prince, Seuthes was his name, who employed them to reduce some rebellious tribes. Seuthes was more perfidious than Anaxibius, for he cheated them of the pay which they had actually

Employed by Sparta, 399 *B.C.* earned. But better times were coming. War broke out—as we shall presently see—between Lacedaemon and Persia, and the Lacedaemonians wanted fighting men. The impoverished army of Cyrus, now reduced to the number of 6000, crossed back into Asia, and received an advance of pay. Here our interest in them ends, if it did not already end when they reached Trapezus,—our interest in all

Career of Xenophon. of them, at least, except Xenophon. Once and again Xenophon had intended to leave the army since its return to civilisation, and he had steadfastly refused all proposals to elect him commander ; but his strong ascendency among the soldiers and his consequent power to help them had rendered it impossible for him on each occasion to abandon them in their difficulties. Now he was at last released, and returned to Athens with a considerable sum of money. It is probable that his native city, where his master Socrates had recently suffered death, proved uncongenial to him ; for he soon went back to Asia to

Xenophon lives at Scillus in Triphylia till 370 *B.C.* fight with his old comrades against the Persians. When Athens presently became an ally of Persia against Sparta, Xenophon was banished, and more than twenty years of his life were spent at Scillus, a Triphylian village, where the Spartans gave him a home. Afterwards the sentence of exile was revoked, and his last years were passed at Athens.

On a country estate near that Triphylian village, not far from Olympia, Xenophon settled down into a quiet life, with abundant leisure for literature ; and composed, among other things of less account, the narrative of that memorable adventure in which Xenophon the Athenian had played such a leading part. Of the environment of his country life in quiet Triphylia he has given a glimpse, showing us how he imprinted his own personality on the place. He had deposited in the great temple of Artemis at Ephesus a portion of a ransom of some captives taken during the retreat, to be reserved for the service of the goddess. This deposit was restored to him at Scillus, and with the money Xenophon bought a suitable place for a sanctuary of Ephesian Artemis. "A river Selinus flows through the place, just as at Ephesus a river Selinus flows past the temple ; and in both streams there are fishes and shellfishes, but in the place at Scillus there is also all manner of game. And Xenophon made an altar and a temple, with the sacred money, and henceforward he used every year to offer to the goddess a tithe of the fruits of his estate, and all the citizens and neighbours, men and women, took part in the feast. They camped in tents, and the goddess furnished them with meal, bread, wine, and sweetmeats, and with a share of the hallowed dole of the sacrifice, and with a share of the game. For Xenophon's lads and the lads of the neighbours used to hunt quarry for the feast, and men who liked would join in the chase. There was game both in the consecrated estate and in Mount Pholoe, wild swine, and gazelles, and stags. That estate has meadowland and wooded hills—good pasture for swine and goats, for cattle and horses ; and the beasts of those who fare from Sparta to the Olympian festival—for the road wends through the place— have their fill of feasting. The temple, which is girt by a plantation of fruit trees, is a small model of the great temple of Ephesus ; and the cypress-wood image is made in the fashion of the Ephesian image of gold." Here Xenophon could lead a happy, uneventful life, devoted to sport and literature and the service of the gods.

At a casual glance the expedition of Cyrus may appear to belong *Signifi-* not to Greek but to Persian history ; and the retreat of the Ten *cance* Thousand may be deemed matter for a book of adventures, and a *of the* digression which needs some excuse in a history of Greece. But the *expedition* story of the upgoing and the home-coming of Xenophon and his *of Cyrus.* fellows is in truth no digression. It has been already pointed out how vitally the interests of Hellas, according to human calculation, were involved in the issue of Cunaxa ; and how, if the arbitrament of fortune on that battlefield had been other, the future of Greece might have been other too. But the whole episode—the upgoing, the battle, and the home-coming—has an importance, by no means problematical, which secures it a certain and conspicuous place in the procession of Grecian history. It is an epilogue to the invasion of Xerxes and a prologue to the conquest of Alexander. The Great King had carried his arms into Greece, and Greece had driven him back ; that was a leading epoch in the combat between Asia and Europe. The next epoch will be the retribution. The Greeks will carry their arms into Persia, and Persia will fail to repel them. The success of Alexander will be the answer to the defeat of Xerxes. For this answer the world has to wait for five generations ; but in the meanwhile the expedition of the soldiers of Cyrus is a prediction, vouchsafed as it were by history, what the answer is to be. Xenophon's *Anabasis* is the continuation of Herodotus ; Xenophon and his band are the reconnoitrers who forerun Alexander. And this significance of the adventure, as a victory of

Greece over Persia, was immediately understood. A small company
of soldiers had marched unopposed to the centre of the Persian
empire, where no Greek army had ever won its way before ; they
had defeated almost without a blow the overwhelming forces of the
king within a few miles of his capital ; and they had returned
safely, having escaped from the hostile multitudes, which did not
once dare to withstand their spears in open warfare. Such a display of Persian impotence surprised the world ; and Greece might
well despise the power whose resources a band of strangers had
so successfully defied. No Hellenic city indeed had won a triumph
over the barbarian ; but all Hellenic cities alike had reason to be
stirred by pride at a brilliant demonstration of the superior excellence
of the Greek to the Asiatic in courage, discipline, and capacity.
The lesson had, as we shall see, its immediate consequences. Only
a year or two passed, and it inspired a Spartan king—a man,
indeed, of poor ability and slight performance—to attempt to achieve
the task which fate reserved for Alexander. But the moral effect of
the Anabasis was lasting, and of greater import than the futile
warfare of Agesilaus. Considering these bearings, we shall have not
said too much if we say that the episode of the Ten Thousand, though
a private enterprise so far as Hellas was concerned, and though
enacted beyond the limits of the Hellenic world, yet occupies a more
eminent place on the highway of Grecian history than the contemporary transactions of Athens and Sparta and the other states of Greece.

SECT. 3. WAR OF SPARTA WITH PERSIA

The enterprise of Cyrus had immediately affected the position
and prospects of the Greek cities of Ionia. In accordance with their
contract the Spartans had handed over the Asiatic cities to Persia,
retaining only Abydus, on account of its strategic importance.
Cyrus, however, bidding for Greek support, had instigated the Ionian
cities to revolt from their satrap, Tissaphernes, and to place them-
Tissa- selves under his protection. Tissaphernes was in time to save
phernes, as Miletus ; but all the other cities received Greek garrisons, and
commander thus, when Cyrus disappeared into the interior of Asia, they had
of Asia, practically passed out of Persian control. After the defeat of Cyrus
plans to at Cunaxa, Tissaphernes returned to the Aegean coast as governor
recover the of all the districts which had been under Cyrus, and with the
Greek general title of commander of Further Asia, implying supremacy
cities, over the adjacent satrapies. His first concern was to recover the
which Greek cities of the coast, and he attacked Cyme. The Asiatic
appeal to Greeks were greatly alarmed, and they sent to Sparta an appeal for
Sparta. her protection.

The relations of Sparta to Persia were no longer the same ; since the help given to Cyrus was an act of war against the king. The successful march of the Ten Thousand inspired Greece with a *Sparta* feeling of contempt for the strength of the Persian empire. The *sends an* opportunity of plundering the wealthy satrapies of Pharnabazus and *army,* Tissaphernes was a bait for Spartan cupidity ; the prospect of *400 B.C.,* gaining signal successes against Persia appealed to Spartan ambition. These considerations induced Sparta to send an army to Asia, and this army was increased by the remains of the famous Ten Thousand, who (as already stated) crossed over from Thrace and entered the service of Sparta. Much might have been accomplished with a *under* competent commander, but the general Thibron was unable to *Thibron* maintain discipline among his men, and the few successes achieved *(400-399* fell far short of Sparta's reasonable hopes. Thibron was super- *B.C.),* seded by Dercyllidas, a man who had the repute of being unusually *who is* wily. Taking advantage of a misunderstanding between the two *succeeded* satraps, Dercyllidas made a truce with Tissaphernes and marched *by Der-* with all his forces into the province of Pharnabazus, against whom *cyllidas* he had a personal grudge. A recent occurrence rendered it possible *(399 B.C.)* for him to get into his hands the Troad—or Aeolis, as it was called *The* —with speed and ease. The government of this region had been *Troad.* granted by Pharnabazus to Zenis, a native of Dardanus. When he died, leaving a widow, a son, and daughter, Pharnabazus was about *Mania,* to choose another subsatrap ; but the widow, whose name was Mania, presented a petition that she should be permitted to fill the post which her husband had held. " My husband," she argued, " paid his tribute punctually, and you thanked him for it. If I do as well, why should you appoint another ? If I am found unsatisfactory, you can remove me at any moment." She fortified her arguments by large presents of money to the satrap, his officers, and concu- bines ; and won her request. She gave Pharnabazus full satisfaction by her regular payments of tribute, and under her vigorous administra- tion the Aeolid became a rich and well-defended land. A body of Greek mercenaries was maintained in her service, and immense treasures were stored in the strong mountain fortresses of Scepsis, Gergis, and Cebren. She even reduced some coast towns in the south of the Troad, and took part herself, like the Carian Artemisia, in military expeditions. But she had for son-in-law an ungrateful traitor, Meidias of Scepsis, whom she treated with trust and affec- tion. In order to possess himself of her power, he strangled her, *murdered* then killed her son, and laid hold of the three fortresses which con- *by her* trolled the district, along with all the treasure. But Pharnabazus *son-in-law.* refused to recognise the murderer of Mania, and sent back the gifts of Meidias with the message : " Keep them till I come to seize both them and you. Life would not be worth living if I avenged not the death of Mania."

Dercyllidas gains the Troad;

As Meidias was expecting with alarm the vengeance of Pharnabazus, the Spartan army appeared on the scene. Dercyllidas became master of the Aeolid without any opposition, since the garrisons of the cities did not acknowledge Meidias,—excepting only the forts of Scepsis, Gergis, and Cebren. The garrison of Cebren soon surrendered; at Scepsis, Meidias came forth to a conference, and Dercyllidas, without waiting to confer, marched up to the gates of the town, so that Meidias, in the power of the enemy, could do nothing but order them to be opened; and his unwilling orders likewise threw open the gates of Gergis. His own private property was restored to Meidias, but all the treasures of Mania were appropriated by the Spartan general; for the property of Mania belonged to her master Pharnabazus, and was therefore the legitimate booty of the satrap's enemy. This booty supplied Dercyllidas with pay for his eight thousand soldiers for nearly a year; and it was noticed that the conduct of the heroes of the Anabasis showed a signal improvement from this time forward. The Aeolid now served the Spartans against the satrapy of Pharnabazus somewhat as Decelea had served them in Attica; it was a fortified district in the enemy's country. Sparta, hoping that these successes would induce Persia to make terms and (398 B.C.) acquiesce in the freedom of the Greek cities, concluded truces with Tissaphernes and Pharnabazus, and sent up ambassadors to Susa (398 B.C.) to treat with the Great King. Dercyllidas meanwhile crossed into Europe and occupied himself with restoring the cross-wall which *besieges and* defended Sestos and the other cities of the Chersonese against the *captures* incursions of the Thracians, the inhabitants gladly furnishing pay *Atarneus* (398-7 B.C.); and food to the army. On returning to Asia, the Spartan commander *goes to Caria* captured, after a long siege, the strong town of Atarneus. Then by (397 B.C.). special orders from home he proceeded to Caria.

The Spartan overtures were heard unfavourably at Susa, for the king had been persuaded by his able satrap Pharnabazus to prosecute the war by sea. The Spartans could not cope in mere numbers with the fleet which Phoenicia and Cyprus could furnish him; but everything would depend on the commander. Here fortune played into his hands. There was an enemy of Sparta, an experienced naval officer, who was ready to compass heaven and earth to work the *Conon,* downfall of her supremacy. The Athenian admiral Conon, whom we last saw escaping from the surprise of Aegospotami, was burning to avenge the disgrace of that fatal day. He had found hospitality and protection at the court of Evagoras, king of the Cyprian Salamis; and through him had entered into communication with Ctesias, the Greek physician, whom we already met at Cunaxa.

Ctesias had the ear of the queen-mother Parysatis, and through her influence and the advice of Pharnabazus Conon was appointed to command a fleet of 300 ships which was prepared in Phoenicia and Cilicia.   Under his command, such a numerous navy was extremely formidable, but the Lacedaemonian government does not seem to have realised the danger, owing perhaps to their experience of the ineffectiveness of previous Persian armaments ; and they committed the mistake of throwing all their vigour into the land warfare, and neglecting their sea-power, which was absolutely vital for the maintenance of their supremacy.   But when Conon, not waiting for the complete equipment of the fleet, sailed to Caunus in Caria with forty ships, the Spartans were obliged to move.   They sent a fleet of 120 ships under Pharax from Rhodes to blockade Caunus and Conon's galleys in the harbour, and ordered Dercyllidas to Caria.   The joint forces of Tissaphernes and Pharnabazus first raised the siege of Caunus and then confronted Dercyllidas in the valley of the Maeander.   A panic which seized some of the troops of the Spartan general might have been fatal, but the reputation of the Ten Thousand, whose valour Tissaphernes had experienced, rendered that satrap unwilling to risk a battle, and a conference issued in an armistice.   [Conon meanwhile was able to win over Rhodes, which had given useful service to Sparta since 411.   At his instigation the leading oligarchs were cut down and an anti-Spartan democracy instituted.]   But Sparta had now decided to conduct the war with greater vigour ; and Dercyllidas had to make way for no less a successor than one of the kings.

appointed commander of a Persian fleet.

Armistice.

Agesilaus, who now comes upon the scene, had been recently raised to the regal dignity in unusual circumstances.   When Lysander retired from public affairs to visit the temple of Zeus Ammon, he had neither discarded ambition nor lost his influence.   He conceived the plan of making a change in the Spartan constitution which can hardly be described as less than revolutionary.   The idea was that the kingship should be no longer confined to the Eurysthenid and Proclid families in which it was hereditary by law, but that the kings should be elected from all Heraclids.   The scheme to make the office elective, instead of hereditary, was momentous.   It meant immediately that Lysander should hold the military functions which belonged to the kings, the command of the army abroad, *for life ;* he could no longer be deposed or recalled at the end of a term of office.   And in the hands of a man like Lysander this permanent office might become something very different from what it was in the hands of the ordinary Proclid or Eurysthenid ; the proportion between the power of king and ephor might be considerably shifted.   Lysander's project might well have proved the first step to a sort of *principate ;* which might have partially adapted Spartan institutions to the require-

*Agesilaus.
Revolutionary scheme of Lysander.*

ments of an imperial state. Lysander did not conceive the possibility of carrying this bold innovation by a *coup d'état;* his plan was to bring religious influence to bear on the authorities ; and he secretly employed his absence from Sparta in attempting to enlist the most important oracles in favour of his design. But the oracles received his proposal coldly ; it sounded far too audacious. He succeeded, however, in winning over some of the Delphic priests, who aided him to invent oracles for his purpose : a rumour was spread that certain sacred and ancient records were preserved at Delphi, never to be revealed until a son of Apollo appeared to claim them ; and at the same time people began to hear of the existence of a youth named Silenus, whose mother vouched that Apollo was his sire. But the ingenious plot broke down at the last moment ; one of the confederates did not play his part ; and the oracles bearing on the *The plot* Spartan kingship were never revealed. Lysander then abandoned *abandoned.* his revolutionary idea, and took advantage of the death of king Agis to secure the sceptre for a man whom he calculated he could direct and control. The kingship descended, in the natural course, on Leotychidas, the son of Agis ; but it was commonly believed that this youth was illegitimate, being really the son of Alcibiades. *Accession of* There were doubts on the matter ; but the suspicion was strong *Agesilaus,* enough to enable the half-brother of Agis, Agesilaus, supported by 398 *B.C.* the influence of Lysander, to oust his nephew and assume the sceptre.

His Lysander was deceived in his man ; the new king was not of the *character.* metal to be the kingmaker's tool. Agesilaus had hitherto shown only one side of his character. He had observed all the ordinances of Lycurgus from his youth up ; had performed all duties with cheerful obedience ; had shown himself singularly docile and gentle ; had never asserted or put himself forward among his fellow-citizens. But the mask of Spartan discipline covered a latent spirit of pride and ambition which no one suspected. Agesilaus, though strong and courageous, was of insignificant stature and lame. When he claimed the throne, an objection was raised on the ground of his deformity ; for an oracle had once solemnly warned Lacedaemon to beware of a halt reign. But like all sacred weapons this oracle could be blunted or actually turned against the adversaries. The god did not mean, said Lysander, physical lameness ; but the reign of one who was not truly descended from Heracles. Yet those Spartans who believed in literal interpretation of divine words were ill content with the preference of Agesilaus.

The new king displayed remarkable discretion and policy by his general demeanour of deferential respect to the other authorities. This had the greater effect, as the kings were generally wont to make up by their haughty manners for their want of real power.

Agesilaus made himself popular with everybody, and he maintained as king the simplicity which had marked his life as a private citizen. He was unswervingly true to his friends ; but this virtue declined to vice, when he upheld his partisans in acts of injustice.

Not long after his accession, a serious incident occurred which *Domestic* gives us a glimpse of the social condition of the Lacedaemonian state *condition of* at this period and shows that while the government was struggling *Sparta.* to maintain its empire abroad, it was menaced at home by dangers which the existence of that empire rendered graver every year. Commerce with the outside world and acquisition of money had promoted considerable inequalities in wealth ; and in consequence the number of Peers or fully enfranchised Spartan citizens was constantly diminishing, while the class of those who had become too poor to pay their scot to the *syssitia* was proportionally growing. These disqualified citizens were not degraded to the rank of Perioeci ; *The* they formed a separate class and were named Inferiors ; a stroke of *Inferiors* luck might at any moment enable one of them to pay his subscription, *(Hypo-* and restore him to full citizenship. But the Inferiors naturally formed *meiûs).* a class of malcontents ; and the narrow, ever narrowing, oligarchy of Peers had to fear that they might make common cause with the Perioeci and Helots and conspire against the state.   Such a conspiracy was hatched, but was detected in its first stage through the efficient system of secret police which was established at Sparta. The prime mover seems to have been a young man of the Inferior *Conspiracy* class named Cinadon, of great strength and bravery.   The ephors *of Cinadon,* learned from an informer that Cinadon had called his attention in the *397 B.C.* market-place to the small number of *Spartans* compared with the multitude of their *enemies*—one perhaps in a hundred.   All alike, Inferiors, Neodamodes, Perioeci, Helots, were, according to Cinadon, his accomplices ; "for hear any of them talk about the Spartans, he talks as if he could eat them raw."   And when Cinadon was asked where the conspirators would find arms, he pointed to the shops of the ironsmiths in the market-place, and added that every workman and husbandman possessed tools.   On the ground of information which was perhaps more precise than this, the ephors sent for Cinadon, whom they had often employed on police service, and sent him on a mission of this kind, but with an escort which arrested him on the road, put him to the torture, and wrung from him the names of his accomplices.   It would have been dangerous to arrest him in Sparta and so spread the alarm before the names of the others were known.   Asked why he conspired, Cinadon said : " I wished to be inferior to none in Sparta."   He was scourged round the city, and put to death with his fellows.

Recollecting the histories of other states we cannot forbear wondering that an ambitious general like Lysander did not attempt to use for his own purposes this mass of discontent, into which Cinadon's abortive conspiracy opens a glimpse. There was something in the Spartan air which made a peer rarely capable of disloyalty to the privileges of his own class.

SECT. 4. ASIATIC CAMPAIGNS OF AGESILAUS. BATTLE OF CNIDUS

396 B.C.

It was arranged that Agesilaus should take the place of Dercyllidas ; that he should take with him a force of 2000 Neodamodes, and a military council of thirty Spartans, including Lysander.

In the Spartan projects at this juncture we can observe very clearly the effect of the episode of the expedition of Cyrus and the Ten Thousand in revolutionising the attitude of Greece towards Persia and spreading the idea that Persia was really weak. The Spartan leaders seemed to have regarded the lands of the Great King as a *Highflying* field of easy conquest for a bold Greek. King Agesilaus, especially, *plans of* who now began to disclose the consuming quality of ambition, *Agesilaus;* dreamed of dethroning the Great King himself, and felt no doubt that he would at least speedily deliver the Asiatic coast from Persian control. But he lived sixty years too soon ; and in any case this respectable Spartan was not the man to settle the " eternal question." He regarded himself as a new Agamemnon going forth to capture a new Troy ; and, to make the illusion of resemblance complete, he sailed with part of his army to Aulis, to offer sacrifice there in the temple of Artemis as the " king of men " had done before the sailing of the Greeks to Ilium. If Agesilaus had subverted the Persian empire, the sacrifice at Aulis would have seemed an interesting instance *his display* of a great man's confidence in his own star. But the performance *at Aulis.* of Agesilaus can only provoke the mirth of history, especially as the solemnity was not successfully carried out. The Spartan king had not asked the permission of the Thebans to sacrifice in the temple ; and a body of armed men interrupted the proceedings and compelled him to desist. It was an insult which Agesilaus never forgave to Thebes.

Lysander expected that the real command in the war would devolve upon himself, and on arriving in Asia he acted on that assumption. He was soon undeceived. Agesilaus had no intention of being merely a nominal chief ; and he checked his councillor's self-sufficiency by invariably refusing the petitions which were presented to him through Lysander. This policy was effectual ; Lysander, smarting under the humiliation, was sent at his own request on a separate mission to the Hellespont, where he did useful work for *396 B.C.* Sparta. The satraps in the meantime had renewed with Agesilaus the truce they had made with Dercyllidas, but it was soon broken by Tissaphernes.   Agesilaus made a feint of marching into Caria, and *Campaign* then suddenly, when Tissaphernes had completed his dispositions for *of Agesi-* defence, turned northwards to Phrygia and invaded the satrapy of *laus in* Pharnabazus.   Here he accomplished nothing of abiding importance *Phrygia* but secured a vast quantity of booty, with which he enriched his *(autumn).* friends and favourites—it was no temptation to himself.   The historian Xenophon, who has left us a special work on the life and character of Agesilaus, tells many anecdotes of this campaign, to illustrate the merits of his hero.   Those incidents which bring out *Anecdotes* his humanity have more than a personal interest for us ; they must *of* be taken in connexion with the general fact that the Greeks of the *Agesilaus.* fourth century were more humane than the Greeks of the fifth.   We are told that Agesilaus protected his captives against ill-usage ; they were to be treated as men, not as criminals.   Sometimes slave-merchants, fleeing out of the way of his army, abandoned on the roadside little children whom they had bought.   Instead of leaving these to perish by wolves or hunger, Agesilaus had them removed and given in charge to natives who were too old to be carried into captivity.   But Agesilaus did not scruple to use the captives, without regard to their feelings, as " object-lessons " for his own soldiers. At Ephesus, where the winter was passed in drill, he conceived the idea of showing his troops the difference between good and bad training.   He caused the prisoners to be put up for auction naked, so that the Greek soldiers might see the inferior muscles, the white skin, and the soft limbs of the Asiatics whose bodies were never exposed to the weather nor hardened by regular gymnastic discipline. The spectacle impressed the Greeks with their own superiority ; but it was an outrage, though not intended as such, on the captives ; for, while all Greeks habitually stripped for exercise, Asiatics think it a shame to be seen naked.

Having organised a force of cavalry during the winter, Agesilaus *Campaign* took the field in spring, and gained a victory over Tissaphernes on *in Lydia,* the Pactolus, near Sardis.   The general ill-success of Tissaphernes *395 B.C.* was made a matter of complaint at Susa.   The queen - mother *(spring).* Parysatis, who had never forgiven him for the part he played in the disaster of her beloved Cyrus, made all efforts to procure his downfall ; and Tithraustes was sent to the coast to succeed him and *Death of* put him to death.   An offer was now made by Tithraustes to Agesi- *Tissa-* laus, which it would have been wise to accept.   He was required to *phernes.* leave Asia, on condition that the Greek cities should enjoy complete autonomy, paying only their original tribute to Persia.   Agesilaus could not agree without consulting his government at home, and an armistice of six months was concluded,—an armistice with

Tithraustes, not with Persia ; for Agesilaus was left free to turn his arms against Pharnabazus.

Second invasion of the satrapy of Pharnabazus by Agesilaus (autumn). In his second campaign in Phrygia, the Spartan king was supported by a Paphlagonian prince named Otys, as well as by Spithridates, a Persian noble whom Lysander had induced to revolt. The province was ravaged up to the walls of Dascylion, where Pharnabazus resided, and the Spartan troops wintered in the rich parks of the neighbourhood, well supplied with birds and fish. The train of Pharnabazus, who moved about the country with all his furniture, was captured ; but a dispute over the spoil alienated the oriental allies of Agesilaus, who was the more deeply chagrined at their departure, as he was warmly attached to a beautiful youth, the son of Spithridates. The Greek occupation of Phrygia was brought to an end by an interesting scene—an interview between the Persian satrap and the Lacedaemonian general. Agesilaus arrived first at the appointed place and sat down on the grass to wait. Then the servants of Pharnabazus appeared and began to spread luxurious carpets for their master. But Pharnabazus seeing the simple seat of Agesilaus went and sat down beside him. They shook hands, and Pharnabazus made a speech of dignified remonstrance. " I was the faithful ally of Sparta when she was at war with Athens ; I helped her to victory ; I never played her false, like Tissaphernes ; and now, for all this, you have brought me to such a plight that I cannot get a dinner in my own province save by picking up what you leave. All my parks and hunting grounds and houses you have ravaged or burnt. Is this justice or gratitude ? " After a long silence, Agesilaus explained that being at war with the Great King he had to treat all Persian territory as hostile ; but invited the satrap to throw off his allegiance and become an ally of Sparta. " If the king sends another governor and puts me under him," said Pharnabazus, "then I shall be glad to become your friend and ally ; but now, while I hold this post of command for him, I shall make war upon you with all my strength." Agesilaus was delighted with this becoming reply. " I will quit your territory at once," he said, "and will respect it in future, so long as I have others to make war upon." Farewells were said and Pharnabazus rode away; but his handsome son, dropping behind, said to Agesilaus, " I make you my guest," and gave him a javelin. Agesilaus accepted the proffered friendship and gave in exchange the ornaments of his secretary's horse. The incident had a sequel. In later years this young Persian, ill-treated by his brothers, fled for refuge to Greece, and did not seek in vain the protection of his guest-friend Agesilaus.

His success in Phrygia rendered Agesilaus more than ever disposed to attempt conquests in the interior of Asia Minor. But in the meantime he had mismanaged matters of greater moment.   Before he marched against Pharnabazus, he had received a message from Sparta, committing to him the supreme command by sea.   The preparation of an adequate fleet was urgent.   Conon, with eighty sail—the rest of the armament was not yet completed—had induced (395 B.C.) Rhodes to revolt and had captured a corn fleet which an Egyptian prince had dispatched to the Lacedaemonians.   Agesilaus took measures for the equipment of a fleet of 120 triremes at the expense of the cities of the islands and coast-land ; but he committed the blunder of entrusting the command to Pisander, his brother-in-law, a man of no experience.   After his Phrygian expedition, Agesilaus had been himself recalled to Europe for reasons which will presently be related ; while Pharnabazus went to discharge the functions of joint-admiral with Conon, who had visited Susa in person, to stimulate Persian zeal and obtain the necessary funds.   In the middle of the summer *Battle of* the fleet of Conon and Pharnabazus, having left *Cnidus* Cilician waters, appeared off the coast of the *(Aug.* Cnidian peninsula.   The numbers are uncertain, *394 B.C.)* but the Persian fleet was overwhelmingly larger than that of Pisander, who sailed out from Cnidus to oppose it with desperate courage. The result could not be doubtful.   Pisander's Asiatic contingents deserted him without fighting, and of the rest the greater part were taken or sunk.   Pisander fell in the action.   The Greek cities of Asia expelled the Spartan garrisons and

FIG.   139.—Coin of Cnidus   (obverse). Head of Aphrodite.

acknowledged the overlordship of Persia.   Thus Conon, in the guise of a Persian admiral, avenged Athens and undid the victory of the Aegospotami in a battle which was almost as easily won.   The maritime power of Sparta was destroyed, and the unstable foundations of her empire undermined.

SECT. 5. SPARTA AT THE GATES OF THE PELOPONNESUS (THE "CORINTHIAN WAR")

At the same time, she was suffering serious checks nearer home. While Agesilaus was meditating his wonderful schemes against Persia, war had broken out in Greece between Sparta and her allies ; and the turn it took rendered it imperative to recall him from Asia. It is necessary to go back a little to explain.

After the battle of the Goat's River, Sparta had kept for herself all the fruits of victory.   She had taken over the maritime empire of her prostrate foe, and enjoyed its tribute.   Her allies had got nothing ; and yet they had made far greater sacrifices than Sparta herself throughout the Peloponnesian war. Any demands made by Corinth and other allies who had borne the burden and heat of those years were haughtily rejected. Lacedaemon felt herself strong enough to treat her former friends with contempt. She further exhibited her despotic temper by her proceedings within the Peloponnesus against those who had displeased her. Elis had given her repeated and recent *Fate of* grounds of offence, and Elis was now chastised. King Agis invaded *Elis,* and ravaged the country, and imposed severe conditions on the *399 B.C.* Eleans. They were deprived of their Triphylian territory, of Cyllene their port, and of other places; and were compelled to pull down the incomplete fortifications of their city. The only grace accorded to them was that they should still have the privilege of conducting the *The Mes-* Olympian festival. The Spartans indulged another grudge by ex-*senians.* pelling from Naupactus and Cephallenia the residue of the Messenians, who had settled in those places.

Spartan The exercise of authority within the Peloponnesus was regarded *activity* by Sparta as an ordering of her own domain; but she also began *north of* vigorously to assert her power in the north of Greece. She re-*Ther-* suscitated into new life her colony of Heraclea, near Thermopylae, *mopylae.* and pushing into Thessaly she placed a Lacedaemonian garrison and harmost in Pharsalus.

Mission of When war broke out between Persia and Sparta, it was the policy *Timo-* of Persia to excite a war in Greece against her enemy, and fan the *crates,* smouldering discontent of the secondary Greek powers into a flame. *396 B.C.* The satrap Pharnabazus sent a Rhodian agent, named Timocrates, with fifty talents to bribe the leading statesmen of the chief cities to join Persia in a league of hostility against Sparta. Timocrates visited Argos, Corinth, Thebes, and Athens, and gained over some of the most influential people. But it really required only an assurance of Persian co-operation, and then a favourable occasion, to raise a general resistance to the ascendency of Lacedaemon. [Already the anti-Spartan elements were strong at Argos, Corinth, and Thebes; and at Athens feeling was rising. While the oligarchs opposed any action against Sparta, extreme democrats, led by Epicrates and Cephalus, urged a bold policy: the more moderate Thrasybulus, conscious of the Spartan harmost at Aegina, preserved an uneasy balance. But when news came of Conon's activities, a ship with arms and equipment was sent off to him secretly: the action was publicly disowned, but further support was sent to Conon. The issue was forced by the anti-Spartan group in Thebes. A border dispute arose between Phocis and Western Locris; the Phocians appealed to Sparta, the *Outbreak* Locrians to Thebes. The Thebans invaded Phocis, and when *of war in* required by Sparta to submit the case to arbitration, refused to *Boeotia.* negotiate. Sparta accepted the challenge. A double invasion of

Boeotia was arranged, king Pausanias advancing from the south, and Lysander coming down from Heraclea, on the north.]

Thus threatened, Thebes turned for aid to her old enemy. The prospect of Persian support, and the increasing activity of Conon, had strengthened the war party at Athens ; and the protection that Thebes had afforded to Thrasybulus and his men was still remembered. *Athens combines with Thebes.* The assembly seized the opportunity for attempting to break free from Spartan rule. The decision was felt to be bold, since the Piraeus was unfortified ; but there was also a feeling that the tide was at the flood —Conon was sailing the south-eastern seas, Rhodes had revolted,— the moment must not be lost. So there was concluded an " eternal alliance between the Boeotians and Athenians " ; the phrase, pregnant with the irony of history, has been preserved on a fragment of the original treaty-stone, and it shows the hopes of the hour.

When Lysander approached Boeotia, he was joined by Orchomenus, which was always bitterly hostile to Theban supremacy in Boeotia. He and Pausanias had arranged to meet near Haliartus, which is about half-way between Thebes and Orchomenus. It is uncertain whether Lysander was too soon or Pausanias too late ; but *Siege of Haliartus.* Lysander arrived in the district of Haliartus first and attacked the town. From their battlements the men of Haliartus could descry a band of Thebans coming along the road from Thebes, some time before the danger was visible to their assailants ; and they suddenly sallied forth from the gates. Taken by surprise and attacked on both sides, Lysander's men were driven back, and Lysander was slain. His death was a loss to Sparta, which she could not make good. He had made her empire such as it was ; and she had no other man of first-rate ability. But the death of the Spartan Lysander was no loss to Greece. *Death of Lysander.*

Pausanias soon came up, and his first object was to recover the corse of his dead colleague. He was strong enough to extort this from the Thebans and Haliartians, but an Athenian army came up at the same moment to their assistance, under the leadership of Thrasybulus. Pausanias was in a difficult predicament. To fight meant to incur defeat ; but to acknowledge weakness by asking for a burial truce was galling to Spartan pride. A council of war, however, decided to beg for a truce ; and, when the Thebans, contrary to usage, would grant it only on condition that the Peloponnesian army should leave Boeotia, the terms were accepted. The Spartans vented their sorrow for the loss of Lysander in anger against their king. He was condemned to death for having failed to keep tryst with Lysander and for having declined battle. It is not clear whether the first charge was well founded ; as for the second, no prudent general could have acted otherwise. Pausanias, who had discreetly refrained from returning to Sparta, spent the rest of his life as an exile at Tegea.

The result of this double blow to the Spartans—their prestige tarnished and their ablest general fallen—was the conclusion of a league against her by the four most important states. Thebes and Athens were now joined by Corinth and Argos. This alliance was soon increased by the adhesion of the Euboeans, the Acarnanians, the Chalcidians of Thrace, and other minor states. Perhaps the most active spirit in this insurgent movement was the Theban Ismenias. This leader succeeded in expelling the Spartans from their northern post Heraclea, and spreading the Theban alliance among the peoples of those regions. Sparta lost her foothold in Thessaly, and the Phocians, who were under the protection of a Spartan harmost, were defeated. [Sympathy with Thebes against Sparta was also shown in the Aegean. The revolt of Rhodes and the victory of Cnidus were followed by the formation of a Maritime League. At this period a number of cities issued alliance coins with a common obverse type derived

FIG. 140.—Alliance coin of Ephesus, *c.* 394-3 B.C. Obverse: Young Heracles strangling snakes [legend: ΣΥΝ(μαχι- κόν)]. Reverse: bee [legend: ΕΦ, and below ΠΕ].

from Thebes, the infant Heracles strangling the snakes; the reverse was reserved for each city's civic device. Rhodes, Iasus, Cnidus, Ephesus, Samos, Byzantium, Cyzicus, Lampsacus are known to us and there may have been others. The same pro-Theban type is also found at this time in the west on coins of Zacynthus and Croton.]

The Con-
federates
at the
Isthmus,
spring,
394 B.C. Thus the situation of Greece and the prospects of Sparta were completely changed. The allies, when spring came, gathered together their forces at the Isthmus, and it was proposed by one bold Corinthian to march straight on Sparta and

FIG. 141.—Coin of Lampsacus, *c.* 394-3 B.C. Obverse: Young Heracles strangling snakes. Reverse: winged horse.

"burn out the wasps in their nest." But there were too many strategists present, and valuable time was wasted. The Lacedaemonians were able to advance through Arcadia to Sicyon, from which place they crossed over, by Nemea, to the southern shores of the Saronic gulf—

a movement somewhat hampered by the allies, who had reached Nemea. The allies then took up a post near Corinth, and a battle *Battle of* was fought. The number of combatants on each side was unusually *Corinth* large for a Greek battle. [The Lacedaemonian hoplite contingent *(July).*

FIG. 142.—Alliance coin of Samos, *c.* 394-3 B.C. Obverse: Young Heracles strangling snakes [legend: ΣΥΝ(μαχικόν)]. Reverse: scalp of lion [legend: ΣΑ].

totalled 6000, and was supported by some 10,000 allies from Elis, Sicyon, Epidaurus and its neighbours, Tegea, and Pellene: the Confederates had mustered some 24,000 hoplites, with a correspondingly larger force of cavalry and light-armed. The Confederates' right defeated the Spartan allies, but the Spartans outflanked and broke the Athenians on the left. The Spartan divisions kept good order, checked their pursuit, wheeled round and caught the Argives, Boeotians, and Corinthians, returning from victory. The one-sided action that followed decisively confirmed the Spartan victory.] The losses of the Confederates were more than twice as great as those of their foes. Some unrecorded feat of arms was achieved in this battle by five Athenian horsemen who lost their lives; and in the burying-ground outside the Dipylon Gate of Athens we may still see the funeral monument

FIG. 143.—Coin of Elis (obverse). Head of Hera [legend: *F*A].

of one of these " five knights," Dexileos, a youth of twenty, who is pourtrayed, according to Greek habit, not in the moment of his death but in the moment of victory, spearing a hoplite who has fallen under his horse's hoofs. Strategically, the Confederates lost nothing, the victors gained nothing by the battle of Corinth. The Isthmus was left under the control of the Confederates, who were now free to oppose Agesilaus in Boeotia.

For Agesilaus was bearing down on Boeotia. The battle of *Return of* Haliartus and the events which followed had decided the ephors to *Agesilaus* recall him from Asia, his presence being more pressingly needed in *to Europe.*

T

Europe ; and with a heavy heart he was constrained to abandon his dazzling visions of Persian conquest. Agamemnon had to return to Mycenae without having taken Troy. He marched overland by a route which no army had traversed since the expedition of Xerxes, through Thrace and Macedonia. At Amphipolis he received the news of the victory of Corinth, not excessively inspiriting. But even as he *Eclipse of* marched the fate of his country's empire was being decided. The *sun, Aug.* victory of Conon at Cnidus was the knell of the ambitions of Agesilaus. *14, 394 B.C.* When his army reached Chaeronea the sun suffered an eclipse ; and the meaning of the phenomenon was explained by the news, which presently arrived, of the battle of Cnidus. To conceal from his army the full import of this news was the first duty of the general ; and the second was to hasten on a battle, while it could still be concealed. Agesilaus had been reinforced by some contingents from Lacedaemon, as well as by troops from Phocis and Orchomenus ; but his main force consisted of the soldiers whom he had brought from Asia, among whom were some of the famous Ten Thousand, including Xenophon himself. The Confederate army which had fought at Corinth was now in Boeotia, though hardly in the same strength, as a garrison must have been left to defend their important position near the Isthmus. The Confederates established their camp in the district of Coronea, a favourable spot for blocking against a foe the road which leads to Thebes from Phocis and the valley of *Battle of* the Cephisus. On the field where the Boeotians had thrown off *Coronea,* Athenian rule half a century before, Athenians and Boeotians now *394 B.C.* joined to throw off the domination of Lacedaemon. Agesilaus advanced from the Cephisus. He commanded his own right wing, and the Argives who were on the Confederate left fled before him without striking a blow. On the other side, the Thebans on the Confederate right routed the Orchomenians on the Lacedaemonian left. Then the two victorious right wings wheeling round met each other, and the real business of the day began. The object of Agesilaus was to prevent the Thebans from joining and rallying their friends. The encounter of the hoplites is described as incomparably terrible by Xenophon, who was himself engaged in it. Agesilaus, whose bodily size was hardly equal to such a fray, was trodden underfoot, and rescued by the bravery of his bodyguard. The pressure of the deep column of the Thebans pushed a way through the Lacedaemonian array. Agesilaus was left master of the field ; he erected a trophy ; and the Confederates asked for the burial truce. But though the battle of Coronea, like the battle of Corinth, was a technical victory for the Spartans, history must here again offer her congratulations to the side which was, superficially, defeated. In the chief action of the day, the Thebans had displayed superiority and thwarted the attempt of their enemy to cut them off. It was a great moral encouragement to Thebes for future warfare with Lacedaemon. And immediately, it was a distinct success for the Confederates. When an aggressor cannot follow up his victory, the victory is strategically equivalent to a repulse. Agesilaus immediately evacuated Boeotia—that was the result of Coronea. He crossed over to the Peloponnesus from Delphi, as the Confederates commanded the road by Corinth.

It was round Corinth that the struggle of the next years mainly *Spartans* centred, in fitting accordance with the object of the war. Sparta was *blockaded* fighting for domination beyond the Peloponnesus; her enemies were *in the Pelo-* fighting to keep her within the Peloponnesus. The most effective *ponnesus.* way of accomplishing this design was to hold the gates of the peninsula, between the Corinthian and Saronic gulfs, and not let her pass out. With this view long walls were built binding Corinth, on the one hand with its western port Lechaeon, and on the other with its eastern port at Cenchreae. Thus none could pass from the Peloponnesus into Northern Greece without dealing with the defenders of these fortifications. Never had Lacedaemon been more helpless; almost a prisoner in her peninsula, and her maritime empire dissolved. This momentary paralysis of Lacedaemon proved the salvation of Athens.

The restoration of Athens to her place among the independent *393 B.C.* powers of Greece at this juncture came about by curious means. *Pharna-* The satrap Pharnabazus who had done so much to aid Lysander in *bazus on* destroying her, now helped to bring about her resurrection. He *the Greek* had not forgiven Sparta for the injury which Agesilaus had inflicted *coast.* on his province, and this rankling resentment was kept alive by the circumstance that, while the other Asiatic cities had unanimously declared against Sparta after the battle of Cnidus, Abydus alone held out against himself under the Spartan Dercyllidas. He exhibited his wrath by accompanying Conon and the fleet, in the following spring, to the shores of Greece, to ravage the Spartan territory and to encourage and support the Confederates. A Persian satrap within sight of Corinth and Salamis was a strange sight for Greece. His revengefulness stood Athens in good stead. When he returned home, he allowed Conon to retain the fleet and make use of it to rebuild the Long Walls of Athens and fortify the Piraeus. He even *Rebuilding* supplied money to inflict this crushing blow on Sparta, a blow which *of the Long* completely undid the chief result of the Peloponnesian war. The *Walls of* two long parallel walls connecting Athens with the Piraeus were *Athens.* rebuilt;[1] the port was again made defensible; and the Athenians

[1] The building of the walls was begun before the battle of Cnidus; the completion was due to Conon.

could feel once more that they were a free and independent people in the Grecian world. Conon who had wrought out their deliverance erected a temple to the Cnidian Aphrodite in the Piraeus, as a monument of his great victory. Never since the day of Salamis was there such cause for rejoicing at Athens as when the fortifications were completed at the end of the autumn. As rebuilder of the walls Conon might claim to be a second Themistocles. But the comparison only reminds us of the change which had come over Greece in a hundred years. It was through Persian support that Athens now under the auspices of Conon regained in part the position which she had won by her championship of Hellas against Persia under the auspices of Themistocles. She did not regain her former ascendency or her former empire, but she was restored to an equality with the other powerful states of Greece ; she could feel herself the peer of Thebes, Corinth, and Argos, and of Sparta, now that Sparta had fallen from her high estate. The Athenians could now calmly maintain that defiance which they had boldly offered to Sparta by their alliance with Thebes. About the same time the northern islands of Lemnos, Imbros, and Scyrus seem to have been reunited to Athens, and she recovered her control of Delos which the Spartans had taken from her. Chios too became her ally.

It was of vital importance to the Lacedaemonians to gain command of the gates of the Peloponnesus by capturing some part of the line of defence ; and thus Corinth becomes the centre of interest. The Lacedaemonians established their headquarters at Sicyon, and from this base made a series of efforts to break through the lines of Corinth—efforts which were ultimately successful. Unluckily the chronology is obscure ; and it cannot be decided whether these operations were partly concurrent with, or altogether subsequent to, the rebuilding of the Long Walls of Athens. In Corinth itself there was a considerable party favourable to Sparta. This party seems to have arranged a plot for violently overthrowing the oligarchy which was in power ; but the design was suspected and prevented by the government, who caused the friends of Sparta to be massacred in cold blood, in the market-place and theatre, on the last day of the *Union of* feast of Euclea. The Corinthian government at the same time drew *Corinth* closer the bonds which attached it to the enemies of Sparta. By *and Argos* a remarkable measure Corinth and Argos united themselves into a *(392 B.C.).* federal state ; the boundary pillars were pulled up ; the citizens enjoyed common rights. It would be interesting to know how this federal constitution was framed ; but such an union had no elements of endurance ; it was merely a political expedient.

Praxitas A considerable number of the philo-Laconian party had escaped ; *at Corinth.* some still remained in the city ; and these now managed to open a gate in the western wall and admit Praxitas, the commander at Sicyon, with a Lacedaemonian *mora* of 600 hoplites. Praxitas secured his position between the two walls by constructing a ditch and palisade, across the intermural space, on the side of Corinth. The Corinthians and their allies came down from the city; the palisade was torn up; a battle was fought; and the Lacedaemonians, completely victorious, captured the town of Lechaeon, though not the port. Praxitas then pulled down part of the walls, and made incursions into the Corinthian territory on the side of the Saronic bay. But when winter set in, he disbanded his army, without making any provision for keeping the command of the Isthmus; and the Athenians came, with carpenters and masons, and repaired the breach in the walls.

Battle of the Long Walls.

A warfare of raids was at the same time constantly carried on by the hostile parties, from their posts at Corinth and Sicyon. In this warfare a force of mercenaries, trained and commanded by the Athenian Iphicrates, was especially conspicuous. They were armed as peltasts, with light shield and javelin, and this armour was far better suited for the conditions of camp life and the duties of the professional soldier, than the armour of a hoplite. The employment of mercenaries had been growing,—destined ultimately to supplant the institution of citizen armies. It was the wilder parts of Greece, like Crete, Aetolia, Acarnania, that chiefly supplied the mercenary troops. Iphicrates of Rhamnus, an officer of great energy and talent, recognised the importance of the professional peltast as a new element in Hellenic warfare, and immortalised his name in military history by reforming the peltast's equipment. His improvements consisted in lengthening the sword and the javelin, and introducing a kind of light leggings, known as "Iphicratid" boots. It is difficult to appreciate the full import of these changes; but they were clearly meant to unite effectiveness of attack with rapidity of motion.

Mercenary troops: their growing importance.

Reforms of Iphicrates.

This enterprising officer and his peltasts won the chief honours of the "Corinthian War." Agesilaus had been sent out to gain some more permanent successes than those which had been achieved by Praxitas. His brother Teleutias co-operated with him by sea; the Long Walls were stormed, and the port of Lechaeon was captured. In the following year he went forth again. It was the time of the Isthmian festival, and the games were about to be held in the precincts of Poseidon at Isthmus. Agesilaus marched thither, interrupted the Corinthians and Argives who were beginning the celebration, and presided at the contest himself. When he retired, the Corinthians came and celebrated the festival over again; some athletes won the same race twice.

Agesilaus captures Lechaeon, 391 B.C.

(390 B.C., spring.)

Agesilaus then captured the port of Piraeon, on the promontory

Spartans
capture
Piraeon.
which forms the northern side of the inmost recess of the Corinthian gulf. The importance of this capture lay in the fact that Piraeon connected Corinth with her allies in Boeotia ; its occupation was a threat to Boeotia ; and the Boeotians immediately sent envoys to Agesilaus. The position was now reversed ; the Spartans commanded the Isthmus passage, and by possessing Sicyon, Piraeon, Lechaeon, as well as Sidon and Crommyon on the Saronic gulf, they entirely closed in Corinth, except on the side of Argolis. If Agesilaus felt himself the arbiter of Greece, his triumph was short. The situation was rescued by Iphicrates.

The light
troops of
Iphicrates
vanquish
Spartan
hoplites.
In the garrison at Lechaeon there were some men of Amyclae, whose custom and privilege it was to return to their native place to keep the local feast of Hyacinthus. The time of this feast was now at hand, and they set out to return home by Sicyon and Arcadia, the only way open to them. But as it was not safe for a handful of men to march under the walls of Corinth, they were escorted most of the way to Sicyon by a *mora* of 600 Lacedaemonian hoplites. As this escort was returning to Lechaeon, Iphicrates and his peltasts issued from the gates of Corinth and attacked them. The heavy spearmen were worn out by the repeated assaults of the light troops with which they were unable to cope, and a large number were destroyed. This event, though less striking and important, bore a resemblance to the famous calamity of Sphacteria. In both cases, Spartan warriors had been discomfited in the same way by the continuous attacks of inaccessible light troops ; and in both cases a blow was dealt to the military prestige of Lacedaemon. The success of Iphicrates was a suggestive sign of the future which might be in store for the professional peltast. To Agesilaus the news came at a moment when he was regarding with triumphant arrogance his captives and the Theban envoys. His pride was changed into chagrin ; the army was plunged into sorrow ; and only the relatives of those soldiers who had fallen in the battle moved about with the jubilant air of victors. Leaving another division as a garrison in Lechaeon, Agesilaus returned home, skulking through Sicyon and the Arcadian cities at night, in order to avoid unkind remarks. Piraeon, Sidon, and Crommyon were soon recovered by Iphicrates ; and the garrison of Lechaeon seems to have done no more than keep the gates of the Peloponnesus open. This was the result of the " Corinthian " war. Sparta had succeeded in breaking down the barrier which was to shut her out from North Greece ; but she had sustained a serious loss and damage to her reputation.

Sect. 6. The King's Peace

We must now turn from the Isthmus of Corinth to the eastern *Efforts* coasts of the Aegean.   The Lacedaemonians ascribed the success of *towards* their opponents to the support of Persia, and drew the conclusion *a peace,* that their chance lay in detaching Persia to their own side.   With *392 B.C.* this view they had dispatched Antalcidas to open negotiations with Tiribazus.   The proposals of Sparta were (1) that the Hellenic cities of Asia should be subjects of the king ; this was the price of Persian help ; (2) that all other Hellenic cities should be independent ; this was aimed at the Confederates—at the supremacy of Thebes in Boeotia, and at the union of Corinth with Argos.   The Athenians and their allies sent Conon and other envoys to counteract the mission of Antalcidas, and perhaps it was at this time also that they sent the orator Andocides to Sparta to consider terms of peace. Both the mission of Andocides and the mission of Antalcidas were alike unsuccessful.   Tiribazus, who was favourable to Sparta and threw Conon into prison, was recalled ; and his successor Struthas had no Spartan leanings.   The object of Antalcidas was indeed ultimately reached, but its attainment was postponed for four or five years, and the war went on as before.

The military events of these years are not of great interest ; our *Warfare* knowledge of them is meagre.   In Asia, the Spartan cause revives. *in Asia;* Thibron is sent out once more, and though he sustains a severe defeat at the hands of Struthas, it is not until he has won over Ephesus, Magnesia, and Priene.   Soon Cnidus and Samos follow the example of these cities.   Agesilaus invades Acarnania, and *in Europe.* forces the Acarnanians to join the Lacedaemonian league ; his colleague Agesipolis carries out one of those invasions of Argolis which lead to nothing.   Then the Spartans use Aegina as a base for harassing Attica, and a warfare of surprises is carried on between the harmosts of Aegina and Athenian admirals.   The harmost Gorgopas captured four ships of an Athenian squadron ; the Athenian Chabrias then landed in Aegina, laid an ambush, and killed Gorgopas. Teleutias, the brother of Agesilaus, was sent to Aegina soon after-wards.   He made an attack on the Piraeus at daybreak, and towed away some of the galleys lying in the harbour.   In old Greece the war was on the whole advantageous to Sparta, though no decisive success was gained.

But the most important event was the recovery of Athenian *Taxation* dominion on the Propontis.   At this moment Athens was in great *at Athens:* financial straits, for she had ceased to receive Persian subsidies. *(1)* When an indirect impost of $\frac{1}{40}$th had been tried and found in- *Euripides' tax of $\frac{1}{40}$th;*

(2) *war tax*, 390, 389 B.C.

sufficient, a direct war-tax was levied. For the Athenians had determined to operate both in the south and in the north; in the south to assist their friend Evagoras who was revolting from the Great King, in the north to recover control of the road to the Euxine

389 B.C.

Sea. Thrasybulus, the restorer of the democracy, sailed with a fleet of forty ships to the Hellespont, and gained over to the Athenian alliance the islands of Thasos and Samothrace, the Chersonesus, and the two cities which commanded the Bosphorus, Byzantium and Chalcedon. Proceeding to Lesbos, he defeated and slew the Spartan harmost, and established Athenian supremacy over most of the island. He also won Clazomenae. The original object for which

he had been sent out was to assist Rhodes in maintaining her independence against the efforts of Sparta to regain the mastery of the island. But to act with effect it was necessary to raise money, and the Athenian fleet coasted round Asia Minor, levying contributions. These exactions appear to have been

FIG. 144.—Coin of Clazomenae (obverse). Head of Apollo laureate.

a renewal of the tax of 5 per cent which Athens imposed on the commerce of her allies towards the end of the Sicilian expedition. It seemed like the beginning of a new empire. Aspendus in Pamphylia was one of the places visited, and the visit was fatal to Thrasybulus. The violent methods of his soldiers enraged the inhabitants; they surprised him at night in his tent

Death of Thrasybulus (388 B.C.).

and slew him. Athens had now lost the two men of action to whom, since the death of Pericles, she owed most, Conon and Thrasybulus. Conon, who soon after his imprisonment by Tiribazus died in Cyprus, had broken down the maritime dominion of the Lacedaemonian oppressor and had given Athens the means of recovering her independence and her sea-power. Thrasybulus had given to the Athenian democracy a new life and breathed into it a new spirit of conciliation and moderation. He strikes us—we know too little of him—as an eminently reasonable citizen, one of those men who command general confidence, and are not biassed by prejudice or ambition. The virtues of Thrasybulus were moral rather than intellectual. After his death insinuations were made against his integrity; and one of his friends named Ergocles was found guilty of embezzlement of money collected on the expedition of Thrasybulus and was put to death. But the statements of an advocate—and we have no other evidence—carry no weight.

The success of Thrasybulus in re-establishing a toll for the advantage of Athens on merchandise passing through the Bosphorus was almost immediately endangered by Anaxibius, whom Sparta promptly sent out to act against Athens and Pharnabazus. He

deprived Athens of her tolls by seizing the merchant vessels. 388 *B.C.*
Iphicrates was dispatched to oppose him with 1200 peltasts, and the
Hellespont became the scene of the same kind of warfare of raids
and surprises which we saw carried on at Aegina.   At last Iphicrates
saw a favourable opportunity for a decisive blow.   Anaxibius had
gone to place a garrison in Antandrus, which he had just gained
over.   Iphicrates crossed by night from the Chersonese and laid an
ambush on the return route, near the gold mines of Cremaste.   The
troops of Anaxibius marched in careless order, traversing the narrow
mountain passes in extended single file, without the slightest suspicion
that an enemy lay in the way.   Suddenly, as they were coming down
from the mountains into the plain of Cremaste, the peltasts of
Iphicrates leaped out.   Anaxibius saw at a glance that the case
was desperate.   The scattered hoplites had no chance against the
peltasts.   " I must die here," he said to his men, " my honour
demands it ; but do you save yourselves."   A devoted youth who
constantly accompanied him fell fighting by his side.   This exploit of
Iphicrates ensured the command of the Hellespont and Bosphorus to
Athens.

Unfortunately for Athens, the political situation changed and other
great powers intervened.   At the beginning of the fourth century
there were three great powers which aimed at supremacy over
portions of the Greek world—Persia, Sparta, and the tyrant of
Syracuse, Dionysius.   At first, however, it was not a case of these
three great powers uniting in a sacred alliance for the suppression of
liberty.   Dionysius did not intervene in the east ; and Persia and
Sparta contested the supremacy over the Asiatic Greeks.   Thus Persia,
in the cause of her own supremacy in Asia, made common cause
with liberty elsewhere.   The general military failure of Sparta forced
her to seek a reconciliation with Persia on the basis of abandoning
Asia.   One of the obstacles to the accomplishment of this object was
the influence of the satrap Pharnabazus who cherished bitter hostility
to the country of Dercyllidas and Agesilaus.   On the other hand,
Athens had taken an ambiguous step which could not fail to create
distrust and resentment at the Persian court.   If Athens was *Athens*
indebted to Persia for the restoration of her walls, she had also been *votes to*
befriended and supported by Evagoras, prince of Salamis, the friend *assist*
of Conon, and she had bestowed upon him her citizenship in *Evagoras,*
recognition of his services.   Thus, when he revolted from Persia, *390 B.C.*
Athens was in an embarrassing position.   The support of Persia
against Sparta was all-important to her.   Artaxerxes was her ally ;
but Evagoras was her citizen too, and a Greek.   Against her *Spartan*
own apparent interests, Athens sent ten ships to assist her Cypriote *diplomacy*
friend ; and, though they were captured by a Lacedaemonian *at Susa.*

admiral and never actually served against the Persians, the incident was calculated to dispose the Great King to entertain the overtures of Sparta. The diplomatist Antalcidas went up to Susa and renewed his proposals. Backed by the influence of Tiribazus he overcame the reluctance of Artaxerxes, who was personally prepossessed against Sparta, and induced him to agree to enforce a general pacification, on the same conditions which had been proposed before. Opposition on the part of Pharnabazus was removed by summoning him to court to marry a daughter of Artaxerxes.

Sparta supported by Syracuse.

The diplomacy of Sparta was successful not only at Susa; it was successful also at Syracuse, and obtained an auxiliary force of twenty triremes from the tyrant Dionysius.

With the support of the west and the east, Sparta was able to force the peace upon Hellas. When Antalcidas and Tiribazus returned to the coast, they found Iphicrates blockading the Spartan fleet at Abydus. Antalcidas dexterously rescued the fleet from this predicament, and was able, when the Syracusan vessels joined him, as well as Persian reinforcements, to blockade the Athenians in the Hellespont and prevent corn vessels from reaching Athens. The coasting trade of Attica was at the same time suffering grievously through the raids from Aegina, which have already been mentioned. Hence peace was expedient for Athens; and the allies could not think of continuing the war without her. The representatives of the belligerents were summoned to Sardis, and Tiribazus read aloud the edict of his master, showing them the royal seal. It was to this effect:—

387 B.C.

The peace which the King sent down, 387-6 B.C.

"King Artaxerxes thinks it just that the cities in Asia, and the islands of Clazomenae and Cyprus, shall belong to him. Further, that all the other Greek cities, small and great, shall be autonomous; except Lemnos, Imbros, and Scyrus, which shall belong to Athens, as aforetime. If any refuse to accept this peace I shall make war on them, along with those who are of the same purpose, both by land and sea, with both ships and money."

(386 B.C.)

The representatives were to report to the cities the terms of the peace, and then meet at Sparta to declare their acceptance. All accepted; but the Thebans raised a difficulty by claiming to take the oath on behalf of all the Boeotian cities as well as of themselves. Such a proposal would clearly place the Boeotian cities in a different class from the other cities of Greece, which took the oath each for itself. It was an attempt to assert the dependence of the Boeotian communities on Thebes, whereas one of the chief objects of the peace was to assert their autonomy. Agesilaus was secretly pleased with the opposition of Thebes: he hoped that the Thebans would persist in it and give him the opportunity of attacking and subduing

FIG. 145.—Sepulchral Monument of Dexileos.

their detested city. But they submitted in time and disappointed his vengeance.

The King's Peace was inscribed on stone tablets, which were set up in the chief sanctuaries of the Greek states. There was a feeling among many that Greece had suffered a humiliation in having to submit to the arbitration of Persia. Both Spartans and Athenians had alike used Persian help, when they could get it, but never before had the domestic conflicts of Hellas been settled by barbarian dictation and under a barbarian sanction. It was Sparta's doing. She constituted herself the minister of the Great King's will in order to save her own position; and the Greeks of Asia were left to endure oriental methods of government. Athens, though she had lost what Thrasybulus had won for her, was allowed to retain her old insular dependencies in the North Aegean; a concession which shows that it was thought necessary to bribe her into accepting the peace, and that Sparta was more eagerly bent on weakening the other confederates. In truth, the main objects were to break up the Boeotian league and to separate the Argives from Corinth.

CHAPTER XIII

THE REVIVAL OF ATHENS AND HER SECOND LEAGUE

SECT. I. HIGH-HANDED POLICY OF SPARTA

THE gates of the Peloponnesus were again open to Sparta without dispute; she was supported by Persia, and she had no complications in Asia to divide her energy. Accordingly she was able to renew the despotic policy which had been inaugurated for her by Lysander. Arcadian Mantinea was the first to suffer. The Mantineans were accused of various acts of disobedience and disloyalty to Sparta, and commanded to pull down their walls. When they refused, king Agesipolis—son of the exiled Pausanias—marched out against them. The city of Mantinea stood in a high plain, without any natural defences, depending entirely on its walls of unburnt brick. The river Ophis flowed through the town; and, a blockade proving tedious, Agesipolis dammed the stream at the point of issue. The water rose and undermined the walls; and when one of the towers threatened to fall, the people surrendered. Their punishment was severe. Mantinea ceased to be a city, and was broken up into its five constituent villages. Those who originally belonged to the *village* of Mantinea remained on the site of the city; the rest had to pull down their houses and move each to the village where his property was. The loss of civic life meant to a Greek the loss of all his higher interests.

The dissolution of the city of Mantinea (386-5 B.C.).

Agesilaus, who had once gone forth to destroy the Persian power, zealously supported the King's Peace. When some one suggested that it was at least curious to find the Spartans medizing, he rejoined, "Rather say that the Persians are laconizing." Each way of putting it expressed a measure of the truth. But some of the Lacedaemonians, including king Agesipolis, were opposed to the recent policy of their government, and thought it ill-done to abandon the Greeks of Asia. Some years after the Peace, there seems to have been floating in the air a vague idea, which might or might not take

*The
Panegyric
of Isocrates
(composed
381),* 380. shape, of organising another Asiatic expedition. It was to animate this idea that the Athenian orator Isocrates published a festal speech when the Greek nation was assembled at the Olympian festival. He advocated a grand Panhellenic union against Persia, under the common headship of Sparta and Athens—Sparta taking the command by land, Athens by sea. It was the third occasion on which a renowned master of style had broached the same idea at the same *(See above,
p. 499 ;
and below,
p. 560.)* gathering-place. Nearly thirty years ago, it had been recommended by the florid eloquence of Gorgias ; more recently it had been advocated with gracious simplicity by Lysias ; and now the rich periods of Isocrates urged it once more upon Greece. The project —in the ideal form in which Isocrates imagined it—was at this moment chimerical. A hundred years before, it had been hard enough to compass a practical co-operation between Greek powers of equal strength and pretensions, in a war of defence ; it was hopeless to think of such co-operation now for a war of aggression. Sparta and Athens were quarrelling, as the orator complains, over the tribute of the Cyclad islands ; and neither was likely to yield to the other without a clear award of war. And other troubles were brewing in another quarter.

*Evagoras
of Cyprus.*　　　The contest of east and west had been going on meanwhile in Cyprus, an island whose geographical situation has marked it out, like Sicily, to be a meeting-place of races. We have already met a man who played an eminent part in that struggle, Evagoras the prince of Salamis. He belonged to the Teucrid family which had reigned there in the days of Darius and Xerxes, but had been supplanted by a Phoenician dynasty about the middle of the fifth *411-10 B.C.* century. Evagoras, crossing over from the Cilician Soli, won back the sceptre of his race by a daring surprise. He governed with conspicuous moderation, discretion, and success ; setting himself to the work of reviving the cause of Hellenism, which had lost much ground during the past half-century ; and pursuing this task by entirely peaceful means. After Aegospotami, the city of Evagoras became the refuge for large numbers of Athenians who had settled down in various parts of the Athenian empire and could no longer remain securely in their homes. For the first sixteen years of his reign Evagoras was a faithful tributary of the Great King, and we have seen how his influence at Susa assisted Conon. But soon after the battle of Cnidus he became involved in war, both with Persia *386 B.C.* and with some of the Phoenician cities in the island. The Peace expressly recognised the sovereignty of Artaxerxes over Cyprus, and as soon as it was concluded, Persia began to concentrate her forces *(Acoris.)
386-4 B.C.* against Evagoras and a recalcitrant king of Egypt, with whom Evagoras was leagued. A severe defeat at sea shut Evagoras

up in Salamis ; but he held out so dauntlessly, and the war had already cost Persia so much, that Tiribazus agreed to leave him his principality, on condition that he should pay tribute "as a slave to his lord." Evagoras refused ; he would only pay it as one king to another. The negotiations were ruptured for a moment on this 381 *B.C.* point of honour, but a dispute between the satrap and his subordinate general resulted in the removal of Tiribazus, and his successor permitted Evagoras to have his way.

The Salaminian despot had thus gained a moral triumph. He *His death.* did not survive it many years, and the story of his death is curious. A certain man named Nicocreon formed a plot against his life, and being detected was forced to fly. He left a daughter behind him in Salamis under the care of a faithful eunuch. This servant privily acquainted both Evagoras and his son Pnytagoras with the existence of this young lady and her uncommon beauty, and undertook to conduct them to her bedchamber, each without the knowledge of the other. Both kept the assignation and were slain by the eunuch, 374 *B.C.* who thus avenged his master's exile. Another son of Evagoras, named Nicocles, succeeded him, and pursued the same Hellenizing policy. One of the great objects of these enlightened princes was to keep their country in touch with the intellectual and artistic movements of Greece. Nicocles was a student of Greek philosophy, and a generous friend of the essayist, Isocrates, to whose pen we are indebted for much of what we know of the career of Evagoras.

Towards the close of the almost single-handed struggle of *Macedonia,* Salamis against Persia, the eyes of Greece were directed to a 383 *B.C.* different quarter of the world. Events were passing in the north of the Aegean, which riveted the attention of Sparta and Athens ; their Greek brethren of Cyprus and the Asiatic coast seem to be quite forgotten ; for a while the oriental question almost passes out of the pages of Greek history. Yet it was destined that from that very region on the north-west corner of the Aegean should issue the force which should not only reclaim for European influence Cyprus and all the Greek cities of Asia, but bear Greek light into lands of which Agesilaus had never dreamed. That force was being forged in the Macedonian uplands ; and some who were children when Isocrates published his Panegyric against the Barbarian lived to see the Barbarian succumb to a Greek power.

It was indeed only indirectly that the southern Greeks had now to concern themselves with their backward brethren of Macedonia. One of the chief obstacles to the development of this country was its constant exposure to the attacks of its Illyrian neighbours. For protection king Amyntas—he was the great-grandson of Alexander—had, soon after his succession, concluded a close defensive and com- ? 392 *B.C.*

mercial alliance for fifty years with the Chalcidian league, which had been formed by Olynthus and comprised the towns of the Sithonian promontory. Almost immediately, however, he was forced to with-draw before an Illyrian in-vasion ; but at the moment of his retreat Amyntas handed over to the Chal-cidians the lower districts of Macedonia and the cities lying round the Thermaic gulf. The Macedonian cities readily embraced an union which could protect them against the Illyrians, and the league spread from the maritime towns up the country and included even Pella. Perfect

The Chalcidian Con-federacy.

FIG. 146.—Coin of Chalcidice. Obverse : head of laureate Apollo. Reverse : lyre bound with fillet [legend : ΧΑΛΚΙΔΕΩΝ].

equality and brotherhood between the members was the basis of this Chalcidian confederacy. All the cities had common laws, common rights of citizenship, intermarriage, and commerce ; Olynthus did not assume a privileged position for herself. The neighbouring Greek cities were also asked to join, and some of them, Potidaea for instance, accepted the offer. But it was always a sacrifice for a Greek city to give up its hereditary laws and surrender any part of its sovereignty, whatever compensating advantages might be pur-chased ; and there was consequently more reluctance among the Chalcidians than among the less developed Macedonians to join the league. The Olynthians, as their work grew, conceived the idea of a confederate power which should embrace the whole Chalcidic peninsula and its neighbourhood. Once this ambition took form, it became necessary to impose by force their proposition upon those who declined to accept it freely. The strong cities of Acanthus and Apollonia resisted, and sent envoys to Sparta to obtain her help. Moreover Amyntas had recovered his throne, and when the Olyn-thians refused to abandon the cities which he had handed over to them, he too looked for aid to Sparta. These appeals directed the eyes of Greece upon the Chalcidian confederacy. It was the Lace-daemonian policy to oppose all combinations and keep Greece dis-united—a policy which was popular, in so far as it appealed to that innate love of autonomy which made it so difficult to bring about abiding federal unions in Greece. The ambassadors had little difficulty in persuading the Lacedaemonians and their allies that the move-ment in Chalcidice was dangerous to the interests of Sparta, and should be crushed at the outset ; and they argued that the very liberality of the principles on which it was founded made the league more attractive and therefore more dangerous. Whether the league was a party to the King's Peace is not known, nor is the legal position important; Sparta and her allies considered that their interests were involved. A vote of assistance to Acanthus and Apollonia was passed, and a small advance force was immediately sent under Eudamidas. Though unable to meet the confederate army in the field, this force was sufficient to protect the cities which had refused to join the league, and it even induced Potidaea to revolt.

The expedition against the Chalcidian Confederacy led unex- *The citadel* pectedly to an important incident elsewhere. Phoebidas, the brother *of Thebes* of Eudamidas, was to follow with larger forces, and, as the line of *seized by* march lay through Boeotia, a party in Thebes favourable to Sparta *the* *Spartans,* thought to profit by the proximity of Spartan troops for the purpose *382 B.C.* of a revolution. Leontiadas, the most prominent member of this party, was then one of the polemarchs. He concerted with Phoebidas a plot to seize the Cadmea—the citadel of Thebes—on the day of the Thesmophoria; for on that day the citadel was given up to the use of the women who celebrated the feast. The plot succeeded perfectly; the acropolis was occupied without striking a blow; the oligarchical Council was intimidated by Leontiadas; and his colleague, the other polemarch, Ismenias was arrested. The leading anti-Spartans fled from Thebes, and a government friendly to Sparta was established. This was a great triumph for Sparta, a great satisfaction to Agesilaus, although, as a violation of peace, it caused a moment's embarrassment. Was the government to recognise the action of Phoebidas and profit by it? Spartan hypocrisy compromised the matter; Phoebidas was heavily fined for his indiscretion, and the Cadmea was retained. Then Ismenias was tried by a body of judges representing Sparta and her allies, and was condemned on charges of Medism and executed. That Sparta, after the King's Peace, should condemn a Theban for Medism, was a travesty of justice.

With the fortress of Thebes in her hands, Sparta had a basis for extending her power in central Greece and might regard her supremacy as secured. She restored the city of Plataea, which she *Restoration* had herself destroyed well-nigh fifty years agone, and gathered *of Plataea,* all the Plataeans who could be found to their old home. But her *382-1 B.C.* immediate attention was fixed on the necessity of repressing the dangerous league in the north of Greece, and continuing the measures which had been interrupted by the enterprise of Phoebidas in Boeotia. The popular brother of Agesilaus, Teleutias, was sent to conduct the war; but, although he was aided by Amyntas, and by Derdas, a prince of Upper Macedonia, who supplied good cavalry, it proved no easy matter to make head against the league. In front

(381 B.C.) of the walls of Olynthus, Teleutias sustained a signal defeat and was himself slain.   The war was fatal to a king as well as to a king's brother.   Agesipolis, who was next sent out at the head of a very (380 B.C.) large force, caught a fever in the intolerable summer heat.   He was carried to the shady grove of the temple of Dionysus at Aphytis, but he died there ; and his body, stowed in honey, was brought home *Suppres-* for burial.   His successor, Polybiadas, was more successful.   He *sion of the* forced the Olynthians to sue for peace and dissolve their league. *Chalcidian* They and all the Greek cities of the peninsula were constrained to *League,* join the Lacedaemonian alliance, and the maritime cities of Mace- *379 B.C.* donia were restored to the sway of Amyntas.   Thus Sparta put down an attempt to overcome that system of isolation, which placed Greek cities at a great disadvantage, when they had barbarian neighbours.   If Sparta had not happened to be so strong at this moment, the Chalcidian league might have grown into a power, which would have considerably modified the development of Mace- donia.   All that Sparta did, although for a moment it made her power paramount in northern Greece, fell out ultimately to the advancement and profit of Macedon.

Sparta About the same time, the Lacedaemonians were making their *tyrannises* heavy hand felt in the Peloponnesus.   Soon after the K ng's Peace *over* they had forced the Phliasians to recall a number of banished *Phlius ;* *blockade,* aristocrats.   Disputes arose about the restoration of confiscated *381-79 B.C.* property, and the exiles appealed to Sparta, where they had a zealous supporter in Agesilaus.   War was declared ; Agesilaus reduced the city of Phlius by blockade, and compelled it to receive a Lacedaemonian garrison for six months, until a commission of one hundred, which he nominated, should have drawn up a new constitution.

Thus the Lacedaemonians, in alliance with the tyrant Dionysius and the barbarian Artaxerxes, tyrannised over the Greeks for a space.   Some demonstrations were made, some voices of protest (388 B.C.) were raised, in the name of the Panhellenic cause.   At the Olympian *Olympiac* festival which was held just before the King's Peace, the Athenian *oration of* orator Lysias warned the assembled Greeks of the dangers which *Lysias.* loomed in the east and in the west, from Persia and from Sicily, and uttered his amazement at the policy of Lacedaemon.   A magni- ficent deputation had been sent by Dionysius to this festival, and the inflammatory words, perhaps the direct instigation, of the speaker incited some enthusiastic spectators to attack the gorgeous pavilion of the Syracusan envoys.   The outrage was prevented ; but the occurrence shows the beginning of that tide of feeling to which Isocrates appealed, eight years later, when in his festal oration he denounced the Lacedaemonians, as sacrificing the freedom of Greece to their own interests and treacherously aiding foreigners and tyrants

Even Xenophon, the friend of Sparta's king, the admirer of Sparta's institutions, is roused to regretful indignation at Sparta's conduct, and recognises her fall as a just retribution. "The Lacedaemonians, who swore to leave the cities independent, seized the acropolis of Thebes, and they were punished by the very men, single-handed, whom they had wronged, though never before had they been vanquished by any single people. It is a proof that the gods observe men who do irreligious and unhallowed deeds." In this way the pious historian introduces the event which prepared the fall of Sparta and the rise of Thebes.

SECT. 2. ALLIANCE OF ATHENS AND THEBES

The government of Leontiadas and his party at Thebes, main- *The* tained by 1500 Lacedaemonians in the citadel, was despotic and *deliverance* cruel, like that of the Thirty at Athens. Fear made the rulers *of Thebes.* suspicious and oppressive; for they were afraid of the large number of exiles, who had found a refuge at Athens and were awaiting an opportunity to recover their city. Athens was now showing the same goodwill to the fugitives from Thebes which Thebes, when Athens was in a like plight, had shown to Thrasybulus and his fellows. One of the exiles, named Pelopidas, of more than common daring and devotion, resolved to take his life in his hands and found six others to associate in his plans. No open attack was to be thought of; Thebes must be recovered by guile, even as by guile it had been won. There were many in Thebes who were bitter foes of the ruling party, such as Epaminondas, the beloved friend of Pelopidas, but most of them deemed the time unripe for any sudden stroke for freedom. Yet a few were found ready to run the risk; above all, Phyllidas, who was the secretary of the polemarchs and therefore the most useful of confederates, and Charon, a citizen of good estate, who offered his house as a place of hiding for the conspirators. The day on which the two polemarchs, Archias 379-8 *B.C.* and Philippus, were to go out of office was fixed for the enterprise. *(winter)*. On the day before, Pelopidas and his six comrades crossed Cithaeron in the guise of huntsmen, and, nearing Thebes at nightfall, mixed with the peasants who were returning from the fields, got them safely within the gates, and found safe hiding in the abode of Charon. The secretary Phyllidas had made ready a great banquet for the following night, to which he had bidden the outgoing polemarchs, tempting them by the promise of introducing them to some high-born and beautiful women, whose love they desired. During the carouse a messenger came with a letter for Archias, and said that it concerned serious affairs. "Business to-morrow," said Archias, placing it under his pillow. On the morrow it was found that this letter disclosed the conspiracy. The polemarchs then called for the women, who were waiting in an adjoining room. Phyllidas said that they declined to appear till all the attendants were dismissed. When no one remained in the dining hall but the polemarchs and a few friends, all flushed with wine, the women entered and sat down beside the lords. They were covered with long veils ; and even as they were bidden lift them and reveal their charms, they buried daggers in the bodies of the polemarchs. For they were none other than Pelopidas and his fellows in the guise of women. Then they went and slew in their houses Leontiadas and Hypatas, the two other chief leaders of the party, and set free the political prisoners. When all this was done, Epaminondas and the other patriots, who were unwilling to initiate such deeds themselves, accepted the revolution with joy. When day dawned, an assembly of the people was held in the Agora, and the conspirators were crowned with wreaths. Three of them, including Pelopidas, were appointed polemarchs, and a democratic constitution was established.

The rest of the exiles and a body of Athenian volunteers presently arrived, on the news of the success. The Spartan commander of the Cadmea had sent hastily, on the first alarm, for reinforcements to Thespiae and Plataea, but those that came were charged and repelled, outside the gate. Then in the first flush of success the *Cadmea sur- rendered.* patriots resolved to storm the Cadmea, strong as the place was. But the labour and the danger were spared them. Amazing as it may seem, the Lacedaemonian harmosts decided to capitulate at once. Two of these commanders were put to death on their return to Sparta, and the third was banished. The chagrin of the ephors and Agesilaus was intense ; king Cleombrotus was immediately sent with an army to Boeotia, but accomplished nothing.

Athens disowns the action of the Athenian volunteers, and punishes the generals. Athens was formally at peace with Sparta, and was not disposed to break with her, however great may have been the secret joy felt at the events in Boeotia. But the march of the Athenian volunteers to Thebes was an awkward incident, the more so as there were two strategi among them. Lacedaemonian envoys arrived to demand explanation and satisfaction ; and their statements were reinforced by the neighbourhood of the army of king Cleombrotus. There was indeed nothing to be said for the conduct of the two strategi. They had abused their position and brought their city into danger and embarrassment. We can only approve the sentence of the Athenians, which executed one and banished the other.

But if these Athenian generals were indiscreet, it was as nothing beside the indiscretion of a Lacedaemonian commander, which now *The raid of* precipitated the breach between the two states.   A not ignoble *Sphodrias.* sympathy might have been pleaded by the two Athenians ; but no excuse could be urged for the rash enterprise of the Spartan harmost of Thespiae, who aspired to be a second Phoebidas.   His name was Sphodrias, and he conceived the plan of making a night march to Athens and surprising Piraeus on the landside.   To seize Piraeus, the seat of Athenian merchandise, would be a compensation for the loss of Thebes.   But the plan was, if not ill-considered, at least ill carried out.   Day dawned when he had hardly passed Eleusis ; and there was nothing to do but to turn back.   He retreated, laying waste the districts through which he passed.

Great wrath was kindled in Athens by this unprovoked deed of hostility.   The envoys had not yet gone ; they were immediately thrown into prison, but escaped by declaring that the Spartan government was not responsible for the raid, and would speedily prove its innocence by the condemnation of Sphodrias.   The assurance was belied ; Sphodrias was not condemned.   His son and the son of Agesilaus were lovers, and the king's influence saved him.   Agesilaus is reported to have said : " Sphodrias is guilty, of course ; but it is a hard thing to put to death a man who, as child, stripling, and man, lived a life of perfect honour ; for Sparta needeth such soldiers." This miscarriage of justice was a grave mistake of policy ; and the high-handed insolence of the Spartan oligarchs was set in a more glaring light by contrast with the fair-mindedness which the Athenian people had displayed in promptly punishing its own generals for a similar though certainly less heinous act.   The Athenian generals had at least not invaded Lacedaemonian territory.   It was debated at the time, and has been debated since, whether Sphodrias acted wholly of his own accord ; some thought that the suggestion came from king Cleombrotus, and the theory was started that the Thebans were the prime instigators—an unlikely theory, which was evidently based on the fact that Thebes was the only gainer by the raid.   It seems most probable that the private ambition of Sphodrias, who thought he had a chance of emulating Phoebidas, was alone responsible.

The raid and acquittal of Sphodrias drove Athens, against her *Alliance of* will, into war with Sparta and alliance with Thebes ; it stirred her *Athens* for a while to leave her rôle of neutral spectator and assume that *with Thebes,* of an active belligerent.   For the next six years, Athens and Sparta *378 B.C.* are at war, though such a war was contrary to the interests of both states, but especially to the interests of Sparta.

SECT. 3. THE SECOND ATHENIAN LEAGUE AND THE THEBAN REFORMS

The raid of Sphodrias was the direct occasion of the Second Athenian Confederacy. For many years back, ever since the battle of Cnidus, Athens had been gradually forming bonds of alliance with various states in Thrace, the Aegean, and the coasts of Asia Minor. *Second Athenian Con-federacy.* The breach with Sparta induced her now to gather together these separate connexions into a common league, with the express object of protecting the independence of the Greek states against the oppression of Sparta. When men thought of the old Confederacy of Delos, they might fear that the second Athenian league would be soon converted into a second Athenian empire. But Athens anticipated such alarms by establishing the confederacy on a different system, which provided safeguards against the dangers of Athenian 378-7 *B.C.* preponderance and Athenian encroachment. In the archonship of Nausinicus, Aristoteles of the deme of Marathon proposed in the Assembly a decree which embodied the principles of the league. The sway of Persia over the Greeks of Asia was explicitly recognised, so that the field of operations was to be European Greece and the Islands. The league, which was purely defensive, was constituted in two parts, Athens on one side, her allies on the other. The allies had their own synedrion or congress which met in Athens, but in which Athens had no part. Both the synedrion of the Confederates and the Athenian Assembly had the right of initiating measures, but no measure passed by either body was valid until it had been approved by the other body also. While this system gave Athens a weight and dignity equal to that of all her allies together, it secured for the allies an independence which they had not possessed under the old league, and they had the right of absolute veto on any Athenian proposal which they disliked. It was necessary for the members of the league to form a federal fund ; their payments were called *syntaxeis* (" contributions "), and the word *phoros* (" tribute"), which had odious memories connected with the confederacy of Delos, was avoided. It was especially enacted that the practice of Athenian outsettling in the lands of the allies, which had formerly helped and supported the Athenian empire, was not to be permitted. No Athenian was to acquire home or farm, " by purchase or mortgage, or any other means whatever," in the territory of any of the confederates. But the administration of the federal fund and the leadership of the federal army were in the hands of Athens.

Good fortune has preserved to us the original stone, shattered in about twenty pieces, with the decree which founded the confederacy, and we find the purpose of the league definitely declared : " To force the Lacedaemonians to allow the Greeks to enjoy peace in freedom and independence, with their lands unviolated." It was no doubt Callistratus, the ablest statesman and orator of the day, who did *Calli-* most to make the new scheme a success ; but, though he may be *stratus.* called the Aristides of the Second Confederacy, Callistratus certainly did not mean the combination against Sparta as seriously as Aristides meant the combination against Persia. The policy which Callistratus generally pursued was based on harmony with Sparta and antagonism to Thebes. It is sometimes said that at this period there were two parties contending for the guidance of the foreign policy of Athens, one friendly and the other obstinately hostile to Boeotia. But, though Thebes had some friends at Athens, we have no good grounds for speaking of a Theban or Boeotian party. It might be truer to say that there was an anti-Spartan faction, which might often seek a Theban alliance as a means to an end. At this juncture Callistratus was astute enough to see not only that it would be useless to oppose the feeling against Sparta, but also that an opportunity which might never recur was offered for increasing the power of Athens. He therefore abandoned for the time his permanent policy, and threw himself heartily into a scheme of which the most remarkable feature was union with Thebes.

The chief cities which first joined the new league were Chios, Byzantium, Mytilene, Methymna, and Rhodes, with whom Athens already had alliances ; then most of the towns of Euboea joined, and, what was most important and wonderful, Thebes enrolled her name in the list of confederates. The Thracian cities, the Chalcidic League, and several other states, including Corcyra, Jason the despot of Pherae in Thessaly, and Alcetas a prince of Epirus, presently brought up the whole tale of members to about seventy. But though the league, drawn on such liberal lines, evoked some enthusiasm at first, and the adhesion of Thebes gave its inauguration a

FIG. 147.—Coin of Euboea (obverse). Head of nymph.

certain *éclat*, it had no vital elements of growth or permanence, and never attained high political importance. The fact is, that the true interest of Athens, as Callistratus knew, was peace with Sparta, and was consequently repugnant to the avowed object of the confederacy. Hence the confederacy was doomed either to fall asunder, or to become the tool of other designs of Athens as soon as Sparta had been taught a lesson and the more abiding interest of Athens could safely assert itself again over the temporary expedient of an unnatural alliance with Thebes.

It was a moment at which the chief Greek states were setting their houses in order. Thebes was making herself ready and dight for a new career ; Sparta was remodelling her league[1] and Athens her

Eisphora or property tax at Athens.

finances. The property tax, which had been introduced in the fourth year of the Peloponnesian War, was revived, and a new assessment of property was made. [The tax was voted, as special need arose, in the form of a percentage of the total assessment, usually one per cent. But Athenian capital had declined sharply since the fifth century. In 428 alone the tax had realised 200 talents : between 378 and 355 little more than 300 talents was collected.] For the purpose of levying the tax the whole body of burghers was divided into 20 symmories, and the richest citizens in each symmory were responsible to the treasury for the total sum due on the properties of all the citizens who belonged to it. By this means the State relieved itself from the friction which is generally caused by the collection of direct imposts, and the revenue accruing from the tax was realised more promptly and easily than if the government had to deal immediately with the individual burghers. Thus Athens tried the novel experiment of a system of joint responsibility, such as in later days was to be introduced and

(Roman Empire.)

established in an empire of which Athens was only an insignificant town.

Sacred Lochos.

At Thebes the attention of the government was chiefly bestowed on military affairs. A ditch was dug and a rampart raised round part of the Theban territory as a defence against the inevitable Lacedaemonian invasions. But this precaution was of small moment in comparison with the creation of a new troop of 300 hoplites, all chosen young men of the noblest families, who had proved their eminent strength and endurance in a long training in the wrestling school. Each man had his best friend beside him ; so that the Sacred Band, as it was called, consisted of 150 pairs of comrades, prepared to fight and fall together. In battle, it was to be the spearhead of the attack. At the same time, we may be sure, much was done to improve the army in other points. Opportunely for Thebes

Epaminondas.

there had arisen, to guide her to success when her chance came, a man of rare ability, in whom nature seemed to have united the best features of Greek character and discarded the defects. This was Epaminondas, the friend of Pelopidas. He was a modest, unambitious man, who in other circumstances would probably have remained in obscurity, unobtrusively fulfilling the duties of a citizen and soldier. But the revolution stimulated his patriotism and lured him into the field of public affairs, where his eminent capacity, gradually revealing itself, made him, before eight years had passed,

[1] In nine divisions :—1, 2, Arcadia ; 3, Elis ; 4, Achaea ; 5, Corinth and Megara ; 6, Sicyon, Phlius, the Acte of Argolis ; 7, Acarnania ; 8, Phocis, Locris ; 9, Olynthus and other Thracian cities.

the most influential man in his city.   He had devoted as much time
to musical as to gymnastic training ; unlike most of his countrymen,
he could play the lyre as well as the Theban flute ; and he had a
genuine interest in philosophical speculation.   A Tarentine friend,
who had been much in his company, assevered that he never met a
man who knew more and talked less than Epaminondas.   But the
Theban statesman could speak when he chose, or when the need demanded ; and his eloquence was extremely impressive.   Exceptional
in his indifference to the prizes of ambition, he was also exceptional in
his indifference to money, and he died poor.   Not less remarkable
was his lack of that party spirit, which led to so many crimes in
Greece.   He could not share in strong political hatred or lust for
revenge ; and we have already seen that his repugnance to domestic
bloodshed kept him from taking a part in the fortunate conspiracy of
Pelopidas.

SECT. 4.   THE BATTLE OF NAXOS AND THE PEACE OF CALLIAS

The following eight years are marked by a successful defensive *378-1 B.C.*
war of Thebes against Spartan invasions ; by a decrease of Spartan
prestige ; by the extension of the Theban supremacy over the rest
of Boeotia.   At the same time, Athens prosecutes a naval war
against the Lacedaemonian Confederacy, and gains considerable
successes ; but the strain on her resources which this war entails,
and a growing jealousy of Thebes, combine to induce her to come to
terms with Sparta.

Two invasions of Boeotia conducted by Agesilaus himself in *Boeotia*
successive summers achieved nothing ; and the Thebans had the *invaded by*
satisfaction of slaying Phoebidas, who had won his fame by the *Agesilaus,*
capture of their acropolis.   The other king, Cleombrotus, did even *378, 377*
less than Agesilaus, for he found the passes of Cithaeron held by the *Defeat and*
foes, and could not enter Boeotia.   After this, the Thebans had *death of*
time to attack the Boeotian cities and drive out the Spartan garrisons ; *Phoebidas,*
so that by the end of four years the Boeotian confederacy once more *Cleombrotus*
extended over all Boeotia, the local governments being overthrown *marches to*
and the foreign harmosts expelled.   Only in the extreme west, in *Cithaeron,*
Orchomenus and Chaeronea, were the Lacedaemonians able to hold *373 B.C.*
their ground.   In the course of this resuscitation of the Boeotian
league one notable exploit was wrought by Pelopidas and the
Sacred Band.   At Tegyra, on the road from Orchomenus to Locris,
in a narrow pass, the Thebans routed twice as many Lacedaemonian
troops, and slew both the Spartan generals.   As in the case of all
Spartan defeats, the moral effect was of far greater import than the
actual loss in the field.   Perhaps it was about this time that Athens

won back Oropus, which had been lost to her in the year of the Four Hundred.

Battle of Naxos, 376 (September).

In the meantime there had been war too on the seas. When the invasions of Boeotia fell out so badly, Sparta had bethought herself of equipping a naval armament to cut off the corn ships which bore grain to Attica from the Euxine. The ships reached Geraestus, the south point of Euboea ; but a fleet of sixty galleys under the Spartan Pollis hindered them from rounding the Cape of Sunium, and Athens was menaced with famine. Eighty triremes were speedily fitted out and sent forth from the Piraeus, under the command of Chabrias, to recover the mastery of the sea. Chabrias sailed to Naxos, important at this time to Sparta as her chief ally among the Cyclades, and beleaguered the city. Pollis hurried to the rescue, and a battle was fought in the sound between Paros and Naxos. The Athenians gained a complete victory, and only eleven of the Lacedaemonian vessels escaped. Even these would have been disabled, had not Chabrias desisted from the action, for the purpose of saving some of his own men who were overboard or in disabled ships. The lesson which the Athenian people taught its generals after the battle of Arginusae had not been forgotten. Though the battle of Naxos had not the important consequences of the battle of Cnidus, it was more gratifying to Athens. The Cnidian victory had been won indeed under the command of an Athenian, but by Persian men and ships ; the victory gained by Chabrias was entirely Athenian. It led immediately to an enlargement of the Confederacy. The triumphant fleet sailed round the Aegean, enrolled seventeen new cities, and collected a large sum of money. Athens had also to reassert her authority at Delos. For the inhabitants of the island who chafed at the administration of their temple by the Athenian *amphictiones*, as the sacred overseers were entitled, had attempted, doubtless with Lacedaemonian help, to recover control of the sanctuary. An interesting entry in the Delian accounts of these years, preserved on a stone, tells how seven ringleaders of the movement were punished by fines and perpetual banishment " for having led the amphictiones forth from the temple and beaten them."

Insurrectionary movement a' Delos, 376 B.C.

376 B.C. Expedition of Timotheus.

Next year, the fleet was sent to sail round the Peloponnesus under the command of Timotheus, son of Conon. This circumnavigation of the Peloponnesus was an assertion by Athens that her naval power was once more dominant ; it was intended to frighten Sparta, to extend Athenian influence in western Greece, and to act in the Corinthian Gulf, in case the Spartans tried to throw an army into Boeotia by the port of Creusis. The islands of Corcyra and Cephallenia, the king of the Molossi, some of the Acarnanians, were won over to the Athenian alliance by the discreet policy of Timotheus, who also gained a trifling victory over some hostile ships. But there was a darker side to this triumphant expedition. The cost of the war was proving to be greater than Athens could well bear, and Timotheus failed to obtain from home the money requisite to pay his seamen. In this strait, he was obliged to ask each trierarch to advance seven minae for the payment of his crew; and Athens herself sent a request to Thebes for some contribution towards the expense of the naval operations, on the ground that the enterprise of Timotheus had been undertaken partly at Theban instigation. The refusal of this demand, along with a growing jealousy of Theban success, and the somewhat grave financial difficulties of the moment, combined to dispose Athens towards peace with Sparta; and this was in fact her wisest policy. Negotiations were opened and carried *Peace*, 374 to a successful issue; but the peace was no sooner made than it was broken. For Timotheus, who was ordered to return home from Corcyra and reluctantly obeyed, halted at Zacynthus on his way, landed some Zacynthian exiles who were with him, and fortified a post for them on the island.[1] The Zacynthians straightway complained to Sparta; Sparta demanded satisfaction from Athens; and when this was refused, the incident was treated as a breach of contract and the war was resumed.

The first object of Sparta was to regain her power in the west, *Lacedae-* and undo the work of Timotheus. The best of the winnings of that *monian* general had been Corcyra, and Corcyra once more became the scene *attack on* of a "Peloponnesian" war. With the help of their confederates, *Corcyra,* including Corinth, the Lacedaemonians launched an armament of *374-3 B.C.* sixty ships, conveying 1500 mercenary hoplites, to gain possession of the island; and at the same time a message was dispatched to Dionysius of Syracuse requesting his aid, on the ground that Sicily had her interests in Corcyraean politics. The armament was commanded by the Spartan Mnasippus. He drove the Corcyraean fleet into the harbour, which he blocked with his own ships, and he invested the city by land, so that the supplies of the inhabitants were cut off. The island was a rich prize for the soldiers to whose depredations it was now given over. The tillage was goodly, the crofts and farmhouses exceeding fair; and so plentiful was the wine that the troopers would drink none that was not of the finest sort. Urgent messages were sent to Athens by the Corcyraeans, who soon began to feel the pinch of famine. So great was the misery that slaves were cast out of the gates; even some citizens deserted, but were whipped back to the walls by the Lacedaemonian commander. But he deeming that

[1] The settlement of democratic exiles was enrolled in the Athenian Confederacy; and "the people of the Zacynthians at Nêllon" appears as the last of the additions to the list of members on the Confederacy stone.

he had the city in his hands grew careless in his confidence ; and from the watch-towers on their walls the besieged could observe that the watch was sometimes relaxed. An opportune moment was seized for a sally, which resulted in a completer success than they looked for. The professional soldiers, who had not been paid and detested their general, showed no zeal in withstanding the hot onslaught of the desperate men who poured forth from the gates. Mnasippus was slain, and the besiegers fell back to their camp. The beleaguerment was thus broken up, and the Corcyraeans were safe until the coming of the expected help from Athens. But they were delivered from all constraint even before that tardy help came ; for the Lacedaemonians evacuated the island almost immediately after the defeat. Then at last the Athenian fleet sailed into the roads of Corcyra.

It was from no want of goodwill on the part of the Athenian people that the help had not come in time to save Corcyra much of the misery which she had suffered. A tale hangs by the delay of the fleet. On the first appeal, it was resolved to send sixty ships at once, and 600 peltasts were sent in advance and successfully intro-
Difficulties and delays of Timotheus. duced into the city. It was befitting that Timotheus should return to the scene of his former achievements, and the command of the fleet was entrusted to him. He found himself in an awkward position, owing to one of the gravest defects in the machinery of Athenian administration. The people had voted a certain measure, appointing him to carry it out ; but had omitted to vote or consider the necessary ways and means. It consequently devolved upon Timotheus to find the men and the money. For this purpose he cruised with some of his ships in the Northern Aegean, visiting Thessaly, Macedonia, and Thrace, while the main part of the fleet awaited his return at the island of Calauria. But meanwhile the need of Corcyra was sore, and more pressing messengers were arriving in Athens. The long tarrying of the general excited public indignation ; his appointment was annulled ; and Iphicrates, in conjunction with Chabrias and Callistratus, was charged to sail at once to Corcyra.

Iphicrates in Thrace.

(c. 378 B.C.)

Callistratus was the most eloquent orator of the day. Chabrias, a tried soldier who had served under Cypriote and Egyptian kings, we have already met as the victor of Naxos. Iphicrates, who had come to the front by his boldness and success in the Corinthian war, had for the last fifteen years served as a captain of peltasts under the princes of Thrace, and had married a daughter of king Cotys. A comic poet gives a picturesque description of his barbaric wedding. In the market-place a plentiful feast is set out for a throng of wild-haired Thracians. There are immense brazen cauldrons of broth, and the king, girding himself up, serves it with his own hands in a golden basin. Then the wine and water are tempered in the mixing-bowls, and the king goes around tasting each bowl, until he is the first drunk. But an adventurous life among the " butter-eating " barbarians does not seem to have wholly satisfied Iphicrates. He served the King of Persia in Egypt and then returned to Athens, and this expedition to Corcyra seems to have been his first service after his return. It was well and capably performed. The people in their excitement gave him a freer hand than they had given to Timotheus. He was able to put hard pressure on the trierarchs ; he was allowed to impress seamen, and to make use of the galleys which guarded the Attic coast, and even the two sacred vessels, the *Salaminia* and *Paralus*. By these unusual efforts a fleet of seventy triremes was put together, but before it was quite ready to sail Timotheus returned. His cruise had been successful in raising money and men, and adding new members to the Confederacy ; but it was thought that neither necessity nor success could excuse the singular inopportune-ness of the delay. Ill-luck seemed to wait upon Timotheus. The funds which he brought back proved insufficient to meet the obliga-tions which they ought to have defrayed, and a fraud was suspected. Iphicrates and Callistratus, his political rivals, lodged an indictment against him, but as they had to sail immediately to the west, the trial was postponed till the autumn.

(375-4 B.C.)

Return of Timotheus.

On his way out Iphicrates learned the news of the deliverance of Corcyra, so that he was able to send back those ships whose true duty was the defence of Attica. But there was still work to be done. The appeal which the Lacedaemonians sent to the tyrant Dionysius had not been in vain, and ten Syracusan triremes were even then approaching Corcyra. They stopped at a point in the north of the island, that the crews might rest after the long voyage ; and there Iphicrates whose scouts had watched for their approach captured them, all but one vessel. This prize raised the welcome sum of sixty talents, but it was not long before Iphicrates, even as Timotheus, found himself embarrassed for want of money. Callistratus went back to Athens, promising to persuade the people either to keep the fleet regularly paid or to make peace. Meanwhile the crews of Iphicrates obtained subsistence by labour on the Corcyraean farms.

372 B.C.
Capture of the reinforce-ments from Syracuse.

If Corcyra had fallen, there can be little question that Timotheus would have been sacrificed to the displeasure of the Athenian people. But the good tidings from the west restored the public good-humour, and this was fortunate for the discredited general. His trial came on towards the end of the year. His military treasurer was tried at the same time, found guilty of malversation, and condemned to death. But Timotheus himself was acquitted. He had indeed unusually powerful support. Two foreign monarchs had condescended to

Trial of Timotheus,
373 (Nov.).

come to Athens to bear testimony in his favour, the Epirot king Alcetas, and Jason the despot of Thessalian Pherae. It was through Timotheus that these potentates had joined the Athenian league; and it was through them that he had been able to transport across Thessaly and Epirus the 600 peltasts who had been sent in advance to Corcyra. The interest of Jason—of whom more will have to be said presently—was particularly effective. Timotheus entertained these distinguished guests in his house in Piraeus, but he was obliged to borrow bedding, two silver bowls, and other things from his rich neighbour, the banker Pasion, in order to lodge them suitably. Though acquitted, Timotheus was discredited in public opinion, and he soon left Athens to take service in Egypt under the Great King.

Sparta had lost heart at the decisive check which she had received in Corcyra, and the discouragement was increased by a series of terrible earthquakes, in which Poseidon seemed to declare his wrath. She was therefore disposed to peace, and she thought to bring peace about, as before, through the mediation of Persia. Antalcidas was once more sent up to the Persian court. But this intervention from without was not really needed. Athens, uneasy under the burdens of the war and feeling rather jealousy of Thebes than bitterness against Sparta, was also well inclined to peace, and the influential orator Callistratus made it the object of his policy. The recent aggressions of Thebes against the Phocians, who were old allies of Athens, tended to estrange the two cities; and to this was added the treatment of that unfortunate little frontier town, Plataea, *Plataea seized by Thebes.* by her Theban enemies. Restored Plataea had perforce been enrolled in the Boeotian confederacy, but she was secretly scheming annexation to Attica. Suspecting these plots, Thebes determined to forestall them, and a small Theban force, surprising the town one day when the men were in the fields, took possession of it and drove all the Plataeans forth from Plataean soil. Many of the people, thus bereft of land and city, found a refuge at Athens; where the publicist Isocrates took up their cause and wrote his *Plataeic Discourse,* a denunciation of Thebes. This incident definitely, though not formally, loosened the bonds between the two northern powers.

371 B.C. Peace of Callias The overtures came from Athens and her Confederacy. When the Lacedaemonian allies met at Sparta in spring, three Athenian envoys appeared at the congress. Of these the chief spokesman was Callistratus, and one of his associates was Callias, Torchbearer of the Eleusinian Mysteries, who had also worked to bring about the abortive peace three years before. Thebes likewise sent ambassadors, one of whom was Epaminondas. The basis of the peace which was now concluded was the principle which had been affirmed by the King's Peace, the principle of the autonomy of every Hellenic city. The

Athenian and Lacedaemonian Confederacies were thus both rendered invalid.   No compulsion could be exercised on any city to fulfil engagements as member of a league.   Cities might co-operate with each other freely so far as they chose, but no obligation could be contracted or enforced.   Yet while Athens and Sparta resigned empire, they mutually agreed to recognise each other's predominance, that of Athens by sea, that of Sparta on land—a predominance which must never be asserted by aggression and must always be consistent with the universal autonomy.

The question immediately arose whether the Boeotian League *The* was condemned by this doctrine of universal autonomy.   Sparta *Boeotian* and Athens, of course, intended to condemn it.   But it might be *question* pleaded that the Confederacy of Boeotian cities under the presidency of Thebes was not on the same footing as the Confederacies which had been formed, for temporary political purposes, without any historical or geographical basis of union, under the presidencies of Athens and Sparta.   It might be contended that Boeotia was a geographical unity, like Attica and Laconia, and had a title to political unity too, especially as the League was an ancient institution. The question came to the issue when it was the turn of Thebes to take the oath.   Her representative Epaminondas claimed to take it on behalf of the Boeotian cities ; and Thebes, represented by him, was not so easily cowed as when she made the same claim at the conclusion of the King's Peace.   He seems to have developed the view that Boeotia was to be compared to Laconia, not to the Lacedaemonian Confederacy ; and when Agesilaus asked him, curtly and *Thebes* angrily : "Will you leave each of the Boeotian towns independent ?" *excluded.* he retorted : "Will *you* leave each of the Laconian towns independent?" The name of Thebes was thereupon struck out of the treaty.

There was an argument as well as a sting in this retort of Epaminondas.   The argument was : Sparta has no more right to interfere in the internal affairs of Boeotia than we have to interfere in the domestic administration of Laconia ; Laconia, Boeotia, Attica, each represents a distinct kind of constitution, and each constitution is justified ; the union of Boeotia in a federation is as natural as the union of Attica in a single city, as legitimate as the union of Laconia in its subjection to the Spartan oligarchy.   The union of Boeotia, like the union of Laconia, could not have been realised and could not be maintained without the perpetration of outrages upon the freewill of some communities.   Yet it is hardly legitimate for one state to say to another : "We have committed certain acts of violence, but you must not interfere ; for at a remote period of history which none of us remember, your ancestors used even more high-handed methods for similar purposes, and you now maintain what they established." But the tyrannical method by which Laconia was governed was certainly a weak point in the Spartan armour ; and the reply of Epaminondas may have well set Greece thinking over a question of political science. Setting aside the arguments of diplomacy, the point of the situation was this : Thebes could never become a strong power, the rival of Sparta or of Athens, except at the head of an united Boeotia, and it was the interest of Athens and Sparta to hinder her from becoming such a power.

Positions of Athens and Sparta. So far as the two chief contracting parties were concerned, this bargain—which is often called the " Peace of Callias "—put an end to a war which was contrary to the best interests of both. They were both partly to blame, but Sparta was far more to blame than her old rival. Her witless policy in overlooking the raid of Sphodrias had caused the war ; for it left to Athens no alternative but hostility. At the end of four years, they seemed to have come to their senses ; they made peace, but they were stupid enough to allow the incident of Zacynthus to annul the bargain. Three more years of fighting were required to restore their wits. But, although Athens was financially exhausted by her military efforts, the war had brought its compensations to her. The victory of Naxos, the circumnavigation of the Peloponnesus and revival of her influence in Western Greece, were achievements which indisputably proved that Athens was once more a first-rate Hellenic power, the peer of Sparta ; and this fact was fully acknowledged in the Peace of Callias. But the true policy of Athens—from which the raid of Sphodrias had forced her—was that of a watchful spectator ; and this policy she now resumes, though only for a brief space, leaving Sparta and Thebes in the arena. As for Sparta, she had lost as much as Athens had gained ; the defeat of Naxos, the defeat of Tegyra, the failure at Corcyra, had dimmed her prestige. After the King's Peace, she had begun her second attempt to dominate Greece ; her failure is confessed by the Peace of Callias. If a third attempt was to be successful, it was obvious that it must begin by the subjugation of Thebes.

SECT. 5. ATHENS UNDER THE RESTORED DEMOCRACY

When Pericles declared that Athens was the school of Greece, this was rather his ideal of what she should be than a statement of a reality. It would have surprised him to learn that, when imperial Athens fell from her throne, his ideal would be fulfilled. This was what actually happened. It was not until Athens lost her empire that she began to exert a great decisive influence on Greek thought and civilisation. This influence was partly exerted by the establishment of schools in the strict sense—the literary school of Isocrates *Influence of* and the philosophical school of Plato—which attracted to Athens *Athens on* men from all quarters of the Hellenic world.   But the increase in the *Greece.* intellectual influence of Athens was largely owing to the fact that she was becoming herself more receptive of influence from without.   She was becoming Hellenic as well as Athenian ; she was beginning to become even something more than Hellenic.   This tendency towards cosmopolitanism had been promoted by philosophical speculation, which rises above national distinctions ; and it is manifested variously in the pan-Hellenism of Isocrates, in the attitude of such different men as Plato and Xenophon towards Athens, in the increasing number of foreign religious worships established at Athens or Piraeus, in a general decline of local patriotism, and in many other ways.   There was perhaps no institution which had a wider influence in educating Greek thought in the fourth century than the theatre ; its importance in city life was recognised by practical statesmen.   It was therefore a matter of the utmost moment that the old Athenian comedy, turning mainly on local politics, ceased to be written, and a new school of comic poets arose who dealt with subjects of general human interest. Here Athens had a most effectual instrument for spreading ideas. And the tragedies of the fourth century, though as literature they were of less note and consequence than the comedies, were not less significant of the spirit of the time.   They were all dominated by the influence of Euripides, the great teacher of rationalism, the daring critic of all established institutions and beliefs.   And the comic poets were also under his spell.

It can easily be seen that the cultivation of these wider sym- *Growth of* pathies was connected with the growth of what is commonly called *indi-* " individualism."   The citizen is no longer content to express his *vidualism.* religious feelings simply as one member of the state, and, since his own life has thus become for him something independent of the city, his attitude to the city is transformed.   His duty to his country may conflict with his duty to himself as a man ; and thus patriotism ceases to be unconditionally the highest virtue.   Again, men begin to put to themselves, more or less explicitly, the question whether the state is not made for the individual and not the individual for the state.   It followed that greater demands were made upon the state by the citizen for his own private welfare ; and that the citizen, feeling himself tied by no indissoluble bond to his country, was readier than formerly to seek his fortune elsewhere.   Thus we find Athenian officers acting independently of their country, in the pay of foreign powers.

A vivid exaggerated description of this spirit has been drawn by Plato in one of his famous contributions to political science, the *Republic.*   " The horses and asses," he says, " have a way of marching along with all the rights and dignities of freemen; and they will run at anybody whom they meet in the street if he does not leave the road clear for them: and all things are just ready to burst with liberty." [1] When he describes the excessive freedom of democracy, he is dealing with the growth of individualism, as a result of freedom in its constitutional sense; but his argument that individualism is the fatal fruit of a democratic constitution rests largely on the double sense of the word "freedom." The notable thing is that no man did more to promote the tendencies which are here deplored by Plato than Plato himself and his fellow philosophers. If any single man could be held responsible for the inevitable growth of individualism, it would be perhaps Euripides; [2] but assuredly, next to Euripides, it would be Plato's revered master, Socrates, the son of Sophroniscus.

Socrates, the sculptor, son of Sophroniscus (born c. 469 B.C.).

When the history of Greece was being directed by Pericles and Cleon, Nicias and Lysander, men little dreamed either at Athens or elsewhere that the interests of the world were far more deeply concerned in the doings of one eccentric Athenian who held aloof from public affairs. The ideas which we owe to Socrates are now so organically a part of the mind of civilised men that it is hard to appreciate the intellectual power which was required to originate them.

His spirit.

Socrates was the first champion of the supremacy of the intellect as a court from which there is no appeal; he was the first to insist that a man must order his life by the guidance of his own intellect. Socrates was thus a rebel against authority as such; and he shrank from no consequences. He did not hesitate to show his companions that an old man has no title to respect because he is old, unless he is also wise; or that an ignorant parent has no claim to obedience on the mere account of the parental relation. Knowledge and veracity, the absolute sovereignty of the understanding, regardless of consequences, regardless of all prejudices connected with family or city—this was the ideal of Socrates, consistently and uncompromisingly followed.

His method.

But men using their intellects often come to different conclusions. The command issued by an authority which Socrates may reject has been, directly or ultimately, the result of some mental process. It is manifest that we require a standard of truth and an explanation of the causes of error. The solution of Socrates is, briefly, this. When we make a judgment, we compare two ideas; and in order to do so correctly it is obvious that these ideas must be clear and distinct;

---

[1] Transl. Jowett.

[2] Euripides first; for, though he did not exert nearly as great influence on the world as Socrates, he reached a larger public in his own and the two next generations.

FIG. 148.—Socrates.

Defini-
tions.

error arises from comparing ideas that are undefined and vague. Definition was thus the essential point—and it was an essential novelty—in the Socratic method for arriving at truth. Its necessity is a commonplace now ; and we have rather to guard against its dangers.

Founder
of utili-
tarianism.

The application of this method to ethics was the chief occupation of Socrates, for the interests of human life and its perplexities entirely absorbed him. In the history of ethics his position is supreme ; he was the founder of utilitarianism. He arrived at the doctrine by analysing the notion of "good"; the result of his analysis was that "the good is the useful." Closely connected was the principle that virtue is happiness, and this was the basis of the famous Socratic paradox that no man willingly does wrong, but only through ignorance, for there is no man who would not will his own happiness. It is easy to point out the errors of this startling statement ; it is perhaps easier to forget how much wrong-doing is due to the confused thinking of clouded brains and the ignorance of untrained minds.

Attitude to
theology.

The man who had no respect for authority was not likely to except the gods from the range of his criticism ; and the popular religion could not sustain examination. Socrates was as little orthodox as Anaxagoras and other "impious" philosophers ; but he made no new departure in the field of theology. He doubtless believed in the existence of a God ; but as to the nature of the divine principle he was probably what we call an "agnostic," as he certainly was in regard to the immortality of the soul.

His
scepticism
and irony.

Socrates then was the originator of a new logical method, the founder of utilitarianism, and, above all, the unsparing critic of all things in heaven and earth—or rather on earth only, for he disdained things in heaven as uninteresting and irrelevant,—a fearless critic, undeterred by any feeling of piety or prejudice. He never wrote anything, he only conversed. But he conversed with the ablest young men of the day who were destined afterwards to become immortal themselves as thinkers ; he communicated to them—to Plato, to Aristippus, to Euclides—his own spirit of scepticism and criticism ; he imbued them with intellectual courage and intellectual freedom. He never preached, he only discussed ; that was the Socratic method—dialectic or the conversational method. He did not teach, for he professed to have no knowledge ; he would only confess that he was exceptional in knowing that he knew nothing : this was the Socratic irony. He went about showing that most popular notions, as soon as they are tested, prove to be inconsistent and untenable ; he wished to convince every man he met that his convictions would not stand examination. We can easily conceive how stimulating this was to the young men, and how extremely irritating to the old. Haunting the market-places and the gymnasia

Socrates was always ready to entrap men of all ages and ranks into argument, and many a grudge was owed him by reverend and conceited seniors, whose foggy minds he exposed to ridicule by means of his prudent interrogations.   Though no man ever taught more effectually than Socrates, he was not a teacher, he had no course of lectures to give, and therefore he took no fee.   Herein lay his distinction from the sophists, to whom by his speculation, his scepticism, his mastery of argument, his influence over young men, he naturally belongs, and with whom he was generally classed.   He soon became a notorious figure in the streets of Athens ; nature had marked him out among other men by his grotesque satyr-like face.

Though he was the child of democracy, born to a heritage of *Criticism* freedom in a city where the right of free discussion was unrestrained, *of demo-* the sacred name of democracy was not more sheltered than anything *cracy.* else from the criticism of Socrates.   He railed, for instance, at the system of choosing magistrates by lot, one of the protections of democracy at Athens.   He was unpopular with the mass, for he was an enemy of shams and ignorance and superstition.   Honest democrats of the type of Thrasybulus and Anytus, who did their duty but had no desire to probe its foundations, regarded him as a dangerous freethinker who spent his life in diffusing ideas subversive of the social order.   They might point to the ablest of the young *His* men who had kept company with him, and say : " Behold the fruits *teaching* of his conversation !   Look at Alcibiades, his favourite companion, *suspected* who has done more than any other man to ruin his country.   Look *and un-* at Critias, who, next to Alcibiades, has wrought the deepest harm to *popular.* Athens ; who, brought up in the Socratic circle, first wrote a book against democracy, then visited Thessaly and stirred up the serfs against their masters, and finally, returning here, inaugurated the reign of terror.   Look, on the other hand, at Plato, an able young man, whom the taste for idle speculation, infused by Socrates, has seduced from the service of his country.   Or look at Xenophon, who, instead of serving Athens, has gone to serve her enemies.   Truly Socrates and his propaganda have done little good to the Athenian state."   However unjust any particular instance might seem, it is easy to understand how considerations of this kind would lead many practical unspeculative men to look upon Socrates and his ways with little favour.   And from their point of view, they were perfectly right. His spirit, and the ideas that he made current, were an insidious menace to the cohesion of the social fabric, in which there was not a stone or a joint that he did not question.   In other words, he was the active apostle of individualism, which led in its further development to the subversion of that local patriotism which had inspired the cities of Greece in her days of greatness.

He receives   And this thinker, whose talk was shaking the Greek world in its
the foundations, though none guessed it, was singled out by the Delphic
approval priesthood for a distinguished mark of approbation. In the truest
of Delphi. oracle that was ever uttered from the Pythian tripod, it was declared
that no one in the world was wiser than Socrates. We know not at
what period of the philosopher's career this answer was given, but, if
it was seriously meant, it showed a strange insight which we should
hardly have looked for at the shrine of Delphi. The motive of the
oracle concerning the wisdom of Socrates is an unsolved problem.
If it were an attempt to enlist his support, in days when religion was
threatened by such men as Anaxagoras, it shows an unexpected perception of his importance, united with a by no means surprising
blindness to the significance of his work.

Trial of   Socrates died five years after the fall of the Athenian empire, and
Socrates, the manner of his death set a seal upon his life. It was thought that
399 B.C. the philosopher, who had been the friend of Critias, was a danger to
the democracy, and should be removed ; but the political motive was
kept in the background. Anytus, the honest democratic politician
who had been prominent in the restoration of the democracy, came
forward, with some others, as a champion of the state religion, and
accused Socrates of impiety. The accusation ran : " Socrates is
guilty of crime, because he does not believe in the gods recognised
by the city, but introduces strange supernatural beings ; he is also
guilty, because he corrupts the youth." The penalty proposed was
death ; but the accusers had no desire to inflict it ; they expected that,
when the charge was lodged in the archon's office, Socrates would
leave Attica, and no one would have hindered him from doing so.
But Socrates was full of days—he had reached the age of seventy—
and life spent otherwise than in conversing in the streets of Athens
would have been worthless to him. He surprised the city by remaining to answer the charge. The trial was heard in a court of 501
judges, the king-archon presiding, and the old philosopher was found
guilty by a majority of sixty. It was a small majority, considering
that the general truth of the accusation was undeniable. According
to the practice of Athenian law, it was open to a defendant when
he was condemned to propose a lighter punishment than that fixed
by the accuser, and the judges were required to choose one of the
two sentences. Socrates might have saved his life if he had proposed
an adequate penalty, but he offered only a small fine, and was conse-
His death. quently condemned, by a much larger majority, to death. He drank
the cup of doom a month later, discoursing with his disciples as eagerly
as ever till his last hour. " I am persuaded that it was better for me to
die now, and to be released from trouble."

    The actual reply of Socrates at his trial has not been preserved, but we know its tone and spirit and much of its tenor. For it supplied *Plato's* his companion Plato, who was present, with the material of a work Apology which stands absolutely alone in literature. In the *Apology of Socrates*, Plato has succeeded in catching the personality of the master and conveying its stimulus to his readers. There can be no question that this work reproduces the general outline of the actual defence, which is here wrought into an artistic form. And we see how utterly impossible it was for Socrates to answer the accusation. He enters into an explanation of his life and motives, and has no difficulty in showing that many things popularly alleged against him are false. But with the actual charge of holding and diffusing *Socrates* heterodox views he deals briefly and unsatisfactorily. He was not *justly con-* condemned unjustly—according to the law. And that is the inten- *demned.* sity of the tragedy. There have been no better men than Socrates ; and yet his accusers were perfectly right. It is not clear why their manifesto for orthodoxy was made at that particular time ; but it is probable that twenty years later such an action would have been a failure. Perhaps the facts of the trial justify us in the rough conclusion that two out of every five Athenian citizens then were religiously indifferent. In any case the event had a wider than a merely religious significance. The execution of Socrates was the protest of the spirit of the old order against the growth of individualism.

Seldom in the course of history have violent blows of this kind failed to recoil upon the striker and serve the cause they were meant to harm. Socrates was remembered at Athens with pride and regret. His spirit began to exercise an influence which the tragedy of his death enhanced. His companions never forgave the democracy for putting their master to death ; he lived and grew in the study of their imaginations ; and they spent their lives in carrying on his work.

They carried forward his work, but they knew not what they were doing. They had no suspicion that in pursuing those speculations to which they were stimulated by the Socratic method they were sapping the roots of Greek city life as it was known to the men who fought at Marathon. Plato was a true child of Socrates, and yet he was vehement in condemning that individualism which it had been the lifework of Socrates to foster. Few sights are stranger than Plato and Xenophon turning their eyes away from their own free country to regard with admiration the constitution of Sparta, where their beloved master would not have been suffered so much as to open his mouth. It was a distinct triumph for the Lacedaemonians when their constitution, which the Athenians of the age of Pericles regarded as old-fashioned machinery, was selected by the greatest thinker of Athens as the nearest existing approach to the ideal. Indeed the Spartan organisation, at the very time when Sparta was making herself detested throughout Greece, seems to have attracted general admiration from political thinkers. It attracted them because the old order survived there,—the citizen absolutely submissive to the authority of the state, and not looking beyond it. Elsewhere they were troubled by the problem of reconciling the authority of the state with the liberty of the individual citizen ; at Sparta there was no such trouble, for the state was absolute. Accordingly they saw in Sparta the image of what a state should be ; just because it was relatively free from that individualism which they were themselves actively promoting by their speculations in political philosophy. How freely such speculations ranged at this time is illustrated by the fact that the fundamental institution of ancient society, slavery, was called in question. It had indeed been called in question by Euripides, and the heterodox "modern" views of Euripides were coming into fashion. One thinker expounded the doctrine that slavery was unnatural. Speculation even went so far as to stir the question of the political subjection of women. The *Parliament of Women*, a comedy of Aristophanes, ridicules women's rights ; and in Plato's ideal *Republic* women are on a political equality with men. Socialistic theories were also rife, and were a mark for the mockery of Aristophanes in the same play. Plato seized upon the notion of communism and made it one of the principles of his ideal state. But his object was not that of the ordinary " collectivist," to promote the material well-being of all ; but rather to make his citizens better, by defending them against poverty and ambition. Before he died, Plato had come to the conviction that communism was impracticable, and in the state which he adumbrated in his old age he recognised private property—though he vested the ownership not in the individual but in the family.

In this period—during the fifty years after the battle of Aegospotami—the art of writing prose was brought to perfection at Athens ; and this is closely connected with the characteristic tendency which has engaged our attention. While Socrates and others had been bringing about a revolution in thought, the Sicilian Gorgias and other professors of rhetoric or style had been preparing an efficient vehicle for diffusing ideas. Prose is the natural instrument of criticism and argument ; it is a necessary weapon for intellectual persuasion ; and therefore the fourth century is an age of prose. The circumstance that the great Athenian poets of the fifth century had no successors in the fourth does not prove any decline in brains or in imagination. If Plato had been born half a century earlier he would have been a rival of Aeschylus and Sophocles. If Aeschylus and Sophocles had been born two or three generations later they would have expressed their genius in prose. Euripides, who has come under the influence of the critical spirit, seems sometimes like a man belated ; he uses the old vehicle to convey thoughts for which it was hardly suited. It must always be remembered that the great dramatic poems of the fifth century bore an inalienable religious character; and, as soon as the day came when the men of the highest literary faculty were no longer in touch with the received religion, drama of the old kind ceased to be written. That is why the fourth century is an age of prose; tragic poetry owes its death to Euripides and the Socratic spirit. The eager individualism of the age found its natural expression in prose, whose rhythmical periods demanded almost as much care and art as poetry; and the plastic nature of the Greek language rendered it a most facile instrument for the purposes of free thought and criticism.

Thus Athens became really a school for Greece, as soon as that individualism prevailed which Pericles had unwittingly foreshadowed in the very same breath: "I say that Athens is the school of Hellas, and that the individual Athenian in his own person seems to have the power of adapting himself to the most varied forms of action with the utmost versatility and grace."[1]

It must never be forgotten that it is to the democratic Athenian law-courts that the perfecting of Attic prose was mainly due. This institution had, as we saw, called into being a class of professional speech-writers. But there were many who were not content *Higher* with learning off, and reciting in court, speeches which a speech-writer *education* like Lysias wrote for them, but wished to learn themselves the art *at Athens:* of speaking. For those who aspired to make their mark in debates *Plato and* in the Assembly, this was a necessity. The most illustrious instructor *Isocrates.* in oratory at this period was Isocrates. But the school of Isocrates had a far wider scope and higher aim than to teach the construction of sentences or the arrangement of topics in a speech. It was a general school of culture, a discipline intended to fit men for public life. Questions of political science were studied, and Isocrates likes to describe his course of studies as "philosophy." But it was to Plato's school in the Academy that the youths of the day went to study "philosophy" in the stricter sense. The discipline of these two rival schools—for there was rivalry between them, though their aims were different—was what corresponded at Athens to our university education. And the pupils of Isocrates, as well as those of Plato, had to work hard. For thoroughness of method was one of the distinctive characteristics of Isocrates. His school attained a pan-Hellenic reputation; pupils came to him from all quarters of the world. "Our city," he says, "is regarded as the established teacher of all who speak or teach others to speak. And naturally so, since

---

[1] Jowett's translation.

men see that our city offers the greatest prizes to those who possess this faculty—provides the most numerous and various schools for those

FIG. 149.—Portrait head of Isocrates

who having resolved to enter the real contests desire a preparatory discipline — and further affords to all men that experience which is the main secret of success in speaking."[1] The tone of the teaching of Isocrates harmonised with the national position which he held. He took a large view of all things; there was nothing narrow or local in his opinions. And not less important than the width of his horizon was the high moral tone in which his thoughts were consistently pitched. Isocrates discharged not only the duties which are in modern times discharged by university teachers, but also the functions of a journalist of the best kind. Naturally nervous and endowed with a poor voice, he did not speak in the Assembly,

Isocrates as a pamphleteer.

but when any great question moved him he would issue a pamphlet, in the form of a speech, for the purpose of influencing public opinion. We may suspect that the Athenians appreciated these publications more for their inimitable excellence of style than for their political wisdom.

Cosmopolitanism in the Panegyric Speech of Isocrates, 381 B.C.

A highly remarkable passage of Isocrates expresses and applauds the wide-minded cosmopolitanism which was beginning to prevail in Greece. He says that "Athens has so distanced the rest of the world in power of thought and speech that her disciples have become the teachers of all other men. She has brought it to pass that the name of Greek should be thought no longer a matter of race but a matter of intelligence; and should be given to the participators in our culture rather than to the sharers of our common origin."[2]

Idealisation of 6th century, Athens.

Thirty or forty years earlier, no one perhaps, except Euripides, would have been bold enough to speak like that. But Isocrates did not see

---

[1] Translated by Jebb.   [2] *Ibid.*

that this enlightenment which he admires was closely connected with the decay of public spirit which he elsewhere deplores. It is curious to find the man who approves of citizenship of the world looking back with regret to the days of Solon and proposing to revive the old powers of censorship which the court of the Areopagus possessed over the lives of Athenian citizens. *(Areopagitikos*, 355-4 *B.C.*)

The form and features of an age are wont to be mirrored in its art; and one effective means of winning a concrete notion of the spirit of the fourth century is to study the works of Praxiteles and compare them with the sculptures which issued from the workshop of Phidias. Just as the citizen was beginning to assert his own individuality as more than a mere item in the state, so the plastic artist was emancipating his art from its intimate connexion with the temples of the gods, and its subordination to architecture. For in the fifth century, apart from a few colossal statues like those which Phidias wrought for Athens and Olympia, the finest works of the sculptor's chisel were to decorate frieze or pediment. In the fourth century the architect indeed still required the sculptor's service ; Scopas, for instance, was called upon in his youth to decorate the temple of Athena Alea at Tegea, in his later years to make a frieze for the tomb of a Carian prince ; but, in general, the sculptor developed his art more independently of architecture, and all the great works of Praxiteles were complete in themselves and independent. And, as sculpture was emancipating itself from the old subordination to architecture, so it also emancipated itself from the religious ideal. In the age of Phidias, the artist who fashioned a god sought to express in human shape the majesty and immutability of a divine being ; and this ideal had been perfectly achieved. In the fourth century the deities lose their majesty and changelessness; they are conceived as physically perfect men and women, with human feelings though without human sorrows ; they are invested with human personalities. The contrast may be seen by looking at the group of gods in the frieze of the Parthenon, and then at some of the works of Praxiteles : the Hermes, which was set up in the temple of Hera at Olympia, and is preserved there ; the Aphrodite of Cnidus— a woman shrinking from revealing her beauty as she enters the bath ; or the Satyr, with the shape of a man and the mind of a beast. Thus sculpture is marked by "individualism" in a double sense. Each artist is freer to work out an individual path of his own; and the tendency of all artists is to pourtray the individual man or woman rather than the type, and even the individual phase of emotion rather than the character. *Individualistic character of the art of 4th century.*

The general spirit of the Athenians in their political life corresponds to this change. Men came more and more to regard the state as a means for administering to the needs of the individual. We might almost say that they conceived it as a co-operative society for making profits to be divided among the members ; this at least was the tendency of public opinion. They were consequently more disinclined to enter upon foreign undertakings which were not either necessary for the protection and promotion of their commerce or likely to fill their purses. The fourth century was therefore for Athens an age of less ambition and glory, but of greater happiness and freedom, than the fifth.

Athenian commerce. The decisive circumstance for Athens was that, while she lost her empire, she did not lose her commerce. This was a cruel blow to Corinth, since it was to destroy Athenian trade that Corinth had brought about the war. The fact shows on how firm foundations Athenian commerce rested. The only rival Athens had to fear was Rhodes, which was becoming a centre of traffic in the south-eastern Mediterranean, but was not destined to interfere seriously with Athenian trade for a long time yet. The population of Attica had declined ; plague and war reduced the number of adult male citizens from at least 40,000 to some 22,000. But that was not unfortunate, for there were no longer outsettlements to receive the surplus of the population ; and even with the diminished numbers there was a surplus which sought employment in foreign mercenary service. The mercantile development of Athens is shown by the increase of the Piraeus at the expense of the city, in which many plots of ground now

Banks. became deserted, and by the growth of private banks. It had long been a practice to deposit money in temples, and the priesthoods used to lend money on interest. This suggested to money-changers the idea of doing likewise ; and Pasion founded a famous house at Athens, which operated with a capital of fifty talents, and had credit at all Greek centres of commerce. Thus business could be transacted by exchanging letters of credit instead of paying in coin ; and the introduction of this system, even on such a small scale, shows the growth of mercantile activity. Money was now much more plentiful, and prices far higher, than before. This was due to the large amount of the precious metals, chiefly gold, which had been brought into circulation in the Greek world in the last quarter of the fifth century. The continuous war led to the coining of the treasures which had been accumulating for many years in temples ; and the banking system circulated the money which would otherwise have been

Rate of interest. hoarded in private houses. But, although the precious metals became plentiful, the rate of interest did not fall ; men could still get 12 per cent for a loan of their money. This fact is highly significant ; it shows clearly that industries were more thriving and trade more active, and consequently capital in greater demand. The high rate of interest must always be remembered when we read of a Greek described as wealthy with a capital which would nowadays seem small.

Communistic ideas were a consequence, perhaps inevitable, of *Socialism.* the growth of individualism and the growth of capital. The poorer burghers became more and more acutely alive to the inconsistency between the political equality of all citizens and the social and economical advantages enjoyed by the rich. Political equality seemed to point to social equality as its logical sequel ; in fact, full and equal political equality could not be secured without social equality also, since the advantages of wealth necessarily involve superiorities in political influence. Thus, just as in modern Europe, so in ancient Greece, capital and democracy produced socialists, who pleaded for a levelling of classes by means of a distribution of property by the state. Aristophanes mocked these speculations in his *Parliament of* Ecclesi-*Women* and his *Wealth*. The idea of communism which Plato azusae, develops on lines of his own in the *Republic* was not an original $389 \ B.C.,$ notion of the philosopher's brain, but was suggested by the current $388 \ B.C.$ communistic theories of the day. It is well worthy of consideration that the Athenians did not take the step from political to social democracy ; and this discretion may have been partly due to the policy of those statesmen who, doubtless conscious of the danger, regarded the theoric fund as an indispensable institution.

The changed attitude of the individual to the state is shown by *Ecclesiastic* the introduction of a fixed remuneration of half a drachma to Athenian *pay* citizens for attending the meetings of the Assembly ; and the rise in (*introduced* prices is illustrated by the subsequent increase of this remuneration. *before* 389 For the regular sessions, in which the proceedings were unattractive, $B.C.$). the pay was raised to a drachma and a half ; for the other meetings, which were more exciting, it was fixed at a drachma. The remuneration for serving in the law-courts was not increased ; it was found that half a drachma was sufficient to draw applicants for the judge's ticket. Payment for the discharge of political duties was part of the necessary machinery of the democracy, but the distribution of "spectacle-money" to the poor citizens was a luxury which involved an entirely different principle. It is uncertain when the practice of giving the price of his theatre ticket to the poor Athenian was first introduced ; it has been attributed to Pericles, but it is possible that it was not introduced till Athens began to recover after the fall of her empire. In any case, the principle became established in the fourth century of distributing "theoric" moneys, which were supposed to be spent on religious festivals ; the citizens came to look forward to frequent and large distributions ; the surplus revenue of the state, instead of being saved for emergencies, was placed in the theoric fund; and this theoric fund became so important that it ultimately required a special minister of finance to manage it. Those statesmen under whose guidance the theoric doles were most liberal had naturally the greatest influence with the mass of the citizens; and consequently finance acquired a new importance, and financial ability was developed in a very high degree. The state thus assumed the character of a commercial society; dividends were a political necessity, and in order to meet it heavier taxation was demanded. We have seen how, when war broke out with Sparta, in the year in which the Second Athenian Confederacy was formed, a property-tax was imposed, and the properties of the citizens were assessed anew for this purpose.

ὁ ἐπὶ τὸ θεωρικόν.

Thus the state provided for the comfort of its poorer burghers at the expense of their wealthier fellows. It is, as it were, publicly recognised as a principle of political science that the end of the state is the comfort and pleasure of its individual members; and everything has to be made subordinate to this principle which is outwardly embodied in the theoric fund. This principle affected the foreign policy of Athens, as we have already observed. When she took the step of sending outsettlers to Samos and elsewhere, in defiance of the public opinion of Greece, her chief motive was doubtless material profit.

The constitution in the 4th century.

Constitutionally, the restored Athenian democracy was a remarkable success. The difficulties which the democratic statesmen encountered after the overthrow of the Thirty had been treated with a wisdom and moderation which are in striking contrast with the violence and vengefulness shown in other Greek states at similar crises. Most democratic men of means had been robbed of property under the tyranny of the oligarchs, and the property had been sold. Were the purchasers to be compelled to restore it without compensation? Were all the acts of the Thirty to be declared illegal? Such a measure would have created a bitter and discontented party in the state. Some of the chief democratic leaders voluntarily resigned all claim to compensation for the property they had lost, and this example promoted a general inclination on both sides to concession and compromise. The wisdom and tact displayed in this matter were not the least of the services which Thrasybulus and his fellows rendered to their country. No oligarchical conspiracy endangered the domestic peace of Athens again; no citizen, if it were not a philosophical speculator, called the democracy in question. Even Isocrates, who had little sympathy with the political tendencies of his day, can hold no public brief for oligarchy. In extolling an earlier Athens he has laboriously to emphasise the true democratic nature of the constitution before the reforms of Ephialtes.

At this epoch the laws were revised, and the register of burghers was revised. A new alphabet also was introduced as the official *Introduc-* script of the state. The old Attic alphabet, with its hard-worked *tion of the* vowels doing duty for more than one sound, was discontinued; and *Ionic* henceforward the stones which record the public acts of the Athenian *alphabet in the* people are inscribed in the Ionic alphabet, with separate signs for the *archonship* long and short *e* and *o*, and distinct symbols for the double consonants. *of Euclides,* The constitution was left practically unaltered, but some 20 years *403-2 B.C.* later a change was made in the presidency of the Assembly, which *Change* had hitherto belonged to the *prytaneis* or board of Ten, selected every *in the* seven days from the presiding tribe in the Council. The close *presidency* organic relation between the Council and Assembly rendered it needful *of the Assembly.* that members of the Council should preside in the Assembly; but the presidency of the Assembly was now divorced from the presidency of the Council and invested in a body of nine, selected one from each *The nine* of the nine tribes which were not presiding. This change was *proedroi.* obviously designed to form a check on the administration. The presiding tribe in the Council could no longer deal directly with the Assembly, but was obliged to present its measures to the people through an intermediate body, which belonged indeed to the Council but not to its own part of the Council.

It is plain that Athens needed, at this period, not men of genius or enthusiasm, but simply men of ability, for the conduct of her affairs. She had no great aims to achieve, no grave dangers to escape, which demanded a Pericles or a Themistocles; a man of genius would have found no scope in the politics of Athens for two generations after the fall of her empire. Men of great ability she had, men who were thoroughly adequate to the comparatively unambitious rôle which she had wisely imposed upon herself—Agyrrhius, Callistratus, and afterwards Eubulus. To us they are all shadowy figures. Agyrrhius *Agyrrhius.* inaugurated the profit-system which afterwards resulted in the institution of the theoric fund; and it was he who opposed and discredited the extreme anti-Spartan policy of the heroes of Phyle. His nephew *Calli-* Callistratus enjoyed a longer career and played a greater part in the *stratus.* affairs of Greece, conspicuous as the founder of the Second Confederacy, as the negotiator of the Peace of Callias, and then as the opponent of Epaminondas. His policy throughout was consistent and reasonable. He aimed at rendering Athens powerful enough to be independent of Sparta; he desired that Sparta and Athens should stand side by side as the two leading states in Greece; and he recognised that the neighbourhood of Attica to Boeotia necessarily laid upon Athens the policy of opposing the aggrandisement of Thebes.

Agyrrhius and Callistratus might once and again fill the office of strategos; but, like Cleon and Hyperbolus, they exercised their

influence as recognised—practically, official—advisers of the Assembly
The art of war became every year more and more an art, and little
could be accomplished except by generals who devoted their life to
Military the military profession. Such were Timotheus, the hero of Leucas;
men. Chabrias, the victor of Naxos; and above all Iphicrates, whom we
have met in so many places and in so many guises. Timotheus was
a rich man; his father Conon had left him a fortune, and he could
afford to serve his country and his country only. But Chabrias and
Iphicrates enriched themselves by taking temporary service under
foreign masters; Iphicrates even went so far as to support the
Thracian king, whose daughter he had wedded, against Athens.
All these military men preferred to dwell elsewhere than at Athens.
Abroad they could live in luxury and ostentation; while at Athens
men lived simply and moderately, and public opinion was unfavourable
to sumptuous establishments. The attitude of the generals to the city
became much more independent when the citizens themselves ceased
to serve abroad regularly, and hired mercenaries instead. The
hiring of the troops and their organisation devolved upon the general,
and he was often expected to provide the means for paying them
too. Here we touch on a vice in the constitutional machine, which
was the cause of frequent failures in the foreign enterprises of Athens
during this period. No systematic provision was made that, when
the people voted that a certain thing should be done, the adequate
moneys at the same time should be voted. Any one might propose
a decree, without responsibility for its execution; and at the next
meeting of the Assembly the people might refuse to allow the
necessary supplies, or no one might be ready to move the grant.
In the same way, supplies might be cut off in the middle of a
campaign. This defect had not made itself seriously felt in the
fifth century, when the leading generals were always statesmen too,
with influence in the Assembly; but it became serious when the
generals were professional soldiers whom the statesmen employed.
During the ten years after the Peace of Callias, Athens was actively
engaged in a multitude of enterprises of foreign aggrandisement;
but she achieved little, and the reason is that her armaments were
hardly ever adequate. The difficulties of her financiers, who had
always to keep a theoric reserve, must be taken into consideration.

CHAPTER XIV

THE HEGEMONY OF THEBES

SECT. I. JASON OF PHERAE; AND THE BATTLE OF LEUCTRA

THE balance of power in Greece had been swayed for a hundred years by the two rivals Sparta and Athens ; and now the Peace of Callias had formally adjusted an equilibrium between them. But this dual system was threatened from the very outset by formidable dangers. It was clear that new forces had arisen within the last few years, which would dispute the leadership of Hellas with the two older states. There had been a development of military power in the north, and two cities had come into dangerous prominence, Thebes and Pherae.

Of the rise of Pherae we know less than of the rise of Thebes. At the time of the Peace of Callias we make the sudden discovery that the Thessalian cities which were usually in a state of feud have been united, and that Thessaly has consequently become one of the great powers of Greece. This was the doing of one man. There *Jason of* had arisen at Pherae a despot, who was not merely vigorous and *Pherae.* warlike, but whose ambition ranged beyond the domestic politics of Thessaly and sought to play a great part on the wider stage of Hellas. Jason had established his dominion by means of a well-trained body of 6000 mercenaries, and also doubtless by able diplomacy. The most influential citizen of Pharsalus exposed at 371 *B.C.* Sparta the ambitious and menacing views of Jason, and urged the importance of checking his career before he became too powerful ; but Sparta, pressed by other more importunate claims, declined to interfere. Then Pharsalus yielded to the solicitations of Jason, and helped to install him as *Tagus* of an united Thessaly. The power of the despot extended on one side into Epirus, where Alcetas, prince of the Molossi, became his vassal ; and on the other side to Macedonia.

A monarch, endowed with uncommon political and military ability, at the head of all Thessaly, with the best cavalry in Greece at his command, seemed likely to change the whole course of Hellenic affairs. That he aimed at becoming the first power in Hellas—at attaining the *hegemony* or leadership, as it was called—there can be no question ; nor, considering the weakness and jealousies of the southern Grecian states, would this object, with his resources, be difficult of achievement. But, if his ambition was not bounded by Thessaly, neither was it confined to Hellas. His dream was to lead Hellas against Persia, and overthrow the power of the Great King. How serious he was in his great projects is shown by the fact that he set about building a navy. Thessaly was again to become a sea-power, as in the days of legendary story, when the Argo ventured forth from the land-locked bay of Iolcus.

The power of Sparta had evidently declined, but she was still regarded as holding the highest position in Greece ; and it was the first object of Jason to weaken her still further and dethrone her from that place. His second immediate object was to gain control of the key of southern Greece—the pass of Thermopylae ; and as this was commanded by the Spartan fortress of Heraclea, these two objects were intimately connected. His obvious policy was to ally himself with Sparta's enemy, Thebes ; and Thebes, in her isolated position, leapt at his alliance. The treaty between the Boeotian and Thessalian federations was probably concluded not long before the Peace of Callias. According to the terms of that Peace, all parties were to recall their armaments from foreign countries and their garrisons from foreign towns. Athens promptly recalled Iphicrates from Corcyra, but Sparta on her side failed to fulfil the contract. King Cleombrotus had, shortly before, led an army to Phocis, and now, instead of disbanding it, he was ordered to march against Thebes and compel that state to set free the Boeotian cities. One voice, perhaps, in the Spartan assembly was raised against this violation of the recent oaths, a violation which was also unfair to the allies who served in the Lacedaemonian army. But in this hour Sparta was led on, as one of her admirers said, by a fatal impulse inspired by the gods ; the feeling of hatred against Thebes, diligently fostered by Agesilaus, swept away all thoughts of policy or justice ; and the voice which was raised for justice and policy was scornfully cried down. The duel between Thebes and Sparta was inevitable ; and all Greece, confident in Spartan superiority, looked to see Thebes broken up into villages or wiped out from among the cities of Hellas. Even Thebes herself hardly hoped for success. But Sparta would have done well to disband the army of Cleombrotus, and organise a new force with the help of those allies who were willing to support her.

Sparta (contrary to treaty) orders Cleombrotus to march against Thebes.
371 B.C.
Protest of Prothous.

The object of Cleombrotus, who was posted near Chaeronea, in the gate between Phocis and Boeotia, was to reach Thebes ; and, as we have seen in the case of former military operations in this country, his direct road lay along the western and southern banks of Lake Copais, by Coronea and Haliartus. The aim of the Thebans was to prevent him from reaching his objective ; and they posted their forces nigh to Coronea, where, nearly a quarter of a century before, a confederate army had waylaid Agesilaus. But Cleombrotus disappointed his enemy ; he marched southward by a difficult road round Mount Helicon to Thisbe, and thence pounced on the port of Creusis, which he captured along with twelve Theban ships in the harbour ; and, by this swift stroke having secured his rear, he advanced northward along the road to Thebes.

When he reached the height of Leuctra, he found that the way *Position of* was barred by the Theban army. Leuctra lies on the hills which form *the armies* the south limit of a small plain, somewhat more than half a mile broad, *at Leuctra.* traversed by the brook of the upper Asopus. The road from the coast to Thebes crosses it and ascends the hills on the northern side, where the Boeotarchs and their army were now drawn up. The round top of one of these low hills, just east of the road, was levelled and enlarged to form a smooth platform. Here the Theban hoplites of the left wing were posted, and the artificial mound marks their place to this day. The numbers of the two hosts are uncertain ; the Lacedaemonians, in any case considerably superior, may have been about eleven, the Theban about six, thousand strong. But the military genius of one of the *Tactics of* Boeotarchs, now for the first time fully revealed, made up for the *Epami-* deficiency in strength. Instead of drawing out the usual long *nondas.* and shallow line, Epaminondas made his left wing deep. This wedge, fifty shields deep, of irresistible weight, with the Sacred Band, under the captaincy of Pelopidas, in front, was opposed to the Spartans who, with Cleombrotus himself, were drawn up on the right of the hostile army. It was on his left wing that Epaminondas relied for victory ; the shock between the Spartans and Thebans would decide the battle ; it mattered little about the Boeotians on the centre and left, whom he could not entirely trust. The Thespians, who were present by constraint, were at the last moment permitted to depart ; but their retreat was cut off and they were driven back to the camp by the Phocians and other of the Lacedaemonian allies, who, by detaching themselves for this purpose, weakened their own army without effecting an useful result.

The battle began with an engagement of the cavalry. In this *Battle of* arm the Lacedaemonians were notoriously weak ; and now their *Leuctra,* horsemen, easily driven back, carried disorder into the line of *July* 371 foot. Cleombrotus, who was confident of victory, then led his *B.C.* right wing down the slopes—the centre and left being probably impeded in their advance by the cavalry ; and on his side Epami-

nondas with the Theban left moved down from their hill, deliberately
keeping back the rest of the line. The novel tactics of Epaminondas
decided the battle. The Spartans, twelve deep, though they fought
ever so bravely, could not resist the impact of the Theban wedge led

FIG. 150.

by Pelopidas. King Cleombrotus fell, and after a great carnage on
both sides the Thebans drove their enemies up the slopes back to
their camp. In other parts of the field there seems to have been
little fighting or slaughter; the Lacedaemonian allies, when they
saw the right wing worsted, retired without more ado.

A thousand Lacedaemonians had fallen, including four hundred Spartans ; and the survivors acknowledged their defeat by demanding the customary truce to take up the dead. It might be thought that they would have immediately retreated to Creusis, the place of safety which the dead king had prudently provided in their rear. It is not likely that the enemy, whom they still considerably outnumbered, would have attempted to stop their way, or even to harass them seriously from behind. The Thebans could hardly realise the victory which they had never expected ; it was more than enough to have defeated the Lacedaemonians in the open field, to have slain their king, and to have compelled them to evacuate Boeotia. But the *Position at* Lacedaemonian army remained in its entrenchments on the hill of *Leuctra* Leuctra, in the expectation of being reinforced by a new army from *after the* Sparta and retrieving the misfortune. A messenger was sent home *battle.* with the inglorious tidings, and the shock was borne there with that studied self-repression which only the discipline of Sparta could inculcate in her citizens. The remaining forces of the city were *Army of* hastily got together, and placed under the command of Archidamus, *relief* son of Agesilaus. Some of the allied states sent aid, and the troops *under* were transported by ship from Corinth to Creusis. *Archi-* *damus.*

But all this took time, and meanwhile Thebes had not been idle. *Reception* Two messengers were sent with the good news, to Athens and to *of the news* Thessaly. At Athens the wreathed messenger was received with an *at Athens.* ominous silence. The Theban victory was distinctly unwelcome there ; it opened up an indefinite prospect of warfare and seemed likely to undo the recent pacification ; while the Athenians were far less jealous of Sparta than of Thebes. At Pherae the tidings had a very different reception. Jason marched forthwith to the scene of *Jason of* action, at the head of his cavalry and mercenaries, flying so rapidly *Pherae* through Phocis that the Phocians, his irreconcilable enemies, did not *marches to* realise his presence until he had passed. He cannot have reached *Leuctra.* Leuctra until the sixth or seventh day after the battle. The Thebans thought that with the help of his forces they might storm the Lacedaemonian entrenchments, dangerous though the task would be. But for the policy of Jason the humiliation already inflicted on Sparta was enough ; the annihilation of the enemy or any further enhance- ment of the Theban success would have been too much. He dis- suaded the Thebans from the enterprise, and induced them to grant a truce to the Lacedaemonians, with leave to retire unharmed. This *Truce.* the Lacedaemonians were now forced to accept, notwithstanding the *The* approach of reinforcements. For their position was totally altered *Lacedae-* through the presence of the seasoned troops of Jason, and it was *monians* clear that the foe would not wait to attack them till the expected *evacuate* reinforcements arrived. The retreat was carried out at night, for the *Boeotia.*

leaders suspected the good faith of their opponents. On the coast
the defeated troops met the army of Archidamus, which had come in
vain, and all the forces were disbanded.

*Another
view of the
evacuation
of Boeotia.*
Such were the circumstances of the Lacedaemonian evacuation of
Boeotia after the battle of Leuctra, according to the historian whose
authority we are naturally inclined to prefer. But the memory of
Xenophon might have misled him in regard to some of the details,
and there was another account from which it might be inferred that
events moved more rapidly. There is something to be said for the
view that the army of Archidamus was not dispatched as a relief
force after the battle of Leuctra, but was already on its way before
the battle was fought; that Cleombrotus had the alternative of
waiting for Archidamus before he ventured on an action, and that
his visit to Creusis was, in fact, connected with the expected arrival
of reinforcements; that Jason too was hastening to support the
Thebans, and that the messenger who bore the news of victory met
him on his southward march. On this view the truce might have
been concluded on the morrow of the battle, and we avoid the
difficulty of supposing that the defeated army decided to remain for
a week on the hill of Leuctra, when the road to Creusis was open
behind them.

The question is of little moment save in so far as it concerns the
movements of the Tagus of Thessaly. The significance of the sequel
of the battle lies in the prominent part which he played as a mediator; and we should like well to know whether his original purpose
*Jason's
fleet.*
was to fight side by side with his Theban allies. We also hear
darkly of his avowed intention to bring help by sea; and we are
tempted to speculate at what point the new Thessalian navy would
have acted at this crisis.

*Jason at
Ther-
mopylae.*
Jason returned to his northern home, but on his way he dealt
another blow at Sparta on his own account, by dismantling Heraclea,
the fort which controlled the pass of Thermopylae. He thus com-
*His
schemes.*
passed an object of great importance for his further designs. These
designs he soon began to unfold. He fixed on the next celebration
of the Pythian festival as a time to display his greatness and his power
to the eyes of assembled Hellas. He sent mandates around to the
Thessalian cities to prepare oxen, sheep, and goats for the sacrifice at
Delphi, offering a gold crown as a prize for the fairest ox. And he
issued commands that the armed host of the Thessalians should be
ready to march with him to keep the feast. He proposed to usurp
the rights of the Amphictyonic board, and preside himself over the
games. A rumour was set afloat that he intended to seize the
treasures of the temple; but it is hard to believe that an aspirant to
the hegemony of Greece would have perpetrated an act so manifestly

impolitic. Apollo told the Delphians, who were fluttered by the report, that he would himself guard his treasure.

But the priests were soon to breathe freely; the Phocians were to be spared the mortification of seeing the hated Thessalian in their land. One day Jason held a review of his cavalry, and afterwards sat to hear petitions. Seven young men, to all appearance wrangling hotly, drew near to lay their dispute before him, and slew him where he sat. The death of Jason was the knell of all his plans. The unity of Thessaly, the high position which it had attained among the Grecian powers, depended entirely on him. The brothers who succeeded to his place were slight insignificant men, without the ability, even if they had possessed the will, to carry out his far-reaching designs. It is the bare truth to say that the blades of the seven young men changed the course of history. Jason was well on his way to attain in eastern Greece the supreme position which his great fellow-despot Dionysius held in the west. Nor is it extravagant to suppose that under him Thessaly might have accomplished part of the work which was reserved for Macedonia. Politically, indeed, his work is to be condemned. He had not laid the foundations of a national unity in Thessaly; the unity which he had compassed was held by military force only and his own genius. We cannot congratulate a statesman on a result of which the stability hangs on the chances of his own life. In this respect Jason stands in the same rank with Epaminondas.

The death of the Thessalian potentate decided that, of the two northern states which had recently risen into prominence, Boeotia, not Thessaly, should take the torch from Sparta.

The significance of the battle of Leuctra is perhaps most clearly revealed in the fact that, during the wars between Sparta and Thebes which followed it, the parts hitherto played by the two states are reversed. Thebes now becomes the invader of the Peloponnese, as Sparta before had been the invader of Boeotia. Thebes is now the aggressor; it is as much as Sparta can do to defend her own land. The significance of Leuctra is also displayed in the effect which it produced upon the policy of Athens, and in its stimulating influence on the lesser Peloponnesian states, especially Arcadia, which was wakened up into new life.

The supremacy of Thebes was the result of no overmastering imperial instinct and was inspired by no large idea, but it brought about some beneficial results. Sparta had grievously abused the dominion which had fallen into her hands; and the period of Theban greatness represents the reaction against the period of Lacedaemonian oppression. The two objects of Theban policy are to hinder Sparta from regaining her old position in the Peloponnesus, and to prevent the revival of Jason's power in Thessaly.

Assassination of Jason, 370 B.C.

Historical significance of this crime;

its consequences for Thebes.

Results of Leuctra and rôle of Thebes.

Although no express record has been handed down as to constitutional changes, there is some evidence which has suggested the belief that the Thebans drew tighter the bond which united the Boeotian communities by transforming the federation into a national state. Thebes, seemingly, became in Boeotia what Athens was in Attica ; the other cities, Coronea, Thespiae, Haliartus, and the rest, were uncitied and became as Marathon and Eleusis ; their citizens exercised their political rights in an Assembly at Thebes. If this be so, we may suspect that Epaminondas played the part of legendary Theseus ; but the new constitution had no elements of stability, and it endured but for a few years.

Sect. 2. Policy of Thebes in Southern Greece, Arcadia and Messenia

The defeat of a Lacedaemonian army in the open field by an enemy inferior in numbers was a thrilling shock to the Greeks, who deemed it part of the order of nature that the Spartan hoplites should be invincible except in front of an overwhelmingly larger force. The event was made more impressive by the death of king Cleombrotus ; a Spartan king had never fallen in battle since Leonidas laid down his life at the gates of Greece. The news agitated every state in the

Democratic movements throughout the Peloponnesus. Peloponnesus. The harmosts, whom Sparta had undertaken to withdraw three weeks before, when she signed the Peace, were now expelled from the cities ; there was an universal reaction against the local oligarchies which had been supported by Sparta and had excited universal discontent ; and these democratic revolutions flooded the

Scytalism, or cudgelling, at Argos. land with troops of dangerous exiles. The contagion spread even to Argos, though Sparta had no influence there, and broke out with such violence that many citizens were cudgelled to death by the infuriated people.

Pan-Arcadian League. But it was in Arcadia that the most weighty political results followed. A general feeling, which had perhaps been growing for some years back, now took definite shape, that the cities of Arcadia must combine together to oppose an united front to Lacedaemonian pretensions. The only way in which each city could hope to preserve her independence against the power of Sparta was by voluntarily surrendering a portion of that independence to a federal union of her sister cities. The most zealous advocate of the Pan-Arcadian idea was the Mantinean Lycomedes, a native of the district which had been more cruelly used than all others by the high-handed policy of Lacedaemon. The fall of Sparta was the signal for the Mantineans to rebuild their walls, desert their villages, and resume the dignity and pleasures of city life. The old king Agesilaus had the insolence to remonstrate ; he requested them at least to ask the gracious permission of Sparta, but he had no power to enforce his request.

The Mantineans resolved that their city should not again be *Rebuilding* captured, as king Agesipolis had captured it, by means of its own *of* river. They dug a new bed, so that the Ophis when it approached *Mantinea,* the south-eastern wall parted into two channels and, having described *370 B.C.,* a great loop, reunited its waters on the north-western side. In this *spring.* loop the city of Mantinea rose again, and by this means the river, which had proved itself a danger, was forced to become a fortification, entirely encompassing the walls. The stone foundations of the wall enable us to trace the circuit of the city ; but they were only the base for a superstructure which, like the buildings of the town, was of brick. The ten gates were curiously constructed, no two alike, yet all elaborations of a principle which was adopted by the builders of the fortress of Tiryns—the principle of exposing the undefended right side of an approaching enemy to the defenders who manned the walls and flanking towers. The general design may be best grasped by conceiving the wall not as a continuous circle but as composed of ten separate pieces, which did not join but overlapped, while the gates connected the overlapping ends.

Mantinea, arisen from her ruins, and the other towns of Arcadia —with the important exceptions of Tegea, Orchomenus, and Heraea —now agreed to form a Pan-Arcadian union and constitute a federal state. Several reasons made it expedient to establish a new seat as *Founda-* the federal capital of the country. The Arcadian cities were too *tion of* small for the purpose. The selection of one of them would have *Megalopolis* excited the jealousies of the other, and it was intended that there *(date un-* should be no Thebes in the Arcadian state. The site chosen for the *371-369* new city was in the western of the two large plains which define the *B.C.).* geographical character of central Arcadia. It lay, in a long narrow irregular shape, on both sides of the river Helisson. Not far off rose Lycaeon, the mountain to which the Arcadian folk attached their most sacred associations ; and in the centre of the market-place was built a shrine of Zeus of that holy hill. The town was entitled to its name of Megalopolis, or Great City, by the large circuit of its double wall, a circuit of five miles and a half—a somewhat rough piece of work, built of stone in the lower courses and brick above, and furnished with towers at intervals.

It must be kept in view that Megalopolis had a double character. It was to be the federal capital, but it was also to be one of the federal cities. Apart from its relation to all Arcadia, it had a special relation to its own plain. The change which had come to pass in the eastern plain, so long ago that no man could tell when, by the founding of Tegea and Mantinea, was now brought to pass in the western plain. The village communities of the surrounding districts were induced to exchange their separate existence for joint life in a city. Lying close to the north-western frontier of Laconia, Megalopolis would be a bulwark against Sparta on this side, corresponding to Tegea on the north. It is natural to compare it with Mantinea, which arose in its new shape at the same time. Both cities seem to have had a similar system of fortification, double walls of stone and brick, strengthened by towers ; but Megalopolis, which was the larger, was also the stronger by nature. For Mantinea lay on a dead level, all its strength was due to art; Megalopolis lay on sloping irregular ground, offering hills of which the architect could take advantage. The difference is illustrated by the fact that the little theatre in Mantinea rested on a stone substructure, while the huge theatre in Megalopolis is cut out of a hill.

Assembly of the Myrioi. The Federal Constitution was modelled on the ordinary type of democratic constitutions. There was an Assembly, which met at stated periods to consider all important questions. Every citizen of the federal communities was a member of this Assembly, of which the official title was the *Ten Thousand.* The name indicates an approximate, not an exact, number, like the Five Thousand in the constitution of Theramenes at Athens. We have no information as to the working of this body, but from the analogy of other ancient federations it is probable that the votes were taken by cities, the vote of each city being determined by the majority of the votes of those of its citizens who were present. The Ten Thousand made war and peace, concluded alliances, and sat in judgment on offenders against *Council of* the League. There was also a *Council,* composed of fifty members *Damiorgoi.* from the various cities, and this body had doubtless the usual executive and deliberative functions which belonged to the Greek conception of a Council.

On the south side of the river stood the Thersilion, the federal building in which meetings of the Arcadian league were held. The foundations of this spacious covered hall have been recently laid bare, and display an ingenious arrangement of the internal pillars, converging in lines whereby as few as possible of a crowded audience might be hindered from seeing and hearing. It is an attempt to apply the principle of the theatre to a covered building. The Thersilion stood close in front of the hill from which the theatre was hewn, and the place of political deliberation seemed part of the same structure as the place of dramatic spectacles. For the Doric portico, which adorned the southern side of the federal house, faced the audience ; the orchestra in which the chorus danced and the actors sometimes played stretched from the circle of seats up to the steps

FIG. 151.—View of Megalopolis, showing the Theatre, the Thersilion, and the River.

of the portico. Such was the original arrangement, changed in later years ; and it illustrates the fact that the stone theatres which began to spring up throughout Greece in the fourth century were intended as much for political assemblies as for theatrical representations.

FIG. 152.—Coin of Arcadia. Obverse : head of Zeus laureate. Reverse : Pan on mountain ; syrinx below [legend : ΑΡΚ (monogram) ; and ΟΛΥ(μπος) on the mountain].

The river Helisson divides Megalopolis into two nearly equal parts ; and it would seem that this division corresponded to the double character of the place. The city of Megalopolis, in the strict sense, was on the northern side ; there was the market-place on the bank of the river, there was the hall *Buleuterion.* in which the Council of the Megalopolitan state met together. But the southern half of Megalopolis was federal ground ; here was the federal Hall of Assembly, here was the theatre, which was in fact *Eparitoi (federal army).* an open-air hall for federal meetings. Here, we may suppose, were the dwellings of the permanent armed force, 5000 strong, which was maintained by the Federation ; here were lodgings for the "Ten Thousand" when they assembled to vote on the affairs of the Arcadian state.

Tegea joins the League, 370 B.C. Tegea had hitherto been a sort of Laconian outpost, and a revolution was necessary to bring about its adhesion to the new federation. With the help of a Mantinean band, the philo-Laconian party was overthrown, and 800 exiles sought refuge at Sparta. This blow stung Sparta to action. She might brook the resuscitation of Mantinea, she might look on patiently at the measures taken by the presumptuous Arcadians for managing their own affairs ; but it was too much to see Tegea, her steadfast ally, the strong warder of her northern frontier, pass over to the camp of the rebels. Agesilaus led an army into Arcadia, and displayed the resentment of Sparta by ravaging the fields of Mantinea ; neither he nor the federal forces risked a conflict.

In view of this Spartan invasion, which came to so little, the Arcadians had sought the help of foreign powers. To Athens their first appeal was made. The tidings of Leuctra had excited in that city mixed feelings of pleasure and jealousy. The humiliation of Sparta opened up a prospect of regaining empire, notwithstanding the undertakings of the recent peace ; but the triumph of Thebes was unwelcome and dangerous. These hopes and fears spurred

Athens to new activity.   Shortly after the battle of Leuctra she *Close of* showed her appreciation of the changed condition of Hellas by 371 *B.C.* inviting delegates from the Peloponnesian cities to pledge themselves anew to the King's Peace (which, it must always be remembered, was the basis of the Peace of Callias) and to pledge themselves to one another for mutual help in case of hostile attack.   Elis, refusing to recognise the autonomy of some of her subjects, was forced to hold aloof; but most of the other states swore to the alliance.   It was a contract between Athens and her allies on one side, and the former allies of Sparta on the other.   By virtue of this act of alliance, Athens was bound to help Mantinea and the Arcadian cities whenever they were threatened by an invasion.   But it appeared that, though ready to usurp the place of Sparta, she was not ready to renew the war with her old rival.   Perhaps a change of feeling had been wrought in the course of the nine or ten months which had run since the congress at Athens ; the violence of the democratic movements in the Peloponnese may have caused disgust ; certain it is that Athens refused the Arcadian appeal ; she seems to have contemplated a policy of neutrality.

The rebuff at Athens drove Arcadia into the arms of Thebes. The battle which had been fought to secure the unity of Boeotia had been the means of promoting the unity of Arcadia ; and there was a certain fitness in the northern state coming to the aid of its younger fellow.   But it was not mere sympathy with federal institutions that induced Thebes to send a Boeotian army into the Peloponnesus. To keep Sparta down and prevent her from recovering her influence was the concern of Thebes, and an united Arcadia was the best instrument that could be devised for the purpose.   At this juncture, the situation in northern Greece permitted Thebes to comply with the Arcadian request.   The Phocians and Ozolian Locrians, the Locrians of Opus, the Malians, had sought her alliance after Leuctra, and even the Euboeans had deserted to her ; so that all central Greece, as far as Cithaeron, was under the Boeotian influence.   But if the request had come some months sooner, it would have been impossible to grant it ; for Jason of Pherae was then alive, preparing to march to Delphi, and the Boeotian forces could not have left Boeotia.

It was already winter when the Theban army, led by Epaminondas, *Boeotians* accompanied by his fellow Boeotarchs, arrived in Arcadia to find that *invade* Agesilaus had withdrawn from the field.   But, though the purpose *Laconia.* of the expedition was thus accomplished, the Arcadians persuaded Epaminondas not to return home without striking a blow at the enemy.   To invade Laconia and attack Sparta herself was the daring proposal—daring in idea at least ; for within the memory of history no foeman had ever violated Laconian soil, the unwalled city had never repelled an assault.   There was little danger, with an army of such size as that which was now assembled ; and a march to the gates of Sparta would drive home the lesson of Leuctra.   The invaders advanced in four divisions by four roads, converging on Sellasia, and met no serious attempt to block their way ; some neodamodes and Tegeate exiles were annihilated by the Arcadians. Sellasia was burnt, and the united army descended into the plain on the left bank of the Eurotas.   The river which separated them from Sparta was swollen with winter rains, and this probably saved the city ; for the bridge was too strongly guarded to be safely attacked. Epaminondas marched southward a few miles further, as far as Amyclae, where he crossed the stream by a ford.   But Sparta was now saved.   On the first alarm of the coming invasion, messages had flown to the Peloponnesian cities which were still friendly ; and these—Corinth, Sicyon, Phlius, Pellene, and the towns of the Argolic coast—had promptly sent auxiliary forces.   The northern roads being barred by the enemy, these forces were obliged to land on the eastern shore of Laconia and make their way across Mount Parnon.   They reached the Eurotas bridge, after the invaders had moved to Amyclae ; and their coming added such strength to the defence of Sparta that Epaminondas did not attack it, but contented himself with marching up defiantly to its outskirts.   It was indeed a sufficient revenge even for Theban hatred to have wounded Sparta as none had wounded her before, to have violated the precinct of the Laconian land.   The consternation of the Spartans at a calamity which, owing to the immunity of ages, they had never even conceived as possible, can hardly be imagined.   The women, disciplined though they were in repressing their feelings when sons or husbands perished in battle, now fell into fits of distress and despair : for, unlike the women of so many other Greek cities, they had never looked upon the face of an enemy before.   Old Agesilaus, who loathed the Theban above all other names, was charged with the defence ; and his task was the harder, since he had to watch not only the foe, but the disaffected.   Freedom had been promised to 6000 helots who came forward to serve ; but this aid was a new danger.

It is needless to say that the loss of a few hundred soldiers on the field of Leuctra had nothing to do with the impotence displayed *Depopula-* by Sparta at this crisis.   And if Leuctra had been won by superior *tion of* generalship, it was not inferior generalship that exposed Laconia. *Sparta.* The disease lay far deeper.   The vigour of Sparta was decaying from the mere want of men ; it has been calculated that at this time there were not more than 1500 with full citizenship.   Not merely constant warfare, but, far more, economical conditions, brought about this dispeopling. Since money had begun to flow into Laconia, and since a new law permitted citizens to alienate their holdings, the inevitable result ensued ; the small lots which meagrely supported each Spartan were gathered into large estates ; and with the lots the citizens disappeared. This disease which was sapping the energies of his enemy cannot have escaped the view of Epaminondas, and his next step is significant.

Having ravaged southern Laconia, from the banks of the Eurotas to the foot of Taygetus, as far as Gytheion—where they failed, we know not why, to take the arsenal—the allies returned to Arcadia. But, though it was midwinter, their work was not over yet ; a far *Foundation of Messene, winter, 370-69 B.C.*

greater blow was still to be inflicted on Sparta. Epaminondas led them now into another part of the Spartan territory, the ancient Messenia. The serfs, who belonged to the old Messenian race, arose at their coming ; and on the slopes of Mount Ithome the foundations of a new Messene were laid by Epaminondas. The ancient heroes and heroines

Fig. 153.—Coin of Messene. Obverse : head of Demeter, corn-crowned. Reverse : Zeus with thunderbolt and eagle [legend : ΜΕΣΣΑΝΙΩΝ].

of the race were invited to return to the restored nation ; the ample circuit of the town was marked out, and the first stones placed, to the sound of flutes. Ithome was the citadel, and formed one side of the town, whose walls of well-wrought masonry descended the slopes and met in the plain below. The Messenian exiles who had been wandering over the Greek world had now a home once more.

Messene, like Megalopolis, was founded by " synoecizing " the districts round about. But its political position was entirely different from that of Megalopolis. Messene was not a federal capital ; it was the Messenian state—a city with the whole country for its territory. Corone and Methone were not cities like Mantinea and Clitor ; they were places like Brauron and Marathon ; their inhabitants possessed the citizenship of Messene, but it was only under Mount Ithome that they could exercise their burgher-rights. The relation of Messene to Messenia was that of Athens to Attica, not that of Megalopolis to Arcadia.

Thus not only a new stronghold but a new enemy was erected against Sparta in Sparta's own domain. All the land west of Taygetus (except the coastal towns of Asine and Cyparissia) was subtracted from the Spartan dominion ; more than half her serfs became the freemen of a hostile state. Under the auspices of Thebes an old

FIG. 154.—The Arcadian Gate of Messene.

act of injustice was undone, and the principle of autonomy was strikingly affirmed. But, besides the glory which Thebes won by so popular an act, besides the direct injury inflicted on Sparta and the establishment of a hostile fort, the policy of Epaminondas was calculated to produce a result of greater importance. The loss of Messenia would accelerate that process of decline in the Spartan state, which had already advanced so far. The fewer the lots, the fewer the citizens, according to the indissoluble connexion between land and burgher-rights on the Lycurgean system. It was high time for Sparta to reform her constitution.

The Arcadians celebrated this memorable invasion of Laconia *The stone* by dedicating with part of the spoil a group of statues to the Delphian *which bears* god. The verses of dedication signify that the indigenous people *witness to* from sacred Arcadia, having laid Lacedaemon waste, set up the *vasion of* monument as a witness to future generations. The statues are *Laconia.* gone, but the verses on their stone have come to light in our own day.

In the meantime Sparta had begged aid from Athens, and Athens had decided to depart from her position of neutrality. A vote was passed, strongly supported by the orator Callistratus, to send the entire force of the city under Iphicrates to assist Sparta. This was evidently the most politic course for Athens to adopt. Sparta was a necessary makeweight against Thebes. Nor is it doubtful that, notwithstanding all their rivalries, no such antipathy parted Athens from Sparta as that which existed between the two states and Thebes. Iphicrates marched to the Isthmus and occupied Corinth and Cen- *Athens* chreae, thus commanding the line of Mount Oneion. His object, it *sends an* must be clearly understood, was not to prevent the enemy from leaving *army to* the Peloponnesus, but to protect the rear of his own army marching *rescue* into a hostile country. He advanced into Arcadia, but found that *Sparta.* the Thebans and their allies had left Laconia, and Sparta was no longer in danger. He therefore drew back to Corinth, and harassed *Theban* the Boeotian army on its return march, without attempting to bar *army* its passage. For the object of the Athenian expedition was simply *returns* to rescue Sparta, not, except so far as Sparta's peril might demand, *home,* to fight with the Thebans. *spring,*
369 B.C.

But the hasty vote to march to the rescue was soon followed *Alliance of* by a deliberate treaty of alliance; and Athens definitely ranged her- *Athens* self with Sparta against Boeotia and Arcadia. She was already *and* meditating schemes of extending her empire; she was nourishing *Sparta,* the hope of recovering the most precious of all her former imperial *369 B.C.* possessions, the Thracian Amphipolis. With such designs it was impossible to remain neutral; and, as we shall see, there was some danger of a collision with Thebes in Macedonia.

*Second
expedition
of Epami·
nondas
into the
Pelopon-
nesus.*
Fighting went on in the Peloponnese between the Arcadians and the allies of Sparta ; and a few months later Epaminondas (who had been re-elected Boeotarch in his absence at the beginning of the year) appeared again at the head of the Boeotian army.   The Spartans and Athenians had occupied the line of Mount Oneion ; this time the object was to keep out the Thebans.   But Epaminondas broke through their lines, joined his allies, won over Sicyon and Pellene, and failed to win Phlius.   A new succour for Sparta arrived at this moment from over-seas.   Twenty ships bearing 2000 Celtic and Iberian mercenaries came from her old ally, the tyrant of Syracuse, to whom she had once sent aid in an hour of peril, and who had more than once sent succour to her.   Their coming seems to have decided Epaminondas to return home, though he had accomplished but little, and his political opponent Meneclidas took advantage of the general disappointment to indict him for treason.   The result was that Epaminondas was not re-elected Boeotarch for the following year.

To establish her supremacy, Thebes was adopting the same policy as Sparta.   She placed a harmost in Sicyon ; as the Boeotian cities had formerly been garrisoned by Sparta, the Peloponnesian cities were now to be garrisoned by Thebes.   Messenia and Arcadia were to be autonomous, but the Thebans desired to be regarded as both the authors and preservers of that autonomy.   As a mistress, distant Thebes might be more tolerable than neighbouring Lacedaemon ; but the free federation of Arcadia determined to be free in very deed. Sparta was now sunk so low that the Arcadians—with friendly Messene on one side, and friendly Argos on the other—could hope to maintain their liberty with their own swords, without foreign aid. Their leading spirit Lycomedes animated them to this resolve of independence and self-reliance.   " You are the only indigenous natives of the Peloponnesus, and you are the most numerous and hardiest nation in Greece.   Your valour is proved by the fact that you have been always in the greatest request as allies.   Give up following the lead of others.   You made Sparta by following her lead ; and now if you follow the lead of Thebes, without yourselves leading in turn, she will prove perhaps a second Sparta."   In this mood the Arcadians displayed a surprising activity and achieved a series of successes.   The two important cities, Heraea in the west, and Orchomenus in the north, which had hitherto stood aloof, were forced to join the league, which now became in the fullest sense Pan-Arcadian.   Some of the northern villages of Laconia were annexed, and the Triphylian towns sought in the league a support against the hated domination of Elis.   The federal forces were active in the opposite quarters of Argolis and Messenia.   Against all this activity

*Spring,
368 B.C.*

Sparta felt herself helpless.   But a second armament of auxiliaries *Sparta*
arrived from her friend, the tyrant of Syracuse, and thus reinforced *receives*
she ventured to take the field, and marched into the plain of *help from*
Megalopolis.   But the expedition was suddenly interrupted ; time *Dionysius.*
had been wasted, and the Syracusan force, in accordance with its *The tear-*
orders, was obliged to return to Sicily.   Its way lay through Laconia, *less battle,*
in order to take ship at Gytheion ; and the enemy tried to cut it off *368 (late*
in the mountain defiles.   The Spartan commander Archidamus, *summer ?).*
who was in the rear, hastened to the rescue, and dispersed the
Arcadians with great loss.   Not a single Lacedaemonian was killed,
and the victory was called the "tearless battle."   The joy displayed
in Sparta over this slight success showed how low Sparta had fallen.

It may be thought that Dionysius might have kept his troops at *Congress*
home, if they were charged to return before they had well time to begin *of Delphi,*
to fight.   But the truth is, that these troops were for some months *368 B.C.*
inactive in Greece, while an attempt was being made to bring about *(summer).*
a general peace.   The initiative came from Ariobarzanes, the Persian
satrap of Phrygia, who sent to Greece an agent well furnished with
money ; and this move on the part of Persia was probably suggested
by Athens.   The Syracusan sovereign also intervened in the interests
of peace, and the stone remains on which the Athenians thanked
Dionysius and his sons for being " good men in regard to the people
of the Athenians and their allies, and helping the King's Peace."
Thus the King's Peace was the basis of the negotiations of the
congress which met at Delphi.   Both Athens, which was doubtless
the prime mover, and Sparta were most anxious for peace ; but each
had an ultimate condition from which she would not retreat.   Sparta's
very life seemed to demand the recovery of Messenia, and Athens
had set her heart on Amphipolis.   But neither
condition would be admitted by Thebes, and
consequently the negotiations fell through.
They led, however, to independent negotiations
of various states with Persia, each seeking to
win from the king a recognition of its own
claims.   Pelopidas went up to Susa on behalf of
Thebes to obtain a royal confirmation of the *Greek*
independence of Messenia.   The Athenians *envoys*
sent envoys to convince the king of their *at Susa,*
rights to Amphipolis.   Arcadia, Elis, and *367 B.C.*
Argos were also represented.   Pelopidas was

Fig. 155. — Coin of
Argos (obverse).
Head of Hera,
crowned.

entirely successful.   The king issued an order to Greece, embodying *Persian*
the wishes of Thebes : Messenia and Amphipolis to be independent, *rescript.*
the Athenians to recall their warships.   The question of Triphylia—
whether it was to be dependent on Elis or a part of Arcadia—was

decided in favour of Elis ; this decision in a matter of absolute indifference to Persia was clearly due to Pelopidas, and indicates strained relations between Thebes and Arcadia. Pelopidas returned with the royal letter, but it found no acceptance in Greece, either at the congress of allies which was convoked at Thebes, or when the document was afterwards sent round to the cities. Arcadia would not abandon Triphylia, and Lycomedes formally protested against the headship of Thebes.

Third expedition of Epaminondas into the Peloponnesus, 366 B.C.

The answer of Thebes to this defiance of her will was an invasion of the Peloponnesus. The line of Mount Oneion was still defended, but negligently ; and Epaminondas passed it with Argive help. His object was not to depress Sparta further, for Sparta was now too feeble to be formidable, but to check the pretensions of Arcadia. And this could only be done through strengthening Theban influence in the Peloponnesus by winning new allies. Accordingly, Epaminondas advanced to Achaea, and easily gained the adhesion of the Achaean cities.

Achaea won and lost, 366 B.C.

But the gain of Achaea was soon followed by its loss. Counter to the moderate policy of Epaminondas, the Thebans had insisted on overthrowing the oligarchical constitutions and banishing the oligarchical leaders ; these exiles from the various cities banded together, and recovered each city successively, overthrowing the democracies and expelling the harmosts. Henceforward Achaea was an ardent partisan of Sparta.

Sicyon : Euphron becomes tyrant, 368 B.C.

The unsettled state of the Peloponnesus was conspicuously shown by the events which happened at Sicyon. When the Theban harmost was installed in the acropolis, the oligarchy had been

FIG. 156.—Coin of Sicyon (obverse). Chimaera and head of Pan.

spared ; but soon afterwards one of the chief citizens, named Euphron, brought about the establishment of a democracy, and then, procuring his own election as general, organising a mercenary force, and surrounding himself with a bodyguard,—the usual and notorious steps of a despot's progress,—made himself master of the city and harbour. The Arcadians had helped Euphron in his first designs, but the intrigues of his opponents were so skilful, that Arcadia again intervened and restored to Sicyon the exiles whom the tyrant had driven out.

Expelled,

Euphron fled from the city to the harbour, which he surrendered to the Lacedaemonians ; but the Lacedaemonians failed to hold

restored. 366-5 B.C.

it. Sicyon, however, was not yet delivered from her tyrant. He was restored by the help of Athenian mercenaries. Afterwards, seeing that he could not maintain himself without the support of

Boeotia, he visited Thebes, and was slain on the Cadmea in front of the Hall of Council, by two Sicyonian exiles who had dogged him. His assassins were tried and acquitted at Thebes, but at Sicyon his memory was cherished and he was worshipped as a second founder of the city. The fact shows that under the rule of Euphron the masses of the people were happier than under the political opponents whom he had so mercilessly treated. His son succeeded to his power.

The expedition of Epaminondas was attended with results which *Thebans* were in the end injurious to Thebes. The relations with Arcadia *seize* became more and more strained. But in the same year Oropus *Oropus,* was wrested from Athens and occupied by a Theban force. The *366 B.C.* Athenians were unable to cope alone with Thebes; they called on their allies, but none moved to their aid. The moment was *Alliance of* seized by Arcadia. Lycomedes visited Athens and induced the *Arcadia* Athenians, smarting with resentment against their allies, to conclude *with* an alliance with the league. Thus Athens was now in the position of *Athens,* being an ally of both Arcadia and Sparta, which were at war with each *366 B.C.* other; and Arcadia was the ally of Athens and Thebes, which were also at war with each other. The visit of Lycomedes incidentally led to a disaster for Arcadia which outweighed the benefit of the alliance. The ambassador, on his way back, was slain by some *Murder of* exiles into whose hands he fell; and the league lost its ablest *Lycomedes.* statesman.

This change in the mutual relations among the Greek states, brought about by the seizure of Oropus, was followed by another change, brought about by an Athenian plot to seize Corinth. The object was to secure permanent control over the passage into the Peloponnesus. But the plot was discovered and foiled by the Corinthians, who then politely dismissed the Athenian soldiers stationed at various posts in the Corinthian territory. But by herself Corinth would have been unable to resist the combined pressure *Partial* of Thebes on one side and Argos on the other; and, as Sparta *peace of* could not help her, she was driven to make peace with Thebes. *366-5 B.C.* She was joined by her neighbour Phlius and by the cities of the Argolic coast; all these states formally recognised the independence of Messene, but did not enter into any alliance with Thebes, or give any pledge to obey her headship. They became, in fact, neutral.

It was a blow to Sparta, who still refused to accept a peace on any terms save the restoration of Messenia. The Messenian question gave political speculators at Athens a subject for meditation. Was the demand of Sparta just? The publicist Isocrates argued the case for Sparta in a speech which he put in the mouth of king Archi-

damus.   Another orator, Alcidamas, vindicated in reply the liberty of
the Messenians and declared a principle which was far in advance of
his time, "God has left all men free ; nature has made no man a
slave."

If we survey the political relations of southern Hellas at this
epoch, we see Thebes, supported by Argos, still at war with Sparta,
who is supported by Athens ; Achaea actively siding with Sparta ;
Elis hostile to Arcadia ; the Arcadian league at war with Sparta, in

alliance with Athens, in alliance with, but cool
towards, Thebes, and already—having lost its leader
Lycomedes—beginning to fall into disunion with
itself.

The peace with Corinth and others of the
belligerent states marks the time at which Peloponnesian affairs cease to occupy the chief place in
the counsels of Thebes, and her most anxious attention
turns to a different quarter.   For Sparta is disabled,
and the mistress of Boeotia recognises that it is with
Athens that the strife for headship will now be.   While events
were progressing in the Peloponnesus, as we have seen, Athens was
busily engaged in other parts of the world with a view to restoring
her maritime empire ; and we have now to see how she succeeded,
and how Thebes likewise was pushing her own supremacy in the
north.

FIG. 157.—Coin
of Cletor (ob-
verse). Radiate
head of Helios.

SECT. 3. POLICY AND ACTION OF THEBES IN NORTHERN GREECE

The same year which saw the death of Jason of Pherae saw the
death of another potentate in the north, his neighbour and ally
Amyntas of Macedonia.   We have seen how
Amyntas had to fight for his kingdom with the
Chalcidian league ; how he was driven out of his
land and restored ; and how the league was
crushed by the power of Sparta.   Both Jason
and Amyntas were succeeded by an Alexander.
At Pherae, the power first passed to Jason's
brothers, of whom one murdered the other and
was in turn murdered by his victim's son,—
Alexander, whose reign was worthy of its
sanguinary inauguration.   The Thessalian cities
refused to bow down to the supremacy of
Pherae, now that Pherae had no man who was worthy to be obeyed ;
and to resist Alexander of Pherae they invoked the aid of Alexander

FIG. 158.—Coin of
Amyntas (ob-
verse). Horse-
man with spear.

of Macedonia. The aid was given, and Larissa, Crannon, and other cities passed under Macedonian sway. But this was not the purpose of the Thessalians, to exchange a native for a foreign ruler ; and accordingly they invoked the help of Thebes against both Alexanders alike. It was sound policy on the part of Thebes to accede to the request. It was impossible to discern yet what manner of man the successor of Jason might prove to be ; and it was important, from the Boeotian point of view, to hinder the reunion of Thessaly under a monarch. The conduct of an expedition was entrusted to Pelopidas, who brought Larissa and other towns in the northern part of Thessaly under a Theban protectorate.

369 B.C.

First expedition of Pelopidas to Thessaly, 369 B.C.

At the same time, the Thessalians sought to strengthen their position by a federal union,—a political experiment which had been tried in Thessaly before. The little we know of the league which was established

Thessalian league.

FIG. 159.—Coin of Larissa, fourth century. Obverse: head of nymph. Reverse : horse feeding [legend : ΛΑΡΙΣΑΙΩΝ].

about this time suggests rather the revival of an old system than a new creation. The country was divided into four political divisions corresponding to the old geographical districts ; at the head of each was a polemarch, who had officers of horse and foot under him ; and at the head of the league was an archon, elected if not for life at least for longer than a year. Thus the organisation was military ; but there are indications that it grew out of an old amphictionic association. There is no reason to think that Pelopidas had more to do with the establishment of the Thessalian federation than Epaminondas with that of the Pan-Arcadian league ; the part of Thebes in either case was simply to support and confirm.

Tetrads.

Archon.

Macedonia offered no obstacles to the operations of Pelopidas in Thessaly, for it was involved in a domestic struggle. One of the nobles, Ptolemy of Alorus, rebelled against the king, and was supported by the king's unnatural mother Eurydice. The two parties called upon Pelopidas to adjudicate between them, and he patched up a temporary arrangement and concluded a Theban alliance with Macedonia. Hardly had he turned his back when Ptolemy murdered Alexander and married Eurydice. But it seemed as if the paramours would not be permitted to reap the profits of their crime. Another pretender to the throne had gathered an army of mercenaries and occupied all the land along the Chalcidian frontier. Help, however, was at hand. An Athenian fleet was cruising in the Thermaic gulf, under the command of Iphicrates. The queen visited

Murder of Alexander of Macedon, 369-8 B.C. Revolt of Pausanias.

Interven-
tion of
Iphicrates.
the admiral on the coast, accompanied by her two sons, Perdiccas and Philip,—the brothers of Iphicrates, since he had been adopted as a son by Amyntas,—and persuaded him to help her in her need. By his exertions the pretender was expelled, and the succession of Perdiccas was secured under the regency of Ptolemy.

The interests of Athens on the Chalcidian and the adjacent coasts had forced that state to keep an ever-watchful eye on political events in Macedonia and to seek influence at the court of Aegae. The intervention of Iphicrates was not the first case in which Athenian power had settled a dynastic question. His settlement was more abiding than that of Pelopidas; we may conjecture that the opportune appearance of the Athenian fleet was due to the circumstance that Thebes had interfered. But Thebes was resolved to continue her interference, and oust the Athenian influence. Pelopidas, again dispatched to the north, compelled the regent Ptolemy to enter into alliance with Thebes and assure his fidelity by furnishing a number of hostages. Among the young Macedonian nobles who were sent as pledges to Thebes was the boy Philip, who was destined to be the maker of Macedonia, and was now to be trained for the work in the military school of Boeotia, under the eye of Epaminondas himself.

Second
expedition
of Pelopidas
to Mace-
donia and
Thessaly,
368 B.C.

Pelopidas
detained by
the despot
of Pherae.
Having thus brought Macedonia within the circle of the Theban supremacy, Pelopidas on his way home visited the camp of the despot of Pherae. But he did not know that Alexander had become the ally of Athens—an inevitable combination, since it was the interest of both to oppose Theban expansion in the north. Supported by Athens, the despot could defy Thebes, and he detained his visitor Pelopidas as a hostage. A Boeotian army marched to rescue the captive; but an armament of 1000 men arrived by sea from Athens, and the invaders, who were commanded by incompetent generals, were out-manœuvred and forced to retreat. Epaminondas was serving as a common hoplite in the ranks, and but for his presence the army would have been lost. The soldiers unanimously invited him to take the command, and he skilfully extricated them from a dangerous position and managed their safe retreat. This exploit secured the re-election of Epaminondas as Boeotarch, and he immediately returned to Thessaly at the head of another army to deliver his friend. It was necessary to apply a compulsion severe enough to frighten the tyrant, but not so violent as to transport him with fury, which might be fatal to his prisoner. This was achieved by dexterous military operations, and Pelopidas was released in return for a month's truce. It seems probable that at the same time Epaminondas freed Pharsalus from the rule of Pherae. But it was not the interest of Thebes to overthrow the tyrant or even limit his authority to his own city.

Theban
invasion
of Thessaly
to rescue
Pelopidas,
368 B.C.
(autumn),
unsuccessful.
Second
invasion
of Thessaly
to rescue
Pelopidas,
367 B.C.
(first
months),
successful.

It was well that he should be there, as a threat to the rest of Thessaly; it was well that Thessaly should be unable to dispense with Theban protection. The power of Alexander extended over Phthiotis and Magnesia, and along the shores of the Pagasaean Bay, and to neighbouring towns like Scotussa. His tyranny and brutality seem to have been extreme, though the anecdotes of his cruelty cannot be implicitly trusted. We read that he buried men alive, or sewed them up in the hides of wild beasts for his hounds to tear. We read that he massacred the inhabitants of two friendly cities. We read that he worshipped as a divine being the dagger with which he had slain his uncle, and gave it the name of "Sir Luck"—an anecdote *Tychon.* indicating a strain of madness which often attends the taste for cruelty. Excellently invented, if not true, is the story that, having seen with dry eyes a performance of the *Troades* of Euripides, a drama unutterably sad, the tyrant sent an apology to the actor, explaining " *What's* that his apparent want of emotion was due to no defect in the *Hecuba to* acting, but to a feeling of shame that tears for the sorrows of *him?"* Hecuba should fall from the eyes of one who had shown no pity for so many victims.

It has been said that the chief desire of Athens at this time was to regain the finest jewel of her first empire, Amphipolis. The fleet, under Iphicrates, was cruising and watching, with this purpose in view; but the hopes of success—which depended much on the goodwill of Macedonia—were lessened by the ties which Ptolemy had contracted with Thebes. And, besides losing Macedonian support, Athens was impeded by the cities of the Chalcidian league, who now broke away from the Athenian alliance and made a treaty with Amphipolis.

Meanwhile Athens began to act in the Eastern Aegean. The *366 B.C.* opportunity was furnished by the revolt of her friend Ariobarzanes, *(367 B.C.)* the satrap of Phrygia. It was the policy of Athens to help the satrap without breaking with the Great King, from whom she still hoped to obtain a recognition of her claim to Amphipolis. A fleet of thirty *Timotheus* galleys and 8000 troops was sent under her other experienced *sent to Asia* general Timotheus, and he accomplished more in the east than *Minor,* Iphicrates had accomplished in the north. He laid siege to Samos, *366 B.C.* on which Persia had laid hands, contrary to the King's Peace; and *He captures* took it at the end of ten months. At the same time he lent *365 B.C.* assistance to Ariobarzanes, who had to maintain himself against the satraps of Lydia and Caria; and as a reward for these services Athens obtained the cession of two cities in the Thracian Chersonese —Sestos and Crithote.

Of these acquisitions Sestos was of special value, from its position *Athens gets* on the Hellespont, securing to Athens control at this point over *Sestos.*

the ships which supplied her with corn from the Euxine coasts. But more than this, she now regained a foothold in the peninsula which Miltiades had won for her, and she hoped to make it entirely her own up to a line drawn across the isthmus north of Cardia, marked at one point by an altar of "Zeus of Boundaries." Timotheus himself began the work of expansion by annexing Elaeus near the southern extremity. Thus Athens began to revive her old empire, but in Samos she revealed her designs even more clearly. This island was not treated as a subject ally, but was appropriated as Athenian territory. Outsettlers were sent from Athens to occupy Samos, and thus the system of cleruchies, which had been the most unpopular feature of the first Confederacy, and had been expressly guarded against at the formation of the second Confederacy, was renewed. It did not indeed violate the letter of the constitution of the league, which only bound Athens not to force outsettlers upon members of the league ; but it was distinctly a violation in spirit. The treatment of Samos showed Greece that Athens was bent on rising again to her old Imperial position ; while the second Confederacy was based on the principle that she had renounced such pretensions for ever.

Delighted with the achievements of Timotheus, the Athenians appointed him to command the fleet which had been operating for years on the Macedonian coast under Iphicrates, whose failure was strikingly contrasted with the success of Timotheus. It must be remembered that while Iphicrates was hindered by the hostility of the regent of Macedon, Timotheus was helped by the friendship of the satrap of Phrygia ; but Timotheus possessed a diplomatic *Murder of* dexterity which Iphicrates never displayed. And now fortune *the regent* favoured the diplomatist. Shortly before his new appointment, the *Ptolemy ;* regent Ptolemy was assassinated by the young king Perdiccas, who *Perdiccas* thus avenged his brother Alexander. The change in the holders of *in power,* power led to a change in policy. Macedonia freed itself from the *365 B.C.* influence of Thebes, and the young king sought the support of Athens. And so Timotheus, not only untrammelled by Macedonian *Successes of* opposition, but even aided by Macedonian auxiliaries, set about the *Timotheus* reduction of towns around the Thermaic gulf. He compelled *in the* Methone and Pydna to join the Athenian confederacy ; and in the *Chalcidic* Chalcidic peninsula he made himself master of Potidaea and Torone. *region* The acquisition of these Chalcidic towns was valuable in itself and *(364-2 B.C.).* Potidaea was occupied by Athenian outsettlers ; but the main purpose of the general was to weaken the resources of Olynthus, which, at the head of the Chalcidian states, gave powerful support to its ally Amphipolis, the supreme object coveted by Athens, whose rights to it had been recently recognised by the Persian king. A famous mercenary captain named Charidemus, who had previously served under Iphicrates, was now secured again by Timotheus ; but two efforts to capture Amphipolis were repelled. The work of Brasidas was not destined to be undone.

It was high time for Thebes to interfere. If the successes of Timotheus were allowed to continue, Athens would soon recover Euboea, and the adhesion of that island was, from its geographical position, of the highest importance to Boeotia. But in order to check the advance of her neighbour it would be necessary for Thebes to grapple with her on her own element. By the advice of Epaminondas, *Boeotian* in spite of the advice of Meneclidas, it was resolved to create a navy *navy.* and enter upon the career of a sea-power. This was a momentous decision, which demanded a careful consideration of ways and means. Given the problem, to break the power of Athens, there can be no question that Epaminondas advised the only possible method of solving it. But it might be well to consider whether its solution was a necessity for Thebes. The history of Boeotia had marked it out as a continental power ; and it would have been wiser to consolidate its sway on the mainland. The maintenance of a navy involved financial efforts which could not be sustained by any but a great commercial state ; and the cities of Boeotia had no trade. It was the natural antipathy of the two neighbours far more than any mature consideration of her own interests that drove Boeotia to take this indiscreet step. Yet the step had immediate success. A hundred triremes *364 B.C.* were built and manned and sent to the Propontis under the Boeotarch, Epaminondas.

The sailing of this fleet was a blow to Athens, not from any victory that it gained—there was no battle—but from the support and encouragement which it gave to those members of the Confederacy which were eager to break their bonds. The establishment of the cleruchs of Samos had created great discontent and apprehension among the Athenian allies, and they wanted only the support of a power like Thebes to throw off the federal yoke. Byzantium openly *Revolts of* rebelled ; Rhodes and Chios negotiated with Epaminondas ; and *Athenian* even Ceos, close to Attica itself, defied Athens. When the Theban *allies,* fleet returned home, Chabrias recalled Ceos to its allegiance, and a *364 B.C.* new act of treaty was drawn up ; but a second rebellion had to be *Revolts* put down at Iulis before the island acquiesced in Athenian sway. *of Ceos,* The expedition of Epaminondas also served to support the enemies *364 and* of Athens, who opposed her advance in the Chersonese ; namely, *362 B.C.* the free city of Cardia, and the Thracian king Cotys, who was aided by his son-in-law Iphicrates. This general, superseded by Timotheus, had not ventured to return to Athens, and now sided with her enemies.

Third ex-
pedition of
Pelopidas
to Thessaly,
364 B.C.
While the young Theban navy went forth to oppose Athens in the Propontis, a Theban army had marched against the ally of Athens, Alexander of Pherae, whose hand, strengthened by a mercenary force, had been heavy against the Thessalians.   Once more, but for the last time, Pelopidas entered Thessaly at the head of an army to assist the Federation.   Before he left Thebes, the sun

Eclipse of
the sun,
July 13.
suffered an eclipse, and this celestial event, interpreted by the prophets as a sign of coming evil, cast a gloom over his departure.

Battle of
Cynos-
cephalae.
At Pharsalus he was joined by forces of the Thessalian league, and immediately advanced against Pherae itself.   Alexander came forth to meet him with a large force, and it was a matter of great importance, for the purpose of barring the Theban advance, to occupy the heights known as the Dog's Heads, on the road from Pharsalus to Pherae.   The armies reached the critical spot nearly at the same time, and there was a rush for the crests.   The Theban cavalry beat off the cavalry of the foe, but lost time in pursuing it, and in the meantime the infantry of Alexander seized the hills.   In the battle which followed the object of the Thebans was to drive the enemy from this position.   Having been repeatedly repelled, Pelopidas, anticipating the tactics of Alexander, by a combined assault of horse and foot, at length won the summit and forced the enemy to give way.   But in the moment of victory the impetuous general espied the hated despot in whose dungeon he had languished, and yielding to an irresistible fit of passion, he forgot the duties of a general and rushed against his enemy.   Alexander withdrew into

Death of
Pelopidas.
the midst of his guards, and Pelopidas, plunging desperately after him, was overwhelmed by numbers.   It was even so that Cyrus threw away his victory at Cunaxa.   The death of Pelopidas was not fatal to his followers, who routed the enemy with heavy loss ; but it

Thessaly
becomes a
Boeotian
dependency,
363 B.C.
was a sore blow both to his own Thebes, of which he had been the deliverer and strong pillar, and to Thessaly, of which he had been the protector.   In the following year an army was sent against Pherae, and avenged his death.   Alexander was obliged to relinquish all his possessions except his own city and submit to the headship of Thebes.

The
destruction
of Orcho-
menus,
364 B.C.
It was about this time that Thebes shocked the Hellenic world by the destruction of her venerable rival, the Minyan Orchomenus. Some Theban exiles induced the horsemen of Orchomenus to join them in a plot to subvert the constitution.   But, the hearts of the principal conspirators failing them before the day of action came, they informed the Boeotarchs ; the horsemen were promptly seized and condemned to death ; and the Assembly passed a resolution to rase Orchomenus and enslave its people.   The Thebans rejoiced at a fair pretext to wreak the hatred of ages upon their unhappy

neighbour.   They marched forth and executed the doom ; the men
were slain because they resisted, the rest of the folk were enslaved.
It was a deed on which Greece cried shame ; and, if the moderate
and humane Boeotarch, who was then in the Hellespontine regions,
had been present to control the counsels of his country, it would
possibly never have been committed.

SECT. 4.   THE BATTLE OF MANTINEA

While Thebes was intent on opposing Athens, now her only
serious rival, she had kept aloof from the Peloponnesus.   But the
course of affairs there was soon to demand a new intervention.   The
interest now centres on the relations of Elis
with Arcadia ; and the decisive element in the
situation is the rift in the Arcadian league,
perceptibly widening every month.

Her rights over Triphylia were the chief
question of political importance for Elis.   They
had been recognised in the Persian rescript, but
Arcadia refused to admit them and Thebes did
not interfere.   Thus Elis found herself in the
same plight as Sparta in regard to the Arcadian
league.   It had always been a principle of
Lacedaemonian policy to preserve against Elis the independence of her
two southern neighbours, the Pisatans and the Triphylians.   But now
Sparta was only too ready to renounce this policy and recognise the
Elean claim, for the sake of winning an ally.   It was in the nature of
things that the two states should combine to recover Messenia and
Triphylia.   Thus there came to pass a change for the better in the
prospect of Sparta : enemies had risen up against Arcadia on the
north and on the west, and Thebes held aloof.   The Spartans had
recently gained a welcome success in the recovery of Sellasia, with
the help of a force which had been sent to their aid by the second
Dionysius of Syracuse.

The Triphylian question.

FIG. 160.—Coin of Elis
(obverse). Eagle tear-
ing a hare on shield.

Besides Triphylia there were certain places on the mountainous *Outbreak*
frontier between Elis and Arcadia to which Elis professed to have *of war*
claims.   One of these was Lasion, in the high plateau of Pholoe, *between*
north-east of Olympia.   The Eleans occupied the district, but were *Elis and*
speedily driven out by the Pan-Arcadian *eparitoi*, who were always *Arcadia,*
ready for such emergencies.   The plains of Elis were far more assail- *365 B.C.*
able than the highlands of Arcadia, and the Arcadians were able to *First*
carry the war to the very heart of their foe.   The Olympian festival *Arcadian*
would fall next year, and they were resolved that it should not be *invasion of*
celebrated under the time-honoured presidency of Elis.   They marched *Elis, 365 B.C.*

to Olympia, and occupied and fortified the Hill of Cronus, which looks down upon the Altis. Then they made an attack on the unwalled city of Elis, in concert with the democratic faction. But the *Second* attempt at a revolution failed and the Arcadians were repulsed. In *Arcadian* the following year a second invasion reduced the Eleans to such dis-*invasion,* tress that they implored Sparta to make a diversion and draw off the *364 B.C.* Arcadian forces. In answer to this prayer Archidamus occupied Cromnon, a fort which commands the road from Megalopolis to Messenia, with a garrison of 200 men. The importance of this step is shown by the fact that not only did the Arcadians promptly leave Elis, but they were also joined by allies, Argives as well as Messenians, to besiege Cromnon. A Spartan post there cut off the communication between the Arcadian and the Messenian capitals and was a threat to both. Archidamus at first tried to create a second diversion by ravaging northern Laconia, which was now politically part of Arcadia. When this failed, he made an attempt to relieve Cromnon, but was driven back with some loss. A second attempt at rescue would have been successful, if it had been better concerted, but it led

to the capture of almost the whole garrison ; an event which ten years before would have sent a shock through the Hellenic world, but now seemed an ordinary occurrence.

The The Arcadians were again free to continue *Olympian* their designs in Elis. The time of the Olym-*games,* pian games was approaching, and the people of *364 B.C.,* Pisa, the ancient possessors of the sanctuary, *July,* who had by no means forgotten the rights *celebrated* which Elis had usurped in days long gone by, *by the* were installed as presidents of the festival. *Pisatans* It was fully expected that the feast would *(Ol. 104).* not pass without battle and bloodshed. The

FIG. 161.—Coin of Elis (reverse). Seated Victory with palm; olive twig below [legend : *FA*].

hill of Cronus had been occupied for a year by the Arcadian garrison, but now the whole army of the federation, as well as 2000 spearmen from Argos and 400 cavalry from Athens, arrived to protect the solemn celebration. The day came round and the games began. The horse race was run and won. The next contest was the pentathlon, which demanded excellence in five different kinds of athletic prowess—in running, wrestling, hurling the javelin, throwing the disc, and leaping. The first event, the race, was over when the company became aware that the men of Elis were marching up to the bank of the Cladeus, which bounded the western side of the Altis. The soldiers took up their position on the opposite bank, but the games went on. Those competitors who had not failed in the race proceeded to the wrestling ; but as the spectators, when the alarm was given, moved from the race-course into the Altis, to be nearer the scene of action, the wrestling match was held in the open space between the race-course and the Great Altar, under the terrace of the Treasure-houses. The Eleans, who were supported by an Achaean force, performed a sacrifice, and then, charging across the stream with unexpected boldness, drove back the Arcadian and Argive line into the Altis. A battle ensued in the southern part of the holy pre- *Battle in* cinct, between the Hall of Council and the great Temple of Zeus. *the Altis.* But the colonnades of these and other adjacent buildings gave shelter and points of vantage to the defenders ; and the Eleans, when their captain fell, retired across the stream to their camp. The Arcadians improvised a fortification on the western side of the Altis, using for this purpose the tents of the spectators ; and the men of Elis, seeing that it would be useless to repeat their attack, returned home, obliged to content themselves with declaring the festival to be null and void, and marking the year in their register as an "An-Olympiad." The religious sentiment of Greece was outraged by these violent scenes at a sanctuary which belonged to all Greece rather than to any single state ; and there can be no question that the general sympathy—independently of all political considerations —was on the side of Elis, whose presidency was regarded in Hellas as part of the order of nature, and was strongly adverse to the Arcadian intruders supporting with arms the antiquated rights of Pisa. But it was far worse when the Arcadians began to make *Spoliation* free use of the sacred treasures of Olympia, for the purpose of *of the* paying the federal army. This was an act of sacrilegious spoliation *Olympian* which could not be defended, and it was disastrous to the Arcadian *treasures.* Federation.

It was inevitable that, when the first impulse of enthusiasm which *Divisions* drove the Arcadian cities to unite together had spent itself, the old *in the* jealousies would emerge again and imperil the Pan-Arcadian idea. *Arcadian* So it was that the two neighbours, Mantinea and Tegea, whose *League.* common action had been the chief cause of the federal union, began to resume something of their traditional enmity. The scandal of Olympia gave Mantinea, who was jealous of Megalopolis also, a fair opportunity to secede from the League, which had put itself so signally in the wrong. This step necessarily involved the consequence that Mantinea would definitely range herself with the other camp in the Peloponnesus—with Sparta, Elis, and Achaea. And thus the traditional policies of Mantinea and Tegea were reversed. Tegea, the support of Sparta, had become the life and soul of the anti-Spartan movement ; Mantinea, the state which Sparta had uncitied, was now Sparta's support. Though the Arcadian Assembly resented and tried to punish the protest of Mantinea, the pressure of public opinion induced it to forbid any further plundering of the Olympian sanctuaries.

When this resolution was taken, the weakness of the Arcadian League was exhibited. There was no money in the federal treasury to pay the standing army, and without this army it would be impossible for Arcadia to maintain herself against enemies on three sides—not to speak of disaffected Mantinea—without the protection of Thebes. But there was a strong feeling throughout the country against a Theban protectorate, and a large number of wealthy Arcadians, who shared this feeling, proposed to solve the difficulty by enrolling themselves in the corps of *Eparitoi* and serving without pay. Occupying this position they would be able to dictate the policy of the League. There was little doubt that the predominance of this party would soon bring Arcadia into alliance with Sparta, which was no longer dangerous to Arcadian liberty. But such a political revolution would be fatal to Theban influence, which rested on the antagonism between Arcadia and Sparta; it might even imperil the independence of Messenia.

Fourth Theban invasion of the Peloponnesus, 362 B.C.
To meet this danger of an alliance between Sparta and Arcadia, Thebes was constrained to send a fourth expedition into the Peloponnese. It was imperative to support the Theban party in Arcadia. Both parties alike were probably satisfied with the resolution of the Assembly to make peace with Elis and acknowledge her rights at Olympia. Each city swore to the peace. At Tegea the solemnity of the oath led to an incident. Arcadians from other places had gathered together for the occasion, which they celebrated by feast and merriment. The commander of the Boeotian garrison ordered the gates to be shut and arrested the leaders of the anti-Theban party. Most of the Mantineans present had left the town at an early hour, but there were a few among the prisoners; and the energetic protests of Mantinea frightened the faint-hearted harmost into releasing all his prisoners and excusing his act by a false explanation. The *coup* had doubtless been planned long beforehand, and consent obtained from the highest quarter. Epaminondas, when complaint was made at Thebes, approved the act of arrest, and condemned the act of release. At the same time he declared to the Arcadian League that it had no right to make peace with Elis without consulting Thebes. "We will march into Arcadia," he said, "and assist our friends."

The quintuple alliance, summer, 362 B.C.
The threat was seriously meant, and the friends and enemies of Thebes prepared for war. Athens, the ally of both Sparta and Arcadia, could now fulfil without difficulty the double obligation, by supporting those Arcadians who were on Sparta's side. The common dread of Thebes was reflected in the quintuple alliance which Athens

(with her allies), Mantinea, Elis, Achaia, and Phlius formed for the sake of mutual protection.[1] Part of the text of this treaty is preserved to us on fragments of one of the original marble copies. It is worthy of remark that the Mantineans, who seem to have been the only Arcadian community that entirely dissociated itself from the government at Megalopolis, appear in the treaty as "the Arcadians" —thus claiming to be the true representatives of their country.

The Boeotian force in its full strength, accompanied by all the allies of central Greece who were pledged to follow Thebes into the field, went forth under Epaminondas to bring back the unruly Peloponnesians under Boeotian control. The Phocians alone refused to go ; the terms of the alliance which bound them to Boeotia obliged them to bear aid only if Boeotia were itself attacked. When he reached Nemea, Epaminondas halted his army, with the hope of intercepting the forces which Athens prepared to send to her allies. But the Athenian forces came not and he advanced to Tegea, the chief centre of Theban influence in the peninsula, which he had appointed as the meeting-place for all his allies—Arcadian, Argive, and Messenian. His enemies were also gathering to the rival city of Mantinea, and a Spartan army under old Agesilaus was expected there. Epaminondas marched to attack them before the Spartans and Athenians arrived, but found their position too strong and retired to his camp in Tegea. Learning that Agesilaus had already *March of* set out, he determined to strike a second blow at Sparta. He *Epami-* would have found the place as unprotected as "a nest of young *nondas* birds," if his plan had not been thwarted by a Cretan runner who *to Sparta.* carried the news to Agesilaus. The king immediately returned on his steps ; and when Epaminondas after a night's march reached Sparta, he found it prepared and defended. Baffled in this project by an incalculable chance, Epaminondas promptly resolved to attempt another surprise. He foresaw that the army at Mantinea would immediately march to the rescue of Sparta, and that Mantinea would consequently be inadequately guarded. His camp at Tegea commanded the direct road from Mantinea to Sparta, so that the enemy would be obliged to march by the longer western road. Moving rapidly he reached Tegea, where he rested his *He returns* hoplites, but he sent on his cavalry to surprise Mantinea. The *to Tegea.* army had departed, as he calculated, and the people were out in the fields, busy with the harvest. But in the same hour in which the Theban horse approached from the south, a body of Athenian cavalry had reached the city. They had not yet eaten or drunk, *Cavalry* but they rode forth and drove the assailants back. The conflict *battle at* *Mantinea.*

[1] The preliminaries must have been arranged in the early summer, but the date of the final treaty was later than the battle of Mantinea.

between the two weary troops of horsemen was sharp, and was marked by the death of Gryllus, the son of Xenophon the historian.

The allied army, learning that Sparta was no longer in danger, soon returned from its fruitless excursion to its former post, now reinforced by both the Spartan and Athenian contingents. Foiled in his two projects of surprise, Epaminondas was obliged to attack the united enemy at Mantinea ; the difficulty of supplying his army with provisions, and the anxiety of his allies to return home as soon as possible, rendered it imperative to bring the campaign to a swift decision. The enemy occupied the narrow part of the plain, south of Mantinea, where ridges of the opposite mountains approach each other ; the object of Epaminondas was to sweep them out of his way and take the city. But instead of marching straight for the gap, he adopted a strategical movement which puzzled his antagonists. He led his army north-westwards to a point in the hills near the modern Tripolitza, and then moved a short distance along the skirts of the mountain so as to approach the right wing of the foe. He then halted and formed in battle array. The enemy were deceived by the indirect advance. Seeing him march obliquely towards the hills, they concluded that he would not attack that day, and even when he changed his direction and advanced towards them, persisted in their false opinion.

Disposi-tions of Epami-nondas.

Epaminondas adopted the same tactics by which he had won at Leuctra. On the left he placed the Boeotian hoplites, under his own immediate command, in a deep column, destined to break through the right wing of the enemy before the rest of the armies could come to blows. The oblique advance, besides its chief purpose of deceiving the foe, had the further advantage of assisting the peculiar tactics of the general ; for, when he formed his line, there was obviously a far greater distance between his right and the hostile left than that which divided his left from the hostile right. The Mantineans (since it was their territory) had the place of honour on the extremity of the enemy's right wing, and the Lacedaemonians were next them ; the Athenians were on the farthest left ; and both wings were protected by squadrons of horse. Epaminondas placed his own cavalry in deep column in front of the deep column of infantry. But there was one danger against which he had to guard. When the Boeotian column charged, the Athenian left might wheel round and attack it on the unshielded side—a movement which could be executed owing to the distance dividing them from his own right. To meet this danger, he sent a body of horse and foot to occupy a rising ground, out in the plain, considerably in advance of his line ; this body could attack the Athenians in the rear if they tried such a movement.

With an extraordinary lack of perception, the Lacedaemonians
and their allies witnessed these manœuvres without understanding
their drift ; and it was not until Epaminondas began to advance in
full march against them, that they realised his meaning and rushed
tumultuously to arms.   All fell out as he designed.   His cavalry
routed their cavalry, and the force of his wedge of hoplites, led by
himself, broke through the opposing array and put the Lacedaemonians
to flight.   It is remarkable indeed how the tactical lesson of Leuctra
seems to have been lost on the Spartans.   The men of Achaea and
Elis and the rest, when they saw the flight of the right wing,
wavered before they came into collision with their own opponents.
It is not quite clear what happened, but here again Mantinea seems
to repeat Leuctra : the charge of the Theban left decided the
battle ; with the exception of cavalry engagements, there was but
little and desultory fighting along the rest of the line.

It was a great Theban victory, and yet a chance determined that
this victory should be the deathblow to the supremacy of Thebes.
As he pursued the retreating foe, at the head of his Thebans, Epami- *Death of*
nondas received a mortal thrust from a spear.   When the news *Epami-*
spread through the field, the pursuit was stayed and the effect of the *nondas.*
victory was undone ; the troops fell back like beaten men.   " So
striking a proof has hardly ever been rendered, on the part of
soldiers towards their general, of devoted and absorbing sentiment.
All the hopes of this army, composed of such diverse elements, were
centred in Epaminondas ; all their confidence of success, all their
security against defeat, were derived from the idea of acting under
his orders ; all their power, even of striking down a defeated enemy,
appeared to vanish when those orders were withdrawn." [1]   And
there was no one to take his place.   In his dying moments, before
the point of the fatal spear was extracted, Epaminondas asked for
Iolaidas and Daiphantus, whom he destined as his successors.   He
was told that they were slain.   " Then," he said, " make peace with
the enemy."   Peace was made on condition that things should
remain as they were ; Megalopolis and Messenia were recognised—
the abiding results of Theban policy.   In this peace Sparta would
not acquiesce ; she still persisted in refusing to recognise the
independence of Messenia, but her allies would not listen to her
protests.

The military genius of Epaminondas, the qualities of mind and *The work*
character which distinguished him among his countrymen, and the *of Epami-*
actual work which he accomplished in the deliverance of Messenia *nondas.*
and the support of Arcadia, must not be suffered to obscure the fact

[1] Grote.

that his political faculty was mediocre. What could be done by the energy and ability of a general, or by the discretion of a magistrate, that he did ; but he failed to solve the fundamental problems which demanded solution at the hands of a statesman who aimed at making his country great. It was necessary to create an efficient machinery, acting on definite principles, for conducting the foreign affairs of Boeotia—like the machinery which existed at Sparta. This was the only possible substitute for brains, which were not plentiful in Boeotia ; Epaminondas could not hope to communicate any part of his own virtue to his successors. It was necessary to decide whether it was possible or desirable for Boeotia to enter into competition with Athens as a maritime power. If the decision were affirmative, it was of capital importance to organise the navy on a sound financial foundation. There is no sign that Epaminondas grappled with the problems of government and finance; his voyage to the Propontis was an experiment which had no results. Nor does he seem to have taken steps to secure Boeotia on the side of her dangerous Phocian neighbours, though he had the insight to organise anew the Amphictionic League and make it an instrument of Theban policy. Above all, he did not succeed in accomplishing the first thing needful, the welding together of Boeotia into a real national unity. He aspired to expand Boeotia into an empire ; the worst of it was that no one had come before him to make it into a nation. That which mythical Lycurgus and Theseus had done for Sparta and Athens had never been done for Thebes by any of her numerous heroes. Epaminondas seems to have attempted to unify Boeotia ; if he had known how to build such an unity on solid foundations, he might have bestowed on Thebes a future of glory which he would not have lived to see. But his ambition—for his country, not for himself—was too impatient and imaginative. The ardour of his patriotism impelled him to enter upon paths of policy which his countrymen felt no resistless impulse to pursue ; the successes of Thebes were achieved by his brains, not by her force. He bore his country aloft on the wings of his genius, but did not impart to her frame the principle of that soaring motion ; so that when the shaft pierced the heart of her sustainer, she sank to the earth, never to rise again. Epaminondas was a great general ; he was not a great statesman.

SECT. 5. THE LAST EXPEDITION OF AGESILAUS

To no one in Greece can the supremacy of Thebes have come as a sorer trial than to the Spartan king Agesilaus. He who had once dreamed of conquering Persia had lived to see his own inviolable

land twice trodden by an invader, his own city quake twice before
an enemy at her doors.   But he had at least the consolation of
outliving the triumph of the Theban, and seeing the brief supremacy
pass away.   The death of Epaminondas, of which he could not
mistake the significance, did not restore Messenia or give Sparta any
immediate power ; but, Epaminondas dead and Arcadia spent,
Sparta had now a prospect of regaining something of her old
influence.   With her own diminished population she could do little ;
it would be necessary to follow the general example and take *Sparta in*
mercenary forces into her pay ; but to do this a well-filled treasury *want of*
was needful.   Accordingly we find Sparta, as well as Athens, busy *money.*
beyond the sea, taking part in the troubles which in these years
agitated the western portion of the Persian kingdom, and lending
help to the satraps and dynasts who were rebelling against the Great
King.   The object of Athens was territory, the object of Sparta was
money.   While Timotheus had been engaged in winning Samos, *365 B.C.*
Agesilaus had visited Asia Minor and done his utmost in support
of Ariobarzanes—for the sake of gold.   And after the battle of
Mantinea, he again went forth in a guise which differed little from
that of a mercenary in foreign service.

The borders of Western Asia, from the Hellespont to the Nile, *The revolt*
were in revolt against the Great King.   The expedition of Cyrus *in the*
was only the first of a series of rebellions which troubled the reign of *Persian*
Artaxerxes.   We have seen how Cyprus rebelled and was subjugated, *empire.*
but Egypt still defied the Persian power, and its success set a bad
example to the satraps of the adjoining countries.   The Athenian
general Chabrias had helped the Egyptians to strengthen their
country by a scientific system of defences, but he was recalled to
Athens after the King's Peace ; and the Athenian whom we next *373 B.C.*
find in Egypt is fighting on the other side—the free-lance Iphicrates,
giving sound military advice to the Persian commander, which the
Persian commander does not follow.   Soon after this the satraps of
Asia began to rebel—first in Cappadocia, then in Phrygia, then
successively in Ionia, Caria, and Lydia—and the insurrection extended to Phoenicia and Syria.   A scheme of co-operation was
formed between the satraps and the Egyptian king Tachos, who had
recently come to the throne, and Sparta decided to support this
coalition.   Athens held aloof, but Chabrias went once more to
Egypt as a volunteer.

At the head of a thousand men, and accompanied by thirty *Agesilaus*
Spartans as advisers, Agesilaus set sail for the Nile.   It is said that *in Egypt,*
the small figure, the lame leg, and the plain dress of the experienced *361 B.C.*
old soldier made a bad impression in Egypt ; in any case he was
not given the supreme command of the army as he expected.   When

a sufficient force was gathered, Tachos, accompanied by Agesilaus and Chabrias, made an expedition to Phoenicia, to act there against the Persian troops ; but they were obliged to return almost immediately in consequence of a revolt against Tachos, headed by his cousin Nektanebos. The Spartan king, who considered that he had been slighted by Tachos, supported the rival ; and Tachos fled to Susa and made his peace with the Persian monarch. Another competitor then arose, but was defeated by the effective support which Agesilaus gave to Nektanebos. In consequence of these struggles for the Egyptian throne nothing was done against Persia, and the great coalition signally failed. Ariobarzanes of Phrygia, the friend of Timotheus, was betrayed and crucified ; another satrap was murdered ; the rest made their submission to their king. By 358 Western Asia was entirely subject to Artaxerxes.

But Sparta had won from the futile project what she really wanted. She might shelter her dignity under the pretext that she had gone forth to punish the Persian king for recognising the independence of Messenia, but every one knew that her motive was to replenish her treasury. Nektanebos presented her with 230 talents, in return for the support of Agesilaus. It was the last service the old king was destined to perform for his country. Death carried

Death of Agesilaus, winter, 361-0 B.C. (?).

FIG. 162.—Coin of Cyrene (reverse). Four-horsed chariot, driven by Victory [legend : KΥΡΑΝΑΙΟΝ].

him off—he was eighty-four years old—at the Harbour of Menelaus on the way to Cyrene, and his embalmed body was sent home to Sparta.

Though not in any sense a great man, though not in the same rank as Lysander, Agesilaus had been for forty years a prominent figure in Greece. There is something melancholy about his career. He could remember the outbreak of the Peloponnesian War; he had seen the triumph of Sparta, and had conducted her policy during a great part of thirty years of supremacy ; and then, as an old man, he shared in her humiliation. He had begun by dreaming of the conquest of Persia ; he had been forced to abandon such dreams ; and he had translated his ardour into a bitter hatred against an Hellenic city. It is tragic to see him, at the age of eighty-three, going forth against Persia once more, not now for conquest or glory, but to earn by any and every means the money needed by his indigent country.

CHAPTER XV

THE SYRACUSAN EMPIRE AND THE STRUGGLE WITH CARTHAGE

WE have seen how the war in Greece, in its last stage, after the *Parallel* collapse of the Sicilian expedition, ceased to be a mere domestic *between* struggle among Greek states and became part of the greater struggle *struggle of* between Greek and barbarian. We have now to see how the strife *western* of Greek and barbarian was renewed at the same moment in the *with* west. It is indeed remarkable how these two episodes in the great *Carthage* conflict between Asia and Europe run parallel though separate *and* courses in the fifth century. The victory of Himera, which beat *eastern* back the Carthaginian invader from the shores of Sicily, was won *with* in the same year which saw the repulsion of the Persian invader *Persia.* from the shores of Attica. After these triumphs of Hellas, both Persia and Carthage had long lain quiescent, and left the Greek cities of east and west to live undisturbed at war or in peace among themselves. It was not till the mightiest city of eastern and the mightiest city of western Hellas came to blows and wore one another out in the conflict, that the barbarian foes, discerning the propitious hour, once more made their voices heard in the Grecian world. Sicily with an exhausted Syracuse, the Aegean with an exhausted Athens, invited Carthage and Persia alike to make an attempt to enlarge their borders at the expense of the Greek.

SECT I. CARTHAGINIAN DESTRUCTION OF SELINUS AND HIMERA

After she had achieved the repulse and utter confusion of *Results of* Athens, it might have seemed likely that Syracuse would succeed *the Syra-* in founding a Sicilian empire. Her first task would be to reduce *cusan* Catane and Naxos ; and, when this was done, the other cities, in- *victory.* cluding luxurious Acragas, would hardly be able to resist. This prospect was disappointed by the intervention of a foreign enemy. But, though the victory of Syracuse over Athens did not lead to a Syracusan empire, as the victory of Athens over Persia had led to an Athenian empire, it was followed, as in the case of Athens, by a *Advance in* further advance in the development of democracy. Had Hermo-*democracy.* crates remained at Syracuse, in possession of his old influence, a change in this direction would hardly have come to pass. But he was appointed to command the auxiliary fleet which Syracuse sent to Sparta's help in the Aegean ; and, when he had gone, the democratic mood of the citizens, excited by their recent efforts, vented itself in a decree pronouncing the deposition and banishment of *Diocles :* Hermocrates. This was the work of his political opponent Diocles, who was a thoroughgoing democrat. Diocles bore the same name as a far earlier lawgiver—belonging to the same class and age as Charondas and Zaleucus—who had drawn up the laws on which the Syracusan constitution rested. The accidental identity of name led in subsequent ages to a confusion, and we find later writers ascribing to the democratic reformer, who rose into prominence now, the *his* legislation of his ancient namesake. In his popular innovations *reforms.* Diocles borrowed ideas from the enemy whom his country had just

overthrown. The Athenian use of lot in the appointment of magistrates was adopted. Hitherto the generals were also the presidents of the sovereign assembly, and had the unrestricted power of dismissing it at discretion. Diocles seems to have taken away this political function from the generals, and assigned the presidency of the assembly to the new magistrates, but with much smaller powers. The presidents, as we shall

Fig. 163.—Coin of Syracuse, *c.* 410 B.C., engraved by Cimon (obverse). Head of Arethusa, amid dolphins [legend : ΣΤΡΑΚΟΣΙΩΝ ; signature of ΚΙΜΩΝ on dolphin below].

presently see, were able only to fine a speaker who was out of order ; they could not silence him or break up the assembly.

Such was the position of the greatest Sicilian city—a full-blown democracy, but without her chief citizen to whom above all others she owed the deliverance from her danger— when the island was exposed for the second time to a Cartha-*Pretext* ginian invasion. The occasion of the war was the same which *and cause* had brought about the Athenian invasion—the feud between *of the war* Selinus and Segesta concerning some fields on their common *with* *Carthage.* frontier. In both cases, the dispute of these towns was a pre-

text, not the deeper cause. As Athens thought that the time
had come for extending her commerce in the west, so Carthage
deemed that the day had dawned for asserting anew her power
in Sicily ; and there were those who had not let fade the memory
of the humiliation endured at Himera seventy years before and
longed to take a late revenge.

Segesta, with no Athens to protect her now, ceded the disputed 410 *B.C.*
lands ; but Selinus went on to exact further cessions, and the
Elymian city appealed to Carthage. One of the two shophets or
judges in that republic was Hannibal, the grandson of Hamilcar,
who had been slain at Himera. The desire of vengeance, long
deferred, dominated Hannibal, now almost an old man ; and his
influence persuaded the Senate to accept Segesta's offer to become a
Carthaginian dependency in return for Carthaginian help. A grand
expedition was fitted out, and Hannibal was named commander.
Sixty warships were got ready, with a large convoy of transports and
strong forces of foot and horse. The fleet was not intended to take *Second*
a part in the offensive warfare ; it was stationed at Motya to be a pro- *Cartha-*
tection for Phoenician Sicily and a security in case of discomfiture. *ginian*
The army landed at Lilybaeum and marched straight to Selinus. *invasion,*
This city had never been besieged before within the memory of its *409 B.C.*
folk ; immunity had made it secure ; the fortifications had been *Siege of*
neglected. For more than two generations the Selinuntines had been *Selinus.*
building a temple of vast proportions to Apollo, or perhaps Olympian
Zeus, when they were brought face to face with the sudden danger
from Carthage. The house of the god was never completed ; of the
" pillars of the giants " which were to support the massive roof some
stand in their places on the eastern hill, but the great drums and the
capitals of others must be looked for, some miles away, in the quarries
from which they were hewn, left there when the Carthaginian destroyer
came. There was no time to repair adequately the walls of the acropolis, on the central hill. Hannibal surrounded it and a breach was
soon made ; but the place was not in the foe's hands for nine days,
owing to the stubborn resistance which the inhabitants were able to
offer in the narrow streets. The Siceliot sister cities were not prompt
in aid ; Syracuse promised to come to the rescue, and sent a force
under Diocles, which arrived too late. Selinus was the first *Destruc-*
Siceliot city which was stormed and sacked by the barbarian ; she *tion of*
was not to be the last. The people were slaughtered without *Selinus.*
mercy ; only some women and children who took refuge in the
temples were spared (not from any respect of the holy places)
and carried into bondage. Those who escaped from the sack
fled to Acragas. Thus Selinus fell, after a brief life of two centuries
and a half.

Hannibal as avenger. Hannibal had now done the work which Carthage had given him to do ; but he had still to do the work which he had imposed upon himself. His real motive, in undertaking the public duty of the Selinuntine war, was to carry out the private duty of ancestral vengeance. Against Selinus he had no personal grudge, and there he did not carry the work of destruction further than military considerations required. The buildings on the western hill, where he had pitched his camp, suffered much ; but the injuries sustained by the temples on the acropolis and on the eastern hill are due, not to Hannibal's army, but to the earthquakes of later ages. It was to be different in the case of the city which he now turned to attack. At Selinus, Hannibal was merely the general of Carthage ; at Himera, he was the grandson of Hamilcar.

Siege of Himera. Hannibal designed to capture Himera by his land forces alone ; and in this absence of a Carthaginian fleet Hannibal's siege of Himera differs from Hamilcar's. The Greeks of Sicily were now bestirring themselves ; the terrible fate of one of their chief cities had aroused them to a sense of their peril. The naval power which was supporting Sparta in the Aegean had been long ago recalled ; and a force of 5000, including 3000 Syracusans, under Diocles, came to the relief of Himera. This city had time to prepare for the danger which she must have foreseen. But the besiegers, by means of mines, opened a breach in the wall ; and, although they were repelled and the defenders made a successful sally, the prospects of Himera looked black, when the fleet of 25 ships, which had returned from the Aegean, appeared in front of the city. Hannibal saved the situation by a stratagem. He spread abroad a report that he intended to march on Syracuse and take it unprepared. Diocles, thoroughly deceived, decided to return home and carry off the citizens of Himera, leaving the empty town to its fate. He induced half the population to embark in the ships, which, as soon as they had set the passengers in safety at Messana, were to return for the rest. Diocles and his army departed in haste, not even waiting to ask Hannibal for the dead bodies of those who had fallen in fight outside the walls ; and for this neglect he was greatly blamed. When Hannibal saw that half his prey had escaped him, he pressed the siege more vehemently, determined to force an entry before the ships returned. The fate of thousands, the vengeance of Hannibal, might *Third day of the siege.* turn on the event of a few minutes. On the third day, the vessels of safety hove in sight of the straining eyes of the Himeraeans. It seemed that Hannibal was to be baulked of his revenge. But the gods of Canaan prevailed in that hour of suspense. Before the ships of rescue could reach the harbour, the Spanish troops of Hannibal burst through the breach, and the town was in the hands of the avenger. On the spot where Hamilcar, according to the story, had offered up his life to the gods of his country, a solemn rite was held ; 3000 men, who had survived the first indiscriminate slaughter, were sacrificed with torture to appease his shade. Himera, the offending city, was swept utterly out of the world and its place knew it no more.

Having thus accomplished his duty to his country and his gods, Hannibal returned triumphant to Africa. The position which Carthage won in Sicily by this year's work, and her new policy of activity there, are reflected in the coinage of Segesta and Panormus. The transformation of Segesta into a Carthaginian dependency was displayed by the fact that she ceased to coin her own money. But Carthage also showed that she intended to keep a firmer hand on her Phoenician dependencies.

These cities had hitherto paid homage to Hellenic influences by adopting a coinage of Hellenic character, with Hellenic inscriptions. This coinage now comes to an end at Panormus, and is replaced by a coinage, of Greek type indeed, but with a Phoenician legend—the word *Ziz*. The change seems to have been made just before the invasion,

FIG. 164.—Silver coin of Panormus. Obverse : female head with sphendone. Reverse : dog ; mussel above [Punic legend : ΖΙΖ].

New coinage at Panormus with mysterious legend— Ziz.

and it was significant of an anti-Greek movement. But the curious thing is that Himera—the city which was to be one of the first victims of the new policy heralded in this numismatic reform— abandoned her old coinage with the cock, and struck a new coinage with a sea-horse, on the Punic model of Panormus. Are we to *Change in* suppose that Himera, aware of the peril which menaced her, *Himera's* thought to avert it by a timely approach of friendship to her *coinage.* Phoenician neighbour, and that this coinage was part of a policy of Punicism, intended to be only temporary ?

Syracuse, although she had sought to do something for Selinus and had done something for Himera, felt no call to come forward as a champion against the new aggressive policy of Carthage. It was reserved for one of her citizens to attempt on his private responsibility the warfare which she declined to undertake against the Phoenician foe. The exile Hermocrates returned to Sicily, enriched by the gifts *Return of* of the satrap Pharnabazus. His own city refused to withdraw the *Hermo-* sentence of banishment, for a man of his views and abilities seemed *crates,* dangerous to the democratic constitution. Hermocrates then *408 B.C.* resolved to earn his recall by performing conspicuous services to the Hellenic cause in Sicily,—by winning back the Greek territory which the Phoenician had taken, by carrying Greek arms into *His* Phoenician territory itself. He had built five triremes, he had *warfare* hired 1000 mercenaries, and he was joined by 1000 Himeraean *against the* fugitives. With these he marched to the spot where Selinus had *Phoenician cities.* once been, and made the place a centre for a "crusade" against *Selinus* the Phoenician. He repaired the fortifications of the acropolis *reoccupied.* on the central hill ; and the remains of the well-built wall betray, by the capitals of columns used in the building, the circumstances of its erection. The adventure prospered ; the band of Hermocrates soon increased to 6000, and he was able to devastate the lands of Motya and Panormus, and to drive back the forces which came out to meet him. In the same way he ravaged the territory of Solus and the now Carthaginian Segesta. These successes of Hermocrates were of greater significance than the actual injury dealt to the enemy. He had done what had not been done before (since the days of Dorieus [1]) ; he had broken into the precincts of Phoenician Sicily, and set an example to many subsequent leaders.

Hermo- Hermocrates was bent, above all things, on regaining his own *crates at* country. Diocles and his political opponents were still powerful in *Himera,* the city, and able to hinder the revulsion of feeling which his successes *407 B.C. :* caused from having any practical effect. Accordingly he made another *he sends* attempt to soften the hearts of his fellow-citizens. It was a well-*the bones* calculated move. He marched to the ruins of Himera, collected *of the dead* the unburied bones of the soldiers of Diocles which Diocles had *to Syra-* neglected, and sent them on waggons to Syracuse, himself remaining *cuse ;* as an exile outside the Syracusan borders. He hoped to awaken the religious sentiment of the citizens in his own favour and at the same time to turn it against his rival. The bones were received and Diocles was banished ; but Hermocrates was not recalled. *he breaks* Having failed to compass his restoration by persuasion, the exile *into Syra-* resolved to compass it by force ; and he was encouraged by his *cuse and* numerous partisans in Syracuse. He was admitted with a small *is slain.* band at the gate of Achradina, and posted himself in the adjacent agora waiting for the rest of his forces to arrive. But they tarried too long ; the people, learning that Hermocrates was in the city, rushed to the market-place ; the small band was soon overcome and Hermocrates was slain. The Syracusans in these days were inspired with an instinctive rather than well-founded dread of tyranny ; and this dread was stronger than admiration for Hermocrates. Their instinct was right ; tyranny was approaching, but *he* was not the

[1] See above, p. 208.

man. They little guessed that their future master was an obscure *(Diony-*
follower of Hermocrates, who was wounded that day in the agora *sius.)*
and left for dead.

FIG. 165.—Coin of Syracuse, engraved
by Cimon (obverse). Head of
Arethusa [legend : ΑΡΕΘΟΣΑ ;
signature of ΚΙΜΩΝ on headband].

FIG. 166.—Coin of Acragas
(obverse). Eagle tearing hare ;
shell as symbol of the seashore
[legend : ΑΚΡΑΓΑΝΤΙΝΩΝ].

SECT. 2. CARTHAGINIAN CONQUEST OF ACRAGAS

The private warfare of Hermocrates in western Sicily had
naturally provoked the wrath of the Carthaginians.   Embassies
passed between Carthage and Syracuse, Carthage regarding
Syracuse as answerable for the acts of a Syracusan.   But diplomacy
was merely a matter of form ; the African
republic had resolved to make all Greek Sicily
subject to her sway.   She made ready another
great expedition—as great as if not greater
than that which had been sent against Selinus ;
and at the same time she took the novel step of
founding a colony on Sicilian soil.   If Hermocrates had lived, Himera might have been partially
restored like Selinus ; but the destroyers of
Himera now founded a city in the neighbourhood which was to take Himera's place.   On
the hill above the " hot baths of the Nymphs,"
whereof Pindar sings, the Carthaginian colonists
built their town. But it was not destined to retain

*Founda-
tion of
Cartha-
ginian
colony at
Thermae,
407 B.C.*

FIG. 167.—Coin of
Acragas   (obverse).
Hare on rocks, under
two eagles ; head of
Pan [legend : ΣΤΡΑ-
ΤΩΝ].

*(Ter-
mini.)*

its Phoenician character. The Greek strangers who were admitted to *mini.)*
dwell in it transformed it before long into a Greek city ; the *Thermae*
of Himera preserved the memories of Himera, and the people were
known as Thermites or Himeraeans indifferently.

Acragas, the city which faces Carthage, was the first object of *Prepara-*
attack to the invaders who now came to conquer and enslave all *tions of*
Greek Sicily. Since the days of Theron, Acragas had held aloof from *Acragas.*

all struggles in the island and was now at the height of her prosperity. But she was enervated by peace and luxury, and, when the day of trial came, she was found wanting. How far her citizens were prepared to endure the hardships of military life may be inferred from the law—passed with a view to the present peril—that none of the men in the watch-towers should have more than a mattress, two pillows,

The Siege of
ACRAGAS,
B.C. 406.

English Miles

Walker & Boutall sc.

FIG. 168.

and a quilt. Such were the austerities of the men of Acragas. But at least they paid homage to the different discipline of Sparta. They invited Dexippus, a Spartan who was then at Gela, to undertake the conduct of the defence. A body of Campanian mercenaries was hired ; and they could rely on the assistance of their old rivals the Syracusans, as well as of the other Greek cities, who were fully conscious that the peril of Acragas was their own. And Acragas herself behaved well. Notwithstanding her habits of ease, and her old practice of holding aloof, she refused the tempting offer of the invader that she should now purchase immunity by remaining neutral. She was true to her own race ; she might remain indifferent when it was a struggle between Dorian and Ionian, but it was another case when the whole of Sicilian Hellas was threatened by the Phoenician.

The army of Carthage was again under the command of Hannibal, *406 B.C.* who felt that he was too old for the work, and was assisted by his cousin Himilco. They pitched their main camp on the right bank *Siege of* of the river Hypsas, south-west of the city, and stationed some forces *Acragas.* in another small camp on the eastern hill, beyond the river Acragas, to act against Greek aids coming from the east. The point of attack was the part of the western wall close to the chief western gate. But the ground, though lower here, was still difficult for a besieger, and Hannibal determined to raise an immense causeway from which the *The* wall could be more effectively attacked. The tombs of the neighbouring *causeway.* necropolis supplied stones for the work ; but, as the tomb of Theron was being broken down, it was shaken by a thunderbolt, and the seers advised that it must be spared. Then a pestilence broke out *Plague.* in the Carthaginian camp, and carried off Hannibal himself. It *Death of* seemed that the gods were wroth and demanded a victim ; Himilco *Hannibal.* lit the fires of Moloch and sacrificed a boy. The causeway was then completed, but no further injury was done to the sepulchres.

An army was already on its way to the relief of Acragas— *Relief* 30,000 foot and 5000 horse from Syracuse, Gela, and Camarina. *army* When they approached the city they were met by the forces which *arrives.* had been placed for this purpose on the eastern hill ; a battle was fought, a victory gained, and the Greek army took possession of the lesser Carthaginian camp. Meanwhile the routed barbarians fled for refuge to the main camp, and their flight lay along the road beneath the southern wall of the city. There was a general cry to sally forth and cut them off ; but the generals refused. The moment was lost ; but presently the people, yielding to an impulse which the generals could not resist, went forth from the eastern gates to meet their victorious allies. A strange scene followed. A tumultuous *Acragan-* assembly was held outside the walls ; the Acragantine commanders *tines* were accused of failing in their duty ; and, when they essayed to *murder* defend themselves, the fury of the people burst out and four generals *their* were stoned to death. The direction of the defence seems now to *generals.* have been shared by Dexippus within the city and Daphnaeus, the commander of the Syracusan troops, without. Though the hostile camp was too strong to be attacked, the prospect looked favourable for Acragas. The Punic army, diminished though it had been by the plague, was sore bestead for lack of supplies, and it seemed certain that hunger and mutinous soldiers would soon force Himilco to raise the siege. But he learned that provision-ships were coming from Syracuse to Acragas; he sent in haste for the Carthaginian vessels at Panormus and Motya, put out to sea with forty triremes, and intercepted the supplies. This not only saved his leaguer, but even reversed the situation. The besieged city now began to suffer from scarcity of food. And as soon as supplies began to run short, the weak point in the position of the Acragantines was displayed. They had found it needful to rely on mercenaries, and hirelings were not likely to serve long when rations ran short. The Campanians were easily induced to transfer their services from Acragas to Carthage. But this was not all. It was commonly believed that Dexippus—like most Spartans abroad, incapable of resisting a bribe—received fifteen talents from Himilco and induced the Italiot and Siceliot allies to desert Acragas as a sinking ship. But, whatever the conduct of Dexippus may have been, the discredit of this desertion cannot rest entirely with him.

Mercenaries and allies desert Acragas.

The defence, which had been maintained for eight months with foreign aid, was now left to the men of Acragas alone. They showed at once that they were shaped of different stuff from the men of Selinus. Overcome with despair, they resolved to save their lives and abandon their city and their gods. Such a resolution, taken by the people of a great city, is unique in Greek history. It did not befit the men who had rejected the overtures of Hannibal, but it was what we might expect from the men who murdered their generals. They marched forth at night, men, women, and children, without let or hindrance from the foe; "they were compelled to leave, for the barbarians to pillage, those things which made their lives happy." [1] The old and sick could not set out on the long journey to Gela, the place of refuge, and were left behind; some too remained who chose to perish at Acragas rather than live in another place. The army of Himilco entered the city in the morning and sacked it, slaying all whom they found, and despoiling and burning the temples. The great house of Olympian Zeus—the largest Greek temple in Europe—was still unfinished, and the sack of Himilco decided that it should never be completed. But Acragas was not to be destroyed like Selinus; it was intended to be a Carthaginian city in a Carthaginian Sicily. Himilco made the place his winter quarters; Gela would be the next object of his attack, when the spring came round.

Flight of the Acragantines.

406-5 *B.C.*

---

[1] Diodorus, from Philistus.

Sect. 3. Rise of Dionysius

For the catastrophe of Acragas the chief blame was laid upon the Syracusan generals, who deserted her in the critical hour. The Acragantines were not slow to make them responsible for their own unheroic flight. At Syracuse itself there was a feeling that these generals were hardly the men to meet the great jeopardy in which Sicily now stood ; and there was one man who saw in the jeopardy the opportunity of his own ambition. It was Dionysius, a man *Dionysius :* of obscure birth, who had been a clerk in a public office. He had been a partisan of Hermocrates, by whose side he had stood in the last fatal fray, and had been wounded and left for dead. Recently he had marked himself out by his energy and bravery before the walls of Acragas. He saw the incompetence of the democratic government of his city ; he saw that in the present peril it might be overthrown, and he determined to overthrow it. An assembly was held to consider *comes for-* the situation. Dionysius arose and in a violent harangue accused *ward for* the generals of treachery. His language was intended to stir up the *the first* hearers to fury ; he called upon the people to rise up themselves and *violent* destroy the traitors without trial. His violence transgressed the *speech.* constitutional rules of the assembly, but the presidents had no power to bridle him ; they imposed a fine—the only resource they had ; but a wealthy friend, Philistus the historian, came forward and *Philistus* paid the fine, bidding the speaker go on, for as often as a fine was *the* imposed he would pay it. Dionysius carried his point. The generals *historian.* were deposed, and a new board was appointed, of which Dionysius *The despot's* was one. This was only the first step on the road which was to *progress :* lead to the *tyrannis.* His next success was to procure the recall of the *nysius* partisans of Hermocrates who had been condemned to exile ; these *general ;* old comrades might be useful to him in his designs. At the same time he sought to discredit his colleagues ; he kept entirely apart from them and spread reports that they were disloyal to Syracuse. Presently he openly accused them, and the people elected him sole *(2) Dio-* general with sovereign powers to meet the instant danger. This *nysius* office, held before, as we have reason to think, by Gelon and *στρατηγὸς* Hiero, did not set him above the laws ; nor was the office *αὐτοκρά-* illegal, though extraordinary ; it may be compared to the Roman *τωρ ;* dictatorship. But it was the second step to the tyranny. The next step, as history taught him—the story of Pisistratus, for instance— was to procure a bodyguard. The Assembly at Syracuse, which had perhaps begun to repent already of having placed so much power in the hands of one man, would certainly not have granted such an instrument of tyranny. But Dionysius was ingenious ; he saw that

Y

the thing might be done elsewhere. He ordered the Syracusan army to march to Leontini, which, it will be remembered, was now a Syracusan dependency. He encamped near the town, and during the night a rumour was spread abroad that the general's life had been attempted and he had been compelled to seek refuge in the acropolis. An assembly was held next day, nominally an assembly of Syracusan citizens, which, when Dionysius laid bare the designs of his enemies, voted him a bodyguard of 600; this he soon increased to 1000; and he had won over the mercenaries to his cause.

(3) gets a bodyguard.

These were the three steps in the "despot's progress" which rendered Dionysius lord and master of Syracuse. His intrigues had won him first a generalship, then sole generalship with unlimited military powers, and finally a bodyguard. Syracuse, unwilling and embarrassed, submitted with evident chagrin, but was dominated by the double dread of the mercenaries and the Carthaginians. The democracy of course was not formally overthrown ; Dionysius held no office that upset the constitution. Things went on as at Athens under Pisistratus ; the Assembly met and passed decrees and elected magistrates.

Democratic constitution formally continues.

The justification of the power of Dionysius lay in the need of an able champion to oppose Carthage, and his partisans represented him as a second Gelon. But, though Dionysius was in later years to prove himself among the chief champions of Hellenic Sicily against the Punic power, his conduct at this crisis did not fulfil the hopes of those who thought to compare him with the hero of Himera. The Carthaginians were already encamped at Gela. Their first act was to remove a colossal brazen statue of Apollo which stood, looking over the sea, on the hill to the west of the city. The Geloans defended their walls with courage and zeal, and when Dionysius arrived with a large army of Italiots and Siceliots, and a fleet of fifty ships to co-operate, it seemed as if Gela would escape the doom of Acragas.

Siege of Gela, 405 B.C.

An excellent plan was arranged for a combined attack on the Carthaginian camp, which lay on the west side of the town. The plan failed, because the concert was not accurately carried out. The Siceliots who were to assault the eastern side of the camp arrived late on the spot, and found the enemy, who had already repelled the attack of the Italiots and the fleet on the southern and western sides, free to meet them in full force. This hitch in the execution of the plan was hardly a mere blunder. Dionysius with his mercenaries had undertaken to issue from the western gate of Gela and drive away the besiegers, while the rest of his army were attacking the camp. It seems, however, that Dionysius took no part in the fighting, and alleged that he was retarded by difficulties in crossing the town from the eastern to the western gate. We shall probably do no

Plan of concerted attack ; its failure.

Strange conduct of Dionysius.

injustice to Dionysius if we conclude that it was through his dispositions that the Siceliots failed to act in concert with the Italiots. The action which he took after the defeat shows that he was half-hearted in the work. He decided in a private council, as Diocles had decided at Himera, that the defence must be abandoned and the whole people of Gela removed. At the first watch of the night he *Gela and* sent the multitude forth from the city, and followed himself at *Camarina* midnight. His way to Syracuse led by Camarina, and here too *dispeopled.* Dionysius ruled that the whole people must forsake their home. The road to Syracuse was full of the crowds of helpless fugitives from the two cities.

It was generally thought that these strange proceedings of *Suspicions* Dionysius were carried out in collusion with the barbarians ; that he *of good* had deliberately betrayed to them Gela, which might have been *faith of* defended, Camarina, which had not yet been attacked. The Italiot *Dionysius.* allies showed not their disgust only, but their apprehension that the war was practically over, by marching immediately home. The *Revolt of* horsemen of Syracuse seized the occasion for a desperate attempt to *the horse-* subvert the new tyrant. They rode rapidly to the city, plundered *men,* the house of Dionysius, and maltreated his wife although she was the daughter of Hermocrates. When Dionysius heard the news, he hastened to Syracuse with a small force. He reached the gate of Achradina by night and, being refused admittance, burned it down with a fire of reeds supplied by the neighbouring marsh. In the *put down by* market-place he easily overmastered a handful of opponents ; the *Dionysius.* remnant fled to Aetna, which now became, " in a better cause, what *Aetna.* Eleusis was to Athens after the overthrow of the Thirty." [1]

In what concerns the charge that the Syracusan tyrant had a secret *Policy of* understanding with Carthage, there is a strong case against him ; the *Dionysius.* events are scarcely intelligible on any other view. But it was no more than a temporary disloyalty to the cause of Hellas and Europe, for which he was hereafter to do great feats. His first motive was the selfish motive of a tyrant. He wanted time to lay stable foundations for his still precarious power at Syracuse ; and he judged that it would be a strong support to obtain a recognition of his power from the Carthaginian republic. The Punicism of the lord of Syracuse was not more unscrupulous than the Medism of the ephors of Sparta, to which it is the western parallel.

The treaty, which was now agreed upon between Himilco and *The treaty* Dionysius, was drawn up on the basis of *uti possidetis*. Each party *between* retained what it actually held at the time. Syracuse acknowledged *Carthage* Carthage as mistress of all the Greek states on the northern and *and* *Dionysius,* *405 B.C.*

[1] Freeman.

*Cartha-
ginian
Sicily :*
southern coasts, and also of the Sican communities. Acragas, what was left of Selinus, Gela, and Camarina, were all to be henceforward under Punic sway ; and, on the north coast, Carthage had advanced her frontier to include the territory of Himera in which she had planted her first colony.[1] But all these cities were not to hold the same relation to their mistress. Acragas and Selinus, like Thermae, were subjects in the full sense of the word ; but Gela and Camarina were to be only tributary and unwalled cities. The Elymian towns are not mentioned ; but we have seen how Segesta became a subject of Carthage by her own act, and we can hardly doubt that Eryx was forced into the same condition.

*subjects
and tribu-
taries.*

*Independent
states :
position of
Leontini.*
The terms of the treaty provided for the independence of the Sicel communities and of the city of Messana. But it provided also for the independence of Leontini, and this was a point in which it departed from the basis *uti possidetis*, Leontini being a dependency of Syracuse. It was clearly a provision extorted from Dionysius, and intended by Himilco to be a source of embarrassment to Syracuse. On the other hand, as a counter-concession, nothing was said about the dependence of Naxos or Catane, so that Syracuse might have a free hand to deal with her old enemies, without fear of violating the treaty. Such was the new arrangement of the map of Sicily at the end of the second Carthaginian invasion. An accidental consequence of that invasion had been to establish Dionysius as tyrant of Syracuse. This consequence enabled Himilco to bring his work to a conclusion more easily and quickly than he had hoped ; he could not foresee that the undoing of his work would be the ultimate result. The

*Clause of
guaranty.*
Carthaginians guaranteed to maintain the rule of Dionysius, who was soon to prove one of their most powerful foes. For Dionysius this guaranty, "the Syracusans shall be subject to Dionysius," was the most important clause in the treaty,—some suppose that it was a secret clause. It was for the sake of this recognition and the implied promise of support that he stooped to betray Sicilian Hellas. We shall see how he redeemed this unscrupulous act of expediency by creating the most powerful Hellenic state in the Europe of his day.

SECT. 4. FIRST YEARS OF DIONYSIUS

For half a century after the fall of Athens it seemed likely that the destinies of Europe would be decided by a Greek city in the western Mediterranean. Under her new lord Dionysius, Syracuse had become a great power, a greater power than any that had yet arisen

[1] In the treaty, the old Phoenician colonies, sisters of Carthage, seem to have been spoken of as if they were her own daughter colonies.

in Europe.   In strength and dominion, in influence and promise, she *Great posi-* outstripped all the cities of the mother-country ; and, in a general *tion of* survey of the Mediterranean coasts, she stands out clearly as the leading *Syracuse.* European power.   The Greek states to which the Persian King sent down his Peace were now flanked on either side by two great powers, and a political prophet might have been tempted to foretell that the communities of old Greece were doomed to perish between the monarchies of Susa and Syracuse, which threatened their freedom on the east and on the west.   Those who were tempted to spy into the future might have conjectured that the ultimate conflict with Persia was reserved for a Sicilian conqueror, who should one day extend his dominion over eastern Greece and the Aegean and, as autocrat of Europe, oppose the autocrat of Asia.   Though this was not to be, though the expansion of Sicily was arrested, and the power which was to subdue Asia arose on the borders of Old Greece, yet we shall see that in many ways the monarchy of Dionysius foreshadowed the monarchy of Philip and Alexander.   It is in Sicily, not in Old Greece, that we see the first signs of a new epoch, in which large states are to take the place of small, and monarchy is to supersede free institutions.

The tyranny of Dionysius lasted for thirty-eight years, till the *The state-* end of his life.   All that time it was maintained by force ; all that *craft of* time it was recognised as a violation of the constitution and an *Dionysius,* outrage on the freedom of the people.   The forms of the consti- *and the* tution were still maintained ; the folk still met and voted in the *his long* Assembly ; and Dionysius was either annually re-elected, or perma- *reign.* nently appointed, general with absolute powers.   But all this was pure form ; his position was a fact, which had no constitutional name, and which made the constitution of none effect.   And it was by compulsion and not of their freewill that the mass of the citizens continued to obey him ; his bodyguard of foreign mercenaries was the support of his power.   More than one attempt was made to throw off the yoke, but his craft and energy defeated the most determined efforts of his adversaries.   Yet the unusual ability of Dionysius would not have availed, more than the spearmen who were ever within call, to extend his unlawful reign to a length which a tyrant's reign seldom reached, if he had not discovered and laid to heart what may be called a secret of tyranny.   While he did cruel and oppressive deeds for political purposes. he never committed outrages to gratify personal desires of his own.   He scrupulously avoided all those acts of private insolence which have brought the reigns of Greek tyrants into such ill repute.   Many a despot had fallen by the hand of fathers or lovers, whom the dishonour of their nearest and dearest had spurred to the pursuit of vengeance at the risk of their own lives. Dionysius eschewed this mistake; his crimes and his enemies were political. When his son seduced a married woman, the discreet tyrant rebuked him. "It is well for you to chide me," said the young man, "but you had not a tyrant for your father." "And if you go on doing this sort of thing," retorted Dionysius, "you will not have a tyrant for your son." This notable moderation of Dionysius in private life was perhaps the chief cause of the duration of his tyranny; beyond the common motive of patriotism, men had no burning personal wrongs to spur them to encounter the danger of driving a dagger to the despot's heart. But, besides this discretion which made his government tolerable, his successes abroad counted for something, and it was more than once borne in on Syracuse that his rule was necessary to protect her against her enemies. And we shall see that Dionysius was fully conscious that it conduced to his own safety that there should be enemies against whom she needed a protector.

Fortifica-tion of the Island.
The first concern of the new tyrant was to establish himself in a stronghold. As we have seen, the acropolis of Syracuse was not, as in other cities, the hill, but the Island; and it was the Island which Dionysius made his fortress. He built a turreted wall on the north side of the isthmus so as to bar the Island off from the mainland, and he built two castles, one close to, if not on, the isthmus, the other at the southern point of the island. Whoever entered the Island from Achradina had to pass under five successive gates; and no one was allowed to dwell within the island fortress except those whom Dionysius regarded as his own friends and supporters. The scheme of fortifications took in the Lesser Harbour, which, with its new docks, became under Dionysius the chief arsenal of the Syracusan naval power. The mouth of this port was entirely closed by a mole, the galleys passing in and out through a gate, which was only wide enough to allow one to pass at a time.

Besides these defences of stone, Dionysius strengthened his position by dealing rich rewards to confirm in their allegiance his friends and hirelings, and by forming a class of New Citizens out of enfranchised slaves. The forfeited estates of his enemies supplied him with the means of carrying out both these acts of policy.

Revolt against Dionysius.
It was not long before he had an unwelcome occasion of putting to the test both the walls of his fortress and the hearts of his followers. The most favourable opportunity for any attempt to overthrow the tyrant was when the Syracusan army was in the field. When the citizens had arms in their hands and were formed in military ranks, the word of a patriot could more easily kindle them to action than when they were engaged in their peaceable occupations at home. Dionysius led out the army against Herbessus, one of the cities of

the Sicels.   Mutinous talk passed from mouth to mouth, and the disaffected citizens slew one of the tyrant's officers who rebuked them.   Then the mutiny broke out loud and free.   Dionysius hastened to Syracuse and shut himself up in his fastness ; the revolted citizens followed and laid siege to their own city.   They sent *Siege of* messages to Messana and Rhegium, asking these cities to help them *Syracuse,* to win back their freedom ; and a succour of eighty triremes came *403 A.D.* in answer to their help.   By sea and land they pressed Dionysius so hard in his island fortress that his case seemed desperate, and some of his mercenary troops went over to the enemy.   Dionysius called a council of his most trusted friends.   Some bade him flee on a swift horse ; others counselled him to stay till he was driven out.   Heloris used a phrase which became famous : " Sovereign power is a fair winding-sheet."   Dionysius followed the counsel of those who bade him stay, but he resorted to a piece of craft which was more successful than he could well have hoped.   He entered into negotiation with his besiegers and asked for permission to quit Syracuse with his own goods.   They willingly agreed to the proposal and allowed him five triremes, and they were so convinced of his good faith that they dismissed a company of cavalry which had come to their aid from Aetna.   But, meanwhile, Dionysius had sent a secret message to *Revolt* the Campanian mercenaries of Carthage, who had been left by *suppressed* Himilco in some part of Sicily.   Twelve hundred in number, they *by Cam-* were permitted to come to the help of the tyrant, whose lordship had *panian* been recognised and guaranteed by Carthage in the recent treaty. *help.* The besiegers, thinking that the struggle was over, had half broken up their leaguer, and were in complete disorder ; the Campanians occupied the hills of Epipolae without resistance ; Dionysius sallied forth, and decisively, though without much shedding of blood, defeated the rebels in the neighbourhood of the theatre—a quarter of the city which we now find for the first time called *Neapolis.*   Dionysius used his victory mildly.   Many of the rebels fled to Aetna and refused to return to Syracuse, but those who returned were received kindly and not punished.   As for the Campanians, to whom Dionysius owed his rescue, they did not return to the service of Carthage, but made a new home in the west of Sicily, in the Sican town of Entella.   They *Entella ;* induced the inhabitants to admit them as new citizens, and one *first* night they arose and slew all the men and married the women. *Italian* Thus was formed the first Italian settlement on Sicilian soil. *settlement in Sicily.*

When the revolt broke out, we saw Dionysius aiming an attack *Designs of* at a Sicel city.   The first step in the expansion of Syracusan power, *Dionysius* which was the object of the tyrant's ambition, was the reduction of the *on the* Greek cities of the eastern coast and the neighbouring Sicel towns. *Sicels.* The Sicel towns were putting on more and more of an Hellenic character, and the reign of Dionysius marks a stage of progress in their Hellenization. We get a glimpse of political parties striving in Sicel just as in Greek cities ; and we find Henna ruled by a tyrant of Greek name. To attack the Sicels was indeed a breach of the treaty with Carthage ; but for the present Dionysius gained no success which obliged Carthage to intervene. He entered Henna indeed, but only to overthrow the local tyrant and leave the inhabitants to enjoy their freedom ; he attacked Herbita, but his attack was fruitless. With the Greek cities which stood in his way he was more *Aetna taken.* successful. First of all he captured Aetna, the refuge of Syracusan exiles and malcontents, and these dangerous enemies dispersed we know not whither. Then he turned against the two Ionian cities, Catane and Naxos. In fear of such an attack Catane had taken the

FIG. 169.—Alliance coin (hemidrachm, enlarged) of Leontini and Catane. Obverse : head of Apollo wreathed with bay ; bay leaf and berry [legend : ΛΕΟΝ($\tau\iota\nu\omega\nu$)]. Reverse : bull (river Simaethos) ; fish below [legend : KATANAION].

Alliance of Catane and Leontini, 404 B.C. precaution of allying herself with Syracuse's former vassal, Leontini. The sole record we have of this alliance is a beautiful little silver coin, with a laurelled head of Apollo and the names of the two cities—one of an issue which was struck in token of the treaty. But the *Catane and Naxos taken by treachery.* support of Leontini did not avail. Both Catane and Naxos were won by gold, not by the sword ; traitors opened the gates to the Dorian tyrant.

Fate of Catane and Naxos. In his treatment of these cities Dionysius showed himself in his worst light. All the inhabitants of Naxos and Catane alike were sold as slaves in the Syracusan slave-market. Catane was given over to Campanian mercenaries as a dwelling-place, and thus became the second Italian town in Sicily. But the city of Naxos, the most ancient of all the Siceliot cities, was not even given to a stranger to dwell in ; the walls and the houses were destroyed ; the territory was bestowed upon the Sicels, the descendants of the original possessors ;

and a small settlement near the old site barely maintained the memory *(The*
of the name.   Dionysius was one of the ablest champions of Greek *Naxian*
Sicily against the Phoenician ; yet here he appears in the character *Neapolis.)*
of a destroyer, dealing to Greek civilisation blows such as we should
expect only from the Phoenician foe.   It is certain indeed that
the severity of the doom which he meted out to these cities was
meant to serve a purpose, for wanton severity was never practised by
Dionysius.   We may suspect what that purpose was.   The conquest *Recovery*
of Naxos and Catane was of far less consequence to the lord of *of Leontini.*
Syracuse than the recovery of Leontini.   To win back this lost Syracusan possession was the first object of all in the eyes of a Syracusan
ruler.   Dionysius had already called upon the Leontines to surrender,
but in vain ; and perhaps he thought that the siege of the place would be
long and tedious.   When he pronounced the doom of Naxos and Catane,
he was in truth besieging Leontini with most effectual engines ; and
when he approached with his army and summoned the Leontines to
migrate to Syracuse and become his subjects under the name of
Syracusan citizens, they did not hesitate to prefer that unwelcome
change to the risk of faring still worse than the folks of Catane and
Naxos.

If we glance over Sicily at this moment, it comes upon us as a
shock to discover that of all the cities of Greek Sicily which enjoyed
sovereign powers at the time of the Athenian invasion, there remained
now not a single independent community, outside Syracuse herself,
with exception of Messana, who still kept watch upon her strait.
The Carthaginians and Dionysius between them had swept all away.

The recovery of the Leontine territory was a success which probably gratified the Syracusans as well as their master.   It was indeed
a direct defiance of Carthage, for the treaty had guaranteed the
independence of Leontini.   But Dionysius knew that a struggle *Fortifica-*
with Carthage must come, and was not unwilling that it should come *tion of*
soon.   He determined to equip Syracuse against all enemies who should *Epipolae.*
come against her, and we next find him engaged in fortifying the
city on an enormous scale.   The fortification of the Island had been
intended mainly for his own safety against domestic enemies ; but
the works which he now undertook were for the city and not for
the tyrant.   The Athenian siege of Syracuse taught him lessons
which he had taken to heart.   It taught him that the commanding heights of Epipolae must not be left for an enemy to seize,
and therefore that it must become part of the Syracusan city, enclosed within the circuit of the Syracusan wall.   It taught too
the decisive importance of the western corner at Euryalos, and the
necessity of constructing a strong fortress at that point, which has
been called " the key of Epipolae and of all Syracuse."   The walls

were built in an incredibly short space of time by 60,000 freemen, under the supervision of Dionysius himself. He seems to have inspired the citizens with the ambition of making their city the most strongly fortified place in the whole Greek world. The northern wall, from Tycha to Euryalos, a distance of more than three miles, was completed in twenty days. The striking ruins of the massive castle of Euryalos, with its curious underground chambers, are a memorial indeed of a tyrant's rule ; but they are more than that ; they are a monument of Greek Syracuse at the period of her greatest might—when she became for a moment the greatest power in Europe.

Improvements of Dionysius in warfare.

It was no small thing to have carried out this enormous system of fortifications which made Syracuse the vastest of all Greek cities ; but Dionysius showed his surpassing energy and resource in preparing for offensive as well as for defensive warfare. In military innovations he is the forerunner of the great Macedonians and the originator of the methods which they employed. He first thought out and taught how the heterogeneous parts of a military armament —the army and the navy, the cavalry and the infantry, the heavy and the light troops—might be closely and systematically co-ordinated so as to act as if they were a single organic body. He first introduced, his engineers first invented, the catapult, which, if it did not revolutionise warfare in general like the discovery of gunpowder, certainly revolutionised siege warfare, and introduced a new element into military operations. An engine which hurled a stone of two or three hundredweight for a distance of two or three hundred yards was extremely formidable in close quarters. In naval warfare he has been credited with the invention of quadriremes and quinqueremes, but this must remain doubtful. He largely increased the fleet, which seems to have numbered about 300 galleys.

Sect. 5. First Punic War of Dionysius

First Punic War, 398-7 B.C.

When his preparations were complete, Dionysius went forth to do what no Greek leader in Sicily had ever done before. He went forth not merely to deliver Greek cities from Phoenician rule, but to conquer Phoenician Sicily itself. Marching along the south coast he was hailed as a deliverer by the Greek dependencies of Carthage, both by the tributary towns Gela and Camarina, and the subject town of Acragas. Thermae on the northern coast likewise joined him, and of the two Elymian towns, Eryx received his overtures, while Segesta remained faithful to her Punic mistress. At the head of a host, which for a Greek army seems immense—80,000 foot, it is said, and more than 3000 horse—Dionysius advanced to test his *Siege of* new siege engines on the walls of Motya. This city, which now for *Motya.* the first and for the last time becomes the centre of a memorable episode in history, was like the original Syracuse, an island town ; but, though it was joined to the mainland by a causeway, the town did not like Syracuse spread to the mainland. It was surrounded entirely by a wall, of which traces still remain ; and the bay in which it lay was protected on the sea side by a long spit of land. The men of Motya were determined to withstand the invader to the uttermost, and the first measure they took was to insulate themselves completely by breaking down the causeway which bound them to the mainland. Thus they hoped that Dionysius would have to trust entirely to his ships to conduct the siege, and that he would be unable to make use of his artillery. But they knew not the enter- *The mole.* prise of Dionysius nor the excellence of his engineer department. The tyrant was determined to assault the city from solid ground, and to bring his terrible engines close to the walls. He set the crews of his ships to the work of building a mole far greater than the causeway which the Motyans had destroyed ; the ships them- selves, which he did not destine to play any part in the business of the siege, he drew up on the northern coast of the bay. The mole *(Compare* of Dionysius at Motya forestalls a more famous mole which we *the mole of* shall hereafter see erected by a greater than Dionysius at another *Alexander* Phoenician island town, older and more illustrious than Motya. *the Great at Tyre.)*

While the mole was being built, Dionysius made expeditions in the neighbourhood. He won over the Sicans from their Carthaginian allegiance, and he laid siege to Elymian Segesta and Campanian Entella. Both these cities repelled his attacks, and leaving them under blockade he returned to Motya when the solid bridge was completed. In the meantime, Carthage was preparing an effort to rescue the menaced city. She tried to cause a diversion by sending a few galleys to Syracuse, and some damage was caused to ships that were lying in the Great Harbour. But Dionysius was not to be diverted from his enterprise ; he had doubtless foreseen such an attempt to lure him away, and knew that there was no real danger. Himilco, the Carthaginian admiral, seeing that Dionysius was immovable, sailed with a large force to Motya and entered the bay, with the purpose of destroying the Syracusan fleet, which was drawn up on the shore. Dionysius seems to have been taken by surprise. For whatever reason, he made no attempt to launch his galleys ; he merely placed archers and slingers on those ships which would be first attacked. But he brought his army round to the peninsula which forms the western side of the bay, and on the shores of this strip of land he placed his new engines. The catapults hurled deadly volleys of stones upon Himilco's ships, and the novelty of these crushing missiles, which they were quite unprepared to meet, utterly disconcerted the Punic sailors, and the Carthaginians retreated. Then Dionysius, who was no less ready to treat earth as water than to turn sea into land, laid wooden rollers across the neck of land which formed the northern side of the bay, and hauled his whole fleet into the open sea. But Himilco did not tarry to give him battle there; he went back to Carthage, and the men of Motya were left unaided to abide their fate.

As the site of the island city required a special road of approach, so its architecture demanded a special device of assault. Since the space in the city was limited, its wealthy inhabitants had to seek dwelling-room by raising high towers into the air; and to attack *(The* these towers Dionysius constructed siege towers of corresponding helepoleis.) height, with six storeys, which he moved up near the walls on wheels. These wooden *belfries*, as they were called in the Middle Ages, were not a new invention, but they had never perhaps been built to such a height before, and it is not till the Macedonian age, which Dionysius in so many ways foreshadows, that they came into common use. It was a strange sight to see the battle waged in mid-air. The defenders of the stone towers had one advantage; they were able to damage some of the wooden towers of the enemy by lighted brands and pitch. But the arrangements of Dionysius were so well ordered that this device wrought little effect; and the Phoenicians could not stand on the wall which was swept by his catapults, while the rams battered it below. Presently a breach was made, and the struggle began in earnest. The Motyans had no thought of surrender; dauntless to the end they defended their streets and houses inch by inch. Missiles rained on the heads of the Greeks who thronged through, and each of the lofty houses had to be besieged like a miniature town. The wooden towers were wheeled within the walls; from their topmost storeys bridges were flung across to the upper storeys of the houses, and in the face of the desperate inhabitants the Greek soldiers rushed across these dizzy ways, often to be flung down into the street below. At night the combat ceased; both besiegers and besieged rested. The issue was indeed certain; for however bravely the Motyans might fight, they were far outnumbered. But day after day the fighting went on in the same way, and Motya was not taken. The losses on the Greek side were great, and Dionysius became impatient. Accordingly he planned a night assault, which the Motyans did not look for, and this was successful. By means of ladders a small band entered the part of the town which was still defended, and then admitted the rest of the army through a gate. There was a short and

N

Wooden Shipway

Ships of Dionysius

Causeway

Motya

Harbour

Ditch

Ditch

Lilybaeum

The Siege of

MOTYA,

B.C. 398.

English Miles

0   ½   1   2

Walker & Boutall sc.

To face page 650.

sharp struggle, which soon became a massacre. The Greeks had no *Capture of* thought of plunder, they thought only of vengeance. Now for the *Motya, and* first time a Phoenician town had fallen into their hands, and they *massacre,* resolved to do to it as the Phoenicians had done to Greek cities. *398 B.C.* They remembered how Hannibal had dealt with Himera. At length Dionysius stayed the slaughter, which was not to his mind, since every corpse was a captive less to be sold. Then the victors turned to spoil the city, and its wealth was abandoned to them without any reserve. All the prisoners were sold into slavery, except some Greek mercenaries, whose treachery to the Hellenic cause was expiated by the death of crucifixion. A Sicel garrison was left in the captured city.

After this achievement, the like of which had not been wrought *Second* before in Sicilian history, Dionysius retired for the winter to *campaign* Syracuse. Next spring he marched forth again to press the siege of *of Diony-* Segesta, which was still under blockade. In the meantime the fall *sius, 397* of Motya had awakened Carthage into action ; she saw that she *B. C.* must bestir herself, if she was not to let her whole Sicilian dominion slip out of her hands. Himilco was appointed Shophet and *Cartha-* entrusted with the work of saving Punic Sicily. He collected a *ginian* force, which seems to have been at least as large as that which *expedition* Dionysius had brought into the field, and set sail with sealed orders *to Sicily,* for Panormus. A small portion of the armament was sunk by *397 B. C.* Leptĭnes, brother of Dionysius, who was in command of the Syracusan fleet ; but the main part disembarked in safety. And then events happened in rapid succession, which are hard to explain. Himilco first gains possession of Eryx by treason ; then he marches *Himilco* to Motya and captures it ; and when Motya is lost, Dionysius raises *takes Eryx* the siege of Segesta and returns to Syracuse. The loss of Eryx *and Motya.* could not be provided against ; but it is hard to discern why Dionysius should have made no attempt to relieve Motya, whose capture had cost him so much the year before, or why he should have allowed the Carthaginian army to march from Panormus to Eryx and Motya without attempting to intercept it. He could not have more effectually pressed the siege of Segesta than by dealing a decided check to Himilco. Not knowing the exact circumstances, not knowing even the number of the two armies, we can hardly judge his action ; but it may be suspected that Dionysius was by nature a man who did not care to risk a pitched battle, unless the advantage were distinctly on his own side. It is to be remembered that he won nearly all his successes by sieges and surprises, by diplomacy and craft, and that the name of this great military innovator is not associated with a single famous battle in the open field. When he had once allowed Motya to be taken, his retreat is not surprising ;

for he had no base in the western part of the island, and we are told
that his supplies were failing.   He had now lost all that he had

*End of
Motya.
Founda-
tion of
Lilybaeum
(Marsala).*
won in the first campaign.   Motya, however, was wiped out as a
Phoenician city, though it was not to be a Greek or Sicel stronghold.   Himilco, instead of restoring the old colony, founded a new
city hard by to take its place.   On the promontory of the mainland
which forms the south side of the Motyan bay arose the city of
Lilybaeum, which was henceforward to be the great stronghold of
Carthaginian power in the west of the island.   The sea washed two
sides of the town, and the walls of the other two sides were protected
by enormous ditches cut in the rock.   The history of Lilybaeum is
the continuation of the history of Motya ; but it was not destined to
be taken either by a Greek or a Roman besieger.

*Himilco
takes and
destroys
Messana.*
Having driven the invader from Phoenician Sicily, and having
laid the foundations of a new city, Himilco resolved to carry his
arms into the lands of the enemy and to attack Syracuse itself.
But he did not go directly against Syracuse.   Before he attempted
that mighty fortress, he would try the easier task of capturing
Messana.   The fall of this city would be a grievous blow to Hellas,
and it would be no mean vengeance for the fall of Motya.   The
walls of Messana had been allowed to fall into decay, and the
place was an easy prey for the Carthaginians ; but the greater
part of the inhabitants escaped into fortresses in the neighbouring
hills.   The Carthaginian general had to wreak his vengeance on
the stones.   He rased the walls and the edifices, and the work
was done so well that no man, we are told, would have recognised
the site.

If the triumphant demolition of the Sicilian city which watched
the strait was a sore blow to the Hellenic cause, Himilco sought at
the same moment to deal another blow to that cause by the foundation of a new Sicilian city in another place.   It was his policy to
cultivate the friendship of the Sicels and to foment the dislike which
they felt towards the lord of Syracuse.   Dionysius too had sought
to win influence over the native race, and we saw how he gave them

*Founda-
tion of
Tauro-
menium.*
the territory of Naxos.   The Carthaginian general grasped at the
idea of erecting a new town for these very Sicels of Naxos, on the
heights of Taurus which rise above the old site.   Such was the
strange origin of the strong city of Tauromenion, with its two rock
citadels, one of the fairest sites in Sicily.   It was the second foundation of Himilco in the same year ; and both his foundations were
destined signally to prosper.   Lilybaeum became more famous than
Motya, and Tauromenion has had a greater place in history than
Naxos.   As a founder of cities Himilco has a high title to fame ; he
was, like Dionysius, a creator as well as a destroyer.   The creation

of new cities and the destruction of old, by Greeks and Phoenicians alike, was a characteristic feature of this epoch.

Dionysius was preparing in the meantime to protect Syracuse. He committed the command of the fleet, which appears to have been now about 200 strong, to his brother Leptines ; and fleet and army together moved northward to Catane. In the waters near the shore *Sea-fight at* of Catane a naval battle was fought, and the Greek armament was *Catane.* defeated with great loss. It was indeed far outnumbered by the fleet of the Phoenicians, who also used their transport vessels as warships ; but the cause of the disaster was the bad generalship of Leptines, who did not keep his ships together. The rout was witnessed by Dionysius from the shore, and it might have been retrieved by a victory on the land. Himilco and his army had not yet arrived on the scene, for an eruption of Aetna had made the direct road impassable and forced them to make a long détour. Dionysius again shrank from risking a battle, though the men of *Retreat of* Sicily were eager to fight ; he retreated to the walls of Syracuse. *Dionysius.* This city was the last bulwark of Greek Sicily, and with it the cause of Greek civilisation was in jeopardy. It was a moment at which the Siceliots might well sue for help from their fellow-Greeks beyond the sea. Dionysius dispatched messages to Italy, to Corinth, and to Sparta, imploring urgently for succour.

It was not long before the victorious Carthaginian fleet sailed *Punic* into the Great Harbour, and the Carthaginian army encamped hard *siege of* by, along the banks of the Anapus. The mass of the host encamped *Syracuse.* as well as it could in the swamp, but the general pitched his tent on the high ground of Polichna, within the precinct of the Olympian Zeus. This insult to the religion of Hellas was followed up by a more awful sacrilege, when Himilco pillaged the temple of Demeter and Kore on the southern slope of Epipolae. When the barbarians began to perish in the plague-stricken marsh, the pestilence was imputed to the divine vengeance for these acts of outrage. The besiegers must have sat for no brief space before the walls of Syracuse. The messengers of Dionysius had time to reach the Peloponnesus and return with succour — thirty ships under a Lacedaemonian admiral. Himilco had time to build three forts to protect his army and his fleet — one near his own quarters at Polichna, one at Dascon, on the western shore of the harbour, and one at Plemmyrion. After the arrival of the auxiliaries, the capture of a Punic cornship was the occasion of a small naval combat in the harbour ; only a few of the Carthaginian ships were engaged, and the Syracusans were victorious.

Within the town there was deep dissatisfaction with Dionysius and his conduct of the war, and the citizens thought that they might

Feeling in Syracuse against the tyrant. reckon on the sympathy of their Peloponnesian allies with an attempt to cast off the tyrant's yoke. At an assembly which the tyrant convened the feeling of dissatisfaction broke openly forth, and the lord of Syracuse could not only read in the faces but hear in the words of the citizens the depth of their hatred. But the movement of revolution was checked by the Peloponnesians, who said that their business was to help Dionysius against the Carthaginians, not to help the Syracusans against Dionysius. So the danger passed over, but the tyrant had a warning, and he put on winning manners and courted popularity.

Plague in Carthaginian camp. The deadly airs of the swamp, in the burning heat of summer, were doing their work. The army of Himilco was ravaged by pestilence ; soon the soldiers fell so fast that they could not be buried. The hour had now come for the men of the city to complete the destruction which their fens had begun. It was just such a case as called forth the energy and craft of the ruler of Syracuse and showed *Dionysius attacks the Carthaginians.* him at his best. He devised his attack with great skill. Eighty galleys, under Leptines and the Spartan captain, were to attack the Carthaginian fleet, which was anchored off the shore of Dascon. He himself led the land forces, marching by a roundabout road on a moonless night, and suddenly appeared at dawn on the west side of the Punic camp. He ordered his horsemen and a thousand mercenaries to attack the camp here ; but the horsemen had secret commands to abandon the hired soldiers once they were in the thick of the fight, and ride rapidly round to the east of the camp, where the true attack was to be made. The attack on the west was only a feint, to distract the attention of the enemy from the other side ; and for this purpose Dionysius sacrificed the lives of the hirelings whom he did not trust. The real attack on the east was made on the forts of Dascon and Polichna. Dascon was assailed by the horsemen along with a special force of triremes which had been sent across the bay ; *Defeat of Carthaginians.* Dionysius himself went round to lead the attack on Polichna. The plan was carried out with perfect success. The thousand hirelings were cut to pieces, the forts were captured, and the victory on the land was crowned by the destruction of the Carthaginian fleet. The Syracusan galleys bore down upon the enemy, before they had time fully to man their vessels, much less to row well out to sea, and the beaks of the triremes crashed into defenceless timber. There was slaughter, but hardly a fight ; and then the land troops, fresh from *their* victory, rushed down to the beach and set fire to the transports and all vessels which had not left the shore. A wild scene followed. A high wind propagated the flames ; the cables were burnt asunder ; and the bay of Dascon was filled with drifting fireships, while amid the waters despairing swimmers were making for the shore.

Fate had indeed delivered the barbarians into the hands of the *Double-* Greeks ; and the Greeks were determined to wreak their vengeance *dealing of* to the uttermost and extirpate the destroyers of Messana.   Dionysius *Dionysius* had approved himself the successor of Gelon ; the double victory of Dascon was worthy to be set beside the victory of Himera.   But Dionysius was not capable of absolute sincerity in the part he played as the champion of Hellas ; he could not act to the end as a Syracusan patriot with singleness of heart.   This was the fatality of his position as a tyrant, conscious that his autocracy rested on unstable foundations.   He fought against Carthage, but it was always with the resolve that the power of the Carthaginians should not be annihilated in Sicily.   The Punic peril was a security for his tyranny, by making him necessary to Syracuse.   The Syracusans must look to him as *His policy* their protector against the ever-present barbarian foe.   This was *in regard* another secret of tyranny discovered by Dionysius.   The Punic *to Car-* subtlety of Himilco, enlightened by passages in the tyrant's past *thage.* career, formed no doubt a shrewd idea of this side of his policy ; the Carthaginian saw that his hope of safety lay in bargaining with Dionysius.   Secret messages passed ; and Dionysius agreed to allow Himilco along with all those who were Carthaginian citizens to sail away at night.   In payment for this collusion he received three *Escape of* hundred talents.   Dionysius recalled his reluctant army from their *Himilco by* assaults on the camp, and left it in peace for three days.   On the *collusion of* fourth night Himilco set sail with forty triremes, leaving his allies *Dionysius.* and his mercenaries to their fate.   It was an act of desertion which was likely to repel mercenary soldiers from the Carthaginian service in the future ; and this was doubtless foreseen by the crafty tyrant. But the squadron of fugitive triremes did not escape untouched. The noise of the oars as they sailed out of the Harbour was detected by the Corinthian allies, and they gave the alarm to Dionysius.   But Dionysius was purposely slow in his preparations to pursue, and the impatient Corinthians sailed out without his orders and sank some of the hindmost of the Punic vessels.   Having connived at the escape of Himilco, the tyrant was energetic in dealing with the remnant of Himilco's host.   The Sicel allies had escaped to their own homes, and only the mercenaries were left.   These were slain or made slaves, with the exception of a band of strong and valiant Iberians who were taken into the service of the tyrant.

Thus ended the first struggle of Dionysius with Carthage, and it ended in a complete triumph for the Greek cause.   The dominion of the African city was now circumscribed within its old western corner ; and the greater part of the rest of Sicily was subject, directly or indirectly, to the rule of the lord of Syracuse.   Both from Greek and from barbarian Sicily, a famous city had been blotted out ; but

Motya had been revived in Lilybaeum, and Messana was soon to rise again upon her ruins.

Sect. 6. Second Punic War, and Sicel Conquests of Dionysius

The equivocal policy of Dionysius in his hostilities to Carthage was manifested clearly enough in the course which he pursued after his great victory. It was the most favourable moment that had yet come in the struggle of centuries, for driving the barbarians out and making Sicily a Greek island from the eastern to the western shore. Carthage could not readily gather together such another armament as that which had been destroyed. No patriot leader who was devoted to the Greek cause heart and soul, with singleness of aim, would have failed to follow up the great success by an invasion of western Sicily. But the preservation of his own precarious despotism was the guiding principle of Dionysius; and he saw in the barbarian corner of the island a palladium of his power.

Sicel conquests of Dionysius (between 396 and 393 B.C.)

The next Punic War broke out five years later, and part of the meantime had been occupied by Dionysius in extending his power over the Sicels. He annexed to his dominion Morgantina, Cephaloedion, and Henna itself; he made treaties with the tyrants of Agyrion and Centuripa, and with other places. But among all the Sicel towns, that which it was most important for him to win was the new foundation of the Carthaginian on the heights of Taurus. He laid siege to Tauromenium in the depth of winter. Operations of war in the winter season are one of the features of the reign of Dionysius, which separate it from the habits of older Greece and link it to the age of the Macedonian monarchy. The tyrant himself led his men on a wild and moonless night up the steep ascent to the town. One of the citadels was taken, and the assailants entered the place. But the Syracusan band was outnumbered and surrounded, six hundred were killed, and the rest were driven down the cliffs. Of these Dionysius was one; he reached the bottom barely alive, after that precipitous descent.

Unsuccessful assault on Tauromenium.

Conquest of Solus.

In the course of the extension of his power on the northern coast, Dionysius had advanced to the limits of the Phoenician corner, and had won possession, through domestic treachery, of Solus, the most easterly of the three Phoenician cities. Of the circumstances we know nothing, but the conquest would seem to have been rather a piece of luck than part of any deliberate plan of aggression on the part of the Greek tyrant. No treaty appears to have been concluded between Carthage and Syracuse after the defeat of Himilco, so that the capture of Solus was not a violation of peace, but only an occasion for the reawakening of hostilities which had been permitted to sleep by tacit consent. At all events, it must have had something to do with the renewal of the war,—a renewal for which our records assign no causes.

At the opening of the second war we find a Carthaginian general *Second* commanding the Phoenician forces of the island, but without any *Punic* troops, so far as we know, from Africa. The general was Mago, *War,* who in the previous war had been commander of the fleet. His *392 B.C.* army was doubtless considerably inferior to the forces which Diony- sius could muster ; certain it is that on this occasion Dionysius did not hesitate to give him battle and did not fail to defeat him. Carthage saw that she must make a more vigorous effort, and she *Victory of* gave Mago a large army—80,000 men, it is said,—to retrieve his *Dionysius.* ill success. To meet the invader, Dionysius entered into a close *League of* league with the strongest Sicel power in the land, his fellow-tyrant *Dionysius* Agyris of Agyrium. This is the special feature of the second Punic *with* War : the cause of Europe is upheld by a federation of the two *Agyris.* European powers of the island, Sicel and Greek. The Carthaginian army advanced into Sicel territory, seeking to win the Sicel towns. But Agyris and his men waged a most effectual manner of warfare, cutting off all the foraging parties of the enemy and thus starving them by degrees. This they were able to do from their knowledge of their native hills. But it seems that the Syracusans were dis- satisfied with this slow method, which was thoroughly to the taste of Dionysius. What happened is not clear ; but we learn that the Syracusans marched away from the camp, and that Dionysius replaced them by arming the slaves. Then the Greeks and the Sicels must have won some unrecorded success, or the Carthaginian host must have been already terribly deplenished by the want of food ; for we next find Mago suing for peace.

This peace, although it is said to have been based on the *Terms of* treaty which Dionysius had made twelve years before, was in truth *the Peace.* altogether different ; for the parts of the two powers were reversed. All the Greek communities of Sicily were now placed under the direct or indirect power of Syracuse. The Carthaginian power was confined to the western corner. Nothing is said of Solus ; it must have been now handed over to Carthage, if Mago had not already recovered it by arms. But the most striking provision of the treaty is that which placed "the Sicels" under the rule of Dionysius. Nothing is said of Agyrium, and we are almost driven to wonder whether there was here any treachery to Agyris, of whom we hear nothing further. But there was a special clause touching *Dionysius* Tauromenium ; and acting on this clause Dionysius immediately *wins* took possession of the town, expelled the Sicels, and established in *Tauro-* *menium*

the fortress one of those mercenary settlements which were characteristic of his age. Such was the end of the two Punic wars, which
were in truth rather but a single war broken by an interval of
quiescence.

SECT. 7. THE EMPIRE OF DIONYSIUS

Having made himself master of all Greek Sicily, the lord of
Syracuse began to extend the compass of his ambition beyond the
bounds of the island. He began to plan the conquest of Greek
Italy. Hitherto the Sicilian cities, though they had constant dealings
with the colonies of the Italian mainland, had never sought there, or
anywhere out of their own island, a field for conquest or aggression.
The restriction of Siceliot ambition to Sicilian territory was the
other side of the doctrine preached by Hermocrates that the Siceliots
should not allow Greeks from beyond the sea to interfere in the affairs
of Sicily. We are reminded of the policy which has been followed
on a greater scale by the United States on the American continent.
Here, as in other things, Dionysius was an innovator; he set the
example of enterprises of conquest beyond the sea. Into the enterprise
of Italian conquest he was naturally led on by his dealings with the
fellow-cities of the strait, Messana and Rhegium.

Messana restored 396 B.C. (Messenians driven from Naupactus, 400-1 B.C.) Foundation of Tyndaris by Dionysius, 395 B.C. For Messana was a city once more; it had been rebuilt by
Dionysius himself. He settled in it colonists from Locri and
Medma in Italy, and 600 Messenians from old Greece, who had
been wandering about homeless since Sparta had driven them from
Naupactus. But this favour to the Messenians displeased the
Spartans, and as Dionysius clave to the friendship of Sparta he
yielded to their protests. He removed the exiles from Messana, but
he made for them a secure though less illustrious home. He founded
the city of Tyndaris on a high hill to the west of Mylae, and fortified
it strongly; the walls and towers, which still remain, are a good
specimen of the fortifications of Dionysius.

Foundation of Mylae, 394 B.C. The restoration of Messana and the foundation of Tyndaris were
no pleasant sight to the Ionian city across the strait; these new
cities seemed to Rhegium a Syracusan menace. The men of
Rhegium sought to make a counter-move by founding a city themselves between Tyndaris and Messana. They gathered together the
exiles from Catane and Naxos and settled them on the peninsula of
Mylae; but the settlement lasted only for a moment; almost
immediately the town of Mylae was captured by its neighbours of
Messana, and the exiles were driven out to resume their wanderings.

Apart from his political hostility to Rhegium, Dionysius is said
to have borne it a private grudge. He had asked the men of

Rhegium to give him one of their maidens to wife, and they had answered that they would give him none but the hangman's daughter. Locri, Rhegium's neighbour, then granted him the request which Rhegium refused ; Locri was his faithful ally ; and now, when the conclusion of peace with Carthage left him free to pursue his Italian designs, it was Locri that he made his base of operations. The first object was to capture Rhegium ; its position on the *Rhegium* strait dictated this, apart from all motives of revenge or hatred. *besieged,* Accordingly starting from Locri with army and fleet, he laid siege to *391 B.C.* Rhegium by land and sea. But the confederate cities of the Italian coast came to the assistance of a member of their league ; the Italiot *Naval* armament worsted the fleet of Dionysius in or near the strait, and *defeat of* Dionysius escaped with difficulty to the opposite coast. *Dionysius.*

Rhegium was thus relieved, and Dionysius now directed his *Alliance of* hostilities against the Italiot federation. He made an alliance with *Dionysius* the Lucanians, to the intent that they and he should carry on war in *with the* common against the Italiot cities, they by land and he by sea. In *Lucanians:* accordance with this treaty, the Lucanians invaded the land of Thurii. *joint* The men of Thurii retorted by invading Lucania in considerable *operations,* force ; but they sustained a crushing defeat at the hands of the bar- *390 B.C.* barians. Most of the Thurians were slain, but some escaped to the *Thurians* shore and swam out to ships which they descried coasting along. *defeated by* By a curious chance, the ships were the fleet of Syracuse, and *Lucanians.* Leptines, the tyrant's brother, was once more the commander. He received the fugitives, and did more ; he landed and ransomed them from the Lucanians. He did even more than this ; he arranged *Leptines* an armistice between the Lucanians and the Italiots. In acting thus, *concludes* he clearly went beyond his powers ; he had been sent to co-operate *an* with the Lucanians against the Italiots, and he had no right to con- *armistice* clude an armistice in such circumstances, without consulting his *and is* brother. It is not surprising that Dionysius deposed him from the *deposed.* command.

In the following year Dionysius took the field himself. He *Dionysius* opened the campaign by laying siege to Caulonia, the northern neigh- *besieges* bour of Locri. The Italiots, under the active lead of Croton, col- *Caulonia,* lected an army of 15,000 foot and 2000 horse, and entrusted the *389 B.C.* command to Helōris, a brave exile of Syracuse, who burned with hatred against the tyrant who had banished him. The federal army marched forth from Croton to relieve Caulonia, and when Dionysius learned of its approach, he decided to go forth to meet it ; for his own forces, 20,000 foot and 3000 horse, were considerably superior. Luck favoured him. Near the river Elleporus which flows into the sea between Caulonia and Croton, the tyrant heard that the enemy were encamped within a distance of five miles, and he drew up his men in

Battle of the Elleporus, 389 B.C. battle array. Heloris, less well-informed, rode forward in front of his main army, with a company of 500 men, and suddenly found himself in the presence of the Syracusan host. He did not quail or flee. Sending back a message to hasten the rest of his army, he and his little band stood firm against the onset of the invaders. Heloris fell himself, and the main army, coming up company by company, in haste and disorder, was easily routed by Dionysius. Ten thousand fugitives escaped to a high hill, but it was a poor hill of refuge, for there was no spring of water and they could not hold out. The next morning they besought Dionysius, who kept watch around the hill throughout the night, to set them free for a ransom. Dionysius *Dionysius' politic act of mercy.* refused ; he would accept only unreserved surrender. But he was cruel only to grant them a greater mercy than they could themselves have dared to ask. When they came down the hill, Dionysius himself told their number with a wand as they filed past him, and each man deemed that his doom would be bondage if not death. But Dionysius let them all depart, without even exacting a ransom. This act of mercy, which was notable as compared not only with other acts of the tyrant, but with the ordinary practice of the age, produced a great sensation. There is no reason for imputing it to a magnanimous impulse ; it was a deliberate act of policy. *His treaties with the Italiot cities.* Dionysius did not wish to be generous, but he wished to be regarded as generous and win over the Italiot cities. For this purpose he made up his mind to sacrifice 10,000 ransoms. His wisdom was soon approved. The communities to which the captives be- *Sub- mission of Rhegium : capture of Caulonia, 389 B.C. Capture of Hipponion, 388 B.C.* longed gratefully voted him golden crowns, and made separate treaties with him. In this way he accomplished his purpose ; with Rhegium, Caulonia, and Hipponion he still remained at war, but these states were now isolated and the league was broken up. Rhegium bought off his hostilities for the time by surrendering its fleet. Caulonia was captured and abolished, and its territory given to Locri ; Hipponion was likewise taken and destroyed ; but the peoples of both these cities were transplanted to Syracuse and became Syra- cusan citizens.

Capture of Rhegium, 387 B.C. But Dionysius had not yet finished with Rhegium. He created a pretext for renewing hostilities and he laid siege to the city. The men of Rhegium had now no friends to help them, but, under their general Phyton, whom the tyrant vainly endeavoured to bribe, they held out for ten months, and were reduced to surrender in the end by starvation. Dionysius accepted ransoms for those who could find the money ; the rest of the inhabitants were sold. Phyton was selected for special vengeance. He was scourged through the army, and then drowned with all his kin. Thus Dionysius gained what hitherto had been one of his most pressing desires—possession of the city

which had so long hated and defied him. He was now master of
both sides of the strait, and held the fortress which was the bulwark
of Greek Italy.   Eight years later he captured Croton, and his
power in Italy reached its greatest height.

But in the meanwhile the unresting lord of Syracuse had turned *The*
his eyes to a region of enterprise further afield. The needs of his *Hadriatic*
treasury, if nothing else, bent his attention to commerce. We touch *schemes of*
here upon that side of ancient enterprise which has been per- *Dionysius.*
sistently and provokingly withdrawn from our vision, because the
writers of antiquity never thought of lingering on the ordinary business transactions which were happening every day before their eyes.
Many things that are now dark would be cleared up if we had more
knowledge of the operations of Greek trade. Dionysius saw an opening
for Sicilian commerce along the eastern and western coasts of the
Hadriatic sea, in whose waters the ships of Corcyra, Athens, and Taras
hitherto had chiefly plied. He set about making the Hadriatic a Syracusan lake, by means of settlements and alliances. He founded settlements in Apulia, which he probably hoped ultimately to incorporate
in his dominion.   He settled a colony and fixed a naval station
in the island of Issa, whose importance as a strategic post has been *Issa.*
more than once illustrated in subsequent history. He took part with
the Parians in colonising Pharos, on an island not far from Issa. A *Pharos.*
Syracusan colony was planted at Ancon, and, even if the colonists *Ancona.*
were, as they are said to have been, exiles and foes of Dionysius,
we may be sure that the merchant ships of Syracuse were welcome
at the wharfs of Ancon. The northern goal of these merchant ships
was near the mouth of the Po, at a spot where there was already a
mart for diffusing Greek merchandise in Cis-Alpine Gaul, and beyond
the Alps into northern Europe. This was the Venetian Hadria, city *Hadria.*
of marshes and canals, which was now colonised by Dionysius, to be
in some sort—as has been aptly observed—a forerunner of Venice
itself.   It was in one of these outlying posts of the Hellenic world
that the historian, to whom we owe our best knowledge of the
Sicilian history of this time, probably wrote his works.   Philistus
had held posts of high trust under Dionysius, and had even been the
commandant of the Syracusan citadel ; but in later years he incurred
his master's displeasure or suspicion, and chose as his place of
banishment some city on the Hadriatic, possibly Hadria.   In connexion with these Hadriatic designs, touching which we have only
the most fragmentary records, Dionysius formed an alliance with
Alcetas of Molossia, whose unstable position in his own kingdom *Molossia.*
made him willing to be a dependent on the strong ruler of Syracuse.
Thus Dionysius made his influence predominant at the gates of the
Hadriatic.

Greatest extent of Syracusan Empire.
Its character.
I. Immediate dominion.
(a) Territory of Syracuse.
(b) Military Colonies
(c) Allied cities.

The Syracusan empire—we may survey it, when it reached its widest extent—consisted, like most other empires, partly of immediate dominion and partly of dependent communities. The immediate dominion was both insular and continental; it included the greater portion of Sicily and the southern peninsula of Italy, perhaps as far north as the river Crathis. But this dominion was not homogeneous, in the relations of its various parts to the government at Syracuse. There was first of all the old territory of the Syracusan republic. There were secondly, a number of military settlements; an institution of Dionysius which has been compared to the military colonies of Rome. Such, for example, was Croton on the mainland; such in Sicily were Henna and Messana; such was Issa in the Hadriatic. Outside these direct subjects was the third class of the allied cities, which, though absolutely subject to the power of Dionysius, had still the management of their less important affairs in their own hands. To this class belonged the old Greek cities of Sicily—like Gela and Camarina; new colonies, like Tyndaris; some Sicel states like Agyrium and Herbita.

II. Dependencies.

Beyond the sphere of direct dominion stretched the sphere of dependencies—the allies, whose bond of dependence was rather implied than formally expressed. Here belonged the cities of the Italiot league, Thurii and the rest, north of the Crathis river; here belonged some of the Iapygian communities in the heel of Italy; and here the kingdom of Molossia beyond the Ionian sea, and some Illyrian places on the Hadriatic coast. The Crathis may be regarded as the line between the two, the outer and the inner, divisions of the empire of Dionysius. But it is remarkable that at one time he planned a wall and ditch, which should run across the isthmus from Scylletion to the nearest point on the other sea—a distance of about twenty miles—and thus sever, as it were, the toe of Italy from the mainland and make it a sort of second Sicily.

Scheme of fencing off the extremity of Italy.

The finances of Dionysius.

The acquisition and maintenance of this empire, the building of ships and ship-sheds, the payment of mercenary soldiers, the vast fortifications of Syracuse, both of the island and of the hill—all this, along with the ordinary expenses of government and the state of a despot's court, demanded an enormous outlay. To meet this outlay Dionysius was forced to resort to extraordinary expedients. He oppressed the Syracusans by a burdensome taxation. He imposed special taxes for war, special taxes for building ships; and he introduced an onerous tax on cattle. It is said that the citizens paid yearly into the treasury at the rate of twenty per cent of their capital. [Later sources embellished the financial theme. He issued, they said, debased tetradrachms of tin instead of silver and, in one case of financial need, paid a debt by placing on each coin an

Walker & Boutall sc.

To face page 662.

Dominions of DIONYSIUS, B.C. 379.

Direct Dominion shaded thus:—
Dependencies outline shaded thus:—
Allied tribes and cities underlined.

Stadia 500 1000

English Miles
50 100 150

16° Longitude East 18° of Greenwich 20°

official mark which made it worth the double of its true value. But the most that the numismatists can confirm is the issue of electrum pieces which in the west amounted to the employment of adulterated gold.] There is, however, little doubt that Dionysius was an un-scrupulous rifler of temples. Thus, when he took Croton, he carried off the treasures of a temple of Hera. In an earlier year he sailed like a pirate to Etruria, swooped down on a rich temple at the port of Agylla, and bore off booty which amounted to the value of 1500 talents. The plunder of a sanctuary on distant barbarian shores might seem a small thing, but no awe of divine displeasure restrained Dionysius from planning a raid upon the holiest place of Hellenic worship. He formed the design of robbing the treasury of Delphi itself, with Illyrian and Molossian help ; but the plan miscarried. It is little wonder that the tyrant had an evil repute in the mother country.

SECT. 8. DEATH OF DIONYSIUS. ESTIMATE OF HIS WORK

It was only for a moment that the dominion of the Syracusan *Outbreak* despot reached its extreme limits. He had hardly won the city and *of Third* lands of Croton, when his borders fell back in the west of his own *Punic* island. A new war with Carthage had broken out, and this time if *War,* Dionysius was not the first to draw the sword, he at least provoked *383 B.C.* hostilities. He entered into alliances with some of the cities dependent on Carthage—possibly Segesta or Eryx. Of the cam-paigns we know almost nothing, except their result. First we find Carthage helping the Italiots with whom the tyrant was at war. Next we find a Carthaginian force in Sicily commanded by Mago. In a battle fought at Cabala—a place unknown—the Syracusans won *Battle of* a great victory and Mago was killed. While negotiations for peace *Cabala.* were proceeding, another battle was fought at Cronion near Panormus, *Battle of Cronion,* and fate reversed her award. Dionysius was defeated with terrible *379 B.C.* loss, and compelled to make a disadvantageous peace. The boundary *Peace,* of Greek against Punic Sicily was withdrawn from the river Mazarus *378 B.C.* to the river Halycus. This meant that the deliverer of Selinus and Thermae gave back those cities to the mercies of the barbarian. At the mouth of the Halycus, the old Greek foundation of Heraclea *Ras* Minoa now became, under the corresponding Punic name Ras *Melkart.* Melkart, one of the chief strongholds of Punic power.

Just ten years later, ten years in which the history of Sicily is a *Fourth* blank, Dionysius essayed to retrieve the losses which the disastrous *Punic* battle of Cronion had brought upon him. He made war once more *War,* upon Carthage, and for the second time he invaded Punic Sicily. *368 B.C.* He delivered Greek Selinus ; he won Campanian Entella ; and captured Elymian Eryx along with its haven Drepanon. He then attempted, we may almost say, to repeat the great exploit of his first war. There was no more a Motya to capture, but he laid siege to Lilybaeum, which had taken Motya's place. But he was compelled to abandon the attempt; the fortress was too strong; and his ill-success was soon crowned by the loss of a large part of his fleet, which was carried out of the harbour of Drepanon by an enterprising Carthaginian admiral.

Death of Dionysius, 367 B.C.

It was the last undertaking of the great "ruler of Sicily." He did not live to conclude the peace which probably confirmed the Halycus as the boundary between Greek and barbarian. His death was connected with a side of his character which has not yet come before us. The tyrant of Syracuse has a place, though it is a small place,

Dionysius as a tragic poet.

in literary history. He was a dramatic poet, and he frequently competed with his tragedies in the Athenian theatre. He won third, he won even second, prizes; but his dearest ambition was to be awarded a first place. That desire was at length fulfilled; his failure at Lily-baeum and the loss of his ships at Drepanon were compensated by the tidings that the first prize had been assigned to his *Ransom of Hector* at the Lenaean festival. He celebrated his joy by an un-wonted carouse; his intemperance was followed by a fever; and a soporific draught was administered to him which induced the sleep of death.

Relations of Sicily to Eastern Greece in time of Dionysius.

Dionysius did not stand wholly aloof from the politics of elder Greece. His alliance with Sparta, and the help which he received from her at the siege of Syracuse, involved him in obligations to her which he fulfilled on more than one occasion; and in the regions of Corcyra his empire came into direct contact with the spheres of some of the states of the mother-country. But these political relations are an unimportant part of his reign. His reign, as a whole, lies apart from the contemporary politics of elder Greece. Yet, from some points of view, it possesses more significance in Grecian, and in European, history than the contemporary history of Sparta and Athens.

Signifi-cance of Dionysius in history. Champion of Europe against the Semite.

Extra-Sicilian Empire.

In the first place, Dionysius stands out as one of the most prominent champions of Europe in the long struggle between the Asiatic and the European for the possession of Sicily. He did what no champion had done before; he carried the war into the enemy's precinct. He well-nigh achieved what it was reserved for an Italian commonwealth to achieve actually, the reclaiming of the whole island for Europe, the complete expulsion of the Semitic in-truder. In the second place, he stands out as the man who raised his own city not only to dominion over all Greek Sicily but to a transmarine dominion, which made her the most powerful city in the Greek world, the most potent state in Europe. The purely Sicilian policy is flung aside, and Syracuse becomes a continental power, laying one hand on that peninsula to which her own island geographically belongs, and stretching out the other to the lands beyond the Hadriatic. And, thirdly, this empire, though it is thinly disguised *Anticipa-* like the later empire of Rome under constitutional forms, is really a *tion of the* monarchical realm, which is a foreshadowing of the Macedonian *Mace-* *donian* monarchies and an anticipation of a new period in European history. *mon-* Again in the art of war Dionysius inaugurated methods which did *archies.* not come into general use till more than half a century later ; some *Military* of his military operations seem to transport us to the age of Alexander *improve-* *ments.* the Great and his successors. In another way too Dionysius antici- *Deifica-* pated the age of those monarchs ; statues were set up representing *tion.* him in the guise of Dionysus, the god by whose name he was called. Here indeed he did not stand alone among his contemporaries ; the Spartan Lysander also had been invested with attributes of divinity.

But in one respect Dionysius was far from being a forerunner of *Dionysius* the Macedonian monarchs : he was not an active or deliberate diffuser *not a* of Hellenic civilisation. On the contrary he appears rather as an *Hellen-* *izer :* undoer of Hellenic civilisation. He destroys Hellenic towns, and he *First signs* replaces Hellenic by Italian communities ; he cultivates the friend- *of the ex-* ship of Gauls and Lucanians, to use them against Greeks, not to *pansion of* make them Greeks. This side of the policy of Dionysius, the estab- *the Italian* *race.* lishment of Italian settlements in Sicily, points in a different direction ; it points—unintentionally, indeed, so far as he was concerned—to the expansion of Italy, it points to the Italian conquest of Sicily which was to be accomplished more than a century after his death.

Dionysius then has the significance of a pioneer. But there is *Why* something else to be said. Original and successful as he was, great *Dionysius* things as he did, we cannot help feeling that he ought to have done *did not do* *more.* greater things still. A master of political wisdom, an originator of daring ideas, a man of endless energy, remarkably temperate in the habits of his life, he was hampered throughout by his unconstitutional position. The nature of tyranny imposed limitations on his work. He had always to consider first the security of his own unchartered rule ; he could never forget the fact that he was a hated master. He could therefore never devote himself to the accomplishment of any object or the solution of any problem with the undivided zeal which may animate a constitutional prince who need never turn aside to examine the sure foundations of his power. We saw how the tyrant's warfare against Carthage was affected by these personal calculations. The Syracusan tyranny accomplished indeed far more than could have been accomplished by the Syracusan democracy ; Dionysius as a tyrant wrought what he could never have wrought as a mere statesman governing by legitimate influence the counsels of a free assembly. But he illustrates—and all the more strikingly, as the pioneer of the great monarchies of the future—the truth to which attention has been called before, that the tyrannies and democracies of Greek cities were in their nature not adapted to create and maintain large empires.

SECT. 9. DIONYSIUS THE YOUNGER

Dionysius II., 367 B.C.

The empire of Dionysius, which he had made fast, to use his own expression, " by chains of adamant "—a strong army, a strong navy, and strong walls—descended to his son, Dionysius, a youth of feeble character, not without amiable qualities, but of the nature that is easily swayed to good or evil and is always dependent on advisers.

Dion, brother-in-law and son-in-law of Diony-sius the elder.

At first he was under the influence of Dion, who had been the most trusted minister of the elder Dionysius in the latter part of his reign, holding the office of admiral, and allied by a double marriage with the tyrant's family. The tyrant had espoused Dion's sister Aris-tomache ; and Dion married one of the daughters of this marriage, Arete, his own niece. The other daughter was given to Dionysius, her half-brother. Another man, possessing the pride, wealth, and ability of Dion, might have sought to fling aside Dionysius, and if he did not seize the tyranny himself, at all events to secure it for the sons

His political aspirations.

of his sister, the brothers of his wife, Hipparinus and Nysaeus. But Dion was not like other men ; his aspirations were loftier and less selfish. His object was not to secure tyranny for any man, but to get rid of tyranny altogether. But this was not to be done by a revolution ; the democracy which would have risen on the ruins of the despotism would have been in Dion's eyes as evil a thing for

Plato's influence on Dion.

Syracuse as the despotism itself. For Dion had imbibed, and thoroughly believed in, the political teaching of his friend, Plato the philosopher. His darling project was to establish at Syracuse a constitution which would so far as possible conform to the theoretical views of Plato, and which would probably have taken the shape of a limited kingship, with some resemblance to the constitution of Sparta. And this could never have been brought about by a pure vote of the Syracusan people ; the ideal constitution must be imposed upon them for their own good. The sole chance lay in persuading a tyrant to impose limitations on his own absolute power and introduce the required constitution. " Give me," says Plato himself, " a city governed by a tyranny, and let the tyrant be young, with good brains, brave, and generous, and let fortune bring in his way a good lawgiver "—then a state has a chance of being well governed. Dion saw in young Dionysius a nature which might be moulded as he wished,—a nature, perhaps, which he missed in his own nephews, Hipparinus and Nysaeus. He devoted himself loyally to Dionysius,

who looked up to his virtue and experience, and he set himself to
interest the young ruler in philosophy and make him take a serious
view of his duties.   But his chief hope lay in bringing the tyrant
under the attraction of the same powerful personality which had
exercised a decisive and abiding influence over himself.   Plato must
come to Syracuse and make the tyrant a philosopher.   The treatment which Plato had experienced on the occasion of a previous visit *c.* 388 *B.C.*
to Sicily, at the hands of the elder Dionysius, was not indeed such
as to encourage him to return.   But he yielded, reluctantly, to the *Plato's*
pressing invitation of the young ruler and the urgent solicitations of *second visit*
Dion, who represented that now at last the moment had come to *to Sicily.*
call an ideal state into actual existence.

It was the vision of a "dreamer dreaming greatly"; and that a *Serious*
statesman of Dion's practical experience and knowledge of human *intention to*
nature should have allowed himself to be guided by such a dream *form an*
ideal state.
may seem strange to us; to us to whom the history of hundreds of
societies throughout a period of more than two thousand years has
brought disillusion.   It has indeed seemed so curious that some
have concluded that Dion was throughout plotting to dethrone
Dionysius, that the philosophical scheme was part of the plot,
and Plato an unconscious tool of the conspiracy.   But the good
faith of Dion seems assured.   We must remember that a state
founded on philosophical principles was a new idea, which was not at
all likely to seem foredoomed to failure to any one who was enamoured
of philosophy; for such a state had never been tried, and consequently there was no example of a previous failure.   On the
contrary, there was the example of Sparta as a success.   The
political speculators of those days always turned with special
predilection to Sparta, as a well-balanced state, and it was believed
that her constitution and discipline had been called into being and
established for all time by the will and fiat of a single extraordinarily wise lawgiver.   Why then should not Dionysius and Dion,
under the direction of Plato, do for Syracuse what Lycurgus had
done for Lacedaemon?   And Dion doubtless thought that his own
experience would enable him to adjust the demands of speculation
to the rude realities of existence.

No welcome could have been more honourable and flattering than
that which Plato received.   He engaged the respect and admiration
of Dionysius, and the young tyrant was easily brought to regard
tyranny as a vile thing and to cherish the plan of building up a
new constitution.   The experiment would probably have been tried,
if Plato, in dealing with his pupil, had acted otherwise than he did.
The nature of Dionysius was one of those natures which are
susceptible of impressions and capable of enthusiasm, but incapable

z

*Plato's
course of
instruction.*
of persevering application.   If Plato had contented himself with
inculcating the general principles which he has expounded with such
charm in his *Republic*, Dionysius would in all likelihood have
attempted to create at Syracuse a dim adumbration of the ideal
state.   It is hardly likely that it would have been long maintained :
still, it would at least have been essayed.   But Plato insisted on
imparting to his pupil a systematic course of philosophical training,
and began with the science of geometry.   The tyrant took up the
study with eagerness ; his court was absorbed in geometry ; but he
presently wearied of it.   And then influences which were opposed to
the scheme of Dion and Plato began to tell.

*Philistus
recalled :
opposed to
Dion's
scheme.*
One of the first acts of the new reign had been to recall from
exile the historian Philistus.   He was entirely adverse to the proposed
reforms, and wished that the tyranny should continue on its old lines.
He and his friends insinuated that the true object of Dion was to
secure the tyranny for one of his own nephews, as soon as Dionysius
had laid it down.   They did everything to turn Dionysius against
Dion, and at last an indiscreet letter of Dion gave them the means
of success.   Syracuse and Carthage were negotiating peace, and
Dion wrote to the Carthaginian Judges not to act without first consulting him.   The letter was intercepted, and though its motive was
*Banishment
of Dion.*doubtless perfectly honest, it was interpreted as treason.   Dion was
banished from Sicily, but was allowed to retain his property ; and the
party of Philistus won the upper hand.   Plato remained for a while
in the island ; Dionysius was jealous of the esteem which he felt for
Dion, and desired above all things to win the same esteem for himself.
*Plato
returns to
Athens.*
But the philosopher's visit had been a failure ; he yearned to get
back to Athens, and at length Dionysius let him go.

So ended the notable scheme of founding an ideal state, the
realisation of which would have involved the disbandment of the
mercenary troops and thereby the collapse of the Syracusan empire.
It is easy to ridicule Plato for want of tact in his treatment of the
young tyrant ; it is easy to flout him as a pedant for not distinguishing between an Academy and a Court.   But Plato was
perfectly right.   The only motive which had brought him to Sicily
was to prepare the way for founding a state fashioned more or less
according to his own ideal.   Now the first condition of the life of
such a state was that a king should be a philosopher.   Therefore,
as Dionysius—not Plato—was to be king in the new state, it was
indispensable that Dionysius should become a philosopher.   Plato
had not the smallest interest in imparting to the tyrant a superficial
smattering of philosophy, enough to beguile him into framing a
Platonic state.   For that state would have been still-born, since it
lacked the first condition of life, a true philosopher at its head.   If

Dionysius had not the stuff of a true, but only of a sham, philosopher, it was useless to make the experiment. Plato adopted the only reasonable course ; he was true to his own ideal.

SECT. 10. DION

Strange as it may appear, after such experiences, Plato seems to have returned once more to Sicily, at the urgent invitation of Dionysius. He can have had no more expectations of making a philosopher out of the tyrant, and his chief motive must have been to bring about the recall of Dion and reconcile him to Dionysius, who appears to have lured the philosopher by the hope that this might be accomplished. Plato was received and entertained with as great honour as before, but his visit was fruitless. Probably the tyrant ascertained that Dion was in the meantime using his wealth to make silent preparations for winning his way back to Syracuse and overthrowing the tyranny. Dionysius therefore took the precaution of confiscating Dion's property ; and then Plato returned to Athens as soon as he could. Dion also betook himself to Old Greece and made Athens his headquarters. Presently the tyrant committed a needless act of tyranny ; he compelled Dion's wife Arete to marry another man. At length Dion deemed that the time for action had come. With a very small force, packed into not more than five merchant ships, he set sail from Zacynthus, to encounter the mighty armaments of Dionysius. His coming was expected, and the admiral Philistus had a fleet in Italian waters to waylay him. But Dion sailed straight across the open sea to Pachynus. His plan was to land in Western Sicily, collect what reinforcements he could, and march on Syracuse. It was a bold enterprise, but Dion knew that the character of the tyrant was feeble, and that the Syracusans pined to be delivered from his tyranny. Driven by a storm to the Libyan coast, the ships of the deliverer finally reached Heraclea Minoa, now a Carthaginian port, in south-western Sicily. Here they learned that Dionysius had departed for Italy with eighty ships, and they lost no time in marching to Syracuse, picking up reinforcements, both Greek and Sicel, on their way. The Campanian mercenaries who were guarding Epipolae were lured away by a trick ; and, making a night march from Acrae, Dion and his party entered Syracuse amid general rejoicings. The Assembly placed the government in the hands of twenty generals, Dion among them. The fortress of Epipolae was secured ; no part of Syracuse remained in possession of Dionysius except the Island, and against this Dion built a wall of defence from the Greater to the Lesser Harbour. Seven days later Dionysius returned.

Third visit of Plato to Syracuse.

Dion at Athens.

357 *B.C.*

Dion sails for Sicily, August.

Enters Syracuse.

Dionysius holds the Island.

While Syracuse was rocking with the first enthusiasm at her deliverance, the deliverer was the popular hero. But Dion was not a man who could hold the affections of the people, for he repelled men by his exceeding haughtiness. And it was seen too that he was determined masterfully to direct the Syracusans how they were to use their freedom. Dionysius, shut up in the Island, resorted to artifices to raise suspicion against him in the minds of the citizens. And a rival appeared on the scene who possessed more popular *Heraclides.* manners than Dion. This was a certain Heraclides, whom the tyrant had banished, and who now returned with an armament of ships and soldiers. The Assembly elected him admiral. Dion undid this act on the ground that his own consent was necessary; and then came forward himself to propose Heraclides. This behaviour alienated the sympathies of the citizens; they did not want another autocrat. Soon afterwards Heraclides won an important sea-fight, defeating Philistus, who had returned from Italy with his *Death of* squadron. The old historian himself was captured and took his own *Philistus.* life. Dionysius thus lost his best support, and presently he escaped from the Island, taking his triremes with him, but leaving a garrison of mercenaries and his young son Apollocrates in command, an unenviable position.

Soon after this the influence of Dion waned so much that the Syracusans deposed him from the post of general, and appointed twenty-five new generals, among them Heraclides. They also refused to grant any pay to the Peloponnesian deliverers who had *Dion* come with Dion. The Peloponnesians would have gladly turned *withdraws* against the Syracusans if Dion had given the signal; but Dion, *to Leontini,* though self-willed, was too genuine a patriot to attack his own city, 356 B.C. and he retired to Leontini with 3000 devoted men.

The Syracusans then went on with the siege of the island fortress, and so hard pressed was the garrison that it determined to surrender. Heralds had been already sent to announce the decision to the *Arrival of* Syracusans, when in the early morning reinforcements arrived— *Nypsius* soldiers and provisions, brought by a Campanian of Naples, by name *(Numsius).* Nypsius, who, eluding the notice of the enemy's ships, sailed into the Great Harbour. The situation was changed, and negotiations were immediately broken off. At first fortune favoured the Syracusans. Heraclides put out to sea, and won a second sea-fight, sinking or capturing whatever warships had been left behind by Dionysius or were brought by Nypsius. At this success the city went wild with joy and spent the night in carousing. Before the dawn of day, when soldiers and generals were alike sunk in a drunken sleep, Nypsius and his troops issued from the gates of the island, and surmounting the cross wall of Dion by scaling-ladders, slew the guards and took possession of Lower Achradina and the Agora. All this part of the city was sacked ; full leave was given to the mercenaries to do as they listed ; they carried off women and children and all the property they could lay hands on. Next day all the citizens who had taken refuge in Epipolae and the Upper Achradina, looking helplessly at what had been done, and seeing that the barbarians were beginning their horrible work again, voted to call Dion to the rescue. Messengers riding as swiftly as they could reached *Dion* Leontini towards evening. Dion led them to the theatre, and *recalled,* there before the gathered folk the envoys told their tale and implored Dion and the Peloponnesians to forget the ingratitude of Syracuse and come to her help. Dion made a moving speech ; he would in any case go, and, if he could not save his city, he would bury himself in her ruins ; but the Peloponnesians might well refuse to stir for a people which had entreated them so ill. A shout went up that Syracuse must be rescued ; and for the second time Dion led the Peloponnesians to her deliverance. They set out at once, and a night march brought them to Megara, five or six miles from Syracuse, at the dawn of day. There dreadful tidings reached them. Nypsius, knowing that the rescue was on its way and deeming that no time was to be lost, had let loose his barbarians again into the city at midnight. They no longer thought of plunder, but only of slaying and burning. At this news the army of rescue hurried on to save what might still be saved. Entering by the Hexapylon on the *rescues* north, Dion cleared his way before him through Achradina, and *Syracuse.* reached the cross-wall which he had himself built as a defence against the Island. It was now broken down, but behind its ruins Nypsius had posted a body of his mercenaries, and this was the scene of the decisive struggle. Dion's men carried the wall, and the foe was driven back into the fortress of Ortygia.

The opponents of Dion, who had not fled, were humbled. Heraclides besought his pardon, and Dion was blamed for not putting him to death. It was at all events foolish magnanimity which consented to the arrangement that Dion should be general with full power on land, and Heraclides by sea. The old dissensions soon broke out, and presently we find a Spartan named Gaesylus reconciling the rivals and constraining Heraclides to swear solemnly to do nothing against Dion.

Nypsius seems to have disappeared from the scene, and it was *Surrender* not long before the son of Dionysius, weary of the long siege, made *of the* up his mind to surrender the Island to Dion. During all these *Island.* dreadful events Dion's sister Aristomache and his wife Arete had been kept in the Island. Dion now took back his wife.

The time at last came for Dion to show what his political aims

Dion's political aim: really were. He professed to have come to give Syracuse freedom; but the freedom which he would have given her was not such as she herself desired. The Syracusan citizens wanted the restoration of their democracy; but to Dion democracy seemed as bad a form of government as tyranny. If, taught by experience, he no longer *a modified* dreamed of a Platonic state, he desired to establish an aristocracy, *aristocracy.* with some democratic limitations, and with a king, or kings, as in Sparta. With this purpose in view he sent to Corinth for helpers and advisers; and he expressed his leanings to the Corinthian oligarchy by an issue of coins, with a flying horse, modelled on the Pegasi of Corinth. But though Dion hoped to establish a state in which the few should govern the many, he made a grave mistake in not immediately placing himself above the suspicion of being a selfish power-seeker—a possible tyrant. The Syracusans longed to see the fortress of the tyrant demolished, and if Dion had complied with their wish he might have secured for himself abiding influence. But though he did not live in the fortress he allowed it to remain, *Dion* and its existence seemed a standing invitation to tyranny. Dion *becomes a* had no intention of allowing the Syracusans to manage their own *tyrant.* affairs, and the enjoyment of power corrupted him. His authority was only limited by the joint command of Heraclides, and at last he was brought to consent that his rival should be secretly assassinated. After this he was to all purposes tyrant, though he might repudiate tyranny with his lips.

Plot of Among those who had come with him from elder Greece to *Callippus;* liberate Syracuse was a pupil of Plato named Callippus; and this man plotted to overthrow Dion, who trusted him implicitly. Aristomache and Arete suspected him and taxed him with treachery; nor *his oath.* were they assured until he had taken the most solemn oath that a mortal could take. He went to the precinct of the great goddesses Demeter and Persephone; the priest wrapped him in the purple robe of the queen of the underworld and gave him a lighted torch; in this guise he swore that he plotted no evil design against Dion. *Murder* But so little regard had Callippus for religion that he chose the *of Dion,* festival of the Maiden by whom he had sworn for the execution of *354 B.C.,* his plot. He employed some men of Zacynthus to murder Dion, and *June.* then seized the power himself.

Tyranny of The tyranny of Callippus lasted for about a year. Then, while *Callippus,* he was engaged in an attack on Catane, the two sons of the elder *354-3 B.C.;* Dionysius by his second wife, Hipparinus and Nysaeus, came to *of Hip-* Syracuse and won possession of Ortygia. These brothers were a *parinus,* worthless pair, drunken and dissolute. Hipparinus held the island *353-1 B.C.;* for about two years; then he was murdered in a fit of drunkenness, *of Nysaeus,* and was succeeded by Nysaeus, who ruled Ortygia five years longer. *351-46 B.C.*

It is not certain how far these tyrants were able to assert their authority over Syracuse outside the precincts of the Island.

During all these changes Dionysius was living at Locri, the *Second* native city of his mother, and ruling it with a tyrant's rod.   His *tyranny of* cruelty and the outrages which he committed on the freeborn *Dionysius,* maidens of the city provoked universal hatred.   At length he saw *346 B.C.* the chance of recovering Syracuse.   Leaving his wife and daughters at Locri with a small garrison, he sailed to Ortygia and drove out Nysaeus.   As soon as he had gone the Locrians arose and easily overcame his mercenaries.   The enormities of which the tyrant *Fate of his* had been guilty may best be measured by the brutal thirst of *wife and* vengeance which now consumed the citizens of Locri.   No supplica- *daughters.* tions, no intervention, no offers of ransom could turn them away from wreaking their pent-up hatred on the wife and daughters of Dionysius.   The women were submitted to the most horrible tortures and insults before they were strangled ; the sea was sown with their ashes.

SECT. 11. TIMOLEON

At this moment tyrannies flourished in Sicily.   Besides Syracuse, the cities of Messana, Leontini, and Catane, and many Sicel towns were under the yoke of tyrants.   Syracuse was at least half free ; Dionysius held only the Island.   But the Syracusans, for lack of another leader, looked for help and guidance, in their struggle against their own tyrant, to the man who had made himself lord of Leontini. This was a certain Hiketas, a man ill to deal with, who was a follower *Hiketas.* of Dion, but after Dion's death caused his wife and sister to be drowned while they were sailing to the Peloponnesus.   This Hiketas was aiming at becoming himself lord of Syracuse, and he hoped to accomplish his purpose with the help of Carthage.   But he veiled *Sicilian* his designs, and he supported an appeal which the Sicilian Greeks *appeal to* now addressed to Corinth.   It was an appeal for help both against *Corinth.* the plague of tyranny which was rampant in Sicily and against the Carthaginians, who were preparing a great armament to descend upon the troubled island.   The Syracusans selected Hiketas as their general.

Corinth, ever a solicitous mother to her colonies, was ready to *Corinth's* respond to the appeal ; and the only difficulty was to find a suitable *response.* commander.   Some one in the assembly, by a sudden inspiration, arose and named Timoleon, the son of Timodemus.   Belonging to a *Timoleon.* noble family, and notable by his personal qualities, Timoleon was living under a strange cloud, through a deed which some highly praised and others severely blamed.   He had saved his brother's life in battle at the risk of his own; but, when that brother afterwards plotted to make himself tyrant, Timoleon and some friends put him to death. His mother and many others abhorred him as guilty of a brother's blood; while others admired him as the slayer of a tyrant. In the light of his later deeds, we know that Timoleon was actuated by the highest motives of duty when he consented to his brother's death. Ever since that terrible day he had lived in retirement, but when his name was mentioned in the Assembly all approved, and Teleclides, a man of influence, expressed the general thought by saying, "We shall decide that he slew a tyrant, if he is successful; that he slew his brother, if he fails." The enterprise was to be Timoleon's ordeal.

The sailing of Timoleon, 344 B.C. With ten ships of war, a few fellow-citizens, and about 1000 mercenaries, Timoleon crossed the Ionian sea, guided, it was said, by the track of a flaming torch, the emblem of the Sicilian goddesses Demeter and Persephone. At Rhegium, now free from the rule of tyrants, he met with a warm welcome. But he found a Carthaginian fleet awaiting him there, and likewise ambassadors from Hiketas, who demanded that the ships and soldiers should be sent back to Corinth, since the Carthaginians would not permit them to cruise in Sicilian waters. As for Timoleon himself, Hiketas would be pleased to have his help and counsel. Timoleon had no thought of heeding such a message. It was not to set up the rule of Hiketas at Syracuse that he had come, or to submit to the dictation of the foes of Hellas. But the difficulty was to leave the roadstead of Rhegium in face of the Punic fleet. Here Timoleon showed caution and craft. He pretended to agree to the proposals, but he asked that the whole matter and the intentions of Hiketas should be clearly stated in the presence of the Rhegine people. With the connivance of the Rhegines, time was wasted, and the Carthaginians and the ambassadors of Hiketas were detained in the Assembly, until the Corinthian ships had put out to sea, Timoleon himself slipping away just in time to embark in the last of them. He made straight for Tauromenium.

Timoleon comes to Tauromenium. It will be remembered that Tauromenium, planted by Himilco to be a Sicel city, had been taken by Dionysius to be an abode for his mercenaries. Amid the troubles after the tyrant's death it had gained its independence, and a citizen named Andromachus had become the foremost man in its public affairs. Andromachus induced his fellow-citizens to offer a home to the homeless Naxians whose parents Dionysius had so cruelly dispossessed. The Naxians came back to the hill which looked down on the place of their old city; Naxos revived in Tauromenium. And the Naxians were the first Sicilians to welcome the deliverer of Sicily to her shores. Timoleon's

Settlement of Naxians there by Andromachus.

first success was at Hadranum, the Sicel town where the great Sicilian fire-god Hadranus had his chief abode. The men of Hadranum *Battle of* were at discord among themselves ; some would summon Hiketas, *Hadra-* others invited Timoleon ; and both Hiketas and Timoleon came. It *num.* was a race between them to get to Hadranum first. Timoleon, the later to arrive, surprised the enemy as they were resting outside the town, and defeated them, although in numbers they were five to one. The gates of the city were then thrown open and Hadranum became the headquarters of Timoleon's army. Soon afterwards Hiketas suborned two men to assassinate the Corinthian leader, but the plot was frustrated at the last moment ; and henceforth the belief gained ground that Timoleon was hedged about by some divine protection. The fire-god of Hadranum too had shown by miraculous signs that he approved of the stranger's enterprise. Other cities now allied themselves with Timoleon ; and presently Dionysius sent a message to him, proposing to surrender the Island, and asking only to be allowed to retire in safety to Corinth, with his private property. The offer was at once accepted ; the fortress, and the mercenaries who guarded it, and all the war gear were transferred to Timoleon. Dionysius lived the rest of his life at Corinth in harmless obscurity. *The end of* Many anecdotes were told of the trivial doings of the fallen lord of *Dionysius.* Sicily and his smart sayings. When some one contrasted his fortune with that of his father, he remarked, " My father came into power when democracy was hated, but I when tyranny was envied."

Having won Ortygia sooner and more easily than could have been hoped, it remained for Timoleon to liberate the rest of Syracuse, which was in the hands of Hiketas. But Hiketas had powerful *Cartha-* allies. A hundred and fifty Carthaginian ships, under the command *ginians at* of Mago, sailed into the Great Harbour, and a Carthaginian force *Syracuse* was admitted into Syracuse. The Corinthian commander in the *supporting* Island — Timoleon himself still abode at Hadranum — was hard *Hiketas.* pressed ; but presently Mago and Hiketas went off to besiege Catane, and Neon making a successful sally occupied Achradina. At the same time reinforcements from Corinth, which had been for some time delayed in Italy by the Carthaginian fleet, arrived in Sicily. It was now time for Timoleon himself to appear at Syracuse. He pitched his camp on the south side, on the banks of the Anapus. Then another piece of luck befell him. The Greek mercenaries, both his own and those of Hiketas, used to amuse their idle hours by fishing for eels at the mouth of the river ; and as they had no cause of quarrel, though they were ready to kill each other for pay, they used to converse amicably on such occasions. One of Timoleon's soldiers observed that the Greeks ought to combine against the barbarians, and the words coming to the ears of Mago caused him to conceive suspicions of Hiketas; he suddenly sailed off with all his fleet; but when he reached Carthage he slew himself and his countrymen crucified his corpse. This story, however, can hardly be the whole explanation of Mago's strange behaviour.

Thus freed from his most formidable foe, Timoleon soon drove Hiketas from Epipolae, and Syracuse was at length completely free. The Syracusans had found a deliverer who did not, like Dion, seek to be their master; and the fortress of Dionysius was pulled down. This act of demolition seemed the seal and assurance of their deliverance. But the city was dispeopled and desolate, grass grew in the market-place; and the first task of the deliverer was to *Syracuse* repopulate it with new citizens. The Corinthians made proclama-*repeopled.* tions at the festivals of elder Greece, inviting emigrants to resettle Syracuse; men whom the tyrants had banished flocked back; and 60,000 men in all gathered both from west and east, with women and children, and restored the strength of the city. The laws of Diocles were issued anew, and the democratic constitution was revived *Democracy.* and in some respects remodelled. The most important innovation was the investing of the *amphipolos* or priest of Olympian Zeus with the chief magistracy. The priest was annually elected and gave his name to the year; but, as he was chosen by lot out of three clans, his promotion to be the first magistrate of the republic was a limita-tion of the democracy. Such was the renovation of Syracuse; and *Coinage.* her debt to Corinth in the winning of freedom was reflected in the issue of coins with the Corinthian Pegasus on the obverse.

Tyrants Timoleon then went on to do for other towns in Sicily what he *suppressed* had done for Syracuse. Many tyrants submitted; even Hiketas, *in Sicily.* who had withdrawn to Leontini. There was also work to be done against the Carthaginians, who were intent upon recovering lost ground and were preparing for another great effort to drive the *Cartha-* Greeks out of Sicily. Five years after Timoleon had landed in the *ginian* island, a large armament sailed from Carthage and put in at *expedition* Lilybaeum. It consisted of 200 galleys and 1000 transports; there *against* were 10,000 horses—some for war chariots; and the total number *Sicily,* of the infantry was said to be 70,000. The flower of the host was *339 B.C.* the "Sacred Band" of 2500 Carthaginian citizens, men of birth and wealth. Hamilcar and Hasdrubal, the commanders, decided to march right across Sicily against Syracuse. But Timoleon did not await them there; he would try to encounter them west of the Halycus, in Punic not in Grecian territory. Collecting such an army as he could—it amounted to no more than 10,000—he set out. On the march he was deserted by 1000 mercenaries who clamoured for arrears of pay and murmured at being led against such over-whelming odds; and with difficulty could he persuade the rest to go

on.   The Carthaginians were encamped on the west bank of the
Crimisus, a branch of the river Hypsas, not that which washes
Acragas, but that which flows through the territory of Selinus.   The
city of Entella, now held by Campanians, was situated on the
Crimisus, and it may be that the Punic army had halted with the
hope of taking it.

The field of the battle which was now fought between the Greeks *Battle of*
and Phoenicians on the banks of the Crimisus is unknown.   In the *the Crimi-*
morning the Greeks ascended a hill which divided them from the *sus (June).*
river, and on their way they met mules laden with wild celery, a *(σέλινον.)*
herb which was used to wreathe sepulchral slabs.   The soldiers were
depressed by an incident which seemed ominous of evil ; but of the
same herb were wrought the crowns of victors in the Isthmian games,
and Timoleon hastened to interpret the chance as an augury of
victory.   He wreathed his head with the celery, and the whole host
followed his example.   Then two eagles appeared in the sky, one
bearing a serpent—another fortunate omen.   The Greeks halted on
the hilltop, striving to pierce the mist which enveloped the ground
below them ; and when it melted away they saw the enemy crossing
the stream.   The war-chariots crossed first, and behind came the
Sacred Band.   Timoleon saw that his chance lay in attacking before
the whole army had crossed.   He sent down his cavalry to lead the
attack and himself followed with the foot.   The war-chariots prevented the horses from approaching the Sacred Band ; so Timoleon
ordered the cavalry to move aside and assail the flank of the foe,
leaving the way clear for the infantry.   It is not recorded how the
infantry swept away the war-chariots, but they succeeded in reaching
the Sacred Band.   The Carthaginians, firm and immovable, withstood
the onset of the spears ; and the Greeks, finding that all their thrusting could not drive back or pierce the shield wall, flung down their
spears and drew their swords.   In the sword fight it was no longer
a matter of weight and courage; skill and lithesome movements told ;
and the Greeks, superior in these qualities, utterly smote the Sacred
Band.   Meanwhile the rest of the Punic army had crossed the river,
and although the flower of it was destroyed, there were still enormous
numbers to deal with.   But fortune followed Timoleon.   Clouds had
gathered and were hanging over the hills, and suddenly there burst
forth a tempest of lightning and wind-driven rain and hail.   The
Greeks had their backs to the wind ; the rain and hail drove into the
faces of the enemy, who in the noise could not hear the commands
of their officers.   When the ground became muddy, the lighter
armour of the Greeks gave them a great advantage over their foes,
who floundered about, weighed down by their heavy mail.   At length
the Carthaginians could no longer stand their ground, and when they

turned to fly they found death in the Crimisus. Rapidly swollen by the rain, the river was now rushing along in a furious torrent, which swept men and horses to destruction. It is said that 15,000 prisoners were secured ; that 10,000 men had been killed in the fight, not counting those who perished in the river ; rich spoils of gold and silver were taken in the camp. The choicest of the arms were sent to the Isthmus to be dedicated in the temple of Poseidon.

The battle had fallen out clean contrary to what was like to have been. Timoleon had gained a victory which may be set beside Gelon's victory at Himera. But he did not follow it up ; he made no attempt to cut short the Phoenician dominion in Sicily. Perhaps his inaction was due less to unwillingness than to embarrassments *Tyranny* which threatened Syracuse. The tyrant of Catane, who had gone *reviving is* over to Timoleon, declared against him. Hiketas seems to have *suppressed.* seized again the tyranny at Leontini ; and Timoleon found himself engaged in a war with these two tyrants, Mamercus and Hiketas, who were aided by Carthaginian mercenaries. At last both the tyrants were captured. The Syracusans put them both to death, and slew the wife and daughter of Hiketas, in retaliation for the murder of the wife and sister of Dion. The Messanians also put to death their oppressor, Hippon, with torture, and the school-boys were taken to the theatre to witness a tyrant's death. Other cities under the yoke of tyranny were likewise liberated, and some *Peace with* dispeopled towns, like Acragas and Gela, were colonised. After *Carthage.* twenty years of troubles Sicily was to have a respite now. Carthage made peace, the Halycus being again fixed as the frontier, and she undertook to do nothing to uphold tyrants in Greek cities.

Timoleon had now delivered Sicily both from domestic despots and from foreign foes, and having achieved his task he laid down the powers which had been granted to him for its performance. Among the great men in Greek history he holds a unique place ; for the work which he accomplished was inspired neither by selfish ambition nor by patriotism. He sought no power for himself; he laboured in a strange land for cities which might adopt him but were not his own. Patriotism, indeed, in the widest sense, might stimulate his ardour, when he fought for Hellas against the Phoenician. But of Greek leaders who achieved as much as he, there is none whose conduct was, like Timoleon's, wholly guided by simple devotion to duty. The Syracusans gave him a property near Syracuse, and there he dwelt till his death, two years after his crowning victory. Occasionally he visited the city when the folk wished to ask for his counsel, but he had become blind and these visits were rare. He was lamented *The Timo-* by all Greek Sicily, and at Syracuse his memory was preserved by a *leonteion.* group of public buildings called after him.

The land had rest for twenty years after Timoleon's death ; the direct results of his work did not amount to more than that.   A tyrant arose then of a worse type than the elder Dionysius, and his hand was heavy upon Sicily.   But the career of Agathocles lies outside the limits of this history.

SECT. 12. EVENTS IN GREAT GREECE

In these days, troubles and dangers beset the Greeks of Italy no less than their brethren of Sicily.   On the mainland, as in the island, the Hellenic name seemed like to have been blotted out,—there by the Phoenicians and the Italian mercenaries, here by the native races. The power of the elder Dionysius had kept at bay the Lucanians, the Messapians, the Iapygians, and other neighbours who pressed on Great Greece ; but when his son was attacked by Dion, the Syracusan empire dissolved of itself, and the barbarians of Italy, having no great power to fear, began anew to descend from the mountains on the Greek settlements of the coast.   A number of tribes in the toe of the *The Bret-* peninsula banded themselves together in a league with their federal *tian league.* capital at Consentia ; and this Brettian league, as it was called, aimed at subduing all the Greek cities of the promontory.   Terina, Hip- *c. 356 B.C.* ponion, New Sybaris on the Traeis, and other places were captured. Men were not blind to the danger which menaced Western Hellas, of being sunk under a tide of barbarism ; one of the objects of Plato and Dion had been to drive all the barbarian mercenaries out of Greek Sicily.   But in Italy the peril was greatest, and there was sore need of help from without.   The appeal of Syracuse to her mother Corinth and the coming of Timoleon put it into the mind of Taras, hard bestead by the neighbouring peoples, to ask succour of her mother Sparta.   The appeal came at a favourable moment.   Sparta was not *King* in a position to undertake any political scheme at home, and king *Archida-* Archidamus eagerly embraced the chance of going forth to fight for *mus sails* Hellas against the barbarians of the West, even as his father Agesi- *to Italy,* laus, sixty years ago, had fought against the barbarians of the East. *343 B.C.* He got together a band of mercenaries, chiefly from the Phocian survivors of the Sacred War,[1] and sailed to Italy.   For four or five years seemingly he strove against the barbarians, but without winning any decisive success, and was finally killed at Mandonium in a battle *Battle of* with the Lucanians.   The ineffectual expedition of Archidamus was *Man-* a striking contrast to the brilliant achievements of Timoleon.   But *donium,* Taras was not ungrateful for his efforts.   She had commemorated her *338 B.C.* appeal to Sparta by minting beautiful gold pieces, on which the infant

---

[1] See below, p. 700.

Taras was shown supplicating Poseidon of Cape Taenarus. The tragic issue of that appeal suggested a motive for another series of coins, and called forth one of those pathetic allusions which Greek art could achieve with matchless grace. Taras is represented riding on his dolphin and sadly contemplating a helmet ; it is the helmet of the Spartan king who had fallen in his service.

Expedition of Alexander of Epirus, 334 B.C. Taras was soon forced to seek a new champion. She invited Alexander of Molossia, the uncle of Alexander the Great, and this king saw and seized the chance of founding an empire in the West—of doing there on a small scale what his nephew was accomplishing on a mighty scale in Asia. He was an able man and success attended his arms. On the east coast of Italy he subdued the Messapians, and pushed as far north as Sipontum, which he captured. In the west he smote the Brettian league, seizing Consentia and liberating Terina. His power was so great in the south that Rome made a treaty with him ; and it is possible that his designs reached to Sicily.

[But a coin issue from Taras shows that Alexander was taking firm hold of his allies. On the obverse is the oak-crowned head of Zeus of Dodona, on the reverse a thunderbolt and spear-head with the legend " Alexander, son of Neoptolemos." Taras, her freedom menaced, renounced her alliance.] War ensued, Thurii upholding Alexander. The barbarians profited by these struggles to rise against their con-

Battle of Pandosia, 331-30 B.C. Alexander's death. queror, and a battle was fought at Pandosia. During the engagement, a Lucanian exile in the Tarentine army stabbed the king in the back, and the design of an Epirote empire bestriding the Hadriatic perished with him. This befell not long after the overthrow of the Persian monarchy on the field of Gaugamela. But Alexander's work had not been futile ; henceforward Taras was able to keep the upper hand over her Italian neighbours.

FIG. 170.—Gold coin of Taras (reverse). Taras on dolphin; contemplating helmet [legend : ΤΑΡΑΣ ; below ΚΑΛ].

FIG. 171.—Gold coin of Taras (reverse). Infant Taras supplicating Poseidon on throne [legend : ΤΑΡΑΝ-ΤΙΝΩΝ].

CHAPTER XVI

THE RISE OF MACEDONIA

AFTER the battle of Mantinea, when Thebes retired from her aggressive policy, Athens stood forth the most important state in Old Greece. She would have been free to devote all her energies to re-establishing her power on the coasts of the northern Aegean and by the gates of the Pontic waters, and would doubtless have successfully achieved this main object of her policy, if two outlying powers had not suddenly stepped upon the scene to thwart her and cut short her empire. These powers, Caria and Macedon, lay in opposite quarters of the Greek world. Both were monarchies, both were semi-Hellenic. Macedon was a land-power; Caria was both a land-power and a sea-power, but it was as a sea-power that she was formidable to Athens. Of the two, it was Caria which seemed to Greece the country with a future and to Athens the dangerous rival. Of Macedonia little account was taken by the civilised world, and Athens expected that she could always manage it. No prophet in his happiest hour of clairvoyance could have predicted that within thirty years Caria would have sunk back into insignificance, leaving nothing to posterity save the sepulchre of her prince, while Macedon would bear the arts and wisdom of Hellas to the ends of the earth.

SECT. 1. ATHENS REGAINS THE CHERSONESE AND EUBOEA

The death of Epaminondas delivered Athens from her most dangerous and active enemy; but the intrigues which he had spun against her in the north bore results after his death. Alexander of Pherae, who had become the ally of the Thebans, seized the island of Peparethus with his pirate ships and defeated an Athenian armament under Leosthenes. He then repeated the daring enterprise of the Spartan Teleutias, sailing rapidly into the Piraeus, plundering the shops, and disappearing as rapidly with ample spoil. The Athenians *Thessalian* replied by making a close defensive and offensive alliance with the *alliance of Athens.*

federal state of the Thessalians.   The stone of the treaty is preserved. The allies of both parties are included.   The Thessalians bind them- selves not to conclude the war against Alexander without the Athenians,

and the Athenians in like wise " without the president (archon) and league of the Thessalians " ; and the treasurers of Athens are directed to pull down the stêlê on which the former alliance with Alexander had been inscribed.

FIG. 172.—Coin of Alexander of Pherae (re- verse).   Lion head [legend : ΑΛΕΞΑΝ].

But the Athenians vented their indignation within their own walls.   Since the capture of Oropus there had been signs of smouldering discontent at the conduct of affairs.   Callistratus had been indicted and acquitted in the matter of Oropus ; but his credit had been roughly shaken, and Alexander's insult to the city at her very doors excited the popular

Condemna- tion and exile of Calli- stratus, 361 *B. C.*

wrath to such a pitch that the statesman as well as the defeated admiral was condemned to death, and escaped only by a timely flight.   Thus the ablest Athenian statesman of the fourth cen- tury passed from the stage, and no sympathy followed him.   Some years later he ventured to return from his Macedonian exile, hoping that the wrath of his countrymen would have passed away.   Their wrath had passed, but it had not been replaced by regret.   On reach- ing Athens he sought the refuge of suppliants at the altar of the Twelve Gods ; but no voice was raised to save him, and the execu- tioner carried out the doom of the people.   The Athenians were always austere masters of their statesmen, and it sometimes appears to us—though in truth we seldom have sufficient knowledge of the circumstances to justify a confident judgment—that they unreasonably expected an ingathering where no seed had been sown.

The Thracian Chersonese.

The public indignation which had been aroused by the daring stroke of the tyrant of Pherae was enhanced by the bad tidings which came from Thrace.   King Cotys, the reviver of the Odrysian power, had succeeded in laying hold of Sestos and almost the whole peninsula which guards the entrance to the Propontis, in spite of the

Death of king Cotys, 360-59.

Athenian fleet.   Soon afterwards the old king was murdered and his son Cersobleptes was challenged by two rivals.   This was advan- tageous to Athens, as she could play off one Thracian prince against

Cersobleptes and his brothers succeed Cotys.

another.   The territory on the Propontis fell to Cersobleptes, who was supported by the Euboean Charidemus, a mercenary captain who had frequently been employed in the service of Athens, and had married, like Iphicrates, a daughter of the Thracian king.   Cersobleptes engaged to hand over to Athens the entire Chersonese, except Cardia, " the enemy of Athens," which was to remain independent.   But there was no fleet on the spot to enforce the immediate fulfilment of the promise ;

and, when an admiral was presently sent out, he was defeated by
Charidemus. At length a capable man was sent, Chares, a daring, 357 *B.C.*
dissolute, and experienced son of Ares, who speedily captured Sestos *Recovery of*
and punished the inhabitants for their unfaithfulness by an unmerciful *the Cherso-*
slaughter. Cersobleptes was forced to change his attitude, and the *nesus and*
peninsula was recovered. The Athenians, adopting the same policy *settlement*
which they had followed in Samos, sent outsettlers to the Cher- *of cleru-*
sonese. In the same year Euboea was won back to the Athenian *chies.*
league, and there even seemed a fair prospect of accomplishing what *Recovery of*
of all things would have rejoiced them most, the recovery of long-lost *Euboea,*
Amphipolis. But their new scheme against Amphipolis may be said *357 B.C.*
to open, in a certain way, a new chapter in the history of Greece.

SECT. 2. PHILIP II. OF MACEDONIA

The man for whom Macedonia had waited long came at last.
We have met once and again in the course of our history kings of
that ambiguous country—Hellenic, and yet not Hellenic : Alexander
playing a double part at Plataea ; Perdiccas playing, with consummate
skill, a double part in the war of Sparta and Athens. But now the
hour of Macedonia has come, and we must look more closely at the
cradle of the power which was destined to change the face not only
of the Greek but of the oriental world.

In their fortress of Aegae the Macedonian kings had ruled for *Macedonia.*
ages with absolute sway over the lands on the northern and north-
western coasts of the Thermaic Gulf, which formed Macedonia in the
strictest sense. The Macedonian people and their kings were of
Greek stock, as their traditions and the scanty remains of their
language combine to testify. They were a military people, and they
extended their power westward and northward over the peoples of
the hills, so that Macedonia in a wider sense reached to the borders of
the Illyrians in the west and of the Paeonians in the north. These hill
tribes, the Orestians, Lyncestians, and others, belonged to the Illyrian
race, and they were ever seeking to cast off the bond of subjection
which attached them to the kings of Aegae. In Illyria and Paeonia
they had allies who were generally ready to support them in rebellion ;
and the dangers which Macedonia had constantly to encounter and
always to dread from half-subjugated vassals and warlike enemies
had effectually hindered her hitherto from playing any conspicuous
part in the Greek world.

Thus the Macedonian kingdom consisted of two heterogeneous
parts, and the Macedonian kings had two different characters. Over
the Greek Macedonians of the coast the king ruled immediately ;
they were his own people, his own " Companions." Over the Illyric

folks of the hills he was only overlord; they were each subject to its own chieftain, and the chieftains were his unruly vassals. It is clear that Macedonia could never become a great power until these vassal

peoples had been completely tamed and brought under the direct rule of the kings, and until the Illyrian and Paeonian neighbours had been taught a severe lesson. These were the tasks which awaited the man who should make Macedonia. The kings had made some efforts to introduce Greek civilisation into their land.

King Archelaus. FIG. 173.—Coin of Archelaus I. (obverse). Horseman with two spears.

Archelaus, who succeeded Perdiccas, had been a builder and a roadmaker, and, following the example of Greek tyrants, he had succeeded in making his court at Pella a centre for famous artists and poets. Euripides, the tragic poet, Timotheus, the most eminent leader of a new school of music, Zeuxis the painter, and many another, may have found pleasure and relief in a change from the highly civilised cities of the south to a new and fresher atmosphere, where there were no politicians. It is sometimes said that Macedonia was still in the Homeric stage of development. The position of the monarch, however, was different from that of the Homeric king. [Though the Macedonian monarch was the religious head of the state and led the army in war, his power was not absolute. He had to observe traditional law. Moreover it was the assembled Macedonians who decided the succession, and it was only on their authority that a capital charge could be heard.] This was the charter of Macedonian liberty. Fighting and hunting were the chief occupations of this vigorous people. A Macedonian who had not killed his man wore a cord round his waist; and until he had

slain a wild boar he could not sit at table with the men. Like the Thracians, they drank deep; Bacchic mysteries had been introduced; it was in Macedonian air, on the banks of Lake Ludias, that Euripides drew inspiration for his *Bacchae.*

Perdiccas sole king, 365 B.C.;

slain 359 B.C.

We have seen how Perdiccas slew his guardian and stepfather Ptolemy and reigned alone. Six years later the Illyrians swooped down upon Macedonia, and the king was slain in battle. It was a critical moment for the kingdom; the land was surrounded by enemies, for the Paeonians at the same time menaced it in the north, and

FIG. 174.—Coin of Perdiccas III. (obverse). Head of Heracles.

from the east a Thracian army was advancing to set a pretender on the throne. The rightful heir, Amyntas, the son of the slain king, was a child. But there was one man in the land who was equal to

the situation—this child's uncle, Philip ; and he took the government *Philip,*
and the guardianship of the boy into his own hands. We have *guardian*
already met Philip as one of the hostages who were carried off to *of Amyntas,*
Thebes. He had lived there for a few years, and drunk in the *359 B.C.*
military and political wisdom of Epaminondas and Pelopidas. We *Philip*
know not why he was allowed to return to his home soon after the *returns to*
death of Ptolemy ; perhaps *Macedonia,*
364 B.C.
it was thought that his
affections had been firmly
won by Thebes and that
he would be more useful
to her in Macedonia.

Philip was twenty-four
years old when he was
called upon to rescue his
country and the dynasty
of his own house. The
danger consisted in the

FIG. 175.—Coin of Philip II. Obverse : head
of laureate Zeus. Reverse : horse and jockey ;
thunderbolt below [legend : ΦΙΛΙΙΙΙΟΥ].

number of his enemies,—foreign invaders, and domestic pretenders,
and pretenders supported by foreign powers. Philip's first step *Philip dis-*
was to buy off the Paeonians by a large sum of money, his next *poses of the*
to get rid of the pretenders. One of these, Argaeus, was assisted by *pretenders,*
Athens with a strong fleet. Philip defeated him, and did all in his *359 B.C. ;*
power to come to terms with Athens. He released without ransom
the Athenians whom he had made prisoners in the battle ; and he
renounced all claim to the possession of Amphipolis, which his
brother king Perdiccas had occupied with a garrison. Gold
easily induced the Thracians to desert the pretender whom they had
come forth to support.

But the Paeonians were quieted only for the moment, and the
Illyrians were still in the land, besetting Macedonian towns. It
was necessary to deal with these enemies once for all, and to assert
decisively the military power of Macedon. Philip had new ideas on
the art of war, and he spent the winter in remodelling and training
his army. When the springtide came round he had 10,000 foot-
soldiers and 600 horsemen, thoroughly disciplined and of great
physical strength. With this force he marched against the Paeonians *defeats the*
and quelled them in a single battle. He then turned against the *Paeonians,*
Illyrians, who refused to evacuate the towns they held in the Lynces- *358 B.C.*
tian territory. A great battle was fought, in which Philip tested his *(spring) ;*
new military ideas ; the Illyrians left 7000 on the field ; and the *the Illyrians,*
vassals of the highlands, who had supported the invaders, were *358 B.C.*
reduced to abject submission.

When he had thus established his power over his dependencies and cleared the land of foes, Philip lost little time in pushing eastward, on the side of Thrace. The motive for this rapid advance was the imperative necessity of obtaining gold. Without gold Philip could not develop his country or carry out his military schemes; the Macedonians were not a commercial folk; and therefore his prospects depended on possessing land which produced the precious ore.

Thasian settlement at Crenides, 359 B.C. In Mount Pangaeus on his eastern frontier there were rich sources of gold; and, incited by him, a number of people from the opposite island of Thasos, where the art of mining was well understood, had crossed over to Crenides near the mountain and formed a settlement. But in order to control the new mines it was indispensable to become master of the great fortress on the Strymon, the much-coveted Amphipolis. The interests of Philip thus came into direct collision with the interests of Athens. Here Philip revealed his skill in

Philip's treaty with Athens, and secret agreement. diplomacy. When he released the Athenian prisoners, he professed to resign all claim to Amphipolis; and on this basis negotiated a peace with Athens. When the treaty was concluded, a secret article was agreed upon, by which Philip undertook to conquer Amphipolis for Athens, and Athens undertook to surrender to him the free town of

Philip attacks Amphipolis, 357 B.C. Pydna. It is probable that this secret engagement was not made until Philip had actually attacked Amphipolis, and the Amphipolitans —preferring Athens to Macedon—had sent a request for Athenian succour. The moment was inconvenient, as the forces of Athens could not be spared from the Chersonese; and the Athenians, failing to grasp the situation, trusted the promises of Philip. Of course Philip deceived them, and they deserve no sympathy; for their own part of the agreement was a shameful act of treachery to Pydna,

FIG. 176.—Gold coin of Philippi. Obverse: head of Heracles. Reverse: tripod; palm above; Phrygian cap [legend: ΦΙΛΙΠ-ΠΩΝ].

their ally. Their orators might cry out against the perfidy of the Macedonian; but the truth is that they thought to make Philip a tool of their own designs and he showed them that in diplomacy he was not their dupe but their master.

When Philip had taken Amphipolis, he converted the Thasian settlement of Crenides into a great fortress, which he called after his own name, Philippi. He had thus two strong stations to secure Mount Pangaeus; and the yield of the gold mines, which were soon actively worked, amounted to at least 1000 talents a year. No Greek state was so rich. The old capital, Aegae or Edessa, was now definitely abandoned, and the seat of government was established at Pella, the favourite residence of Archelaus. This coming down from Aegae to

Pella is significant of the opening of a new epoch in Macedonian history.

Not long afterwards Philip captured Pydna. If the seizure of *Philip* Amphipolis was an injury to Athens, the capture of Pydna was an *takes* insult. He then took Potidaea, but instead of keeping it for himself, *Pydna and* handed it over to the Olynthians, to whom he also ceded Anthemus. *c. B.C. 356;* The Olynthians, alarmed by his operations on the Strymon, had made *his alliance* proposals to Athens for common action against Macedon. The *with* Athenians, trusting Philip, had rejected the overtures. But when *Olynthus.* they found that they had been duped, they would have been ready and glad to co-operate with Olynthus ; and it was to prevent such a combination that Philip dexterously propitiated the Olynthians — intending to devour them on some future day. With the exception of Methone, the Athenians had no foothold now on the coasts of the Thermaic Gulf.

They formed alliances [1] with the Thracians of the west, who were indignant at the Macedonian occupation of Crenides, and with the Paeonian and Illyrian kings, who were smarting under their recent discomfitures. But Philip prevented the common action of the allies. He forced the Paeonians to become his vassals ; his ablest general *Defeat of* — his only general, he used to say himself — Parmenion inflicted *Illyrians,* another overwhelming defeat on the Illyrians ; and the Thracians, *356 B.C.,* again bought off, renounced their rights to Mount Pangaeus. *autumn.*

But the successes cost Philip little. Having established his mining town, he assumed the royal title, setting his nephew aside, and devoted himself during the next few years to the consolidation of his kingdom, and the creation of a national army. It was in these years *The mak-* that he made Macedonia. His task, as has been already indicated, *ing of* was to unite the hill tribes, along with his own Macedonians of the *Macedonia.* coast, into one nation. The means by which he accomplished this was military organisation. He made the highlanders into professional soldiers and kept them always under arms. Caught by the infection of the military spirit, seduced by the motives of emulation and ambition, they were to forget that they were Orestians or Lyncestians, and blend into a single homogeneous Macedonian people. To complete this consummation would be a work of years, but Philip conceived the project clearly and set about it at once. " A professional army with a national spirit—that was the new idea." Both infantry and cavalry were indeed organised in territorial regiments ; perhaps Philip could not have ventured at first on any other system. But common pride and common desire of promotion, common hope

[1] A treaty of alliance in summer 356, between Athens, the Thracian king Cetriporis and his brothers (who ruled in western Thrace), Lyppeios the Paeonian, and Grabos the Illyrian, is extant.

Hetairoi.

Hyp-aspists.

of victory, tended to obliterate these distinctions, and they were done away with under Philip's son. The heavy cavalry were called " Companions " of the king and " Royal " soldiers, and they were more honourable than the infantry. Among the infantry there was a special corps of *Hypaspistae*, including a royal guard.

The famous Macedonian phalanx, which Philip drilled, was merely a modified form of the usual battle-line of Greek spearmen. The men in the phalanx stood freer, in a more open array, and used a longer spear ; so that the whole line, though still cumbrous enough, was more easily wielded, and the effect was produced not merely by the sheer pressure of a heavy mass of men but by the skilful manipulation of weapons. Nor was the phalanx intended to decide a battle, like the deep columns of Epaminondas ; its function was to keep the front of the foe in play, while the cavalry, in wedge-like squadrons, rode into the flanks. It was by these tactics that Philip had won his victory over the Illyrians.

But Greece paid little heed to the things which Philip was doing. The Athenians might indeed encourage his Illyrian and Paeonian enemies, and urge the Thracians to drive him from Mount Pangaeus, but though he had outwitted them, they could not yet see that he was an enemy of a different stamp from a Cotys or a Cersobleptes ; having managed Macedonia for a hundred years, they had little fear that as soon as they had the time to spare they would easily manage it again.

Birth of Alexander, summer, 356 B. C.

When Philip married Olympias, the daughter of an Epirot prince, the event could cause no sensation ; the birth of a son a year later stirred no man's heart in Greece ; for who, in his wildest dreams, could have foreseen in the Macedonian infant the greatest conqueror who had yet been born into the world ? If it had been revealed to men in that autumn that a power had started up which was to guide history into new paths, they would have turned their eyes not to Pella but to Halicarnassus.

SECT. 3. MAUSOLUS OF CARIA

Caria, like Macedonia, was peopled by a double race, the native Carians and the Greek settlers on the coast. But the native Carians were further removed than the Illyrians from the Greeks : the Illyrians spoke a tongue of the same Indo-Germanic stock as the Greeks ; the Carians belonged to an older race which held the region of the Aegean before Greeks and Illyrians came. Yet the Carians were in closer touch with Greece than the Greeks of Macedonia. The Greeks of Caria were always abreast of Greek civilisation, and they had assimilated and tutored the natives of the land. Tralles and Mylasa were to all appearance Greek towns ; Greek was the dominant language of the country. A province of the Persian empire, Caria had yet a certain independent bond of union among her cities in an Amphictionic League which met in the temple of Zeus at Lagina. It was a religious union, though it might be used for purposes of common political action. But political unity was given to Caria not by federation but by monarchy. A citizen of Mylasa named *Heca-* Hecatomnus succeeded in establishing his rule over the whole land, *tomnus,* soon after the death of Tissaphernes, and the Great King esteemed *c.* 395-90 it his most prudent policy to acknowledge the "dynast of Caria" as *to* 377 *B.C.* his official satrap. Both Hecatomnus and his son Mausolus,[1] who succeeded to his power, never failed to pay their tribute to the treasury of Susa or to display the becoming submission to the Persian king ;

only once—as we have seen—when all the western satraps rebelled, did Mausolus fall short in his loyalty. The Carian Dynasts—they never assumed the royal title—thus secured for themselves a free hand. With the constitutions of the Carian cities their sovereignty did not interfere. Thus even in their own city, Mylasa, the popular Assembly still passes decrees, and these decrees are ratified not by Mausolus but by the "Three Tribes"—perhaps a sort of aristocratic council. In fact Hecatomnus and Mausolus held in relation to the Carian states an analogous position to that which Pisistratus and his sons held in the Athenian

Extra-constitutional position of the Carian tyrants.

Fig. 177.—Coin of Mausolus (reverse). Zeus labrandeus with double axe; wreath [legend: ΜΑΥΣΣΩΛΛΟ].

state ; they were the actual rulers but officially they did not exist. The differences were that the Carian dynast held the official position of Persian satrap, and was "tyrant" of a number of states which were independent of each other.

These native satraps brought the Greek towns of the coast, Halicarnassus, Iasus, Cnidus, perhaps Miletus itself, gradually under their power ; and Mausolus annexed the neighbouring land of Lycia. Thus at the time of Philip's accession to the throne of Macedonia, a rich and ambitious monarchy had arisen on the south-eastern shores of the Aegean. To develop his power, it was desirable for Mausolus to win the lordship of the islands adjacent to his coasts, and it was clearly necessary to form a strong navy. The change of the satrap's residence from inland Mylasa to Halicarnassus on the sea is thus politically significant ; Caria was to become a sea-power. Mausolus built himself a strong castle on the little island of Zephyrion in front of the city, and constructed two harbours, one for ships of war, the other for ships of trade.

[1] The true form is Maussôllos, but for literary purposes Mausolus is consecrated by *Mausoleum*.

The great islands of Rhodes, Cos, and Chios, which Mausolus especially coveted, belonged to the Athenian alliance. But recently there was much discontent at the Athenian supremacy, and there were good grounds for this feeling. The reversion to the policy of cleruchies in neighbouring Samos, as well as in distant Potidaea, excited apprehensions for the future ; and the exactions of the rapacious and irresponsible mercenaries whom Athens regularly employed, but did not regularly pay, caused many complaints. There were moreover strong oligarchical parties in these states which would

Revolt of Chios, Cos, and Rhodes, 357 B.C.

be glad to sever connexion with Athens. The scheme of the Carian prince was first to induce these islands to detach themselves from Athens and then to bring them under his own sway. He fanned the flame of discontent, and the three islands jointly revolted from the Athenian alliance and were supported by Byzantium.

Athenian attack on Chios ; death of Chabrias 357 B.C.

Athens immediately sent naval forces to Chios under Chabrias and Chares, two of the generals of the year, and the town was attacked by land and sea. But in trying to enter the harbour, Chabrias, who led the way, was assailed on all sides and fell fighting. Thus the Athenians lost the most gallant of their soldiers—a commander of whom it was said that he never spared himself and always spared his men. The attack on Chios was abandoned, and the Chians, much elated, and commanding a fleet of 100 ships, proceeded to aggressive warfare against the outsettlers of Athens, and

356 B.C.

blockaded Samos. With only sixty ships Chares could do nothing ; and as many more were hastily sent under the command of Timotheus and Iphicrates. Under three such generals much might be expected from such a fleet ; but more would probably have been accomplished under any one of them alone. They relieved Samos and made an unsuccessful diversion to the Propontis, hoping to take

Battle of Embata.

Byzantium. Then they sailed to Chios, and concerted a plan of attack in the strait between the island and the mainland. But the day proved stormy, and the two veteran admirals, Iphicrates and Timotheus, deemed that it would be rash to fight. Chares, however, against their judgment, attacked the enemy, and being unsupported was repulsed with loss.

Trial of Timotheus and Iphicrates, 355 B.C. (?).

The ineffectual operations of two such tried and famous generals were a cruel disappointment to the Athenians, who had given them an adequate fleet. Chares, furious at the behaviour of his colleagues, formally accused them of deliberate treachery, and was supported by the orator Aristophon. The charge was that they had received bribes from the Chians and the Rhodians. Counter-charges were brought against Chares by Timotheus and Iphicrates, but the sympathies of Athens were altogether given to the commander who erred on the side of boldness. Iphicrates, however, had less political influence and therefore fewer enemies than Timotheus, and he knew how to conciliate the people ; he was accordingly acquitted. Timotheus, always haughty and unpopular, probably assumed a posture as haughty and unbending as ever, Aristophon probably pressed him hard, and he was fined 100 talents. Rich as he was, he was unable to pay this enormous sum, and he withdrew to Chalcis where he died soon afterwards. Thus within twelve months the Athenians lost the two men, Chabrias and Timotheus, who had built up their second empire. They afterwards recognised that the measure which they had dealt out to Timotheus was hard, and they permitted his son—who had himself been tried and acquitted on the same charge—to settle the fine by a payment of ten talents.

Condemna- tion of Timotheus (£27,000); his death.

Chares now went forth as sole commander to sustain the war against the recreant allies ; but he went unfurnished with money to pay his troops. He found the means of supplying this deficiency in the disturbed state of Asia Minor. The satrap of Hellespontine Phrygia, Artabazus, had rebelled, but was not strong enough to hold his own against the king's troops. Chares came to his rescue, gained a brilliant victory over the satraps who were arrayed against him, and received from the grateful Artabazus money which enabled him to pay and maintain the army. The victory and the money pleased the Athenians, but Artaxerxes was deeply incensed. The news presently reached Athens that the Great King was equipping a vast armament in Syria and Cilicia to avenge the audacity of Chares. How much truth there was in this report it is impossible to say ; but it evoked an outburst of patriotism and supplied the Athenian orators with material for invectives and declamations. Men began to talk in earnest of realising the dream of Isocrates, of convoking a pan-Hellenic congress and arming Hellas against the barbarian. Demosthenes, who was now beginning to rise into public notice, delivered in these days a speech which was more to the point than many of his later more famous orations. He showed that the alarm was premature ; and that the notion of sending round appeals to the cities of Greece was foolish ; "your envoys will do nothing more than rhapsodise in their round of visits." The truth was that Athens could in no case think of embarking at this juncture on a big war ; she had not the means. Isocrates himself raised his voice for peace in a remarkable pamphlet, distinguished by the nobility of tone and the width of view which always mark his writings. It was a scathing condemnation of Imperialism. Passing from the momentary state of affairs, he looked out into the future and boldly declared that the only salvation for Athens lay in giving up her naval empire. "It is that," he said, "which brought us to this pass ; it is that which caused the fall of our democracy." He showed the calamities which the

Chares in Asia Minor, 355 B.C.

Demosthenes' speech On the Symmories

Isocrates on the Peace, 355 B.C.

(404 B.C.)

empires of Athens and Sparta had drawn upon themselves and Greece. But it is to be observed that, when a moment had come at which his favourite plan of a common attack on Persia seemed at length feasible, he was wise enough not to advise it. He looks to Thrace, not to Persia, to find lands for endowing those needy Greeks who were roving about for subsistence.

Peace,
354 B.C.
In the end prudent counsels prevailed ; Chares was recalled ; negotiations were opened with the revolted allies, and a peace was made.[1] Athens recognised the independence of the three islands, Chios, Cos, and Rhodes, and of the city of Byzantium. It was not long before Lesbos also severed itself from the Athenian alliance, which thus lost all its important members in the eastern Aegean ; and in the west Corcyra fell away about the same time.

All happened as Mausolus foresaw. He helped the oligarchies to overthrow the popular governments, and then gave them the pro-
Death of
Mausolus,
353 B.C.
tection of Carian garrisons. But the prince did not live to develop his empire. Soon after the success of his policy against Athens, he died, leaving his power to his widow Artemisia. The opportunity was seized by the democrats of Rhodes to regain their freedom, and they appealed to Athens. After what had passed they had little right to expect a hearing ; and under the influence of the wise and pacific statesmen who now controlled the Assembly, their appeal was refused —in spite of the hot and somewhat sentimental pleadings of Demo-
353 B.C.
sthenes, who upheld the extraordinary doctrine that Athens was bound, whenever she was called upon, to intervene to support democracy against oligarchy. Artemisia soon recovered her grip on Rhodes.

Caria remained for another twenty years under dynasts of the house of Hecatomnus, until it submitted to Alexander the Great. The expansion of the Carian power, which seemed probable under
The statues
of Mau-
solus and
Artemisia
(in the
British
Museum).
the active administration of Mausolus, was never fulfilled. Though we know nothing of his personal character, the outward appearance of Mausolus is familiar to us, the islanders of the north, who possess in our capital his genuine portrait, and the headless figure of his queen. The colossal statue, made, at latest, soon after his death, re-presents a man of a noble cast of face, of a type presumably Carian, certainly not Greek, and with the hair curiously brushed back from the brow. This statue stood, along with that of Artemisia, within the sepulchral tomb which he probably began and which she
The tomb
of Mau-
solus.
certainly completed. Such a royal tomb seems to take us back to the days of prehistoric Greece ; it strikes one almost like a glorified resurrection of one of the old chamber sepulchres of the Leleges

---

[1] The war which this peace brought to an end is generally called, by a mis-leading translation of ὁ συμμαχικὸς πόλεμος, the Social War. This Latinism might well disappear from histories.

which are strewed about the Halicarnassian peninsula. It rose
above the harbour at Halicarnassus, conspicuous from the sea,
crowned with a chariot on its apex. The building was adorned with

FIG. 178.—Statue of Mausolus (British Museum).

friezes, wrought by four of the most illustrious sculptors of the day, *Sculptures*
of whom Scopas himself was one. The precious fragments of these *(in British*
works of art are the legacy which the Carian realm has bequeathed *Museum).*
to mankind—these and a new word which the tomb of Mausolus *Origin of*
added to the vocabularies of Europe. *"Mau-soleum."*

SECT. 4. PHOCIS AND THE SACRED WAR

In the meantime, another of the states of northern Greece seemed likely to win the position of supremacy which Thessaly had seemed on the eve of winning, and which Boeotia had actually held for a few years. Phocis now came forward in her turn and enjoyed a brief moment of expansion and conquest—a flashlight which vanished almost as soon as it appeared. In succession to the national leaders, Jason of Pherae and Epaminondas of Thebes, we now meet Onomarchus of Elatea.

Position of Phocis. Into this career of aggrandisement Phocis was thrust by the aggression of her neighbours rather than lured by the lust of conquest. The Phocians had never been zealous adherents of the Boeotian alliance, which they were forced to join after the battle of Leuctra, and they cut themselves loose from it after the death of Epaminondas. But though Thebes could no longer maintain her wider supremacy in Greece, an independent Phocis was a source of constant danger to her in her narrower supremacy in Boeotia, as the western cities of the land could always find in Phocis a stay and support for their own independence. It was therefore deemed necessary by the politicians of Thebes to strike a blow at their western neighbours. One of the instruments of which Epaminondas had made use to promote his city's influence in the north was the old Amphictionic League, which for a hundred years had never appeared on the scene of history. At an assembly of this body, soon after Leuctra, the Thebans accused the Spartans of having seized the Cadmea in time of

FIG. 179.—Coin of Delphic Amphictiony (fourth century). Obverse: Demeter, with veil and crown of corn. Reverse: Apollo, sitting on omphalos, leaning on lyre [legend: ΑΜΦΙΚΤΙΟΝΩΝ].

Sparta fined. peace. The Spartans were sentenced to pay a fine of 500 talents; the fine could not indeed be exacted, but they were doubtless excluded from the temple of Delphi. The Thebans resolved to wield against Phocis the same engine which they had wielded against Sparta. The nature of the pretext is uncertain, but it was not difficult to find a misdemeanour which would seem grave enough to the Thessalians and Locrians, inveterate enemies of Phocis, to *Phocians fined.* justify a sentence of condemnation. A number of rich and prominent Phocians were condemned to pay large fines for sacrilege, and when these sums were not paid within the prescribed time, the Amphictions decreed that the lands of the defaulters should be taken from them and consecrated to the Delphian god, and a tablet with the inscribed decree was set up at Delphi.

The men who were implicated in the alleged sacrilege determined to resist, and they appealed to their fellow-countrymen, in whatever form of federal assembly the Phocian cities used to discuss their common interests, to protect themselves and their property against the threatened danger. The man who took the lead in organising the resistance was Philomelus, a weathy citizen of Ledon. *Philo-* He discerned clearly that mercenaries would be required to defend *melus.* Phocis against her enemies—Boeotians, Locrians, and Thessalians— and made the bold and practical proposal that Delphi should be seized, since the treasures of Delphi would supply at need the sinews of war. It is hardly likely that he openly avowed the true reason of the importance of seizing Delphi ; it was enough to assert the old rights of the Phocians over rocky Pytho—rights for which he could appeal to the highest authority, the sacred text of Homer [1]—and to point out that the Delphians were implicated in the unjust decrees of the Amphictions. The proposals of Philomelus were adopted, and he was appointed general of the Phocian forces, with full powers. His first step was to visit Sparta, not only as the enemy of Thebes, but as being in the same case as Phocis, lying under an Amphictionic sentence which had recently been renewed and confirmed. King Archidamus welcomed the proposals of the Phocian plenipotentiary, but Sparta stood in a rather awkward position. Hitherto she had 450 *B.C.* always supported the Delphians in maintaining their independence *sqq.* against Phocian claims, as, for instance, when in the days of Pericles she restored them to their shrine after the Phocians with Athenian aid had dispossessed them. It would consequently have been a flagrant inconsistency in Spartan policy to turn against the Delphians now ; so that Archidamus did not openly avow his sympathy with the Phocian cause, but privately he supported it by placing fifteen talents in the hands of Philomelus. With this sum and fifteen talents from his *Phocians* own purse, Philomelus was able to hire some mercenaries, and with *seize* their help to seize Delphi. The Locrians of neighbouring Amphissa, *Delphi,* whom the Delphians had summoned to their aid, arrived too late and 356 *B.C.* were repulsed. Philomelus did no hurt to the people of Delphi, excepting only the clan of the Thracidae, bitter anti-Phocians, whom he put to death.

The first object of Philomelus was to enlist Hellenic opinion in his favour. He had the secret sympathy of Sparta, and he might count

[1] In the Homeric Catalogue, Pytho is said to be possessed by two Phocian chiefs.

on the friendship of Athens, who had always been an ally of Phocis and was now an enemy of Thebes. He sent envoys to Sparta, to Athens, to Thebes itself, to explain the Phocian position. These envoys were instructed to say that in seizing Delphi the Phocians were simply resuming their rights over the temple, which belonged to them and had been usurped by others, and to declare that they would act merely as administrators of the Panhellenic Sanctuary, and were ready to allow all the treasures to be weighed and numbered, and to be responsible to Greece for their safety. In consequence of these embassies Sparta came forward from her reserve and openly allied herself with Phocis, while Athens and some smaller states promised their support. The Thebans and their Amphictionic friends resolved to make war.

Philomelus fortifies Delphi; In the meantime, Philomelus had fortified the Delphic sanctuary by a wall, and had collected an army of 5000 men, with which he could easily hold the position. It was his wish that the oracular responses from the mystic tripod should continue to be given as usual to those who came to consult Apollo, and he was anxious above all to receive some voice of approval or encouragement from the god. But the Delphian priestess was stubborn to the Phocian intruder, and refused to prophesy. He tried to seat her by force upon the tripod, and in her alarm she bade him do as he would. He eagerly seized these words as an oracular sanction of his acts. It soon became necessary to raise more money for paying the mercenaries, and for this purpose Philomelus, refraining as long as he could from touching the treasures of the shrine, levied a contribution from the rich Delphians. *and defeats the Locrians.* At first he had to deal only with the Locrians, whom he finally defeated in a hot battle near the Phaedriad cliffs which rise sheer above Delphi. The loss of the Locrians was heavy; some of them, driven to the edge, hurled themselves down the cliffs.

Thebes prepares to act. This victory forced the Thebans to prepare actively to intervene. The Amphictionic assembly met at Thermopylae, and it was decided that an Amphictionic army should enforce the decree of the league against the Phocians, and rescue Delphi from their power. Philomelus, with the forces which he had, might hold his own against the Locrians, but not against the host which would now be arrayed against him. There were only two means of saving Phocis. One was the active support of Athens or Sparta, or both; the other was the organisation of a large army of mercenaries. As neither Athens nor Sparta showed willingness to give any immediate assistance, nothing remained but the other alternative. And that alternative, as Philomelus must have foreseen from the beginning, would not be possible without the control of far larger sums of money than could either be contributed by the Phocian cities or extorted from the Delphian proprietors.

No resource remained but to make use of the treasures of the temple. At first Philomelus was scrupulous. He only *borrowed* from the god enough to meet the demand of the moment ; but, as habitude blunted the first feelings of scrupulousness, and as needs grew more pressing, the Phocians dealt as freely with the sacred vessels and the precious dedications as if they were their own. By offering large pay Philomelus assembled an army of 10,000 men, who cared little whence the money came. An indecisive war with the Thebans and *Battle of* Locrians was waged for some time, till at length the Phocians under- *Neon,* went a severe defeat near Neon on the north side of Mount Par- 354 *B.C. ;* nassus. The general fought desperately, and, covered with wounds, he *death of* was driven to the verge of a precipice where he had to choose between *melus.* *Philo-* capture and self-destruction. He hurled himself from the cliff and perished.

The Thebans imagined that the death of Philomelus meant the *Onomar-* doom of the Phocian cause, and they retired after the battle. But *chus* it was not so. In Onomarchus of Elatea, who had been associated *succeeds* with him in the command of the army, he had a successor as able as *Philo-* himself. The retreat of the enemy gave Onomarchus time to re- *melus.* organise the troops and collect reinforcements ; and he not only coined the gold and silver ornaments of the temple, but beat the bronze and iron donatives into arms for the soldiers. He then entered upon a short career of signal successes. Westward, he forced Locrian Amphissa to submit ; to northward he reduced Doris, and crossing the passes of Mount Oeta he made himself master of Ther- mopylae, and captured the Locrian Thronion near the eastern gate of the pass. Eastward, he took possession of Orchomenus and re- stored those of the inhabitants who had escaped the sword of the Thebans ten years before.

The Thebans meanwhile were hampered by want of money, and, having neither mines like Philip nor a rich temple like Phocis, they decided to replenish their treasury by sending out a body of troops on foreign service. We have already seen Sparta and Athens raising money by the same means, and the Theban soldiers who now went forth under Pammenes hired themselves out to the same Persian satrap Artabazus, for whom the Athenian Chares had won a victory over the army of the king. Pammenes was equally successful, but it does not seem that his expedition profited the Boeotian treasury ; for he presently became suspected by Artabazus, who threw him into prison.

Among the most important uses to which Onomarchus applied the gold of Delphi was the purchase of the alliance of the tyrants of Pherae. By this policy Thessaly was divided ; and the Thessalian league, beset by the hostility of Pherae, was unable to co-operate with the Thebans against Phocis. But the Thessalians, being hard pressed, turned for help to their northern neighbour, Philip of Macedon, and his intervention south of Mount Olympus marks a new stage in the course of the Sacred War.

Philip's capture of Methone, 353 B.C. He enters Thessaly; 352 B.C. Philip had lately deprived Athens of her last ally on the Thermaic Gulf by the capture of Methone, the Athenian expedition of relief coming too late to save it. He readily acceded to the request of the Thessalians to act as their general; it was a convenient occasion to begin the push southward, and lay the foundation of Macedonian supremacy in Greece, plans which were now coming within the range of practical effort. Against the forces which Philip led to the support of the Thessalian league, it was hopeless for Lycophron of Pherae to stand alone; the tyrant was lost unless he were succoured *defeats a Phocian army;* by the arm of those who had already furnished him with gold. Nor did the Phocians leave him unsupported. The strength of Onomarchus was now so great that he could spare a force of 7000 men for a campaign in the north. But his brother Phayllus, to whom he en*suffers two defeats and is expelled from Thessaly by Onomarchus.* trusted the command, was beaten out of Thessaly by Philip. Then Onomarchus went forth himself, at the head of the whole Phocian host (about 20,000), to rescue his ally. Far superior in numbers, he defeated the Macedonian army in two battles with serious loss; Philip was compelled to withdraw into Macedonia; and Onomarchus delivered Thessaly into the hands of Lycophron.

Height of the Phocian supremacy, 353-2 B.C. *Coronea.* At this moment, the power of the Phocians was at its height. Their supremacy reached from the shores of the Corinthian Gulf to the slopes of Olympus. They were masters of the pass of Thermopylae, and they had two important posts in western Boeotia, for, in addition to Orchomenus, they won Coronea immediately after the Thessalian expedition. If all these things had befallen at some other epoch, the Phocian power might have endured for a time, and the name of their able leader might have been more familiar to posterity. But Onomarchus had fallen on evil days. He and his petty people were swept away in the onward course of a greater nation and a greater chief.

Philip drives the Phocians from Thessaly. Philip of Macedon speedily retrieved the humiliation which he had suffered at the hands of his Phocian foes. In the following year he descended again into Thessaly, and Onomarchus went forth again to succour his ally or dependent. In the preceding campaign Philip had captured the port of Pagasae, and placed in it a Macedonian garrison. It was important not only for Pherae, but for Athens, that this post should not remain in his hands, and Chares was sent with an Athenian fleet to assist the Phocians in recovering it. The decisive battle was fought at a place unknown, near the Pagasaean Gulf. The numbers of the infantry were nearly equal, but Philip's cavalry and his tactics were far superior. More than a third of the Phocian army was slain or made prisoners, and Onomarchus was killed. Pherae was then captured and Lycophron driven from the land; and Philip, having thus become master of Thessaly, prepared to march southward for the purpose of delivering the shrine of Apollo from the possession of the Phocians, whom he professed to regard as sacrilegious usurpers.

Phocis was now in great need, and her allies—Sparta, Achaea, and Athens—at length determined to give her active help. The Macedonian must not be permitted to pass Thermopylae. The *Eubulus* statesman Eubulus, whose influence was now predominant at Athens, *rescues* and was chiefly directed to the maintenance of peace, acted promptly *Phocis.* on this occasion, and sent a large force under Nausicles to defend the pass. Philip at once recognised that it would be extremely hazardous to attempt to force the position, and he retired. He was a prince who knew when to wait and when to strike. Thus Phocis was rescued for the time ; she was indebted both to Sparta and Achaea who had sent her aid, but most of all to Athens.

In supporting Phocis, the Spartans had objects of their own in view. They had not abandoned their hopes of winning back Messenia and destroying Megalopolis. It was therefore their policy to sustain Phocis, in order that Phocis might keep Thebes so fully occupied that they would have a free hand in the Peloponnesus without fear of Theban interference. The successes of Onomarchus in his first *Megalo-* Thessalian campaign encouraged Sparta to prepare for action, and *polis applies* Megalopolis, made aware of the danger, applied to Athens for help. *to Athens,* It was a request which no practical statesman could have entertained, *end of* and it had no chance of being granted under the régime of as wise *353 B.C.* a head as Eubulus. Orators like Demosthenes, who constituted *Demo-* themselves the opponents of Eubulus, might invoke the old principle *sthenes'* that it was the policy of Athens to keep Sparta weak. But this *speech for* was an obsolete maxim, for there was now no serious prospect *the Megalo-* of Sparta becoming formidably strong. It was no concern of Athens *politans.* to meddle in the Peloponnesus now. Her true policy was to keep on friendly terms with Sparta, and, in conjunction with her, to support the Phocian state against Thebes, Thessaly, and Macedon. This was the policy which Eubulus followed.

The war broke out in the Peloponnesus soon after the check of *War in* Philip at Thermopylae. While Athens held aloof, Achaea and Elis, *the Pelo-* Phlius and Mantinea, supported Sparta, and the Phocians sent 3000 *ponnesus,* men to her help. But all these forces were outnumbered by the *352 B.C.* Messenians, Arcadians, and Argives, to whom the Thebans had sent a considerable aid. A series of engagements were fought ; they were almost all indecisive ; but they rescued Messenia and the Arcadian capital, and frustrated the plans of Lacedaemon.

2 A

Phayllus.   The death of Onomarchus devolved the leadership of the Phocian league upon his brother Phayllus. At first the Phocians barely maintained their posts in western Boeotia; but presently—after the return of the auxiliaries whom they had sent to the Peloponnesus— they invaded Epicnemidian Locris and laid siege to Naryx, which 352-1 *B.C.* they ultimately captured. Thus Phayllus maintained the power of Phocis for about two years; then he was carried off by disease, and was succeeded by his nephew, Phalaecus, son of Onomarchus.

Phalaecus.   Under Phalaecus the war dragged on for a few more years, without any notable achievement, the Thebans winning battles of no import- ance and ravaging Phocis, the Phocians retaining their grip on western Boeotia.

The posi- tion and policy of Phocis.   The rise of Phocis to its momentary position as one of the lead- ing powers in Greece depended on two conditions—the possession of Delphi and the possibility of hiring mercenaries. It is therefore clear that Phocis could not easily have come to the front before the fourth century, when mercenary service had come widely into vogue. But these two essential features of the Phocian power, the occupation of Delphi and the employment of mercenary troops, gave it a bad name. Historians echo the invectives of the enemies of Phocis, and give the impression that during the Sacred War the sanctuary of Apollo was in the hands of sacrilegious and unscrupulous barbarians. Tales were told how the dedicatory offerings were bestowed upon the loose favourites of the generals—how Philomelus gave a golden wreath to a dancing girl, or Phayllus a silver beaker to a flute-player. It matters little whether such scandals are true or false; if true, they would only show that the generals were not above petty peculations. But the Phocians were not alien desecrators of the shrine of Apollo. They could establish as good a claim to Delphi as many claims founded on remote events in the past; and they certainly desired to maintain the Panhellenic dignity and sanctity of the shrine and the oracle as high as ever under their own administration. But they regarded Delphi not only as a Panhellenic sanctuary, but as a national sanctuary of Phocis; somewhat in the same way as Athens employed the treasures of her temples for national purposes of defence in the Peloponnesian war, so Phocis felt justified in employ- ing the treasures of Apollo for the national interest of Phocis. Throughout all, the Phocian statesmen could have maintained that they were only borrowing from the god loans which would be gradu- ally paid back after the restoration of peace.

    Recently there has come to light, among the original documents inscribed on the stones of Delphi, a striking disproof of the old view which conceived the Phocians of Onomarchus and Phayllus as a band of robbers holding their orgies in a holy place. The temple of the god which had been built by the Alcmaeonids was destroyed *The build-* by an earthquake nearly twenty years before the Phocian usurpation. *ing of the* The work of rebuilding had been begun, perhaps soon after, but had *temple of* advanced slowly, and when Philomelus seized Delphi the completion *Apollo not* of the temple was still far off. The work was carried out under a *during the* commission of "Temple-builders," in which all the Amphictionic *Phocian* states were represented; and this body administered a fund set *occupation.* apart for the building. During the Phocian usurpation the council *Destruc-* of Temple-builders still held their meetings; the *tion of the* work still went on; the skilful artisans in Corinth *Second* and elsewhere wrought the stone material and *Temple of* transferred it to Delphi, as if nothing had *Delphi,* befallen; the payments were made, as usual, *373 B.C.* from the fund; and the accounts were kept—we *Council of* have some of them still. Those Amphictionic *Naopoioi.* states which were at war with Phocis, like Thebes and Thessaly, were naturally not repre- FIG. 180.—Coin of sented at the meetings of the board of the Opuntian Locrians Temple-builders, but Delphian members were (reverse). Ajax, son always present; and after Locris had been of Oïleus, charging; conquered by Phayllus we find Locrians also spear [legend: attending the meetings.[1] Thus the completion ΟΠΟΝΤΙΩΝ]. of the temple of Apollo was not suspended while the Phocians held the sanctuary; and the Dorian and Ionian states continued to take their part in the Panhellenic work of supervising the structure, as if nothing had happened to alter the centre of the Greek world.

Sect. 5. The Advance of Macedonia

The Macedonian monarch was now master not only of the Thermaic Gulf and the mouth of the Strymon, but of the basin of Pagasae, and he was beginning to create a fleet. His marauding vessels, let loose in the northern Aegean, captured the cornships of Athens, descended on her possessions and dependencies—Lemnos, Imbros, and Euboea —and once even insulted the coast of Attica itself. The most important interests of Athens centred round the Hellespont and Propontis; and it was obviously her policy to form a close combination with the Thracian king Cersobleptes, with a view to offering common resistance to the advance of the new northern power on the Thracian

[1] Thus in B.C. 351-50 the members present are a Delphian, a Sicyonian, a Corinthian, and two Argives; in B.C. 349-48, a Delphian, an Athenian, two Locrians, a Megarian, an Epidaurian, a Lacedaemonian, a Corinthian, two Phocians.

*Demo-
sthenes'
speech
against
Aristo-
crates,
352 B.C.*
side. It was an effort in this direction when Aristocrates proposed a resolution in honour of Charidemus, the adventurer who had become the brother-in-law and the chief minister of the Thracian king. The resolution was impeached as illegal, and the accuser was supplied with a speech by the young politician Demosthenes. The legal objections were probably cogent, but the opponents of the proposal might wisely have confined themselves to this aspect of the question. They went on to impugn the expediency of the measure ; and the speech of Demosthenes against Aristocrates was calculated, so far as a single speech could have a political effect, to alienate a power which it was distinctly the interest of Athens to conciliate.

*Philip in
Thrace,
352 B.C.,
autumn.*

*Submission
of Cerso-
bleptes to
Philip.*
But it mattered little. No sooner had Philip returned from Thessaly than he moved against Thrace. Supported by a rival Thracian prince and by the cities of Byzantium and Perinthus, he advanced to the Propontis, besieged Heraeon-Teichos the capital of Cersobleptes, and forced that potentate to submit to the overlordship of Macedon. The movements of Philip had been so rapid that Athens had no time to come to the rescue of Thrace. When the news arrived there was a panic, and an armament was voted to save the Chersonese. But a new message came that Philip had fallen ill ; then he was reported dead ; and the sending of the armament was postponed. Philip's illness was a fact ; it compelled him to desist from further operations, and the Chersonesus was saved.

*Position of
Philip at
the end of
352 B.C.*
Eight years had not elapsed since Philip had mounted the throne of Macedon ; and he had shifted the balance of power in Greece, and altered the whole prospect of the Greek world, for those who had eyes to see. He had created an army, and a thoroughly adequate revenue ; he had made himself lord of almost the whole sea-board of the northern Aegean from the defile of Thermopylae to the shores of the Propontis. The only lands which were still excepted from his direct or indirect sway were the Chersonesus and the territory of the Chalcidian league. He was ambitious to secure a recognised hegemony in Greece ; to hold such a position as had been held by Athens, by Sparta, and by Thebes in the days of their greatness ; to form, in fact, a confederation of allies, which should hold some such dependent relation towards him as the confederates of Delos had held towards Athens. Rumours were already floating about that his ultimate design was to lead a Panhellenic expedition against the Persian king—the same design which was ascribed to Jason of

*His
Hellenism.*
Pherae. Though the Greek states regarded Philip as in a certain sense an outsider, both because Macedonia had hitherto lain aloof from their politics and because absolute monarchy was repugnant to their political ideas, it must never be forgotten that Philip desired to identify Macedonia with Greece, and to bring his own country up

to the level of the kindred peoples which had so far outstripped it in civilisation. Throughout his whole career he regarded Athens with respect; he would have given much for her friendship, and he showed that he deemed it one of his misfortunes that she compelled him to be her foe. He was himself imbued with Greek culture; and if the robust Macedonian enjoyed the society of the somewhat rude boon companions of his own land with whom he could drink deep, he knew how to make himself agreeable to Attic philosophers or men of letters whom he always delighted to honour. He chose an accomplished man of letters, Aristotle of Stagira, who had been educated at Athens, to be the instructor of his son Alexander. This fact alone sets Philip in the true light, as a conscious and deliberate promoter of Greek civilisation.

Greece saw with alarm the increase of the Macedonian power, though men were yet far from apprehending what it really meant. No state had been directly hit except Athens—though the day of Chalcidice was at hand; and it was now too late for Athens to retrieve her lost position, either alone or with any combination she could form, against a state which possessed an ample revenue and a well-drilled national army, under the sovereign command of the greatest general and diplomatist of the day. The only event which could now have availed to stay the course of Macedon would have been the death of Philip. But the Athenians did not apprehend this; they still dreamed of recovering Amphipolis. Their best policy would have been peace and alliance with Macedonia. There can be little question that Philip would have gladly secured them the Chersonese and their cornships; for the possession of the Chersonese had not the same vital importance for him as Amphipolis, or as the towns around the Thermaic Gulf. *Position of Athens.*

In these years, Athens was under the guidance of a cautious statesman, Eubulus, who was a marvellously able minister of finance. He was appointed chancellor of the Theoric Fund for four years, and this office, while it was specially concerned with the administration of the surplus of revenue which was devoted to theoric purposes, involved a general control over the finances of the state. He pursued a peace policy; yet it was he who struck the one effective blow that Athens ever struck at Philip, when she hindered him from passing Thermopylae. But Eubulus wisely refused to allow Athens to be misled into embarking in unnecessary wars in the Peloponnesus or Asia Minor; and frankly accepted the peace which had concluded the war of Athens with her allies. The mass of the Athenians were well contented to follow the counsel of a dexterous financier, who, while he met fully all the expenses of administration, distributed *Eubulus, in charge of the Theoric Fund, 354-50 B.C., and probably, 350-346 B.C.*

large dividends of festival-money. The news of Philip's campaign in Thrace may have temporarily weakened his influence ; it was felt that there had been slackness in watching Athenian interests in the Hellespontine regions ; and his opponents had a fair opportunity to inveigh against an inactive policy.

Demosthenes, born c. 384 B.C.

The most prominent among these opponents was Demosthenes, who had recently made a reputation as a speaker in the Assembly.

Fig. 181.—Portrait head of Demosthenes.

The father of Demosthenes was an Athenian manufacturer, who died when his son was still a child; his mother had Scythian blood in her veins. His guardians dealt fraudulently with the considerable fortune which his father had left him; and when he came of age he resolved to recover it. For this purpose he sat at the feet of the orator Isaeus, and was trained in law and rhetoric. Though he received but a small portion of his patrimony, the oratory of Demosthenes owed to this training with a practical purpose many qualities which it would never have acquired under the academic instruction of Isocrates. He used himself to tell how he struggled to overcome his natural defects of speech and manner, how he practised gesticulation before a mirror and declaimed verses with pebbles in his mouth. In the end he became as brilliant an orator as the Pnyx had ever cheered; perhaps his only fault was a too theatrical manner. His earlier political speeches are not monuments of wisdom. He came forward as an opponent of the policy of Eubulus, and so we have already met him supporting the appeals of Rhodes and Megalopolis. The advance of Philip to the Propontis gave him a more promising *His first* occasion to urge the Athenians to act, since their own interests *Philippic.* were directly involved. And the effort of Demosthenes was more than adequate. The harangue, which is known as the First Philippic, one of his most brilliant and effective speeches, calls upon the Athenians to brace themselves vigorously to oppose Philip "our enemy." He draws a lively picture of the indifference of his countrymen and contrasts it with the energy of Philip "who is not the man to rest content with that he has subdued, but is always adding to his conquests, and casts his snare around us while we sit at home postponing." Again : "Is Philip dead ? Nay, but he is ill. What does it matter to you? For, if this Philip die, you will soon raise up a second Philip by your apathy." Demosthenes proposed a scheme for increasing the military forces of the city ; and the most essential part of the scheme was that a force should be sent to Thrace of which a quarter should consist of citizens, and the officers should be citizens. At present the numerous officers whom they elected were kept for services at home : "You choose your captains, not to fight but to be displayed like dolls in the market-place." Demosthenes was applauded, but nothing was done. His ideal was the Athens of Pericles ; but he lived in the Athens of Eubulus. In the fourth century the Athenians were quite capable of holding their own among their old friends and enemies, the Spartans and Thebans and the islanders of the Aegean ; with paid soldiers and generals like Iphicrates and Chares they could maintain their position as a first-rate power. But against a large, vigorous landpower with a formidable army their chances were hopeless ; for, since the fall of their empire, the whole spirit of the people had tended to peace and not to war ; they were no longer animated by the idea of empire ; and the memories of the past, which Demosthenes might invoke, were powerless to stir them to action. The orations of Demosthenes, however carefully studied, however imbued with passion, could not change the character of his countrymen ; their spirit did not respond to his, and, not being under the imperious dominion of an idea, they saw no reason for great undertakings. Nor was the condition of Athens as ill as the opponent of Eubulus painted it. Under the administration of Eubulus the fleet was increased, the building of a new arsenal was begun, new ship-sheds were made, and the military establishment of Athens was in various ways improved. She was still the great sea-power of the Aegean, and strong enough to protect her commercial interests.

The next stage in the development of Macedonia was the incorporation of Chalcidice, and as soon as Philip recovered from his illness he turned his attention to this quarter. If the Olynthians had treated Philip honourably, they would probably have been left a self-governing community, with their territory intact, dependent on *Peace* Macedonia. But they treated both Athens and Philip badly. They *of the* first made a close alliance with Philip to rob Athens; and *Chalcidian* then, when they had received from Philip Anthemus and Potidaea, *league with* *Athens,* they turned round and made peace with Athens, a power with *352 B.C.* which Philip was at war, and recognised the right of Athens to Amphipolis. At the time Philip was otherwise engaged; but three years later he sent a requisition to Olynthus, demanding the surrender of his half-brother, a pretender to the Macedonian throne, to whom *Philip* they had given shelter. The demand was refused and Philip marched *reduces* against Chalcidice. One after another the cities of the Olynthian *Chalcidice,* confederacy opened their gates to him; or if they refused, like *349 B.C.* Stagira, they were captured.

Alliance In her jeopardy Olynthus sought an alliance with Athens, and on *of Athens* this occasion both the leaders of the Athenian Assembly and the *with the* advocates of a war policy found themselves in harmony. It was *Olynthians.* during the debates on the question of alliance that Demosthenes pronounced his Olynthiac orations, which were animated by the same spirit as his Philippic, and were in fact Philippics. At this juncture the Athenians seem to have been awakened to the necessity of action sufficiently to embolden Demosthenes to throw out the unpopular suggestion that the Theoric Fund should be devoted to military purposes; and he repeats his old plea for citizen-soldiers. An alliance was concluded and mercenaries were dispatched to the Chalcidian peninsula under Chares and Charidemus (who had left the service of Cersobleptes). More troops would certainly have followed, and Philip might have been placed in some embarrassment, especially as Cersobleptes had rebelled. But he diverted the concern *Revolt of* of Athens in another direction, and so divided her forces. He had *Euboea.* long been engaged in intrigues in Euboea, and now Eretria revolted and drove out Plutarch, the tyrant who held the city for Athens. Neighbouring Chalcis, and Oreos in the north, followed the example; Euboea was in a state of revolt. It is just possible that, if Athens had left Euboea alone, and concentrated all her military power in Chalcidice, she might have saved Olynthus for the time. The division of her forces was certainly fatal ; and Demosthenes deserves great credit for opposing any interference in Euboea. But the Athenians would have been strong-minded indeed if they had done nothing to regain the neighbouring island, while they dispatched all their troops to succour an ally. The expedition to Euboea, which *Expedition* was now entrusted to the general Phocion, might better never have *to Euboea,* been sent ; but beforehand there seemed no reason why it should not *spring,* succeed. Phocion's only exploit was to extricate himself from a *348 B.C.* dangerous position at Tamynae, by winning a battle, but he returned to Athens without having recovered any of the rebellious cities. The enemy had taken a number of prisoners, for whose ransom Athens had to pay fifty talents ; and it was decided that there was nothing *Euboea* for it but to acknowledge the independence of Euboea, with the *declared* exception of Carystus, which remained loyal. *independent.*

Meanwhile Philip was pressing Olynthus hard, and urgent appeals were sent to Athens. This time Demosthenes had his way, and 2000 citizen-soldiers sailed for the north. But it was too late. *Fall of* Olynthus was captured before they reached it ; and Philip showed *Olynthus,* no mercy to the city which had played him false. The place was *348 B.C.* destroyed and the inhabitants scattered in various parts of Macedonia, some set to work as slaves in the royal domains. The other cities of the confederacy were practically incorporated in Macedonia ; but they still continued to exist as cities and manage their local affairs. There was no question of their extermination.

Demosthenes had opposed the expedition to Euboea, and thereby hangs a story. He had a bitter foe in a rich man, named Meidias, who was a supporter of Eubulus. Their personal hostility was *Demosthenes* reawakened in the debates over the Euboean question, and Meidias *insulted* seized the occasion of the great Dionysiac feast to put a public affront *by Meidias,* on his enemy. Demosthenes had undertaken the duty of supplying *348 B.C.* a chorus for his tribe, and on the day of the performance, when he appeared in the sacred robe of a choregus, Meidias struck him in the face. The outrage involved contempt of a religious festival, and Demosthenes instituted proceedings against his insulter. The speech which he composed for the occasion contains fine scathing invective. The description of Meidias vulgarly displaying his wealth may be quoted to illustrate contemporary manners. " Where," Demosthenes asks, " are his splendid outlays ? For myself, I cannot see unless it be in this—that he has built a mansion at Eleusis large enough to darken all the neighbourhood—that he keeps a pair of white horses from Sicyon, with which he conducts his wife to the mysteries or any-where else he fancies—that he sweeps through the market-place with three or four lackeys all to himself, and talks about his bowls and drinking-horns and saucers, loud enough to be heard by the passers-by." [1] But Demosthenes consented to compromise the matter for a small sum before it was brought to an issue, and there can be little question that his consent was given from political motives. On the capture of Olynthus the different parties drew together and agreed to co-operate; and this new political combination rendered it necessary for Demosthenes, however reluctant, to patch up the feud with Meidias.

SECT. 6. THE PEACE OF PHILOCRATES

Her recent military efforts had exhausted the revenue of Athens; there was not enough money in the treasury to pay the judges their daily wage. Peace was clearly a necessity, and this must have been fully recognised by Eubulus. But there was great indignation at the fall of Olynthus, and the feeling that a disaster had been sustained was augmented by the fact that there were a considerable number of Athenians among the captives. Accordingly the pressure of popular opinion, which was for the moment strongly aroused against Philip, induced Eubulus to countenance the dispatch of envoys to the cities of the Peloponnesus, for the purpose of organising a national resistance in Hellas against the man who had destroyed Olynthus. It is probable that this measure was advocated by Demosthenes; in later years, a national resistance to Philip was his favourite idea. It was an effort foredoomed to failure, as Eubulus knew perfectly well; yet it served his purpose, for it protected him against suspicions of being secretly friendly to Philip. On this occasion the orator Aeschines, famous as the antagonist of Demosthenes, first came prominently forward. He had begun life as an usher in a school kept by his father, he had then *Aeschines* been a tragic actor, and finally a public clerk. He was now sent to *at Megalo-* rouse the Greeks of the Peloponnesus against Macedonia, and he *polis*, 347 used such strong language in disparagement of Philip, especially at *B.C.* Megalopolis, that no one could accuse him of "philippizing." The mere fact that envoys were sent to Megalopolis—whose application for help had so recently been rejected by Athens—is enough to cast suspicion on the whole round of embassies as a farce, got up to satisfy public opinion at home. Demosthenes, like other politicians, saw the necessity of peace and worked towards it.

Philip desired two things, to conclude peace with Athens and to *Philip's* become a member of the Amphictionic Council. Towards this *intervention* second end a path was prepared by the Thebans, who, along with *sought by* the Thessalians addressed an appeal to Philip that he would under- *Thebes.*

---

[1] Translation by Professor Butcher.

take the championship of the Amphictionic League and crush the
Phocians. In Phocis itself there had recently been domestic strife;
Phalaecus had been deposed from the generalship, but he had a
party of his own and he held Thermopylae with the strong places in
its neighbourhood. When it was noised abroad that Philip was about
to march southward in answer to the Theban prayer, the Phocians
invited Athens and Sparta to help them once again to hold the gates
of Greece. Both Athens and Sparta again responded to the call; *The
but the call had come from the political opponents of Phalaecus, ambiguous
and he refused to admit either Spartan or Athenian into the pass. position of
Phalaecus seems to have previously assisted the enemies of Athens in Phalaecus.*
Euboea; and statesmen at Athens might now feel some uneasiness,
whether he would not turn traitor and surrender the pass to Philip.
It was another reason for acquiescing in the necessity of making
peace.

The first overtures came from Athens. Ten Athenian envoys, *First
and one representative of the Synedrion of Athenian allies, were sent embassy
to Pella to negotiate terms of peace with the Macedonian king. to Philip,
Among the envoys were Philocrates, who had proposed the embassy, end of
Aeschines, and Demosthenes. The terms to which Philip agreed 347 B.C.*
were that Athens and Macedon should each retain the territories of
which they were actually in possession at the time the peace was
concluded; the peace would be concluded when both sides had
sworn to it. Both the allies of Macedonia and those of Athens were
to be included, with two exceptions: Philip refused to treat with
Halus in Thessaly—a place which he had recently attacked—or *(Halon-
with the Phocians, whom he was determined to crush. nesus.)*

By these terms, which were perfectly explicit, Athens would
surrender her old claim to Amphipolis, and on the other hand Philip
would recognise Athens as mistress of the Chersonese. The two
exceptions which Philip made were inevitable. Halus indeed was a
trifle which no one heeded; but it was an essential part of the
Macedonian policy to proceed against Phocis. To the envoys, whom
the king charmed by his courteous hospitality at Pella, he privately
intimated that he was far from being ill-disposed to the Phocians;
and perhaps a few of them hoped that there was something in the
assurance. But in truth the Athenian statesmen troubled themselves
little about Phocis; some of them, like the Theban proxenos Demosthenes, were more disposed to lean towards Thebes. It would be
necessary to keep up the appearance of protecting an ally,—though
relations with that ally had recently grown somewhat strained; but
neither Eubulus nor Demosthenes would for a moment have dreamed
of forgoing the peace for the sake of supporting Phocis against her
enemies.

Peace
accepted
and
sworn to
at Athens,
346 B.C.,
March.
There were a few Thracian forts, belonging to Cersobleptes, which Philip was anxious to capture before the peace was made ; and, when the envoys left Pella, he set out for Thrace, having given them an undertaking to respect the Chersonese. The envoys returned home bearing with them a friendly letter from Philip to the Athenian people, and they were followed in a few days by three Macedonian delegates, appointed to receive the oaths from the Athenians and their allies. How important this negotiation was for Philip is proved by the fact that two of these deputies were the two greatest of his subjects, Parmenio and Antipater. On the motion of Philocrates, the Peace was accepted by Athens on the terms which Philip offered, though there were dissentient voices against the exclusion of Phocis and Halus ; but the murmurs of the opposition were silenced by the plain speaking of Eubulus, who showed that if the terms were rejected the war must be continued. And some of the ambassadors disseminated the unofficial utterances of Philip, that he would not ruin the Phocians and that he would help Athens to win back Euboea and Oropus. The upshot was that Phocis was not mentioned in the treaty ; she was tacitly, not expressly, excluded.[1]

The Peace was now concluded on one side, and it remained for the envoys of Athens to administer the oath to Philip and his allies. It was to the interest of Athens that this act should be accomplished as speedily as possible, for Philip was entitled to make new conquests until he swore to the Peace, and he was actually engaged in making new conquests in Thrace. The same ambassadors who had visited Macedonia to arrange the terms of a treaty now set forth a second time to administer the oaths.

Second
embassy
from Athens
to Philip
sets out
in April,
346 B.C.
Meanwhile Philip had taken the Thracian fortresses which he had gone to take, and had reduced Cersobleptes to be a vassal of Macedonia. When he returned to Pella, he found not only the embassy from Athens, but envoys from many other Greek states also, awaiting his arrival with various hopes and fears. He was beginning to be recognised as the arbiter of northern Hellas.

So far as the formal conclusion of the Peace went, there was no difficulty. But the Athenian ambassadors had received general powers to negotiate further with Philip, with a view to some common decision on the settlement of the Phocian question and northern Greece. The treaty was a treaty of " peace and alliance," and, if Philip could have had his way, the alliance would have become a bond of close friendship and co-operation. And it was in this direction that Eubulus and his party were inclined cautiously to move.

[1] The express exclusion was not necessary, since Phocis did not belong to the Athenian symmachy or confederacy in the strict sense, and had no voice in the Synedrion of the Athenian allies.

Athens might have now taken her position as joint arbitrator with Philip in the settlement of the Amphictionic states. Both Philip and Athens had a common interest in reducing the power of Thebes; and, if it was the interest of Athens that Phocis should not be utterly destroyed, Philip had no special enmity against Phocis, whose strength was now exhausted; the Phocian "sacrilege" was a convenient pretext to interfere and step into the place of Phocis in the Delphian Amphictiony. A common programme was discussed, and might easily have been concerted between Philip and the ambassadors. To treat the Phocians with clemency and to force Thebes to acknowledge the independence of the Boeotian cities would have been the basis of common action; the restoration of Plataea was mentioned; and while Philip promised to secure the restitution to Athens of Euboea and Oropus, Athens would have supported the admission of Macedonia into the Amphictionic Council. Aeschines was the chief mouthpiece of the counsels of Eubulus. But the project of an active alliance was opposed strenuously by Demosthenes, and as Demosthenes had great and daily increasing influence with the Athenian Assembly, it would have been unsafe for Philip to conclude any definite agreement with the majority of the embassy. The policy of Demosthenes was to abandon the Phocians to their fate and to draw closer to Thebes; so that, when his city had recovered from her financial exhaustion, Thebes and Athens together might form a joint resistance to the aggrandisement of Macedonia. In consequence of this irreconcilable division, which broke out in most unseemly quarrels among the ambassadors, nothing more was done than the administration of the oath. The envoys accompanied the king into Thessaly, and at Pherae the oath was administered to the Thessalians, his allies. A peace was then arranged with Halonnesus, *Embassy* and the envoys returned to Athens, leaving Philip to proceed on *returns to* his own way. *Athens,*

It now remained to be seen whether Eubulus would carry the *June,* Assembly with him in favour of a rational policy of co-operation with *346 B.C.* Macedon, or would be defeated by the brilliant oratory of his younger rival. Philip's course of action would depend on the decision of the Assembly.

It was a calamity for Athens that at this critical moment there was no strong man at the helm of the state. The Assembly was swayed between the opposite counsels of Demosthenes, whose oratory was irresistible, and of Eubulus, whose influence had been paramount for the past eight years. When the ambassadors returned, Demosthenes lost no time in denouncing his colleagues, as having treacherously intrigued with Philip against the interests of the city. His denunciation was successful for a moment, and the usual vote of thanks to the embassy was withheld. But the success was only for a moment; Aeschines and his colleagues defended their policy triumphantly before the Assembly; and it was clear that the programme which they had discussed with Philip would have been satisfactory to the people. The Assembly decreed that the treaty of peace and alliance should be extended to the posterity of Philip. It further decreed that Athens should formally call upon the Phocians to surrender Delphi to the Amphictions, and should threaten them with armed intervention if they declined. Demosthenes appears to have made no opposition to this measure against the Phocians; and it seemed that the policy of co-operation with Philip was about to be realised.

Thermo-
pylae
opened to
Philip,
July.

Philip in the meantime advanced southward. The pass of Thermopylae was held by Phalaecus, who had been reinforced by some Lacedaemonian troops; but Phalaecus had opened secret negotiations with Pella some months before; and the hostile vote of the Athenians decided him to capitulate on condition of departing unhindered where he would.

Before he reached Thermopylae, Philip had addressed two friendly letters to Athens, inviting her to send an army to arrange the affairs of Phocis and Boeotia. Indisposed as the Athenian citizens were to leave Athens on military service, they lent ready ears to the absurd terrors which Demosthenes conjured up, suggesting that Philip would detain their army as hostages. Accordingly they contented themselves with sending an embassy (on which Demosthenes declined to serve) to convey to Philip an announcement of the decree which they had passed against the Phocians. Thus swayed between Eubulus and Demosthenes, the Athenians had done too much or too little. They had abandoned the Phocians, and at the same time they resigned the voice which they should, and could, have had in the political settlement of northern Greece.

As it was clear that Philip could not trust Athens, owing to the attitude of Demosthenes, he was constrained to act in conjunction with her enemy, Thebes. The cities of western Boeotia, which had been held by the Phocians, were restored to the Boeotian confederacy. The doom of the Phocians was decided by the Amphic-

Fate of the tionic Council which was now convoked. If some of the members
Phocians. had had their way, all the men of military age would have been cast down a precipice; but Philip would not have permitted this, and the sentence was as mild as could have been expected. The Phocians were deprived of their place in the Amphictionic body; and all their cities (with the exception of Abae) were broken up into villages, so that they might not again be a danger to Delphi. They were obliged to undertake to pay back, by instalments of sixty talents a

year, the value of the treasures which they had taken from the
sanctuary. The Lacedaemonians were also punished for the support
which they had given to Phocis, by being disqualified to return either
of the members who represented the Dorian vote. The place which
Phocis vacated in the Council was transferred to Macedonia, in
recognition of Philip's services in expelling the desecrators of the
temple.

The Athenian declaration against Phocis exempted Athens from the
penalty which was inflicted on Sparta at this Amphictionic meeting.
But this was small comfort, and when the Athenians realised that
they had gained nothing and that Thebes had gained all she
wanted, they felt with indignation that the statesmanship of their city
had been unskilful. The futility of their policy had been mainly due
to Demosthenes, who had done all in his power to thwart Eubulus;
and he now seized the occasion to discredit that statesman and his
party. He encouraged his fellow-countrymen in the unreasonable fear
that Philip would invade Attica, and the panic was so great that they
brought their families and movable property from the country into
the city. The fear was soon dispelled by a letter from Philip himself; but Demosthenes had succeeded in creating a profound distrust of Philip, and there was soon an opportunity of expressing this
feeling.

An occasion offered itself to Philip almost immediately to display
publicly to the assembled Greek world the position of leadership
which he had thus won. It so happened that the celebration of the *Pythian games*,
Pythian games fell in the year of the Peace. It will be remembered
how the despot of Pherae, when he had made himself ruler of *346 B.C.: Philip president.*
Thessaly, was about to come down to Delphi and assume the pre-
sidency of the Pythian feast, when he was cut down by assassins.
The ambitions and plans of Pherae had passed to Pella, and
Greece, which had dreaded the claims of the Thessalian tyrant, had
now to bend the knee before the Macedonian king. Athens sulked;
she sent no deputy to the Amphictionic meeting which elected Philip
president for the festival, no delegates to the festival itself. This
marked omission was a protest against the admission of Macedonia
to the Amphictionic League, and Philip understood it as such. But
he did not wish to quarrel with Athens; he hoped ultimately to gain
her good-will; and instead of marching into Attica, whither his
Thessalian and Theban friends would have only too gladly followed
him, he contented himself with sending an embassy to notify to the
Athenian people the vote which made him a member of the Amphictiony and to invite them to concur. The invitation was in fact an
ultimatum. Eubulus and his party had lost their influence in the out- *Incon-sistency of Athens.*
burst of anti-Macedonian feeling which Demosthenes had succeeded in

*Demo-
sthenes'
speech on
the Peace.* stirring up. But the current had gone too far, and Demosthenes had
some difficulty in allaying the spirits which he had conjured up. The
Assembly was ready, on the slightest encouragement, to refuse its
concurrence to the Amphictionic decree, and Demosthenes was forced
to save the city from the results of his own agitation by showing
that it would be foolish and absurd "to go to war now for the
shadow at Delphi." Rarely had Athens been placed in such an
undignified posture—a plight for which she had to thank the brilliant
orator whom a malignant fate had sent to guide her on a futile path.
From this time forward Demosthenes was the most influential of her
counsellors.

Neither Demosthenes, the eloquent speaker, nor Eubulus, the able
*The
political
insight and
foresight
of Isocrates* financier, saw far into the future. The only man of the day perhaps
who grasped the situation in its ecumenical aspect, who descried, as
it were from without, the place of Macedonia in Greece and the
place of Greece in the world, was the nonagenarian Isocrates. He
had never ventured to raise his voice in the din of party politics ; he
had kept his garments unspotted from the defilement of public life ;
and when he condescended to give political advice to Greece, it was
easy for the second-rate statesman as well as the party hack to
laugh at a mere man of study stepping into a field where he had no
practical experience. But Isocrates discerned the drift of events,
where the orators who madly declaimed in the Pnyx were at fault ;
and the view which he took of the situation after the conclusion of
the Peace of Philocrates simply anticipated the decrees of history.
He explained his view in an open letter to king Philip. He had,
long since, seen the endless futility of perpetuating that international
system of Greece which existed within the memory of men : a number of small sovereign states, which ought by virtue of all they had in
common to form a single nation, divided and constantly at feud.
The time had come, he thought, to unite Greece, now that there had
arisen a man who had the brains, the power, and the gold to become
the central pivot of the union. Sovereign and independent the city
states would of course remain ; but they might be drawn together
into one fold by a common hope and allegiance to a common leader.
And under such a leader as Philip there was a great programme for
Greece ; and not a mere programme of ambition, undertaken for the
sake of something to do, but an enterprise which was urgently
needed to meet a pressing social danger. We have already seen how
Greece was flooded for many years past with a superfluous population
who went about as armed rovers, attached to no city, hiring themselves out to any state that needed fighting men, a constant menace
to society. A new country to colonise was the only remedy for
this overflow of Greece, as Isocrates recognised. And the new

country must be won from the barbarian. The time had come for
Hellas to take the offensive against Persia, and the task appointed for
Philip was to lead forth the hosts of Hellas on this splendid enterprise.
If he did not destroy the whole empire of the Great King, he might
at least annex Asia Minor "from Cilicia to Sinope" to the Hellenic
world and appropriate it to the needs of the Hellenic folk.

Ten years later the fulfilment of this task which Isocrates laid
upon Philip was begun, not indeed by Philip himself, but by his
successor. We shall see in due time how the fulfilment surpassed
the utmost hopes of the Athenian speculator. But it is fair to note
how justly Isocrates had discerned the signs of the times and the
tendency of history. He saw that the inveterate quarrel between
Europe and Asia, which had existed since the "Trojan war," was the
great abiding fact; he foresaw that it must soon come to an issue;
and throughout the later part of his long life he was always watching for the inevitable day. The expedition of Cyrus and the campaign of Agesilaus were foreshadowings of that day; and it had
seemed for a moment that Jason of Pherae was chosen to be the
successor of Agamemnon and Cimon. Now the day had come at
last; the choice of destiny had fallen upon the man of Macedonia.
And Isocrates knew that this expansion of Greece would meet
Greece's chief practical need. It is instructive to contrast his sane
and practical view of the situation of Greece with the chimerical
conservatism of some of his contemporaries. This conservatism,
to which the orator Demosthenes gave a most noble expression, was founded on the delusion that the Athens of his day
could be converted by his own eloquence and influence into the form
and feature of the Periclean city. That was a delusion which took
no account of the change which events had wrought in the Athenian
character; it was a noble delusion which could have misled no great
statesman or hard-headed thinker. It did not mislead Isocrates; he
appreciated the trend of history, and saw the expansion of Greece, to
which the world was moving.

Sect. 7. Interval of Peace and Preparations for War (346-1 B.C.)

Having gained for Macedonia the coveted place in the religious
league of Greece, Philip spent the next year or two in improving his
small navy, in settling the administration of Thessaly, and in acquiring influence in the Peloponnesus. It may fairly be said that
Thessaly was now joined to Macedonia by a personal union. The *Philip*
Thessalian cities elected the Macedonian king as their *archon*—the *elected*
old name of tagus with its Pheraean associations was avoided,—and *archon of Thessaly;*

four tetrarchies of Thessaly. he set four governors over the four great divisions of the country. South of the Corinthian Isthmus, Philip adopted the old policy of Thebes, offering friendship to those states which needed a friend to stand by them against Sparta. His negotiations gained him the adhesion of Messenia and Megalopolis, Elis and Argos. In Megalopolis they set up a bronze statue of Philip, while Argos had a special tie with Macedon, since she claimed to be the original home of the Macedonian kings.

Nor did Philip yet despair of achieving his chief aim, the conciliation of Athens. No one knew how to bribe better than he, and we may be sure that he gave gold without stint to his Athenian sup-

The Peace-party at Athens. porters. The Athenians naturally preferred peace to war ; and the political party which was favourable to friendly relations with Philip was still strong and might at any moment regain its power. The influence of the veteran Eubulus, who seems to have withdrawn somewhat from public affairs, was on that side ; there were Aeschines and Philocrates who had been active in the negotiation of the Peace ; and there was the incorruptible soldier Phocion, who was a remarkable figure at Athens, although he had no pretensions to eminence either as a soldier or as a statesman. He was marked among his contemporaries as an honest man, superior to all temptations of money ; and, as the Athenians always prized this superhuman integrity which few of them attempted to practise, they elected him forty-five times as strategos, though in military capacity he was no more than a respectable sergeant. But his strong common sense, which was impervious to oratory, and his exceptional probity made him an useful member of his party.

The War-party. There was one man in Athens who was firmly resolved that the peace should be no abiding peace, but a mere interval preparatory to war. Demosthenes, supported by Hypereides, Lycurgus, and others, spent the time in inflaming the wrath of his countrymen against Philip and in seeking to ruin his political antagonists. These years are therefore marked by a great struggle between the parties of war and peace ; the influence of Demosthenes being most often in the ascendency and ultimately emerging victorious.

Demosthenes impeaches Aeschines, 346-5 B.C. After Philip's installation in the Amphictionic Council, Demosthenes lost no time in striking a blow at his opponents. He brought an impeachment against Aeschines for receiving bribes from the Macedonian king and betraying the interests of Athens in the negotiations which preceded the Peace. Men's minds were irritated by the triumph of Thebes, and Demosthenes might have succeeded in inducing them to make Aeschines a scapegoat, if he had not committed a fatal mistake. He associated with himself in the prosecution a certain Timarchus, whose early life had been devoted to vices which disqualified him from the rights of a citizen ; and thus Aeschines easily *Aeschines* parried the stroke by bringing an action against Timarchus and sub- *against* mitting his private life to an annihilating exposure. The case of *Timar-chus.* Demosthenes was thereby discredited, and he was obliged to let it drop for the time.

A year or so later we find Demosthenes going forth on a mission *Demo-* to the cities of the Peloponnesus, to counteract by his oratory the *sthenes in* influence of Philip. But his oratory roused no echoes, and Philip *the Pelo-ponnese,* had good reason to complain of invectives which could hardly be *344 B.C.* justified from the lips of the representative of a power which was at peace and in alliance with Macedonia. An embassy came from Pella to remonstrate with the Athenians on their obstinate misconstruction of Macedonian motives, and Demosthenes seized the occasion to *The Second* deliver one of his uncompromising anti-Macedonian harangues. The *Philippic.* basis of his reasoning in this Philippic, and in the political speeches which followed it during the next few years, is the proposition that Philip desired and purposed to destroy Athens. It was a proposi-tion of which he had no valid proof ; and it was actually untrue, as the sequel showed.

We are not told what answer Athens sent to Pella, but it would seem that she complained of the terms of the recent Peace as unfair, and specially mentioned her right to Halus. This *Halus.* island off the coast of Thessaly, a place of no value whatever, had belonged to the Athenian Confederacy, but it had been seized by pirates, and the pirates had been expelled by Philip's soldiers. Philip sent an embassy with a courteous message, requesting Athens to propose emendations in the terms of the Peace, and offering to give her Halonnesus. But the place was of so little consequence to Athens or any one, that it served as an excellent pretext for diplomatic wrangling, and Demosthenes could persuade the people to refuse Halonnesus as it was offered, and demand that it should not be " given " but " given back." Besides the " restoration " of this worthless island, Athens made the proposal that the basis of the Peace should be altered, and that each party should retain, not the territories which were actually in its possession when the treaty was concluded, but the territories which lawfully belonged to it. This proposal was preposterous ; no peace can be made on a basis that leaves open all the debated questions which it is the object of the treaty to settle. Athens also complained of the Thracian fortresses which Philip captured and retained after the negotiation had begun. On this question Philip was legally in the right, but he offered to submit the matter to arbitration. Athens refused the offer on the plea that suitable arbiters could not be found. She thus showed that she was not in earnest ; her objection was as frivolous as her proposal.   Demosthenes was responsible for the attitude of the city, and his intention was to keep up the friction with Macedonia and prevent any conciliation.

Impeachment and flight of Philocrates, 343 B.C.

The ascendency which Demosthenes and his fellows had now won emboldened them to make a grand attack upon their political opponents, and thereby deal Philip a sensible blow.   Hypereides brought an accusation of treachery against Philocrates, whose name was especially associated with the Peace, and so formidable did the prospect of the trial seem, in the present state of popular opinion, that Philocrates fled, and he was condemned to death for contempt of

Impeachment of Aeschines, 343 B.C.

court.   Encouraged by this success, Demosthenes again took up his indictment against Aeschines, but Aeschines stood his ground ; and one of the most famous political trials of antiquity was witnessed by the Athenian public.   We can still hear the two rivals scurrilously reviling each other and vying to deceive the judges ; for they published their speeches after the trial, to instruct and perplex posterity.   It is in these documents, burning with the passions of political hatred, that the modern historian, picking his doubtful way through lies and distortions of fact, has to discover the course of the negotiations which led to the Peace of Philocrates.

Demosthenes on the malversation of the embassy.

The speech of Demosthenes, in particular, is a triumph in the art of sophistry.   No politician ever knew better than he how short is the memory of ordinary men for the political events which they have themselves watched and even helped to shape by their votes and opinions ; and none ever traded more audaciously on this weakness of human nature.   Hardly four brief years had passed since the Peace was made, and Demosthenes, confident that his audience will remember nothing accurately, ventures lightly to falsify facts which had so lately been notorious in the streets of Athens.   Disclaiming all responsibility for a peace which he had himself worked hard to bring about but now seeks to discredit, he discovers that the Phocians were basely abandoned and imputes their fate to Aeschines.   Against Aeschines there was in fact no case ; the charge of receiving bribes from Philip was not supported by any actual evidence.   The reply of Aeschines, which as an oratorical achievement is not inferior to

Aeschines acquitted.

that of his accuser, rings less falsely.   Eubulus and Phocion, men of the highest character, supported Aeschines, but the public feeling was so hostile to Philip at this juncture, that the defendant barely escaped.

That Aeschines and many others of his party received money from Philip we may well believe — though the reiterations of Demosthenes are no evidence.   But to receive money from Philip was one thing and to betray the interests of Athens was another. It must be proved that a politician had sacrificed the manifest good of his country, or deserted his own political convictions, for a sackful of silver or gold, before he could be considered unconditionally a traitor. Public opinion in Greece thought no worse of a man for accepting a few talents from foreigners who were pleased with his policy ; although those few public men—Demosthenes was not among them—who made it a rule never to accept an obol in connexion with any political transaction were respected as beings of superhuman virtue. Philip, who unlocked many a city by golden keys, was doubtless generous to the party whose programme was identical with his own interests ; and it may be that Aeschines and others, who were not in affluent circumstances, would have been unable to devote themselves to public affairs if the king had not lined their wallets with gold.

Meanwhile Philip was seeking influence and intriguing in the countries which lay on either side of Attica,—in Megara on the west, and Euboea on the north-east. An attempt at a revolution in Megara was defeated, and the city allied itself with its neighbour and old enemy Athens. But in Euboea the movements supported by Macedonia were more successful. Both in Eretria and in Oreus oligarchies were established, really dependent on Philip. But in Chalcis, which from its strategic position was of greater importance, the democracy held its ground, and sought an equal alliance with Athens, to which Athens gladly consented. *Alliances of Athens with Megara and Chalcis, 343-2 B.C. Philo-Macedonian oligarchies in Euboea.*

Events in another quarter of Greece now caused a number of lesser Greek states to rally round Athens, and so bring within the field of near possibilities a league such as it was the dream of Demosthenes to form against Macedonia. By his marriage with an Epirot princess, it naturally devolved upon Philip to intervene in the struggles for the Epirot throne which followed her father's death. He espoused the cause of her brother Alexander against her uncle Arybbas, marched into the country, and established Alexander in the sovereignty. Epirus would now become dependent on Macedonia, and Philip saw in it a road to the Corinthian Gulf and a means of reaching Greece on the western side. His first step was to annex the region of Cassopia (between the rivers Acheron and Oropus) to the Epirote league of which his brother-in-law was head ; and his eyes were then cast upon Ambracia, which stood as a barrier to the southward expansion of Epirus. But the place which he desired above all was doubtless Naupactus, the key to the Corinthian Gulf, now in the hands of the Achaeans. For compassing his schemes in this quarter his natural allies were the Aetolians. They too coveted Naupactus and would have held it for him ; and they were the enemies of the Ambraciots and Acarnanians, whom he hoped to render dependent on Epirus. The evident designs of Philip alarmed all *Philip in Epirus.*

these peoples, and not only Ambracia, Acarnania, and Achaea, but Corcyra also, sought the alliance of Athens.

Philip, however, judged that the time had not come for further advances on this side, and some recent movements of Cersobleptes decided him to turn now to one of the greatest tasks which were imposed upon the expander of Macedonia — the subjugation of Thrace. Since the Persians had been beaten out of Europe, Thrace had been subject to native princes, some of whom—Teres, Sitalces, Cotys—we have seen ruling the whole land from the Strymon's to the Danube's mouth. It was now to pass again under the rule of a foreigner, but its new lords were Europeans who would lead Thracian soldiers to avenge upon Asia the oriental yoke which had been laid upon their ancestors. Of the Thracian expedition of Philip we know as little as of the Thracian expedition of Darius. Unlike Darius, he did not cross the rivers of the north or penetrate into any part of Scythia, but his campaign lasted ten months, and he spent a winter in the field in that wintry land, suffering from sickness as well as from the cold. In war Philip never spared himself either hardship or danger. Demosthenes in later years described his reckless energy, ruthless to himself, in a famous passage : "To gain empire and power he had an eye knocked out, his collar-bone broken, his arm and his leg maimed ; he abandoned to fortune any part of his body she cared to take, so that honour and glory might be the portion of the rest."

Thracian expedition of Philip, summer, 342 B.C. ; spring, 341 B.C.

The Thracian king was dethroned, and his kingdom became a tributary province of Macedon. There is still in the land a city which bears Philip's name, and is the most conspicuous memorial of that great and obscure campaign. Philippopolis on the Hebrus was the chief of the cities which the conqueror built to maintain Macedonian influence in Thrace.

Philippo-polis founded.

This conquest was not an infringement of the Peace, for Cersobleptes had not been admitted to the treaty as an ally of Athens. But it affected nearly and seriously the position of Athens at the gates of the Black Sea. The Macedonian frontier was now advanced to the immediate neighbourhood of the Chersonese, and Athens had no longer Thracian princes to wield against Philip. The prospect did not escape Demosthenes, and he resolved to force on a war,—though both his own country and Philip were averse to hostilities. Accordingly he induced Athens to send a few ships and mercenaries under a swashbuckler named Diopeithes, to protect her interests in the Chersonese. There had been some disputes with Cardia touching the lands of the Athenian outsettlers, and Diopeithes lost no time in attacking Cardia. Now Cardia had been expressly recognised as an ally of Philip in the Peace, and thus the action of

Diopeithes was a violation of the Peace. The admiral followed up this aggression by invading some of Philip's Thracian possessions, and Philip then remonstrated at Athens. Their admiral was so manifestly in the wrong that the Athenians were prepared to disown his conduct, but Demosthenes saved his tool and persuaded the people to sustain Diopeithes. He followed up his speech on the Chersonese question, which scored this success, by a loud call to war —the harangue known as the Third Philippic. The orator's thesis is that Philip, inveterately hostile to Athens and aiming at her destruction, is talking peace but acting war; and, when all the king's acts have been construed in this light, the perfectly sound conclusion is drawn that Athens should act at once. The proposals of Demosthenes are to make military preparations, to send forces to the Chersonese, and to organise an Hellenic league against "the Macedonian wretch."

Demosthenes' speech on the Chersonese, 341 B.C.

Third Philippic.

Envoys were sent here and there to raise the alarm. Demosthenes himself proceeded to the Propontis and succeeded in detaching Byzantium and Perinthus from the Macedonian alliance. At the same time Athenian troops were sent into Euboea; the governments in Oreus and Eretria were overthrown, and these cities joined an independent Euboeic league, of which the Synod met at Chalcis. The island was thus liberated from Macedon without becoming dependent on Athens.

Demosthenes at Byzantium, 341 B.C.

The Euboeic Federation, 341 B.C.

All these acts of hostility were committed without an overt breach of the Peace between Athens and Philip. But the secession of Perinthus and Byzantium was a blow which Philip was not prepared to take with equanimity. When he had settled his Thracian province, he began the siege of Perinthus by land and sea. There was an Athenian squadron in the Hellespont which barred the passage of the Macedonian fleet, but Philip caused a diversion by sending land troops into the Chersonese, and by this stratagem got his ships successfully through. The siege of Perinthus marks, for eastern Greece, the beginning of those new developments of the art of besieging, which in Sicily had long since been practised with success. But all the engines and rams, the towers and the mines of Philip failed to take Perinthus on its steep peninsular cliff. His blockade on the seaside was inefficient, and the besieged were furnished with stores and men from Byzantium. The Athenians were still holding aloof. They had addressed a remonstrance to Philip for violating the Chersonese and capturing some of their cruisers. Philip replied by a letter in which he rehearsed numerous acts of Athenian hostility to himself. But the decisive moment came when the king suddenly raised the siege of Perinthus and marched against Byzantium, hoping to capture it by the unexpectedness of his attack. Athens could no

Philip lays siege to Perinthus, 340 B.C.

then to Byzantium.

longer hold aloof when the key of the Bosphorus was in peril. The marble tablet on which the Peace was inscribed was pulled down ; it was openly war at last. A squadron under Chares was sent to help Byzantium, and Phocion presently followed with a second fleet. Other help had come from Rhodes and Chios, and Philip was compelled to withdraw into Thrace, baffled in both his undertakings. It was the first triumph of Demosthenes over the arch-foe, and he received a public vote of thanks from the Athenian people.

But one wonders that the naval power of Athens had not made itself more immediately and effectively felt. The Macedonian fleet was insignificant ; it could inflict damage on merchant-vessels or raid a coast, but it had no hold on the sea. The Athenian navy was 300 strong and controlled the northern Aegean ; and yet it seems that in these critical years there was no permanent squadron of any strength stationed in the Hellespont. Naval affairs had been by no means neglected. Eubulus had seen to the building of new ship-sheds and had begun the construction of a magnificent arsenal, close to the harbour of Zea, for the storage of the sails and rigging and tackle of the ships of war. But these luxuries were vain, if the ships themselves were not efficient, and the group-system on which *The naval* the ships were furnished worked badly. Demosthenes had long ago *reform of* desired to reform this system, which had been in force for seventeen *Demo-* years. The 1200 richest citizens were liable to the trierarchy—each *sthenes.* trireme being charged on a small group, of which each member contributed the same proportion of the expense. If a large number of ships were required, the group might consist of five persons ; if a small, of fifteen. This system bore hardly on the poorer members of the partnership, who had to pay the same amount as the richer, and some were ruined by the burden. But the great mischief was that these poorer members were often unable to pay their quota in time and consequently the completion of the triremes was delayed. The influence of Demosthenes was now so enormous that he was able, in the face of bitter opposition from the wealthy class, to introduce a new law, by which the cost of furnishing the ships should fall on each citizen in proportion to his property. Thus a citizen whose property was rated as exceeding thirty talents, would henceforward, instead of having to pay one-fifth or perhaps one-fifteenth of the cost of a single trireme, be obliged to furnish three triremes and a boat.

So popular was Demosthenes, by the successes of Euboea and Byzantium, that he was able to accomplish a still greater feat. Years before he had cautiously hinted at the expediency of devoting the Festival Fund to military purposes ; he now persuaded the Athenians to adopt this highly disagreeable measure. The building of the arsenal and ship-sheds was interrupted also, in order to save the expenses.

Philip in the meantime had again withdrawn into the wilds of *Philip in* Thrace. The Scythians near the mouth of the Danube had rebelled, *Thrace,* and he crossed the Balkan range to crush them. In returning to Mace- 340-339 don through the land of the Triballi, in the centre of the peninsula, he *B.C.* had some sore mountain warfare and was severely wounded in the leg. But Thrace was now safe, and he was free to deal with Greece.

SECT. 8. BATTLE OF CHAERONEA

Philip had no longer the slightest prospect of realising the hope, which he had cherished both before and after the Peace of Philo- crates, of establishing friendly relations with Athens. The influence *Philip* of the irreconcilable orator was now triumphant ; through the per- *makes up* sistent agitation of Demosthenes, coldness and quarrelling had issued *his mind* in war ; and Macedonia had received a distinct check. There was *to the war* nothing for it now but to accept the war and bring the Macedonian *Athens.* cavalry into play. There were two points where Athens could be attacked effectively, at the gates of her own city, and at the gates of her granary in the Euxine. But a land-power like Macedonia could not operate effectively in the Propontis, unless aided by allies which possessed an effective navy ; and Philip had experienced the truth of this when he laid siege to Perinthus and Byzantium. And in that quarter he had now to reckon not only with the Athenian sea-power but with the small navies of the Asiatic islands, Rhodes, Cos, and Chios, which had recently come to the rescue of the menaced cities. For these island states calculated that, if Philip won control of the passage between the two continents, he would not only tax their trade, but would soon cross over to the conquest of Asia Minor, and their fleets would then be appropriated to form the nucleus of a Macedonian navy. Now that Athens had been awakened from her slumbers, it was abundantly evident that the only place where Macedonia could inflict upon her a decisive blow was Attica.

On her side Athens had lightly engaged in a war, for which she *Dangerous* had not either fully counted the cost or meditated an adequate pro- *position of* gramme. In truth the Athenians had no craving for the war ; and *Athens.* they were not driven to it by an imperious necessity, or urged by an irresistible instinct, or persuaded by a rational conviction of its ex- pediency. The persistent and crafty agitation of Demosthenes and his party had drawn them on step by step ; their natural feeling of irritation at the rise of a new great power in the north had been sedulously fed and fostered by that eloquent orator and his friends, till it had grown into an unreasoning hatred of the Macedonian king, whose character, aims, and resources were totally misrepresented. But now that war was declared, what was to be the plan of action ? Athens had not even an able general who could make an effective combination. She controlled the sea, and it was something that Euboea had shaken off the Macedonian influence. In Chalcis, Athens had a point of vantage against Boeotia, and from Oreus she could raid the Thessalian coast and operate in the bay of Pagasae. But when Philip advanced southward, and passed Thermopylae, which was in his hands, the Athenian superiority at sea was of no use, for his communications were independent of the sea. There was no means of offering serious opposition if he marched on Attica ; and the citizens were hardly likely at the bidding of Demosthenes to ascend their ships as they had done at the bidding of Themistocles. If events fell out according to the only probable forecast which could be made—on the assumption of Demosthenes that the invasion of Attica and ruin of Athens were the supreme objects of Philip—the Athenians had to look forward to the devastation of their country and the siege of their city. How was this peril to be met ? They were practically isolated ; for they had no strong continental power to support them ; what could Megarians or Corinthians, Ambraciots or Achaeans, do for them against the host of Philip and his allies? "Ah, if we were only islanders !" many an Athenian must have murmured in these critical years. It was the calamity of Athens, as it has been the calamity of Holland, that she was solidly attached to the continent. Now that the crisis approaches nearer, it is borne in upon us more and more how improvident the policy of Athens had been. If she had accepted Macedonian friendship and kept a strong naval force permanently in the Propontis, assuring herself of undisputed control of her own element, she would have been perfectly safe. The constant presence of a powerful fleet belonging to a predominant naval state may be in itself a strategic success equivalent to a series of victories. But, though we have almost no notices of the movements of the Athenian galleys at this time, we cannot help suspecting that the naval power of Athens was inefficiently handled.

Demosthenes had never had a free hand until the siege of Byzantium ; till then, he could do little more than agitate. When at length he became in the full sense of the word the director of Athenian policy, his energy and skill were amazing. But we cannot help asking with what hopes he was prepared to undertake the responsibility of bringing an invader into his country and a besieger to the walls of his city. The answer is that he rested his hope on a single chance. From the beginning of his public career Demosthenes had a strong leaning to Thebes ; it has been already mentioned that he

Theban leanings of Demosthenes.

was Theban proxenos at Athens. This was a predilection which it behoved him to be very careful of airing ; for the general feeling in his city was unfriendly to Thebes. The rhetorical tears which Demosthenes shed over the fate of the Phocians were not inconsistent with his attachment to the enemies of Phocis ; for he never raised his voice for the victims of Theban hatred until their doom was accomplished. The aim of his policy was to unite Athens in alliance with Thebes. It was a difficult and doubtful game. Could Thebes be induced to turn against her Macedonian ally, who had recently secured for her the full supremacy of Boeotia, and who, she might reasonably reckon, would continue to support her as an useful neighbour to Attica ? On this chance, and a poor chance it seemed, rested the desperate policy of Demosthenes. If Thebes joined Philip, or even gave him a free passage through Boeotia, the fate of Attica was sealed. But if she could be brought to desert him, her well-trained troops, joined with those of Athens, might successfully oppose his invasion.

The invasion was not long delayed ; and it came about in a *Meeting of* curious way. During the recent Sacred War, the Athenians had *the Am-* burnished anew and set up again in the sanctuary of Delphi the *phictionic* donative which they had dedicated after the victory of Plataea, being *Council,* gold shields with the inscription, "From the spoils of Persians and *autumn,* 340 *B.C.* Thebans, who fought together against the Greeks." Such a re-dedi-cation, while Delphi was in the hands of the Phocians, who had been condemned as sacrilegious robbers, might be regarded as an offence against religion ; at all events, the Thebans and their friends had an excellent pretext to revenge themselves on Athens for that most offensive inscription, which had perpetuated the shame of Thebes for a century and a half. The Thebans themselves did not come forward, but their friends of the Locrian Amphissa arranged to accuse the Athenians at the autumn session of the Amphictionic Council and propose a fine of fifty talents. At this session Aeschines was *Speech of* one of the Athenian deputies and he discovered the movement which *Aeschines,* was afoot against his city. He was an able man and he forestalled *who retorts* the blow by dealing another. The men who had been incited to *sacrilege* charge Athens with sacrilege had been themselves guilty of a sacri- *Locrians.* lege far more enormous. They had cultivated part of the accursed field which had once been the land of Crisa. Aeschines arose in the assembly and, in an impressive and convincing speech which carried his audience with him, called upon the Amphictions to punish the men who had wrought this impious act. On the morrow at break of day the Amphictions and the Delphians, armed with pickaxes, marched down the hill to lay waste the places which had been unlawfully cultivated, and, as they did so, were assaulted by the

Amphissians, whose city is visible from the plain. The Council then resolved to hold a special meeting at Thermopylae, in order to consult on measures for the punishment of the Locrians, who, to their former crime, had added the offence of violating the persons of the Amphictionic deputies.

By his promptness and eloquence the Athenian orator had secured a great triumph. He had completely turned the tables on the enemies, Amphissa and Thebes, who must have been prepared to declare an Amphictionic war against Athens, in case she declined, as she certainly would have done, to pay the fine. They calculated of course on the support of Philip of Macedon. But it was now for Athens to take the lead in a sacred war against Amphissa ; and it was a favourable opportunity for her to make peace with Philip—so that the combination should be Philip and Athens against Thebes, instead *Athens does* of Philip and Thebes against Athens. It was not to be expected *not follow* that this advantage which Aeschines had gained would be welcome *up the* to Demosthenes ; for it was the object of Demosthenes to avoid an *stroke of* embroilment with Thebes. Accordingly he persuaded the people to *Aeschines.* send no deputies to the special Amphictionic meeting and take no part in the proceedings against Amphissa. He upbraided Aeschines with trying to " bring an Amphictionic war into Attica " : a strange taunt to the man who had prevented the declaration of an Amphictionic war against Athens.

Thus, although the attack upon Athens must have been prepared at Theban instigation, the incident was converted, through the policy of Demosthenes, into a means of bringing Athens and Thebes closer together. Athens and Thebes alike abstained from attending the *The Am-* special meeting. The Amphictions, in accordance with the decisions *phictions* of that meeting, marched against the Amphissians, but were not *proceed* strong enough to impose the penalties which had been decreed. *against* Accordingly, at the next autumn session, they determined to invite *Amphissa,* Philip to come down once more to be leader in a sacred war. *339 B.C.*

The Am- Philip did not delay a moment. An Amphictionic war, from *phictions* which both Athens and Thebes held aloof, was a matter which *call in* needed prompt attention. When he reached Thermopylae, he prob- *Philip,* ably sent on, by the mountain road which passes through Doris to *338 B.C.,* Amphissa, a small force to occupy Cytinion, the chief town on that *spring.* road. Advancing himself through the defile of Thermopylae into northern Phocis, he seized and refortified the dismantled city of Elatea. The purpose of this action was to protect himself in the rear against Boeotia, and preserve his communications with Ther- mopylae, while he was operating against Amphissa. But while he halted at Elatea, he sent ambassadors to explore the intentions of Thebes. He declared that he intended to invade Attica, and called upon the Thebans to join him in the invasion, or, if they would not do this, to give his army a free passage through Boeotia. This was a diplomatic method of forcing Thebes to declare herself; it does not prove that Philip had any serious intention of marching against Attica, and his later conduct seems to show that he did not contemplate such a step.

But in Athens, when the news came that the Macedonian army was at Elatea, the folk fell into extreme panic and alarm. It would seem that Philip's rapid movements had brought him into central Greece far sooner than was expected; and the news of his arrival, which must have been transmitted by way of Thebes, was accompanied by the rumour that he was about to march on Athens. And thus the Athenians in their fright connected the seizure of Elatea with the supposed design against themselves, although Elatea had no closer connexion than the pass of Thermopylae with an attack on Athens. For a night and a day the city was filled with consternation, and these anxious hours have become famous in history through the genius of the orator Demosthenes, who in later years recalled to the people the scene and their own emotions by a picturesque description which no orator has surpassed. *Alarm at Athens.*

On the advice of Demosthenes, the Athenians dispatched ten envoys to Thebes; everything depended on detaching Thebes from the Macedonian alliance. And it seemed at least possible that this might be effected. For, though there were probably few in Thebes who were inclined to be friendly to Athens, there was a party of some weight which was distinctly hostile to Macedonia. Moreover, there was a feeling of soreness against Philip for having seized Nicaea, close to Thermopylae, and replaced its Theban garrison by Thessalians. The envoys, of whom Demosthenes was one, were instructed to make concessions and exact none. *Athens sends ten envoys to Thebes.*

The ambassadors of Athens and Macedon met in the Boeotian capital, and their messages were heard in turn by the Theban assembly. It would be too much to say that the fate of Greece depended on the deliberations of this assembly, but it is the mere truth that the Theban vote not only decided the doom of Thebes itself, but determined the shape of the great event to which Greece had been irresistibly moving.

In considering the situation which the rise of Macedon had created we have hitherto stood in Pella or in Athens; we must now for a moment take our point of view at Thebes. The inveterate rivalry and ever-smouldering hate which existed between Thebes and Athens was a strong motive inducing Thebes to embrace an opportunity for rendering Athens harmless. But it would require no great foresight to see that, by weakening her old rival, Thebes would gravely endanger her own position. So long as Philip had a strong Athens to *Situation of Thebes.*

reckon with, it behoved him to treat Thebes with respect, but, if Athens were reduced to nothingness, Thebes would be absolutely in his power, and probably his first step would be to free the cities of Boeotia from her domination. To put it shortly, the independent attitude which Thebes had hitherto been able to maintain towards her friend Macedonia depended on the integrity of Athens. Thus the positions of Thebes and Athens were remarkably different. While Athens could with impunity stand alone as Philip's enemy, when Thebes was Philip's friend, Thebes could not safely be Philip's friend unless Athens were his enemy. The reason of this difference was that Athens was a sea-power, less dominant than in the fifth century, but still formidable.

To a Theban statesman then, possessing any foresight, the subjugation of Athens would have been feared as the prelude to the depression of Thebes ; and it would have seemed wiser to join in a common resistance to Philip. This sound reasoning was quickened by the eloquence of Demosthenes and the offers of Athens. The Athenians were ready to pay two-thirds of the expenses of the war ;

Thebes forms an alliance with Athens against Philip, 338 B.C., spring.

they abandoned their claim to Oropus, and they recognised the Boeotian dominion of Thebes—a dominion which they had always condemned before as an outrage on the rights of free communities. But professing now, through the mouth of Demosthenes, to be the champion of Hellenic liberty, Athens scrupled little to sacrifice the liberties of a few Boeotian cities. By these concessions she secured the alliance of Thebes, and Demosthenes won the greatest diplomatic success that he had yet achieved—the consummation to which his policy had been directed for many years.

Philip captures Amphissa, summer, 338 B.C.

[The allies occupied the passes leading from Phocis into Boeotia and detached a strong force under Chares to bar the road from the Gulf of Corinth through Amphissa and Doris. In the summer Philip, reinforced, made a lightning campaign through Phocis, defeated Chares, captured Amphissa, and seized Naupactus to gain direct access to the Gulf. The Greeks, now threatened in their rear, fell back to the plain of Chaeronea. Philip, advancing through the pass of Parapotamii from which the allies had withdrawn, found them guarding the way to Thebes, and prepared to give him battle. He had 30,000 foot soldiers and 2000 horse, perhaps slightly outnumbering his foes.]

Battle of Chaeronea, August (Meta-geitnion 7), 338 B.C.

Their line extended over about three and a half miles, the left wing resting on Chaeronea and the right on the river Cephisus. The Theban hoplites, with the Sacred Band in front, under the command of Theagenes, did not occupy the left wing, as when Epaminondas led them to victory at Leuctra and at Mantinea, but were assigned the right, which was esteemed the post of honour. In the centre were ranged the troops of the lesser allies, Achaeans, Corinthians, Phocians, and others, whom Demosthenes boasted of having rallied to the cause of Hellenic liberty. On the left stood the Athenians under three generals, Chares, Lysicles, and Stratocles, of whom Chares was a respectable soldier with considerable experience and no talent, while the other two were incompetent. Demosthenes himself was serving as a hoplite in the ranks.

Of the battle we know less perhaps than of any other equally important engagement in the history of Greece. But we can form a general notion of the tactics of Philip. The most formidable part of the adverse array was the Theban infantry ; and accordingly he posted on his own left wing the phalanx, with its more open order and long pikes, to try its strength against the most efficient of the old-fashioned hoplites of Greece. On the flank of this wing he placed his heavy cavalry, to ride down upon the Thebans when the phalanx had worn them out. The cavalry was commanded by Alexander, now a lad of eighteen, and, many hundred years after, "the oak of Alexander" was shown on the bank of the river. The right wing was comparatively weak, and Philip planned that it should gradually give way before the attack of the Athenians, and draw them on, so as to divide them from their allies. This plan of holding back the right wing reminds us of the tactics of Epaminondas ; but the use of cavalry to decide the combat is the characteristic feature of Philip's battles.

The Athenians pressed forward, fondly fancying that they were pressing to victory, and Stratocles in the flush of success cried, "On to Macedonia !" But in the meantime the Thebans had been broken by Alexander's horsemen : their leader had fallen, and the comrades of the Sacred Lochos were making a last hopeless stand. Philip could now spare some of his Macedonian footmen, and he moved them so as to take the Athenians in flank and rear. Against the assault of these trained troops the Athenians were helpless. One thousand were slain, two thousand captured, and the rest ran, Demosthenes running with the fleetest. But the Sacred Band did not flee. They fought till they fell, and it is their heroism which has won for the battle of Chaeronea its glory as a struggle for liberty. When the traveller, journeying on the highway from Phocis to Thebes, has passed the town of Chaeronea, he sees at the roadside the tomb where those heroes were laid, and the fragments of the lion which was set up to keep a long ward over their bones.

An epitaph which was composed in honour of the Athenian dead suggested the consolation that God alone is sure of success, men must be prepared to fail. It is true, but in this case the failure cannot be imputed to the chances of war. When the allies opened the campaign the outlook was not hopeless ; if they had been led by

Signifi-cance of battle of Chaeronea.
(1) mili-tary ;

a competent general they might have reduced the Macedonian army to serious straits amid the valleys of Phocis and the hills of Locris. But to oppose to a Philip, the best they had was a Chares. The war

FIG. 182.—The fragments of the Lion of Chaeronea

was really decided in Locris by the strategical inferiority of the Athenian and Theban generals; and the inevitable sequel of the blunders there was the catastrophe in Boeotia. The advantage in numerical strength with which the allies started had been lost, and when they stood face to face with the advancing foe at Chaeronea, all the chances were adverse to any issue save defeat, in a battle in the open against a general of such pre-eminent ability. Men must be prepared to fail when they have no competent leader.

If the chances of another issue to the battle of Chaeronea have *(2) politi-* been exaggerated, the significance of that event has been often mis- *cal.* represented. The battle of Chaeronea belongs to the same historical series as the battles of Aegospotami and Leuctra. As the hegemony or first place among Greek states had passed successively from Athens to Sparta, and to Thebes, so now it passed to Macedon. The statement that Greek liberty perished on the plain of Chaeronea is as true or as false as that it perished on the field of Leuctra or the strand of the Goat's River. Whenever a Greek state became supreme, that supremacy entailed the depression of some states and the dependency or subjection of others. Athens was reduced to a secondary place by Macedon, and Thebes fared still worse ; but we must not forget what Sparta, in the day of her triumph, did to Athens, or the more evil things which Thebes proposed. There were, however, in the case of Macedonia, special circumstances which seemed to give her victory a more fatal character than those previous victories which had initiated new supremacies.

For Macedon was regarded in Hellas as an outsider. This was *Greek* a feeling which the southern Greeks entertained even in regard to *feelings* Thessaly when Jason threatened them with a Thessalian hegemony ; *towards* and Macedonia, politically and historically as well as geographically, *Macedon.* was some steps further away than Thessaly. If Thessaly was hardly inside the inner circle of Hellenic politics, Macedonia was distinctly outside it. To Athens and Sparta, to Corinth and Argos and Thebes, the old powers, who, as we might say, had known each other all their lives as foes or friends, and had a common international history, the supremacy of Macedonia seemed the intrusion of an upstart. And, in the second place, this supremacy was the triumph of an absolute monarchy over free commonwealths, so that the submission of the Greek states to Macedon's king might be rhetorically branded as an enslavement to a tyrant in a sense in which subjection to a sovereign Athens or a sovereign Sparta could not be so described. For these reasons the tidings of Chaeronea sent a new kind of thrill through Greece. And the impression that there was something unique in Philip's victory might be said to have been confirmed by subsequent history, which showed that the old Greek commonwealths had had their day and might never again rise to be first-rate powers.

SECT. 9. THE SYNEDRION OF THE GREEKS. PHILIP'S DEATH

Isocrates just lived to hear the tidings of Chaeronea, and died consoled for the fate of his fallen fellow-citizens by the thought that the unity of Hellas was now assured. But a Greek unity, such as he dreamed of, was by no means assured. The hegemony of Macedonia did as little to unite the Greek states or abolish the separatist tendency as the hegemony of Athens or of Sparta. But we must see how Philip used his victory.

Philip harsh to Thebes ;

He treated Thebes just as Sparta had treated it when Phoebidas surprised the citadel. He punished by death or confiscation his leading opponents ; he established a Macedonian garrison in the Cadmea, and broke up the Boeotian league, giving all the cities their independence, and restoring the dismantled towns of Orchomenus and Plataea.

lenient to Athens.

But if his dealing with Thebes did not go beyond the usual dealing of one Greek state with its vanquished rival, his dealing with Athens was unusually lenient. The truth was that Athens did not lie defenceless at his feet. He might invade and ravage Attica, but when he came to invest Athens and Piraeus, he might find himself confronted by a task more arduous than that which had thwarted him at Perinthus and Byzantium. The sea-power of Athens saved her, and not less, perhaps, the respect which Philip always felt for her intellectual eminence. Now, at last, by unexpected leniency, he might win what he had always striven for, the moral and material support of Athens. And in Athens men were now ready to listen to the voices which were raised for peace. The policy of Demosthenes had failed, and all desired to recover the 2000 captives and avert an invasion of Attic soil. There was little disposition to hearken to Hyperides, who proposed to arm all disenfranchised citizens, metics,

Demades.

and slaves. Among the captives was an orator of consummate talent, named Demādes, who belonged to the peace party and saw that the supremacy of Macedon was inevitable. An anecdote was noised abroad that Philip, who spent the night after the battle in wild revelry, came reeling drunk to the place where his prisoners were and jeered at their misfortune, making merry, too, over the flight of the great Demosthenes. But Demades stood forth and ventured to rebuke him : " O king, fortune has given you the rôle of Agamemnon, and you play the part of Thersites ! " The words stung and sobered the drunken victor ; he flung away his garlands and all the gear of his revel, and set the bold speaker free. But whether this story be true or not, Demades was politically sympathetic with Philip and was sent by him to negotiate peace at Athens.

Philip offered to restore all the prisoners without ransom and not

to march into Attica.   The Athenians on their side were to dissolve *Terms*
what remained of their confederacy, and join the new Hellenic union *of Peace*
which Philip proposed to organise.   In regard to territory, Oropus *between*
was to be given to Athens, but the Chersonesus was to be surrendered *Athens and*
to Macedonia.   On these terms peace was concluded, and the *Macedonia.*
Athenian people thought that they had come off well.   Philip sent
his son and two of his chief officers to Athens, with the bodies of the
Athenians who had been slain.   They were received with great
honour, and a statue of the Macedonian king was set up in the
market-place, a token of gratitude which was probably genuine.
Demosthenes himself afterwards confessed with a snarl that Philip
had been kind.

It was now necessary for Macedonia to win the recognition of her *Philip in*
supremacy from the Peloponnesian states.   Philip marched himself *the Pelo-*
into Peloponnesus, and met with no resistance.   Sparta alone refused *ponnese.*
to submit, and the conqueror bore down upon her, with the purpose
of forcing on her a reform of the constitution and the abolition of her
peculiar kingship, which seemed to him like a relic of the dark ages.
But something mysterious happened which induced him to desist *Isyllus of*
from his purpose, and a poet of Epidaurus, who was at that time a *Epidaurus.*
boy, told in later years how the god Asklêpios had intervened to save
the Spartan state—

> What time king Philip unto Sparta came,
> Bent on abolishing the royal name.

But Sparta, though her kings were saved, had to suffer at the hands
of Philip what she had before suffered at the hands of Epaminondas,
the devastation of Laconia and the diminution of her territory.   The
frontier districts on three sides were given to her neighbours, Argos,
Tegea, Megalopolis, and Messenia.   Having thus displayed his arms *Synedrion*
and power in the south, the Macedonian king invited all the Greek *at Corinth,*
states within Thermopylae to send delegates to a congress at Corinth ; *338 B.C.*
and, with the sole exception of Sparta, all the states obeyed.

It was a Federal congress : the first assembly of an Hellenic
Confederacy, of which the place of meeting was to be Corinth, and
Macedonia the head.   The aim of the Confederacy was understood *Second*
from the first ; but it would seem that it was not till the second *Synedrion*
meeting, a year later, that Philip announced his resolve to make war *at Corinth,*
upon Persia, in behalf of Greece and her gods, to liberate the Greek *337 B.C.*
cities of Asia, and to punish the barbarians for the acts of sacrilege
which their forefathers had wrought in the days of Xerxes.   It was
the formal announcement that a new act in the eternal struggle
between Europe and Asia was about to begin, and Europe, having
found a leader, might now have her revenge for many a deed of

insolence. The federal gathering voted for the war and elected Philip general with supreme powers. It was arranged what contingents in men or ships each city should contribute to the Panhellenic army ; the Athenians undertook to send a considerable fleet.

Comparison of the Synedrion of the Isthmus of 480 B.C. with that of 338 B.C. The league which was thus organised under the hegemony of Macedon had the advantage of placing before its members a definite object to be accomplished, and, it might be thought, a common interest. But if Themistocles found it hard to unite the Greek states by a common fear, it was harder still for Philip to unite them by a common hope ; and the idea which Macedon promulgated produced no Panhellenic effort, and awakened but small enthusiasm. Yet the Congress of Corinth has its significance ; it is the counterpart of that earlier congress which met at the Isthmus, when Greece was trembling at the thought of the barbarian host which was rolling towards her from the east. She had so long since ceased to tremble that she had almost forgotten to remember before the day of vengeance came ; but with the revolution of fortune's wheel, that day came duly round, and Greece met once more on the Isthmus to concert how *Unity of Greece not achieved.* her ancient tremors might be amply avenged. The new league did not unite the Greeks in the sense in which Isocrates hoped for their union. There was a common dependency on Macedon, but there was no zeal for the aims of the northern power, no faith in her as the guide and leader of Greece. Each state went its own private way ; and the interests of the Greek communities remained as isolated and particular as ever. A league of such members could not be held together, the peace which the league stipulated could not be maintained, without some military stations in the midst of the country ; *Philip's garrisons in Greece.* and Philip established three Macedonian garrisons at important points : at Ambracia to watch the west, at Corinth to hold the Peloponnesus in check, and at Chalcis to control north-eastern Greece.

Parmenio, Amyntas, and Attalus invade Asia Minor, 336 B.C. The designs of Philip probably did not extend beyond the conquest of western Asia Minor, but it was not fated that he should achieve this himself. In the spring after the congress, his preparations for war were nearly complete, and he sent forward an advance force under Parmenio and other generals to secure the passage of the Hellespont and win a footing in the Troad and Bithynia. The rest of the army was soon to follow under his own command.

But Philip, as a frank Corinthian friend told him, had filled his own house with division and bitterness. A Macedonian king was not expected to be faithful to his wife ; but the proud and stormy princess whom he had wedded was impatient of his open infidelities. Nor was her own virtue deemed above suspicion, and it was even whispered that Alexander was not Philip's son. The crisis came when Philip fell in love with a Macedonian maiden of too high a station to

become his concubine—Cleopatra, the niece of his general Attalus. *Philip*
Yielding to his passion, he put Olympias away and celebrated his *divorces*
second marriage. At the wedding feast, Attalus, bold with wine, *Olympias*
invited the nobles to pray the gods for a *legitimate* heir to the throne. *and*
Alexander flung his drinking-cup in the face of the man who had *marries*
insulted his mother, and Philip started up, drawing his sword to *Cleopatra.*
transpierce his son. But he reeled and fell, and Alexander jeered,
"Behold the man who would pass from Europe to Asia, and trips in
passing from couch to couch!" Pella was no longer the place for
Alexander. He took the divorced queen to Epirus, and withdrew
himself to the hills of Lyncestis, until Philip invited him to return.
But the restless intrigues of the injured mother soon created new
debates, and when a son was born to Cleopatra, it was easy to arouse
the fears of Alexander that his own succession to the throne was
imperilled. Philip's most urgent desire was to avoid a breach with
the powerful king of Epirus, the brother of the injured woman. To
this end he offered him his daughter in wedlock, and the marriage
was to be celebrated with great pomp in Pella, on the eve of Philip's
departure for Asia. But it was decreed that he should not depart.
Olympias was made of the stuff which does not hesitate at crime, and
a tool was easily found to avenge the wrongs of the wife and assure
the succession of the son. A certain Pausanias, an obscure man of
no merit, had been grossly wronged by Attalus, and was madly
incensed against the king, who refused to do him justice. On the *Murder of*
wedding day, as Philip, in solemn procession, entered the theatre a *Philip,*
little in advance of his guards, Pausanias rushed forward with a *336 B.C.*
Celtic dagger and laid him a corpse at the gate. The assassin was *(summer).*
caught and killed, [but the real authors of the plot were not discovered. Her enemies later accused Olympias of the crime, but the
charge comes from tainted sources. Alexander reaped the fruits but
was not responsible. There were dark whispers against him, but
the loyalty of Philip's two leading generals, Antipater and Parmenio, is sufficient evidence of his innocence.]

To none of the world's great rulers has history done less justice *Injustice*
than to Philip. This failure in appreciation has been due to two *done to*
or perhaps to three causes. The overwhelming greatness of a son *Philip by*
greater than himself has overshadowed him and drawn men's eyes to *posterity.*
achievements which could never have been wrought but for Philip's
lifetime of toil. In the second place, we depend for our knowledge
of Philip's work almost entirely on the Athenian orators, and especially
on Demosthenes, whose main object was to misrepresent the king.
And we may add, thirdly, that we possess no account of one of the
greatest and most difficult of his exploits, the conquest of Thrace.
Thus through chance, through the malignant eloquence of his

opponent, who has held the ears of posterity, and through the very results of his own deeds, the maker and expander of Macedonia, the conqueror of Thrace and Greece, has hardly held his due place in the history of the world. The importance of his work cannot be fully understood until the consequences which it devolved upon his son to carry out have been studied. The work of Alexander is the most authentic testimony to the work of Philip.

The Philippic Histories of Theopompus.

But there was one notable man of the day whose imagination grasped the ecumenical importance of the king of Macedon. A pupil of Isocrates, Theopompus of Chios—who played some part in the politics of his own island—was inspired by the deeds of Philip to write a history of his own time, with Philip as its central figure. In that elaborate work, the loss of which is irreparable, Theopompus exposed candidly and impartially the king's weaknesses and misdeeds ; but he declared his judgment that Europe had never produced so great a man as the son of Amyntas.

It is part of the injustice to Philip that the history of Greece during his reign has so often been treated as little more than a biography of Demosthenes. Only his political opponents would deny that Demosthenes was the most eloquent of orators and the most patriotic of citizens. But that oratory in which he excelled was one of the curses of Greek politics. The art of persuasive speech is indispensable in a free commonwealth, and, when it is wielded by a statesman or a general,—a Pericles, a Cleon, or a Xenophon,—is a noble as well as useful instrument. But once it ceases to be a merely auxiliary art, it becomes dangerous and hurtful. This is what had happened at Athens. Rhetoric had been carried to such perfection that the best years of a man's youth were absorbed in learning it, and when he entered upon public life he was a finished speaker, but a poor politican. Briefly, orators took the place of statesmen, and Demosthenes was the most eminent of the class. They could all formulate striking phrases of profound political wisdom ; but their school-taught lore did not carry them far against the craft of the Macedonian statesman. The men of mighty words were as children in the hands of the man of mighty deeds. The Athenians took pleasure in hearing and criticising the elaborate speeches of their orators ; and the eloquence of Demosthenes, though it was thoroughly appreciated, imposed far less on such connoisseurs than it has imposed upon posterity. The common sense of a plain man could easily expose his sophistries ; he said himself that the blunt Phocion was the "chopper" of his periods.

Demosthenes as an orator.

Demosthenes used his brilliant gift of speech in the service of his country ; he used it unscrupulously according to his light—the light of a purblind patriotism. He could take a lofty tone ; he professed to regard Philip as a barbarian threatening Hellas and her gods. There is no need to show that, judged from the point of view of the history of the world, his policy was retrograde and retarding. We cannot fairly criticise him either for not having seen, even as fully as Isocrates, that the day for the expansion of Greece had come, and that no existing Greek commonwealth was competent to conduct that expansion ; or if he did vaguely see it, for having looked the other way. All he saw, or at least all he cared, was that the increase of Macedonia meant the curtailment of Athens ; and his political life was one long agitation against Macedonia's resistless advance. But it was nothing more than a busy and often brilliant agitation, carried on from day to day and from month to month, without any comprehensive plan. A fervent patriot does not make a great statesman. Demosthenes could devise reforms in special departments of the administration ; he could admonish his fellow-citizens to be up and doing ; but he did not grapple seriously with any of the new problems of the day ; he did not originate one fertile political idea. A statesman of genius might conceivably have infused fresh life into Athens by effecting some radical change in her constitution and finding for her a new part to play. The fact that no such statesman arose is perhaps merely another side of the fact that her part as a chief actor was over. It has often been said that the Demosthenic Athenians were irreclaimable. They certainly could not have been reclaimed by Demosthenes ; for Demosthenes, when all is said, was a typical Demosthenic Athenian.

The policy of Demosthenes.

CHAPTER XVII

THE CONQUEST OF PERSIA

SECT. I. ALEXANDER'S FIRST DESCENT ON GREECE

Alexander surrounded by foes. ON his accession to the throne of Macedon, Alexander found himself menaced by enemies on all sides. The members of the Confederacy of Corinth, the tributary peoples of the province of Thrace, the inveterately hostile Illyrians, all saw in the death of Philip an opportunity, not to be missed, for undoing his work ; and in Asia, Attalus, the father of Cleopatra, espoused the claim of Cleopatra's infant son. Thus Alexander stood within a belt of dangers like that by which his father, at the same crisis in *his* life, had been encompassed ; and the difference of the means which sire and son adopted to deal with the jeopardy showed the difference in temperament between the two men.

His methods unlike Philip's. If Alexander had followed the slow and sure methods of his father, he would have bought off the barbarians of the north, effected a reconciliation with Attalus, and deferred the Greek question till he had thoroughly established his power in Macedonia ; then, by degrees, he could have recovered in a few years the dominion which Philip had won, and undertaken the expedition against Persia which Philip had planned. But such cautious calculation did not suit the bolder genius of Philip's son. He refused to yield to any of his foes ; he encountered the perils one after another, and overcame them all.

First of all, he turned to Greece, where the situation looked serious enough. Athens had hailed the news of Philip's death with undisguised joy, and at the instance of Demosthenes had passed a decree in honour of his murderer's memory. Trumpets were sounding for war ; messengers were flying to Attalus and to Persia ; and Greece was incited to throw off the Macedonian yoke. Ambracia expelled her garrison, and Thebes attempted to expel hers.

Importance of Thessaly. But the insurrection of Thessaly was of far greater importance than the hostile agitations in the southern states. The Thessalian cavalry was an invaluable adjunct to the Macedonian army, and it was of more material consequence to a Macedonian king to be the archon of the Thessalian Federation than to be acknowledged as general of the Confederacy of Corinth.   Yet it was hardly altogether the need of quickly securing Thessaly that urged Alexander to deal with Greece before he dealt with any other portion of his empire.   He wished above all things to save Greece from herself.   His timely appearance, before the agitation could develop into a fully declared rebellion, might prevent the cities from committing any irreparable action, which would necessitate a condign punishment, or even harsh measures.   He would march south, not to chastise or judge the Greeks, but to conciliate them and obtain recognition as successor to his father's place in the amphictiony of Delphi and in the league of Corinth.

FIG. 183.—Alexander the Great.

336 B.C., late summer.

He advanced to the defile of Tempe, but found it strongly held by the Thessalians.   Instead of attempting to carry a position which was perhaps impregnable, he led his army farther south along the coast, and cutting steps up the steep side of Ossa he made a new path for himself over the mountain and descended into the plain of the Peneus behind his enemy.   Not a drop of blood was shed.   A Thessalian assembly elected Alexander to the archonship, and he guaranteed to the communities of the land the same rights and privileges which they had enjoyed under his father.   The conciliation of Thessaly led, without a blow, to the adhesion of its southern neighbours, Malis and Dolopia.   At Thermopylae the young king was recognised by the amphictiony, and as he marched southward not a hand was raised against him ; he had swooped down so quickly that nothing was ready to resist.   The Athenians sent a repentant embassy, which the king received kindly without any reference to the public jubilations over his father's murder ; and the Congress of the Confederacy met at Corinth to elect Alexander general in his father's place.

Alexander   Alexander was chosen supreme general of the Greeks for the invasion
elected   of Asia ; and it was as head of Hellas, descendant and successor of
General of Achilles, rather than as Macedonian king, that he desired to go forth
the Greeks. against Persia.   But his election by the Greek Confederacy at
Corinth had more of historical fitness than political significance.   The
contingents which the Greek states furnished as members of the
league were small, and the idea of the expedition failed to arouse
any national feeling.   Yet the welcome, though half-hearted and hypo-
critical, which was given to Alexander at Corinth, and the vote, however perfunctory, which elected him leader of the Greeks, were the
fitting prelude to the expansion of Hellas and the diffusion of
Hellenic civilisation, which destiny had chosen him to accomplish.
He was thus formally recognised as what he in fullest verity was,
the representative of Greece.   Of all those who thronged at
Corinth round the royal youth, to observe him with curious gaze
or flatter him with pleasant words, some may have foreseen that he
would be a conqueror of many lands, but none can have suspected
how his conquests would transform the world ; for few realised
that the world was waiting to be transformed.   Outside the gates
of Corinth, according to a famous story, the king found the
eccentric philosopher Diogenes, sitting in the barrel, which served
him as a home, and asked him to name a boon.   " Stand
out of the sun," was the brief reply of the philosopher.   " Were
I not Alexander," said the king to his retinue, " I should like to be
Diogenes."   The incident may never have happened, but the anecdote
happily brings face to face the enthusiast who carried individual
liberty to the utmost verge of independence and the enthusiast who
dreamed of making his empire conterminous with the globe.   For
the individualism which Diogenes caricatured was sister to the spirit
of cosmopolitanism which Alexander's empire was to promote.[1]

Meanwhile some domestic dangers had been cleared violently out
of his path.   His stepmother, her father, and her child had all been
done away with.   Attalus had been murdered in Asia, in accordance
with the king's commands.   But Alexander was not responsible for the
death of Cleopatra and her infant.   This was the work of Olympias,
who, thirsty for revenge, caused the child to be slaughtered in its
mother's lap, and forced Cleopatra to hang herself by her own belt.

SECT. 2. ALEXANDER'S CAMPAIGNS IN THRACE AND ILLYRIA

There were symptoms of disquietude in Thrace ; there were signs
of a storm brewing in the Illyrian quarter ; and it would have been

[1] Cp. above, p. 575.

impossible for the young king to invade Asia, with Thrace ready to *Alexander*
revolt in his rear, and Macedonia exposed to attack from the west. *marches*
It was indispensable to teach the Thracians a lesson, and especially *against the*
the Triballi, who had never been chastised for the check which they *Triballi,*
had inflicted on Philip.   The Triballi lived beyond the Haemus, and *335 B.C.*
when Alexander, having crossed Mount Rhodope, reached the foot
of one of the western passes of Mount Haemus, he found the steep *Shipka*
defile defended by mountaineers.   They had hauled up a multitude *Pass.*
of their war-chariots to the top of the pass, in order to roll them
upon the Macedonians and then, rushing down themselves, to fall upon
the disordered array.   There was no other way of crossing the
mountain, and the mountain must be crossed.   Alexander showed
here again the same temper and the same resource which he had
shown at Tempe ; when he had made up his mind that an object
must be attained, he never hesitated to employ the boldest or most
novel means.   He ordered the infantry to advance up the path, opening the ranks when possible to let the chariots roll through, but
when that was impossible, he directed them to fall on their knees
and, holding their shields locked together, to form a roof on which
the chariots could fall and roll harmlessly away.   The device was
successful.   The volleys of the cars rattled over the locked shields,
and notwithstanding the shock not a man was killed.   When the
barbarians had exhausted these ponderous missiles, the pass was
easily taken, and the Macedonians descended into the country of
the Triballi.   At the news of Alexander's approach the Triballi
had sent their wives and children to an island named Peuce, in the
Danube ; and then, waiting until he advanced into their land, stole
behind him to seize the mountain passes in his rear.   Learning of
this movement, Alexander marched rapidly back, forced the enemy
to fight and dispersed them with great loss.   He then proceeded on *On the*
his way to the bank of the Danube.   He had foreseen that it might *Danube,*
be necessary to operate on that river, perhaps to make a demonstra- *May.*
tion in the country of the Getae on the northern bank ; and he had
prepared for this emergency by adopting the same plan as Darius in
his famous Thracian expedition.   He instructed his ally Byzantium
to dispatch ships to sail up the river.   The garrison in the island
of Peuce were supported by a host of Scythian friends on the left
bank of the stream, and Alexander saw that with his few Byzantine
galleys it would be hopeless to attack the island until he had secured
the Scythian shore.   The problem was to throw his troops across
the river without the enemy's knowledge, and this must be done in
the darkness of one night.   The ships were too few in number ;
but all the fishing-boats in the neighbourhood were collected, and
tent-skins filled with hay were tied firmly together and strung across

the stream. Landing on the other bank, led by the king himself, a large band of horse and foot advanced under the cover of the long corn at dawn of day, and the barbarian host arose to see the Macedonian phalanx unfolded before them. Startled as much by the terrible promptitude of their foe as by the formidable array which faced them, they withdrew into their poorly fortified town, and when Alexander followed them at the head of his cavalry, they fled with all their horses could carry into the wilds of the north. Empire beyond the Danube was not sought by Alexander, and he did not pursue. He marked the term of his northern conquest by sacrificing solemnly on the banks to Zeus Soter, Heracles, and the river-god himself.

The embassy of the Celts.
This exploit led to the surrender of the Triballi in the island, and all the neighbouring tribes south of the river hastened to assure the king of their submission. There came also from unknown homes far up the river, or perhaps in the Dalmatian mountains, an embassy of Celts, huge-limbed, self-confident men, who had heard of Alexander's deeds and were fain to be his friends. [They swore alliance with him in a form still used by the Irish Gaels a thousand years later. " We will keep faith unless the sky fall and crush us or the earth open and swallow us or the sea rise and overwhelm us.] " Braggarts ! " said Alexander afterwards. But before two generations had passed away these men of mighty limbs and mighty words were destined to roll down in a torrent upon Greece and Asia, and to wrest for their own habitation a part of Alexander's conquests.

[Subsequent settlement of Celts in Galatia.]

The Illyrian danger.
Alexander's work was done in Thrace, but as he marched homewards he learned that the Illyrians were already in the gate of Macedonia, and that not a moment must be lost if the country was to be saved from an invasion. Philip had secured the Macedonian frontier on the Illyrian side by a number of fortresses, near the sources of the Haliacmon and Apsus ; and Pelion, which was the strongest of these strongholds, the key-fortress of the mountain gate, had now fallen into the hands of Clitus, the Illyrian chief. To reach Pelion as quickly as possible, before the arrival of the Taulantines, a folk in alliance with Clitus, was the object of Alexander. His march was threatened by the Autariats, another hostile folk, whom Clitus had engaged to waylay him ; but this danger was prevented by the friendly king of the Agrianes, who invaded the Autariat territory and fully occupied the fighting-men. Marching rapidly up the valley of the Erigonus, Alexander encamped near Pelion. The heights around were covered with Illyrians, and Clitus, as was the custom of his people before a battle, sacrificed three boys, three maidens, and three black rams. But before they came to the actual attack, the hearts of the Illyrians failed them, and deserting all their points of vantage

Alexander marches to Pelion.

and leaving their sacrifice incomplete, they retired into the fastness. Alexander intended to blockade the place next day by a circumvallation, but the Taulantines arrived in a large force, and he saw that his men were too few to deal at once with the foes within and the foes without the walls, nor were his provisions sufficient for a protracted siege.   It was absolutely necessary to withdraw from his present *The Mace-* position ; but it was a task of extreme peril to retreat in these defiles, *donian* with hostile Pelion in the rear and Taulantine troops occupying the *troops* slopes and heights.   This task, however, was carried out success- *themselves* fully, through the amazingly swift and skilful manœuvring of the *from a* highly drilled Macedonian soldiers ; the enemy were driven from their *dangerous* flanking positions, and the river was crossed with much trouble yet *position.* without the loss of a man.   At the other side of the river, Alexander's communications were safe ; he could obtain provisions and reinforcements as he chose, and might wait, at his ease, for an opportunity to strike.   The moment soon came.   The enemy, seeing in Alexander's retreat a confession of fear, neglected all precautions and formed a camp without rampart or outpost before the gates of the fortress.   Taking a portion of his army and bidding the rest follow, Alexander set out at night and surprised the slumbering camp of the barbarians.   A carnage followed and a wild flight, and the Mace- *Mace-* donians pursued to the Taulantine mountains.   At the first alarm, *donian* Clitus rushed into the gates of Pelion and set the town on fire, before *victory.* he joined the flight.

This discomfit of the Illyrians was a no less striking proof of Alexander's capacity than his exploits in Thrace.   These months of incessant toil had earned him a rest, but there was to be no rest yet for the young monarch.   Even as the tidings of the Illyrian danger had reached him before he left Thrace, so now, while he was still at Pelion, the news came that Thebes had rebelled.   He must now speed to Greece as swiftly as seven days agone he had sped to the Illyrian hills.   No need was more pressing than to crush this revolt before it spread.

Sect. 3. Alexander's Second Descent on Greece

The agitation against Macedon had not ceased during the past *Greek* year in the cities of Greece, and it was now fomented by the gold *cities* and the encouragement of Persia.   Five years before, at the out- *negotiating* break of the war, Athens had sent ambassadors to Susa begging for *against* subsidies from Artaxerxes, but the Great King would not break with *Macedonia.* Philip then, and sent them away with "a very haughty and barbarous letter " of refusal.   The Phrygian satrap, however, perhaps on his own responsibility, sent useful help to Perinthus in its peril, and

Persia gradually awoke to the fact that Macedonia was a dangerous neighbour. The new king, Darius, saw the necessity of embarrassing Alexander in Europe, so as to keep him as long as possible from crossing into Asia, where the Macedonian forces under Parmenio were holding their own. For this purpose he stirred up thoughts of war in Greece and sent subsidies to the Greek states. To many cities these overtures were welcome, but especially to Thebes, under the shadow of the Macedonian garrison. Three hundred talents were offered to Athens and publicly declined ; but Demosthenes privately accepted them, to be expended in the interests of the Great King. It is not probable that any city entered into a formal contract with Persia, but the basis of the negotiations was the King's Peace, of fifty years ago, the Greeks admitting the rights of the Persian empire over their brethren in Asia, who on their part were awaiting with various feelings the approach of the Macedonian deliverer.

Report of Alexander's death. As the patriots had often prayed for the death of Philip, so now they longed for the death of his youthful son, an event which might have hurled back Macedon into nothingness for ever. Rumours soon spread that the wish was fulfilled. Alexander was reported to have been slain in Thrace ; Demosthenes produced a man who had seen him fall ; and the Theban fugitives in Athens hastened to return to their native city and incite it to shake off the Macedonian yoke. Two captains of the garrison were caught outside the Cadmea *Thebans blockade the Cadmea.* and murdered, and the Thebans then proceeded to blockade the citadel by a double rampart on the south side, where there was no city wall outside the wall of the citadel. Greece responded to the Theban leading, which Demosthenes, Lycurgus, and the other Athenian patriots had prompted and encouraged. There were movements against Macedon in Elis and Aetolia ; the Arcadians marched forth to the Isthmus ; and the Athenians sent arms to Thebes, though they sent no men. The hopes of the patriots ran high ; the fall of the Cadmea seemed inevitable.

Alexander at Onchestus. Suddenly a report was whispered in Thebes that a Macedonian army was encamped a few miles away at Onchestus. As Alexander was dead, it could only be Antipater—so the Theban leaders assured the alarmed people. But messengers soon came, affirming that it was certainly Alexander. Nay, then, said the leaders, since King Alexander is dead, it can only be Alexander of Lyncestis.

But it was indeed the king Alexander. In less than two weeks he had marched from Pelion to Onchestus, and on the next day he stood before the walls of Thebes. He halted first on the north-eastern side of the city, near the sanctuary of the Theban hero, Iolaus ; he would give the citizens time to make their submission. But they were in no mind to submit, and some of their light-armed

THEBES.

Scale of Feet

0   500   1000   2000

Walker & Boutall sc.

To face page 744.

troops, rushing out of the gates, attacked the outskirts of the Macedonian camp. On the morrow Alexander moved his whole army to the south side of the city, and encamped close to the Cadmea, without making any attack on the walls, still hoping that the city would surrender. But the fate of Thebes was precipitated by one of his captains, by name Perdiccas, who was in charge of the troops which guarded the camp on the side of the Cadmea. Stationed *Capture of* within a few yards of the Theban earthworks, Perdiccas, without *Thebes,* waiting for orders, dashed through the outer rampart and fell upon the *beginning of Sept.* Theban guards. He was supported by a fellow-officer ; and Alex- 335 B.C. ander, when he observed what had happened, sent archers and light troops to their aid. The Thebans who manned the rampart were (*The* driven along the gully, which, running along the east side of the *Hollow Way.*) Cadmea, passes the temple of Heracles outside the walls. When they reached this temple they rallied and turned on their assailants and routed them back along the "hollow road." But, as they pursued, their own ranks were broken, and Alexander, watching for the moment, brought his phalanx into action and drove them within the Electran gate. They had no time to shut the gate before some Macedonians pushed in along with the fugitives ; and there were no men on the walls to shoot the enemy down, for the men who should have defended the walls had been sent to the blockade of the citadel. Some of the Macedonians, who thus entered, made their way to the Cadmea, and joining with the garrison they sallied out close to the Ampheion, where the main part of the Theban (*Tomb of* forces was drawn up. Others, having mounted the bastions, helped *Amphion* their friends without to climb the walls, and the troops thus admitted *and Zethus.*) rushed to the market-place. But the gate was now in the possession of the Macedonians ; the city was full of them ; and the king himself was everywhere. The Theban cavalry was broken up, and fled through the streets and the open gates into the plain ; the foot soldiers saved themselves as they could ; and then a merciless butchery began. It was not the Macedonians who were zealous in the work of slaughter, but the old enemies of Thebes, the Phocians, the Plataeans and other Boeotian peoples, who now wreaked upon the proud city of the seven gates vengeance for the wrongs and insults of many generations. Six thousand lives were taken before Alex- *The* ander stayed the slaughter. On the next day he summoned the *destruction* Confederates of Corinth to decide the fate of the rebellious city. The *of Thebes.* judges meted out to Thebes the same measure which Thebes would have once meted out to Athens. The sentence was that the city should be levelled with the dust and her land divided among the Confederates ; that the remnant of the inhabitants, with the women and children, should be sold into bondage, except the priests and priestesses of the gods, and those burghers who had bonds of guest-right with the Macedonians; and that the Cadmean citadel should be occupied by a garrison. The severe doom, showing how deeply the masterful city was abhorred, was carried out; and among the ruined habitations, on which the Macedonian warders looked down from the fortress walls, only one solitary house stood, making the desolation seem more desolate, the house of Pindar, which Alexander expressly spared.

The Boeotian cities were at length delivered from the yoke of their imperious mistress; Plataea and Orchomenus re-arose from their ruins. The fall of Thebes promptly checked all other movements in Greece; the Arcadian forces withdrew from the Isthmus; Elis and Aetolia hastened to retrieve their hostile attitude. The news reached *Athens* Athens during the festival of the Mysteries. The solemnity was *congratu-* interrupted, and in a hurried meeting of the Assembly it was resolved, *lates* on the proposal of Demades, to send an embassy to welcome Alex- *Alexander* *on the fall* ander on his safe return from his northern campaign, and to con- *of Thebes.* gratulate him on the just chastisement which he had inflicted upon Thebes. The same people passed this decree who, a few days before, on the proposal of Demosthenes, had resolved to send troops to the aid of that luckless city. Alexander demanded—and it was a fair demand — that Demosthenes and Lycurgus and the other agitators who kept the hostility to Macedonia alive, and were largely responsible for the disaster of Thebes, should be delivered to him; for so long as they were at large there was no security that Athens would not entangle herself in further follies. When the demand was laid before the Assembly, Demosthenes epigrammatically expressed his own view of the situation by advising the people not to hand over their sheep-dogs to the wolf. Phocion said in downright words that Alexander must be conciliated at any cost; let the men whose surrender he demanded show their patriotism by sacrificing them-selves. But it was finally decided that Demades, who had in-gratiated himself with the Macedonian king, should accompany another embassy and beg that the offenders might be left to the justice of the Athenian people. Alexander, still anxious to show every consideration to Athens, withdrew his demand, insisting only on the banishment of the adventurer Charidemus, of Thracian notoriety.

With the fall of Thebes Alexander's campaigns in Europe came to an end. The rest of his life was spent in Asia. The European campaigns, though they filled little more than a year, and though they seem of small account by the side of his triumphs in the east, were brilliant and important enough to have won historical fame for any general.   In his two descents into Greece, first to conciliate and afterwards to punish, in his expedition to the Danube, and in his Illyrian campaign, he had given tokens of the rare strategic capacity, the originality of conception, the boldness of resolution, the rapidity of action, and those other qualities which served Alexander's genius and soon found a more spacious sphere for their manifestation when they bore him toward the unknown limits of the eastern world.

Sect. 4. Preparations for Alexander's Persian Expedition. Condition of Persia.

Having spent the winter in making his military preparations and setting in order the affairs of his kingdom for a long absence, Alexander set forth in spring for the conquest of Asia.   Of his plans *The* and arrangements we know almost nothing, but we may say with *scheme of* confidence that his scheme of conquest was well considered, and *Alex-* that he did not go forth as an adventurer to take whatever came in *ander's* his way.   His original scheme of conquest was afterwards merged in *conquests.* a second and larger scheme, of which he had no conception when he went forth from Macedonia, for he had not the requisite geographical knowledge of central Asia.   But in the first instance his purpose was to conquer the Persian kingdom, to dethrone the Great King and take his place, to do unto Persia what Persia under Xerxes had essayed to do unto Macedonia and the rest of Hellas.   To carry out this design the first thing needful was to secure Thrace in the rear, and that had been already done.   In the conquest itself there were three stages.   The first step was the conquest of Asia Minor ; the second was the conquest of Syria and Egypt ; and these two conquests, preliminary to the advance on Babylon and Susa, would mean not merely acquisitions of territory, but strategic bases for further conquest.   The weak point in Alexander's enterprise was the *Want of* lack of a fleet capable of coping with the Persian navy, which was *a fleet.* 400 strong.   Here the Confederacy of Corinth should have come to his help ; Athens alone could have furnished over 200 galleys.   And Alexander doubtless counted on obtaining the support of Athens and the other Greek cities ultimately.   But he desired aid rendered with goodwill, and he made no effort to extort ships or men.   The loosely organised league of Corinth had undertaken to supply fixed contingents, but the fulfilment of these promises was not strictly exacted.

To secure Macedonia against her neighbours and subjects during his absence, Alexander was obliged to leave a large portion, perhaps as much as one half, of the national army behind him.   The govern-

Provisions for the government of Macedonia. ment was entrusted to his father's minister, Antipater. It is said that the king made dispositions before his departure as one who expected never to return. He divided all his royal domains and forests and revenues among his friends ; and, when Perdiccas asked what was left for himself, he replied, Hope. Then Perdiccas, rejecting his own portion, exclaimed, " We who go forth to fight with you need share only in your hope." The anecdote at least illustrates the enthusiasm with which Alexander infected his friends and officers on the threshold of a venture, of which the conception was almost as wonderful as its success.

State of Persia. The Persian empire was weak and loosely knit, and it was governed now by a feeble monarch. Two generations had passed since Greece beheld its weakness memorably demonstrated by the adventures of Xenophon's Ten Thousand ; and since then we have *Ochus (acceded, 358 B.C.) conquers Egypt.* seen it, on the western side, rent and riven by revolts. Artaxerxes Ochus displayed more strength than his predecessors. He re-established his power in Asia Minor, he quelled rebellions in Phoenicia and Cyprus, and even conquered Egypt, which had long set at nought the Persian efforts to regain it. The king, Nektanebos, was driven back from Pelusium to Memphis, and from Memphis he fled to Ethiopia. The Persian king had no thought of holding the land of the Nile by kindness ; as soon as he had Memphis in his power he displayed the intolerance of the fire-worshipper. He drowned the holy bull, Apis, and inaugurated the ass as the sacred animal of Egypt. This stupid outrage made the Persian rule more *Murder of Ochus, 338 B.C. Accession of Darius, 335 B.C.* detested than ever. Ochus was assassinated, the victim of a palace conspiracy ; and after two or three years of confusion the throne passed to a distant member of the Achaemenid house, Darius Codomannus, destined to be the last successor of his great name-sake. He was a mild and virtuous prince, beloved by his followers, but too weak, both in brains and will, for the task to which fate had doomed him.

Advantages on the side of Persia in the approaching struggle. It cannot be gainsaid that, if Darius had been able and experienced in war and capable of leading men, he had some enormous advantages. In the first place, he had the advantage in the sheer weight of human bodies. Though the size of his forces has been wildly exaggerated by ancient writers, at every stage of the war he heavily outnumbered Alexander's army. In the second place, while the coffers of Pella are said to have been emptied before Alexander set foot in Asia, the Great King commanded untold wealth. The treasury of Susa was full, and in the palace of Persepolis were hoarded inexhaustible stores of gold. In the third place, he had a navy which controlled the seaboard of Asia Minor, Syria, and Egypt, and ought, if it had been handled ably, to have placed insuperable obstacles in the way of an invader who had no adequate sea-power. And fourthly, although there was no cohesion in the vast empire or unity of centralisation, there was, for that very reason, little or no national discontent in the provinces. Egypt was an exceptional case. The revolts which occurred from time to time were not national movements, but the disaffections of ambitious satraps. If the Persian monarch was not loved, at least he was not hated ; and the warlike barbarians of the east, from far Hyrcania or the banks of the Oxus, were always ready to follow him and glad to fight in his cause. It was quite feasible, so far as the state of feeling in the provinces was concerned, to organise an effective defence of the empire. But all these advan- *Fatal* tages were as naught, for lack of a master mind and a controlling *short-* will. Multitudes were useless without a leader, and money could not *comings of* create brains. Moreover Persia was behind the age in the art of *Persia.* warfare. She had not kept pace with the military developments in Greece during the last fifty years, and, though she could pay Greek mercenaries, and though these formed in fact a valuable part of her army, they could have no effect on the general character of the tactics of an oriental host. The Persian commanders had no notion of study-ing the tactics of their enemy and seeking new methods of encountering them. They had no idea of shaping strategic plans of their own ; they simply waited on the movements of the enemy. They trusted, as they had always trusted, with perfect simplicity, in numbers, individual bravery, and scythe-armed chariots. The only lesson which the day of Cunaxa had taught them was to hire mercenary Greeks. Tradition gives their number as 50,000, but it was probably substantially less.

The strength of the army which Alexander led forth against *Alex-* Persia is said to have been 30,000 foot and 5000 horse, thus pre- *ander's* serving the large proportion of cavalry to infantry which was one of *army.* the chief novelties of Philip's military establishment. We have seen how Philip organised the national army of Macedonia, in the chief divisions of the phalanx, the special corps of hypaspists, and the heavy cavalry. Alexander led to Asia six regiments of the phalanx, *Heavy* and in the great engagements which decided the fate of Persia these *infantry.* formed the centre of his array. They were supported by Greek hoplites, both mercenary and confederate ; the mercenary were com-manded by Menander, the confederate by Antigonus. The hypaspists, *Light* led by Nicanor, son of Parmenio, had their station on the right wing, *Mace-* and the first regiment of these was the royal guard, called the *agēma*. *donian* Philҭotas, another son of Parmenio, was commander of the heavy *infantry.* cavalry, in eight squadrons ; one of which, the " royal squadron," *Cavalry.* under Clitus, corresponded to the *agēma* of the hypaspists. This Macedonian cavalry was always placed on the right, while on the

Light troops.   left rode the splendid Thessalian cavalry under Callas, with a corps of other Greek horse attached. Both the right and the left wings were strengthened by light troops, horse and foot, accoutred according to their national habit, from Thrace, Paeonia, and other countries of the Illyrian peninsula.

SECT. 5. CONQUEST OF ASIA MINOR

Successes of Parmenio, 335 B. C.   The forces which had been operating in Asia under Parmenio while Alexander was detained in Europe had been endeavouring to establish a footing in Aeolis and Mysia, and secure a base on the Propontis for further advance. The Great King had empowered

Memnon of Rhodes, an able mercenary captain, who in recent years had come to the front, to oppose the van of the Macedonian invasion. The most pressing need of the Persians was to recapture Cyzicus, which was in the hands of Parmenio. In this Memnon failed ; but he occupied Lampsacus, he forced the Macedonians to raise the siege of Pitane and beat them back to the coast of the Hellespont. But he could not or did not press his advantage, and the shores where Alexander's host would land were safe in Macedonian possession.

Fig. 184.—Coin of Lampsacus (obverse). Head (perhaps a Kabeiros) with laureate hat.

The crossing of the Hellespont, 334 B.C.   The fleet transported the army from Sestus to Abydus, while Alexander himself proceeded to Elaeus, where he offered a sacrifice on the tomb of Protesilaus, the first of the mythical Greeks who landed on the shore of Asia in the Trojan war, and the first who fell. Praying that he might be luckier than Protesilaus, Alexander sailed across to the " Harbour of the Achaeans," and in the mid-strait made libations to Poseidon and the Nereids from a golden dish. The first to leap upon the Mysian strand, he crossed the plain of Troy and went up to the hill of Ilion, where he performed a sacrifice in the temple of Athena, in the poor town which stood on the ruins of seven prehistoric cities. It is said that he dedicated his own panoply in the shrine, and took down from the wall some ancient armour, preserved there as relics of the war of Priam and Agamemnon. He sacrificed to Priam to avert his anger from one of the race of Neoptolemus ; he crowned the tomb of Achilles his ancestor ; and his bosom-friend Hephaestion cast a garland upon the grave of Patroclus, the beloved of Achilles. He commanded that Ilion should rise again from its ruins, as a favoured city enjoying the rights of self-government and immunity from taxation. These solemnities on the hill of Troy are significant as revealing the spirit which the young king carried into his enterprise. They show how he was imbued with Greek scrip-

Alexander at Troy.

tures and Greek traditions ; how his descent from Achilles was part of his life, part of his inspiration ; how he regarded himself as chosen to be the hero of another episode in the drama, whereof the first act had been illustrated by the deeds of that glorious ancestor.

Meanwhile the satraps of the Great King had formed an army of *Advance of* about 40,000 men to defend Asia Minor.   If he had entrusted the *a Persian* command to the Rhodian Memnon, it is possible that some effec- *army to the* tive defence might have been made ; but he committed the character- *Granicus.* istic blunder of a Persian monarch, and consigned the army to the joint command of a number of generals, including Memnon and several of the western satraps.   The Persian commanders were jealous of the Greek, and against his advice they decided to risk a battle at once.   Accordingly they advanced from Zelea, where they had mustered, to the plain of Adrastea, through which the river Granicus flows into the Propontis, and posted themselves on the steep left bank of the stream, so as to hinder the enemy from crossing. Alexander and his army advanced eastward from Abydus, and *Advance of* received the submission of Lampsacus, and then of Priapus, a town *Alexander.* near the mouth of the Granicus.   It was impossible for him to avoid the combat, which the Persians desired ; he could not march south- ward, leaving them in his rear.   But he courted the combat even more than they ; for the worst thing that could have befallen him (as Memnon knew well) was that the hostile army should persistently retire before him, eating up the provisions of the country as it re- treated.

With his heavy infantry in two columns and his horse on the *Position of* wings, Alexander marched across the Adrastean plain.   The Persians *the armies.* had made the curious disposition of placing their cavalry along the river bank and the Greek hoplites on the slopes behind.   As cavalry in attack has a great advantage over cavalry in defence, Alexander saw that the victory could best be won by throwing his own squadrons against the hostile line.   Parmenio advised him to wait till the fol- lowing morning and cross the river at daybreak before the foe were drawn up in array.   " I should be ashamed," said the king, " having crossed the Hellespont, to be detained by a miserable stream like the Granicus " ; an answer such as Alexander loved to give, veiling under the appearance of negligent daring a self-confidence which was perfectly justified by his strategic insight.

Drawing up his army in the usual way (which has been described *Battle* above), with the six regiments of the phalanx in the centre, entrust- *of the* ing the left wing to Parmenio and commanding the right himself, *Granicus* Alexander first sent across the river his light cavalry to keep the *(334 B.C.,* extreme left of the enemy engaged, and then led his heavy Macedon- *May-June).* ian cavalry against the Persian centre.   Alexander himself was in the thickest of the fight, dealing wounds and receiving blows. After a sharp mellay on the steep banks, the Persian cavalry was broken and put to flight. The phalanx then advanced across the river against the Greek hoplites in the background, while the victorious cavalry cut them up on the flanks.

This victory, in winning which Alexander drank to the full the mad excitement of battle, cost few lives to the Macedonians and cleared out of their way the only army which was to oppose their progress in Asia Minor. But it was very far from laying Asia Minor at the conqueror's feet. There were strong places, which must be taken one by one—strong places on the coast, which could be supported by the powerful Persian fleet. Of all things, the help of the Athenian navy would have best bestead Alexander now, and he did not yet despair. After the skirmish of the Granicus, when he divided the spoil, he sent 300 Persian panoplies to Athens, as an offering to Athena on the Acropolis, with this dedication : " Alexander, son of Philip, and the Greeks (except the Lacedaemonians), from the barbarians of Asia." But Athens had no zeal for the cause of the Greeks and Alexander against the barbarians.

The victor entrusted the satrapy of Hellespontine Phrygia to Callas, making no change in the method of the Persian administra-
Submission of Lydia. tion ; and marched southward to occupy the satrapy of Lydia and the rock of Sardis, girt with its threefold wall. It was a little more than 200 years since Cyrus had overthrown the Lydian kingdom and Sardis had become the chief burg of Persian power in the west. The citadel was strong and capable of a stout defence, but it now passed with its treasures unresistingly into the hands of the Greek conqueror. For this prompt submission the Lydians received their freedom and the ancestral constitution, which had been suspended during the long period of Persian domination. Alexander resolved to build a temple to the Olympian Zeus on the citadel. It was said that a thunder shower falling on the site of the royal palace showed him the fitting place for the sanctuary ; the spot where a more famous thunder shower had quenched the pyre of the last Lydian king.

Parmenio's brother, Asander, was appointed satrap of Lydia, and Alexander turned to deal with the Ionian cities. Here, as was to be expected, everything depended on the strength of the political parties. The democrats welcomed the Greek deliverer ; but the oligarchs supported the Persian cause, and wherever they were in power, admitted Persian garrisons. In Ephesus the oligarchy had got the upper hand, but on the approach of Alexander's army the garrison left the city and the people began to massacre the oligarchs. Alexander pacified these troubles and established a democratic constitution. He abode some time in the city, and during this sojourn the painter Apelles executed a famous picture of the king, wielding lightning in his hand, which was set up in the temple of Artemis.

The next stage in the advance of Alexander was Miletus, and *Siege and* here for the first time he encountered resistance. The Persian *capture of* garrison was commanded by a Greek, who had at first meditated *Miletus,* surrender, but learning that the Persian fleet was at hand in full force, *334 B.C.* decided to brave a siege. In an earlier episode of the struggle between Europe and Asia, we witnessed memorable operations in the Latmian gulf and the Milesian harbours, which the retreat of the sea has blotted from the map. The isle of Lade, then associated with the triumph of Asia, was now to play a part in the triumph of Europe. The Macedonian fleet, of 160 galleys, sailed into the bay and occupied the harbour of Lade, before the great fleet of the enemy arrived. When the Persian vessels came and saw that they had been forestalled, they anchored off the promontory of Mycale. The city of Miletus consisted of two parts, an outer city which Alexander easily occupied as soon as he came up, and an inner city strongly fortified with wall and fosse. Alexander threw up a rampart round the inner city, and placed troops in the island of Lade. Miletus was easily stormed by the Macedonian siege engines, and the fleet blocking the harbour hindered the Persian squadron from bringing help.

Parmenio had urged the king to risk a battle on the water, though the enemy's ships were nearly three to one, but Alexander rejected the advice. He had judged the whole situation, and he had made up his mind that the Persian sea-power would have to be conquered on land. If Athens had sent him naval reinforcements it might have been otherwise, but he now despaired of active help from Greece, and he decided that it was an useless drain on his treasury to maintain 160 galleys, too few to cope with the 400 of the enemy. Accordingly *Alexander* he disbanded the fleet, after the fall of Miletus, and proceeded to *disbands* blockade the sea by seizing all the strong places on the shores of the *his fleet.* Eastern Mediterranean. The execution of this design occupied him for the next two years, but it brought with it the conquest of Asia Minor, Syria, and Egypt.

The manifest objection to the dissolution of the naval force was that, in case a decisive defeat at the hands of the Great King should compel him to retreat, he would have no fleet to transport his army from Asia to Europe, and the fleet of the enemy, by occupying the straits at either end of the Propontis, could entirely cut him off. But Alexander trusted his own strategy ; he knew that he would not be compelled to retreat.

As for Asia Minor, the next and the hardest task was the reduction of Caria and the capture of Halicarnassus.   The remnant of the host which fled from the Granicus, and the Rhodian Memnon himself, had rallied here and rested their last hopes in the strong city of Mausolus, with its three mighty citadels.   The Great King had now entrusted to Memnon the general command of the fleet and the coasts, and Memnon had dug a deep fosse round Halicarnassus, furnished the place with food for a long siege, and placed garrisons in the smaller neighbouring towns.   Halicarnassus was to be the centre of a supreme resistance.

The last rulers of the dynasty of Mausolus.   There had once been a chance that Alexander himself might have been, by a personal right, lord of Halicarnassus.   The prince Pixodarus, one of the brothers of Mausolus, had wished to form an alliance of marriage with the house of Macedon, and Alexander had thought of offering himself as a bridegroom for his daughter.   But Philip would not hear of such a match, and Pixodarus had given the maiden to a Persian noble, who had succeeded to the dynasty after his father-in-law's death.   There was indeed another claimant to the dynasty, Ada, wife and sister of Idrieus.   She had succeeded her husband as ruler, and had been driven out by her brother Pixodarus.   She now sought the protection of Alexander, and when he captured Halicarnassus, he assigned to her the satrapy of Caria.   It was destined that women should represent Caria in the two great collisions of Greece with Persia, in the days of Alexander as in the days of Xerxes ; the submission of Ada atoned for the bravery of Artemisia.

Ada.   FIG. 185.—Gold coin of Pixodarus.   Obverse : head of Apollo.   Reverse : Zeus Labrandeus with double axe (labrys) and sceptre [legend : ΠΙΞΩ-ΔΑΡΟΥ].

Siege of Halicarnassus, autumn, 334 B.C.   Having made a futile attack on Myndus, Alexander filled up the moat with which Memnon had encompassed Halicarnassus, and brought his towers and engines against the walls.   A breach was made on the north-east side near to the gate of the road to Mylasa, but Alexander, who hoped to induce the town to surrender, forbore to order an attack.   His hands were almost forced by two soldiers of the phalanx, who, one day drinking together in their tent and bragging of their prowess, flushed with wine and the zeal of rivalry, put on their armour, and marching up to the wall, challenged the enemy to come out.   The men on the wall seeing them alone rushed out in numbers, and the twain were hard pressed till their comrades came to the rescue, and there was a sharp fight under the walls.   But even now, Alexander would not order an attack on the breach, and the besieged built a new crescent wall connecting the two points between which the wall had been broken down, and maintained themselves

behind it for a time.   At length they made a great excursion against
the camp of the besiegers at two different places.   On both sides they
were driven back in confusion, and in their haste to shut the gates
they left many of their fellows to perish.   At this moment an assault
would doubtless have carried the Macedonians within the walls, but
Alexander gave the signal to retire, still intent on saving the city.
Memnon saw that the prospect of holding out longer was hopeless,
and he determined to withraw the garrison to the citadel of Salmacis
and the royal fortress on the island in the harbour.   He fired the
city at night before he withdrew, and the place was in flames when
the Macedonians entered.   Alexander destroyed what the fire spared,
and left a body of mercenary soldiers under Ptolemy to blockade
Salmacis and support the princess of Caria.

The cold season was approaching and Alexander divided his army *Division of*
into two bodies, one of which he sent under Parmenio to winter in *the army.*
Lydia, while he advanced himself with the other into Lycia.   He gave
leave to a few young officers who had been recently wedded to return
to their Macedonian homes, charging them with the duty of bringing
reinforcements to the army in spring, and appointing Gordion in
Phrygia as the mustering-place of the whole host.

Alexander met with no resistance from the cities of the Lycian *Lycia*
League, and he left the constitution of the confederacy intact.   From *submits.*
the rich frontier town of Phasēlis he advanced along the coast *Advance through*
of Pamphylia, receiving the submission of Perge and Aspendus *Pam-*
and other maritime cities ; and then he turned inland from Perge, *phylia and*
and fought his way through the Pisidian hills, taking with some *Pisidia.*
trouble Sagalassus, the chief fastness of the Pisidian mountaineers.
He descended to Celaenae, the strong and lofty citadel of the Phrygian
satrapy, and leaving a garrison there, he marched on to Gordion on
the Sangarius, the capital of the ancient kingdom of Phrygia.

While he was winning the Lycian and Phrygian satrapies, he *Trans-*
lost, for the moment, some points in the Aegean.   Memnon, ap- *actions in*
pointed commander of the Persian fleet, had taken Chios, reduced *the Aegean.*
the greater part of Lesbos, and laid siege to Mytilene.   He died
during the siege, but Mytilene soon surrendered, and then Tenedos
was compelled to recognise the " Peace which the king sent down."
The great danger for Alexander was that these successes might encourage the Greeks to revolt, and ten Persian ships sailed as far west as
Siphnos for the purpose of exciting a movement in Hellas.   But
eight of these vessels were captured by some Macedonian triremes
which ran over from Chalcis, and the project of a Greek rising was
not carried out.

At Gordion, the appointed mustering-place, Alexander's army re- *At Gordion,*
united, and new troops arrived from Macedonia to replace those who 333 *B.C.*

had been left to garrison the subjugated countries and cities. On the citadel of Gordion stood the remains of the royal palaces of Gordius and Midas, and Alexander went up the hill to see the chariot of Gordius and the famous knot which fastened the yoke. Cord of the bark of a cornel-tree was tied in a knot which artfully concealed the ends, and there was an oracle that he who should loose it would rule over Asia. Alexander vainly attempted to untie it, and then drawing his sword cut the knot and so fulfilled the oracle. From Gordion *Advance* Alexander marched by Ancyra into Cappadocia. Having received *to Cilicia.* the submission of Paphlagonia and asserted rather than confirmed his authority over the Cappadocian satrapy, he marched southward to Tyana and the Cilician gates. It was well that Alexander should show himself for a moment in the centre of Asia Minor, but the reduction of these wild regions and of the southern coast of Pontus was a task which might safely be postponed. The Cilician gates might have easily been defended by the garrison which the satrap Arsames had posted in the pass. Alexander, with the hypaspists and other light troops, leaving the rest of his army in camp, marched up at

night to surprise the station. As soon as the guards heard the footfalls of the approachers they fled; and then Alexander at the head of his cavalry moved so rapidly on Tarsus that Arsames, amazed at his sudden appearance, fled without striking a blow.

FIG. 186.—Silver coin of Tarsus. Obverse: *At Tarsus.* enthroned Zeus [Aramaic legend: Baal Tars]. Reverse: lion [obscure legend].

Here a misadventure happened which well-nigh changed the course of history. After a long ride under a burning sun, the king bathed in the cool waters of the Cydnus, which flows through Tarsus. He caught a chill which resulted in violent fever and sleepless nights, and his physicians despaired of his life. But Philip of Acarnania, who was eminent for his medical skill, recommended a certain purgative. As he was preparing the draught in the king's tent, a letter was placed in Alexander's hands. It was from Parmenio, and was a warning against Philip, alleging that Darius had bribed him to poison his master. Alexander taking the cup, gave Philip the letter to read, and, while Philip read, Alexander swallowed the medicine. His generous confidence was justified, and under the care of Philip he soon recovered from his sickness.

Sect. 6. Battle of Issus

The Great King had already crossed the Euphrates at the head of a vast host. He had let the invader subjugate Asia Minor, but he now came in person to bar his further progress. Alexander did not hurry to the encounter, and his delay, as we shall see, turned to his profit in an unexpected manner. Sending forward Parmenio with part of the army to secure the passes from Cilicia into Syria, Alexander himself turned to subdue western Cilicia. He first visited *Reduction* Anchialus, noted for the statue of the Assyrian king Sardanapalus, *of Cilicia.* and the famous inscription : " Sardanapalus founded Anchialus and *At* Tarsus on the same day. But thou, O stranger, eat, drink, and *Anchialus.* sport ; all else is worthless." Having seen this comment on his own ambitious dreams, Alexander went on to Soli, the city of " solecisms," *At Soli.* an ultimate Greek outpost, where men had almost forgotten Greek institutions and Greek speech. From here he made an excursion against the Cilician hill-folks, and reduced the whole district in seven days. He then returned eastward, and advanced to Issus under *At Issus,* Mount Amanus.   *333 B.C.,*

Darius was on the other side of the mountains, in the plain of *Oct.* Sochoi, on ground which was highly favourable for deploying his host. There were two roads from Issus into Syria. One led directly over difficult mountain-passes, while the other wound along the coast to Myriandros and then crossed Mount Amanus. The second road, along which we formerly accompanied Cyrus and Xenophon, was now chosen by Alexander. Leaving his sick at Issus, he marched forward *At Myri-* to Myriandros, but was detained there by a violent storm of rain, for *ander.* it was already the beginning of winter. The Great King, informed by Arsames of the rapid approach of Alexander, expected every day to see him descending from the mountains. And when he came not, owing to the delays in Cilicia, it was thought that he held back through fear, and did not venture to desert the coast. Accordingly Darius and his nobles decided to seek Alexander. The Persian army *Advance* crossed the northern passes of Amanus and reached Issus, where *of the* they tortured and put to death the sick who had been left behind. *Persians* Alexander cannot be blamed for this disaster, for he could not foresee *to Issus,* that his enemies would commit such an incredible military error as to abandon the open position in which their numerical superiority would tell for a confined place where the movements of a multitude would be cramped. To Alexander the tidings that Darius was at Issus was too good to be true, and he sent a boat to reconnoitre. When he was *and return* assured that the enemy had thus played into his hands, he marched back *of Alex-* from Myriandros through the sea-gates into the little plain of Issus. *ander.*

Position of the armies at Issus. The plain of Issus is cut in two by the stream of the Pinarus, which was to play the same part in the coming battle as the Granicus had played in the plain of Adrastea. Here, as in that first skirmish, it fell to Alexander to attack the Persians, whose plan was defensive ; and here as there the Persians were defended by the natural entrenchment of a steep-banked river. The Macedonian columns defiled into the plain at dawn, and when Darius learned that they were approaching he threw across the river his main cavalry force and light troops to cover the rest of the army while it arrayed itself for battle and to threaten the enemy's rear. The Persian front was composed of hoplites—some 15,000 Greek mercenaries, and regiments of orientals called *Kardakes*. Archers were stationed on the left in front of the *Kardakes* and light-armed on the extreme left wing, which touched the lower slopes of the mountains and curved round, following the line of the hill, so as to face the flank of the enemy's right wing. Darius himself was behind the centre of the line. When the array was formed, the cavalry was recalled to the north of the river, and posted on the right wing, near the sea, where the ground was best adapted for cavalry movements.

Arrangement of Alexander's troops. Alexander advanced, his army drawn up on the usual plan, the phalanx in the centre, the hypaspists on the right. At first he placed the Thessalian as well as the Macedonian cavalry on the right wing, in order to strengthen his own cavalry attack, but when he saw that all the Persian cavalry was concentrated on the sea side, he was obliged to transfer the Thessalians to their usual position on his own left. In order to meet the danger which threatened the flank and rear of his right wing from the Persian forces on the slope of the mountain, he placed a column of light troops on the extreme right, to form a second front. As in the engagement on the Granicus, the attack was to be made by the heavy cavalry on the left centre of the enemy's line. But it was a far more serious and formidable venture. Those who had read the story of the battle of Cunaxa might despise an Asiatic multitude, but Darius had 15,000 Greek mercenaries who knew how to stand and to fight. And if Alexander was defeated, his retreat was cut off.

Battle. The Persian left did not sustain Alexander's onset at the head of his cavalry. The phalanx followed more slowly, and in crossing the stream and climbing the steep bank the line became dislocated, especially at one spot, and the Greek hoplites pressed them hard on the river-brink. If the phalanx had been driven back, Alexander's victorious right wing would have been exposed on the flank and the battle lost ; but the phalangites stood their ground obstinately, until the hypaspists were free to come to their help by taking their adversaries in the flank. Meanwhile Alexander's attack had been directed

The Battle of
ISSUS, B.C. 333.

Persian Army.
A. *Greek hoplites*
B. *Cavalry*
C.C. *Oriental hoplites (kardakes)*
D.D. *Other Asiatic light troops*

Macedonian Army.
φ. *Phalanx*
α. *Hypaspists*
β. *Greek hoplites*
δ. *Greek cavalry*
γ. *Macedonian cavalry*
ε. *Line of light troops*
Other light troops on the wings

Walker & Boutall sc.

FIG. 187.

upon the spot where the Great King himself stood in his war-chariot, surrounded by a guard of Persian nobles. There was a furious mellay, in which Alexander was wounded in his leg. Then Darius turned his chariot and fled, and this was the signal for an universal flight on the left. On the sea side the Persian cavalry crossed the river and carried all before them ; but in the midst of their success the cry that the king was fleeing made them waver, and they were soon riding wildly back, pursued by the Thessalians. The whole Persian host was now rushing northward towards the passes of Amanus, *Flight of* and thousands fell beneath the swords of their pursuers. Darius did *Darius.* not tarry ; he forgot even his mother and his wife who were in the camp at Issus ; and when he reached the mountain he left his chariot, his shield, and his royal cloak behind him, and mounting a swift mare rode for dear life.

Having pursued the Great King till nightfall and found his relics by the wayside, Alexander returned to the Persian camp. He supped in the tent of Darius, and there fell upon his ears a noise and the wailing of women from a tent hard by. He asked who the women were, and why they were lodged so near, and learned that it was the mother and wife and children of the fugitive king. They had been told that Alexander had returned with the shield and cloak of Darius, and, supposing that their lord was dead, had broken out into lamentation. Alexander sent one of his companions to comfort them with the assurance that Darius lived, and that they would receive, while they were in Alexander's power, all the respect and consideration due to royal ladies ; for Alexander had no personal enmity against Darius. No act of Alexander, perhaps, astonished his contemporaries more than this generous treatment of the family of his royal rival. His ideal hero Achilles would not have resisted the charm of the captive queen Statira, the most beautiful of women. But the charms of love had no temptation for Alexander ; and his behaviour to the captives was prompted not only by his natively humane and generous feelings, but by the instinct and policy of a royal invader to display respect for royalty as such.

Foundation of Alexandria at Issus (Alexandretta). Thus was the Persian host, which had come to "trample down" Alexander and his little army, annihilated on the plain of Issus. A city, which still retains the name of Alexander, was built in commemoration of the battle, at the northern end of the sea-gates. The road was now open into Syria ; this was the immediate military result of the battle of Issus. Just as the small fight on the Granicus had cleared the way for the acquisition of Asia Minor, so the fight on the Pinaros cleared the way for the conquest of Syria and Egypt. The rest of the work would consist in tedious sieges. But the victory of Issus had, beyond its immediate results, immense importance through the prestige which it conferred on the victor. He had defeated an army considerably larger than his own, led by the Great King in person, whom he had driven back over the mountains in ignominious flight ; he had captured the mother of the Great King, and his wife and his children. Darius himself unbent his haughty Persian pride, when he had reached safety beyond the Euphrates, so far as to make the first overtures to the conqueror. He wrote a letter, in which he complained that Alexander was an unprovoked aggressor, begged that he would send back the royal captives, and professed willingness to conclude a treaty of friendship and alliance. It was much for a Persian king to bring himself to write this, but such a condescending appeal required a stern reply. We are fortunate enough to possess the text of Alexander's answer, which seems to have been published as a sort of manifesto to Europe as well as Asia. It was to this effect :—

" Your ancestors invaded Macedonia and the rest of Greece, and *A state* without provocation inflicted wrongs upon us. I was appointed *document* leader of the Greeks, and crossed over into Asia for the purpose of *of Alexander:* avenging those wrongs ; for ye were the first aggressors. In the *letter to* next place, ye assisted the people of Perinthus, who were offenders *Darius,* against my father, and Ochus sent a force into Thrace, which was *333 B.C.* part of our empire. Further, the conspirators who slew my father were suborned by you, as ye yourselves boasted in your letters. Thou with the help of Bagoas didst murder Arses [son of Ochus] and seize the throne unjustly and contrary to the law of the Persians, and then thou didst write improper letters regarding me to the Greeks, to incite them to war against me, and didst send to the Lacedaemonians and others of the Greeks, for the same purpose, sums of money (whereof none of the other cities partook, but only the Lacedaemonians) ; and thine emissaries corrupted my friends and tried to dissolve the peace which I had brought about in Greece. Wherefore I marched forth against thee, who wert thus the aggressor in the quarrel. I have overcome in battle, first thy generals and satraps, and now thyself and thine host, and possess thy land, through the grace of the gods. Those who fought on thy side and were not slain, but took refuge with me, are under my protection, and are glad to be with me, and will fight with me henceforward. I am lord of all Asia, and therefore do thou come to me. If thou art afraid of being evilly entreated, send some of thy friends to receive sufficient guarantees. Thou hast only to come to me to ask and receive thy mother and wife and children, and whatever else thou mayest desire. And for the future, whenever thou sendest, send to me as to the Great King of Asia, and do not write as to an equal, but tell me whatever thy need be, as to one who is lord of all that is

2 C

thine. Otherwise I will deal with thee as an offender. But if thou disputest the kingdom, then wait and fight for it again, and do not flee; for I will march against thee wherever thou mayest be."

The treasures which Darius had brought with him into Syria had been sent for safety to Damascus when he crossed the passes of Mount Amanus. Accordingly Alexander sent Parmenio to take posses-*Greek* sion of them. Parmenio found at Damascus some Greek envoys who *intrigues* had arrived at the camp of Darius a short time before the battle— *with the* one Spartan, one Athenian, and two Thebans. Alexander detained *Persian* the Spartan as a prisoner, kept the Athenian as a friend, and let the *king.* Thebans go free. His clemency to the Thebans was due to a certain compunction which he always felt for the hard measure dealt out to their city; while a personal motive dictated his favour to the

FIG. 188.—Coin of Phaestus in **Crete** (obverse). Resting Heracles; bow and quiver on tree; vase behind [legend: ΦΑΙΣΤΙ(ων)].

FIG. 189.—Coin of Cydonia (obverse). Ivy-crowned head of Dionysus.

FIG. 190.—Coin of Cnossus (obverse). Head of Argive Hera.

Athenian, Iphicrates, son of the great general of the same name, whose memory was highly esteemed in Macedonia. The incident showed that Greece, which had openly chosen Alexander for her leader, was secretly intriguing with Persia. When it was known that Darius was crossing the Euphrates, men were hoping and praying at Athens that the Macedonians would be trodden down by the Persian host. *Persian* A hundred fast-sailing Persian ships appeared at Siphnos, and Agis *squadron* the Spartan king visited the commanders, asking for money and *at Siphnos.* galleys to carry out a project of rebellion against Macedonia. At *Activity of* *Agis.* Athens, Hypereides agitated for open war, but Demosthenes prudently counselled his fellow-citizens to wait until the expected catastrophe *Disappoint-* of Alexander had become an accomplished fact. Then the news *ment in* came that the leader of the Greeks had won a brilliant victory, and *Greece at* *the news of* Greece had to cloak her disappointment. The Persian squadron *Issus.* hurried back to save what could be saved on the Asiatic coast, and only thirty talents and ten vessels could be spared to Agis, who used them to secure the island of Crete, which might prove a useful recruiting ground for the fleet.

SECT. 7. CONQUEST OF SYRIA

It might seem that the course plainly marked out for the victor *Strategic* of Issus was to pursue and overwhelm Darius before he should have *plan of* time to collect another army ; and this is what Darius himself would *Alex-* have done if he had been Alexander. But it would have been a *ander's* *conquest.* strategical error to plunge into the heart of the Persian empire, leaving Syria and Egypt unsubdued behind him and a Persian fleet controlling the coast. The victory of Issus did not seduce Alexander into swerving from his inevitable course ; the strategic value of that victory was simply that it opened the gates to Syria and Egypt. As the subjugation of Asia Minor was the strategic condition of subjugating Syria and Egypt, so the conquest of Syria and Egypt was the strategic condition of conquering Mesopotamia and Iran. It was the more imperative to follow this logical order of conquest, since Phoenicia supplied the main part of the hostile navy, and nothing but the reduction of the Phoenician towns would effectually break down the sea-power of Persia. No one could swoop more swiftly than Alexander when it was the hour to swoop ; but never did he display his superior command of the art of war more signally than when he let the royal prey escape him and quietly carried out the plan of conquest which he had predestined.

The Persian kings had allowed the Phoenician traders to go on their own way, and meddled little with their prosperous cities, so long as the Phoenician navy was at the disposal of Persia. If these strong

Condition of Phoenicia.

FIG. 191.—Silver coin of Sidon (400-384 B.C.). Obverse : galley in front of city wall ; below two lions. Reverse : king and charioteer in chariot ; below goat (incuse).

and wealthy semi-insular cities of the coast, cut off as they were from the inner country by the high range of Lebanon, had formed a solid federal union, they might have easily succeeded in winning complete independence in the days of Persian decadence. But though Tyre, Sidon, and Aradus were bound together by a federal bond, their commercial interests clashed and their jealousies hindered a hearty national effort. This had been illustrated by a recent experience. When Sidon revolted from Persia, in the reign of Artaxerxes Ochus, her two sister cities promised at a federal meeting to stand by her. But both Tyre and Aradus selfishly calculated that if Sidon were crushed and punished, her trade would come to themselves, and they left her to maintain the struggle alone. She succumbed to the power of Ochus, her town was burnt down, and she lost her rights as a city.

The divisions, which prevented the Phoenicians from becoming a nation, were profitable to Alexander. If their united fleet, which was now acting ineffectually in Aegean waters, had acted energetically in defence of their own coast against the Macedonian, their cities would have been impregnable even to Alexander. But those cities could not trust each other. Byblus, which had in some measure taken the place of Sidon, and Aradus sent their submission to the conqueror of Issus ; while dismantled Sidon, which still contributed some ships to the fleet, hoped to be reinstated in her old position by the favour of Persia's foe. Her hope was not disappointed. Alexander restored to Sidon her constitution and her territory.

The sarcophagus (vulgarly called of Alexander).

FIG. 192.—Silver coin of Sidon (330 B.C.). Obverse : king in chariot ; servant with sceptre and flask behind [Phoenician legend : 'AB (? Abdalonymus)]. Reverse : galley ; waves.

It cannot have been long after this that a kingling of Sidon was laid in a resting-place worthy of the great conqueror himself. His sculptured sarcophagus, recently dug up in a burying-ground of the Sidonian kings, is one of the most beautiful achievements of Greek art. But we may well associate this monument with Alexander, rather than with the obscure Phoenician for whose ashes it was made. For in two of the vivid scenes which are represented in coloured relief upon its sides, Alexander appears on horseback. One of these is a passage from the battle of Issus. There is a mellay in the centre ; the king charges on this side ; a general, perhaps Parmenio, on that. The other scene is a lion-hunt, and here, if Alexander were not marked out by the royal fillet, we might almost recognise him by his eager straining face.

Tyre defies Alexander, 333 B.C., Dec.

Alexander advanced southward towards Tyre. Ambassadors from this city met him on the road, professing the readiness of the Tyrians to do his will. Alexander expressed his intention of visiting the city, in order to sacrifice in the famous temple of Heracles. But a Macedonian visit was far from the wish of the men of Tyre.

FIG. 193.—Battle-scene on the great Sarcophagus of Sidon : Alexander in the centre.

Persia was not yet subdued, and their policy was to await the event, and avoid compromising themselves by a premature adhesion to Macedonia. They felt secure on their island rock, which was protected by eighty ships, apart from the squadron which was absent in the Aegean. Accordingly they invited Alexander to sacrifice in

Fig. 194.

Old Tyre on the mainland, but refused to "receive either Persian or Macedonian into the city."

To subdue Tyre was an absolute necessity, as Alexander explained to a council of his generals and captains which he called together. It was not safe to advance to Egypt, or to pursue Darius, while the Persians were lords of the sea; and the only way of wresting their sea-power from them was to capture Tyre, the most important naval station on the coast ; once Tyre fell, the Phoenician fleet, which was the most numerous and strongest part of the Persian navy, would come over to Macedon, for the rowers would not row or the men fight when they had no habitations to row or fight for. The reduction of Cyprus and Egypt would then follow without trouble.   Alexander grasped and never let go the fact that Tyre was the key to the whole situation.

It was easy to say that Tyre must be captured ; but it was not *Siege of* easy to say how, without a powerful navy, its capture could be *Tyre, Jan.* achieved.   This was perhaps the hardest military task that Alexander's *to July,* genius ever encountered.   The city, girt by walls of great height and *332 B.C.* magnificently strong masonry, stood on an island severed from the continent by a sound of more than half a mile in width.   On the side which faced the mainland were the two harbours : the northern or Sidonian harbour with a narrow mouth, and the southern or Egyptian. It might seem utterly hopeless for an enemy, vastly inferior at sea, to attempt a siege of the island Rock.   And in truth there was only one way for a land-power to set about the task.   Those thousand yards of water must be bridged over and the isle annexed to the mainland.   Without hesitation Alexander began the building of the causeway.   The first part of the work was easy, for the water was shallow ; but when the mole approached the island, the strait deepened, the workmen came within range of the walls, and the difficulties of the task began.   Triremes issued from the havens on either side to shoot missiles at the men who were at work.   To protect them Alexander erected two towers on the causeway, and mounted engines on the towers to reply to the missiles from the galleys.   He attached to these wooden towers curtains of leather to screen both towers and workmen from the projectiles which were hurled from the city walls.   But the men of Tyre were ingenious. They constructed a fire-ship filled with dry wood and inflammables, and choosing a day on which a favourable wind blew, they towed it close to the dam and set it on fire.   The device succeeded ; the burning vessel soon wrapt the towers and all the engines in flames, and the triremes which had towed it up discharged showers of darts at the Macedonians who attempted to extinguish the fire.   The Tyrians too rowed across from their island in boats and tore up the stakes at the unfinished part of the mole.

Undismayed by this disaster, which seemed to show the hopelessness of the enterprise, Alexander only went to work more vigorously. It was necessary to take Tyre, and he was determined that Tyre should be taken.   He widened the causeway throughout its whole length, so that it could accommodate more towers and engines, before he attempted to complete it.   He saw that it would be needful to support his operations from the causeway by operations from shipboard ; and he went to Sidon to bring up a few galleys which were stationed there. But at this moment the aspect of affairs was suddenly changed by the accession to Alexander of naval forces which enabled him to cope with Tyre at an advantage on her own element. The squadrons of Aradus and Byblus which were acting in the Aegean, learning that their cities had submitted to Alexander, left the fleet and sailed to Sidon, which the Macedonians had chosen as their naval station. These Phoenician ships were about eighty ; and at the same time there came nine galleys from Rhodes and ten from Lycia and Cilicia. The adhesion of the kings of Cyprus presently followed, and reinforced the fleet at Sidon by 120 ships. With a fleet of about 250 triremes at his command, Alexander was now far stronger at sea than the merchants of Tyre, and though the siege of the mighty stronghold was still a formidable task, it was no longer superhuman.

While the fleet was being made ready in the roads of Sidon, and the engineers were fabricating new siege-engines to batter down the walls of Tyre, Alexander made an expedition, at the head of his light troops, to punish the native brigands who infested the hills of Antilibanon, and made the traffic between the coast and the hinter-

Embassy from Darius.

land unsafe. Perhaps it was now that he received an embassy from the Great King, offering an immense ransom for the captives of the royal house, and the surrender of all the lands west of the Euphrates ; proposing also that Alexander should marry the daughter of Darius and become his ally. The message was discussed in a council, and Parmenio said that if he were Alexander he would accept the terms. "And I," said the king, "would accept them if I were Parmenio." Alexander was resolved to carry out his plan of conquest to the end ; he would agree to no compromise. He bade the ambassadors say that he would receive neither money nor provinces in lieu of the whole empire of Darius, for that all the land and possessions of Darius were his ; he would marry the daughter of Darius if he chose, whether Darius willed it or not ; and if Darius wished for any boon he must come himself and ask it.

From Sidon Alexander bore down upon Tyre with his whole fleet, hoping to entice the Tyrians into an engagement. He commanded the right wing, while the left was committed to the charge of Craterus, and Pnytagoras the king of Cypriote Salamis. When the fleet hove in sight, the men of Tyre were astonished and dismayed. Before, they would gladly have given battle, but they saw that they had no chance against so many, and they drew up their triremes in close array to block the mouths of their harbours. Alexander set the Cyprian vessels on the north side of the mole to blockade the

Sidonian harbour, and the Phoenician on the south side to blockade the Egyptian harbour. It was opposite this harbour, on the mainland, that his own pavilion was placed.

The mole had now been carried up to the island, and engineers, the best that Phoenicia and Cyprus could furnish, had prepared the engines of war. All was ready for a grand attack on the eastern wall. Some of the engines were placed on the mole, others on transport ships or superannuated galleys. But little impression was made on the wall, which on this side was 150 feet high and enormously thick ; and the besieged replied to the attack with volleys of fiery missiles from powerful engines, which were mounted on their lofty battlements. Moreover, the machine-bearing vessels could not come close enough to the walls for effective action ; huge stones lying under the water hindered their approach. Alexander decided that these must at all cost be removed ; and galleys with windlasses were anchored at the spot in order to drag the boulders away. It was a slow task, and was thwarted by the Tyrians. Covered vessels shot out of the havens and cut the anchor-ropes of the galleys, so that they drifted away. Alexander tried to meet this by placing boats similarly decked close to the anchors ; but even this failed, since Tyrian divers swam under water and cut the cables. The only resource was to attach the anchors with chains instead of ropes, and by this means the stones were hauled away and the ships could approach the wall.

The Tyrians now resorted to a last device. They spread the sails of all the ships which were riding at the entrance of the northern harbour, and behind this curtain of canvas, which screened them from the observation of the enemy, they manned seven triremes, three five-oared and three four-oared boats, with the coolest and bravest of their seamen, and waiting for the hour of noon, when the sailors of the besieging vessels used generally to disembark and Alexander himself used to retire to his tent, they rowed noiselessly towards the Cyprian squadron, which was taken completely by surprise, sank some of the vessels at once, and drove the rest on the strand. It happened that on this day Alexander remained for a shorter time than usual in his pavilion ; and when he returned to his station with the Phoenician ships on the south side of the mole, discovering what had happened, he stationed the main part of these ships close to the Egyptian harbour to prevent the enemy from making any movement on this side, and taking with him some five-oared boats and five swift-sailing galleys he sailed round the island. The men in the city saw Alexander and all that he did, and signalled to their own crews who were engaged in battering the stranded Cyprian vessels ; but the signals were not seen or heard until Alexander was close upon them. When they saw him coming, they desisted from their work and made all speed for the haven, but the greater number of their boats were disabled by Alexander's vessels before they reached the harbour mouth. Henceforward the ships of Tyre lay useless in the harbours, unable to do anything for the defence of the island.

It was now a struggle between the engineers of Tyre and the engineers of Alexander. The wall opposite to the mole defied all machines of battery and methods of assault, and the northern part of the same eastern wall, though the big stones had been cleared away from the water below it, proved equally impracticable. Accordingly the efforts of the besiegers were united upon the south side near the Egyptian harbour. Here at length a bit of the wall was torn down, and there was fighting in the breach, but the Tyrians easily repelled the attack. It was an encouragement for Alexander, it showed him the weak spot, and two days later he prepared a grand and supreme assault.

Capture of Tyre, August 332 B.C. The vessels with the siege engines were set to work at the southern wall, while two triremes waited hard by, one filled with hypaspists under Admetus, the other with a phalanx regiment, ready as soon as the wall yielded to hurl their crews into the breach. Ships were stationed in front of the two havens, to force their way in at a favourable moment, and the rest of the fleet, manned with light troops and furnished with engines, were disposed at various points round the island, to embarrass and bewilder the besieged and hinder them from concentrating at the main point of attack. A wide breach was made, the two triremes were rowed up to the spot, the bridges were lowered, and the hypaspists, Admetus at their head, first mounted the wall. Admetus was pierced with a lance, but Alexander took his place, and drove back the Tyrians from the breach. Tower after tower was captured ; soon all the southern wall was in the hands of the Macedonians, and Alexander was able to make his way along the battlements to the royal palace, which was the best base for attacking the city. But the city had been already entered from other points. The chains of both the Sidonian and the Egyptian harbours had been burst by the Cyprian and Phoenician squadrons ; the Tyrian ships had been disabled ; and the troops had pressed into the town. The inhabitants made their last stand in a place called the Agenorion. Eight thousand are said to have been slain, and the rest of the people, about 30,000, were sold into slavery, with the exception of the king, Azemilco, and a few men of high position, who were set at liberty.

The siege had been long and wearisome, but the time and the labour were not too dear a price. The fall of Tyre gave Alexander Syria and Egypt, and the naval supremacy in the eastern Mediterranean. He performed the sacrifice to Heracles in the temple to which the Tyrians had refused him access, and celebrated the solemnity with a torch procession and games. The communities of Syria and *Southward* Palestine, that had not submitted, like Damascus, after the victory *advance of* of Issus, submitted now after the capture of Tyre, and he encountered *Alexander.*

no resistance in his southern march to Egypt, until he came to the great frontier stronghold, Gaza, the city of the Philistines.

Girt with a stout wall Gaza stood on a high rising-ground, and more than two miles of sand lay between the city and the seashore, so that a fleet was no help to a besieger. The place had been committed by Darius to

Siege of Gaza, Oct.-Nov. 332 B.C.

FIG. 195.—Silver coin of Tyre (331 B.C.). Obverse : Melkart with bow on sea-horse ; waves ; dolphin. Reverse : owl with crook and flail (Egyptian emblems of royalty).

the care of Batis, a trusty eunuch, and had been well furnished with provisions for a long siege. Batis refused to surrender, trusting in the strength of the fortifications, and at the first sight the engineers of Alexander declared that the wall could never be stormed on account of the height of the hill on which it stood. But Alexander was now accustomed to overcome the insuperable, and the conqueror who sacked Tyre was not ready to turn away from the walls of Gaza. He could not leave such an important post on the line from Damascus to Egypt in the hands of the enemy. He ordered ramparts to be thrown up round the city, in order that the siege engines mounted on this elevation might be on a level with the wall. The best chance seemed to be on the south side, and here the work was pushed on rapidly. When the engines were placed in position, Alexander offered a sacrifice, and a bird of prey flying over the altar dropped a stone on the king's garlanded head. The soothsayer interpreted the meaning of the sign : " O king, you will take the city, but you must take good heed for your own safety on this day." Alexander was cautious for a while, but when the besieged sallied forth from the gates and attacked the Macedonians who were working the engines on the rampart, and pressed them hard, he rushed to their aid, and was wounded in the shoulder by a dart from a catapult. Thus part of the sign had come true ; the other part was in time fulfilled. The engines which had been used in the siege of Tyre arrived by sea ; the rampart was widened and raised to a greater height ; and underground mines were dug beneath the walls. The walls yielded in many places to the mines and the engines, but it was not till the fourth attack that the Macedonians succeeded in scaling the breaches and entering the city. The slaughter was greater than in Tyre ; the women and children were sold into bondage ; and the place became a Macedonian fortress.

SECT. 8. CONQUEST OF EGYPT

Alexander enters Egypt, c. Nov. 332 B.C.

Egypt was now absolutely cut off from Persia ; the gate to that sequestered land was open, and Alexander had only to march in. The Egyptians had not the vigour to offer any national resistance to the Greek invader ; and Mazaces the Persian satrap, seeing Phoenicia and Syria in Alexander's power, the Macedonian navy in the roadstead of Pelusium, and no help at hand, thought only of making his submission and winning the conqueror's grace. Sending his fleet up the Pelusiac branch of the Nile to meet him at Memphis, Alexander

At Memphis.

journeyed thither by way of Heliopolis. In the capital of the Pharaohs, where he was probably proclaimed king, he sacrificed to Apis and the other native gods, and thereby won the goodwill of the people, who contrasted his piety with the bigotry of the Persian monarch Ochus, who had killed the sacred bull. But while the new king showed that he would treat the native religion and customs with respect, he also made it clear that Greek civilisation was now to pour into the exclusive regions of the Nile. He held athletic games and a poetical contest at Memphis ; and the most famous artists from Greece came to take part in it.

Foundation of Alexandria, 331 B.C. Jan. (?).

From Memphis he sailed down the river to Canopus, and took a step which, if he had never performed another exploit in his life, would have made his name memorable for ever. He chose the ground, east of Rhacotis, between Lake Mareotis and the sea, as the site of a new city, over against the island of Pharos, famous in Homeric song, and soon to become more famous still as the place of the first lighthouse, one of the seven wonders of the world. The king is said to have himself traced out the ground plan of *Alexandria*—the marketplace and the circuit of the walls, the sanctuary of Isis and the temples of the Hellenic gods. He joined the mainland with the island by a causeway seven stades (nearly a mile) in length, and thus formed two harbours. The subsequent history of Alexandria, which has held its position as a port for more than 2000 years, proves that its founder had a true eye in choosing the site of the most famous of his new cities. The greatness of the place as a mart of the world far surpassed any purposes or hopes that Alexander could have formed ; but his object in founding it can hardly be doubted. Alexandria was not intended to supersede Memphis as the capital of Egypt ; it was intended to take the place of Tyre as the commercial centre of Western Asia and the Eastern Mediterranean. And there was a good reason for diverting the lines of traffic from the Phoenician to the Egyptian coast. For it was naturally the policy of Alexander to transfer the trade of the world, so far as might be, into the hands of Greeks; but any new emporium rising on the ruins of Tyre or Sidon would have soon become predominantly Phoenician, owing to the Phoenician genius for trade; whereas on the Egyptian coast Greek traders would encounter no such rivalry. It was thus with a view to the commercial interests of his own race that Alexander founded the port of Egypt.

In the official style of the Egyptian monarchy the Pharaohs were sons of Ammon, and as the successor of the Pharaohs Alexander assumed the same title. It was therefore necessary in order to regulate his position that an official assurance should be given by Ammon himself that Alexander was his son. To obtain such a declaration and satisfy fully the formalities required by the priests, Alexander undertook a journey to the oracular sanctuary of Ammon in the oasis of Siwah. And this motive is alone sufficient to explain the expedition. But it may well be that in Alexander's mind there was a vague notion that there

Amen Ra.

Fig. 196. — Coin of Cyrene (obverse). Head of Zeus Ammon; olive spray.

was something divine about his own origin, something mystical in his mother's conception, and that, like Achilles, he was somewhat more than an ordinary man. Proceeding along the coast to Paraetonion, he was there met by envoys who conveyed the submission of Cyrene. By this acquisition the western frontier of the Macedonian empire extended to the border of the Carthaginian sphere of rule. Alexander then struck across the desert to visit that Egyptian temple which was most famous in the Greek world, the temple as it was always called of Zeus Ammon. There were no tracks to guide the travellers, for the south wind had ploughed up the sand and obliterated the road-marks; and stories were told in the camp of miraculous guidance vouchsafed to the favourite of the god. Ptolemy, son of Lagus, who was destined hereafter to rule over Egypt and Libya, recorded in his Memoirs that two snakes moved in front of the troops and showed the way; while Aristobulus, another companion of the king, spoke of

Fig. 197. — Coin of Barce (reverse). Three silphion plants; owl, jerboa, and chameleon between them [legend: BAPKAIΩN].

Alexander's visit to temple of Zeus Ammon (first months of 331 B.C.).

the guidance of two crows. A certain mystery enveloped this expedition. It is said that Alexander told no man what he asked the god or what the god replied, save only that the answer pleased him. But it is certain that the priests had made such dispositions that Ammon spoke and recognised him as his son. The very route by which Alexander returned to Memphis is uncertain, for the same two companions differ; Ptolemy stating that he fared direct across the desert, and Aristobulus that he returned by Paraetonion.

Organisation of Egypt. At Memphis he organised the government of Egypt, entrusting it to two native nomarchs, and appointing separate Greek governors for the adjoining districts of Arabia and for Libya. But the control of the finances was placed in the hands of a special minister, Cleomenes of Naucratis. Several military commanders were also appointed, and it would seem that Alexander instituted this divided command as a safeguard against the danger of a rebellion. For, geographically situated as Egypt was, an ambitious commander might have a fair prospect of holding the country against his lord; and its recent history as a Persian province had illustrated the difficulty of dealing with it. If this be so, Alexander inaugurated a policy which was followed, in later days and in another form, by his Roman successors.

SECT. 9. BATTLE OF GAUGAMELA, AND CONQUEST OF BABYLONIA

The new lord of Egypt and Syria returned with the spring to Tyre. The whole coastland was now in his possession, and he controlled the sea; the time had come to advance into the heart of the Persian empire. Having spent some months in the Phoenician city, busied with various matters of policy and administration, as well as with *Alexander crosses the Euphrates and marches to the Tigris.* plans for his next campaign, he set forth at the head of 40,000 infantry and 7000 horse, and reached Thapsacus on Euphrates at the beginning of August. The building of two bridges had been already begun, but the Persian Mazaeus, who was stationed with troops on the further shore, had hindered their completion. When Alexander arrived, he withdrew; the bridges were finished, and the army passed over. The objective of Alexander was Babylon. At that time of year it would have been mad to follow the direct route down the Euphrates which was traversed by Cyrus and the Ten Thousand. Alexander chose the other road, across the north of Mesopotamia and down the Tigris on its eastern bank. Throughout the Asiatic campaigns of Alexander we are struck by the perfect organisation of his transports and supplies; but we are struck even more by the certainty of his movements through strange lands, as if he had a map of the country before him. His intelligence department must have been excellent, and though our records give us no intimations on the subject, it has been supposed with much plausibility that here the invader received help from the Jews, who ever since the Captivity were scattered about Media and Babylonia. It is certain that Alexander had shown special favour to the race of Israel at the foundation of Egyptian Alexandria ; he had invited a Jewish colony to settle there, enjoying the rights of citizens, and yet living in a separate quarter and keeping their own national customs.

From some Persian scouts who were captured it was ascertained that Darius, with a yet larger multitude than that which had succumbed at Issus, was on the other side of the river, determined to contest the passage. Alexander crossed the Tigris, not at Nineveh, the usual place of crossing, but higher up at Bezabde. On *Eclipse of* the same night the moon went into eclipse, and men anxiously sought *the moon,* in the phenomenon a portent of the issue of the coming struggle for *Sept.* 20, the lordship of Asia. *331 B.C.*

Marching southward for some days, Alexander learned that *Alexander* Darius was encamped in a plain near Gaugamela on the river *reaches the* Bumōdus. The numbers of the army have again been grossly *plain of* exaggerated but they were considerably larger than at Issus. Having *Gauga-mela.* given his men four days' rest, Alexander moved on by night and halted on a hill looking down on the plain where the enemy lay. A council of war was held, and the question was discussed whether the attack should be made immediately ; but Parmenio counselled a day's delay, for the purpose of reconnoitring fully the enemy's position and discovering whether perchance covered pits had been dug or stakes laid in the ground. Parmenio's counsel was followed, and the troops pitched their camp in the order in which they were to fight. Alexander rode over the plain and found that the Persians *Sept.* 30. had cleared it of all bushes and obstacles which might impede the movements of their cavalry or the effect of their scythed chariots.

The following night was spent by the Persians under arms, for *Night* their camp was unfortified and they feared a night attack. And *before* a night attack was recommended by Parmenio, but Alexander preferred *the battle.* to trust the issue to his own generalship and the superior discipline of his troops, and not to brave the hazards of a struggle in the dark. He said to Parmenio, " I do not steal victory," and under the gallantry of this reply he concealed, in his usual manner, the prudence and policy of his resolve. A victory over the Persian host, won in the open field in the light of day, would have a far greater effect in establishing his prestige in Asia than an advantage stolen by night.

The Great King, according to wont, was in the *centre* of the *Battle of* Persian array, surrounded by his kinsfolk and his Persian body- *Gaugamela,* guard. On either side of them were Greek mercenaries, Indian *331 B.C.* *Oct.* 1, auxiliaries with a few elephants, and Carians whose ancestors had been settled in Upper Asia. The centre was strengthened and deepened by a second line, composed of the Babylonian troops, and the men from the shores of the Persian Gulf, and the Uxians who dwelt east of Susa, and the Sitacenes. On the *left* wing, the Cadusians from the shores of the Caspian and the men of Susa were nearest the centre ; next came a mixed host of Persian horse and foot ; and at the extreme left were the troops from the far east, from Arachosia and Bactria. This wing was covered by 1000 Bactrian cavalry, 100 scythe-armed chariots, and the Scythian cavalry from the desert districts of Lake Aral. On the *right* were the contingents of the Caucasian folks ; the Hyrcanians and Tapurians from the south-eastern shores of the Caspian ; the Parthians, who were destined in the future to found a new oriental monarchy ; the Sacae from the slopes of the Hindu-Kush ; the Medes, and the dwellers in Mesopotamia and northern Syria.

Against this host, of which the cavalry alone is said to have been as numerous as all the infantry of the enemy, Alexander descended the hill in the morning. On his *left* wing—commanded as usual by Parmenio—were the cavalry of the Thessalian and confederate Greeks ; in the *centre* the six regiments of the phalanx ; and on the *right*, the hypaspists, and the eight squadrons of the Companions, the royal squadron of Clitus being at the extreme right. Covering the right wing were some light troops, spear-throwers and archers. The line was far outflanked on both sides by the enemy, and the danger which Alexander had most to fear, as at the battle of Issus, was that of being attacked in rear or flank ; only that, whereas in the plain of Issus his right alone was threatened, here both wings were in peril. He sought to meet these contingencies by forming behind each wing a second line, which by facing round a quarter or half circle could meet an attack on flank or rear. Behind the *left* wing were placed Thracian foot and horse, some Greek confederate cavalry, and Greek mercenary cavalry; behind the *right*, the old Greek mercenaries under Cleander, the Macedonian archers, some of the Agrianian spear-throwers, the mounted pikemen, the light Paeonian cavalry ; and, at the extreme right, to bear the brunt of a flank assault, the new Greek mercenaries under Menidas.

As he advanced, Alexander and his right wing were opposite to the centre of the enemy's line, and he was outflanked by the whole length of the enemy's left. He therefore bore obliquely to the right, and, even when the Scythian horsemen riding forward came into contact with his own light troops, he continued to move his squadrons of heavy cavalry in the same direction. Darius saw with anxiety that this movement would soon bring the Macedonian right outside the ground which he had carefully levelled and prepared for the action of his scythed chariots, and, as he had set no small part of his hopes in the deadly effect of these chariots, he commanded the Scythian and Bactrian cavalry to ride round and deliver a flank-charge, in order to hinder any further advance towards the right. The charge was met by the new mercenaries of Menidas; but they were too few, they were driven back, until the Paeonians and the old mercenaries were bidden to come to their support. Then the barbarians gave way, but in a short while, reinforced by more troops, they returned to the charge. The battle raged, and it was well if the Macedonians, far outnumbered, could hold their ground. *Cavalry battle on the extreme right.*

Meanwhile Darius had loosed his scythed cars, to whirl destruction into the ranks of the Companions and the hypaspists. But the archers and the Agrianian spear-throwers received them with showers of spears and arrows; some of these active hillsmen seized the reins of the horses and pulled the drivers from their seats, while the hypaspists, swiftly and undismayed, opened their ranks, and the terrible chariots rattled harmless down the intervals. *The attack of the scythe-chariots frustrated.*

The whole Persian line was now advancing to attack, and Alexander was waiting for the moment to deliver his cavalry charge. He had to send his mounted pikemen to the help of the light cavalry, who were being hard pressed on the right by the Scythians and Bactrians; and as a counter-check to this reinforcement, squadrons of Persian cavalry were dispatched to the assistance of their fellows. By the withdrawal of these squadrons a gap was caused in the left wing, and into this gap Alexander plunged at the head of his cavalry column and split the line in two. Thus the left side of the enemy's centre was exposed, and turning obliquely Alexander charged into its ranks. Meanwhile the bristling phalanx was moving forward and was soon engaged in close combat with another part of the Persian centre. The storm of battle burst with wildest fury round the spot where the Persian king was trembling, and what befell at Issus befell again at Gaugamela. The Great King turned his chariot and fled. His Persians fled with him, and swept along in their flight the troops who had been posted in the rear. *Charge of Alexander. Flight of Darius.*

Thus the Persian centre and the neighbouring part of the left wing were cut down or routed by the phalanx, the hypaspists, and the Companions. And in the meantime, the severe struggle of the light cavalry on the uttermost left had also ended in victory for the Macedonians.

The regiments of the phalanx in their rapid advance had failed to keep abreast, and it would seem that when the regiment of Craterus, on the extreme left, was already far forward in the thick of the fight, the regiment commanded by Simmias, second from the left, was *Gap in the phalanx.*

considerably in the rear. From his position Simmias saw that the
Thessalian cavalry on the left wing were pressed hard by their
adversaries, and he halted his regiment, in order apparently to make
Attack on the Macedonian camp. a movement to assist them. The Indian and Persian cavalry of the
hostile centre rushed through the gap in the phalanx, but instead of
exploiting their tactical advantage and attacking the phalanx in the
rear they rode straight on the Macedonian camp to set the royal
captives free. This gave the Greek mercenaries and Thracians of
the rear line time to recover and regroup ; they turned round, attacked
the plunderers in the rear, and saved the camp. The enemy cavalry
turned and in good order tried to cut their way back through the
lines.

Meanwhile Parmenio was hard bestead. The Mesopotamians and
Syrians of the extreme Persian right had attacked his cavalry in the
flank or rear. Parmenio sped a messenger to Alexander entreating
aid, and Alexander desisted from the pursuit of his fleeing rival, to
restore the battle on his left wing. Riding back with his Companions
he encountered a large body of cavalry, Persians, Parthians, and
Indians, in full retreat, but in orderly array. A desperate conflict
ensued, perhaps the most fearful in the whole battle, the Persians
fighting not for victory but for life. Sixty of the Companions fell,
but Alexander was again victorious and rode on to the help of
Victory on the Macedonian right. Parmenio. But Parmenio no longer needed his help. Not the least
achievement of this day of great deeds was the brilliant fighting of
the Thessalian cavalry, who not only sustained the battle against the
odds which had wrung from Parmenio the cry for aid, but in the end
routed their foemen before Alexander could reach the spot. The
battle was won, and the fate of the Persian empire was decided.

Pursuit of Darius as far as Arbela. Alexander did not tarry on the field. He lost not a moment in
resuming the chase which he had abandoned, and, riding eastward
throughout the night on the tracks of the Persian king, he reached
Arbela on the morrow. It befell now as it had befallen after Issus.
He did not take the king, but found at Arbela his chariot, his shield,
and his bow. Darius fled into the highlands of Media, and
Ariobarzanes with a host of the routed army hastened southward to
Persia. Alexander did not follow either king or satrap, but pursued
his way to Babylon.

Babylon submits to Alexander. It might have been expected, and Alexander seems to have
expected, that the men of Babylon, trusting in their mighty walls,
would have offered to the victor of Gaugamela the same defiance
which the men of Tyre offered to the victor of Issus. He was disappointed. When he approached the city, with his army arrayed for
action, the gates opened and the Babylonians streamed out, led by
their priests and their chief men. The satrap Mazaeus, who had

fought bravely in the recent battle, surrendered the city and citadel. In Babylonia, Alexander followed the same policy which he had already followed in Egypt. He appeared as the protector of the national religions which had been depressed and slighted by the fire-worshippers. He rebuilt the Babylonian temples which had been destroyed, and above all he commanded the restoration of the marvellous temple of Bel, standing on its eight towers, on which the rage of Xerxes had vented itself when he returned from the rout of Salamis. The Persian Mazaeus was retained in his post as satrap of Babylonia.

SECT. 10. CONQUEST OF SUSIANA AND PERSIS

Having rested his army in the luxurious and wonderful city of the *Alexander* Euphrates, the conqueror advanced south-eastward to Susa, the *at Susa,* summer residence of the Persian court. Susa had been already secured *Dec.* 331 for him by Philoxenus, whom he had dispatched thither from Arbela *B.C.* with some light troops. In the citadel he found enormous treasures of gold and silver and purple. Among other precious things at Susa *Statue-* was the sculptured group of the tyrant-slayers, Harmodius and *group of* Aristogiton, which Xerxes had carried off from Athens ; and Alexander *Harmodius and Aristo-* had the pleasure of sending back to its home this historical monu- *giton.* ment, now more precious than ever through its own strange history.

Though it was mid-winter, Alexander soon left Susa to accomplish one of the most arduous adventures that he ever undertook. He had won the treasures of Susa, but there were immense treasures still in the palaces of Cyrus and Darius in the heart of the Persian highlands, and these were guarded not only by the difficulties of the mountainous approaches, but by the army which Ariobarzanes had rescued from the overthrow of Gaugamela. Perhaps the reason for Alexander's haste in pressing on to Persis was the fear that Darius might descend with a new force from Media, if time were given him before Ariobarzanes was crushed. But whatever were his reasons, it seemed to him of the greatest moment to secure Persis immediately. *(Kārūn.)* His road lay south-eastward, and when he had crossed the river Pasitigris, the first obstacle that he encountered was the independent tribe of the Uxian hillsmen, on whom the Persian kings themselves were accustomed to bestow gifts for their goodwill. The barbarians held the *The Uxian* passes through which the road lay, but a night march by a difficult *pass.* mountain path enabled Alexander to surprise them, and the Uxians henceforward were forced to pay yearly gifts to the lord of Asia—a hundred horses, five hundred draught oxen, and thirty thousand sheep.

The Macedonian army was now in the midst of a region which was unknown to Greek charts. Alexander's advance is a march not only of conquest but of discovery, and opens a new epoch in the history of geographical science by revealing Central Asia to the knowledge of Europe.

Storming of the Persian Gates, Jan. 330 B.C.   Leaving half of his army with Parmenio to proceed more slowly along the main road, Alexander led the other half (including the Macedonians, both horse and foot) by a shorter path through the hills to the narrow defile which formed the entrance to Persis and was called the Persian Gates. Ariobarzanes was posted there with 40,000 foot and 700 horse, guarding the rocky pass which he had fortified by a wall. An attack, easily repelled, showed Alexander that the pass was impregnable ; yet it must be carried, for this was the only road to the royal cities of Persia. For a moment Alexander was baffled ; never perhaps—not even before Tyre—was he encountered by a problem more desperate to all seeming. But he learned from a prisoner of some extremely perilous paths leading round, through the forests which covered the mountains, to the back of the pass. At this season the snow made these paths more dangerous than ever, and they might well seem hopeless to men weighed down with heavy armour ; but they were the only hope and Alexander did not hesitate. He left Craterus with part of the troops in front of the pass, with orders to attack as soon as he heard the Macedonian trumpets sounding from above on the other side. With the rest of his force, including most of the cavalry, three regiments of the phalanx, the hypaspists, and other light troops, he set forth at night, and marched quickly eleven miles along the precipitous snowy track, intersected frequently by deep gullies. When the point was reached at which he was to turn in order to descend on the Persian camp, he again divided his forces, and sent one division forward to bridge the river Araxes and cut off the Persian retreat. Taking the hypaspists, the royal squadron of the Companions, one regiment of the phalanx, and some light troops, he raced down upon the camp and destroyed or routed three successive sets of outposts before the day dawned. Instead of raising the alarm, the sentinels scattered on the mountain, and when the Macedonian trumpets pealed on the brink of his entrenchments, Ariobarzanes was taken completely by surprise. Attacked on both sides, in front by Craterus who stormed up the wall of rock, and in the rear by Alexander, the Persians were cut to pieces or fell over precipices in their flight. Ariobarzanes with a small band escaped into the mountains.

The palaces of Persia (Persepolis).   The royal palaces of Persia, to which Alexander now hurried with the utmost speed, stood in the valley of Mervdasht, fertile then but desolate at the present day, and close to the city of Istachr, which the Persians deemed the oldest city in the world. In Istachr itself there was a royal house too, but the great palaces stood some miles away, close beneath the mountain, upon a lofty platform

FIG. 198.—Propylaea of Xerxes, at Persepolis.

against a background of black rock. The platform was mounted by magnificent staircases, and it bore, besides massive propylaea, four chief buildings, the small palace of Darius, the larger palace of Xerxes, and two great pillared halls. The impressive ruins tell a trained eye how to reconstruct the general plan of the royal abode, and there can be no question that Achaemenian architecture had wrought here its greatest achievements, greater than the palace of Susa which Alexander had seen, greater than that of Ecbatana which he was soon to see. This cradle of the Persian kingdom, to which, city and palace together, the Greeks gave the name of *Persepolis*, was "the richest of all the cities under the sun." It is said that 120,000 talents were found in the treasury ; an army of mules and camels were required to remove the spoils. This store of gold, so long withdrawn from use, was now suddenly to be restored to circulation and perturb the markets of the world.

Pasargadae.   Not far off, two days' journey northward up the winding valley of the Murghab, was Pasargadae, the city of Cyrus. The maker of Persia built it close to the field where he had shattered the host of the Median king ; and the place is still marked by his tomb, and the stones of other buildings, on some of which the traveller may read the words "I am Cyrus the king, the Achaemenian." In Pasargadae too Alexander found a store of treasure.

Jan.-April,   For four months he made the Persian palaces his headquarters,
330 B.C.   during which time he received the submission of Caramania or Kirman, and made some excursions to punish the robbers who infested the neigh-
Burning of bouring mountains. But the most famous incident connected with
the palace the sojourn at Persepolis is the conflagration of the palace of Xerxes.
of Xerxes. [This was a spectacular act of calculated policy. It symbolised the achievement of an objective. The Persian invasion of Greece had been avenged ; the rule of the Achaemenids was ended. Later gossip embroidered the tale to detract from Alexander and heighten the moral.] The story is that one night when Alexander and his companions had drunk deep at a royal festival, Thais, an Attic courtesan, who was of the company, flung out among the tipsy carousers the idea of burning down the house of the malignant foe who had burned the temples of Greece. The mad words of the woman inspired a wild frenzy, and whirled the revellers forth, armed with torches, to accomplish the barbarous deed. Alexander hurled the first brand, and the cedar wood-work of the palace was soon in flames. But before the fire had done its work the king's head was cool, and he commanded the fire to be quenched. The great Xerxes had burnt the Acropolis, his palace was to be burnt by a humble Athenian flute-girl.

SECT. 11. DEATH OF DARIUS

In the meantime king Darius remained in Ecbatana, surrounded
by the adherents who were faithful to him, chiefly the satraps of
those lands which were still unconquered—Media itself and Hyrcania, Areia and Bactria, Arachosia and Drangiana.   It is probable
that after the Gaugamela battle Alexander hoped to receive some
proposal from his defeated foe, more submissive and acceptable than
that which had been sent after Issus.   He would have been ready
perhaps to leave to Darius the eastern part of his dominions, with
the royal title, though as a dependent vassal, and to content himself
for a while with the empire which he had won, including Susa and
Persepolis.   It may have been with the hope of receiving overtures
that he tarried so long in Persis.   But Darius gave no sign.   Media
was defensible ; he had a large army from the northern satrapies ;
and he had Bactria as a retreat, if retreat he must.

The spring was advanced when Alexander left Persis for Ecbatana.
The direct road did not lie by Susa, but much farther east through
the land of Paraetacene.   He made all speed, when the news reached
him by the way, that Darius was at Ecbatana with a large army, prepared to fight.   But when after a succession of forced marches he
drew nigh to the city, he found that Darius had flown eastward,
following the women and heavy baggage which had been sent on to
the Caspian Gates, and taking the treasures with him.   When he *Alexander*
reached the Median capital, Alexander was detained by the need of *at*
arranging certain matters before he pursued his rival into the northern *Ecbatana.*
wilds.   The purpose of the League had now been achieved, and the
League forces had the right to withdraw.   He paid off the Thessalian
troops and the other Greek confederates, giving them a handsome
donative and a conduct to the Aegean ; but any who chose to enrol
themselves anew in his service and share in his further course of conquest might stay, and not a few stayed.   Parmenio was entrusted with
the care of seeing that the treasures of Persis were transported and
safely deposited in the strong keep of Ecbatana, where they were to
remain in charge of the treasurer Harpalus and a large body of
Macedonian troops.   Parmenio was then to proceed northward to
Cadusia, and along the shores of the Caspian Sea, where he was to
meet the king.

With the main part of the army Alexander hurried on, merciless
to men and steeds, bent on the capture of Darius.   His way lay by
Ragae, and when he reached that place, a little to the south of the *(Rayy).*
modern capital of Persia, he found that the fugitive was already well
beyond the Caspian Gates, which lie a long day's journey to the
east.   Despairing of overtaking him, Alexander rested some days

at Ragae before he advanced towards Parthia through the Caspian

Darius seized by Bessus. pass. But meanwhile doom was stealing upon Darius by another way. His followers were beginning to suspect that ill-luck dogged him, and when he proposed to stay and risk another battle instead of continuing his retreat to Bactria, none were willing except the remnant of Greek mercenaries, who were still faithful to the man who had hired them, and perhaps dreaded punishment as recusants to the Greek cause. Bessus, the satrap of Bactria, was a kinsman of the king, and it was felt by many that he might be able to raise up again the Achaemenian house, which Darius had been unable to sustain. A plot was formed ; Darius was seized and bound in the middle of the night, set in a litter, and hurried on as a prisoner along the road to Bactria. This event disbanded his army. The Greek mercenaries went off northwards into the Caspian mountains, and many of the Persians turned back to find pardon and grace with Alexander. They found him encamped on the Parthian side of the

The pursuit of Darius. Caspian Gates, and told him the new turn of events. When he learned that his old rival was a prisoner and that Bessus was now his antagonist, Alexander resolved on a swift and hot pursuit. Leaving the main body of the army to come slowly after, he set forth at once with his cavalry and some light foot, and sped the whole night through, not resting till next day at noon, and then another evening and night at the same breathless speed. Sunrise saw him at Thara. It was the place where the Great King had been put in chains, and it was ascertained from his interpreter, who had remained behind ill, that Bessus and his fellows intended to surrender Darius if the pursuit were pressed. There was the greater need for haste. The pursuers rode on throughout another night ; men and horses were dropping with fatigue. At noon they came to a village where the pursued had halted the day before, and Alexander learned that they intended to force a march in the night. He asked the people if there was no short way, and was told that there was a short way, but it was waterless. Alexander instantly dismounted five hundred of his horsemen and gave their steeds to the officers and the strongest men of the infantry who were with him. With these he started in the evening, and having ridden about forty-five miles came up with the enemy at break of day. The barbarians were straggling, many of them unarmed ; a few who made a stand were swept away, but most of them fled when they saw that it was Alexander. Bessus and his fellow-conspirators bade their prisoner—no longer, seemingly, in chains—mount a horse ; and when Darius refused, they stabbed him and rode their ways, wounding the litter-mules too and killing the drivers. The beasts, sore and thirsty, strayed about half a mile from the road down a side valley, where they were found at a spring

by a Macedonian who had come to slake his thirst. The Great
King was near his last gasp. If he could have spoken Greek, or if
the stranger had understood Persian, he might have found words to
send a message of thanks to his conqueror for the generous treatment
of his wife and mother who were then assuredly in his thoughts ;
afterwards men had no scruple in placing appropriate words in the
mouth of the dying monarch. It is enough to believe that he had
the solace of a cup of water in his supreme moments and thanked
the Macedonian soldier by a sign. Alexander viewed the body, and
is related to have thrown his own cloak over it in pity. It was part
of his fair luck that he found Darius dead ; for if he had taken him
alive, he would not have put him to death, and such a captive would
have been a perpetual embarrassment. He sent the corpse with all
honour to the queen-mother, and the last of the Achaemenian kings
was buried with his forefathers at Persepolis.

SECT. 12. SPIRIT OF ALEXANDER'S POLICY AS LORD OF ASIA

Before we follow Alexander on his marches of conquest and dis- *Change*
covery into the regions which were then in European eyes the Far *in Alex-*
East, we may pause to observe his attitude as ruler and king ; for *ander's*
the months which passed between the battle of Gaugamela and the *aims.*
pursuit of Darius were a critical period, which witnessed a remarkable change in his conception of his duty and in his political aims.

From the very beginning he had shown to the conquered pro- *His*
vinces a tolerance, which was not only prompted by generosity but *tolerant*
based on political wisdom. He had not attempted to apply an *policy.*
artificial scheme to all countries, but had permitted each country to
retain its national institutions. One general principle, indeed, he
did adopt—the division of power ; and this was a notable improvement on the Persian method. Under the Persian kingdom the satrap
was usually sole governor, controlling not only the civil administration,
but the treasury and the troops. Alexander in most cases committed
only the internal administration to the governor, and appointed
beside him, and independent of his authority, a financial officer and
a military commander. This division of authority was a security
against rebellion. We have already seen, in Egypt and Babylonia,
how in matters of religion Alexander was, like all the Greeks, broad-
minded and tolerant.

But the Macedonian king, the commander-in-chief of the Greek *His policy*
confederates, had set forth as a champion of Greeks against mere *as successor*
barbarians, as a leader of Europeans against effeminate Asiatics, as *of the Great*
the representative of a higher folk against beings lower in the human *King.*
scale. All the Greeks and Macedonians who followed him regarded

the east as a world to be plundered and rifled by their higher intelligence and courage, and considered the orientals as inferiors meant by nature to be their own slaves. " Slaves by nature " they seemed to the political wisdom of Aristotle himself, Alexander's teacher ; and the victories of Issus and Gaugamela were calculated to confirm the Europeans in their sense of unmeasured superiority. But, as Alexander advanced, his view expanded, and he rose to a loftier conception of his own position and his relation to Asia. He began to transcend the familiar distinction of Greek and barbarian, and to see that, for all the truth it contained, it was not the last word that could be said. He formed the notion of an empire, both European and Asiatic, in which the Asiatics should not be dominated by the European invaders, but Europeans and Asiatics alike should be ruled on an equality by a monarch, indifferent to the distinction of Greek and barbarian, and looked upon as their own king by Persians as well as by Macedonians. The idea begins to show itself after the battle of Gaugamela. The Persian lords and satraps who submit are received with favour and confidence ; Alexander learns to know and appreciate the fine qualities of the Iranian noblemen. Some of the eastern provinces are entrusted to Persian satraps, for example Babylonia to Mazaeus, and the court of Alexander ceases to be purely European. With oriental courtiers, the forms of an oriental court are also gradually introduced; the Asiatics prostrate themselves before the lord of Asia ; and presently Alexander adopts the dress of a Persian king at court ceremonies, in order to appear less a foreigner in the eyes of his eastern subjects. The idea which prompted this policy was new and bold, and it harmonised with the great work of Alexander,— the breaking down of the barriers between west and east ; but it was accompanied by a certain imperious self-exaltation, which we do not find in the earlier part of Alexander's career, and it involved him in troubles with his own folk. The Macedonians strongly disapproved of their king's new paths ; they disliked the rival influence of the Asiatic nobles, and their prejudices were shocked at seeing Alexander occasionally assume oriental robes. The Macedonian royalty was indeed inadequate for Alexander's imperial position ; but it is unfortunate that he had no other model than the royalty of Persia, hedged round by forms which were so distasteful to the free spirit of Greece. The life of Alexander was spent in solving difficult problems, political and military ; and none was harder than this, to create a kingship which should conciliate the prejudices of the east without offending the prejudices of the west.

CHAPTER XVIII

THE CONQUEST OF THE FAR EAST

SECT. I. HYRCANIA, AREIA, BACTRIA, SOGDIANA

THE murderers of Darius fled, Bessus to Bactria, Nabarzanes to *Conquest of* Hyrcania; and the direction of their flight determined the course of *Hyrcania* Alexander's advance. He could not pursue Bessus while there was *(Tabaristan* an enemy behind him in the Caspian region, and therefore his first *and Mazen-* movement was to cross the Elburz chain of mountains which separate *deran).* the south Caspian shores from Parthia, and subdue the lands of the 330 *B.C.* Tapuri and Mardi. The Persian officers who had retreated into these regions submitted, and were received with favour; the life of Nabarzanes was spared. The Greek mercenaries who had found refuge in the Tapurian mountains capitulated. All who had entered the Persian service, before the Synedrion of Corinth had pledged Greece to the cause of Macedon, were released; the rest were compelled to serve in the Macedonian army for the same pay which they had received from Darius. The importance of the well-wooded southern coast of the Caspian was understood by Alexander, and he sent orders to Parmenio to go forth from Ecbatana and take possession of the Cadusian territory on the south-western side of the sea. He himself could not tarry. Having rested a fortnight at Zadracarta *(Astrabad.)* and held athletic games, he marched eastward to Susia, a town in *(Near* the north of Areia, and was met there by Satibarzanes, governor of *Meshed.)* Areia, who made his submission and was confirmed in his satrapy. Here the news arrived that Bessus had assumed the style of Great King with the name of Artaxerxes, and was wearing his turban "erect." Alexander started at once on the road to Bactria. His way would have lain by Merv; in the wilds of Central Asia the beaten ways of traffic remain the same for thousands of years. But he had not gone far when he was overtaken by the news that Satibarzanes had revolted behind him. There was nothing to be done but to return and secure the province of Areia; for this province did not stand

alone ; it would certainly be upheld in its hostility by the neighbouring countries of Arachosia and Drangiana, which formed the satrapy
of Barsaentes, one of the murderers of Darius.　Hurrying back in
forced marches with a part of his army, Alexander appeared before

Alexandria Artocoana, the capital of Areia, in two days ; Satibarzanes galloped
Areiôn away to seek Bessus in Bactria, and his troops who fled to the
(Herat). mountains were pursued and overcome.　There was no further
Occupation resistance, and the conqueror marched southwards to Drangiana.
of Drangi- His road can hardly be doubtful—the road which leads by Herat
ana. into Seistan.　And it is probable that Herat is the site of the city
which Alexander founded to be the capital and stronghold of the new
Execution province, Alexandria of the Areians.　The submission of Drangiana
of was made without a blow ; the satrap, who had fled to the Indians,
Barsaentes. was given up by them and put to death.

(Near Nad At Prophthasia, the capital of the Drangian land, there befell a
Ali in tragedy, whereof we know too little to judge the rights and wrongs of
Seistan.) the case.　It came to Alexander's ears that Philotas, the son of
The Parmenio, was conspiring against his life.　The king called an
conspiracy assembly of the Macedonians and stated the charges against the
of Philotas. general.　Philotas admitted that he had known of a plot to murder
Alexander and said nothing about it ; but this was only one of the
charges against him.　The Macedonians, although many of them
were ill-content with the developments of their king's policy in
the east, found Philotas guilty, and he was pierced by their
javelins.　The son dead, it seemed dangerous to let the father live,
whether he was involved or not in the treasonable designs or
Fate of Philotas.　A messenger was despatched with all speed to Media,
Parmenio. bearing commands to some of the captains of Parmenio's army to
put the old general to death.　If the guilt of Philotas was assured—
and we have no reason to doubt it—we can hardly, so far as Philotas
is concerned, blame Alexander for his rigorous measures, which it
must have been painful for him to adopt.　A crime which might
have been pardoned in Macedonia could not be dealt gently with in
a camp in distant lands, where not only success but safety depended on loyalty and discipline.　But the death of Parmenio was
an arbitrary act of precaution against merely suspected disloyalty;
there seem to have been no proofs against him, and there was
certainly no trial.

　　In the meantime Alexander had changed his plans.　Instead of
retracing his steps and following the route to Bactria, which he had
originally intended to take, he resolved to fetch a circle, and marching through Afghanistan, subduing it as he went, he would cross the
Hindu-Kush mountains and descend on the plain of the Oxus from
the east.　First he advanced southwards to secure Seistan and the

north-western regions of Baluchistan, then known as Gedrosia. The *Alexander*
Ariaspae, a peaceful and friendly people whom the Greeks called *winters in*
" Benefactors," dwelt in the south of Seistan. Alexander passed *Seistan,*
part of the winter among them, and gratified them by a small *330-29 B.C.*
increase of territory, and made them free, subject to no satrap.
The neighbouring Gedrosians volunteered their submission, and
a Gedrosian satrapy was constituted with its capital at Pura.
When spring came, Alexander pushed north-eastward up the valley
of the Halmand to Candahar. And in pronouncing the name of
Candahar, we are perhaps pronouncing the name of the great conqueror ; for the chief city which he founded in Arachosia was *Alexandria*
probably on the site of Candahar, which seems to be a corruption of *in*
its name, Alexandria. The way led on over the mountains, past *Arachosia.*
Ghazni, into the valley of the upper waters of the Cabul river, and
Alexander came to the foot of the high range of the Hindu-Kush. The
whole massive complex of mountains which diverge from the roof of the
world, dividing southern from central, eastern from western Asia—
the Pamirs, the Hindu-Kush, and the Himalayas—were grouped by
the Greeks under the general name of Caucasus. But the Hindu-
Kush was distinguished by the special name of Paropanisus, while
the Himalayas were called the Imaus. At the foot of the Hindu- *Alexandria*
Kush he spent the winter, and founded another Alexandria to secure *of the*
this region, somewhere to the north of Cabul ; it was distinguished *Caucasus*
as Alexandria of the Caucasus. While he was in these parts he *Houpian),*
learned that Satibarzanes was still abroad in Areia, inflaming a *329-8 B.C.*
rebellion ; some forces were sent to crush him ; a battle was fought
and Satibarzanes was killed.

The crossing of the Caucasus, undertaken in the early spring,
was an achievement which, for the difficulties overcome and the
hardships of cold and want endured, seems to have fallen little
short of Hannibal's passage of the Alps. The soldiers had to content themselves with raw meat and the herb of silphion as a substitute
for bread. At length they reached Drapsaca, high up on the *(? Kun-*
northern slope—the frontier fortress of Bactria. Having rested his *duz.)*
way-worn army, Alexander went down by the stronghold of Aornus *(Tash-*
into the plain, and marched through a poor country to Bactra, the *kurgan.)*
chief city of the land, which has preserved its old site but has
changed its name to Balkh.

The pretender, Bessus Artaxerxes, had stripped and wasted *Occupation*
eastern Bactria up to the foot of the mountains, for the purpose of *of Bactria.*
checking the progress of the invading army ; but he fled across the
Oxus when Alexander drew near, and his native cavalry deserted
him. No man withstood the conqueror, and another province was
added without a blow to the Macedonian empire. Alexander lost no

BACTRIA
and
SOGDIANA.

Stadia   Parasangs
0 200 400 600 800 0 10 20   40   60

English Miles
0   50   100   150

(Tashkend)

R. Jaxartes Tanais

Alexandria Eschate
(Khojend)

R. (axus) Darya (SYr FERGANA)

(Kashgar)

R. Sogd (Saravschan)

SOGDIANA

Maracanda
(Samarcand)

Nautaca

(Hissar)

PARAETACENE

(Karshi)

Sogdiana
(Bochara)

Kilif

R. Oxus

Aornus
(Tashkurgan)

Drapsaca
(Indus?)

PAROPAMISUS

HINDU KUSH

Zariaspa
(Char-jui)

R. Oxus

Bactra
(Balkh)

B   A   C   T   R   I   A

(Merv)

Nicaea
(Kabul?)

Alexandria
ad
Paropamisum

Alexandria Areion
(Herat)

A   R   E   I   A

62°   64°   66°   Longitude East 68° of Greenwich   70°   72°

Walker & Boutall sc

FIG. 199.

time in pursuing the fugitive into Sogdiana.   This is the country
which lies between the streams of the Oxus and the Jaxartes.   It
was called Sogdiana from the river Sogd, which flows through the
land and, passing near the cities of Samarcand and Buchara, loses
itself in the sands of the desert before it approaches the waters of the
Oxus.   Bessus had burned his boats, and when Alexander, after a *(R. Sarav.*
weary march of two or three days through the hot desert, arrived at *shan.)*
the banks of the Oxus, he was forced to transport his army by the
primitive vehicle of skins, which the natives of Central Asia then used
and still use to-day.   Alexander's soldiers, however, instead of in-
flating the sheep-skins with air, stuffed them with rushes.   They
crossed the river at Kilif, where its banks contract to the width of
about two-thirds of a mile, and advanced on the road to Maracanda,
the chief city of the country, easily recognised as Samarcand.

Bessus had no support north of the Oxus.   He had some
Sogdian allies, at the head of whom were Spitamenes and Data-
phernes ; but these men had no intention of sacrificing their country
to the cause of the pretender.   Thinking that Alexander's only
object was to capture Bessus, and that he would then withdraw from
Sogdiana and fix the Oxus as the northern boundary of his dominion,
they sent a message to him offering to surrender the usurper.   The
king sent Ptolemy, son of Lagus, with 6000 men to secure Bessus,
whom they found in a walled village, deserted by his Sogdian
friends.   By Alexander's orders he was placed, naked and fettered,
on the right side of the road by which the army was marching.
Alexander halted as he passed the captive, and asked him why he
had seized and murdered Darius, his king and benefactor.   Bessus
replied that he had acted in concert with other Persian nobles, in the
hope of winning the conqueror's favour.   He was scourged and sent
to Bactra to await his doom.

But Alexander did not arrest his march ; he had made up his *River*
mind to annex Sogdiana.   Not the Oxus but the Jaxartes was to be *Jaxartes*
the northern limit of his empire.   The children of the waste called *(Syr*
this river the Tanais.   It is said that the Greeks were deceived into *Darya).*
imagining that it was the same river as the familiar Tanais which *(Don.)*
discharges its waters into the Maeotic lake, and hence regarded it as
the boundary between Asia and Europe, and thought that the
herdsmen of the north, who dwelt beyond it, were "the Scythians
of Europe."   But they can hardly have fallen into this error, for they
imagined that the Caspian Sea was a gulf of the ocean, and the two
errors are inconsistent.   Having seized and garrisoned Samarcand,
the army pushed on north-eastward by the unalterable road which
nature has marked out, and occupied seven strongholds which the
Sogdians had built as defences against invaders from the north.

The road reaches the Jaxartes where that river issues from the chilly vale of Fergana and deflects its course to flow through the steppes. It was a point of the highest importance; for Fergana forms the vestibule of the great gate of communication between south-western Asia and China—the pass over the Tian-shan mountains, which *Alexandria* descends on the other side into the land of Kashgar. Here Alexander, *Eschate* with strategic insight, resolved to fix the limit of his empire, and on *(Khodjend),* the banks of the river he founded a new city which was known as 328 B.C. Alexandria the Ultimate. There is no doubt about the situation; it is the later Khodjend.

The conqueror, judging from the ease with which he had come and conquered Arachosia and Bactria, seems not to have conceived that it might be otherwise beyond the Oxus. But the chiefs of *Sogdiana* Sogdiana were not as the Persian grandees; they were ready to dare *rises* greatly for their freedom against the European invader. As he was *against* designing his new city, Alexander received the news that the land *Alexander.* was up in arms behind him. Spitamenes was the leader of the movement, and was supported by Oxyartes and other leading Sogdians. The few Macedonian soldiers left in the seven strongholds had been overpowered, and the garrison of Samarcand was besieged in the citadel. A message had gone forth into the western wastes, and the Massagetae and other Scythian tribes were flocking to drive *Summer,* out the intruder. It was a dangerous moment for Alexander. He 328 B.C. first turned to recover the fortresses, and in two days he had taken *(Uratübe.)* and burned five of them. Cyrupolis, the largest and strongest, caused more trouble; but Alexander, with a few companions, contrived to creep under the wall by the bed of a dry stream, and threw open a gate to the troops. The resistance of the inhabitants was furious, and the king was wounded in the mellay. The fall of Cyrupolis was followed by the capitulation of the seventh town, and the remnant of the indwellers of all these places were led in chains to take part in peopling the new Alexandria.

The next task should have been the relief of Samarcand, but Alexander found himself confronted by a new danger, and could send only a few thousand troops to succour the besieged garrison. The herdsmen of the north were pouring down to the banks of the Jaxartes, ready to cross the stream and harass the Macedonians in the rear. It was impossible to move until they had been repelled and the passage of the river secured. The walls of Alexandria were hastily constructed of unburnt clay and the place made fit for habitation in the short space of twenty days. Meanwhile the northern bank was lined by the noisy and jeering hordes of the barbarians, and Alexander determined to cross the river. The offerings were not favourable; they betokened, said the seer, personal danger to the king; but Alexander would be mocked no longer. Bringing up his missile-engines to the shore, he dismayed the shepherds, who, when stones and darts began to fall among them from such a distance and unhorsed one of their champions, retreated some distance from the bank. The army seized the moment to cross; the Scythians were routed, and Alexander, at the head of his cavalry, pursued them far into the steppes. Parched by the intense summer heat, the king was tempted to drink of the foul water of the desert, and he fell dangerously ill. Thus was the presage of the offerings fulfilled.

Luckily Alexander soon recovered, for ill tidings came from the south. When the relieving force approached Maracanda, Spitamenes had fled westward to the town of Sogdiana, which probably answers to Buchara. The Macedonians marched after him, hoping to drive him utterly out of the land, but they were indiscreet, and the whole detachment was cut off. Learning of this disaster, Alexander hurried to Samarcand with cavalry and light troops, covering the distance, it is said, in three days,—a forced march of between fifty and sixty miles a day, which seems almost impossible for foot soldiers, however lightly equipped, in the heat of a Sogdian summer. At his coming, Spitamenes, who had returned to the siege of Samarcand, again darted westward, and Alexander followed in pursuit. Visiting the spot where the unlucky corps had been cut down on the banks of the Sogd, the king buried the dead; then crossing the river, he pursued the fugitive chieftain and his Scythian allies to the limits of the waste. He swept on to Sogdiana, ravaging the land; then *Alexander* marching south-westward to the Oxus, he crossed into western *in western* Bactria and spent the winter at Zariaspa. The Bactrian cities of *Sogdiana; winters,* Zariaspa and Bactra bore somewhat the same relation to one another *328-7 B.C.* as the Sogdian cities of Maracanda and Sogdiana. *at Zari-*

At Zariaspa, Bessus was formally tried for the murder of Darius, *aspa* and was condemned to have his nose and ears cut off and be taken *(Charjui).* to Ecbatana to die on the cross. The Greeks, like ourselves, regarded mutilation as a barbarous punishment, and it is not pleasant *Fate of* to find Alexander violating this sentiment. But the adoption of *Bessus.* oriental punishments in dealing with orientals must be judged along with the adoption of other oriental customs. Every conqueror of an alien race finds himself in a grave embarrassment. Is he to offend his ideals and fall away from his convictions by acquiescing in outlandish usages antagonistic to his own? Or is he, stiffnecked and inflexibly true to the principles of his own civilisation, to remain out of touch with his new subjects? Is he to adopt the policy which will be most effective in administering the conquered land, or is he to impose a policy which works and is approved in his home-country, but may be useless or fatal elsewhere? Alexander did not adopt the second method. It was the task of his life to spread Greek civilisation in the East. But he saw that this could not be done by an outsider—a general of Hellas or basileus of Macedonia,—he must meet the orientals on their own ground; he must become their king in their own way. The surest means of planting Hellenism in their midst was to begin by taking account sympathetically of their prejudices Alexander therefore assumed the state of Great King, surrounded himself with Eastern forms and pomp, exacted self-abasement in his presence from oriental subjects, and adopted the maxim that the king's person was divine. He was the successor of Darius, and he regarded the murder of that monarch as a crime touching himself, inasmuch as it was a crime against royalty. It was therefore an act of deliberate policy that he punished the king-slayer in Eastern fashion, as an impressive example to his Eastern subjects.

The misfortune was that Alexander's assumption of oriental state, and the favour which he showed to the Persians, were highly unpopular with the Macedonians. It was hard always to preserve a double face, one for his Companions, another for his Persian ministers. Nor was it Alexander's policy to maintain this difference for ever. He hoped ultimately to secure uniformity in the relations of Macedonians and Persians to their common king. Meanwhile, in the intervals of rest between military operations, discontent smouldered among the Macedonians. Though they were attached to their king, and proud of the conquests which they had helped him to achieve, they felt that he was no longer the same to them as when he had led them to victory at the Granicus. His exaltation over obeisant orientals had changed him, and the execution of his trusted general Parmenio was felt to be significant of the change.

These feelings of discontent accidentally found a mouthpiece about this time. Rebellious movements in Sogdiana brought Alexander over the Oxus again before the winter was over, and he spent some time at Samarcand. One of the most unfortunate consequences of the long-protracted sojourn in the regions of the Oxus was the increase of drunkenness in the army. The excessively dry atmosphere in summer produces an intolerable and frequent thirst; and it was inevitable that the Macedonians should slake it by wine—the strong wine of the country—if they would not sicken themselves by the brackish springs of the desert or the noisome water of the towns. One night in the fortress of Samarcand the carouse lasted far into the night. Greek men of letters, who accompanied the army, sang the praises of Alexander, exalting him above the Dioscuri, whose feast he was celebrating on this day. Clitus, his foster-brother, flushed with wine, suddenly sprang up to denounce the blasphemy, and once he had begun, the current of his feelings swept him on into a denunciation and disparagement of Alexander.   It was to the Macedonians, he said—to men like Parmenio and Philotas—that Alexander owed his victories ; he himself had saved Alexander's life at the Granicus.   These were the two sharpest stings ; and they stirred Alexander's blood to fury.   He started to his feet and called in Macedonian for his hypaspists ; none obeyed his drunken orders ; Ptolemy and other banqueters forced Clitus out of the hall, while others tried to restrain the king.   But presently Clitus made his way back and shouted from the doorway some insulting verses of Euripides, signifying that the army does the work and the general reaps the glory.   The king leapt up, snatched a spear from the hand of a guardsman, and rushed upon his foster-brother.   Drunk though *Murder of* he was, the aim was sure—Clitus sank dead to the ground. *Clitus.* An agony of remorse followed.   For three days the murderer lay in his tent, without sleep or food, cursing himself as the assassin of his friends.   The army sympathised with his grief ; they tried the dead man and resolved that he had been justly slain.   The tragedy was attributed to the anger of Dionysus, because the day was his festival and the Dioscuri had been celebrated instead.

The tragic issue of this miserable drunken brawl is a lurid spot in Alexander's life, but it was a slight matter compared with an act which is said to have marked his invasion of Sogdiana.   When we saw him first cross the Oxus in pursuit of Bessus, we did not pause to witness his treatment of a remarkable town which lay on his *The town* way.   The Branchidae, who had charge of the temple and oracle *of the* of Apollo twenty miles from Miletus, are charged with having *Branchidae* betrayed the treasures of the sanctuary.   Their lives were not *(near* safe from the anger of the Milesians, and Xerxes transported them *Kilif).* into Central Asia, where no Greek vengeance could pursue them. They were established in Sogdiana, not far from the place where Alexander   crossed, —a solitary little settlement, which, though severed so long from Hellas, preserved its Greek religion and Greek customs, and had not forgotten the Greek speech.   It is easy to imagine what excitement was stirred there by the coming of a Greek army.   The folk come forth joyously to bid Alexander welcome and offer him their fealty.   But Alexander remembered only one thing—the ancestors of this people had committed a heinous crime against Apollo, and had sided with Persia against Greece.   That crime had never been forgotten by the men of Miletus, and the king called upon the Milesians in his army to pronounce sentence upon the Branchidae.   The Milesians could not agree, and Alexander himself decided the fate of the town.   Having surrounded it with a cordon of soldiers, he caused all the inhabitants to be massacred and the place to be utterly demolished. Few of the children of the children's children of the original transgressors could have been still alive ; most of the victims would have belonged to the fifth degree of descent. We cannot imagine a fouler enforcement of the savage principle that crimes of the fathers should be visited to distant generations. Such is the shocking story which has blackened Alexander's fame ; fortunately we can safely reject it as untrue ; it was not related in the memoirs of the two oldest and best authorities, Ptolemy and Aristobulus. Alexander committed some cruel deeds, but none so appalling as this massacre would have been.

There were more hostilities in western Bactria and western Sogdiana, until at last, overawed by Alexander's success, the Scythians, in order to win his favour, slew Spitamenes. With this chieftain the resistance expired, and it only remained to reduce the rugged south-eastern regions of Sogdiana, which were called Paraetacene. The Sogdian Rock, which commands the pass into these regions, was occupied by Oxyartes, and a band of Macedonian soldiers captured it by an arduous night-climb. Among the captives was Roxane, the daughter of Oxyartes ; and the love of Alexander, who had been always indifferent to women, was attracted by the beauty and manners of the Sogdian maiden. It was characteristic of him that, notwithstanding the adverse comment which such a condescension would excite among the proud Macedonians, he resolved to make her his wife, and, on his return to Bactra after subjugating other fortresses in Paraetacene, he divided a loaf of bread with his bride according to the fashion of the country, and celebrated the nuptials. There was policy in this marriage as well as inclination. It was symbolic of the union of Asia and Europe, of the breaking down of the barrier between barbarian and Hellene, and of Alexander's position as an oriental king.

Reduction of Paraeta-cene (Hissar).

Marriage of Alexander with Roxane, 327 B.C.

About this time an attempt seems to have been made to render uniform the court ceremonial. The Persian nobles were not well pleased that, whereas they were compelled to abase themselves to the ground before the divinity of the king, the Macedonians and Greeks were excused from the obeisance. Most of the Greeks would have been pliant enough, but there was one prominent man of letters who stood out against the usage and drew upon himself displeasure by the utterance of bold truths. This was Callisthenes, a nephew of Aristotle. He was composing a history of the campaigns of Alexander, whose exploits he ungrudgingly lauded ; he had joined the army, he used to say, to make *him* famous, not to win fame himself. It is related that Hephaestion and a number of others arranged a plan for surprising the king's guests at a banquet into making the

Callisthenes of Olynthus,

obeisance. Alexander, raising his golden cup, drank to each guest in order,—first to some of those who were privy to the plan ; each arose and prostrated himself and was then kissed by the king. Callisthenes, when his turn came, drained the cup and went to *refuses* receive the kiss, without doing obeisance ; Alexander would not kiss *to do* him ; and he turned away, saying, " I go the poorer by a kiss ! " *obeisance.* Incidents of this kind created a coolness between the king and his historian. One of the duties of Callisthenes and the other philo- sophers and literary men who accompanied Alexander's progress was to educate the pages, the noble Macedonian youths who at- tended on the king's person ; and over some of these Callisthenes had great influence. One day at a boar-hunt a page named *Conspiracy* Hermolaus committed the indiscretion of forestalling the king in *of the pages.* slaying the beast ; and for this breach of etiquette he was flogged and deprived of his horse. Smarting under the dishonour, Hermolaus plotted with some of his comrades to slay Alexander in his sleep. But on the appointed night Alexander sat up carousing till dawn, and on the next day the plot was betrayed. The conspirators were arrested, and put to death by the sentence of the whole army. Callisthenes was also handfasted on the charge of being an accom- *Callisthenes* plice, and was afterwards hanged. Hermolaus was indeed one of *charged* his warmest admirers, but it is not clear what the evidence against the *with* historian was. On the one hand, Ptolemy and Aristobulus asserted *treason and* independently that the pages declared under torture that Callisthenes *executed.* had incited them ; on the other hand, Alexander is said to have stated in a letter that the torture had failed to elicit the name of any accomplice.   The deeper cause may be that Alexander suspected Callisthenes as an agent of the anti-Macedonian party in Greece.

Before the end of summer, Alexander bade farewell to Bactria *Alexander's* and set forth to the conquest of India.   Three years had passed *position* since the death of Darius, three unique years in the annals of the *among* world.   In that time the western conqueror, disarranging the cycles *western* of Asiatic history, had subdued Afghanistan, and cast his yoke over *conquerors* the herdsmen of the north as far as the river Jaxartes. He was the first *of Asia.* and last western conqueror of Afghanistan ; he was the first but not the last invader. He was the first European invader and conqueror of the regions beyond the Oxus, anticipating by more than two thousand years the conquests which have been achieved by a European power in modern times.   His next enterprise forestalled our own conquest of north-western India.   But England made her conquests from the south, Russia hers from the north ; Alexander was the only European conqueror who marched straight from the west to the Indus and the Oxus.

The Macedonian monarch's work in Bactria and Sogdiana was an unavoidable sequel of his succession to the Persian empire. He had to set up a barrier against the unsettled races of the waste, who were a perpetual menace to the civilisations of the south. He founded a number of settlements in these regions, not only for the purpose of military garrisons, but also probably with the hope of gradually training the herdsmen to more settled ways of life. If so, it was a vain hope. History has shown that there is only one means of forcing the shepherd races to become reluctant tillers of the soil. Not until they have been encompassed on all sides by civilisation, and driven within a narrow geographical area, will they adopt, under the stress of necessity, the regular and laborious life of agriculture. In the days of Alexander they had endless space behind them and an indefinite future before them.

SECT. 2. THE CONQUEST OF INDIA

In returning to Afghanistan, Alexander seems to have followed the main road from Balkh to Cabul, crossing the Hindu-Kush by a pass more westerly than that by which he had come. Reaching Alexandria in ten days, he went on to another town, which, if he had not refounded, he had at all events renamed, Nicaea, and which is possibly to be sought in Cabul itself. Here he stayed till the middle of November, finding much to do both in organising the province and in preparing for further advance. He had left a large detachment of his army in Bactria, but he had enrolled a still larger force—30,000—of the Asiatics of those regions,—Bactrians, Sogdians, Dahae, and Sacae. The host with which he was now to descend upon India must have been at least twice as numerous as the army with which he had crossed the Hellespont seven years before. It had increased as it rolled on, and the augmentations far more than counterbalanced the reductions caused by leaving detachments in each new province, and the losses due to warfare or disease.

Halt at Nicaea (Cabul or Bagram ?), 327 B.C.

During these years Alexander's camp was his court and capital, the political centre of his empire,—a vast city rolling along over mountain and river through Central Asia. Men of all trades and callings were there, some indispensable for the needs of the king and his army, others drawn by the prospect of making profits out of the spoil-laden soldiers : craftsmen of every kind, engineers, physicians, and seers ; cheapmen and money-changers ; literary men, poets, musicians, athletes, jesters ; secretaries, clerks, court attendants ; a host of women and slaves. In many of the halting-places athletic and musical contests were held, serving both to cheer the

Alexander's camp.

North-Western
INDIA.

Stadia
0   600   1200   1800

Parasangs
0   10   20   30   40   50

English Miles
0   100   200

*Ancient confluence of Indus with joint stream of the rivers, near Ucch.

Walker & Boutall sc

FIG. 200.

Greeks by reminding them of their home country and to impress the imagination of the barbarians. A Court Diary was regularly kept —in imitation of the court journal of Persia—by Eumenes of Cardia, who conducted all the political correspondence of Alexander.

State of India.

(R. Cabul.)

Alexander had no idea of the shape or extent of the Indian peninsula, and his notion of the Indian conquest was probably confined to the basins of the Cophen and the Indus. He was not the first invader speaking an Aryan language who went down through the north-western hills into the plains of India. Centuries and centuries before, Aryan herdsmen had flowed down in successive waves and found an abiding home there. From Central Asia, from the regions of the Hindu-Kush, bringing with them their old hymns, some of which we still possess, they came down into the lands of the Indus, "the glorious giver of wealth," and turned to a settled agricultural life. Strangely different was the civilisation which grew up in northern India among the men who called upon *Dyaus pitar* from that of their speech-brethren who worshipped *Zeus patêr* on the shores of the Aegean. The castes of the Brahmans and the warriors, the inhuman asceticism of the Brahman's life, the political influence of these religious men, must have seemed repulsive and outlandish to the free and cheerful temper of the Greeks. The great Darius had partially annexed the lands of the Indus, and they constantly supplied troops to his successors. Scylax of Caryanda had sailed down the Indus by his orders and probably published an account of the voyage. The stories that were told about the wonders of India excited the curiosity of the Greek invaders. It was a land of righteous folks, of strange beasts and plants, of surpassing wealth in gold and gems. It was supposed to be the ultimate country on the eastern side of the world, bounded by Ocean's stream.

Omphis.

(Takka çila.)
(The Paurava.)
(Asikni.)

At this time north-western India was occupied by a number of small heterogeneous principalities and village communities. The northern districts of the land between the Indus and the Hydaspes—the stream which we now call the Jhelum—were ruled by Omphis, a prince whose capital was at Taxila near the Indus. His brother Abisares was the ruler of Hazara and the adjacent parts of Cashmir. Beyond the Hydaspes was the powerful kingdom of Porus, who held sway as far as the Acesines or "dark-hued," which we know as the Chenab, the next of the "Five Rivers." East of the Chenab, in the lands of the Ravee and the Bëas, were other small principalities, and also free "kingless" peoples, who owned no master. These principalities and free communities differed much in manners and religion; they had no tendency to unity or combination; the free tribes feared and hated the princes; the princes strove with one another. And these states

Aryans, were not all of the same race. Most perhaps were Aryan; but

some, like the Malli, belonged to the old "Dravidian" stock, whom *and Dra*
even in the Punjab the Aryans had not entirely dispossessed or sub- *vidians.*
dued.   An invader, therefore, had no common resistance to fear ; he
had to deal with the states one by one ; and he could be assured
that many would welcome him out of hatred for their neighbours.
The prince of Taxila hoped great things from the Macedonian conqueror, especially the downfall of his rival Porus.   He visited Alexander at Nicaea, laid himself and his kingdom at the great emperor's
feet, and promised his aid in subduing India.   Other chiefs on the
hither side of the Indus also made submission.

Alexander's direct road from the high plain of Cabul into the
Punjab lay along the right bank of the Cophen or Cabul river, through
the great gate of the Khyber Pass.   But it was impossible to advance
to the Indus without securing his communications, and for this purpose it was needful to subjugate the river-valleys to the left of the
Cabul, among the huge western spurs of the Himalaya mountains.

It was perhaps not far from Jelalabad that the army came to *Nysa*
a city which was called Nysa.   The name immediately awakened in *(Nanghen-*
the minds of all the Greeks the memory of their god Dionysus.   For *har).*
Mount Nysa was the mythical place where he had been nursed by
nymphs when he was born from the thigh of Zeus.   The mountain
was commonly supposed to be in Thrace ; but an old hymn placed it
" near the streams of Nile " ; it had no place on the traveller's chart.
But here was an actual Nysa ; and close to the town was a hill whose
name resembled *mêros*, the Greek word for " thigh," and whose slopes
were covered with the god's own ivy.   Therefore Nysa, they said, was
founded by Dionysus ; the god had fared eastward to subdue India ;
and now Alexander was marching on his tracks.   Everywhere on
their further march the Greeks and Macedonians were alert to discover traces of the progress of the bacchic god.

For the purposes of this campaign Alexander divided his army. *Alex-*
Hephaestion, taking three regiments of the phalanx, half the Mace- *ander's*
donian cavalry, all the mercenary cavalry, advanced by the Khyber *campaigns*
Pass, with orders to construct a bridge across the Indus.   The king, *etc.*
with the rest of the army, including the light troops, plunged into
the difficult country north of the river ; and the winter was spent in
warfare with the hardy hill-folks, especially the Aspasians and
Assacenes, and in capturing their impregnable fortresses, in the dis- *(Açrakas.)*
trict of the Kunar, in remote Chitral, and in the Panjkar and Swat
valleys.   Massaga, of the Assacenian people, in the Swat valley,
was one of the most important strongholds that Alexander captured ;
we cannot point it out on the map, but Dyrta, another fortress of the
same people, may be fairly sought in Dir. [The most wonderful
exploit of all was the scaling and taking of the rock of Aornus, to *Aornus.*

which the Assacenes had fled for refuge after Alexander's successful operations in the Swat valley. Perched high on the summit of Pir-sar, some 5000 feet above the Indus, this natural fortress had defied, so tradition ran, even Heracles. Using a local guide Alexander made the difficult ascent to an attacking base, filled in with a mound the ravine below the rock, brought his catapults into play and stormed the fortress. Even now a brief campaign in Buner was needed before the Assacenes could be safely left.]

Crossing of the Indus near Attock, 326 B.C.
After this severe winter campaign the army rested on the hither bank of the Indus until spring had begun, and then, with the solemnity of games and sacrifices, crossed the river and marched a three days' journey eastward to Taxila. The rich country of these Aryan husbandmen was a striking and pleasant contrast to the barren abodes of the shepherds of Bactria and Sogdiana. The prince of Taxila met Alexander with obsequious pomp, and other lesser princes assembled at the city to do him homage. The administration of the recent conquests was now arranged. A new satrapy, embracing the lands west of the Indus, was established and entrusted to Philip, son of Machatas ; Macedonian garrisons were placed in Taxila and some other places east of the Indus, and Philip was charged with the general command of these troops. This shows the drift of Alexander's policy. The Indus was to be the eastern boundary of his direct sway ; beyond the Indus, he purposed to create no new provinces, but only to form a system of protected states.

Alexander then marched by a southward road to the Hydaspes, where he was to meet the only power in the land which could hope to resist his progress. Prince Porus had sent a defiance, and having gathered an army from thirty to forty thousand strong, was encamped on the left bank of the river, to contest the crossing. Moreover, Abisares of Cashmir promised him aid, although he had sent marks of homage to Alexander. The boats which had been constructed on the Indus for transporting the troops were, by Alexander's orders, sawn in two or three pieces according to their size *Alexander and Porus encamped on the Hydaspes.* and conveyed on carts to the Hydaspes. After a march, which was made slow and toilsome by the heavy tropical rain, the invaders encamped on the right bank of the river, near Jalalpur, and saw the lines of Porus on the opposite shore, protected by a multitude of elephants, his most formidable weapon of war. It was useless to think of crossing in the face of this host ; for the horses, who could not endure the smell and noise of the elephants, would certainly have been drowned ; and the men would have found it almost impossible to land, amid showers of darts, on the slimy, treacherous edge of the stream. All the fords in the neighbourhood were watched. Alexander adopted various measures to deceive and puzzle the enemy.

He collected large stores of corn, as if he had made up his mind to remain for many days where he was ; he spread the rumour that he intended to wait till the season of rains was over ; and he kept his troops in constant motion, sending detachments hither and thither. Then one night his trumpets blew, his cavalry rode down to the edge of the water, and to the eyes of the enemy it seemed that the whole army was about to cross. Porus moved his elephants up to the bank and set his host in array. But it proved to be a false alarm. The same feint was repeated again and again. Each night the Macedonian camp was in motion as if for crossing ; each night the Indians stood long hours in the wind and rain. But when he saw that the noise was never followed by action, Porus became weary of these useless nightly watches and disregarded the alarms of a faint-hearted foe. Alexander meanwhile was maturing a plan which he was able to carry out when he had put Porus off his guard.

About sixteen miles upwards from the camp, the Hydaspes makes a bend, changing its course from south to westward, and opposite the jutting angle a thickly wooded island rose amid the stream, while a dense wood covered the right shore. Here Alexander determined to cross. He caused the boats to be conveyed thither and remade in the shelter of the wood close to a deep ravine ; he had prepared skins stuffed with straw, such as he had used in passing the Oxus. When the time came, he led a portion of his troops to the wooded promontory, marching at a considerable distance from the river in order to avoid the observation of the enemy. A sufficient force was left in the camp under the command of Craterus, with orders not to cross, unless Porus either moved his entire army from its present position or was defeated and routed. Other forces were posted at points between the camp and the island, to cross and help at the right moment. The king arrived at the appointed spot later in the evening, and throughout the wet stormy night he directed the preparations for passing the swollen stream. Here, on the right bank, he posted the regiments of heavy infantry which he had brought with him,—a precaution, probably, against the possible arrival of Abisares.

Alexander's artifice.

The wind and rain, which had effectually concealed all the noise from the ears of hostile outposts on the bank, abated before dawn, and the passage began. Alexander led the way in a barque of thirty oars ; and the island was safely passed ; but land was hardly reached before they were descried by Indian scouts, who galloped off at full speed to warn their chieftain. The king, who was the first to leap ashore, waited till the cavalry had been disembarked and marshalled, but on advancing he discovered that he had landed not on the bank but on an island which was parted from the bank by a small channel now swollen with rain. It was some time before a passage for wading could be found, and the water was breast-high. At last the whole force was safely landed on the bank, and Alexander ordered his men for the coming battle—the third of the three great battles of his life. It was to be won without any heavy infantry ; he had with him only 6000 hypaspists, about 4000 light foot, 5000 cavalry, including 1000 Scythian archers. Taking all the cavalry with him, he rode rapidly forward towards the camp of Porus, leaving the infantry to follow. If the whole host of Porus should come out to meet him, he would wait for the infantry, but if the enemy showed symptoms of retreating, he would dash in among them with his superior cavalry. Presently he saw a troop coming ; it was the son of Porus at the head of 1000 horsemen and sixty war-chariots, too late to impede the landing of the Macedonians. As soon as he perceived the small number of the foe, Alexander charged and easily drove them back, slaying the prince and four hundred of his men.

Battle of the Hydaspes. But Porus himself was advancing with his main army, having left a small force to guard the river-bank against Craterus. When he reached sandy ground, suitable for the movements of his cavalry and war-chariots, he drew up his line of battle. In front of all he arranged two hundred elephants at intervals of 100 feet, and at some distance behind them his infantry, who numbered 20,000 if not more. On the wings he placed his cavalry—perhaps 4000. Alexander waited for the hypaspists, and drew them up opposite to the elephants. It was impossible to attack in front, for neither horse nor foot could venture in between these beasts which stood like towers of defence, the true strength of the Indian army. The only method was to begin by a cavalry attack on the flank ; and Seleucus and the other captains of the infantry were bidden not to advance until they saw that both the horse and the foot of the foe were tumbled into confusion by the flank assault. Alexander determined to concentrate his attack on the left wing ; perhaps because it was on the river-side and he would be within easier reach of his troops on the other bank. Accordingly he kept all his cavalry on his right wing. One body was entrusted to Coenus, who bore well to the right, and was ready to strike in the rear, and to deal with the body of horse stationed upon the enemy's right wing, in case they should come round to assist their comrades on the left. The mounted Scythian archers rode straight against the front of the enemy's cavalry—which was still in column formation, not having had time to open out—and harassed it with showers of arrows ; while Alexander himself, with the rest of the heavy cavalry, led the charge upon the flank. Porus—who had committed the fatal mistake of allowing the enemy to take the offensive—brought up

Battle of the
HYDASPES.
(J. B. B. *fecit.*)

R. Hydaspes

K

I

H

L

B

C

C

C

B′

A

A

A

AAA. *Infantry*
BB′. *Cavalry* ⎫ **INDIAN**
CCC. *Elephants* ⎭

H. *Hypaspists*
I. *Heavy cavalry led by Alexander* ⎫
K. ,, ,, ,, ,, *Coenus* ⎬ **MACEDONIAN**
L. *Mounted Archers* ⎭

Walker & Boutall sc.

FIG. 201.

FIG. 201A.—Decadrachm, minted at Babylon (obverse). Alexander attacking Porus.

his remaining squadrons from the right wing as fast as he could. Then Coenus, who had ridden round close to the river-bank, fell upon them in the rear. The Indians had now to form a double front against the double foe. Alexander seized the moment to press hard upon the adverse squadrons; they swayed backwards and sought shelter behind the elephants. Then those elephant riders who were on this side of the army drove the beasts against the Macedonian horses; and at the same time the Macedonian footmen rushed forward and attacked the animals which were now turned sidewards towards them. But the other elephants of the line were driven into the ranks of the hypaspists, and dealt destruction, tramp- *The* ling down and striking furiously. Heartened by the success of *Indian* the elephants, the Indian cavalry rallied and charged, but beaten *rally.* back by the Macedonian horse, who were now formed in a serried mass, they again sought shelter behind the elephantine wall. But many of the beasts were now furious with wounds and beyond control; some had lost their riders; and in the mellay they trampled on friends and foes alike. The Indians suffered most, for they were surrounded and confined to the space in which the animals raged; while the Macedonians could attack the animals on side or rear, and then retreat into the open when they turned to charge. At length, when the elephants grew weary and their charges were feebler, Alexander closed in. He gave the order for the hypaspists to advance in close array shield to shield, while he, re-forming his squadrons, dashed in from the side. The enemy's cavalry, already weakened and dislocated, could not withstand the double shock and was cut to pieces. The hypaspists rolled on upon the enemy's infantry, who, though they had hitherto taken no serious part in the fight, soon broke and fled. Meanwhile the generals on the other side of the river, Craterus and the rest, discovering that fortune was declaring for Alexander, crossed the river without resistance and arrived in time to consummate the victory by pursuing the fugitives. Porus, who had shown himself a mediocre general but a most valiant soldier, when he saw most of his forces scattered, his elephants lying dead or straying riderless, did not flee—as Darius had twice fled—but remained fighting, seated on an elephant of commanding height, until he was wounded in the right shoulder, the only part of his body unprotected by mail. Then he turned round and rode away. Alexander, struck with admiration at his prowess, sent messengers who overtook him and induced him to return. The victor, riding out to meet the old prince, was impressed by his stature and beauty, and asked him how he would fain be treated. "Treat me like a king," said Porus. "For my own sake," said Alexander, "I will do that; ask a boon for thy sake." "That," replied Porus, "containeth all."

And Alexander treated his captive royally. He not only gave
him back his kingdom, henceforward to be a protected state under
Macedonian suzerainty, but largely increased its borders. This royal
treatment, however, though it pleased the generous impulses of Alexander, was inspired by deep policy. He could rest the security of
his rule beyond the Indus on no better base than the mutual jealousy
of two moderately powerful princes. He had made the lord of
Taxila as powerful as was safe ; the reinstatement of his rival Porus
would be the best guarantee for his loyalty. But on either side of *Alexander's*
the Hydaspes, close to the scene of the battle, two cities were founded, *cities on the*
which would serve as garrisons in the subject land. On the right *Hydaspes.*
hand, the city of Bucephala, named after Alexander's steed, which
died here—probably shortly before the battle—of old age and weariness ; on the left, Nicaea, the city of victory.   *(Mong.)*

Leaving Craterus to build the cities, Alexander marched north- *Alexander's*
wards to subdue the Glausae, a hill-folk on the border of Cashmir, *advance*
and at the same time to intimidate Abisares. Then keeping near *through the*
the skirts of the hills, he crossed the Acesines, more than a mile *Punjab.*
and a half broad, with great peril and some loss, into the territory
of a namesake and nephew of Porus. This Porus was at enmity
with his uncle, who probably claimed overlordship over him ; he
had sent messages of submission to Alexander before the battle ;
but, disappointed and frightened at the favour which the conqueror
had shown his uncle, he fled eastward. Alexander himself hastened
in pursuit, crossing the Hydraotis, which, unlike the Acesines, was *(Ravee.)*
easily passed, but he left Hephaestion to march southward and subdue
the land of the younger Porus, as well as the free communities
between the two rivers,—all this northern portion of the " doab " or
interfluvial tract to be added to the realm of the elder Porus. The
news that the Cathaeans, a free and warlike people, whom Porus
and Abisares had, some time before, failed to conquer, were determined to give him battle, diverted Alexander from the pursuit. He *Capture of*
advanced against their chief town Sangala, strongly walled and pro- *Sangala.*
tected on one side by a hill and on the other by a lake. It was
probably near Amritsar, to the north-west of Lahore. The Cathaeans,
supported by some neighbouring tribes, had made a stockade with a
triple line of waggons round the hill. After a severe struggle the
entrenchment was carried and the defenders retreated into the city.
They tried to escape through the lake under the cover of night, but
Alexander discovered the plan and lined the shores with soldiers.
Then the place was stormed, and slighted ; the neighbouring peoples
submitted ; and all this land was likewise placed under the lordship
of Porus. Thus of the four river-bounded tracts which compose the
Punjab, the largest, between Indus and Jehlum, belonged to Omphis

of Taxila, while the three others, between Jehlum and Bëas, were assigned to Porus.

The term of Alexander's march.

Alexander now advanced to the Hyphasis, or Bëas, and reached it higher up than the point where it joins the Sutlej to form the Çatadru or "Hundred Streams." It was destined to be the landmark of his utmost march. He wished to go farther and explore the lands of the Ganges, but an unlooked-for obstacle occurred. The Macedonians were worn out with years of hard campaigning, and weary of this endless rolling on into the unknown. Their numbers had dwindled; the remnant of them were battered and grown old before their time. The terrible rains which had beaten incessantly upon them since the crossing of the Indus and had made their labours doubly laborious were the last weight in the scale. Their gear was worn out; the hoofs of their horses, as one of the campaigners described, were rubbed away by the long rough journeys; their arms were blunted and broken in hard combats; the bodies of the veterans were enveloped in Indian rags, for their Greek clothes were worn out. All yearned back to their homeland in the west. They had won glory enough; why heap up toil on toil and peril upon peril?

The army refuses to advance.

On the banks of the Hyphasis the crisis came; the men resolved to go no farther, and their resolution was strengthened by the information that they would have to cross the Indian desert, a journey of eleven days, before they reached the fertile regions of the Ganges. At a meeting of the officers which Alexander summoned, Coenus was the spokesman of the general feeling. The king, not a little vexed, dismissed them, and summoning them on the morrow, declared that he purposed to advance himself, but would constrain no man to follow him; let the Macedonians go back to Macedonia and tell how they abandoned their king in a hostile land. He retired to his tent, and for two days refused to see any of his Companions, hoping that their hearts would be softened. But though his resentment made them unhappy, the Macedonians did not relent or go back from their purpose. On the third day, Alexander offered sacrifices preliminary to crossing the river. But the victims— and this was assuredly no freak of chance—gave unfavourable signs. Then the king yielded, and signified to the obdurate army that he had decided to return. When his will was made known, the way-worn veterans burst into wild joy; the more part of them shed tears. They crowded round the royal tent, blessing the unconquered king, that he had permitted himself to be conquered for once, by his Macedonians. On the banks of the Hyphasis Alexander erected twelve towering altars to the twelve great gods of Olympus, as a thank-offering for having strewn his wonderful path with victories and led him safely within reach of the world's end.

Within reach of the world's end, and not to reach it—this was the disappointment which befell Alexander at the Hyphasis. To understand fully the measure of this disappointment we must realise *Alexander's* his geographical conceptions. Of the southern extension of Asia in *conception* the great Indian promontory, and Further India with its huge islands, *of the* he knew nothing ; of the vastness of China, of the existence of Siberia *geography* he had not the least suspicion. He supposed that the Ganges *of Asia.* discharged its waters into the ocean which bounded the earth on the east, as the Atlantic bounded it on the west ; and he imagined that this eastern sea, washing the base of the further slopes of the Hindu-Kush and Pamir mountains, and rounding the northern shores of Scythia, was continuous with the Caspian. And just as he planned to navigate the southern ocean, from the mouth of the Indus to the Arabian Gulf, or perhaps even round Libya to the Pillars of Heracles, —plans of which we shall presently speak,—so he probably dreamed of navigating the eastern ocean from the mouth of the Ganges and winning round to the shores of Scythia and Hyrcania. On annexation or effective conquest beyond the Hyphasis the mind of Alexander does not seem to have been bent. He had only a small army with him, for he had dropped large detachments on his way from the Jehlum to the Bëas ; and he expected no hostilities from the tranquil dwellers of the Ganges. His expedition would have been in the first instance a journey of exploration ; circumstances might have made it a march of conquest.

Alexander is often represented as a madman, dazzled by wild and whirling visions of dominion and glory, impelled by an insatiable lust of conquest for conquest's sake. But in judging his schemes, which in themselves seem wild to us who know the configuration of the earth, we must contract our imagination to the compass of his false notions and imperfect knowledge. If the form and feature of the earth were what he pictured it to be, twenty years would have sufficed to make his empire conterminous with its limits. He might have ruled from the eastern to the western ocean, from the ultimate bounds of Scythia to the shores of Libya ; he might have brought to pass in the three continents an universal peace, and dotted the habitable globe with his Greek cities. Alexander was ambitious, but ambition did not blind him ; he was perfectly capable of discerning shine from substance. The advance to the Indus was no mere wanton aggression, but was necessary to establish secure routes for Indian trade, which was at the mercy of the wild hill-tribes ; and the subjugation of the Punjab was a necessity for securing the Indus frontier. The solid interests of commerce underlay the ambitions of the Macedonian conqueror. It is not without significance that Phoenician merchants accompanied his army.

Alexander retraced his steps to the Hydaspes, on his way picking up Hephaestion, who had founded a new city on the banks of the Acesines. On the Hydaspes, Craterus had not only built the two cities at the scene of the great battle, but had also prepared a large fleet of transports, which was to carry part of the army down the river to reach the Indus and the ocean. The fleet was placed under the command of Nearchus, and the king's own ship was piloted by Onesicritus, who afterwards wrote a book on Alexander's expedition. The rest of the army, divided into two parts, marched along either bank, under Hephaestion and Craterus.

As they advanced they swept the southern portions of the doabs, reducing the tribes which did not submit. The only formidable resistance that they encountered was from the free and warlike tribe of the Malli, whose territory stretched on both sides of the Ravee. Having routed a large host of these Indians on the southern bank of the river, Alexander pursued them to their chief city, Sangala, whose site has not yet been identified. Since then the Ravee has changed its bed ; in the days of Alexander it used to flow into the Chenab below Multan. Here he met with a grave adventure. The city had been easily taken, and the Indians had retreated into the *Siege of* citadel. Two ladders were brought to scale the earthen wall, but *Sangala.* it was found hard to place them beneath the shower of missiles from above. Impatient at the delay, Alexander seized a ladder and climbed up under the cover of his shield. Peucestas, who bore the sacred buckler from the temple of Ilion, and Leonnatus followed, and Abreas ascended the other ladder. When the king reached the battlement, he hurled down or slew the Indians who were posted at that spot. The hypaspists, when they saw their king standing upon the wall, a mark for the whole garrison of the fortress, made a rush for the ladders, and both ladders broke under the weight of the crowd. Only those three—Peucestas, Leonnatus, and Abreas— reached the wall before the ladders broke. His friends implored Alexander to leap down ; he answered their cries by leaping down among the enemy. He alighted on his feet. With his back to the wall he stood alone against the throng of foes, who recognised the Great King. With his sword he cut down their leader and some others who ventured to rush at him ; he felled two more with stones ; and the rest, not daring to approach, pelted him with missiles. Meanwhile his three companions had cleared the wall of its defenders and leapt down to help their king. Abreas fell slain by a dart. Then *Alexander* Alexander himself received a wound in the breast. For a space he *wounded.* stood and fought, but at last sank on his shield fainting through loss of blood. Peucestas stood over him with the holy shield of Troy, Leonnatus guarded him on the other side, until rescue came. Having no ladders, the Macedonians had driven pegs into the wall, and a few had clambered up as best they could and flung themselves down into the fray. Some of these succeeded in opening one of the gates, and then the fort was taken. No man, woman, or child in the place was spared by the infuriated soldiers, who thought that their king was dead. But though the wound was grave, Alexander recovered. The rumour of his death reached the camp where the main army was waiting at the junction of the Ravee with the Chenab, and it produced deep consternation and despair. Reassuring letters were not believed ; so Alexander caused himself to be carried to the banks of the Ravee and conveyed by water down to the camp. When he drew near, the canopy which sheltered his bed in the stern of the vessel was removed. The soldiers, still doubting, thought it was his corpse they saw, until the barque drew close to the bank and he waved his hand. Then the host shouted for joy. When he was carried ashore, he was lifted for a moment on horseback, that he might be the better seen of all ; and then he walked a few steps for their greater reassurance.

This adventure is an extreme case of Alexander's besetting *Alexander's* weakness, which has been illustrated in many other of his actions. *rashness in* In the excitement of battle, amid the ring of arms, he was apt to *endanger-* forget his duties as a leader. Though one of the most consummate *ing his person.* generals that the world has seen, he took a far keener delight in fighting in the thickest of the fray, or heading a charge of cavalry, than in manœuvring an army or contriving strategical operations. His eyes and ears were ever filled

With the brilliance of battle, the bloom and the beauty, the splendour of
    spears.

He could not resist the temptations of danger, and he had hardly conducted a single campaign in which he had not been wounded. On the last and most flagrant occasion, when some of his intimate friends upbraided him for acting as a soldier instead of acting as a general, he was deeply hurt ; for his conscience pricked him. To have endangered his own safety was a crime against the whole army.

The Malli made a complete submission, and their example was 325 *B.C.* followed by the Oxydraces, their southern neighbours, who were also renowned for their warlike character. These lower parts of the Punjab were not added to the dominion of Porus, but were placed in direct dependence on the satrapy which had been committed to Philip. When Alexander had recovered from his wound, the fleet sailed downward past the junction of the Hyphasis, and the Indian tribes submitted, presenting to the conqueror the characteristic

products of India, gems, fine draperies, tame lions and tigers.
(The Panj- At the place where the united stream of the four lesser rivers joins
nab.) the mighty flow of the Indus, the foundations were laid of a new
Alexandria Alexandria, to be the great trade centre between the Punjab and the
(Uchh). territory of the lower Indus, and to be the bulwark of the southern
Foundation of Sogdian* frontier of the province of Philip. The next stage of the southward
Alexandria advance was the capital town of the Sogdi, which lay upon the river.
(? Alor, or, Alexander refounded it as a Greek colony, and built wharfs ; it was
higher up, known as the Sogdian Alexandria and was destined to be the
Sirwahi). residence of a southern satrapy which was to extend to the sea-
coast. This province was committed to Peithon, the son of
Agenor.

The principalities of the rich and populous land of Sind were
distinguished from the states of the north by the great political
power enjoyed by the Brahmans. Under the influence of this
caste, which was vehemently opposed to the intrusion of the outlanders, the princes either defied Alexander or, if they submitted
at first, speedily rebelled. The spring was spent in reducing these
regions, and it was nearly midsummer when the king reached
Patala Patala at the vertex of the Indus delta. On the tidings of an
(Hydera- insurrection in Arachosia, he had dispatched Craterus with a con-
bad). siderable portion of the army to march through the Bolan Pass into
southern Afghanistan and put down the revolt. Alexander himself
designed to march through Baluchistan, and Craterus was ordered
to meet him in Kirman, near the entrance of the Persian Gulf.
Another division of the host was to go by sea to the mouth of the
Tigris. The king fixed upon Patala to be for the Indian empire
what the most famous of his Alexandrias was for Egypt. He charged
Hephaestion with the task of fortifying the citadel and building an
ample harbour. Then he sailed southward himself to visit the
southern ocean. It was the season at which the monsoons blow
from the south-west, and the Macedonians, accustomed to the tideless
midland sea, were at first sorely perplexed by the ebb and flow of
the oceanic tide, at this time especially high and violent in the main
Alexander arm of the river. Several ships were lost, but the sailors soon
sails in mastered the secret of the times and tides, and Alexander fared out
the Indian into the open sea. He sacrificed to Poseidon ; he poured drink-
Ocean. offerings from a golden cup to the Nereids and Dioscuri, and to
Thetis the mother of his ancestor Achilles, and then hurled the cup
into the waves. This ceremony inaugurated his plan of opening a seaway for commerce between the West and the Far East. The enterprise
of discovering this seaway was entrusted to Nearchus, an officer who
was an intimate companion of his own and possessed the confidence
of the troops. Alexander started on his land-march in the early

autumn, but Nearchus and the fleet were to wait till October, in order to be helped forward by the eastern monsoons.

FIG. 202.—Coin of Alexander.   Obverse : head of Heracles, in lion s skin. Reverse : eagle - bearing Zeus, and prow of galley in field [legend : ΑΛΕΞΑΝΔΡΟΥ].

SECT. 3. ALEXANDER'S RETURN TO BABYLON

No enterprise of Alexander was so useless, and none so fatal, as the journey through the desert of Gedrosia, the land which is now known as the Mekran.   Of the inhospitable character of the country he must have had general information, but he had no idea of the hardships and terrors of the march which awaited him.   His guiding motive in choosing this route was to make provisions for the safety of the fleet, to dig wells and store food at certain places along the coast.   He also had in view the subjugation of the Oritae, a hardy warlike people who dwelled in the mountains on the eastern limit of the wilderness.   But if it had been only a matter of subduing the Orites, this could easily have been accomplished by an expedition from Patala.   The march through the Mekran and the voyage of Nearchus were interdependent parts of the same adventure ; and so timid were the mariners of those days that the voyage into unknown waters seemed far more formidable than the journey through the waste.

With perhaps thirty thousand men, Alexander passed the *March of* mountain wall which protects the Indus delta, and crossing the river *Alexander through the* Arbis, he reduced the Oritae to subjection.   He chose their chief *Mekran* village Rambacia for the foundation of a colony, the Orite Alexandria ; *(August,* it was important to have stations on his projected ocean-route.   Then *Sept., Oct.),* he descended into the waste of Gedrosia.   No resistance met him *325 B.C.* here, for there was no folk to resent his intrusion ; only a few miserable villages in the hills, or more miserable fishing hamlets on the coast.   The army moved painfully through the desert of rocks and sand, waterless and barren ; and part of the scanty provisions that the foragers obtained had to be stored on the shore for the coming of the fleet. It was often almost impossible to step through the deep sinking sand; the pitiless heat rendered night marches necessary; and those marches were frequently of undue length, owing to the need of reaching a spring of water. Alexander himself is said to have trudged on foot and shared all the hardships of the way. It was doubtless the non-combatants and camp-followers who suffered most. At length the waste was crossed; and, leaving the coast regions, the remnant of the army marched north to Pura, the residence of the satrapy of Gedrosia. It is said that the survivors, exhausted and dishevelled, were the smaller part of the army which had set forth from India two months before; and the losses of that terrible Gedrosian journey exceeded the losses of all Alexander's campaigns. But this is probably a heightened statement of the calamities of the march.

The voyage of Nearchus, Oct.-Dec. 325 B.C.

(? Karachi.)

Having rested at Pura, the king proceeded to Kirman, where he was joined by Craterus, who had suppressed the revolt in Arachosia. Presently news arrived that the fleet had reached the Kirman coast, and soon Nearchus arrived at the camp and relieved Alexander's anxiety. He too had a tale to tell of hardships and perils. The hostile attitude of the Indians, when Alexander's back was turned, had forced him to start a month before the season of the east winds; and contrary south winds kept him for twenty-four days in a haven at some distance to the west of the delta. Then a storm wrecked three of his ships near Cocala. During the rest of their voyage the seafarers were sore bestead by want of sweet water and provisions. But the king was overjoyed that they had arrived at all. Nearchus was dismissed to complete the voyage by sailing up the Persian Gulf and the Pasitigris river to Susa; Hephaestion was sent to make his way thither along the coast; while Alexander himself marched through the hills by Persepolis and Pasargadae.

Misconduct of Alexander's governors, and his dealings with them.

It was high time for Alexander to return. There was hardly a satrap, Persian or Macedonian, in any land, who had not oppressed his province by violence and rapacity; and some, in the expectation that the king would never come back from the Far East, had formed plots for establishing independent principalities. In Kirman, in Persis, and at Susa, the most pressing business of the king was to re-establish his authority by punishing without favour or mercy the governors and officers who were found guilty of treason and oppression. Many satraps were deposed or put to death; Atropates of Media was one of the few who had been faithful to his charge. But the military garrison of Media had not behaved so well; and none of Alexander's dooms at this juncture was more effective than the execution of two officers and six hundred soldiers for having plundered the temples and sepulchres of that province. Of all evil deeds, that perhaps which most vexed the king was the opening and plundering of the sepulchre of Cyrus at Pasargadae; it was more than a common sacrilege, it was an outrage against the majesty of kings. He tortured the Magians who were the guardians of the tomb, but did not discover the author of the outrage.

One guilty minister fled at Alexander's approach. This was *Flight of* Harpalus, who had once before been disloyal but had been forgiven *Harpalus.* and placed in charge of the financial administration of the empire. He squandered his master's money in riotous living at Babylon, and as the news of these scandals reached Alexander in India, he deemed it prudent to move westward. Taking a large sum of money, he went to Cilicia, and hiring a bodyguard of 6000 mercenaries, he lived in royal state at Tarsus with Glycera, an Athenian courtesan. On Alexander's return, Tarsus was not safe, and he fled to Greece, where we shall meet him presently.

Having punished with a stern hand the misrule of his satraps, *Alexander's* Macedonian and Persian alike, Alexander began to carry out *policy:* schemes which he had formed for breaking down the barrier which *the fusion* divides the East from the West. He had unbarred and unveiled the *of Greeks* Orient to the knowledge and commerce of the Mediterranean peoples, *Asiatics;* but his aim was to do much more than this; it was no less than to fuse Asia and Europe into a homogeneous unity. He devised various means for compassing this object. He proposed to transplant *means for* Greeks and Macedonians into Asia, and Asiatics into Europe, as *accomplish-* permanent settlers. This plan had indeed been partly realised by *ing this:* the foundation of his numerous mixed cities in the Far East. The *(1) trans-* second means was the promotion of intermarriages between Persians *and colon-* and Macedonians, and this policy was inaugurated in magnificent *isation;* fashion at Susa. The king himself espoused Statira, the daughter *(2) inter-* of Darius; his friend Hephaestion took her sister; and a large *marriage;* number of Macedonian officers wedded the daughters of Persian grandees. The nuptials were celebrated on the same day and according to the Persian fashion; Alexander is said to have feasted 9000 guests. Of the general mass of the Macedonians 10,000 are said to have followed the example of their officers and taken Asiatic wives; all those were liberally rewarded by Alexander. He looked forward to the offspring of these unions as a potent instrument for the further fusing of the races. It is to be noticed that Alexander, already wedded to the princess of Sogdiana, adopted the polygamous custom of Persia; and he even married another royal lady, Parysatis, daughter of Ochus. These marriages were purely dictated by policy; they were meant as an example; for Alexander never came under the influence of women. The bridals of Susa were a lesson in political marriages on a vast scale.

(3) *equal military service.*

But the most effective means for bringing the two races together was the institution of military service on a perfect equality. With this purpose in view, Alexander, not long after the death of Darius, had arranged that in all the eastern provinces the native youth should be drilled and disciplined in Macedonian fashion and taught to use the Macedonian weapons. In fact, Hellenic military schools were established in every province, and at the end of five years an army of 30,000 Hellenized barbarians was at the Great King's disposition. At his summons this army gathered at Susa, and its arrival created a natural, though unreasonable, feeling of discontent among the Macedonians, who divined that Alexander aimed at making himself independent of their services. His schemes of transforming the character of his army were also indicated by the enlistment of Persians, Bactrians, Areians, and other orientals in the Macedonian cavalry regiments, and the enrolling of nine distinguished Persians in the royal Agema itself. The general dissatisfaction was not allayed by the king's liberality in defraying all the debts of the soldiers—amounting perhaps to two millions.

Alexander left Susa for Ecbatana in spring. He sailed down the river Pasitigris to the Persian Gulf, surveyed part of the coast, and sailed up the Tigris, removing the weirs which the Persians had constructed to hinder navigation. The army joined him on the way, *Macedonian* and he halted at Opis. Here he held an assembly of the Macedonians, *mutiny* and formally discharged all those—about 10,000 in number—whom *at Opis.* old age or wounds had rendered unfit for warfare, promising to make them comfortable for life. He fondly thought that his words would be welcomed with delight, but he was disappointed. The smouldering discontent found a voice now. The cry was raised, "Discharge us all"; and some tauntingly added, "Go and conquer with your father Ammon." The king may well have been taken aback. The men who on the banks of the Hyphasis had declared themselves worn out with war and toil and sick with yearning for their homes, were now indignant when he honourably discharged their veterans. Alexander leapt down from the platform into the shouting throng; he pointed out thirteen of the most forward rioters, and bade his hypaspists seize them and put them to death. The rest were cowed. Amid a deep silence the king remounted the platform, and in a bitter speech he discharged the whole army. Then he retired into his palace, and on the third day summoned the Persian and Median nobles and appointed them to posts of honour and trust which had hitherto been filled by Macedonians. The names of the Macedonian regiments were transferred to the new barbarian army. When they heard this, the Macedonians, who still lingered in their quarters, miserable and uncertain whether to go or stay, appeared before the gates of the palace. They laid down their arms submissively and implored admission to the king's presence. Alexander came out, and there was a tearful reconciliation, which was sealed by sacrifices and feasts. This dramatic incident possesses no historical importance like the action of the troops on the Hyphasis, and it is only significant in so far as it marks the last futile explosion of Macedonian sentiment against the liberal policy of the king, the final protest of men who knew that they would have to acquiesce in a new order of things.

The veterans started for home under the leadership of Craterus *Veterans* and Polyperchon ; they left behind the children whom Asiatic women *sent back to* had borne to them, the king promising to bring them up in Macedonian *Macedonia.* fashion. Craterus was to supersede Antipater as regent of Macedonia, and Antipater was to come out to Asia with a fresh supply of troops. This arrangement was desirable, on account of the estranged relations which existed between Antipater and the queen-mother, whose letters to Alexander were always teeming with mutual accusations.

The summer and early winter were spent at the Median capital. *Alexander* Here a sorrow, the greatest that could befall him, befell Alexander. *at Ecba-* Three thousand professional players or " Dionysiac artists," as they *tana.* were called, had arrived from Greece ; and Ecbatana was festive with revels and dramatic exhibitions. In the midst of the gaiety, *Death of* Hephaestion fell ill, languished for seven days, and died. Alexander *Hephaes-* was plunged into despair at losing the friend of his bosom ; he fasted *tion ; Alex-* three days, and the whole empire went into mourning ; it is said that *ander's* *grief.* he crucified the miserable physician whose skill had been found wanting. Inconsolable the lonely monarch might well be. He could have other boon companions, other faithful counsellors and devoted servants ; but he knew that he would never find another to whom he would be simply " my friend Alexander " and not " my lord the king." The body was sent to Babylon to be burned ; 10,000 talents were set apart for a funeral of unsurpassed magnificence.

Alexander set out for Babylon towards the end of the year, and *Subjuga-* on his way he enjoyed the excitement of hunting down the Cossaeans, *tion of the* a hill-folk of Luristan, who made brigandage their trade. The slaughter *Cossaeans,* *winter,* of these robbers, who were chased to their mountain nests, was *324-3 B.C.* described as an offering to the spirit of Hephaestion. [As Alexander *The em-* advanced to Babylon, ambassadors came to him from Libya, from the *bassies* Lucanians and Bruttians of south Italy who feared vengeance for the *from the* *west and* death of Alexander of Epirus, his brother-in-law, and from the Etrus- *south.* cans. These embassies are attested by Arrian from a good source. He also adds the story (from inferior authorities) that Carthaginians also came and envoys from the Aethiopians, Scythians of Europe, Celts and Iberians. They brought their differences to Alexander : " then espe- cially did he appear to be lord of the whole earth and sea." Certain

Greek writers even included Rome in the list : "when Alexander saw the bearing, the endurance and the free spirit of the Romans and learnt about their form of government, he prophesied something of their future greatness." Rome, preoccupied with wars in Italy, can have sent no mission to Alexander. The invention is due to Greek flattery.]

Arrival at Babylon. The warning of the Chaldeans ; and the temple of Bel. When Alexander approached within sight of Babylon, he was met by a deputation of priestly star-gazers who counselled him not to enter the city, for their god Bel had revealed to them that it would not be for his profit. He replied to the Chaldaeans with a verse of Euripides—" The best seer he who guesseth well," and entered at the head of his army. One of his first cares was to take measures for the rebuilding of the temple of Bel, unduly retarded by the wilful neglect of the Chaldaean priests, who were unwilling to appropriate their revenues to the purpose. It has been thought that their attempt to divert the king from entering Babylon may have had a motive connected with their negligence.

SECT. 4. PREPARATIONS FOR AN ARABIAN EXPEDITION. ALEXANDER'S DEATH

Alexander's designs on Arabia ; Ever since the successful voyage of Nearchus, the brain of Alexander was filled with maritime enterprises. He was bent on the exploration of the northern and the southern oceans. He had already sent Heraclides and a company of shipwrights to the Hyrcanian mountains, to cut wood in the forests and build a fleet to navigate the Caspian Sea and discover its supposed communication with the eastern ocean. But his more immediate and serious enterprise was the circumnavigation and conquest of Arabia. His eastern empire was not complete so long as this peninsula lay outside it. He knew of the rich spice-lands of Arabia Felix, but he had no conception of the vast extent of the desert which renders a land invasion so difficult and so unremunerative. The possession of this country of sand, however, was not his main object ; it was only an incident in the grand range of his plans. His visit to India and the voyage of Nearchus had given him new ideas ; he had risen to the conception of making the southern ocean another great commercial sea like the Mediterranean. He proposed to make the seaboard of the Persian Gulf a second Phoenicia, and he sent to the Syrian coast for seamen to colonise the shores of the mainland and the islands. He hoped to establish a regular trade route from the Indus to the Tigris and Euphrates, and thence to the canals which connected the Nile with the Red Sea. If he had lived to accomplish this he might have renewed the project of king Necho and hewn a water-way through the neck of Suez. Mighty Babylon would then

be in close connexion with the new oceanic trade ; argosies from
Alexandria or Patala could sail into her wharves.   Alexander destined
Babylon to be the capital of his empire, and doubtless it was a wise
choice.   But its character was now to be transformed.   It was to
become a naval station and a centre of maritime commerce.   Alexander
set about the digging of a great harbour, with room for a thousand
keels, and designed the building of shipsteads.

The fleet of Nearchus sailed up the Euphrates and met the king *his pre-*
at Babylon.   But this fleet was not sufficient for the approaching *parations,*
enterprise.   Orders had been sent to Phoenicia for the building of
new warships : twelve triremes, three quadriremes, four quinqueremes,
and thirty of the smaller thirty-oared barques.   These were constructed
in pieces, conveyed overland to Thapsacus on Euphrates, and there put
together.   Other ships, of cypress wood, were also built in Babylonia.
The expedition was to set forth in the summer, and the king occupied
part of the intervening time in a voyage down the Euphrates to visit *his voyage*
the Pallacopas canal.   The snows of winter melting in the late spring- *to the*
tide on the north slopes of the Armenian mountains used to swell the *Babylonian*
waters of the Euphrates and force it to overflow its banks in the *marshes.*
Babylonian plain.   About ninety miles below Babylon a canal had been
dug to drain the superfluous waters into the marshes which stretched
for leagues and leagues south-westward.   In the autumn the canal
was closed by a sluice to prevent the water leaving its bed.   But the
sluice was out of working order, and Alexander devised a better
place, connecting the canal with the river at a different point.   He
sailed up the canal, lost his way for a while among the swamps, and
selected a site for a new city, whose building was immediately begun.
We may guess that the city was meant to be the first of a string of
fortresses stretching across the desert from Babylonia to the Red Sea.

On his return to Babylon, he found some new western troops
which had arrived from Caria and Lydia, and also a body of 20,000
Persians who had been recruited by Peucestas.   He proceeded to *Reform*
carry out a sweeping military reform, at which his mind must have *of the*
been working for some time past.   It was nothing less than a com- *phalanx.*
plete transformation of his father's phalanx,—in fact, of the Hellenic
hoplite system.   Alexander had done much with the well-drilled
phalanx ; but his experience had taught him that it was far from
being the ideal infantry.   The advantages of its sheer weight and
solid strength were more than counterbalanced by its want of
mobility.   Alexander invented a means of increasing the mobility
with as little as possible diminution of the weight.   He inserted the
fresh body of 20,000 Persians into the Macedonian phalanx in the
following way.   The old depth of the file, namely sixteen men,
was retained, but of these only four were Macedonian pikemen—

the men of the first three ranks and the hindmost man of all. The twelve intervening places—the fourth to the fifteenth ranks— were filled by Persians lightly armed with their native bows and javelins. This new phalanx required a new kind of tactics, which must have consisted in opening out the ranks, so as to allow the archers and javelin-men to deploy into the intervals and discharge their missiles, and then closing up again, in order to advance in a serried mass, each file bristling with three, no longer with five, spear-points. It was a thoroughly original idea, this combination of heavy and light troops into a tactical unity ; but it would need all the skill of the great master to bring it to perfection. The strange thing is to find Alexander introducing this new system, which implied a complete change in the drill, on the very eve of his setting forth on the Arabian expedition. We are tempted to think that he had already made experiments—perhaps with that army of 30,000 orientals, drilled in Macedonian fashion, who had come to him at Susa. The tactical reform had also its political bearings. It was another step in the direction of fusing the Macedonian and Persian together, and marrying Europe with Asia.

Funeral of Hephaestion, May 323 B.C. There was one thing, very near to the king's heart, still to be accomplished before he set out—the funeral of Hephaestion. The oracle of Ammon had been consulted touching the honours which should be paid to the dead man, and had ordained that he might be honoured as a hero. In accordance therewith, Alexander ordered that chapels should be erected to Hephaestion in Egyptian Alexandria and other cities. Never were obsequies so magnificent as those which were held at Babylon ; the funeral pyre, splendidly decked with offerings, towered to the height of 200 feet.

Illness of Alexander, 16th day of Daesius (June 1?) ; All was in readiness at length for the expedition to the south. On a day in early June a royal banquet was given in honour of Nearchus and his seamen, shortly about to start on their oceanic voyage. As Alexander was retiring to his chamber at a late hour, a friend named Medius carried him off to spend the rest of the night *17th ;* in a bout of hard drinking. On the morrow he slept long ; in the evening he dined with Medius, and another carousal followed. After *18th ;* a bath and a meal in the early hours of the morning, he fell into a feverish sleep. On awaking, he insisted upon preparing the daily sacri- fices according to his wont; but the fever was still on him, he could not walk, and was carried to the altar on a couch. He spent the day in bed, actively engaged with Nearchus in discussing the expedition, which he fixed for four days hence. In the cool of the evening he was con- veyed to the river and rowed across to a garden villa at the other *19th-24th ;* side. For six days he lay here in high fever, but regularly perform- ing the sacrifices, and daily perforce deferring the departure of the

expedition for another and yet another day.   Then his condition grew *25th ;*
worse, and he was carried back to the palace, where he won a little
sleep, but the fever did not abate.   When his officers came to him
they found him speechless ; the disease became more violent, and a
rumour spread among the Macedonian soldiers that Alexander was
dead.   They rushed clamouring to the door of the palace, and the
bodyguards were forced to admit them.   One by one they filed past *27th.*
the bed of their young king, but he could not speak to them ; he
could only greet each by slightly raising his head and signing with
his eyes.   Peucestas and some others of the Companions passed the
night in the temple of Serapis and asked the god whether they should
convey the sick man into the temple, if haply he might be cured there
by divine help.   A voice warned them not to bring him, but to let
him remain where he lay.   He died on a June evening, before the *Death of*
thirty-third year of his age was fully told.   Such is the punctilious *Alexander,*
and authentic account of the last illness of Alexander, as it was re- *28th of*
Daesius
corded in the Court Diary ; but it is not sufficient to enable us to dis- *(= June*
cover the precise nature of the fatal disease. *13).*

The untimely deaths of sovereigns at particular junctures have *His work*
often exercised an appreciable influence on the course of events ; but *and what*
no such accident has diverted the paths of history so manifestly and *he might*
have done.
utterly as the death of Alexander.   Twelve years had sufficed him to
conquer western Asia, and to leave an impress upon it which centuries
would not obliterate.   And yet his work had only been begun.
Many plans for the political transformation of his Asiatic empire had
been initiated,—plans which reveal his originality of conception, his
breadth of grasp, his firm hold of facts, his faculty for organisation,
his wonderful brain-power,—but all these schemes and lines of policy
needed still many years of development under the master's shaping
and guiding hand.   The unity of the realm, which was an essential
part of Alexander's conception, disappeared upon his death.   The
empire was broken up among a number of hard-headed Macedonians,
capable and practical rulers, but without the higher qualities of the
founder's genius.   They maintained the tolerant Hellenism which he
had initiated,—his lessons had not been lost upon them ; and thus
his work was not futile ; the toils of even those twelve marvellous
years smoothed the path for Roman sway in the East, and prepared
the ground for the spread of an universal religion.

It is impossible to write the history of Alexander so as to produce
a true impression of his work, because, in the records which we have,
the general and soldier fills the whole stage and the statesman is, as
it were, hustled out.   The details of administrative organisation are
lost amidst the sounding of trumpets and the clashing of spears.   But
it is the details of administration and political organisation which the

historical inquirer craves to know, and especially the constitution of the various new-founded cities in the Far East, those novel experiments which set Macedonian, Greek, and oriental inhabitants side by side. By their silence on these matters the Companions of Alexander, who wrote memoirs about him, unwittingly did him a wrong, and hence there has largely prevailed an unjust notion that he only knew and only cared how to conquer.

Pyrrhus.) It is hardly open to question that this brilliant lord of well-trained myriads would have advanced to the conquest of the West ; nor can we affect to doubt that, succeeding where one of his successors failed, he would have annexed Sicily and Great Hellas, conquered Carthage, and overrun the Italian peninsula. To apprehend what his death meant for Europe we need not travel farther in our speculations. To the Indies he would certainly have returned and carried out with fresh troops that project of visiting the valley of the Ganges which had been frustrated by his weary army. As it was, he had left no lasting impression upon Indian civilisation ; and his successors soon abandoned their hold upon the Punjab. It is needless to add that if Alexander had lived another quarter of a century, he would have widened the limits of geographical knowledge. The true nature of the Caspian Sea would have been determined ; the southern extension of the Indian peninsula would have been discovered ; and an attempt would have been made to repeat the Phoenician circumnavigation of Africa. Nor could Alexander have failed, in his advanced position on the Jaxartes, to have learned some facts about the vast extension of the Asiatic continent to the east and north, and the curiosities of Chinese civilisation.

His sudden death was no freak of fate or fortune ; it was a natural consequence of his character and his deeds. Into thirteen years he had compressed the energies of many lifetimes. If he had been content with the duties of a general and a statesman, laborious and wearing though those duties would have been both to body and to brain, his singularly strong constitution would probably have lasted him for many a long year. But the very qualities of his brilliant temper which most endeared him to his fellows, a warrior's valour and a love of good fellowship, were ruinous to his health. He was covered with scars ; and he had probably never recovered from that terrible wound which had been the price of his escapade at Multan. Sparing of himself neither in battle nor at the symposion, he was doomed to die young.

SECT. 5. GREECE UNDER MACEDONIA

The tide of the world's history swept us away from the shores of Greece ; and, borne breathlessly along from conquest to conquest in the triumphant train of the Macedonian, we could not pause to see what was happening in the little states which were looking with mixed emotions at the spectacle of their own civilisation making its way over the earth. Alexander's victory at the gates of Issus and his ensuing supremacy by sea had taught many of the Greeks the lesson of caution ; the Confederacy of the Isthmus had sent congratulations and a golden crown to the conqueror ; and when, a twelvemonth later, the Spartan king Agis, a resolute man without any military ability, renewed the war against Macedonia, he got no help or countenance outside the Peloponnesus. Some hot spirits at Athens proposed to support the movement, but the people were discreetly restrained not only by Phocion and Demades but by Demosthenes himself. Agis induced the Arcadians, except Megalopolis, the Achaeans, except Pellene, and the Eleians, to join him ; and having mercenary troops besides, he got together a considerable army. It was easy to gain a few successes, before the regent of Macedonia, then occupied with a rising in Thrace, had time to descend on the Peloponnesus. The chief object of the allies was to capture Megalo- *Battle of* polis, and the federal capital of Arcadia was in the strange position of *Megalo-* being besieged by the Arcadian federates. Antipater, as soon as the *polis,* situation in Thrace set him free, marched southward to the relief of *331 B.C.* Megalopolis, and easily crushed the allies in a battle fought hard by. Agis fell fighting, and there was no further resistance ; Sparta sent up hostages to Alexander, who accorded the conquered Greeks easy terms.

So long as Darius lived, many of the Greeks cherished secret hopes that fortune might yet turn against Alexander, and maintained clandestine intrigues with Persia. But on the news of his death such hopes expired, and tranquillity prevailed in Hellas. It was not till Alexander's return from India that anything happened to trouble the peace. And in the meantime Greece was experiencing a relief which she had needed for two generations. A field had been opened to her superfluous children, who were pouring by thousands, or rather tens of thousands, into Asia, to find careers, if not permanent homes.

For Athens the twelve years between the fall of Thebes and the *Athens.* death of Alexander were an interval of singular well-being. The conduct of public affairs was in the hands of the two most honourable statesmen of the day, Phocion and Lycurgus. Supported by the

Attitude of Demosthenes. orator Demades, Phocion was able to dissuade the people from embarking in any foolhardy enterprises; and Demosthenes was sufficiently clear-sighted not to embarrass, but, when needful, to support, the policy of peace. Phocion probably did not grudge him the signal triumph which he won over his old rival, Aeschines; for this triumph had only a personal, and not a political, significance. Shortly before Philip's death, Ctesiphon had proposed to honour Demosthenes, both for his general services to the state and especially for his liberality in contributing from his private purse towards the repair of the city-walls, by crowning him publicly in the theatre with a crown of gold. The Council had passed a resolution to this effect; but Aeschines lodged an accusation against the proposer, whose motion technically exposed him to the Graphe Paranomon, and consequently the Council's resolution was not brought before the people. The matter remained in abeyance for about six years, neither party venturing to bring it to an issue, Aeschines by following up his indictment or Ctesiphon by forcing him to bring it into court. The collapse of the attempt of Agis to defy Macedonia probably encouraged Aeschines to face his rival at last. In a speech of the highest ability Aeschines reviewed the public career of Demosthenes, to prove that he was a traitor and responsible for all the disasters of Athens. The reply of Demosthenes, a masterpiece of splendid oratory, captivated the judges; and Aeschines, not winning one-fifth part of their votes, left Athens and disappeared from politics. It is not unfair to say that it was Demosthenes the orator, not Demosthenes the statesman, who convinced the Athenian judges. Apart from his Speech on the Crown, which has been described as the funeral oration on Greek freedom, Demosthenes fell almost silent during these years; he saw that public action on his part would be useless; but perhaps he worked underground.

Speeches on the Crown, 330 B.C.

Aeschines on the strange events of his time. In these two speeches in the matter of the crown, the most interesting passage is where Aeschines reflects on the changes which had recently come to pass over the face of the earth. We want to know what the Greeks thought of those startling changes, what they felt as they saw the fashion of the world passing and the things which had seemed of great weight and worth in Hellas becoming of small account. Aeschines thus utters their surprise :—

" All manner of strange events, utterly unforeseen, have befallen in our lifetime. Our extraordinary experiences will seem to those who come after us like a curious tale of marvels. The king of the Persians, who dug the canal through Athos, who bridged the Hellespont, who demanded earth and water from the Greeks, who dared in his letters to declare, 'I am the lord of all the world from the rising to the setting of the sun,' is at this moment struggling

not for domination over other men, but to save his own life and
limb.   Thebes, even Thebes our neighbour, has been snatched, in
the space of a single day, out of the midst of Hellas—justly, for her
policy was false ; but assuredly she was rather blinded by a heaven-
sent infatuation than misled by human perversity.   And the poor
Lacedaemonians, who once lifted themselves up to be leaders of the
Greeks, must now go up to Alexander as hostages and throw themselves upon the mercy of the potentate whom they wronged.   Our
own city, once the asylum of the Greek world, whither all men looked
for help, has now ceased to strive for the leadership of the Greeks,
for the very ground of her home is in danger."

The Macedonian empire had not yet lasted long enough to turn *Athenian*
the traffic of the Mediterranean into new channels, and Athens still *activity in*
enjoyed great commercial prosperity.   She sent a colony to some *the west.*
unknown place on the Hadriatic seaboard, to be a base of protection
against the Etruscan rovers, the big menacing eyes of whose pirate
crafts were a constant terror to traders in those seas.   And although
peace was her professed policy, she did not neglect to make provision for war, in case a favourable opportunity should come round,
in the revolution of circumstance, for regaining her sovereignty on
sea.   Money was spent on the navy, which is said to have been
increased to well-nigh 400 galleys, and on new ship-sheds.   The *Skeuotheke*
handsome "marble storehouse for the hanging shipgear," designed *of Philo.*
by the architect Philo, was completed at the harbour of Zea.   It was
expressly provided that the cases which lined the walls and pillars of
this cool triple-aisled arcade should be open, "in order that those
who pass through may be able to see all the gear that is in the gear-
store."

The man who was mainly responsible for this naval expenditure *Financial*
was Lycurgus.   It is significant of the spirit of Athens at this time *ministry*
that while Phocion and Demades were the most influential men *of Lycur-*
in the Assembly, the finances were in the charge of a statesman *gus.*
who had been so signally hostile to Macedonia that Alexander had
demanded his surrender.   In recent years considerable changes had
been made in the constitution of the financial offices.   Eubulus had
administered as the president of the Theoric Fund.   But now we
find the control of the expenditure in the hands of a Minister of the
Public Revenue, who was elected by the people and held office for
four years, from one Panathenaic festival to another.   Lycurgus was *338-326*
entrusted with this post for twelve years ; for the first period in his *B.C.*
own name ; for the two succeeding periods his activity was cloaked
under the names of his son and another nominal minister.   He
acted, of course, in conjunction with the Council, but the influence of
the more permanent and experienced minister upon that annual body

2 E

was inevitably very great. The new system, it is evident, was a distinct improvement on the old. It was much better that the administration of the revenue should be managed by one competent statesman, unhampered by colleagues, and that his tenure of office should not be limited to a year. The post practically included the functions of a minister of public works, and the ministry of Lycurgus *The stadion; the gymnasium at the temple of Apollo Lyceus;* was distinguished by building enterprises. He constructed the Panathenaic stadion on the southern bank of the Ilisus. He rebuilt the Lycean gymnasium, where in these years the philosopher Aristotle used to take his morning and evening "walks," teaching his "peripatetic" disciples. It lay somewhere to the east of the city, under Mount Lycabettus. But the most memorable work of Lycurgus was the reconstruction of the theatre of Dionysus. It was *theatre;* he who built the rows of marble benches, climbing up the steep side of the Acropolis, as we see them to-day ; and his original stage-buildings can be distinguished, amidst the ruins, from the mass of *canonical copies of the tragic poets.* later additions and improvements. He canonised, as it were, the three great tragic poets, Aeschylus, Sophocles, and Euripides, by setting up their statues in the theatre, and by carrying a measure that copies of their works should be officially prepared and preserved by the state.

Working of the Laurion silver mines. In connexion with the prosperity of Athens and her large public outlay, it is important to observe that the silver mines of Laurion, which had been closed when the Spartans occupied Decelea and had been neglected—for want of capital and enterprise—throughout the whole first half of the fourth century, had been reopened and were working vigorously. They seem to have been managed largely on *Xenophon, De Vecti-gal., 355 B.C.* a new principle, namely by private companies. The historian Xenophon had written a pamphlet on the subject of the mines as a neglected source of revenue, and it would be interesting to know whether the revival of the industry is to be ascribed directly or indirectly to the influence of his exhortations.

The re-organisation of the ephebi, c. 336 B.C. No sign of the times, which followed the defeat of Chaeronea, is more striking than the framing of a new system for drilling the young burghers of Athens in the duties of military life. The training began when the youth, having completed his eighteenth year, came of age and was enrolled in the register of his deme ; and it lasted for two years. During these two years the young citizen was known as an *ephēbos*, and might not appear either as prosecutor or defendant in the law-courts except in a few cases expressly specified. The general supervision over all the Attic ephebi was committed to a marshal (*kosmētēs*), who was elected by the Athenian Assembly ; and under him were ten masters of discipline (*sōphrŏnistai*), one for each tribe. The institution had a religious consecration. The first act in the service of the ephebi was solemnly to "go round the temples" under the conduct of the masters.   Then they served for a year on duty in the guard-houses at Munychia and along the coast, receiving regular military instruction from special drill-masters, who trained them in the exercises of the hoplites, and taught them how to shoot with bow and javelin and to handle artillery.   The ephebi of each tribe ate together at barrack messes which were managed by the masters of discipline.   At the end of the first year they appeared

FIG. 203.—Plato.

before an Assembly in the theatre, and when they had made a public display of their proficiency in the art of warfare, each received from the city a shield and a spear.   The second year was spent in patrolling the frontiers of the land and guarding the prisons.   The garrison and patrol duties had always devolved upon the young men of Attica, but they were now organised into a new and thorough scheme of discipline,—a mild Attic approach to the stern system of Sparta.   It almost strikes one as a conscious effort to arrest the decline of the citizen army in the face of the encroachments of the mercenary system.   The ephebi in their characteristic dress, the dark mantle and the broad-brimmed hat, are a graceful feature in Athenian life and art from this time forward.

It is significant that the whole revival, stimulated by the disaster of Chaeronea, was marked by a religious character. Lycurgus, who belonged to the priestly family of the Eteobutads, was a sincerely pious man, and impressed upon his administration the stamp of his own devotion. Never for a hundred years had there been seen at Athens such a manifestation of zealous public concern for the worship of the gods. The two chief monuments of the Lycurgean epoch—the Panathenaic stadion and the theatre of Dionysus—were, it must always be remembered, religious, not secular, buildings.

Thus Athens discreetly attended to her material well-being, and courted the favour of the gods, and the only distress which befell her was a dearth of corn. But on the return of Alexander to Susa, two things happened which imperilled the tranquillity of Greece.

The exiles.

324 B.C.

Alexander promised the Greek exiles—there were more than 20,000 of them—to procure their return to their native cities. He sent Nicanor to the great congregation of Hellas at the Olympian festival, to order the states to receive back their banished citizens. A general reconciliation of parties was a just and politic measure ; but it could be objected that, by the terms of the Confederation of Corinth, the Macedonian king had no power to dictate orders to the confederates in the management of their domestic affairs. Only two states objected, Athens and Aetolia ; and they objected because, if the edict were enforced, they would be robbed of ill-gotten gains. The Aetolians had possessed themselves of Oeniadae and driven out its Acarnanian owners ; by Alexander's edict the rightful inhabitants would now return to their own city and the intruders be dislodged. The position of Athens in Samos was similar ; the Samians would now be restored to their own lands, and the Athenian settlers would have to go. Both Athens and Aetolia were prepared to resist.

Alexander's divinity.

Another desire was expressed by Alexander at the same time, which was readily acquiesced in. He demanded that the Greeks should recognise his divinity. Sparta is reported to have replied indifferently, " We allow Alexander to call himself a god, if he likes." There was not a sensible man at Athens who would have thought of objecting ; even the bitterest patriots would have allowed him to be " the son of Zeus or Poseidon, or whomever he chose." If the Greeks of Corinth looked up to Alexander as their chieftain and protector—and this was actually their position in regard to him—there was no incongruity in the idea of officially acknowledging his divinity. Ever since the days in which an Homeric king " was honoured as a god by the people," there was nothing offensive or outlandish to a Greek ear in predicating godhood of a revered

sovereign or master.   Divine honours had been paid to Lysander;
and the Greeks, in complying with Alexander's desire, did not commit themselves more than the pupil of the Academy who erected
an altar to his master Plato.

Sect. 6. The Episode of Harpalus and the Greek Revolt

Meanwhile an incident had happened which might induce some *Harpalus*
of the patriots to hope that Alexander's empire rested on slippery *in Greece,*
foundations.   Harpalus had arrived off the coast of Attica with *spring,*
5000 talents, a body of mercenaries, and thirty ships.   He had come *324 B.C.;*
to excite a revolt against his master.   A gift of corn had formerly
secured him the citizenship of Athens, but the Athenians prudently
refused to harbour him, coming in this guise.   He sailed away to
Cape Taenaron, always a refuge of adventurers, and leaving his men
and ships there, returned to Athens with a sum of about 700 talents.
He was now received, since he did not come with an armed array, *his recep-*
but after a while messages arrived both from Macedonia and from *tion at*
Philoxenus, Alexander's financial minister in western Asia, demand- *Athens;*
ing his surrender.   It would have been an act of war to protect the
runaway treasurer and his stolen moneys; but the Athenians, on the
proposal of Demosthenes, adopted a clever device.   They arrested
Harpalus, seizing his treasure, and said that they would surrender
him to officers expressly sent by Alexander; but declined to give
him up to Philoxenus or Antipater.   It was not long before Harpalus *his death.*
escaped; he returned to Taenaron, and was shortly afterwards
murdered by one of his fellow-adventurers.

The stolen money was deposited in the Acropolis, under the *The*
charge of specially-appointed commissioners, of whom Demosthenes *Harpalus*
was one.   It was known by report that the sum was about 700 *scandal:*
talents, but Demosthenes and his fellows had strangely omitted to
make any official entry or report of the amount.   Suddenly it was
discovered that only 350 talents were actually in the Acropolis.
Charges immediately circulated against the influential politicians, *bribery and*
that the other 350 talents had been received in bribes by them *peculation.*
before the money was deposited in the citadel.   Men of opposite
sides were suspected; Demades, for example, as well as Demosthenes.   But, apart from the suspicion of bribery, manifest blame
rested upon Demosthenes for having grossly neglected his duty.
He was responsible for the custody of the treasure, for which Athens
was responsible to Alexander.   He was bound to demand an investigation, and on his motion the people directed the Council of
Areopagus to hold an inquiry.   Philoxenus furnished the account-
book of Harpalus, which had come into his hands.   By this evi-

dence it was proved that 700 talents had been delivered for safe-keeping in the Acropolis ; the entries ceased at this point. It was also shown that certain Athenians had previously been bribed ; but Demosthenes was not among them. Other evidence was necessary to show how the missing half of the 700 talents had disappeared. We know not what this evidence was, but the court of Areopagus satisfied themselves that a number of leading statesmen had received *Demo-* considerable sums. Demosthenes appeared in their report as the *sthenes a* recipient of twenty talents. The proofs against him were irrefutable, *receiver of* for he confessed the misdemeanour himself, and sought to excuse it *twenty* by the paltry and transparent subterfuge that he had taken it to *talents.* repay himself for twenty talents which he had advanced to the Theoric Fund. But why should he repay himself, without any authorisation, out of Alexander's money, for a debt owed him by the Athenian state ? There can be little doubt that Demosthenes took the money not for personal gratifications, but for the good of his party. It was all the more necessary for his party to clear themselves from implication in such corrupt transactions. We therefore find Hypereides coming forward as a public prosecutor of Demosthenes. We possess considerable portions of his speech ; and we have in its complete form another speech, written for one of the other prosecutors by a miserable hack named Dinarchus. The charges against Demosthenes were twofold : he had taken money, and he had culpably omitted to report the amount of the deposit and the neglect of those who were set to guard it. For the second offence alone he deserved a severe sentence. The judges were not excessively severe, if we consider that his behaviour had placed the *Condemna-* city in a most embarrassing position towards Alexander. He was *tion of* condemned to pay a fine of fifty talents. Unable to pay it, he was *Demo-* imprisoned, but presently effected his escape. It was a venial *sthenes.* offence in the eyes of Greece for a statesman to take a bribe, pro-vided he did not take it to injure his country ; and in the view of public opinion the moral character of Demosthenes was little damaged by this tortuous transaction. He was not on a level with men like Nicias and Phocion, whom millions would not have tempted ; but then nobody ever supposed that he was incorruptible. Yet there were two circumstances which aggravated the case. The money of which Demosthenes partook was stolen money. which Athens was about to sequester for Alexander ; and he was himself a commissioner responsible for its safety. It was far from being an ordinary case of corruption.

If Alexander had lived, the Athenians might have persuaded him to let them remain in occupation of Samos ; for he was always dis-posed to be lenient to Athens. When the tidings of his death came,

men almost refused to credit it ; the orator Demades forcibly said,
" If he were indeed dead, the whole world would have smelt
of his corpse." The patriots had been building on the slender hopes
of some disaster ; and the greatest disaster of all had befallen. It
had been recognised as madness to defy the power of Alexander ;
but it did not seem rash to strike for freedom in the unsettled condition of things after his death. Athens revolted from Macedonia ; *The Greek*
she was joined by Aetolia and many states in northern Greece, and *revolt*
she secured the services of a band of 8000 discharged mercenaries who *against*
Macedonia,
had just returned from Alexander's army. One of their captains, the *323 B.C.*
Athenian, Leosthenes, occupied Thermopylae, and near that pass
the united Greeks gained a slight advantage over Antipater, who
had marched southward as soon as he could gather his troops
together. The Thessalian cavalry had deserted him, and no state
in north Greece except Boeotia remained true to Macedonia. The
regent shut himself in the strong hill-city of Lamia, which stands *Antipater*
over against the pass of Thermopylae under a spur of Othrys ; and *besieged in*
Lamia,
here he was besieged during the winter by Leosthenes. These suc- *323-2 B.C.*
cesses had gained some adherents to the cause in the Peloponnesus ;
and, if the Greeks had been stronger at sea, that cause might have
triumphed, at least for a while. But the strange thing was that, notwithstanding the improvements of recent years in her naval establishment, Athens seems to have been able to set afloat no more than
170 warships against 240 of Macedon. The brave general Leosthenes was hampered by a Council of War, in which the various allies
were represented—reminding us of the days of the Persian invasion ;
yet, if a fatal stone had not put an end to his life during the
beleaguerment, more would probably have been effected for the
cause of the allies. In spring the arrival of Leonnatus, governor
of Hellespontine Phrygia, at the head of an army, raised the siege of
Lamia. The Greeks marched into Thessaly to meet the new army
before it united with Antipater ; a battle was fought, in which the
Greeks had the upper hand, and Leonnatus was wounded to death.
Antipater arrived the next day, and, joining forces with the defeated
army, withdrew into Macedonia, to await Craterus, who was approaching from the east. When Craterus arrived, they entered *Battle of*
Thessaly together, and in an engagement at Crannon, in which *Crannon,*
the losses on both sides were light, the Macedonians had a slight *322 B.C.,*
Aug.
advantage. This battle apparently decided the war, but the true cause
which hindered the Greeks from continuing the struggle was not the
insignificant defeat at Crannon, but the want of unity among themselves, the want of a leader whom they entirely trusted. They were
forced to make terms singly, each state on its own behoof.

Hypereides pronounced a funeral oration, distinguished by that

Funeral speech of Hypereides. lucidity of which he was a perfect master, over those who had fallen in this hopeless war ; and gave his due—it is not for us to say that he gave more than his due—to Leosthenes, who "succeeded in what he undertook, but not in escaping fate." There is a fine passage which distorts indeed the historical perspective, but well displays the spirit of the patriots. " In the dark underworld—suffer us to ask—who are they that will stretch forth a right hand to the captain of our dead ? May we not deem that Leosthenes will be greeted with welcome and with wonder by those half-gods who bore arms against Troy ? Ay, and there, I deem, will be Miltiades and Themistocles, and those others who made Hellas free to the glory of their names." [1]

Athens submitted when Antipater advanced into Boeotia and prepared to invade Attica. She paid dearly for her attempt to win back her power. Antipater was not like Alexander. He was an able man, warmly devoted to the royal house of Macedon ; but he did not share in Alexander's sympathies with Greek culture, he had no soft place in his heart for the memories and traditions of Athens. He saw only that, unless strong and stern measures were taken, Macedonia would not be safe against a repetition of the rising which *Terms im-* he had suppressed. He therefore imposed three conditions, which *posed on Athens.* Phocion and Demades were obliged to accept : that the democratic constitution should be modified by a property qualification ; that a Macedonian garrison should be lodged in Munychia ; and that the agitators, Demosthenes, Hypereides, and their friends, should be surrendered.

Demosthenes had exerted eloquence in gaining support for the cause of the allies in the Peloponnesus, and his efforts had been rewarded by his recall to Athens. As soon as the city had submitted, he and the other orators fled. Hypereides with two companions sought refuge in the temple of Aeacus at Aegina, whence they were taken to Antipater and put to death. Demosthenes fled to the temple *Death of* of Poseidon in the island of Calauria. When the messengers of *Demo-* Antipater appeared and summoned him forth, he swallowed poison, *sthenes, 322 B.C., Oct.* which he had concealed, according to one story, in a pen, and was thus delivered from falling into the hands of the executioner.

Introduc-tion of property qualifica-tion at Athens. (£80.) The constitutional change which was carried out at the dictation of the Macedonian general would have been judged by Aristotle an improvement. The institutions were not changed, but the democracy was converted into a " polity " or limited democracy—such as Thera-menes had striven for—by a restriction of the franchise. All citizens whose property amounted to less than 2000 drachmae were deprived

---

[1] Translated by Professor Jebb.

of their civic rights.   It is said that this measure erased 12,000
names from the burgher lists, and that 9000 citizens remained.   A
large number of the poorer people thus disfranchised left Attica and
settled in Thrace, where Antipater gave them land ; perhaps these
settlers included some of the outdwellers of Samos, who were now
turned adrift, being obliged to quit the island and make way for the
rightful possessors.

SECT. 7. ARISTOTLE AND ALEXANDER

It was through an accident that Alexander was brought into
contact with the one other man of his time whose genius was destined
to move the world.   Aristotle's father had been court physician of *Aristotle,*
Amyntas II., and Aristotle was meant to follow his father's pro- *born* 384-3
fession.   At the age of seventeen he went to Athens, where he was *c.* 367 *B.C.*
under the guardianship of a certain Proxenus, to whose son Nicanor
—the same Nicanor who made public Alexander's edict at Olympia—
he afterwards betrothed his only daughter.   At first Aristotle studied
in the school of Isocrates, but when Plato returned from Sicily he
came under the influence of that philosopher's idealism, and this
decided him for the " life of speculation," which he regards—and it
is the deliberate judgment of his mature years—as the only life that
is perfectly happy.   After Plato's death he spent some years on the
north-eastern coasts of the Aegean, at Assos and Mytilene, and then
received the call from Philip to undertake the education of the crown *Called to*
prince.   As yet he had won no eminent reputation for wisdom or *Pella,*
learning, and Philip probably chose him because his father had been 343-2 *B.C.*
connected with the Macedonian court.   The instruction which
Aristotle imparted to Alexander was perhaps chiefly literary and
philological ; he came as a tutor, not as a philosopher.   We know
nothing of the mutual relations between the brilliant master and his
brilliant pupil ; they were men of different and hardly sympathetic
tempers ; we may suspect that Aristotle was fainer to curb than spur
the ardent straining spirit of Alexander.   Certainly the episode led to
no such maintenance of intimacy afterwards as it might have led
to if Plato had been the teacher.   On his return to Athens, *c.* 335 *B.C.*
Aristotle founded his school of philosophy, and the Lyceum soon
took the place formerly occupied by the Academy, which ever
since the discomfiting adventures in Sicily had withdrawn itself
more and more from the public attention.   He taught for twelve
or thirteen years—and these years were doubtless the time of his
most effective philosophical activity—and died not long after the *Death,*
death of Alexander.   322 *B.C.*

Never were there more wonderful years than these in which the

Debt of
Europe to
Aristotle.

brains of Alexander and Aristotle were ceaselessly working. It is not an overstatement to say that there is no one to whom Europe owes a greater debt for the higher education of her peoples than to Aristotle. The science of the laws of thought is still taught mainly as he first worked it out. There are no better introductions to ethical and political speculation than his fundamental treatises on ethical and political science. Nor was it a small thing that his system controlled the acutest minds of the Middle Ages, whose reasoning faculties,

FIG. 204.—Aristotle.

though cabined by the imminence of a narrowly interpreted theology, were amazingly powerful and subtle.

Aristotle's
prejudices,

But Aristotle, supreme as he was in abstract reasoning, zealous as he was in collecting and appreciating concrete facts, was not without prejudices. As a boy, in the narrow self-satisfied community of little remote Stagira, he had imbibed the dislike which was openly

against
Athens

or secretly felt towards Athens in all the Chalcidian regions. And, though he established his abode at Athens, he never overcame this distrust; he always remained a citizen of Stagira and lived in Athens as a stranger. This initial prejudice prevented him from ever judging with perfect impartiality the Athenian institutions, which he took as

and
Macedonia,

the type of democracy. He was also prejudiced against Macedonia. The Chalcidians looked upon their Macedonian neighbours as far

below themselves in civilisation; and Aristotle's experience of the
court of Pella, where he must have been a spectator of the scandalous
quarrels between Philip and Olympias, did not create a favourable
impression.   He was thus disposed to hold his sympathies entirely
aloof from the enterprises of Alexander.   But not only did he not
sympathise, he disapproved.   For he was wedded to the idea of the
small Greek republic; he condemned the large state.   Moreover,
he held firmly to the Hellenic conviction that Hellenes were superior *and*
by nature to peoples of other race, and he was thus opposed to the *barbarians.*
most original and enlightened feature of Alexander's policy—the
ruling of Greeks and barbarians on an equality.   Owing to this attitude of coldness and distrust towards the Macedonians, he missed
a great opportunity.   Alexander's expedition threw open to science
a new field of discovery in natural history; and we can imagine what
endless pains the king would have given himself, if Aristotle had
urged him to collect extensive observations on the animal and
vegetable kingdoms in the various countries and climates through
which he passed.

It is a strange sensation to pass from the view of the state which *His ideal*
Alexander was fashioning to the sketch of an ideal state which was *state.*
drawn by the most thoughtful of men at the same time.   Aristotle
desires a little north-country city, situated in a compact, defensible
territory; close to the sea and yet not on the coast, having a harbour
within easy reach, but quite disconnected, so that the precincts of the
city may not be contaminated and its indwellers troubled by the
presence of a motley crowd of outlanders, cheapmen, and mariners,
such as throng a seaport's quays.   He will not have his city a centre
of trade; it is to import and export only for the purposes of its own
strict needs.   It is to be a tiny city, the number of the burghers so
limited that each one may be able to know all about each of the
others.   The burghers are to have equal rights; their early manhood
is to be spent on military duties; when they come to middle life they
are to be eligible for political offices; in their old age they are to act
as priests.   Subject to this citizen aristocracy, but entirely excluded
from the franchise, are to be the artisans and merchants.   Part of
the land is to be public—the yield to be devoted to maintaining the
worship of the gods and providing the public meals of the city; part
is to be the private property of the citizens; and the fields are to be
tilled by slaves or labourers of non-Hellenic race.   Such was the
little exclusive community which Aristotle designed, while his former
pupil was setting in motion schemes for world-wide commerce,
shattering the barriers which sundered nation from nation, building
an empire which should include millions, founding cities composed
of men of divers races, hewing his way through a maze of new political

problems which were beyond Aristotle's horizon.   The republic of
Aristotle's wish is not quickened like Plato's by striking original ideas ;
it is a commonplace Greek aristocracy with its claws cut, carefully
trimmed and pruned, refined by a punctilious education, without
any expansive vitality, and like Sparta leaving no room for the free
development of the individual citizens.   If the cities of Hellas had
been moulded and fashioned on the model of the city of the
philosopher's wish, they would hardly have done what they did for
European civilisation.

We may wonder whether Aristotle divined before his death that
the Hellenic cities were not to have the last word in the history of
men.   More probably the untimely end of Alexander reassured him
that the old fashion of things would soon go on again as before.   The
brilliant day of the Greek city states had indeed drawn to a close so
suddenly that they could not be expected to grasp the fact ; and no
people that has ever borne the torch of civilisation has been willing,
or even able, to recognise that the hour of relinquishing sovereignty
has come.   The Greeks may well be excused if they were reluctant
to acquiesce in the vicissitude which forced them to sink into a subordinate place.   But it is thus that the austere laws of history reward
the meritorious.   The republics of Greece had performed an im-
perishable work ; they had shown mankind many things, and, above
all, the most precious thing in the world, fearless freedom of thought.

FIG. 205.—Syracusan Demaretean, 480 B.C. (reverse). Head of
Victory surrounded by dolphins.

CHRONOLOGICAL TABLE

B.C.

c. 3000	Beginning of " Minoan " civilisation in Crete.
c. 2200	Building of first palaces at Cnossus and Phaestus.
c. 2200—1400	Crete leading power in Aegean. Trade relations with Egypt and Syria.
c. 2000—1300	Hittites leading power in Asia Minor.
c. 2000	Greek-speaking peoples enter Greece.
c. 1700	Destruction of palaces of Cnossus and Phaestus by earthquake. Palaces rebuilt.
c. 1600—1400	Strong Cretan influence in Greece. The shaft-grave dynasty at Mycenae.
c. 1400	Destruction of palaces at Cnossus and Phaestus. Eclipse of Cretan power.
c. 1400—1200	The great age of Mycenae. Development of Mycenaean trade in Egypt and Eastern Mediterranean. Relations with Hittites. Mycenaean settlements in Rhodes, Cyprus, etc. Trade with the West.
1287	Battle of Cadesh between Egypt and Hittites; decline of both powers.
c. 1230—1150	Breakdown of settled conditions.
1223	Achaeans join in raid on Egypt.
c. 1200	Phrygians invade Asia Minor.
c. 1180	Troy destroyed by Mycenaeans.
c. 1150	Destruction of Mycenaean centres in Greece.
c. 1000	Main Dorian invasion of Peloponnese, followed by invasions of Thessaly and Boeotia.
c. 1000—900	Aeolian, Ionian, Dorian colonisation of Asia Minor.
c. 800—700	Rise of aristocracies throughout Greece.
c. 750—700	Homer composes the *Iliad* and *Odyssey*.

B.C.	
c. 700	Hesiod.
776	Traditional date of First Olympiad.
735	,, ,, foundation of Naxos (Sicily).
734	,, ,, ,, Corcyra.
734	,, ,, ,, Syracuse.
728	,, ,, ,, Catane and Leontini.
728	,, ,, ,, Megara (Hyblaean).
721	,, ,, ,, Sybaris.
715	,, ,, ,, Zancle.
707	,, ,, ,, Taras.
703	,, ,, ,, Croton.
688	,, ,, ,, Gela
648	,, ,, ,, Himera.
c. 730—10	Spartan conquest of Messenia.
709	King Sargon of Assyria sets up stele in Cyprus.
c. 700	Midas king of Phrygia. Deioces founds Median monarchy.
	Athenian conquest of Eleusis.
678—52	Reign of Gyges king of Lydia.
683—2	List of annual archons at Athens begins.
681—68	Reign of Assarhaddon king of Assyria.
679	Assarhaddon defeats the Cimmerians under their leader Teuspa.
c. 672	Assyrian conquest of Egypt.
668—26	Reign of Assurbanipal king of Assyria.
c. 675—55	Pheidon of Argos dominant in Peloponnese.
668	Traditional date of battle of Hysiae, in which Argos defeats Sparta.
664	Traditional date of ancient sea-battle of Corinth with Corcyra.
664	Fortress of Defenneh (Daphnae) in Egypt built by Psammetichus I.
650—600	Age of law-givers in Greece.
	Rise of tyrannies in Ionia. Foundation of tyrannies in Sicyon, Corinth, and Megara.
	Ardys and Sadyattes reign in Lydia. Ardys drives out the Cimmerians.
c. 650—25	Reign of Phaortes king of Media.
645	Egypt throws off yoke of Assyria.
c. 632	Cylon attempts to seize tyranny at Athens.
c. 630	Foundation of Cyrene.
625	Nabopolassar founds new Babylonian kingdom.
c. 621	Legislation of Dracon at Athens.
c. 620	Sparta crushes Messenian revolt.
612	Fall of Nineveh. Nabopolassar of Babylonia and Cyaxares of Media conquer and divide Assyria.
c. 610	Foundation of Naucratis.
c. 610	Thrasybulus tyrant of Miletus.
605	Nebucadnezar succeeds Nabopolassar.
c. 600	War of Athens and Mytilene on the coast of the Hellespont.
	Sappho, Alcaeus, Pittacus, flourish at Mytilene.
	Periander tyrant of Corinth.

B.C.	
594—89	Nubian expedition of Psammetichus II. Inscription of Greek mercenaries at Abu Simbel.
594—3	Archonship of Solon. *Seisachtheia.*
590—89	Sacred War against Crisa.
	Cleisthenes of Sicyon flourishes.
585	May 28: Eclipse of sun. Drawn battle of Cyaxares king of Media with Alyattes king of Lydia.
	Thales flourishes.
583—1	Archonship of Damasias at Athens.
582	First Pythiad.
572	Eleans win control of the Olympian games.
c. 570	Athenian war with Megara.
569	Accession of Amasis to throne of Egypt.
562	Death of Nebucadnezar.
560	Croesus succeeds to throne of Lydia.
c. 560—50	War of Sparta with Tegea.
561—60	Archonship of Comeas. Pisistratus seizes tyranny.
c. 559—6	Miltiades becomes tyrant in Thracian Chersonese.
556—5	First exile of Pisistratus.
550—49	? Restoration of Pisistratus ; and his second exile.
c. 550	Spartan conquest of Thyreatis.
548—7	Temple of Apollo at Delphi burnt down.
546	Cyrus king of Persia conquers Lydia, and captures Sardis.
546—5	Persian conquest of Asiatic Greeks.
540—39	Second restoration of Pisistratus.
538	Cyrus takes Babylon.
528—7	Death of Pisistratus.
526	Polycrates, tyrant of Samos, abandons alliance with Amasis and joins Persia.
525	Death of Amasis king of Egypt.
	Persian conquest of Egypt : battle of Pelusion.
c. 525	Spartans attack Samos.
c. 523	Death of Polycrates.
522	Death of Cambyses king of Persia.
521	Accession of Darius.
520	First capture of Babylon by Darius.
519	Second capture of Babylon by Darius.
514	Conspiracy of Harmodius and Aristogiton.
c. 512	First European expedition of Darius : conquest of Thrace
510	Fall of the Pisistratid tyranny. Spartans in Attica. Athens joins Peloponnesian league.
	War of Sybaris and Croton.
508—7	Archonship of Isagoras. Spartans under Cleomenes invade Attica ; besieged in the Acropolis. Beginning of reforms of Cleisthenes.
507	Peloponnesian army invades Attica.
	Athenians defeat (1) Boeotians, (2) Chalcidians : acquire Chalcidian plain
506	Athens acquires Oropus (land of the Graeans).
? 503—2	First civil year on the Cleisthenic system.

B.C.	
501	Institution of the *Ten* stratêgoi of the tribes at Athens.
499	Outbreak of Ionic revolt.
c. 498	Ionians and allies at Sardis : burning of Sardis.
c. 497	Crushing of revolt in Cyprus.
496	(?) Revolt of Thrace; Scythians drive Miltiades from Chersonese.
496—5	Hipparchus archon at Athens.
494	Battle of Lade ; Persians capture Miletus.
c. 494	Battle of Sêpeia (Spartans under Cleomenes defeat Argives).
493—2	Archonship of Themistocles.
c. 492	Athens coerces Aegina. Battle of the Helorus.
492	Mardonius subdues Thrace and Macedonia.
c. 492	Trial of Miltiades.
c. 491	Gelon becomes tyrant of Gela.
490	Expedition of the Persians under Datis against Greece. Destruction of Eretria. Battle of Marathon.
489	Expedition of Miltiades to Paros.
c. 489	Death of Cleomenes.
488	Victory of Gelon in chariot-race at Olympia.
487	Ostracism of Hipparchus the Pisistratid. War of Athens with Aegina.
487—6	Archons begin to be appointed by lot. Strategoi supersede the Polemarch.
486	Ostracism of Megacles. Pindar's *7th Pythian.*
486—5	Egypt revolts against Persia.
485	Death of Darius. Accession of Xerxes.
484	Ostracism of Xanthippus son of Arriphron.
484—3	Persia recovers control of Egypt.
483	Persians hew canal through Mount Athos.
483—2	Discovery of a new vein of silver in mine-fields of Laurion.
482	Ostracism of Aristides. Increase of Athenian fleet. Pythian victory of Hieron in horse-race.
481	Xerxes comes down to Sardis.
480	Spring : Athens recalls ostracized citizens. August : Xerxes enters Greece. Battles of Artemisium and Thermopylae. September : Battle of Salamis. Olynthus given to the Chalcidians. Carthaginians invade Sicily. Battle of Himera.
479	Mardonius in Attica. August : Battle of Plataea ; and battle of Mycale. Ionians revolt from Persia. Athenians capture Sestos at end of 479.
478	Pausanias' expedition to Cyprus, Byzantium. Death of Gelon : his brother Hieron succeeds to his power. Pythian victory of Hieron in horse-race. *3rd Pythian Ode* of Pindar.
477	Foundation of Confederacy of Delos. Pausanias driven from Byzantium by Cimon.
478—6	Fortification of Athens.

B.C.	
476	Lacedaemonian expedition to Thessaly (?). Victory of Hieron in horse-race at Olympia (1st *Olymp. Ode* of Pindar ; 5th *Ode* of Bacchylides).
476—5	Cimon captures Eion.
474	Battle of Cyme.
474—3	Cimon conquers Scyrus.
472	Olympian victories of Hieron in horse-race and Theron in chariot-race. 2nd and 3rd *Olympians* of Pindar. The *Persae* of Aeschylus.
472—1	Athenians reduce Carystus. Ostracism of Themistocles. Death of Theron of Acragas. Synoecisms of Elis and Mantinea.
c. 471	Flight of Themistocles. Battle of Dipaea (?).
471—70	War of Hieron with Thrasydaeus of Acragas.
470	Pythian victory of Hieron in chariot-race. Pindar's 1st *Pythian.* 4th *Ode* of Bacchylides (?).
470—69	Revolt and reduction of Naxos (?).
468	Olympian victory of Hieron in chariot-race. 3rd *Ode* of Bacchylides. Olympian victory of a boy of Tiryns in boxing.
	Battle of the Eurymedon (?).
468—7	Argos reduces Tiryns (?).
467	Death of Hieron.
465	Revolt of Thasos.
465—4	Attempt to colonise the Nine Ways.
464	Earthquake at Sparta. Revolt of helots. Siege of Ithome. Accession of Artaxerxes to throne of Persia.
463	Surrender of Thasos.
463—2	Cimon in Messenia.
463—1	Ephialtes influential at Athens. The Areopagus deprived of its powers.
462—60	Argos reduces Mycenae (?). Pay introduced at Athens for the judges of the heliaea. Influence of Pericles begins.
461	Ostracism of Cimon.
461—60	Alliance of Athens and Argos.
459	Athens wins Megara. Long Walls of Megara built. Athenian expedition to Egypt.
	Capture of Ithome. Messenians settled at Naupactus. Capture of Memphis.
459—8	Battle of Halieis. Battle of Cecryphalea.
458	*Oresteia* of Aeschylus. Zeugitae admitted to archonship. Battle of Aegina. Battle in the Megarid.
	Building of Long Walls of Athens.
457	Lacedaemonian expedition to Phocis and Boeotia. Battle of Tanagra.
	Athenian conquest of Boeotia (battle of Oenophyta ; autumn).
457—6	Athenian conquest of Aegina.
456	Megabyzus arrives in Egypt with army and fleet.
456—5	Expedition of Tolmides to Corinthian Gulf.
454	Catastrophe of Egyptian expedition.

B.C.	
454	Treasury of confederacy of Delos transferred from Delos to Athens.
453	Expedition of Pericles to Corinthian Gulf.
453—46	Inclusion of Achaea in Athenian empire.
451	Five years' Truce between Athenians and Peloponnesians. Thirty years' Peace between Argos and Lacedaemon.
451—50	Law of citizenship at Athens.
450—49	Cimon in Cyprus. Death of Cimon.
449—8	Peace with Persia. Sacred War. Athens invites the Greeks to restore the temples.
447	Parthenon begun. Athens loses Boeotia (battle of Coronea). Cleruchies sent to the Chersonese, Euboea, etc.
447—6	Revolt and reduction of Euboea. Athens loses Megara.
446—5	Thirty years' Peace between Athens and Peloponnesians. Foundation of New Sybaris.
443	Foundation of Thurii. Ostracism of Thucydides, son of Melesias.
440—39	Revolt of Samos, and Byzantium.
438	Chryselephantine Athena set up in the Parthenon.
436	Foundation of Amphipolis.
c. 435	Pericles' expedition to Euxine.
436—5	Sedition at Epidamnus.
435	Sea-victory of Corcyra over Corinth (spring).
433	Defensive alliance of Athens with Corcyra. Battle of Sybota (autumn). Treaties of Athens with Rhegion and Leontini renewed.
432	Revolt of Potidaea. The " Megarian decree " passed at Athens. Battle of Potidaea (c. Sept.).
432—1	Assemblies at Sparta decide on war.
431	*First year of the Peloponnesian War.*—Theban attack on Plataea (March). First Peloponnesian invasion of Attica (May). Athens wins Sollion and Cephallenia; takes Thronion and Atalanta; expels Aeginetans from Aegina.
430	*Second year of the War.*—Outbreak of plague at Athens. Second invasion of Attica. Expedition of Pericles to Argolis and his failure at Epidaurus. Pericles deposed from strategia, tried, fined, and reappointed strategos. Phormio operates in the west. Surrender of Potidaea.
429	*Third year of the War.*—Peloponnesians besiege Plataea. Sea-victories of Phormio. Death of Pericles (autumn).
428	*Fourth year of the War.*—Third invasion of Attica. Revolt of Mytilene.
427	*Fifth year of the War.*—Fourth invasion of Attica. Surrender of Mytilene. Surrender of Plataea. Civil war breaks out in Corcyra. Athens captures Minoa. Expedition of Laches to Sicily.
426	*Sixth year of the War.*—Aetolian expedition of Demosthenes. Battle of Olpae. Purification of Delos.

B.C.

425 *Seventh year of the War.*—Fifth invasion of Attica. Athenians send reinforcements to Sicily. Occupation of Pylos; and capture of Spartans in Sphacteria. Triumph of the democracy in Corcyra. Athens wins Anactorion, and occupies Methone. Athens raises the tribute of her allies. Introduction of the triobolon for jurors. *Acharnians* of Aristophanes. Antiphon's *De Choreuta.* Congress of Gela.

424 *Eighth year of the War.*—Athens wins Oeniadae; captures Nisaea, with the Long Walls of Megara, and Cythera. Athenian invasion of Boeotia; battle of Delion. Brasidas in Thrace. Revolt of Acanthus, Amphipolis, and other cities. Banishment of Thucydides, the historian. *Knights* of Aristophanes.

423 *Ninth year of the War.*—Negotiations for peace. One year's truce (March). Revolt of Scione. *Clouds* of Aristophanes. Leontini annexed by Syracuse.

422 *Tenth year of the War.*—Battle of Amphipolis. Death of Brasidas and Cleon. Peace negotiations. *Wasps* of Aristophanes.

421 Peace of Nicias (March). *Peace* of Aristophanes. Capture of Scione.

421—20 Defensive alliance between Athens and Sparta.

420 Alliance of Athens with Argos, Elis, and Mantinea.

418 Battle of Mantinea. Argos forms alliance with Sparta. Eleusinian decree.

417 Ostracism of Hyperbolus. Nicias in Chalcidice.

416 Conquest of Melos. Embassy of Segesta to Athens.

415 Mutilation of the Hermae at Athens. Athenian expedition to Sicily. Recall of Alcibiades.

414 Spring: *Birds* of Aristophanes. Siege of Syracuse. Gylippus arrives in Sicily.

413 Spartans occupy Decelea. Second Athenian expedition to Sicily. Great battle in the Syracusan Harbour (Sept. 9). Disaster of the Athenians.

412 Revolt of Athenian allies. Treaty of Miletus (between Sparta and Persia). Alcibiades leaves Sparta.

411 Battle of Syme (Jan.). Revolt of Rhodes. Pisander at Athens (c. Feb.). Revolt of Abydus and Lampsacus (April). Assembly at Colonus and provision made for a new Constitution (May). Council of Four Hundred comes into office (early in June), and governs till September. Revolt of Euboea (Sept.). Four Hundred overthrown and Polity established (Sept.). Battle of Cynossema. *Lysistrate* and *Thesmophoriazusae* of Aristophanes. Evagoras becomes king of Salamis.

410 Battle of Cyzicus. Restoration of Democracy at Athens. Athens recovers Thasos. [Pseudo-Lysias] *For Polystratus.*

409 Athens recovers Colophon; loses Pylos and Nisaea. Carthaginian invasion of Sicily. Destruction of Selinus and Himera.

B.C.	
408	Athens recovers Chalcedon and Byzantium. Gorgias at Olympia. Warfare of Hermocrates in western Sicily.
407	Cyrus comes down to the coast. Alcibiades at Athens.
	Battle of Mytilene. Death of Hermocrates. Foundation of Thermae.
406	Battle of Notion. Alcibiades deposed.
	Battle of Arginusae. Trial of the Generals. Siege of Acragas.
406—5	Conspiracy of reed-bearers at Chios.
405	Lysander navarch. Cyrus called to Susa. Battle of Aegospotami (end of summer).
	Dionysius becomes tyrant of Syracuse ; and makes peace with Carthage.
405—4	Blockade of Athens.
404	Surrender of Athens. Long Walls pulled down (April). Psephism of Dracontides (summer) and rule of the Thirty. Thrasybulus seizes Phyle (Dec.). Alliance of Catane and Leontini.
404—3	First expedition of Thirty against Thrasybulus. Death of Theramenes.
403	Lacedaemonian garrison at Athens. Second expedition against Thrasybulus (May).
	Thrasybulus seizes Piraeus. Battle of Munychia. King Pausanias at Athens. Fall of Thirty (Sept.). Recall of Lysander. Lysias' *Against Eratosthenes*.
	Revolt at Syracuse against Dionysius.
403—2	Archonship of Euclides.
403—400	Sicel war of Dionysius. His reduction of Naxos and Catane
401	Expedition of Cyrus. Battle of Cunaxa (summer).
400	Thimbron in Asia Minor (end of summer).
399	Dercyllidas succeeds Thimbron, and gains the Troad. War of Sparta and Elis. Death of Socrates.
398	Sparta makes truce with the satraps ; sends embassy to Susa. Accession of Agesilaus. Dionysius captures Motya.
398—7	Dercyllidas in the Chersonese ; takes Atarneus (397, first months).
397	Dercyllidas in Caria ; makes truce with the satraps. Conon appointed commander of Persian fleet. Conspiracy of Cinadon at Sparta.
	Himilco's expedition to Sicily. Siege of Syracuse. Foundation of Lilybaeum.
396	First campaign of Agesilaus in Phrygia (autumn). Restoration of Messana. Acoris becomes king of Egypt.
396—3	Sicel war of Dionysius.
395	Campaign of Agesilaus in Lydia. Death of Tissaphernes. Second campaign of Agesilaus in Phrygia. Revolt of Rhodes. War breaks out in Boeotia. Battle of Haliartus and death of Lysander. Accession of Agesipolis at Sparta. Athens begins to rebuild her Long Walls. Foundation of Tyndaris.
395—4	Confederation of Athens, Thebes, etc., against Sparta.

B.C.

394 Battle of Corinth (July). Battle of Cnidus (Aug.). Eclipse of sun (Aug. 14). Battle of Coronea (Aug.). Foundation of Mylae.

393 Completion of Long Walls of Athens.

392 Union of Corinth and Argos. Battle of the Long Walls (of Megara). First embassy of Antalcidas to Susa. Second Punic War of Dionysius.

391 Spartans capture Lechaeon. Dionysius besieges Rhegion.

390 Agesilaus celebrates Isthmian games and captures Piraeon. Iphicrates gains a victory over Spartan hoplites. Teleutias captures an Athenian squadron. Evagoras revolts from Persia. Alliance of Athens with Evagoras and Acoris. Hecatomnus has become satrap of Caria (between 395 and 390).

390—89 Tax of $\frac{1}{40}$th ; and a war-tax introduced at Athens.

389 Successes of Thrasybulus in the Hellespont. Dionysius besieges Caulonia. Battle of the Elleporus. *Ecclesiazusae* of Aristophanes.

388 Death of Thrasybulus (first months). Warfare of Anaxibius and Iphicrates in the Hellespont.

Speech of Lysias at Olympic games (July-Aug.).

388—7 Second mission of Antalcidas to Susa.

387 Capture of Rhegion by Dionysius. Chabrias sent to help Evagoras.

387—6 The King's Peace.

386 Evagoras defeated at Cition. Chabrias in Egypt.

386—4 Persian siege of Cypriote Salamis.

386—5 Breaking up of Mantinea.

384 Orontes makes peace with Evagoras.

384—2 Formation of the Chalcidian Confederacy.

383—78 Third Punic War of Dionysius.

383 Death of Acoris.

382 Spartans seize citadel of Thebes (summer).

382—1 Restoration of Plataea.

381 Defeat of Spartans at Olynthus. Siege of Phlius begins. Persia concludes Peace with Evagoras. Accession of Nektanebos I. in Egypt.

380 Accession of king Cleombrotus at Sparta. Olympic games for which Isocrates wrote his *Panegyric*.

379 Suppression of Chalcidian League. Battles of Cabala and Cronion in Sicily.

379—8 Spartans expelled from Theban citadel (winter). Raid of Sphodrias.

378 Alliance of Athens with Thebes. Boeotia invaded by Agesilaus. Iphicrates in Thrace ; his marriage (?). Peace of Syracuse with Carthage.

377 Foundation of Second Athenian Confederacy. Property tax at Athens.

377 Boeotia invaded by Agesilaus. Defeat of Phoebidas. Mausolus becomes satrap of Caria.

B.C	
376	Battle of Naxos. Western expedition of Timotheus. Rebellion at Delos. Iphicrates in Persian service.
375—3	Iphicrates and Pharnabazus in Egypt. Jason of Pherae a member of Athenian League.
374	Peace between Athens and Sparta. Death of Evagoras; accession of Nicocles.
374—3	Peace broken. Lacedaemonians at Corcyra.
373	Iphicrates sent to Corcyra. Trial of Timotheus.
	Earthquakes in Greece; destruction of temple of Delphi (?).
371	Peace of Callias (June). Battle of Leuctra (July). Accession of Agesipolis II. at Sparta.
371—69	Foundation of Arcadian League, and of Megalopolis.
370	[Epaminondas a Boeotarch.] Rebuilding of Mantinea. Death of Jason of Pherae. Accession of Cleombrotus II. at Sparta.
370—69	First Boeotian invasion of Peloponnesus.
369	[Epaminondas a Boeotarch.] Foundation of Messene (first months). Alliance of Athens and Sparta (spring). Second Boeotian invasion of Peloponnesus. First Thessalian expedition of Pelopidas.
369—8	Murder of Alexander of Macedon, and intervention of Iphicrates.
368	Heraea and Orchomenus join Arcadian League. Congress of Delphi (summer). Tearless Battle. Euphron tyrant of Sicyon. Second Thessalian expedition of Pelopidas, and his captivity. First expedition to rescue him. Fourth Punic war of Dionysius.
367	[Epaminondas a Boeotarch.] Greek envoys at Susa. Second expedition to rescue Pelopidas. Death of Dionysius I.
	Ariobarzanes revolts from Persia.
366	Third Boeotian invasion of Peloponnesus. Thebans seize Oropus. Alliance of Athens with Arcadia. Death of Lycomedes. Timotheus in eastern Aegean. Isocrates' *Archidamus*.
366—5	Partial peace in Peloponnesus.
365	Timotheus wins Samos. Murder of Macedonian regent Ptolemy. Timotheus wins Potidaea and other towns of Chalcidian region. War breaks out between Arcadia and Elis.
364	[Epaminondas a Boeotarch.] Naval expedition of Epaminondas. Third Thessalian expedition of Pelopidas. Eclipse of sun, July 13. Battle of Cynoscephalae. Destruction of Orchomenus. Pisatans celebrate Olympian games; battle in the Altis. Athens obtains Sestos. Timotheus besieges Amphipolis.
363	Timotheus recovers Byzantium. Nektanebos I. succeeded by Tachos.
363—2	Timotheus again besieges Amphipolis. Revolts of satraps against Persia.

B.C.	
362	[Epaminondas a Boeotarch.] Battle of Mantinea. Athenian fleet sent to Hellespont. Ariobarzanes crucified.
361	Agesilaus in Egypt. Accession of Nektanebos II. Battle of Peparethus.
361—60	Death of Agesilaus (?).
360—59	Death of king Cotys, and division of Thrace.
359	Death of Perdiccas and accession of Amyntas.
358	Victories of Philip over Paeonians and Illyrians. Death of Artaxerxes II. ; accession of Artaxerxes III. Ochus.
357	Athens recovers the Chersonese and Euboea. Philip captures Amphipolis. Revolt of Chios, Cos, and Rhodes from Athens. Death of Chabrias. Dion returns to Sicily.
356	Illyrian victory of Philip. Battle of Embata. Phocians seize Delphi. Revolt of Artabazus and Orontes. Arrival of Nypsius at Syracuse.
356—5	Philip captures Pydna and Potidaea. Birth of Alexander. Composition of Xenophon's *De Vectigalibus.*
355	Chares in Asia Minor ; defeats Tithraustes. Isocrates' *De Pace.* Trial of Timotheus and Iphicrates (?).
355—4	Peace of Athens with Rhodes, Cos, etc. Isocrates' *Areopagiticus.*
354	Battle of Neon. Death of Philomelus. Murder of Dion.
354—3	Demosthenes' *On the Symmories.* Tyranny of Callippus at Syracuse.
354—50	Eubulus in charge of the Theoric Fund.
353	Philip captures Methone. Power of Onomarchus in Thessaly. Eubulus hinders Philip from attacking Phocis. Demosthenes' *For the Megalopolitans.* Death of Mausolus. Demosthenes' *For the Freedom of the Rhodians.*
353—1	Hipparinus tyrant of Syracuse.
352	Cersobleptes of Thrace submits to Macedon. Demosthenes' *Against Aristocrates.* Artabazus flees to Macedonia, and Artaxerxes makes peace with Orontes.
351	Revolt of Phoenicia against Persia ; revolt in Cyprus. Demosthenes' *First Philippic.* Idrieus succeeds Artemisia in Caria. Nysaeus becomes tyrant at Syracuse.
350	Phocion in Cyprus helping to suppress revolt.
349	Phocion in Euboea. Philip reduces Chalcidice. Alliance of Athens with Olynthus. Demosthenes' *Olynthiacs.*
348	Euboea acknowledged independent. Philip captures Olynthus.
347	First Athenian embassy to Philip (end of year). Death of Plato.
346	The Peace of Philocrates. Second embassy to Philip (spring). Philip at Thermopylae. The Phocians crushed. Philip presides at Pythian games. Demosthenes' *De Pace.* Isocrates' Letter to Philip. Second tyranny of Dionysius II.
346—5	Demosthenes impeaches Aeschines. Aeschines' *Against Timarchus.*

B.C.	
345—3	Persia recovers Egypt.
344	Demosthenes in the Peloponnesus. His *Second Philippic*.
	Timoleon sails for Sicily. Battle of Hadranum.
343	Impeachments of Philocrates and Aeschines.
	King Archidamus II. sails to Italy.
343—2	Alliance of Megara with Athens. Philip in Epirus.
	Aristotle goes to Macedonia as tutor of Alexander.
342—1	Philip's conquest of Thrace.
341	Athens sends Diopeithes to the Chersonese. Demosthenes' *On the Chersonese*, and *Third Philippic*. Demosthenes at Byzantium. The Euboic League.
340	Sieges of Perinthus and Byzantium. Naval reform at Athens. Violent proceedings at Amphictionic Council (autumn).
339	Thracian expedition of Philip. Amphictions determine to make war on Amphissa.
	Battle of the Crimisus.
338	Philip descends into Greece. His campaign in Phocis and Locris. Battle of Chaeronea (Aug.).
	Philip in the Peloponnesus. Synedrion of Corinth. Death of Isocrates. Battle of Mandonia.
338—7	Murder of Artaxerxes Ochus and accession of Arses.
338—4	Lycurgus minister of finance at Athens.
337	Second meeting of Synedrion of the Greeks at Corinth.
336	Macedonian forces sent into Asia Minor. Murder of Philip and accession of Alexander (summer).
	Alexander's first descent into Greece ; his election as general of the Greeks.
335	Alexander's campaign in Thrace and Illyria, and his second descent into Greece. Destruction of Thebes (Oct.). Accession of Darius III. Codomannus. Memnon opposes the Macedonians in Asia Minor. Aristotle begins his teaching at Athens.
334	Alexander starts on his expedition against Persia (spring). Lattle of the Granicus (Thargelion). Conquest of Lydia. Siege of Miletus. Siege of Halicarnassus. Expedition of Alexander of Epirus to Italy.
334—3	Conquest of Lycia, Pamphylia, Pisidia.
333	Alexander at Gordion. Conquest of Cilicia. Battle of Issus (Nov.).
332	Siege of Tyre (Jan.-July). Submission of Syria and Judaea. Siege of Gaza (Oct.). Conquest of Egypt.
331	Foundation of Alexandria. Submission of Cyrene. Lunar eclipse, Sept. 20 ; battle of Gaugamela (Oct. 1). Alexander at Babylon (Oct.) ; at Susa (Dec.). Battle of Megalopolis.
331—30	Battle of Pandosia.
330	Alexander in Persis (Jan.-April) ; at Ecbatana. Death of Darius (July). Conquest of Hyrcania, Areia, and Drangiana. Foundation of Alexandria Areion and Prophthasia. Execution of Philotas and Parmenio.

B.C.	
330	Aeschines' *Against Ctesiphon* and Demosthenes' *On the Crown*. Lycurgus' *Against Leocrates*.
330—29	Alexander winters in Drangiana.
329	Partial submission of Gedrosia. Conquest of Arachosia. Foundation of the Arachosian Alexandria.
329—8	Alexander winters in the Cabul region. Foundation of Alexandria under Caucasus.
328	Alexander comes to the Hindu-Kush ; conquers Bactria and Sogdiana. Foundation of Alexandria Eschate.
328—7	Alexander winters at Zariaspa.
327	Alexander at Samarcand (first months) ; murder of Clitus. Conquest of eastern Sogdiana.
	Alexander marries Roxane. Conspiracy of the pages, and execution of Callisthenes.
	Alexander recrosses the Hindu-Kush, and prepares for Indian expedition.
327—-6	Winter campaigns in the Kunar, Chitral, and Swat regions.
326	Alexander crosses the Indus. Battle of the Hydaspes. Conquest of the Punjab.
325	Conquest of the Malli. Foundation of towns on the Lower Indus. Alexander sails in the Indian Ocean. His march through Gedrosia (Aug.-Oct.). Voyage of Nearchus (Oct.-Dec.).
324	Macedonian mutiny at Opis. Alexander at Ecbatana Death of Hephaestion. Harpalus in Greece (spring). Restoration of exiles proclaimed at Olympic games (July-Aug.). Harpalus' trial at Athens ; speeches of Hypereides and Dinarchus.
324—3	Subjugation of the Cossaeans.
323	Alexander at Babylon. Funeral of Hephaestion (May). Death of Alexander (June 13). Greece revolts against Macedonia.
323—2	Siege of Lamia.
322	Battle of Crannon. Funeral oration of Hypereides. Change of the Athenian Constitution. Death of Demosthenes (Oct.). Death of Aristotle. Death of Lycurgus (?).

FIG. 206.—Coin of Metapontion (reverse). Ear of corn, bird on leaf [legend : META ; below leaf, AMI].

FIG. 207.—Coin of Terina (obverse). Head of nymph Terina ; wreath [legend : Φ].

FIG. 208.—Coin of Croton (reverse). Apollo shooting Python, tripod between.

FIG. 209.—Coin of Heraclea in Italy (reverse). Heracles strangling lion; club; owl [legend: ҺHPA-ΚΛΗΙΩΝ; ΚΑΛ above club].

NOTES AND REFERENCES

The following notes are partly illustrative, partly justificatory. Only in the case of the first sections of Chapter I., where the material is chiefly archaeological, is a select bibliography given. The following abbreviations are used :—

A.J.A. = American Journal of Archaeology.

A.T.L. = B. D. Meritt, H. T. Wade-Gery, M. F. McGregor, The Athenian Tribute Lists (3 vols., 1939-50).

B.S.A. = Annual of the British School at Athens.

C.Q. = Classical Quarterly.

C.R. = Classical Review.

Hicks and Hill = E. L. Hicks and G. F. Hill, Greek Historical Inscriptions (1901).

I.G. = Inscriptiones Graecae : I.G. i². etc. = Editio Minor.

J.H.S. = Journal of Hellenic Studies.

S.E.G. = Supplementum Epigraphicum Graecum.

S.I.G. = Dittenberger, Sylloge Inscriptionum Graecarum (3rd edition, 1915-24).

Tarn = W. W Tarn, Alexander the Great (2 vols., 1948).

Tod = M. N. Tod, A Selection of Greek Historical Inscriptions, to the end of the fifth century (2nd edition, 1946). Tod, ii = Vol. II, from 403 to 323 B.C. (1948).

CHAPTER I

[*Sect.* 1.—A comprehensive review of the problems: Sir John Myres, Who were the Greeks ? (1930).]

P. 6.—Pre-Hellenic names on both sides of the Aegean : Kretschmer, Einleitung in die Geschichte der griechischen Sprache.

[P. 6.—Thessaly : H. O. Hansen, Early Civilization in Thessaly (1933).

P. 7. *Sect.* 2.—The comprehensive results of Sir Arthur Evans' excavations are set out in his work, The Palace of Minos (4 vols.). A technical survey of Cretan problems in J. D. S. Pendlebury, The Archaeology of Crete (1939), which includes a select bibliography (381-383). A useful collection of photographs in H. Bossert, The Art of Ancient Crete (1937). Popular introduction : C. H. and H. B. Hawes, Crete the Forerunner of Greece (1909).

P. 8.—Fig. 2B, vase from Cnossus. The vase is decorated with three naturalistic octopuses amid rocks. The three handles are in the form of figure-of-eight shields. Early in the Late Minoan period.]

P. 9.—Cretan writing: Sir A. J. Evans, Scripta Minoa i (1909); to be continued by Sir John Myres.

P. 10.—Melos. Four settlements have been explored at Phylakopi, the earliest unwalled, the second and third " pre-Mycenaean " fortresses, the fourth of the Mycenaean Age: Excavations at Phylakopi in Melos (British School at Athens) (1904).

[P. 10.—Fig. 3, ivory statuette. The Boy God has short hair, after offering up his childhood's locks. He wears gold loin plates and probably once had a biretta of gold.

Pp. 10 and 11.—Troy. The conclusions from Schliemann's excavations have to be modified in the light of recent American work on the site. Detailed reports in A.J.A. xxxvi (1932) to xliii (1939). Effect on chronology summarised by W. Blegen, B.S.A. xxxvii. 8.

P. 12.—Cretan pottery. There is a change in fashion in Cretan pottery from decorative to pictorial at the end of the Middle Minoan period; but the pictorial is succeeded in turn by a more formal style. Marine and plant motifs in the latter stages of Late Minoan become highly stylised. For Cretan pottery: D. Mackenzie, J.H.S. xxiii (1903), 157, xxvi (1906), 243. See also Sir E. J. Forsdyke, Minoan Art (1929).

P. 12.—Note 2, Chronology. Sir Arthur Evans' dates have been modified to conform with new evidence set out by S. Smith, A.J.A. xlix (1945), 1.]

P. 18.—Hagia Triada. This residence flourished in Middle Minoan 3 and Late Minoan 1. This was also the period of the prosperity of Zakro, a small port on the east coast of the island (a few miles south of Palaikastro), where ships trading with Egypt and Libya called. It was excavated by D. G. Hogarth in 1901, B.S.A. vii. 121, J.H.S. xxii. 6, 333. 500 seal impressions in clay were found in a house which seems to have belonged to a gold merchant. [The buildings seem to have been destroyed at the same time as the great palaces at Cnossus and Phaestus (c. 1400).]

[P. 20.—Cretan trade. Trade contacts with Syria and Egypt become important in the first half of the second millennium. There is perhaps evidence of Cretan settlement at Ugarit (Ras-Shamra) (cf. A. Schaeffer, The Cuneiform Texts of Ras Shamra, 1939). Cretan designs influence Egyptian; perhaps textiles as well as vessels of metal and pottery were traded. This Cretan trade with the east declines sharply in the Late Minoan period (from c. 1600 B.C.) and appears to be increasingly supplanted by the Greek mainland. See H. J. Cantor, A.J.A. ii (1947), 17.] For purple-dyeing in Crete: B.S.A. ix. 276, J.H.S. xxiv (1904), 321.

P. 20.—Minos. Ridgeway, in his Minos the Destroyer rather than the Creator of the so-called " Minoan Culture of Cnossus " (Proceedings of the British Academy, iv.), insists on the tradition (preserved in the Parian Chronicle, also in Diodorus and Plutarch) that there were two kings of the name Minos, the earlier c. 1406 B.C., the later c. 1229 B.C., out of whom Herodotus has made one person (i. 171 and 173, iii. 122). He finds Minos I. in Iliad xiv. 321, Minos II. in Odyssey xi. 322 and xix. 169. He regards Minos I. as an Achaean and the destroyer of Cnossus; Minos II. as the king of the traditional thalassocracy and perhaps the leader of the Achaeans who invaded Egypt in 1223 B.C.

P. 20.—Minoa. For places of this name: Fick, Vorgriechische Ortsnamen (1905), 27. It is uncertain whether the name Minoa in Sicily is of early origin, but there is an old legend that Minos went to Sicily to seek Daedalus (Herodotus vii. 169).

P. 20, *Sect.* 3.—[H. Schliemann describes his excavations in Mycenae (Preface by W. E. Gladstone), 1878; Tiryns (1886); Troja (1884). A general account of his work in Schliemann's Excavations by Dr. C. Schuchhardt. A popular account of Schliemann's career: Emil Ludwig, Schliemann (1931). A detailed description of the monuments of Mycenae: A. J. B. Wace, Mycenae (1949). General works on the Mycenaean Age: C. Tsountas and J. I. Manatt, The Mycenaean Age (1897); H. R. Hall, The Civilization of Greece in the Bronze Age (1928); M. P. Nilsson, Homer and Mycenae (1933). A historical review of the discussion of Aegean problems during this period: Sir John Myres, The Cretan Labyrinth (Huxley Memorial Lecture, 1933).

P. 23.—Shaft graves. Very fully illustrated in G. Karo, Schachtsgräber von Mykenai.

P. 23.—Fig. 9B. Dagger-blade, from the fifth shaft grave. Similar design on both sides—wild cats stalking wild ducks amid papyrus by a river with fishes. The cats, the papyrus, and the bodies of the ducks are inlaid with gold; the wings of the ducks and the river are silver; the fish are in some dark substance.

P. 24.—Relation of Crete to Mycenae. Cretan dominance over Greece was championed by Sir Arthur Evans. Later opinion has tended to emphasise the independence of the mainland. A review of the controversy included in Sir John Myres, The Cretan Labyrinth (1933).

P. 24.—Mycenaean pottery. A. Furumark, The Mycenaean Pottery: Chronology; Analysis and Classification (1941); Chronology (1942). Distribution in the East: Wace and Blegen, Klio xxxi (1939), 131; H. J. Cantor, A.J.A. li (1947), 17.

P. 25.—New walls and palace at Mycenae: A. J. B. Wace, Mycenae, 49.

P. 27.—Treasury of Atreus. Dated by pottery from test digs under the *dromos* and by the entrance: evidence and detailed description, A. J. B. Wace, *op. cit.* 119.

P. 30.—Dendra-Midea: A. W. Persson, The Royal Tombs at Dendra (1931); New Tombs at Dendra (1945).

P. 31.—Tiryns. Early occupation is revealed by the remains of a large circular building underneath the palace. For this and other remains at Tiryns, G. Karo, Führer durch Tiryns (1934).

P. 31.—Smaller megaron. The suggestion that this was the women's megaron was made by Dörpfeld.

P. 34.—Orchomenus. The site and excavations described in Bulle and Kunze, Orchomenus (3 vols.) (1907-34).

P. 34.—Mycenaean remains in the territory of Corinth. An important site during this period was Korakou on the coast a little west of Corinth; excavations described by W. Blegen, Korakou (1921). The rest of Corinthian territory has not been fully explored. Little trace of Mycenaean remains has yet been found on the actual site of Corinth.

P. 34.—Fig. 15. Gold cup. From one of two gold cups found in a tholos tomb at Vapheio, near Sparta. The illustration shows two men tossed by a bull. The other two scenes on this cup show (*a*) a bull stampeding; (*b*) a bull caught in a net.

P. 35.—Fig. 16B, from a Mycenaean shaft grave. Note the thrusting sword of the attacker and the large body shield of his victim.

P. 38.—Fig. 18. Gem. This gold signet ring was found by Schliemann south of the Shaft Grave Circle at Mycenae. It represents a typical Mycenaean cult scene. On the right is a sacred tree (such as frequently recurs in cult scenes and has been compared with the olive tree of Athena on the Athenian Acropolis). Seated in front of the tree is the goddess holding poppy heads, probably presented by the leading votary. On the left a second votary carries a bouquet in her left hand and two iris-like flowers in her right hand. The sun and moon crescent above probably indicate that the sacred area is open to the air. In the centre the symbolic double-axe (see p. 19); to the left and above, a figure-of-eight shield with head and arms, the religious significance of which is very uncertain. See A. W. Persson, The Religion of Greece in Prehistoric Times, 70.

P. 38.—Chamber Tombs : A. J. B. Wace, Chamber Tombs at Mycenae (1932).

P. 38.—Burial customs : G. E. Mylonas, A.J.A. lii (1948), 56.

P. 38.—Mycenaean religion : M. P. Nilsson, The Minoan-Mycenaean Religion (second edition, 1950).

P. 39.—Fig. 19. Ivory group. Identification with Eleusinian goddesses suggested by Wace, *op. cit.* 86. This is perhaps the finest surviving example of Mycenaean ivory carving in the round.

P. 39.—Mycenaean writing. American publication of the Pylos tablets is awaited.

P. 41.—Mycenaean trade with the east : Wace and Blegen, Klio xxxi (1939), 131 ; H. J. Cantor, A.J.A. li (1947), 17.

P. 41.—Fig. 21. Ivory box. The style of the work, particularly of the galloping hounds and their quarry, is typically Mycenaean ; the dress of the hunters is probably eastern. Probably thirteenth century. See R. D. Barnett, Palestine Exploration Quarterly (1939), 11.

P. 41.—Settlement of Rhodes. Settlement shown by typical Mycenaean chamber tombs. Much of the pottery is of local manufacture, though inspired by mainland models. Rhodes owed its importance to its position on the route to Cyprus and Egypt. Recent excavations have shown that, as at Ugarit, the Mycenaean phase was preceded by a period of strong Cretan influence (fifteenth century), most clearly revealed in remains of frescoes on house walls. See A. Maiuri, Ialysos (1926), and G. Monaco, Clara Rhodos x (1941), 41.

P. 41.—Ugarit. An account of the settlement in C. F. A. Schaeffer, The Cuneiform Texts of Ras Sharma Ugarit (1939).

P. 42.—Fig. 22. Siege-scene. At the back a fortified city. On its walls women and men watch the struggle. In front defenders, slingers and archers, and two men protected by large shields. At the bottom right corner an upright man, possibly with boar's tusk helmet. In front of him two other helmets can be seen. Perhaps these are ship-borne attackers. The regular bricks of the fortification are not Greek and suggest the east. This may represent a characteristic eastern raid by Achaeans. Egypt has been suggested : A. W. Persson, New Tombs at Dendra (1942), 166.

P. 42.—Mycenaean remains in western Asia Minor. References to Miletus, Colophon, etc. collected: G. M. A. Hanfmann, A.J.A. lvii (1948), 145.

P. 42.—Lesbos. Excavations described: W. Lamb, Thermi (1936).

P. 43.—The Hittites. An early account: J. Garstang, The Hittite Empire (1929). Much new evidence, however, has since accumulated. See L. Delaporte, Les Hittites (1936); J. Contenau, La Civilisation des Hittites et des Hurrites du Mitanni (1948); O. R. Gurney, The Hittites (Penguin, 1951).

P. 43.—Achaeans in Hittite archives. A balanced review of the problem in F. Schachermeyer, Hethiter und Achäer (1938). I am grateful to Dr. O. R. Gurney for the translation of passages of one of the most revealing of these documents, the so-called " Tawagalawas " Letter. Tawagalawas is an Achaean chieftain, claiming a principality within the Hittite sphere of interest. He must recognise Hittite overlordship, but insists on being treated with full respect. He interferes with Hittite subjects; the Hittite king protests to the King of Ahhiyawa (" my brother ").

Col. i, 6-21. " Now when I came to Sallapa, he (Tawagalawas) sent a [ma]n to meet me | (saying) ' Take me into vassalage, and send me the " tuhkantis " | and he will conduct me to MY SUN ! ' And I sent him | the ' tartenu ' (saying) ' Go, set him beside you | on the chariot and bring him here ! ' But [he] | he snubbed the ' tartenu ' and said ' no.' But is not a ' tartenu ' | the proper representative (?) of the King ? He ha[d] my hand but he | answered (?) him ' no,' and humiliated him before the lands ; | and moreover he said this : ' Give me a kingdom here | on the spot ! If not, I will not come.' | But when I reached Waliwanda, I wrote to him : | ' If you desire my overlordship, see now, | when I come to Iyalanda, let me not find | any of your men in Iyalanda ; and [yo]u shall not let anyone go back (there), and you shall not | trespass in my dom[ain].' " Tuhkantis and Tartenu are the titles of Hittite military officials.

The rest of the letter is concerned with a Hittite vassal who has " escaped by ship " to the kingdom of Ahhiyawa.

Col. ii, 65-70. " Come, make an appe[al] | to me, and I will set you on the road (to promotion) ; and how I will set you on (that) road | that I will write to my brother (the king of Ahhiyawa). If you are | satisfied, let it be so. But if you are not | satisfied, then one of my men will bring you back, | just as you came, into the land of Ahhiyawa."

P. 44.—Danuna. Their eighth-century capital has recently been found at Kara Tepe. Excavations have yielded interesting sculptures showing strong Hittite influence, and inscriptions in Hittite hieroglyphics, but others in Phoenician script. For a general account: U. B. Alkin, Revue hittite et asianique ix (1948-9), 1.

P. 44.—Raids on Egypt. The sources for the invasion by Libyan and Mediterranean peoples translated in J. H. Breasted, Ancient Records of Egypt, iii (nos. 592-617). The main inscription is on a wall in the great temple at Karnak. (580) " They have halted, they have spent whole days and months dwelling. . . . They spend their time going about the land, fighting, to fill their bodies daily. They came to the land of Egypt, to seek the necessities of their mouths. . . . Their chief is like a dog, a man of boasting, without courage." A decisive Egyptian victory is described and a list of prisoners is added : they include Libyans, Sherden (identified by some with Sardinians), Shekelesh (? Sicels), Ekwesh (Achaeans), Teresh (? Etrus-cans). For the raids of Egypt under Rameses III.: Egerton and Wilson, Medinet Habu (1936). An extract (p. 53): " As for the foreign countries, they made a conspiracy in their isles. Removed and scattered in the fray were the lands at one time. No land could stand before their arms, from Hatti, Kode, Carchemish, Yereth, and Yeres on, (but they were) cut off at [one time]. A camp [was set up] in one place in Amor. They desolated its people, and its land was like that which has never come into being. They were coming, while the flame was prepared before them, forward toward Egypt. Their confederation was the Peleset (Philistines), Theker, Shekelesh, Denye⟨n⟩ (Danuna), and Weshesh. They laid their hands upon the land to the (very) circuit of the earth, their hearts confident and trusting : ' Our plans will succeed ! ' " This destructive raid passes along the south coast of Asia Minor and down the Syrian coast to Egypt. The identification of the peoples in these documents is very controversial, but they seem to come mainly from the fringes of Asia Minor. See G. A. Wainwright, Journal of Egyptian Archaeology, xxv (1939), 148.

P. 45.—Rhodes evacuated : Maiuri, Ialysos, 165.

P. 45.—Fig. 23. Gallery in the palace, Tiryns. This gallery dates from the strengthening of the palace fortifications in the thirteenth century.

P. 46.—Strengthening of the Acropolis at Athens : O. Broneer, A.J.A. lii (1948), 113.

P. 46.—Thucydides i. 11, trans. Jowett.

P. 47.—Troy dates : W. Blegen, B.S.A. xxxvii. 8. The view that in the period immediately following the sack of Troy (VIIa) a new people, using a radically different type of pottery, occupied the site must now be abandoned. The burnt layer of VIIa is covered by a deep stratum containing pottery of local fabrication and a few late Mycenaean pieces. It is only in the layer above this that the new pottery (knobbed ware, or Buckelkeramik) appears. This new pottery is generally associated with a Balkan origin, but it has affinities elsewhere. The view that it was introduced by invaders from the north, though still probable, cannot yet be proved. See J. L. Caskey, A.J.A. vii (1948), 122.

Sects. 5 and 6.—Chief source : Homer. For the relation of Homer to History : M. P. Nilsson, Homer and Mycenae (1933) ; W. Schadenwaldt, Von Homers Welt und Werk (1944) ; H. L. Lorimer, Homer and the Monuments (1950).

P. 50.—Herodotus' date for Homer : Her. ii. 53. " I think that Hesiod and Homer were 400 years before my time, not more." Perhaps this view was based on genealogical reckoning.

P. 50.—Fig. 25. Dagger-blade, from fourth shaft grave at Mycenae. On the left are five men, the leading hunter on his back from the charge of the leading lion. Note the deliberate variety in the lions (one attacking, one in full flight, the middle lion flying but his head turned back) to give life to the design. Lions and naked parts of the men in gold ; men's clothing and shields in silver ; the rest dark.]

P. 51.—Catalogue of Greek forces against Troy : Iliad ii. Genuineness defended by T. W. Allen, The Homeric Catalogue of Ships (1921).

P. 51.—The helmet of Meriones : Iliad x. 261. An example in A. W. Persson, New Tombs at Dendra (1942), 126.

P. 52.—Writing in the Iliad vi. 168. Perhaps the symbols were pictorial.

P. 53.—Brooch of Odysseus : Odyssey xix. 216 *sqq.*

P. 53 *sqq.*—For comparison of early Greek institutions with Roman and Teutonic, cp. Freeman, Comparative Politics (2nd ed. 1896). But though I have adopted in the text the view which regards these institutions as characteristically Aryan, I own that I feel grave doubts as to its truth, since we find similar institutions (the Council, and the assembly of the folk) among primitive non-Aryan peoples (*e.g.* in South Africa).

P. 54.—Family property in land : P. Guiraud, La Propriété foncière en Grèce, 1893.

Sects. 7, 8, and 9.—Chief sources : *Primary:* Homer ; Hesiod's Theogony ; fragments of Cyclic and Hesiodic poems. *Derivative:* (1) fragments of Hecataeus, Acusilaus, Charon, Pherecydes of Athens, Hellanicus, Herodotus ; Thucydides i. 1-21 ; (2) fragments of Ephorus ; Diodorus ; Strabo ; Pausanias. For detailed bibliography : Cambridge Ancient History ii (to be revised).

[P. 58.—Herodotus on Dorian invasions, i. 56.

P. 58.—Dialect distribution : C. D. Buck, Introduction to the Study of the Greek Dialects (1928).

P. 60.—Dorian Laconia. The archaeological evidence in Artemis Orthia (1929).

P. 60.—Dorian Corinth : T. J. Dunbabin, J.H.S. lxviii (1948), 59.

P. 61.—Archaeological evidence for Dorian invasion : T. C. Skeat, The Dorians in Archaeology (1934).

P. 61.—Fig. 27. Attic Protogeometric vase, from a grave in the Kerameikos at Athens.

P. 62.—Destruction of the Mycenaean palace. Wace, Mycenae, 23, 101. Similar evidence of destruction at Homeric Sparta (on the east bank of the Eurotas), B.S.A. xvi. 7.

P. 62.—Introduction of cremation : H. L. Lorimer, J.H.S. liii (1933), 131.

P. 63.—Herodotus and the Ionian colonisation, i. 143-148.

P. 64.—Mimnermus : Diehl, Anthologia Lyrica Graeca, 12.

P. 65.—Boeotia and Aeolian settlement : Thucydides iii. 2. The Lesbians (in 428) plotted revolt from Athens with the Lacedaemonians and " their Boeotian Kinsmen."

P. 68.—Shield of Achilles : Iliad xviii. 478. For a reconstruction of the shield : Sir John Myres, Who were the Greeks ?, 517.

P. 69.—Orientalising bronze shields from Crete : E. Kunze, Kretische Bronzereliefs (1931).

P. 70.—Halicarnassus : Herodotus (i. 144) attributes the exclusion of Halicarnassus from the Dorian festival to an individual's offence. The cause was certainly deeper.

P. 72.—Cyprus : See Sir George Hill, A History of Cyprus, vol. i (1940).]

Sect. 10.—Chief sources : passages in Homer ; Herodotus i. 1-5, 105, and other passages.

P. 77.—For mining in Greek islands : Ardaillon, Les Mines du Laurion (1899).

[P. 78.—Al Mina. Excavations described, Sir Leonard Woolley, J.H.S. lviii (1938), 1 and 131 ; for the history of the site, S. Smith, The Antiquaries

2 F

Journal, xxii (1942), 89-112. For Ionian trade with Tyre in the early sixth century, Ezekiel xxvii.

P. 78.—The Greek alphabet. That the Greeks adopted their alphabet from the Phoenician is certain. The forms of the letters correspond closely, and the names. The Phoenician names have a meaning—aleph (ox-head), beth (house), gimel (throw-stick); the corresponding Greek words, alpha, beta, gamma have no meaning. The date of transmission is controversial and Bury's view, retained in the text, is still widely held; but the arguments in favour of an eighth-century date are growing stronger. There are two main lines of enquiry. (1) At what date do Phoenician and the earliest Greek letter forms most closely correspond? This question has been answered differently, for, while some Greek letters correspond more closely to tenth-century or earlier Phoenician letters, some of the Greek letter forms (such as kappa and mu) do not appear in Phoenician inscriptions until after the ninth century. This evidence cannot be decisive until more Phoenician inscriptions of the ninth and eighth centuries are found. (2) What is the earliest evidence for Greek writing? Though much early writing on pottery has been discovered since Bury wrote, the Attic vase which he quotes is still probably the earliest surviving example, and it should be noted that its letter forms are primitive and that the alpha is closer to the Phoenician than any other example known. It is just possible that the alphabet was adopted by the Greeks some two centuries before the earliest surviving example, but the absence of writing on ninth-century pottery is a strong argument against such a view. The reopening of the eastern Mediterranean in the eighth century, when Greeks were trading in Phoenician ports, is the most probable historical setting for the transmission. See R. Carpenter, A.J.A. xxxvii (1933), 8, xlii (1938), 58, xlix (1945), 452. For letter forms, Phoenician and Greek, G. R. Driver, Semitic Writing (1948); Facsimiles of the earliest Greek inscriptions in H. Roehl, Imagines Inscriptionum Graecarum Antiquissimarum (1907).]

P. 78, *note* 1.—The reading of the second verse of the inscription is very uncertain.

[P. 78.—Byblos and papyrus: H. L. Lorimer, A.J.A. lii (1928), 21.]

Sect. 11.—Chief sources: *Primary:* (1) Hesiod and " Hesiodic " fragments; (2) fragments of Hecataeus, Acusilaus, etc.; Herodotus; Thucydides i. 1-21. *Derivative:* Diodorus iv, v, fragments of vi, vii; the Bibliotheca of Pseudo-Apollodorus; Pausanias.

P. 78, *note* 2.—Grote, History of Greece, Pt. i. ch. xvii.

P. 80.—The Ionians are mentioned once in the Iliad (xiii. 685), where the Athenians are meant.

CHAPTER II

[P. 86.—Trade and colonisation. The evidence has been systematically studied only in Sicily and Italy, for the early archaeological evidence from the Euxine and its approaches, and from the Thracian coast, is very meagre. The western evidence is set out by A. Blakeway, B.S.A. xxxiii (1935), 170 and, even if some of his early pottery dating has to be lowered, his main conclusions stand. Blakeway shows that there was a substantial export of Greek pottery, and presumably of other more perishable goods, to the west before colonies were established, and that, in many cases, Greeks were trading with natives in or near sites that they were later to colonise. It does not necessarily follow that the Greeks established colonies to secure more trade, but it is at least certain that they knew where they were going; and, though land hunger was in most cases probably the primary cause, merchants will have been very ready to support the ventures.]

P. 87.—Influence of land-system on colonisation: P. Guiraud, La Propriété foncière en Grèce (i. 6), who, however, exaggerates it.

P. 89.—The Euxine was also called the Axine or inhospitable ("Αξενος, Pind. Pyth. iv. 203); and it has been conjectured (by E. Meyer) that the sea was called the " Ascanian " from the (Phrygian) Ascanians, and that "Αξενος was a Greek corruption of this name. For recent controversy (which is likely to continue) on the name, cp. C.Q. xxxiv (1940), 123; xli. 8; xlii. 59 and 60.

P. 90.—Dates of colonies in Pontus and Propontis. The dates assigned seem untrustworthy. Thus 757-6 is given for both Cyzicus and Trapezus (and in the Parian Marble for Syracuse). Sinope: 1st colony, 676, and 2nd colony of Cyzicus, 676; 2nd colony of Sinope, 631, same year as colonisation of Cyrene. The dates for Chalcedon vary between 687 and 677; the date for Byzantium is 660-59. Other dates are: Astacus, 712-1; Acanthus, Stagira, Abdera, and Lampsacus, 654; Istrus, 656; Olbia, 645; Perinthus, c. 600; Odessus, in the reign of the Median king Astyages, c. 585. [For a convenient table of dates given by the various sources, R. M. Cook, J.H.S. lxvi (1946), 77.]

P. 93, *Sect.* 3.—Sources: *Primary:* coins; [traditions]. *Derivative:* (1) [Antiochus of Syracuse]; (2) Thucydides vi. 1-5; fragments of Philistus and Ephorus; (3) fragments of Timaeus; Diodorus iv and v, and fragments of viii; Strabo v and vi; Pseudo-Scymnus. The evidence fully discussed by T. J. Dunbabin, The Western Greeks.

P. 94.—[Cyme. It is possible that the Cyme from which settlers were drawn was Aeolian Cyme, the home of Hesiod's father. The approximate date of foundation is established by the pottery in the earliest colony graves. Natives on the site had previously imported Greek ware.

P. 94.—Cyme's harbour. The need for sheltered harbours developed comparatively late. Athens was content with the open sandy bay of Phalerum until the early fifth century. The Samian harbour was not protected by a mole until the tyranny of Polycrates (c. 530 B.C.).

P. 94.—Pithecusae. It is interesting to note that, in a native settlement of the Bronze Age on the island, fragments of Mycenaean pottery have been found (not yet published), showing an earlier connexion with the Aegean.

P. 98.—Dating of Sicilian colonies. The dates are based on Thucydides whose source is not known (Antiochus and Hellanicus have been suggested). His dates seem to be precise and not guesses based on a calculation of generations. Archaeological evidence confirms the main sequence of colonies as given by Thucydides, but cannot yet provide absolute dates, since the dating of the pottery is mainly based on the assumed colonisation dates. Dunbabin, *op. cit.* Appendix I.

P. 100.—Eretrians in Corcyra. Plutarch (Greek Questions 11 = Moralia 293B) records that the Eretrians were driven out of Corcyra by the Corinthians; their attempt to return to Eretria was violently resisted and they could not

land (hence the name given to them " οἱ ἀποσφενδόνητοι," the slung-out).
They then sailed north and established Methone on the Thermaic gulf.

P. 101.—Acragas: Dunbabin, *op. cit.* 305-325.

P. 103.—Poseidonia. The three surviving temples of Poseidonia (Paestum) are of striking scale and impressive workmanship. The earliest, the so-called basilica, may date from the early sixth century, the temple of Ceres *c.* 510 B.C., and the temple of Poseidon *c.* 460 B.C. They suggest considerable wealth, probably derived from the overland trade route. Photographs and description in F. Krauss, Paestum.]

P. 106.—Name Hellenes: Bury, J.H.S. xvi. 217.

P. 110.—[Triremes. Thucydides (i. 13) seems to imply that the trireme was invented by Corinth *c.* 700, but such an early date is difficult to reconcile with the long survival of penteconters. Herodotus implies that Polycrates, tyrant of Samos (from *c.* 535), began his rule with penteconters but later built triremes. The case for dating the invention of the trireme in the sixth century is argued by Davison, C.Q. xli (1947), 18. For the reconstruction of a trireme, Morrison, The Mariner's Mirror, xxvii (1941), 14. An illustration, p. 264.]

P. 110.—Battle between Corinth and Corcyra. Dated by Thucydides (i. 13).

P. 110, *Sect.* 5.—Sources: *Primary:* fragments of Callinus and Archilochus; cuneiform inscriptions of Assarhaddon and Assurbanipal; coins. *Derivative:* (1) Herodotus i. 6-15; [Xanthus]; (2) fragments of Nicolaus of Damascus.

P. 112.—Fig. 42. East Greek vase. Orientalising style, probably Rhodian. The frieze of wild goats is a recurrent motif among east Greeks.

P. 112.—Sardanapalus has been identified with other Assyrian kings; but he was doubtless suggested by Assurbanipal (E. Meyer, *op. cit.* i. 481).

P. 112.—Sarcophagus with Cimmerians (sixth cent.): A. S. Murray, Terracotta Sarcophagi, Greek and Etruscan, in the British Museum, 1898.

P. 112.—" It was some satisfaction to Assurbanipal to record ": The account given by Assurbanipal of the submission, the revolt, and the death of Gyges is as follows (translated from the Assyrian by G. Smith, History of Assurbanipal, p. 64; cp. p. 73) :—Gyges, king of Lydia, a district which is across the sea, a remote place of which the kings my fathers had not heard speak of its name. The account of my grand kingdom in a dream was related to him by Assur, the God my creator . " Of Assurbanipal, king of Assyria, the beloved of Assur, king of the Gods, lord of all, his princely yoke take." The day [he saw that] dream his messenger [he sent to pray for my friendship]. That dream [which he saw] by the hand of his envoy he sent and repeated [to me]. From the midst of the day when he took the yoke of [my kingdom], the Cimmerians, wasters of [his] people, who did not fear my fathers and me, and did not take the yoke of my kingdom, he captured, in the service of Assur and Ishtar, the Gods my lords. From the midst of the chiefs of the Cimmerians, whom he had taken, two chiefs in strong fetters of iron and bonds of iron, he bound, and with numerous presents he caused to bring to my presence. His messengers whom, to pray for my friendship, he was constantly sending, he wilfully discontinued; as the will of Assur, the God my creator, he had disregarded; to his own power he trusted and hardened his heart. His forces to the aid of Psammetichus (king) of Egypt, who had thrown off the yoke of my dominion, he sent; and I heard [of it] and prayed to Assur and Ishtar thus: " Before his enemies his corpse may they cast, and may they carry captive his attendants." When thus to Assur I had prayed he requited me. Before his enemies his corpse was thrown down, and they carried captive his attendants. The Cimmerians, whom by the glory of my name he had trodden under him, conquered and swept the whole of his country. . . . (Ardys) his son sat on his throne, that evil work at the lifting up of my hands, the Gods my protectors in the time of the father his begetter had destroyed. By the hand of his envoy he sent [word] and took the yoke of my kingdom thus: " The king whom God has blessed art thou; my father from [thee] departed and evil was done in his time; I am thy devoted servant, and my people all perform thy pleasure."

P. 113.—Coin of Phanes of Halicarnassus. This Phanes may be the grandfather of Phanes, son of Glaucus (mentioned in Herodotus iii. 4), who dedicated a costly bowl found at Naucratis.

P. 113.—[Greek coinage: C. Seltman, Greek Coins. The date of the earliest Greek coins is disputed. The primary evidence comes from a sealed deposit in the temple of Artemis at Ephesus, containing early crude coins with other objects. This deposit used to be dated *c.* 700, which was consistent with the attribution of the first mainland coinage to Pheidon of Argos, minting in Aegina *c.* 670. But the attribution of the Aeginetan turtles to Pheidon may be an arbitrary expansion by Ephorus of Herodotus who refers to Pheidon a system of weights and measures, but does not mention coins. Archaeologists now incline to date the objects associated with the early coins in the temple of Artemis later. This would imply *c.* 650 for the first coins and roughly a generation later for the Aeginetan coinage. The new chronology has not yet been discussed in print.

P. 114.—Italian cities' use of Corinthian coins. For a good example of an overstruck Corinthian Pegasus, Sutherland, American Numismatic Society, Museum Notes, iii (1948), Pl. iv. 2.]

P. 114, *Sect.* 6.—Sources: *Primary:* inscription of Abu Simbel; inscriptions of Naucratis; archaeological remains at Naucratis and Defenneh. *Derivative:* Herodotus ii; Strabo 801, 808.

P. 115.—[Naucratis and Defenneh: Relation of archaeological evidence to literary sources, R. M. Cook, J.H.S. lvii (1937), 227.

P. 115.—Abusimbel inscription: Tod, 4. The Greeks were under the command of Psammetichus, son of Theocles: the father may have served under the first Psamatik and named his son after the Egyptian king. Three of the Greeks give their origins as Ialysus, Teos, Colophon.]

P. 116, *Sect.* 7.—Sources: *Primary:* fragments of Eugammon. Inscription. *Derivative:* Herodotus iv; Pindar, Pyth. iv, v, ix; Callimachus, Hymn 2.

[P. 116.—Colonisation of Cyrene. An early fourth-century decree discovered in Cyrene (S.E.G. ix. 3) throws light on the original settlement. It confers citizenship on resident Theraeans κατὰ τὰ πάτρια, τὰ οἱ πρόγονοι ἐποιήσαντο and records the oath of the settlers: " It was resolved by the ecclesia: since Apollo unprompted bade Battus and the Theraeans colonise Cyrene, the Theraeans are resolved to send Battus as leader and king; and the Theraeans shall sail as his companions. They shall sail with equal rights from each household, one son from each, and the young men (shall be drawn

from all the districts), and any other free Theraean who wishes may sail.
And if the colonists establish their settlement any kinsman who sails afterwards to Libya shall be entitled to citizenship and office and to a share in
land that has no owner.   But if they do not establish their settlement and
the Theraeans cannot help them, and they are hard pressed by necessity for
five years, then they may leave the land without fear for Thera, and they
may take again their property and be citizens.   And whoso refuses to sail
when the city despatches him he shall be condemned to death and his property
shall be state property. . . . On these terms they made oaths, both those
that remained in Thera and those who sailed to establish the colony, and
they made curses against those who transgressed the oath and did not abide
by it. . . . They fashioned images of wax and burnt them, all standing in a
circle, men, women, boys and girls, chanting imprecations, that he who did
not abide by these oaths should be consumed and should dissolve like the
images, himself, his descendants, and his property."   The main substance
of the document seems to be original and is close to the version of Herodotus
(iv. 153).   Herodotus (iv. 156) also records that when, after their first disappointment, the colonists sailed home, the Theraeans refused to let them
land (cp. the Eretrians, note to p. 100).   Colonisation was here the alternative to starvation.

P. 116.—Cyrene's trade.   Importance of sheep, Homer, Odyssey 85 *sq.*:

καὶ Λιβύην, ἵνα τ᾽ ἄρνες ἄφαρ κεραοὶ τελέθουσι.
τρὶς γὰρ τίκτει μῆλα τελεσφόρον εἰς ἐνιαυτόν.

Cp. next note.   Silphium, used as a purgative and also as a vegetable, Aristophanes, Knights, 895.   Horses: Pindar's Fourth and Fifth Pythian Odes
celebrate Arcesilas, last king of Cyrene, for his victory of 462 B.C., in the
horse race at Delphi.

P. 117.—Arcesilas vase.   Formerly regarded as Cyrenaean, but excavations at Sparta have shown it to be Laconian (cp. Lane, B.S.A. xxxiv. 161).
The artist has been to Cyrene and recalls a vivid scene.   The material which
is being weighed and packed has been thought to be silphium, but silphium
was packed in jars and kept moist : almost certainly wool is represented.
The king's name is painted by his head.   In the field are various animals, a
tame cat under the chair, to the left a lizard, above a flying stork, and, on
the awning, a tame monkey with collar.   Sparta had natural connexions with
Cyrene through her colony, Thera.   Samos, also connected with Sparta
(Her. iii. 47), has also strong commercial connexions with Cyrene.]

P. 118, *Sect.* 8.—Sources : *Primary :* fragments of Archilochus.   *Derivative :* passages in Aristotle's Politics iv and v.

[P. 118.—Slave trade : cp. Ezekiel xxvii. 13, a vivid picture of Tyre in
the early sixth century.   "Javan (the name extended by the Phoenicians
from the Ionians to all Greeks), Tubal and Meshech, they were thy traffickers :
they traded the persons of men and vessels of brass for thy merchandise."

P. 119.—Archilochus.   Eclipse of the sun, frag. 74 (Diehl).   The passage
has been thought by some to refer to the eclipse of March 14, 711, by others
to that of April 6, 648.   The latter is more probable, Jacoby, C.Q. xxxv
(1941), 97.]   The lines of Archilochus are :

Ζεὺς πατὴρ Ὀλυμπίων
ἐκ μεσημβρίης ἔθηκε νύκτ᾽ ἀποκρύψας φάος
ἡλίου λάμποντος.

CHAPTER III

P. 120, *Sects*. 1 and 3.—Sources: *Primary :* fragments of laws quoted in Plutarch's Lycurgus; fragments of Tyrtaeus and Alcman; excavations described in Artemis Orthia. *Derivative :* (1) Herodotus (i. 65; iv. 147, etc.; vi. 51, etc.); Xenophon's Polity of the Lacedaemonians; Aristotle, **Pol.** ii and fragments of Polity of Lacedaemonians; (2) Strabo viii; Diodorus vii (frags.); Plutarch's Lycurgus; Pausanias iii.

[**P. 123.**—Spartan statute: Preserved in Plutarch, Lycurgus vi, the text in places uncertain. Tyrtaeus (cited by Plutarch) paraphrased this document, probably in his poem, Eunomia; but presented it as an oracle. It is probably a statute of the Spartan assembly, perhaps based on or confirmed by an oracle. The main power rests with the γερουσία σὺν ἀρχαγέταις. The people can discuss and ratify proposals; but the Gerousia with the kings retains the right of veto. This document has been associated with reform following the Messenian revolt (late seventh century), Wade-Gery, C.Q. xxxvii (1943), 62 and C.Q. xxxviii. 1, 115; but both date and precise significance are very uncertain. The ephors are not mentioned, which may suggest an earlier date, for the power of the ephors is full grown by the middle of the sixth century.]

P. 124, *note* 3.—Names of kings of Eurypontid house significant (Anaxidamus, Damaratos, etc.): E. Meyer, *op. cit.* ii. 562.

P. 125, *Sect.* 2.—Sources: *Primary:* fragments of Tyrtaeus. *Derivative:* (1) Herodotus iii. 47; (2) [Rhianus]; (3) Diodorus xv. 66; Pausanias iv; Justin iii. 4-5.

P. 127.—[First Messenian War. Tradition connected the founding of Rhegium (*c.* 730) with the beginning of the war; the founding of Taras (*c.* 707) with its end. The last Messenian victory at Olympia was dated to 736, the first Spartan victory to 716. Tyrtaeus says that Theopompus led the Spartans; a date towards the end of the eighth century suits his place in the Spartan king list. The only valuable ancient source for the conquest of Messenia is Tyrtaeus.

P. 128.—Messenian revolt. Tyrtaeus, a contemporary, says that the war of conquest was fought by our fathers' fathers. This might date the revolt to the middle of the seventh century, but the phrase cannot be pressed. The revolt reflects the general reaction against Dorians in the Peloponnese, clearly expressed also in the tyrannies of Corinth and Sicyon. The revival of Messenian independence in the fourth century stimulated "traditions" about the great revolt. Pausanias and other late sources have been particularly infected by a romantic epic composed by Rhianus, a third-century Alexandrian scholar.

P. 129.—Land problem at Sparta. Aristotle (Politics 1306 b) speaks of " a state of society which is most often the result of war, as at Lacedaemon in the days of the Messenian War (ὑπὸ τὸν Μεσσηνιακὸν πόλεμον, meaning perhaps just after the war); this is proved from the poem of Tyrtaeus, entitled ' Good Order '; for he speaks of certain citizens who were ruined by the war and wanted to have a redistribution of the land."

P. 129.—Phalanx: H. L. Lorimer, B.S.A. xli (1947), 76.

P. 130.—Archaeological evidence for early Sparta: Artemis Orthia, the account of British excavations on the site of a Spartan temple. Laconian pottery, Lane, B.S.A. xxxiv (1933-4), 99.

P. 131.—Military reforms at Sparta. The Spartan army system was probably reformed at some time after the crushing of the Messenian revolt. Tyrtaeus, frag. i. 12 (Diehl), speaks of the Spartans as brigaded in three Dorian tribal divisions:

> Χωρὶς Πάμφυλοί τε καὶ Ὑλλεῖς ἠδ[ὲ Δυμᾶνες:
> ἀνδροφόνους μελίας χερσὶν ἀν[ασχόμενοι.]

It is possible, however, from the context that Tyrtaeus is referring to an earlier period than the Messenian revolt. According to Herodotus (ix. 53²) there was a λόχος Πιτανήτης at Plataea, and Pitana was one of the villages which composed Sparta.]

P. 132.—Spartan boys. They were divided into " herds " (βοῦαι), and each herd consisted of a certain number of " pens " or troops (ἴλαι). The youth who commanded the *bua* was a *buagor*, the captain of the *ila* an *ilarch*.

P. 132.—Iranes. The elder youth from eighteen to twenty was called a *melliran*, for he was soon, on completing his twentieth year, to enter into the ranks of the *iranes*, or young men over twenty and under thirty. The younger members of this class were called *first iranes* (*protiranes*); the eldest, who were about to become " men," were *sphaireis*; and there were probably intermediate classes.

P. 136.—Lycurgus. Apollo himself debated whether Lycurgus was god or man in an oracle cited by Herodotus (i. 65), which was to this effect:

> Well-come, Lycurgus, come to my rich shrine,
>   Whom Zeus loves well, and all celestials love;
> Shall I declare thee human or divine?
>   Surely a god, if I know aught thereof.

P. 136, *Sect.* 4.—Sources: *Primary:* (1) Laws of Gortyn; (2) Aristotle, Pol. ii. 7; passages in Plato's Republic and Laws. *Derivative:* Strabo x. 4.

[P. 137.—Gortyn: Laws of Gortyn, Tod, 36.]

P. 139, *Sect.* 5.—Sources: *Primary:* architectural remains at Olympia. *Derivative:* Herodotus vi. 127; Ephorus (in Strabo, 358); Aristotle, Pol. ii. 6, v. 10; 'Aθ. Πολ. 10 and frags. 480, 481; Pausanias v and vi.

P. 140.—[Pheidon of Argos. There is much confusion in the ancient sources concerning the date of Pheidon. Ephorus called him the tenth from Temenos, which to Ephorus would be *c.* 800-770; but while the king list might be genuine the date assumed for Temenos might be wrong. In another tradition, reflected in the Parian Marble, he is placed 100 years earlier (900-870); but this dating probably derives from the fiction that Pheidon was brother of Karanus, the founder of the Macedonian Kingdom, whose date was pushed back into a more remote past for reasons of prestige. Herodotus speaks of Pheidon as father of a suitor for Agariste of Sicyon (*c.* 570). These various traditions are set out in How and Wells, Herodotus ii. 117. In view of the wide divergence the best approach is to attempt to fit the actions attributed to Pheidon with the historical setting that best fits them. The fullest account is given in Strabo, 358 (from Ephorus). Pheidon was the strongest man of his day. He reasserted the heritage of Temenus. He established a system of weights and measures and a coinage (Herodotus, who mentions weights and measures, says nothing of a coinage, which may have been added arbitrarily by the rationalising Ephorus; for it is doubtful whether silver coinage was current in Greece when Pheidon died, cp. note on p. 114). He presided over the Olympic festival. He robbed Sparta of the leadership of the Peloponnese.

It is probable that Pheidon's Olympiad fell in 668 (amending Pausanias' 8th to 28th). The Spartan defeat at Hysiae in 669-8 is not explicitly connected with Pheidon but would fit in well with his presidency at Olympia in 668. Megarian activity in colonisation at this time may owe something to Argive help. It was perhaps also in Pheidon's time that Argos helped Aegina to defeat Athens (Her. v. 82-88). A strong Argos shortly before the middle of the seventh century is an attractive hypothesis. Sparta had perhaps grown soft after the conquest of Messenia. For a generation Argos became the strongest power in the Peloponnese, weakening Sparta, Corinth and Athens, supporting Megara and Aegina. With the death of Pheidon and the rise of tyrannies in Sicyon and Corinth, partly perhaps in protest against the dominance of Dorian Argos, power shifted to the isthmus cities.] For extent of Argive power to the south, Herodotus i. 82.

P. 140.—The story of the struggle of the Eleans and Pisatans for Olympia rests on Elean tradition. The certain facts seem to be that the Elean control of the games dates from 572 B.C., and that for some years before then was a struggle. The Eleans represented this struggle as begun by the Pisatans (Pausanias vi. 22. 4), they themselves having been in possession of Olympia since the Olympiad of Pheidon. But it may be questioned whether this is true. The mere fact that the Elean control of the festival is dated from 572 B.C. (Eusebius i. 198, ed. Schöne) makes it probable that till then the festival was administered by the Pisatans.—The institution of the Ἑλλανο-ζίκαι, as umpires, may be referred to 572 B.C. or shortly after.—The struggle between Elis and Pisa may probably be illustrated by a treaty, graven on a bronze tablet discovered at Olympia (now in the British Museum), between the men of Elis and the men of Arcadian Heraea. We may guess (cp. Busolt, Griechische Geschichte, i². 706; von Scala, Staatsverträge, No. 27) that it belongs to a year shortly before 572 B.C.; the aid of Heraea would have been very valuable to Elis in the war with Pisa. As this is the earliest extant treaty between two Greek states, I may add a translation of it here :—

" The treaty (*vratra*) between the Eleans and Heraeans.

" There shall be an alliance for a hundred years; this year shall be the first. If any need arise, either in word or deed, they shall help one another, both in other matters and in war. But if they do not so help, the transgressors shall pay a talent of silver to Zeus of Olympia as a fine. If any injure this writing, whether a private man (*Fέτας*) or magistrate (*τελεστά*) or deme, he (or it) shall be liable to the sacred penalty herein written " (Text : Tod, 5).

[P. 141.—Olympia. The site, history, and monuments in Pausanias v. 7-vi.]

P. 142.—The first Olympiad : Records of the Olympian victors seem to have been kept by the Eleans since the early part of the sixth century; but the Olympian list, as a whole, with the dates of the eighth and seventh centuries, seems to have been first worked out by Hippias of Elis at the very end of the fifth century. The Olympiads were first used as a system of chronological reckoning in the third century by the Siceliot Timaeus. The untrustworthy character of the Olympian list and of the generally accepted early dates in Greek history was pointed out by Professor Mahaffy. See Problems in Greek History, 217 *sqq.* Appendix. His arguments have been reinforced by Busolt, *op. cit.* 2nd ed. i. 586 *sqq.*

[P. 143.—Temple of Hera : Dated to the late seventh century, replacing an earlier temple in timber and sun-dried brick.]

P. 144, *Sect.* 6.—Sources : *Primary:* fragments of Archilochus, Alcaeus, Sappho. *Derivative:* Thuc. i. 13 ; Aristotle, Pol. iv and v.

P. 148, *Sect.* 7.—Sources : *Primary:* fragments of Theognis. *Derivative:* (1) Herodotus iii. 48-53 ; v. 67-68, 92 ; vi. 126-130 ; (2) Aristotle, Pol. iv and v ; frags. of Nicolaus of Damascus : Pausanias, v. 17 ; Diogenes Laertius, i. 72.

P. 149.—[Fig. 56. So-called Chigi vase, found in Etruria. The upper panel shows two lines of hoplites meeting (one of the earliest representations of phalanx tactics) : note the flute-player, whose function is to maintain rhythm For Corinthian pottery (and other crafts), H. G. G. Payne, Necrocorinthia ; also the account of British excavation in Perachorâ.]

P. 152.—Chest of Cypselus : Described by Pausanias, v. 17²-19. Interesting restoration by Stuart Jones in J.H.S. xiv (1894), 30 and Pl. I.

P. 153.—[Temple of Apollo at Corinth. Formerly thought to be a monument of the tyranny. Excavation has shown it to date from *c.* 550-530, Weinberg, Hesp. viii (1939), 191. Fig. 58 : in the background, Acrocorinth.

P. 154.—Periander's relations with Corcyra. Corcyra had fought against Corinth shortly before the tyranny. Some Bacchiad nobles fled from the tyranny to Corcyra. Cypselus' colonisation in the north-west may have been opposed by Corcyra, cp. Tod, **2,** the epitaph of Arniades of Corcyra whom " Ares slew as he fought at the ships by the streams of Aratthus " (a river which flows into the Ambraciot Gulf). Later, Corinth and Corcyra seem to have come to terms, for Epidamnus (625) was a joint foundation. The period of co operation did not last long. Periander seems to have brought the independent island under direct control (Her. iii. 52).]

P. 155.—Orthagoras : Aristotle, Pol. v. 12. Presumably Andreas took the name Orthagoras when he became tyrant, *c.* 665. Cleisthenes probably ruled *c.* 600-570.

[P. 156.—Wooing of Agariste : Her. vi. 126-131. It is interesting to see how Athenian noble families sought marriage alliances with tyrants. Cylon was the son-in-law of Theagenes, tyrant of Megara : a member of the Philaid house, which produced Miltiades and Cimon, married into the family of Cypselus. In the struggle for power at home influence abroad might be useful.]

P. 157, *Sect.* 8.—Sources : *Primary:* Homeric Hymn to Pythian Apollo. *Derivative:* Aeschines, c. Ctes. 107-112 ; Marmor Parium, 37 ; Strabo ix. 3 ; Plutarch, Solon 11 ; Pausanias x. 37 ; Hypothesis to Pindar's Pythian Odes.

[P. 157.—Delphi. An admirable collection of photographs of the site and remains in G. de Miré and P. de la Coste-Messelière, Delphes. The photograph (fig. 59) was taken before excavation began. The village occupied the site and had first to be moved. For the Delphic oracle, H. W. Parke, A History of the Delphic Oracle. The site and monuments described by Pausanias x. 9-32.]

P. 157.—Date of Homeric Hymn to Pythian Apollo : prior to the Sacred War, as its tenor shows.

P. 159, *note.*—The part ascribed to Solon in the Sacred War is very doubtful. [According to Plutarch (Solon, 11), Delphic records showed that Alcmaeon led the Athenian contingent. The Alcmaeonid connexion with Delphi was to be of considerable importance later.]

P. 159.—" Crisaean Gulf " : the name remained in common use long afterwards ; it is always used by Thucydides.

P. 159.—First Pythiad = 582 B.C. (not 586) : the scholiasts on Pindar calculated the Pythiads on this assumption.

P. 159.—Old stadion in the plain below Crisa : cp. Pindar, Pyth. xi. 49.

[P. 160.—Sicyan Treasury metopes : Delphes, Plates 40-43.

P. 161.—League of Italian cities. A distinctive type of coin appears in south Italy near the middle of the sixth century. The reverse repeats, incuse, the design of the obverse, and the coins are very thin. Seltman (Greek Coinage, 76-9) has ingeniously suggested that this was a reflection of Pythagoreanism, but the coins probably begin earlier than the arrival of Pythagoras in Italy and the importance of luxury-loving Sybaris in the series seems to be inconsistent with an influence derived from stern Pythagorean doctrines.]

CHAPTER IV

P. 163.—Sources : *Primary:* Homeric Hymn to Demeter ; fragments of Solon ; [laws of Solon] ; [register of Archons]. *Derivative:* (1) Herodotus (various passages) ; Thucydides ii. 15 ; Aristotle, Politics and 'Aθ. Πολ. ; fragments of Atthidographers ; (2) Plutarch, Theseus and Solon ; Pausanias i. Solon's poems translated in K. Freeman, The Work and Life of Solon.

P. 169. — For kings and regents and position of the Medontids, Willamowitz-Möllendorf, Hermes (1898), 126. Acastus and his successors beside the *basilês fainéants* correspond to the Pippins and Charles Martel in the days of the last Merovingian kings of Gaul.

P. 173.—The Eumolpids, who traced themselves to Poseidon, were the royal house of Eleusis, and they retained the priesthood after the incorporation in Attica. Their Thracian descent was a legend which had obtained credence as early as the fifth century. There may, however, have been Thracian settlers at Eleusis ; this is an obscure question. For Thracians in Phocis : Thuc. ii. 29. There was a clan of Thracidae at Delphi, Diodorus xvi. 24.

[P. 174.—Hektemoroi. The position of these sixth-parters is unknown. The name occurs in ancient accounts of Solon's measures, but is not found later. The status was probably abolished by Solon ; later classical writers may have received the name from Solon's poems or tradition and themselves not known the precise meaning. According to Plutarch and Aristotle the hektemor system was widespread. In one of his poems Solon (24, Diehl) claimed : " Black earth, formerly enslaved, now free, from whom I once uprooted the horoi fixed in many places." It is natural to connect the uprooting of horoi (markers) with the end of the hektemor system. The hektemors may have been small-holders who got into debt to the wealthy landowners and, when they could not pay, were reduced to virtual serfdom, paying one-sixth of their produce to their creditors (or possibly five-sixths, if the nobles provided seed corn and equipment). The horoi marked the transaction and their uprooting followed naturally from the cancellation of debts. The hektemors became again free farmers.]

P. 175.—Timocracy before Solon. Three classes, not four; Solon made the citizens who had a smaller income than two hundred medimni into a fourth class, called the Thêtes. Pentacosiomedimni *may* have been a name invented officially for the highest class when the timocracy was organised; but it may also, as I suggest, have been a popular name for the rich (like our millionaire, though applied to income, not to capital).

P. 176.—The Demiurgi. Their political position both under the timocracy and under Solon's constitution is obscure. Yet that they had political rights, whether they acquired land or not, I consider certain. The mere fact that they stand out as a distinct social class, and are not simply merged in the Thêtes, shows their importance.

P. 177.—Athenian navy in second half of seventh century. That the Athenians had then a small fleet of penteconters is not only a necessary inference from the institution of the naucraries, but is implied by the Athenian occupation of Sigeum before 600 B.C.

P. 178.—[Temple of Poseidon on Calauria. The foundations of the stone temple date from the end of the sixth century, but there was probably an earlier building in sun-dried brick. G. Welter, Troizen und Kalauria, 43 ff.

P. 180.—Dracon. Constitutional reforms are attributed to him by Aristotle ('Aθ. Ποл. 4). This Draconian constitution contains clear anachronisms and is invented by later oligarchic propaganda. Dracon's political work, as the other sources imply, was confined to a codification of the laws.

P. 182.—Limitation of land tenure. That Solon fixed a limit to the land which could be owned by one person is inferred from Aristotle, Pol. 1266 b. No other ancient evidence for such a law exists, and Aristotle's words are ambiguous. It is possible that he is citing Solon's liberation of the small farmers as an example of a measure which produced greater equality, not unlike the effect produced by laws in other states to limit the acquisition of land.

P. 182.—Ban on export of Attic products. This measure would further stimulate the growing of olives, which, with their products, were easily marketed abroad. Solon, however, was probably more anxious to ensure that all Attic corn was reserved for Attica. Landowners, especially in the Eleusinian plain, might be tempted to sell their corn at a higher price to traders from Aegina or Megara. Athens was probably not yet dependent on imported corn but she needed all she could produce.]

P. 183.—Monetary reform of Solon : the conclusions of P. Gardner are here adopted. [Much has since been written on the subject but conclusions are still very uncertain.]

[P. 184.—Solon's Heliaea. To speak of " the institution of popular courts " by Solon is perhaps an anachronism. Solon's Heliaea was probably the assembly of the whole people meeting in judicial capacity. But an increase in such judicial business led logically to the delegation of jurisdiction to smaller courts. The popular law courts, however, only reached full maturity and full political power as a result of the reforms of Ephialtes (462-1).

P. 185.—The Council of four hundred. Many scholars have doubted whether a popular council existed before Cleisthenes' reforms. But Plutarch's words (Solon 19), οἰόμενος ἐπὶ δυσὶ βουλαῖς ὥσπερ ἀγκύραις ὁρμοῦσαν ἧττον ἐν σάλῳ τὴν πόλιν ἔσεσθαι, seem to be taken directly or indirectly from an actual poem (Wade-Gery). The appeal of the oligarchic reformers in 411 to tradition in establishing a Council of 400 implies that late fifth-century Athenians thought that the Cleisthenic Council of 500 was preceded by a Council of 400. Plutarch implies that the councillors were chosen and not selected by lot, but his words cannot be pressed ; election would seem more natural in an age which was still primarily aristocratic.

P. 185.—Use of the lot : Aristotle ('Aθ. Πολ. 8) says that Solon "made the nine archons to be appointed by lot from (40) previously elected." Later (22) he says that in 488-7 " they appointed the nine archons by lot from 500 previously elected by the demesmen, then for the first time after the tyranny." These two passages can be reconciled by assuming that the lot, introduced by Solon, was abandoned under the tyranny and reintroduced in 488-7. But the main struggle for power in the period following Solon's reforms centred round the archonship, which was still the most important office in the state. It is probable that archons were elected until their power was substantially diminished in the period following Cleisthenes' reforms.

P. 189.—Fig. 65. This Attic Kouros, now in the Metropolitan Museum of New York, is one of a long series. Such statues were a favourite form of dedication by the nobility to Poseidon and were used also as funerary monuments. They are striking testimony to the early achievement of Attic sculpture.]

CHAPTER V

P. 190.—Sources, as for Chapter IV, with a few inscriptions, architectural remains, etc.

P. 191.—[Conquest of Salamis. The accounts of Athens' wars with Megara are confused in the ancient sources. Plutarch (Solon, 9-10) associates Pisistratus with Solon in the conquest. Herodotus (i. 59) refers the capture of Nisaea to Pisistratus, but makes no mention of Salamis. Aristotle ('Aθ. Πολ. 17²), drawing on a standard history of Athens, denies that Pisistratus had any part in Solon's war. Solon certainly wrote a poem rousing the Athenians to fight (2, Diehl):

> ἴομεν ἐς Σαλαμῖνα μαχησόμενοι περὶ νήσου
> ἱμερτῆς χαλεπόν τ' αἶσχος ἀπωσόμενοι.

This may well have been before his archonship and may in part account for his pre-eminence. Perhaps Salamis was won c. 600 : further fighting broke out c. 570 with Megara in which Nisaea was captured and the Athenian hold on Salamis confirmed, largely as a result of Pisistratus' generalship.

P. 191.—Spartan arbitration. Connected by Plutarch with Solon's conquest of Salamis, but probably much later. Plutarch includes among the five arbitrators a Cleomenes, who may be the Spartan king (c. 516-490). The short period after the expulsion of the tyrants from Athens (510), when both Megara and Athens accepted Spartan leadership, provides the most probable historical setting.

P. 192.—Salamis decree : Tod, 11, S.E.G. x. 1. There are crucial gaps in the decree as preserved. The subject of the main provisions has been restored to mean (a) the original Salaminians (οἰκοντας), (b) all Athenians who have acquired land on Salamis ('Aθεναιος), (c) new Athenian settlers (κλεροχος). Since hoplite service is demanded it is probable that the native population is not concerned, for they were not enrolled in the Attic demes and did not serve in the hoplite ranks. The regulations are similar to those adopted for later cleruchs ; probably the decree is concerned with new Athenian settlers. The date can be inferred only from letter forms, probably late sixth century. It is tempting to believe that, when the Cleisthenic democracy broke with Sparta, the Athenians felt anxious about Salamis, to which their main title was a recent Spartan arbitration. They may have sent settlers to strengthen their hold on the island.

P. 192.—Stele of Aristion from his tomb near Brauron, I.G. i². 1024. But the sculpture is considerably later than 560 and the name is common.

P. 194.—Dates of Pisistratus' tyranny. The beginning of Pisistratus' tyranny (561/0) and his death (528/7) are securely established. The dates of his two exiles are controversial. The figures in Aristotle's 'Aθ. Πολ. are inconsistent and require amendment. An alternative chronology, more consistent with the indications of Herodotus, dates the second exile 556-546. This scheme has the further advantage of giving Pisistratus a long period of continuous rule before his death.]

P. 195.—Land-taxes. Thus we may reconcile Aristotle 'Aθ. Πολ. 16 (δεκάτην) with Thucydides vi. 54 (εἰκοστὴν μόνον).

P. 195.—Mines of Laurion : Ardaillon, Les Mines du Laurion.

P. 197.—The presence of the Athenians on the Hellespontine shores in the first (?) half of the sixth century is illustrated by an inscription found at Sigeum (now in the British Museum), *in the Attic dialect and in the Attic alphabet*, on a pillar which supported the sculptured portrait of a certain Phanodicus of Proconnesus—probably the tyrant of that city—who presented the city hall (πρυτανεῖον) of the Sigeans with a mixing-bowl, a stand for it, and a strainer. Phanodicus sent the pillar with his bust, and an Ionic inscription recording his gift ; the men of Sigeum added an Attic version below (Hicks and Hill, 8).

P. 198.—The story of the Pisistratean commission on the Homeric poems has been definitely disproved by T. W. Allen, C.Q. vii. 33.

P. 199.—Pisistratus also built a temple to the Pythian Apollo S.W. of the temple of Zeus. [Pisistratus, son of Hippias, dedicated an altar in the temenos to commemorate his archonship (probably 522/1). Thucydides (vi. 54) quotes the inscription and two fragments have been recovered, Tod, 8. The lettering is strikingly handsome and mature and for that reason some scholars have dated it much later and attributed the archonship of Pisistratus to 497/6. But it is highly improbable that the eldest son of Hippias should be left in Athens when his father was expelled and Thucydides implies that Pisistratus' archonship was during the tyranny. The tyrant's house would naturally employ one of the best craftsmen of the day. A dedication by Hipparchus (? brother of Hippias) in the Ptoan sanctuary near Thebes is probably by the same hand (Meritt in Hesp. viii (1939), 65).]

P. 203.—Tegea to harbour no Messenians: Aristotle (Plutarch, Greek Questions 5 = Moralia, 292 B), who quotes from the stele on which the treaty was engraved, and which was set up on the banks of the Alpheus (at Olympia?).

P. 204.—[Athens and Aegina. For the early war, Her. v. 82-88, see Dunbabin, B.S.A. xxxvii (1936-7), 83.

P. 204.—Hippias' tyranny. A recently discovered fragment of an Athenian archon list, inscribed in the late fifth century, Hesp. viii (1939), 59, shows that Hippias, Cleisthenes (the first letter is missing), Miltiades were archons in successive years from 526 to 524, and perhaps Pisistratus, son of Hippias, in 522 (. . . . . στρατος). It seems that Hippias began his rule with a general political reconciliation and the return of hostile nobles from exile. The reconciliation, however, did not last long. The Alcmaeonids were again in exile by 514.

P. 205.—Temple of Apollo at Delphi. Subscriptions were also obtained from foreign peoples in contact with the Greeks. Herodotus (ii. 180) says that Amasis, king of Egypt, contributed 1000 talents of alum.]

P. 207.—1 represents a portion of the north side of the frieze, which was occupied with the battle of the Gods and Giants: Cybele in her lion-drawn car is conspicuous. 2 is the central portion of the battle of Greeks and Trojans over the body of Sarpedon.

P. 208.—[Statue group of Harmodius and Aristogiton. The original group, by Antenor, was carried to Persia in 480, and restored by Alexander or one of his successors (the sources differ). A new group, by Critias and Nesiotes, was set up at Athens immediately after the Persian War. For the base of this group see Hesp. v (1936), 355. The illustration is taken from a Roman copy in Naples, and the figures have been heavily restored. Most misleading is the new head of Aristogiton (left) which should be bearded. The upraised right hand of Harmodius held a sword. The original position of the figures is uncertain, cp. Richter, Sculpture and Sculptors of the Greeks, 150. A Greek copy in relief, Seltman in J.H.S. lxvii (1947), 24.]

P. 216.—Date of alliance between Athens and Plataea (Thuc. iii. 55). According to the text of Thuc. iii. 68 the date would be 519/8, which can hardly be right. Busolt proposes a slight emendation (Gr. Geschichte, ii. 399), which would give 510/9.

P. 217.—[Inscription on Athenian stoa at Delphi: Tod, 18. Date and occasion are controversial, since letter forms are not a decisive criterion. The colonnade commemorates a naval victory between 510 and 465. Many scholars have attributed it to the Persian Wars, and it has been recently suggested that the ὅπλα of the inscription are not arms but the cables of the Persian bridges over the Hellespont, P. Amandry, B.C.H. lxxii (1946), 1. These with the beaks of captured ships would commemorate the operations which ended in the capture of Sestos, 479.]

CHAPTER VI

P. 219, *Sect.* 1.—Sources: *Primary:* inscriptions of Assarhaddon and Assurbanipal. *Derivative:* (1) Herodotus i; [Xanthus]; Bacchylides, Ode 3; fragments of Ctesias; (2) fragments of Nicolaus of Damascus; Diodorus, fragments of ix; Justin i.

P. 220.—Sargon stele: Schrader, Die Sargonstele des Berliner Museums, in the Abhandlungen of the Berlin Academy, 1881.

[P. 221.—Fall of Assyria. Detailed account of events preceding and following the fall of Nineveh in a cuneiform text in the British Museum, C. J. Gadd, The Fall of Nineveh.

P. 222.—Greek mercenaries serving Babylon: Poem of Alcaeus to his brother Antimenidas (50, Diehl).

P. 223.—Croesus inscription at Ephesus: Tod, 6.

P. 224.—Fig. 73. The male figure is probably the eunuch priest of Artemis in ceremonial costume, known from literary sources as Megabyzos. His name and femininity reflect the oriental origin of the cult. The female figure is probably a priestess. See Excavations at Ephesus, 155.

P. 227.—Fall of Sardis. Croesus had not expected Cyrus to follow him, and had disbanded his mercenaries. The date of the fall of Sardis in ancient sources is variously given, 546-541.]

P. 228.—Fig. 74. The date of this red-figured vase (in the Louvre) is early fifth century.

P. 229, *Sect.* 2.—Sources: Herodotus i; Justin and fragments as in Sect. 1.

P. 232, *Sect.* 3.—Sources: Herodotus iii; Justin and fragments as in Sect. 1.

P. 234, *Sect.* 4.—Sources: *Primary:* inscripton of Behistun (Rawlinson, The Persian Cuneiform Inscription at Behistun); fragments of Hecataeus. *Derivative:* Herodotus iii. 61-96, 133 *sqq.*; v. 52, etc.

P. 236.—Maps: cp. J. L. Myres, An attempt to reconstruct the maps used by Herodotus, Geographical Journal, Dec. 1896.

P. 236.—" Text of Anaximander's map ": phrase of E. Meyer.

P. 238, *Sect.* 5.—Sources: *Derivative:* Herodotus iv; cp. fragments of Ctesias, and Strabo vii. 2.

[P. 239.—Scythian expedition. It is perhaps more likely that Darius had strategic rather than economic objectives. His empire was already wealthy and he did not lack gold. Invasion from Scythia had earlier brought considerable unrest into Asia Minor; he may have had the double objective of advancing along the north Aegean and ensuring that no strong power developed north of the Euxine.

P. 242.—Naxian expedition. Our only source is Herodotus who explains the expedition and its failure by personal motives. It is perhaps unlikely that the Persians warned the Naxians in advance; but friction between Greeks and Persians may have accounted for the failure.

P. 243.—Ionian revolt. The political motive was undoubtedly strong. The Greeks resented tyrannies imposed by an outside power. Probably also their economic prosperity had declined under Persian domination and this decline had increased political discontent.

P. 243.—Confederate coinage: Seltman, Greek Coins, 87-88.

P. 246.—Letter of Darius to Gadates: Tod, 10. Darius also praises the satrap for planting Syrian fruit trees in his satrapy, an interesting parallel to Roman activity in giving a wide distribution to the trees that they found in their provinces.

P. 247.—Fig. 77. There are other contemporary representations of Athenian nobles in similar oriental costume at this time, suggesting that it was a temporary fashion. The costume might be Scythian, Amazonian, or, more probably, Persian. The καλος-names on vases imply admiration of an outstanding youth. This Miltiades was the later victor of Marathon.]

P. 247, *Sect.* 7.—Sources: *Primary:* inscriptions. *Derivative:* (1) Herodotus vi. 43 *sqq.*; (2) Plato, Menexenus; [Lysias] Epitaphios; fragments of Ctesias; Justin ii; Nepos, Miltiades; Plutarch, Aristides 5; Parallels 305; De malignitate Herodoti; Pausanias i. 15 and 32.

P. 250.—Decree to march to Marathon: τὸ Μιλτιάδου ψήφισμα, Demosthenes, De Fals. Leg. 303 with schol., and Aristotle, Rhet. iii. 10.

P. 252.—[Battle of Marathon. Herodotus gives the earliest and fullest account; later ancient writers add little but exaggeration. The central problem is to explain why the battle took place. The most radical view is that the Persians had divided their force: while one division reduced Eretria, the other landed at Marathon to contain the Athenians. The Athenians attacked when Eretria fell so that they should not have to fight the united Persian force (F. Maurice, J.H.S. xlix (1929), 100). This interpretation is dangerously different from Herodotus and is not supported by any ancient evidence. As an alternative to the view in the text it might be suggested that the Athenians attacked because they knew that there was serious danger of political collapse in Athens.

P. 255.—Memorial of Callimachus: Inscription, Tod, 13. Monument, A. E. Raubitschek, Dedications from the Athenian Acropolis, no. 13.

P. 255.—Athenian treasury at Delphi. It is thought by some that the treasury and the trophy base added to it are contemporary, commemorating Marathon. The view accepted in the text is based on W. B. Dinsmoor in Studies in Culture, 188.

P. 255.—Marathon memorial in Athens: J. H. Oliver in Hesp. ii (1933), 480. Text and interpretation are very controversial. See S.E.G. x. 404 for full bibliography. (The first epigram has been restored:

ἀνδρὸν τόνδ' ἀρετῆ[ς λάμφσει κλέος ἄφθιτον]αἰεί[:]
[εὔτολμοι Πε]ρ[σῶν hοι στόρεσαν δύναμιν]·
ἔσχον γὰρ πεζοὶ τε[ν ἄλκιμον Ἀσιδος hίππο]ν:
hελλά[δα μ]ὲ πᾶσαν δούλιο[ν ἔμαρ ἰδὲν].)

P. 255.—Old Parthenon and Propylon: W. B. Dinsmoor, *op. cit.* 205-206. The date of the commencement of the building is given by fragments of pottery found at the foundation level. This temple and its successor, the Parthenon, were built on the site of the old Hecatompedon, or hundred-footer; the name remained attached to the site.

P. 255.—Commemoration of Marathon on coinage: Seltman, *op. cit.* 91.

P. 258, *Sect.* 8.—Sources: Herodotus, passages in v and vi.

P. 259.—Athens and the Peloponnesian League. It is probable that Athens became a member of the Peloponnesian League when Cleomenes expelled Hippias. Cleisthenic democracy, however, was nationalist and anti-Spartan. Sparta attempted first to overthrow the democracy, then to restore Hippias: it is probable that Athens did not remain in the Peloponnesian League. The appeal to Sparta in 490 may follow from the rise to power of the aristocratic Miltiades and the needs of the emergency.]

P. 261, *Sects.* 9, 10.—Sources: Pindar, Pyth. 7 (486 B.C.); Herodotus

viii. 104, and other passages; Thucydides i. 93; Aristotle, 'Aθ. Πολ.; Plutarch's Themistocles and Aristides.

P. 262.—Ostracism: J. Carcopino, L'Ostracisme athénien. Annual Procheirotonia whether an " ostrakophoria " should be held, Arist. 'Aθ. Πολ. 43⁵.

P. 264.—Maronea identified with Camareza: Ardaillon, Les Mines du Laurion.

[P. 264.—Fig. 80. Dated *c.* 400. There is a continuous deck over the rowers. The rowers of the top bench have outriggers. The oars of the two lower benches can be seen. Probably the relief was painted, making the line of the oars clearer. The relief fully described by Morrison (cp. note on p. 110), 27.]

CHAPTER VII

P. 265, *Sects*. 1-8.—*Primary:* Aeschylus, Persae; contemporary epigrams (ascribed to Simonides); passages in Pindar. *Derivative*: (1) Herodotus vii-ix; fragments of Ctesias; (2) Diodorus xi; Justin ii; Nepos, Themistocles and Aristides; Plutarch, Themistocles and Aristides.

P. 265.—The whole story of the Persian Invasion has been fully and critically treated in G. B. Grundy, The Great Persian War; R. W. Macan, Herodotus vii-ix, Appendix volume; Cambridge Ancient History iv.

[P. 269.—Persian numbers: F. Maurice, J.H.S. l (1930), 210.

P. 272.—Thessaly: A strong additional motive for abandoning Thessaly was the active Medism of the powerful Aleuadae (Her. vii. 6).

P. 273.—Persian tactics at Artemisium: A more radical reconstruction suggests that the Persian squadron which sailed round Euboea was despatched much earlier and was wrecked by the same storm which destroyed a large part of the main fleet. The reconstruction in the text, based more closely on Herodotus, is to be preferred.]

Pp. 273 *sqq*.—Thermopylae and Artemisium: criticism of the account of Herodotus, Bury, B.S.A. ii. 83.

[P. 276.—Last stand at Thermopylae. Herodotus (vii. 219-220) says: " After this (the news that the Immortals had forced the mountain pass) they divided. Part of the army left and dispersed to their various states. The remainder made ready to stand with Leonidas. There is another story that Leonidas sent them away, anxious that they should not be destroyed." Herodotus prefers the more charitable version, but it is more probable that Leonidas intended to hold off the Immortals with the larger part of his force.

P. 278.—Action of Areopagus. Aristotle ("Aθ. Πολ. 23¹) introduces this story to explain the increased power and prestige of the Areopagus after the Persian War. Both the story and the sequel have been doubted, but it is probable that, in the crisis and confusion of dispersal, the Areopagus assumed a directing control and provided finance where it was needed.

P. 281.—Tactics at Salamis. Herodotus seems to have no clear mental picture of the position of the fleets. He implies that the Persians lined the Attic coast, the Greeks facing them along the shore of Salamis. He makes the Corinthians, stationed in the middle of the line, withdraw in the middle of the battle, an operation which, if the fleets occupied the positions he gives them, would have been impossible. He does not mention the Persian turning squadron (Egyptians according to Diodorus). Aeschylus was an eye-witness and his account should be decisive. In his drama the Persians before the battle are outside the straits in three columns (στοῖχοι): they sailed in expecting easy victory and were confounded in the narrow waters. Other ships, he says, were sent round the island of Ajax. The Corinthians were probably detached to meet this turning squadron. Herodotus may, however, be right when he says that, even before Themistocles' message, Xerxes intended to sail in. He was full of confidence and a decisive action would have suited his mood better than a wiser but more delaying strategy.]

P. 284.—Corinthian epitaph : Tod, 16.

P. 289.—Battle of Plataea : G. B. Grundy, The Topography of the Battle of Plataea.

P. 295.—The tripod at Delphi : Tod, 19.

P. 296, *Sects*. 9-11.—Sources : *Primary:* Sicilian Odes of Pindar and Bacchylides. *Derivative:* (1) Herodotus vii. 153-167 ; (2) Pindaric scholia ; Diodorus xi ; Xenophon's Hiero.

[P. 298.—Carthaginian control of Sardinia. Traditions were preserved of early Greek colonies in Sardinia at Calaris (Cagliari) and Olbia. After Malchus' invasion of Sicily Carthaginian armies operated in Sardinia (before 550). At the time of the Persian conquest and again during the Ionian revolt (Her. i. 170, v. 106, 124) eastern Greeks still regarded the island, rich in corn and metals (the S.W. district round Iglesias), as a possible land for conquest and settlement ; but no attempt was made. During the fifth century the Carthaginians had firm control of the island.]

P. 305.—Hiero's victories in the games were : Horse-races at Delphi, 482, 478 B.C. ; horse-races at Olympia, 476, 472 B.C. ; chariot-race at Delphi, 470 B.C. ; chariot-race at Olympia, 468 B.C. (cp. Oxyrhynchus Papyri, ii. 87-88).

P. 306.—Fig. 90 : " Hiero, son of Deinomenes, and the Syracusans (dedicated) to Zeus Etruscan spoils won at Cyme," Tod, 22.

[P. 306.—Golden tripods. A tripod base has been found at Delphi, the dedication of Gelo. Three other similar bases were found nearby, one bearing an inscription of Hiero. They may have been dedicated by the four brothers, but not necessarily at the same time. See Tod, 17.

P. 306.—Charioteer dedicated by Polyzalus : probably commemorating a Pythian victory in 478. The first line now extant was cut on an erased surface and traces of the earlier lettering survive. It has been suggested that in 477 Polyzalus described himself as King of Gela. He combined with Theron against Hiero, but when Theron made his peace with Hiero, Polyzalus renounced the title, and it was erased from his dedication at Delphi. See Wade-Gery, J.H.S. liii (1933), 102.

P. 310.—Fig. 94. From the so-called Ludovisi Throne, in the National Museum (in the Baths of Diocletian) at Rome. Reliefs of similar style and date (early fifth century), probably from the same monument, acquired by the Boston Museum (U.S.A.). Both were found in Rome, probably transported from a Greek site during the Roman period. The closest parallels in style and subject come from Locri in south Italy, where there was an important cult of Persephone. The popular title " Birth of Venus " is less probable. See B. Ashmole, J.H.S. xlii (1922), 248.]

P. 311, *Sects*. 12, 13.—Homeric Hymn to Demeter : Orphicorum Fragmenta (ed. Kern); material collected in Lobeck's Aglaophamus [cp. Kern, De Orphei, Epimenidis, Pherecydis theogoniis; and Rohde's Psyche.].

P. 316.—[Orphic Theology: cp. W. K. C. Guthrie, Orpheus and Greek Religion.

P. 319, *Sect.* 14.—Sources: *Primary:* H. Diels, Die Fragmente der Vorsokratiker, 3 vols. 5th ed. 1934-8 (cp. K. Freeman, Companion to the Pre-Socratic Philosophers, and Ancilla to the Pre-Socratic Philosophers, a translation of the fragments in Diels). *Derivative:* Lives of the philosophers in Diogenes Laertius.

For a select bibliography of works on early Greek philosophy, A. H. Armstrong, An Introduction to Ancient Philosophy, 226-227.]

CHAPTER VIII

Pp. 322 and 346.—Sources: *Primary:* inscriptions; scattered notices in Herodotus; Thucydides i. 89-117, 128-138; fragments of Timocreon, Ion, Stesimbrotus, Cratinus, Eupolis; [Hellanicus]. *Derivative:* (1) [Cleidemus]; [Ephorus]; [Androtion]; (2) Aristotle, 'Αθηναίων Πολιτεία; Diodorus xi. 37– xii. 28; Plutarch: Themistocles, Aristides, Cimon, Pericles; Nepos: Themistocles, Aristides, Pausanias, Cimon. [The sources are collected in G. F. Hill's Sources for Greek History, 478-431 B.C. (revised edition, 1951).

[For chronology: Gomme, Thucydides, i. 389. For tribute problems: Meritt, Wade-Gery, McGregor, The Athenian Tribute Lists (vols. i and ii, evidence; vol. iii, historical conclusions).

P. 322.—Fig. 96, Themistocles. Roman copy of an early Greek head, recently found at Ostia.]

P. 327.—Argos recovers Tiryns: Date seems to be later than Aug. 468, for in the recently discovered List of Olympian Victors (Oxyrhynchus Papyri, ii. 89) we find that in that year the Boys' boxing-match was won by a Tirynthian (. . . ης Τιρύνθιο[ς παιδων π]ύξ). The conclusion is not indeed quite certain: the victor might have been an exile.

P. 327.—[The battles of Tegea and Dipaea cannot be securely dated. They are mentioned by Herodotus in a list of five Spartan victories, and fall between Plataea (479) and the Helot revolt (464). Themistocles, who stirred up anti-Spartan feeling in the Peloponnese when, after his ostracism, he lived at Argos, may have been responsible.

P. 328.—Aristides' assessment. 460 talents seems a high figure for the first assessment. The tribute received by Athens after 454 in no year before 430 seems to have exceeded 400 talents; and, by the middle of the century, the League had been considerably enlarged and some states, such as Thasos, which had originally provided ships, were by then contributing money. It has therefore been suggested that 460 talents included both money payments and the money equivalent of ship contributions. Thucydides (i. 96), how- ever, seems to imply clearly that 460 talents represented the money payments only and his figure, repeated by secondary ancient sources, should be accepted. Some of the original assessments may have been lowered by the mid-century (but cf. A.T.L. iii. 234).

P. 334.—Ostracism of Themistocles. Sherd deposit, Hesp. x (1941), 2.

P. 335.—Themistocles issued coins in his own name as governor of

Magnesia. It is interesting, in view of his reputation, to note that two of the four specimens known are ancient forgeries, copperplated with silver: Seltman, Greek Coinage, 108.

P. 337.—Eurymedon account based on Thucydides, supplemented by Plutarch (Callisthenes): Cimon, 12-13. Diodorus [Ephorus], misled by a commemorative epigram, has confused with the Eurymedon later operations in Cyprus.

P. 339.—Erythrae, A.T.L. ii. 53. Erythrae had probably medised and been recovered by Athens (the date, ?453-2, depends on the restoration of the archon's name). An oath is to be taken by members of the new Erythraean democratic Boule: " I will serve as a councillor in the best and most just interests of the people of Athens and her allies ; and I will not revolt from the people of Athens and her allies, nor will I follow anyone else so doing ; and I will not desert nor follow anyone else deserting ; and I will not receive back any of those who have taken refuge with the Medes without the authority of the Council and people of Athens ; nor will I drive out any of those who remain in Erythrae without the authority of the Council and people of Athens."

P. 340.—Tribute Quota Lists. The heading of the first list (454-3) describes the procedure: " These offerings to the goddess were received from the Hellenotamiae and were submitted to the thirty Logistae (public auditors), from the tribute which the cities brought in the archonship of Ariston to the Athenians, a mina in each talent."

Pp. 340-41.—Jurisdiction. A distinction should be drawn between private, including commercial, cases (based on agreements) and political cases. For the summoning of political cases to Athens: Ps. Xen. Ἀθπ. 1¹⁶⁻¹⁸ ; Aristophanes, Birds, 1046, 1422-6.

P. 343.—Death of Aristides. ? Alive in 467: Plutarch, Aristides 3⁵. According to Plutarch, Arist. 26¹ one account said that he died in the Euxine. Perhaps Athens was attempting in the 'sixties to include the Greek cities of the Euxine in the Delian League.

P. 344.—Sparta : Thasos. According to Thucydides the Spartans promised to invade Attica. This was probably not a public state decision but an undertaking by anti-Athenians, perhaps on the board of Ephors.

P. 345.—The date of the settlement of Messenians at Naupactus is disputed. According to our text of Thucydides Ithome fell in the tenth year of the siege. Diodorus attributes the capture of Naupactus and the settlement of Messenians to Tolmides in 456-5. The advance of Athenian influence in central Greece after the victory of Oenophyta would provide a good context. But Thucydides seems careful to maintain chronological sequence, suggesting that the settlement preceded the alliance of Athens with Megara. Perhaps the numeral in Thucydides is corrupt.

CHAPTER IX

P. 346.—Sources : see sources for Chapter VIII.

P. 348.—Aeschylus, Eumenides. See especially 681-710.

P. 349.—Payment of courts. Many scholars prefer a later date for the introduction of jurors' pay: cp. Gomme, Thucydides i. 327. The sources are indecisive. But administrative officers were paid when the Athena Promachos was constructed, S.E.G. x. 243, ii. 67, and this statue was begun in the early 'fifties at latest. Payment for jury service was probably an essential condition for the effectiveness of fully democratic courts.

P. 352.—The Argive alliance: Aeschylus, Eumenides, 290-91.

P. 355.—Erechtheid inscription: Tod, 26.

P. 357.—Spartan dedication for Tanagra: Tod, 27. Argos sent a contingent to the battle, and her dead were commemorated at Athens, S.E.G. x. 407.

P. 357.—Egyptian disaster. Thucydides implies that 200 ships went to and stayed in Egypt. It is probable, however, that a large part of the fleet returned, after the initial naval victory, for the naval operations in the Saronic gulf.

P. 359.—Cimon's recall from ostracism. Theopompus (fr. 88) says that Cimon was recalled by the people before five years of his ostracism were completed, and put an end to the war. Plutarch, Cimon 17[8], adds that Pericles moved the decree recalling him. Theopompus' passage implies recall after Tanagra, but the war did not end then, nor is there any firm evidence of Cimon's presence in Athens in the years following Tanagra. Plutarch's language, however, suggests that a decree was preserved in Pericles' name. The most probable combination is that Cimon was specially recalled, but only towards the end of his ten years' ostracism.

P. 360.—Peace with Persia. There is good evidence that a formal peace was made with Darius II., successor of Artaxerxes: Wade-Gery, Athenian Studies, 127. It is probable that this Peace was a renewal of a definite peace made with Persia after Cimon's death.

P. 362.—March of Andocides: Tod, 41.

P. 362.—Settlement with Chalcis: Tod, 42. The oath to be taken by Chalcis is more stringent than the oath imposed on Erythrae, and no mention is made of Athenian allies: " I will not revolt from the people of Athens by any manner or means, either by word or deed, nor will I follow anyone else revolting, and if anyone stirs up revolt I will denounce him to the Athenians, and I will pay to the Athenians the tribute which I persuade the Athenians to impose, and I will be an ally of the Athenian people to the best of my ability and as justly as I can, and I will help and defend the people of Athens, if anyone harms the people of Athens, and I will obey the will of the people of Athens." Land was also confiscated from Chalcis on the Lelantine plain: Aelian, Varia Historica vi. 1. A fragment of the settlement with Eretria also survives (S.E.G. x. 35); the form of the oath imposed is identical.

P. 363.—Restored memorial of Athenian victories: Tod, 43. It is possible, however, that the restoration of this memorial commemorates the victory over the Boeotians at Oenophyta (457). The only evidence for the date is the letter forms of the inscription, which are inconclusive.

P. 364.—Panhellenic Congress: Plutarch, Pericles, 17, is our only source. His language, however, seems to be a close paraphrase of an actual decree, which he may have found in a published collection of Attic decrees.

P. 364.—Opposition to Pericles' building policy: Plutarch, Pericles, 12, a vivid passage, possibly drawn from a contemporary source.

P. 365.—Discontent in the Empire. For the tribute crisis: Wade-Gery,

Hesp. xiv (1945), 212. Decree tightening up tribute collection: A.T.L. ii. 50; the decree begins: " The Boule and the (Athenian) officers in the allied cities and the visiting commissioners are to see that the tribute is collected in the course of each year; and they are to agree seals with the cities so that those who carry the tribute cannot defraud."]

Pp. 364, 365.—For the feeling in the allied cities against the great statesmen of the democracy, especially Themistocles and Pericles, the lost work of Stesimbrotus of Thasos, entitled Concerning Themistocles, Thucydides, and Pericles, may be cited as evidence. We know the tone of the work (composed *c.* 430 B.C.) from quotations and references; the author collected all the stories, true and untrue, that he could hear of, to the disadvantage of Pericles and Themistocles. But there is no doubt that his political views were oligarchical; and therefore he cannot be used as evidence for the sentiments of the democrats or the mass of the citizens in Thasos or anywhere else.

[P. 365.—The missing quota list. For the epigraphic argument for believing that in one year no quota list was recorded, Wade-Gery, *op. cit.* An alternative explanation might be that the whole tribute of the year was assigned to another purpose (? perhaps a gift to Athena Nike for her temple which was decreed about this time). The waiving of tribute for a year by Athens would have been a dangerous admission.

P. 366.—Brea: Tod, 44.

P. 366.—Coinage decree: A.T.L. ii. 61. Reconstructed from a series of fragments found in different parts of the Athenian empire: formerly dated *c.* 420 on the strength of a parody in Aristophanes' Birds, 1040 (produced in 414). A new fragment from Cos, however, is inscribed in Attic on Pentelic marble and can be compared with a long series of Attic inscriptions: it is now dated in the early 'forties. The importance attached by Athens to the decree is emphasised by the addition of a clause to the Bouleutic oath: " If anyone mints silver coinage in the cities or does not use Athenian coins or weights or measures, but uses non-Athenian coins and weights and measures, I will punish and penalise him according to the terms of the former decree of Clearchus." For the effects of this decree on allied coinages: Robinson, Hesp. Suppl. viii (1949), 324.

P. 367.—Athena Promachos. The accounts for this statue have been identified: S.E.G. x. 243 , they include payments for tin, charcoal, logs for burning, wages.

P. 369.—Parthenon. The accounts have been in part preserved and include payments for quarrying, transport, sculptures. They show that the main payments to the commissioners in charge of the work came from the Treasurers of Athena. An example in Tod, 52.

P. 369.—Athena Parthenos. Tod, 47, gives one of the year's accounts : 100 talents was received during the year by the commissioners from the Treasurers of Athena. Gold (weighing 6 talents, 1618 drachmae, and half an obol) was bought for 87 talents, 4652 drachmae, 5 obols. The ivory bought during the year cost only 2 talents, 743 drachmae. S.E.G. x. 257 is probably a summarised account of the whole work, showing a total cost of over 700 talents.

P. 371.—Temple of Athena Nike. The decision to build a temple was taken very soon after the Peace of Callias: Tod, 40. The temple was not, however, built until the later 'thirties, possibly not before the Peloponnesian War. Cp. D. S. Robertson, Greek and Roman Architecture², 125.

P. 372.—Temple of Hephaestus. Evidence for date and identification: Dinsmoor, Hesp. Suppl. v.

P. 373.—Cost of buildings. Heliodorus, who wrote a description of the monuments of the Acropolis, gave 2012 talents for the cost of the Propylaea alone. This seems much too high, judging by what we know of ancient building costs, but the figure has been reasonably held to represent the total cost of the major works on the Acropolis—Parthenon, Parthenos, Propylaea. What is probably the summary of the Parthenos accounts, S.E.G. x. 257, gives a total cost of over 700 talents. For the Parthenon the Commissioners twice, in 446 and 441, hand over a balance of more than 30 talents on the year's working: it seems clear that continuous heavy expenditure was involved.

P. 373.—Social building programme. Ps. Xen. 'Aθπ. 2¹⁰: " Some of the wealthy have their own gymnasia and baths ; but the common people builds for itself many wrestling schools and baths ; and the mob profits more from these than the few and the fortunately placed."

P. 374.—Propylaea. Original plan and modifications: Robertson, Greek and Roman Architecture², 118.

P. 378.—Population of Attica: Gomme, The Population of Athens in the Fifth and Fourth Centuries B.C.

P. 379.—Themistocles and the west. Themistocles at Salamis threatened an Athenian emigration to Siris if the Peloponnesians deserted: Her. viii. 62. He named two of his daughters Sybaris and Italia. His interest in the west before the Persian invasion was probably due mainly to the threat to Athenian supplies of corn from the Euxine and of ship timber from Thrace, now occupied by Persia. The fleet which fought at Salamis may have been built of timber from south Italy.

P. 379.—Alliance with Segesta. The date depends on the restoration of the archon's name. Formerly dated 454/3: Tod, 31; now 458/7: S.E.G. x. 7. Athens was probably interested in Segesta's cornfields ; Segesta hoped that Athens' reputation would protect her from neighbouring Selinus.

P. 380.—Thurii. The Panhellenic character of the colony is well illustrated by the ten tribes which took their names from Arcadia, Achaea, Elis, Boeotia, the Amphictiony, Doris, Ionia, Athens, Euboea, the islands: Diodorus xii. 11³. The Athenian nucleus was small, but Pericles probably thought that the non-Athenian colonists, very mixed in origin and owing their prospects of a new and better life to Athens, would follow Athenian leadership, and that Thurii would be an important centre of Athenian cultural, and therefore political, influence in the west. Herodotus may have been one of the original settlers.

P. 380.—Hippodamus was also the propounder of an ideal symmetrical state of 10,000, divided into craftsmen, farmers, warriors, with a threefold division of the land and a threefold division of the laws : Aristotle, Politics, 1267 b 22.

P. 381.—Pericles' expedition to the Euxine is mentioned by Plutarch (Pericles, 20) only. Lamachus is said to have participated, which suggests a date later than 440, since Lamachus was still a vigorous general in the Sicilian expedition of 415. Sinope was colonised by 600 settlers from Athens.

P. 382.—Amphipolis. Economic importance: Thuc. iv. 108[1]: "The place was useful to them (the Athenians), because it sent ship timber and a revenue of money."

P. 382.—Pericles' position. The generals took part in the deliberations of the Boule and alone among officers of state could propose decrees before the assembly. A large number of Pericles' decrees are reflected in the sources, most of them probably moved by Pericles as general. His pre-eminence is reflected in the election of a second general from his tribe in 441-0, 439-8, 433-2, 432-1, 431-0 (evidence for other years is lacking). This departure from the normal principle of equal tribal representation may have been introduced after the ostracism of Thucydides (443).

P. 384.—Samian revolt. A fragmentary record on stone is preserved of money paid out by the Treasurers of Athena, showing a total between 1400 and 1500 talents: Tod, 50; revised text, S.E.G. x. 221. This might represent payment for operations against Byzantium and Samos (as restored by Meritt), leaving over 1200 talents for Samos; or for Samos alone. It is possible also that, in addition to these sums paid out by the Treasurers of Athena from the reserve, part of the year's tribute was also used for the fleet. Terms of the settlement imposed on Samos have been in part preserved: A.T.L. ii. 73. The settlement seems to have been lenient. In addition to exacting an oath of loyalty from the Samians, Athens binds herself by oath to act honourably towards the Samian people.]

CHAPTER X

P. 390.—Sources: *Primary:* inscriptions; Thucydides i-v; Aristophanes: Acharnians, Knights, Wasps, Peace. *Derivative:* [Ephorus]; Plutarch, Pericles and Nicias; Diodorus xii. 31-74.

P. 392.—[Payments to Athenian squadrons sent to Corcyra: Tod, 55. Payment to the first squadron was made on the thirteenth day of the first prytany of Apseudes' archonship, mid-July 433. The second squadron received its grant three weeks later. The battle of Sybota was therefore fought at the end of August, or early September.

P. 393.—Revolt of Potidaea. Payments: S.E.G. x. 223.

P. 393.—Athenian epitaph (Potidaea): Tod, 59.

P. 394.—Grievances against Athens. Aegina also complained secretly "that she was not autonomous as the terms of the Peace demanded." Perhaps Athens had interfered in jurisdiction or had imposed a security garrison.

P. 396A.—Financial policy. The main source for the measures outlined are the two decrees of Callias, Tod, 51 (revised text, A.T.L. ii. 46), passed by the assembly in 434-3, probably early in 433. That steps were taken to concentrate Athens' resources before war was patently imminent suggests that Pericles was not prepared to compromise to maintain peace. It is significant that under the first decree money is to be spent on the walls of Athens and on her naval arsenal.

P. 402.—Treaties with Rhegium and Leontini renewed: Tod, 57 and 58. The prescript of both decrees is inscribed on an erased surface, and is in a different hand from the main text of the alliance, suggesting that both treaties were now renewed and not made for the first time. The date of the original alliances can be inferred only from letter forms, *c*. 450-40. Shortly after the Syracusan defeat of Acragas in 445 is perhaps the most probable setting.

P. 403.—Athenian ships round the Peloponnese. Payments to the generals: S.E.G. x. 223.

P. 408.—Population, Gomme, *loc. cit*.]

P. 408.—Expedition to Epidaurus: it has been suggested that the very brief and inadequate treatment of this episode by Thucydides, his omission to explain how and why the enterprise failed—in contrast with his full accounts of events of less moment—is an instance of partiality; and that it is one of those rare cases in which he allowed his personal prepossessions to influence his presentation of history. In his treatment of the statesmen, Cleon and Hyperbolus, he failed to control his prejudice against them. But I doubt whether admiration of Pericles was his motive for passing so lightly over the failure at Epidaurus.

P. 408.—[The expedition of Phormio to Amphilochian Argos is mentioned only by Thucydides (in retrospect, ii. 68^{7-8}): the date is uncertain. Phormio's strong action, in a district within the Corinthian sphere of influence, might suggest a late stage in the incidents leading to the war, after Sybota, in 432. But Thucydides' account of this period is detailed and he could be expected to have mentioned the campaign in its context, if so late. A date between the end of the Samian revolt (when Corinth opposed help to Samos) and the outbreak of trouble at Epidamnus seems more probable.

P. 408.—Athenian colonists sent to Potidaea: Record of this on a stone: Tod, 60.

P. 409.—Attacks on Pericles' friends. According to Philochorus (schol. Aristoph. Peace, 605) Pheidias was tried in 438-7. The main attacks came later, on the eve of war. Diopeithes, a handler of oracles, moved a decree (Plutarch, Pericles, 32^2) " that those who did not accept the divine powers or taught doctrines about the heavenly bodies should be impeached." Thucydides does not mention these attacks. They were made the main cause of the war by Ephorus (as reflected in Diodorus). They probably represent an attempt by the opponents of war to discredit Pericles and his policy. They were not of decisive importance.

P. 414.—Cleon's position in 428. Cleon moved the decree to put all male Mytilenians to death, probably before the end of 428-7, and was therefore a member of the Boule. In Aristophanes, Knights, 774, the Paphlagonian (Cleon) boasts: " When I was your Councillor I could show an abundance of money in the public treasury." From this it is reasonable to infer that Cleon was active in increasing Athens' revenues in 428.

P. 415.—Fleet of Alcidas. An inscription (Tod, 62) may record donations for Alcidas' fleet (financing naval operations was a crucial problem for Sparta). The contributors include friends of Sparta in Chios and Ephesus (members of the Athenian empire), and Melos which was neutral.

P. 417.—Cleruchy on Lesbos. Normally cleruchs occupied the land allotted to them. In Lesbos it was probably thought better to concentrate them as a garrison. A fragmentary inscription (Tod, 63; revised text, A.T.L. ii. 76) records the regulations between Mytilenians and cleruchs. The tone is conciliatory. Private cases between Athenians and Mytilenians are to be governed by the same agreements as obtained before the revolt. There is no trace of these cleruchs in the later stages of the war : they were probably withdrawn through weakness in man-power, perhaps for the campaigns of 424.]

P. 419.—The " peninsula " of Leucas : The canal of Periander, which had completely insulated it, seems to have been silted up, for Thucydides mentions that ships were hauled across the isthmus.

P. 422.—Aetolian campaign of Demosthenes : Woodhouse, Aetolia, 57 *sqq.*, 340 *sqq.* Identification of Aegition : *ib.* 363.

P. 425, *Sect.* 9.—Additional sources : Pseudo-Xenophon, Constitution of the Athenians ; Antiphon, de Choreuta and fragment of Contra Philinum.

P. 427.—[Pseudo Xenophon. The date is uncertain and not of vital importance, between 431 and 415, probably early in the war (? 430). For the character of the treatise : Gomme, Athenian Studies, 211.

Pp. 428-9.—Athenian finances. Borrowing from the reserve, 433-22 : Tod, 64. This document is the report of the state auditors drawn up in the summer of 422, the end of a four-year financial period. It gives a summary of borrowings from 433 to 426, and a detailed account of the yearly borrowings from 426 to 422. The entry for 426-5 begins : " The treasurers (of Athena), Androcles of the deme Phlyeus and his colleagues paid out to the hellenotamiae . . . for (the general) Hippocrates and his colleagues, in the prytany of Cecropis, when four days had passed, in the session of the Boule in which Megacleides was the first secretary, in the archonship of Euthynos, 20 talents. The interest accumulated on this payment (in the four-year period) was 5696 drachmae." Annual borrowings in the first years of the war had averaged over 700 talents : by 426-5 they had been reduced to just over 260 talents.

P. 429.—Assessment of 425 : Tod, 66 (revised text, A.T.L. ii. 40). The total is in part preserved, either 960-1000 talents or 1460-1500 talents. Sufficient details survive to confirm the higher figure. The island figures are best preserved and may be compared with the pre-war assessments, given in brackets : Paros, 30 talents (18) ; Naxos, 15 (6⅔) ; Andros, 15 (6) ; Siphnos 9 (3) ; Eretria, 15 (3) ; Ceos, 10 (3), etc. The highest pre-war assessment was 30 talents (Thasos, Aegina). One Thracian town, probably Abdera, now had to pay 75 talents.]

P. 430.—Topography of Pylos and Sphacteria : see G. B. Grundy, Thucydides and his Age, ii. 122.

P. 438.—425-4 B.C. : An inscription (imperfect) is preserved of Athenians and soldiers in Athenian service who fell during this year. One citizen fell at Pylos : I.G. i². 949.

P. 438.—[Victory of Paeonius. Inscribed base (Tod, 65) : " Messenians and Naupactians dedicated (this statue) to Olympian Zeus, a tithe from the enemy."

P. 442.—Athens and Boeotia. The Athenians had made a demonstration in force in Boeotia in 426 : Thuc. iii. 91. The main Athenian army marched out of Athens to meet at Tanagra a force landed from the sea. A victory was won over the Tanagraeans and some Theban reinforcements but was not followed up. Later in the year Demosthenes had hoped to advance through Aetolia into Boeotia, but was blocked by the Aetolians.

P. 442.—Boeotian constitution. A detailed description is provided by a historian of the early fourth century, fragments of whose work have been recovered on papyri found in Egypt: Hellenica Oxyrhynchia, xi.[2-4]. Boeotia was divided into eleven districts, each of which provided a Boeotarch and 60 representatives to a Federal Council which was responsible for foreign policy. Thebes' position at the time was preponderant as she provided 4 Boeotarchs (2 on her own account, 2 on behalf of the Plataean and adjoining district). The individual states in Boeotia also had their own local governments for internal affairs, based on a hoplite franchise and four rotating Councils.

P. 444.—Athens in 424-3. In view of the failure of the offensive in Greece the Athenians were lucky in confirming, during the year, peace with Darius II., the new king of Persia. See Andocides, De Pace 29, and the inscriptions reviewed by Wade-Gery in Athenian Studies, 127.

P. 445.—Methone decrees: Tod, 61. Methone was probably first brought into the Athenian empire in the campaign that preceded the siege of Potidaea (432). In return for help given to the Athenian forces in Chalcidice she is given diplomatic protection against Perdiccas; her tribute is remitted, apart from the *aparche* to Athena; she is allowed to import corn through the Hellespont up to a stated amount each year.

P. 452.—Athenian alliance with Bottiaean cities: Tod, 68.

P. 456.—Peace negotiations. In the Peloponnesian League each state had an equal vote. Though the most powerful members were opposed to the terms, the small states, especially in Arcadia, stood to gain nothing from war and probably voted solid for the Peace.]

CHAPTER XI

P. 458.—Sources: *Primary:* inscriptions; Thucydides v-viii; Xenophon, Hellenica, i-ii; [Philistus]; Andocides, De Mysteriis, De Reditu; Pro Polystrato (=Pseudo-Lysias, 20). Aristophanes, Birds, Lysistrata, Thesmophoriazusae. *Derivative:* [Ephorus]; Aristotle, ᾿Αθ. Πολ.; [Timaeus]; Diodorus xii. 75, xiii. 104, xiv. 3-5, 32, 33; Plutarch: Nicias, Alcibiades, Lysander.

P. 460.—[Quadruple alliance: Tod, 72.

P. 461.—Mantinea campaign. Alcibiades was probably not elected general at the annual election in spring 418; but he seems to have become general after the battle (his name is probably to be restored in the accounts of the year 418-17, Tod, 75[18]), perhaps in place of the dead Nicostratus. Athenian policy was a typical democratic compromise. Laches and Nicostratus, who were in command of the Athenian force, had been continuously associated with Nicias and presumably did not approve the offensive policy; but Alcibiades, the prime mover, was sent with the force officially as ambassador and forced an offensive.

P. 462.—Ostracism of Hyperbolus. Thucydides does not mention the ostracism in its context. Later accounts differ and are confused. One tradition introduces Phaeax, a prominent speaker with aristocratic connexions, as one of the principles: Plutarch, Alcibiades, 13. It seems to derive from a speech attributed in antiquity to Andocides (iv). This speech, however, is probably a rhetorical exercise of the early fourth century and cannot be trusted. Whatever part Phaeax played, the main issue was probably thought to lie between Nicias and Alcibiades.

P. 462.—Melos. Contribution to Alcidas' fleet : Tod, 62. It is significant also that Melos continued to mint coins independently until her fall.

P. 463.—Eleusinian decree : Tod, 74.

P. 464.—Hyperbolus and the west. Aristophanes, Knights, 1300 : " They say that the triremes held a session and one of them, an elder soul, said : ' Haven't you heard, my dears, what is on in the city ? They say that there's a demand for a hundred of us to sail to Carthage, from sourpuss Hyperbolus, wicked citizen.' "

P. 465.—Cleon's attack on Laches. The case is parodied by Aristophanes : Wasps, 924.

P. 469.—Mutilation of the Hermae. A full, but tendencious, account in Andocides iii. Since the earlier sources make no mention of Corinth it is perhaps doubtful whether the plot was instigated from outside Athens. Those who were convicted were condemned to death and their property confiscated. Fragments of the records of the public sale of these properties have survived : Tod, 79. Interesting is a list of slaves, with the prices they fetched, belonging to the metic Cephisodorus : (prices in drachmae, f. = female) Thracian (f.), 165 ; Thracian (f.), 135 ; Thracian, 170 ; Syrian, 240 ; Carian, 105 ; Illyrian, 156$\frac{1}{6}$; Thracian (f.), 220 ; Thracian, 115 ; Scythian, 144 ; Illyrian, 121 ; Colchian, 153 ; Carian boy, 174 ; Carian child, 72 ; Syrian, 300 ; Maltese, 106 ; Lydian (f.), 170.

Pp. 471-3.—Plan of Syracuse, based on Knud Fabricius, Das antike Syrakus (1932). Earlier plans placed Achradina at the eastern end of Epipolae and assumed that Dionysius later built his wall round Epipolae to protect a city which had expanded over the whole terrace. Fabricius has shown conclusively, from the disposition of cemeteries and other evidence, that the city of Syracuse at no time extended on to Epipolae but was confined to the lower ground. The sources speak of three districts on the mainland. Achradina was the first and most important ; later were added Tyche to the north-east, Temenitis to the north-west. Achradina alone was surrounded by a wall in 415. In winter 415/4 the Syracusans " built a wall, enclosing the shrine of Apollo Temenites, all along that side of Syracuse which looks towards Epipolae." A very small stretch of this wall remains, near the theatre, but there are no other traces of mainland walls of this period. The lines suggested on the plan are conjectural. The location of Trogilus is accepted from H. W. Parke (J.H.S. lxiv (1944), 100), who bases his argument on Livy's account of the Roman capture of Syracuse, 25. 33[10]. The general line of the third and successful Syracusan counter-wall is clear, but its terminal point is uncertain. From Thucydides, vii. 4[1] and vii. 43[3], it is assumed that this wall was not intended to reach as far as Euryalos.

P. 485.—Emergency finance. Silver objects from the Parthenon were first converted into coin in 409-8. In 406 the people decreed that the golden statues of Victory should be melted down (schol. Aristophanes, Frogs 720), the first gold coinage of Athens. By the end of the war most of Athena's dedications had been taken, Ferguson, Treasurers of Athena, 85.

Pp. 489-93.—The oligarchic revolution. We have two main accounts, in Thucydides and in Aristotle's Athenian Constitution. They cannot be reconciled. Aristotle represents the revolution as a constitutional reform: the 5000 are selected and appoint 100 commissioners who draft a provisional and a permanent constitution. Thucydides, who is to be preferred, presents the revolution as a coup. The 400 are appointed under intimidation at Colonus (deliberately chosen for the assembly as being outside the protection of the walls and dangerous to all but hoplites owing to the threat from Spartan forces); the 5000 are not enrolled; the extremists outwit the moderates. From Thucydides' vivid and convincing account it seems clear that the 5000 never played a significant part, except in propaganda. A little further evidence is provided by the speech in defence of Polystratus (wrongly attributed to Lysias) delivered in 410. From this speech it is at least clear that men were actually appointed to enrol the 5000.

P. 490.—The constitution of Dracon, included in Aristotle's Athenian Constitution, 4, is a reflection of oligarchic propaganda. It bases office on a money qualification, a clear anachronism, and is inconsistent with the main tradition which attributes to Dracon a codification of the laws, but not a constitution.]

P. 495.—Assassination of Phrynichus: Tod, 86.

P. 497.—" Our success is over," adopting the reading ἔρρει τὰ καλά (so Grote): ἔρρει τὰ κᾶλα is the other reading: " our timber (ships) is rotting." [For this use of κᾶλα cp. the Spartan speaker in Aristophanes, Lysistrata 1253.]

P. 497.—[Restoration of democracy: Andocides i. 96, preserves the first action of the restored democracy, determined to prevent a repetition of oligarchic revolution: " If anyone overthrows the democracy at Athens or holds any office if the democracy is overthrown he shall be an enemy of the Athenians and he shall die." To solemnise the resolution all Athenians were required, by tribes and demes, to take an oath over burning victims to abide by its provisions.

P. 498.—Two-obol payment. This diobelia is recorded first in the payments by the Treasurers of Athena in 410-9: Tod, 83.

P. 498.—Erechtheum. A report was presented to the people in 409 detailing the present state of the building (I.G. i² 372): " The commissioners of the temple on the Acropolis in which is the ancient image . . . recorded as follows the state of the work on the temple, in obedience to the decree of the people proposed by Epigenes, according as they found it complete or incomplete, in the archonship of Diokles . . .

" The following parts of the temple we found unfinished. At the corner towards the Cecropium (the south-west corner): four wall blocks not placed, four feet long, two feet wide, one foot and a half thick. . . . On the Porch adjoining the Cecropium the upper surfaces of three of the ceiling blocks over the maidens, thirteen feet long, five feet wide, needed to be dressed."

It is clear from the very detailed report that the building had been abandoned when nearing completion.

Large fragments of the expenditure on the completion of the temple are also preserved. They are considerably more detailed than the earlier accounts of the Parthenon (a sign of a more radical democracy). ix. 10: " To sawyers working by the day, to two men, each receiving a drachma a day, 12 days, to Rhadios living in Kollytos and his assistants, 24 drachmae. For sawing 14 eight-foot timbers, 84 cuts, at two obols a cut, to Rhadios living in Kollytos, 28 drachmae." xiii. col. ii. 32 : " For taking down and carrying away the scaffolding from the north wall, from which the figures of the frieze were fastened in place (3 obols apiece to 6 men)." The normal day rate was one drachma as in the navy, and it is interesting to note that the sculptors of the frieze are paid on roughly the same level as skilled craftsmen and according to the piece at a standard rate. xvii. col. i. 4 : " Praxias, living in Melite, the horse and the man appearing behind it and striking it in the flank, 120 drachmae ; Antiphanes of Kerameis, the chariot and the youth, and the two horses being harnessed, 240 dr. ; Phyromachus of Kephisia, the man leading the horse, 60 dr. . . . Iasos of Kollytos, the woman with the little girl leaning against her, 80 dr." (" Living in Melite " = a metic resident in the deme Melite ; " of Melite " = an Athenian citizen enrolled in that deme, but not necessarily living in it.)

There is a general medieval flavour about the following entry, xvii. col. ii. 28 : " Paid for offerings at the new moon, with the workmen—4 dr. 3 ob." Translations from Paton, The Erechtheum (a detailed account of the temple including translations of all the relevant documents).

P. 498.—Recovery of Selymbria. The very conciliatory settlement made by the generals was ratified by the people on Alcibiades' return in 407 : Tod, 88. The Selymbrians are allowed to shape their own constitution : Athenian moveable property lost during the war is not to be recoverable.]

P. 501.—The indignation of the Athenians at the time of the trial of the Generals was inflamed by the circumstance that it was the season of the festival of the Apaturia, a time for family reunions, and the relatives of the doomed men put on black. This trial was an instructive example of the evils of having no court of revision to correct the dooms of the Assembly.

[P. 502.—Conspiracy in Chios. Xen. Hell. ii. 1$^{1-4}$. The key word is κάλαμος, translated by Bury " straw." Professor Wace points out to me that the word normally means a "reed," such as grows by ponds and watercourses, long and stiff. The reed is used for roofing sheds, byres, etc., but can also be used as a walking-stick. This seems clearly to be the meaning here. It would be natural for the blind man to use a stick to find his way.

P. 505.—Samos. After the disaster of Aegospotami the Samians alone had remained faithful to Athens and had been given exceptional privileges: Tod, 91. The Athenians resolved " that the Samians shall be Athenians, while maintaining whatsoever constitution they choose . . . and when peace is made then they shall take common counsel about all other matters." This conferment of Athenian citizenship on a whole independent community was unprecedented, but the collapse of Athens made it impossible to work out and apply the practical application of this revolutionary step.]

P. 507, *Sect.* 10.—Additional sources : Lysias, Against Eratosthenes, and Περὶ τῆς πολιτείας (403 B.C.), Δήμου καταλύσεως ἀπολογία (c. 402 B.C.), Against Agoratus (400-398 B.C.), Against Philo (before 395 B.C.), Περὶ δημεύσεως τῶν τοῦ Νικίου ἀδελφοῦ (c. 396 B.C.), For Mantitheus (c. 392 B.C.) ; Isocrates, Against Callimachus (399 B.C.). For the chronology of 404-3 B.C., see Busolt, Aristoteles und Xenophon, in Hermes, 1899.

P. 510.—Law passed before the execution of Theramenes : Aristotle, 'Αθ. Πολ. 37.

P. 513.—Idea of making landed property a condition of political rights :

This was proposed by Phormisius, and we have a fragment of a speech of Lysias opposing it (Περὶ πολιτείας, Or. 34).

CHAPTER XII

P. 514, *Sects.* 1 and 3-6.—Sources: *Primary:* inscriptions; Andocides, On the Peace (391 B.C.); Lysias, Against Alcibiades I. and II. (395 B.C.), Against Ergocles and Against Philocrates (389 B.C.), Against Epicrates (*c.* 389 B.C.), On the Property of Aristophanes (*c.* 387 B.C.), Against Evandrus (382 B.C.); Hellenica Oxyrynchia (? Cratippus); Xenophon, Hellenica iii, iv, v. 1. *Derivative:* [Ephorus]; Diodorus xiv. 12–xv. 110; Plutarch, Lives of Lysander, Agesilaus, Artaxerxes; Nepos, Lives of Conon, Thrasybulus, Agesilaus, Iphicrates.

P. 517, *Sect.* 2.—Sources: *Primary:* Xenophon's Anabasis; fragments of Ctesias. *Derivative:* Plutarch's Life of Artaxerxes.

P. 517.—March of the Ten Thousand. Fully recounted in the Anabasis. Xenophon cloaked his authorship under the pseudonym " Themistogenes of Syracuse ": Xen. Hell. iii. 2.

[Numbers. Xenophon puts the number of Asiatics with Cyrus at 100,000, and Artaxerxes' army at the battle of Cunaxa at 900,000. These figures are impossibly high, but typical of the irresponsibility of most ancient writers when dealing with large armies, especially oriental armies. Similar exaggerations appear in the description of Xerxes' invasion and of the forces opposed to Alexander.

P. 533.—Recovery of Rhodes. The best account in Ox. Hell., which dates the revolution in Rhodes to 395. Probably the Spartans attacked Caunus in 396.

P. 540.—Persian gold. According to Xenophon Timocrates was sent by Tithraustes, who succeeded Tissaphernes as satrap of Ionia and Lydia in 395, but this allows too short an interval before the outbreak of war. The account of Ox. Hell. is to be preferred. This author makes Pharnabazus responsible and dates the commission to 396 (or, possibly, 397). He also gives the best account of the party tensions in the various states. According to him, as against Xenophon, the leaders of the war party in Athens, Cephalus and Epicrates, accepted money. But he emphasises that deep-lying causes of resentment against Sparta were more important than Persian gold in shaping the alliance and bringing on war.

P. 541.—Athenian alliance with Boeotia (395): Tod, ii. 101.

P. 542.—Athenian alliance with Euboeans. Eretria: Tod, ii. 103.

P. 542.—Maritime League coinage. Seltman, Greek Coinage, 157.

P. 543.—Figures of the forces from Xenophon, Hell. iv. 2[16-17]. He gives a total of 7500 Spartan allies, but in his review of the forces he does not include the men of Tegea and Pellene (in Achaea) whom he mentions in the fighting. Different figures in Diodorus xiv. 82.

P. 543.—Battle of Corinth. Monument of Dexileos (fig. 145, p. 553) (Tod, ii. 105); he is described as τῶν πέντε ἱππέων. Memorial of Athenian cavalry killed at Corinth and Coronea (including Dexileos): Tod, ii. 104. Ten cavalrymen and a phylarch are listed for the battle of Corinth, one for Coronea. Possibly the memorial commemorated the dead of only one tribe.]

P. 545.—Building of the walls had begun in the archonship of Diophantus = 395-4 : Tod, ii. 107.

P. 546.—Temple to Cnidian Aphrodite (near Eetionea), Pausanias i. 1³ : " for the Cnidians honour Aphrodite more than all the other gods . . . and they call her Aphrodite of the Fair Voyage."

P. 546.—Athens recovered her control of Delos. Delos had been freed from Athens after Aegospotami : Lacedaemonian decree, Tod, ii. 99. Athens had recovered control by 390-89, I.G. ii². 1634.

P. 550.—Exactions of Thrasybulus = 5% on commerce. This seems to follow from the phrase τὴν ἐπὶ Θρασυβούλου εἰκοστήν in the Athenian decree recording an agreement with Clazomenae in 387 : Tod, ii. 114.⁸

P. 551.—Unfortunately for Athens: the King's Peace was a blow to Athens, since she was gradually recovering confidence. Negotiations with Clazomenae in 387 (Tod, ii. 114) probably had to be broken off.

P. 551.—Evagoras of Salamis. Evagoras had become king c. 411, and had helped Athens in the last phase of the Peloponnesian War. He was made an Athenian citizen in 410-9: I.G. i². 113. An Athenian decree of 393 honours him : Tod, ii. 109.

CHAPTER XIII

P. 555, *Sects.* 1-4.—Sources: *Primary:* inscriptions; Isocrates, Panegyricus, Plataeicus, Evagoras, Nicocles; Lysias, Against Evandrus (382 B.C.), Olympiacus (388 B.C.); Xenophon, Hellenica, v. 2–vi. 3; [Ephorus]. *Derivative:* Diodorus xv. 2-50; Plutarch, Lives of Agesilaus, Pelopidas; Nepos, Lives of Timotheus, Chabrias, Pelopidas.

P. 558.—Amyntas concluded an alliance with the Chalcidians. [A fragmentary copy of the decree: Tod, ii. 111. The Chalcidians are to be allowed to import from Macedon pitch, constructional timbers of all species and shipbuilding timber, except firs. If the Chalcidian state (as opposed to private traders) needs firs they may import them after first notifying Amyntas and paying the necessary dues. Firs (ἔλαται) for shipbuilding were throughout her history one of Macedon's greatest economic assets, since the Aegean world was extremely poor in softwoods that provided long lengths.]

P. 558.—Amyntas recovered his throne. The Athenians helped him (schol. Aesch. De Falsa Leg. 26), but the inscription relating to an alliance between Amyntas and Athens is probably to be dated near the end of his reign : Tod, ii. 129.

P. 564.—The decree founding the Confederacy: Tod, ii. 121. Passed in the seventh prytany of 478-7, *i.e.* Feb. or March 477. The list of allies is as follows :—Chios, Mytilene, Methymna, Rhodes, Byzantium, Thebes; Chalcis, Eretria, Arethusa, Carystus, Icus, Perinthus, Peparethus, Sciathus, Maronea, Dion ; Paros ; O——, Athenae Diades (in Euboea) ; P—— ; Tenedos ; Poeessa in Ceos ; Pal—— ; the demos of Corcyra, Abdera, Thasos, Chalcis (at Mt. Athos), Aenus, Samothrace, Dicaeopolis, Acarnania, Pronnoi in Cephallenia, Alcetas, Neoptolemus, Jason (erased), Andros, Tenos, Hestiaea, Myconos, Antissa, Eresus, the Astraiousioi (?), Iulis in Ceos, Carthaea, Coresia in Ceos, Elaeus, Amorgos, Selymbria, Siphnos, Sicinos, Dion in Thrace, Neapolis in Thrace ; the demos of Zacynthus in Nellon.

[The first five names are cut at the same time and by the same hand as the decree : they are the original members with whom Athens had already alliances (Byzantium, Tod, ii. 121 ; Methymna, Tod, ii. 122 ; Chios, Tod, ii. 118). The other states were added in groups, a Euboean group first, cut by different hands, as they were brought into the Confederacy.

P. 565.—Additions to the League. Alliance with Chalcis (377): Tod, ii. 124. The safeguards are clearly formulated : " The Chalcidians shall maintain what is theirs, in freedom and autonomy . . . they shall not be subjected to a garrison from Athens, they shall not pay tribute, they shall not receive a resident overseer contrary to the decrees of the allies."

P. 565.—Incorporation of Corcyra, Acarnania and Cephallenia (375): Tod, ii. 126. This decree illustrates procedure : " In order that the necessary action may be taken, they shall bring the envoys before the demos and they shall put forward the resolution of the Boule, that the secretary of the Boule shall record the names of the cities that have come on the common stele of the allies, and the Boule and the Generals and the Knights shall give oaths to the cities that have come ; and in the same way the allies shall swear the oath. And when these things are done the demos shall choose men, in such manner as shall be approved by the council of the allies, who shall receive oaths from the cities." This was the preliminary stage, followed by detailed alliance : for Corcyra, Tod, ii. 127.

P. 567.—For the yield of the *eisphora* and its relative importance in Athenian finance the evidence is good. The method of raising the tax is controversial. According to Polybius (ii. 62²) the new assessment of Attica (private property, landed and moveable) totalled 5750 talents. His figure is confirmed by Demosthenes (xiv. 19) who rounds it off to 6000 talents. Many scholars have considered this figure much too low for the assessment of private capital in Attica ; Böckh suggested that it represented not the total capital but taxable capital and that Polybius had misunderstood his source. Demosthenes implies (xxvii. 17, xxix. 59) that for the richest citizen the taxable capital was one-fifth of their total assessment ; of Demosthenes' private fortune of 15 talents, 3 talents was the taxable proportion (xxvii. 9). On this basis Böckh estimated the capital value of private property in Attica at 30,000 to 40,000 talents. Such evidence, however, as we have, including a late parallel from Messene (I.G. v. 1. 1433) is against such a high figure, and Polybius should not be assumed to have made such a mistake unless there is firm evidence against him, cp. A. M. Andreades, History of Greek Public Finance, 334. It is possible that the passages cited from Demosthenes have been misunderstood, that a fifth of the richest citizens' property represents not the taxable capital but the maximum amount which they could be required to pay in property tax during later levies. At each individual levy all who were liable may have equally paid 1 or 2 per cent of their total assessment. The poorest citizens may have been exempt ; metics paid.

For levies of 1 and 2 per cent, Dem. xiv. 27 ; 300 talents collected, Dem. xxii. 44.]

P. 568.—Delian accounts (for 377-4 B.C.) : Tod, ii. 125. Anti-Athenian action (quoted in text), lines 134-140.

P. 570.—A comic poet : Anaxandrides in the Protesilaus (Kock, Comicorum Att. Frag. ii. 41).

P. 574, *Sect.* 5.—Sources : *Primary:* works of Isocrates and Plato ;

Xenophon's Memorabilia and Apologia Socratis; Aristophanes' Ecclesiazusae and Plutus; fragments of " Middle Comedy " ; Aristotle, Politics and Ethics.

P. 576.—Athenian officers in the pay of foreign powers. Conon, Xenophon, Iphicrates, Chabrias and others. Such men were often looked on with disfavour when they returned home rich, and were suspected of dishonesty and treachery: Lysias, On the Property of Aristophanes (c. 387 B.C.).

[P. 580.—The political aspect of the trial has been introduced to conform with what Bury later wrote in the Cambridge Ancient History, v. 390.]

P. 586.—On commerce, prices, banks, etc.: cp. H. Michell, The Economics of Ancient Greece.

P. 586.—In regard to the high rate of interest, the great risk of trade in ancient times must be borne in mind.

[P. 587.—Ecclesiastic pay. The earliest evidence in Aristophanes' Ecclesiazusae (produced in 389). Possibly introduced when money was accepted from Persia in 396.]

P. 588.—Democratic leaders resigned claim to compensation. Especially Thrasybulus and Anytus: Isocrates, Callimachus, 23.

P. 589.—[Ionic alphabet. The change from Attic to Ionic alphabet was official and general from 403-2; but many Attic documents of the fifth century, especially during the last quarter, have some Ionic letters. Attic had used the long e as the aspirate, φς for ψ and χς for ξ.

P. 589.—Presidency of the Assembly. The new procedure is first illustrated in the alliance with Chalcis (377): τῶν προέδρων ἐπεψήφιζεν Παντάρετος.]

CHAPTER XIV

P. 591.—Sources: *Primary:* inscriptions; Xenophon, Hellenica vi. 4-vii; [Ephorus]. *Derivative:* Diodorus xv. 51-89; Plutarch: Pelopidas, Agesilaus; Nepos: Pelopidas, Epaminondas; Pausanias, passages in viii and ix.

P. 591.—The rise of Thessaly: cp. H. D. Westlake, Thessaly in the fourth century.

P. 591.—The name of Jason of Pherae, who had joined the Athenian Confederacy in 375, is erased on the stone (Tod, ii. 123[111]); it must have been erased between 373 (when he was at Athens for the trial of Timotheus) and his death in 370; perhaps in 372.

P. 593.—It may be noted that the tactics of Delium (424) were in some measure an anticipation of the tactics of Leuctra. An epigram commemorating Leuctra, set up by a Boeotarch and two companions (Tod, ii. 130) includes: " The trophies of victory won by the spear proclaim ' The Thebans are mightier in war.' "

P. 596.—Another account of the events after Leuctra: I infer this account from Diodorus xv. 54; his authority was doubtless Ephorus.

P. 598, *Sect.* 2.—Additional sources: architectural remains of Mantinea, Megalopolis, and Messene.

P. 598.—Many citizens cudgelled to death. More than 1200 according to Diodorus xv. 58. The number seems incredible.

P. 600.—Constitution of the Arcadian League. A decree honouring an

Athenian, probably from the sixties, begins : ἔδοξεν τῆι βουλῆι τῶν Ἀρκάδων and ends with a list of 50 Δαμιοργοί, headed by 10 from Megalopolis. The number 10,000 suggests some limitation on membership of the Assembly. The inscription also suggests that the Damiorgoi were distinct from the Boule ; perhaps they were the main executive body.

P. 600.—The Thersilion : cp. Excavations at Megalopolis (1892), 17.

P. 602.—The two parts of the city of Megalopolis : Bury, J.H.S. xviii., 1898, 15.

P. 607.—Decline of Sparta. Concentration of landed property in a few hands had already begun. Law permitting alienation of the κλῆρος : law of the ephor Epitadeus, Plutarch, Agis 5 (from the context, c. 400).

P. 607.—Arcadian statues to Apollo, Paus. x. 9. 5. The inscription has been recovered ; it ends :

Τῶνδέ σοι ἐκγίνεται Λακεδαιμονίους δη[ιώσαντες]
Ἄρκαδες ἔστησαν μνῆμ᾽ ἐπιγινομένοις.

P. 616.—The Athenian occupation of Samos and the consequent imitation there of Athenian institutions are illustrated by Hicks and Hill, 114, a list of treasures in the temple of Hera (346-5).

P. 616.—The operations of Timotheus in Chalcidice and against Amphipolis are illustrated by a decree honouring Menelaus the Pelagonian (probably King of the Lyncestians) who assisted him. The decree passed in the sixth prytany of 363-2 shows that operations were protracted into 362.

P. 617.—[Athenian relations with Ceos : Tod, ii. 142. The first revolt was signalised by the murder of an Athenian proxenos and the exile of pro-Athenians. When Chabrias withdrew, the new alliance stele was overthrown and supporters of Athens suppressed. The decree gives the terms of the new settlement in 362. Those who had been responsible for the second revolt are to be exiled from Ceos and Athens, and their property confiscated. But the general terms are generous : the Athenians and their allies (still important in the constitution of the Confederacy) take an oath to bury the past : Οὐ μνησικακήσω τῶν παρεληλυθότων πρὸς Κείους οὐδενός.]

P. 620.—Arcadian occupation of Olympia. Pisatan presidency illustrated by an inscription conferring privileges on certain Sicyonians, Hicks and Hill, 115.

P. 622.—Text of quintuple alliance treaty : Tod, ii. 144.

P. 623.—Phocians refuse to join Epaminondas. Anti-Theban Phocian group in Delphi : cp. Hicks and Hill, 116 ; a decree recording the reception by Athens of men expelled from Delphi, where Theban influence was now dominant.

P. 625.—Effects of Battle of Mantinea. Xenophon (vii. 5²⁶⁻⁷) sums up admirably the unsettling effects of the battle :

ἀκρισία δὲ καὶ ταραχὴ ἔτι πλείων μετὰ τὴν μάχην ἐγένετο ἢ πρόσθεν ἐν τῇ Ἑλλάδι.

P. 626, Sect. 5.—Sources : Diodorus xv. 90-94 ; Xenophon, Agesilaus ; Plutarch, Agesilaus ; Nepos, Agesilaus.

P. 627.—Chabrias in Egypt. Ambassadors of Tachos seeking help at Athens : Hicks and Hill, 121. Inscription (from Memphis) of Greek mercenaries, possibly serving under Chabrias : Hicks and Hill, 122. Strabo

(760, 803) mentions Χαβρίου χάραξ and Χαβρίου κώμη in the Delta, named presumably after the Athenian general.

CHAPTER XV

P. 629.—Sources: *Primary:* [Philistus]; Platonic and Pseudo-Platonic Epistles. *Derivative:* Diodorus xiii, xiv, xvi; Plutarch, Dion, Timoleon; Nepos, Dion, Timoleon; Justin xx, xxi.

[P. 631.—Temple of Apollo, Selinus. Bury's view derives from Freeman, History of Sicily, iii. 457. The current view of archaeologists is that work on the temple was discontinued *c.* 470.

P. 631.—Hannibal's force. According to Diodorus (xiii. 54[1]), 1500 transports. The size of his force was " according to Ephorus 200,000 infantry, 4000 horse; according to Timaeus not many more than 100,000." Greek writers in dealing with high numbers almost always exaggerate highly.]

P. 646.—Alliance coin of Catane and Leontini (fig. 169): A. J. Evans, Num. Chron. xvi., 1896, 128.

[P. 647.—For Epipolae, cp. p. 472. Dionysius fortified Epipolae to deny it to the enemy and to provide protected camping ground for his large army.

P. 647.—Quadriremes and quinqueremes. The new principle in these ships, which dominated Hellenistic naval warfare, was the assignment of 4, 5 (or more) men to a single large oar. It is unlikely that they were invented by Dionysius, since they are not used in the Aegean until the last third of the fourth century: Tarn, Hellenistic Military and Naval Developments, 129.

P. 658.—Escape of Carthaginians. The view that the Carthaginians escaped by collusion with Dionysius is based on the account of Diodorus. It is, however, doubtful whether it was in Dionysius' interest to let the Carthaginians escape. And while they held Plemmyrion and so commanded the entrance to the harbour they were not trapped: cp. Beloch, Gr. Gesch. iii. 1. 60.]

P. 658.—Ruler of Sicily. Dionysius is called ὁ Σικελίας ἄρχων in Athenian decrees honouring him: Tod, ii. 108 (393 B.C.), 133 (368 B.C.); 136 (367 B.C.).

P. 679.—" Archidamus eagerly embraced," etc. It may be noted that in 356 B.C. Isocrates had urged Archidamus inopportunely to lead an expedition against Persia: Isocrates, Letter 9 (to Archidamus).

P. 680.—Tarentine coins alluding to appeal to Sparta and death of Archidamus: A. J. Evans, Horsemen of Tarentum (Pl. v. 1; Pl. iv. 9, 10).

CHAPTER XVI

P. 681.—Sources: *Primary:* inscriptions; speeches of Demosthenes and Aeschines, and works of Isocrates (see below under separate sections); fragments of Theopompus; [Ephorus]. *Derivative:* Diodorus xv. 95, xvi; Plutarch, Demosthenes, Phocion; Justin vii–ix; Pseudo-Plutarch, Lives of Ten Orators (Demosthenes and Aeschines).

P. 682.—Athenian alliance with Thessaly: Tod, ii. 147.

[P. 682.—Thracian kingdom. Cersobleptes was challenged by Berisades and Amadocus, both probably members of the royal house. By Athenian mediation the Kingdom was divided, Berisades taking the west and Amadocus the centre.

P. 683.—Recovery of Chersonese. Two unfavourable agreements had been made by Athens with Cersobleptes (Dem. xxiii. 167 and 171). Chares secured more satisfactory terms: Tod, ii. 151 (Dem. xxiii. 173). The cities of the Chersonese were recognised as Athenian allies: they had to pay contributions to the Confederacy, but also tribute to the Thracian kings, a double obligation which may go back to the fifth century.

P. 683.—Recovery of Euboea. The Euboean cities had joined the Athenian Confederacy early (377-6), but, after Leuctra, they followed Thebes. In 366 it was the tyrant of Eretria who seized Oropus and handed it to Thebes. With the decline in Theban prestige the pro-Athenian elements in Euboea became stronger. In 357 the Thebans sent a force to support their partisans, but the Athenians intervened and drove them out. Eretria, Chalcis, Carystus and Hestiaea came over to Athens: Tod, ii. 153. Another decree (Tod, ii. 154) records a new alliance with Eretria, guaranteeing her the protection of Athens and the allies if she is attacked. Cp. I.G. ii². 149.]

P. 683, Sect. 2.—Additional sources: *Primary:* [Thrasybulus]. *Derivative:* Herodes Atticus, Περὶ πολιτείας; Arrian's Tactics.

[P. 684.—Position of Macedonian kings: Hampl, Der König der Makedonen.

P. 686.—Secret engagement. It has been suggested that this understanding was the diplomatic invention of Philip.]

P. 686.—Philip's capture of Amphipolis. For the proceedings against the pro-Athenian party in Amphipolis on its capture: Tod, ii. 150; a decree from Amphipolis of perpetual exile against Stratocles, who had been sent as an envoy to secure Athenian help, and Philon (unknown).

P. 687, *note.*—Thracian alliance: Tod, ii. 157. [The Athenian oath includes: " And I will not end the war against Philip without the agreement of Cetriporis and his brothers and I will join with Cetriporis and his brothers in reducing the other places which Philip holds and I will join with Cetriporis and his brothers in destroying Crenides." Crenides, the centre of Philip's gold mines, was of vital importance.]

P. 687.—" A professional army with a national spirit": Hogarth, Philip and Alexander of Macedon, 51.

P. 688, Sect. 3.—Special sources: Demosthenes, On the Trierarchic Crown (359), Against Androtion, Against Timocrates, Against Leptines (355-4), On the Symmories (354), For the Rhodians (353); Isocrates, On the Peace (353), Areopagiticus (355-4), Περὶ ἀντιδόσεως (353).

P. 688.—The fact that the Carians saw much of the world in mercenary service, since the days of Psammetichus and Amasis, helped to keep the country abreast of civilisation.

[P. 688.—*Hypaspistae.* Alexander had three battalions of hypaspists, each 1000 strong. One of them was a royal guard, *agema.* In what respects they differed from the hoplites of the phalanx is not clear from the sources. It is misleading to call them light-armed, because they often share the work of the phalanx (Tarn, ii. 148). But they seem to have been more mobile and were probably not armed with the long *sarissa.*

P. 689.—Position of the Carian princes: Tod (ii. 138) records three decrees passed by Mylasa in 367-6, 361-0, 355-4, dealing severely with conspiracies against Mausolus. The first decree's prescript runs : " In the thirty-ninth year of Artaxerxes' reign, when Mausolus was satrap, it was resolved by the people of Mylasa at a regular assembly meeting, and confirmed by the three tribes." A similar document from Iasus, S.I.G. 169, quoted by Tod.

P. 690.—Mausolus and Athenian allies : cp. Tod, ii. 155 ; honours paid to Mausolus, including citizenship, by Erythrae.

P. 690.—Revolt of Athenian allies. This led to the introduction of Athenian garrisons into some of the allied cities which had not revolted, contrary to the original guarantees when the Confederacy was formed, as at Andros : Tod, ii. 156. " That Andros may be preserved for the demos of Athens and for the demos of Andros." There are clear signs of financial difficulties ; Archedemos is sent " to exact the moneys that are owed from the islands for the troops in Andros . . . that the troops may have pay." Cf. Arcesine in Amorgos, Tod, ii. 152.

P. 690.—Chares in the Hellespont, 356. Chares seems to have prevented the Byzantines from joining forces with the Aegean rebels : cp. S.I.G. 199, a decree which honours a Sestian " for reporting the expeditionary force prepared by Byzantium."]

P. 691.—It is noteworthy that in the speech on the Symmories there is no mention of Philip.

P. 692.—Pleadings of Demosthenes for Rhodes. The received date (from Dionysius of Halicarnassus) is 351-0 ; but the difficulties of this date have been pointed out by Judeich (Kleinasiatische Studien, 186-189). There can be hardly any doubt that the true date is 353, second half of the year.

P. 694, *Sect.* 4.—Special source : Demosthenes, For the Megalopolitans (353).

P. 694.—Thebes and Amphictiones make war. An account of moneys paid to the Boeotians for urging this war " against those who profane the sanctuary of Pythian Apollo " : Tod, ii. 160. The payments cover three years (perhaps 355-2) and are not substantial. The largest contributions came from Byzantium which had made an alliance with Thebes, on revolting from Athens. A Boeotian proxenos in Tenedos (loyal to Athens) contributed 1000 drachmas.

P. 701.—Accounts of the Naopoioi : S.I.G. 236-253. Soon after the beginning of the war the building seems to have been interrupted for a few years. Accounts of 346-4 : Tod, ii. 169.

P. 701, *Sect.* 5.—Special sources : Demosthenes, Against Aristocrates (352), First Philippic (351), Olynthiacs (349), Against Meidias (348).

P. 706.—Treaty of Chalcidians with Athens (? 351-0) : cp. Tod, ii. 119, but the date of the decree is very uncertain.

P. 708, *Sect.* 6.—Special sources : Demosthenes, On the Peace (346), On the Embassy (343), On the Crown (330) ; Aeschines, Against Timarchus (346-5), On the Embassy (343), Against Ctesiphon (330) ; Isocrates, Philip (346) ; Hypereides, For Euxenippus, 39, 40.

P. 712.—Phocians obliged to repay. Accounts of payments : Tod, ii. 172. For five years the Phocians paid 30 talents half-yearly (343-338). In spring 337 they paid 10 talents only : perhaps the fine was reduced when Philip restored the Phocian κοινόν in 338. The last payment, making a total of 460 talents, was probably made in spring 322.

P. 714.—Isocrates. In 370 Isocrates seems to have looked to Dionysius of Syracuse to be the saviour of Greece : Isocrates, Letter 1 (to Dionysius).

P. 715, *Sect.* 7.—Special sources : Demosthenes, Second Philippic (344), On the Chersonese and Third Philippic and Fourth Philippic (341), On the Embassy, On the Crown ; Hegesippus (Pseudo-Demosth.), On Halonnesus ; Aeschines, as for *Sect.* 6, Letter of Philip ; Isocrates, Panathenaicus (339).

P. 722.—Chares sent to Byzantium. He had already, earlier in 340, been operating in the Hellespont : cp. Tod, ii. 174; honour paid by Athens to Elaeus for loyalty.

P. 722.—Siege of Byzantium. Important help was given to Athens by Tenedos : Tod, ii. 175.

P. 732, *Sect.* 9.—Special sources: *Primary:* Isocrates, Letter 3 (to Philip) ; Pseudo-Demosthenes, On the Treaty with Alexander (335) ; Circular Letter of Philip Arrhidaeus (319), in Diodorus xviii. 56 ; fragments of Hypereides, In reply to Aristogeiton ; Isyllus. *Derivative:* Justin ix.

P. 733.—Philip at Sparta : Isyllus of Epidaurus : Wilamowitz-Möllendorff, Isyllos von Epidauros, 30 *sqq.*

The lines are :—

> ἐγ κείνοισι χρόνοις ὅκα δὴ στρατὸν ἦγε Φίλιππος
> εἰς Σπάρτην, ἐθέλων ἀνελεῖν βασιληΐδα τιμήν.

P. 733.—Synedrion of 338. Fragment of the oath taken by the members : Tod, ii. 177. [This oath probably accompanied the peace settlement and preceded the alliance and declaration of war against Persia. The members swear to maintain the new peace and resist war and revolution. After the oath the members are listed, with the number of votes assigned to them in the League Council.]

CHAPTERS XVII AND XVIII

SOURCES : *Primary:* [Aristobulus], [Ptolemy], [Callisthenes], [Onesicritus], [The Court Journal of Alexander], [Journal of Nearchus], [Chares of Mytilene], [Anaximenes of Lampsacus]. *Derivative:* [Cleitarchus] ; Arrian's Anabasis ; Plutarch's Life of Alexander ; Quintus Curtius ; Diodorus xvii ; Justin xi, xii ; passages in Strabo. (Fabulous, but containing a fact or two : Pseudo-Callisthenes.)

[The best surviving ancient account is in Arrian who governed Cappadocia under Hadrian. His account is based on Ptolemy, one of Alexander's marshals, later King of Egypt, who had access to the official Journal. Ptolemy is supplemented from Aristobulus, a Greek architect and engineer who was with the army, and from other less reliable sources (usually indicated by λέγεται δέ, οἱ δὲ λέγουσι, etc.). The fullest and best modern account in W. W. Tarn, Alexander the Great ; vol. i, narrative ; vol. ii, sources and studies. The sources critically examined in Tarn, ii. 1-127.

P. 740.—Alexander and the Greeks. A possible fragment of the treaty between Alexander and the Greeks : Tod, ii. 183.

P. 742.—Celtic oath : Tarn, i. 5-6.

P. 748.—Persian numbers. The ancient authors grossly exaggerate throughout. It is impossible to estimate even approximately the numbers involved.

P. 752.—Alexander and the Greeks of Asia. Dedication by Alexander at Priene: Tod, ii. 184, cp. 185. For the establishment of democracies: Tod, ii. 192. This decree from Chios lays down " that all the exiles from Chios shall return and the constitution in Chios shall be a democracy. Law drafters shall be appointed to draft and correct the laws in order that there be nothing in the way of the democracy nor of the return of the exiles. And the laws, corrected or drafted, shall be referred to Alexander." For the relationship of Alexander to these Greeks: Tarn, ii. 199; but see also V. Ehrenberg, Alexander and the Greeks.

P. 756.—The Gordian Knot. Tarn (ii. 262) argues from the sources that the cutting of the knot with a sword is the malicious invention of the hostile tradition, inconsistent with Alexander's respect for gods and oracles. Aristobulus (Arrian, ii. 3[1]) makes Alexander draw out the pole to find the end of the cord, implying that the knot was then untied.]

P. 757, *Sect.* 6.—Special source: *Derivative* (from Callisthenes): Polybius xii. 17-22.

[P. 757.—Persian advance to Issus. The Persian move to Issus might have been dangerous, as threatening Alexander's lines of communications.]

P. 758.—Battle of Issus. The resemblance of the tactics of Alexander to the tactics of Cromwell has been instructively pointed out by Mahaffy (Greek Life and Thought[2], 32). " Each of them fought most of his battles by charging with his heavy cavalry on the right wing, overthrowing the enemy's horse, and then, avoiding the temptation to pursue, charging the enemy's infantry in flank, and so deciding the issue."

P. 771.—The submission of the Jews is a certain inference from the situation, though the account of his visit to Jerusalem by Josephus (Ant. xi. 8) is a fable.

[P. 775.—Diodorus gives the Persian numbers at Gaugamela as 1,000,000 foot and 40,000 horse. Such an immense army could not have been contained in the battle area.

P. 782.—Burning of the palace: Arrian iii. 18[11] attributes the act to policy: cp. Tarn, ii. 47.]

P. 785.—The satrapies. But it seems to have become ultimately the policy of Alexander to appoint only Macedonian governors. At his death only three satrapies (Media, Parthia, Paropamisadae) were held by orientals.

[P. 791.—The Caspian. The Caspian was certainly regarded as a gulf of ocean by some Greeks for some time after Alexander. Aristotle, like Herodotus, knew it to be a lake; but whether his knowledge was widely spread among his contemporaries (including Alexander) is uncertain. See Tarn, ii. 16.]

P. 794.—Intemperance promoted by the dryness of the air, and want of good water: cp. F. v. Schwarz, Alexander des Grossen Feldzüge in Turkestan (1893), 44-45, who points out the similar experience of the Russians in these regions. Drunkenness among the Europeans in Turkestan was shocking until General v. Kauffmann introduced the use of tea in the army.

P. 795.—We must unquestionably reject the episode of the Branchidae, because the act was so unlike Alexander, and the sources for the story are late. The story may be regarded as definitely exploded by Mr. Tarn's paper in the Classical Review, xxxvi (1922), 63. [Cp. Tarn, Alexander the Great, ii. 272.]

P. 796.—Alexander's indifference to women. Little importance need be attached to the passing connexion with Barsine, daughter of Memnon, after the capture of Damascus (Plut. Al. 22).

[P. 798.—The conquest of India. Alexander's route : Sir A. Stein, On Alexander's Track to the Indus.]

P. 800.—The extant Periplus, ascribed to Scylax, is a later work under a false name.

P. 801.—Massaga. According to Diodorus (xvii. 84), Alexander was guilty of gross treachery on this occasion. This does not appear in the narrative of Arrian.

[P. 802.—Aornus. Identified by Sir Aurel Stein, op. cit. chs. xvi-xxi.

Pp. 803-6.—Battle of the Hydaspes. This, the most interesting of Alexander's battles, is the most difficult to reconstruct from the sources. Arrian's account analysed : Tarn, ii. 190. The main problems are (1) the part played by the battalions of the phalanx ; (2) the tactics assigned to Coenus. (1) Two battalions were left with Craterus, three were stationed at intervals between camp and crossing point ; two were taken with him by Alexander. Arrian's text implies, but does not state, that these two battalions were left on the right bank, and that only the hypaspists (3000) and light infantry were taken across—a total of c. 6000. The text, however (v. 18⁴), is awkward and Tarn is probably right in holding that the two battalions of the phalanx remained with Alexander. Tarn also holds that the three battalions posted between crossing and camp joined Alexander as he marched past them ; this is more controversial and cannot be extracted from the sources. (2) The tactics assigned to Coenus depend largely on the meaning of Arrian vi. 16³. Alexander ἐπὶ τὸ εὐώνυμον κέρας τῶν πολεμίων παρήλαυνεν, ὡς ταύτῃ ἐπιθησόμενος. Κοῖνον δὲ πέμπει ὡς ἐπὶ τὸ δεξιόν. Most historians, including Bury, have assumed that Coenus was intended to ride round Alexander's right flank. Tarn is almost certainly right in insisting that while Alexander moved on the enemy's left, Coenus was instructed to move as though against the enemy's right. This was intended to draw the Indians' left wing to attack Alexander's reduced force ; their attack gave Coenus his opportunity to change direction, cut through and attack in the rear.

P. 809.—Caspian. See note on p. 791.

P. 817.—Banquet at Opis. Tarn (ii. 434) attaches considerable importance to the banquet of reconciliation at Opis. He believes that Alexander prayed there for the brotherhood of man. The crucial passage is in Arrian vii. 11⁹, εὔχετο δὲ τά τε ἄλλα ἀγαθὰ καὶ ὁμόνοιάν τε καὶ κοινωνίαν τῆς ἀρχῆς Μακεδόσι καὶ Πέρσαις. Tarn translates " he prayed for the other good things, and for Homonoia, and for partnership in the realm between Macedonians and Persians." But ὁμόνοια and κοινωνία τῆς ἀρχῆς are closely linked. Homonoia here seems not to be a general conception of the brotherhood of man, but harmony between Macedonians and Persians.

P. 817.—Embassies to Alexander : cp. Tarn, ii. 374.]

P. 821.—Date of Alexander's death : Court Journal (in Plutarch, Al. 77), τῇ τρίτῃ φθίνοντος (Δαισίου) = 28th (27th if a short month) of Daesius. The correspondence of the Macedonian with Roman months is uncertain ;

but we have a statement in a MS. of Pseudo-Callisthenes, which may well be trustworthy, and would enable us to interpret the date. According to one reading (ed. Müller, 151), Alexander " died on the 4th of Pharmuthi " ; and in 323 the 4th of the Egyptian month Pharmuthi fell on the 13th of June (Unger, Philologus, 1882, 82).

[P. 822.—Seventy cities are said to have been founded by Alexander, but less than twenty are certain. They were all named Alexandria and most of them were east of the Tigris where cities were rare. The list has been swollen by the inclusion of military colonies which only later became cities and a few cities which Alexander projected such as Alexandria Troas and Ilium. See Tarn, ii. 232-259.

P. 822.—Alexander and the west. Diodorus xviii. 4 says that specific plans were left by Alexander. He intended to build 1000 warships larger than triremes in Phoenicia, Syria, Cilicia, Cyprus for an expedition against Carthage and the coastal peoples of Africa and Spain ; and to build a road along the coast of Africa to the pillars of Hercules. Tarn (ii. 378) has shown that Diodorus' account has very suspicious elements (e.g. road-building, which is a prominent feature of imperialism under the Romans, but not in the time of Alexander or his successors). The story probably arose in the second century B.C., when the rise of Rome focussed interest in the west. Livy (ix. 18) speculates interestingly on how Alexander would have fared against Rome. But though he probably did not formulate specific plans, Alexander may well have thought of Carthage and the west.]

P. 823.—In Alexander's camp the war in Arcadia was likened to a war of mice (Plut. Ages. 15).

P. 823, Sect. 5.—Sources : Primary: inscriptions ; Aeschines, Against Ctesiphon ; Demosthenes, On the Crown ; Lycurgus, Against Leocrates ; Aristotle, Constitution of the Athenians ; architectural remains. Derivative: Life of Lycurgus ; Plutarch, Lives of Demosthenes and Phocion ; Diodorus xvii. 62-63.

P. 824.—Aeschines, quotation : Against Ctesiphon, 132-4.

[P. 825.—Etruscan rovers. A report of the curators of the Attic dock yards (325-4 B.C.) refers to a decree establishing the colony (I.G. ii.² 1629; a long extract in Tod, ii. 200). The report includes (217-232) : " In order that the people may also safeguard its own trade and corn transport and that, by the establishment of its own naval station, it may have protection against the Etruscans, and in order that Miltiades the oekist and the settlers may have a fleet of their own and that Greeks and barbarians who sail the sea may also sail into the Athenian naval station, with protection for their merchantmen. . . ." It is interesting to note that this Miltiades is of the same deme and genos as the earlier oekist of the Chersonese and the victor of Marathon.]

P. 826.—Ephebic oath : Tod, ii. 204.

P. 828.—[Dearth of corn, 330-326 B.C. An interesting stele was found in Cyrene in 1922 (Tod, ii. 196) giving a list of states to which Cyrene sent grain, with the amounts sent, totalling 805,000 medimni. Athens received, and probably needed, the largest allocation, 100,000 medimni. Other epigraphic evidence for the famine cited by Tod, loc. cit.

P. 828.—Restoration of exiles. Decrees arising from Alexander's instruction: Tod, ii. 201 (Mytilene), 202 (Tegea). The latter represents the revision of an earlier draft submitted to Alexander. Careful provision had to be made, especially for property disputes.

P. 828.—Alexander's divinity. Tarn (ii. 370) suggests that Alexander had a political purpose, to enable him to do as god what he could not do as Hegemon of the League, bound by his oath. It is very doubtful whether the Greeks would have drawn this conclusion from his deification.

P. 829.—Harpalus affair. The responsibility of Demosthenes is difficult to determine and has been hotly debated. His defence is lost; Hypereides' speech for the prosecution (a careful introduction in the Budé edition by G. Colin, 1946) is only in parts preserved. Tarn (Cambridge Ancient History, vi. 453) emphasises that Demosthenes' admission is not proved. It is referred to by Hypereides (Col. x. 111), but only as hearsay: "At first, *apparently* (ὡς [ἔοι]κεν) he admitted that he had taken the money, but had used it for you, borrowing it for the Theoric fund. And Cnosion and his other friends went round saying that the prosecution would compel him to disclose what he did not wish to make public, that he had borrowed the money for the needs of government." This is hearsay, but it sounds circumstantial. It is difficult to believe that Demosthenes, whatever his motives, was completely innocent.]

INDEX